A STUDY OF SAVING
IN THE UNITED STATES

A STUDY OF SAVING IN THE UNITED STATES

A STUDY OF SAVING
IN THE
UNITED STATES

VOLUME I

Introduction;
Tables of Annual Estimates of Saving
1897 to 1949

BY

RAYMOND W. GOLDSMITH

GREENWOOD PRESS, PUBLISHERS
NEW YORK

Published 1955, by Princeton University Press
Reprinted by permission of
Princeton University Press

First Greenwood Reprinting 1969

Library of Congress Catalogue Card Number 69-13910

S.E.G. soli —
sapienti sat

FOREWORD

BY THE CHAIRMAN OF THE ADVISORY COMMITTEE
OF THE SAVING AND CAPITAL MARKET STUDY

Under the terms of the grant made for the Saving and Capital Market Study by the Life Insurance Association of America, it was provided that the Chairman of the LIAA Investment Research Committee should appoint a nine-man committee to assist the research of Dr. Goldsmith and his staff. It was stipulated that six members of this committee were to be economists who by training and experience were capable of advising on research in the proposed field of study. These six, one of whom was to be selected by the Chairman of the LIAA Investment Research Committee to serve as Chairman, were to be drawn from academic, government, and nonprofit research positions outside the life insurance business. The remaining three members of the Advisory Committee were to be appointed from among the officers of member companies of the LIAA. It was further provided that the Advisory Committee was to meet at least quarterly and more frequently if deemed necessary by its Chairman.

Under the terms of the grant the functions of the Advisory Committee were:

(1) To determine, in collaboration with Dr. Goldsmith, the specific areas in the field of study outlined by Dr. Goldsmith which were to be explored and the emphasis to be placed on each;

(2) To approve the methods and techniques to be followed;

(3) To review progress reports to be submitted quarterly by Dr. Goldsmith;

(4) To make suggestions to Dr. Goldsmith with respect to the execution of his work; and

(5) To advise the LIAA Investment Research Committee on the progress of the Study.

The Advisory Committee which was appointed and which has served during the course of the Study is as follows: Dr. Winfield W. Riefler, Assistant to the Chairman of the Board of Governors of the Federal Reserve System (Chairman); William W. Bodine, Chairman of the Board of the Penn Mutual Life Insurance Company; Dr. Arthur F. Burns, Director of Research, National Bureau of Economic Research, and Professor of Economics, Columbia University (presently on leave of absence from these positions to serve as Chairman of President Eisenhower's Council of Economic Advisers); Frederic W. Ecker, President, Metropolitan Life Insurance Company; Dr. Simon Kuznets, Professor of Economics, University of Pennsylvania, and member of the research staff, National Bureau of Economic Research; Gerard S. Nollen, Chairman of the Board of the Bankers Life Company, Iowa; Dr. Summer H. Slichter, Lamont University Professor of Economics, Harvard University; Dr. Jacob Viner, Professor of Economics, Princeton University; Dr. Theodore O. Yntema, Financial Vice President, Ford Motor Company, and formerly Director of Research, Committee for Economic Development, and Professor of Business and Economic Policy, University of Chicago.

Dr. Ralph A. Young, Director of the Division of Research and Statistics of the Board of Governors of the Federal Reserve System, served as alternate to the Chairman of the Committee. In the late stages of the work Mr. Nollen, due to retirement from his position at Bankers Life, was obliged to resign from the Committee and Robert B. Patrick, Financial Vice President, Bankers Life Company, Iowa, was appointed to replace him. Dr. James J. O'Leary, Director of Investment Research of the LIAA, met with the Committee and served as Secretary.

During the period of the Study, the Advisory Committee met regularly and meetings were generally well attended. In the first year, meetings were held quarterly; subsequently, three meetings per year proved sufficient to follow the progress of the Study.

In accordance with the terms of the grant, Dr. Goldsmith has submitted regular progress reports to the Advisory Committee well in advance of meetings. In addition, he has circulated nearly seventy voluminous research memoranda to the Committee to permit it to follow currently the work under way. The Committee has thus been able to review continuously the results of the Study as they have developed, and to advise Dr. Goldsmith on the general coverage of the Study as well as on the areas of emphasis. It has likewise consulted with Dr. Goldsmith on methods of approach. It should be clearly understood that the many decisions with respect to research techniques have rested with Dr. Goldsmith. Dr. Goldsmith has consulted with the Committee on matters involving the research technique, but the voluminous nature of the research memoranda has made it impossible for the Advisory Committee to consider many of the technical aspects of the work.

The Advisory Committee feels that Dr. Goldsmith has made a fundamental contribution in this study to our knowledge of saving and the American capital market. We believe that his work represents by far the most comprehensive and detailed study that has been made to date in this field. Dr. Goldsmith has broken new ground. He has provided rich new data on savings and has shown remarkable ingenuity in weaving together hitherto scattered sources of data. The results provide basic material for future students in the field of saving and the capital markets and indicate clearly areas requiring further primary research.

Due to time and budget limitations, it has proved necessary for Dr. Goldsmith to reduce greatly the original plans for analysis of the data. Much of this analytical job remains to be done, and it is our hope that Dr. Goldsmith and other students will be encouraged to go forward with the analysis.

WINFIELD W. RIEFLER

New York City
September 1, 1953

Chairman, Advisory Committee on Study of Saving and the American Capital Market

AUTHOR'S PREFACE

(*Apologia pro opere suo*)

The Saving Study, the principal statistical results of which are reported in the three volumes now being published, was undertaken with the objective of providing a comprehensive quantitative description as well as an analysis of the saving process in the United States in the first half of this century, i.e. of the process of financing the country's economic growth. The Study, as so often happens in such endeavors, has proven more laborious than expected; has taken more time than anticipated; and yet falls short of the goal, even in the author's eyes.

As the Study now stands Volume I contains an Introduction, which provides a summary of the main findings; two sets of summary tables (one on an annual, the other on a period or quadrennial, basis); and 550 tables—accounting for the bulk of the volume—which show in fair detail the derivation of the annual estimates of national saving and its components. In accordance with the "principle of reproducibility" the figures are shown in the tables and explained in the accompanying notes in sufficient detail to enable the reader to retrace the derivation of the final estimates from the basic data.[1] Adherence to this principle makes it necessary to present more basic data and intermediate calculations than has been customary in similar publications. No apologies are offered for this approach. On the contrary, it is felt that even the detail now presented, both in the tables and in the notes, is at times not entirely sufficient; and that excuses are in order where—as occasionally in this study or as in other publications presenting the results of similarly elaborate and complicated calculations—the principle of reproducibility has not been fully adhered to, with the result that the serious reader is not able to follow the derivation of the estimates in detail, and thus often cannot rearrange or adjust the figures to suit his own purposes.

Volume II consists, first, of a discussion of the principles involved in measuring saving within a system of social accounts and of the accuracy of the estimates described in Volume I, and a comparison with other relevant data; and, secondly, of a set of chapters reviewing the problems encountered in the derivation of the main components of national and personal saving.

Volume III, finally, is made up of four special studies, supplementing both the Introduction and the statistical tables of Volume I. The first of these studies presents and briefly discusses estimates of national wealth and national balance sheets; the second and third—contributed by Dr. Dorothy Brady and Dr. Horst Mendershausen, respectively—analyze the information on saving contained in two important bodies of information not used in the time series of Volumes I and II: household expenditure studies and estate tax returns. Dr. Brady in her summary actually goes further, formulating a theory intended to explain differences in the volume of saving and in saving ratios among families. Dr. Brady's contribution unfor-

---

[1] See Volume II, Chapter III, Section 10 for some discussion of the principle and explanation of deviations from it.

tunately could not be completed on the scale originally envisaged due to her return to government service in 1951. The text and appendices which now constitute this part of Volume III should therefore be considered as working memoranda, prepared during a period of more than four years, which it has not been possible to integrate completely, either one with another or with the summary. An additional section on "Family Savings in Relation to Changes in the Level and Distribution of Income" has been published in Volume xv of *Studies in Income and Wealth*. The fourth special study in Volume III reports briefly on some simple econometric experiments with the new estimates of saving. Though time for a thorough treatment was lacking and though the author's competence in this field is quite limited, even the preliminary and tentative results obtained appeared worth reporting if only in the hope that this imperfect attempt will spur other investigators to launch a more elaborate attack with more decisive results to supersede what is offered here.

A process as fundamental to a country's economic development as saving, and so little known in its details, is not likely to be reduced with ease to quantitative terms; it is even less likely that its mode of operation and the motivations of the participants can as yet be adequately explained. What would be required is an attack with the combined resources of social accounting, economic theory, econometrics, economic history, and psychology. However, the time is not yet ripe for such an exhaustive analysis of the saving process of the American economy, an analysis that would attempt, with reasonable expectation of success, to explain in detail the course of saving over half a century in terms of a general theory of economic behavior and growth. We lack many of the quantitative and other factual data required for such an undertaking and we are in many cases without the theoretical tools for attacking the problems effectively, though significant steps have been taken in both directions during the last two decades. The development of a statistical basis, though as yet not sufficiently detailed, for the current observation of the saving process; the promising approach to the study of habits and motivations of savers through sample interviews; and the better understanding of the function and effects of saving in a modern economy which has come from the Keynesian controversies—these are probably the most important of the steps.

From the beginning, therefore, this study could at best be expected to make an advance in two directions. Its first objective was to increase the factual knowledge of the saving process in the United States—and thus to some extent in modern dynamic economies in general—by providing measurements of saving by the main saver groups over a longer period, in more detail, and more nearly in accord with the principles of social accounting than previously had been available. The second objective was twofold: To subject these new estimates to analysis with the tools of econometrics and economic theory, and to integrate the findings with what we know about savers and the saving process from other sources, notably from household budget studies and national balance sheets. The volumes now published are devoted almost exclusively to the first objective, that of providing basic data not only on saving but incidentally on several other subjects, data which should be of use in different fields of financial research. These volumes also aim to make some contribution to the second objective, but again mainly by providing additional facts on subjects relevant to the saving process, such as the compilation of national balance sheets, or by comparing the information on specific aspects of saving obtained by different approaches. Statistical analysis of the new estimates, their integration with other data bearing on the saving process, and their utilization within the framework of economic theory essentially remain to be done.

The Study as published thus falls short of the original goal with respect both to basic data and to their interpretation. Careful readers will discover the shortcomings for themselves and will judge them with a degree of severity that depends upon their temperament as well as their familiarity with the conditions of financial research. These shortcomings have also been discussed in some detail, and I trust with sufficient frankness, throughout Volume II, but particularly in Chapters III and IV.

Warning signals are hoisted throughout the three volumes concerning the degree of accuracy that can be expected from material of the type with which this study has had to work, and a specific though probably not quite satisfactory and conclusive discussion of margins of error is given in Volume II, Chapter IV. The reader of these volumes—as well as the user of virtually all estimates of national income and other social accounting data now available—must be constantly aware that he is dealing with imperfect approximations to often very complicated concepts. The unavoidable shortcomings of these approximations are no reason to abandon work on them and with them. It is only through constant experimentation that the conceptual structure of the estimates may be clarified, and that the margin of error in the actual figures can be reduced to a tolerable size.

Because the Study of necessity had to cover a good deal of territory untouched by previous research workers or only roughly surveyed by them, it cannot hope to have escaped the special risks which beset explorations. The main function and value of such attempts often is to provide a dartboard on which later students may practice their critical skill and—no less important—improve the game. This process may be hard on the author, but it is good for the progress of science. Elsewhere, and particularly in the estimates for the last one or two decades, I was in the more favorable position of making use of predecessors' work. It is but natural that in such cases the difference between the present and the earlier estimates may be stressed at the expense of their similarity, but where this seems to involve criticism of earlier estimates it should not be interpreted as a slight to their contribution.

In projects as complex as this study it is necessary to "freeze" the basic figures well before the manuscript is finished and a still longer time before it is made available to users. It has thus not been possible to extend the statistics beyond 1949 or to take account, except by way of occasional notes, of basic statistical data or analytical studies published or circulated later than the fall of 1951.

Some readers may be interested primarily in the figures for recent years and may consult the Study chiefly to look for differences between them and the existing estimates. I should very much regret it if this were the general attitude, and at least for three reasons. First, the emphasis throughout the Study is on long-term trends and structural changes, and not on short-term movements and current estimates. Secondly, the figures for the last few years necessarily are in many cases based on preliminary figures. Thirdly, the estimates for these years differ more from the commonly utilized figures of the Department of Commerce and the Securities and Exchange Commission than those for earlier years. These differences, which are explained in detail in Appendix B of Volume II, are mainly the result of differences in concepts, and are only secondarily due to different estimates of the same items. The basic similarity in approach of this study and the statistics of the Securities and Exchange Commission is, of course, hardly astonishing, as I had the privilege more than fifteen years ago of initiating the Commission's statistics on saving, though in a less detailed and much rougher form than that now available.[2]

My chief apologies are not so much for the scope or the detail of the estimates or even their reliability and accuracy, as for the nature of the Introduction to Volume I, which constitutes the only general discussion of the saving process in the United States included in this study.

An attempt at a full analysis of the saving process in the United States during the past half century which was originally scheduled in place of the Introduction had to be abandoned as the derivation of the basic data necessary for such a synthesis proved more difficult and time-consuming than had been anticipated. Consequently, much of the statistical material now included in these three volumes is not fully utilized in the Introduction; the analysis presented, as a rule, stops short of its possibilities; and the body of collateral material on the saving process beyond the data assembled in Volumes I to III has not been drawn upon, material which though not too scarce is as yet generally unorganized and not processed to suit the purposes of an economic study of saving. What is offered in the Introduction is, therefore, far from the comprehensive analysis of the saving process in the United States originally envisaged as the capstone of the Study, and such an analysis remains the goal even though it entirely transcends what is presented in these volumes. I expect to treat some subjects not covered here, particularly some of the institutional aspects of the saving process and of the capital market, in a study of financial institutions now in process as part of a more comprehensive investigation of the demand for capital in the United States by the National Bureau of Economic Research. Others will have to wait for other occasions and other students.

Virtually all previous studies of saving have been limited to the period beginning in 1929 or 1933. Some cover only the last few years. Such relatively short series are quite inadequate for a study of trends or cyclical movements of saving, or for an evaluation of the structural changes in the saving process. They

[2] See "Volume and Components of Saving in the United States, 1933–1937" in *Studies in Income and Wealth*, Volume III, 1939, pp. 217ff.

are of limited value even for the standard econometric analysis of the relations between saving and income. For these purposes it was deemed imperative to go back to the "watershed of the nineties."[3] Extension of the statistics back to 1897 provides an opportunity for studying the quantitative characteristics of saving during periods as different as America's economic coming of age in the two decades before World War I; the New Era of the twenties; the Great Depression; the New Deal; the two World Wars; and the years 1946 to 1949, which may constitute the first part of a longer period of Midcentury Prosperity, or form a short interlude before another epoch of armed conflict or protracted preparation for it. The broader perspective thus made possible was not bought, it is hoped, at too high a price in terms of diversion of the available resources of the Study and the probably larger margin of error in the estimates for the earlier part of the period.

Most previous statistical investigations in this field lack separate figures for the main groups of economic units within the nation, or for more than a few broad forms of saving. This study represents the first attempt to provide estimates for extended periods of time for the saving or dissaving of federal, state, and local governments; and to prepare separate figures for saving of agriculture, unincorporated business enterprises, and nonagricultural households, figures which are usually combined in one total figure for personal saving. The Study also goes considerably beyond its predecessors in supplying estimates on specific forms of saving. It provides, e.g. the first continuous estimates of saving in the form of consumer goods, of saving through common as distinguished from preferred stock, of saving through stocks of smaller corporations not passing through the investment banking machinery, of personal saving in the form of mortgage holdings and of multi-family and commercial buildings, and of saving through private self-administered pension funds.

Whatever material is available—over-all time series as well as sample household budgets, estate tax returns, and probate records—points to great differences in saving habits among different groups of the population, individuals as well as business enterprises, and to differences in the effect of changes in income, and income distribution, interest rates, prices, tax rates, and other economic and non-economic factors on different forms of saving. The danger of overlooking significant aspects of the problem and, worse, of accepting erroneous conclusions is great if we are limited to broad undifferentiated aggregates like total personal saving. Indeed this study may well not have gone as far in this direction as is desirable, though it has moved as far as appeared possible with the limited amount of basic data available for any period except the last few years. All the additional detail provided by this study, both on saver groups and on forms of saving, is, therefore, regarded as worth its cost, even though the margin of error may be larger in many of the separate estimates presented here than in the broader aggregates to which analysis was formerly limited.

The Study also tries to take a step forward in supplementing the estimates of saving with balance sheets for the main saver groups and the nation as a whole

[3] Commager, *The American Mind*, pp. 41–53.

at eight benchmark dates (1900, 1912, 1922, 1929, 1933, 1939, 1945, and 1949). As this is virtually the first attempt in this field these balance sheets hardly can be anything but rough and imperfect. The attempt has nevertheless been made and the results exposed to scrutiny in Volume III because of the conviction that group and national balance sheets constitute an important tool in the analysis of the saving process, and the hope that the estimates presented here will stimulate work in this field and thus render these first attempts obsolete.

Analysis of national income and similar aggregates over the last decade has come to be conducted increasingly within an integrated system of national accounts on both the theoretical and the practical level. This tendency, however, has not been carried through fully in previous estimates of saving. The Study has attempted to adhere as closely as possible to the concepts of a consistent system of national accounts which follows in its essential structure and many of its conventions the principles of modern business accounting.

As a result the estimates of this study differ, to mention only points of substantial quantitative importance, from previous work in basing capital consumption allowances on replacement rather than original cost; in a more consistent elimination of capital gains and losses from saving and dissaving; in the treatment of business expenditures on plant and equipment charged to current expense and of depletion in a manner parallel to the treatment of capitalized expenditures; in the coverage of saving through consumer durable goods; in the inclusion of estimates of cost of turnover of existing assets, such as commissions on individuals' purchases of real estate and securities; in the allowance for changes in individuals' tax liabilities; and in the substitution of business accounting methods for cash flow accounting in the case of revenues and expenditures of federal, state, and local governments.

This stricter and more consistent adherence to a set of principles of national accounting—a set regarded as in accord with both economic theory and modern business accounting standards—has called for a good deal of spadework, and has resulted in many new estimates, often of a kind to which substantial margins of error necessarily attach, or which may occasionally appear strange to readers, even economists, not familiar with social accounting conventions. These difficulties have been regarded as compensated by the greater consistency of the final estimates.

In addition to estimates of total national saving and of saving by the main saver groups and through the main forms of saving which follow the standard social accounting concept which underlies the Study, comparable figures are given, at least for the main totals, on the basis of two chief alternative definitions, business accounting and cash saving. This has been done for two purposes which I regard as important and, I hope, justify the extra effort involved. The first is to enable the reader to observe the actual differences between estimates and to evaluate how much the interpretation of events may be influenced by the choice of concept. A second purpose is to make possible comparison and integration of the new estimates with figures which happen to be compiled on a different basis. This is particularly important because the national income estimates of the Department of Commerce are still essentially on what is designated here as a business accounting basis, and the new and promising money flow estimates of Professor Copeland and the Federal Reserve Board are naturally on a cash basis.[4]

Most of the data from which the estimates in this volume are derived are taken from published sources which are specified in the notes. In a number of cases, however, it was necessary to have recourse to unpublished material. The most important sources of this type are, on the one hand, certain studies which have been circulated in mimeographed form, such as *Corporate Financial Data for Studies in Business Finance* of the National Bureau of Economic Research's Financial Research Project, the revised banking statistics for the period 1896 to 1933 of the Federal Reserve Board, and Friend and Natrella's manuscript *The Volume and Composition of Individuals' Saving* (which the authors kindly made available before its publication);[5] and on the other hand, worksheets of certain federal agencies—particularly the Board of Governors of the Federal Reserve System, the Bureau of Agricultural Economics, the National Income Division of the Department of Commerce, and the Securities and Exchange Commission—and of the National Bureau of Economic Research. Wherever figures have been taken from unpublished sources the fact is indicated in the notes, and the use of the material has been authorized. Any errors in manipulation or interpretation of course are mine. The readiness of these agencies, as well as of several other organizations mentioned at the proper place in the notes, to make these unpublished figures available is gratefully acknowledged.

To facilitate the use of the tables and the tracing of sources, two indexes have been added to the usual subject index which covers the Introduction. The one is an index indicating in which tables of Volume I figures on a given subject—e.g. assets of life insurance companies or saving through commercial banks—may be found. The other index, in the form of a bibliography, permits the reader to ascertain at a glance in which tables use has been made of a given source, whether one of the standard comprehensive statistical publications which are used in dozens of separate tables, or a monograph or other source which has been utilized but once.

In a statistical enterprise utilizing data as varied as that covered by the Saving Study, it is especially important to have the benefit of review by persons who are familiar with the figures used but are not connected with making the estimates. Such a review was provided in the Saving Study in two ways. First, as the estimates of saving were completed in draft form, the tables with notes and explanatory text were sent to members of the Advisory Committee, which included six econo-

---

[4] Copeland, *A Study of Moneyflows in the United States*, 1952.

[5] Now published, with some revisions that could not be utilized in this study, as *Individuals' Saving: Volume and Composition*, by Irwin Friend with the assistance of Vito Natrella, John Wiley and Sons, Inc., New York, 1954.

mists with extensive experience in quantitative economic research. Secondly, copies of these reports were sent to experts, in universities and government agencies, having special knowledge of the subject matter. Each report dealing with one of the most important component series of saving was submitted to at least two experts outside the Advisory Committee—sometimes four to six—while the reports on minor series were sent to at least one outside expert. Not all the experts who received the drafts found it possible to review them. In view of the bulk and complicated nature of the reports, it is gratifying that most of those who received the manuscripts took the trouble to review them and comment on them, sometimes spending a considerable amount of time on this task.

Since the responses to the memoranda varied a good deal, both within and outside the Advisory Committee, the effective scrutiny which different segments of the estimates have received ranges all the way from intensive independent examination by three or four experts to virtually nothing. Broadly speaking, the estimates of saving through bank deposits, life insurance, consumer and producer durable goods, and residential real estate benefited most from review; those of saving through securities, nonresidential real estate, savings and loan associations, and fraternal orders, and of saving by federal, state, and local governments and by unincorporated business enterprises least. It is probably fair to say that improvement resulting from review was roughly proportional to the amount of work previously done in the field, with the unfortunate but not unexpected result that the sectors least known and the estimates subject to the largest margins of error benefited least.

All comments made by the reviewers received careful attention. Whenever comments pointed to errors or inconsistences in underlying figures, methods of estimation, or logic, or indicated sources which had been overlooked, they were taken into account. Where actual data were unavailable to decide on a point, but where an expert's opinion, even if unsupported, was regarded as better than an equally unsupported opinion of the author, the former was generally adopted. The numerous suggestions which did not fall into these categories could not, unfortunately, be handled in the same way. These comments generally either cast doubt as to whether certain estimates, although not subject to refutation by available data, were sufficiently reliable to be used; or suggested alternative approaches without definite promise of more accurate results. In some cases, suggested alternative methods of estimation were explored and, if their results appeared superior, were substituted for the original estimates. To treat all suggestions in this way was impossible as it would have required far more resources than were available, without certainty, or even a high degree of probability, of improving the figures. A number of suggestions called for the collection of additional primary materials, but limitations of time and resources usually ruled out steps in that direction.

Clearly, then, neither the Advisory Committee nor the other experts who have commented on the figures are responsible for the estimates. As the estimates stand after revision they probably often still fail to satisfy the reviewers, and they

xvi

certainly in many cases fail to satisfy me. How serious their shortcomings are, whether they can be remedied, and what the alternatives are to using the estimates in their present form—these questions are discussed in some detail in Volume II, Chapter IV. What may be claimed for the review procedure adopted is that it goes at least as far as, and possibly well beyond, what is customary in studies of this kind; and that the final estimates are in many cases better because of the reviews. Unfortunately, but necessarily, the sins of omission remain. Likewise, the additional testing and alternative estimating suggested by some reviewers were impossible of achievement. Even where the final estimates have not been changed, the doubts or suggestions of the reviewers in many cases have found their way into the notes of Volume I or into Volume II and thus will benefit users.

Conduct of the Study was made possible through generous grants from the Life Insurance Association of America. The Study was sponsored by the Association as a contribution to the common fund of knowledge of the saving process. It is a tribute to the life insurance business that through the Investment Research Committee of the LIAA it recognized the need for a basic study of the saving process. In keeping with this spirit the Association has given me full freedom in conducting the Study. While enjoying it, I have greatly benefited from approximately quarterly meetings for nearly five years with the Advisory Committee consisting of six economists and three officers of life insurance companies. I am much indebted to the members of the Committee listed in Dr. Riefler's Foreword, and to Dr. Ralph A. Young, who served as an alternate member, for the patience with which they have read drafts and redrafts of parts of the manuscript; for the numerous suggestions they have made—some of which I have disregarded probably at my peril; and for the constant interest they have taken in the Study. My debts are particularly heavy to the Committee's Chairman, Dr. Winfield W. Riefler, who became interested in the project when a member of the Institute for Advanced Study at Princeton, and remained with it notwithstanding his arduous duties as Assistant to the Chairman of the Board of Governors of the Federal Reserve System; and to Dr. James J. O'Leary, Director of Investment Research of the Life Insurance Association of America, who acted as the Committee's Secretary. Not the least of their services to the Study is the fact that they lifted it over some rough spots such as are encountered in every research venture of this character and duration. Dr. Riefler's Foreword describes briefly the activities of the Advisory Committee and makes it clear that its members should not be held responsible either for the general plan of the Study or for the content or form of the three volumes which are published.

In any project of the size and complexity of this study the author needs help from two directions: first, from his immediate assistants, who work with him on the preparation of the estimates, and secondly, from experts in the various fields of financial statistics touched intensively or casually by the Study, who contribute information, advice, and criticism.

xvii

Among the first group my greatest debt is to Charlotte Hanley Scott who has been with the Study from beginning to end and has contributed in one way or another to most of it. I am indebted for assistance with one or more sections of Volumes I and II during shorter association with the Study, sometimes in addition to their other duties, to Ruth Aull, Nathan Belfer, Josef Berolzheimer, Carl P. Blackwell, Lawrence Bridge, Lucy Cohen, Joel Darmstadter, Lena J. Fine, Selma F. Goldsmith, Benjamin Handler, Maynard M. Hufschmidt, Theodore Levin, Laura Lokke, Milton A. Margolis, Hyman P. Minsky, Eva L. Mueller, Leonard D. Nierenberg, Bertram E. Rifas, Robert L. Sammons, S. Grant Saunders, David Schwartz, and Harry Shulman. Parts II and III of Volume III, of course, are as indicated the work of Dorothy S. Brady and Horst Mendershausen, to whom I am greatly indebted for their collaboration. A glance at the tables will tell what a task the typing and retyping has been; it has been shouldered, together with a heavy load of other secretarial work, efficiently and without complaint by Elsie Jennings and Adelaide Duvall.

The list of experts who have helped me to a greater or lesser degree in the five years this study has been in progress is too long to be set forth here in full. Apart from the Advisory Committee I want at least to mention the members of the National Income Division of the Department of Commerce, the Statistical Sections of the Securities and Exchange Commission, the Research Division of the Board of Governors of the Federal Reserve System, the Bureau of Agricultural Economics, and the Statistical Section of the Bureau of Internal Revenue, who have answered innumerable enquiries, but, if this need be added, bear no responsibility for any errors that remain in the figures presented here.

I am very grateful, finally, to the staff of Princeton University Press, who have had more than the usual share of problems in getting these volumes through the press. I also am obliged to the Dutch printers for doing a creditable job with what for them must often have been a strange and perplexing manuscript.

Washington, D.C.   RAYMOND W. GOLDSMITH
August 1953

LOCATION OF TABLES IN VOLUMES I, II, AND III

Identifying letter	Subject	Location
A	Agricultural Saving	Volume I, pp. 752–851
B	Supplementary Tables on the Derivation of Annual Estimates of Saving	Throughout Volume II
C	Corporate Saving	Volume I, pp. 912–971
D	Nonfarm Individuals' Non-Real Estate Debt	Volume I, pp. 698–719
E	Wealth of the Estate Tax Population	Volume III, Part III
F	Saving of the Federal Government	Volume I, pp. 972–1043
G	Saving of State and Local Governments	Volume I, pp. 1044–1077
H	Household Saving	Volume III, Part II
I	Saving through Life Insurance and Pension Funds	Volume I, pp. 448–471
J	Individuals' Saving through Savings and Loan Associations	Volume I, pp. 434–447
K	Net Foreign Investment of the United States	Volume I, pp. 1078–1093
L	Nonfarm Individuals' Cash Saving	Volume I, pp. 378–433
M	Nonfarm Individuals' Saving through Mortgages	Volume I, pp. 720–751
N	National and Personal Income	Volume III, Part V
P	Nonfarm Saving through Producer Durable Goods and Inventories	Volume I, pp. 870–911
Q	Nonfarm Saving through Consumer Durable Goods	Volume I, pp. 674–697
R	Nonfarm Saving through Real Estate	Volume I, pp. 582–673
S	Period Averages of Annual Estimates of Saving	Volume I, pp. 259–321
T	National Saving by Major Saver Groups; Personal Saving by Major Components	Volume I, pp. 344–377
U	Saving by Unincorporated Business Enterprises	Volume I, pp. 852–869
V	Individuals' Saving through Securities	Volume I, pp. 472–581
W	National Wealth and Balance Sheet Statements	Volume III, Part I
X	Assets of Private Nonfinancial Nonprofit Institutions	Volume III, Part VI
Y	Econometric Analysis of Relation of Saving and Income	Volume III, Part IV
Z	Supplementary Tables to Introduction	Volume I, pp. 229–258

VOLUME I

CONTENTS

PART I

TABLES IN INTRODUCTION

TABLES IN APPENDIX TO INTRODUCTION

CHARTS

XXX

PART I
INTRODUCTION

I

SUMMARY OF FINDINGS
AND PROBLEMS

1.01. This Introduction is intended as a reader's guide to (a) the annual estimates of saving in the United States from 1897 to 1949 which are presented in Part II of this volume and the derivation of which is described in Volume II, and (b) the special studies of Volume III. It is not a substitute for a comprehensive analysis of the saving process in the United States during the first half of the twentieth century, but represents at best a first step towards that goal. Due to limitations of time and resources after completion of the basic estimates, this Introduction deals only with those aspects of the figures that are deemed of general interest and that do not require the use of elaborate statistical methods of analysis. For the same reasons the treatment is of a summary nature, foregoes detailed documentation with the exception of references to the tables in which the underlying data may be found, and omits many of the qualifications and elaborations sometimes required for a full understanding of the statements made and for placing them in their proper perspective.

1. SCOPE OF CHAPTER

1.02. A country's economic growth is a complicated process which we are far from understanding thoroughly and in detail. Among the circumstances that accompany and condition economic growth hardly one is more striking than the increase, in the aggregate or per head, of the stock of tangible reproducible assets, i.e. structures, equipment, inventories, and net soil improvement. This increase is the result of the use of resources—the services of labor, capital, and land—in the production of durable goods in excess of the wear and tear on the existing stock, instead of their application to the production of currently consumed goods and services.

The process by which current resources are shifted to the creation of reproducible durable tangible assets may be viewed from two sides. We may, first, look at the results of the process, i.e. at the amounts and forms of reproducible tangible assets which are produced or added to the stock. This means measurement or analysis of real capital formation or investment and of national wealth. We may, on the other hand, direct our attention to the contribution of the various economic units which supply the current resources used in the production of reproducible tangible assets, and to the channels through which current resources flow until they emerge as additions to the stock. In that case we are studying saving. Saving

3

is thus the process of financing economic growth insofar as it is reflected as an increase in the stock of reproducible durable tangible assets.

1.03. The crucial characteristics of the saving process, and hence the essential questions to be asked in an investigation of the process, can be summed up in four queries: Who saves; how much; in what forms; and why? These are the four questions around which this chapter is built.

The first question identifies those economic units who provide the resources for an increase in the nation's stock of reproducible assets by withholding part of current income from current consumption. The second question is meant to include the statistical analysis of observable determinants of the volume of saving. The third seemingly deals with the types of assets, tangible or intangible, in savers' balance sheets, in which saving is embodied. Much of its significance, however, stems from the fact that it provides a map of the channels through which saving flows and identifies the ultimate recipients of funds saved. The fourth question concerning the motives of saving—why economic units of different type save as much as and in the particular forms they do—is of a different nature, and is not open to a straightforward statistical answer. Insofar as it involves the psychological aspects of individuals' behavior it is entirely beyond the scope of this study. It is only insofar as saving is rationally motivated that the considerations which enter into its determination are open to economic and statistical investigation, and even then with our present knowledge to only a very limited extent.

2. Main Characteristics of Saving in the United States in the Twentieth Century

1.04. During the past fifty years the volume of national saving in the United States has shown an upward secular trend at a rate of approximately $1\frac{3}{4}$ percent a year if the figures are adjusted for changes in the price level and allowance is made for population growth.[1] This means that real saving per head has doubled every forty years. Aggregate current saving, of course, has increased at a much more rapid rate—approximately 7 percent a year—as the price level has risen throughout most of the last half century, and the population has increased.

1.05. The trend of real national saving per head during the nineteenth century taken as a whole does not seem to have differed much from that of the past fifty years. There is, however, some evidence that the rate of growth of real saving per head was at a peak in the 1870's and 1880's. The growth of aggregate real saving (which is obviously influenced by the rate of population growth) shows a slightly declining trend, if the analysis begins with the last quarter of the nineteenth century. This movement is not peculiar to saving, but reflects a major turning

[1] The figures used throughout this section follow what is being called in this study the standard social accounting concept of saving, i.e. they include saving through consumer durables but exclude saving through military durables; they calculate capital consumption allowances on replacement cost basis; and they exclude all realized and unrealized capital gains and losses.

4

point in American economic history in the 1890's, and more specifically mirrors a change in the long-term rate of growth of real national income.

1.06. Following a deep and extended trough in the 1930's the level of saving after World War II appears to be back on the trend line established during the three decades preceding 1930. There is thus no reason to reject the hypothesis that this trend, which implies a rate of growth of real national saving per head of a little less than 2 percent a year, is still in effect.

1.07. The variability of saving is quite marked, both in absolute terms and in comparison with other basic economic magnitudes. During the last half century one year's national saving has in at least one-half of the cases been 50 percent higher or lower than that of the preceding or the following year. The movements have been even more violent for different saver groups and for particular forms of saving.

This extreme short-term variability of total saving and its components points to two important characteristics. First, saving is a residual in many respects, determined for large groups of savers by the factors which govern the level of their income and consumption more than by independent motives and considerations specifically related to saving. Secondly, there is a high degree of substitutability of one form of saving for another, as evidenced by the much lower variability of a group's total saving than of most of the specific forms of its saving.

1.08. The volume of saving has shown sharp short-term cyclical fluctuations, and the swings have been considerably wider than in most other basic economic series. The turning points correspond well to those in business cycles. As far as can be judged by annual data saving has not shown definite and consistent leads or lags compared with the movements in general business activity.

1.09. In addition to these short-term fluctuations, there is evidence, though it is not yet sufficient for a definite conclusion, of long swings in saving of approximately twenty years' duration but of much smaller amplitude. One of these long cycles, counting from trough to trough, seems to have lasted from the mid-nineties until shortly before World War I. The next cycle extended from then to the mid-1930's. A third long cycle apparently is still in progress, and its upward phase may have terminated about the middle of the century.

3. Who Saves?

1.10. During any given period some households, business enterprises, and governmental units save, i.e. spend less than their current income and thus add to their net assets, while others dissave. In the United States in an average year approximately two out of three households save while one dissaves. This relation is based on observations made during a recent period (1946 to 1950),[2] but there is no reason to assume that the proportions of savers and dissavers were very

---

[2] *Federal Reserve Bulletin*, 1951, p. 1,073. The proportion of savers would be higher if purchases of consumer durables were included. For an analysis of the proportion of dissavers and their characteristics see Garvy, "The Role of Dissaving in Economic Analysis," *Journal of Political Economy*, 1948, pp. 416ff., and Katona, *Psychological Analysis of Economic Behavior*, 1951, Chapters 7 and 8.

different in other prosperous years during the past half century. When times are bad and incomes fall the proportion of dissavers is naturally higher and their number may well exceed that of savers. Most of the dissavers are people with small incomes. However, even among the 10 percent of households at the top of the income pyramid, one out of eight fails to show any net saving.[3]

The net result of a household's saving and dissaving over longer periods is evident in its earned net worth. The fact that at the end of 1949 only one-tenth of all households had no net worth[4] indicates that most households save at some time or other, and that only few households fail to save to an extent sufficient to offset the dissaving to which most of them apparently are subject from time to time.

Most households thus contribute to the process of financing economic growth, but they do so with varying regularity—an aspect of the saving process as yet insufficiently known—and the contribution they make varies greatly in absolute size as well as in relation to their income.

1.11. The situation is similar for other saver groups, though comparable statistics are generally lacking. In years when the economy operates close to capacity the majority of business enterprises and of local governmental units retain part of their current income, i.e. increase their earned net worth. The proportion of units unable to save, however, increases sharply—and probably more than that of households—in periods of recession and depression. The proportion of units with negative earned surplus, indicating cumulative dissaving during the entire period of operation, is considerable among business enterprises. It may be put at approximately one-third for corporations,[5] even in prosperous periods, and is probably even higher for unincorporated business enterprises.[6]

4. The Saving-Income Ratio [7]

1.12. During the entire period covered by this study, i.e. from 1897 through 1949, households—including farms and unincorporated business enterprises—saved on the average a little more than one-eighth of their income. This figure is influenced by the extraordinarily high saving ratios during war periods. If these years, as well as the particularly low ratios of the Great Depression, are excluded the average personal saving ratio for what may be called the "normal" period (1897–1916; 1919–1929; 1934–1941; 1946–1949) amounts to approximately one-ninth. In periods of practically full employment during peacetime (1902, 1905, 1925, 1929, 1948) the ratio has been substantially higher, saving averaging approximately one-seventh of personal income after taxes. These ratios include saving through con-

---

[3] *Federal Reserve Bulletin*, 1950, p. 1,448.

[4] Appendix Table Z-23; also see Volume III, Part I.

[5] Roughly estimated on basis of proportion of surplus and deficit corporations in different size classes as reported in *Statistics of Income* for 1947. After a prolonged depression the proportion of corporations with negative earned surplus probably was well above one-half.

[6] The short life of the average unincorporated business—three to five years—points to a high proportion of firms that dissave rather than save during their entire life.

[7] For details see Chapter III, Section 4.

sumer durables. Without it all ratios are between one-tenth and one-fourth lower. For example, the personal saving ratio excluding consumer durables averages approximately one-twelfth for the normal period.

1.13. The personal saving ratio including consumer durables has failed to show a marked upward or downward trend during the past half century. In particular, the average level of the personal saving ratio has been approximately the same in the four to seven years after World War II as during the twenties and during the two decades before World War I. Although the evidence is much less satisfactory for the nineteenth century the average level of the personal saving ratio from the Civil War to the end of the century does not seem to have differed considerably from the level of the past fifty years.

If consumer durables but not consumer debt are excluded the personal saving ratio probably has undergone a very slow secular decline during the past 50 to 100 years. In particular the ratio is slightly lower after World War II than during the three decades prior to 1930.

1.14. The personal saving ratio has exhibited marked cyclical variations, rising sharply during prosperity and falling steeply during depressions.

The relation of the personal saving ratio to economic fluctuations appears to have been of the same form throughout the period, viz. a change in the personal saving ratio by slightly less than one percentage point for a change of one point in the ratio of actual employment to normal labor force, a ratio which may be regarded as a rough indicator of the distance of the economy from full employment of resources. This relation implies that aggregate personal saving disappears when the unemployment ratio approaches one-fifth.

1.15. The over-all personal saving ratio is the resultant of very different ratios of the various groups of households. Probably the most pronounced and at the same time the most significant of these differences is the higher saving ratio associated at a given time or place with higher income. For all dates for which observations are available the average saving ratio for households shows a marked and uninterrupted increase with income before and after taxes. There remain, however, substantial differences at a given date in the saving ratio among households of the same income level. They reflect, in addition to random variations among households, differences in the saving ratios of households which vary with the occupation or age of the head of the household, the household's location and race, and its net worth and liquid assets.

1.16. The saving ratio of corporations (e.g. the proportion of income after taxes not distributed as dividends) averaged slightly over 30 percent for the three decades 1897 to 1929, and during this period showed a slight tendency to decline. The ratio was negative during the thirties, but averaged nearly 40 percent during the forties, and was at least as high after World War II as in prosperous years prior to 1930.[8] Whether a definite trend in the corporate saving

[8] These ratios are lower for most of the period than those derived from published corporate reports because in social accounting calculations corporate profits exclude inventory gains and losses and capital consumption allowances are based on replacement rather than original cost.

ratio has existed during the past half century is in doubt. The ratio has, however, varied sharply with the business cycle throughout the period, and hence with total net income of all corporations, or major groups of them.

1.17. Differences in the saving ratio among corporations are pronounced, but they are not primarily connected with the level of income of an individual corporation, as is the case with households, but rather with the industry to which the corporation belongs, and with factors peculiar to the individual enterprise. In particular, saving ratios have been considerably lower for railroad, public utility, and financial corporations than for corporations engaged in manufacturing, mining, and trade.

1.18. The saving ratio of state and local governments, i.e. the excess of their current income above their current expenditures divided by their income, has been substantial, averaging approximately 10 percent for the period as a whole (20 percent for state and 5 percent for local governments). While the saving ratio of state governments increased sharply from the turn of the century to the twenties and remained at a fairly high level through World War II, the ratio has been more erratic and has tended generally downwards for local governments. After World War II the combined saving ratio of state and local governments averaged not much over 5 percent compared with nearly 20 percent in the 1920's and approximately 10 percent in the first decade of the century.

1.19. The federal government is the only sector of the economy which shows net dissaving for the period as a whole, dissaving which primarily reflects the very large deficits of World War II. If we consider the periods when the ratio was predominantly positive, it reached a peak of approximately 25 percent during the twenties, but averaged between 5 and 10 percent for the two decades prior to World War I and for the period since World War II.

1.20. The national saving ratio has differed but little from the personal saving ratio during the normal period, when personal saving has accounted for approximately three-fourths of national saving. For this period national saving has averaged approximately one-eighth of net national product. The two ratios, however, have diverged widely during the wars, particularly World War II, when the large dissaving of the federal government reduced the national saving ratio to almost zero while the personal saving ratio was at a peak of approximately one-fourth. As a result the national saving ratio of 9 percent for the entire period is considerably below the personal saving ratio of 13 percent. [9]

5. Distribution of National and Personal Saving [10]

1.21. The distribution of national saving among the main saver groups shows little secular trend. Before 1930—excluding the war years 1917–1918—personal

[9] This difference is due mainly to the fact that the dissaving of the federal government is concentrated in the later part of the period, when all absolute figures are large. On the basis of unweighted averages of annual ratios both national and personal ratios are very close to 10 percent.

[10] For details see Chapter v.

8

saving, including agriculture and unincorporated business enterprises, accounted for approximately 70 percent of national saving, corporate saving for nearly 20 percent, and government saving for the remaining 10 percent. Approximately the same distribution reappeared after World War II.

If saving through social security and other governmental trust funds is transferred from personal saving, where it belongs if classification is determined by ultimate beneficiaries, to government saving because of the argument that it is compulsory and under the government's control, then the share of government in national saving shows a marked increase from only 1 percent in the first decade of the century to 8 percent in the 1920's and to as much as 16 percent from 1946 to 1949.

1.22. Since national saving is the sum of the saving of all saver groups it is considerably below personal or private saving in periods when the federal government's current expenditures are far in excess of its income, as is the case during wars. Actually the federal government's dissaving was so large, particularly during World War II, that for the full period 1897–1949 it offsets three-fifths of the saving of all other groups. Hence private saving and personal saving are approximately 50 and 30 percent, respectively, in excess of national saving for the entire period.

1.23. By far the largest part of personal saving is attributable to nonfarm households. For the period as a whole, farmers and unincorporated business enterprises together account for less than one-sixth of personal saving. [11]

1.24. All indications point to a marked concentration of personal saving. In recent periods more than four-fifths of current personal saving has been contributed by the tenth of households having the highest income in the year in question. [12] It is, therefore, unlikely that the share of upper income groups in total personal saving has shown a marked or continuous downward trend since the turn of the century, even though a movement in this direction is indicated between the 1920's and 1940's.

There is reason to believe that the degree of concentration is less pronounced if based on aggregate net saving of the same household for periods longer than one year. This surmise is supported by the lesser degree of concentration of net worth, a magnitude which is the result of cumulated saving or dissaving, net realized capital gains and losses, and net inheritances, gifts, and bequests. At the end of 1949 the 10 percent of households with the highest income in that year accounted for almost all of personal net saving but for only approximately two-fifths of total net worth of all households. [13] Even the 10 percent of households with highest net worth held only a little more than one-half of aggregate net worth. The proportion may, moreover, be lower if based on earned net worth alone.

[11] The saving estimates on which these ratios are based include both household and business saving of farmers, but only that part of saving of unincorporated business which is reflected in changes in business assets and liabilities, excluding all other forms of saving of proprietors.

[12] Appendix Table Z-24. The figures exclude all consumer durables from current saving, and exclude consumer durables other than automobiles from net worth.

[13] See note 12.

6. Composition of Personal Saving [14]

1.25. For the entire period and for all households together, including agriculture and unincorporated business, the increase in liabilities has amounted to only one-sixth of the increase in assets (excluding valuation changes).

Real estate has accounted for one-tenth of the total increase in assets, and other tangible assets, mostly consumer durables, for almost one-seventh. Among intangible assets—which in the aggregate represent three-fourths of personal saving before offsetting liabilities—the most important outlets for saving have been commercial bank deposits (15 percent of total increase in assets), U.S. Government securities (12 percent), life insurance reserves (11 percent), corporate stock (9 percent), equity in government trust funds (7 percent), savings bank deposits ($4\frac{1}{2}$ percent), currency (4 percent), mortgages (3 percent), corporate bonds (3 percent), savings and loan and other deposits (3 percent), state and local government securities ($1\frac{1}{2}$ percent), and private pension fund reserves (1 percent).

1.26. Changes in the distribution of personal saving among forms of saving, except for the two wars and the Great Depression, are characterized by a considerable increase in the share of saving through consumer durables, life insurance, and pension and retirement funds, and by a decline in the share of saving through corporate stocks and bonds, mortgages, and real estate. The share of saving in the form of deposits with financial institutions has not shown pronounced long-term changes, but has exhibited some tendency to decline since World War I. The distribution of personal saving during war periods is quite different and is marked by a high share of saving through U.S. Government securities and commercial bank deposits and a low share of saving through real estate and consumer durables.

If we focus attention on economic types of saving rather than on individual forms, we find that the shares of relatively illiquid forms of saving, of contractual saving, and of saving through financial intermediaries, which include government and private pension and retirement funds, have shown an increasing trend. Saving transferred directly from savers to ultimate users of funds, primarily in the form of purchases of securities and mortgages, on the other hand, has shown a tendency te decline in relative importance. The share of saving to be used in the saver's own household or business has not changed significantly.

1.27. Only a small part of domestic saving has been invested abroad. During the past half century slightly more than 5 percent of national saving was made available to foreigners. In addition the equivalent of another 5 percent of national saving was used to increase the country's gold stock by importation of metal from abroad. On the other hand capital imports have added not much over 2 percent to the national supply of saving. Thus net capital exports (including acquisition of gold) has been equal to approximately one-tenth of national saving. Most of the net capital exports have been attributable to the federal government in the form of additions to its gold stock or of loans to foreign governments and international

[14] For details see Chapter VI.

financial institutions. [15] Private capital exports have been very small. For the period as a whole they have amounted to only 2 percent (net), to 3 percent (gross), of private domestic net saving. They were of substantial importance, on a net basis, only for 1915-1921, when they accounted for nearly 10 percent of private saving, and for 1922-1929, when their share was 6 percent. From the Great Depression to the end of World War II there was even a net capital import balance on private account which was substantial in comparison to private saving during the latter half of the thirties.

7. SAVING AND WEALTH CHANGES [16]

1.28. Saving has been responsible for only a little more than one-half of the $800 billion increase in the current value of national wealth from 1897 to 1949, while the other half has reflected net capital appreciation. The share of saving in changes in national wealth was highest in the 1920's and lowest—below one-fifth—from the Great Depression to the end of World War II.

The share also differs considerably among saver groups. More than three-fifths of the increase in the net worth (at current asset values) of nonfarm households during the past half century, but not much more than one-third of that of agriculture, is attributable to cumulated saving. The share is low—less than one-third—for corporations, but high for federal, state, and local governments.

These differences in the share of saving in net worth changes are primarily due to differences in the movements of asset prices, in the proportion of price-sensitive assets (tangibles and equity securities), and in the debt-asset ratio. Saver groups with high ratios of price-sensitive assets and of debt, such as business enterprises, are bound to show a lower share of saving in net worth changes during a period of generally rising prices, as in the past half century, than groups with lower debt ratios and a higher proportion of price-insensitive assets (claims), such as nonfarm households.

8. THE STATISTICAL DETERMINANTS OF SAVING [17]

1.29. After these brief answers to two of the four basic questions—Who saves? and In what form?—and to some simple aspects of the third question—How much?—we turn to the statistical measurement of the determinants of saving. This econometric approach centers on the saving function, i.e. an algebraic relationship of reasonable regularity and closeness between volume or composition of saving (of an economic unit, of groups of units, and finally of the entire nation), regarded as the independent variable, and measurable characteristics of the savers or of their environment (e.g. income, occupation or age of savers, or employment,

[15] Loans to allied governments during and immediately after World War I have been treated as contributions rather than as capital exports and therefore are not included in saving.

[16] For details see Chapters V and VIII.

[17] For details see Parts II and IV of Volume III.

11

prices or interest rates), which are treated as independent or explanatory variables. Attention may be directed to the relation prevailing during one and the same period of time between saving of a number of economic units, each taken individually, and the explanatory variables applicable to them. Alternatively it may be centered on the relation of saving of a group of units, e.g. total personal and national saving, and the explanatory variables for a number of successive or separate periods, usually of annual length. In the first case we are looking for a cross-section saving function, which is derived from data for a small number of sample units; in the second we are interested in a historical saving function, obtained from statistical time series of saving and explanatory variables. Since this study is concerned mainly with annual estimates of saving for the period 1897–1949, discussion in general is limited to historical saving functions for the past half century.

1.30. Although the econometric analysis of the new estimates of national and personal saving has as yet been very limited and although the results must be regarded as quite preliminary and tentative, they appear to justify the following conclusions and suggestions, which are based mainly on what may be called the elementary saving function, i.e. the expression: $S = a\,(Y - b)$, where S is saving, Y is income, and a and b are constants, a indicating the marginal propensity to save, i.e. the average change in saving per unit change in income, and b the zero saving point: [18]

(a) Changes in current income are the most important single determinant of variations in current national and personal saving. This is but a confirmation of the results obtained from previous analyses of time series or cross-section data of saving. Variations in current income alone account for more than two-thirds of the year-to-year changes in current personal saving for the entire period 1897–1949, and a similar proportion of the changes in national saving if the war years 1917–1918 and 1942–1945 are excluded.

(b) The proportion of variations in saving accounted for statistically by income is smaller if the calculations are based on deflated or per head values rather than if current aggregate values of both saving and income are used.

(c) The proportion of variations in saving accounted for by changes in income alone is higher from 1929 to 1941 than for the three preceding decades, and appears to decline as we go back to the turn of the century. [19] (This, however, may be due to deterioration of the quality of the estimates.) The movement is more marked for personal than for national saving.

(d) There has been a pronounced and continuous shift to the right in the saving function, i.e. at the same absolute level of either personal disposable income or national income, saving has been progressively smaller as we move forward in time. [20] This is true not only for aggregate current values of saving and income,

[18] For details see Volume III, Part IV.

[19] Not enough time has elapsed since World War II to determine the relation for a more recent period.

[20] This and the following three paragraphs are taken from "Trends and Structural Changes in Saving in the Twentieth Century," *Savings in the Modern Economy*, 1953, pp. 144–145.

CHART I

RELATIONSHIP BETWEEN PERSONAL SAVING AND PERSONAL DISPOSABLE INCOME: 1897 to 1952

Standard Social Accounting Concept; 1929 Values per Head

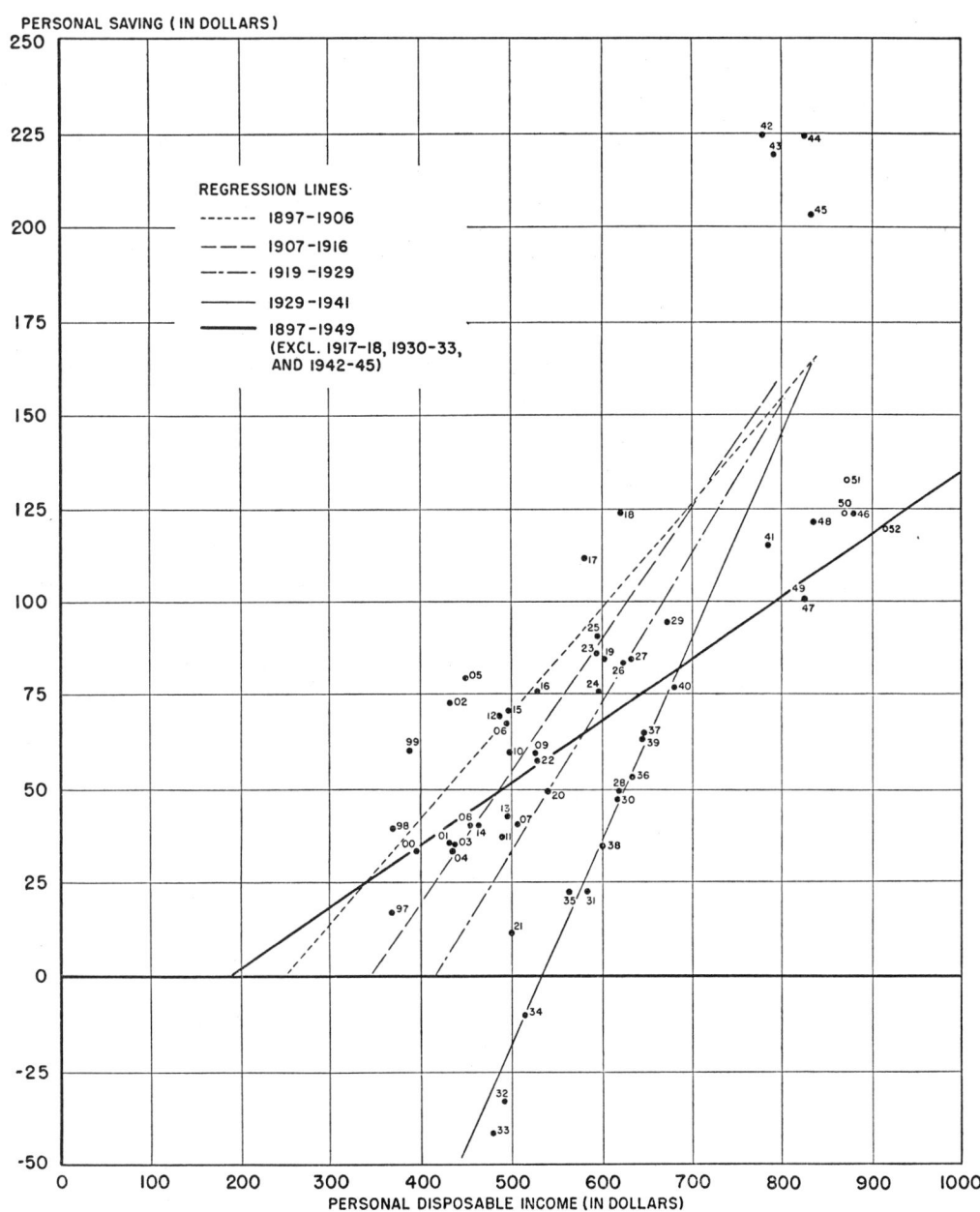

but also for deflated aggregate or per head values, which are used in Chart I. This shift involves an increase over time of the break-even point of saving, i.e. the level of income at which aggregate national or personal saving is zero. It means that the average household must have an ever-increasing nominal or real disposable income per head before it does any saving; or, to put it differently, that an increasing level of real consumption has been necessary throughout the past half century to elicit the same proportion of saving. [21]

While the fact of this shift to the right of the saving function is scarcely open to doubt, the question remains whether the process has been continuous, involving a shift of the curve by approximately equal distances in every year; or whether, as seems more likely, it must be regarded as proceeding by jumps at points of time when a break in economic structure occurs, e.g. after World War I, after the Great Depression, and after World War II. If due allowance is made for this shift in the elementary saving function by the introduction of time as an independent variable, the function statistically accounts for almost seven-eighths of the observed variations in deflated personal saving per head for the entire period 1897–1949.

(e) The slope of the personal saving function, which indicates the marginal propensity to save, i.e. the proportion of an increase in income that is saved, was considerably higher during the thirties than for any of the three preceding decades.

(f) As a result of the shift to the right and the variations in slope of the saving function, a misleading picture is obtained if we secure the long-term saving function from the period 1897–1949 as a whole without making allowance for the shift, or if we derive it from sections such as the years 1929 to 1941. Use of the marginal propensity implied in the saving function for the past fifty-year period as a whole leads to a substantial understatement of the marginal propensity for practically every subperiod of the past, and may be assumed also to lead to an understatement if applied to the future. The explanation is that the saving function for the entire period is a combination of a family of functions for subperiods with increasing break-even points.

(g) If a simple long-term saving function is sought that fits the last fifty years and that may be expected to continue in force in the future, the dependent variable should in all probability be cast in the form of a saving-income ratio. From an inspection of the distribution of the actual ratios for the period 1897–1949 it appears that the formula for a long-term function for the saving ratio should contain at least two components, the first a constant and the second a cyclical factor depending on something like the ratio of actual to full employment income. The

[21] If the estimates for the seven years following World War II, particularly the very preliminary figures for 1950 to 1952 obtained by somewhat simplified procedures, could be treated as the basis for a postwar regression line, it would be less steep than that for any of the four preceding periods illustrated in Chart I. Indeed, if the regression included the preliminary estimates for 1952 (but not if limited to 1946–1951) the zero-saving point would lie only slightly to the right of that for the decade 1907 to 1916 and to the left of those for 1919 to 1929 and 1929 to 1941, thus interrupting its previously regular rightward shift. It may, however, be the better part of valor to wait for final estimates for a few more years before committing oneself about the slope and location of the elementary saving function after World War II.

14

exact form of the cyclical component will require careful study since it is evident that the cyclical variations of the saving ratio around its long-term average are very substantial.

(h) In addition to changes in current income and the shift in the break-even point which have determined year-to-year variations in personal and national saving, attention has been given to the following as independent variables in the saving function: previous peak income or consumption, holdings of liquid assets, and the ratio between actual employment and the normal labor force, a ratio which may be used as an indicator of the distance of the economy from full employment of resources. Numerous other explanatory variables suggested by economic theory or by the statistical material at hand might have been examined and subjected to experiment if resources had been available.

Each of the three factors listed was found to have some influence on those variations in saving that are not statistically attributable to changes in current income. This influence is relatively small for the entire period, but is of greater importance for subperiods. Analysis has not progressed sufficiently far to enable us to assess the differential influence of each of the three—and of other—factors on variations in saving during different periods.

1.31. Similar econometric analysis directed towards the discovery of saving functions of stable character is required, and is made possible by the new estimates for saving of major saver groups—particularly nonfarm households, agriculture, and corporations—as well as for the major forms of personal saving. There has been no opportunity as yet to undertake the comprehensive calculations that would be required for such an analysis on a systematic scale. Scattered experimentation, however, suggests that the determinants of saving, and hence the form of the saving functions as well as the explanatory variables included, differ considerably among saver groups and among forms of saving.

1.32. The econometric analysis of time series and cross-section data on saving lead to an apparent contradiction between the increase in the saving ratio with income found in all cross-section studies and the absence of a similar relation—an increasing trend in the national saving ratio as national income rose over the past fifty years—in time series. What seems to be the most satisfactory theory, or at least one of the most promising, resolves this difficulty by assuming that a household's saving ratio is determined primarily not by the household's absolute level of income but by its relative position in the national income pyramid. [22] The theory is based on the hypothesis that consumption standards are a group phenomenon, and that the level of consumption of an individual family depends on its economic position within the group. Savings are accumulated by families that happen to enjoy a current income more than sufficient to finance the customary manner of living in their environment—if customary expenditures are understood to include some that must be regarded in part as saving from the national point of view, viz. life insurance premiums, social security contributions, home mortgage

[22] For formulation of the theory, due largely to Professor Brady, and statistical evidence see Volume III, Part II.

amortization, and acquisition of consumer durables. The amount of saving done by an individual family in a given year is thus almost a random variable, but the number of families is large enough to make the average excess of income over customary expenditures a fairly stable proportion of income when average income changes but little.

To harmonize the theory with the facts it is further necessary to assume that the customary manner of living of a group is determined by its average income during a period of years; more specifically, that as a rule the "typical" family in any environment tends to spend the entire income common to that environment. If this is so, and both observation and statistics tend to corroborate the hypothesis, consumption in the long run will increase in step with income. There is, in particular, no reason why the percentage difference between the customary standard of consumption and the average income should widen, i.e. why the saving-income ratio should rise as income increases. There is likewise no reason to expect a change in the saving ratio in the future so long as the basic social structure and the basic mass psychological attitudes implied in the theory persist. What the theory fails to explain is why the long-term level of the personal saving ratio has been of the order of one-eighth to one-tenth. Considerations of length of working life and retirement, of the relation between working and retirement income, and of yield rates help to account for this level, but only in very broad terms, and they do not fully explain the degree of stability during the past half century.

9. Saving Motives

1.33. Volume and composition of saving of individual households, business enterprises, and governments, and hence personal and national saving, are influenced consciously and unconsciously by motives very different in kind. Their identification and analysis is a matter for individual and mass psychology. In this section only a narrow group of motives can be discussed, however briefly, viz. the motives that are connected rationally with definite objectives of the saver. It must always be borne in mind that such rational considerations actually are applied by only a portion of savers, probably even by a minority.

The rational motives of saving are basically of three types: (a) acquisition of certain durable tangible assets to be used in saver's household; (b) provision for certain future expenditures; and in cases where saver is, or intends to become, an independent businessman, farmer, or professional, (c) provision of an equity fund necessary to establish and maintain him in business. Objective (b) may in turn be particularized under the headings of (i) funeral and related expenses—even in twentieth century America still one of the few contingencies for which most people of small means make conscious provision, (ii) maintenance of saver and dependents after retirement, (iii) estate of surviving spouse, children, and other dependents, (iv) specific anticipated expenditures of substantial size compared to current income, e.g. children's education, and (v) establishment of a reserve for undesignated contingencies, that is, a "rainy day."

16

1.34. All these requirements are determined partly by objective factors; partly, like current consumption, by group standards; and partly by idiosyncrasies which have to be ignored here. Among the objective factors which may be presumed to have the greatest influence on rational requirements for saving are length of working life and retirement (so far as they lie outside the saver's individual decision), yields obtainable on different forms of saving, level of income, movements of cost of living, availability of insurance against certain contingencies such as death or invalidism, cost of education and medical care, and minimum equity required for starting in a business or profession. Saving requirements determined or at least strongly influenced by group standards include, to mention only important ones, the desired relation of average real income during retirement and working life, the types and qualities of durable consumer goods regarded as part of the group standard of living, the value put upon home ownership, and—in the long run possibly of greatest influence—the relative attraction of hired employment and entrepreneurial status.

1.35. The mere enumeration of the main factors which influence rational saving requirements indicates the complexity of the problem. Difficulties multiply when an effort is made to quantify these factors and to combine them in a formula which measures rational saving requirements. But even without taking such an ambitious approach it is evident that the required saving ratio (i.e. the ratio between required saving and income averaged for the saver's working life) will move in the same direction as the following factors, and will be the higher or lower the larger or smaller they are: (a) ratio of desired retirement income to average working life income, (b) ratio to average income of estate desired to be left to dependents at saver's death, (c) outlay for consumer durables required by custom, expressed as multiple of average income, and (d) length of retirement life. The required saving ratio, on the other hand, is inversely related to two important factors, i.e. it rises as they decline and falls as they increase: (e) yield on different forms of saving and (f) length of working life.

1.36. During the fifty years since the turn of the century the length of the retirement period has shown a rising trend, reflecting earlier retirement as well as increased longevity; length of working life seems to have declined slightly for people living until retirement age; the cost of the customary complement of consumer durables has increased considerably in proportion to average income, chiefly as a result of the advent of the automobile; and the proportion of desired retirement income to average working life income has probably risen—all four factors calling for a rise in the required saving ratio. The downward movement of yields has worked in the same direction. The only factor that may have contributed to a reduction in the required ratio is a decline in desired estate (in relation to average income), a movement about which not much can be said with confidence, but which certainly cannot have been sufficient to counteract the factors which tend in the opposite direction.

Thus, the conclusions—based in part on factors and quantitative considerations not specifically set forth—apparently must be that the required personal saving ratio has shown a tendency to increase during the last fifty years, and that the increase may have been substantial. These conclusions are borne out by the figures as far as saving through tangible assets used in consumer's household are concerned. [23] Saving through intangible assets, however, which is designed to meet requirements of type (b) of Division 1.33 and which one would expect to have increased in relation to income, actually shows a decline, which is substantial if compulsory saving is excluded. [24] This discrepancy may be explained by two developments. The first is entirely rational from the individual saver's point of view: The more specific contingencies are either covered by insurance [25] or without direct cost to the saver by public bodies, the smaller the requirements for which the individual must provide by saving. The spread of private life insurance, private pension plans, federal old age insurance, federal and private sickness and invalid benefits, and governmental unemployment benefits all have tended to reduce the individual household's rational saving requirements. The second development, which must be surmised and cannot be documented, is less rational and less unequivocal—a feeling that the contingencies for which no explicit provision is made through insurance or public assistance and for which rationally specific provision would have to be made by saving will somehow be taken care of by public bodies, even though—and this is a consideration working in the opposite direction—much less reliance can now be placed in such contingencies on support from children, relatives, neighbors, or friends.

1.37. The combination of objective factors and shifts in mass psychology thus appears to have led to four important changes in the motives behind personal saving: increased emphasis on saving in the form of durable tangible assets used in saver's household, i.e. home and consumer durables; [26] reduced stress on individual

[23] Saving through consumer durables (disregarding consumer debt) has increased from $1\frac{1}{2}$ percent of disposable income around the turn of the century to $2\frac{1}{2}$ percent in the twenties and over $4\frac{1}{2}$ percent after World War II. For all durable tangible assets the rise is from less than $5\frac{1}{2}$ to 8 to 9 percent (Table S-50). The increase in the proportion of families living in owned homes (from 37 percent in 1900 to 46 percent in 1930 and 54 percent in 1950) is another indication of this tendency (Table R-36 and *Federal Reserve Bulletin*, 1951, p. 771).

[24] The ratio of saving through intangibles to disposable income on a gross basis moved from 9 percent in the first decade of the century, to 10 percent in the twenties, and back to 9 percent from 1946 to 1949. A decline is apparent on a net basis, i.e. after deducting increases in debt, viz. from $5\frac{1}{2}$ to $4\frac{1}{2}$ percent in the twenties and after World War II. It is still more pronounced if compulsory saving (government trust and independent pension funds) are excluded. In that case the decline is from $5\frac{1}{2}$ to $4\frac{1}{2}$ to 2 percent of disposable income.

[25] Insurance drastically reduces saving rationally required from every individual—or more correctly makes irrational oversaving unnecessary—because he now needs to cover only the average and no longer the maximum contingency, e.g. he needs to save only enough to provide for maintenance from retirement until actuarial date of death—say, at 75 years—instead of having to provide for maintenance until latest possible date of death, at approximately 100 years.

[26] This applies not only to people of small means but also to executives, as attested by the results of Professor Sanders' interviews (Sanders, *Effects of Taxation on Executives*, 1951, pp. 190–192): "The cost of buying and financing a suitable home has come to represent a substantial part of an executive's total saving for a considerable period of time" and "...these family necessities (ownership of house, insurance, retirement pay, ready liquid reserve) are not regarded as investment, and in the thinking of many executives investment begins only after these things have been attended to."

18

provision for old age in favor of collective arrangements; considerably less accent on leaving a substantial estate—a possibility at any time and in any country open only to a minority of the nonagricultural population; [27] and the necessity of providing within a shorter working life for a substantially longer period of retirement. [28]

10. Saving Plans and Their Realization

1.38. There is no opportunity here (or elsewhere in this Introduction) of discussing in appropriate detail the economic implications of the facts summarized in Divisions 1.03 to 1.37, particularly their bearing on the process of economic growth in the United States.

It seems necessary, however, even if we limit ourselves to brief answers to the four basic questions of who saves, how much, in what forms, and why, to deal summarily with two problems of general and chiefly theoretical character, but of substantial importance for every analysis of statistics of saving, viz. the relation of observed actual saving to saving plans and decisions, and the primacy of saving or investment.

1.39. Any analysis of estimates of saving of the type on which this study is based must distinguish between planned and realized saving. All available data refer to the results of the saving process as observed when the process is completed. They show, more specifically, which economic units increased their holdings of a particular asset or liability during a given year, disregarding changes in holdings which reflect valuation changes rather than acquisitions or dispositions of assets. Not all of these changes can be termed "planned," either in the strict sense that they were provided for in a deliberate and articulated schedule of income and expenditures made before the beginning of the year or even in the more restricted sense that they were made consciously at the time they occurred. [29] Realized, or observed, saving thus does not permit direct and unequivocal inferences regarding planned or spontaneous saving, i.e. regarding the character of saving decisions.

[27] See Commager, *The American Mind*, 1950, p. 423: "And though thrift was no longer cultivated for moral reasons, insurance and banking statistics showed that Americans continued to provide, as best they could, for the future. If there was a change here from the nineteenth to the twentieth century, it was in the future that was envisioned: where an earlier generation had saved in order to leave an estate, the new generation was inclined to save for more immediate and personal purposes—an automobile, vacations, education, or retirement."

[28] It is easy to overlook how potent this force is. At the beginning of this century the average man (white) had to provide actuarially for only about 3 years of retirement out of saving that could be spread over a working life of 39 years. Recently (1940) 42 working years must provide for 6 years of retirement. In other words, the number of years of retirement to be provided for by saving during each year of working life has approximately doubled (see Spengler, *Journal of Finance*, Volume VII, 1951, p. 20).

[29] Both planned and unplanned changes in assets and liabilities may, of course, be compulsory (contributions to social security and pension funds are examples), contractual (e.g. life insurance premium payments or debt repayment), or entirely spontaneous, i.e. entered into or refrained from without a directly connected economic penalty.

1.40. The possible discrepancies between planned and realized saving (between expected and actual results of saving decisions) would be of no great importance from the point of view of the nation if they were random, i.e. if the discrepancies, while occurring in the case of many individual households or other economic units, were of a nonsystematic nature and thus had a tendency to cancel out for larger groups of units. Many of the discrepancies between planned and actual saving undoubtedly are of this character. For many units the problem will not arise at all, because they do not have specific saving plans, and saving is simply the undesignated residual between actual income and customary expenditures. Nevertheless, there are cases, and for large groups of savers, in which actual saving differs significantly from what savers had intended it to be. Such cases are essentially limited to periods when current income or taxes change sharply and unexpectedly, or when current expenditures are increased or reduced unexpectedly to a marked extent by *force majeure*. Practically speaking, planned and realized saving will differ significantly during periods of sharp inflation and deflation; and the discrepancy will be most pronounced during wars, when income is affected simultaneously by unexpected increases in nominal receipts and by limitations on expenditures in many directions imposed by government.

Sharp rises in nominal or real income are almost always accompanied—and indeed partly caused—by large increases in the volume of liquid assets, particularly bank deposits, increases that must, of course, appear as components of saving for some of the economic units. These increases occur, without being planned or even desired by any group of savers, simply as the result of lending operations of the banking system and the Treasury. Sharp declines in income have similar effects in the opposite direction. Individual savers, or even groups of savers, cannot easily undo these additions to or reductions in liquid assets, though their reactions may offset them in part or may aggravate them, and may influence saving and dissaving in other forms. The often very involved chains of actions and reactions form a major subject of monetary theory and are much too complicated to be discussed here. All that is required is the realization that at times a considerable part of saving or dissaving is unplanned and may thus be regarded as involuntary from the point of view of the community of savers though not of an individual, who remains in a position to decide whether to spend or to save.

1.41. If the volume and distribution of saving were uniquely determined by the volume and distribution of investment there would be no point in inquiring into the determinants of saving or in tracing the effects of structural changes in saving. All explanations and interpretations would then have to be expressed in terms of investment and the factors that influence it.

For any economy—though, of course, not for every economic unit or every group—a period's actual saving is numerically equal to its investment. The question, however, is whether it is investment that determines saving; or whether it is saving that determines investment; or whether both are simultaneously determined by other factors. The answer to this question, unfortunately, is not subject to direct empirical proof, but depends essentially on the assumptions

20

made regarding the form and stability of certain relations in the economic system, particularly the reactions of individual economic units regarding their saving and investment to changes in certain economic variables. Up to the last generation the theory that the volume of national investment depends upon national saving was hardly challenged. Under the influence of Lord Keynes the opposite view that it is national investment that determines both national income and national saving has gained ascendancy among theoretical economists, possibly only for a time.[30] As so often, the truth seems to lie between the two extreme positions. The relations among saving, investment, and income are so intricate and many-sided that it is impossible to regard the one as the cause and the other as the effect; and, what is equally important, the relations depend on the length of the period taken into account. The subject is altogether too complex to be adequately discussed here. Suffice it to say that the more rigid, regular, and complete the reaction of individual units' saving to changes in their income, the more reason there is to regard saving as dependent on investment; and that the looser, slower, and more variable the reaction the more reason to look upon saving as the determinant of investment. This statement is based on the assumption, which is not yet proven, that changes in income are determined primarily by autonomous variations in investment expenditures. The more we doubt that assumption, the less the reason to accept the theory of the causal primacy of investment in relation to saving.

1.42. The question of the primacy of investment or of saving thus brings us back to the problem of the existence and character of a stable saving function for the nation and for significant groups of economic units. The time is certainly not ripe for a confident answer. The possibility cannot be ruled out that further analysis may yield formulas for the saving function of the nation and for major components in which saving as the dependent variable is so closely determined, or statistically speaking so completely explained, by income and possibly by a few other independent variables that theoretical and observed values of saving for any year, or shorter period, differ only randomly by insignificant amounts, and that the differences are small and random not only in years of wide swings in income but also in periods of mild changes, and not only for the period to which the function is fitted but also for years before the period starts and after it ends. Thus far, however, such functions have not been found. The variations in observed saving from calculated values are still so large, particularly if long periods are considered, that considerable doubt is cast on the primacy of investment or the purely passive, self-adaptive nature of saving postulated or implied by that point of view. The doubts concerning the stability of the saving function, particularly in the short run, which are suggested by an analysis of time series of saving are reinforced by the investigations into the behavior of samples of households. These investigations seem to have led to the conclusion that there is a considerable degree of autonomy, i.e. of independence from close adaptation to changes in in-

[30] For a review of the literature see, e.g., Mack, "Economics of Consumption," in *A Survey of Contemporary Economics*, Volume II, 1952.

come or other economic variables, in saving decisions and in actual saving, not only for individual households, but also for all households taken together.

11. Recapitulation

1.43. The main enduring characteristics and the chief structural changes of saving in the United States during the past half century (disregarding distortions during wars) may be restated with the utmost brevity and not without unavoidable oversimplification as follows:

(a) Long-term stability of aggregate personal saving at approximately one-eighth of income, and of national saving at approximately one-seventh;

(b) Sharp year-to-year variations in total saving which correspond in timing fairly closely to the business cycle, variations that depend primarily on changes in income;

(c) Considerable insensitivity of saving to gradual but prolonged declines in the purchasing power of money, i.e. existence of a "money illusion," which means that so long as inflation is kept in bounds saving is determined to a considerable extent by the level of and change in nominal incomes, prices, and other magnitudes rather than the level of and change in their real (stable price) equivalents;

(d) Stability in the division of private saving between individuals and business enterprises in the ratio of approximately four to one;

(e) Increase since the 1930's in the proportion of saving by government, particularly if additions to the assets of social security and similar funds are regarded as government saving;

(f) Pronounced concentration of personal saving (i.e. the proportion supplied by the relatively small number of individuals of large income and wealth), although this concentration has decreased at least since the 1920's and probably throughout the period;

(g) Increase in the proportion of individuals' saving which is embodied in durable tangible assets used in the saver's own household;

(h) Increase in the proportion of individuals' saving of contractual or compulsory nature, or entrusted to financial institutions;

(i) Sharp decrease in the proportion of individuals' saving transferred directly from savers to borrowers for ultimate investment in structures, equipment, and inventories, particularly saving made available to nonfinancial corporations in the form of bonds and stocks;

(j) Continued small proportion of private saving that is transferred abroad.

II

SCOPE, METHODS, AND ARRANGEMENT OF SAVING STUDY [1]

1. Basic Relationships

2.01. For each economic unit three simple relationships (which exclude all revaluations) define and describe saving:

(1) Saving = current income — (current consumption + capital consumption allowances).

(2) Saving = change in assets — change in liabilities.

(3) Saving = change in earned net worth.

Relations 2 and 3 can immediately be rearranged into (and are indeed derived from) an additional relation:

(4) Change in assets = change in liabilities + change in earned net worth.

Distinguishing tangible and intangible assets, we obtain the supplementary relationship:

(5) Change in earned net worth = change in tangible assets + change in intangible assets — change in liabilities.

The essential feature of relation 5 is the indication that for an individual household or business the change in earned net worth, which is the same thing as its saving, is not equal to the change in tangible assets, which is what economists call investment; but that the two differ by the excess (or deficit) of the change in intangible assets over (under) the change in liabilities, i.e. by the change in net intangibles.

2.02. Combination of these relations for a group of economic units and ultimately for the nation yields the following relations:

(6) National saving = national income — (national consumption + national capital consumption allowances).

(7) National saving = change in national assets — change in national liabilities.

(8) National saving = change in national earned net worth.

(9) Change in national assets = change in national liabilities + change in national earned net worth.

To understand these relationships on the national level it is necessary to distinguish, first, tangible and intangible assets; and secondly, to separate among intangible assets the claims against and liabilities to nationals from claims against and liabilities to foreigners. We then obtain the following picture:

[1] This section may be omitted by readers interested only in substantive findings.

23

a. Change in domestic tangible assets	*d.* Change in liabilities to nationals [a]
b. Change in claims against nationals [a]	*e.* Change in foreign liabilities [b]
c. Change in foreign assets	*f.* Change in earned net worth

$$a + b + c = d + e + f$$

[a] Includes stock of domestic corporations and equity of unincorporated business enterprises.
[b] Includes domestic tangible assets owned by foreigners.

Since changes in claims against nationals are necessarily equal to changes in liabilities to nationals, both being only two sides of the same relation; since the difference between changes in foreign assets and foreign liabilities is equivalent to the change in net foreign balance; and since the change in nonreproducible tangible assets must be zero by definition if valuation changes are excluded, this statement can be consolidated into the following more compact relation:

g. Change in domestic reproducible tangible wealth	*i.* Change in earned net worth
h. Change in net foreign balance	

$$g + h = i$$

The left hand side of this statement is nothing but net national investment, while the right hand side is the same thing as national saving. Hence,

(10) National saving = national investment.

2.03. It is important to realize (1) that the equality applies only to the nation as a whole and not to an individual economic unit or any group of them; and (2) that the equality holds only if we look at any closed period of the past (ex post), and does not apply to plans and anticipations as they may exist before, at the beginning of, or during a period (ex ante). Indeed, the differences between saving and investment by individual savers and groups of them and the discrepancies between their planned and actual (realized) saving constitute some of the most important influences on the saving process. The difference between gross saving and investment determines the amounts which a unit, or a group of them, is making available or requiring from the capital market, and thus influences the flow of capital funds and the level of yields. Discrepancies between planned and realized saving in one period may lead to changes in spending and saving in the next period and thereby determine that period's level of income and saving. More importantly, the fact that some units' actual saving differs from what they had expected makes it hazardous to infer saving motives (both with respect to the aggregate level of saving and to its distribution by forms and saver groups) from the statistics of saving, which necessarily refer only to actual, realized, ex post saving.

24

2. Alternative Approaches to the Measurement of Saving

2.04. To understand the saving process adequately we need to know, for the present as well as for a relevant stretch of the past, (a) which economic units save or dissave at different times, (b) how much they save or dissave, (c) in what forms their saving or dissaving occurs, (d) how saving is related to characteristics of the saving unit, such as its income, assets, age, and occupation, and to factors affecting the entire economy, such as movements in prices and interest rates, and (e) why different economic units save or dissave to the extent and in the forms they do.

2.05. Some of the facts necessary to answer these questions—the last of which is beyond the scope of this study—can be obtained without the cooperation or even the knowledge of the savers themselves. Other relevant facts can be determined only through questioning individual savers, and as a practical matter must be obtained from a small representative sample of savers rather than from all of them. Thus there are basically two ways of building up estimates of saving of groups of savers and of national saving—the aggregative and the sample approach. The first approach is the combination of aggregative statistical time series. This method, in turn, can proceed either from series each of which measures the amount of saving or dissaving by a broad group of savers in one specific form of saving (balance sheet measurement of saving), or from aggregative series for current income and current expenditures of a saver group (income account measurement). The second approach consists of "blowing up" the results of sample inquiries to group or national totals, and can again work from either the balance sheets or the income accounts of the sample population.

The Saving Study proceeds by the aggregative balance sheet method, i.e. by building up estimates of saving from aggregative series measuring year after year the different forms of saving and dissaving for all saver groups with the exception of corporations, the saving of which is calculated by the aggregative income account method. Since sufficiently detailed sample inquiries of saving have been made only at rare intervals and only for private households, the aggregative balance sheet method is the only way of obtaining annual estimates of saving of the main saver groups through the main forms of saving for an extended period—the objective of this study. The results of the occasional sample inquiries of household saving provide, however, important checks on the estimates derived from aggregative time series. They also furnish additional information on the saving of groups within the universe of all households, particularly on the saving of households of different income levels, information which cannot be obtained by the aggregative method. The results of these sample inquiries are discussed in Volume II, Chapter V, and in Volume III, Part II of this study. Volume I, however, deals almost exclusively with the figures obtained from a combination of aggregative annual time series.

2.06. In addition to the over-all and sample approach to the study of the saving process there is a choice between the individualized and the standardized

25

method of measuring saving. If we follow the first method we measure what the economic units themselves—households, business enterprises, and government—regard as their "saving"; under the second, we have recourse to the methods of social accounting, i.e. to the application of the principles of business accounting on a national scale,[2] from which certain rules can be derived regarding the calculation of saving.

2.07. The individualized approach has the advantage of motivational significance. There is reason to assume that what determines an individual economic unit's decision to save or dissave is, together with other factors, what the unit itself regards as saving, rather than a magnitude calculated by accounting methods with which the unit is often unfamiliar, and many aspects of which it could not understand even if aware of them. The individualized approach, however, is quite inapplicable in practice. We simply do not know what different groups of economic units typically regard as their own saving or dissaving and how they measure it. We have, however, reason to believe that the differences are great not only among groups of savers, but also within such groups. We may also assume that the unit's own estimate of saving is closer to the figure derived in accordance with an economic or accounting definition in the case of business enterprises than in that of households or governments; and that within each group the difference is smaller for the units with high income and saving than for the others. It is also probable that the individual unit's concept of saving is, on the one hand, narrower than the economic or accounting concept, disregarding, for example, items like increases in pension and retirement fund reserves and accruing interest on U.S. savings bonds; but broader in other respects, particularly making no or insufficient allowance for depreciation. All these possibilities, however, are matters of speculation. What is fairly certain is the wide variation among units and the wide divergence of saving as understood by many units from the economic or accounting concept of saving. Therefore, no practical alternative exists to taking the second approach to the measurement of saving, i.e. to developing a definition of saving from the logic of social accounting and applying it to groups of economic units and to the nation as a whole. This is also the only way to obtain a measure of saving which is reasonably uniform as between different economic units and is consistent over time. Thus the concept of saving used in a comprehensive study of saving must be a social accounting concept.

3. Some Problems of the Social Accounting Approach

2.08. To cast estimates of saving into the mould of social accounting has both advantages and drawbacks. The advantages obviously have been regarded as decisive and the drawbacks as remediable, or another approach would have been taken in this study.

The most important advantages of integrating the estimates of saving into

[2] The concept of social accounting and its relation to business accounting is discussed in Volume II, Chapter I, Section 2.

a system of social accounts are (a) the methodical tie-in of saving with income, consumption, and the national balance sheet, a tie-in which permits use of a logically consistent and comprehensive system of defining and recording transactions and holdings, and (b) the checks on actual estimates inherent in such a system, exemplified by the requirement that the estimates of national saving and investment must be equal. The importance of these advantages probably will be more evident to the estimator himself and to those who intensively utilize the results of his labor than to the casual reader.

Possibly the most serious apparent drawback of treating the estimates of saving as a part of a system of national accounts is the rigidity in concepts and measurement which it may, but need not, induce. In such a system a concept like saving must be defined identically for all groups and for all years within a period, though its subjective meaning may differ as between groups and may vary over time. In other words, social accounting definitions are not always motivationally the most meaningful concepts that can be used. The answer to this problem is the development of variant concepts, each of which fits into a system of social accounts, and the use in a given case of that concept which appears to correspond best to the purpose of analysis. The following section will show, it is hoped, that the Saving Study has gone as far in providing alternative estimates as can reasonably be expected in view of the limitation of resources and the need of avoiding confusion. The Study certainly has proceeded further in this direction than most previous investigations in the field. The reader who prefers to use a different variant of saving, at some point or throughout the discussion, will generally find the figures he needs in the basic tables or should be able to derive them from these tables without undue difficulty.

In textual discussion or statistical analysis of the estimates of saving it is obviously impossible to take account of all variants that have been developed, or even of all those that are specifically shown in the tables. It is primarily in order to keep the discussion of this Introduction within reasonable length and to emphasize the main results rather than the detail that attention is centered on one definition of saving, which has been called the standard social accounting concept. This concept is described in the following division and compared, in quantitative terms, with the main other variants. Throughout the remainder of the Introduction differences between the standard and other variants will be pointed out whenever they appear to be significant. This may have been done too often rather than too rarely if simplicity of presentation is the goal.

2.09. The standard social accounting concept is nevertheless not regarded as simply one of many equally significant variants, but has been selected because it appears to be the concept most useful for many analytical purposes, and the one most nearly in line, given the data now available, with the essence of social accounting as a systematic record of economically relevant facts, or more precisely as the systematic comparison of income and cost.[3] The reasons for this selection will become apparent, it is hoped, as the story unfolds, but may be briefly summarized here.

[3] See Volume II, Chapter I.

Under the standard social accounting concept saving is defined as the change in earned net worth, including consumer durables but excluding net soil improvement and military assets, omitting all valuation changes, making allowance for accruals, and taking account of capital consumption allowances by basing them on replacement cost and straight line depreciation.

Some of the attributes of this definition are inherent in the use of the principles of accounting, e.g. allowances for capital consumption and accruals and omission of unrealized valuation changes. Others reflect the limitation of available data or lack of agreed procedures, e.g. the use (with only few exceptions) of straight line depreciation. Military assets are omitted from the standard definition both for the conceptual reason—admittedly not wholly convincing, though widely accepted—that war is not among the objectives of the economic society, and because of the extreme difficulty of obtaining reliable and economically meaningful estimates of changes in the stock of military assets. Saving through net soil improvement (i.e. the difference between soil improvement and deterioration) has been omitted from the standard concept, notwithstanding its great practical and conceptual interest, because as yet it can be measured only in very rough terms and with a very wide margin of error. Elimination of realized capital gains and losses and substitution of replacement cost for original cost as the basis of capital consumption allowances result almost necessarily from the consistent application of the principles of social accounting. The first of these two adjustments is already generally accepted.

This leaves the inclusion of saving through consumer durables as probably the most controversial feature of the standard saving concept used. It has been influenced by three considerations. The first is the desire to preserve a tie between cumulated saving and national wealth. Since the stock of consumer durables is always included in national wealth this consideration argues for their inclusion in saving. Secondly, many consumer durables, e.g. passenger cars, are now as essential to the functioning of the economy as some structures and producer durables, and without them output would be different from and probably lower than what it actually is. Their financing is therefore an integral part of the saving process. Thirdly, estimates of saving including consumer durables seem generally to provide a more satisfactory explanation of variations in saving than those excluding them. This is not to deny that a case can be made for excluding consumer durables, particularly on the grounds that they do not directly contribute to production—in the sense that factory buildings, machines, and railroads do—and that their acquisition is not governed by consideration of return. But if these criteria are valid, saving through owner-occupied residences and most of the saving of governments and private nonprofit institutions must also be eliminated from the saving concept, and we shall be left with a magnitude having but little connection with changes in national wealth.

2.10. The standard social accounting concept is thus regarded as the most useful all-purpose measure of saving that can be contrived at the present time. The concept obviously is not equally well fitted for all purposes of analysis. It is just this realization of the situation which led to presenting also estimates corresponding to numerous alternative definitions. This variety of estimates may create an impression of confusion, and will not please readers who look for simple and unequivocal answers to all questions. But the need for variant concepts of saving is unfortunately inherent in the problems which statistics of saving are designed to illuminate. In many cases limitation to one concept—here the standard social accounting definition—may be entirely satisfactory. In other cases resort must be had to alternative definitions, sometimes even to definitions as far different from the standard concept as gross saving (without allowance for capital consumption) or changes in total current net worth (including realized and unrealized valuation changes). Selection of the appropriate definition for a specific problem is a matter of judgment. All that an author can do is to supply—within reasonable limits—those who disagree with his judgment with the figures needed to translate the argument into their own terms. It is hoped that the presentation in the Introduction and in the tables that follow will be found to meet this requirement.

4. Variant Concepts of Saving Used in the Study

2.11. The saving concept underlying this study is that of the change in earned net worth during an accounting period, usually a year. This basic concept is able to accommodate numerous variant definitions, depending on the scope of assets, the method of calculating capital consumption allowances, and the treatment of certain types of transactions. The most important alternative concepts of saving which are used in this study are shown in Table I and are illustrated by a comparison in Divisions 2.12 to 2.19 of the estimates of national saving following the various concepts for the full period covered by the Study (1897–1949) and for the so-called "normal period," which excludes the six years of war and the Great Depression (1917–1918, 1930–1933, 1942–1945).

2.12. Thanks to the formalism of double-entry bookkeeping, the change in net worth can be determined both from the income acount and from the balance sheet of every economic unit. Thus there always exist two measures of saving for every economic unit and every accounting period, one derived from the income account and one from the balance sheet. Saving is calculated from the income account as the difference between current income and current expenditures, including among the latter capital consumption allowances and distributions to owners in the form of profit withdrawals and dividends. It excludes realized as well as unrealized capital gains and losses, in particular inventory profits and losses. Saving is measured from the balance sheet as the net result of changes (generally excluding valuation changes such as inventory profits and losses, realized capital gains and losses, and write-ups and write-downs) in all types of assets and liabilities, with paid-in capital included among the latter. The numerical results of the two measurements of saving are necessarily equal if consistent methods of accounting are employed.[4] Hence, the saving of some economic units calculated

[4] See Volume II, Chapter I, Section 4, and Appendix A.

from their income account can be combined with the saving of other units measured from their balance sheet without danger of gaps, overlaps, or discrepancies.

2.13. National saving is the result of the combination of the saving, or dissaving, of all saver groups within the nation, while group saving, e.g. of households or corporations, is the result of the combination of all units belonging to the group. Both national and group saving are net in the sense that the dissaving of some groups or units is treated algebraically as an offset against the saving of others.

CHART II

NATIONAL (NET) SAVING: 1897 to 1949
Social Accounting Concept; Estimates of Varying Scope

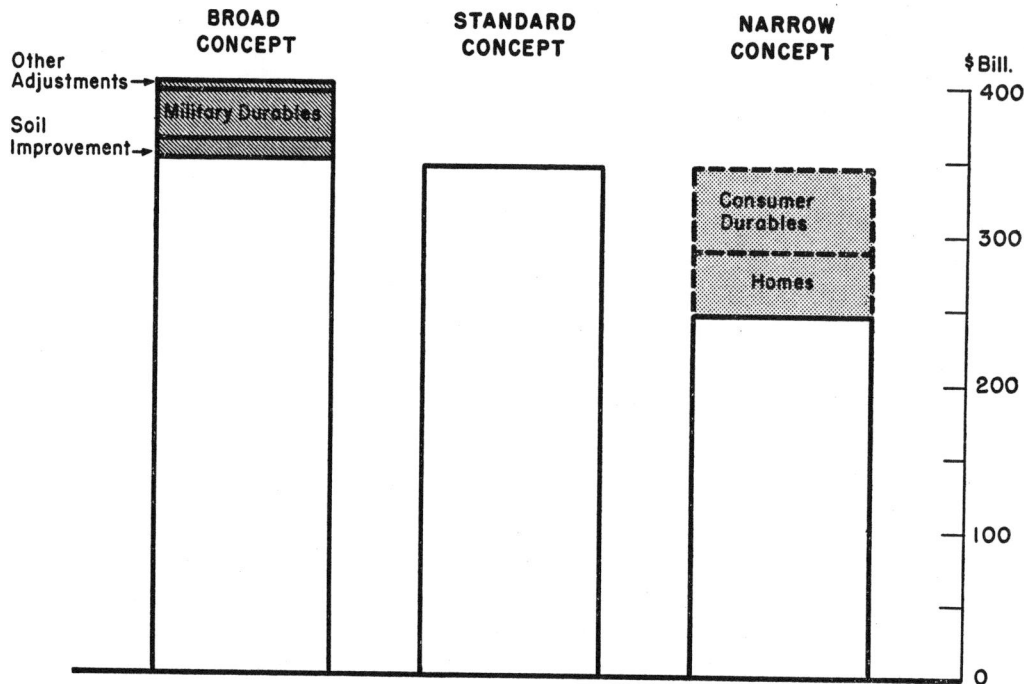

2.14. Saving may be estimated on either a gross or a net basis, the difference representing capital consumption allowances, the calculation of which probably presents the most difficult single problem in the measurement of saving, both conceptually and practically.

This problem arises basically (1) because there is no unequivocal or satisfactory way of separating the reduction of the value of assets that is due to wear and tear and lapse of time, which is measured by capital consumption allowances, from other changes in value, e.g. from losses reflecting faulty investment, and (2) because the amount of the reduction attributable to a given accounting period can be determined only at the end of the asset's life. Business accounting overcomes or, rather, sidesteps these problems by treating capital consump-

80

TABLE I

RELATION BETWEEN VARIANT DEFINITIONS OF SAVING

	Saving (change in earned net worth)				Gross (cash) saving	Change in total net worth
	Net saving			Business accounting		
	Social accounting					
	Standard	Narrow	Broad			
1. Residences	I	E	I	B	B	B
2. Consumer durables	I	E	I	B	B	B
3. Inventory valuation adjustment	I	I	I	E	E	E
4. Realized capital gains and losses (other than line 3)	E	E	E	I	I	I
5. Unrealized capital gains and losses (other than line 3)	E	E	E	E	E	C
6. Accruals	I	I	I	I	E	C
7. Soil improvement and deterioration	E	E	I	B	B	C
8. Military assets	E	E	I	B	B	B
9. Depreciation: original cost	N	N	N	A	N	N
10. Depreciation: replacement cost	A	A	A	N	N	C
11. Dealers' commissions on transactions in assets	I	E	I	I	I	C

A = Applicable.
N = Not applicable.
I = Explicitly included in saving estimate.
E = Explicitly excluded from saving estimate.
B = Both I and E applicable depending on whether the narrow or broad base is used.
C = Included by implication.

tion allowances essentially as the regular prorating of an asset's original cost over its anticipated useful life. This treatment leads to the prevalence of straight line depreciation allowances in actual accounts, based on original dollar cost and a conservatively estimated length of life, i.e. a life often below the asset's actual utilization.

While this treatment is far from satisfactory, it has been accepted in the Study except in one important point: Capital consumption allowances have been based in the social accounting concept of saving on an asset's replacement cost rather than on its original cost. This shift at least ensures that a year's depreciation charges are commensurable with expenditures on depreciable assets made during the same year; in other words, that the minuend and the subtrahend in the calculation of net saving are expressed in the same price level. How important the shift is will be seen from the facts that for the entire period from 1897 to 1949 national capital consumption allowances were $89 billion, or 15 percent, higher on a replacement than on an original cost basis, and that the difference was as high as 35 percent in 1949.

Not enough data are available to depart from the straight line basis of depreciation except in a few cases, particularly that of automobiles; or to abandon the commonly accepted rates of depreciation and the length of life they imply, except for residential structures. As a result capital consumption allowances estimated in the Study are probably somewhat higher, and estimates of net saving lower, than they would be if they could have been based systematically on the actual length of life of the different types of assets while adhering to straight line depreciation.

Every calculation of capital consumption allowances, and consequently every estimation of net saving, is thus unavoidably affected by the arbitrariness involved in using conventional straight line rates of depreciation. Estimates of gross saving do not have to contend with these difficulties. They are, however, quite unable to provide information, as net saving can, on the growth of tangible assets of a saver group or the nation since, whatever question may be raised regarding the "best" method of taking account of capital consumption, there is no doubt that tangible assets are used up as time goes on and that capital consumption is at any time equal to a large portion of capital expenditures.

2.15. Of the definitions of saving which differ conceptually (rather than solely in scope of assets) to a significant degree from the basic social accounting definition only two have been used, viz. the business accounting concept and the cash flow concept of saving.

The business accounting concept does not eliminate realized capital gains and losses, calculates depreciation on the basis of original cost, and accepts all depletion allowances made by owners. While inferior from a theoretical point of view to the standard social accounting concept, it is of practical importance because it corresponds to prevailing business practices. It therefore provides estimates which are reasonably comparable to saving and income figures derived from the actual accounts of business, and may be assumed to be more significant in the analysis of the motives underlying business behavior than similar figures calculated in accordance with the standard social accounting concept.

The cash flow, or gross, concept of saving ignores capital consumption allowances and other accruals. Cash saving thus is approximately equal to gross expenditures on durable tangible goods plus net expenditures (cost of acquisition less proceeds from sales) on intangible assets. This concept is of use primarily in money flow analysis.

2.16. For the entire period from 1897 through 1949 national saving expressed in current dollars and calculated in accordance with the standard social accounting concept amounts to $345 billion (Chart III and Table II). The total for the "normal" period (1897–1916, 1919–1929, 1934–1941, 1946–1949) is slightly higher, viz. $364 billion, because national saving was negative for the ten remaining years taken together and for six of them (1931–1933 and 1943–1945) taken separately.

Use of alternative estimates, incorporating two technical adjustments of lesser importance [5] and including saving through net soil improvement, which is particularly difficult to estimate, increases the period total only by moderate amounts—together by a little more than $20 billion or 6 percent. A larger increase is brought about by inclusion of saving through durable military assets, which is both controversial in theory and subject to a wide margin of error of estimation.[6] It would

---

[5] One of the two adjustments is an alternative and probably preferable estimate of expenditures on residential construction; the other is an adjustment for the understatement of individuals' bank deposits on account of call loans by nonfinancial corporations.

[6] This adjustment has been calculated only for the period after 1940 as it is relatively small for earlier years and data for estimating it are still more tenuous.

32

CHART III

NET AND GROSS NATIONAL SAVING: 1897 to 1949
Reconciliation of Three Basic Concepts

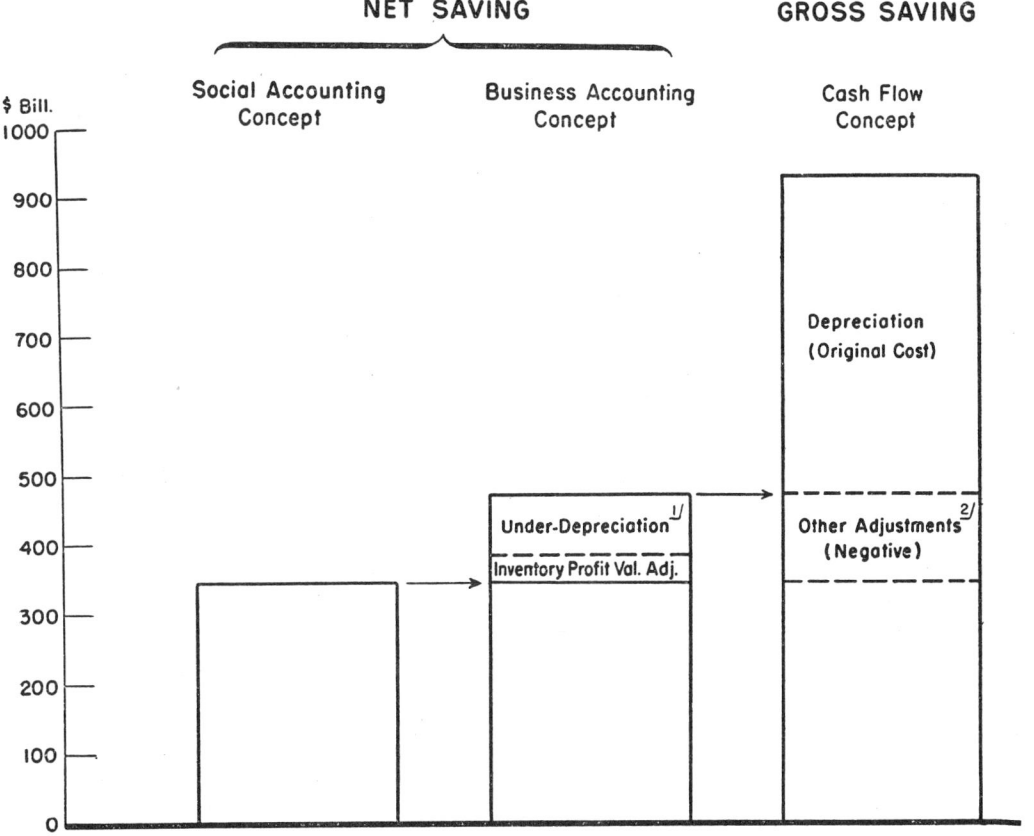

NET SAVING

GROSS SAVING

Social Accounting
Concept

Business Accounting
Concept

Cash Flow
Concept

$ Bill.

Depreciation
(Original Cost)

Under-Depreciation [1]

Inventory Profit Val. Adj.

Other Adjustments [2]
(Negative)

¹ Original cost minus replacement cost basis.
² Chiefly interest credits and tax accruals.

add $33 billion or nearly 10 percent for the entire period, but would reduce the total for the normal period by $23 billion or 6 percent since depreciation allowances on military assets exceed current expenditures on them except during war years. In the "broad" concept (i.e. including military assets, net soil improvement, and technical adjustments) aggregate saving would then amount to $400 billion for the full period and to about $360 billion for the normal period.

2. 17. Exclusion of saving through consumer durables makes a considerable difference, as will be seen in Chart IV—indeed a larger difference than any of the adjustments discussed so far. It reduces national saving by $56 billion or 16 percent for the period as a whole, and by even a little more for the normal period. Saving through consumer durables is often eliminated on the ground that it does not contribute to an expansion of the country's productive equipment. If that argument is accepted one might also exclude saving through one- to four-

33

TABLE II

NATIONAL SAVING ESTIMATES REFLECTING VARIANT SAVING CONCEPTS
1897 to 1949

	Entire period (53 years)	Excluding wars and Great Depression [a] (43 years)	Entire period (53 years)	Excluding wars and Great Depression [a] (43 years)
	$ bill.		Percent of standard concept	
	1	2	3	4
I. Current Values				
1. Social accounting concept; standard	345	364	100	100
2. Social accounting concept; including two technical adjustments [b, c]	354	373	103	102
3. Social accounting concept; including net soil improvement [b]	358	373	104	102
4. Social accounting concept; including military assets [b]	378	341	110	94
5. Social accounting concept; broad	399	358	116	98
6. Social accounting concept; excluding consumer durables [b]	289	298	84	82
7. Social accounting concept; narrow	245	247	71	68
8. Business accounting concept; standard	472	468	137	129
9. Business accounting concept; excluding consumer durables	390	380	113	104
10. Cash flow concept; standard	931	814	270	224
11. Cash flow concept; excluding consumer durables	602	544	174	149
II. Deflated (1929) values; standard social accounting concept				
1. Deflated by index of general price level	360	380	104	104
2. Deflated by group purchasing power indices	415	395	120	109
3. Deflated by index of wage level	397	407	115	112

[a] 1917–1918, 1930–1933, and 1942–1945.
[b] Not including adjustments set forth in other lines.
[c] See Table T-4.

Line I-1 – Table T-1, col. 1.
Line I-2 – Sum of Table T-1, col. 1, Table R-3, col. 6, and adjustment for understatement of individuals' bank deposits on account of call loans by nonfinancial corporations obtained by taking successive difference of Tables D-8, col. 5 minus col. 9 for the period 1920–1942.
Line I-3 – Table T-1, col. 1 plus net soil improvement costs obtained by equally distributing within the period totals given in Volume II, Table B-61, col. 1 plus col. 2 minus col. 3.
Line I-4 – Table T-1, col. 1 plus Table F-31, col. 8.
Line I-5 – Sum of Table T-1, col. 1, Table R-3, col. 6, call loan adjustment (line 2), net soil improvement costs (line 3), and military assets from Table F-31, col. 8.
Line I-6 – Table T-1, col. 1 minus Table T-6, col. 5.
Line I-7 – Table T-1, col. 1 minus sum of Table T-6, col. 5, Table R-6, cols. 1–4 less cols. 5 and 7, and Table A-6, col. 6 raised 55 percent (see notes to Table A-1, col. 3).
Line I-8 – Table T-2, col. 1.
Line I-9 – Table T-2, col. 1 minus Table T-7, col. 5.
Line I-10 – Table T-3, col. 1.
Line I-11 – Table T-3, col. 1 minus sum of Table T-10, col. 4 and Table A-66, col. 3.
Line II-1 – Table T-12, col. 1.
Line II-2 – Table T-14, col. 1.
Line II-3 – Table T-13, col. 1.

family residential construction. In that case saving would be further reduced by $44 billion, or 13 percent of the standard concept, to what may be called the "narrow" concept of national saving of only $245 billion both for the period as a whole and the normal period. This figure probably corresponds to what many nineteenth century economists would have called "capital formation," which limits investment to reproducible means of production in the narrow sense of the word. It is also close, although not yet quite equivalent to the concept of capital formation in use in the Soviet Union.[7] For an analysis of the operation of the American economy in the twentieth century such a narrow concept appears to be of little use.[8]

2.18. Thus, even within the social accounting concept, estimates of saving for the entire period from 1897 through 1949 range from less than $250 billion to approximately $400 billion. Larger differences appear when we leave the social accounting definition for the business accounting or the cash definition, but retain the scope of the standard concept which includes consumer durables while excluding military assets and soil improvement.

For the entire period business accounting saving totals $472 billion, i.e. it exceeds social accounting saving by 37 percent. The difference is the result primarily of two factors. The first is that original cost depreciation allowances, which are used in the business accounting concept, are substantially lower than replacement cost allowances of the social accounting concept, because the level of prices has risen almost without interruption throughout the period. The second is the inclusion in the business accounting concept of realized capital gains and losses, particularly net inventory profits, which have been substantial and which again reflect the rising trend of prices over the period.

Cash saving naturally is still higher since it makes no allowance at all for capital consumption and, what is less important, ignores accrued liabilities such as taxes. For the entire period cash saving is 170 percent larger than social accounting saving and exceeds even business accounting saving by almost 100 percent.[9]

2.19. If the estimates of saving are expressed in 1929 prices to reduce the figures to a stable basis, they are, as a rule, slightly higher than in terms of current prices (Chart IV and Table II, section II). That the difference is so small is due to the fact that the price level of 1929 is close to that for the average of the entire period. Using an index of the general price level as deflator, national saving in 1929 prices is only 4 percent above saving in current prices for the entire period from 1897 through 1949. The difference is somewhat larger—15 to 20 percent—if indices of the wage level or of the purchasing power of the different saver groups are employed as deflators. The relation of deflated to current values of saving for the period as a whole is not greatly influenced by the elimination of war years and the Great Depression, although there is a tendency for the difference to be smaller if these years are excluded.

[7] See, e.g., Studenski, "Methods of Estimating National Income in Soviet Russia" in *Studies in Income and Wealth*, Volume VIII, 1946, pp. 199ff.; and Bergson, "Soviet National Income and Product in 1937," in *Quarterly Journal of Economics*, Volume LXIV, 1950, pp. 237ff.

[8] See Division 2.09.

[9] The ratio of cash to social or business accounting saving necessarily increases—in contrast to the ratio of social to business accounting saving—other things being equal, with the length of the period covered, as long as cash saving increases. This is the main reason why the ratio is substantially higher for the full than for the normal period.

5. CHARACTER OF FACTUAL EVIDENCE UNDERLYING THE STUDY

2.20. The statistical basis of the Saving Study is characterized by two features: the consistent use of the social accounting approach, and the comprehensive and composite nature of the estimates.

2.21. The Saving Study proceeds on the assumption, discussed earlier, that the most appropriate and indeed the only satisfactory way of analyzing the process of saving in a modern market economy is to look at its operation through the balance sheets and income accounts of its constituent units, individually or combined into groups, all arranged on the basis of, but not necessarily rigidly bound by, the rules of modern business accounting.[10]

CHART IV

NATIONAL SAVING: 1897 to 1949

Standard Social Accounting Concept; Current and Deflated Values

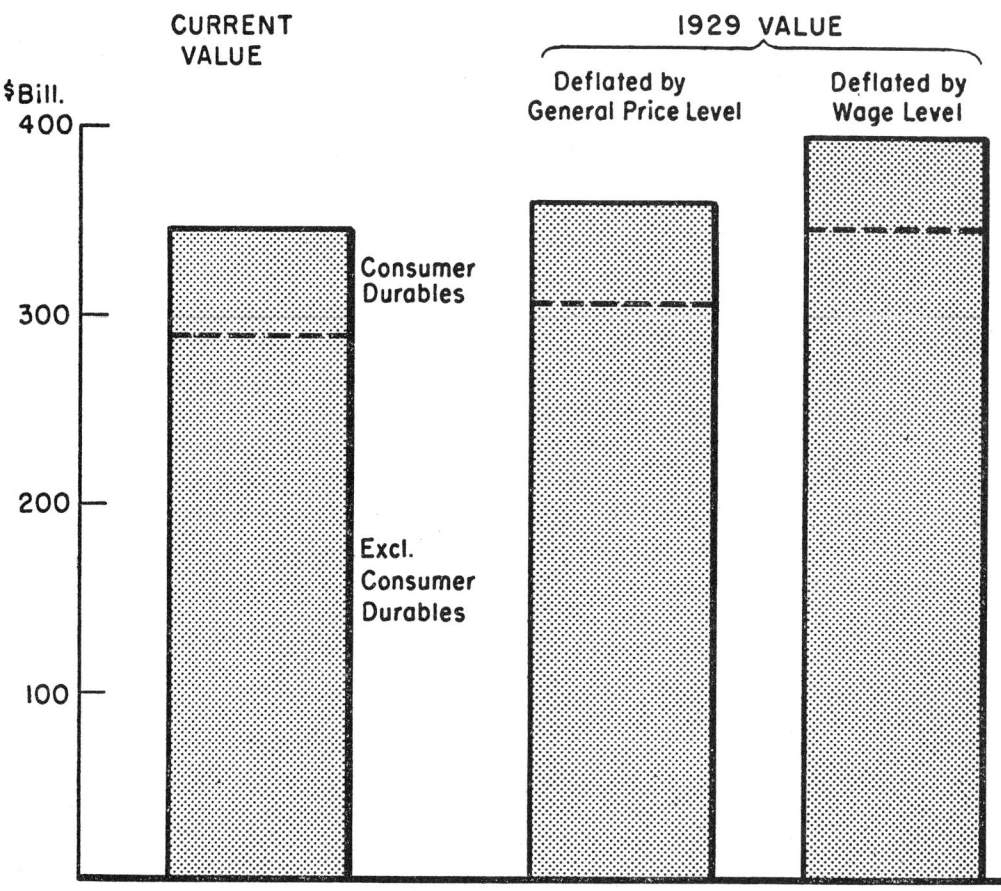

[10] The characteristics of the social accounting approach and its applicability to the different types of economic units are discussed in Volume II, Chapters I and II.

36

Such a theoretical framework taken seriously in many cases requires modifications of existing measurements, and calls for inclusion of a number of components of saving or dissaving which might be omitted if a more conventional approach were chosen. Strict adherence to the theoretical framework in each and every case, however, has proved impossible. Such consistency would have required a prohibitive amount of labor, even if the necessary data could always have been procured. In practice the problem, as in every study in the field of social accounting, is solely whether or not departures from the theoretical framework in favor of simpler procedures have been limited to cases of small substantive importance.

2.22. The estimates are comprehensive insofar as they cover in principle all forms of saving or dissaving by all groups of savers domiciled in the United States. This means that we are precluded from picking and choosing our series, as is so often done in economic research. He who works within a framework of social accounting is not granted this privilege. The system of social accounts presents us for each year with a square array of empty boxes, one for the saving or dissaving of each of the half dozen saver groups which have been distinguished, in each of the one to three dozen forms into which each group's total saving has been split. Each of these boxes, many of which have quite a number of compartments, must be filled for each year lest the resulting estimates for total national saving be incomplete and the objective of integrating the figures into a system of social accounts be frustrated. Unavoidably, the figures to be put in some of the boxes will be of doubtful reliability and affected with a wide margin of error, while the figures entered in some other boxes will be of little interest because of their small absolute size. All these figures must nevertheless be calculated and exposed to scrutiny. This state of affairs is not an argument against the procedure adopted so long as we recognize what is being done, and so long as no use is made, except for the purpose of deriving certain needed aggregates, of the boxes in which numbers of doubtful reliability or of little substantive significance have been written. In other words, the procedure is legitimate so long as what is intended as an integrated entry within a system of accounts is not given independent status, and is not treated indiscriminately as if it were a figure able to stand on its own and able to furnish an answer to substantive questions.

2.23. The estimates are composite in the sense that they are the result of the combination of a large number of basic figures, some long-term series, some short consecutive runs, and some benchmark data at irregular intervals; some of known and honorable ancestry and considerable accuracy, others of doubtful reliability and without pedigree or constituting little more than informed guesses; some interrelated, but most of them independent of each other. This composite character is a source of both weakness and strength of the estimates.

2.24. To start with the weaknesses of the estimates, the multitude of sources, the variety of material, and the wide range of subject matter—from over-all statistics of capital formation to detailed aspects of production statistics, intricacies of corporate balance sheets and income accounts, and fine points of financial statistics—have made it impossible to examine each basic figure used with meticulous care as to coverage, methods of derivation, changes in both over time, and comparability with other data.

Recourse to material prepared by experts in specialized fields, involving the utilization of secondhand sources, may seem a way out of the dilemma. There are two reasons why this has not been used except in a few instances. The first and compelling one is the scarcity of reliable studies which might have been used. The second reason is the experience, repeated over and over, that unless one goes back to primary sources, even if only cursorily, it is not possible to acquire sufficient familiarity with the material to manipulate it with the freedom which is necessary to adapt it to the requirements of comprehensive estimates. To these limitations, which might be overcome by the teamwork of a group of experts if time and money were no objects, there are added the unavoidable difficulties encountered in combining heterogeneous statistical data, difficulties which are common to practically all work in social accounting and which apply to most work in macroeconomics.

2.25. The composite approach, however, has at least two advantages. It is not dependent on the shortcomings of any one set of figures, and it is to a certain degree self-checking, both characteristics being common to social accounting. First, because the final estimates are the result of combining literally hundreds of series, most of which are independent of each other with respect to sources, methods of collection, coverage, and concepts, errors in individual component series are likely to offset each other to a substantial extent in the estimates of national saving or the saving of large saver groups.[11] The final estimates are therefore not too seriously dependent on the weaknesses of any one component series. Secondly, because the composite estimates are made up of many components of which most are independent the method provides numerous opportunities for internal checks. These, however, are not automatic, but call for use of all relevant material and often require a good deal of ingenuity.[12]

6. RELIABILITY OF ESTIMATES

2.26. In a study which is based so preponderantly on statistical data and on estimates cast into the mould of a system of social accounts, an evaluation of the accuracy, reliability, and margin of error of the figures used, such as is common in the physical sciences, is most desirable. Unfortunately, not much can be said about these matters in precise quantitative terms, if only because the measurement of the margin of error in economic statistics is still in its infancy.

2.27. The first difficulty in the evaluation of reliability and error margins is conceptual. Obviously, there is no "true" figure for saving in the United States in a given year in the sense that a true figure can be said to exist for the number of inhabitants of the country at a given date. The latter figure may be established by an exhaustive count—subject in practice to certain minimum errors—as it is

[11] This important feature of composite estimates is discussed in Volume II, Chapter IV, Section 3.

[12] The most important checks of this type are discussed in Chapter V of Volume II.

possible to define rather precisely who should be counted as an inhabitant of the United States at any given moment. Not so with an estimate of saving. A period's saving cannot be defined as simply or unequivocally as the number of inhabitants, or the production of pig iron ingots, or the sale of new passenger automobiles. All that can be done is to regard as the "true" value of saving the figure which would be obtained if all economic units within a country kept accounts, if they kept them by the same methods, and if such accounts could be combined or consolidated consistently. The "error" in any estimate of saving is thus nothing but the difference between the estimate actually made and the value which would be obtained on the assumption of universal uniform social accounting. Hence, any discussion of true values or errors of estimates of saving presupposes the acceptance of a definite method of measurement or accounting.

2.28.   Once this is granted four basic approaches become available by which the reliability of any one estimate of saving can be evaluated. The first is the comparison with estimates derived by other investigators who use essentially the same basic method, making allowance for any differences in concept or coverage among the estimates compared. The second approach is the comparison of the estimates with other magnitudes which conceptually show a predetermined relation to saving—for instance, with investment, which on a national scale should be equal to saving. The third method is the evaluation of the possible errors inherent in each component of saving or arising in their combination into groups or national aggregates. The fourth is the comparison of aggregate estimates with those derived from a blow-up of saving determined from samples of groups of economic units. All four approaches have been followed in Volume II, Chapter V, so far as data were available and so far as the amount of labor involved was not excessive. The procedures are too complicated to be described here and the results do not lend themselves easily to summarization.

2.29.   Comparison with the results of other investigators does not provide a satisfactory check on the estimates presented here, partly because none of the other estimates covers nearly as long a period; and partly because the other estimates are narrower in scope, generally omitting saving by the government and through consumer durables. So far as any conclusion can be drawn—and this can be done only for the period since 1929—the estimates of saving developed by this study tend to be somewhat above other estimators' figures (of course after adjustment for differences in concept and coverage), particularly for the period after World War II.

2.30.   Comparison with estimates of investment made by this study, a comparison which obviously must be limited to the national level, shows virtually no difference between saving and investment for the period as a whole. [13] Annual differences, however, are substantial and average about 15 percent, disregarding the sign of the difference. Until the 1930's the estimates of saving are generally above those of investment, while the difference is irregular in the last two decades, but generally in the direction of an excess of investment over saving. This com-

[13] See Volume II, Chapter V, Section 6.

parison, taken by itself, may thus point to a slight overestimation of saving before the thirties. There may be a similar slight understatement for the thirties. The comparison does not point to a systematic error in the level of the estimates of saving for the forties.

Analysis of the statement of sources-and-uses-of-funds of corporations, which can be shown to be implied in the comparison between investment and saving, [14] also fails to point to a substantial discrepancy for the period as a whole, but discloses considerable differences for individual years and for subperiods, differences which are generally of the same direction and size as those shown between the estimates of saving and investment.

2.31. Comparison with blown-up data on saving derived from budget studies, possible only for the saving of nonfarm households and for a few scattered years since the midthirties, is inconclusive, partly because of the great practical differences of adequately adjusting for differences in coverage and methods. [15] To date the differences between the results of the two approaches remain considerable, the blow-up of the budget study data generally showing lower saving or higher dissaving than the estimates derived from aggregate data, in particular those developed in this study. No entirely satisfactory explanation of the remaining differences has as yet been given. It is possible, though not proven, that the differences are due at least in part to an undercoverage in budget studies of saving of upper income households, which account for a large part of total saving of individuals.

2.32. Evaluation of the possible errors in the individual series from which the estimates of group and national saving have been constructed indicates that the margin of error is hardly under 10 percent for any given year or for the average annual figure in any series, that it is probably in the order of magnitude of 20 to 30 percent in many of them, that it may run even higher in not a few cases, but that the relative margin of error in most cases is reduced for sequences of several years and generally the smaller the longer the period. This is due partly to the existence of periodic benchmark data which prevent errors from accumulating for more than the years between benchmarks, generally five or ten years; and partly to erratic fluctuations, many of which disappear when groups of several years are combined.

2.33. Most of the components utilized in building the estimates of saving of any of the major saver groups are statistically independent; and the estimates for the major saver groups are very largely independent of each other except for those of nonfarm households and unincorporated business enterprises. Accordingly since the number of components of saving is large for each of the groups, running to several dozen even if only those of substantial quantitative importance are taken into account, there is reason to assume that errors in one direction, i.e. overstatements or underestimates of saving, made in any one year in some of the component series will be offset by errors in the opposite direction in other series. As a result, the relative error in the estimates of saving by the major groups, and still more the

[14] See Volume II, Chapter II, Section 9.
[15] See Volume II, Chapter V, Section 4 and Volume III, Part II.

40

estimates of broad aggregates such as national or personal saving, may be expected to be considerably lower than the average of the relative errors in the component series. Indeed, it is quite possible that, if we take account of the number of independent component series and their relative size, and even take a pessimistic view of errors in constituent series, the relative error of national or personal saving in any one year does not on the average exceed something like 10 percent.

2.34. The quality of most of the individual series used in the measurement of saving has undoubtedly improved. It would seem to be substantially poorer for the period before the thirties than for the last two decades, and within the earlier period, in turn, to be particularly poor for the years before approximately 1905. Nevertheless, there is no statistical evidence, such as might be provided by the difference between estimates of saving and investment, that the estimates of aggregate saving have larger relative errors in the earlier part of the period than in the later part. Indeed, from that point of view, the relative error in the estimates would have to be regarded as substantially the same through the thirties, and as considerably lower only for the last decade. There is, however, evidence, as has already been indicated, that the error is in different directions before and after 1929, viz. in the direction of an overstatement of saving in the first three decades and an understatement during the thirties.

7. Period Covered by the Study [16]

2.35. The annual estimates of saving, which form the backbone of this study, cover the years 1897 through 1949. The national balance sheet and the estimates of national wealth, appearing in Volume III, span the same period, although in the case of the balance sheet not on an annual basis but only for eight benchmark years (1900, 1912, 1922, 1929, 1933, 1939, 1945, and 1949).

2.36. Selection of the period 1897–1949 is necessarily a compromise between the desire to develop figures covering as long a period as possible and the availability of data. The choice of 1897 as the starting point of the estimates was determined by the fact that the middle nineties constitute a turning point in the long cycles in American economic development, and possibly also in the country's political and cultural life. This consideration finally outweighed the increasing scarcity and diminishing reliability of basic data which become obvious as we approach or go back beyond the turn of the century. Termination of the Study with the year 1949, except for a few preliminary aggregate figures for 1950–1952, was virtually predetermined by the data available at the time the basic estimates were completed, i.e. the fall of 1950.

2.37. For purposes of analysis the fifty-three years covered by the Study have been combined into eight periods which are reasonably homogeneous with regard to basic economic conditions and which generally include an integral number—one, two, or three—of business cycles. The periods selected are:

[16] See Volume II, Chapter III, Section 1.

(1) 1897–1908: America's economic coming of age;
(2) 1909–1914: Consolidation of advance;
(3) 1915–1921: World War I and its aftermath;
(4) 1922–1929: The New Era;
(5) 1930–1933: The Great Depression;
(6) 1934–1938: The New Deal;
(7) 1939–1945: World War II;
(8) 1946–1949 (continuing into at least 1953): Midcentury prosperity.

8. Grouping of Savers and Forms of Saving

2.38. Throughout the Study seven saver groups have been distinguished and separate estimates of saving have been prepared for each of them, viz.:
(1) Nonagricultural households and unattached individuals;
(2) Agricultural households and individuals;
(3) Unincorporated business enterprises;
(4) Corporations;
(5) State governments;
(6) Local governments;
(7) Federal government.
Because of the general lack of sufficiently detailed basic data it has been necessary to include saving of private nonprofit institutions (such as churches, hospitals, foundations, and educational institutions) and of personal trust funds with that of nonagricultural households. In most of the calculations the agricultural saving of those owners of farms who do not live on farms—but, of course, not their saving in other forms, particularly through intangibles—has been included with the saving of agriculture. Estimates, however, have also been derived in Table T-11 in which these amounts are transferred from group 2 to group 1; these estimates, therefore, give a closer approximation to the saving attributable to nonfarm and farm households, respectively.

2.39. The group totals are combined into a number of broader aggregates, shown below, which depend on the purpose of the analysis. The most comprehensive of these, of course, is the total of all seven groups, which is identical with national saving. The next in order is the total of all groups except the federal government. This aggregate is of importance particularly because of the different behavior of the federal government's saving during war periods. It is also justified by the fact that the motives and forms of saving and dissaving by the federal government are often quite different from those of any of the other six groups, while these six groups show a much greater degree of affinity among themselves. The other aggregates, some of which overlap, are self-explanatory.

42

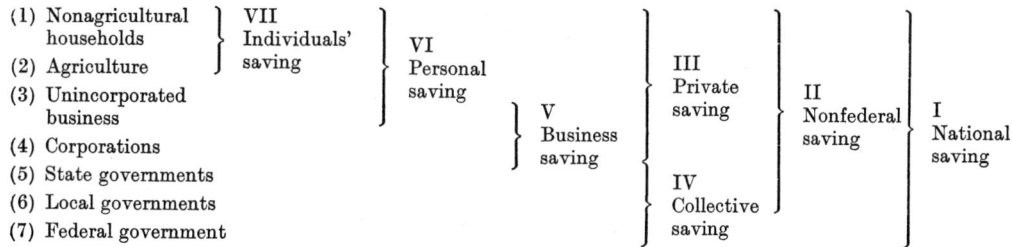

(1)	Nonagricultural households	} VII Individuals' saving	} VI Personal saving		} III Private saving		} II Nonfederal saving	} I National saving
(2)	Agriculture							
(3)	Unincorporated business			} V Business saving				
(4)	Corporations							
(5)	State governments				} IV Collective saving			
(6)	Local governments							
(7)	Federal government							

2.40. It is one of the main advantages of the balance sheet measurement of saving that it necessarily yields estimates of the different types of tangible and intangible assets in which saving appears and of liabilities which constitute negative components of saving. The number and scope of the forms of saving distinguished for each saver group depend primarily on the nature of the primary data from which the estimates are constructed. They also depend on the estimator's willingness to make use of possibly less reliable material in order to obtain figures for a finer breakdown of forms of saving which may disclose economically significant relationships or differences.

The distinction among separate forms of saving has been pushed furthest for individuals' saving, both because the available data are more plentiful and because saving of this group accounts for over two-thirds of total national saving. Separate estimates have been prepared for approximately three dozen forms of saving of nonfarm households and for approximately two dozen forms of agricultural saving, not counting the further breakdown of saving through consumer and producer durables into a dozen components. For unincorporated business enterprises and governments a scant dozen forms of saving and dissaving could be distinguished, but all the important ones are included. Corporate saving, being derived by the income account rather than the balance sheet method, did not permit a comparable breakdown by forms of saving.

9. ARRANGEMENT OF THE STUDY

2.41. The Study as now published consists of three volumes:
    (1) Volume I: Introduction, Tables of Annual Estimates of Saving
    (2) Volume II: Nature and Derivation of Annual Estimates of Saving
    (3) Volume III: Supplementary Studies
2.42. The tables of Volume I are divided into three groups:
    (1) Period (Economic and Quadrennial) Summary Tables (in Part I)
    (2) Annual Summary Tables } (in Part II).
    (3) Annual Detail Tables
2.43. The fifty period summary tables, identified by the letter S, combine annual figures, either taken without change from the basic annual tables in this volume, or transformed by deflation, by reduction to a per head basis, or by similar statistical manipulations. Three groupings of annual data have been used. The first covers the full period 1897–1949, including or excluding the ten

43

"abnormal" years 1917–1918, 1930–1933, and 1942–1945. For the second grouping, the fifty-three years from 1897 through 1949 have been arranged into the eight economic periods extending over four to twelve years listed in Division 2.37. The third grouping is more mechanical, and uses thirteen four-year periods beginning with 1898 and ending with 1949.

There are three main reasons for operating with period totals or averages—as has been done throughout this Introduction—in preference to annual data. The first is the reduction of statistical errors and the smoothing of incidental movements. The second is the fact that arrangement into periods, particularly into periods of varying length but relatively homogeneous economic character, helps the salient features and changes in the figures to stand out more clearly. The third is the impossibility of the reader's grasping fifty-three separate values rapidly. As any arrangement into periods is to some extent subjective and no single arrangement will suit all purposes, some readers will still want to consult the annual tables either for information on individual years or for the purpose of grouping the data differently. In doing so they should always remember that the figures for individual years must be treated with more circumspection than those for period totals or averages.

2.44.   The sixteen annual summary tables, identified by the letter T, contain estimates of national saving, of aggregate saving by the six main groups of savers distinguished throughout the Study, and of the various forms of total personal saving (which covers saving of nonfarm individuals, farmers, and unincorporated business enterprises) and saving of nonfarm individuals. These tables show figures expressed in deflated as well as current values.

2.45.   The 497 detailed annual tables, expressed with few exceptions in current prices, start with those dealing with the components of nonfarm individuals, saving, and are followed by tables on the saving of other groups of savers—farmers, unincorporated business enterprises, corporations, state and local governments, and the federal government. Each table is identified by a capital letter which indicates the saver group (e.g. A for Agriculture, C for Corporations), or in the case of nonfarm individuals the forms of saving to which it refers (e.g. R for nonfarm individuals' saving through real estate and V for their saving through securities), followed by an arabic numeral indicating the position of the table in the set of estimates of the saver group or form of saving to which it belongs. [17]

2.46.   In accordance with the "principle of reproducibility" [18] the figures are shown in the tables and explained in the footnotes in sufficient detail to enable the reader to retrace the derivation of the final estimates from the basic data. Ad-

[17] Following the same principle, tables in Volume II are identified by the letter B; those in Volume III by a letter appropriate to the subject of the section, namely, W for the national wealth and balance sheet data, E for the estate tax study, H for the sample household budgets, Y for an econometric study of the relation between saving and income, N for the national income tables, and X for the tables of the assets of private nonprofit institutions.

[18] See Volume II, Chapter III, Section 10 for a discussion of this principle and an explanation of deviations from it.

44

herence to this principle makes it necessary to present more basic data and inter-mediate calculations than has been common in similar publications, but even the detail now presented, both in the tables and in the footnotes, may at times not be entirely sufficient.

2.47. Wherever possible, each table covers the entire period from 1897 through 1949. Exceptions—and they are not rare—had to be made where methods of estimation, sources, or detail available changed substantially during the period. Thus in the section presenting the estimates of saving of the federal government, all tables dealing with the period 1897–1928 precede those devoted to the period 1929–1949.

2.48. The unit of measurement in most tables is $1 million, although figures to the nearest $100,000 have been shown in a few cases when the absolute values involved were very small. The fact that all series have been shown to the nearest $1 million—even though, in the cases of very rough estimates, generally rounded to the nearest $5, $10, or even $100 million—does not, of course, imply that the figures are accurate to that extent. Indeed, in most cases the last digit shown, and in many instances the last two digits, should not be regarded as significant.

2.49. The notes to the annual tables show column by column the sources of the figures and indicate any adjustments made in the original data. It is im-portant to realize that it is not the function of the notes to explain or to justify the selection of series, the choice of sources, or the adjustments made in trans-forming the original data into the estimates fitting into the statistical scheme of the Saving Study. These questions are discussed in Parts II and III of Volume II whenever it appeared necessary.

The scope of the notes varies somewhat depending on the presumed need for explanation. There is, however, one case in which the notes are much more ex-tensive than elsewhere and in which they fulfill many functions usually assigned to Volume II, viz. the section on saving of the federal government. This deviation has been motivated by the particular difficulties involved in this field, which called for detailed discussion but were of a technical nature, difficulties the treatment of which has generally been avoided in Volume I.

2.50. To facilitate use of the tables, two indexes have been added to the usual subject index which covers the Introduction. The first is a subject index indicating in which tables of Volume I figures on a given subject, e.g. assets of life insurance companies or saving through commercial banks, may be found. The second index permits the reader to ascertain at a glance in which tables use has been made of a given source, whether one of the standard comprehensive statistical publications which are used in dozens of separate tables, or a mono-graph or other source which has been utilized but once.

2.51. Volume II consists of three parts of different character. Part I starts with a fairly detailed presentation of the theory of measuring saving within a system of social accounts, and is completed by a discussion of the essential features of the derivation and presentation of the basic estimates underlying this study, by an appraisal of the margin of error in the estimates, and by their comparison with

45

other estimates of saving. Part II provides a discussion of the main practical problems encountered in deriving the estimates of the main components of the saving of nonagricultural individuals. Part III does the same for the saving of each of the other six main saver groups.

2.52. Volume III is a collection of special studies dealing with three main subjects, the national balance sheet and national wealth statement (Part I), the information on individuals' saving that can be extracted from sample household budgets (Part II), and the wealth of the estate tax population (Part III). It also contains three supplementary studies: one (Part IV) summarizing a preliminary econometric study of the relation between saving and income, some results of which are used in Chapter I of the Introduction; the second (Part V) presenting the estimates of national and personal income that have been used in the analysis of saving, particularly in Chapter III of the Introduction; and the third (Part VI) giving the estimates of the aggregate value and distribution of nonoperating assets of private nonfinancial nonprofit institutions which are utilized in Chapter VIII of the Introduction.

These studies serve a double purpose. Their primary function, of course, is to provide factual information on the saving process. In doing so they fulfill a function similar to that performed in Volume I and II by the annual estimates of saving from 1897 to 1949, which may be regarded as the statistical backbone of the Study. Beyond this, however, the various parts of Volume III constitute monographs dealing with relatively well-defined subjects and containing a substantial amount of new data or analyses. They may, therefore, be consulted by readers who are interested in the subject of the monograph rather than in the entire Saving Study.

III

THE TREND OF TOTAL NATIONAL
AND PERSONAL SAVING

1. Summary of Findings

3.01. Over the last century saving has increased almost without interruption if the usual cyclical fluctuations and the effects of war are disregarded, the most important exception being the 1930's. This statement applies whether saving is measured in current prices or in constant prices, whether it is based on aggregate or per head figures, whether it refers to total national or to personal saving, and irrespective of the definition of saving which is used. There are, however, considerable differences in the rate of growth between saving estimates of different scope, breadth, and method. (Table IV.)

3.02. No simple algebraic curve has been found which fits national or personal saving, in current or deflated values, reasonably well for the entire fifty-three year period covered by the Study. However, for the first thirty years, i.e. from 1897 to 1929, the actual values are fairly close to a logarithmic straight line, a fact which implies stability in the long-term trend of growth during these three decades. (Subsection 3d.)

3.03. The very scanty evidence on the trend of saving during the nineteenth century points to an average rate of growth of deflated national saving per head of approximately 2 percent a year, i.e. the same order of magnitude as that observed during the first half of the twentieth century. Although very little is known about long-term fluctuations in the rate at which saving grew during the nineteenth century, it is very unlikely that the rate showed a steadily declining trend. On the contrary, it is quite possible that growth was most rapid in the two decades following the Civil War. The rate of growth of aggregate deflated saving probably declined over the nineteenth century, though not spectacularly. (Section 5.)

3.04. Most of the flattening in the trend of aggregate deflated saving which is observable since late in the nineteenth century reflects the slowing down of population growth. Deflated saving per head, including consumer durables, shows no definite evidence of long-term deceleration since the end of the nineteenth century, or of departure from an average rate of growth of almost 2 percent a year. The rate of growth of personal saving per head excluding consumer durables, however, appears to have been declining slowly. (Subsection 3d.)

3.05. The proportion of income saved fails to show a long-term trend in either direction over the past half century if consumer durables are included, but has declined slightly if they are excluded. For longer periods the saving ratio has averaged approximately one-eighth of national and one-tenth of personal saving if consumer durables are included but the two World Wars and the Great De-

CHART V

THE CONTOUR OF NATIONAL SAVING

Standard Social Accounting Concept

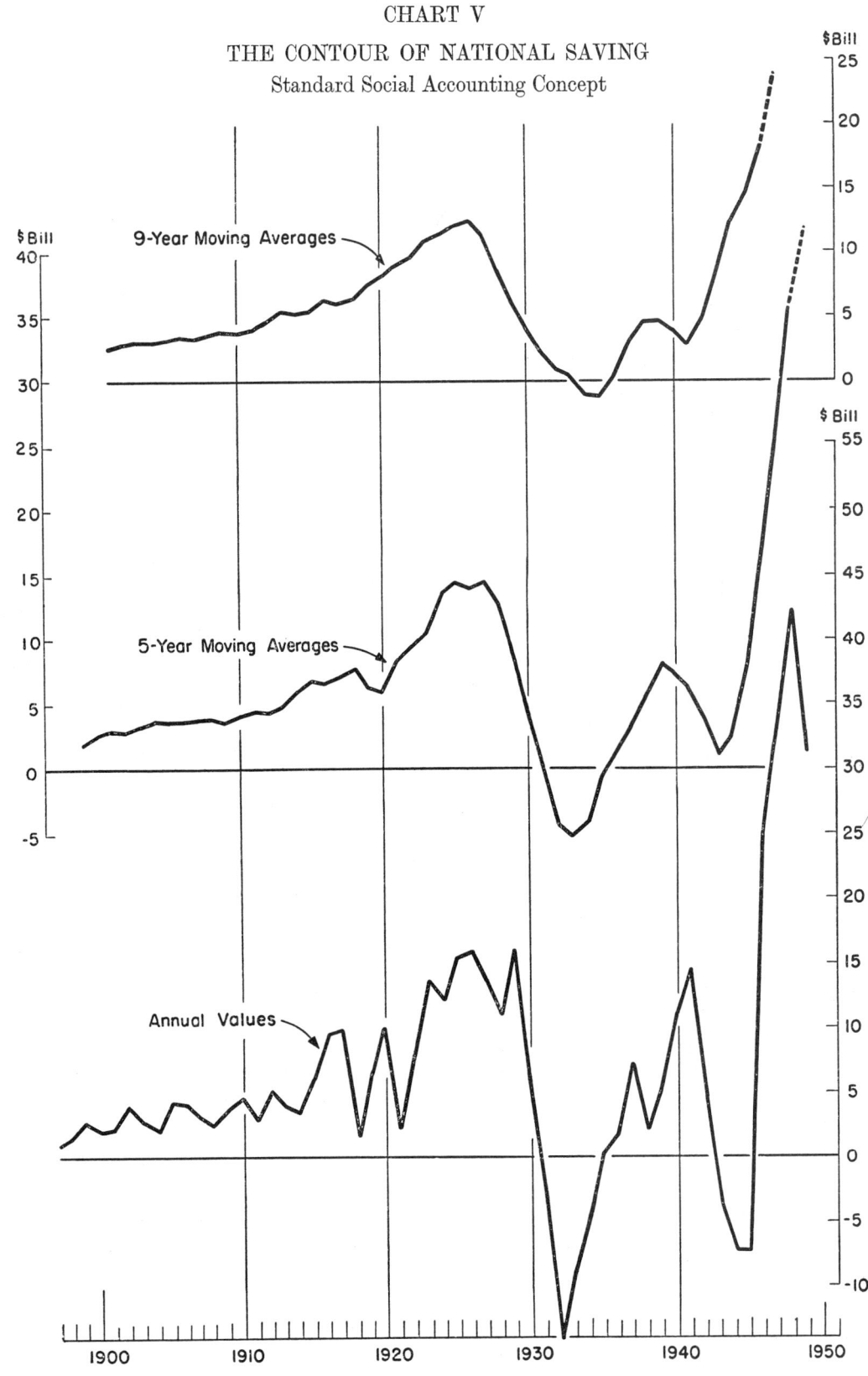

pression disregarded. This ratio has, of course, been somewhat higher for periods of full employment during peacetime—approximately one-sixth for national and one-seventh for personal saving. (Section 4.)

3.06. If the level of the saving ratio in the half dozen years after World War II can be taken as typical of the situation at midcentury, no break with the pre-1930 level is observable so long as attention is directed towards aggregate national or personal saving, in the former case even if consumer durables are excluded. (Subsection 3d.)

2. A First Look at the Basic Movements of Saving, 1897 to 1952

3.07. Before starting to analyze the basic movements in total saving, it is well to have a look at the broad contour of the series. Even for such a preliminary exploration two different series must be considered—national saving and personal saving, both estimated following the social accounting concept. They must be viewed, moreover, from different distances, first closely enough to distinguish annual features and then from farther away where only the main ups and downs remain visible.

3.08. The close-range view obtained from the annual data in the bottom panel of Chart v discloses the following features of national saving: First a jagged but fairly regular upward movement from 1897 to 1914; then two mountains with sharp peaks—at approximately the same height—in 1917 and 1920, and deep but narrow valleys in 1918 and 1921; after that an irregular high plateau from 1923 to 1929; then a wide trough of great depth with the bottom in 1932–1933 but extending through most of the thirties; after the precarious peak of 1941 another trough, equally deep but much narrower, from 1942 to 1945; and finally, beginning in 1946, a sharp rise to a level much higher than any reached before.

3.09. The moving five- and nine-year averages, which are shown in the upper panels of Chart v, remove or greatly reduce the influence of cyclical fluctuations and of incidental movements other than wars. In the nine-year average the basic contour of national saving is a fairly smooth upward slope from the beginning of the century to the late twenties, considerably steeper from about 1912 on than for the preceding decade; followed by a deep and broad trough extending over almost two decades; and ending with a sharp rise to a new level, the position and slope of which will not become clear before at least the midfifties, but which in absolute terms will be well above the previous peak of the twenties.

3.10. Up to 1915 the picture presented by the annual estimates of personal saving in the lower panel of Chart vi hardly differs from that for national saving. [1] However, the bulge of personal saving during World War I is much more pronounced than in the case of national saving, and its peak in 1918 exceeds the level

---

[1] While the picture refers specifically to the aggregate saving of three groups—nonfarm individuals, farmers, and unincorporated business enterprises—the contour would be essentially similar if the chart represented two more comprehensive totals, viz. nonfederal saving and private saving; or one slightly less comprehensive total, viz. saving by nonagricultural individuals.

CHART VI

THE CONTOUR OF PERSONAL SAVING
Standard Social Accounting Concept

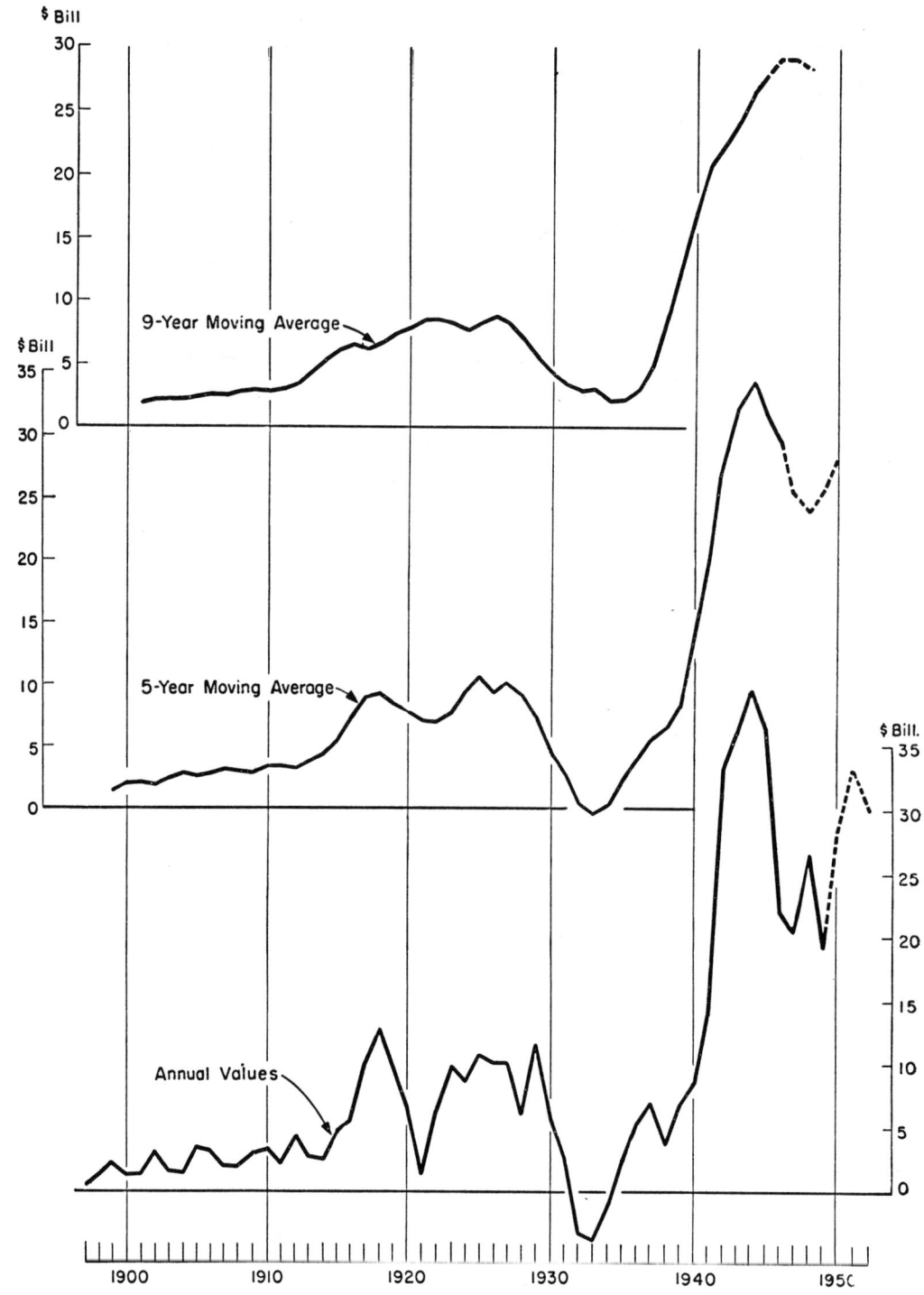

of the plateau of the twenties while for national saving it keeps well below it. The peak of 1920, on the other hand, disappears altogether. The plateau of the twenties is an equally outstanding feature, but its evenness is more pronounced. The trough of the Great Depression, while still conspicuous, is definitely less marked than in the case of national saving. The most striking difference between the two series, however, occurs in the forties. The trough during World War II visible in the series of national saving disappears entirely, and is replaced by a sharp peak in personal saving. As a result the level of 1946-1949 is now well below the World War II peak, though it is still twice as high as the level of the highlands of the twenties.

Comparison of Charts V and VI will indicate several differences in the turning points, slope, amplitude, and sometimes even the direction of the curves of national and personal saving. Most of these differences, and all of the conspicuous ones, are traceable to the fact that personal saving is affected less—and in the opposite direction—by the large dissaving of the federal government in both World Wars. It is this dissaving, reflecting deficits due to military expenditures, [2] which is responsible for a good deal of the irregularities in aggregate national saving. As a result the contour of personal saving is smoother than that of national saving.

3.11.   Nine years probably constitute a period prolonged enough to eliminate the influence of all movements except long-term trends and extraordinary movements such as the Great Depression and World War II. The contour traced by the nine-year moving average of saving may, therefore, be regarded as a reasonable approximation to its basic movement, at least preliminarily. It is therefore of some interest that the movements of this series are compatible with the swings of about twenty years' duration distinguished by Kuznets in national income and other basic economic series. [3] The first wave, which probably started in the mid-1890's, although it can be followed in our figures only from the turn of the century, ends shortly before World War I, probably in 1912. Its peak, not easily located in the nine-year average, appears to have occurred in 1905–1906. The second wave is fairly well defined, starting around 1912, reaching a peak in 1926, and ending in a deep trough in 1935. It is too early to date the third wave, particularly because of the distortions introduced by World War II and the Korean War. If these are allowed for, its peak appears to have been reached in the late forties or early fifties.

3.12.   Presentation of these curves of current national and personal saving—unadjusted for price changes and growth of population—has two main purposes. The first is to fix the contours of the curves in the reader's mind. The second may

[2] Allowance for expenditures on durable military assets, i.e. inclusion of changes in stock of durable military assets among saving, would slightly reduce the difference between the contours of national and personal saving, but would by no means eliminate them, as Chart IX shows.

[3] These waves will be analyzed in Kuznets' forthcoming volume on *Capital Formation and Financing in the United States, Trends and Prospects*. An earlier discussion will be found in his *Secular Movements in Production and Prices*, 1930.

be more important. It is to suggest that the movements of saving up to the late twenties follow a sufficiently even course to be regarded as fluctuations around a steady upward trend, but that the movements between 1930 and 1945 cannot be so interpreted.

3. The Trend of Saving from 1897 to 1949

3.13. There is no one algebraic method of determining long-term trends which is always applicable and productive of significant results. This is particularly true for saving because the series includes negative values which rule out the direct application to the entire period of some common methods of trend analysis, such as the fitting of logarithmic trends. We therefore must experiment with different approaches and tread warily. From the numerous approaches which may be thought of, five have been selected which appear to be most promising and which are applied in the following sections to the principal estimates of national and personal saving developed by this study.

We shall start with a comparison of the level of saving near the beginning of the period, at the middle of the period in the twenties, and at the end of the period, i.e. the years after World War II. This, of course, is the simplest—and possibly an oversimplified—approach, since it disregards the path by which the levels are connected. We shall then proceed to measure trends by changes between period averages, using the eight economic periods of four to twelve years distinguished throughout this Introduction. This approach is equivalent to measuring trends as a series of steps, and seeing whether the steps form a reasonably regular pattern. The third method, that of moving averages, differs in that trends are represented not by a series of steps but by a relatively smooth curve, although not one following a simple mathematical form. This curve is obtained by substituting for each year's actual saving the average of that year's saving and the saving of a given number of preceding and succeeding years. This method produces a series of values which for any one year obviously differs, possibly even to a substantial extent, from the year's actual saving, but which distributes actual saving for the entire period in a way which eliminates ups and downs of short duration, and thus brings out the basic movements. Fourthly, an attempt is made to fit simple algebraic curves to the annual estimates and to see whether the actual values for the post-World War II period lie reasonably close to the trend lines derived from the period 1897–1929. In the fifth method income is used as the "reference trend" of saving, i.e. it is assumed that the movements of income constitute the matrix of the movements of saving so that the ratios of saving to income may be regarded as reflecting the deviations of saving from its long-term trend, if not for individual years at least for groups of years.

a. *Changes between level of saving at beginning, middle, and end of period*

3.14. A comparison of the level of saving at the beginning, midpoint, and end of the period studied provides an adequate measure of basic movements only if two

52

conditions are met, viz. first, if the path taken by the series from the beginning to the middle level and from the middle to the closing level is reasonably smooth, and secondly, if the cyclical standing of each period—in relation to both short-term cycles and long-term waves—is similar. Even if these conditions are not fully complied with, this method provides at least a starting point for the analysis of trends. In that function it has the advantage that, because of its simplicity, it can be applied easily to a large number of series and hence can be used to winnow out the series which justify more detailed analysis.

The calculations are based throughout on four-year averages in order to eliminate vagaries of the estimates for individual years. The use of such averages is particularly to be recommended when, as is the case here, the years included in the average are of a reasonably homogeneous character economically, and do not show too much variation from year to year. The initial level is that of the years 1906–1909, the central level that of 1926–1929, and the terminal level that of 1946–1949. [4]

3.15. The main purpose of the comparison between these three quadrennial benchmarks is to obtain a first impression of the differences in trend between saving estimates of varying scope, breadth, method, and unit of measurement. This is provided in Table III and summarized in Divisions 3.16 to 3.25. This summarization does not touch upon differences in the rate of growth of saving between the two twenty-year intervals, as such differences are better observed in continuous period averages, moving averages, or fitted trends.

3.16. For the entire period, i.e. for the forty-year span between the initial and terminal benchmarks, saving in current prices has increased, as Table III, section I, shows, between approximately 660 percent (nonagricultural individuals' saving) and somewhat over 800 percent (national, nonfederal, and private saving). These variations, due mainly to a slightly more rapid increase in agricultural, corporate, and state and local government saving, do not seem large enough to indicate significant differences in trends of saving. If a smooth path of saving between the initial and the terminal benchmark periods is assumed, the figures indicate annual rates of growth between 5.2 percent for nonagricultural individuals' saving and 5.8 percent for national saving.

Differences are, however, somewhat larger for the two subperiods. On the same assumption they vary for the twenty-year interval from 1906–1909 to 1926–1929 between 6.5 percent for nonagricultural individuals' saving and 7.4 percent for national saving. For the interval between 1926–1929 and 1946–1949 the rates range from 4.0 percent for nonagricultural individuals' saving to 4.7 percent for private saving. It will be noted that those aggregates, which show a particularly rapid growth in the first period, tend to exhibit a relatively slow increase in the second period. This explains why the

[4] These twenty-year intervals have been selected because the three benchmark periods used are reasonably similar in cyclical standing, representing years of practically full employment and high business activity.

TABLE III

INCREASE IN SAVING BETWEEN QUADRENNIAL BENCHMARKS

1906–1909, 1926–1929, and 1946–1949

Variant Concepts and Methods

Percent

	1906–1909 to 1926–1929	1926–1929 to 1946–1949	1906–1909 to 1946–1949
I. Concepts of varying scope a			
1. National saving	319	132	870
2. Nonfederal saving	293	136	827
3. Private saving	268	150	821
4. Personal saving	265	144	789
5. Nonagricultural individuals' saving	249	118	660
II. Concepts varying in method			
1. National saving			
a. Social accounting concept	319	132	870
b. Business accounting concept	232	218	956
c. Cash flow concept	283	119	739
2. Personal saving			
a. Social accounting concept	265	144	789
b. Business accounting concept	204	209	838
c. Cash flow concept	245	109	621
III. Concepts of varying breadth			
1. National saving			
a. Standard	319	132	870
b. Narrow b	404	102	718
c. Broad c	324	81	667
2. Personal saving			
a. Standard	265	144	789
b. Narrow b	236	99	569
c. Broad c	274	135	779
IV. Current and deflated values			
1. National saving, standard concept			
a. Current values	319	132	870
b. Deflated by index of general price level	134	65	286
c. Deflated by index of group purchasing power	118	63	255
d. Deflated by index of wage level	62	3	67
2. Personal saving, standard concept			
a. Current values	265	144	789
b. Deflated by index of general price level	104	75	256
c. Deflated by index of group purchasing power	90	86	252
d. Deflated by index of wage level	41	9	54
V. Aggregate and unit values			
1. National saving, standard concept			
a. Aggregate, current	319	132	870
b. Aggregate, deflated by index of general price level	134	65	286
c. Deflated, per inhabitant	71	36	133
d. Deflated, per consumption unit	70	35	129
e. Deflated, per household	55	18	84
2. Personal saving, standard concept			
a. Aggregate, current	265	144	789
b. Aggregate, deflated by index of general price level	104	75	256
c. Deflated, per inhabitant	49	44	116
d. Deflated, per consumption unit	47	43	111
e. Deflated, per household	35	25	70

a Standard social accounting concept.   b Excluding consumer durables.
c Including durable military assets, land costs, and two other adjustments.
Source: Tables S-1 to S-4.

rates for the entire period vary considerably less than those for either of the two subperiods.

Some of the reasons for these differences, both as between the two subperiods and as between the aggregates of different scope, will be investigated later, in Chapter IV.

It suffices here to note that the trend, measured by the rate of increase between benchmarks of twenty-year intervals, is approximately the same whether the conclusions are based on personal saving, the estimates of which are analyzed in the rest of this chapter, or on nonfederal, private, or nonagricultural individuals' saving, for which such an analysis is omitted.

3.17. For the entire period as well as for the second subperiod, social accounting saving has increased less than business accounting saving, while the opposite relation prevails in the first subperiod (Table III, section II). The reason for this difference in the behavior of the two series lies mainly in the treatment of depreciation allowances and of inventory profits and losses. Under the social accounting concept, it will be recalled, depreciation allowances are calculated at replacement cost, while they are figured at original cost under the business accounting concept. When prices rise replacement cost depreciation exceeds original cost depreciation and social accounting saving is smaller than business accounting saving. Inventory profits and losses are excluded from social accounting saving and included in business accounting saving. In periods of rising prices business accounting saving will, therefore, exceed social accounting saving, other things being equal. The differences in the rates of increase between benchmark periods, which appear in Table III, are due to a combination of these two factors, as well as to the less important effects of a number of other circumstances. As prices were generally rising during the entire period, replacement cost depreciation may be expected to be in excess of original cost depreciation. If this were the only difference involved, social accounting saving would be lower than business accounting saving. Inventory profits and losses tend in the same direction. They were very substantial in the terminal benchmark period but small in the initial and central periods. The differences may be expected to be more pronounced for national than for personal saving as most inventory profits and losses are attributable to corporations and, hence, do not enter into the calculation of personal saving. These expectations are borne out by the figures in Table III.

3.18. Cash saving, which ignores depreciation altogether but includes capital gains and losses, has increased substantially less than either business accounting or social accounting saving. This holds for the period as a whole and for the second subperiod, and for national as well as personal saving. The relationship, which may at first seem strange since the inclusion in cash saving of inventory profits and losses ought to have lifted its rate of increase above that of social accounting saving, is explained by the increasing importance of depreciation allowances compared to net saving. When the ratio of depreciation allowances to net saving (and hence also the ratio of depreciation allowances to gross saving and the ratio of gross to net saving) increases, as it has throughout the period, a slower increase in cash saving than in either business or social accounting saving is an arithmetic consequence.[5]

3.19. The discussion of trends in saving has so far been based on the standard concept which includes consumer durable goods but excludes durable military assets. For some purposes, however, we want either a narrower alternative from which consumer durables are excluded, or a broader alternative which includes durable military assets and net soil improvement.

3.20. The trend of saving is flatter if consumer durables are excluded, as can be seen from Table III. This is due to the fact that saving through consumer durables has increased more rapidly than the aggregate of other forms of saving, particularly during the second half of the period. The difference is obviously more pronounced for personal than national saving, since the same absolute difference (saving through consumer durables) is compared with a total which is larger in the case of national than of personal saving.

3.21. Inclusion of durable military assets and soil improvement as well as two other technical adjustments makes no difference for the first half of the period, but decreases the rate of increase in saving for the second half and for the period as a whole. This results from the fact that saving through durable military assets was negative for the terminal benchmark period 1946–1949 as expenditures on newly acquired durable military assets were then considerably below the heavy depreciation allowances which must be figured on the large stock of such assets produced during World War II if account is taken of the relatively rapid obsolescence of most types of military equipment.

3.22. Up to this point the rates of increase in different variants of saving, for the entire span or for either of the two subperiods, have all been of the same order of magnitude even though they show considerable variation, i.e. within a range of 1 to $1\frac{1}{2}$. This clustering of the rates of increase, irrespective of the inclusiveness of coverage or the method of calculation, is largely due to the fact that all the estimates were expressed in current prices and, therefore, were all affected by the pronounced rise in prices over the entire period and during both subperiods. The picture changes when we turn to trends in saving expressed in different units of measurement, i.e. the trends of current saving deflated by indices of either the

---

[5] Designating the amounts of gross saving, net saving, and depreciation allowances by G, N, and D, respectively, and the rates of increase in gross saving and depreciation allowances between two periods, indicated by subscripts 0 and 1, by g and d, we have

$$\frac{N_1}{N_0} = \frac{gG_0 - dD_0}{G_0 - D_0}$$

$$\frac{G_1}{G_0} : \frac{N_1}{N_0} = \frac{gG_0 - gD_0}{gG_0 - dD_0}$$

This expression is larger than unity if $d > g$ and so long as the denominator is positive as assumed in the text; and exceeds unity to an extent depending on the ratio $\frac{d}{g}$.

general price level, the wage level, or the purchasing power of the different groups of savers.[6]

3.23. When base-year (1929) rather than current prices are used as a unit of measurement—and this is necessary if the effect of price fluctuations is to be eliminated—all rates of increase are considerably lower. This simply reflects the fact that the trend of prices has been rising between the three benchmark periods. The increase in saving between the initial and the terminal benchmarks is approximately 250 percent if either the general price level or group purchasing power indices are used as deflators, compared to an increase of nearly 900 percent in saving measured in current prices (Table III). The rate of increase per year—again assuming a smooth path between benchmarks—is now about $3\frac{1}{4}$ percent against nearly 6 percent for national saving in current prices. The difference between the trends in deflated and current prices is more pronounced in the first than in the second half of the period, as would be expected since the relative increase in the price level was considerably larger between 1906–1909 and the late twenties than in the following twenty years.

3.24. Still more striking differences appear if the figures are reduced by means of the average level of hourly wages, i.e. if saving is expressed in terms of number of man-hours. The man-hour equivalent of aggregate national or personal saving is then found to have increased by only approximately 60 percent between the initial and terminal benchmark periods. As a result national saving in wage units increased only at the rate of 1.3 percent per year for the entire period compared to a rate of increase of about 5.8 percent for current saving and one of 3.4 percent for saving deflated by the general price level. The much slower growth of aggregate saving in terms of man-hours, of course, is nothing but a reflection of the rise in real wages, i.e. the fact that wages have increased substantially in terms of the general price level or the consumer price index.

3.25. During the period covered by the Study not only has the price level changed markedly, generally upwards, strongly influencing all magnitudes which are expressed in current prices, but the basis of the American economy, as measured by the number of inhabitants or the size of the labor force, has also grown considerably, and much more regularly than any basic economic magnitude such as saving or national income, even if the latter are adjusted for price fluctuations. It is, therefore, necessary to determine the trend of saving not only expressed in a relatively stable unit of measurement but also reduced to an average per economic unit. This is achieved, in effect, if aggregate real saving, using the general price level as deflator, is divided by the number either of inhabitants, or of households, or of equivalent full consumers, or of members of the labor force, and the resulting trends in real saving per unit are studied.

It is immediately evident that the trends in real saving per unit are of an

[6] In deflation by group purchasing power indices, current saving of each major saver group is reduced to the 1929 level by means of an index of purchasing power of that specific group. Deflated national or personal saving is obtained by totalling the components so deflated. The details of the procedure are explained in the notes to Table T-14.

57

order of magnitude which differs from aggregate saving either in current or 1929 prices. While national saving increased between the initial and terminal benchmarks by approximately 870 percent in current prices and 285 percent in terms of the general price level, the increase in real saving per unit is only between approximately 80 and 130 percent, depending on the divisor used.[7] Both halves of the period are about equally affected, i.e. the relative increase per unit is close to half of that in aggregate real saving.[8] For the total period the annual rate of increase in real national saving per head varies between 1.5 percent (real saving per household) and 2.1 percent (real saving per inhabitant or equivalent consumer unit), against rates of 5.8 percent for current and 3.4 percent for deflated aggregate saving.

b. *Changes in level of saving between subperiods*

3.26. The preceding section was based on the assumption that the average level of saving during four-year periods separated by a distance of twenty years could be used to measure the trend of saving, i.e. that a trend line existed and that the benchmark averages lay on or at least near this line. Even if this assumption is correct one would want the level of saving in the intervals to lie on or reasonably symmetrically around the line joining the benchmark periods. Otherwise the deviations from the assumed trend line may be so large as to create doubt about its economic meaning or to raise the question whether any simple trend exists. Tables S-1 to S-4 permit us to investigate these possibilities by showing averages, both for four-year periods and for economic periods of four to twelve years, in the dozen series of national and personal saving, differing in scope, method of calculation, and unit of measurement, which have been used in the analysis of trends of saving. Charts VII and VIII, based on the eight economic periods, illustrate the trends for national and personal saving, following the social accounting concept, in aggregate current, aggregate deflated, and deflated per head values. There is no need to discuss here each of the variants of saving and to explain the differences in their behavior, as was done in the preceding section.

3.27. A summary of the characteristics of the different series shows that:

(1) Period-to-period changes vary considerably from what would be expected if total changes between benchmarks were evenly distributed over the interval, i.e. if the path between benchmarks were a smooth one. This is particularly true of the second half of the period.

(2) Differences between variants of saving are generally more pronounced than they appear in the benchmark comparisons. There are even considerable differ-

---

[7] The differences between the rates of increase in real saving per inhabitant, per household, and per equivalent full consumer solely reflect differential rates of growth of these three magnitudes. Which of the three magnitudes should be used to reduce aggregate real saving depends on the purpose of the analysis. At this point the differences resulting from the application of the one rather than the other divisor are immaterial.

[8] This relation is based on the percentage increase between benchmark periods as it is shown in Table III.

58

CHART VII

NATIONAL SAVING

Standard Social Accounting Concept; Period Averages

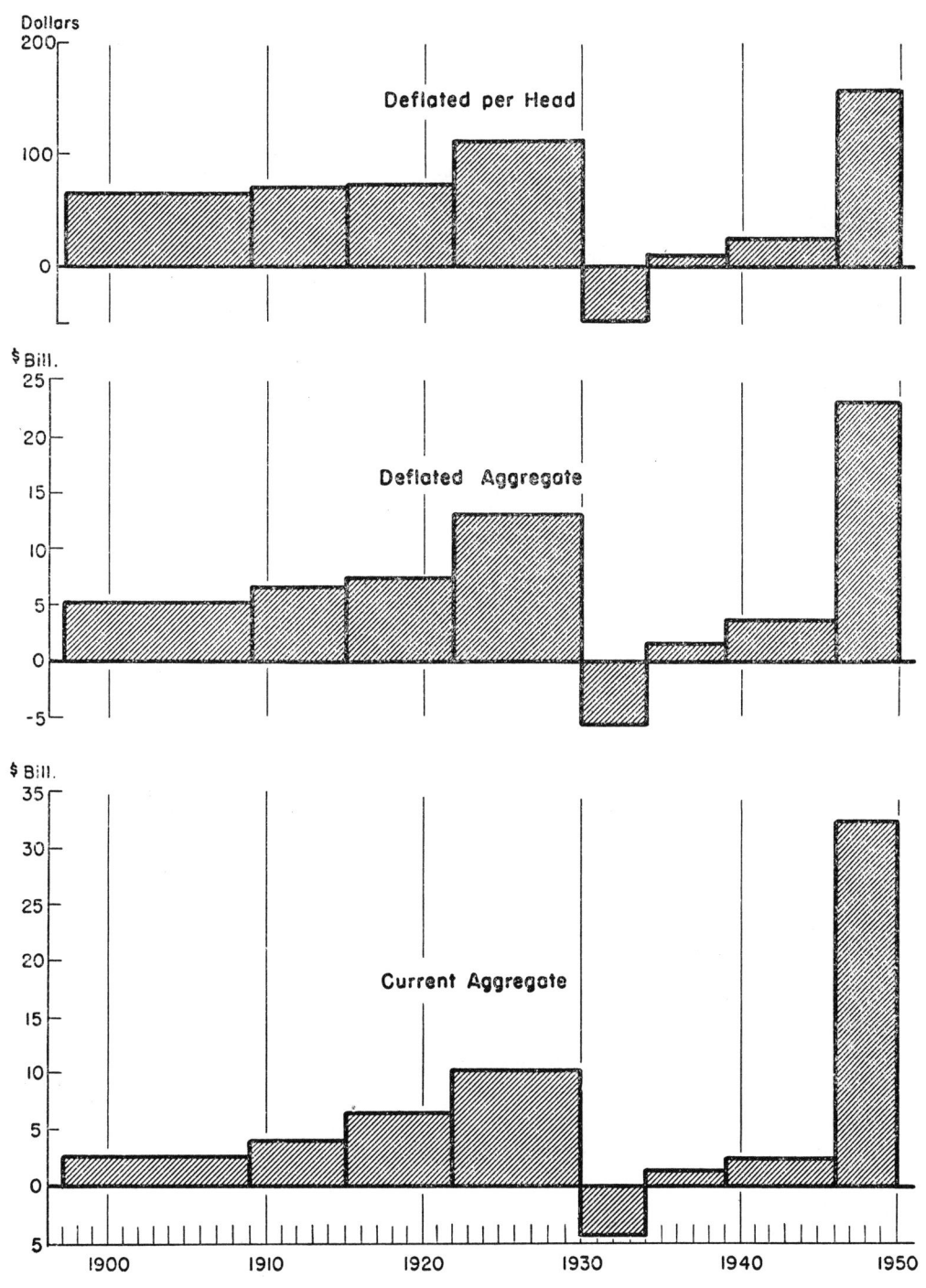

CHART VIII

PERSONAL SAVING

Standard Social Accounting Concept; Period Averages

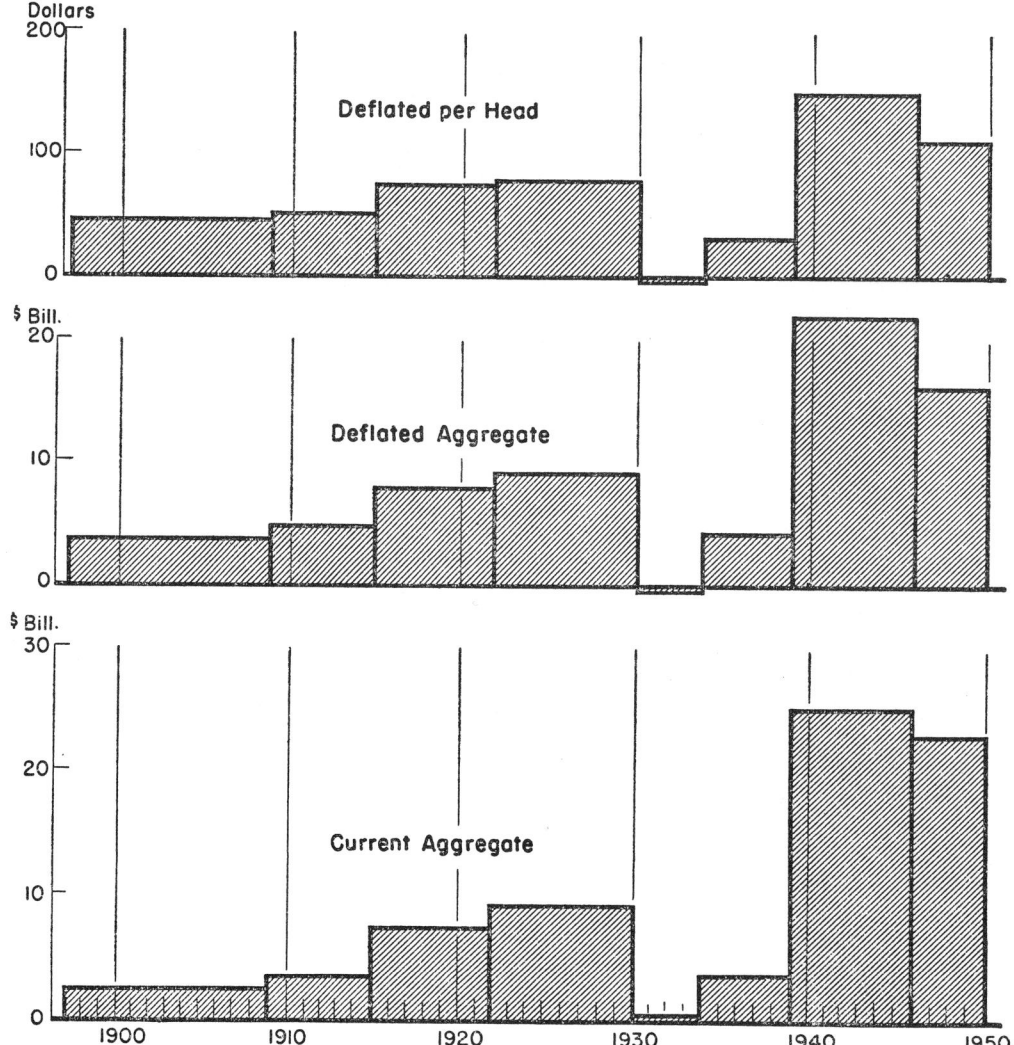

ences between national and personal saving which were not noticeable when the analysis was limited to the three benchmark periods.

(3) The rates of change follow a more regular pattern for personal than for national saving, particularly during the first part of the period. This points to the fact that federal saving and corporate saving are the most volatile components of national saving.

(4) The regularity, or irregularity, in period-to-period changes is about the same whether saving is calculated according to the social accounting or the

business accounting concept. Cash saving, however, as a rule shows smaller relative variations than either of the other concepts.

(5) Exclusion of consumer durables produces a somewhat less variable pattern for economic periods; in the case of four-year periods the difference is hardly noticeable.

3.28. The main conclusion which can be drawn from the period-to-period changes in the different variants of saving is that the figures delineate a movement sufficiently regular to be regarded as a long-term trend only for the first half of the period. Even in this case the steps, which represent the period-to-period changes, do not trace a straight or simple path. The period-to-period rate of increase is more rapid in the middle of the first subperiod than at either the beginning or the end.

No simple trend is visible after 1929. Sharp, rather short movements showing some cyclical pattern dominate. The pattern is quite different between national and personal saving, and considerable differences are shown for the variants of each. National current saving (Chart VII), for instance, shows a sharp decline in the period-to-period rates of change in the early thirties, and two periods of rapid increase—in the late thirties and after World War II. The same rhythm can be distinguished in aggregate and per unit deflated saving, although the movements are less violent than in current values.[9] Personal saving also shows two periods of increasing and one of declining rates of change, but they are not quite identical with those evident in national saving (Chart VIII). Changes are upward both in the late thirties and, contrary to the movements in national saving, in the first half of the forties. They are downward in the early thirties, as in national saving, but also after World War II.

c. *The trend as reflected in moving averages of annual values*

3.29. The use of moving averages as indicators of trend is justified by two of their characteristics. First, if the length of the averaging period is equal to the length of the cycles in the original data (or to an integral multiple thereof) moving averages entirely eliminate cyclical movements. Secondly, moving averages are under such circumstances flexible enough to depict a trend truthfully and closely even if it is not a simple curve. Full realization of these possibilities of moving averages, however, depends on at least two conditions, regularity in length and amplitude of the cycles and absence of strong incidental movements in the underlying data.[10]

[9] Some of the violence in the movements of the rates of change between four-year or economic period averages is due to the nature of the calculation. If saving in any one period is of small absolute amount, whether positive or negative, changes from the preceding or to the succeeding period may yield very high percentages even when the absolute changes are not particularly large. In judging the significance of period-to-period changes one must therefore take account of both the relative and the absolute changes.

[10] When the length of the cycles in the original data varies, use of an unchanging averaging period necessarily will lead to the inclusion of either more or less than one full cycle. Depending on whether the missing or additional periods belong to a cyclical upswing or downswing the moving

The movements of saving during the period from 1897 to 1949 obviously do not meet either of the two conditions which make moving averages an easy and flexible means of disclosing trends. We shall see in Chapter VII that cyclical movements in the saving series have shown considerable variation in length and amplitude. It is also known that the series are affected by at least two strong incidental movements, viz. those reflecting the two World Wars. We therefore cannot expect to benefit as much from the use of moving averages in our attempt to determine trends of saving as might be possible under more favorable circumstances. Nevertheless, moving averages are still able to produce a much smoother picture of the movements of saving than can be obtained from an inspection of annual data, and, moreover, a picture that is essentially truthful. They therefore bring us one step nearer to deciding whether or not saving since the turn of the century has shown movements which can be regarded as long-term trends; and if so, to determining the form of such trends.

3.30. Differences between the movements of the nine-year moving averages of national and personal saving following the standard social accounting concept have already been reviewed in Section 2 of this chapter. Differences in movement of either national or personal saving appear when nine-year moving averages of estimates of different breath, scope, or unit of measurement are compared, as will be done in the following divisions.

3.31. Chart IX shows that the differences between the standard, the narrow, and the broad social accounting concepts are relatively small, at least in the case of personal saving. They consist mostly in a slightly steeper slope of the standard and the broad as compared to the narrow estimate. The main reason for this difference, of course, is the particularly rapid growth of saving through consumer durables, which is excluded from the narrow concept.

3.32. Other differences appear in Chart X, where the standard social accounting concept of saving is compared with the business accounting and cash concepts. The increase in cash saving appears to be much larger than that in business accounting saving, and the increase in business accounting saving in turn appears to exceed that of social accounting saving. On a relative basis, as they would appear on a logarithmic scale, the trends differ considerably less, but the differences are still visible. The result of these differences may be seen by a comparison of the levels early in the century and in 1945, the last year for which nine-year averages can be calculated.[11] During this period of more than forty years cash saving has increased to more than 6 times its level at the beginning of the century, and business accounting saving to more than 7 times, while social accounting saving has expanded to less than 5 times its earlier size.

---

average will then show the influence of cyclical movements by being higher or lower than an average for full cycles. If the peak and trough of one cycle are much more below or above the trend line than those of another the residual influence of cyclical movements on the moving averages will be reinforced.

[11] Rough estimates have been made for personal saving, social accounting concept, in 1950–1952; hence in this case it is possible to extend the nine-year moving average to 1948.

CHART IX

NATIONAL AND PERSONAL SAVING

Variant Definitions of Saving
Social Accounting Concept
Nine-Year Moving Averages

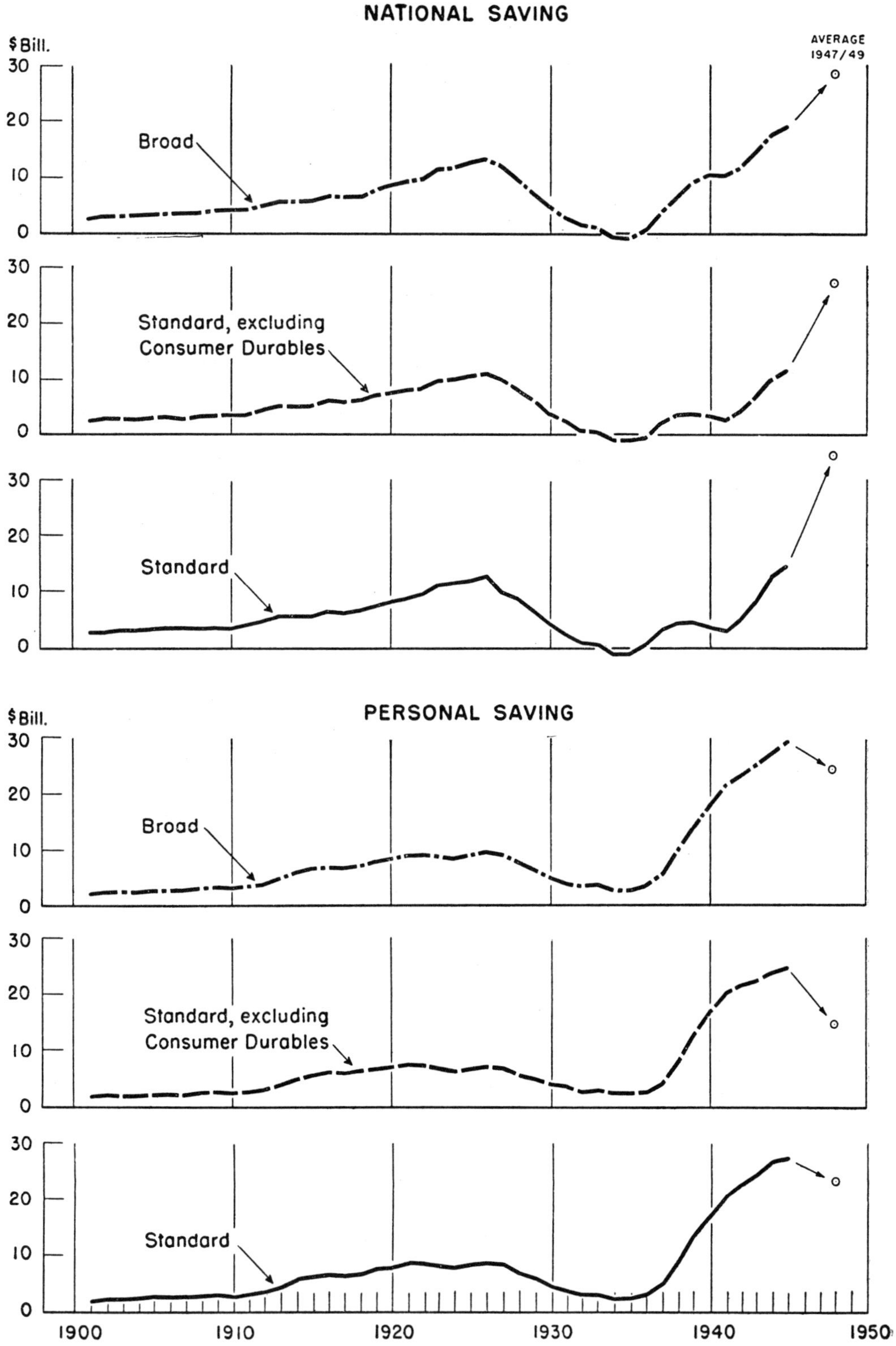
NATIONAL SAVING
$ Bill.
AVERAGE 1947/49
30
20
10
0
Broad
Standard, excluding Consumer Durables
Standard
PERSONAL SAVING
$ Bill.
Broad
Standard, excluding Consumer Durables
Standard
1900
1910
1920
1930
1940
1950

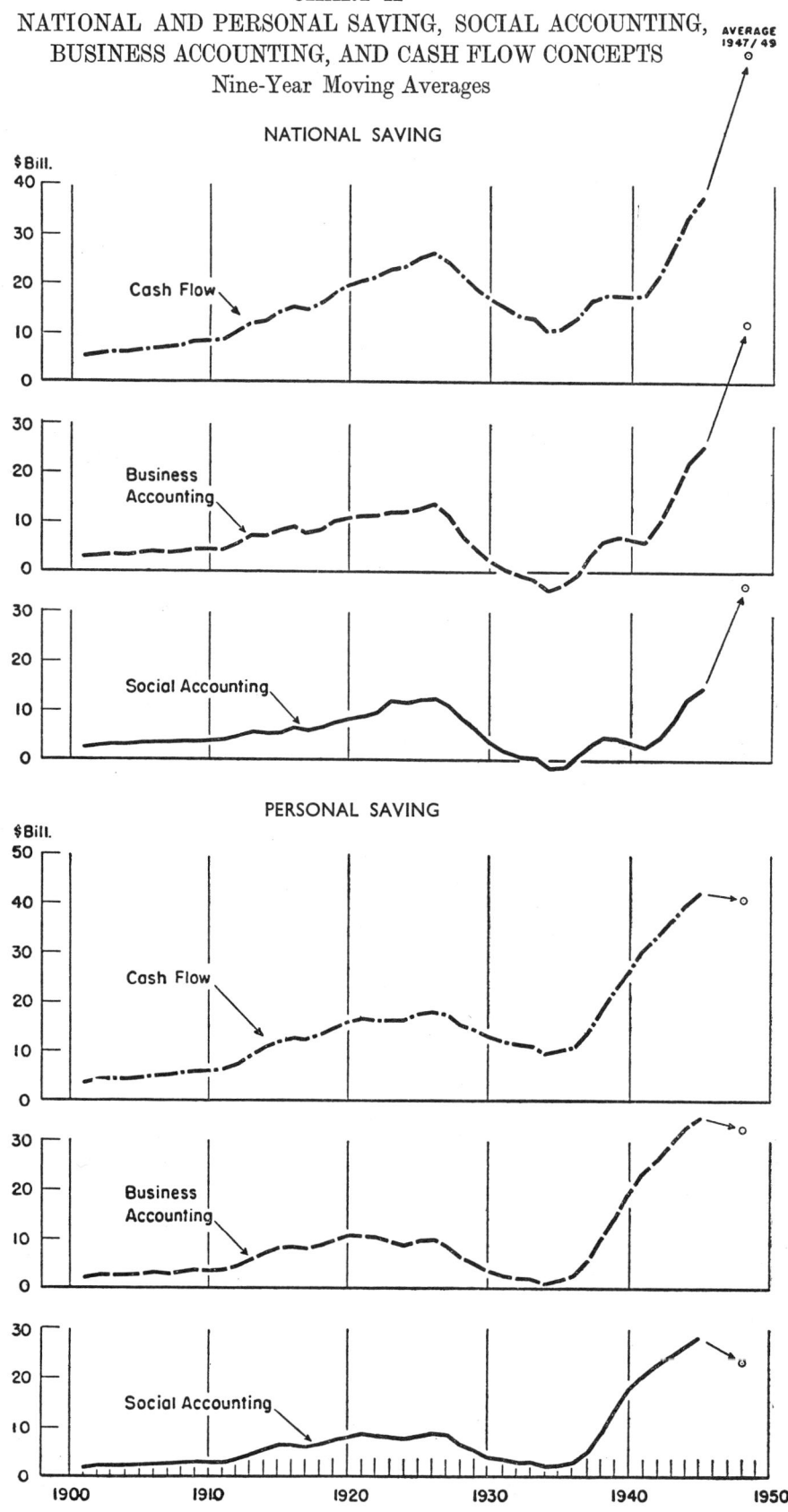

CHART X

NATIONAL AND PERSONAL SAVING, SOCIAL ACCOUNTING,
BUSINESS ACCOUNTING, AND CASH FLOW CONCEPTS

Nine-Year Moving Averages

AVERAGE
1947/49

NATIONAL SAVING

$Bill.

Cash Flow

Business
Accounting

Social Accounting

PERSONAL SAVING

$Bill.

Cash Flow

Business
Accounting

Social Accounting

1900   1910   1920   1930   1940   1950

3.33. More significant differences are visible in Chart XI, which permits comparison of the nine-year moving averages of aggregate saving in current prices, aggregate saving deflated by means of an index of the general price level, and deflated saving per head. The differences in the averages are not in the direction of the entire curves or parts of them or in the location of the turning points, but are visible in the slopes of the upward and downward movements. Up to the late twenties the increase is most pronounced in aggregate current saving and smallest in deflated saving per head, with aggregate deflated saving in the middle. All three curves agree in showing a more rapid increase from about 1912 to the middle twenties than in either the preceding or the following decade. Differences in slope among these three subperiods are less pronounced in deflated than in current values. The variations in the slope are indicated by the fact that between early in the century and the midtwenties aggregate current personal saving increased by approximately 400 percent, aggregate deflated saving by 100 percent, and deflated saving per head by approximately 50 percent. The form and depth of the trough of the Great Depression are quite similar for all three curves. Differences reappear from the midthirties on. Again, the increase is sharpest for aggregate current saving and smallest for deflated saving per head. As a result of these differences the level of personal saving in the midforties (1945), measured by nine-year moving averages, was approximately $3\frac{1}{4}$ times as high as in the midtwenties in the case of aggregate current saving, $2\frac{3}{4}$ times as high for aggregate deflated saving, and twice as high for deflated saving per head.

d. *Fitted trends*

3.34. (1) *Basic problems.* Systematic analysis of economic time series directed towards the discovery of long-term trends, initiated hardly more than twenty years ago, has tended towards the conclusion that the growth or the decline of the output of an individual commodity or a single industry as a rule follows a curve which is characterized by a declining rate of growth and by a tendency to approach a fixed upper limit (logistic curve) or to turn downwards after having reached it (logarithmic parabola).[12] These curves have also been found to be characteristic of the growth or the decline of populations, human, animal, or vegetal. While these curves differ considerably in their early and late stages from an exponential (straight line logarith-

[12] This is approximately the sense of the summary as it appears in the most recent and, on an international scale, most comprehensive investigation of long-term trends, Dupriez's *Des Mouvements Economiques Généraux:* "Examination of the facts has shown that secular expansions are of two types, exponential expansions corresponding to the concept of a phenomenon that grows without being impeded by its surroundings; and logistic expansions corresponding to developments in surroundings that after a period of increasing ease offer resistance which grows with the level attained by the curve. Expansion along broken exponential lines, the successive breaks corresponding to braking effects, falls between these two formulas, the first of which generally holds good for shorter periods than the second. Indeed the curves tend to take this form when the braking effect in the logistic formula is still weak and the saturation level distant. Analysis, however, does not disclose any secular expansion which follows an arithmetic straight line...." (Translated from Volume I, 1951, p. 273.)

CHART XI
NATIONAL AND PERSONAL SAVING
Current Aggregate, Deflated Aggregate, and Deflated Per Head
Standard Social Accounting Concept
Nine-Year Moving Averages

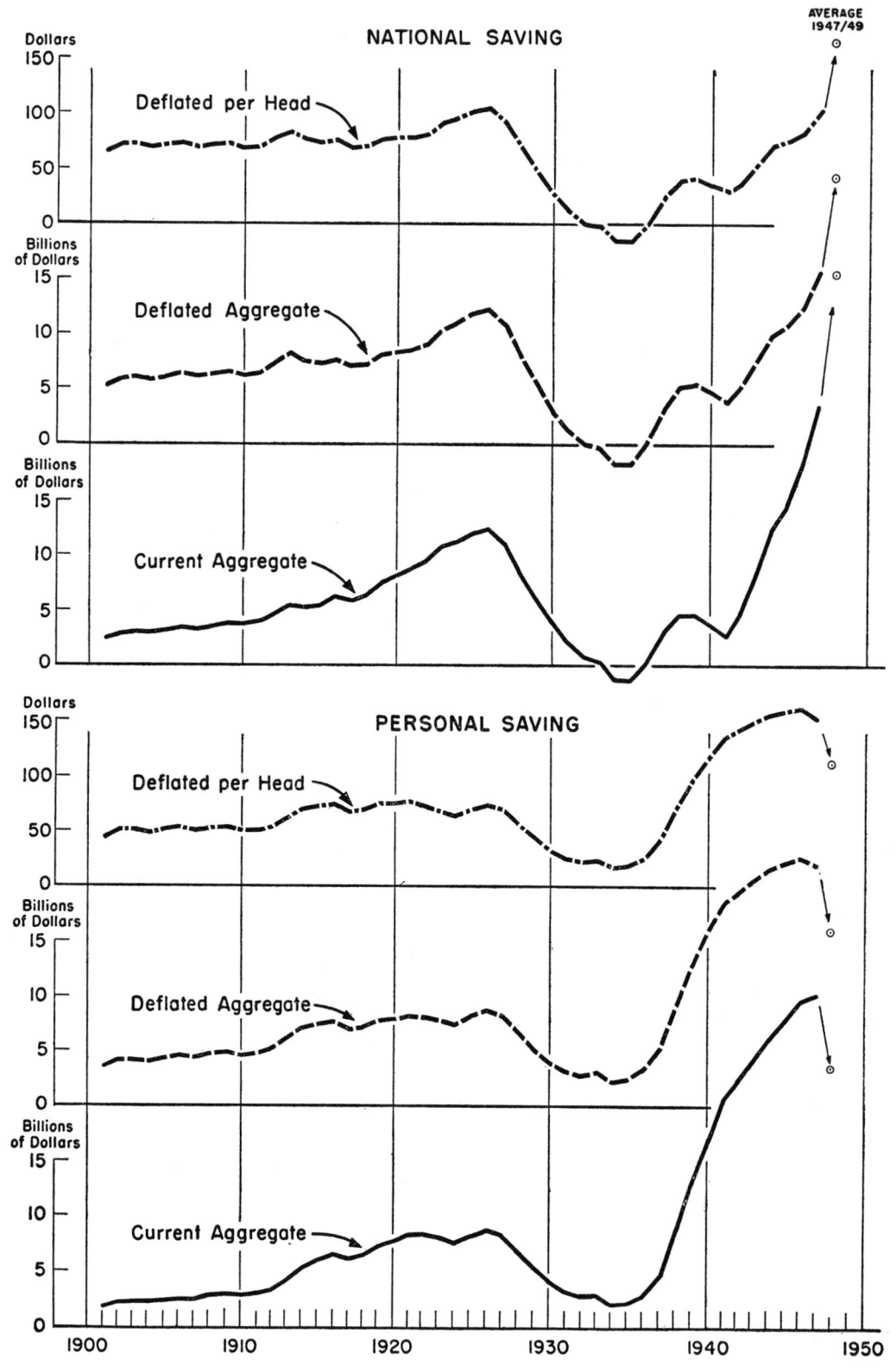

mic) trend, which implies a constant rate of growth, the divergence is small over the middle part of the curve. This fact makes it difficult to choose between forms of trend when the available figures, as usually is the case, do not cover the entire life of an industry or population, in particular when they do not include its infancy and old age.

3.35. The application of these findings to trends in over-all economic magnitudes, such as national income or saving, is far from simple. These magnitudes are the results of three factors: movements in real income (or saving) per head, trends in population, and movements in the price level.

No satisfactory evidence has as yet been presented to support the hypothesis that the growth of real national income per head in the United States shows the deceleration characteristic of the later phases of logistic curves. On the contrary the data for the last fifty to one hundred years suggest an increase in output per head or per man-hour along a logarithmic straight line, i.e. a constant rate of growth.[13] Whether better figures for the second half of the nineteenth century and a more thorough examination of the figures for the past fifty years would modify this finding it is impossible to anticipate. There are, however, considerations, although they are partly speculative, which make it unlikely that growth at the constant rate of the past fifty to one hundred years, or a rate close to it, could continue indefinitely. They are based on the fact that the rate of increase in output per head or per man-hour which the American economy has experienced during the past century has been due partly to a shift within the labor force from sectors with lower to those with higher output per man-hour, particularly from agriculture to industry. As a result the rate of increase in national output per head has been higher than the rate of increase in any of the major sectors, even in the manufacturing industries. These gains from a change in the composition of the labor force cannot continue indefinitely. The time is bound to come, although it still may be quite distant, when only a small proportion of the total labor force will be working in the industries with high and formerly growing productivity—just because high productivity reduces labor requirements. Most of the labor force will then be engaged in occupations which by their very nature do not lend themselves to substantial increases in productivity, primarily the service industries. When this point is reached—in the extreme case, when production of commodities has become entirely automatic—the rate of increase of output per head will necessarily decline, although this movement may be offset for a while by increase in hours worked per week, a development which would reverse the trend of the past century. Thus in the very long run output per man-hour would also have to follow a logistic trend. But we do not know enough about these secular movements to rule out the possibility that, starting from the present level, output per man-hour in the United States will continue to grow for several generations at the fairly constant rate of the last fifty to one hundred years.

[13] See, e.g., Kuznets, *Income and Wealth*, Series II, 1952, p. 55; Kendrick, "National Productivity and Its Long-term Projection" in *Long-Range Economic Projection*, Studies in Income and Wealth, Volume XVI, 1954; or Clark, *The Conditions of Economic Progress*, 1951, p. 47.

Still less can be said about the trend in the price level. Obviously, the physical constraints which force the output of individual commodities, as well as the growth of populations, into the form of a logistic or similar curve are not at work here; or if they are, the experiences with hyperinflation after both World Wars show that the upper boundary to a rise in the price level is so high as to be without practical significance. We cannot, therefore, deny the possibility of a rise in the price level sufficient to compensate not only for any decline in the rate of growth of output per head but also for a slowing down of population growth, a rise which will thus enable national income, or saving, in current prices to follow a path along an exponential curve if not indefinitely then for a very long period. The chance of such a configuration, however, would appear to be small, primarily because of the explosive and, therefore, shortlived character of inflation involving an accelerating rise in the price level.

3.36. The conclusion, then, is that in selecting the form of trend to be fitted to data on saving in current prices we are without a theoretical guide, i.e. the trend must essentially be limited to a description of data of the past. In the case of real saving (saving in constant prices) per head we are free to choose between exponential, logistic, and possibly parabolic curves if we want to use fitted trends and desire to avoid complicated formulas which lack an economic rationale. Aggregate real saving naturally occupies an intermediate position as its trend is a combination of those of population growth and the movement of real saving per head. Its trend, therefore, may be assumed to follow either a logistic or an exponential curve, although the population factor makes a logistic curve the first choice for very long periods.

3.37. (2) *Trend movements.* Determination of trends fitted by means of simple algebraic formulas to the actual estimates of saving has been essentially limited to trends in the form of arithmetic and logarithmic straight lines, i.e. curves which grow each year by either the same absolute amount or by the same proportion; and to arithmetic or logarithmic parabolic trends which assume a regularly declining or increasing rate of increase. The reason for this restriction is threefold. First, limitation of resources made it impossible to experiment comprehensively with a large number of different forms of fitted trends, particularly those requiring a substantial amount of computation. Secondly, visual inspection of the curves of the different variants of saving did not provide a clear indication of trends that deviated from arithmetic or logarithmic straight lines or parabolas but seemed to follow other relatively simple formulas. Thirdly, there is no good theoretical reason to expect saving to show trends of a different form. Experiments with other curves and a study of charts, only a few of which are shown, however, have been carried far enough to permit the conclusion that a comprehensive analysis by means of more elaborate fitted curves is unlikely to produce much additional significant knowledge about the secular trend of saving.

3.38. The results of experimentation, within these limits, with fitted trends may be summarized as follows:

68

CHART XII

LOGARITHMIC TRENDS IN NATIONAL SAVING

Standard Social Accounting Concept

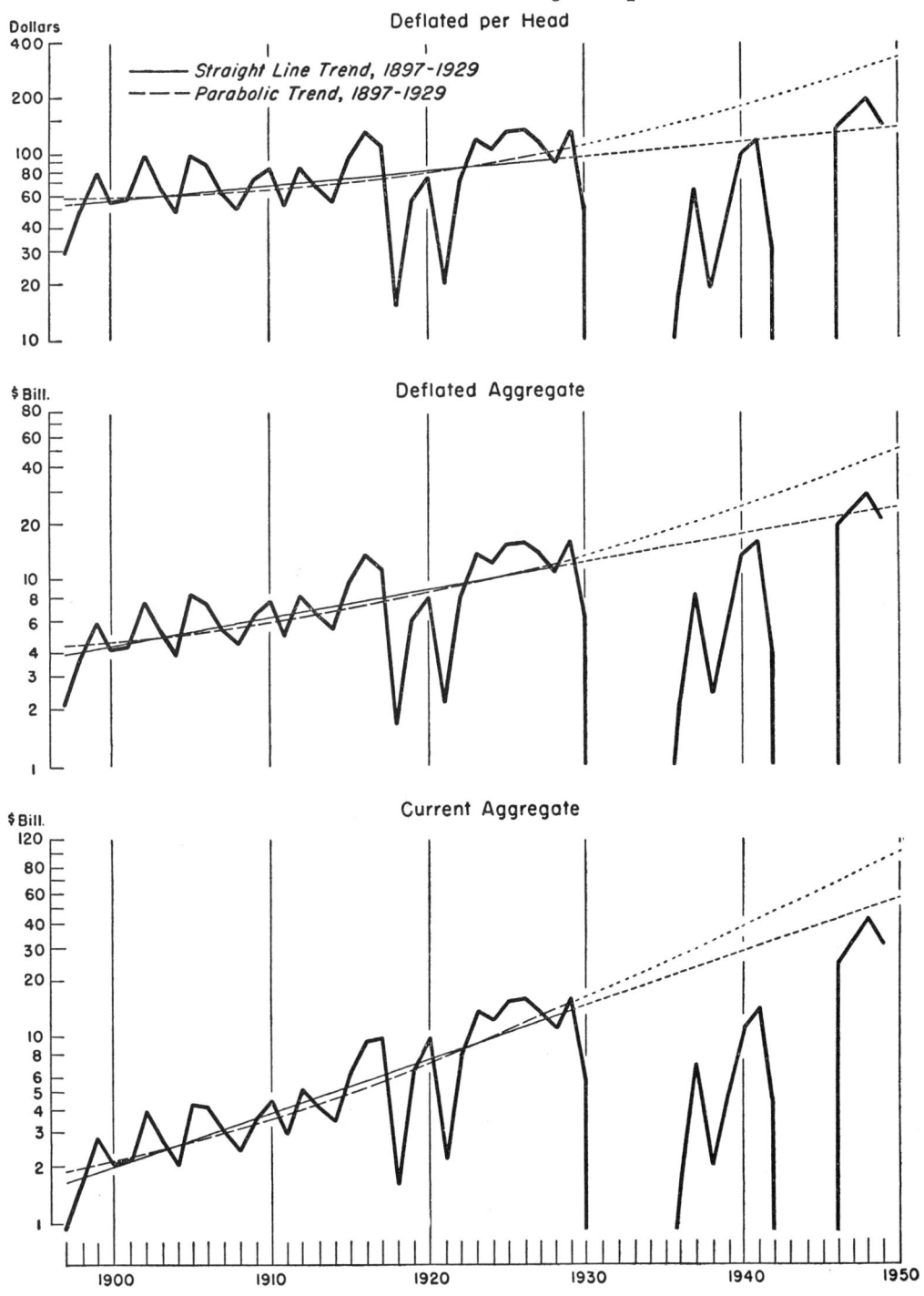

CHART XIII

LOGARITHMIC TRENDS IN PERSONAL SAVING

Standard Social Accounting Concept

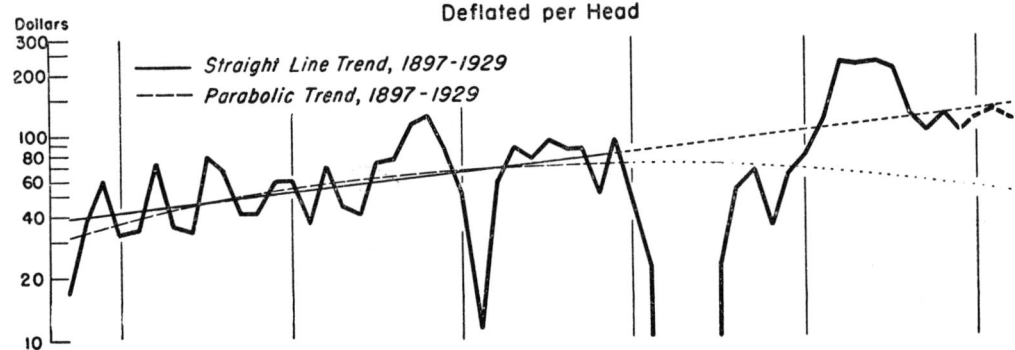

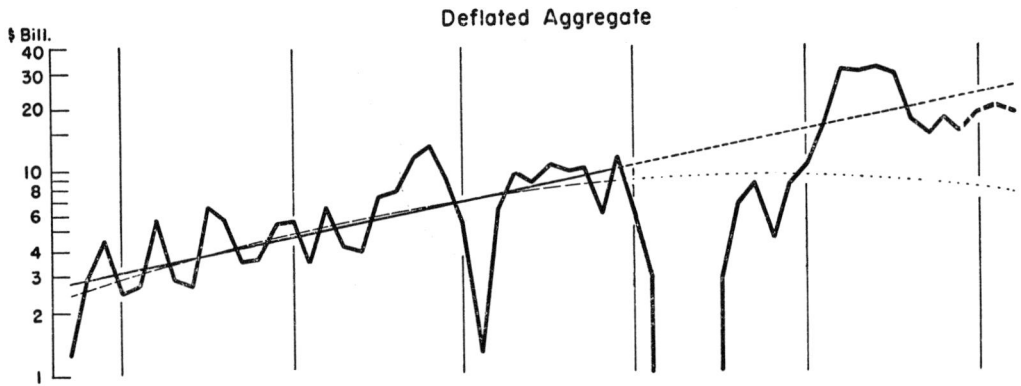

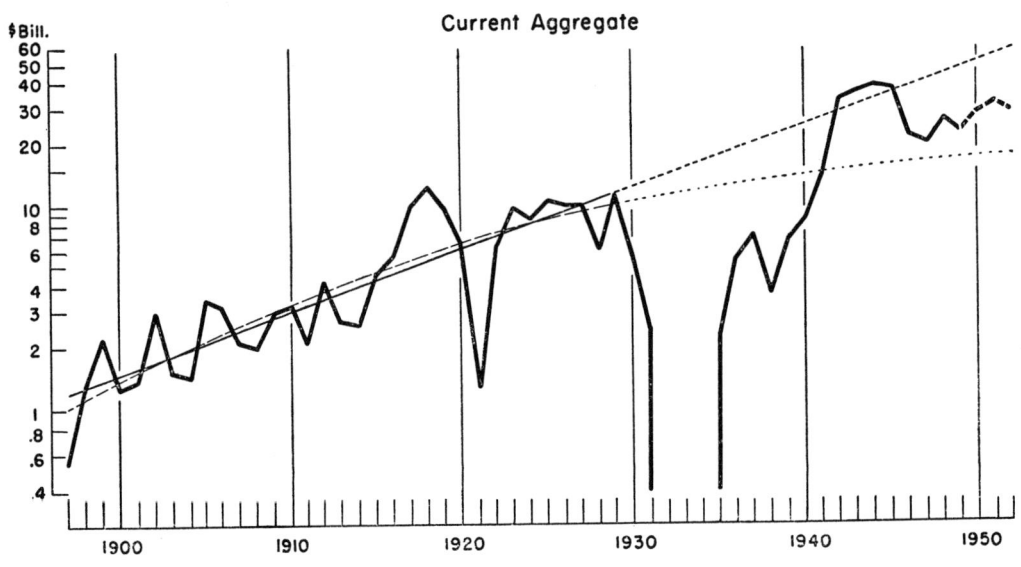

(a) No one trend fits aggregate national or personal saving in current values for the entire period.

(b) The trend of aggregate national saving for the period 1897–1929, on the other hand, can be approximated with fairly satisfactory results (i.e. particularly without undue concentration of positive or negative deviations from the trend line) either by an arithmetic parabola or by a logarithmic straight line or parabola (Chart XII). In the case of personal saving the logarithmic straight line or parabola likewise provides a reasonably good fit (Chart XIII), but none of the simple arithmetic trends is able to do so.

(c) Fitted trends, as a rule, provide a better approximation if applied to aggregate deflated or deflated per head saving rather than to aggregate saving in current values. Even in this case, however, no simple trend is able to fit the entire period satisfactorily.

(d) All long-term trends are upward, but there is considerable difference in steepness among trends in aggregate current, aggregate deflated, and deflated per head saving; in national and personal saving; and in social accounting, business accounting, and cash saving.

3.39. The characteristics of logarithmic straight line trends for the period 1897–1929, which generally yield the best results,[14] particularly from the point of view of extrapolation, are summarized below and can be followed in more detail in Table IV and Appendix Tables Z-1 to Z-5.

(a) The rate of increase in personal saving (7.4 percent) is somewhat higher than that in national saving (6.8 percent). This difference may not look large, but it becomes significant when trends in deflated and per unit values of saving are studied.

(b) Exclusion of consumer durables does not make a substantial difference in the rate of growth, except in the case of personal saving calculated according to the business accounting and cash concepts.

(c) The rate of growth in national business accounting saving is higher than that of social accounting saving. The rate of increase of cash saving is not far from that of social accounting saving.

(d) Deflated aggregate saving increased at a considerably lower rate than current saving. In the case of national saving the difference is between 3.5 percent a year for deflated saving, using an index of the general price level as deflator, and 6.8 percent for undeflated figures. There is no significant further difference when group purchasing power indices are used as deflators. Reduction to wage units, however, leads to a lower rate of growth, viz. 2.2 percent for aggregate national saving.

(e) The shift to per unit values provides a further marked reduction in the

---

[14] Parabolic trend lines, which necessarily fit the data for the period of observation at least as closely as straight lines, have in the case of personal saving the basic drawback that they imply a continuous decline in the absolute trend values rather soon after the end of the period (i.e. 1929), a development which is contradicted by the actual figures, particularly those for 1946–1952, for all variants of saving. For national saving, where the parabolic trends are convex to the time axis, they lead to extrapolations which outrun actual values to such an extent as to preclude the use of logarithmic parabolas as measures of secular trends.

TABLE IV

NATIONAL AND PERSONAL SAVING, RATES OF GROWTH
OF VARIANT ESTIMATES: 1897 to 1929

Percent per year

	National saving	Personal saving
I. Social accounting saving		
1. Current, aggregate, standard	6.80	7.35
2. Current, aggregate, adjusted	6.82	7.34
3. Current, aggregate, excluding consumer durables	6.78	7.04
4. Deflated, general price level, aggregate, standard	3.49	4.01
5. Deflated, general price level, aggregate, excluding consumer durables	3.46	3.94
6. Deflated, wage level, aggregate, standard	2.16	2.68
7. Deflated, group purchasing power, aggregate, standard	3.39	3.88
8. Deflated, general price level, per inhabitant, standard	1.80	2.32
9. Deflated, general price level, per inhabitant, excluding consumer durables	1.77	2.25
10. Deflated, general price level, per household, standard	1.32	1.84
11. Deflated, general price level, per consuming unit, standard	1.72	2.24
II. Business accounting saving		
1. Current, aggregate, standard	7.57	6.58
2. Current, aggregate, excluding consumer durables	7.06	7.35
III. Cash saving		
1. Current, aggregate, standard	6.97	6.87
2. Current, aggregate, excluding consumer durables	6.12	5.18

Source: Appendix Tables Z-1 and Z-2.

rate of growth. For national saving per inhabitant, deflated by the general price level, the rate of increase is only 1.8 percent a year against 3.5 percent for the comparable aggregate figure. Reduction to equivalent full consumers does not yield a substantially different rate of growth. A considerably lower rate of increase —1.3 percent per year—however, is obtained when the number of households is used as divisor, the result of the decline in the average number of persons per household.

3.40. The relation between the annual growth rates of approximately 7 percent for aggregate current saving, fully 3½ percent for deflated aggregate saving, and approximately 2 percent for deflated saving per head is important. These figures show the relative contribution to the observed trend in aggregate current saving made by the three main components, the increase in real saving per head, the growth in population, and the rise in the price level. Of the total increase about one-half was due to a rise in the price level, i.e. a change in the unit in which saving is measured; fully one-fifth reflected growth in population, i.e. a broadening of the base of the economy; less than one-third was the effect of an increase in real saving per head.

3.41. There is a fairly clear break in trend around the beginning of World War I, but it is of different character for national than for personal saving. The

72

rates of growth of national saving are considerably higher for the period 1915 to 1929 than for the years 1897 to 1914, at least for the variants for which fitted trends for the two subperiods have been calculated. The difference is somewhat less pronounced in current than in deflated saving. The reason for this break lies mostly in the sharp drop in national saving during World War I and in the depression of 1920–1921, the first of which reflects the federal government's dissaving while the second is due largely to the low level of saving of business and agriculture. In the case of personal saving the war was accompanied by a sharp upward jump with the result that the trend for the subperiod 1915–1929 is much flatter than that for 1897–1914, just the opposite of the pattern observed in national saving. As a consequence, in the first subperiod (as well as for the entire period) the rates of growth are higher for personal than for national saving, though only slightly so; while the opposite relation prevails, and to a much more pronounced extent, in the second subperiod.

3.42. (3) *The relation of the level of saving after World War II to extrapolated pre-1930 trends in saving.* As we have not succeeded in finding one trend line representing the course of saving over the entire period 1897–1949 we cannot say whether the values of saving which we observe for the years after World War II are below or above the long-term trend. Indeed, we are unable even to assert that a long-term trend has existed since the thirties; or that the values for the years beginning with 1946 form a part of a new trend which will become evident only as we are able to include in our observations a sufficient number of years after World War II. So long as we are thus uncertain about the existence or form of the trend applicable to the late forties, we are obviously unable to extrapolate the trend into the fifties.

3.43. We may, however, make an experiment. We may ascertain how the estimates of saving for the years 1946–1949 and the cruder figures for 1950, 1951, and 1952 compare with values obtained by extrapolation of the trend which prevailed in the thirty years before 1930. Such a comparison will show the differences between actual and extrapolated values for various forms of trends and for trends fitted to various concepts of saving. The relative size of the differences between actual and extrapolated values will give an indication as to which of the trends comes closest, by coincidence or otherwise, to encompassing the period after World War II in addition to fitting the values of saving during its own life. Even if the extrapolation of one or more pre-1930 trends should closely approximate the actual level of saving observed from 1946 to 1949 or 1952, it may not be concluded that all or any pre-1930 trends which produce such a result can be regarded, on the strength of this performance alone, as representing a true long-term trend for the entire first half of the century, and presumably also for the near future insofar as it is unaffected by extraneous forces such as war. One reason why even a close coincidence between values extrapolated from pre-1930 trends and actual values for the years following World War II cannot be regarded as confirming the validity of the pre-1930 trends through and beyond the middle of the century is that we may not, without further evidence, regard the years 1946 to

1949 or 1952 as "normal" in the sense that they are situated on or close to a true long-term trend.

TABLE V

NATIONAL AND PERSONAL SAVING, RATIO OF VALUES EXTRAPOLATED
FROM 1897–1929 TRENDS TO ACTUAL 1946–1952 VALUES
FOR THREE BASIC ESTIMATES

Standard Social Accounting Concept; Annual Averages: 1946 to 1949 and 1946 to 1952

	Straight line trend				Parabolic trend			
	Arithmetic		Logarithmic		Arithmetic		Logarithmic	
	1946–1949	1946–1952	1946–1949	1946–1952	1946–1949	1946–1952	1946–1949	1946–1952
	1	2	3	4	5	6	7	8
I. National saving								
1. Current aggregate	0.64	.	1.47	.	1.19	.	2.58	.
2. Deflated aggregate	0.79	.	0.98	.	1.27	.	1.80	.
3. Deflated per head	0.87	.	0.84	.	1.31	.	1.80	.
II. Personal saving								
1. Current aggregate	0.99	0.91	1.88	1.85	1.20	1.10	0.73	0.66
2. Deflated aggregate	0.86	0.82	1.27	1.24	0.84	0.80	0.51	0.47
3. Deflated per head	0.98	0.95	1.09	1.07	0.72	0.68	0.51	0.47

Source: Appendix Tables Z-3 to Z-5.

3.44. A study of the ratios between extrapolated trends and actual values of saving after World War II, based primarily on Table V and on the more detailed Tables Z-3 to Z-5 in the Appendix, leads to four conclusions, which are corroborated by Charts XII and XIII:

(a) Some very simple formulas derived exclusively from the observed values for the period 1897–1929 yield extrapolated figures for the period 1946–1949 or 1946–1952 that come quite close to the actual values of saving—say within 5 percent for the aggregate of the four or seven years and within 15 percent if each of the four or seven years is taken individually.

(b) We therefore cannot reject the hypothesis that the trend in the absolute values of saving observed from 1897 to 1929 is still in force. This statement, of course, is not equivalent to claiming actual continuation of pre-1930 trends, but only to maintaining the possibility of such persistence.

(c) Provided it is assumed that the same trend underlies the course of saving in the first and second quarters of the century, then it is probably of exponential form (logarithmic straight line) if only relatively simple curves are considered. For most variants of saving it certainly does not take the form of an arithmetic straight line.

(d) The trend should be sought in deflated rather than in current values of saving, and in per head rather than aggregate values, although the evidence on the last point is not conclusive.

4. Trends in the Saving Ratio

3.45.   Current income and its change is without doubt the main single determinant of personal, and, except in wartime, also of national, saving. Changes in the proportion of saving to income may therefore be regarded as expressions of the specific movements of saving, i.e. the movements which go beyond the reflection of changes in income due to trends in population, capital equipment, and the price level. Long-term changes in the national or personal saving ratio thus provide a second basic approach to the determination of trends in saving, which supplements and in some respects supersedes that based exclusively on the absolute values of saving.

The problems and methods of measuring trends in the saving ratio are basically the same as those already dealt with in the determination of trends in absolute saving. Actually four methods, which differ but little from those applied in the previous section to the absolute values of saving, will be used to measure trends in the saving ratio: cycle averages; nine-year moving averages; comparison of saving ratios during years of virtually full employment; and fitted straight line trends.

3.46.   A brief review of the results of these four approaches will indicate that all of them are compatible with the hypothesis that the secular trend of the basic ratios (i.e. the proportion of national or personal saving, including consumer durables, to net national product or personal disposable income, all calculated by comparable social accounting methods) has been horizontal for the period 1897–1929, and has also been level for the entire first half of this century.

This hypothesis is tentative. It may be upset insofar as it deals with secular trend by the experience of the 1950's. It may also have to be modified by revisions in the estimates for earlier years, particularly for the period before World War I. This hypothesis, therefore, should not be taken as a positive assertion that there actually was no secular upward or downward trend in the national or personal saving ratios. It only means that on the basis of the evidence now available absence of a long-term trend appears to be the most acceptable hypothesis.

a. Cycle averages

3.47.   A flexible indicator of the movement of the saving ratio over a long period which is not dominated by large cyclical variations is provided by cycle averages, i.e. averages including the ratios for all years in a cycle dated from trough to trough or from peak to peak. [15] Such averages, of course, do not eliminate the influence of incidental movements such as wars or of particularly severe depressions.

3.48.   Up to World War I cycle averages deviated, as Table VI shows, only little from the average level of the cycle averages for this period of approximately 13 percent for the national saving ratio and $10\frac{1}{2}$ percent for the personal saving

[15] Trough to trough cycles based on the chronology of the National Bureau of Economic Research (Burns and Mitchell, *Measuring Business Cycles*, 1946, p. 78) have been used.

TABLE VI

CYCLE AVERAGES OF NATIONAL AND PERSONAL SAVING-INCOME RATIOS
Social Accounting Concept: 1896 to 1949
Percent

Cycle (reference trough to reference trough)	National saving ratio		Personal saving ratio		Saving ratio of nonfarm households	
	Including	Excluding	Including	Excluding	Including	Excluding
	Consumer durables		Consumer durables		Consumer durables	
	1	2	3	4	5	6
1896 to 1900	11.7	10.5	9.4	8.1	.	.
1900 to 1904	14.4	13.1	10.5	9.0	13.6	11.9
1904 to 1908	14.4	12.9	12.0	10.4	14.8	12.9
1908 to 1911	12.7	11.4	10.5	9.1	14.2	12.7
1911 to 1914	12.9	11.7	10.3	9.0	13.3	11.8
1914 to 1919	13.6	12.9	16.1	15.2	19.3	18.6
1919 to 1921	9.2	8.8	8.8	8.4	12.5	11.6
1921 to 1924	13.2	11.5	11.0	9.0	13.1	10.5
1924 to 1927	17.7	14.9	13.9	10.6	15.8	12.1
1927 to 1932	5.9	5.7	7.4	7.1	11.3	10.7
1932 to 1938	-3.9	-3.8	2.0	2.0	1.8	1.8
1938 to 1946	4.0	3.3	19.4	18.5	18.6	17.7
1946 to 1949	15.5	11.7	13.4	8.5	14.8	9.3
Mean	10.9	9.6	11.1	9.6	13.6	11.8
Coefficient of variation	0.51	0.53	0.37	0.40	0.31	0.34

Averages of annual values, first and last year of cycles weighted one-half; ratio for 1896 assumed equal to that for 1897. Annual values obtained as follows:

Column 1 – Table T-1, col. 1 divided by Table N-1 (Volume III), col. 6.

Column 2 – Table T-1, col. 1 minus Table T-6, col. 5 divided by Table N-1, col. 6.

Column 3 – Table T-1, col. 2 divided by Table N-1, col. 9.

Column 4 – Table T-6, col. 1 minus col. 5 divided by Table N-1, col. 9.

Column 5 – Table T-1, col. 3 divided by the residual of Table N-3, col. 8 and estimates of the income of unincorporated business derived as follows: 1899–1918, Martin, *National Income in the United States, 1799–1938*, p. 39 (figures exclude agriculture and miscellaneous categories); 1919–1928, Volume II, Table B-79, col. 2; 1929–1949, Table B-79, col. 4.

Column 6 – Table T-8, col. 1 minus col. 5 divided by the same denominator as in col. 5 of this table.

ratio (including in both cases saving through consumer durables). The variations between cycle averages become larger in the period 1914–1927, and are particularly evident in the low level of both ratios for the 1919–1921 cycle and the high level of the personal saving ratio for the 1914–1919 cycle, which reflects the World War I bulge. The values of the three long cycles between 1927 and 1946, on the other hand, are entirely out of line. The national saving ratio is far below the average of the preceding thirty years for all three cycles. The personal saving ratio likewise is unprecedentedly low for the two cycles between 1927 and 1938, but is at a maximum for the 1938–1946 cycle, reflecting the extraordinarily high personal saving ratios for the years 1942–1945. For the only complete post-World War II cycle, that of 1946–1949, both the national and the personal saving ratios are about two percentage points above the 1896–1927 average, but do not exceed the values reached in the 1924–1927 cycle, which shows the highest saving ratios for any nonwar cycle during the past half century.

3.49. Exclusion of saving through consumer durables lowers the level of the ratios by 1½ percentage points on the average, but does not impart a definite slope to either the national or the personal saving ratio. On the contrary, it eliminates the increase which appears in the national and personal saving ratios including consumer durables, between the five cycles ending with 1914 and the four cycles ending with 1927, on the one hand, and the only post-World War II cycle, on the other. The saving ratio of nonfarm households, which is horizontal if consumer durables are included, now shows a declining trend from 12.3 percent for the four cycles between 1900 and 1914, to 11.4 percent for the three cycles between 1919 and 1927, and to 9.3 percent for the single post-World War II cycle of 1946–1949.

3.50. The course of the cycle averages of national, personal, and nonfarm saving-income ratios thus would seem to justify two conclusions: (1) No trend is visible for the period 1896–1927; (2) if the 1946–1949 cycle is regarded as a typical midcentury cycle there is no reason to postulate a break in long-term trends after 1927 as long as saving through consumer durables is included.

b. *Nine-year moving averages*

3.51. If attention is concentrated on the entire span from the turn of the century to the late twenties, what stands out in Chart XIV is the absence of a continuous or consistent movement upwards or downwards. In other words, the saving ratios during that period do not seem to reflect a primary trend of secular character. A slight downward trend, however, may have been present in national saving, particularly if consumer durables are excluded.

During the Great Depression and most of the thirties, the nine-year moving average of all ratios falls deeply below the comparatively stable pre-1930 level, and then recovers rapidly. Personal saving reached a high in 1945, the last year for which the figures can be calculated. It is fairly certain that nine-year moving averages, when available for a few more years, will show values considerably below the 1945 level. For national saving the postwar ratios will probably be substantially above the 1945 figure. If the three-year average of 1947–1949 or the seven year average of 1946–1952 [16] is typical for the postwar period, all the ratios which include consumer durables would be close to the pre-1929 level, while those excluding them would be slightly below it. The movements of the ratios since the late twenties obviously do not reflect a simple long-term trend. It is likewise difficult to detect an underlying movement for the entire span 1897–1949 along any simple curve.

c. *Full employment years*

3.52. Cycle averages, moving averages, and fitted trends all fail to make specific allowance for differences in the approach of the economy to full employment. For some purposes, particularly the extrapolation of saving ratios under conditions of full employment, it is preferable to base the evaluation of trends on only those

[16] This average, like all averages using data for years beyond 1949, cannot be obtained exclusively from figures utilized in this study, but can be roughly approximated by extrapolating the Saving Study estimates with the help of the Department of Commerce's figures for total personal saving.

CHART XIV

THE TREND OF SAVING-INCOME RATIOS

Social Accounting Concept

Nine-Year Moving Averages

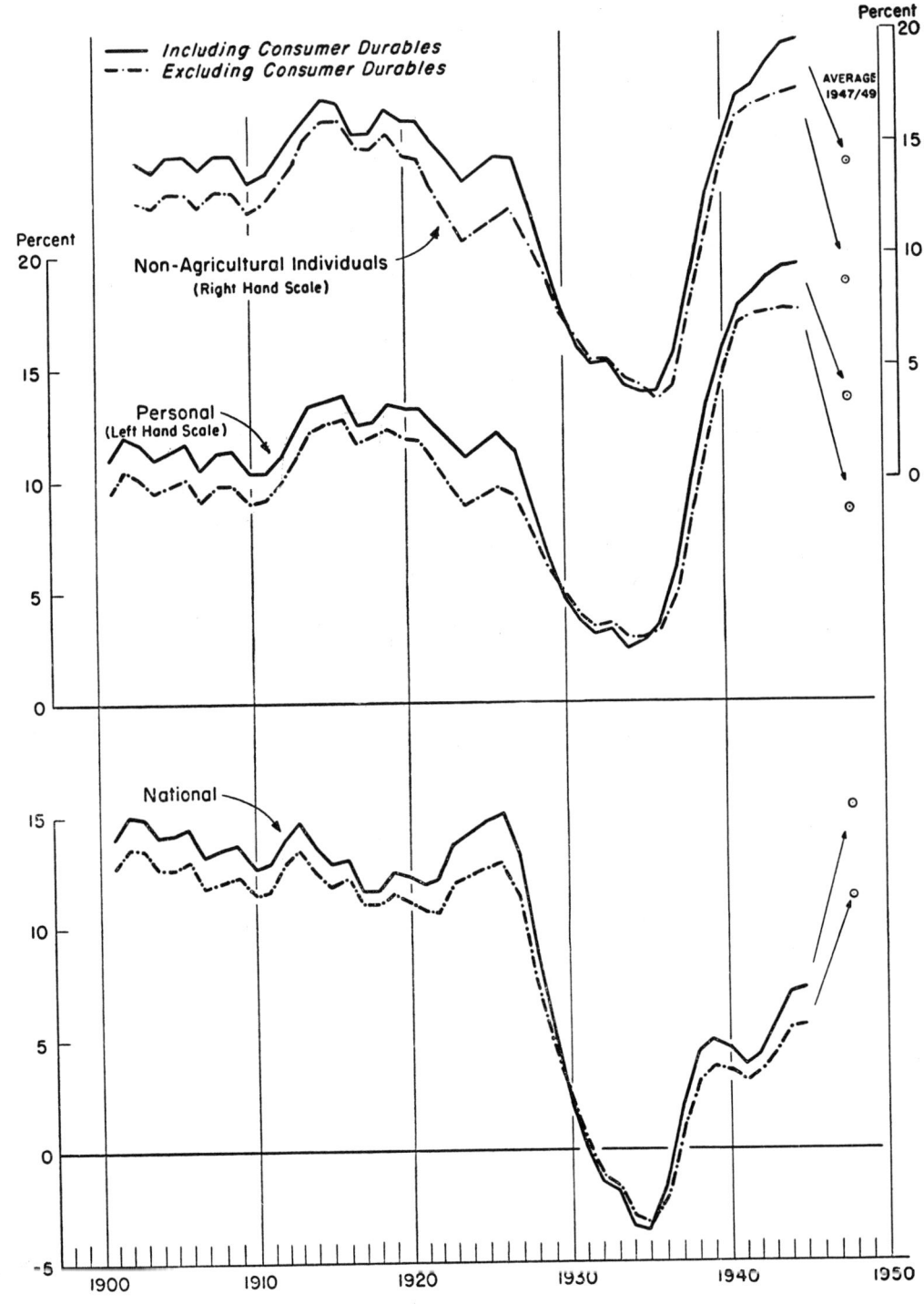

years for which there is little doubt that practically full employment of resources existed. These are usually also years in which business cycles culminated and in which the volume of saving is at a peak.

Table VII shows the saving ratios for a number of years, excluding war years, since 1897 which have been selected because they meet the conditions of constituting both cyclical peaks and periods of full employment. The list does not include all years which form the peak of a cyclical movement or in which unemployment was at or near its practical minimum. [17]

TABLE VII

SAVING-INCOME RATIOS FOR SELECTED (CYCLICAL TOP NONWAR) YEARS

Social Accounting Concept: 1900 to 1950

Percent

Year	National saving ratio		Personal saving ratio		Saving ratio of nonfarm households	
	Including	Excluding	Including	Excluding	Including	Excluding
	Consumer durables		Consumer durables		Consumer durables	
	1	2	3	4	5	6
1902	20.7	19.3	17.3	15.7	18.2	16.2
1905	19.9	18.2	17.7	15.8	19.6	17.3
Average	20.3	18.8	17.5	15.8	18.9	16.8
1925	19.1	15.9	15.2	11.5	18.1	13.9
1929	17.1	15.0	14.1	11.7	15.9	13.3
Average	18.1	15.5	14.6	11.6	17.0	13.6
1948	18.1	14.4	14.6	9.9	15.6	10.3
1950	.	.	14.2	7.7	.	.
Average	.	.	14.4	8.8	.	.

Source: Same as for Table VI.

3.53. The main features of Table VII are the facts that for national and personal saving including consumer durables the saving ratios for the forties are on the same level as those for the twenties, and that both are somewhat below the ratios for the first decade of the century.

The decline in the ratio between the first and third decades amounts to between 2 and 3 percentage points for an interval of nearly twenty-five years. It is smallest for nonfarm individuals' saving and largest for personal saving, the difference reflecting a sharper decline in the saving ratio of agriculture and of unincorporated business enterprises.

The differences in the ratios which include consumer durables for the twenties and forties are astonishingly small—undoubtedly to some extent a coincidence—

[17] In general the years in which cyclical peaks occur are also those in which unemployment is at a minimum and saving at a maximum. The peak of saving in 1905, however, slightly anticipated the peaks in business activity and employment which occurred in 1906 and 1907. For the purpose of establishing the trend in the saving ratio at full employment this discrepancy may be disregarded.

79

except for nonagricultural individuals' saving. In that case the ratio seems to have fallen 1 to 2 percentage points, continuing a smaller decline observable over the preceding thirty years.

3.54. The figures create a presumption that the trend of the full employment saving ratios over the last half century has been slightly downward, particularly for nonfarm households, if the cyclical peaks of Table VII can be regarded as typical of the full employment level of the saving ratios for their decades or similar periods, and if the figures are equally reliable throughout the past fifty years. This conclusion, however, is precarious. Trends based on saving ratios for individual years are less reliable than those derived from composites for longer periods, such as cycle or moving averages, particularly for the early part of the century. The decline between the full employment saving ratios of the first and third decades may, therefore, be more apparent than real. The figures may, however, with equal likelihood correctly reflect changes in the saving ratios at full employment, particularly since there is at least one reason to expect the decline which they indicate. Cyclical fluctuations were much more pronounced in the first decade of this century than in the twenties or late forties, and it is likely that the saving ratio in years when full employment is reached (or closely approximated) from a deep depression trough is higher than if the same situation is the result of only a small bulge beyond the level of activity over several years or if virtually full employment prevails for protracted periods. There is, then, good reason to expect the full employment saving ratio to be lower if full employment is the rule rather than the exception. In that case the decline of the ratio in full employment years between the first and the fifth decade of this century does not necessarily indicate a trend that can be expected to continue.

3.55. The problems encountered in interpreting the movements of the saving ratios between full employment periods in the first, third, and fifth decades are met with in even more pronounced form when attention is directed to saving excluding consumer durables. In that case there appears a definite downward trend in all three saving ratios—national, personal, and nonfarm individual. The decline is somewhat sharper between peak years in the first decade of the century and the twenties than between the twenties and the forties, and sharper for non-agricultural and personal than for national saving, but it is quite pronounced in all cases. In fact the average decline per decade is of the order of 1 to $1\frac{1}{2}$ percentage points or 10 percent. This movement is so pronounced that it strongly reinforces the much less clear-cut conclusion suggested by moving averages. It is not the existence of a downward trend in the saving ratio which is in doubt, but only its continuation, i.e. the question whether the movement of the ratio over the past four decades can be extrapolated into the future.

d. *Fitted trends*

3.56. Inspection of graphs of annual values or of nine-year or cyclical averages of the saving ratios indicates that if simple trends are to be fitted to the ratios this probably can be done only for the period 1897–1929, and that it is unprofitable to use forms other than arithmetic straight lines.

80

The characteristics of straight line trends for the period 1897–1929 are shown in Table VIII. The positive value of the coefficient for all three saving ratios—national, personal, and nonagricultural—indicates an increasing trend in the ratios of saving (including consumer durables) to income for the three decades before 1930 of 0.02 to 0.10 percentage points per year. The increase is smallest for the nonagricultural individuals' saving ratio and largest for the personal saving ratio. The values of the coefficients are large enough to produce substantial changes in the saving ratios over periods of several decades.

TABLE VIII

FITTED TRENDS IN SAVING-INCOME RATIOS

Social Accounting Concept: 1897 to 1929

Straight line arithmetic trends

	Value of ratio at midpoint (1913)	Average annual change over period	Annual rate of change at midpoint
	Percent of income		Percent of col. 1
	1	2	3
I. Including consumer durables			
1. National saving	13.68	0.047	0.34
2. Personal saving	11.78	0.085	0.72
3. Nonagricultural individuals' saving	14.84 [a]	0.022	0.15
II. Excluding consumer durables			
1. National saving	12.30	0.022	0.18
2. Personal saving	10.23	0.055	0.54
3. Nonagricultural individuals' saving	13.00 [a]	—0.015	—0.12

[a] Trend line fitted to 1899–1929, hence origin at 1914.
Source: Appendix Tables Z-1 and Z-2.

The coefficients, however, are not statistically significant at the 5 percent level. This means that the calculated average increase in the saving ratios might have arisen by chance in one out of twenty cases. Hence the hypothesis that the coefficients express true rather than spurious relationships is regarded as not proven. Following the rules of statistical induction the hypothesis is rejected and the alternative hypothesis that the saving ratios fail to show a trend movement along a straight upward- or downward-sloping line is accepted.

3.57.   This elementary analysis of fitted trends, therefore, hardly modifies the conclusions drawn from the cycle and nine-year moving averages. A slight upward trend in the saving-income ratios appears for the entire period 1897–1929, but its significance is in doubt and it remains to be seen whether this trend may be regarded as continuing beyond 1929. This may be tested by comparing extrapolated values for the period after World War II with the actual values.

Table IX then indicates that for the years 1946–1949 the extrapolated values are in excess of the actual values for all three saving ratios. The excess is rather small for the national saving ratio, for which it amounts to approximately $\frac{1}{2}$ percentage point. It is slightly more substantial for the personal and nonagricultural individuals' saving ratios, which are around 1 percentage point or less than one-tenth too high.[18] All these differences are larger for saving excluding consumer durables. In this case the excess of the calculated over the observed saving ratio is so large, at least for personal and nonagricultural saving, that continuation of the trend of the data for 1897 to 1929 to the middle of the century must be ruled out.

TABLE IX

ACTUAL AND EXTRAPOLATED SAVING-INCOME RATIOS

Annual Averages: 1946 to 1949 and 1946 to 1952

Percent

	National saving	Personal saving	Non-agricultural individuals' saving	National saving	Personal saving	Non-agricultural individuals' saving
	Including consumer durables			Excluding consumer durables		
	1	2	3	4	5	6
I. 1946–1949						
1. Extrapolated ratio	15.3	14.7	15.6	13.1	12.1	13.5
2. Actual ratio	14.9	13.4	14.6	11.2	8.6	9.3
3. Base (1897–1929) ratio	13.7	11.8	14.8	12.3	10.2	13.0
4. Difference, extrapolated minus actual ratio						
a. Absolute	0.4	1.3	1.0	1.9	3.5	4.2
b. Relative	3	9	6	15	29	31
5. Difference, base minus actual ratio						
a. Absolute	—1.2	—1.6	0.2	1.1	1.6	3.7
b. Relative	—9	—14	1	9	16	28
II. 1946–1952						
1. Extrapolated ratio	.	14.8	.	.	12.2	.
2. Actual ratio	.	13.7	.	.	9.1	.
3. Base (1897–1929) ratio	.	11.8	.	.	10.2	.
4. Difference, extrapolated minus actual ratio						
a. Absolute	.	1.1	.	.	3.1	.
b. Relative	.	7	.	.	25	.
5. Difference, base minus actual ratio						
a. Absolute	.	—1.9	.	.	1.1	.
b. Relative	.	.—16	.	.	11	.

Sources:
Lines 1 and 3 – Derived from arithmetic straight line trend equations for 1897 to 1929 as shown in Appendix Tables Z-1 and Z-2.
Line 2 – See notes to Appendix Tables Z-1 and Z-2.
Line 4a – Line 1 minus line 2.
Line 4b – Line 4a divided by line 1.
Line 5a – Line 3 minus line 2.
Line 5b – Line 5a divided by line 3.

[18] If the same comparison is made for the longer period 1946–1952—this is possible only for personal saving and only on the basis of rough preliminary figures—the differences are small, and are about the same order of magnitude as for the period 1946–1949.

3.58. These results may be compared with those obtained by assuming that the trend was horizontal in the three decades before 1930 so that the values for 1946–1949, or those for 1946–1952, are equal to the average of the base period 1897 to 1929. It is then found that with two exceptions (national and personal saving including consumer durables) deviation from observed values is smaller for base than for extrapolated ratios, and that the difference is pronounced for ratios excluding consumer durables.

3.59. The comparison of actual values of the saving ratios after World War II with extrapolated trend or base values thus does not lead to conclusive results. We need the evidence of additional years before we can make a decision with a reasonable degree of confidence. At this moment we can neither reject nor definitely accept either the assumption of a horizontal or that of a slightly upward trend in the national and personal saving ratios including consumer durables calculated in accordance with the standard social accounting concept. For saving excluding consumer durables, however, an upward trend is ruled out and a downward trend is more likely than a horizontal one if the period covered is extended from the three decades ending in 1929 to the middle of the century.

5. The Trend of Saving before 1897

3.60. As no direct estimates of national saving or its components are available before 1897, estimates of national investment, which, however, do not extend beyond 1869,[19] and changes in national wealth provide the only basis for even a rough estimate of the volume of saving during the nineteenth century. These indirect estimates, it is hardly necessary to add, are of a very rough nature and should be used only to establish the order of magnitudes involved.

3.61. Utilizing the estimates of reproducible real national wealth (1929 prices) for the years 1805, 1850, 1880, 1890, and 1900 [20] the following rough period averages are obtained for annual national saving:

> 1806 to 1850: $ 200 million
> 1851 to 1880: $1,400 million
> 1881 to 1890: $4,300 million
> 1891 to 1900: $3,900 million

[19] There is apparently only one exception, an estimate made by David Wells (*Report of Special Commissioner of Revenue for 1869*, p. xxii). Wells estimated aggregate saving, described as the "annual increase of active capital in the U.S. arising from the excess of production over expenditure" at $546 million for 1869—a year of prosperity—or "8 percent of the gross annual product." (This implies an estimate of gross national product of over $6.8 billion, which compares with Kuznets' unpublished figure of $5.8 billion.) Since the method by which this estimate of saving was derived is not known and since we do not know its coverage (it probably does not include consumer durables), not much can be done with this figure. For what it is worth, the estimate is somewhat lower than, although of the same order of magnitude as, the ratio of net capital formation to national product prevailing during the first thirty years for which estimates are now available, and considerably lower than the national saving ratio for years of prosperity since 1900.

[20] For derivation of these figures see Goldsmith, *Income and Wealth*, Series II, 1952, pp. 307, 315–323.

These are the figures which underlie the step curve of saving before 1897 at the bottom of Chart xv. [21]

3.62. An estimate of national saving in current prices, comparable to the annual figures developed for the period beginning with 1897, can be obtained only indirectly, viz. by multiplying the figures in constant prices, derived from national wealth statements, by a price index for the average of the period. Using an index of the general price level—though there is some question whether this is the most appropriate series and any price index used will have a wide margin of error for the earlier part of the period—the following very rough approximate period averages of national saving in current prices emerge:

> 1806 to 1850: $ 100 million
> 1851 to 1880: $ 600 million
> 1881 to 1890: $1,900 million
> 1891 to 1900: $1,700 million [22]

3.63. These figures can be supplemented for the three decades 1869–1898 by estimates of investment, which on the national level is necessarily equal to saving. It is also possible to approximate personal saving by subtracting from national saving, equated with either national investment or the change in national wealth, estimates for the saving of all other saver groups, i.e. corporations and governments. No specific estimate of the saving of these two groups is available for the period before 1897, but it is certain that the proportion of personal saving to national saving declined in the course of the nineteenth century. This assumption leads to the following very rough indirect estimates of personal saving derived from changes in reproducible national wealth: [23]

Period	Base (1929) prices	Current prices	Base (1929) prices	Current prices
	\$ mill. per year		\$ per head	
1806 to 1850	190	95	16	8
1851 to 1880	1 250	550	36	16
1881 to 1900	3 250	1 400	52	22

3.64. This excursion into the badlands of the statistics of saving in the nineteenth century has been undertaken primarily for the purpose of ascertaining whether the trend of saving observed after 1896 represents a continuation of earlier basic movements, and, if it does not, how it differs from previous trends.

[21] The estimates for the last two decades together, though not separately, agree fairly well (see Appendix Table Z-10) with estimates for the same period derived from statistics of investment (capital formation).

[22] This compares with an average of about $1,800 million for the years 1897 to 1900 derived from the annual estimates of saving.

[23] For an application of this method to data on national investment for the period 1869–1898 see Appendix Table Z-10.

84

The first tentative conclusion that can be drawn from this material is that the rate of increase of aggregate real national saving was approximately the same in the first and the second half of the nineteenth century, viz. close to 5 percent per year. This statement can be made only with reservations with respect to the first half of the century, for which the rate of increase between very rough benchmark estimates of reproducible tangible wealth is almost the only source available.

3.65. From the decadal data on investment available since 1869 it appears that the rate of growth of real national saving (correcting for price changes) was very high—over 6 percent a year—from the midseventies to the late eighties, but rather steady, though at a distinctly lower rate—approximately $2\frac{3}{4}$ percent a year—from then to World War I. [24] Fragmentary material leads to the surmise that the rate was relatively high in the fifties, and low in the sixties under the influence of the Civil War. This would mean that the rate of growth which apparently prevailed during the first half of the century continued for another generation, but that a break in trend occurred around 1890.

3.66. We are thus led to the conclusion that, concentrating attention on basic long-term movements and disregarding the effects of business cycles, there is no evidence that the trend of aggregate national saving in constant prices has shown substantial changes throughout most of the nineteenth century. It rather appears that growth of real (deflated) saving at a rate of approximately 5 percent a year is characteristic of almost the entire century, if attention is focussed only on movements of at least twenty years' duration. The rate of growth of personal saving alone, however, is likely to have decreased slightly, as corporations and government saving accounted for over one-quarter of national saving at the end of the century against only a very small proportion, certainly less than one-tenth, .at the beginning.

3.67. The rate of growth of aggregate deflated saving during the first half of the twentieth century—or more correctly from the 1890's on—was almost certainly lower than during most of the nineteenth century. If it is determined by a comparison of the level of saving at the beginning and the middle of the twentieth century, thus disregarding the trough of the 1930's, or by the trend fitted to the period 1897–1929 alone (Appendix Table Z-1), the rate of increase for national saving in constant (1929) prices is close to $3\frac{1}{2}$ percent per year. This is well below the rate of approximately 5 percent which seems to have prevailed during most of the nineteenth century. On a ratio (logarithmic) scale this trend will therefore appear as a straight line, reflecting steady growth, up to near the end of the nineteenth century, but as a slightly concave parabola, indicating a decreasing rate of growth, for the first half of the twentieth century.

3.68. The rate of increase in deflated national saving per head appears to have averaged slightly above 2 percent for the nineteenth century, but probably was somewhat higher in the first than in the second half. As it amounted to nearly 2 percent in the first half of the twentieth century (excluding the period 1930–

---

[24] Kuznets, *National Product since 1869*, 1946, Table II-15. The discussion in the text is based on allocating Kuznets' values for overlapping decades to the midpoints of the periods.

CHART XV
THE TREND OF SAVING, WEALTH, PRODUCTION, AND POPULATION

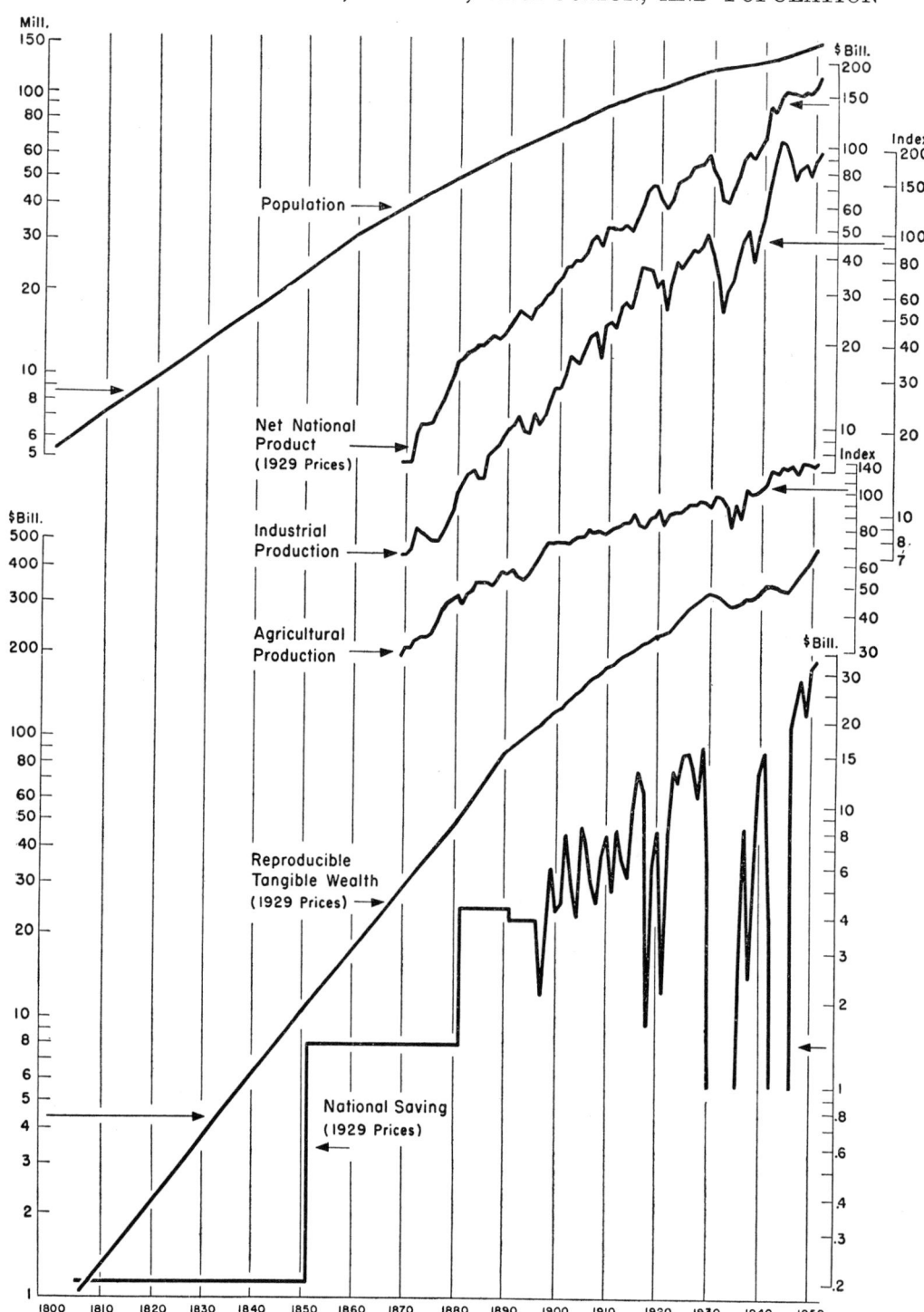

1945), there is no evidence here of a substantial decline in the rate of growth. The slowing down in the rate of growth of aggregate deflated national saving beginning in the neighborhood of 1890 can be regarded as mainly, though not entirely, reflecting the slowing down of the rate of population growth.

3.69.   The national saving-income ratio appears to have been a little higher in the last three decades of the nineteenth century, the only part of it for which reasonably reliable data are available, than during the first half of the twentieth century, even if the years 1930–1945 are excluded. [25] This is indicated in Chart xv by the steeper slope of the curve of net national product compared with that of national saving. It is confirmed by the movements of the ratio of national income including consumer durables to net national product, which averaged 17 percent for the thirty years 1869–1898, compared with 13 percent for the three decades ending 1928. [26]

No data are available for a calculation of the personal saving ratio before 1897. The movements of the national ratio suggest, however, a decline between the last quarter of the nineteenth and the first quarter of the twentieth century, although probably one of rather moderate dimensions. [27]

[25] For reasons for disregarding the national income estimates available for the period before 1869 see Kuznets, *Income and Wealth*, Series ii, 1952, pp. 221ff.

[26] Appendix Table Z-10, and Kuznets, *National Product since 1869*, 1946, Table ii-16, p. 119; the ratios are obtained from estimates of investment and national product in 1929 prices.

[27] A very rough estimate of nonfarm personal saving can be derived from a sample study of urban households in 1888–1890 which is analyzed in Volume iii, Part ii (see particularly Appendix i, Table H-15). Comparison of this sample with the results of a similar study for 1901 indicates that the volume of nonfarm individuals' saving in 1888–1890 was fully one-third below the 1901 level. In evaluating the 60 percent increase between 1888–1890 and 1901 it should be kept in mind that national income outside agriculture was about 55 percent higher in the latter than in the former period (Martin, *National Income in the United States, 1799–1938*, 1939, p.58), and that both samples were taken in periods of prosperity. Insofar as the figures can be regarded as reliable, they thus do not point to a substantial change in the ratio of personal saving to income in the last decade of the nineteenth century.

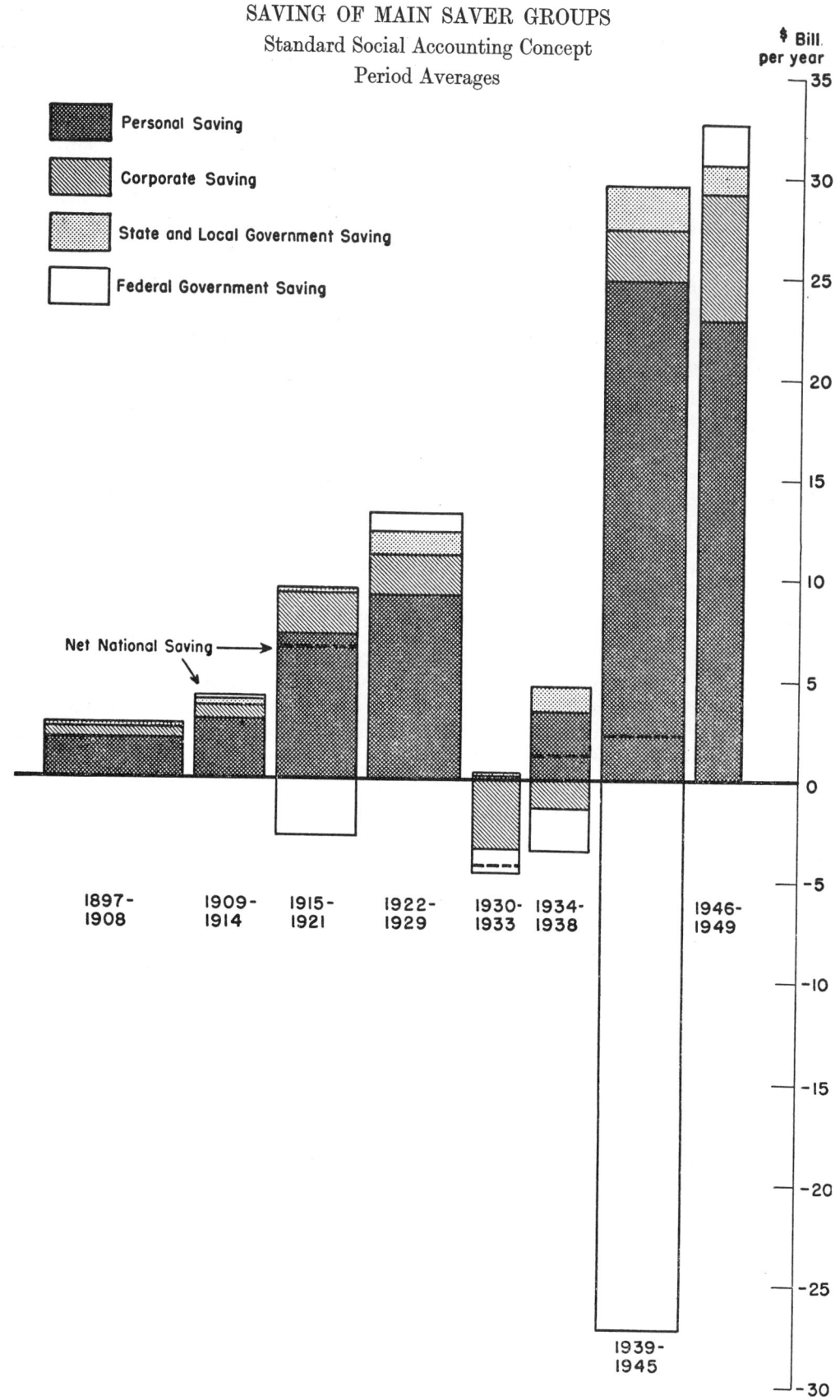

CHART XVI
SAVING OF MAIN SAVER GROUPS
Standard Social Accounting Concept
Period Averages

Personal Saving

Corporate Saving

State and Local Government Saving

Federal Government Saving

Net National Saving ➝

$ Bill.
per year

35

30

25

20

15

10

5

0

-5

-10

-15

-20

-25

-30

1897-
1908

1909-
1914

1915-
1921

1922-
1929

1930-
1933

1934-
1938

1946-
1949

1939-
1945

IV

THE COURSE OF SAVING OF
THE MAIN GROUPS OF SAVERS

4.01. This section is not a substitute for an intensive analysis of the trend in total saving, the structural changes among forms of saving, or the determinants of saving of the seven main saver groups distinguished in this study, an analysis which would require a set of special studies each of book length. The brief summary of the rate of growth of saving and its fluctuations, of the distribution of saving among its principal forms, and of the level and movements of the saving-income ratio of the main saver groups which constitutes this section is of an introductory and tentative, rather than an exhaustive and definitive, character.

1. SUMMARY OF FINDINGS

4.02. There are considerable differences between the main saver groups with regard both to the trend of the absolute values of saving and to the level and trend of the saving-income ratios. Similar differences exist within saver groups, particularly among nonfarm households of different income, wealth, occupation, and age, and among corporations in different industries. Such intragroup differences, however, are outside the scope of this study.

4.03. For the period as a whole corporations have shown the highest and the federal government the lowest—in fact the only negative—saving-income ratio. The ratios of nonfarm households, agriculture, [1] and state and local governments have been of approximately the same order of magnitude—around one-tenth. (Chart XVII.)

4.04. Both absolute saving of agriculture, even in deflated values per head, and its saving ratio have been considerably higher since the late thirties than in the preceding three or four decades. It would appear that the increase represents a level shift rather than a continuing trend.

4.05. The trend of saving of unincorporated business enterprises (excluding personal saving of owners) is in doubt, partly because of the unsatisfactory nature of the available data. It is probable, however, that the secular increase in their saving was small compared to that of most of the other saver groups, and that their saving ratio has shown a downward trend. Heavy accumulations of undistributed earnings are visible only during war years.

4.06. The corporate saving ratio has kept fairly close to an average of approximately one-third if cyclical fluctuations, on the one hand, and the period of

---

[1] The saving ratio of agriculture is considerably lower if either net land costs (soil improvement less soil deterioration) or war years are excluded.

the thirties, on the other, are disregarded. The absolute volume of corporate saving has shown only a slow upward trend if adjusted for price and population changes.

4.07. The volume of saving of state governments increased rapidly through World War II, even after adjustment for price and population changes. Their saving ratio also rose sharply from the turn of the century to the 1920's and stayed at a high level to the midforties. It remains to be seen whether the decline both in absolute values and in the saving ratio observed after World War II represents a change in trend or an ephemeral development.

4.08. The absolute volume of deflated saving of local governments per head has shown an upward trend until the twenties, but a downward trend since. The ratio of saving to income, however, exhibits no definite trend up to 1930, but has been on a definitely lower level during the last two decades.

4.09. The trend of total saving of the federal government has been dominated by heavy dissaving during the two World Wars. During nonwar periods saving has increased considerably, if adjustments are made for price and population changes and if military assets are disregarded.

2. NONAGRICULTURAL HOUSEHOLDS

4.10. No comments are required at this place on the course of saving of the largest single saver group, nonagricultural households, because it is necessarily very similar to that of aggregate personal saving, of which it constitutes about nine-tenths, both for the entire and for the normal period. The trend of total personal saving has already been discussed in Chapter III, while the trends and structural changes in the main components of personal saving will be taken up in Chapter VI. Readers who desire separate figures for the saving of nonagricultural households (i.e. total personal saving less the total saving of agriculture and less the saving through business assets and liabilities of unincorporated business enterprises) will find the necessary data in Tables S-20 through S-23.

3. AGRICULTURE

4.11. The measurement of saving in agriculture is faced with some special difficulties. These are caused not so much by the inability to separate certain assets and liabilities attributable to farmers from those attributable to nonagricultural households, although such difficulties exist, particularly in the case of absentee landlords, as by the treatment and estimation of two forms of saving specific to agriculture, the cost of bringing land into cultivation and the balance of soil improvement and soil deterioration. For a correct evaluation of the role of saving in agriculture and of agriculture in national saving it is necessary to take account of land costs or, in other words, net soil improvement. In the present state of our information the estimates unfortunately must remain most precarious. [2]

4.12. For the entire period 1897–1949 saving of agriculture amounted to $44 billion in current prices, if allowance is made for land costs, and to $31 billion without them. The difference, which may well be an understatement, clearly

[2] See Volume II, Chapter XII, Section 2.

90

CHART XVII

SAVING-INCOME RATIOS OF MAIN SAVER GROUPS

Standard Social Accounting Concept

Period Averages

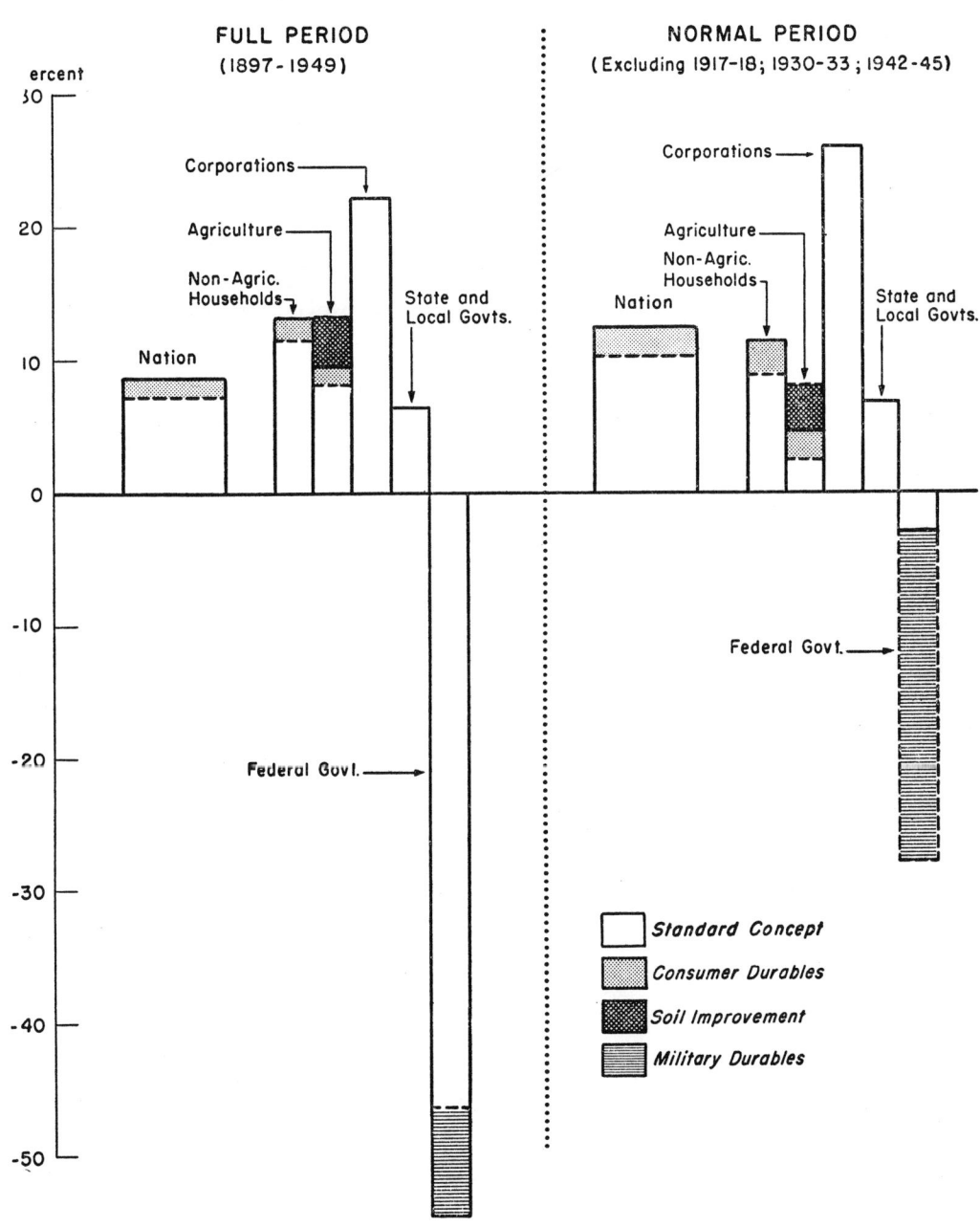

FULL PERIOD
(1897-1949)

NORMAL PERIOD
(Excluding 1917-18; 1930-33; 1942-45)

Corporations

Agriculture

Non-Agric.
Households

Nation

State and
Local Govts.

Federal Govt.

☐ Standard Concept

▨ Consumer Durables

■ Soil Improvement

▤ Military Durables

indicates the great importance of land costs in the saving of agriculture. The figures are not much different when deflated values are used. [3] Saving in agriculture thus represents approximately 6 percent of total personal saving without land costs, and remains under 10 percent even if land costs are included.

4.13. Part of saving of agriculture is attributable not to operating farmers but to nonfarm landlords. This part can be estimated only in a very rough manner by assuming that the share of nonfarm landlords in agricultural assets and liabilities—structures, equipment, inventories, equity in farm cooperatives, mortgage and short-term debt—is equal to the proportion of the value of land which they own, a proportion which has been in the neighborhood of one-third during the period covered by the Study. Because of the derivation of the figures, it may be assumed that the amounts reported or estimated as farmers' liquid assets contain only relatively small amounts belonging to nonfarm landlords. [4] Similarly, reported or estimated expenditures on consumer durables and consumer debt may be regarded as attributable entirely to farm operators. It then appears that for the full period the agricultural saving of nonfarm landlords was in the order of magnitude of $3 billion, or approximately 10 percent of total saving of agriculture excluding land costs.

a. *The structure of agricultural saving for the period as a whole*

4.14. For the full period, saving through tangible assets and saving through intangible assets, as shown in Table x, have been of approximately equal size. Each has come to about 60 percent of total net saving in current prices while the increase in debt has been equal to approximately one-fifth of net saving. These relations are strongly influenced by the war years, in which saving was very large and concentrated in intangible assets, particularly bank deposits, currency, and U.S. Government bonds. As a result the structure of agricultural saving during the normal period differs considerably from that during the period as a whole. For the normal period the increase in debt offset almost one-half of the increase in assets—against only one-fifth for the full period. Likewise tangible assets accounted for over two-thirds, and intangible assets for less than one-third, of the increase in total assets.

4.15. The question immediately arises as to how to allocate the increase in debt, which has offset a substantial part of the increase in assets, among the main forms of saving. This is relatively easy only in the case of consumer debt as it may be assumed that most of it has been incurred in the process of purchasing consumer durables. For all other forms of debt, allocation is difficult. In particular, a con-

---

[3] If all components of saving are reduced by means of an index of the general price level (i.e. the gross national product deflator), as this is usually done throughout the Study, saving of agriculture in 1929 prices amounts to about $42 billion including, and to $27 billion excluding, land costs. (See Table T-12.) In this case, however, an attempt has also been made in Table A-2 to deflate each component of saving by an appropriate special price index, e.g. saving through farm machinery by an index of farm machinery prices. This calculation yields total saving, again in 1929 prices, of $32 billion excluding land costs.

[4] For details of the calculations see Volume II, Chapter XII, Section 2, and notes to Table T-11.

92

CHART XVIII

SAVING OF NONAGRICULTURAL HOUSEHOLDS

Standard Social Accounting Concept

Period Averages

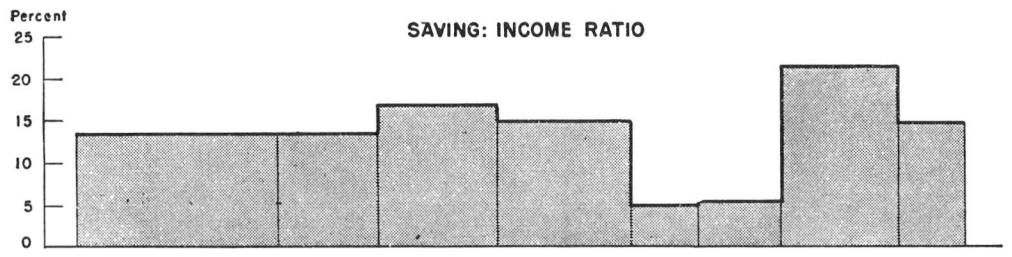

SAVING: INCOME RATIO

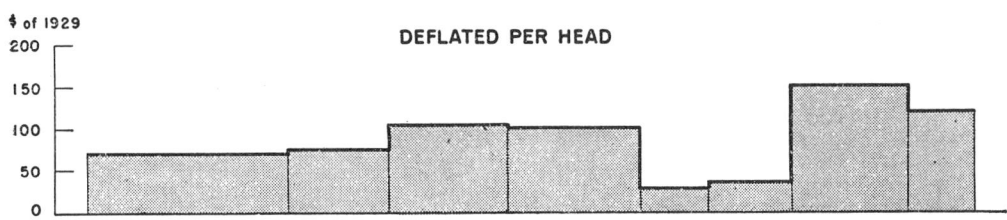

DEFLATED PER HEAD

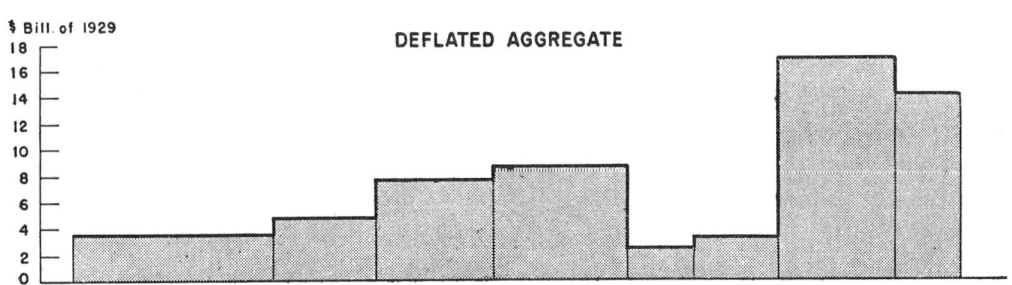

DEFLATED AGGREGATE

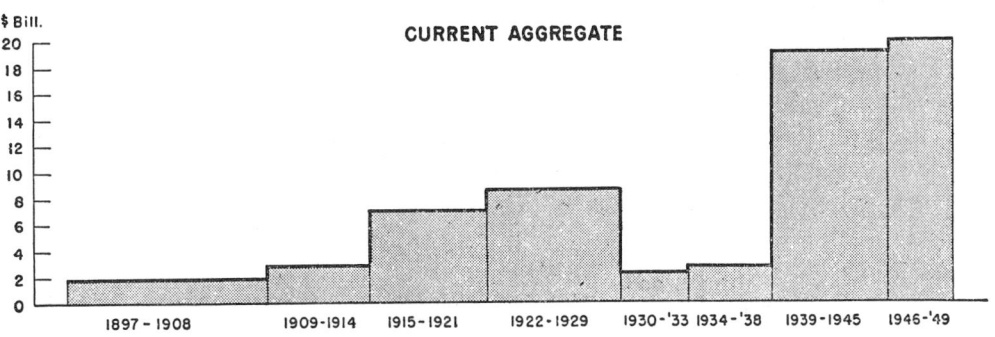

CURRENT AGGREGATE

1897 - 1908   1909-1914   1915-1921   1922-1929   1930-'33 1934-'38   1939-1945   1946-'49

TABLE X

AGRICULTURAL SAVING BY MAJOR COMPONENTS

Standard Social Accounting Concept: 1897 to 1949

	Current values				1929 prices	
	Full period	Normal period	Full period	Normal period	Full period	Normal period
	$ bill.		Percent of total net saving		$ bill.	
1. Structures	6.3	6.9	14.3	36.8	6.6	7.3
2. Equipment	7.8	7.3	17.7	38.4	7.1	7.0
3. Inventories	−1.4	−2.6	−3.2	−13.7	−0.2	−1.5
4. Net sales of farm land a	−1.9	−2.2	−4.3	−11.6	−3.1	−3.2
5. Land costs	12.8	8.7	29.0	45.8	14.1	10.5
6. Consumer durables	4.3	5.1	9.8	26.8	4.2	5.0
7. Tangible assets	27.9	23.4	63.3	123.2	28.7	25.1
8. Intangible assets	26.2	10.7	59.4	56.3	25.3	11.7
9. Total assets	54.1	34.2	122.7	180.0	54.0	36.8
10. Mortgage debt b	4.8	7.4	10.9	38.9	5.0	6.8
11. Other debt c	5.2	7.7	11.8	40.5	7.9	9.9
12. Total debt	10.0	15.2	22.7	80.0	12.9	16.7
13. Net saving, including line 5	44.1	19.0	100.0	100.0	41.2	20.1
14. Net saving, excluding line 5	31.4	10.3	71.0	54.2	27.0	9.7
15. Net saving, excluding line 5, attributable to nonfarm landlords	3.2	1.9	7.3	10.0	2.6	1.6
16. Net saving, excluding line 10	48.9	26.4	110.9	138.9	49.0	30.0
17. Net saving, excluding lines 5, 6, and 10	31.8	12.6	72.1	66.3	27.8	11.5
18. Disposable income	331.2	247.5	751.0	1302.6	361.4	283.6

a Less commissions paid on transactions in land.
b Including write-downs on all debt.
c Including tax accruals.
Source: Tables A-3, A-54; Volume II, Table B-61; and Volume III, Table N-3.

siderable part of the mortgage debt, and probably also some of the short-term debt, has been incurred in order to acquire land, which is not a component of saving at all, rather than in order to finance the construction of farm residences or service buildings, to purchase farm equipment, or to increase crop or livestock inventories. If land changes hands at increasing prices, as it has during most of the period since 1897, mortgage indebtedness incurred for the purchase of farm land rather than to finance the acquisition of reproducible tangible assets is likely to increase. This increase constitutes a negative component of saving, while the rise in the value of land underlying the increase in debt is not regarded as a positive component, being excluded as a realized or unrealized capital gain. The increase in mortgage debt which reflects sales of farm land at rising prices rather than the financing of building, equipment, or inventories is thus one of the main factors which has kept down the level of saving in agriculture before the twenties. From 1897 through 1921 farm mortgage debt increased by nearly $9 billion. If only a little more than one-half of this amount was used to finance the acquisition of land rather than that of reproducible tangible assets, disregard of such debt in the calculation of saving would increase it by approximately $5 billion and thus eliminate the dissaving now shown in Table A-3 for this period. Since part of the increase in short-term debt probably also was incurred in order to acquire land,

CHART XIX
SAVING OF AGRICULTURE
Standard Social Accounting Concept
Period Averages

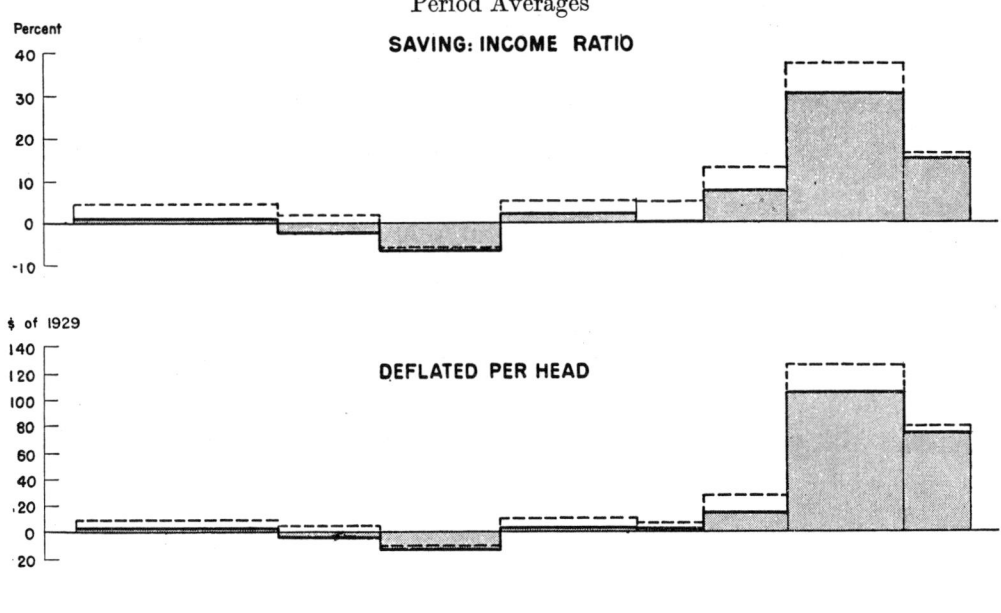

SAVING: INCOME RATIO

Percent

40
30
20
10
0
-10

DEFLATED PER HEAD

$ of 1929

140
120
100
80
60
40
.20
0
20

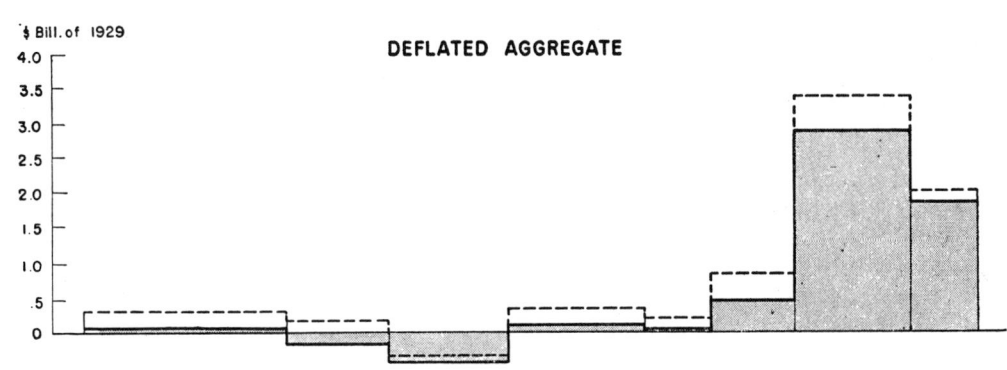

DEFLATED AGGREGATE

$ Bill. of 1929

4.0
3.5
3.0
2.5
2.0
1.5
1.0
.5
0

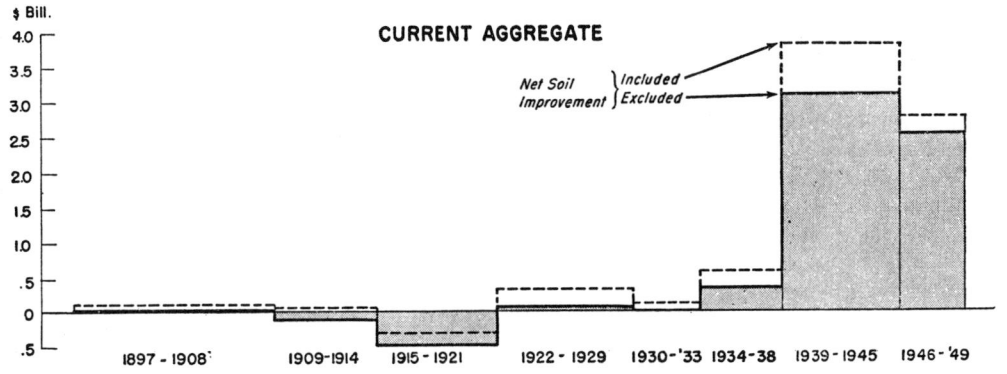

CURRENT AGGREGATE

$ Bill.

4.0
3.5
3.0
2.5
2.0
1.5
1.0
.5
0
.5

Net Soil Improvement { Included Excluded

1897 - 1908   1909-1914   1915 - 1921   1922 - 1929   1930-'33 1934-38   1939 - 1945   1946 - '49

the effect of this form of dissaving on total net saving in agriculture may have been even more pronounced.

4.16. Land costs have been the largest single component of saving through tangible assets if the rough estimates made by this study can be accepted as at least indicative of the order of magnitude involved. They have amounted to approximately one-quarter of the increase in total assets for both the full and the normal period. Saving through farm machinery and equipment has been slightly larger than saving through structures. Each has accounted for about one-eighth of the increase in total assets for the full period, but for as much as one-fifth for the normal period. Saving through consumer durables has been considerably smaller than that through either equipment or structures, representing about one-twelfth of the total increase in assets during the full, and about one-seventh during the normal, period.

4.17. The two remaining components of saving through tangible assets, inventories and net sales of farm land, together have been negative to the extent of offsetting about 5 percent of the increase in assets of agriculture for the full period, but 15 percent for the normal period. They call for some comment not because of their size but because of some peculiarities of the resulting figures, comment which because of its rather technical nature will be relegated to a footnote. [5]

[5] Using the standard social accounting concept there has been a small amount of dissaving through inventories in both the full and the normal period. This means that the sum of the changes in inventories excluding profits and losses, i.e. the sum of the product of quantity changes and year-end prices, for all of the fifty-three or forty-three years included is negative. This result is unexpected, first, because of the substantial expansion of agricultural output between 1897 and 1949; and, secondly, because of the fact that the physical inventory quantities were as a rule larger, although not spectacularly so, at the end than at the beginning of the period. (The calculation of inventory quantities, prices, and values is described in detail in the notes to Tables A-33 to A-49.) The explanation is twofold. First, it so happens that inventory quantities increased when prices were relatively low, particularly before World War I, and decreased when they were high. This pattern will lead to net dissaving through inventories in current prices, if inventory changes are calculated by multiplying quantity changes by year-end prices, even though quantities are the same at, or even though they increase between, the beginning and the end of the period. This apparent anomaly disappears once all figures are reduced to 1929 prices, as is done in Table A-2. In that case saving through inventories is positive to the extent of slightly over $2 billion, or approximately one-fourth of the level of farm inventories at the beginning of the period. The second factor influencing the estimates of saving through farm inventories is the impossibility, due to lack of data, of taking account of the changes in quality of the items included in inventories. This factor is of importance in the case of livestock where it leads—as a result of using the 1929 unit price per species throughout the period—to ignoring the substantial improvement which appears to have taken place in the quality of livestock regarded as instruments of production. The estimates of inventory changes, therefore, disregard the saving that is represented by the development of economically more efficient types of livestock or, to put it differently, do not take account of the fact that the country's livestock inventory in 1949 was economically more valuable—in terms of 1929 prices—head for head than fifty years earlier. This disregard of quality improvements does not affect most of the other types of tangible assets which evidence saving, because the calculation of saving in current prices is not based, as it is in the case of inventories, on physical quantities of changing quality.

Net sales of farm land, which represent a reduction in the assets of agriculture, have constituted a rather small component of dissaving. The figures include net sales to institutions, negligible for the period as a whole; sales of land for purpose of subdivision; and the balance of transactions

96

4.18. Saving through intangible assets differs between the full and the normal period mainly because the heavy purchases of U.S. Government securities represent about one-fifth of all saving through intangible assets for the full period, while sales constitute a small element of dissaving for the normal period. Saving through bank deposits and currency accounts for slightly more than one-half of total saving through intangibles both for the full and for the normal period. The shares of saving through life insurance and of investment in farm cooperatives in total saving through intangibles, however, are much higher during the normal than the entire period. In the case of life insurance the shares amount to about one-quarter for the normal period and one-sixth for the entire period; for investment in farm cooperatives they are one-sixth and one-twelfth respectively.

4.19. The increase in debt, which constitutes a component of dissaving, has been divided about equally between long-term and short-term debt, both for the full and for the normal period. For the period as a whole bank borrowing has accounted for about 17 percent of total debt, other commercial debt for about 20 percent, consumer debt for about 8 percent, and tax accruals for about 6 percent.

4.20. No account has been taken in the figures of some minor forms of saving by farmers, particularly their saving through securities other than U.S. Government bonds, and through nonfarm real estate. There is evidence, however, that these omitted forms of saving are of relatively small importance and that their inclusion would not substantially change the picture here given of the structure of agricultural saving for the period as a whole.

b. *Trends in aggregate saving of agriculture*

4.21. The characteristic movements of saving in agriculture are wide fluctuations—sometimes at variance with those in the rest of the economy—which almost submerge the long-term trend.

What distinguishes the course of saving in agriculture from that of most other saver groups is that the basic movement, as shown in Table XI, was downward for

---

between operating farmers and nonfarm landlords. These sales have been partially offset in the calculations by amounts paid as commissions on transactions in farm land. The latter have been regarded, as has been argued in Volume II, Chapter IX, as capitalizable expenditures and, hence, as part of saving.

Net sales of farm land during the entire period have been estimated (see Table A-1, cols. 10 and 11) at slightly over $3 billion. This figure includes an estimate of net sales for the 1946–1949 period of $0.4 billion, made before the results of the Census of Agriculture of 1950 became available. The newer data indicate that there was a considerable net purchase of land by farmers from absentee landlords after 1945. Use of the same methods of estimation as for the rest of the period—admittedly very rough and not too satisfactory—leads to an estimate of about $2½ billion of net purchases of land by farmers. Total saving of agriculture for both 1946–1949 and 1897–1949 would therefore increase by about $3 billion. This would mean a rise for the years 1946–1949 from about $10½ billion to over $13 billion excluding land costs. Dissaving through net sales of land, in particular, would be reduced for both the entire and the normal period from a little over $3 billion to almost zero. This revision, of course, does not affect total personal or national saving as it entails a reduction of equal size in the saving of nonfarm individuals.

TABLE XI

MAIN FORMS OF AGRICULTURAL SAVING

Standard Social Accounting Concept; Economic Period Averages: 1897 to 1949

Period	Tangible assets			Intangible assets	Liabilities	Net land sales	Net saving	Net soil improvement	Saving including net soil improvement
	Expenditures	Depreciation	Saving						
	1	2	3	4	5	6	7	8	9

I. Current prices ($ bill.)

1897–1908	0.73	2.49	0.24	0.09	0.23	0.08	0.03	0.10	0.13
1909–1914	1.21	0.80	0.41	0.10	0.49	0.12	−0.09	0.18	0.09
1915–1921	2.01	1.65	0.36	0.56	1.35	0.05	−0.49	0.09	−0.39
1922–1929	1.72	1.73	−0.01	−0.04	−0.30	0.15	0.10	0.23	0.33
1930–1933	0.78	1.47	−0.69	−0.27	−0.98	0.01	0.01	0.14	0.15
1934–1938	1.15	1.28	−0.13	0.42	−0.06	0	0.36	0.30	0.66
1939–1945	2.21	1.76	0.45	2.30	−0.29	−0.07	3.11	0.75	3.86
1946–1949	5.97	3.30	2.67	0.89	0.83	0.11	2.63	0.18	2.81

II. 1929 prices ($ bill.)

1897–1908	1.43	0.95	0.48	0.18	0.44	0.15	0.07	0.21	0.28
1909–1914	1.98	1.31	0.67	0.17	0.80	0.19	−0.15	0.30	0.15
1915–1921	2.11	1.71	0.40	0.64	1.38	0.08	−0.42	0.13	−0.29
1922–1929	1.70	1.71	−0.01	−0.04	−0.30	0.14	0.10	0.23	0.33
1930–1933	0.89	1.75	−0.86	−0.31	−1.20	0.01	0.02	0.17	0.19
1934–1938	1.38	1.56	−0.18	0.52	−0.08	0	0.42	0.37	0.79
1939–1945	2.14	1.65	0.49	1.99	−0.24	−0.06	2.78	0.58	3.36
1946–1949	4.18	2.32	1.86	0.69	0.59	0.08	1.88	0.13	2.01

III. Percent of total saving including net soil improvement

1897–1908	608	408	200	75	192	67	17	83	100
1909–1914	1 512	1 000	512	125	612	150	−125	225	100
1915–1921	−515	−423	−92	−144	−346	−13	123	−23	100
1922–1929	521	524	−3	−12	−91	45	30	70	100
1930–1933	520	980	−460	−180	−653	7	7	93	100
1934–1938	177	197	−20	65	−9	–	54	46	100
1939–1945	57	46	12	60	−8	−2	81	19	100
1946–1949	213	118	95	32	30	4	94	6	100

Section I:

    Column 1 – Table A-66, col. 2 plus Table A-3, col. 12.

    Column 2 – Table A-3, col. 2 minus col. 1 of this table.

    Column 3 – Col. 1 minus col. 2.

    Column 4 – Table A-3, col. 7.

    Column 5 – Table A-3, cols. 8 and 9.

    Column 6 – Table A-3, cols. 10 and 11.

    Column 7 – Cols. 3 and 4 minus cols. 5 and 6.

    Column 8 – Derived according to procedure described in Table II, line 3.

    Column 9 – Col. 7 plus col. 8.

Section II:

    Columns 1 to 9 – Annual figures of Section I of this table, cols. 1–9 respectively, divided by gross national product deflator as given in Table T-16, col. 1.

Section III:

    Columns 1 to 9 – Derived from Section I of this table.

the first twenty-five years of the period, irrespective of whether account is taken of net soil improvement (land costs) and of whether current or deflated values and aggregate or per head values are used. This decline culminates in the depression of 1919–1921, which hit agriculture with particular severity. As a result the level of agricultural saving was not much higher in the twenties, if account is taken of changes in prices and farm population, than at the turn of the century.

From the twenties on, the trend of agricultural saving has been definitely upward, and quite sharply so since the early thirties. The effect of the Great Depression is much less visible than in the saving of most other groups, another distinguishing feature of saving in agriculture. The contour of the movements since the twenties is the same whatever the scope of the estimates and irrespective of whether current or deflated and aggregate or per head values are used. The slope of the curve, however, is steeper for figures excluding land costs than for those including them, and steeper for current than for deflated values.

Apart from these two basic long-term movements two large bulges stand out which reflect the effect of the two wars, particularly the farm prosperity accompanying World War II, and the deep trough during the depression of 1919–1921.

c. *Trends in main components of agricultural saving*

4.22. The trend in aggregate saving of agriculture will be easier to understand after a look at the structure of total agricultural saving and at the trends of the main forms of saving.

Net expenditures on tangible assets have shown an increasing trend which is evident over most of the period, i.e. from 1897 through World War I and again from the midthirties on, both in current and in deflated (1929) prices. From 1897–1908 to 1946–1949 saving through tangible assets in current prices has increased more than eleven times. It has nearly tripled even if adjustment is made for price changes. The movement, however, was interrupted for about two decades, during the twenties and thirties, when capital consumption allowances, calculated on the basis of replacement cost, exceeded current expenditures on new reproducible durable tangible assets. Between the turn of the century and World War I net saving through reproducible durable tangible assets (excluding land costs) was increasing rapidly—at a rate of about 9 percent per year in current, and 7 percent in 1929, prices.

As a result of the rapid increase in both gross and net saving through reproducible durable tangible assets their value at the end of World War I, after adjusting for price changes, was about 50 percent higher than in 1896.[6] By 1949 the deflated value of reproducible durable tangible assets was twice as high as it had been fifty years earlier, and even two-and-one-half times as high per head of the farm population. This is equivalent to growth of aggregate tangible assets at an average rate of 2.3 percent a year from 1896 to 1918 and at a rate of a little under $1\frac{1}{2}$ percent for the entire period of fifty-three years, even though growth virtually stopped for two decades following World War I. These rates of growth of saving

[6] These estimates of reproducible tangible wealth of agriculture will be found in Volume II, Table B-62; for derivation see Volume III, Table W-7.

99

through reproducible tangible assets are thus not only far from negligible, but were also considerably in excess of the rate of growth of agricultural output before World War I. Between 1897 and 1917, for instance, farm output increased by only 20 percent [7] compared to an increase of about 50 percent in deflated reproducible tangible wealth. For the entire period 1897–1949, on the other hand, agricultural output increased by about 100 percent, while the value of real reproducible durable tangible assets rose little more than this.

4.23.   These findings are about what would be expected from our knowledge of the vicissitudes of American agriculture over the last half century. The inclusion of allowances for changes in farm debt in the calculation, which is a necessary part of any measurement of saving, nevertheless produces some results in the over-all figures which appear astounding at first sight. For both the 1897–1908 and the 1909–1914 periods the increase in long-term and short-term debt together is sufficient to offset not only saving through tangible assets excluding land costs if net sales of farm land to nonfarm owners are taken into account (Table XI, col. 3 plus col. 8), but also virtually all of saving including land costs (Table XI, col. 3 plus col. 8 minus col. 6). In other words, farmers in the two decades ending with World War I borrowed so much that as a group they showed no saving through tangible assets. This means that all the new tangible assets in agriculture—and they were of substantial proportions—were actually financed by the lenders, both individual and institutional. Obviously not all the increase in debt appearing in the statistics was used to finance investment in new tangible assets, although a considerable part was actually so employed. Part of the increase, and one may assume a substantial part even though no specific estimate can be made, reflected borrowing to finance a change of hands of existing farms either among farmers or between farmers and nonfarmers. This large increase in borrowing without counterpart in saving through tangible assets is, as suggested earlier, responsible for much of the seemingly low level of aggregate saving in agriculture up to the end of World War I. In contrast to these developments farmers almost continuously reduced their total indebtedness from the twenties to the end of World War II.[8] The reduction was so pronounced during the Great Depression that it entirely offset the substantial dissaving through tangible assets and the smaller one through intangibles. This leads to the seemingly paradoxical result that dissaving was smaller during the Great Depression of 1930–1933 than in the depression of 1919–1921. The explanation is that farmers had to reduce expenditures on consumption as well as investment in order to meet interest and debt repayments. These reductions lowered their standard of living and led to deterioration of their plant (structures and equipment), but improved their financial position.

[7] Department of Agriculture, *Progress of Farm Mechanization*, Miscellaneous Publication No. 630, 1947, p. 81; also Strauss and Bean, *Gross Farm Income and Indices of Farm Production and Prices in the U.S., 1869–1937*, Department of Agriculture, Technical Bulletin No. 703, 1940, p. 126.

[8] All statements in the text on changes in debt as well as the underlying figures in Tables S-24 and S-25 have been adjusted for the reduction in reported debt outstanding which reflects write-downs rather than repayments. (See Volume II, Chapter IX, Section 2; and Table A-65.)

4.24. The movements of saving through intangible assets have been, as Table XI shows, almost the inverse of those of saving through tangible assets disregarding attaching liabilities. Saving through intangible assets was highest during the two wars. It was negative to a substantial extent during the Great Depression. These statements probably would not be substantially modified if information, now missing, were available on a few secondary forms of farmers' saving through intangible assets, particularly securities other than U.S. savings bonds. Whether the increase in the share of saving through intangible assets which can be observed from the midthirties to the end of World War II is permanent or temporary and whether, subsequently, the relatively low share of the years 1946–1949 is an exception cannot yet be said.

4.25. Three changes in the structure of agricultural saving thus seem to merit attention:

(1) The importance of debt as an offset to an increase in assets has declined considerably. Even in 1946–1949, a period of high investment in agriculture and of generally sharp expansion of credit in the private economy, net borrowing offset less than one-third of saving through tangible assets after allowance for capital consumption, a ratio much lower than that observed before World War I.

(2) Saving through intangibles has increased in importance, at least from World War I to the end of World War II.

(3) Within saving through tangible assets the importance of machinery and equipment, both for farm operations and for household use, has increased as in other sectors of the economy. On the other hand, saving in the form of inventories and land costs have declined in importance. This is as expected in the case of saving through land costs, since expenditures on bringing additional land into cultivation have been reduced as the expansion of farm acreage has more or less come to an end. Saving through structures (including farm residences, farm service buildings, and improvements such as fencing, ditching, and tiling) seems to have approximately maintained its share in total net expenditures on reproducible tangible assets.

d. *The saving-income ratio of agriculture*

4.26. For the entire period the saving of agriculture has averaged, as seen in Table XII, nearly one-tenth of agricultural disposable income if the standard social accounting concept of saving is used, i.e. if land costs (net soil improvement) are excluded, saving through consumer durables is included, depreciation is calculated on a replacement cost basis, and capital gains and losses are disregarded. Excluding consumer durables, the saving ratio averages approximately 8 percent. Inclusion of land costs raises it to over 13 percent. These figures are greatly influenced by the very high level of saving during World War II. For the normal period the saving-income ratio averages only 5 percent under the standard social accounting concept, 3 percent if consumer durables are excluded, and 8 percent even if land costs are taken into account.

4.27. Like the absolute figures of agricultural saving the saving-income ratios

TABLE XII

SAVING-INCOME RATIO OF AGRICULTURE

Social Accounting Concept; Economic Periods: 1897 to 1949

Percent

Period	Standard social accounting concept	Including net soil improvement	Excluding consumer durables
	1	2	3
1897–1908	1.1	4.6	0
1909–1914	−2.2	2.2	−3.8
1915–1921	−6.8	−5.5	−6.9
1922–1929	1.8	5.8	1.2
1930–1933	0.4	5.3	7.9
1934–1938	7.5	13.7	5.8
1939–1945	30.7	38.0	30.5
1946–1949	15.1	16.2	10.2
1897–1949	9.5	13.3	8.2
1897–1949, excluding 1917–1918, 1930–1933, 1942–1945	4.6	8.1	2.5

Column 1 – Table T-1, col. 4 divided by disposable income as given in Volume III, Table N-3, col. 7.
Column 2 – Same procedure as for col. 1 except that land costs (see Table II, line 3) are added to Table T-1.
Column 3 – Same procedure as for col. 1 except that Table A-3, col. 5 is subtracted from Table T-1.

are characterized by low and even declining values from the turn of the century through the depression of 1919–1921, and by substantial increases from the twenties on, particularly in the forties. It may be rather unexpected to find that the saving ratio was fairly substantial in the late thirties. This is true even during the Great Depression—mainly as a result of debt repayment—if we exclude consumer durables, which at that time contributed heavily to dissaving, since current purchases were considerably smaller than depreciation allowances. During World War II the saving ratio of agriculture rose to the unprecedented level of almost one-third, even excluding land costs. For the four years 1946–1949 the ratio averages about one-seventh including, but only one-tenth excluding, saving through consumer durables, both values well above those for any period before World War II.[9]

[9] For these years the ratio derived from Saving Study estimates can be compared with the median saving ratio of farm operator households shown in the Federal Reserve Board's Survey of Consumer Finances. It happens that for the four years 1946–1949 the median saving ratio of farm operators, which excludes saving through consumer durables, averages 10 percent, or the same value as shown in Table XII. Differences in concepts and scope between the Survey and this study and differences between mean and median values are, however, sufficiently substantial to reduce the value of the close correspondence of the two figures as a confirmation of the average level of the estimates used here. No similar comparison is possible for earlier periods, for which it would be even more desirable because this study's figures contradict the popular impression of a high saving ratio in agriculture before 1930.

4.28. The question obviously arises whether the saving ratio of the four years after the end of World War II or the ratios for the three decades before 1930 should be regarded as typical. The answer would seem to be that the ratios for the period before 1930, and particularly those for the two decades before the depression of 1919–1921, apply to a phase in American agriculture which has passed. It was a phase characterized by substantial expansion of farm acreage, rapid movements of operators from farm to farm, and the belief in the continuous rise in land values. These characteristics appear to be much less applicable, if at all, to American agriculture in the middle of the twentieth century. Agriculture now operates within an essentially unchanging area, and has become highly mechanized, less volatile, and less speculative. The saving-income ratios of the first two decades of this century, which are strongly affected by the rapid accumulation of debt to finance change of hands of farm land, and that of the third decade, which is still under the influence of the agricultural crisis of 1919–1921 and the milder depression of the twenties, should therefore probably be regarded as having historical interest only, and as being without indicative value for the long-term level and trend of the saving-income ratio of agriculture in the mid-twentieth century. Whether the ratio observed in the last few years since the end of World War II is representative it is much too early to tell. It certainly has been subject to many factors not likely to be of enduring character, particularly the need to make up deficiencies in buildings, machinery, and equipment which had accumulated in the preceding twenty years as the result first of financial stringency and then of the unavailability of labor and materials during World War II. Nevertheless, the ratio of the past four years is more likely to give an idea of the average level for the next one or two decades than the relationships which prevailed in the generation before 1930.

4. Unincorporated Business Enterprises

4.29. Even a summary discussion of the estimates of saving of unincorporated business enterprises must be prefaced by two warnings. The first is that because of our scandalous ignorance of the financial situation and history of unincorporated business, repeatedly stressed in this study, the estimates of its saving are rougher and less reliable than those for any of the main saver groups.[10] Whatever confidence can be placed in the figures derives largely from the fact that they yield estimates of the present net worth of unincorporated business enterprises which are reasonably close to the few independent data available.[11] The second warning is to the effect that the figures cover not only retained net profits but also net investment or disinvestment by proprietors, i.e. what corresponds to net sales or redemptions of their own equity securities by corporations. The impossibility of

[10] Familiarity with Volume II, Chapter XIII, Section 3, in which the nature and limitation of the estimates of saving of unincorporated business enterprises are discussed at some length, is essential for an evaluation of the discussion in this section.

[11] Volume II, Chapter XIII, Section 5.

separating these two components is a considerable drawback to any analysis of the financial history of unincorporated business. It is of less importance for the study of national or personal saving since it only means that there is no separate information on one of the forms of saving of nonfarm individuals, viz. their net investment or disinvestment in unincorporated business enterprises, and that this component must be combined with the profits retained in unincorporated businesses. The sum of the two items may thus be treated either as a component of nonfarm individual and personal saving, or, as is done in this study, as a measure of saving of unincorporated business enterprises.

a. *The structure of saving of unincorporated business for the period as a whole*

4.30.   For the entire period 1897–1949 saving of unincorporated business enterprises, including throughout this section the net investment (or disinvestment) by proprietors, has totalled slightly over $20 billion in current prices and a little over $18 billion in 1929 prices. Since saving was very high during World War II, the total for the normal period amounts to only about $13 billion in current or $15 billion in 1929 prices, or approximately $300 million per year.

These are rather small figures, constituting only approximately 4 percent of total national saving for the normal period. They appear particularly small if it is remembered that they include not only retained net earnings but also net investment by proprietors. The estimates are probably too low because no adjustment could be made for the unincorporated enterprises which are transformed into or absorbed by corporations and no account could be taken of a few secondary forms of saving.[12] The figures also appear modest in relation to the total net income of unincorporated businesses, a comparison which will be carried through in Divisions 4.36 and 4.37.

4.31.   The outstanding feature in the distribution of total saving among forms, shown in Table XIII, is the small positive saving through buildings in both full and normal periods, which turns to dissaving if allowance is made for the increase in mortgage debt. This feature calls for explanation since it would seem obvious that the equity of unincorporated business enterprises in buildings must have been much higher at the end of 1949 than at the end of 1896, particularly if it is remembered that all nonresidential real estate owned by individuals is included in that of unincorporated business.[13] Much of the explanation is provided by the very substantial revaluations, indicative of both realized and unrealized capital gains, which reflect the rise in the price level of real estate and which are excluded from the social accounting concept of saving. The extent of these revaluations cannot be measured directly, but consideration of the age distribution of nonresidential buildings standing at the end of 1949 and of the trend of real

---

[12] Volume II, Chapter XIII, Section 2.

[13] The current (replacement cost) value of all nonresidential structures not owned by corporations, nonprofit institutions, or governments totalled approximately $2 billion in 1896 and $20 billion in 1948 (Table U-2). Deduction of the mortgage debt attributable to these structures (Table U-1, col. 9) leads to estimates of owners' equity of about $1 billion and $14 billion respectively.

TABLE XIII

CHANGE IN NET WORTH OF UNINCORPORATED BUSINESS
BY MAJOR COMPONENTS
Standard Social Accounting Concept: 1897 to 1949

$ bill.

Saving	Full period	Normal period [a]	Dissaving	Full period	Normal period [a]
1. Buildings	4.5	5.6	8. Mortgage debt	6.2	6.2
2. Producer durables	7.0	7.5	9. Bank loans	6.0	7.9
3. Inventories	4.8	5.4	10. Net accounts payable	3.5	.
4. Cash	14.2	6.2	11. Undistributed profits and		
5. U.S. Government securities	5.5	−0.4	net investment by pro-		
6. Net accounts receivable	.	2.6	prietors	20.4	12.8
7. Increase in assets	36.1	26.9	12. Increase in liabilities and		
			earned net worth	36.1	26.9

[a] Excludes 1917–1918, 1930–1933, and 1942–1945.
Source: See notes to Table U-3, col. 3.

estate prices for the past half century suggests that revaluations may well account for the apparent difference between the small saving through commercial and industrial structures owned by unincorporated business which is indicated by the estimates and the obvious fact of a substantial increase in the current value of the equity in buildings.

4.32. A second characteristic of the distribution is the fact that saving through producer durable goods, i.e. machinery and equipment, is the largest component of saving through tangible assets by unincorporated business enterprises. Without making allowance for that part of the bank debt which was incurred to finance the acquisition of such durables, an allowance which can be only conjectural, saving through producer durables accounts for nearly one-fourth of the total increase in assets. Increases in inventories have represented about one-sixth of the total increase in assets. Saving through producer durables and inventories together, less increases in bank loans, has accounted for about 30 percent of total net saving for the full period and 40 percent for the normal period.

4.33. The importance of saving through intangible assets differs greatly between the full and the normal period. Cash saving, mostly in the form of bank balances, accounted for about 40 percent of the total increase in assets for the full period, as a result of the particularly heavy accumulations of cash during World War II, but for less than 25 percent for the normal period. Saving through U.S. Government securities, which represented over 15 percent of the total increase in assets for the full period, was even slightly negative for the normal period alone. For the full period the estimates—particularly precarious for this item—indicate that unincorporated business enterprises were on balance net borrowers from corporations, the increase in their accounts payable exceeding that in accounts receivable to an extent equal to approximately one-tenth of the total increase in assets. For the normal period, on the other hand, the increase in accounts receiv-

105

able from corporations was larger than that in accounts payable to them, and the difference amounted to about one-tenth of the total increase in assets. This discrepancy is due mostly to the sharp deterioration of the position of unincorporated business enterprises in their debtor and creditor relations to corporations other than banks during the Great Depression.

b. *Trends in saving of unincorporated business*

4.34. The saving of unincorporated business enterprises—or more correctly the change in their net worth, since the figures include net investment by proprietors—has, as Chart xx indicates, shown an upward trend over the period like that of all other saver groups. This movement, however, has been very irregular. The most characteristic features are the sharp increases in saving during both wars and the precipitous decline during the Great Depression.

Apart from the bulges reflecting the two wars, aggregate saving of unincorporated business enterprises, as shown in Table xiv, exhibits no upward trend once the figures are adjusted for changes in the price level. It even moves irregularly downwards if allowance is made for the increase in population. The picture is a little brighter if saving (or dissaving) through nonresidential real estate is eliminated on the assumption that to a considerable extent it does not reflect unincorporated business activities in the narrower sense, but represents a form of investment by individuals. Even then the increase in deflated saving of unincorporated business enterprises is moderate, and does not do much more than keep

TABLE XIV

TRENDS IN THE CHANGE IN NET WORTH OF
UNINCORPORATED BUSINESS

Standard Social Accounting Concept; Economic Period Averages: 1897 to 1949

Period	Total			Excluding real estate		
	Aggregate saving		Deflated saving per head	Aggregate saving		Deflated saving per head
	Current	Deflated		Current	Deflated	
	$ bill.		$	$ bill.		$
	1	2	3	4	5	6
1897–1908	0.10	0.20	2.6	0.02	0.04	0.6
1909–1914	0.15	0.24	2.5	0.15	0.23	2.4
1915–1921	0.62	0.60	5.7	0.63	0.62	6.0
1922–1929	0.20	0.20	1.7	0.15	0.15	1.3
1930–1933	−2.23	−2.62	−21.1	−2.17	−2.53	−20.4
1934–1938	0.44	0.56	4.5	0.61	0.76	6.0
1939–1945	2.54	2.18	16.5	2.65	2.27	16.7
1946–1949	0.33	0.24	1.6	0.61	0.43	3.0

Columns 1 and 4 – See notes to Table U-3, col. 3.

Columns 2 and 5 – Cols. 1 and 4 respectively divided by gross national product deflator. (From Table T-12, col. 5.)

Columns 3 and 6 – Cols. 2 and 5 respectively divided by total population (1900–1945 *Historical Statistics*, p. 26; 1946–1949 *Statistical Abstract*, various issues).

CHART XX

CHANGE IN NET WORTH OF UNINCORPORATED BUSINESS
Standard Social Accounting Concept
Period Averages

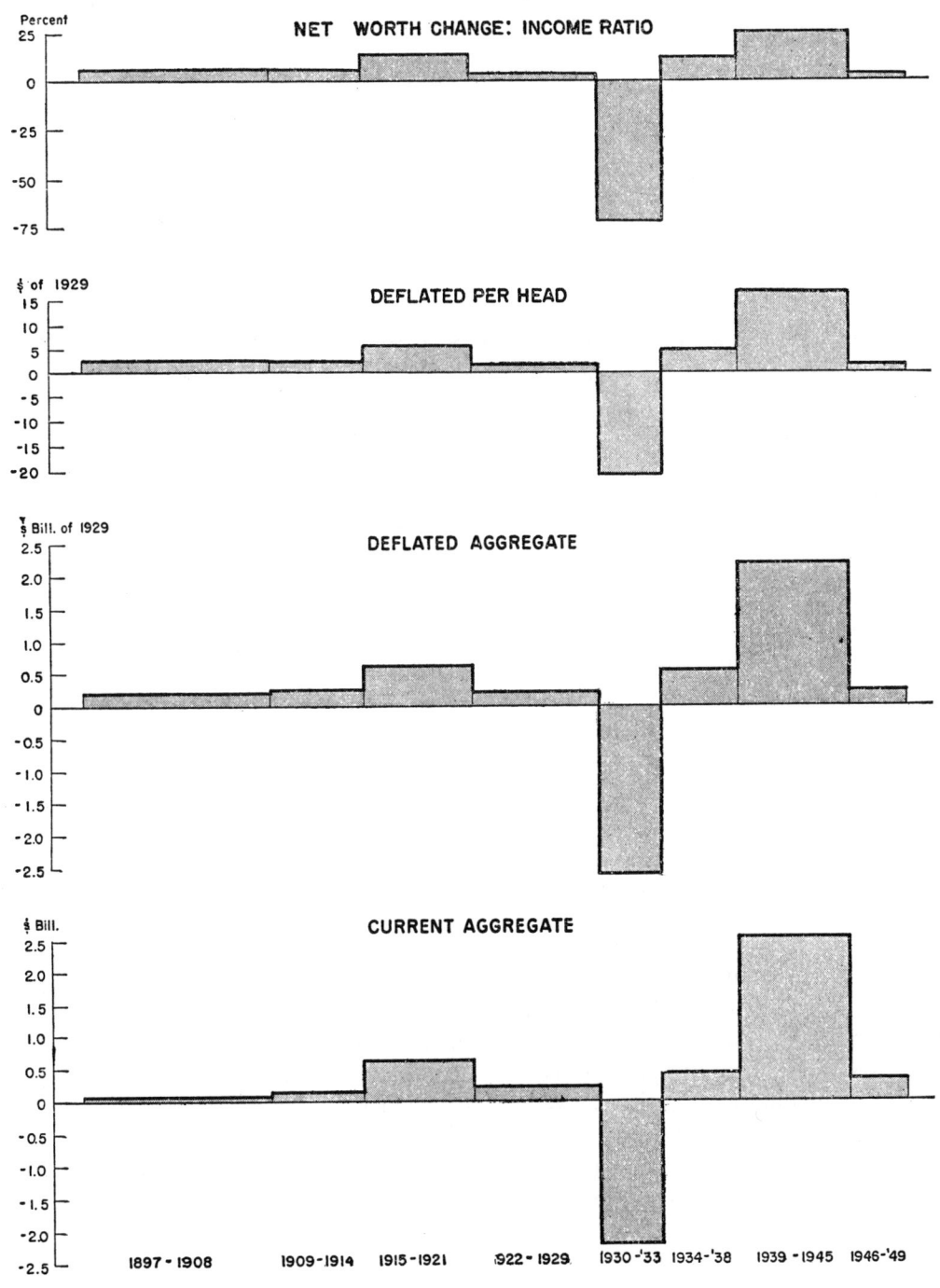

in step with the increase in population. The increase therefore still lags considerably behind the rate of growth of national income or total saving. This lag is not astonishing in view of the decline of the importance of unincorporated business within the economy, particularly in the fields of manufacturing and retail trade. These broad and tentative conclusions represent about all that can be justified in view of the very rough nature of the estimates and the somewhat erratic character of the figures.

4.35. Considerable changes have occurred in the distribution of saving by forms between periods (Tables S-26 and S-27), but no pronounced long-term trends are visible except the declining share of net saving through structures. In the first period, from 1897 through 1908, net saving through structures accounted for about three-quarters of the total. Since that time the share of saving through structures has been negative in most years as the increase in mortgage debt has been larger than the excess of new construction expenditures over depreciation allowances on a replacement cost basis.

If real estate is excluded, cash and U.S. Government securities provide the most important outlet for saving. It is only in the Great Depression and after World War II that these liquid assets do not represent at least one-third of total net saving excluding real estate. The high share of saving through cash, (primarily bank deposits) before World War II is rather astonishing, but may in part reflect shortcomings in the estimates. Saving through producer durables was particularly high in the two postwar periods. The share of inventories has fluctuated less, falling generally between one-sixth and two-fifths of total net saving or dissaving. The proportion of net receivables has moved rather erratically, possibly a reflection of the poor quality of the underlying data. Increases in bank loans have in most periods offset a considerable part of saving through tangible and intangible assets, particularly in the first decade of the century and after World War II. The Great Depression is the only period in which bank loans declined consistently and thus offset one-fourth of the large dissaving of those years.

c. *The saving-income ratio of unincorporated business*

4.36. In contrast to the rather confused picture obtained for the distribution of saving by forms, the movements of the saving ratio, as they are shown in Table XV, are reasonably clear-cut and in accordance with expectations. The highest ratios are registered for the two war periods and the only negative ratio—a very high one—for the Great Depression. This pattern is similar to that for corporate saving except for the bulge during World War II, which is partly due to the fact that no allowance is made in the estimates for taxes on the net income of unincorporated business enterprises since they are paid by the proprietors and, hence, are not separately reported in income tax statistics. What may need comment is the apparent declining trend in the ratio since World War I and, still more, the relatively low level of the ratio for the normal periods, averaging only a little over 6 percent and ranging between 2 and 11 percent. This low level is particularly remarkable as it is arrived at before allowance for taxes and includes net investment by proprietors.

108

TABLE XV

SAVING-INCOME RATIO OF UNINCORPORATED BUSINESS

Standard Social Accounting Concept; Economic Periods: 1899 to 1949

Period	Income			Saving	Saving-income ratio
	Martin	Kuznets	Department of Commerce		
	$ bill.				Percent
	1	2	3	4	5
1899–1908	18.3	.	.	1.1	6.0
1909–1914	14.2	.	.	0.9	6.3
1915–1921	26.1	.	.	4.3	16.5
1922–1929	41.8	45.1	.	1.6	3.5
1930–1933	18.1	14.9	12.1	−8.9	−73.6
1934–1938	.	20.4	20.2	2.2	10.9
1939–1945	.	.	71.7	17.8	24.8
1946–1949	.	.	67.7	1.3	1.9
Entire period	.	.	275.4	20.4	7.4
Normal period	.	.	203.2	12.8	6.3

Column 1 – *National Income in the United States 1799–1938*, p. 39. Figures are differences between total for all industries and agriculture and miscellaneous.

Column 2 – From Volume II, Table B-79, col. 2.

Column 3 – From Table B-79, col. 4. Figures for entire and normal periods are sum of col. 1 for 1899–1921, col. 2 for 1922–1929, and col. 3 for 1930–1949.

Column 4 – Table T-1, col. 5. Includes proprietors' net investment or disinvestment.

Column 5 – Col. 4 divided by col. 1 to 1921, col. 2 to 1929, and col. 3 for 1930 to 1949 and for entire and normal periods.

4.37. No satisfactory explanation of what appears at first sight to be an astonishingly low level for the ratio of saving to income is possible with the present dearth of reliable data. Nor is it possible, again mainly for lack of data, to compare and reconcile the estimates derived from time series of selected assets and liabilities, which have been used in this study, with the information on the saving of the proprietors of unincorporated businesses—including without distinction both their business and personal saving, particularly saving through homes, consumer durables, life insurance, securities other than U.S. Government, and personal bank and other deposits—which have been developed through sample household budget studies.[14] Two factors provide at least a partial explanation of why saving by all unincorporated business enterprises taken together is small, both absolutely and in comparison to their income. The first is the large share of unincorporated businesses which are unprofitable over most or all of their existence and are liquidated, generally after a rather short life, involving losses which appear as dissaving in our calculations. The second is the tendency of proprietors to withdraw most, and often more than the entirety, of current profit, particularly if profits are calculated after elimination of inventory profits and by using depreciation allowances based on replacement cost, as is done in this study.

[14] See particularly Morgan, in *Journal of Political Economy*, Dec. 1951.

5. Corporations

a. *Trends in corporate saving*

4.38. The basic trend of corporate saving has been upward throughout the period, although it was interrupted for a full decade, 1930–1940. The movement is probably seen most clearly when estimates of corporate saving following the social accounting concept and adjusted for changes in the price level are used,[15] as is done in Chart XXI.

4.39. Between 1898–1901 and 1926–1929 corporate saving increased by about 300 percent in current prices, but by only about 100 percent if the rise in the price level is taken into account. This increase corresponds to a growth of corporate saving in deflated prices at a rate of nearly $2\frac{1}{2}$ percent a year. The variations of corporate saving from the trend line are clearly related to the business cycle.[16] The widest upward deviation occurs in 1916–1917 and reflects the extraordinary profits of World War I. Similarly, the wide downward deviation of 1918 is apparently connected with reconversion at the end of World War I.

4.40. Corporate saving was negative from 1930 to 1939, primarily as a result of a sharp decline in total corporate profits and in some years the emergence of net losses, and secondarily, as a consequence of a relatively smaller reduction in dividend payments. Dissaving during this decade, totalling about $20 billion in current prices, was equal to the entire cumulated corporate saving of the twenties.[17]

4.41. During World War II corporate saving rose to twice the level of the twenties in current prices, and was 50 percent above that level even if account is taken of the rise in prices. That the increase was not as pronounced as during World War I is attributable primarily to price control and the high level of corporate taxation. From 1946 to 1949 corporate saving was on the average three times as high as in the twenties in current, and a little more than twice as high in deflated, prices notwithstanding continued high rates of taxation. It is interesting to note that if the trend of deflated corporate saving observed from 1897 to 1929 is extrapolated for the succeeding two decades the actual level of corporate saving during the forties is on the average fairly close to the extrapolated trend values. However, it is considerably below the trend line in 1940–1941 and above it in 1948–1949.[18]

[15] This means that, compared to the published figures, capital gains and losses, including inventory profits and losses, are eliminated; capital consumption allowances are calculated on the basis of replacement cost rather than original cost; depletion is reduced to writing off actual cost; and allowance is made for profits disclosed by Bureau of Internal Revenue audits—to mention only the adjustments of greatest quantitative importance.

[16] See Chapter VII, Section 4.

[17] If all estimates are reduced to 1929 prices, dissaving during the thirties amounts to about $25 billion and equals cumulated saving back to 1917.

[18] The estimates of this study end with 1949, but it is known that corporate saving continued on a very high level in 1950–1952, and thus was well above the extrapolated pre-1930 trend in these years too.

CHART XXI

CORPORATE SAVING
Standard Social Accounting Concept
Period Averages

SAVING: INCOME RATIO

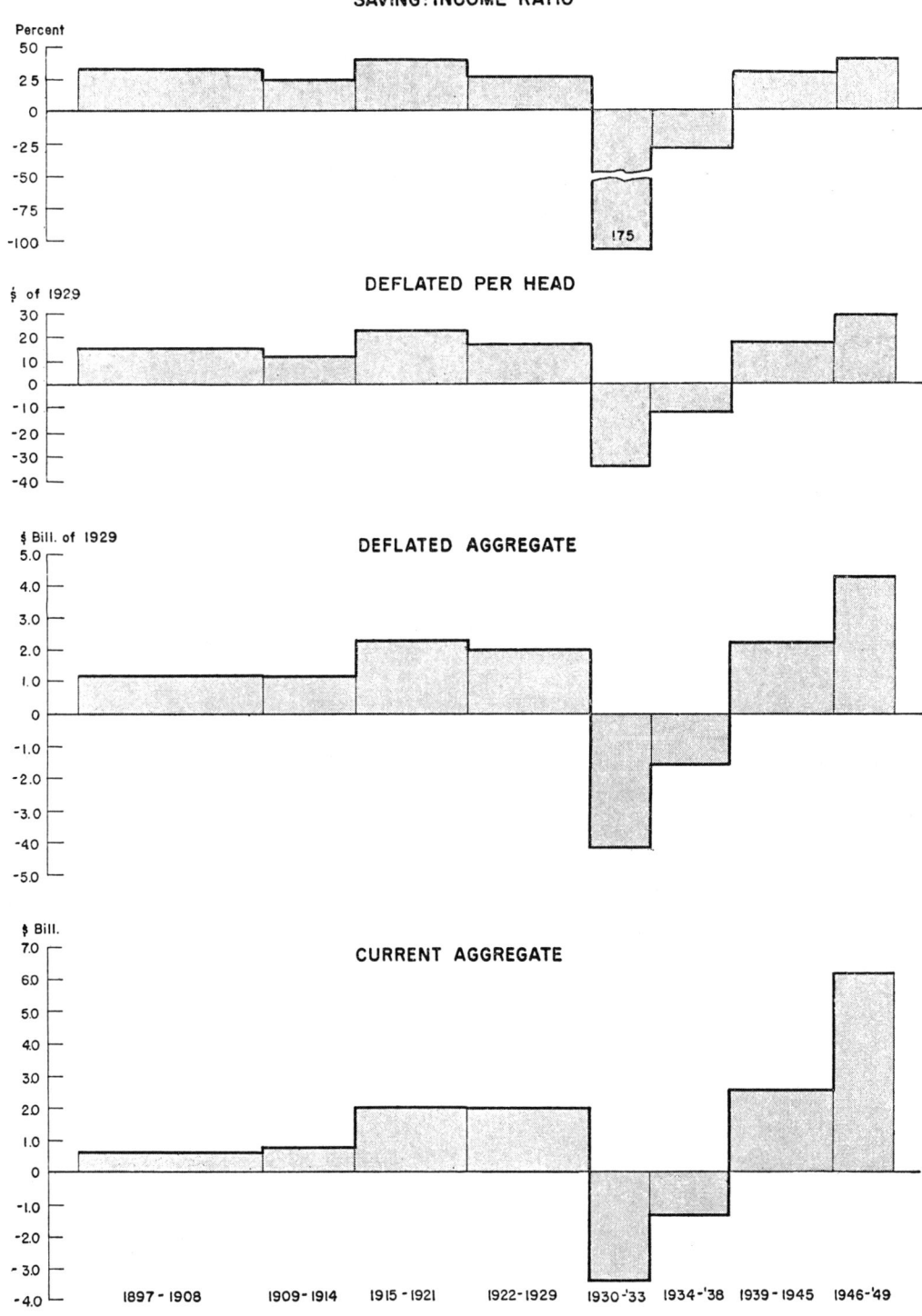

Percent
50
25
0
-25
-50
-75
-100

175

DEFLATED PER HEAD

$ of 1929
30
20
10
0
-10
-20
-30
-40

DEFLATED AGGREGATE

$ Bill. of 1929
5.0
4.0
3.0
2.0
1.0
0
-1.0
-2.0
-3.0
-40
-5.0

CURRENT AGGREGATE

$ Bill.
7.0
60
5.0
40
3.0
2.0
1.0
0
-1.0
-2.0
-3.0
-4.0

1897 - 1908   1909 - 1914   1915 - 1921   1922 - 1929   1930 -'33   1934 -'38   1939 - 1945   1946 -'49

b. *The corporate saving-income ratio*

4.42. The absolute amount of corporate saving is the result of three main factors: net profits; the rate of taxation; and the distribution ratio, i.e. dividend payments divided by total net profits. Corporate profits are known to depend mostly on the level of the national product and changes in it, although the amplitude of the fluctuations is wider in profits than in national product. The share of net profits taken by taxation has increased over the period. The distribution ratio appears to have been stable in the long run until 1930, but to have moved to a higher level in the forties. As dividends have always fluctuated less than net profits, corporate saving naturally has varied from year to year even more than profits.[19] This is shown by the fact that the average variation in corporate saving (i.e. the median percentage of change from year to year disregarding sign) for the period 1898–1949 is 48 percent for corporate saving against only 25 percent for corporate net income, 14 percent for dividend payments, and 9 percent for net national product.

4.43. As shown in Chart XXI, for the period 1897–1929 the corporate saving ratio averaged slightly over 30 percent. Quadrennial averages, however, varied between a low of 24 percent (1906–1909 and 1926–1929) and a high of 45 percent (1898–1901). The ratio showed a tendency to decline from the turn of the century to the period 1906–1913. It was on a higher level, averaging 40 percent, from 1915 to 1921, but considerably lower—with an average of only little over 25 percent—during the twenties. In general the corporate saving ratio was high when total corporate profits and national income were high.

4.44. During the thirties the saving ratio was negative. In the forties it was positive again and high, averaging about 40 percent. This rate is considerably above the 1897–1929 average, and is equal to the ratio for the highest decade before the Great Depression (1915–1924), a figure which was influenced by the high saving ratios of World War I. What is probably more significant, the saving ratio for the years 1946–1949 of more than 40 percent is the highest for any normal period of equal length except 1898–1901, a span for which the figures are naturally much less reliable.[20] The increase in the retention ratio in the forties, which may turn out to be an enduring structural change, is probably attributable to two

[19] The most careful statistical study of this subject available (Dobrovolsky, *Corporate Income Retention, 1915–1943*, 1951, p. 2) concludes that "An increase in net income of one dollar (per hundred dollars of net worth) has been associated, on the average, with a rise in retained income of 70–80 cents, on the one hand, and a rise of dividends of 20–30 cents (per hundred dollars of net worth), on the other... In the language of economic theory, it can be said that the average corporate propensity to save has varied with the level of net income, but that the marginal corporate propensity to save has remained the same at different levels of net income."

[20] It should be remembered that these retention ratios are based on net profit figures adjusted to the social accounting concept, which differ considerably from the unadjusted figures of tax returns and from published corporate reports. The ratios may, therefore, be presumed to differ also from those which corporate managers use in making their decisions about the division of net corporate profits between dividends and retained income. In recent years, for instance, the retention ratios

factors. The first is the high rate of taxation, which requires a high retention ratio (retained profits divided by total net profits after taxes) to produce the same ratio of retained income to profits before taxes.[21] The second is the greater difficulty of obtaining equity funds from outside.

c. *The structure of corporate saving*

4.45. As the estimates of corporate saving were derived from the income account rather than from the balance sheet, in contrast to the derivation for all other saver groups, it is not possible to utilize the estimates for an analysis of the structure of saving and of changes in it over the period. The income account estimates necessarily provide only one undivided total for corporate saving. The reader interested in the structure of corporate saving, i.e. the changes in specific assets and liabilities, or the forms in which corporate saving has appeared, therefore must resort to the very rough statement of sources-and-uses-of-corporate-funds which has been developed in Volume II, Table B–19, not as an integral part of the measurement of corporate or national saving, but in an attempt to check the estimates of national saving against calculations of national investment. This statement is available, even in rough form, only for all corporations taken together and, what is a more serious drawback, had to be prepared on a consolidated rather than a combined basis. It consequently does not show creditor-debtor relationships among corporations nor one corporation's holdings of the securities of another.

6. State and Local Governments

4.46. Before reviewing in very summary fashion the course of saving of state and local governments over the past half century it is well to recall that an attempt has been made in this study to calculate the saving of these organizations in a manner as parallel as possible to that in use by business enterprises though modified to fit into a system of social accounts. This means that expenditures on durable assets, in particular the cost of construction of public buildings and roads, have been treated as capitalizable rather than as current expenditures, and that depreciation has been charged at replacement cost. The saving estimates on which this discussion is based, therefore, may be regarded as "constructed," and do not always correspond to items that can be found in the published accounts of state and local governments.

---

used here are considerably lower than those obtained from corporate reports or from income tax statistics, and probably also lower than those which guided corporate managers in their decisions. On the other hand, the difference between the ratios for the period after World War II and the twenties or earlier decades is smaller in the adjusted than in the unadjusted figures.

[21] Compare the situation under average levels of taxation of 10 percent and 40 percent, which are roughly representative of the twenties and the late forties respectively. Assuming a net income before taxes of $1 million, a retention ratio of one-third of total net income after taxes is needed in the first case to yield corporate saving of $300,000, while a ratio of one-half is necessary in the second case to obtain the same result.

It should also be noted that the estimates cover utility and other enterprises of state and local governments as well as their strictly governmental activities. Those trust funds administered by state and local governments the beneficiaries of which are well defined (primarily the pension and retirement funds for state and local government employees, but also workmen's compensation funds) have been excluded from the calculations, the increase in the funds having been regarded as a part of the saving of the beneficiaries. The other trust funds, of which unemployment compensation funds are quantitatively the most important example, have been regarded as part of the financial operations of state governments with the result that changes in the assets of these funds contribute to saving or dissaving of state governments. Since the change in assets of unemployment compensation funds is shown separately, an adjustment can easily be made by those readers who prefer to treat these funds as part of individuals' saving.

a. *State governments*

4.47. The trend of saving by state governments, shown in Chart XXII, is characterized by a sharp and almost continuous increase throughout the period, or at least through World War II, irrespective of whether the estimates are expressed in current values or adjusted for changes in the price level.

From 1898–1901 to 1926–1929 the saving of state governments increased, starting from a very low level, at an average annual rate of approximately $15\frac{1}{2}$ percent in current prices, $12\frac{1}{2}$ percent in 1929 prices, and 9 percent in deflated values per head. All three rates are extraordinarily high compared to rates for other saver groups. Furthermore, the rapid increase suffered hardly any interruption, not even in World War I and during the subsequent depression.

The upward movement continued after 1929, though not as rapidly. From 1926–1929 to 1946–1949 saving increased by 130 percent in current prices, by 65 percent if adjusted for price changes, and by 40 percent if adjusted also for population changes. The corresponding annual rates of growth are somewhat over 4 percent for current saving, approximately $2\frac{1}{2}$ percent for aggregate deflated saving, and about $1\frac{1}{2}$ percent for deflated saving per head. These rates are obviously much lower than those prevailing before 1930, but they are still quite high compared to the rates observed for the same period for other saver groups. In particular they are considerably higher than the rates for local governments.[22] World War II is reflected in a sharp bulge in saving, particularly if unemployment compensation funds are included. If they are not, saving during the years 1946–1949 is on about the same level as during the war and about 60 percent above the level of the late thirties in terms of current prices, but hardly at all ahead of it if allowance is made for the rise in the price level.

[22] Part of the increase in the saving of state governments during this period is due to the inclusion of the assets of unemployment compensation funds, which began to be of importance in the middle thirties. If they are eliminated the increase in saving between 1926–1929 and 1946–1949 is reduced to 88 percent for current aggregate saving, 36 percent for deflated aggregate saving, and 12 percent for deflated saving per head.

CHART XXII
SAVING OF STATE GOVERNMENTS
Standard Social Accounting Concept
Period Averages

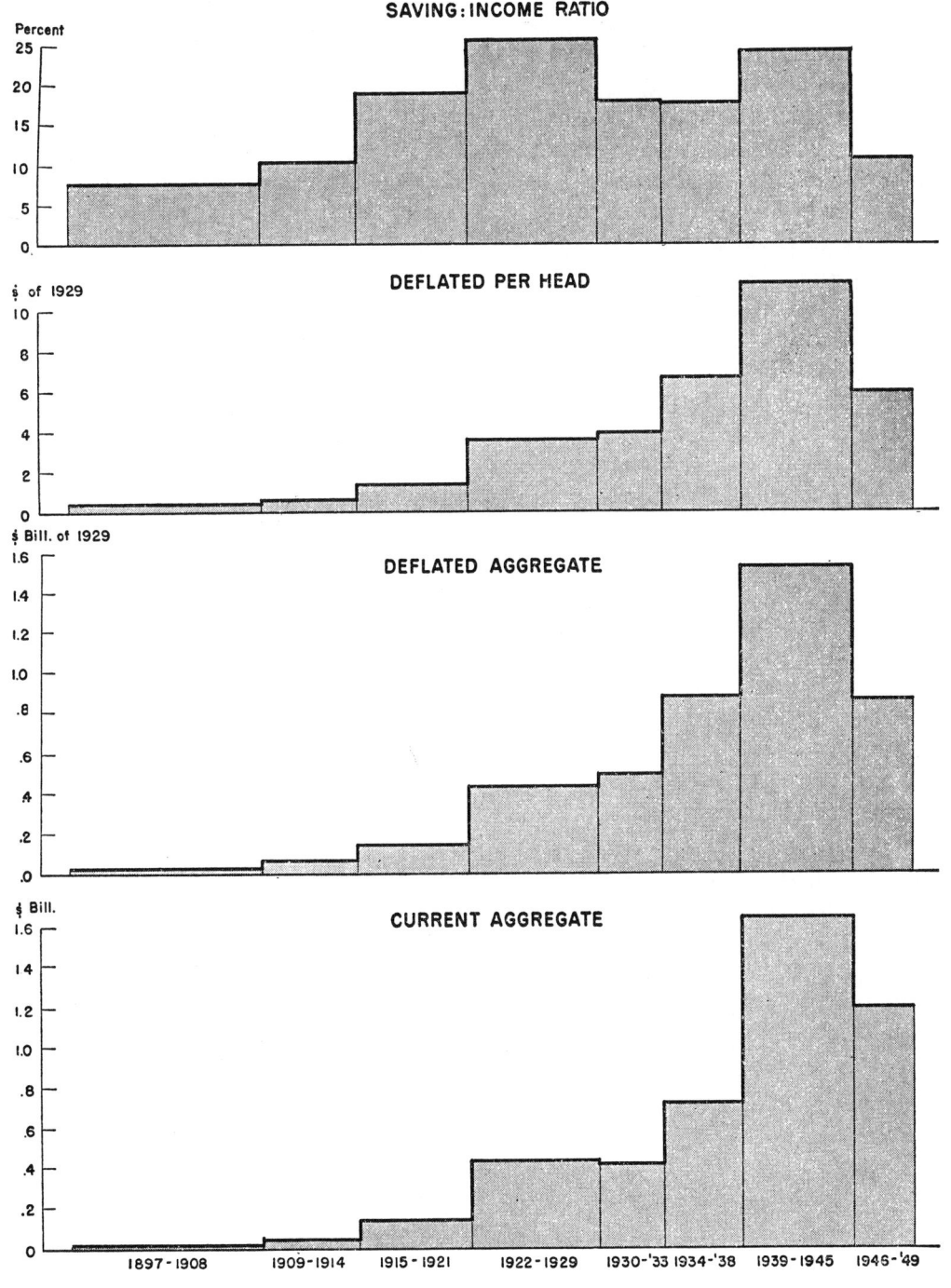

SAVING : INCOME RATIO

Percent

25
20
15
10
5
0

DEFLATED PER HEAD

$ of 1929

10
8
6
4
2
0

DEFLATED AGGREGATE

$ Bill. of 1929

1.6
1.4
1.2
1.0
.8
.6
.4
.2
.0

CURRENT AGGREGATE

$ Bill.

1.6
1.4
1.2
1.0
.8
.6
.4
.2
0

1897-1908   1909-1914   1915-1921   1922-1929   1930-'33 1934-'38   1939-1945   1946-'49

4.48. The sharp and fairly continuous growth in the saving of state governments reflects primarily the rapid increase in their total revenues, which in turn is due to both the growth of the American economy, particularly in monetary terms, and the expansion of the economic activities of state governments during the past fifty years, particularly their prominent role in the building and financing of roads. The increase in the proportion of revenue saved, however, has been a second important factor in the spectacular rise of saving by state governments, at least before the Great Depression. The saving-income ratio rose steadily from 6 percent in 1898–1901 to 27 percent in 1926–1929 with only two minor interruptions, one around 1913 and the other reflecting the depression of 1920–1921. From 1930 on, the movement has been less regular, but the level of the ratio has remained fairly high compared to that of other groups. Including unemployment compensation funds it was slightly below 20 percent from 1930 to World War II, somewhat higher during the war, and considerably lower—not much over 10 percent—since 1946. If unemployment compensation funds are excluded the downward trend becomes clearer, and the bulge during World War II less pronounced. Great caution must be exercised in determining the trend of the saving-income ratio of state governments by any procedure which puts heavy weight on the figures for 1946–1949 because they are in part preliminary. There is, nevertheless, little doubt that the high rates of the twenties are not typical of the situation prevailing around the middle of the century.

4.49. The reasons for the high level of saving of state governments, particularly in comparison with the lower level of local governments, are worth careful exploration, which cannot be undertaken here. It may well be that thye are not the result of a deliberate policy, but stem from a combination of the need for heavy capital requirements, particularly in the development of automobile highways, and a disinclination to borrow, which in turn is partly rooted in constitutional debt limitations. If the tendency towards financing through separate highway authorities should be applied to a considerable proportion of the country's highway system, the volume of saving and the saving-income ratio of state governments in the future may well be considerably lower than they have been in the past since these authorities cover a considerably larger proportion of construction costs through the issuance of debt than state governments appear to have done.

4.50. Turning to the structure of saving of state governments, it is seen from Table XVI that for the entire period 1897–1949 tangible assets accounted for slightly more than 40 percent of total saving, and intangible assets for nearly 60 percent. For the normal period total net saving was about equally divided between tangible and intangible assets.[23] The increase in debt offset less than one-fifth of the increase in assets for the entire, and more than one-quarter for the normal, period. These differences are due mainly to the low level of capital expenditures and considerable debt retirement during World War II.

[23] Exclusion of unemployment compensation funds, the assets of which are kept entirely in intangible items, necessarily increases the share of saving through tangible assets, viz. to about 55 percent for the full, and fully 70 percent for the normal, period.

116

TABLE XVI

SAVING OF STATE GOVERNMENTS BY MAJOR COMPONENTS
Standard Social Accounting Concept: 1897 to 1949

	Absolute amount		Share	
	Full period	Normal period	Full period	Normal period
	$ bill.		Percent of line 8a	
1. Structures	9.9	8.7	38	54
a. Expenditures	21.2	16.4	81	101
b. Depreciation allowances	11.3	7.7	43	48
2. Acquisition of real estate	0.7	0.5	3	3
3. Liquid assets	10.9	6.7	41	41
a. Cash	4.0	2.9	15	18
b. U.S. Government securities	5.6	2.2	21	14
c. State and local government securities	0.9	1.3	3	8
d. Other	0.4	0.3	2	2
4. Taxes receivable	1.8	1.6	7	10
5. Unemployment compensation funds	7.4	3.3	28	20
6. Total assets				
a. Including } Unemployment compensation	30.7	20.8	117	128
b. Excluding } funds	23.3	17.5	89	108
7. Debt	4.4	4.6	17	28
8. Net saving				
a. Including } Unemployment compensation	26.3	16.2	100	100
b. Excluding } funds	18.9	12.9	72	80

Source: See notes to Table S-28.

4.51. The figures may be more instructive if we deduct the increase in debt from saving through tangible assets on the supposition that most of the debt (excluding the Bonus issues after World War II and borrowing to cover deficits during the Great Depression) was incurred to finance construction or the acquisition of real estate. It then appears that up to the twenties saving through tangible assets hardly exceeded the increase in debt. For the period 1922–1929, however, the excess averaged almost $300 million a year. It was even higher in the thirties —approximately $350 million a year—particularly if allowance is made for the decline in the price level. The excess would be still more impressive if the increase in debt reflecting current deficits could be taken into account separately. In the forties the situation was similar to that before the twenties in that there was no excess of saving through tangible assets over the increase in debt. Even if the Bonus issues after World War II were excluded the excess would be small, possibly in the order of $1 billion for the four years 1946–1949. This is certainly less in absolute amount than in the twenties or thirties, particularly if the figures are adjusted for the increase in the price level.

4.52. In comparison with the excess of saving through tangible assets over debt increases, saving through intangible assets has gained in importance since the twenties. From 1922 to 1929 saving through tangible assets adjusted for changes in total debt was $1 billion higher than saving through intangible assets. The excess amounted to about $600 million for the period 1934–1941 if unemploy-

117

ment compensation funds are excluded, but it is turned into a deficit of $2 billion if they are included. In the four years after World War II, finally, saving through intangible assets was larger by $4 billion than the excess of saving through tangible assets over the increase in debt if unemployment compensation funds are excluded, and by $5 billion if they are included.

b. *Local governments*

4.53. Like the saving of most of the other groups, that of local governments shows an upward trend to 1929 both in current and deflated values, evident in Chart XXIII. Between 1898–1901 and 1926–1929 it rose from nearly $90 million a year to approximately $800 million. Even after adjustment for price changes an increase by about 350 percent remains, which is reduced to about 120 percent if a further adjustment is made for the increase in the total urban population on the assumption that virtually all of the saving of local governments is attributable to cities and nonagricultural counties. This rate of growth—over 8 percent a year for aggregate current saving—is higher than that for most other groups, but substantially lower than that for state governments.

4.54. The increase in the saving of local governments, however, has been rather irregular. It was interrupted from 1906 to 1909, during World War I, and still more seriously during the depression of 1920–1921. Only in the latter period, however, was the saving of local governments negative. A particularly rapid increase in saving occurred in the twenties. The 1922–1929 average of nearly $700 million a year compares with one of only $150 million in the two decades before World War I, an increase by 260 percent in current values and by slightly more than 150 percent in deflated values. According to the balance sheet method—which underlies all the figures in this section unless the contrary is specifically indicated—saving during the four years 1930–1933 became negative to the extent of $1½ billion. Since the income account shows a small positive saving—not quite $1 billion for the same period—one must be careful in asserting how much the Great Depression affected the saving of local governments, but there is no doubt that it sharply reduced it from the level of the twenties. The saving of local governments was positive during most of the thirties, but continued to be considerably below the level of the twenties. It increased somewhat during World War II, but less than the saving of many other groups. Assessment of the situation after World War II is particularly difficult because of the discrepancy between the estimates made by the balance sheet and income account methods. [24] Saving according to the balance sheet method was rather low, continuing at about the same absolute level as in the thirties, and hence was considerably smaller in deflated values. The estimates based on the income account are more than twice as high, and are equal in current values to the previous peak reached in the twenties, although they are still considerably lower if account is taken of price increases.

4.55. The saving-income ratio of local governments was approximately the same—one-sixth to one-eighth—before World War I and during the twenties. It

[24] On this difference see Volume II, Chapter XVII, Section 5.

118

CHART XXIII

SAVING OF LOCAL GOVERNMENTS
Standard Social Accounting Concept
Period Averages

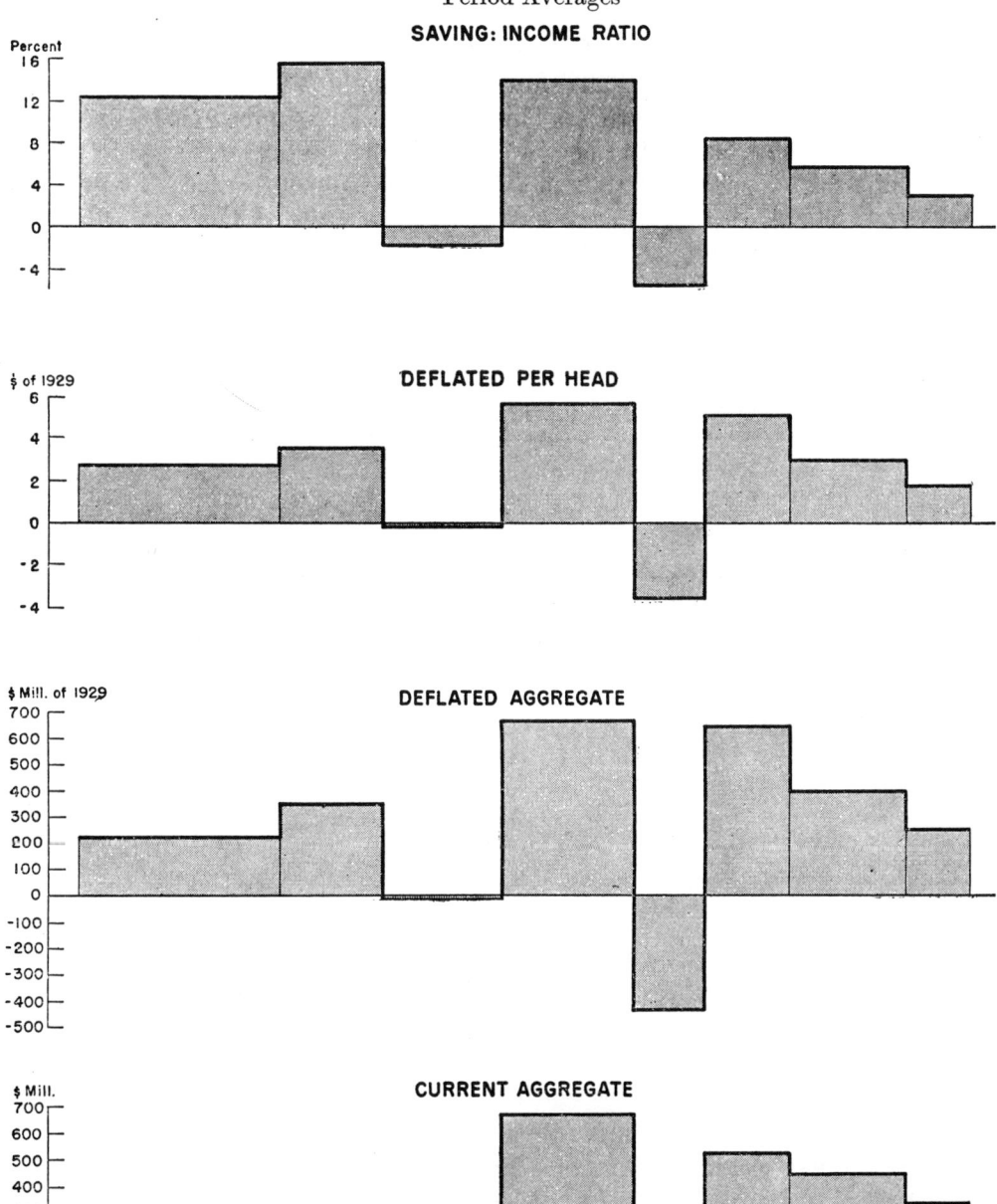

SAVING: INCOME RATIO

Percent

DEFLATED PER HEAD

$ of 1929

DEFLATED AGGREGATE

$ Mill. of 1929

CURRENT AGGREGATE

$ Mill.

1897-1908   1909-1914   1915-1921   1922-1929   1930-'33   1934-'38   1939-1945   1946-'49

was considerably lower between the Great Depression and the end of World War II, averaging 6 percent. Since then it either has been lower than during any previous normal period—if the estimates by the balance sheet method are accepted—or has continued at the level of the thirties, if the income account estimates are followed.

There is no doubt, however, that during the last two decades the saving-income ratio of local governments has shifted from the high level which prevailed until 1930 to a considerably lower one. This has been due mainly to the failure of the absolute volume of saving to rise above the very high levels of the twenties in the face of a fairly continuous though decelerating increase in the total income of local governments.

4.56. For the period as a whole the increase in indebtedness has, as Table XVII shows, offset about one-half of the increase in assets of local governments, a

TABLE XVII

SAVING OF LOCAL GOVERNMENTS BY MAJOR COMPONENTS

Standard Social Accounting Concept: 1897 to 1949

	Absolute amount		Share	
	Full period	Normal period	Full period	Normal period
	$ bill.		Percent of net saving	
1. Structures	10.9	11.5	80	91
a. Expenditures	42.6	34.5	313	272
b. Depreciation allowances	31.7	23.0	233	181
2. Acquisition of real estate	3.6	3.3	26	26
3. Liquid assets	9.8	8.8	72	69
a. Cash	5.0	4.9	37	39
b. U.S. Government securities	2.4	0.4	18	3
c. State and local government securities	1.6	2.8	12	22
d. Other	0.7	0.7	5	6
4. Taxes receivable	5.4	5.4	40	43
5. Total assets	29.7	29.0	218	228
6. Debt	16.1	16.3	118	128
7. Net saving	13.6	12.7	100	100

Source: See notes to Table S-30.

ratio much higher than that for state governments and well above that for most other saver groups. [25] Of the total increase in assets about one-half has been accounted for by saving in the form of durable tangible assets, primarily construction expenditures less depreciation allowances, and, to a lesser extent, by acquisition of land and structures. In the other half the main components have been increases in holdings of cash amounting to approximately one-third of the total increase in intangible assets; accumulation of U.S. Government securities, mostly during World War II, equivalent to approximately one-sixth of saving through intangible assets; acquisition of state and local government securities to the extent

[25] The structure of saving for the normal period is sufficiently similar to that for the full period described in the text to justify omission of separate discussion. The relevant figures can be found in Table XVII.

120

of approximately one-tenth; and an increase in tax accruals equal to approximately one-third of total saving through intangible assets, an increase which in a sense is the necessary accompaniment to the rise in tax levies and can hardly be regarded as the result of deliberate saving.

4.57. There is a clear distinction between the structure of saving of local governments before and after the Great Depression. Up to 1930, excluding the years of World War I, the increase in debt accounted for slightly more than one-half of the increase in assets. Of total asset acquisitions tangible assets represented more than two-thirds and intangible assets (including tax accruals) less than one-third.

No generalizations are possible about the structure of saving of local governments after the Great Depression. It is, rather, necessary to separate three periods, the years 1934 to 1941, World War II, and the period 1946–1949, and to follow developments shown in Tables S-30 and S-31. There is, however, one characteristic which all three periods have in common and which distinguishes them from the period before 1930—the low level of saving through tangible assets. This is due primarily to the reduction of construction expenditures. Even in 1946–1949 construction expenditures were only 10 percent above the average of 1922–1929 in current prices, and approximately 30 percent below if the increase in the price level is taken into account. Since depreciation allowances continued to rise, particularly if calculated on a replacement cost basis, saving through tangible assets, being the difference between construction expenditures and depreciation allowances, declined even more. Indeed, depreciation allowances exceeded construction expenditures by a small amount for 1934–1937 and very substantially during World War II, while the excess of expenditures over depreciation allowances in 1946–1949 was negligible. A second common characteristic which distinguishes the period 1934 on from that before 1930 is the higher share of saving through liquid assets. While liquid assets, excluding tax accruals, accounted for only about one-fifth of the total increase in assets before 1930, they have represented two-fifths or more of total asset increases since the midthirties.

7. Federal Government

a. *Aggregate saving of the federal government*

4.58. In the case of the federal government's saving there is not much point in discussing trends extending over the last fifty years since the picture has been so completely dominated by the effects of this country's participation in the two World Wars. Mostly as the result of very large deficits in the war years, the federal government shows a dissaving of $209 billion for the full period 1897–1949 if military assets are disregarded, and $177 billion if allowance is made for them. For the normal period there was a dissaving of $7 billion if military assets are excluded, and one of $30 billion if they are included. [26] The smallness of the

[26] It may be well to recall some of the characteristics of the calculation of the saving of the federal government which have a bearing on these figures. First, the estimates cover federal agencies and corporations as well as the Treasury. Secondly, the liabilities include guaranteed obligations,

dissaving by the federal government during the normal period taken as a whole is the result of three factors: small but fairly regular surpluses before World War i; large surpluses which were used for debt retirement in the years immediately following both World Wars; and sizable deficits during the thirties.

4.59. If the comparison is limited to normal periods and military assets are excluded, the level of saving is shown in Chart xxiv to have increased considerably from the beginning to the end of the period, even if adjusted for changes in the price level. From 1897 to 1914 saving averaged a little under $50 million a year. From 1922 to 1929 it was slightly in excess of $900 million a year. From 1946 to 1949 the annual average approximated $2,000 million. Reduced to 1929 prices the increase is still substantial, viz. from about $80 million in 1897–1914 to $900 million in 1922–1929 and $1,300 million in 1946–1949. A large part of the substantial saving of 1946–1949, however, is due to a nonrecurrent factor, the lag of the reduction of taxes behind the falling off of military expenditures to what proved to be a temporary trough. Moreover, not only the level but the very existence of federal saving during that period is dependent on the use of a concept which ignores the dissaving in military assets caused by the excess of depreciation allowances over current expenditures. The average saving during the years 1946–1949, therefore, cannot be given much weight in determining long-term trends. It remains, nevertheless, worth noticing that for the periods not affected by war expenditures or the Great Depression the federal government has saved rather than dissaved, once its expenditures on durable goods are capitalized and depreciated as in business accounting, and provided military assets are excluded from the calculation.

4.60. The ratio of saving to income of the federal government for the period as a whole has, of course, been negative and very strongly so, dissaving amounting to 50 percent of income. The dissaving ratio was highest during World War ii, when it stood at 140 percent of current income, and during World War i, when it all but equalled current income. The ratio was also quite high during the thirties, with about 50 percent of income. Within the normal periods the saving ratio, while positive except for a few years, has varied considerably from period to period, but has been quite substantial compared to the saving ratio of other groups. It has averaged 8 percent for 1897–1914, 25 percent for 1922–1929, but only 6 percent for 1946–1949. [27]

but not contingent guarantees, such as those on home mortgages and deposits. Thirdly, military assets are defined broadly to include war plants and merchant vessels built during the wars, with the result that the estimates excluding military assets can be regarded as minimum figures. Fourthly, loans made to foreign governments, chiefly made during World Wars i and ii, have not been capitalized with the exception of Export-Import Bank and surplus property loans and, hence, have been regarded as part of current expenditures. This omission strengthens the conservative character of the estimates. Fifthly, all trust funds, including social security and veterans' funds, are excluded since their assets have already been treated as part of individuals' saving.

[27] If military assets are included the dissaving ratio during World War ii is reduced to about 100 percent. In that case, however, 1946–1949 also shows a dissaving ratio, averaging about 14 percent.

CHART XXIV

SAVING OF FEDERAL GOVERNMENT
Standard Social Accounting Concept
Period Averages

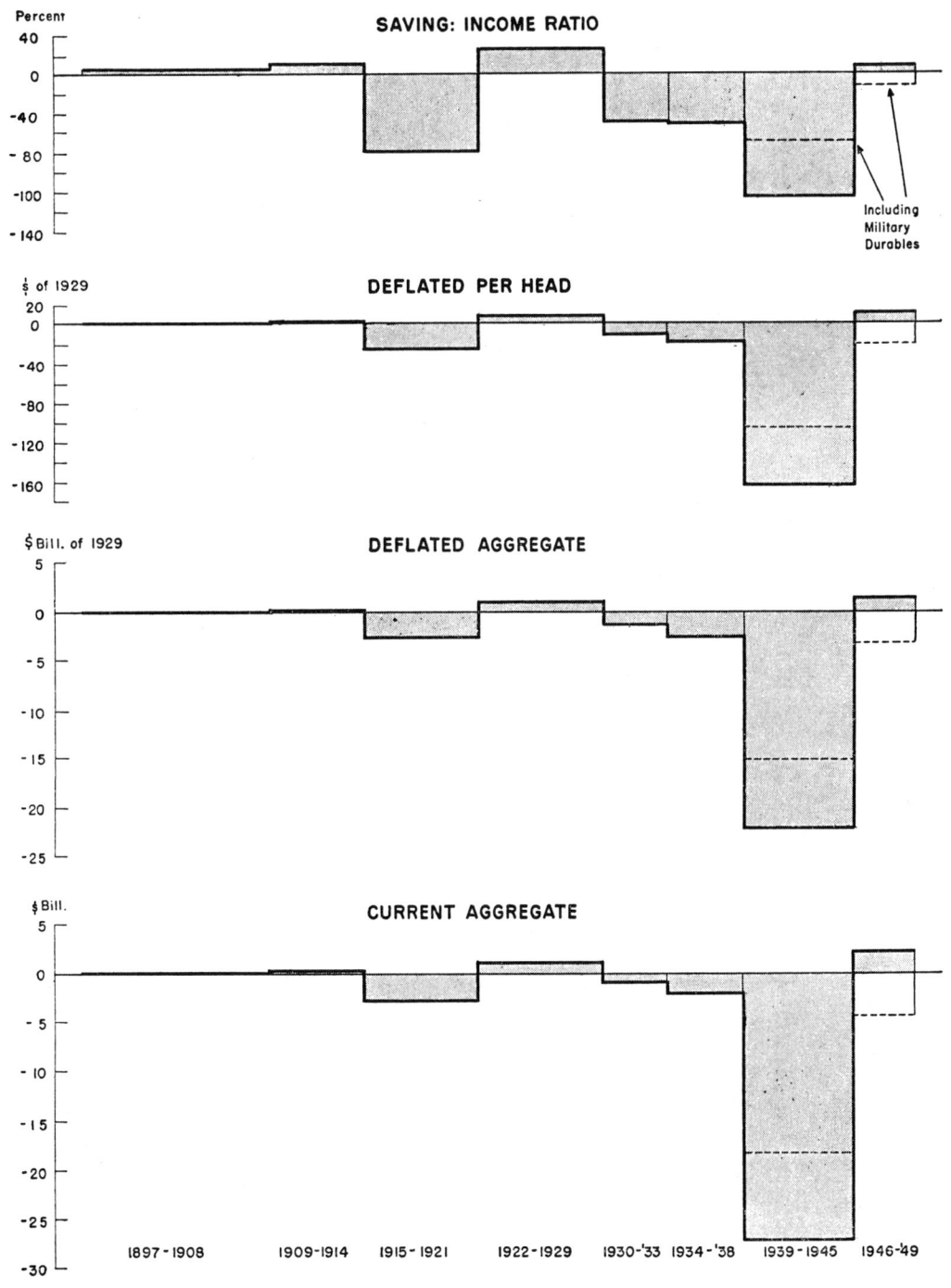

b. *Forms of saving and dissaving of the federal government*

4.61. The federal government differs from all other saver groups not only by the fact that its saving is negative for the period as a whole, but also in that the increase in its liabilities has, as Table xviii shows, been vastly in excess of the increase in its assets. For the entire period the increase in assets, including military durables, has been slightly below $110 billion, compared to an increase in liabilities —almost all in the form of Treasury securities—of about $290 billion. Liabilities thus have increased by more than two-and-one-half times the increase in assets, a ratio strikingly higher than for any other major saver group. The ratio is still less favorable if military assets are disregarded, and gold and silver, as well as the certificates issued against them, are eliminated from both assets and liabilities. In that case the increase in liabilities is five times as large as the increase in assets.

TABLE XVIII

SAVING OF FEDERAL GOVERNMENT BY MAJOR COMPONENTS

Standard Social Accounting Concept: 1897 to 1949

	Absolute amount		Share	
	Full period	Normal period	Full period	Normal period
	$ bill.		Percent of line 9	
1. Bank deposits	4	−21	4	−210
2. Loans and investments	13	12	12	120
3. Personal tax accruals and miscellaneous	21	9	19	90
4. Inventories	4	2	4	20
5. Structures (including equipment)	12	5	11	50
6. Land	2	1	2	10
7. Gold and silver	21	24	19	240
8. Military durable assets	32	−24	29	−240
9. Total assets	109	10	100	100
10. Total assets, excluding military assets	77	34	71	340
11. Liabilities	286	40	262	400
12. Liabilities, excluding gold and silver certificates	261	13	239	130
13. Saving i (line 10 minus line 11)	−209	−7	−192	−70
14. Saving ii (line 9 minus line 11)	−177	−30	−162	−300
15. Saving iii (line 10 minus lines 7 and 12)	−205	−3	−188	−30

Source: See notes to Table S-32.

4.62. Since most of the increase in liabilities has occurred during wars, when it was not accompanied by a comparable increase in assets, even if we take account of military durables, there is more interest in the increase in assets taken by itself.

Saving through civilian nonmonetary tangible assets (i.e. the excess of expenditures on civilian structures, equipment, inventories, and land over depreciation allowances), which are the assets of most interest for the saving process, has been rather small, amounting to only $18 billion for the entire period of more than half a century. This is less than the increase in the stock of monetary metals or of military durables. The position of civilian nonmonetary tangible assets, however, is more favorable if the figures are reduced to 1929 prices, because most of the military assets were acquired at relatively high prices during World War ii.

The increase in intangible assets for the period as a whole amounted to $38 billion even excluding foreign loans. This is more than twice saving through civilian nonmonetary tangible assets, and is almost equal to saving through nonmonetary tangibles including military assets. About half of the total, however, is represented by tax accruals which are treated in this study as receivables by the government, as they would be in the books of a business concern, since most corporation taxes and part of personal direct taxes are received by the Treasury in the year after the income on which they are assessed is earned. These accruals obviously cannot be regarded as the result of deliberate saving by the federal government. The same applies, though to a lesser extent, to increases in bank deposits which are kept mainly as a revolving fund for current operations. Loans and investments, held mostly by federal agencies and corporations, on the other hand, are as a rule the result of deliberate action by the government, although often in situations where choice is restricted. They account for about $13 billion for the period as a whole, only about one-eighth of the total increase in assets including military durables, but approximately one-fourth if both military durables and monetary metals are excluded.

4.63. The distribution of saving among the different forms of assets has fluctuated considerably from period to period, as Tables S-32 and S-33 show. No definite trends or structural changes are, however, visible. Only a few movements are worth noticing, most of them being connected with the two World Wars.

Compared to the level of the following fifteen years saving through federal government construction was high from 1897 to 1914, considerably influenced by expenditures on the Panama Canal. It reached a peak, in terms of stable prices, in the middle thirties.

Saving in the form of inventories has been of importance only since the thirties and reflects mainly the accumulation of surplus farm products. It is, of course, not the result of a deliberate policy to increase saving, but is incidental to the program of raising the level of agricultural prices and farm income. [28]

Acquisition of loans and investments was concentrated in the thirties and in the period after World War II. In the thirties it was mainly the result of the reorganization of the country's financial structure exemplified in the home and farm mortgage loans taken over by the Home Owners' Loan Corporation and the Federal Farm Mortgage Credit Corporation, and in the operations of the Reconstruction Finance Corporation. After World War II the increase was due primarily to the federal government's contribution to international financial agencies like the International Monetary Fund and the International Bank for Reconstruction and Development, and to the international loans made by the Export-Import Bank. [29]

[28] Stockpiles of strategic commodities which might be included with military assets were of no quantitative importance through 1949.

[29] The share of loans and investments would be considerably higher—and the federal government's net dissaving over the entire period covered by the Study slightly lower—if all foreign loans made during and after World War II were included, e.g. the British loan, which has not been capitalized (as it probably should have been), or if the loans to our allies during World War I had not been treated as part of current war expenditures.

Saving through bank deposits shows very large fluctuations during the forties, but they are without much significance. The increase during World War II reflects primarily the unspent portion of the last war loan, which was large. The sharp reduction during 1946–1949, on the other hand, represents in effect the use of this accumulation in the retirement of debt.

Increases in receivables (mostly tax accruals) were concentrated in the two war periods. Both reflect sharp increases in tax rates on rapidly rising incomes.

The fluctuations in the accumulation of monetary metals, of course, are the result of the movements in the balance of payments of the United States, and not of deliberate saving or dissaving by the federal government. The increases are largest in absolute amounts during the thirties and forties. For the period as a whole this accumulation accounted for slightly over one-fourth of the increase in total civilian assets of the federal government. It was much smaller, or even negative, during World War II and the Great Depression, but represented at least one-fourth, and in the aggregate more than two-thirds, of the total asset increase in normal periods.

126

V

DISTRIBUTION OF NATIONAL SAVING
AMONG SAVER GROUPS

5.01. Up to this point the discussion has been limited, with only few exceptions, to estimates of saving defined as the change in earned net worth. When it comes to the relation of the saving of one saver group to the saving of others, i.e. the distribution of national saving among them, it is advisable to supplement the discussion (Section 1) with an analysis of the distribution among these groups of changes in total national combined net worth at current prices (Section 2). This is done, first, because the results of the two approaches differ significantly in some points, and, secondly, because the distribution of unearned increments or decrements in net worth—which is what essentially distinguishes the distribution of changes in total net worth and cumulated saving—is of considerable economic and social importance and interest as it contributes to intergroup shifts in purchasing power and to changes in their relative economic status.

1. DISTRIBUTION OF CURRENT SAVING

a. *Distribution for full and normal periods*

5.02. The need for distinguishing between the full period of fifty-three years, from 1897 to 1949, and the "normal" period, from which the ten years of war and the Great Depression are excluded, is nowhere better illustrated than in the distribution of total national saving among saver groups, which is shown in Charts XXV and XXVI and in Tables S-8 to S-10. For the full period the dissaving of the federal government is so large that it offsets three-fifths of the saving of other groups; private saving exceeds national saving by approximately 50 percent; and personal saving is about 30 percent above national saving. These relationships, all based on the standard social accounting concept and current prices, obviously are not typical of the distribution of national saving over the last half century.

5.03. If the war years and the Great Depression are excluded from the calculations federal saving is still negative, mainly as a result of deficits in the thirties, but federal dissaving is so small that it offsets less than 2 percent of the saving of other groups. Nonfarm individuals' saving now accounts for just over 70 percent of national saving. The shares of agriculture and unincorporated business enterprises are quite small, only a little over 3 percent for either group. [1] Corporate

---

[1] In the case of saving by unincorporated business enterprises, it is well to keep in mind that the figures include only those assets and liabilities which are clearly identified with business activities and hence do not measure total saving of proprietors. In fact proprietors' total saving is probably

CHART XXV

SHARE OF MAIN SAVER GROUPS IN NATIONAL SAVING

Standard Social Accounting Concept

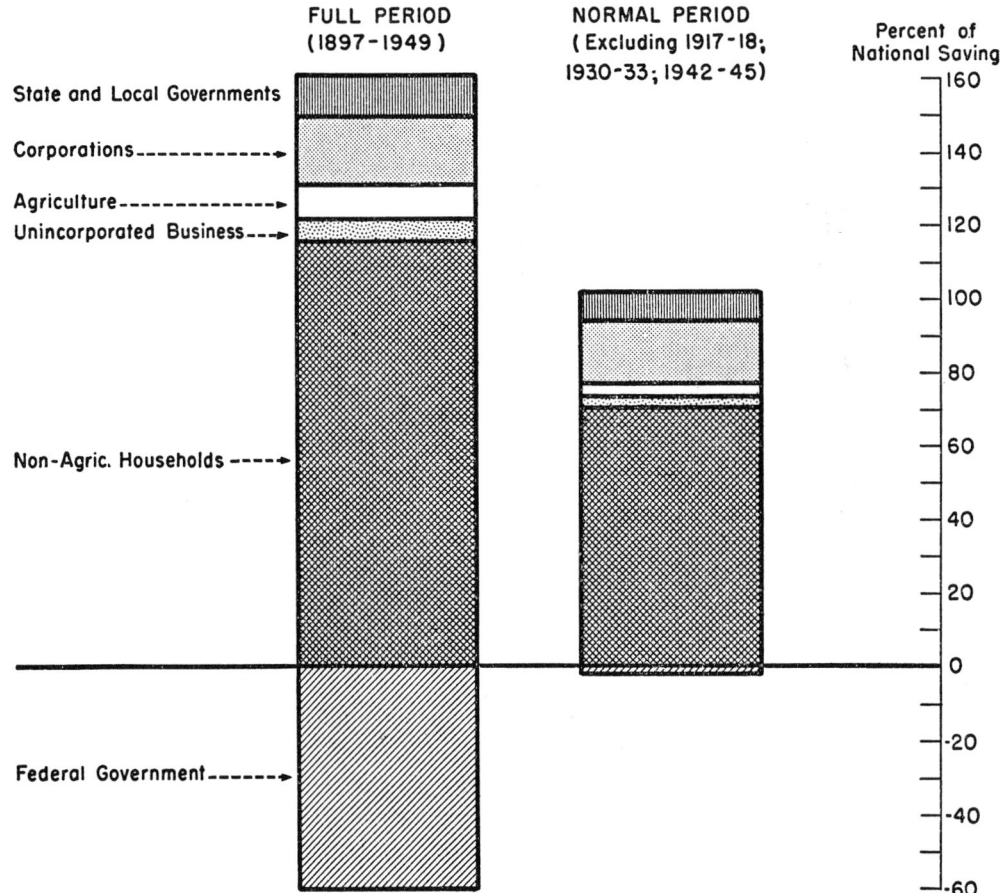

saving accounts for approximately one-sixth of national saving in the normal period. State and local governments contribute the remaining one-twelfth.

5.04. The time series of economic statistics on which these estimates of saving are based do not permit the segregation of saving of groups within the universe of households, and there are no other sources available for the entire period covered by the Study or for a large part of it which can make up for this deficiency. We are therefore unable to make statistically founded statements about the distribution of personal saving during the first half of this century among households of

---

several times as large as what is here measured as the saving of unincorporated business enterprises, although the present figures include not only the undistributed earnings of such business but also the net investment or withdrawals by proprietors. (See the analysis of data collected by the Survey of Consumer Finances for the years 1947–1949 by J. N. Morgan in *Journal of Political Economy*, 1951, p. 530.)

128

CHART XXVI

SHARE OF FEDERAL[a] AND NONFEDERAL SAVING IN NATIONAL SAVING

Standard Social Accounting Concept

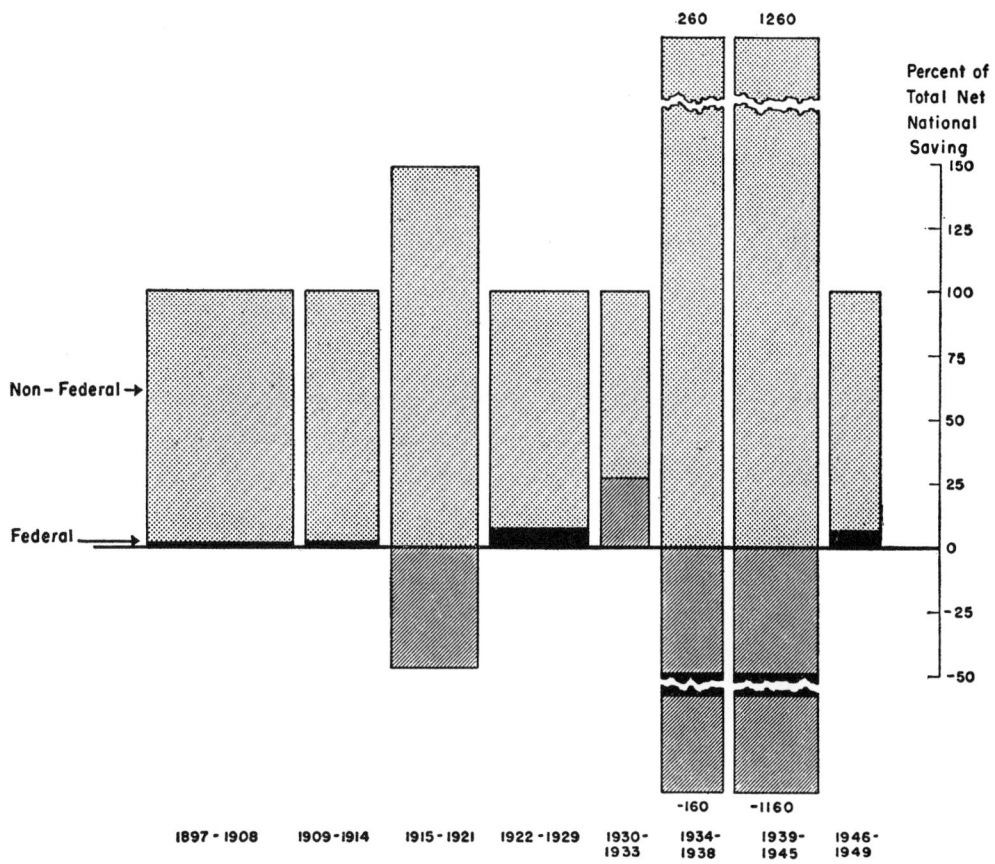

[a] Federal saving in black; federal dissaving hatched.

different income level, occupation, age of head, race, location, and wealth; nor can we distinguish between households which, in a given year or over a long period, have saved and those which have dissaved.

Enough material is available for recent years, however, particularly from the annual Surveys of Consumer Finances of the Federal Reserve Board, and from similar inquiries for a few scattered years before World War II,[2] to state that a large proportion of total personal saving is accounted for by a relatively small fraction of households at the top of the income or wealth pyramid. Since World War II, for instance, the 10 percent of households with the highest income in any one year—of course not the same households year after year—have accounted for over 80 percent of the year's total net saving of all households.[3]

Saving is also concentrated in certain occupational and age groups, partly

[2] An analysis of this material will be found in Volume III, Part I.
[3] *Federal Reserve Bulletin*, 1951, p. 1,067. The figures refer to the years 1947–1950.

because the proportion of income saved varies from group to group, and partly for no other reason than that average income itself, the main determinant of saving, differs among age and income groups. Thus managers and self-employed persons accounted for not less than one-half of total personal net saving although they represented only one-eighth of the number of households. Households with the head between 35 and 55 years of age contributed about two-thirds of total net personal saving though representing only approximately two-fifths of all households. [4]

No comparable information is available for earlier years other than 1935–1936. There is little doubt, however, that the basic characteristics of the distribution of aggregate saving among nonfarm households, disclosed by these recent surveys, apply also to the entire period 1897–1949 and to the normal period alone, viz. that most of total saving is done by households with incomes or assets well above the national average, by households with the head of middle age, and by households of businessmen, independent or hired.

5.05. Exclusion of saving through consumer durables naturally decreases in total national saving the share of households, the only group with a substantial amount of saving of this type, and increases that of all other groups (Tables S-12 to S-14). For the normal period exclusion of consumer durables reduces the share of households from 74 percent to 68 percent. Exclusion of saving through homes further lowers the share of households and raises that of all other groups.

The only saver group substantially affected by inclusion of saving through soil improvement is, of course, agriculture. Its share in national saving is increased from 9.1 percent to 12.3 percent for the full period, and from 3.1 percent to 5.1 percent for the normal period.

Inclusion of military assets likewise affects only one group, and that group to a substantial extent, viz. the federal government. The effect is to increase the share of the federal government in national saving from —61 percent to —47 percent for the period as a whole, but to decrease it from —2 percent to —9 percent for the normal period. That the change is in the opposite direction for the full and the normal period is due to the fact that saving through military durables is positive during war periods, but negative in other years as the depreciation allowances on the accumulated stock of weapons exceed current expenditures on them.

5.06. Considerable differences appear if the basis of the calculation is shifted from social accounting to business accounting or cash saving. The main effect of this shift—apart from the fact that the saving of all groups other than the federal government is higher under the business than under the social accounting concept and higher again under the cash than under the business accounting concept—is an increase in the share of business enterprises in total national saving at the expense of nonfarm households and governments. This shift reflects the relatively larger importance of capital consumption allowances and inventory profits for business enterprises.

5.07. The picture remains unchanged in its main characteristics if it is based on deflated (1929) saving, as in Table S-16, rather than on current saving, as in

[4] *Ibid.*, p. 1,074.

130

Table S-8. For the period as a whole the shares of the main saver groups in national saving are all lower; for the normal period the shares of nonagricultural households, unincorporated business, and state and local governments are slightly higher and those of agriculture, corporations, and the federal government slightly lower when each year's saving is reduced to the 1929-base level by means of an index of the general price level. All the differences are, however, small. For the full period 1897–1949 the share in national saving of the three business groups together (agriculture, unincorporated business, and corporations) declines only from 33.7 to 29.4 percent. Differences are generally equally small for subperiods, with the exception of the years 1939–1945. For this period both the negative share of the federal government and the positive shares of all other saver groups are considerably lower on the basis of deflated figures, reflecting the fact that within this subperiod the federal government's largest dissaving occurred in the years of highest prices.

b. *Trends in distribution of national saving among saver groups*

5.08. No definite significant long-term trends are visible in the distribution of national saving among the main saver groups during the past half century as it is shown in Chart XXVII.

5.09. The tendency towards an increase in the share of government saving and a decrease in the share of nonagricultural households, which is far from clear-cut if the standard social accounting concept of saving including consumer durables is used, becomes much more pronounced if (a) saving through consumer durables is excluded and (b) saving through government pension and retirement funds is transferred from the category of personal saving, where it belongs if classification is determined by ultimate beneficiaries, to government saving, on the ground that these funds represent accumulations administered by government agencies without any positive action by individual contributors or even against their will. If these adjustments are made the share of personal saving in total national saving declines from 69 percent in 1897–1908 and 63 percent in 1922–1929 to 47 percent in 1946–1949. The share of government saving, on the other hand, then rises sharply from 7 percent in 1897–1908 to 19 percent in 1922–1929 and to 28 percent in 1946–1949.

5.10. The short-term noncyclical movements in the shares of the various saver groups are dominated by the effects of the World Wars and reflect the large dissaving of the federal government during these periods. These movements take the form of a relatively high level, in comparison to its average for the entire period, of the shares of unincorporated business and agriculture. [5] War inflations strengthen the position of these two groups with respect to their share in national income and saving. The first World War had the same effect on the share of saving by corporations, but in World War II corporate saving remained at a relatively low level, reflecting the much more effective taxation of wartime profits. The share of state and local governments shows the opposite movement, being

[5] These movements are better seen in the annual values (Table T-1) than in the quadrennial or economic period averages.

131

CHART XXVII

SHARE OF MAIN SAVER GROUPS IN NONFEDERAL SAVING
Social Accounting Concept

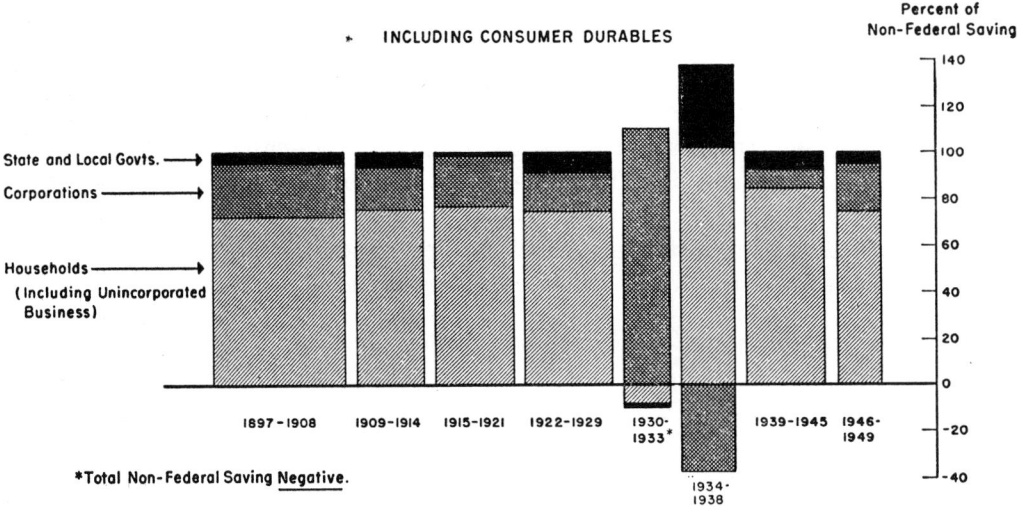

INCLUDING CONSUMER DURABLES

Percent of
Non-Federal Saving

State and Local Govts.

Corporations

Households
(Including Unincorporated
Business)

1897-1908   1909-1914   1915-1921   1922-1929   1930-1933*   1939-1945   1946-1949

1934-1938

*Total Non-Federal Saving Negative.

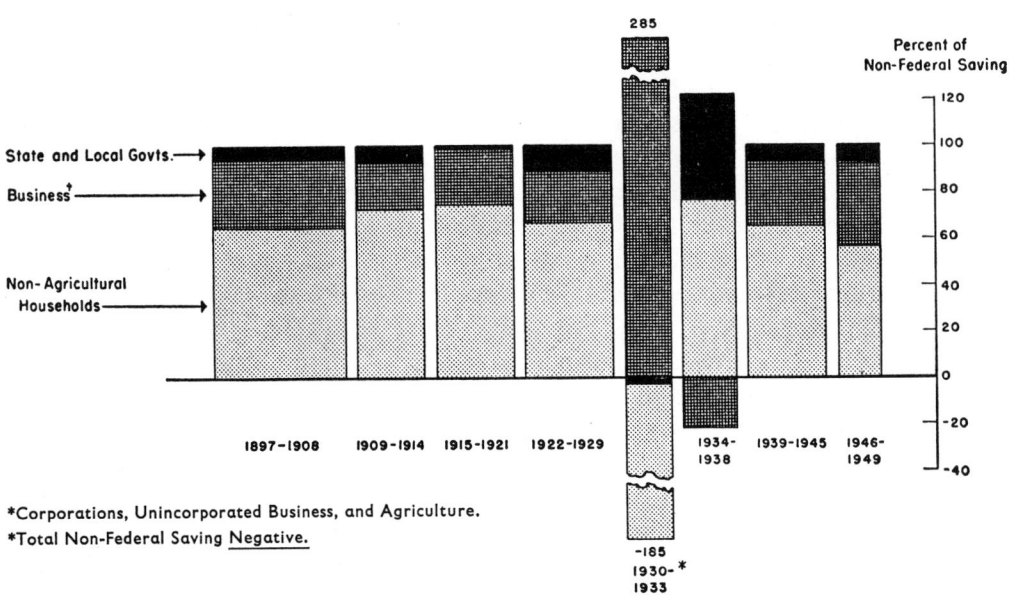

EXCLUDING CONSUMER DURABLES

285

Percent of
Non-Federal Saving

State and Local Govts.

Business*

Non-Agricultural
Households

1897-1908   1909-1914   1915-1921   1922-1929   1934-1938   1939-1945   1946-1949

*Corporations, Unincorporated Business, and Agriculture.
*Total Non-Federal Saving Negative.

-185
1930-*
1933

very low during World War I, but rather high during World War II. The share of nonfarm households in total nonfederal saving, finally, does not seem to have been greatly affected by war inflation.

5.11. The other movement which has left a distinct mark on the figures is the Great Depression. It is characterized by large dissaving on the part of the federal government, corporations, and unincorporated business enterprises and, hence, by an unusually high share of nonfarm households in total saving.

5.12. Apart from the effects of the wars and the Great Depression a number of movements of ten to twenty years' duration can be observed, but they do not fall into a clear-cut pattern and do not seem to reflect systematic changes in the distribution of national saving among the main saver groups.

5.13. The general conclusion, then, is that if periods affected by extraneous forces like wars and the Great Depression are disregarded and saving through government pension and retirement funds is treated as part of personal saving, there has been little change in the distribution of saving over the past half century among the three main saver groups of nonfarm households, business, and governments. Nonfarm households have accounted throughout the period for slightly more than two-thirds of total national saving, business for about one-fifth, and only the governments' share has exhibited something that might be regarded as a trend, viz. a slow increase to about one-tenth of total saving. The figures, therefore, do not clearly point to substantial structural changes in the distribution of saving among the main saver groups.

2. Distribution of Changes in Current Net Worth

5.14. Before one can understand the distribution of changes in current net worth among saver groups and compare this distribution with a similar distribution of current saving it is necessary to look at the share of current saving in net worth changes for different saver groups. This will be done briefly in Divisions 5.15 to 5.19, but unfortunately it is possible only for rather broad saver groups since no material has yet become available on the asset structure or on the relation between cumulated saving and net worth changes of large numbers, or of scientifically selected small samples, of individual economic units.

a. *The share of current saving in net worth changes*

5.15. Of the total increase in individuals' net worth between 1900 and 1949, amounting to over $880 billion, about three-fifths represents cumulated saving. The remaining two-fifths, approximately $355 billion, is primarily the result of an increase in asset prices, particularly the prices of real estate and common stock owned by individuals.

The variations from period to period in the share of cumulated saving in total change in individuals' net worth depend chiefly on the direction and extent of movements in asset prices. In most periods the share of saving is close to one-half; in other words, valuation changes have contributed as much to the increase in total net worth as cumulated saving. The share is smaller in the periods 1901–

133

1912 and 1934–1939. It reflects in the first period a persistent and substantial rise in the price level and results in the second period from an unusually low volume of saving as well as a modest recovery in asset prices. In the Great Depression, finally, dissaving accounts for only a negligible fraction of a decline in individuals' net worth of over $150 billion, or one-third of its 1929 level.[6]

5.16. Farm and nonfarm households differ considerably in the contribution of saving to aggregate net worth changes, as Chart XXVIII and Table XIX indicate. While saving is responsible for slightly more than three-fifths of the increase in the net worth of nonagricultural households (including unincorporated business enterprises and nonprofit nonfinancial institutions) between 1900 and 1949, it accounts for slightly less than one-half of the sharp rise in the net worth of agriculture if net expenditures on soil improvement are included.

The differences in the share of saving in total net worth changes are particularly pronounced before 1930. In the period 1901–1929 saving contributed hardly anything to the substantial increase in the net worth of farm households, which was due almost exclusively to rising land values, as increases in debt offset net capital formation in agriculture.[7] Among nonfarm households, on the other hand, saving accounted for fully one-half of the increase in net worth. Beginning with the thirties the difference has become much smaller, though it has not disappeared. Saving contributed about one-half of the increase in farmers' net worth between 1933 and 1949 compared to the share of almost three-fifths—the same as before 1930—for nonfarm households.

5.17. Corporate saving has accounted for slightly over one-quarter of the change in corporate net worth. The share has shown hardly any trend over the period.[8] That the share is rather low, and in particular is lower than that of individuals, is due largely to the higher share of price-sensitive assets for some, and to the higher debt-asset ratio for other, groups, both factors which tend to reduce the share of saving in total net worth changes when prices of tangible assets rise.

5.18. From the twenties to the end of World War II, when there was no persistent upward trend in the price level, the net worth change of state and local governments was hardly in excess of cumulated saving. In the first two decades of the century and in the last few years—both periods of rising prices, which imply an upward revaluation of tangible assets in a balance sheet based on replacement cost—the share of cumulated saving in total net worth changes averaged less than two-fifths, approximately the same as for corporations.

[6] This fact is responsible for the apparent anomaly that individuals' cumulated saving is equal to three-fifths of the change in their net worth for the entire period between 1900 and 1949, although the share is below that figure in every single period.

[7] For a discussion of the low level of saving in agriculture before 1929 see Division 4.15, and Volume II, Chapter XII.

[8] These proportions, like all the figures in Table XX, section I, are influenced by the fact that reported capital consumption allowances, which have been accepted in the calculation of corporate saving, are lower—for the period as a whole by about one-fourth—than standardized allowances based on assumed uniform lengths of life for the different types of structures and equipment, which underlie the estimates of the net worth of corporations at benchmark dates.

CHART XXVIII

SHARE OF SAVING IN NET WORTH CHANGES OF MAIN SAVER GROUPS

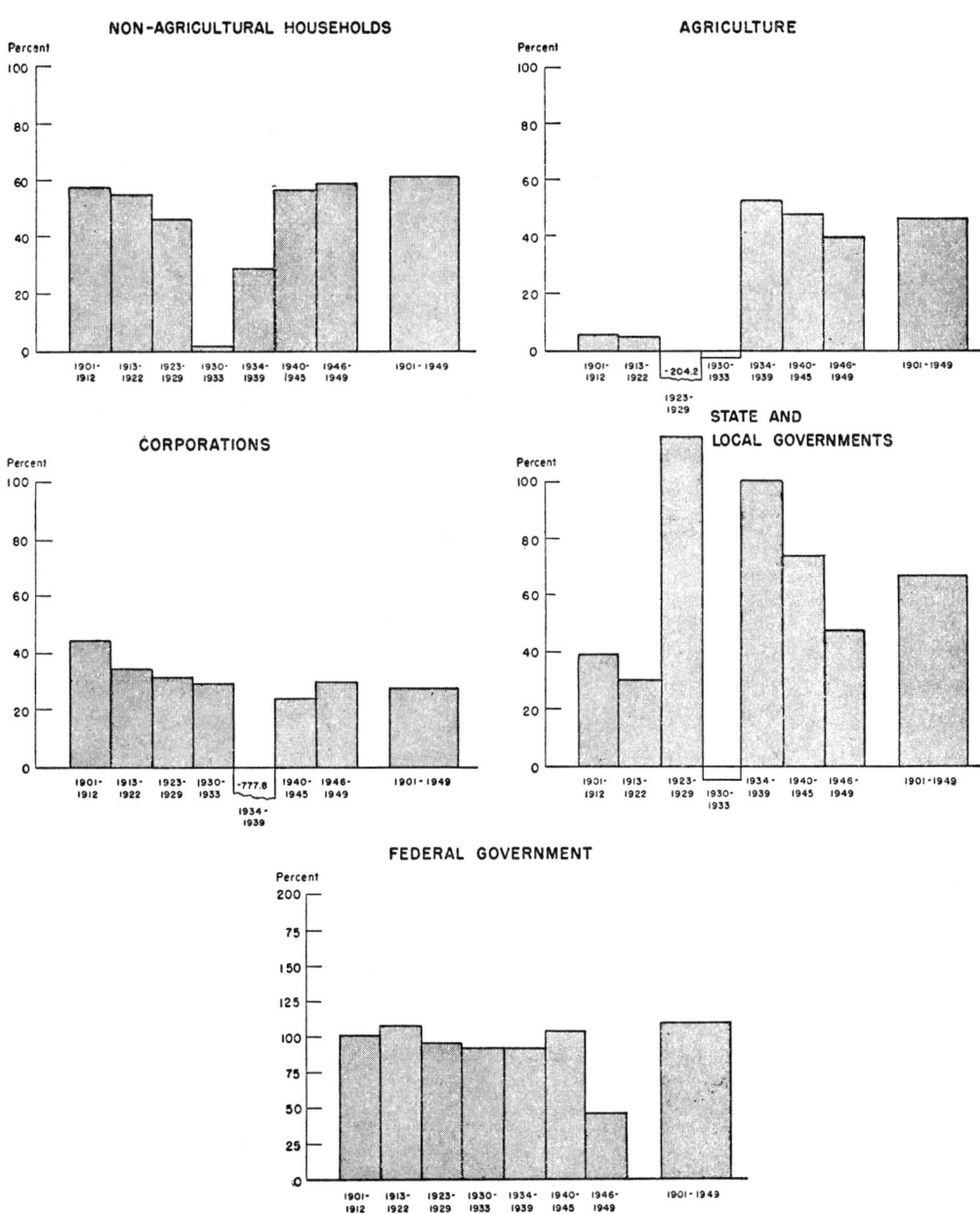

TABLE XIX

SHARE OF SAVING IN NET WORTH CHANGES
OF HOUSEHOLDS

Selected Periods: 1901 to 1949

Period	Change in total net worth	Saving	Difference	Share of saving in net worth changes
	$ bill.			Percent
	1	2	3	4

I. All individuals

1901–1912	79.8	34.5	45.3	43.2
1913–1922	161.7	82.4	79.3	51.0
1923–1929	156.8	78.1	78.7	49.8
1930–1933	−152.2	−2.1	−150.1	1.4
1934–1939	75.1	23.7	51.4	31.6
1940–1945	342.5	187.3	155.2	54.7
1946–1949	219.3	121.7	97.6	55.5
1901–1949	883.0	525.6	357.4	59.5

II. Nonagricultural households (including unincorporated business)

1901–1912	57.4	33.3	24.1	58.0
1913–1922	147.9	81.7	66.2	55.2
1923–1929	159.2	73.2	86.0	46.0
1930–1933	−132.2	−2.5	−129.7	1.9
1934–1939	67.1	19.4	47.7	28.9
1940–1945	284.0	159.5	124.5	56.2
1946–1949	180.8	106.4	74.4	58.8
1901–1949	764.2	471.0	293.2	61.6

III. Agriculture

1901–1912	22.4	1.2	21.2	5.4
1913–1922	13.8	0.7	13.1	5.1
1923–1929	−2.4	4.9	−7.3	−204.2
1930–1933	−20.0	0.4	−20.4	−2.0
1934–1939	8.0	4.3	3.7	53.8
1940–1945	58.5	27.8	30.7	47.5
1946–1949	38.5	15.3	23.2	39.7
1901–1949	118.8	54.6	64.2	46.0

Column 1 – Derived from Volume III, Tables W-22, W-27, and W-29.

Column 2 – Derived from Table T-1 except that original cost depreciation (see Table T-2) is used instead of replacement cost and that agricultural saving includes land costs (Table II, col. 3).

Column 3 – Col. 1 minus col. 2.

Column 4 – Col. 2 divided by col. 1.

TABLE XX

SHARE OF SAVING IN NET WORTH CHANGES OF CORPORATIONS AND GOVERNMENTS

Selected Periods: 1901 to 1949

Period	Change in total net worth	Saving	Difference	Share of saving in net worth changes
	$ bill.			Percent
	1	2	3	4
I. Corporations				
1901–1912	16.3	7.2	9.1	44.2
1913–1922	60.5	20.7	39.8	34.2
1923–1929	53.9	16.9	37.0	31.4
1930–1933	−46.3	−13.7	−32.6	29.6
1934–1939	0.9	−7.0	7.9	−777.8
1940–1945	80.1	19.2	60.9	24.0
1946–1949	97.0	28.8	68.2	29.7
1901–1949	262.4	72.1	190.3	27.5
II. State and local governments				
1901–1912	5.9	2.3	3.6	39.0
1913–1922	11.3	3.4	7.9	30.1
1923–1929	8.3	9.6	−1.3	115.7
1930–1933	−2.4	0.1	−2.5	−4.2
1934–1939	7.2	7.2	0	100.0
1940–1945	21.9	16.2	5.7	74.0
1946–1949	22.0	10.5	11.5	47.7
1901–1949	74.2	49.3	24.9	66.4
III. Federal government				
1901–1912	0.8	0.8	0	100.0
1913–1922	−17.4	−19.2	1.8	110.3
1923–1929	7.8	7.5	0.3	96.2
1930–1933	−4.7	−4.4	−0.3	93.6
1934–1939	−14.4	−13.2	−1.2	91.7
1940–1945	−180.2	−187.2	7.0	103.9
1946–1949	18.7	8.8	9.9	47.1
1901–1949	−189.5	−206.9	17.4	109.2

Column 1 – Derived from Volume III, Tables W-30, W-42, and W-43.

Column 2 – Derived from Table T-1 except that original cost depreciation (see Table T-2) is used instead of replacement cost.

Column 3 – Col. 1 minus col. 2. Government corporations and credit agencies in col. 1 are included under corporations and excluded from the federal government while in col. 2 the reverse is true.

Column 4 – Col. 2 divided by col. 1.

5.19. The differences between cumulated saving and dissaving and net worth changes of the federal government are small and without significance up to the early thirties and during World War II. The excess of dissaving over the decline in total net worth between 1933 and 1939 is due to the revaluation of the Treasury's gold holdings. The substantial excess of net worth increase over cumulated saving in the years 1946–1949—similar to that of all other groups—reflects the effect of the rise in the price level on the estimated replacement cost of the by now rather substantial tangible assets of the federal government.

b. *Distribution of net worth changes among saver groups*

5.20. As a result of differences in the share of saving in total net worth changes, movements in the shares of the main saver groups in combined national (or nonfederal) net worth show a number of divergencies compared with changes in the distribution of national saving. As has been explained in Subsection a, these divergencies reflect the varying effects of advances and declines of asset prices on different saver groups.

5.21. The divergencies are already quite marked for the entire period 1901–1949, for which they are shown in Table XXI. The share of nonfarm households and of state and local governments in cumulated nonfederal saving is higher than that in total net worth change, while the opposite relation prevails for agriculture and corporations. The federal government's offset to other groups' saving is proportionately twice as large as its offset to the increase in their net worth. These differences reflect two factors. The first is the balance of net valuation gains and losses. Groups with relatively high net gains will show a higher share in net worth change than in cumulated saving. This is exemplified by business enterprises and reflects relatively high levels of tangible assets and debt-asset ratios. The second is the distribution of saving and net worth changes over the period. Since the absolute figures of both have increased considerably between the beginning and middle of the twentieth century, a discrepancy of equal proportion will as a rule have greater influence on the difference in the two ratios for the entire period if it occurred near to its end rather than its beginning. This is one of the reasons why the negative share of the federal government for the period as a whole is much higher in saving than in net worth change.

5.22. To separate the effect of the two factors it is necessary to extend the comparison to intervals between all benchmark dates rather than to limit it to the entire period between 1900 and 1949. If this is done, it appears from Table XXI that the differences between a group's share in national saving and that in net worth change are often considerably larger for periods between benchmarks than for the period as a whole. Explanation of these differences requires consideration of the balance sheet structure of the different saver groups, particularly the ratio of price-sensitive assets and the debt ratio, of the trend in asset prices, and of the ratio of saving to total assets. It is not possible here to go into these questions in detail. Most of the necessary basic data are presented elsewhere in this study (particularly in Volume III, Part I) and a brief summary without supporting figures must suffice here.

138

TABLE XXI

SHARE OF MAIN SAVER GROUPS IN SAVING AND
IN NET WORTH CHANGES

Economic Periods: 1901 to 1949

Percent

	1901 to 1912	1913 to 1922	1923 to 1929	1930 to 1933	1934 to 1939	1940 to 1945	1946 to 1949	1901 to 1949
I. Saving [a]								
1. Nonfarm households [b]	75.7	76.7	70.0	15.9	81.2	71.6	66.1	72.8
2. Agriculture	2.7	0.7	4.7	−2.5	18.0	12 5	9.5	8.4
3. Corporations	16.4	19.4	16.2	87.3	−29.3	8.6	17.9	11.1
4. State and local governments	5.2	3.2	9.2	−0.6	30.1	7.3	6.5	7.6
5. Nonfederal, total	100.0	100.0	100.0	100.0	100.0	100.0	100.0	100.0
6. Federal government	1.8	−18.0	7.2	28.0	−55.2	−84.1	5.5	−32.0
II. Net worth changes								
1. Nonfarm households [b]	56.3	63.3	72.7	65.8	80.6	63.9	53.4	62.7
2. Agriculture	22.0	5.9	−1.1	10.0	9.6	13.2	11.4	9.7
3. Corporations	16.0	25.9	24.6	23.0	1.1	18.0	28.7	21.5
4. State and local governments	5.8	4.8	3.8	1.2	8.7	4.9	6.5	6.1
5. Nonfederal, total	100.0	100.0	100.0	100.0	100.0	100.0	100.0	100.0
6. Federal government	0.8	−7.5	3.6	2.3	−17.2	−40.5	5.6	−15.5

[a] Social accounting concept except that original cost depreciation is used.
[b] Includes unincorporated business enterprises.
Source: See Tables XIX and XX.

5.23.   The share of nonagricultural households in total nonfederal saving exceeds their share in net worth change in five of the seven periods distinguished in Table XXI. This relation indicates that for most of the first half of this century (1901–1922 and 1934–1949) the distribution of unearned increments in net worth resulting from changes in the price level of assets was such as to deprive nonfarm households of a part—though not a large one—of national wealth which they might have commanded if asset prices had been stable.[9] Such a development is not astonishing since on the average the debt-asset ratio of nonfarm individuals (Table XLI) is lower than that of most other saver groups, a factor which makes for a shortfall of cumulated saving compared with net worth change when prices rise. It is only for the periods 1923–1929 and 1930–1933 that nonagricultural individuals' share in total nonfederal current net worth changes exceeded their share in saving, and the reason was the same in both periods: the extraordinarily sharp movements in stock prices. Their rise lifted individuals' share in net worth change above that in saving for the period 1923 to 1929, while their fall was responsible for the much greater share of individuals in the decline of total net worth than in dissaving during the Great Depression.

[9] This argument assumes that stability of asset prices would not have affected the share of the different saver groups in saving, i.e. earned net worth changes. This, of course, cannot be rigorously true, but might be sufficiently accurate not to invalidate the comments made in the text on the direction of the difference between the two shares.

5.24. The differences between shares in saving and in net worth changes are much more spectacular for agriculture, at least through World War I. As a result of the sharp fluctuations in land values (upward to 1920, downward during most of the following two decades), low holdings of price-insensitive assets, and a relatively high debt-asset ratio (the latter only up to the Great Depression), agriculture's share in net worth changes customarily exceeded its contribution to national saving. This discrepancy benefited agriculture up to 1920 by giving it a much higher share in the increase in national wealth than corresponded to its saving in the strict social accounting sense. During the two decades following the process was reversed as land values declined more, or rose less, than most of the other asset prices. From 1940 on, finally, agriculture's share in current net worth changes was fairly well in keeping with its contribution to current saving.

5.25. The share of corporations in combined net worth (estimated, it will be recalled, as the excess of assets at market value or replacement cost over liabilities) has generally fluctuated more widely than their share in cumulated net saving, partly because corporations have a relatively high debt-asset ratio (Table XLI). As a result the share of corporations in net worth increase may be expected to have been higher than their contribution to saving in periods of prosperity and rising prices, while they should have accounted for a higher proportion of net worth declines than of dissaving in depressions and price declines. This is borne out in Table XXI. Only the years 1934–1939 clearly fail to conform to this pattern, but this may be attributed to the peculiar character of the period, an economic recovery and a rise in prices—the latter reflected in unrealized appreciation on tangible assets—being accompanied by an extraordinarily low level of corporate saving which is in part explained by the tax on undistributed corporate profits in force during part of the period. Thus corporations generally have been able to command a higher share of increases in national wealth than corresponded to their saving.

5.26. In the case of state and local governments, their share in saving was below that in net worth changes for the first portion of the period (1901–1922) and above it for the later portion (1923–1949). The time distribution of periods of excess or shortfall does not show a clear relationship to the trend of prices. The share in saving is always below that in net worth when tangible asset prices move markedly upwards—in this respect similar to the movement over time of the shares for corporations. The share in saving, however, is above that in net worth change during periods of price rise (1940–1945), of price decline (1930–1933), and of relatively stable prices (1923–1929).

5.27. The differences between the two shares of the federal government are particularly pronounced in the periods in which the government has large deficits involving increases in debt without corresponding increases in assets. These differences, however, are not the result of large discrepancies, in absolute amounts, between the federal government's dissaving and the decline in its net worth. They are due rather to the fact that during these periods the increase in combined national net worth is much larger than cumulated national saving. The federal government's

140

dissaving thus necessarily constitutes a much larger (negative) share of national saving than the ratio which the almost equally large decline in the government's net worth bears to the increase in combined national net worth. The large discrepancy between the two shares of the federal government—which indicates that its negative share in national wealth has generally been smaller than corresponds to its dissaving, with the familiar result that the federal government's real debt burden has been lightened—is thus the result primarily of valuation changes in other sectors of the economy.

VI

DISTRIBUTION OF PERSONAL SAVING
AMONG FORMS OF SAVING

1. APPROACH

6.01. One of the main steps in the analysis of saving which the Saving Study makes possible is the study of trends and structural changes in the forms of saving.

In this discussion the field has been restricted in two directions. First, changes in the forms of saving by state, local, and federal governments are left out. The essential points have been mentioned in Chapter IV, and details are not required for the purpose of this summary. Secondly, the discussion combines saving by nonfarm households, agriculture, and unincorporated business enterprises, and thus deals only with total personal saving. Such a combination appears justified, first, because quantitatively the saving of nonfarm households dominates personal saving to such an extent that the main structural changes in personal saving are not much different from those in the saving of nonfarm households. The second reason is even more compelling. The estimates of saving for all three groups together are more reliable than those for one of them separately, because it is very difficult in some cases (particularly for saving through bank deposits, securities, and nonresidential real estate) to divide total personal saving, which can be measured fairly well, among the three component saver groups. Thirdly, the basic tables (T-8 to T-10 for annual values and S-20 to S-23 for period averages) permit those who so desire to study trends and structural changes in the forms of nonfarm individuals' saving alone.

If we are interested primarily in long-term trends or changes a further limitation of the discussion is both permissible and advisable, viz. the elimination of periods strongly influenced by wars, because they are of an essentially different nature from the rest of the period, and of the years 1930–1938 because for this period personal saving was of small absolute value and percentage distributions are therefore erratic. These considerations lead to concentration on the four economic periods 1897–1908, 1909–1914, 1922–1929, and 1946–1949. This does not mean ignoring the other periods, which after all account for twenty-three of the fifty-three years covered by the Study. It merely reflects the conviction that what the other periods show is relevant to the study of the United States only under abnormal rather than normal economic conditions.

6.02. The discussion is divided into two steps. The first step makes use of the approximately thirty forms of saving from which the total of personal saving has been built up. In the second step the forms of saving are arranged into groups which are made up on the basis of economic considerations. Such groupings lead to figures for forms of saving having a different degree of liquidity; for forms of saving destined for use by the saver himself, for use by the first recipient of the amounts saved, and for use by financial intermediaries; for saving through claims and equities; for tied saving; and for forms of saving typical for upper and lower income groups.

6.03. One very important aspect of the distribution of personal saving by form is discussed neither in this chapter nor in the brief treatment of the cyclical movements in the components of personal saving included in Chapter VII. This is the question of the affinity or substitutability of different forms of saving, particularly with respect to changes in yield rates, a subject which calls for more elaborate econometric methods than used in this Introduction. Hardly anything, finally, is said here on the determinants of the different forms of saving, partly because of limitations of resources and partly again because of the need to bring more elaborate econometric methods into play if these problems are to be treated adequately.

2. Summary of Findings

6.04. The distribution of personal saving among forms is a point on which, similar to the distribution of national saving among saver groups and largely for the same reasons, the distinction between the full period 1897–1949 and the normal period, from which the years of the two World Wars and the Great Depression are excluded, becomes of essential importance. The differences stem by and large from the fact that war periods are characterized by the creation of massive amounts of intangible assets, particularly government securities, bank deposits, and currency, most of which end in individuals' hands. As a result saving through U.S. Government securities, negligible in normal periods, accounts for more than one-third of total personal saving during war periods, and the share of cash saving is twice as high in war as in nonwar periods. By way of contrast, personal saving through tangible assets, in particular real estate and consumer durables, almost disappears during war years.

6.05. If attention is concentrated on nonwar periods, as is done throughout this Introduction, it appears that the share of saving through consumer durables, life insurance, government and private pension and retirement funds, savings and loan associations, and credit unions increased from period to period, and as a rule substantially (Chart XXIX). On the other hand, the share of saving through real estate, bank deposits, and corporate stocks and bonds showed a declining trend, though in no case without interruptions (Chart XXX).

6.06. The share of liquid saving has shown a tendency to decrease while that of illiquid saving has increased markedly, primarily reflecting the increasing share of saving through consumer durables and pension and retirement funds.

6.07. There has been a sharp shift in the shares of personal saving from saving which is transferred directly from the saver to the user (e.g. mortgages and corporate securities) to saving which is entrusted to financial intermediaries and reaches the users of the funds only after one or more additional transfers. The share of saving in

CHART XXXI

FORMS OF PERSONAL SAVING INCREASING IN RELATIVE IMPORTANCE
Social Accounting Concept

CONSUMER DURABLES

LIFE INSURANCE RESERVES

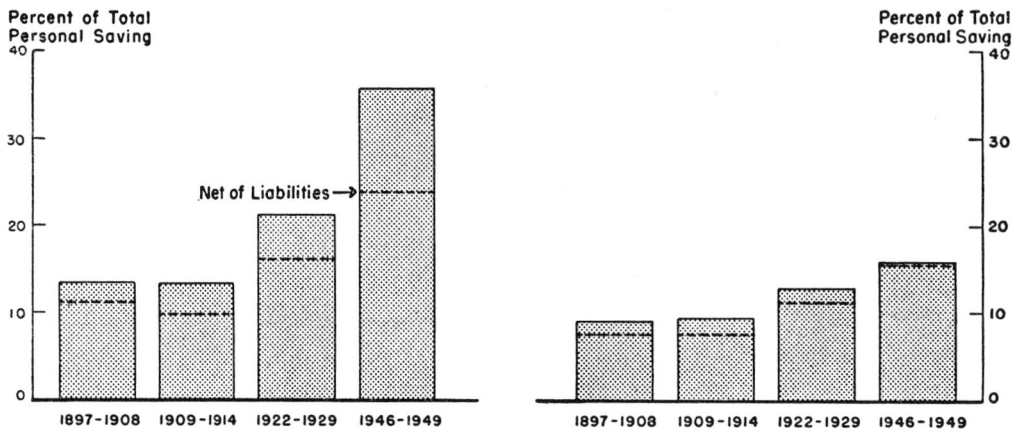

PENSION AND RETIREMENT FUNDS

SAVINGS & LOAN AND CREDIT UNION DEPOSITS

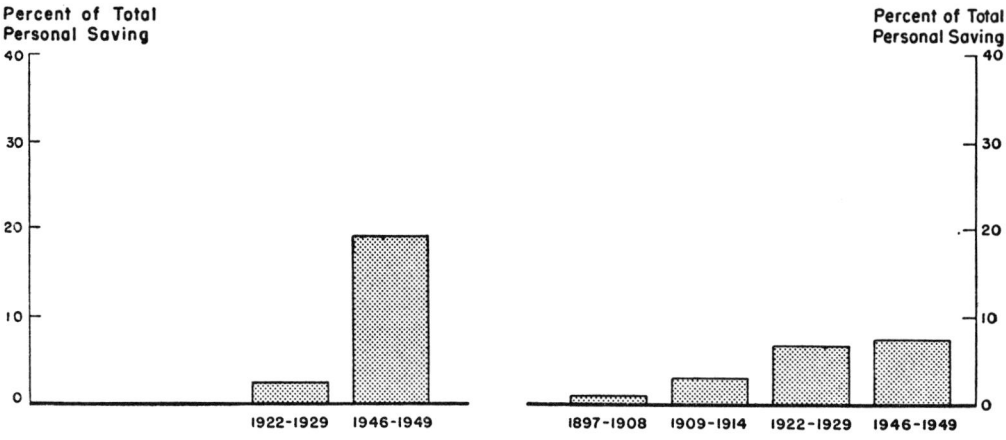

144

CHART XXX

FORMS OF PERSONAL SAVING DECREASING IN RELATIVE IMPORTANCE
Social Accounting Concept

RESIDENTIAL REAL ESTATE   **BANK DEPOSITS**

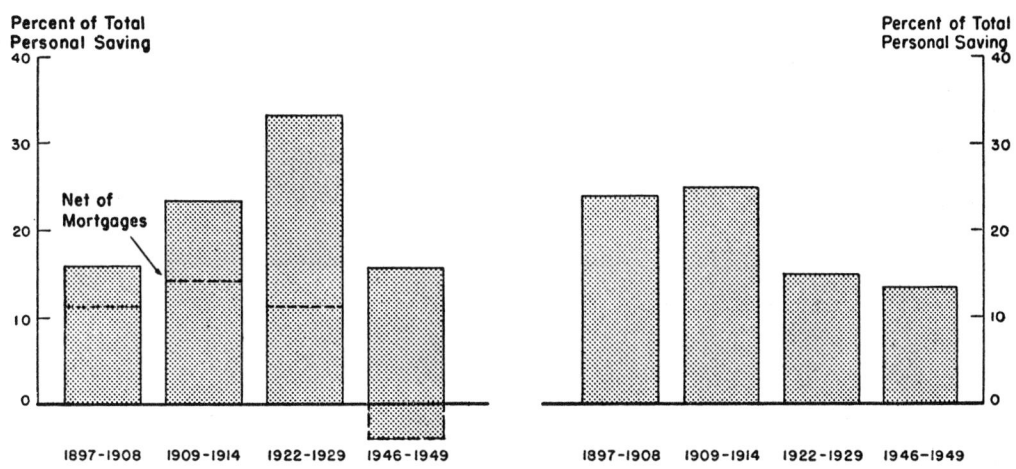

CORPORATE AND FOREIGN BONDS   **CORPORATE STOCKS**
                                       (COMMON AND PREFERRED)

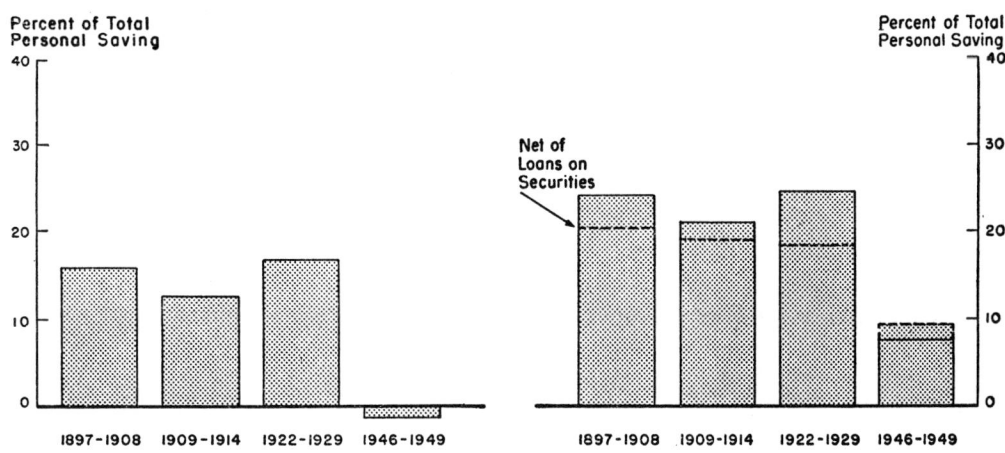

145

forms destined for use in the saver's own household or business, and hence not touching the capital market at all, has shown only a slight upward trend.

6.08. The share of personal saving in the form of long-term claims has increased at the expense of saving through short-term claims and through equities (e.g. corporate stocks, real estate, and consumer and producer durables). The decline in the share of saving through equities would disappear if corporate saving were allocated to stockholders.

6.09. The share of contractual saving through insurance, pension funds, and mortgage amortization has increased sharply from less than one-tenth of total personal saving before World War I to approximately one-half after World War II.

6.10. There is some evidence that the share of the upper income groups in total personal saving has decreased throughout the period, particularly if consumer durables are included. The shift cannot have been radical, however, since even after World War II the 10 percent of households with the highest incomes accounted for over 80 percent of total personal saving excluding consumer durables.

3. Trends in the Distribution of Personal Saving among Forms of Saving

a. *Normal periods*

6.11. Probably the most pronounced trend, if attention is limited to normal periods (1897–1908, 1909–1914, 1922–1929, 1946–1949), is the increase in the share of saving in the form of consumer durables (i.e. value of purchases less accruing depreciation at replacement cost on the stock of consumer durables), as it is shown in Charts XXVII and XXIX.

Without allowance for consumer debt, the share of consumer durables rises from 13 percent of total personal saving in 1897–1908 to 21 percent in 1922–1929 and 36 percent in 1946–1949. Even when increases in consumer debt are deducted the share shows an almost continuous increase from 11 percent in 1897–1908 to 24 percent in 1946–1949. Saving in the form of government and private pension reserves likewise shows a rising trend throughout the period, but most of the increase is limited to the period after the midthirties. Two other forms of saving may also be included in this category, viz. saving through private life insurance reserves and saving through farm construction net of farm mortgage debt, although the rising trend begins only with the period 1909–1914. The increase is substantial and significant in the case of life insurance, its share in total net personal saving rising from about 8 percent in the first two decades of the century to 11 percent in the twenties and to 16 percent after World War II.

Only one of the individual forms of saving shows a continuously decreasing trend over the four normal periods, viz. saving through common stock adjusted for changes in borrowing on securities. Its share in total personal saving declined from about 16 percent in the 1897–1908 period to 12 percent in the twenties and to not much over 5 percent after World War II. If the interruption during the twenties is ignored, the share of saving through corporate bonds and preferred stock also

146

exhibits a generally declining trend over the period. So do mortgages beginning with 1909-1914, and savings bank deposits although the decline ceased in the twenties.

6.12. If we are on the lookout for possible breaks in trends after 1929, which calls for comparison of the distributions for the 1922-1929 and 1946-1949 periods, rather than for trends persisting over the entire five decades, the characteristic movements are:

(1) The sharp decline in the share of net expenditures on real estate;

(2) The precipitous reduction in the share of saving through corporate securities, particularly bonds, from almost two-fifths to less than one-tenth of the total;

(3) The absence after World War II of the pronounced liquidation of holdings of U.S. Government securities, which was an important factor in the saving picture of the twenties;

(4) The rapid increase in the share of saving through consumer durables, and particularly through insurance and pension reserves, both continuations of previous trends but much accentuated in extent.

b. *War periods and the Great Depression*

6.13. While the distribution of personal saving by forms that is indicated for the periods 1915-1921, 1930-1933, 1934-1938, and 1939-1945 can in no way be regarded as indicative of long-term trends, the figures are of interest because they show how war financing and an extraordinarily severe and protracted depression have affected the distribution of personal saving.

6.14. Both war periods are clearly distinguished by two characteristics, viz. first, the high proportion of saving in the form of U.S. Government securities, commercial bank deposits, and currency, and secondly, the correspondingly low proportion of most other forms of saving, particularly saving through tangible durable assets. These tendencies are clearly evident in both war periods, although they are more pronounced during World War II.

The sharp increase in the share of personal saving through U.S. Government securities, commercial bank deposits, and currency from an average level of not much over 10 percent for the normal periods to nearly 80 percent in 1917-1918 and 1942-1945—indicating a still sharper increase in the absolute amounts saved in these forms, as the aggregate volume of personal saving increased greatly during both war periods—clearly reflects the way in which the war expenditures of the U.S. Government have been financed, viz. partly through direct sales of Treasury securities to individuals and financial institutions, and partly through sales to the commercial banking system, which lead to an expansion of bank deposits, most of which are held by individuals. The decrease in the shares and also the absolute amounts of saving through real estate, through consumer durables, and through producer durables used by agriculture and unincorporated business enterprises, a tendency which again is more pronounced during World War II than World War I, is the result of the unavailability of these assets rather than of a shortage of funds or a shift of individuals' predilections for specific types of saving.

147

Purchase of U.S. Government securities insofar as it is ascribable to patriotic rather than pecuniary motives may be regarded as the only important exception, as it reflects a genuine, although temporary, shift in savers' tastes. As a result, saving through tangible assets (disregarding changes in the debt attaching to them) amounted to less than 15 percent of total personal saving in 1917–1918 and was negative to the extent of 6 percent of total personal saving in 1942–1945 against a share varying between one-half to two-thirds for normal periods. The share of saving through intangible assets other than U.S. Government securities, commercial bank deposits, and currency is also lower during the war periods than during normal periods, but the reduction is much less marked than in the case of tangible assets and the absolute amounts saved in several instances show an increase rather than a decrease.

One considerable difference between the two war periods is evident in the behavior of personal debt. World War I apparently did not greatly affect the relation between the increase in assets and the increase in liabilities which had prevailed during the preceding twenty years. During World War II, on the other hand, the increase in liabilities came virtually to a halt and there were even substantial debt reductions, equivalent to additional saving, in consumer debt and most forms of mortgages.

6.15. Compared with the normal periods, the distribution of personal saving during the Great Depression and the rest of the thirties is characterized by the very high share of a few forms of saving which show relatively moderate variations in absolute amount, primarily saving through private life insurance and through government and private pension reserves. This is necessarily accompanied by very low, and in some cases negative, shares of saving through real estate, producer durables, and, for 1930–1933, consumer durables.

Among the more erratic movements of the shares of saving through intangible assets other than life insurance and pension reserves mention may be made of the rather high share—compared to normal periods—of saving through common stock, particularly when allowance is made for reduction in borrowing on securities, most of which are connected with the acquisition or holding of common stocks. For the period 1930–1938 as a whole, individuals' purchases of common stock minus borrowing were equal to more than one-half of total personal saving, and even in absolute amounts were larger, on an annual basis, than saving through common stock in any other period except 1922–1929 and 1946–1949, another example of the occasionally great importance of debt repayment for the distribution of personal saving.

c. *Degree of similarity in distribution during normal periods*

6.16. In addition to following the variegated movements in individual forms of personal saving it is desirable to obtain an idea of the degree of similarity, or of the extent of change, in the distribution of personal saving by forms from one period to another. This can be done in a simple even if not entirely satisfactory way by means of the correlation coefficient between the percentages of personal

148

CHART XXXI

SHARE OF MAIN FORMS OF SAVING IN TOTAL PERSONAL SAVING

Social Accounting Concept

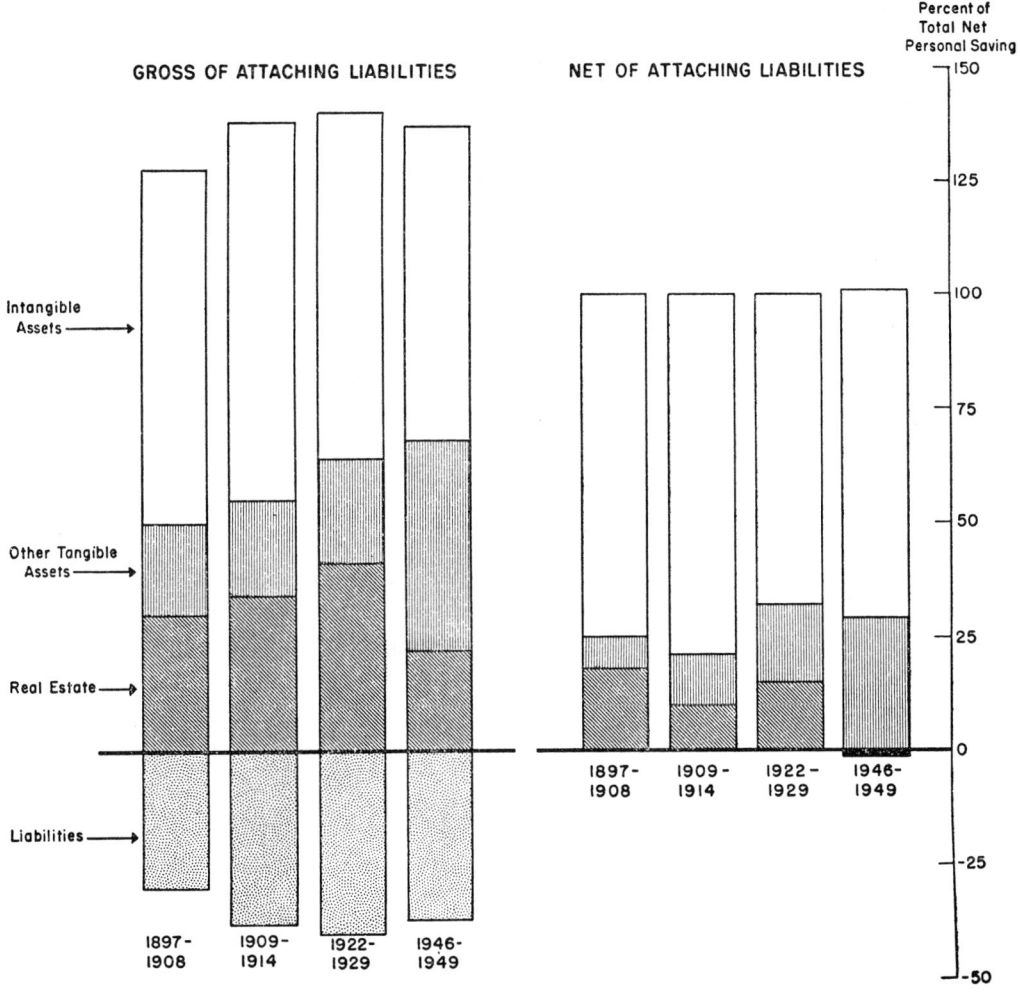

saving represented by the individual forms of saving for the two periods to be compared. If every form of saving accounted for the same proportion of total personal saving in both periods the correlation coefficient would be 1.00; the greater the difference, loosely speaking, between the two distributions the closer the coefficient approaches zero. If this calculation is carried through for the four normal periods, the ones for which it is of most interest, it is found, first, that the longer the interval the smaller the correlation, and secondly, that there is a somewhat closer affinity between the distribution for the three periods before 1930 than among any of them and the distribution for 1946–1949, the correlation being particularly close for the two earliest periods, 1897–1908 and 1909–1914. There is no

149

evidence of a sharp break in the structure of personal saving after the twenties. This is shown by the correlation coefficients between the percentage distributions for the various economic periods of twenty-nine forms of personal saving:

1897–1908 to 1909–1914: 0.93
1909–1914 to 1922–1929: 0.83
1897–1908 to 1922–1929: 0.79
1922–1929 to 1946–1949: 0.69
1909–1914 to 1946–1949: 0.61
1897–1908 to 1946–1949: 0.55

4. Trends in the Distribution of Personal Saving by Form among Variant Estimates of Saving

6.17. The long-term movements in the distribution of personal saving by form depend to some extent on the nature of the estimates used. Textual discussion of these differences, most of which turn out to be neither very pronounced nor economically significant, is rather tedious and has therefore been omitted. The main features are evident in Table xxii. Readers interested in the details can obtain the information they need by comparing Table S-40, which shows the distribution of current personal saving including consumer durables according to the social accounting concept for each economic period, with Tables S-42 and S-44, which present the same picture based on the business accounting concept and cash flow concept respectively, and with Table S-22, which shows the saving of nonfarm households alone.

5. Trends in the Distribution of Personal Saving by Form among Economic Types of Saving

a. *Approach*

6.18. While Divisions 6.11 to 6.16 were based on an operational classification of forms of saving, i.e. they dealt with the main categories of saving from which the estimates of aggregate personal saving have been constructed, an attempt must now be made to arrange these categories (sometimes after further subdivision) into groups which as far as possible show an economically significant breakdown of total personal saving. Such an economic classification of the forms of personal saving must be approximative statistically rather than exact and must remain indicative rather than conclusive in an economic sense. The reasons for these limitations will become obvious once the possible economic classifications of personal saving are reviewed.

6.19. Before this can be done it is necessary to face one difficulty which is encountered by some classifications of saving—the treatment of negative components of saving, i.e. forms of debt the increase in which acts as an offset to saving through an increase in assets. The classification of saving by economic type may,

150

TABLE XXII

SHARE OF MAIN FORMS OF SAVING IN TOTAL PERSONAL SAVING
Variant Concepts; Selected Periods: 1897 to 1949

Percent

	1897 to 1908	1909 to 1914	1922 to 1929	1946 to 1949	1897 to 1908	1909 to 1914	1922 to 1929	1946 to 1949
	I. Social accounting				*II. Business accounting*			
1. Real estate	29.9	33.7	40.9	21.5	26.3	30.5	42.4	25.6
2. Other tangible assets	19.7	21.3	22.5	45.6	32.7	32.5	26.7	51.2
3. Intangible assets	80.1	83.1	76.1	69.5	65.2	68.2	64.5	49.4
4. Liabilities	29.7	38.1	39.5	36.6	24.1	31.3	33.5	26.0
	III. Cash flow				*IV. Excluding agriculture and unincorporated business* [a]			
1. Real estate	30.1	30.7	33.8	27.6	24.6	29.8	37.8	19.3
2. Other tangible assets	50.6	53.7	54.7	71.2	12.8	11.2	21.8	37.0
3. Intangible assets	32.6	32.2	29.3	21.0	77.0	77.3	77.8	77.8
4. Liabilities	13.3	16.6	17.8	19.8	14.4	18.2	37.4	34.0
	V. Deflated values [a]				*VI. Deducting liabilities* [a]			
1. Real estate	29.6	33.8	40.8	21.1	17.8	10.4	14.6	−1.1
2. Other tangible assets	19.8	21.2	22.4	45.2	6.6	10.8	17.2	29.1
3. Intangible assets	80.9	83.2	76.1	70.4	75.5	78.8	68.2	71.9
4. Liabilities	30.2	37.9	39.5	36.9	–	–	–	–
	VII. Excluding consumer durables [a]				*VIII. Excluding consumer durables and deducting liabilities* [a]			
1. Real estate	34.5	38.9	51.9	33.5	20.6	12.1	18.5	−1.6
2. Other tangible assets	7.2	9.2	1.6	15.5	−7.9	−2.9	−5.1	−10.2
3. Intangible assets	92.5	95.7	96.6	108.0	87.2	90.9	86.6	111.8
4. Liabilities	34.3	44.0	50.1	57.0	–	–	–	–

[a] Social accounting concept.

Source: Derived from annual figures as follows:

    I: From Table T-6.

    II: From Table T-7.

    III: From Tables T-10, A-66, and U-11.

    IV: From Table T-8.

    V: From Table T-6 divided by gross national product deflator from Table T-16, col. 1.

VI–VIII: From Table T-6.

on the one hand, be limited to the positive components of saving, grouping them in accordance with their economic characteristics. This may be called a classification of gross saving, although the term "gross" is understood in a special sense and in particular does not imply disregard of capital consumption allowances. Classification of net saving, on the other hand, makes allowance for forms of dissaving. This can be done in two ways. The one is to group all liabilities together and to treat their total as a component of saving with negative sign so that the sum of the shares of the positive forms of saving exceeds 100 percent by the percentage which liabilities are of net saving. The other possibility is to deduct the individual forms of dissaving from the forms of saving with which they are associated. Dissaving through an increase in mortgage debt (residential, nonresidential, or farm), for instance, is deducted from saving through the appropriate form of construction, which in turn is essentially derived as the difference between construction expenditures and depreciation allowances.[1] Similarly, dissaving in the form of an increase in consumer debt is deducted from saving through consumer durables, and an increase in borrowing on securities is subtracted from net purchases of securities. If this is done classification of forms of saving refers to net saving, i.e. acquisition of assets less attaching debt. The main difficulty arising in this approach is the fact there is no perfect correspondence between forms of debt and types of assets. Some of the liabilities classified as consumer debt, for instance, are not used to finance the purchase of consumer durables but for current consumption expenditures or in business ventures. Similarly a part, and possibly at times a considerable one, of what appears as borrowing on securities is not used to acquire stocks or bonds. For some forms of saving, of course, there is no difference between the gross and the net approach, or the difference is negligible. This is the case particularly for most types of saving through intangibles, particularly through currency, deposits, and pension and retirement reserves. To overcome these difficulties, as far as this is possible without a great deal of additional spadework, the classification of forms of personal saving is presented on the gross as well as the net basis, whenever both approaches are appropriate, and significant differences between the two bases are pointed out. The discussion, as a rule, is based on the classification of total personal saving, but parallel tables are provided for nonagricultural individuals' saving.

b. *Saving of different degrees of liquidity*

6.20. Even more than for some other breakdowns the classification of types of saving by degree of liquidity is conventional and arbitrary. To arrange all forms of saving into only two groups, liquid and illiquid, is unsatisfactory although it is often done. It was found that at least four degrees of liquidity had to be distinguished, the probable attitude of savers being taken as the main guidepost.

Class A, the content of which is fairly close to what is usually called liquid saving, includes saving through currency, deposits, and U.S. Government securities. Two criteria were used in forming this group: (1) immediate convertibility

[1] The calculation, as shown in Volume II, Chapter IX, is actually more complicated.

152

into cash, possible loss in the conversion being either of no, or of secondary, importance; and (2) absence, or at least lack of predominance, of intention to hold saving permanently in this form. It is the second criterion that distinguishes Class A from Class B, which covers saving through securities (excluding U.S. Government securities) and life insurance, since some of the forms of saving included in Class B—like life insurance and high grade securities—also are characterized in savers' evaluations by immediate convertibility into cash with no, or with only moderate, loss. Saving through real estate and mortgage holdings make up the bulk of Class C. Difficulty and cost of conversion into cash are as a rule higher than for Class B, but the intended duration of the investment is probably longer for most savers. Class D consists of assets which either cannot be liquidated prematurely, such as social security and private pension fund reserves, or of assets which are not intended to be disposed of at all (except by way of a trade-in) save in emergencies because they form part of the saver's household or business, e.g. consumer durables, livestock, and inventories in agriculture and unincorporated business enterprises. [2] Forms of saving in this class are definitely illiquid in the sense that disentanglement of saving embodied in these assets is not anticipated and, if it becomes necessary, is generally difficult and costly. It is probably fair to say that Classes A and D are reasonably well defined in savers' minds, but that the distinction between the two classes of semiliquid saving, B and C, is fluid and to a great extent arbitrary.

6.21. Classification of personal saving by degrees of liquidity, although it makes sense only on a gross basis and is not without conceptual difficulties, does at least afford a fairly clear-cut statistical picture. The outstanding characteristic of this picture is the difference, which has been noted repeatedly, between normal periods on one side and war and depression periods on the other. During normal periods liquid (Class A) assets have, as Chart XXXII shows, represented not more than 20 percent of total personal saving. Their share has been at least three times as high during war periods and in the Great Depression. [3] During the two World Wars it even exceeded three-fourths of total personal saving. As a result liquid saving has accounted for about 40 percent of total personal saving for the period 1897–1949 as a whole.

6.22. Within normal periods the proportion of liquid (Class A) saving has declined from approximately one-fifth before 1915 to well under 10 percent in the twenties, but has recovered to 15 percent after World War II. The particularly low share of liquid saving during the twenties reflects both the slow increase in the total volume of circulating media and the predilection of savers for investment in corporate securities. This tendency is shown in the fact that the proportion of Class B saving is higher in 1922–1929 than in any other period. Apart from this bulge, and a downward dip during World War II, the share of Class B saving has shown a down-

---

[2] In the case of inventories and livestock the individual elements may turn over rapidly, but liquidation of the entire stock—which may be regarded as a revolving fund—is not anticipated by the saver and only occurs when his household or business comes to an end.

[3] Figures for all economic periods will be found in Table S-46.

153

CHART XXXII

DISTRIBUTION OF PERSONAL SAVING BY LIQUIDITY

Social Accounting Concept

Percent of Total
Personal Saving

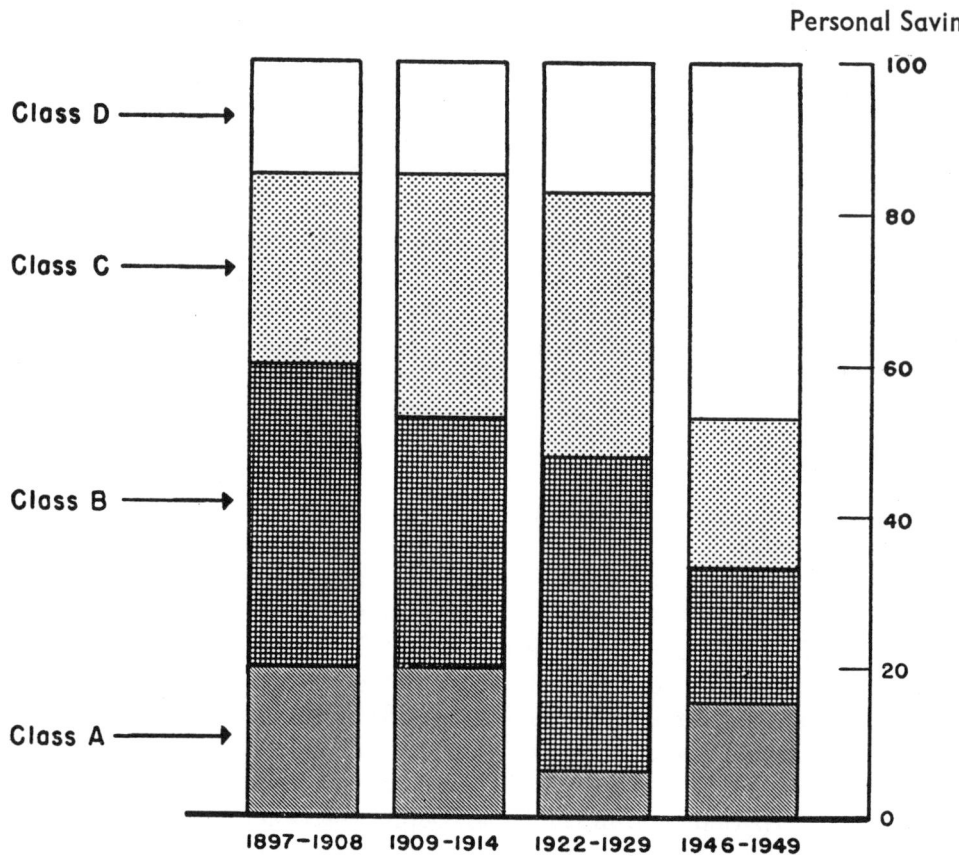

ward trend, falling from about 35 percent before 1915 to only about half as much in 1946–1949. The movements of the share of Class C saving, dominated by saving through real estate, have been erratic. No definite trend is visible for the period as a whole although the share is somewhat lower after World War II than before 1915. The dips, reflecting restrictions on construction during the two World Wars, however, are well marked. The illiquid forms of saving of Class D show the most spectacular movement, rising from about one-sixth of total personal saving before 1930, with a moderately upward trend within the period, to nearly one-half since 1933 with the exception only of World War II. This sharp rise is due chiefly to the increase in the the share of saving through consumer durables and through pension and retirement funds.

The main structural change in the distribution of personal saving over the last fifty years by degree of liquidity, ignoring the special effects of war, thus is

154

the sharp increase in the share of illiquid forms of saving, particularly since the thirties, which is accompanied by a decline in the share of saving in semiliquid forms (mostly corporate securities and real estate), while the share of liquid saving has not changed significantly.

c. *Direct and indirect saving*

6.23.   From the economic point of view possibly the most important classification of forms of saving is the distinction between (1) saving in the form of tangible assets which are used by the saver himself; (2) saving which is invested in tangible assets by the economic unit which receives the funds directly from the saver; and (3) saving which is transferred by the saver to a financial intermediary which, in turn, makes the funds available—after one or more additional steps—to the ultimate investor, i.e. the person who purchases, owns, or operates tangible durable assets. For easy identification, these three forms may be called saving for self-use, direct saving, and indirect saving. In the case of saving for self-use saver and investor are the same person. Examples are household saving in the form of residential real estate [4] and consumer durables, and saving by unincorporated business enterprises and agriculture in the form of nonresidential real estate, producer durables, and inventories. [5] In direct saving there is only one step between the saver and the investor, i.e. the funds flow directly from the individual saver to the investor without interposition of a financial intermediary. [6] Direct saving should exclude not only the purchase of securities the proceeds of which are not destined for investment in tangible durable assets (particularly the acquisition of securities of investment and holding companies, banks, and insurance companies) but also the cases where the proceeds are used to increase liquid assets or to retire debt. This adjustment has not been made here because it would require rather risky manipulation of the figures, and because it is not likely to make a substantial difference in the results, though, of course, it would reduce the share of direct saving and increase that of indirect saving, particularly in periods like the late twenties. Indirect saving includes currency, deposits in financial institutions, and life insurance and pension reserves.

6.24.   For the entire period 1897–1949 saving for self-use and direct saving have each accounted for approximately one-fourth, and indirect saving has repre-

---

[4] It may be recalled that ownership and operation of rental housing has been classified in this study as part of household rather than unincorporated business activities.

[5] There is a question whether cash, as well as some other intangible assets used by agriculture and unincorporated enterprises in their business activities, should not be classified as saving for self-use. This is for many purposes a defensible classification, but it has not been adopted here because it has been regarded as preferable to retain as the criterion the distance between saver and investor.

[6] Financial intermediaries include only organizations which raise a substantial part of their total funds from outside, in other words, institutions which administer "other people's money." The term, therefore, excludes investment and mortgage bankers, who, of course, play a role in bringing together savers and investors in such outstanding examples of direct saving as the purchase of new securities and the acquisition of new mortgage loans.

sented somewhat less than one-half, of total personal saving, disregarding for the time being the liabilities attaching to saving in certain forms. For normal periods alone the share of indirect saving, as shown in Chart XXXIII, is considerably lower—less than one-third—and that of saving for self-use and of direct saving higher. The difference is due partly to the particularly high share of saving through currency and bank deposits during wars and the Great Depression.

CHART XXXIII

DISTRIBUTION OF PERSONAL SAVING BY RELATION BETWEEN SAVER AND INVESTOR

Social Accounting Concept

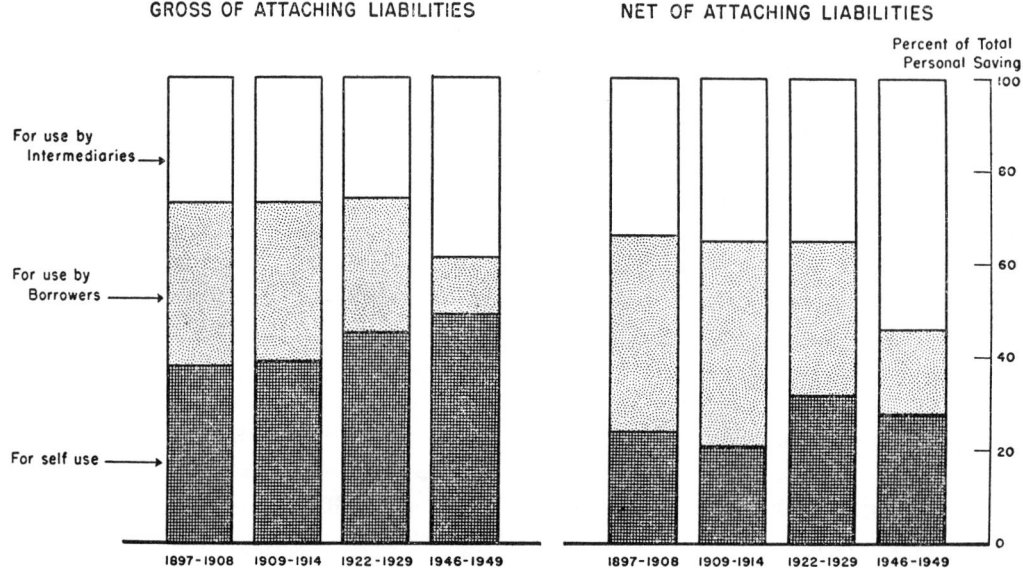

6.25. If allowance is made for attaching liabilities—and this is the less significant approach from the viewpoint of relating saving to investment although it is more in keeping with social accounting procedures—the shares of direct and indirect saving are somewhat increased and that of saving for self-use is sharply reduced. These changes, of course, reflect the fact that the ratio of dissaving in the form of increasing debt to saving in the form of acquisition of assets is much higher for personal saving through tangible assets, all of which are for self-use, than for saving through intangibles. On this basis indirect saving accounts for somewhat over one-half of aggregate personal saving for the full period, direct saving for about one-third, but saving for self-use for only about one-tenth.

6.26. Again disregarding attaching liabilities, within the normal periods the share of saving for self-use shows a slightly rising trend, visible in Chart XXXIII. The rise is from slightly less than 40 percent before 1915 to nearly 50 percent in 1946–1949. This is the result primarily of the increasing share of saving through consumer durables. If figures net of attaching liabilities are used, i.e.

156

if attention is limited to that part of the acquisition of assets (gross acquisition less depreciation allowances) which is financed by the savers themselves, then no trend is visible in the movements of the share of saving for self-use. The average is somewhat over one-fourth of total net personal saving. It is slightly higher after World War II than before 1915, but still a little below the share reached in the twenties.

6.27. The share of direct saving shows a definite trend downwards over the normal periods, both gross and net of attaching liabilities. In the first case the decline is from over one-third of net personal saving before 1915 to only about one-eighth in the period 1946–1949. In the second case, in which the level of the share of direct saving is higher, the decline is from over two-fifths to less than one-fifth.

6.28. No trend is visible up to 1930 in the share of indirect saving through intermediaries, which stays close to one-fourth of total personal saving disregarding liabilities, and to around one-third including them. It has been considerably higher since the midthirties. After World War II it has amounted to about two-fifths disregarding liabilities, and to over one-half allowing for them. Both shares are about one-and-a-half times as high as their pre-1930 level.

6.29. The structural changes in the distribution of personal saving by use thus consist mainly in (1) an increase in the share of indirect saving through intermediaries and in saving for self-use, the latter only if attaching liabilities are disregarded, and (2) a sharp decline, particularly after the thirties, in the share of direct saving, in which savers make funds directly available for investment in tangible assets, of which the purchase of securities and the acquisition of mortgages by individuals are outstanding examples. These structural changes in the distribution of personal saving have, of course, been of great importance in the development of the capital market over the last fifty years.

d. *Saving through claims and equities*

6.30. The distribution of personal saving between claims and equities has probably aroused more public interest in recent years than any other question concerned with the structure of saving. The distribution is fairly clear-cut statistically so long as no account is taken of undivided corporate profits, which may well be regarded as an element of, or at least a supplement to, individuals' saving in equity form, in particular individuals' saving through corporate stock.

6.31. For the period 1897–1949 as a whole approximately one-third of total personal saving took the form of equities and two-thirds that of claims, provided the liabilities attaching to certain forms of saving are disregarded. Of saving through claims two-fifths was in short-term form, and three-fifths in long-term form, the latter being accounted for mostly by net purchases of bonds and by increases in the equity in life insurance and pension contracts. The proportion of saving through claims was substantially higher during the two wars and the Great Depression. As a result personal saving was about equally divided between claims and equities for the normal periods.

157

6.32. Allowance for attaching liabilities makes a considerable difference for the distribution since practically all liabilities other than policy loans, some borrowing on securities, and tax accruals constitute offsets against equity forms of saving, particularly against saving through tangible assets. If the distribution is based on net saving the share of saving through equities is reduced to less than one-fourth for the period as a whole, and a little over two-fifths for the normal periods.

CHART XXXIV

SHARE OF EQUITIES AND CLAIMS IN PERSONAL SAVING
Social Accounting Concept

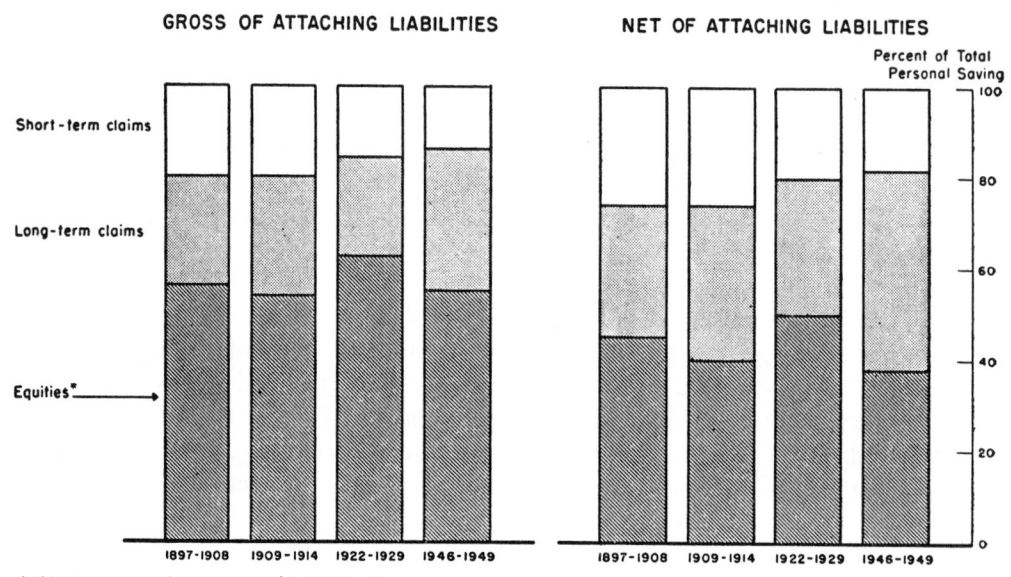

*Without allowance for stockholders' ownership of corporate undivided profits

Treatment of undistributed corporate profits as part of equity saving of individuals has the opposite effect. It restores the proportion of saving through equities to total personal saving (now, of course, including corporate saving) to about one-third for the period as a whole, and increases it to somewhat over one-half for the normal periods. The result for personal saving of including undistributed corporate profits is therefore the same as that of ignoring liabilities attaching to certain forms of saving, but this is a coincidence. If corporate undistributed saving is included, saving through corporate stock accounts for a much larger proportion (20 percent for the full period) than it does if both undivided corporate profits and attaching liabilities are disregarded (10 percent), and saving through real estate and consumer durables account for a correspondingly lower proportion.

6.33. Within normal periods the share of equity saving has been relatively

158

stable, as Chart XXXIV shows. Disregarding attaching liabilities it has amounted to about 55 percent both before 1915 and after World War II, and reached a peak of slightly over 60 percent in 1922–1929. If attaching liabilities are taken into account the level of the share of equity saving is lower, but its movements are similar. The highest proportion is still reached in the twenties. The share after World War II, however, is now a little below that for the period 1897–1914—38 percent against 43 percent.

The movements are less pronounced again if allowance is made for undivided corporate profits. In that case equity saving accounted for 55 percent of total personal and corporate saving before 1915, for nearly 60 percent in 1922–1929, and for slightly over 50 percent in 1946–1949. Thus, if there has been a secular downward trend in the share of total equity saving, which is far from proven, it has been of moderate proportions and it has been in evidence only since the thirties.

6.34. Although the aggregate share of all forms of equity saving in total personal saving has not varied much over the normal periods of the past fifty years, there have been considerable changes within equity saving. The relative importance of saving through consumer durables has increased, while that of saving through real estate has declined, and saving through corporate stock has held its own if undivided corporate profits are taken into account.

6.35. Considerable changes have also taken place as between saving through short-term claims (currency and deposits) and through long-term claims (bonds, mortgages, insurance and pension reserves). They have been in the direction of increasing the share of saving through long-term claims, not only as compared with that through short-term claims, but also in proportion to total personal saving. Up to 1915 personal saving through long-term claims was only slightly larger than that through short-term claims. In the twenties the share of saving through long-term claims already was about one-and-a-half times as large as that of saving through short-term claims. After World War II saving through long-term claims rose to well over twice the level of saving through short-term claims. At the same time the share of saving through long-term claims in total personal saving, after making allowance for attaching liabilities, increased from an average of slightly over one-fourth, from which it deviated only little in the normal periods before 1930, to over 40 percent after World War II.

e. *"Tied" saving*

6.36. No change among the forms of personal saving is more spectacular than the rise in the share of "tied" saving, i.e. the forms of saving which do not depend on a decision of the saver and those which once begun must be carried through to the termination of the contract, often over a period of several decades, unless part of the savers' contributions are to be lost.

Three types of tied saving may profitably be distinguished. The first is represented by voluntary contracts between individuals, on the one hand, and life insurance companies and similar institutions, on the other. The saver may termi-

159

nate these contracts at any time, although this usually entails some loss and termination certainly is not in accordance with the saver's original intentions. In effect, saving through such contracts may also be temporarily suspended by means of policy loans. The second type is exemplified by saving through insurance or retirement plans in which participation is not voluntary, but either is required by law, as is the case with contributions to the federal government's old age and retirement fund, or is a necessary part of the saver's employment, such as saving through private pension and retirement funds. Not only is the saver usually unable to withdraw his funds at will, but he sometimes even forfeits part of his own contributions and those made for his account by his employer unless he continues his contractual payments; he is also as a rule unable to borrow on his equity in the contract either from the insurer or from other lenders. The third type of contractual saving arises in connection with individuals' borrowing. In one sense repayment of any loan which entails the obligation to repay at a stipulated date can be regarded as tied saving. It seems more sensible, however, to limit this concept to the cases in which repayments are regular and predetermined, and renewal of the loan at maturity is either ruled out or not anticipated. The most important examples of tied saving through debt retirement are the repayments on amortizable urban residential mortgages and on installment debt. The second of these has been of importance since the twenties, but the first has essentially developed only from the thirties on. While the share of saving through insurance and pension contracts is usually determinable without much trouble, substantial statistical difficulties arise in the case of tied saving through debt retirement. The available material often provides information only on changes in debt outstanding, lacks separate figures on new loans made and repayments, and, a fortiori, does not give separate data for repayments under contracts. Rough estimates must therefore be utilized.

6.37. Starting with net saving through insurance and pension plans only and disregarding attaching liabilities, it is found that the share of tied saving in total personal saving has increased from 7 percent before 1915 to 11 percent in the twenties, and to approximately 25 percent after World War II. Allowing for attaching liabilities but still disregarding contractual debt repayment, the share of tied saving has risen from 8 percent before 1915 to 35 percent for the period 1946–1949.

Allowance for contractual repayment on mortgages would have only little influence on the figures before 1915. Even for the twenties it probably would only increase the share of tied saving to not much over 15 percent of total personal saving. For the period after World War II, however, inclusion of contractual mortgage repayment makes a considerable difference. It probably raises the share of tied saving in all forms (compulsory and contractual) to well over two-fifths of total personal saving. Inclusion of repayments on installment debt would further increase the shares of tied saving, but installment loans are disregarded here because of their short life.

6.38. The importance of this sharp increase in the share of tied saving is

160

twofold. From the saver's point of view it reduces freedom of action, particularly when income declines. The choice is then between reducing consumption by more than otherwise would be the case, or concentrating the entire cut in saving on the noncontractual forms, particularly liquid saving. From the point of view of the users of funds saved and the economy in general, a high proportion of tied saving provides, on the one hand, a stabilizing element as certain groups of financial intermediaries, particularly life insurance companies and pension and retirement funds, are able to count on a fairly stable inflow of funds and can plan their own placements accordingly. The regularity of the flow of savers' funds into certain financial institutions, however, creates the problem of finding relatively steady outlets for them, a problem which is made more difficult by the fact that most of the institutions which receive contractual saving are limited by law, custom, or policy to certain forms of investment. Discussion of this problem goes well beyond the scope of this Introduction.

f. *Saving of upper and lower income groups*

6.39.   One of the most serious gaps in our knowledge of the structural changes in the saving of households is the absence of information extending over long periods about the distribution of saving among saver groups of different income and wealth levels, different occupations, different ages, and other characteristics. This gap can be bridged by a study of time series for the different forms of saving only to the extent that it is permissible to associate certain forms of saving with certain groups of savers. The only grouping for which an attempt in this direction may be made is a very broad one by income and wealth—say, the upper tenth and the lower nine-tenths of the population. It is known, from cross-section studies of household budgets and balance sheets, and in some cases from other information, such as income and estate tax returns, that certain forms of saving and the holdings of certain forms of assets resulting from saving are predominantly attributable either to the upper or to the lower income and wealth groups. Among the forms of saving predominantly attributable to the upper income groups are corporate stocks and bonds, equity in unincorporated business enterprises, U.S. Government securities other than savings bonds, state and local government bonds, and probably also demand deposits in commercial banks and multi-family dwellings. On the other hand, it is fairly certain that other forms of saving—such as currency, time and savings deposits in banks, deposits in savings and loan associations and credit unions, equity in pension and retirement funds, consumer durables, and one- to four-family homes—are attributable mostly to the lower income groups, if only because some of these forms of saving and assets are fairly evenly distributed among the population and because it has been assumed here that the "lower" income groups include the bottom nine-tenths of the population. [7]

[7] Probably the most important single source of data are the balance sheets of a sample of households as of early 1950 collected by the Survey of Consumer Finances and discussed in Volume III, Part I. These data indicate that the top 10 percent of income receivers held approximately the following percentages of the main types of assets and liabilities:

6.40. In view of the severe limitations of the material we must be content to draw four rather general and tentative conclusions from this study of time series of individual forms of personal saving, and must resist the temptation to give them quantitative expression:

(1) The upper income groups have always accounted for a predominant share of total personal saving, particularly if undistributed earnings of corporations and unincorporated business enterprises are imputed to their owners.

(2) The time series point to a decline in the share of the upper income groups in saving, which not only characterizes the last two or three decades, but also seems to have been at work between the turn of the century and the twenties.

(3) This decline is due largely to an increase in the share of saving through consumer durables and through pension and retirement funds, most of which is attributable to the lower income groups, and part of which is involuntary.

(4) In the more restricted field of voluntary saving excluding consumer durables the share of upper income groups has held up better if allowance is made for their share in the undistributed profits of corporations and unincorporated business enterprises. Even here the share appears to have declined, but possibly not very much.

6.41. These findings are compatible with what other studies in this field have disclosed. All of them have shown, first, that the upper income groups account for most of total personal saving. The budget studies for 1888–1890 and 1901 yield, only with the help of a good deal of estimation it is true, a share for the upper income groups of three-fourths to three-fifths. [8] The Brookings Institution estimated that in 1929 the top tenth of income receivers were responsible for over 85 percent of total personal saving. [9] In 1935–1936 dissaving in the lowest income groups was still so large that the saving of the top tenth exceeded total net personal saving by 5 percent. [10] The Survey of Consumer Finances, finally,

Total assets 40	U.S. Government securities. 40
Total net worth 42	Life insurance reserves 40
Debt 25	Real estate other than homes 40
Homes 30	Demand deposits. 45
Automobiles 30	Equity in unincorporated business and
Farm real estate 30	closed corporations 75
Savings deposits 30	Corporate marketable stock 80

While it cannot be assumed that the share of the top tenth of income receivers in different forms of saving is the same as that in the corresponding asset holdings—beside other factors, changes in asset values, inheritances, and gifts prevent such an identification—the distribution of asset holdings by income groups should still provide an indication of the distribution of saving over longer periods.

[8] See Volume III, Part II, Appendix I, Table H–15. The 1917–1918 budget inquiry data indicate, if similarly treated, a share for the top tenth of income receivers of about one-half of total saving. The saving data of this inquiry, however, are subject to particularly strong reservations.

[9] *America's Capacity to Consume*, p. 95. The figure is increased, compared with the other estimates, by the inclusion of realized capital gains.

[10] National Resources Planning Board, *Family Expenditures in the United States*, p. 51.

162

found that in the years 1947 to 1950 slightly more than 80 percent of personal saving was attributable to the 10 percent of households with the highest incomes. [11] These studies, secondly, point to a decline in the share of the upper income groups, at least for the period since the twenties. [12]

[11] *Federal Reserve Bulletin*, 1951, p. 1,067.

[12] Kuznets, *Shares of Upper Income Groups in Income and Savings*, 1950, Section C, pp. 45ff. Since Kuznets' study provides comparable annual figures for 1919 to 1945 his series has been regarded as a better indicator of movements over time than a comparison of the scattered estimates cited in the text.

VII

CYCLICAL FLUCTUATIONS IN SAVING

1. Approach

7.01. As business cycles in the United States have typically lasted from three to four years, and some have been as short as two years, series of annual data such as the estimates of saving on which this study is based are obviously not well suited for an analysis of cyclical fluctuations. For that purpose quarterly or preferably monthly data are called for. Such data, unfortunately, do not exist for the period before 1939, and even those which are available for the last decade are as a rule considerably less detailed than the annual estimates of this study, and in many cases are not comparable with them. [1]

7.02. If this Introduction nevertheless subjects the annual estimates of saving to cyclical analysis along the methods developed by the National Bureau of Economic Research, it is done for two reasons. First, annual data permit us to compare, although only in a rough way, the patterns of cyclical fluctuations in saving and general business; they thus enable us to form a judgment on whether the cyclical fluctuations in saving are essentially similar to those in other basic economic series. Secondly, such a comparison may be regarded as a test of the short-term movements of the estimates. Theoretical considerations, as well as the data on capital formation, definitely lead us to expect similarity in the cyclical movements of saving and of business in general, although they indicate that fluctuations in saving or capital formation will be wider than those in basic series like national income or industrial production. [2] If such similarity failed to show up in the Saving Study estimates we should either find an explanation for systematic deviations if they existed or suspect the value of the estimates as indicators of year-to-year movements of saving.

7.03. This discussion of cyclical fluctuations of saving will be limited to a few simple questions, primarily because the annual data are such a rough tool of cyclical analysis. The first is the extent to which the turning points in saving coincide with, or differ from, the turning points in the "reference cycles" of general business conditions as determined by the National Bureau of Economic Research. [3] The second is the similarity, or dissimilarity, of cyclical behavior

[1] See quarterly releases (Statistical Bulletin) of the Securities and Exchange Commission on personal liquid saving; and quarterly estimates of aggregate personal saving from the income account in U.S. Department of Commerce, Survey of Current Business, National Income Supplement, 1951 ed., pp. 208–209.

[2] For data on cyclical characteristics of capital formation and other basic economic series see Mitchell, What Happens during Business Cycles, 1951, Tables 15, 16, and 42.

[3] Burns and Mitchell, Measuring Business Cycles, 1946, p. 78.

164

among saving series. The third is the amplitude of cycles, i.e. the extent of upswing or downswing in relation to the average level of the cycle, again comparing series of aggregate saving and its components among themselves and with other basic economic series. All comparisons will be made for aggregate national and personal saving estimated according to variant concepts of saving, for estimates of saving of the main saver groups (standard social accounting concept), and for estimates of the main components of personal saving.

2. SUMMARY OF FINDINGS

7.04. There is a reasonably close similarity over the past half century in the timing of turning points and in the duration of upward and downward movements between national and personal saving and the chronology of business cycles. However, conformity is considerably lower than for comprehensive series like national income, industrial production, bank debits, or prices.

7.05. No significant differences in turning points exist between estimates of saving of different scope and method such as estimates including and excluding saving through consumer durables, estimates according to the social accounting, business accounting, or cash flow concepts, and estimates in current or deflated values.

7.06. No definite change has occurred in the degree of conformity of saving to the reference chronology during the past fifty years. There is some indication, however, that conformity has been somewhat better since 1929.

7.07. Cyclical turning points in saving as a rule match reference cycle turns considerably better at troughs than at peaks.

7.08. While no systematic difference in timing between turning points in saving and business cycles is observable at troughs, there is a tendency at peaks for saving to change its direction, i.e. to decline, a little ahead of the turn in general business activity.

7.09. A considerable proportion of the cases in which turning points in saving and in the reference cycle do not fall in the same calendar year occur during wars or immediately after them.

7.10. Cyclical behavior of saving of most saver groups is more irregular than that of the national total. Among the main groups, nonfarm households and corporations conform at least as well to business cycle chronology as aggregate national saving. Conformity is much less pronounced or practically absent for the saving of agriculture, unincorporated business enterprises, and governments.

7.11. The main components of personal saving show, as a rule, considerably less conformity to business cycle chronology than does aggregate personal saving. Conformity is particularly low for saving through savings and loan associations, state and local government securities, and nonresidential urban real estate. It is in general higher for saving through tangible, than for saving through intangible, assets.

7.12. The amplitude of cyclical movements in saving is very great and

165

exceeds that of practically all other basic economic magnitudes. It was considerably narrower before 1930 than afterwards; considerably wider for the saving of agriculture, unincorporated business, and the federal government than for that of nonagricultural households, corporations, and state and local governments; and considerably higher for most forms of personal saving, particularly for saving through liquid assets, than for the aggregate.

7.13. Annual variability of saving is high for national aggregates, group totals, and individual forms of saving. A year's national saving, for instance, is in more than one-half of the cases 50 percent higher or lower than that of the preceding or the following year. Variability was considerably higher for the period 1930–1945 than for the preceding three decades, but returned to its lower level after World War II.

3. THE CYCLICAL BEHAVIOR OF NATIONAL AND PERSONAL SAVING

a. *Turning points in national saving*

7.14. From 1897 to 1949 the reference cycle chronology of the National Bureau of Economic Research recognizes twenty-five cyclical turning points in business conditions. All twenty-five peaks and troughs—and no other turning points—appear in the annual estimates of national saving, irrespective of the

CHART XXXV

TURNING POINTS IN NATIONAL AND PERSONAL SAVING (STANDARD SOCIAL ACCOUNTING CONCEPT) AND IN REFERENCE CYCLES OF NATIONAL BUREAU OF ECONOMIC RESEARCH

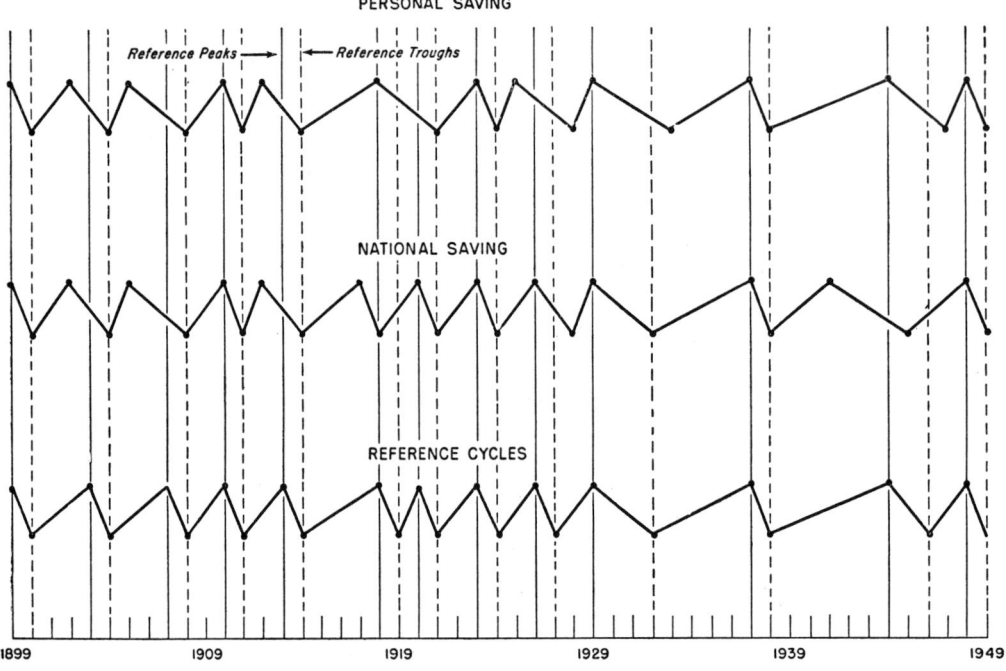

TABLE XXIII

TURNING POINTS IN NATIONAL AND PERSONAL SAVING DIFFERING IN TIMING FROM REFERENCE DATES OF NATIONAL BUREAU OF ECONOMIC RESEARCH
1897 to 1949

	National Bureau reference dates		Saving [a]	Lead (—) or lag (+) of saving (years)	
	Annual	Monthly	Annual	Based on	
				Annual dates	Monthly dates [b]
I. National saving					
Peak	1903	Sept. 1902	1902	−1	−0.3
Peak	1907	May 1907	1905	−2	−1.9
Peak	1913	Jan. 1913	1912	−1	−0.6
Peak	1918	Aug. 1918	1917	−1	−1.2
Trough	1919	Apr. 1919	1918	−1	−0.8
Trough	1927	Nov. 1927	1928	+1	+0.7
Peak	1944	Feb. 1945	1941	−3	−3.7
Trough	1946	Oct. 1945	1945	−1	−0.3
II. Personal saving					
Peak	1903	Sept. 1902	1902	−1	−0.3
Peak	1907	May 1907	1905	−2	−1.9
Peak	1913	Jan. 1913	1912	−1	−0.6
Trough	1919	Apr. 1919	} missed	–	–
Peak	1920	Jan. 1920		–	–
Peak	1926	Oct. 1926	1925	−1	−1.3
Trough	1927	Nov. 1927	1928	+1	+0.7
Trough	1932	May 1933	1933	+1	+0.3
Trough	1946	Oct. 1945	1947	+1	+1.8

[a] Standard social accounting concept. From Table T-1, cols. 1 and 2.
[b] Locating all turning points in saving at midyear.

concept adopted, although the year in which some of the turning points occur is not always the same as the National Bureau's dating. If the standard social accounting concept is used seventeen of the twenty-five turning points in saving fall in the same year as in the reference chronology of the National Bureau. The eight turning points which differ in dating are identified in Chart xxxv and in Table XXIII.

7.15. Study of Table XXIV and of Appendix Tables Z-11 to Z-18, which present measures of (1) the degree of conformity between the timing in reference cycles and the cycles in saving, (2) the average duration of upswings and downswings, and (3) the average lead and lag at cyclical peaks and troughs, leads to the conclusions summarized in Divisions 7.16 to 7.23.

7.16. Four of the eight cases in which the turning points in saving and the reference chronology differ occur during war years or immediately after them (1919 and 1946). In such periods national saving does not correspond well to the level of economic activity because the deficit of the federal government, while contributing to employment and income, tends to offset the saving of all other groups even though the latter may be much higher both relatively and absolutely than in the years preceding and following.

TABLE XXIV
CONFORMITY INDICES OF NATIONAL AND PERSONAL SAVING
1897 to 1949

	Contraction	Expansion	Full cycle
I. National saving, current			
1. Social accounting concept			
a. Standard	50	50	52
b. Broad	50	67	56
c. Excluding consumer durables	50	50	39
2. Business accounting concept	50	33	48
3. Cash flow concept	67	67	83
II. National saving,[a] deflated			
1. Aggregate	50	50	43
2. Per head	50	50	48
III. Personal saving,[a] current			
1. Social accounting concept			
a. Standard	100	83	87
b. Broad	100	83	87
c. Excluding consumer durables	50	83	55
2. Business accounting concept	67	67	56
3. Cash flow concept	67	83	66
IV. Personal saving,[a] deflated			
1. Aggregate	67	67	72
2. Per head	75	67	72

[a] Social accounting concept.

Source: Same as for Table S-1 to S-4. For method of calculation of conformity indices see Burns and Mitchell, *Measuring Business Cycles*, pp. 179–182.

7.17. Of the eleven peacetime peaks in saving eight coincide with the reference chronology and the remaining three lead the corresponding peaks in business activity. All three leads occur before World War I. From 1920 on all peacetime peaks in reference cycles are reflected by a simultaneous peak in national saving.

7.18. All but one of the ten peacetime troughs in business activity are reflected in a simultaneous trough in national saving. The only difference is a one-year lag of saving behind the 1927 reference trough.

7.19. The average lead of saving is slightly over one year for the cases in which any difference exists, irrespective of whether the comparison is made between annual datings for both the reference chronology and saving, or whether the monthly date of the reference chronology is compared with saving on the assumption that its turning points are located uniformly at midyear.[4]

If all the turning points are averaged—not just those at which the timing of saving and the reference chronology differs—the net lead or lag at troughs is negligible. At peaks, however, an average lead of a little over half a year is shown which is the result of an average lead of somewhat over one year at approximately one turning point out of three.

7.20. There are only two instances in which the turning points in saving

[4] On this technique see *ibid.*, pp. 228–229.

and in the reference chronology differ by more than one year. Both are cases of cyclical peaks in the saving series, 1905 and 1941, and in both cases the peak in saving occurs ahead of that in the reference chronology. The three-year difference between the 1941 peak in saving and the 1944 peak in the reference pattern can easily be explained as reflecting the special circumstances of World War II which kept the level of national saving—though not that of personal saving—below the high of 1941 by means of the large dissaving of the federal government. No similarly simple explanation is available for the two-year lead of the 1905 peak in saving. It may be worth noticing, however, that the estimate of national saving for 1905 is so little above that for 1906 that a slight revision of the figures might shift the peak in saving to within one year of that of the reference cycle peak (May 1907).

7.21. Considering the nature and precision of the available data the evidence does not seem sufficient to assert the existence of a typical lead in the turning points of saving over those of the reference chronology. This statement might have to be modified if monthly or quarterly estimates of saving were available. Even if such data should show a reasonably regular lead in saving, particularly at peaks—and it is difficult to imagine that the monthly or quarterly data would differ sufficiently from the annual ones to result in a regular lag, particularly at troughs—such a lead would probably be short.

7.22. The average cycle in saving has lasted just over four years irrespective of the estimate of saving used. On the average, expansions have endured for about $2\frac{1}{4}$ years and contractions for $1\frac{3}{4}$ years. The longer duration of the average expansion is, of course, not peculiar to saving, but reflects a similar difference in the reference cycles.

7.23. Table XXIV indicates that as a rule the standard social accounting concept of saving shows the closest conformity to the reference cycle chronology. It hardly matters in this respect whether current aggregate values of saving are used or whether the figures are adjusted for changes in the price or wage level or for changes in the population, the number of households, or the number of consumer units. The differences between estimates following the social accounting concept, the business accounting concept, or the cash flow concept, while visible in the figures, are not very large and possibly not of significance.[5]

b. *Turning points in personal saving*

7.24. The cyclical behavior of personal saving is essentially similar to that of aggregate national saving, but there are a few significant differences which are visible in Chart XXXV. Of these the failure of personal saving to reflect one short cycle—that of 1919–1920—is possibly the most important. It is the result of the sharp and continuous decline of personal saving from a peak of almost $13 billion in 1918 to a trough of not much over $1 billion in 1921 without an intermediate

[5] The turning points in business accounting and cash flow saving differ in twelve and eleven cases respectively from the annual dating in the reference chronology, compared to eight cases when the social accounting concept is used. (For conformity indices see Table XXIV.)

peak in 1920 or even an interruption in the speed of the downward movement. Secondly, the seven turning points which differ in dating from the reference chronology are about evenly divided between peaks and troughs. Thirdly, only one of the seven instances of difference in timing occurs during war.

7.25. Six of the nine cases in which the annual dating of turning points of personal saving differs from that of the reference chronology (including the two missed turning points) are identical with those found in the case of national saving, as will be seen in Table XXIII. Discrepancies not encountered in national saving appear in the cases of the peak of 1925 and the trough of 1933, although the latter difference is reduced if the monthly dating of the National Bureau is used. On the other hand, the peaks of 1918 and 1944 coincide with those of the reference chronology in personal saving, while they are located in aggregate national saving in 1917 and 1941 respectively. In both national and personal saving the trough of 1946 is shifted, in the former case to 1945 and in the latter to 1947.

7.26. Cases in which turning points in personal saving lead reference turning points are hardly more numerous than those in which they lag, and the average lead or lag for all turning points is insignificant.

7.27. The conformity indices of personal saving are generally higher than those for national saving (Table XXIV), indicating that the correspondence in timing between saving and business cycles is a little closer for personal than for national saving.

7.28. Exclusion of saving through consumer durables leads to shifts in three turning points, generally by one year each. In two of these, the reference troughs of 1908 and 1914, saving including consumer durables coincides with the reference pattern while saving excluding consumer durables leads by one year. In the third case, the reference peak of 1926, the turning point leads by one year if consumer durables are included and lags by two years if they are excluded.

7.29. The turning points in personal business accounting and cash saving differ from those in social accounting saving in six instances, but two of them are not common to the two comparisons. Since the numbers of cases in which business accounting or cash saving is closer to the turning point in the reference chronology, is farther away from it, or is equally close to it are about the same, there is no clear evidence that any of the three concepts conforms more closely to cycles in general business than do the others. The conformity indices, however, indicate a definite advantage of the standard social accounting concept over either the narrower concept excluding consumer durables or the business and cash accounting concepts.

c. *Behavior at more or less pronounced turning points of national and personal saving*

7.30. So far each turning point has been given the same weight. This is justified if what is sought is the typical relationship between general business reference cycles and particular cycles (i.e. cycles in saving) at turning points. Additional insight may, however, be gained by disregarding minor turning points and concentrating on the more important ones. Classification of turning points in the

170

reference chronology by degree of importance is, of course, difficult and can never be accomplished unequivocally. Consideration of the major phases in American economic history during the last fifty years and of the amplitude of cyclical fluctuations suggest separate treatment of the reference troughs of 1908, 1921, 1932, and 1938 and of the peaks of 1907, 1920, 1929, and 1937 as "very pronounced" turning points,[6] leaving the remaining seventeen reference turning points under the label of "less pronounced."

7.31. It is then found that correspondence is considerably better for the very pronounced than for the less pronounced turning points. This is apparent in the behavior of the ratio of turning points in saving which occur simultaneously, on annual reckoning, with those in reference cycles. Of the eight very pronounced reference turning points seven, or 88 percent, are reflected in simultaneous turning points in national saving compared with a ratio of only 59 percent for the less pronounced turning points. The difference, however, almost disappears for personal saving. Here the ratio of simultaneous turning points is 75 percent for very pronounced and 67 percent for less pronounced reference turning points.[7]

These results are hardly unexpected. The chance of a reference turning point's being reflected simultaneously in a turning point in saving should be greater for high and steep peaks or deep and precipitous troughs in the reference pattern than for those of more moderate elevation or depth or softer contour. The stronger the basic forces that form, or deform, the reference chronology the more likely it is that their influence will be felt in saving without substantial anticipation or delay.

d. *Turning points in saving-income ratios*

7.32. The comparisons of turning points in the reference chronology and in saving presented so far are open to at least one objection, viz. that the saving series used are not adjusted for trend and for changes in prices and population. This objection can be met by basing the comparisons on turning points in saving-income ratios rather than on those in aggregate current saving.

It then appears that the number of turning points occurring in the same year in the saving series and in the reference chronology declines slightly (Table XXV). The direction of the differences between current saving and the saving-income ratios is exactly that which would be expected from adjustment of a series for an upward trend. It is likely that some peaks will be shifted backwards and some troughs shifted forwards when the series is adjusted for trend—and division by the appropriate income series is equivalent in this respect to a trend adjustment.

The conclusions based on the dating of the turning points in current aggregate saving and their comparison with the reference chronology thus slightly overstate the degree of conformity if it is to be measured on the basis of trend-adjusted

[6] See Burns and Mitchell, *op. cit.*, p. 455, and Hansen, *Business Cycles and National Income*, 1951, p. 24.

[7] Locating the reference trough at the end of the Great Depression in 1933 (rather equal than equal 1932) on the basis of the monthly rather than the annual chronology.

171

figures. However, the shifts introduced by the substitution of saving-income ratios for the unadjusted figures of current aggregate saving do not seem to be sufficiently large to call for modification of the main findings derived from a study of the turning points in current aggregate saving.

4. THE CYCLICAL BEHAVIOR OF THE SAVING OF MAIN SAVER GROUPS

7.33. If total national and personal saving show pronounced similarity to the cyclical reference chronology we are likely to find it also for at least the quantitatively most important saver groups. As a matter of fact, the saving of one group—corporations—conforms better to the reference chronology than the aggregate. The correspondence is worse for four groups—agriculture, unincorporated business, state and local governments, and the federal government. For the sixth group, nonfarm households, it is about the same, as would be expected since nonfarm households account for over one-half of total national saving. The correspondence is so poor for some of these groups that hardly any systematic positive association can be claimed between the ups and downs in their saving and the general business cycle. For these groups calculation of average leads and lags and similar measures is therefore unlikely to produce significant results, although the figures are shown in the tables for the sake of completeness. No group has been found to show a definite countercyclical pattern, i.e. a pattern the saving of which increases during reference contractions and declines during reference expansions, although such a pattern cannot be ruled out in the case of saving by state and local governments.

7.34. Among all the twenty-five turning points in the reference cycle chronology from 1897 to 1949 there is not a single one in which the saving of all six groups shows a turning point in the same year in which the peak or the trough in the reference chronology occurs (Appendix Table Z-14). The highest degree of conformity is reached in 1929, when five groups—all except the usually erratic state and local governments—reach a peak in their saving curves. There are another six years in which the saving of four groups shows a turning point simultaneously with the reference pattern—the peaks of 1920 and 1937, and the troughs of 1904, 1908, 1921, and 1938. There are thus only two reference cycles the peak and the trough of which are reflected in the saving of four or more saver groups, viz. the cycles of 1920–1921 and of 1937–1938 both "very pronounced" cycles in which the accumulation and liquidation of inventories played a particularly important role. To determine whether this characteristic of the cycle has anything to do with the relatively high degree of conformity of group saving, particularly the saving of the three business groups, would require more intensive investigation and probably would call for more detailed data on saving, particularly on a quarterly basis, than are now available.

7.35. The saving of nonagricultural households shows cyclical characteristics essentially similar to those of personal saving. This may well be expected since nonagricultural households account in most years for well over three-fourths of total personal saving.

172

TABLE XXV

COMPARISON OF TURNING POINTS IN SAVING OF MAIN SAVER GROUPS AND IN REFERENCE CYCLE CHRONOLOGY

Current Aggregates and Saving-Income Ratios
Standard Social Accounting Concept: 1897 to 1949

Number of Turning Points

	Simultaneous		Leading		Lagging		Missing		Additional [a]	
	I	II	I	II	I	II	I	II	I	II
1. National	17	15	7	8	1	2	0	0	0	0
2. Nonfederal	18	14	3	6	2	3	2	2	0	0
3. Personal	16	11	4	10	3	4	2	0	0	0
4. Nonfarm households	15	11	6	8	2	3	2	3	2	2
5. Agriculture	9	6	7	10	7	5	2	4	6	6
6. Unincorporated business	11	11	9	8	4	4	1	2	8	6
7. Corporations	18	13	2	4	4	5	1	3	2	4
8. State and local governments	5	5	13	15	6	3	1	2	6	10
9. Federal government	12	11	9	9	3	4	1	1	4	6

I = Aggregate current saving.   II = Saving-income ratios.

[a] The additional turning points not found in the reference cycle chronology are as follows:

	Aggregate current saving		Saving-income ratio	
	Peak	Trough	Peak	Trough
Nonfarm households	1927	1926	1927	1926
Agriculture	1912, 1932, 1935	1911, 1930, 1936	1914, 1932, 1937	1913, 1930, 1938
Unincorporated business	1924, 1936, 1940 1944	1925, 1935, 1941 1943	1924, 1936, 1940	1925, 1935, 1941
Corporations	1935	1936	1932, 1940	1931, 1941
State and local governments	1907, 1934, 1940	1906, 1935, 1941	1900, 1907, 1936 1938, 1940	1901, 1906, 1935 1937, 1941
Federal government	1933, 1935	1931, 1934	1932, 1934, 1939	1933, 1935, 1940

Basic data given in Table T-1.

TABLE XXVI

CONFORMITY INDICES OF SAVING OF MAIN SAVER GROUPS

Standard Social Accounting Concept: 1897 to 1949

	Contraction	Expansion	Full cycle
1. Nonfarm households	67	83	66
2. Agriculture	−17	17	−14
3. Unincorporated business	33	17	30
4. Corporations	50	67	56
5. State governments	−33	17	−13
6. Local governments	0	50	31
7. Federal government	33	33	48

Basic data given in Table T-1.

173

CHART XXXVI

TURNING POINTS IN SAVING OF MAIN SAVER GROUPS (STANDARD SOCIAL ACCOUNTING CONCEPT) AND IN REFERENCE CYCLES OF NATIONAL BUREAU OF ECONOMIC RESEARCH

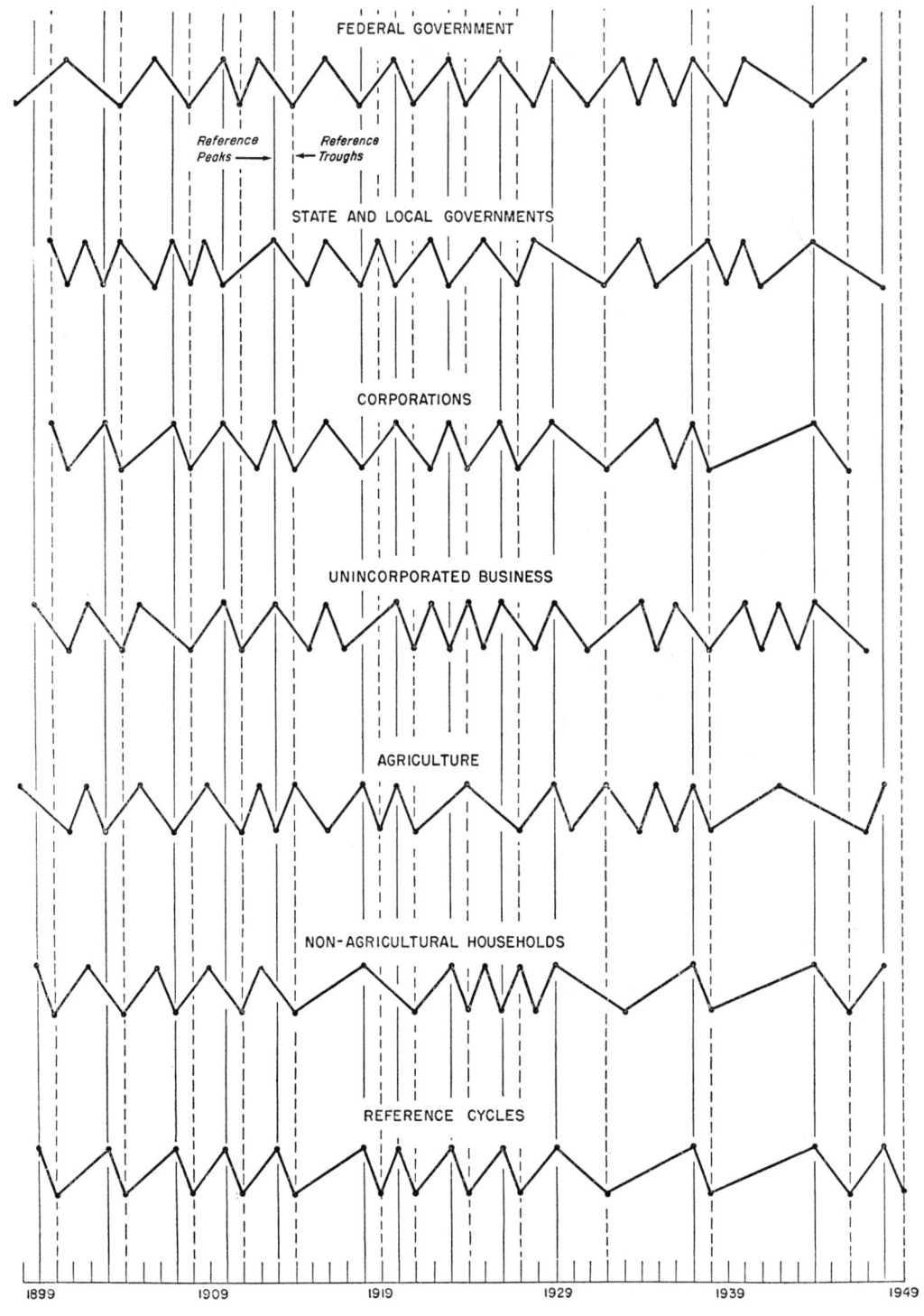

7.36. The cyclical behavior of agricultural saving is rather erratic. Only nine of the twenty-five turning points of the reference pattern are reflected in a peak or trough in the saving of agriculture located in the same year. Moreover, agricultural saving shows six additional turning points not found in the reference chronology. Up to 1910 agricultural saving regularly leads the cyclical reference turns by at least one year except at the trough of 1900. From 1910 on, however, the turning points in agricultural saving are simultaneous, on calendar-year reckoning, with those in the reference chronology in nine of the eighteen cases. Two turning points are missed entirely, 1924 and 1926. In six cases agricultural saving lags by one or even two years, but there is only one case (1944) in which agricultural saving leads. Much more detailed research is necessary before we can venture a guess as to whether this apparent change in relationship is real and of significance.

7.37. The same picture of erratic cyclical behavior is presented by the saving of unincorporated business enterprises, and here any explanation is further complicated by the very rough nature of the estimates which may have smoothed cyclical fluctuations in some components of saving and exaggerated them in others. We cannot, therefore, deny the possibility that the poor quality of the figures hides an actually existing substantial degree of conformity to the reference pattern of business cycles. As the figures stand, however, saving of unincorporated business reflects slightly less than one-half of all reference turning points in the same year, but shows eight additional turning points not found in the reference chronology. This is obviously no basis for claiming any systematic relationship to business cycles.

7.38. Corporate saving shows the highest conformity to the reference cycles of any group with the exception of nonfarm households. Only one of the twenty-five points is missed, the peak of 1948, and here even a small revision of the present preliminary estimate might restore the correspondence. Of the remaining twenty-four reference turning points eighteen are reflected simultaneously in corporate saving and only two turning points are found which do not appear in the reference chronology (1935 and 1936). The degree of conformity seems to have increased slightly over the period, all differences in timing occurring before 1923. From 1897 to 1921 only eight of the fourteen reference turning points were reflected in simultaneous turning points in corporate saving. From 1922 to 1949 only one of the eleven reference turning points (the peak of 1948) failed to be so reflected. These relationships may point to a closer adaptation of corporate saving to the business cycle pattern since the twenties. Unfortunately, however, the possibility cannot be ruled out that the apparent change in behavior is due to an improvement in the statistics, particularly to the availability of the comprehensive figures of the Bureau of Internal Revenue for the later period.

7.39. State and local governments show the least conformity to the reference chronology, and the situation is even worse if state governments and local governments are treated separately. Indeed, it is difficult to find a systematic relation for the period as a whole, or large parts of it, between the estimates of saving of state and local governments and business cycles.

7.40. In view of the large dissaving during war years one would expect little correspondence between the saving or dissaving of the federal government, on the one hand, and the reference cycle chronology, on the other. On the basis of the approach taken here, in which each year has the same weight, the correspondence actually turns out to be reasonably good, probably because federal revenue, though not expenditures, conforms fairly well to the cycle chronology. Only one of the twenty-five turning points (1899) fails to be reflected in the federal government's saving, and twelve of the remaining twenty-four turning points occur in the same year as in the reference pattern. However, the federal government's saving shows four additional turning points not found in the reference chronology. Of the twelve cases in which the turning points occur in different years, the federal government's saving leads in nine and lags in three. Some of the differences are very pronounced. The 1944 reference peak is anticipated in federal saving as far back as 1940, while the 1944 trough in federal saving formally corresponds to the 1946 reference trough.

7.41. Use of saving-income ratios instead of current aggregate saving as the basis of measuring the conformity of a group's saving to the cyclical reference turning points results, as in the case of total national or personal saving, in a slight reduction of the proportion of turns occurring simultaneously, on annual reckoning, in saving and in the reference pattern.

5. The Cyclical Behavior of the Main Forms of Personal Saving

7.42. Of the fifteen main forms of personal saving three (deposits with savings and loan associations; saving through state and local government securities; net saving through nonfarm nonresidential real estate) show so little correspondence to the reference, or any other, cycles that they are better regarded as not exhibiting cyclical characteristics. The degree of correspondence for the other series, however, also leaves much to be desired. (For basic data see Appendix Table Z-18.)

7.43. The remaining twelve forms of personal saving reflect most of the turning points in reference cycles. On the average they miss about one cycle, or two turning points; but some fail to reflect as many as eight of the twenty-five turning points in the reference pattern. Moreover, all but four show additional turning points not found in the reference chronology—three on the average, and in some cases as many as six—which can be identified in Chart XXXVII for the more important series.[8]

7.44. The turning points missed by the individual series are by no means common to all or even most of them as evidenced by the fact that no turning point in the reference pattern is missed by more than one-third of the components of personal saving. Indeed, twelve of the twenty-five turning points (1903, 1904, 1907, 1908, 1910, 1911, 1913, 1914, 1918, 1919, 1932, and 1944) are reflected in all twelve series. This high degree of conformity is limited, with but two exceptions, to turning points in the first half of the period.

[8] Mortgage holdings, inventories, producer durables, and consumer durables show no additional turning points.

CHART XXXVII

TURNING POINTS IN MAIN COMPONENTS OF PERSONAL SAVING (SOCIAL ACCOUNTING CONCEPT) AND IN REFERENCE CYCLES OF NATIONAL BUREAU OF ECONOMIC RESEARCH

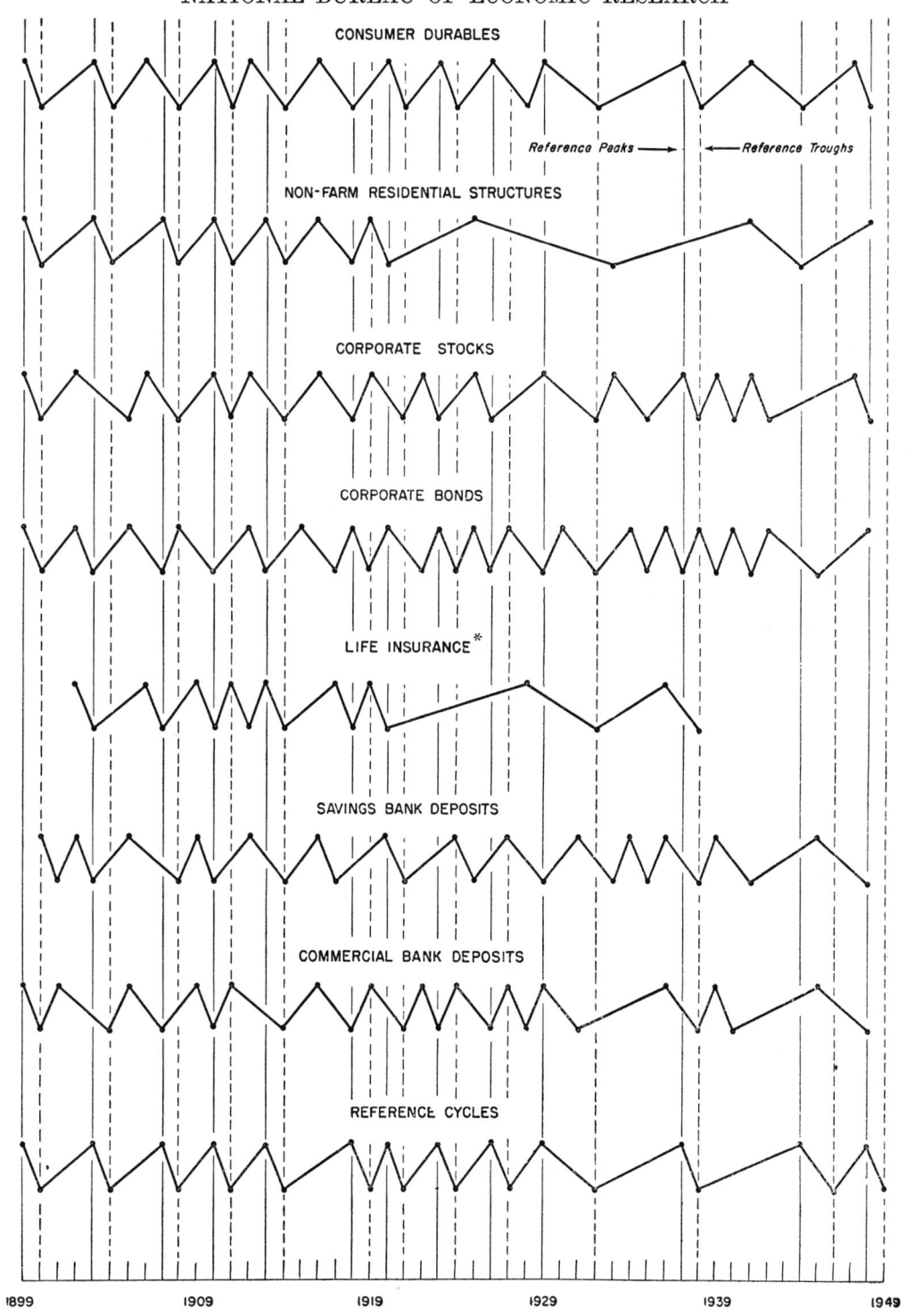

TABLE XXVII

(Part 1)

COMPARISON OF TURNING POINTS IN MAIN COMPONENTS OF PERSONAL
SAVING AND IN REFERENCE CYCLE CHRONOLOGY

1897 to 1949

	Number of turning points				
	Missed	Simulta-neous	Leading	Lagging	Additional
I. Behavior at all turning points					
1. Twelve series; all turning points (twenty-five reference turning points)	25	117	118	40	34
2. Twelve series; excluding war turning points (twenty-one) [a]	22	109	85	36	32
II. Behavior at peaks and troughs					
1. Twelve series, peaks (thirteen)	13	52	78	13	17
2. Twelve series, nonwar peaks (eleven)	13	49	60	10	16
3. Twelve series, troughs (twelve)	12	65	40	27	17
4. Twelve series, nonwar troughs (ten)	9	60	25	26	16
III. Saving through tangible and intangible assets					
1. Eight series of saving through intangible assets (twenty-five)	17	62	86	35	32
2. Four series of saving through tangible assets (twenty-five)	8	55	32	5	2
3. Four series of expenditures on tangible assets (twenty-five)	30	52	15	3	8
IV. Changes over time (twelve series)					
1. 1899 to 1914 (ten)	5	53	54	8	7
2. 1918 to 1929 (nine)	12	39	36	21	7
3. 1932 to 1948 (six)	8	25	28	11	20
4. 1918 to 1929 (seven) } Excluding war [a]	12	34	18	20	12
5. 1932 to 1948 (four) }	5	22	13	8	20

[a] Excluding turning points of 1918, 1919, 1944, and 1946.

Basic data given in Table T-6.

7.45. Only a little over two-fifths of all turning points in the twelve forms of personal saving occur in the same calendar year as those in the reference chronology.[9] Another two-fifths lead the reference chronology, generally by one year. The instances in which the turning points in components of personal saving lag behind those in the reference pattern are rather rare, occurring in only about one of five cases. The predominance of leading over lagging turning points confirms the slight average lead, compared to the reference pattern, observed in total personal saving.[10]

[9] Here, as throughout this section, turning points missed are excluded from the denominator.
[10] Any statement about differences of timing in turning points of personal saving, particularly in individual series, must be severely qualified because of the irregular nature of most of the series. Indeed, under the National Bureau's practice of limiting timing comparisons to series with a full

TABLE XXVII

(Part 2)

COMPARISON OF TURNING POINTS IN MAIN COMPONENTS OF PERSONAL SAVING AND IN REFERENCE CYCLE CHRONOLOGY

1897 to 1949

	Percentage of turning points [b]				
	Missed	Simultaneous	Leading	Lagging	Additional
I. Behaviour at all turning points					
1. Twelve series; all turning points (twenty-five reference turning points)	9	39	39	13	11
2. Twelve series; excluding war turning points (twenty-one) [a]	9	43	34	14	13
II. Behavior at peaks and troughs					
1. Twelve series, peaks (thirteen)	8	33	50	8	11
2. Twelve series, nonwar peaks (eleven)	10	37	45	8	12
3. Twelve series, troughs (twelve)	8	45	28	19	12
4. Twelve series, nonwar troughs (ten)	7	50	21	22	13
III. Saving through tangible and intangible assets					
1. Eight series of saving through intangible assets (twenty-five)	8	31	43	18	16
2. Four series of saving through tangible assets (twenty-five)	8	55	32	5	2
3. Four series of expenditures on tangible assets (twenty-five)	30	52	15	3	8
IV. Changes over time (twelve series)					
1. 1899 to 1914 (ten)	4	44	45	7	6
2. 1918 to 1929 (nine)	11	36	33	20	6
3. 1932 to 1948 (six)	11	35	39	15	28
4. 1918 to 1929 (seven) } Excluding war [a]	14	40	22	24	14
5. 1932 to 1948 (four) }	10	46	27	17	42

[a] Excluding turning points of 1918, 1919, 1944, and 1946.

[b] Number of additional turning points not included in the denominator.

7.46. Conformity is considerably more pronounced at troughs than at peaks. For the twelve series the share of simultaneous turning points is 33 percent for peaks, but 44 percent for troughs. Moreover, the nonconforming cases are about equally divided between leads and lags at troughs, while at peaks the leads predominate over the lags in the ratio of more than three to one.

7.47. The degree of conformity between turning points in components of personal saving and in the reference chronology has declined over time if the war turning points are included in the calculation, but has hardly changed if they are

conformity index of 50 or more, only two or three forms would qualify, viz. corporate stock, producer durables (in agriculture and unincorporated business), and consumer durables. It is only when a sufficiently large number of series is combined that differences in timing may be of significance, although they are not necessarily so.

eliminated. In the latter case approximately one-half of all turning points in components of personal saving occur in the same year as turning points in the reference chronology before World War I as well as from 1918 to 1929, and from 1932 on. The proportion of turning points at which saving leads, however, has definitely declined since World War I, and that in which it lags behind reference turning points has increased. The ratio of leads to lags, which was as high as seven to one for 1899 to 1914, has fallen to not more than two to one from 1918 on. No easy explanation offers itself for this change.

7.48. Saving through tangible assets (after deduction of increases in debt and in capital consumption allowances) conforms considerably better to the reference cycle chronology than saving through intangible assets. Of the turning points in the four components of personal saving through tangible assets (excluding one poorly conforming series) three-fifths occur in the same year as in the reference chronology. In six of the seven remaining cases, the turning point in saving precedes that in the reference chronology. The turning points in the eight components of personal saving through intangible assets, on the other hand, occur in the same year as the turning points in the reference pattern in only a little over one-third of the cases. Saving leads in nearly one-half of all turning points, but lags in only about one of five cases.

7.49. In the case of personal saving through tangible assets it might be thought that cyclical correspondence is hidden or minimized by depreciation allowances, which, of course, exhibit hardly any cyclical variations, or by the behavior of changes in debt. The data, however, show that expenditures on tangible assets fail to correspond considerably better to the reference chronology than net saving through tangible assets, and that the correspondence of changes in debt is also of about the same order.

7.50. Up to this point the discussion has been based on a comparison of the annual dating of turning points in the components of personal saving and in the reference chronology, and its purpose has been to ascertain the conformity of forms of personal saving to the business cycle. In order to bring out similarities and discrepancies between different components of personal saving one might want to compare the turning points in these components with those in aggregate personal saving. It will then be found that the results do not differ much from those derived from a comparison with turning points in the reference chronology.[11]

[11] The comparison for all fifteen series is as follows (as percentages of all turning points, i.e. 25 points for the reference pattern, and 23 points for aggregate personal saving since the peak of 1918 and the trough of 1919 are not reflected in it):

	Based on turning points in:	
	Aggregate personal saving	Reference pattern
Missing	12	12
Simultaneous	40	36
Leading	29	36
Lagging	19	16

180

This is due mainly to the facts that the turning points in aggregate personal saving occur in most cases—eighteen out of twenty-five—in the same year as in the reference pattern, and that when they do not, turning points in components are generally closer to reference turning points than to turning points of aggregate personal saving. Hence, the conformity of individual components of personal saving to aggregate personal saving, of which they are a part, is only slightly more pronounced than their correspondence to turning points in the reference pattern.

7.51. The behavior of the main components of personal saving can be followed in Appendix Table Z-18. It does not seem advisable to analyze the movements for each component. Satisfactory analysis would require a much closer study of the nature of each series and of the factors which influence its cyclical behavior than is possible here, and would hardly be profitable unless additional data on at least a quarterly basis were used.

6. CYCLICAL AMPLITUDE AND ANNUAL VARIABILITY

7.52. Probably the most important aspect of cyclical fluctuations in saving, apart from the location of troughs and peaks in the different saving series and their relationship to those in the reference chronology, is the amplitude of these fluctuations, which may be measured by the relation of the difference between cyclical peaks and troughs to the average value for specific cycles of the series. [12] The larger the amplitude the more pronounced, it may be assumed, the cyclical influences in the series; and the greater the dispersion of the measure of amplitude among individual cycles the less regular the cyclical behavior of a series.

7.53. The amplitude of cyclical fluctuations is, of course, related to the average year-to-year variability of a series, i.e. the average percentage change without regard to sign. If annual variability is high, i.e. if the average change from year to year is high compared to the value in the preceding year, we generally may assume that the cyclical amplitude of the series is also high.[13] Similarly, low annual variability usually is associated with low cyclical amplitude. Therefore this section also discusses the average variability in the estimates of national saving, of the saving of the main saver groups, and of the main forms of personal saving; and compares them with the variability of a few other basic economic series. This brief review of typical variability is useful, too, for giving an idea of the character of fluctuations in series that do not

[12] Specific cycles are delimited by peaks and troughs in the series the amplitude of which is being measured and not by turning points in the reference chronology.

[13] The ratio between average amplitude and average variability is often much higher in the case of saving than in those of other economic series. This is due primarily to the possibility of saving's being positive for some years in the cycle and negative for others, with the result that the cycle average, the denominator of the measure of amplitude, is sometimes extremely small compared with the difference between the positive peak and the negative trough. High (low) annual variability and high (low) cyclical amplitude go together in saving as in other economic series, but the spread between the two measures is often much wider for saving.

show sufficiently pronounced specific cycles to justify the calculation of cyclical amplitudes.

a. *Total national and personal saving*

7.54. The average cyclical amplitude of most of the variants of national and personal saving for the period 1897–1929 is slightly in excess of 100 percent (Table XXVIII). [14] This means that typically the fall from the highest to the lowest annual value within the cycle plus the rise to the next highest value is slightly above the average value of all the years—on the average four years—included in the cycle.

7.55. The values of the amplitudes for most variants of saving are so similar that no significant differences appear between national and personal saving, between saving including and excluding consumer durables, between social accounting and business accounting saving, and between current, deflated aggregate, and deflated per head saving. This similarity reflects the close correlation between measures of cyclical amplitude of the different variants of national or personal saving which refer to the same cycle. Such similarity, of course, is to be expected in the case of current, deflated aggregate, and deflated per head series since the annual changes in the price level and in population, on which the deflated and per head figures depend, are relatively small compared with the typical annual fluctuations in aggregate current saving.

The only variant of saving which differs considerably from the rest is cash saving. Its cyclical amplitude, both for national and personal saving, is only 70 percent, compared with slightly over 100 percent for all other variants. This lower value, however, is only what one would expect as cash saving includes large capital consumption allowances which by their very nature show hardly any cyclical variation.

7.56. The annual variabilities of national and personal saving for the entire period are of the order of 50 and 40 percent respectively. There is a definite difference between the variability of national saving for the period before, and that for the period beginning with, the Great Depression. For the period 1898–1929 the typical (median) annual variability is a little over 30 percent. For the twenty years from 1930 to 1949, on the other hand, it is as high as 85 percent. This increase reflects mainly very high variability during the thirties. For the few years since the end of World War II variability has been closer to the level of the period before 1930

[14] The average or typical amplitude is measured here by the median of the amplitudes for all the specific cycles included in the period, rather than by their mean, in order to reduce the weight of erratic and extreme values. Amplitudes for the cycles beginning with the Great Depression are so high and erratic, mainly because of the alternation of positive and negative values for saving and the small number of cycles (four), that they do not permit the calculation of a significant average. Use of a median percentage is a departure from the practice of the National Bureau, which does not calculate such percentages for series which alternate between positive and negative values. (Burns and Mitchell, *Measuring Business Cycles*, 1946, p. 138.) This departure is made in order, to permit comparison between series. The period 1897–1929 is not affected by this difficulty since all the saving figures involved are positive.

182

TABLE XXVIII

CYCLICAL AMPLITUDE AND ANNUAL VARIABILITY OF NATIONAL AND PERSONAL SAVING

Variant Concepts; Selected Periods: 1897 to 1949

Median percent disregarding sign

	Cyclical amplitude		Annual variability		
	1897 to 1929	1897 to 1949	1898 to 1929	1930 to 1949	1898 to 1949
I. National saving					
1. Social accounting concept					
a. Standard	112	135	33	86	51
b. Excluding consumer durables	105	137	35	74	49
2. Business accounting concept	119	132	36	89	47
3. Cash flow concept	70	84	18	34	25
4. Deflated aggregate ⎱ Standard social	112	135	32	82	48
5. Deflated per head ⎰ accounting concept	114	135	32	81	46
II. Personal saving					
1. Social accounting concept					
a. Standard	113	131	36	43	38
b. Excluding consumer durables	139	159	39	47	40
2. Business accounting concept	117	128	36	43	37
3. Cash flow concept	69	75	22	19	21
4. Deflated aggregate ⎱ Standard social	120	136	40	42	40
5. Deflated per head ⎰ accounting concept	112	130	41	42	41
III. National product and income					
1. Net national product					
a. Current	25	38	9	11	9
b. Deflated	24	24	6	7	6
c. Deflated per head	8	8	5	7	6
2. Disposable personal income	24	38	8	11	8

Basic data given in Tables T-1 to T-12 and Volume III, Tables N-1 and N-2. The calculations underlying Tables XXVIII to XXXI do not always reflect later minor revisions made in the basic tables.

than to that of the last two decades, but it remains to be seen whether this relationship will continue for an extended period.

7.57. The measures of cyclical amplitude used up to this point include the relatively small variations which represent long-term trends. In view of the difficulties in fitting trends to absolute values of saving for the entire period and the long-range stability of the saving-income ratio, a rough indication of cyclical variability may be attempted by using these ratios, instead of absolute figures, as the basis for computing measures of cyclical amplitude. These measures, shown in the lower part of Table XXIX, are, however, only slightly lower than those derived from absolute figures. Most of the variability in the annual estimates of saving is obviously of a cyclical character.

b. *Saving of main saver groups*

7.58. With respect to cyclical amplitude the seven saver groups clearly arrange themselves into two families. The one, comprising nonagricultural households, corporations, and state and local governments, has typical cyclical amplitudes of approximately the same order of magnitude as national saving. The other, composed of agriculture, unincorporated business enterprises, and the federal government, shows values for cyclical amplitudes much in excess of the national total (Table xxix).

TABLE XXIX

CYCLICAL AMPLITUDE AND ANNUAL VARIABILITY OF SAVING
OF MAIN SAVER GROUPS

Standard Social Accounting Concept; Selected Periods: 1897 to 1949

Median percent disregarding sign

	Cyclical amplitude		Annual variability		
	1897 to 1929	1897 to 1949	1898 to 1929	1930 to 1949	1898 to 1949
I. Absolute values of saving					
1. Nation	112	135	33	86	51
2. Nonfederal	101	105	27	47	39
3. Private	105	107	30	53	40
4. Business (lines 7 to 9)	256	256	68	88	68
5. Persons (lines 6 to 8)	113	131	36	43	38
6. Nonagricultural households	92	95	29	36	51
7. Agriculture	1 129	1 119	135	92	117
8. Unincorporated business	575	575	138	104	118
9. Corporations	154	178	47	49	48
10. State governments	75	116	25	16	19
11. Local governments	198	265	46	86	60
12. Federal government	423	427	104	85	100
II. Saving-income ratios					
1. Nation	107	124	32	81	40
2. Persons (lines 3 and 4)	118	134	36	38	36
3. Nonagricultural households [a]	110	110	28	32	28
4. Agriculture	3 000	2 035	137	89	118
5. Corporations	109	111	26	59	33
6. Local governments	193	230	46	87	59
7. State governments	86	89	16	15	16
8. Federal government	400	395	99	64	82

[a] Including unincorporated business enterprises.
Source: I. Basic data given in Table T-1.
  II. Data derived according to procedure described in notes to Appendix Table Z-7.

That the amplitude of total national saving is considerably below the average of that for the seven main groups is due to two factors. The first is that generally the groups with the highest absolute volume of saving have the smallest amplitude. This, in turn, may well be due to the fact that small components of economic aggregates like saving may, and have the tendency to, fluctuate more widely than the aggregates of which they form a part. Secondly, the largest fluctuations do not occur in all groups in the same year or in the same cycle. This lack of correspondence has some dampening effect on the value of the cyclical amplitude of aggregate personal or national saving.

184

c. *Main forms of personal saving*

7.59. The typical value for cyclical amplitude of the main forms of personal saving is high (Table xxx). For the twenty forms of personal saving for which it can be calculated the median is around 200, counting values for the periods 1897–1929 and 1897–1949 separately.

TABLE XXX

CYCLICAL AMPLITUDE AND ANNUAL VARIABILITY OF MAIN FORMS OF PERSONAL SAVING

Standard Social Accounting Concept; Selected Periods: 1897 to 1949

Median percent disregarding sign

	Cyclical amplitude		Annual variability		
	1897 to 1929	1897 to 1949	1898 to 1929	1930 to 1949	1898 to 1949
1. Currency	864	695	93	99	99
2. Commercial bank deposits	350	410	65	40	59
3. Mutual savings bank deposits	86	152	23	45	32
4. Savings and loan association shares	×	×	23	38	27
5. Mortgage holdings	211	240	41	97	57
6. Life insurance reserves	44	45	11	10	11
7. Pension and retirement funds [a]	×	×	37	34	37
8. U.S. Government securities	445	445	110	112	111
9. State and local government securities	199	263	68	96	71
10. Corporate and foreign bonds	213	297	54	79	66
11. Corporate stock	124	168	32	58	42
12. Nonfarm residential real estate	60	71	51	75	40
13. Nonfarm nonresidential real estate	×	134	28	32	31
14. Farm real estate	52	97	16	58	29
15. Inventories (farm and unincorporated business)	2 137	1 760	195	144	168
16. Producer durables	193	176	66	73	70
17. Consumer durables	96	241	28	61	38
18. Nonfarm residential expenditures	28	35	10	37	17
19. Nonfarm residential debt	96	195	27	93	31
20. Nonfarm nonresidential expenditures	×	×	14	35	15
21. Nonfarm nonresidential debt	×	×	21	45	28
22. Farm construction expenditures	×	×	7	25	11
23. Farm mortgage debt	×	×	18	40	29
24. Loans on securities	304	370	107	81	94
25. Consumer debt	124	216	28	84	41
26. Short-term liabilities (farm and unincorporated business)	365	412	81	58	71
27. Tax liabilities [b]	×	×	103	141	121

× = Less than 5 specific cycles.
[a] Beginning in 1918.
[b] Beginning in 1912.
Basic data given in Tables T-6, R-4, and A-7.

7.60. Amplitude is considerably higher for the last two than for the first three decades. The medians for the twelve forms of personal saving are 158 for 1897–1929 and 438 for 1930–1949.

7.61. Amplitude is considerably less for saving through tangible assets than for saving through intangible assets. It is still lower for expenditures on tangible assets alone (i.e. without allowance for changes in attaching debt and for depreciation).

7.62. Amplitude is markedly lower for saving through stocks than through bonds. This rather unexpected finding is partly due to the inclusion of saving through the stocks of small and newly organized corporations. It also reflects the fact that cyclical fluctuations in a properly calculated figure for personal saving through stocks are lower than the figures on new publicly offered stock issues would indicate. Similarly, the relatively high amplitude of personal saving through bonds may be due to the fact that fluctuations in institutional holdings and in retirements aggravate the fluctuations in new publicly offered bond issues alone.

7.63. Liquid assets show very high cyclical amplitudes. Those for currency and commercial bank deposits amount to at least 350 in both the full period and before 1930.

7.64. Essentially the same picture emerges from a study of the values of annual variability (Table xxx) except that all values are on a lower level. The typical (median) value for the seventeen forms of personal saving is 42 for the entire period, only 41 for the years 1898–1929, but as high as 61 for the last two decades. The range of the values for individual forms of personal saving is wide for all three periods. Saving through life insurance shows the lowest variability with only 10, while saving through unincorporated business and agriculture in the form of inventories is at the top of the range with values of 145 to 200. One-half of all the ratios, however, lie between 30 and 75. The annual variability of expenditures on tangible assets, shown in the lower part of Table xxx, is considerably smaller. The median, based on three series, is as low as 15. Although this figure is somewhat affected by the understatement of variations in a few series during the earlier part of the period resulting from the use of interpolated annual values, it is very likely that the amplitude of expenditures on tangibles would still be substantially below that of saving through tangible assets if correction could be made for this defect. Dissaving or saving through changes in debt, on the other hand, shows amplitudes of about the same order of magnitude as those for the components of personal saving.

7. Comparisons with Amplitude and Variability of Other Economic Series

7.65. Comparison of the cyclical amplitude and annual variability of saving with those of other basic economic magnitudes, which is necessary to put the measures studied in the preceding sections into their proper perspective, is hampered by the lack of data on amplitude and variability of annual economic series. The National Bureau of Economic Research has determined the relevant

186

magnitudes for a large number of economic series, [15] but most of these are on a monthly or quarterly basis and in general no separate information has been made available for the same series on an annual basis. Cyclical amplitude is higher when determined from monthly or quarterly data than when calculated from annual data, but it is not possible to say exactly how large a difference to expect for series of the type of saving data. [16] All that can be done here is, first, to compare the amplitude and variability of saving, determined from annual data, with similarly calculated measures for net national product and for a few other comprehensive measures of economic activity, and, secondly, to compare the cyclical amplitude of the different saving series with National Bureau data, making rough allowances on account of the different lengths of the base period underlying the calculations.[17]

7.66. Notwithstanding all the reservations that must be made on account of differences in the length of the base period, in the cycles covered, and in other incomparabilities, one conclusion emerges quite clearly from a comparison of the cyclical amplitudes of saving, on the one hand, and the large number of economic series analyzed by the National Bureau of Economic Research, on the other. The cyclical amplitude of saving, whether for the total or its components, is much larger than that of most other basic economic series. About half a dozen business indices and more than thirty comprehensive economic series, as well as the nearly 800 individual series analyzed by the National Bureau, all show an average amplitude of about 50. (Table XXXI.) This may be compared with a median amplitude of about 100 for aggregate national and personal saving. Actually the difference is even larger since the amplitudes of the saving series are calculated from annual data while those of the other series are based on monthly or quarterly figures and, hence, are considerably higher—possibly twice as high—than they would·be if derived on the less satisfactory basis of annual data, which had to be used for calculating the amplitude of saving.

7.67. Apparently there are only a few economic series with amplitudes of the same magnitude—making allowance for the difference between calculations based on annual or on monthly and quarterly data—as even aggregate national or personal saving. Of the twenty-nine groups of economic series in Mitchell's list, [18] only the three with the highest amplitudes show values of average cyclical amplitude approximating the level encountered for saving. They are corporate security

[15] See Mitchell, *What Happens during Business Cycles*, 1951, Chapter 7.

[16] In six series studied by Burns and Mitchell (*Measuring Business Cycles*, 1946, p. 238; the series are deflated bank clearings, pig iron production, railroad stock prices, railroad bond yields, shares traded, and call money rates) the amplitude in annual data was on the average only three-fifths as large as that in monthly data. Comparison with quarterly data would apparently lead to the same result (*ibid.*, p. 244).

[17] The measures of cyclical amplitude of saving used here and those of other economic series found in Mitchell's book also differ in the cycles they cover. All saving series are based on the period 1897–1949. The period covered by the calculations of the National Bureau of Economic Research varies from series to series and most of them encompass fewer cycles than the saving series. (*What Happens during Business Cycles*, Table 3, p. 24.)

[18] *Ibid.*, Table 11, p. 106.

TABLE XXXI

COMPARISON OF CONFORMITY INDICES AND REFERENCE CYCLE AMPLITUDES
OF SELECTED SAVING AND GENERAL BUSINESS SERIES

	General business monthly or quarterly series (National Bureau)				Annual Saving Study series[a]		
	794 series	184 long series [b]	34 compre-hensive series	7 business indices	14 variants of national and personal saving	7 saver groups	15 compo-nents of personal saving
	1	2	3	4	5	6	7
I. Conformity index							
1. Mean	71	64	89	99	62	34	25
2. Median	78	69	100	100	62	17	17
3. Proportion of perfectly conforming series	37	17	53	86	0	0	0
II. Cycle amplitude							
1. Mean, sign regarded	+40	.	+40	+45	−16	+204	−24
2. Mean, sign disregarded	51	.	53	45	269	421	418
3. Median, sign regarded	+30	.	+45	+48	+81	+119	−7

[a] These figures are based on reference cycles rather than, as is the case in Tables XXIX and XXX, on specific cycles in saving, and cover the period 1897–1949.
[b] Covering 10 or more cycles.

Source: Columns 1 to 4 – Mitchell, *What Happens during Business Cycles*, 1951, pp. 86, 107, 256–257.

Columns 5 to 7 – See Tables XXIV to XXX.

issues (a component of saving), new orders from manufacturers (a notoriously volatile type of series), and private construction contracts (again a type of series which directly or indirectly is reflected in saving). All of the groups which are made up of production, sale, employment, and price series and even those consisting of inventory series have average amplitudes well below those for aggregate saving of any saver group and also for almost all forms of personal saving. It is, therefore, probably justified to say that saving, and particularly its components, shows the largest cyclical amplitude among all groups of important economic series.

7.68. Like cyclical amplitude, the annual variability of saving, particularly its components, appears to be higher than that of most other economic series. This can be asserted with some confidence even though no extensive study seems to have been made of the variability during the last fifty years of annual economic series for the United States.

The annual variability of net national product for the period 1898–1949 averages about 10, against 40 for the different variants of aggregate saving. Similarly, the variability of the income of the main saver groups is considerably lower than that of their saving, as will be seen from the table below.

Thus there is little doubt about the higher variability of saving compared

AMPLITUDE AND VARIABILITY OF INCOME AND SAVING
1897 to 1949

Median percent disregarding sign

Saver groups	Cyclical amplitude		Annual variability	
	Disposable income	Saving	Disposable income	Saving
1. All groups	38	131	9	38
2. Nonagricultural households	x	95	9	51
3. Agriculture	55	1 119	17	117
4. Unincorporated business enterprises	22	575	10	118
5. Corporations	77	178	25	48
6. State governments	x	116	8	19
7. Local governments	x	265	7	60
8. Federal government	31	427	9	100

x Not calculated since annual series distinguish less than 5 cycles.

with comprehensive economic series. No equally positive statement can be made, because of lack of data, about the relative variability of the components of saving, particularly of personal saving, and of economic series of comparable character, such as the production, sales, unfilled orders, or inventories of individual commodities or the income of individual industries. There appears to be little question, however, that series with as high an average annual variability as most of the components of personal saving have, i.e. between 25 and 100, are rare.

VIII

SAVING, NATIONAL WEALTH, AND
THE NATIONAL BALANCE SHEET

1. SUMMARY OF FINDINGS

8.01. Cumulated saving has accounted for not much over one-half of the total increase in the current value of national wealth between 1900 and 1949. The other half is primarily the result of valuation changes, i.e. the net increase in the prices of land and of reproducible tangible assets.

8.02. The share of cumulated national saving in national wealth changes was highest in the 1920's. It slightly exceeded one-half from 1900 to 1922 and after World War II, but was very small—about one-fifth—from 1930 to 1945. These differences reflect variations in the magnitude of asset price changes as well as the influence of wars, during which saving is high but additions to national wealth are small. During peacetime the share of saving in current national wealth changes is high when asset prices move little, and low when price changes are protracted or violent.

8.03. Among main saver groups the share of cumulated saving (or dissaving) in the change in combined net worth at current value of assets was highest, taking the period 1901–1949 as a whole, for governments, and lowest—less than one-half—for corporations and agriculture. The proportion for nonfarm individuals (including unincorporated business) of slightly over three-fifths was close to the national average. These relationships are in line with expectations, inasmuch as groups with relatively high ratios of tangible assets and/or of debt to total assets— like business enterprises and agriculture—may be expected to benefit more from a rise in asset prices, as has prevailed during most of the past fifty years, than groups with relatively low ratios of debt and high ratios of claims in their balance sheets, such as nonfarm households.

8.04. The proportion of liquid assets (currency, deposits, U.S. Government securities) to total assets has increased considerably, and for almost all saver groups, over the last half century. Among major saver groups the increase has been most pronounced for financial intermediaries, unincorporated business, state and local governments, and agriculture, but even for nonagricultural households and nonfinancial corporations it has meant at least a doubling of the ratio prevailing at the turn of the century, e.g. for nonfarm households, from 10 to 20 percent of total assets. Most of the increase has taken place during the war years 1917–1919 and 1942–1945 and reflects the extraordinary expansion of federal government debt and monetary circulation during these periods.

8.05. Within the total assets of households, price-sensitive assets (i.e. tangibles, corporate stock, and equity in unincorporated business) have lost steadily

190

in importance though not uninterruptedly. Their share in total assets has declined from over four-fifths in 1900 to less than two-thirds in 1949, mostly during the two World Wars and the Great Depression. Price-sensitive assets have, by contrast, increased their share in the total assets of nonfinancial business enterprises, though irregularly.

8.06. The ratio of indebtedness to total assets has declined for most saver groups other than the federal government, mostly after 1933. The decline has been much sharper for business (nonfinancial corporations, unincorporated business, and agriculture) and state and local governments than for nonfarm households. As a result of this movement, indebtedness represented at midcentury less than one-tenth of the assets of households, and even for nonfinancial business and state and local governments did not in the group aggregate exceed one-third of assets. The increase in the absolute amount and ratio of federal debt, however, has been so large that for all saver groups together the debt ratio has risen from 30 percent in 1900 to 45 percent in 1949 after having reached a peak of slightly under one-half at the end of World War II.

8.07. It may be inferred from the assets and liabilities of a sample of individuals of different ages early in 1950, from estate tax returns, and from scattered data on saving of households in different age brackets that for the bulk of the population cumulated saving increases until the age of about sixty, although the accumulation of the wealthier groups continues until the seventies. Average absolute amounts saved, as well as the ratio of current saving to income, rise with age until about fifty, but disappear or become negative after sixty-five. Debts are incurred or increased early in adult life and on balance are reduced after the head of the household reaches forty years of age.

2. BASIC RELATIONS

8.08. National and group balance sheets and national wealth statements serve at least four purposes within the framework of this study. They provide, first, an important supplement to estimates of saving cumulated for shorter or longer periods of time by permitting the calculation of changes in total net worth due to valuation changes, primarily price level movements. Secondly, they shed light, in the form of balance sheet ratios, on factors which presumably affect individuals and other economic units in their saving decisions. Thirdly, national and group balance sheets may be used, to a certain extent, as checks on estimates of saving. National wealth statements, finally, constitute at the present time one of the few sources, and sometimes the only source, for estimating the volume of saving during the nineteenth century. [1]

This chapter is limited to a discussion of the first two aspects of national balance sheets. The third aspect is given some attention in Volume II, particularly

[1] See Goldsmith, "A Perpetual Inventory of National Wealth," *Studies in Income and Wealth*, Volume XIV, 1951.

191

in Chapter v, while the fourth aspect has already been taken up in Chapter iii of this Introduction.

8.09. The main bodies of data utilized in this chapter are:

(a) National wealth estimates for 1805, 1850, 1880, and for every year between 1896 and 1949 described in *Studies in Income and Wealth*, Volume xiv; [2] in *Income and Wealth*, Series ii; [3] and in Volume iii, Part i of this study;

(b) National and group balance sheets for eight benchmark dates (1900, 1912, 1922, 1929, 1933, 1939, 1945, and 1949) presented in Volume iii, Part i;

(c) Balance sheets of all households in the United States as of early 1950 derived from sample data collected by the Federal Reserve Board's Survey of Consumer Finances, as described in Volume iii, Part i;

(d) Balance sheets for the year 1944 of the estate tax population, i.e. individuals with total assets of over $60,000, derived from estate tax returns, developed in Volume iii, Part iii.

8.10. Each economic unit's net worth at a given date is equal to:

(a) Cumulated saving in the social accounting sense of the excess of current income over current expenditures. This excess, in turn, is determined by

   (i) Current income } from the beginning of the individual's earning peri-
   (ii) Saving ratio   } od to the balance sheet date;

+ (b) Net capital changes, which consist of the difference between

   (i) Inheritances, gifts, bequests received; and
   (ii) Gifts and bequests made;

+ (c) Net realized capital gains or losses;

+ (d) Net unrealized capital gains or losses, i.e. the difference between current value and original cost of assets (and occasionally also of liabilities) which includes write-ups and write-downs.

Similar relationships apply to the combined balance sheets of groups of economic units, and finally to the combined national balance sheet.

8.11. The problems are at once simpler and more difficult for the consolidated balance sheet of the nation, which is better known as the national wealth statement. [4] On the level of national consolidation, where gifts and similar one-sided transactions may be disregarded and national original cost takes the place of original cost to the owning unit, the following relations hold:

---

[2] See note 1.

[3] Goldsmith, "The Growth of Reproducible Wealth of the United States of America from 1805 to 1950," *Income and Wealth*, Series ii, 1952.

[4] If the balance sheets of all economic units within the nation are consolidated, i.e. if creditor-debtor and owner-issuer relationships are eliminated, there remain only tangible assets and the net foreign balance, i.e. national wealth. For a discussion of problems raised by such consolidation see Goldsmith, "Measuring National Wealth in a System of Social Accounting," *Studies in Income and Wealth*, Volume xii, 1950, pp. 37–42.

(a) National wealth = National original cost of domestic reproducible tangible
    at original cost   assets—accumulated capital consumption allowances on
                         such assets on original cost basis
                         + net foreign assets at national original cost
                      = Cumulated net national saving (eliminating valuation
                         changes but calculating depreciation on national original
                         cost basis).

(b) National wealth = Current value of (domestic reproducible tangible assets
    at current values   + domestic nonreproducible tangible assets
                         + net foreign assets)
                      = Cumulated net national tangible saving
                         + net realized and unrealized capital gains or losses on
                         reproducible and nonreproducible assets.

(c) National wealth = Cost of domestic reproducible tangible assets at base
    at base period   period prices — accumulated capital consumption allow-
    (deflated) values   ances on base period price basis
                         + base period value of domestic nonreproducible tangible
                         assets
                         + net foreign assets at base period values
                      = Base period value of domestic nonreproducible assets and
                         net foreign assets
                         + cumulated net saving in base period prices.

8.12. These relations are easily adapted to a comparison of changes in national wealth between two dates and saving cumulated for the same period. It will then appear that in (c) the change in national wealth becomes equal to cumulated national net saving. However, neither national wealth statements nor the combined balance sheets of groups of economic units permit direct inferences on cumulated saving between balance sheet dates when they are expressed in original or current values.

3. THE SHARE OF SAVING IN CHANGES IN NATIONAL WEALTH AND NET WORTH

8.13. If cumulated saving explained most of the changes in national wealth and in the net worth of groups of economic units, the preparation of national and group balance sheets and their analysis would be of but little interest and importance for this study. Actually, however, the differences have been so large that the process of saving and capital formation in the United States during the past half century cannot be understood without taking account of changes in total net worth and in balance sheet structure which reflect changes in asset prices—primarily of corporate stock, real estate, inventories, and producer and consumer durables—rather than the cumulation of current saving.

8.14. Between 1900 and 1949 national wealth at current prices, i.e. the consolidated net worth of all economic units in the United States, increased by

193

approximately $810 billion. Only 55 percent of this total reflects cumulated saving. [5] The other 45 percent of the increase—approximately $350 billion—is the result primarily of the rise in prices of tangible assets which has taken place over the last fifty years.

The amount and proportion of the changes in national wealth have varied greatly from period to period (Table XXXII and Chart XXXVIII). However, in no period except the 1920's did cumulated saving or dissaving account for much over one-half of the change in national wealth, and the share was considerably lower in the period 1930–1945.

TABLE XXXII

THE SHARE OF NATIONAL SAVING
IN CHANGES IN NATIONAL WEALTH AND COMBINED NET WORTH

Period Totals: 1897 to 1949

Period	Change in wealth	Change in combined net worth	Saving	Share of saving in change in	
				Wealth	Net worth
	$ bill.			Percent	
	1	2	3	4	5
1897–1900	19	.	8	42	.
1901–1912	77	103	45	58	44
1913–1922	169	216	87	51	40
1923–1929	105	227	112	107	49
1930–1933	−109	−206	−20	18	10
1934–1939	65	69	11	17	16
1940–1945	175	264	35	20	13
1946–1949	328	357	170	52	48
1901–1949	810	1 030	439	54	43
1897–1949	830		447	54	.

Column 1 – From Volume III, Table W-1; col. 1, like cols. 2 and 3, excludes military durables.

Column 2 – From Volume III, Table W-18.

Column 3 – Table T-1, col. 1 plus excess of replacement cost over original cost capital consumption allowances (see Table T-2) and net soil improvement (Table II, line 3).

Columns 4 and 5 – Col. 3 divided by cols. 1 and 2 respectively.

8.15. While national wealth changes essentially reflect three factors only —cumulated domestic saving, changes in the prices of tangible assets, and, though much less importantly, the net foreign balance—combined national net worth shows in addition the effects of realized capital gains and losses, and of unrealized appreciation or depreciation due to changes in the prices of equity securities. Combined national net worth is, furthermore, affected by certain duplications, such as the

[5] For this comparison it is preferable to base capital consumption allowances on original cost. If replacement cost allowances had been used, as is done throughout this study when the standard social accounting concept of saving is employed, cumulated saving would have been lower ($338 billion for 1901–1949) and its share in the change in national wealth smaller (42 percent).

194

CHART XXXVIII

SHARE OF NATIONAL SAVING IN CHANGES IN NATIONAL WEALTH AND
COMBINED NATIONAL NET WORTH

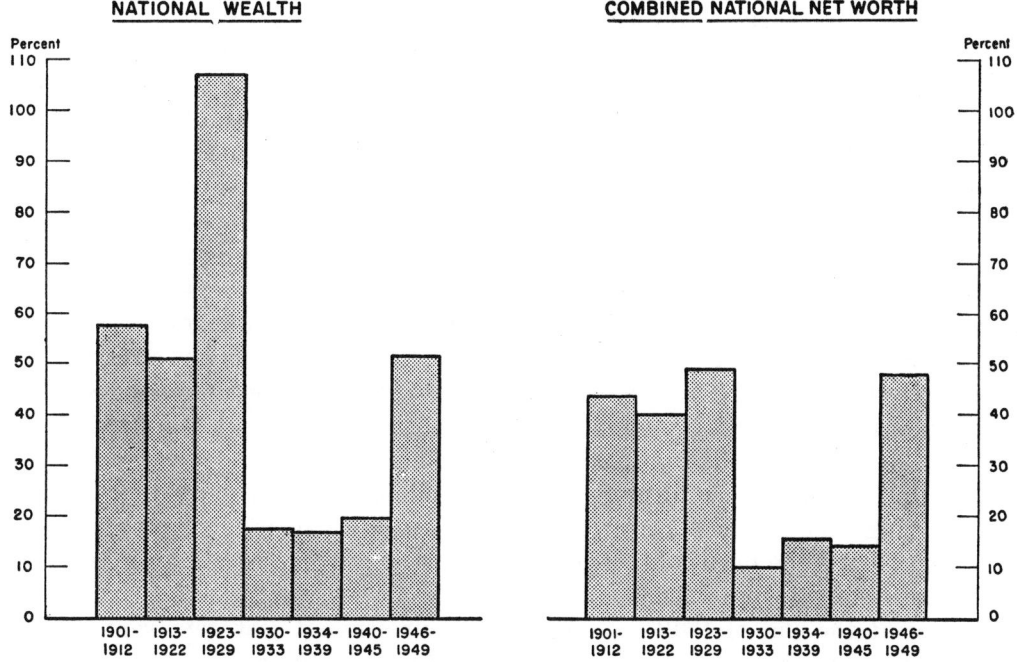

NATIONAL WEALTH   COMBINED NATIONAL NET WORTH

inclusion of the market value of corporate stock and the balance sheet value of participations in unincorporated business enterprises, first in the calculation of the net worth of the owners and then again in that of the balance sheet value of the equity of corporations and unincorporated businesses. Combined national net worth may therefore be expected to show wider fluctuations, at least in absolute terms, than national wealth, with the result that cumulated saving accounts for a smaller proportion of changes in the former than in the latter. This is confirmed by Table XXXII. Of the total increase in combined national net worth between 1900 and 1949 of over $1,000 billion, cumulated saving accounts for only two-fifths, compared with a share of one-half in changes in national wealth.

8.16. Table XXXII and Chart XXXVIII further indicate that the two ratios at times diverge much more substantially. Over the past half century the most significant difference occurred in the 1920's.

Between 1922 and 1929 cumulated national saving accounted for more than the entire increase in national wealth of approximately $100 billion, but for less than one-half of the rise in combined national net worth of $220 billion. The explanation is simple: Since the price level of commodities in general and that of reproducible durable assets in particular did not change substantially over this period, national wealth necessarily increased by approximately the amount of net capital formation, which is numerically equal to national saving. Net worth, on

195

the other hand, rose considerably because the price level of common stocks underwent an extraordinary inflation, and more than doubled within seven years.[6]

8.17. The main purpose of the comparison between changes in national wealth or in the combined net worth of all economic units within the nation, on the one hand, and cumulated national saving, on the other, is to emphasize the importance of inflation and deflation—both in commodity and security prices—for the balance sheet structure of the main saver groups. Volume and distribution of saving of individuals and business enterprises, and possibly even of governmental units, should be influenced by their assets and their debts, and by the structure and interrelations of both. How important this influence is, compared with that of current, past, and expected future income and of other factors, we do not yet know. But the role of these balance sheet relations is not likely to be negligible or even secondary. It is, therefore, necessary to go beyond the comparison of national totals and to look, although briefly, at the relation between changes in net worth and in cumulated saving of at least the main saver groups. This has already been done in Divisions 5.15 to 5.19 in connection with the discussion of changes in the distribution of national saving among the main saver groups. It still needs to be done with respect to the main forms of individuals' saving.

8.18. The difference of more than $350 billion between individuals' cumulated saving and the increase in the current value of their net worth between 1900 and 1949 is the result of increases in the prices of some assets and decreases in the prices of others.[7] Dollar claims and liabilities which have been repaid in full or at the end of 1949 are valued at their original cost represent practically the only—though a very important—item not affected by either price increases or decreases, and the only item for which cumulated saving is necessarily equal to change in value of holdings between benchmark dates. The share of individual assets in the total "valuation difference" (i.e. the difference between net worth changes and cumulated saving) depends on two factors: the asset's price movement compared with that of other assets, and its share in total assets.

8.19. Real estate, as Table xxxiv shows, has been by far the most important source of valuation gains for individuals. Between 1900 and 1949 the current value of real estate held by individuals has increased by about $200 billion more than owners' saving, i.e. the amounts which have been spent for construction and related outlays, after account is taken of depreciation allowances on original cost basis and of increase in mortgage debt. This represents well over one-half of individuals' total unearned increment. The valuation difference of $200 billion, of

---

[6] The increase in net worth, and hence the difference between changes in national wealth and in combined national net worth, would be still larger if it it had been possible to value holdings of real estate at current market prices in determining net worth, while adhering to the practice of valuing all reproducible assets at replacement cost in the calculation of national wealth.

[7] Under the rules of business as well as social accounting, liabilities are subject to "price change" only when they are reduced or eliminated by voluntary agreement or by default and bankruptcy.

196

TABLE XXXIII

COMPARISON OF PERSONAL SAVING AND NET WORTH CHANGES
FOR THE PERIOD 1901 to 1949

$ bill.

	Holdings		Change in net worth	Saving	Difference
	End of 1900	End of 1949	1901–1949		
	1	2	3	4	5
1. Real estate	45.3	349.4	304.1	108.7	195.4
2. Producer durables	2.2	28.8	26.6	20.1	6.5
3. Consumer durables	6.0	99.3	93.3	81.2	12.1
4. Inventories	7.2	31.9	24.7	3.0	21.7
5. Currency	1.3	23.3	22.0	22.3	−0.3
6. Deposits	6.1	120.2	114.1	118.5	−4.4
7. Life insurance reserves	1.6	58.8	57.2	58.1	−0.9
8. Pension and retirement funds	0	45.7	45.7	46.2	−0.5
9. U.S. Government securities	0.6	61.6	61.0	67.4	−6.4
10. Other bonds	3.9	17.7	13.8	25.3	−11.5
11. Stocks	10.7	117.8	107.1	50.2	56.9
12. Mortgage holdings	4.2	25.3	21.1	17.8	3.3
13. Equity in unincorporated business	6.3	68.8	62.5	.	62.5
14. Other assets	4.1	24.2	20.1	1.1	19.0
15. Total assets	99.4	1 072.8	973.4	619.9	353.5
16. Debt	14.9	105.3	90.4	94.7	−4.3

Columns 1 and 2 – Volume III, sum of Tables W-22, W-27, and W-29.

Column 3 – Col. 2 minus col. 1.

Column 4 – From Table T-6 but based on original cost depreciation (see Table T-7) and including net soil improvement (Table II, line 3). Lines 5–10, 12, 14, and 16, which are not substantially, if at all, affected by valuation changes, differ from col. 3 for the following reasons:

Line 5: The $0.3 billion is the difference between Shapiro and the Federal Reserve Board's estimates of corporate currency holdings in 1939, which affects personal holdings since it is derived as a residual. See Tables L-3 and L-12, A and B estimates in 1939.

Line 6: Difference is partly the result of individuals' losses in closed banks; also greater reductions from the total outstanding for corporate deposits have been made on the balance sheet material.

Line 7: Apart from capital gains and losses which are deducted from saving figures, the difference is accounted for by the fact that in the balance sheet material individuals' equity in life insurance is smaller than that derived by cumulation of saving, as larger amounts of "other liabilities" have been subtracted from the total assets of life insurance companies.

Line 8: Balance sheet data are restricted to investments and loans of federal trust funds and do not include cash and other assets which are covered in the derivation of the saving figure.

Lines 9 and 10: Differences are largely the result of net profits or losses on sale of securities, by which the change in holding figures is adjusted to arrive at the saving estimates. For amounts involved see, for example, Tables A-53, V-75, L-36, V-66, and V-68. Also a minor difference arises because foreigners' holdings of U.S. Government securities include government currency and deposit liabilities, which it was not possible to segregate from debt in the form of securities, while their saving figure includes only net purchases of U.S. Government securities.

Line 12: Balance sheet data incorporate the revised Home Loan Bank Board estimates for mortgage holdings (cf. *Statistical Summary*, 1951, p. 18, and 1949, p. 18). Also the change in holding figures have been adjusted for foreclosures and write-downs in arriving at the saving estimates.

Lines 14 and 16: A few of the items in the balance sheet data are on a gross basis and include the offsetting liability on the debt side, while in the saving figures they are reported on a net basis either among assets or among liabilities; for example, change in holdings of assets includes trade and consumer receivables of unincorporated business, which in the saving estimates are given on a net basis on the liability side.

Column 5 – Col. 3 minus col. 4.

which about two-fifths is accounted for by the increase in the value of land while nearly three-fifths reflects the increase in the level of construction costs, is equal to over three-fifths of the current value of all real estate held by individuals at the end of 1949. It corresponds, of course, to a still higher proportion—over three-quarters—of the increase in individuals' equity between 1900 and 1949.[8] These relationships are explained in Table XXXIV.

TABLE XXXIV

COMPARISON OF SAVING AND CHANGE IN VALUE OF REAL ESTATE
OWNED BY INDIVIDUALS: 1901 to 1949

$ bill.

	End of 1900	1901 to 1949	End of 1949
	1	2	3
1. Current value of property	45		349
2. Land	23		105
3. Structures	22		245
4. Expenditures on construction		199	
5. Depreciation allowances		82	
6. Net capital formation		109	
7. Mortgage debt	6	51	51
8. Owners' equity	39		298
9. Owners' net saving		55	
10. Valuation difference		204	
11. Attributable to increase in land values		82	
12. Attributable to change in replacement cost of structures and write-downs on mortgage debt		122	

Columns 1 and 3 – Lines 1–7: Sum of appropriate lines from Tables W-22, W-27 and W-29.
  Line 8: Line 1 minus line 7.

Column 2 – Line 4: See sources to Table S-38. Includes net soil improvement amounting to $11.7 billion.
  Line 5: Calculated on an original cost basis. (See Table S-36.)
  Line 6: Line 4 minus line 5.
  Line 7: See sources to Table S-34. Includes write-downs.
  Line 9: Line 6 minus line 7 and estimate of net purchases of real estate by institutions from individuals as given in Table R-6, col. 7; Table R-9, col. 5; and Table R-12, col. 5.
  Line 10: Line 8, col. 3 minus col. 1, and line 9, col. 2.
  Line 11: Line 2, col. 3 minus col. 1.
  Line 12: Line 10 minus line 11.

8.20. Stocks constitute the next largest source of valuation differences. With a net gain to individuals between 1900 and 1949 of nearly $60 billion they contribute not much over one-sixth, or less than one-third as much as real estate, to the excess of individuals' net worth increase over their cumulated saving.

[8] This, of course, does not mean that the individuals who in 1949 owned real estate had acquired it at a cost of only two-fifths of the current value of the property, but only that this ratio applies to all present and former real estate owners taken together, going back to the original occupation of the territory of the United States so that unimproved land can be regarded as costless.

8.21. Equity in unincorporated business enterprises also accounted for a substantial fraction of the excess in the increase of individuals' net worth over their saving. The figure in col. 5 of Table XXXIII, however, overstates this contribution—and possibly to a substantial extent—as it does not allow for individuals' net investment in unincorporated business.[9]

8.22. Net losses through price changes are small and limited to a few types of claims for which either defaults were considerable or current values at the end of 1949 were still substantially below original sale price. Bonds and deposits with financial institutions show the largest absolute amounts of losses. However, the amounts are small compared either with valuation gains on other assets or, except for bonds, with saving invested in these assets.[10]

8.23. The effect of these revaluation changes on the distribution of indi-

TABLE XXXV

DISTRIBUTION OF INDIVIDUALS' SAVING AND TOTAL NET
WORTH CHANGE AMONG MAIN TYPES OF ASSETS: 1901 to 1949

Percent

	Share in	
	Change in net worth	Saving
1. Real estate	31.2	17.5
2. Producer durables	2.7	3.2
3. Consumer durables	9.6	13.1
4. Inventories	2.5	0.5
5. Currency	2.3	3.6
6. Deposits	11.7	19.1
7. Life insurance reserves	5.9	9.4
8. Pension and retirement funds	4.7	7.5
9. U.S. Government securities	6.3	10.9
10. Other bonds	1.4	4.1
11. Stocks	11.0	8.1
12. Mortgage holdings	2.2	2.9
13. Equity in unincorporated business	6.4	.
14. Other assets	2.1	0.2
15. Total assets	100.0	100.0

Source : Table XXXIII.

[9] The increase in equity in unincorporated enterprises constitutes duplication from the national viewpoint since the increases in the values of real estate and inventories held by unincorporated business are also included in the change in combined individual or national net worth.

[10] In evaluating the estimates shown in Table XXXIII as representing valuation losses on bonds these facts should be kept in mind:

(a) Amounts invested between 1900 and 1949 are much larger than cumulated net saving because a large part of the bonds sold in these fifty years had already been retired before 1949.

(b) Because the valuation difference of col. 5 is the difference between numerators and denominators of much larger size it is subject to relatively high margins of errors.

(c) Individuals' losses are known to have been substantial on at least two types, real estate and foreign bonds.

199

viduals' saving among the main types of assets is visible in Table xxxv, and it is immediately evident that the differences between the two distributions, i.e. between the structure of total current and of earned net worth changes, are substantial. Moreover, the distribution of total net worth changes, including all capital gains and losses, may be more in conformity with popular ideas about the structure of individuals' saving than the distribution following economic or social accounting principles. Tangible assets and equity securities account for a higher share of the increase in current than that in earned net worth, while the opposite relationship prevails for claims of fixed amount like deposits, insurance reserves, and bonds.

8.24. It is unfortunately not possible to make similar comparisons for groups within the broad universe of all 45 million nonagricultural households. The main reason is the absence both of balance sheets for earlier dates comparable to the sample collected by the Survey of Consumer Finances for early 1950, and of estimates of saving over a long period of time for the various groups of households.

It is, however, evident that changes in asset prices have quite different effects on the net worth and balance sheet structure of households of different wealth, income, occupation, and age brackets, since such households differ, as will be shown for age groups in Section 6, in the average or typical proportion of their total assets which is subject to price changes and in the typical debt-asset ratio. The differences between these average values, however, are in most cases rather small. Although no data have been published on the variations in asset structure among households within net worth, income, occupation, and age groups, intragroup variations in asset structure are probably in most cases more pronounced than the intergroup differences. This would mean that an individual household's asset structure (particularly the liquid asset ratio and shares of claims and equities) and its debt-asset ratio depend to a considerable extent on factors specific to the household rather than on the fact that it belongs to a given net worth, income, occupation, or age group.

4. THE STRUCTURE OF ASSETS OF MAIN SAVER GROUPS

8.25. The structure of assets and liabilities of groups of savers and changes in it are relevant to a study of saving primarily because balance sheet relationships, such as the proportion between more and less liquid assets or the proportion between price-sensitive and -insensitive assets (equities and claims) or the ratio of debt to assets, probably have a considerable influence on the allocation of income between spending and saving. They thus constitute one of the significant, although as yet poorly known, determinants of the volume of individual and national saving and of its distribution among forms of saving. They are useful, secondarily, in providing a comparison with the distribution of saving by form as determined from aggregative time series, and likewise as checks on some estimates of saving. This and the following sections will therefore deal mainly with the composition of the aggregate national and group balance sheets, and with the blown-up balance

200

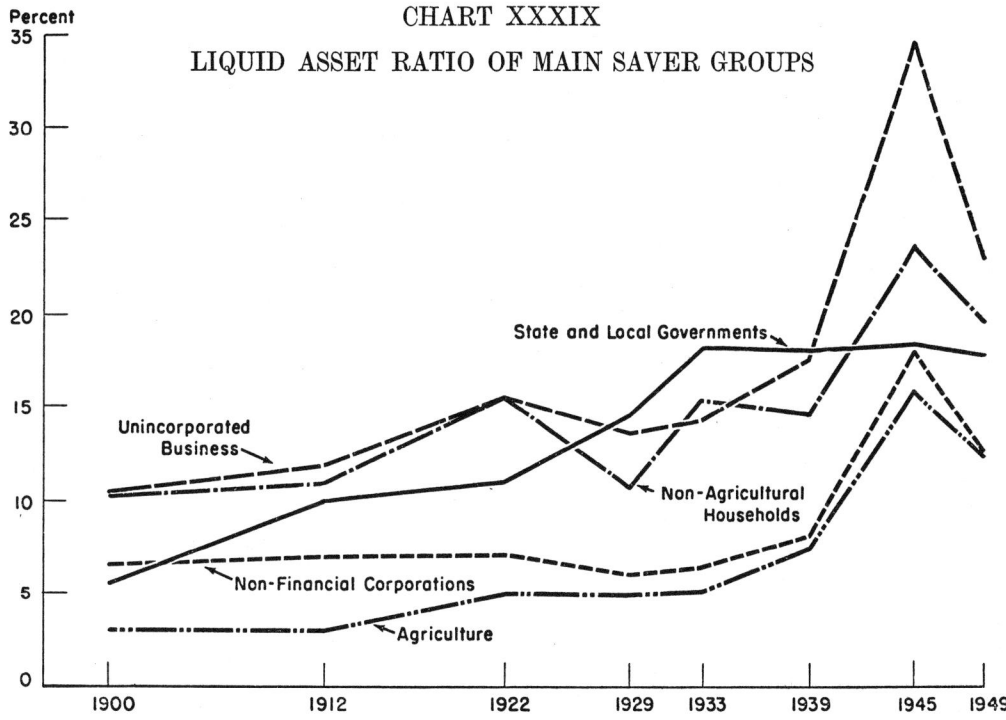

sheets based either on samples of the entire population or on the estate tax population described in Volume III, Parts I and III.[11]

8.26. While it is possible to trace the changes in the structure of assets and liabilities of the main saver groups over the last fifty years, at least in rough outline, and while it is feasible to do the same thing for the estate tax population for the last quarter century, we are limited for groups falling within the broad totals of all farm and nonfarm households to data for the end of the period— early 1950—and even for that date must do without a number of types of assets which together account for as much as one-fourth of total assets.[12] Even with this limitation the data described in Volume III, Part I are of substantial importance for an understanding of the saving process.

8.27. Of the many characteristics of balance sheet structure on which the data can be made to throw light only four will be investigated:

[11] The problem of the influence of balance sheet structure on economic behavior has received considerable emphasis in recent theoretical literature, e.g. in Boulding, *A Reconstruction of Economics*, 1950; Hart, "Uses of National Wealth Estimates and the Structure of Claims," *Studies in Income and Wealth*, Volume XII, 1950, pp. 82ff.; and Klein, "Assets, Debts and Economic Behavior," *ibid.*, Volume XIV, 1951, pp. 197ff.

[12] A comparison of the amounts of individuals' assets derived from the 1950 sample data of the Federal Reserve Board's Survey of Consumer Finances with the estimates for the same assets based on over-all data may be found in Volume III, Table W-44. It shows that notwithstanding substantial differences in a few items the two sets of data give sufficiently similar results to permit their being used together.

TABLE XXXVI

RATIO OF LIQUID ASSETS [a] TO TOTAL ASSETS BY MAJOR SAVER GROUPS
Selected Years: 1900 to 1949
Percent

	1900	1912	1922	1929	1933	1939	1945	1949
I. Households	7.8	8.4	13.1	10.0	14.7	14.5	23.6	19.7
1. Nonagricultural households	10.3	11.0	15.5	10.6	15.3	14.5	23.7	19.5
2. Personal trust funds	6.7	8.6	17.8	16.0	28.4	26.0	41.6	44.0
3. Farm households	3.1	3.1	5.0	4.9	5.1	7.4	15.9	12.4
4. Nonfinancial nonprofit institutions	0	4.8	6.9	5.8	9.9	13.5	25.3	21.9
II. Business enterprises	11.4	11.3	13.7	11.1	15.3	28.7	47.4	35.5
1. Nonfinancial corporations	6.5	6.9	7.0	6.0	6.5	8.2	18.0	12.7
2. Financial enterprises other than line II-3	4.2	5.1	5.6	5.5	4.7	6.1	12.6	10.0
3. Financial intermediaries	23.8	20.7	27.1	20.2	29.8	51.4	70.6	58.6
a. Banks	27.4	23.6	29.2	24.1	41.1	65.5	80.6	70.5
b. Government corporations	–	0	13.3	0	2.2	11.8	11.6	9.1
c. Other	7.4	9.2	20.0	13.1	14.2	34.4	59.5	49.8
4. Unincorporated business	10.5	11.8	15.5	13.6	14.3	17.6	34.7	22.9
III. Governments	20.7	20.0	19.0	17.8	16.6	30.8	35.7	23.8
1. State and local	5.6	10.0	10.9	14.5	18.2	17.9	18.3	17.6
2. Federal	42.3	48.8	40.4	34.7	34.0	57.7	50.4	32.4
IV. Total	9.9	10.1	13.7	10.9	15.2	22.0	34.7	26.6
V. Total, nonfederal (excludes lines II-3b and III-2)	9.3	9.6	13.3	10.7	14.9	20.5	34.0	26.6

[a] Consists of monetary metals, currency, commercial bank deposits, deposits in other financial institutions, U.S. Government and state and local government securities.

Source: Volume III, Tables W-9 to W-16.

(a) The distribution of total assets between liquid and illiquid assets;

(b) The share of tangible and intangible assets;

(c) The relationship of claims to equities among assets;

(d) The ratio of debt to assets.

If attention is limited to broad saver groups probably the most pronounced change in asset structure over the last fifty years is the increase in the share of liquid assets (currency, deposits with financial institutions and government securities). For nonfarm households the liquid asset ratio, as shown less in Chart XXXIX and Table XXXVI, has risen from 10 percent in 1900 to 20 percent in 1949. Sharp increases occurred between 1912 and 1922, and between 1939 and 1945. They reflect primarily the extraordinary expansion of both cash and U.S. Government securities which has characterized American war financing. The only reductions in the ratio appear after the Great Depression and during the two postwar periods (1923–1929, 1934–1939, 1946–1949).

8.28. The increase in the liquid asset ratio is also pronounced for farm households—from approximately 3 percent in 1900 to 12 percent in 1949—though the level of the ratio has always been considerably lower than for nonfarm households. Here, too, practically the entire increase occurred during war periods.

8.29. The upward movement of the liquid asset ratio among nonfinancial business enterprises is even more limited as it is confined almost entirely to the years 1942 to 1945, at least for corporations. The movement was, however, so strong during World War II that the liquid asset ratio of nonfinancial enterprises in 1949 was twice as high as it had been in 1900 and 1929, notwithstanding a sharp decline between 1945 and 1949.

8.30. The trend toward higher liquidity ratios has been marked also for state and local governments. Here it has been in force during most of the period contrary to the experience of other saver groups. The increase in the ratio from 6 percent in 1900 to 18 percent in 1949 occurred mostly before the thirties.

8.31. The largest increase in the liquid asset ratio occurred in the case of financial institutions, mainly reflecting large-scale acquisition of U.S. Government securities from the Great Depression to the end of World War II.[13]

8.32. The increase in the share of liquid assets in an important, but not the only, factor in the rise of the share of intangible assets. For all households the ratio of intangible to total assets, as shown in Table XXXVII, increased from nearly 40 percent in 1900 to approximately 55 percent in 1929, but stayed at that level until 1949, with the exception only of the bulge in World War II. Since most of the increase in the liquid asset ratio occured after 1929, this means that the share of nonliquid intangible assets, i.e. primarily corporate securities and mortgages,

TABLE XXXVII

RATIO OF INTANGIBLE ASSETS TO TOTAL ASSETS BY MAJOR SAVER GROUPS
Selected Years: 1900 to 1949

Percent

	1900	1912	1922	1929	1933	1939	1945	1949
I. Households	37.5	42.3	48.1	56.0	55.4	55.5	60.5	53.5
1. Nonagricultural households	50.3	57.4	57.6	61.8	59.4	58.1	65.3	57.7
2. Personal trust funds	90.0	90.0	92.2	95.0	95.2	94.9	96.9	98.0
3. Farm households	3.9	4.8	8.4	9.6	13.1	16.0	22.5	19.7
4. Nonfinancial nonprofit institutions	28.6	35.7	39.1	39.7	43.2	48.1	51.8	46.0
II. Business enterprises	54.7	55.3	56.6	61.6	62.9	62.7	71.6	64.4
1. Nonfinancial corporations	39.0	36.4	36.5	41.6	42.2	30.0	40.0	31.0
2. Financial enterprises other than line II-3	52.1	57.1	65.3	72.1	73.5	55.9	51.7	55.5
3. Financial intermediaries	95.4	96.6	97.4	97.0	94.7	95.3	96.3	95.7
a. Banks	96.0	96.5	97.3	96.7	94.9	97.6	99.5	99.4
b. Government corporations	–	0	93.3	94.1	97.8	83.5	48.8	51.9
c. Other	92.6	96.9	98.0	97.8	93.8	94.0	99.0	98.9
4. Unincorporated business	44.4	40.0	37.1	32.0	31.8	36.0	49.5	40.5
III. Governments	18.4	16.2	24.2	26.1	25.4	22.8	44.8	35.9
1. State and local	24.6	20.1	23.3	26.2	21.8	22.5	25.2	24.8
2. Federal	3.8	2.4	26.9	25.4	36.7	23.1	59.7	47.6
IV. Total	43.3	45.7	50.0	56.5	56.0	55.0	63.4	56.3
V. Total, nonfederal (excludes lines II-3b and III-2)	43.9	46.3	50.3	56.8	56.2	56.0	63.8	56.8

Source: Volume III, Tables W-9 to W-16.

[13] For a more detailed discussion of changes in the asset structure of financial institutions see Goldsmith, *Financial Intermediaries in the Saving and Investment Process,* to be published by the National Bureau of Economic Research.

advanced quite sharply during the first three decades of this century, but declined with equal sharpness during the last twenty years.

8.33.   There are some differences in this respect between nonfarm and farm households. The most important one is the more regular movement in the share of nonliquid intangibles of farm households, which rises much less between 1900 and 1929 than among nonfarm households, but continues to increase over the next two decades in contrast to the decline among nonfarm households. This difference is due mainly to the much smaller importance (in the estimates: the absence) of holdings of equity securities among farmers' assets.

TABLE XXXVIII

CHANGES IN SHARE OF INTANGIBLES IN TOTAL HOUSEHOLD ASSETS
1900 to 1949

Percentage Points

| | 1900 to 1929 | 1929 to 1949 | 1900 to 1949 | |
| | | | Including | Excluding |
			War periods (1912–1922, 1939–1945)	
I. All intangible assets				
1. All households	18.5	−2.5	16.0	5.2
2. Nonfarm households [a]	11.9	−3.6	8.3	1.5
3. Farm households	5.7	10.1	15.8	5.7
II. Liquid assets				
1. All households	2.2	9.7	11.9	−1.9
2. Nonfarm households	1.1	10.1	11.2	−2.9
3. Farm households	1.8	7.5	9.3	−1.1
III. Other claims				
1. All households	3.5	0.5	4.0	6.3
2. Nonfarm households	1.3	0.5	1.8	−19.3
3. Farm households	2.7	2.1	4.8	5.1
IV. Equities [b]				
1. All households	12.3	−12.7	−0.4	0.4
2. Nonfarm households	9.1	−14.2	−5.1	−1.4
3. Farm households	0.4	0.5	0.9	1.1

[a] Includes nonfinancial nonprofit institutions, and personal trust funds.
[b] Consists of corporate stock, interest in unincorporated business, and equity in financial nonprofit institutions.

Source: Volume III, Tables W-9 to W-16.

8.34.   Trends in the ratio of price-sensitive assets are closely connected with the movements of tangibles, on the one hand, and with those of liquid assets on the other, since this category is a combination of tangible assets and intangible equities (corporate stock and interest in unincorporated business).

8.35.   Within total assets of households price-sensitive assets have lost in importance steadily though not without interruption, as their share declined according to Table XXXIX from over four-fifths in 1900 to below two-thirds

204

TABLE XXXIX

RATIO OF PRICE-SENSITIVE ASSETS ᵃ TO TOTAL ASSETS
BY MAJOR SAVER GROUPS

Selected Years: 1900 to 1949

Percent

	1900	1912	1922	1929	1933	1939	1945	1949
I. Households	81.4	79.8	74.3	75.6	65.1	67.6	61.7	65.4
1. Nonagricultural households	78.2	75.1	71.5	75.3	64.0	67.7	60.1	63.8
2. Personal trust funds	30.0	44.3	42.8	47.0	36.8	42.3	43.1	42.0
3. Farm households	95.3	94.8	91.4	90.3	86.7	83.8	77.3	80.2
4. Nonfinancial nonprofit institutions	71.4	73.8	69.0	71.9	65.8	65.4	64.1	69.2
II. Business enterprises	50.2	51.2	51.0	50.4	51.3	44.9	33.9	40.5
1. Nonfinancial corporations	67.1	72.1	72.5	70.4	75.8	79.5	69.0	74.7
2. Financial enterprises other than line II-3	64.6	65.3	65.3	62.8	71.0	72.5	72.4	68.9
3. Financial intermediaries	4.6	4.9	3.7	9.4	9.4	8.5	6.3	7.1
a. Banks	3.2	3.9	3.2	4.3	5.4	3.1	0.8	0.8
b. Government corporations	–	0	6.7	5.9	8.7	22.0	52.7	48.8
c. Other	11.1	9.2	5.3	20.0	16.2	15.3	9.2	8.5
4. Unincorporated business	55.6	59.4	62.6	68.0	68.5	64.0	50.5	59.4
III. Governments	71.3	73.5	67.2	67.1	68.6	55.2	41.9	50.3
1. State and local	77.0	79.9	76.7	73.8	78.4	77.5	74.9	75.1
2. Federal	57.7	51.2	38.5	40.7	37.4	23.1	16.8	24.2
IV. Total	68.3	68.6	64.3	64.8	59.5	57.0	48.1	53.6
V. Total, nonfederal (excludes lines II-3b and III-2)	68.5	68.8	64.9	65.2	60.3	59.1	50.1	55.2

ᵃ Includes stocks, tangible assets other than monetary metals, and equity in unincorporated business.

Source: Volume III, Tables W-9 to W-16.

in 1949. Most of the decline took place during the two wars and the Great Depression, while the two movements which run counter to the long-term trend occurred in the late twenties and after World War II. Thus the share of price-sensitive assets has increased during peacetime periods of inflation in asset prices. It has decreased during peacetime deflations and during wars when the extraordinary expansion of the claims' structure, combined with commodity price controls in World War II, more than offset the effect of the rise in equity prices.

8.36. The level of the share of price-sensitive assets has been substantially higher for farm than for nonfarm households, particularly during the Great Depression.

8.37. The share of price-sensitive assets has also declined for banks and "other" financial intermediaries, even though the decline was interrupted in the twenties as a result of net purchases of, and a price rise in, stocks, and in the early thirties on account of the accumulation of foreclosed properties.

8.38. In contrast to the decline among households and banks the share of price-sensitive assets in the total assets of nonfinancial corporations has shown an irregular upward movement. It stood at nearly three-fourths in 1949 compared to a little over two-thirds in 1900. However, the trend was downward from 1922 until 1929 and again during World War II. The small net increase for the period as a whole has been due almost entirely to sharp rises in the Great Depression and during the later thirties.

8.39. The structural changes in the first half of this century have thus reduced the share of price-sensitive assets of households, banks, and governments, and have increased the share in the case of nonfinancial business enterprises. This means that, since debt-asset ratios have as a rule decreased substantially over the same period, a change in asset prices of the same proportion has now a relatively smaller effect on the net worth of farm and nonfarm households than fifty years ago, but has still about the same repercussion on the equity of nonfinancial business enterprises, and a larger effect on that of certain financial institutions. In other words the real net worth (i.e. the current net worth divided by an index of the general price level) of individuals is now more susceptible, at least for households in the aggregate, to dilution by inflation than it was twenty or fifty years ago.

8.40. Turning to the data for the end of the period, which are based on samples rather than on aggregates but which permit us to distinguish a number of groups within the universe of individual households, it is found that liquid assets, if defined narrowly, i.e. restricted to deposits in financial institutions and U.S. Government securities, represent a definitely smaller proportion of the total assets of households of very low (less than $50) or very high ($60,000 and more) net worth, as can be seen in Appendix Table Z-23, than for the remaining 86 percent of households, among which the ratio shows only small variations.

Differences in the proportion of liquid to total assets are even less pronounced if households are classified by income, although the ratio is again lowest at the two ends of the scale. Households with incomes of more than $7,500 keep, on the average, only one-eighth of their assets in liquid form, while the proportion varies between 15 and 19 percent for those with incomes between $1,000 and $7,500.[14]

Classification of households by occupation of head leads to more marked differences. Entrepreneurs, whether in agriculture or in other industries, show a considerably smaller proportion of assets in liquid form than other individuals—approximately one-tenth compared with one-fifth. Among nonentrepreneurial

[14] While the differences in the average liquid asset ratio (liquid assets as percentage of total assets) of households of different income levels are small, the differences among individual households within the same income groups are large. Early in 1952, for example, one-half of all households with an income of $7,500 and over had a liquidity ratio (liquid assets as a percentage of money income before taxes) of less than one-eighth or more than two-thirds compared with a median ratio of 30 percent; 11 percent had a ratio of less than 5 percent; while 17 percent had a ratio of over 100 percent (*Federal Reserve Bulletin*, 1952, p. 983). A wide spread of the liquidity ratios among individual households within the same group was also found for other income brackets and for occupational and age groups of households. It is likely that the spread is similarly wide for the liquidity ratio within other groupings of the population, and for other asset and liability ratios for which no tabulations based on the ratios for individual households are available. These individual differences among households are possibly more important in explaining differences in volume and structure of saving among them than their income, occupation, or other broad characteristics.

households the differences, however, are small, except for a slightly higher share of liquid assets among households whose head has retired from work.

8.41. The picture changes drastically if marketable nongovernment securities, which consist mostly of corporate stock, are included in liquid assets. In that case the proportion of liquid assets increases with total net worth and income, particularly for households with net worth above $60,000 or income above $7,500.[15]

8.42. Tangible assets account for approximately one-half of total assets of all households together. The proportion declines with increasing income, particularly for incomes in excess of $7,500. It fails to show a definite trend among households with a net worth of less than $60,000, but is considerably lower—less than 40 percent—for households above that level than for those below it, for which it averages approximately 60 percent (Appendix Table Z-21). The tendency of tangible assets to decline in proportion to total assets as total assets increase is known from estate tax statistics to continue up to the higher estate classes (Volume III, Table E-56). It is entirely in line with expectations inasmuch as all the main forms of assets in which large fortunes are now held, with the exception of real estate other than homes, are of intangible nature, particularly stocks and bonds.

8.43. Differences in the share of tangible assets among occupations are fairly pronounced, but depend to some extent on the treatment of the tangible assets of unincorporated business and closed corporations. If these are attributed to the partners and stockholders, the share of tangible assets is high for farmers and other self-employed individuals, approximately 85 and 75 percent respectively, but is hardly lower for workmen, managers, and clerical and sales personnel, for whom it averages between 60 and 70 percent (Appendix Table Z-20). It is smaller for professional and retired individuals, who on the average keep only approximately one-half of their total assets in tangibles.

8.44. Tangible assets, however, consist of two categories of very different nature—tangibles for consumer use (house, car), on the one hand, and income properties, on the other (farm, livestock and crops, other real estate, equipment, inventories). The share of the first of these categories increases with income up to $5,000 and then declines rapidly. The decline of tangibles for consumer use with net worth starts with net worth of $25,000 and is very pronounced for higher net worth groups, while the ratio fluctuates erratically for lower net worth groups. Business-type tangibles, on the other hand, are of small importance for households with net worth of less than $10,000—simply because at the present time the value of tangible assets of even a moderate sized farm or nonfarm business is above that level—but increase their share so rapidly that they exceed 40 percent for households with a net worth of over $25,000. Although estate tax data are not classified in an entirely comparable manner, there is reason to assume that the increase in the proportion of business tangibles to total assets ceases soon after the estate tax boundary of $60,000 is crossed and decreases among large estates.

[15] See Appendix Tables Z-19 and Z-21 for entire population in 1950 and Table XL for estate tax population in 1944.

8.45. From the point of view of an analysis of saving possibly the most significant classification of assets is in the distinction, illustrated in Table XL and Appendix Table Z-23, between assets which directly or indirectly are subject to substantial price fluctuations (tangible assets, corporate stock, and interest in unincorporated business enterprises), and those which are tied fairly closely to a fixed dollar amount (cash, bonds, mortgages, and receivables). It is primarily the share of price-sensitive assets which determines—together with the ratio of debt to assets—how inflation or deflation affects narrower or broader groups of economic units.

The share of price-sensitive assets increases with total net worth and with income (once it exceeds $3,000), but the connection is more regular and more pronounced for the former. In the case of net worth the relation extends up to near the top—in 1944 up to estates of approximately $1 million—to judge from estate tax returns.

TABLE XL

EQUITİES, CLAIMS, AND DEBT OF ESTATE TAX POPULATION: 1944

Percent of gross estate

	Price-insensitive assets (claims)			Price-sensitive assets (equities)				Debt
	Total	Cash and bonds	Other	Total	Stocks and interest in unincorporated business	Real estate	Other	
	1	2	3	4	5	6	7	8
I. By size of gross estate ($000)								
Under 60	28	19	9	72	43	27	2	16
60 to 80	36	24	12	64	32	28	4	8
80 to 100	36	23	13	64	34	26	4	9
100 to 150	34	23	11	66	38	24	4	11
150 to 200	35	23	12	65	43	18	4	10
200 to 300	34	23	11	66	44	18	4	10
300 to 500	29	19	10	71	53	15	3	11
500 to 1,000	30	23	7	70	56	11	3	10
1,000 to 2,000	36	27	9	64	50	10	4	7
2,000 to 5,000	32	27	5	68	61	4	3	5
5,000 and over	48	45	3	52	45	5	2	5
II. By age								
20 to 30	31	24	7	69	48	17	4	6
30 to 40	33	23	10	67	43	19	5	10
40 to 50	31	22	9	69	48	17	4	12
50 to 55	32	20	12	68	48	16	4	12
55 to 60	40	29	11	60	41	16	3	10
60 to 65	34	23	11	66	45	18	3	8
65 to 70	39	30	9	61	44	14	3	6
70 to 75	34	26	8	66	47	16	3	8
75 to 80	37	29	8	63	45	16	2	5
80 to 85	38	30	8	62	44	16	2	4
85 and over	43	37	6	57	42	13	2	3
Total	35	25	10	65	45	17	3	9

Source. Tables E-56 (for Section I) and E-60 (for Section II), allocating one-half of "other intangible assets" to claims and one-half to equities.

Differences are less pronounced among occupations and in this case quite similar to those noticed for the share of tangible assets. Farmers and nonfarm entrepreneurs show by far the highest average share of price-sensitive assets—almost seven-eighths— while the share of all other groups is close to 70 percent.

5. The Debt Ratio of Main Saver Groups

8.46.   In savers' eyes the proportion of indebtedness to current value of assets is probably the most important single balance sheet ratio, although character and maturity of debt are sometimes as important as the mere amount. It is also the

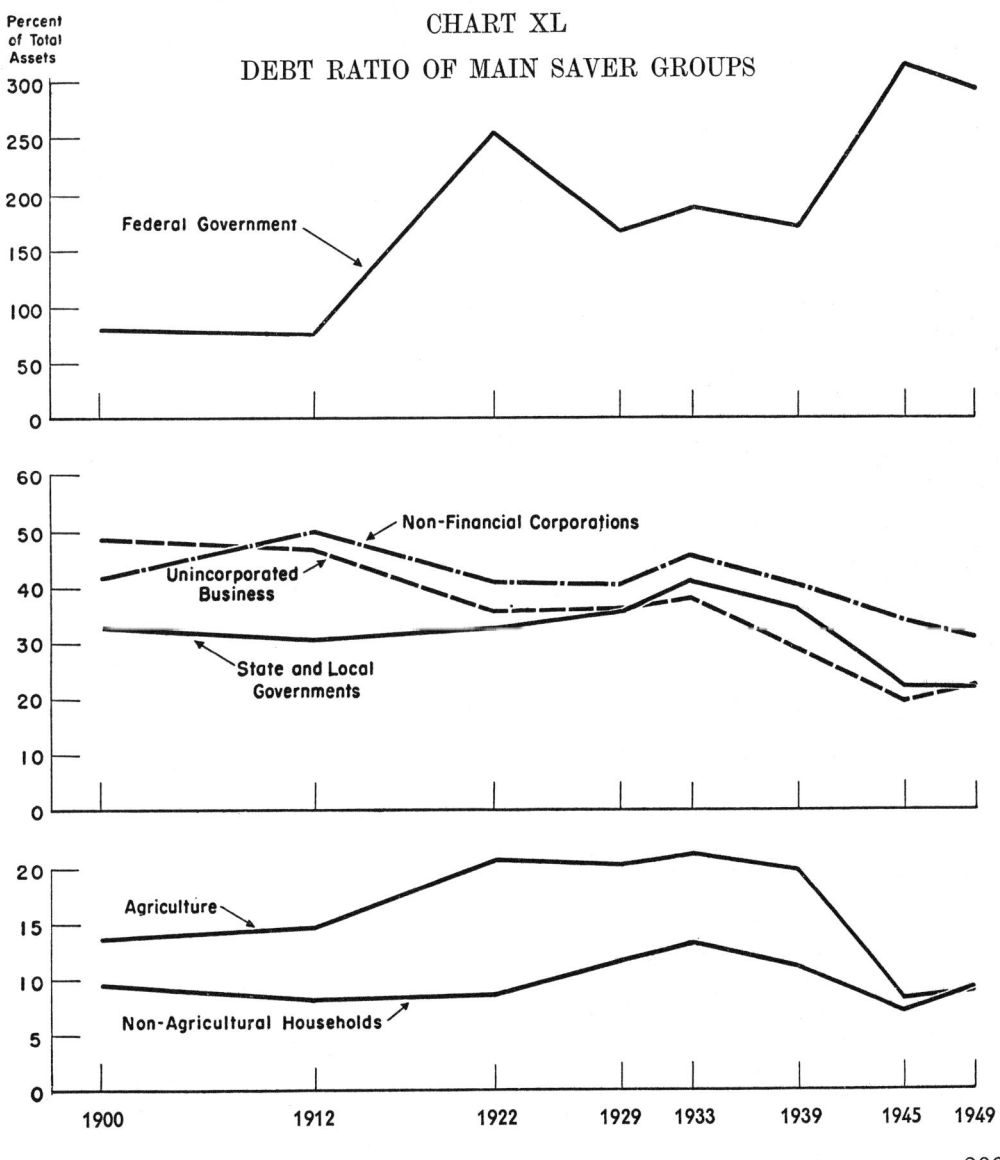

Percent of Total Assets

CHART XL

DEBT RATIO OF MAIN SAVER GROUPS

Federal Government

Non-Financial Corporations

Unincorporated Business

State and Local Governments

Agriculture

Non-Agricultural Households

1900   1912   1922   1929   1933   1939   1945   1949

most significant ratio for an analysis of saving next to or together with the ratio of price-sensitive to total assets. The debt ratio (which might more unequivocally but more clumsily have been called indebtedness ratio) possibly loses more than other ratios by aggregation, since it is the ratio for the individual household or business enterprise rather than averages for broad groups that is significant for the determination of economic behavior, because low ratios for some members do not offset high ratios for others in their effect on spending, investing, and saving decisions. Nevertheless, even the group ratios, the only ones available for most of the period, show a number of clear and significant trends, which may be assumed to reflect changes in the typical, and not only the mean, ratio for individual economic units.

8.47. The main fact which stands out in Table XLI is the decline in the ratio of debt to assets for the nonfinancial saver groups between the beginning and the middle of this century, most of the decline occurring after 1933. The federal government, of course, constitutes the most important exception.

TABLE XLI
DEBT RATIO OF MAJOR SAVER GROUPS
Selected Years: 1900 to 1949
Percent

	1900	1912	1922	1929	1933	1939	1945	1949
I. Households	10.1	10.1	11.6	12.7	13.8	11.5	6.9	8.6
1. Nonagricultural households	9.4	8.1	8.5	11.8	13.0	11.2	7.0	9.2
2. Farm households	13.7	14.8	23.3	21.8	24.2	19.5	8.2	8.9
3. Nonfinancial nonprofit institutions	23.8	21.4	17.2	20.7	20.7	17.3	11.8	8.0
II. Business enterprises	54.0	59.0	54.4	55.0	59.6	62.4	62.6	57.7
1. Nonfinancial corporations	41.9	50.0	40.8	40.5	46.1	40.6	34.2	31.1
2. Financial enterprises other than line II-3	54.2	53.1	54.2	57.5	54.8	59.1	53.7	55.5
3. Financial intermediaries	82.8	83.3	86.3	81.7	84.0	87.3	88.1	85.5
a. Banks	83.1	83.0	88.1	87.1	87.9	91.7	95.2	94.0
b. Government corporations	–	0	53.3	76.5	34.8	65.4	16.9	10.8
c. Other	81.5	84.6	82.7	70.9	83.2	84.5	87.0	87.5
4. Unincorporated business	49.2	47.1	36.2	36.6	38.8	29.3	20.2	22.9
III. Governments	48.3	39.5	88.1	63.6	77.0	92.4	190.2	156.2
1. State and local	32.8	30.6	32.8	36.3	41.8	36.5	22.5	22.2
2. Federal	84.6	70.7	256.7	171.2	189.1	172.9	318.0	296.9
IV. Total	29.7	30.5	34.1	33.0	38.4	40.6	49.6	43.3
V. Total, nonfederal (excludes lines II-3b and III-2)	28.8	30.0	30.4	31.3	35.3	34.2	32.3	31.0

Source: Volume III, Tables W-9 to W-16.

8.48. The debt-asset ratio of nonfarm households remained slightly above 8 percent until 1922, but then increased until 1933, when it reached its peak at 13 percent. The rise in the twenties was due to a rapid increase of installment financing and large-scale borrowing on securities. It continued during the Great

Depression, notwithstanding a sharp reduction in the volume of debt, particularly short-term debt, as the value of individuals' total assets shrank even more seriously. The decline of the debt ratio from 13 to 7 percent in the decade from the middle thirties to the end of World War II is due exclusively to the increase in individuals' total assets as the absolute level of debt increased slightly, though it remained below the 1929 peak. The situation was entirely reversed after the end of World War II. The increase in debt was so rapid—more than 60 percent in four years, mainly in home mortgage and installment loans—that it outran the sharp increase in the value of assets with the result that the debt-asset ratio increased from 7 to 9 percent. Even at that level it was lower than at any time since the midtwenties. It is evident, then, that the debt ratio of individuals is not uniquely related to the level of asset prices or inflation and deflation as they are commonly understood, as the ratio increased both when asset prices rose (1913–1922, 1923–1929, 1946–1949) and when they fell (1930–1933), and decreased when asset prices went up (1901–1912, 1934–1939, 1940–1945).

8.49. Farm households are similar to nonfarm households in the decline in the debt-asset ratio between 1933 and 1945, and in the increases between 1912 and 1922, during the Great Depression, and between 1945 and 1949. They differ, however, by showing a small increase in the ratio between 1900 and 1912 and a small decline between 1922 and 1929. As most of the movements are considerably more pronounced for farm households the decline in the ratio for the period as a whole, or for its later part, is much greater. The reduction from the peak of 24 percent in 1933 to approximately 8 percent in 1945 is remarkable and one of the largest for any major group.

8.50. If attention is centered on the period as a whole, the decline in the debt-asset ratio is most spectacular in the case of nonfinancial business enterprises, as shown in Table XLI. At the turn of the century indebtedness amounted to about two-fifths of total assets, i.e. was a little less than the value of equity if assets are valued at market or depreciated replacement cost. By 1949 this ratio had been reduced to nearly 30 percent of assets, or less than one-half of equity. This was the result, first, of the decline in the relative importance of industries in which the debt-asset ratio is customarily high, particularly railroads; and, secondly, of the decline in the typical debt-asset ratio in manufacturing and trade, which in turn is the result mainly of the rising trend in the prices of tangible assets.

This hypothesis is corroborated by the movements of the ratio between benchmark dates. Most of the decline in the debt-asset ratio took place between 1912 and 1922 and between 1939 and 1949, both periods of rapid rise in the price level. The only substantial increase in the debt ratio of both corporate and unincorporated business occurred between 1929 and 1933, when the price level fell sharply.[16]

---

[16] Nonfinancial corporations also show a substantial increase in the ratio of debt to assets between 1900 and 1912 although tangible asset prices rose. No sufficiently detailed and reliable data are at hand to explain this apparent anomaly. It may be due to an increase during that period of the share of industries with typically high ratios or to an increase in the typical ratio in all or most industries, which would be in contrast to later experience.

211

8.51. The debt-asset ratio of state and local governments has shown an irregular and not very marked downward trend, falling from slightly less than one-third in 1900 to one-fifth in 1949. The decline occurred between 1900 and 1912 and between 1933 and 1949, but was interrupted by a rise from 33 to 42 percent between 1922 and 1933 reflecting the extraordinary expansion of capital formation and debt during the twenties, as well as the combined effect of emergency borrowing and shrinkage of asset values during the Great Depression.

8.52. Two of the groups with rising debt ratios—banks and the federal government—constitute special situations. For banks, debts are of necessity about equal to total assets. The increase in the ratio from 85–90 percent between 1900 and 1933 to about 95 percent since 1939 reflects the inability of the banking system to increase its equity funds—through the retention of earnings or the sale of additional stock— in step with the expansion of its deposit liabilities.

8.53. The federal government is the only group for which liabilities have exceeded assets during most of the period.[17] The two sharp increases in the debt ratio—between 1912 and 1922, and between 1939 and 1945—are the direct result of borrowing for war. The declines between 1922 and 1929 and between 1945 and 1949 are mainly due to debt retirement, assisted after World War II by an increase in asset prices.

8.54. The debt ratios for broad saver groups, shown in Table XLI, to which this discussion has so far been limited, naturally hide substantial differences in the ratios among subgroups and still wider variations among individual units. These are of particular interest, from the point of view of an analysis of saving, insofar as they distinguish among households of different economic characteristics. The necessary data are available only for the end of the period, but it may be assumed that the main features of the picture which they disclose are applicable to a longer period.[18]

8.55. It is only to be expected that the debt ratio should decline with increasing net worth since heavy indebtedness will by itself tend to shift a household into a low net worth class. This tendency is accented, and indeed over-emphasized, for households with small net worth by the omission from the sample data of consumer durables other than cars, notwithstanding the inclusion of all consumer debt. The inverse relation between debt ratio and total net worth is, however, also evident in the upper net worth classes (above, say $5,000), where this inconsistency is of smaller effect. The correlation does not continue among estates of between $60,000 and $1,000,000, if estate tax returns may be trusted (see Table XL). In this group the correlation reappears only among the few estates in the top net worth classes.

[17] This would be true even if military durables were counted among assets.

[18] The over-all debt ratio for all households of 11 percent, shown in the detailed statistics for early 1950 and based on sample data collected by the Federal Reserve Board's Survey of Consumer Finances, compares with the over-all ratio, derived from combined balance sheets, of 9 percent. Direction and extent of the differences are satisfactorily explained by the fact that the combined balance sheet includes a number of assets not covered in the sample, which together account for approximately 21 percent of total assets. The absolute figures for debt in the blown-up sample and the aggregate balance sheet are not far apart.

212

8.56. There is little relation between debt ratios and income before taxes up to $7,500, as the figures stand (Appendix Table Z-19). If allowance could be made for holdings of consumer durables other than cars it is possible, however, that the ratio would rise to incomes of about $5,000, and would then fall, particularly beyond $7,500. Satisfactory analysis requires separation of home owners from renters, which is as yet missing. Even then the debt ratio within the upper income brackets would probably fall with increasing income, but the income level at which the inverse correlation begins may well be considerably higher than the figures show now.

8.57. Variations of debt ratios by occupation are considerable. That the debt ratio is shown to be lowest for retired individuals is only to be expected, since the proportion of ownership of cars and other expensive durables is smaller for them than for groups of middle age, while the opportunity for the repayment of debt on these durables is greater. These tendencies are reinforced for recent dates by the fact that acquisition of most tangible assets now owned by retired persons antedates the sharp increase in their price which has taken place since World War II. That age more than any other factor is responsible for the very low debt ratio of retired individuals is confirmed by the similarly low ratios for households with heads aged more than 55 years (Appendix Table Z-22).

The relatively high debt ratios for workmen, clerks, and salesmen are partly due to the exclusion of consumer durables, which probably are more important in relation to included assets for these than for most other groups. The ratios also reflect the high share of the home—often financed with the help of a mortgage loan—in total assets. The low ratio for the self-employed, the lowest of all groups except retired individuals, is attributable partly to the relatively high level of income and net worth of this group, both characteristics associated with low debt ratios, but may be influenced also by the classification of some debt as business liabilities not included in the statistics. [19]

8.58. The debt ratio is inversely related to age, and markedly so. The apparent exception—a lower ratio for the 18-to-24-than for the 25-to-34-year group —may be due to the relatively high proportion of secondary units in the former group (particularly individuals living with relatives). It is only natural that debts are incurred primarily at the time of marriage and when the first home is purchased. Neither of these two major causes of debt is likely to occur often after the head of the household is over 35 or at most 40 years of age. From then on the contractual repayments on mortgage debt will almost ensure that the absolute volume of debt decreases, even if the decrease is interrupted when a new home or a new car is acquired or an emergency arises. [20] Since average assets tend to increase with age the decline in the debt ratio will be even more rapid than that in the absolute amount of liabilities. At the time the decrease in mean income and in assets sets

[19] This classification may well be offset by the listing of some business obligations as personal debt.

[20] Average debt reaches a peak, at approximately $1,700 per spending unit, in the age group of 35 to 44 years, and for households with head of over 64 years averages only $700.

213

in—at 40 to 50 and at 60 years respectively—debt has generally been reduced to very low levels, on the average to less than $1,000. Whether it increases after retirement we cannot say since the data for the entire population provide no breakdown above age 65. Among the estate tax population the debt ratio changes little between 60 and 75 years, but declines markedly thereafter.

6. LIFE SAVING (ACCUMULATION) CURVES

8.59.   Life saving, or accumulation, curves, i.e. figures describing the gradual building up of an individual's assets, liabilities, and net worth and their later liquidation, constitute an important tool in the analysis of the saving process, though the actual determination of such curves is still largely a matter for the future. [21] Under stationary conditions (i.e. when number and age structure of the population are stable, when disposable income and saving habits remain unchanged, when valuation changes are absent, and when national saving is zero though individual households save and dissave continuously) statistics of household balance sheets classified by age of head would immediately provide a picture of life saving curves. Direct inferences drawn from the structure of estates of individuals of a given age at the time of the inquiry as to the position or the shape of the life saving curves are ruled out in a society in which, as in the United States during the last half century, both the level of income and asset prices show pronounced trend movements. Even in such a situation the balance sheets of individuals in different age groups permit indirect inferences on the shape of the life saving curves, but these are more difficult to draw and must be treated with greater reserve. [22]

8.60.   The only usable picture of the net worth of spending units with heads

[21] For an analysis of the data available on the relation between saving and age, but with only secondary emphasis on life saving curves, see Fisher, *The Economics of an Aging Population: A Study of the Income, Spending and Saving Patterns of Consumer Units in Different Age Groups, 1935–1936, 1945, and 1946,* unpublished Columbia University thesis, 1950; "Postwar Changes in Income and Savings among Consumers in Different Age Groups," *Econometrica,* Volume 20, 1952, pp. 47–70; and "Income, Spending and Saving Patterns of Consumer Units in Different Age Groups," *Studies in Income and Wealth,* Volume xv, 1952, pp. 77–102.

[22] When asset prices rise, realized and unrealized capital gains are likely to constitute a larger proportion, and cumulated saving a smaller proportion, of total assets or net worth for older than for younger people. The extent of the difference will depend on the rate of rise of asset prices, the proportion of assets kept in forms subject to price fluctuations, and the difference in age. Net capital changes probably increase with age to a maximum which may be located for men around fifty years (inheritances from parents are unlikely to occur much later) though later for women, and then decrease continuously until death.

In view of the high proportion of net worth which is not the result of cumulated saving (see Table XXXIII), of the numerous factors which influence the difference between increase in net worth and cumulated saving, and of the difficulty of disentangling their effects, great caution is obviously necessary in drawing inferences from the difference at any one date in net worth of individuals of different age as to the form of the life saving curves of the community or of groups of savers.

of different age which covers the entire population refers to end of the period studied, the beginning of the year 1950.[23]

At that time average net worth increased markedly up to a top of nearly $19,000 in the 55–64 age bracket, but declined slowly thereafter. The increase was small up to the middle thirties, but from then on proceeded at a level equivalent to an average annual increase in net worth of about $500 for three decades until the middle sixties. Total dissaving after age 64 was relatively small compared with net worth at the time it reached its peak. This would indicate that in the aggregate, although not always and not even necessarily in the majority of individual cases, much of the net worth accumulated by the time of retirement is passed on to heirs.

8.61. If the differences in net worth of the different age groups are interpreted as reflecting primarily accumulated saving (or at least as reflecting a fairly constant proportion of saving to net worth changes) and thus are used to construct a life saving curve, the result conforms to the common impression: People save until, or almost until, retirement and then draw slowly upon their accumulated saving. This general correspondence, however, is of little value for a quantitative analysis of saving habits and saving processes. Whatever contribution wealth data may be able to make to such an analysis rests upon what they can tell us about less obvious relations, and upon the quantification of relationships which otherwise would have to remain vague. Only a few of these contributions can even be touched upon here, such as the differences between the curves for different types of assets; the difference between the life saving curves of the entire and of the estate tax population, or of men and women; and changes in life saving curves over the last generation.

8.62. Life saving curves may be approximated by three approaches, but all three in the present state of our knowledge require rather heroic assumptions. The first and entirely unsophisticated approach is to treat differences in the observed average net worth of different age groups as reflecting cumulated saving, thus either disregarding the effects of valuation changes, as well as of the increasing trend in income and of fluctuations in the saving ratio, or hoping that these influences have offset each other. The second approach is to assume that the average level of saving of different age groups in recent years also prevailed in the past, ignoring the fact that the average absolute amount of saving per spending unit has shown an increasing trend during the period except for the 1930's. This

[23] For a description of the data see Volume III, Part I. The data used cover approximately two-thirds of individuals' total assets. They omit among major items holdings of currency, bonds except those of the U.S. Government, equity in social security funds, personal trust funds, and consumer durables other than automobiles. They considerably understate holdings of corporate stock and liquid assets. It is nevertheless unlikely that the relationship between average net worth of the different age groups would be considerably different if it could be based on complete and accurately valued balance sheets, since some of the omitted or understated assets are held mostly by the older age groups (particularly personal trust funds) while others are primarily in the hands of the younger groups (consumer durables). If the available statistics err it is probably in the direction of somewhat understating the increase of average net worth with age.

assumption is avoided in the third approach, which proceeds on the hypothesis that spending units of a given age in 1949 have in the past saved amounts which are determined by the 1948–1950 ratio of saving in that age group to average saving of all spending units, an average which may be obtained from the historical estimates of saving back to 1897 developed in this study. [24]

TABLE XLII

COMPARISON OF OBSERVED NET WORTH AND
CALCULATED CUMULATED LIFE SAVING

End of 1949

Age of head of spending unit	Observed average net worth	Calculated cumulated life saving		Inferred share of cumulated saving in net worth	
		Based on 1948–1950 levels	Based on historical levels	Based on 1948–1950 levels	Based on historical levels
	$000	$000		Percent	
	1	2	3	4	5
18–24	1.4	−0.2	−1.5	.	.
25–34	4.3	1.0	2.4	23	56
35–44	9.5	4.0	6.1	42	64
45–54	14.1	7.8	11.3	55	80
55–64	18.8	11.5	14.3	61	76
65 and over	15.3	11.9	8.1	78	53
All age groups	10.2	5.7	6.5	56	64

Column 1 – Obtained by dividing total assets of spending units in a given age group (Volume III, Table W-48) by number of spending units in that group, derived by applying percentage of Table XLIII, col. 1, to 52 million (*Federal Reserve Bulletin*, 1950, p. 1,441).

Column 2 – Based on the assumption that average 1948–1950 saving for each age group, as estimated in Table XLIII, col. 8, is applicable to earlier periods (i.e. in effect, that asset price rises have offset increases in income). There are, unfortunately, some differences in the definitions of saving and net worth changes in the underlying data. The most important of these are: the omission from saving of cars (both acquisition and depreciation), depreciation on houses, farm machinery owned by tenants, and changes in farm inventories, all of which are implicitly included in net worth; and the treatment of all life insurance premium payments as saving rather than only additions to reserves. These inconsistencies work in different directions, but how near they come to cancelling each other is impossible to say. It is unlikely, however, that the net overstatement, or understatement, of saving is large enough compared with net worth changes to invalidate, or greatly modify, the differences between cols. 1 and 2 or their interpretation.

Column 3 – Estimated on the assumption that saving during earlier years of spending units of a given age in 1949 bore the same ratio to that year's average saving per spending unit as applied in 1948–1950 to a unit of corresponding age. In this calculation an estimate of saving excluding consumer durables and social security funds has been used to make figures in col. 3 more nearly comparable to those in cols. 1 and 2.

Columns 4 and 5 – Cols. 2 and 3 divided by col. 1.

[24] This approach, notwithstanding all its uncertainties, probably yields the least distorted picture of life saving curves that can be fashioned out of the rough over-all data now available, particularly since the underlying assumption of a steady relationship among the saving ratios of spending units of different age does not make undue demands upon our credulity. This approach is, however, subject to the drawback of reflecting the wide swings in total personal saving since 1930, particularly the very low level of saving in the early thirties and the extraordinarily high level during World War II. Application of the same method to periods of less violent fluctuations of total saving may, therefore, be expected to produce smoother life saving curves.

216

8.63. Use of this estimate of cumulated saving at different age levels (Table XLII, col. 3) leads to two conclusions:

First, cumulated saving reaches a peak at about age 60, most of the increase taking place between 35 and 55. Inclusion of consumer durables is not likely to shift the location of the peak, but would probably reduce the steepness of the curve before age 40. A further correction for understatement of liquid assets and stock, the holdings of which increase sharply with age, might, however, restore the curve to approximately the form shown in Table XLII. The shape of the curve is in reasonable agreement with that for average net worth. [25]

Secondly, cumulated saving accounts for less than two-thirds of observed net worth, taking all age groups together. This ratio is only moderately higher than the corresponding proportion derived from over-all statistics (Table XXXII), a fact which may influence our willingness to accept the results of this approach. The share is lowest for people over 64, much of whose saving would have been accumulated before the Great Depression, and for those under 35. It is highest for spending units with heads between 45 and 65. In view of the roughness of the figures it

TABLE XLIII

NET WORTH AND SAVING BY AGE: End of 1949

Age of head of spending unit	Percent of spending units	Number of spending units (mill.)	Average assets	Average net worth	Change in net worth		Average annual saving	
					Total	Per year	1948–1950	For age bracket
					$000			
	1	2	3	4	5	6	7	8
18–24	9.8	5.1	1.8	1.4	1.4	0.47	−0.04	−0.2
25–34	22.4	11.7	5.9	4.3	2.9	0.33	0.12	1.2
35–44	22.3	11.6	11.2	9.5	5.2	0.52	0.30	3.0
45–54	19.3	10.0	15.5	14.1	4.6	0.46	0.38	3.8
55–64	14.2	7.4	19.6	18.8	4.7	0.47	0.37	3.7
65 and over	12.0	6.2	16.0	15.3	−3.5	−0.35	0.04	0.4
All age groups	100.0	52.0	11.7	10.2	−	−	0.22	5.7

Column 1 – From Volume III, Table W-61.

Column 2 – Col. 1 multiplied by 52 million (*Federal Reserve Bulletin*, 1950, p. 1,441).

Column 3 – Total assets (Volume III, Table W-48), divided by col. 2.

Column 4 – Total net worth (Volume III, Table W-48), divided by col. 2.

Column 5 – First differences of col. 4.

Column 6 – Col. 5 divided by number of years in age bracket; for top bracket assumed at 10 years. In calculating value for bottom bracket net worth at age 18 is assumed negligible.

Column 7 – Calculated from distribution of aggregate saving by age groups (*Federal Reserve Bulletin*, 1950, p. 1,442; 1951, p. 1,074).

Column 8 – Col. 7 multiplied by number of years in age bracket; for top bracket assumed at 10 years.

[25] The main difference, the sharper decline in calculated cumulated saving after 64 than in average net worth, may be due in part to the fact that observed net worth of this age group has been relatively most affected by the upward trend of asset prices.

would seem best not to attach great weight to these differences, even though they are not unreasonable, with the possible exception of the low share of saving for the 25–34 age group, in view of the movements in asset prices since the time the accumulations were made.

8.64. Life accumulation curves can be drawn not only for total assets and net worth but also for specific assets and liabilities. They differ considerably both from the aggregate curves and among themselves (Table XLIV and Chart XLI).

TABLE XLIV

HOLDINGS OF MAIN TYPES OF ASSETS BY AGE GROUP: Early 1950

Age of head of spending unit	Liquid assets	Car	House	Farm	Other real estate	Life insur- ance	Retire- ment fund	Stock	Interest in busi- ness	Total assets	Debt	Net worth
	1	2	3	4	5	6	7	8	9	10	11	12

I. Average amount per spending unit ($000)

18–24	0.32	0.37	0.45	0.10	0.18	0.06	0.04	0.02	0.08	1.76	0.35	1.41
25–34	0.83	0.65	2.01	0.41	0.53	0.29	0.18	0.06	0.77	5.90	1.60	4.30
35–44	1.46	0.67	3.59	1.12	1.12	0.67	0.22	0.56	1.46	11.20	1.68	9.52
45–54	2.35	0.62	4.34	1.40	1.40	1.40	0.31	1.08	2.17	15.50	1.40	14.10
55–64	2.35	0.60	4.89	1.76	2.95	1.57	0.19	1.38	3.52	19.60	0.78	18.82
65 and over	3.03	0.32	4.47	1.76	2.39	1.27	–	2.08	0.48	15.96	0.65	15.31
All ages	1.68	0.58	3.36	1.08	1.36	0.87	0.18	0.79	1.48	11.67	1.22	10.45

II. Percent of spending units owning specified asset

18–24	59.4	46.4	7.0	1.4	3.3	68.0	8.5	1.7	2.2	100.0	47.6	100.0
25–34	66.5	62.1	24.1	2.3	8.3	83.0	14.2	4.0	7.7	100.0	63.2	100.0
35–44	73.3	61.6	39.7	5.9	14.6	85.0	14.6	6.0	13.5	100.0	63.4	100.0
45–54	74.8	60.2	47.4	8.0	16.2	81.0	14.4	8.6	12.6	100.0	51.5	100.0
55–64	71.3	53.4	52.2	10.0	20.8	73.0	11.0	9.9	12.0	100.0	39.1	100.0
65 and over	65.2	34.2	50.9	10.4	17.6	55.0	4.4	12.6	4.1	100.0	21.8	100.0
All ages	69.2	55.2	39.3	6.1	15.9	77.0	12.2	6.8	9.5	100.0	51.4	100.0

III. Average amount per spending unit owning specified asset ($000)

18–24	0.54	0.80	6.43	7.14	5.45	0.09	0.47	1.18	3.64	1.76	0.74	1.41
25–34	1.25	1.05	8.34	17.83	6.39	0.35	1.27	1.50	10.00	5.90	2.53	4.30
35–44	1.99	1.09	9.04	18.98	7.67	0.79	1.51	9.33	10.81	11.20	2.65	9.52
45–54	3.14	1.03	9.16	17.50	8.64	1.73	2.15	12.56	17.22	15.50	2.72	14.10
55–64	3.30	1.12	9.37	17.60	14.18	2.15	1.73	13.94	29.33	19.60	1.99	18.82
65 and over	4.65	0.94	8.78	16.90	13.58	2.31	–	16.51	11.71	15.96	2.98	15.31
All ages	2.43	1.05	8.55	17.70	8.55	1.13	1.48	11.62	15.58	11.67	2.37	10.45

Sections I and II – See Volume III, Part I. Data from 1950 Survey of Consumer Finances.
Section III – Obtained by dividing figures of Section I by those of Section II.

In contrast to total assets or total net worth two factors must be distinguished in analyzing life accumulation curves of individual assets and liabilities: first, the proportion of all individuals in a given age group holding the asset, and, secondly, the average value per holding. It is only in rather rare cases where the proportion of holders does not change with age that the life accumulation curves have the same shape whether they are based on averages of all spending units (Section I of Table XLIV) or on averages for actual owners only (Section III). Even then the level of the life accumulation curve is always higher for average actual holdings than for the purely arithmetic result of dividing total holdings

218

by the number of all spending units in the age group, the distance between the two curves being determined by the percentage of owners (Section II).

8.65. Starting with actual average holdings, i.e. taking account only of spending units owning an asset, a striking difference appears between two classes of assets (and liabilities) which might be called "lumpy" and "accumulative," respectively. These terms indicate that units of assets of the first type are typically of high value compared to savers' total assets or income and are not easily divisible, while assets of the second type can be, and usually are, accumulated (or liquidated) more or less continuously and in relatively small amounts.

For most "lumpy" assets the average value of actual holdings is little influenced by age, but the proportion of spending units owning them varies with age, with the result that the arithmetic average of all spending units' holdings also gives the appearance of being correlated with age. Assets of this type are characterized by a relatively small range—say, a value of less than $1\frac{1}{2}$ in column 3 of Table XLV—between average actual holdings of the old and the young. [26] This group is represented by homes, farms, and cars, all assets the "lumpy" character of which

TABLE XLV

RATIO OF AVERAGE HOLDINGS OF MAIN TYPES OF
ASSETS BY UPPER AGE GROUPS TO HOLDINGS BY
LOWER AGE GROUPS: Early 1950

Percent

	Age groups		
	18 to 24 and over 64	25 to 34 and over 64	25 to 34 and 55 to 64
	Average holding in upper age group / Average holding in lower age group		
	1	2	3
1. Stock in publicly held corporations	14.0	16.5	13.9
2. Life insurance	25.7	6.6	6.2
3. Interest in business[a]	3.2	1.2	2.9
4. Liquid assets	8.6	3.7	2.6
5. Other real estate	5.3	2.1	2.5
6. Retirement fund	.	.	1.4
7. House	1.4	1.1	1.1
8. Car	1.2	0.9	1.1
9. Farm	2.3	0.9	1.0
10. Debt	4.0	1.2	0.8
11. Total assets	9.1	2.7	3.3
12. Net worth	10.9	3.6	4.4

[a] Includes interest in closely held corporations.
Source: Derived from Volume III, Table W-48.

[26] On the basis of this criterion alone, retirement fund and debt also belong to this class, which they obviously do not. The reason is, in the case of retirement fund, that the estimates are based on current contributions rather than reserve value. The relation of debt to age is discussed in Division 8.67.

CHART XLI

SIZE OF ASSET HOLDINGS WITHIN DIFFERENT AGE GROUPS

Early 1950

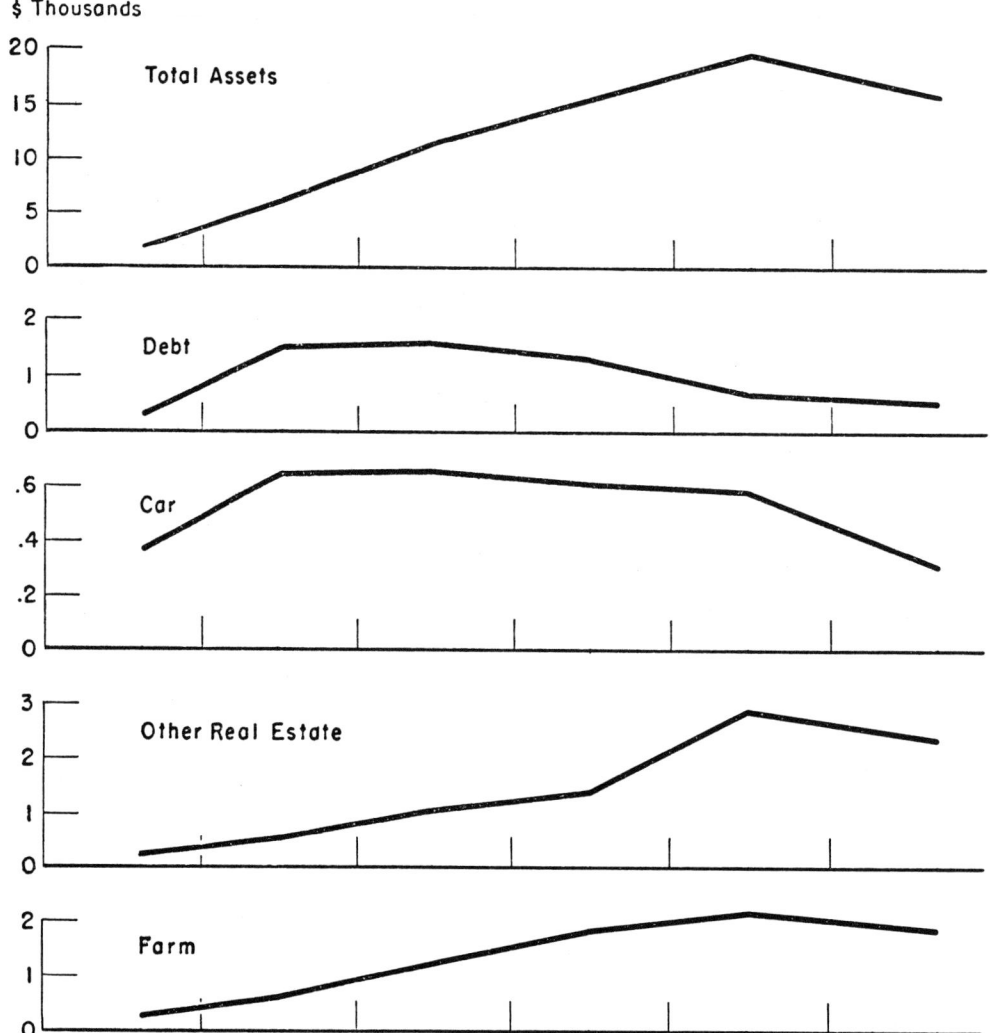

is obvious, most spending units owning either one unit of the asset or none. At the other end of the scale—showing a wide difference between average actual holdings of the young and the old—are life insurance, marketable stocks, interest in business, liquid assets, and real estate other than homes. These assets, except interest in business, in the typical case are accumulated gradually, and in the case of liquid assets and life insurance predominantly in small installments.

8.66. While the average actual holding has a tendency, as shown in Table XLIV, to remain stable or to increase with age (the decline in average value of business interest after 64 is the main exception), the proportion of spending units

CHART XLI *(Continued)*

SIZE OF ASSET HOLDINGS WITHIN DIFFERENT AGE GROUPS

Early 1950

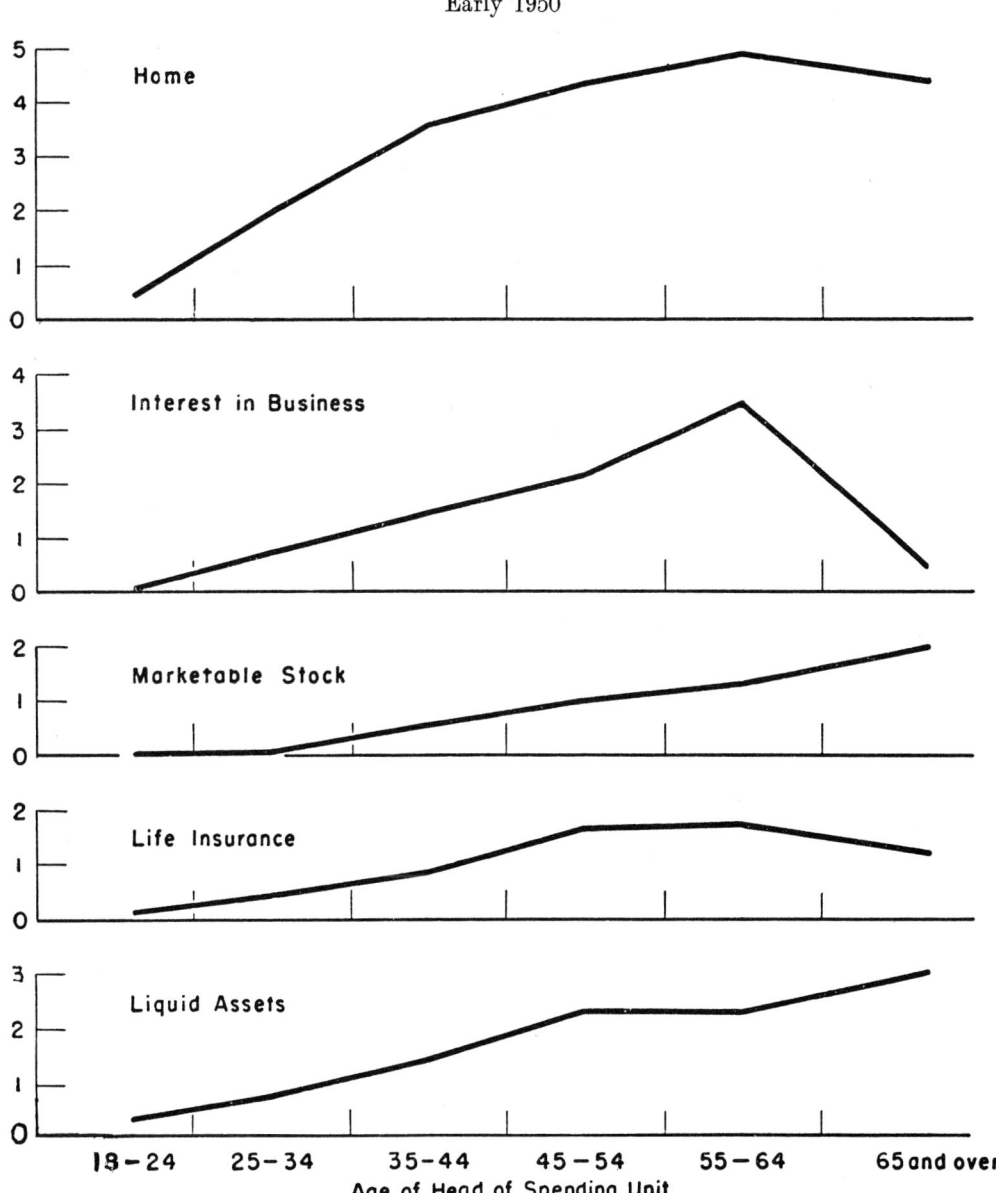

owning different types of assets is typically of parabolic form, first rising and then falling, with the peak usually in the 55–64 age group. Sometimes, however, the peak occurs as early as 45–54 years (liquid assets) or even 35–44 years (life insurance, retirement fund, interest in business, and debt).

8.67. The life accumulation curve for average holdings of an asset among the entire population, shown in Section I of Table XLIV, is thus the combined result of the participation curve and the curve of actual average holdings.

Some of the most important assets are then found to have a life accumulation curve similar to that for total assets and net worth, i.e. accumulation to a peak at age 55–64, and a moderate decline after 64. Holdings of owner-occupied homes, of farms, and of life insurance conform fairly well to this pattern. So do holdings of other real estate except that the increase is particularly pronounced between the 45–54 and 55–64 age groups. Apparently rental housing and other income properties typically are acquired in the decade before retirement.

Some assets, on the other hand, increase even after retirement is reached. Liquid assets and marketable stock are the most important representatives of this group. In the case of liquid assets the increase in average amounts held by the top age groups is due mostly to liquidation of other assets, not to continued current saving in liquid form.

Cars (and presumably other consumer durables not covered by the Survey), interest in business (unincorporated enterprises and closely held corporations), and debt show a pattern of accumulation that differs considerably. The distinguishing characteristic of the life accumulation curve for interest in business is the abrupt decline in the top age group, easily explained by retirement from active management, but also indicative of the fact that such retirement is usually accompanied by outright sale of interest or by transformation into a claim or another form not reached by the Survey. The trapezoidal form of the curves for debt and automobiles (and presumably other consumer durables) reflects the acquisition of consumer durables at or soon after household formation, financed to a large extent by consumer credit in one or more of its numerous forms; and the purchase at the same time of the first home by approximately two-fifths of the new households. [27]

8.68. The life accumulation curve of the entire population in 1950, to which discussion has hitherto been limited, is compared in Chart XLII with that of the estate tax population in 1948, i.e. individuals having a net estate—a concept very similar to net worth—of more than $60,000. [28] This group, though numbering only 976,000 in 1946 (Table E-41) accounted for something like 30 percent of the wealth of all individuals. [29]

The two outstanding differences between the two curves are, first, the milder slope of the curve for the estate tax population, and, secondly, the later peak in the life accumulation curve of the estate tax population. Average net worth of the entire population rises from $4,300 at 30 years to a top of $19,000 at 60 years,

[27] The statistics do not provide a distribution of first home purchases by age, but it can be approximated from the data on home ownership by age (*Federal Reserve Bulletin*, 1950, p. 1,597) and on family status by age (*Statistical Abstract*, 1952, p. 45).

[28] For a discussion of the nature and limitations of estate tax data and estimates of the wealth of the estate tax population see Volume III, Part III, particularly Chapters II and V.

[29] Estate tax wealth in 1945 may be put at approximately $180 billion (average of estimates for 1944 and 1946 in Volume III, Table E-39), while net worth of all individuals is estimated at nearly $550 billion. (Volume III, Table W-48.)

CHART XLII
RELATION OF ESTATE[a] TO AGE

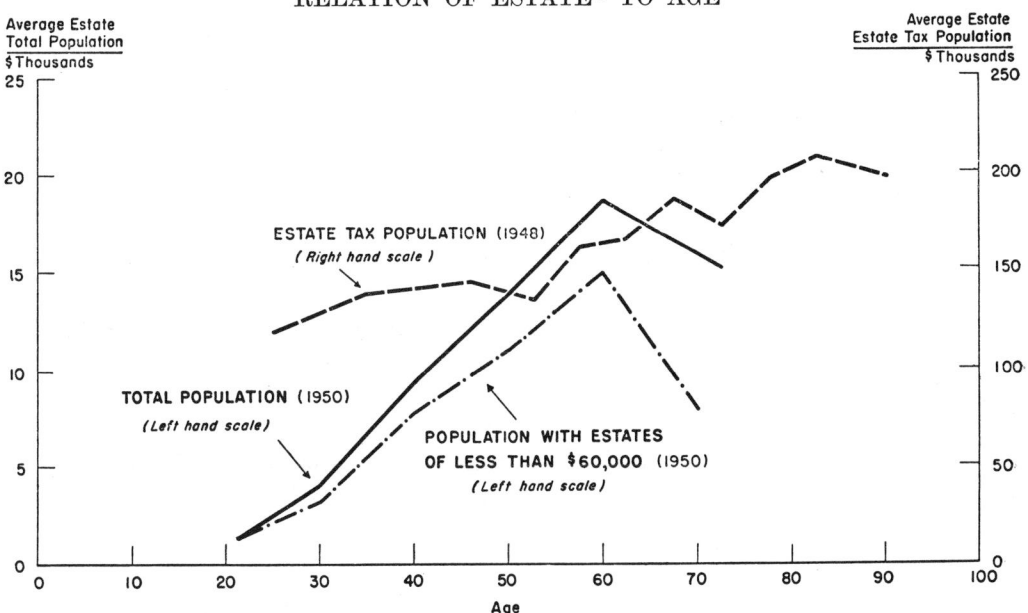

[a] Refers to net taxable estate before specific exemption in the case of estate tax population.

an increase by 340 percent, or at a rate of 5 percent per year. Average net estate of the estate population, on the other hand, increases only from approximately $130,000 at age 30 to a peak of $208,000 at age 80 to 85, i.e. by 60 percent, or at a rate of only 1 percent a year.

These differences remain when the estate tax population is compared not with the entire population but only with that part having estates of less than $60,000. This comparison is more appropriate because it is not affected by the fact that the proportion of people with estates of over $60,000 in the entire population increases with age. The increase in net worth with age is much more pronounced among smaller (less than $60,000) than among larger estate holders, and the peak is reached earlier for the former than for the latter.

The differences between the curves for estates above and below $60,000, however, cannot be regarded as reflecting exclusively differences in the shape of life accumulation curves since many individuals have in the course of their life moved from one to another group, particularly from the lower to the upper group. The differences should nevertheless give some clues to the underlying life accumulation curves. From that point of view both differences conform to expectations. Among the estate tax population inheritances and gifts, which probably do not markedly increase with age, particularly after middle age, as well as realized and unrealized capital gains may be expected to account for a larger proportion of total net worth and a considerably lower proportion of cumulated saving, which necessarily increases with age until retirement, than for the rest of the population. The later peak in the life accumulation curve of the estate tax population

223

probably reflects the absence of the need to draw on capital to defray living expenses, which is an important factor in explaining the decline in average net worth of the entire population after retirement age.

8.69. A similar conclusion is reached by comparing average gross estate for men and women of different age who died in 1948 leaving more than $60,000, as is done in Chart XLIII. While the average estate of male decedents rose from $135,000 for those twenty to thirty years of age to approximately $300,000 for those over eighty years, the average estate of women oscillated about $210,000 without any tendency to increase with age. This difference might be explained by the fact that cumulated saving, which rises with age, accounts for a considerably higher proportion of total estates for men than for women. The estates of women leaving more than $60,000 probably result mostly from inheritances and gifts—and thus in part, though indirectly, from their fathers' or husbands' saving—and from capital appreciation. The life accumulation curves of the two sexes are obviously quite different, at least among the upper wealth groups.

8.70. Very little quantitative information is available on possible changes over time in the slopes of life accumulation curves, and what information there is refers to the relatively small group of individuals leaving fortunes subject to

CHART XLIII

RELATION OF GROSS ESTATE TO AGE AND SEX AMONG ESTATE TAX POPULATION

1948

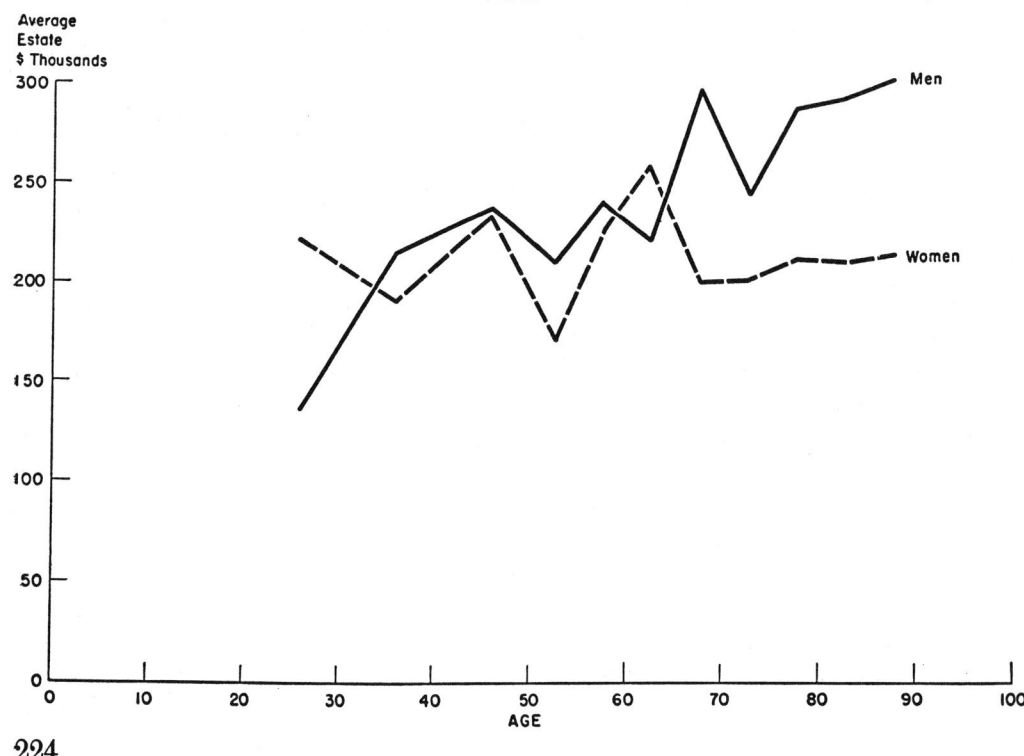

224

CHART XLIV

RELATION OF NET ESTATE TO AGE AMONG ESTATE TAX POPULATION

Selected Years: 1922 to 1949

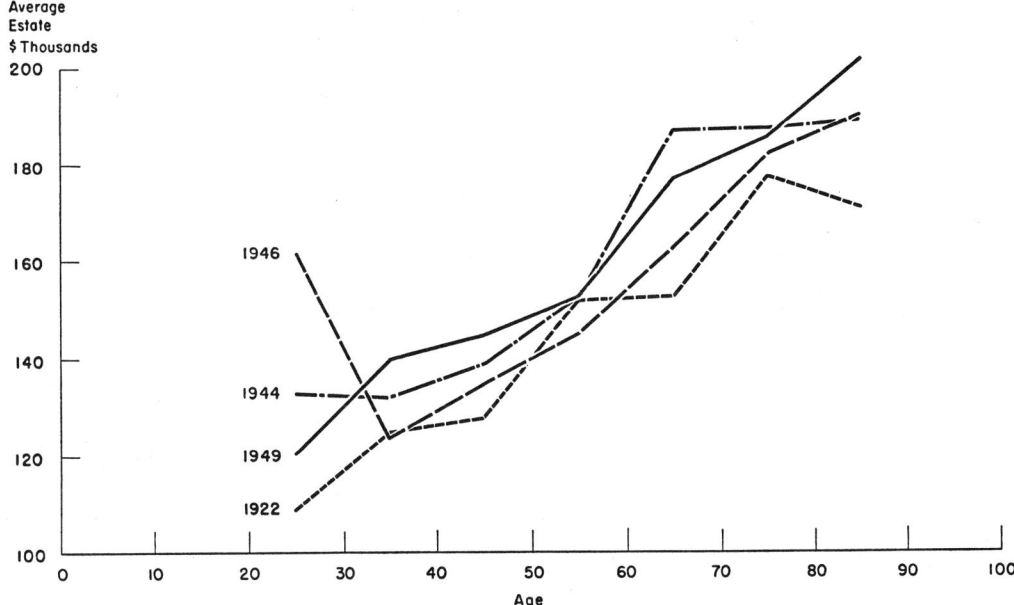

estate tax, i.e. fortunes exceeding $40,000 to $100,000 depending on the year of death.

Analysis of this material leads to only one important, though negative, conclusion: There is no evidence of substantial or systematic changes in the relation between average estate and age over the last thirty years, and hence no presumption that the form of the life saving curve has changed among the upper wealth groups. In the four years which are illustrated in Chart XLIV (1922, 1944, 1946 and 1949) average estate increases with age to the seventies; and at approximately the same rate. The only difference between the curves, apart from occasional irregularities, is the fact that the average for decedents over eighty is below that for those dying between seventy and eighty years in 1922, while it continues upwards in the forties and at a margin increasing between 1944 and 1949. In view of the small number of cases in the top age group this difference may not be significant.

8.71. All that we can now say about life saving curves, though generally in accord with expectations and suggestive of significant insights into the saving process, must remain tentative and a bit vague. Progress in this field is bound to be rather slow as long as we are limited to the type of data now available. Adequate analysis of life saving curves calls for primary data specifically adapted to the objective, i.e. the building up of actual life accumulation curves for a scientifically selected sample of the population, an undertaking of no mean difficulty and of substantial cost, but one holding considerable promise.

APPENDIX TO INTRODUCTION

Tables Z–1 to Z–24 – Supplementary Tables to Introduction

Tables S–1 to S–50 – Period Averages of
Annual Estimates of Saving

Z-1

(Part 1)

Number	Scope of estimate	Period	Form [1]	Equation [2]
N–1		1897–1949	AS	$S = 6{,}507 + 181.41\,t$
N–2		1897–1929	AS	$S = 6{,}313 + 403.30\,t$
N–3		1897–1914	AS	$S = 3{,}218 + 147.86\,t$
N–4		1915–1929	AS	$S = 10{,}116 + 692.39\,t$
N–5	Social accounting, current, aggregate, standard	1897–1929	AP	$S = 4{,}884 + 403.30\,t + 15.77\,t^2$
N–6		1897–1929	LS	$S = 4{,}771\ (1.0680)^t$
N–7		1897–1914	LS	$S = 2{,}997\ (1.0586)^t$
N–8		1915–1929	LS	$S = 8{,}625\ (1.0850)^t$
N–9		1897–1929	LP	$S = 4{,}554\ (1.0680)^t\ (1.0005)^{t^2}$
N–10		1897–1949	AS	$S = 7{,}279 + 247.42\,t$
N–11		1897–1929	AS	$S = 6{,}462 + 413.41\,t$
N–12	Social accounting, current, aggregate, adjusted	1897–1914	AS	$S = 3{,}303 + 156.36\,t$
N–13		1915–1929	AS	$S = 10{,}347 + 713.10\,t$
N–14		1897–1929	LS	$S = 4{,}878\ (1.0682)^t$
N–15		1897–1949	AS	$S = 5{,}453 + 140.00\,t$
N–16		1897–1929	AS	$S = 5{,}613 + 346.58\,t$
N–17	Social accounting, current, aggregate, excluding consumer durables	1897–1914	AS	$S = 2{,}906 + 133.92\,t$
N–18		1915–1929	AS	$S = 8{,}942 + 529.09\,t$
N–19		1897–1929	LS	$S = 4{,}335\ (1.0678)^t$
N–20		1897–1949	AS	$S = 8{,}906 + 341.93\,t$
N–21		1897–1929	AS	$S = 7{,}765 + 460.14\,t$
N–22	Business accounting, current, aggregate, standard	1897–1914	AS	$S = 3{,}916 + 171.72\,t$
N–23		1915–1929	AS	$S = 12{,}847 + 446.04\,t$
N–24		1897–1929 excl. 1921	LS	$S = 6{,}480\ (1.0757)^t$
N–25		1897–1949	AS	$S = 7{,}365 + 257.22\,t$
N–26		1897–1929	AS	$S = 6{,}588 + 371.93\,t$
N–27	Business accounting, current, aggregate, excluding consumer durables	1897–1914	AS	$S = 3{,}485 + 139.49\,t$
N–28		1915–1929	AS	$S = 10{,}396 + 367.34\,t$
N–29		1897–1929 excl. 1921	LS	$S = 5{,}603\ (1.0706)^t$
N–30		1897–1949	AS	$S = 17{,}550 + 623.40\,t$
N–31		1897–1929	AS	$S = 13{,}784 + 864.94\,t$
N–32	Cash flow, current, aggregate, standard	1897–1914	AS	$S = 6{,}837 + 318.87\,t$
N–33		1915–1929	AS	$S = 22{,}311 + 1153.05\,t$
N–34		1897–1929	LS	$S = 10{,}939\ (1.0697)^t$

[1] AS refers to arithmetic straight line, AP to arithmetic parabola, LS to logarithmic straight line, and LP to logarithmic parabola.

[2] For all equations t equals one year; for period 1897–1949 origin is in 1923, for 1897–1929 in 1913, for 1897–1914 in 1906, for 1915–1929 in 1922. Aggregate saving data expressed in $ mill.

229

Number	Scope of estimate	Period	Form [1]	Equation [2]
N–35	Cash flow, current, aggregate, excluding consumer durables	1897–1949	AS	$S = 11{,}343 + 349.29\,t$
N–36		1897–1929	AS	$S = 9{,}770 + 567.29\,t$
N–37		1897–1914	AS	$S = 5{,}129 + 211.20\,t$
N–38		1915–1929	AS	$S = 15{,}466 + 661.67\,t$
N–39		1897–1929	LS	$S = 7{,}703\ (1.0612)^{t}$
N–40	Social accounting, deflated general price level, aggregate, standard	1897–1949	AS	$S = 6{,}783 + 64.15\,t$
N–41		1897–1929	AS	$S = 7{,}840 + 288.25\,t$
N–42		1897–1914	AS	$S = 5{,}762 + 162.52\,t$
N–43		1915–1929	AS	$S = 10{,}432 + 508.24\,t$
N–44		1897–1929	AP	$S = 6{,}948 + 288.25\,t + 9.94\,t^{2}$
N–45		1897–1929	LS	$S = 6{,}771\ (1.0349)^{t}$
N–46		1897–1914	LS	$S = 5{,}488\ (1.0363)^{t}$
N–47		1915–1929	LS	$S = 8{,}901\ (1.0648)^{t}$
N–48		1897–1929	LP	$S = 6{,}440\ (1.0349)^{t}\ (1.0006)^{t^{2}}$
N–49	Social accounting, deflated general price level, aggregate, excluding consumer durables	1897–1949	AS	$S = 5{,}795 + 26.24\,t$
N–50		1897–1929	AS	$S = 7{,}000 + 242.93\,t$
N–51		1897–1914	AS	$S = 5{,}203 + 146.94\,t$
N–52		1915–1929	AS	$S = 9{,}244 + 357.63\,t$
N–53		1897–1929	LS	$S = 6{,}163\ (1.0346)^{t}$
N–54	Social accounting, deflated wage level, aggregate, standard	1897–1949	AS	$S = 7{,}489 - 89.39\,t$
N–55		1897–1929	AS	$S = 10{,}210 + 227.34\,t$
N–56		1897–1914	AS	$S = 8{,}513 + 206.39\,t$
N–57		1915–1929	AS	$S = 12{,}371 + 162.01\,t$
N–58		1897–1929	LS	$S = 9{,}157\ (1.0216)^{t}$
N–59	Social accounting, deflated group purchasing power, aggregate, standard	1897–1949	AS	$S = 7{,}823 + 115.41\,t$
N–60		1897–1929	AS	$S = 8{,}284 + 285.85\,t$
N–61		1897–1914	AS	$S = 6{,}198 + 190.86\,t$
N–62		1915–1929	AS	$S = 10{,}902 + 410.51\,t$
N–63		1897–1929	LS	$S = 7{,}250\ (1.0339)^{t}$
N–64	Social accounting, deflated general price level, per inhabitant, standard	1897–1949	AS	$S = 62.09 - 0.29\,t$
N–65		1897–1929	AS	$S = 78.66 + 1.63\,t$
N–66		1897–1914	AS	$S = 66.87 + 0.79\,t$
N–67		1915–1929	AS	$S = 93.27 + 3.10\,t$
N–68		1897–1929	AP	$S = 72.99 + 1.63\,t + 0.06\,t^{2}$
N–69		1897–1929	LS	$S = 70.88\ (1.0180)^{t}$
N–70		1897–1914	LS	$S = 64.28\ (1.0170)^{t}$
N–71		1915–1929	LS	$S = 80.52\ (1.0497)^{t}$
N–72		1897–1929	LP	$S = 66.61\ (1.0180)^{t}\ (1.0007)^{t^{2}}$

[1] AS refers to arithmetic straight line, AP to arithmetic parabola, LS to logarithmic straight line, and LP to logarithmic parabola.

[2] For all equations t equals one year; for period 1897–1949 origin is in 1923, for 1897–1929 in 1913, for 1897–1914 in 1906, for 1915–1929 in 1922. Aggregate saving data expressed in $ mill.

Number	Scope of estimate	Period	Form [1]	Equation [2]
N– 73		1897–1949	AS	$S = 53.75 - 0.49\,t$
N– 74	Social accounting, deflated gener-	1897–1929	AS	$S = 86.32 + 1.32\,t$
N– 75	al price level, per inhabitant,	1897–1914	AS	$S = 60.39 + 0.71\,t$
N– 76	excluding consumer durables	1915–1929	AS	$S = 82.87 + 1.90\,t$
N– 77		1897–1929	LS	$S = 64.42\,(1.0177)^{t}$
N– 78		1897–1949	AS	$S = 265.25 - 2.88\,t$
N– 79	Social accounting, deflated gener-	1897–1929	AS	$S = 350.64 + 5.57\,t$
N– 80	al price level, per household,	1897–1914	AS	$S = 310.20 + 2.47\,t$
N– 81	standard	1915–1929	AS	$S = 400.65 + 10.86\,t$
N– 82		1897–1929	LS	$S = 318.55\,(1.0132)^{t}$
N– 83		1897–1949	AS	$S = 86.92 - 0.46\,t$
N– 84	Social accounting, deflated gener-	1897–1929	AS	$S = 110.62 + 2.20\,t$
N– 85	al price level, per consuming unit,	1897–1914	AS	$S = 94.57 + 1.02\,t$
N– 86	standard	1915–1929	AS	$S = 130.48 + 4.22\,t$
N– 87		1897–1929	LS	$S = 99.83\,(1.0172)^{t}$
N– 88		1897–1949	AS	$S = 154.25 - 0.98\,t$
N– 89	Social accounting, deflated gener-	1897–1929	AS	$S = 198.39 + 4.06\,t$
N– 90	al price level, per labor force	1897–1914	AS	$S = 167.20 + 1.16\,t$
N– 91	member, standard	1915–1929	AS	$S = 236.51 + 7.71\,t$
N– 92		1897–1929	LS	$S = 178.91\,(1.0175)^{t}$
N– 93		1897–1949	AS	$S = 9.53 - 0.224\,t$
N– 94		1897–1929	AS	$S = 13.68 + 0.047\,t$
N– 95	National saving as percent of	1897–1914	AS	$S = 13.34 - 0.030\,t$
N– 96	net national product	1915–1929	AS	$S = 14.09 + 0.198\,t$
N– 97		1897–1929	LS	$S = 12.58\,(1.0014)^{t}$
N– 98		1897–1949	AS	$S = 8.39 - 0.226\,t$
N– 99	National saving excluding con-	1897–1929	AS	$S = 12.30 + 0.022\,t$
N–100	sumer durables as percent of net	1897–1914	AS	$S = 12.06 - 0.027\,t$
N–101	national product	1915–1929	AS	$S = 12.57 + 0.043\,t$
N–102		1897–1929	LS	$S = 11.37\,(1.0006)^{t}$

[1] AS refers to arithmetic straight line, AP to arithmetic parabola, LS to logarithmic straight line, and LP to logarithmic parabola.
[2] For all equations t equals one year; for period 1897–1949 origin is in 1923, for 1897–1929 in 1913, for 1897–1914 in 1906, for 1915–1929 in 1922. Aggregate saving data expressed in $ mill.

TABLE Z-1

Part 1

N-1 to N-9   – From Table T-1, col. 1.

N-10 to N-14 – From Table T-4, col. 1.

N-15 to N-19 – Table T-1, col. 1 minus Table T-6, col. 5.

N-20 to N-24 – From Table T-2, col. 1.

N-25 to N-29 – Table T-2, col. 1 minus Table T-7, col. 5.

N-30 to N-34 – From Table T-3, col. 1.

Part 2

N-35 to N-39 – Table T-3, col. 1 minus the sum of Table T-10, col. 4 and Table A-66, col. 3.

N-40 to N-48 – From Table T-12, col. 1.

N-49 to N-53 – The residual of Table T-1, col. 1 minus Table T-6, col. 5 divided by Table T-16, col. 1.

N-54 to N-58 – From Table T-13, col. 1.

N-59 to N-63 – From Table T-14, col. 1.

N-64 to N-72 – Table T-12, col. 1 divided by total population (1900–1945 *Historical Statistics*, p. 26; 1946–1949 *Statistical Abstract*, various issues).

Part 3

N-73 to N-77 – Values as described in notes to lines N-49 to N-53 divided by total population.

N-78 to N-92 – Table T-12, col. 1 divided by number of households, number of consuming units, and the labor force (see notes to Table S-3).

N-93 to N-97 – Table T-1, col. 1 divided by Table N-1, col. 6.

N-98 to N-102 – The residual of Table T-1, col. 1 minus Table T-6, col. 5 divided by Table N-1, col. 6.

Number	Scope of estimate	Period	Form [1]	Equation [2]
P–1		1897–1949	AS	$S = 8,483 + 416.49\,t$
P–2		1897–1929	AS	$S = 4,998 + 507.31\,t$
P–3		1897–1914	AS	$S = 2,341 + 115.59\,t$
P–4	Social accounting, current,	1915–1929	AS	$S = 8,257 + 198.73\,t$
P–5	aggregate, standard	1897–1929	AP	$S = 4,621 + 507.31\,t + 4.16\,t^2$
P–6		1897–1929	LS	$S = 3,689\,(1.0735)^t$
P–7		1897–1914	LS	$S = 2,130\,(1.0657)^t$
P–8		1915–1929	LS	$S = 7,410\,(1.0316)^t$
P–9		1897–1929	LP	$S = 3,987\,\dfrac{(1.0735)^t}{(1.0009)^{t^2}}$
P–10		1897–1949	AS	$S = 8,648 + 426.32\,t$
P–11	Social accounting, current,	1897–1929	AS	$S = 5,147 + 316.99\,t$
P–12	aggregate, adjusted	1897–1914	AS	$S = 2,425 + 124.08\,t$
P–13		1915–1929	AS	$S = 8,488 + 219.44\,t$
P–14		1897–1929	LS	$S = 3,800\,(1.0734)^t$
P–15		1897–1949	AS	$S = 7,430 + 361.63\,t$
P–16	Social accounting, current, aggre-	1897–1929	AS	$S = 4,298 + 250.16\,t$
P–17	gate, excluding consumer	1897–1914	AS	$S = 2,028 + 101.65\,t$
P–18	durables	1915–1929	AS	$S = 7,083 + 35.43\,t$
P–19		1897–1929	LS	$S = 3,181\,(1.0704)^t$
P–20		1897–1949	AS	$S = 10,209 + 510.00\,t$
P–21	Business accounting, current,	1897–1929	AS	$S = 6,171 + 361.42\,t$
P–22	aggregate, standard	1897–1914	AS	$S = 2,865 + 138.81\,t$
P–23		1915–1929	AS	$S = 10,222 + 1.60\,t$
P–24		1897–1929	LS	$S = 4,263\,(1.0658)^t$
P–25		1897–1949	AS	$S = 8,668 + 425.29\,t$
P–26	Business accounting, current,	1897–1929	AS	$S = 4,994 + 273.21\,t$
P–27	aggregate, excluding consumer	1897–1914	AS	$S = 2,434 + 106.59\,t$
P–28	durables	1915–1929	AS	$S = 8,130 - 37.10\,t$
P–29		1897–1929 excl. 1921	LS	$S = 3,998\,(1.0735)^t$
P–30		1897–1949	AS	$S = 15,673 + 666.72\,t$
P–31	Cash flow, current, aggregate,	1897–1929	AS	$S = 10,174 + 606.31\,t$
P–32	standard	1897–1914	AS	$S = 5,022 + 236.53\,t$
P–33		1915–1929	AS	$S = 16,497 + 480.15\,t$
P–34		1897–1929	LS	$S = 8,088\,(1.0687)^t$
P–35		1897–1949	AS	$S = 9,465 + 393.23\,t$
P–36	Cash flow, current, aggregate,	1897–1929	AS	$S = 6,160 + 309.66\,t$
P–37	excluding consumer durables	1897–1914	AS	$S = 3,315 + 128.86\,t$
P–38		1915–1929	AS	$S = 9,652 - 11.24\,t$
P–39		1897–1929	LS	$S = 4,687\,(1.0518)^t$

[1] AS refers to arithmetic straight line, AP to arithmetic parabola, LS to logarithmic straight line, and LP to logarithmic parabola.

[2] For all equations t equals one year; for period 1897–1949 origin is in 1923, for 1897–1929 in 1913, for 1897–1914 in 1906, for 1915–1929 in 1922. Aggregate saving data expressed in $ mill.

TREND EQUATIONS OF PERSONAL SAVING

Number	Scope of estimate	Period	Form [1]	Equation [2]
P–40		1897–1949	AS	$S = 8,309 + 285.92\,t$
P–41		1897–1929	AS	$S = 6,103 + 225.03\,t$
P–42		1897–1914	AS	$S = 4,186 + 133.74\,t$
P–43	Social accounting, deflated	1915–1929	AS	$S = 8,484 + 68.82\,t$
P–44	general price level,	1897–1929	AP	$S = 6,129 + 225.03\,t - 0.28\,t^2$
P–45	aggregate, standard	1897–1929	LS	$S = 5,235\,(1.0401)^t$
P–46		1897–1914	LS	$S = 3,899\,(1.0432)^t$
P–47		1915–1929	LS	$S = 7,647\,(1.0124)^t$
P–48		1897–1929	LP	$S = 5,638\,\dfrac{(1.0401)^t}{(1.0008)^{t^2}}$
P–49		1897–1949	AS	$S = 7,321 + 248.05\,t$
P–50	Social accounting, deflated gener-	1897–1929	AS	$S = 5,263 + 179.72\,t$
P–51	al price level, aggregate, ex-	1897–1914	AS	$S = 3,627 + 118.19\,t$
P–52	cluding consumer durables	1915–1929	AS	$S = 7,297 - 81.76\,t$
P–53		1897–1929	LS	$S = 4,523\,(1.0394)^t$
P–54		1897–1949	AS	$S = 8,256 + 113.09\,t$
P–55	Social accounting, deflated wage	1897–1929	AS	$S = 8,053 + 195.30\,t$
P–56	level, aggregate, standard	1897–1914	AS	$S = 6,180 + 174.15\,t$
P–57		1915–1929	AS	$S = 10,405 - 292.99\,t$
P–58		1897–1929	LS	$S = 7,080\,(1.0268)^t$
P–59		1897–1949	AS	$S = 8.996 + 319.32\,t$
P–60	Social accounting, deflated group	1897–1929	AS	$S = 6,457 + 226.40\,t$
P–61	purchasing power, aggregate,	1897–1914	AS	$S = 4,484 + 155.56\,t$
P–62	standard	1915–1929	AS	$S = 898 - 25.29\,t$
P–63		1897–1929	LS	$S = 5,527\,(1.0388)^t$
P–64		1897–1949	AS	$S = 70.81 + 1.55\,t$
P–65		1897–1929	AS	$S = 61.11 + 1.36\,t$
P–66		1897–1914	AS	$S = 48.50 + 0.77\,t$
P–67	Social accounting, deflated gener-	1915–1929	AS	$S = 76.69 - 0.54\,t$
P–68	al price level, per inhabitant,	1897–1929	AP	$S = 63.48 + 1.36\,t - 0.03\,t^2$
P–69	standard	1897–1929	LS	$S = 54.81\,(1.0232)^t$
P–70		1897–1914	LS	$S = 45.67\,(1.0238)^t$
P–71		1915–1929	LS	$S = \dfrac{6918}{(1.0019)^t}$
P–72		1897–1929	LP	$S = 58.34\,\dfrac{(1.0232)^t}{(1.0007)^{t^2}}$
P–73		1897–1949	AS	$S = 62.47 + 1.35\,t$
P–74	Social accounting, deflated gener-	1897–1929	AS	$S = 52.87 + 1.06\,t$
P–75	al price level, per inhabitant,	1897–1914	AS	$S = 42.01 + 0.69\,t$
P–76	excluding consumer durables	1915–1929	AS	$S = 66.31 - 1.75\,t$
P–77		1897–1929	LS	$S = 47.25\,(1.0225)^t$

[1] AS refers to arithmetic straight line, AP to arithmetic parabola, LS to logarithmic straight line, and LP to logarithmic parabola.

[2] For all equations t equals one year; for period 1897–1949 origin is in 1923, for 1897–1929 in 1913, for 1897–1914 in 1906, for 1915–1929 in 1922. Aggregate saving data expressed in $ mill.

234

Number	Scope of estimate	Period	Form [1]	Equation [2]
P– 78	Social accounting, deflated general price level, per household, standard	1897–1949	AS	$S = 291.26 + 4.46\,t$
P– 79		1897–1929	AS	$S = 272.29 + 4.89\,t$
P– 80		1897–1914	AS	$S = 224.83 + 2.72\,t$
P– 81		1915–1929	AS	$S = 330.88 - 4.29\,t$
P– 82		1897–1929	LS	$S = 246.29\,(1.0184)^{\,t}$
P– 83	Social accounting, deflated general price level, per consuming unit, standard	1897–1949	AS	$S = 98.38 + 2.06\,t$
P– 84		1897–1929	AS	$S = 85.92 + 1.86\,t$
P– 85		1897–1914	AS	$S = 68.56 + 1.02\,t$
P– 86		1915–1929	AS	$S = 107.37 - 0.86\,t$
P– 87		1897–1929	LS	$S = 77.18\,(1.0224)^{\,t}$
P– 88	Social accounting, deflated general price level, per labor force member, standard	1897–1949	AS	$S = 170.47 + 3.14\,t$
P– 89		1897–1929	AS	$S = 154.18 + 3.42\,t$
P– 90		1897–1914	AS	$S = 121.14 + 1.34\,t$
P– 91		1915–1929	AS	$S = 194.63 - 1.49\,t$
P– 92		1897–1929	LS	$S = 138.35\,(1.0227)^{\,t}$
P– 93	Personal saving as percent of personal disposable income	1897–1949	AS	$S = 11.50 + 0.077\,t$
P– 94		1897–1929	AS	$S = 11.78 + 0.085\,t$
P– 95		1897–1914	AS	$S = 10.66 + 0.003\,t$
P– 96		1915–1929	AS	$S = 13.13 - 0.284\,t$
P– 97		1897–1929	LS	$S = 10.90\,(1.0072)^{\,t}$
P– 98	Personal saving excluding consumer durables as percent of personal disposable income	1897–1949	AS	$S = 10.17 + 0.062\,t$
P– 99		1897–1929	AS	$S = 10.23 + 0.055\,t$
P–100		1897–1914	AS	$S = 9.26 + 0.008\,t$
P–101		1915–1929	AS	$S = 11.39 - 0.458\,t$
P–102		1897–1929	LS	$S = 9.42\,(1.0067)^{\,t}$
P–103	Nonfederal saving as percent of nonfederal disposable income	1897–1929	AS	$S = 14.27 + 0.071\,t$
P–104		1897–1914	AS	$S = 13.09 - 0.086\,t$
P–105		1915–1929	AS	$S = 15.63 - 0.302\,t$
P–106	Nonfederal saving excluding consumer durables as percent of nonfederal disposable income	1897–1929	AS	$S = 12.88 + 0.045\,t$
P–107		1897–1914	AS	$S = 11.83 - 0.076\,t$
P–108		1915–1929	AS	$S = 14.10 - 0.464\,t$
P–109	Nonagricultural individuals' saving as percent of nonagricultural disposable income	1899–1929	AS	$S = 14.84 + 0.022\,t$
P–110		1899–1914	AS	$S = 13.87 - 0.139\,t$
P–111		1915–1929	AS	$S = 15.81 - 0.437\,t$
P–112	Nonagricultural individuals' saving excluding consumer durables as percent of nonagricultural disposable income	1899–1929	AS	$S = 13.00 - 0.015\,t$
P–113		1899–1914	AS	$S = 12.23 - 0.097\,t$
P–114		1915–1929	AS	$S = 13.78 - 0.660\,t$

[1] AS refers to arithmetic straight line, AP to arithmetic parabola, LS to logarithmic straight line, and LP to logarithmic parabola.

[2] For all equations t equals one year; for period 1897–1949 origin is in 1923, for 1897–1929 in 1913, for 1897–1914 in 1906, for 1915–1929 in 1922. Aggregate saving data expressed in $ mill.

235

TABLE Z–2

Part 1

P-1 to P-9 – From Table T-1, col. 2.

P-10 to P-14 – From Table T-4, col. 4.

P-15 to P-19 – Table T-6, col. 1 minus col. 5.

P-20 to P-24 – From Table T-2, col. 2.

P-25 to P-29 – Table T-2, col. 2 minus Table T-7, col. 5.

P-30 to P-34 – From T-3, col. 2.

P-35 to P-39 – Table T-3, col. 2 minus the sum of Table T-10, col. 4 and Table A-66, col. 3.

Part 2

P-40 to P-48 – From Table T-12, col. 2.

P-49 to P-53 – The residual of Table T-1, col. 2 minus Table T-6, col. 5 divided by Table T-16, col. 1.

P-54 to P-58 – From Table T-13, col. 2.

P-59 to P-63 – From Table T-14, col. 2.

P-64 to P-72 – Table T-12, col. 2 divided by total population (1900–1945 *Historical Statistics*, p. 26; 1946–1949 *Statistical Abstract*, various issues).

P-73 to P-77 – Values as described in notes to lines P-49 to P-53 divided by total population.

Part 3

P-78 to P-92 – Table T-12, col. 2 divided by number of households, number of consuming units, and the labor force (see notes to Table S-3).

P-93 to P-97 – Table T-1, col. 2 divided by Table N-1, col. 9.

P-98 to P-102 – Table T-6, col. 1 minus col. 5 divided by Table N-1, col. 9.

P-103 to P-105 – Table T-1, col. 1 minus col. 8 divided by estimate of nonfederal disposable income obtained by adding personal disposable income (Table N-1, col. 9); corporate income (Table C-1, col. 12 plus corporate dividends from Table C-6, col. 1 for 1897–1915; Table C-29, col. 1 for 1916–1922; and from *Statistics of Income* for 1923–1949); income of state governments (Table G-13, col. 1 converted to calendar year by arithmetic averaging of successive years); and income of local governments (Table G-1, col. 1).

P-106 to P-108 – Table T-1, col. 1 minus col. 8 minus Table T-6, col. 5 divided by same denominator as for P-103 to P-105.

P-109 to P-111 – Table T-8, col. 1 divided by the residual of Table N-3, col. 8 and estimates of the income of unincorporated business derived as follows: for 1899–1918, Martin, *National Income in the United States, 1799–1938*, p. 39 (figures exclude agriculture and miscellaneous categories); for 1919–1928, Volume II, Table B-79, col. 2; and for 1929–1949, Table B-79, col. 4.

P-112 to P-114 – Table T-8, col. 1 minus col. 5 divided by same denominator as for P-109 to P-111.

1946 to 1949

		Form	Number of equation	Ratios			
				1946	1947	1948	1949
1.	Social accounting, current, aggregate, standard	AS	N–2	0.800	0.619	0.485	0.668
2.		AP	N–5	1.441	1.138	0.909	1.278
3.		LS	N–6	1.707	1.383	1.133	1.638
4.		LP	N–9	2.854	2.392	2.032	3.045
5.	Social accounting, current, aggregate, adjusted	AS	N–11	0.967	0.792	0.596	0.882
6.		LS	N–14	2.069	1.773	1.397	2.166
7.	Social accounting, current, aggregate, excluding consumer durables	AS	N–16	0.915	0.747	0.528	0.808
8.		LS	N–19	2.026	1.732	1.280	2.054
9.	Business accounting, current, aggregate, standard	AS	N–21	0.530	0.417	0.427	0.642
10.		LS	N–24	1.545	1.282	1.385	2.197
11.	Business accounting, current, aggregate, excluding consumer durables	AS	N–26	0.548	0.443	0.453	0.781
12.		LS	N–29	1.445	1.226	1.319	2.387
13.	Cash flow, current, aggregate, standard	AS	N–31	0.761	0.645	0.609	0.756
14.		LS	N–34	1.816	1.613	1.598	2.079
15.	Cash flow, current, aggregate, excluding consumer durables	AS	N–36	0.734	0.648	0.613	0.897
16.		LS	N–39	1.408	1.295	1.275	1.942
17.	Social accounting, deflated general price level, aggregate, standard	AS	N–41	0.891	0.758	0.638	0.871
18.		AP	N–44	1.401	1.213	1.039	1.444
19.		LS	N–45	1.077	0.933	0.799	1.112
20.		LP	N–48	1.872	1.681	1.497	2.166
21.	Social accounting, deflated general price level, aggregate, excluding consumer durables	AS	N–50	1.015	0.911	0.691	1.048
22.		LS	N–53	1.279	1.168	0.903	1.394
23.	Social accounting, deflated wage level, aggregate, standard	AS	N–55	1.372	1.186	1.008	1.458
24.		LS	N–58	1.438	1.294	1.075	1.569
25.	Social accounting, deflated group purchasing power, aggregate, standard	AS	N–60	0.850	0.806	0.683	0.897
26.		LS	N–63	1.408	1.007	0.868	1.162
27.	Social accounting, deflated general price level, per inhabitant, standard	AS	N–65	0.959	0.829	0.707	0.979
28.		AP	N–68	1.412	1.241	1.076	1.516
29.		LS	N–69	0.925	0.804	0.689	0.960
30.		LP	N–72	1.835	1.668	1.501	2.194
31.	Social accounting, deflated general price level, per inhabitant, excluding consumer durables	AS	N–74	1.242	1.129	0.867	1.330
32.		LS	N–77	1.098	1.006	0.778	1.204
33.	Social accounting, deflated general price level, per household, standard	AS	N–79	1.048	0.908	0.790	1.110
34.		LS	N–82	0.964	0.837	0.731	1.029
35.	Social accounting, deflated general price level, per consumer unit, standard	AS	N–84	0.968	0.831	0.705	0.972
36.		LS	N–87	0.925	0.798	0.681	0.944
37.	Social accounting, deflated general price level, per labor force member, standard	AS	N–89	1.038	0.891	0.760	1.048
38.		LS	N–92	0.990	0.853	0.732	1.015

Source: Extrapolated values obtained from appropriate equations in Appendix Table Z–1; actual values obtained from sources listed there.

RATIO OF VALUES EXTRAPOLATED FROM 1897–1929 TRENDS
TO ACTUAL VALUES OF PERSONAL SAVING: 1946 to 1952

		Form	Number of equation	Ratios						
				1946	1947	1948	1949	1950	1951	1952
1.	Social accounting, current, aggregate, standard	AS	P–2	0.987	1.102	0.851	1.036	0.834	0.730	0.831
2.		AP	P–5	1.176	1.321	1.028	1.259	1.021	0.899	1.030
3.		LS	P–6	1.738	2.036	1.651	2.109	1.784	1.641	1.964
4.		LP	P–9	0.739	0.818	0.627	0.751	0.597	0.515	0.577
5.	Social accounting, current, aggregate, adjusted	AS	P–11	0.697	0.764	0.587	0.711			
6.		LS	P–14	1.757	2.025	1.636	2.087			
7.	Social accounting, current, aggregate, excluding consumer durables	AS	P–16	0.778	1.153	0.717	0.973	0.875	0.567	0.591
8.		LS	P–19	2.008	3.127	2.048	3.924	2.769	1.891	2.075
9.	Business accounting, current, aggregate, standard	AS	P–21	0.549	0.533	0.548	0.701			
10.		LS	P–24	1.061	1.075	1.155	1.546			
11.	Business accounting, current, aggregate, excluding consumer durables	AS	P–26	0.582	0.651	0.671	0.987			
12.		LS	P–29	1.606	1.891	2.053	3.184			
13.	Cash flow, current, aggregate, standard	AS	P–31	0.768	0.735	0.744	0.826			
14.		LS	P–34	1.840	1.846	1.958	2.279			
15.	Cash flow, current, aggregate, excluding consumer durables	AS	P–36	0.725	0.843	0.932	1.334			
16.		LS	P–39	1.100	1.321	1.508	2.228			
17.	Social accounting, deflated general price level, aggregate, standard	AS	P–41	0.774	0.947	0.785	0.942	0.770	0.719	0.793
18.		AP	P–44	0.758	0.927	0.767	0.920	0.750	0.699	0.771
19.		LS	P–45	1.097	1.373	1.165	1.432	1.197	1.144	1.294
20.		LP	P–48	0.485	0.575	0.461	0.534	0.421	0.378	0.402
21.	Social accounting, deflated general price level, aggregate, excluding consumer durables	AS	P–50	0.875	1.423	0.953	1.279	1.169	0.810	0.820
22.		LS	P–53	1.267	2.109	1.444	1.984	1.857	1.318	1.367
23.	Social accounting, deflated wage level, aggregate, standard	AS	P–55	1.251	1.558	1.304	1.659			
24.		LS	P–58	1.464	1.847	1.567	2.021			
25.	Social accounting, deflated group purchasing power, aggregate, standard	AS	P–60	0.738	0.918	0.775	0.917			
26.		LS	P–63	1.028	1.307	1.128	1.366			
27.	Social accounting, deflated general price level, per inhabitant, standard	AS	P–65	0.857	1.066	0.895	1.091	0.903	0.854	0.956
28.		AP	P–68	0.646	0.790	0.652	0.779	0.632	0.586	0.644
29.		LS	P–69	0.943	1.185	1.005	1.238	1.035	0.989	1.121
30.		LP	P–72	0.474	0.569	0.461	0.540	0.430	0.390	0.418
31.	Social accounting, deflated general price level, per inhabitant, excluding consumer durables	AS	P–74	0.969	1.603	1.087	1.480	1.371	0.963	0.986
32.		LS	P–77	1.088	1.816	1.245	1.714	1.604	1.140	1.183
33.	Social accounting, deflated general price level, per household, standard	AS	P–79	0.947	1.182	1.013	1.252			
34.		LS	P–82	0.982	1.234	1.065	1.326			
35.	Social accounting, deflated general price level, per consumer unit, standard	AS	P–84	0.866	1.070	0.895	1.086			
36.		LS	P–87	0.942	1.176	0.993	1.217			
37.	Social accounting, deflated general price level, per labor force member, standard	AS	P–89	0.930	1.148	0.965	1.170			
38.		LS	P–92	1.008	1.257	1.067	1.370			

Source: Extrapolated values obtained from appropriate equations in Appendix Table Z–2; actual values obtained from sources listed there.

RATIO OF VALUES EXTRAPOLATED FROM 1897–1929 TRENDS TO ACTUAL VALUES OF NATIONAL AND PERSONAL SAVING; ANNUAL AVERAGES
1946 to 1949

	National saving		Personal saving	
	Arithmetic	Logarithmic	Arithmetic	Logarithmic
	Straight line trend		Straight line trend	
I. Current aggregate values				
1. Social accounting, standard	0.64	1.47	0.99	1.88
2. Social accounting, adjusted	0.81	1.85	0.69	1.88
3. Social accounting, excluding consumer durables	0.75	1.77	0.91	2.78
4. Business accounting, standard	0.50	1.60	0.58	1.21
5. Business accounting, excluding consumer durables	0.56	1.66	0.72	2.18
6. Cash flow, standard	0.69	1.78	0.77	1.98
7. Cash flow, excluding consumer durables	0.72	1.48	0.96	1.54
II. Deflated aggregate values, social accounting				
1. By general price level, standard	0.79	0.98	0.86	1.27
2. By general price level, excluding consumer durables	0.92	1.19	1.13	1.70
3. By wage level, standard	1.26	1.34	1.44	1.72
4. By group purchasing power, standard	0.81	1.11	0.84	1.21
III. Deflated by general price level, per unit values				
1. Per inhabitant, standard	0.87	0.84	0.98	1.09
2. Per inhabitant, excluding consumer durables	1.14	1.02	1.28	1.47
3. Per household, standard	0.96	0.89	1.10	1.15
4. Per consumer unit, standard	0.87	0.84	0.98	1.08
5. Per labor force member, standard	0.93	0.90	1.05	1.16

Source: Appendix Tables Z–3 and Z–4.

NATIONAL SAVING-INCOME RATIO
Variant Concepts; Economic Periods: 1897 to 1949

Percent

	1897 to 1908	1909 to 1914	1915 to 1921	1922 to 1929	1930 to 1933	1934 to 1938	1939 to 1945	1946 to 1949	1897 to 1949
I. Social accounting concept									
1. Standard	13.7	12.8	10.7	16.2	−6.8	1.9	1.6	15.0	8.6
2. Including net soil improvement	14.2	13.4	10.9	16.5	−6.6	2.3	2.1	15.1	9.0
3. Including military durables	13.7	12.8	10.7	16.2	−6.8	1.9	7.4	11.9	9.5
4. Broad [1]	14.5	13.8	11.1	16.9	−6.0	2.3	7.9	12.3	10.0
5. Excluding consumer durables	12.4	11.6	10.2	13.8	−4.9	0.8	1.5	11.3	7.2
6. Excluding consumer durables and nonfarm residential construction	10.7	9.3	9.2	10.5	−3.4	1.6	1.5	9.4	6.1
II. Business accounting concept									
1. Standard	16.7	15.4	14.7	18.2	−14.3	1.9	5.0	21.6	11.6
2. Excluding consumer durables	15.1	13.5	11.9	15.4	−10.6	2.3	4.3	16.4	9.6
III. Cash flow concept									
1. Standard	26.1	25.1	24.2	30.0	8.9	18.1	11.3	26.5	21.1
2. Excluding consumer durables	20.1	18.4	17.1	20.6	1.5	10.3	6.2	17.3	13.6

[1] Including lines 2 and 3 and two technical adjustments of lesser importance.

Source: Obtained by dividing the appropriate numerator derived according to procedure described in Table II by the appropriate denominator from Volume III, Table N–1, cols. 1, 2, and 6.

Standard Social Accounting Concept; Economic Periods: 1897 to 1949

Percent

Period	National saving	Personal saving			Corporate saving	Government saving		
		Non-agricultural individuals	Agriculture	Un-incorporated business		State	Local	Federal
	1	2	3	4	5	6	7	8
1897–1908	13.7	14.2 [1]	1.1	6.0 [1]	33.4	7.7	12.1	6.1
1909–1914	12.8	13.3	−2.2	6.3	24.2	10.3	15.3	11.5
1915–1921	10.7	16.7	−6.8	16.5	40.4	18.8	−1.8	−79.7
1922–1929	16.2	14.7	1.8	3.5	26.3	25.8	13.8	25.2
1930–1933	−6.8	4.8	0.4	−73.6	−175.3	17.8	−5.7	−49.2
1934–1938	1.9	5.2	7.5	10.9	−27.0	17.6	8.2	−51.9
1939–1945	1.6	21.3	30.7	24.8	29.5	23.9	5.5	−125.8
1946–1949	15.0	14.5	15.1	1.9	41.4	10.5	2.9	5.7
1897–1949	8.6	14.7 [2]	9.5	7.4 [2]	22.4	18.0	5.8	−54.6
Normal period	12.6	12.9	4.6	6.3	26.1	15.6	7.4	−2.8

[1] 1899–1908.
[2] 1899–1949.

Column 1 – Table T-1, col. 1 divided by Volume III, Table N-1, col. 6.

Column 2 – Table T-8, col. 1 divided by the residual of Table N-3, col. 8 and estimates of the income of unincorporated business derived as follows: for 1899–1918, Martin, *National Income in the United States, 1799–1938*, p. 39 (figures exclude agriculture and miscellaneous categories); for 1919–1928, Volume II, Table B-79, col. 2; for 1929–1949, Table B-79, col. 4.

Column 3 – Table T-1, col. 4 divided by Table N-3, col. 7.

Column 4 – Table xv, col. 5.

Column 5 – Table T-1, col. 6 divided by corporate income obtained as follows: Table C-1, col. 12 plus corporate dividends from Table C-6, col. 1 for 1897–1915; Table C-29, col. 1 for 1916–1922; and from *Statistics of Income* for 1923–1949.

Column 6 – Sum of Table G-13, col. 4 minus col. 5 converted to calendar-year basis by simple arithmetic averaging, Table G-12, col. 5 and first differences of Table G-20, cols. 2, 3, and 4 divided by Table G-13, col. 1 converted to calendar-year basis.

Column 7 – Sum of Table G-1, col. 4 minus col. 5, Table G-12, col. 2, and first differences of Table G-20, col. 5 (figures for 1928–1949 overstated in that they include state property tax accruals) divided by Table G-1, col. 1.

Column 8 – Table T-1, col. 8 divided by federal income obtained as follows: for 1897–1928, Table F-10, col. 11; for 1929–1949, Table F-22, cols. 1 and 6 minus col. 12 and net receipts of social insurance funds from *Survey of Current Business*, various issues.

Lines I-1 to I-10 – In all cases denominator of ratio is Volume III, Table N-1, col. 9. Numerator obtained as follows:

Line I-1 – Table T-6, col. 1.

Line I-2 – Table T-4, col. 4. Includes net soil improvement and two technical adjustments.

Line I-3 – Table T-6, col. 1 minus col. 5.

Line I-4 – Table T-6, col. 1 minus col. 5 plus consumer debt derived as follows: sum of first differences of Table D-1, col. 6 minus col. 8 and first differences of Table U-6, col. 3 minus col. 4 minus first differences of Table D-1, col. 4.

Line I-5 – Table T-6, col. 1 minus sum of Table T-6, col. 5, Table R-6, cols. 1–4 minus cols. 5 and 7, and Table A-6, col. 6, raised 55 percent (see notes to Table A-1, col. 3).

Line I-6 – Table T-6, col. 1 minus sum of cols. 5, 15–17. Excludes reserves in government and private pension and retirement funds as well as consumer durables.

Line I-7 – Table T-6, col. 1 minus cols. 5, 14–17. Excludes saving through consumer durables, government and private pension and retirement funds and life insurance.

Line I-8 – Line I-5 of this table minus Table T-6, col. 18.

Line I-9 – Table T-6, col. 1 plus sum of consumer debt (see note to line I-4), and mortgage debt on one- to four-family structures (Table T-8, col. 20), minus sum of net expenditures on consumer durables (Table T-6, col. 5), and on one-to four-family homes (Table T-8, col. 2), currency (Table T-6, col. 8), and demand deposits (Table L-1, col. 3 and the first differences of Table A-53, col. 3).

Line I-10 – Line I-9 minus reserves in government and private pension and retirement funds from Table T-6, cols. 15–17.

Line II-1 – Table T-2, col. 2 divided by Volume III, Table N-1, col. 5.

Line II-2 – Table T-7, col. 1 minus col. 5 divided by Table N-1, col. 5.

Line III-1 – Table T-3, col. 2 divided by the sum of Table N-1, col. 1 and capital consumption allowances (replacement cost as described in notes to Table N-5).

Line III-2 – Table T-3, col. 2 minus the sum of Table A-66, col. 3 and Table T-10, col. 4 divided by same denominator as for line III-1.

Variant Concepts; Economic Periods: 1897 to 1949

Percent

	1897 to 1908	1909 to 1914	1915 to 1921	1922 to 1929	1930 to 1933	1934 to 1938	1939 to 1945	1946 to 1949	1897 to 1949
I. Social accounting concept									
1. Standard	10.9	10.4	13.3	12.8	0.4	5.7	22.5	13.4	13.5
2. Broad	11.8	11.5	13.7	13.6	1.3	6.1	23.1	13.9	14.1
3. Excluding consumer durables	9.4	9.0	12.7	10.1	2.5	4.5	22.3	8.6	11.8
4. Excluding consumer durables and consumer debt	9.7	9.4	13.0	10.7	1.1	5.4	22.2	10.2	12.3
5. Excluding consumer durables and homes	7.6	6.5	11.6	6.3	4.1	5.3	22.3	6.3	10.5
6. Excluding consumer durables and compulsory saving	9.4	9.0	12.7	9.8	2.4	3.3	19.4	6.0	10.4
7. Excluding consumer durables and contractual saving	8.6	8.2	11.9	8.4	1.3	0.8	17.1	4.0	8.7
8. Excluding consumer durables, homes, and U.S. Government securities	7.6	6.5	8.0	7.9	3.1	5.1	14.8	6.1	8.5
9. Saving through revenue-yielding assets	7.2	6.8	11.1	8.9	2.3	4.3	15.6	10.4	9.9
10. Saving through revenue-yielding assets excluding compulsory saving	7.2	6.7	11.0	8.6	2.2	3.1	12.7	7.9	8.5
II. Business accounting concept									
1. Standard	13.3	12.5	17.2	14.8	−3.5	5.8	25.2	18.4	20.0
2. Excluding consumer durables	11.5	10.5	14.0	11.6	0.6	6.2	24.4	11.8	13.5
III. Cash flow concept									
1. Standard	21.0	19.9	22.8	22.6	11.0	16.0	28.5	20.8	21.9
2. Excluding consumer durables	14.4	12.7	14.9	12.2	3.2	7.3	22.0	9.4	13.3

NATIONAL AND PERSONAL SAVING ESTIMATED FROM CHANGES IN REPRODUCIBLE NATIONAL WEALTH
Period Totals: 1806 to 1929
$ bill.

Period	Period estimates				Annual (Saving Study) estimates			
	Current values		Deflated (1929) values		Current values		Deflated (1929) values	
	National saving	Personal saving	National saving	Personal saving	National saving	Personal saving	National saving	Personal saving
	1	2	3	4	5	6	7	8
1806–1850	3.6	3.4	9.2	8.7	.	.	.	.
1851–1880	20.5	17.9	41.8	36.6	.	.	.	.
1881–1890	18.6	15.2	42.8	35.1	.	.	.	.
1891–1900	17.7	13.8	39.3	30.7	.	.	.	.
1901–1912	50.3	39.4	65.5	45.8	41.5	30.6	74.4	54.7
1913–1922	134.9	135.2	63.4	60.6	61.8	62.1	72.1	69.3
1923–1929	85.2	54.5	85.9	55.6	97.6	66.9	96.4	66.1

Columns 1 and 3 – 1805–1929: First differences of estimates of reproducible tangible wealth at beginning and end of period as given in Goldsmith, "The Growth of Reproducible Wealth of the United States of America from 1805 to 1950," *Income and Wealth*, Series II, Table I, col. 1 and Table I-C, col. 1, respectively.

Columns 2 and 4 – 1805–1900: Obtained by multiplying cols. 1 and 3, respectively, by the estimated proportion of personal to total national saving. This proportion was put at 95 percent for 1805–1850; 87½ percent for 1851–1880; 82 percent for 1881–1890; and 78 percent for 1891–1900. These percentages are only rough approximations and are based on the proportion derived by the Saving Study for the period 1900–1912 (see Table T-1) and on the trend of the share of national wealth held by governments and corporations, which, in turn, was approximated from the data on reproducible tangible wealth given in Goldsmith, *op. cit.* Table I.

1901–1929: Obtained by deducting from cols. 1 and 3, respectively, the estimates of corporate and government saving, given in Tables T-1 and T-12, for the years between the beginning and end of the period.

Columns 5 and 6 – 1901–1929: From Table T-1.

Columns 7 and 8 – 1901–1929: From Table T-12.

Period Totals: 1869 to 1928

Period	National saving				Personal saving			
	Including		Excluding		Including		Excluding	
	Consumer durables				Consumer durables			
	Current prices	1929 prices	Current prices	1929 prices	Current prices	1929 prices	Current prices	1929 prices
	1	2	3	4	5	6	7	8

I. Aggregates; $ bill.

1. 1869–1878	.	14.5	7.8	12.8	.	12.7	6.7	11.0
2. 1879–1888	.	29.6	13.1	26.2	.	25.1	10.9	21.7
3. 1889–1898	.	44.2	16.5	39.2	.	36.4	13.2	31.4
4. 1899–1908	28.9	57.2	24.9	50.6	21.2	41.5	17.2	34.9
5. 1909–1918	53.5	71.3	45.4	65.9	48.1	70.6	40.0	65.2
6. 1919–1928	103.2	84.8	78.6	70.2	80.4	63.0	55.8	48.4

II. $ per head

1. 1869–1878	.	33.3	17.9	29.4	.	29.2	15.4	25.3
2. 1879–1888	.	54.1	23.9	47.8	.	45.8	19.9	39.6
3. 1889–1898	.	65.4	24.4	58.0	.	53.8	19.5	46.4
4. 1899–1908	35.4	70.1	30.5	62.1	26.0	50.9	21.1	42.8
5. 1909–1918	54.7	72.8	46.4	67.3	49.1	72.1	40.9	66.6
6. 1919–1928	91.4	75.1	69.6	62.2	71.2	55.8	49.4	42.9

III. Preceding decade = 100

1. 1879–1888	.	161	132	163	.	157	132	159
2. 1889–1898	.	122	102	121	.	117	98	117
3. 1899–1908	.	107	124	107	.	94	108	92
4. 1909–1918	153	104	153	107	191	142	193	156
5. 1919–1928	168	103	151	93	145	78	121	65

Lines I-1 to I-3 – Column 2: Col. 4 plus estimates of saving through consumer durables derived on the basis of Kuznets' figures for expenditures (*National Product since 1869*, Table II-3, p.95) with depreciation on the basis of an average life of twelve years.

Columns 3 and 4: From *ibid.*, Table II-15 (p. 118), cols. 5 and 10 respectively.

Column 6: Col. 8 plus Saving Study estimates of consumer durables (Tables Q-3, col. 1; Q-14, col. 9; P-17, col. 6; A-22, col. 1; A-29, col. 7 minus Q-15, col. 7).

Columns 7 and 8: Cols. 3 and 4 multiplied by 86 percent for 1869–1878; 83 percent for 1879–1888; and 80 percent for 1889–1898. These ratios are based on very rough estimates of the share of corporate and government saving in national saving.

Lines I-4 to I-6 – Columns 1 and 2: Cols. 3 and 4 plus Saving Study estimates of saving through consumer durables.

Columns 3 and 4: Same source as for lines I-1 to I-3.

Columns 5 and 6: Cols. 7 and 8 plus Saving Study estimates of saving through consumer durables.

Column 7: Col. 3 multiplied by 69 percent for 1899–1908; 88 percent for 1909–1918; and 71 percent for 1919–1928; these ratios derived from Table T-2, cols. 1 and 2, and Table T-7, col. 5.

Column 8: Col. 4 multiplied by 69 percent for 1899–1908; 99 percent for 1909–1918; and 69 percent for 1919–1928; these ratios derived from Tables T-1 and T-6.

Lines II-1 to II-6 – Lines I-1 to I-6 divided by average number of inhabitants of the United States (see *Historical Statistics*, p. 26).

Lines III-1 to III-5 – Derived from lines II-1 to II-6.

TIMING OF TURNING POINTS IN NATIONAL SAVING

Variant Concepts: 1899 to 1948

Number of years lead (−) or lag (+) of saving at reference turning points
(blank = no lead or lag)

Reference turning point	Social accounting concept					Business accounting concept	Cash flow concept
	Current			Deflated aggregate	Deflated per head		
	Standard	Broad	Narrow	Standard		Current standard	
Peak 1899							
Trough 1900							
Peak 1903	−1	−1	−1	−1	−1	−1	−1
Trough 1904							
Peak 1907	−2	−2	−2	−2	−2	−1	−1
Trough 1908							
Peak 1910						−1	−1
Trough 1911							
Peak 1913	−1	−1	−1	−1	−1	−1	−1
Trough 1914							
Peak 1918	−1	−1	−1	−2	−2	−1	−1
Trough 1919	−1	−1	−1	−1	−1	−1	−1
Peak 1920						−1	−1
Trough 1921							
Peak 1923							
Trough 1924							
Peak 1926						−1	−1
Trough 1927	+1	+1	+1	+1	+1	+1	+1
Peak 1929							
Trough 1932							
Peak 1937							
Trough 1938							
Peak 1944	−3	−3	−3	−3	−3	−3	−3
Trough 1946	−1	−1	−1	−2	−2	−2	−3
Peak 1948						−1	
Simultaneous cases	17	17	17	17	17	13	14

Source: See notes to Tables S-1 and S-3.

Variant Concepts: 1897 to 1949

	Turning points		Average lead (—) or lag (+) of saving		Average difference (disregarding sign)	
	All	With differ-ence	On all turning points	On turning points with difference	On all turning points	On turning points with difference
	Number		Years			
I. National saving						
1. Social accounting concept, current						
a. Standard	25	8	−0.36	−1.12	0.44	1.38
b. Broad	25	8	−0.36	−1.12	0.44	1.38
c. Narrow (excluding consumer durables)	25	8	−0.36	−1.12	0.44	1.38
2. Social accounting concept, standard, deflated aggregates						
a. General price level	25	8	−0.44	−1.38	0.52	1.62
b. Wage level	25	8	−0.44	−1.38	0.52	1.62
c. Group purchasing power	25	8	−0.42	−1.25	0.48	1.50
3. Social accounting concept, standard, deflated per unit						
a. Per head	25	8	−0.44	−1.38	0.52	1.62
b. Per household	25	9	−0.48	−1.33	0.56	1.56
c. Per consuming unit	25	8	−0.44	−1.38	0.52	1.62
4. Business accounting concept						
a. Standard	25	12	−0.52	−1.08	0.60	1.25
b. Narrow	25	12	−0.52	−1.08	0.60	1.25
5. Cash flow concept						
a. Standard	25	11	−0.52	−1.18	0.60	1.36
b. Narrow	25	11	−0.52	−1.18	0.60	1.36
II. Personal saving						
1. Social accounting concept, current						
a. Standard	23	7	−0.09	−0.29	0.35	1.14
b. Broad	23	7	−0.09	−0.29	0.35	1.14
c. Narrow (excluding consumer durables)	23	9	−0.09	−0.22	0.43	1.11
2. Social accounting concept, standard, deflated aggregates						
a. General price level	23	8	−0.13	−0.38	0.39	1.12
b. Wage level	23	7	−0.09	−0.29	0.35	1.14
c. Group purchasing power	23	7	−0.09	−0.29	0.35	1.14
3. Social accounting concept, standard, deflated per unit						
a. Per head	23	8	−0.17	−0.50	0.43	1.25
b. Per household	23	7	−0.09	−0.29	0.35	1.14
c. Per consuming unit	23	7	−0.09	−0.29	0.35	1.14
4. Business accounting concept						
a. Standard	23	8	−0.26	−0.75	0.35	1.00
b. Narrow	21	8	−0.19	−0.50	0.38	1.00
5. Cash flow concept						
a. Standard	23	7	−0.13	−0.43	0.30	1.00
b. Narrow	21	7	−0.14	−0.43	0.33	1.00

Source: See notes to Tables S-1 to S-4.

247

TIMING OF TURNING POINTS IN SAVING-INCOME RATIOS
Variant Concepts: 1899 to 1948

Number of years lead (−) or lag (+) of saving at reference turning points
(blank = no lead or lag; × = turning point missed)

Reference turning point	National saving			Personal saving		
	Social accounting		Business accounting	Social accounting		Business accounting
	Standard	Narrow		Standard	Narrow	
Peak 1899						
Trough 1900	+1	+1		+1	+1	
Peak 1903	−1	−1	−1	−1	−1	−1
Trough 1904						−1
Peak 1907	−2	−2	−2	−2	−2	−2
Trough 1908		−1		−1	−1	
Peak 1910			−1			−1
Trough 1911						
Peak 1913	−1	−1	−1	−1	−1	−1
Trough 1914				−1	−1	
Peak 1918	−2	−2	−2	−3	−3	−1
Trough 1919	−1	−1	−1	−3	−3	×
Peak 1920			−1	−2	−2	×
Trough 1921						
Peak 1923						
Trough 1924						
Peak 1926	−1	−1	−1	−1	−1	−1
Trough 1927	+1	+1	+1	+1	+1	+1
Peak 1929						
Trough 1932				+1	+1	
Peak 1937						−1
Trough 1938						
Peak 1944	−3	−3	−3	−2	−2	−2
Trough 1946	−1	−1	−2	+1	+1	×
Peak 1948			−1			×
Simultaneous cases	15	14	13	11	11	11

Source: See notes to Tables Z-6 and Z-8.

248

Standard Social Accounting Concept: 1899 to 1948

Number of years lead (−) or lag (+) of saving at reference turning points
(blank = no lead or lag; × = turning point missed)

Reference turning point	Nonfarm households	Agriculture	Unincorporated business	Corporations	Government	
					State and local	Federal
Peak 1899		−1		+1	+1	×
Trough 1900		+1	+1	+1	+1	−2
Peak 1903	−1	−1	−1		−1	−2
Trough 1904		−1			−1	
Peak 1907	−1	−2	−2		−3	−1
Trough 1908	−1	−1				
Peak 1910	−1	−1			−1	
Trough 1911		+2		+1	−1	
Peak 1913	−1	+1				−1
Trough 1914		+2	+1		+1	
Peak 1918			−2	−2	−2	−2
Trough 1919	×		−2	−1	−1	−1
Peak 1920	×				−1	
Trough 1921				+1	−1	
Peak 1923		+1	−1		−1	
Trough 1924		×	−1		−1	
Peak 1926	−1	×			−1	
Trough 1927	+1		+1			+1
Peak 1929					−1	
Trough 1932	+1	+2	−1			+4
Peak 1937			−3		+1	
Trough 1938					+1	+1
Peak 1944		−2	−2			−4
Trough 1946		+1	+1		+2	−2
Peak 1948			×	×	×	−1
Extra specific cycles	1	3	4	1	3	2

Source: Table T-1.

TIMING OF TURNING POINTS IN SAVING-INCOME RATIOS OF MAIN SAVER GROUPS: 1899 to 1948

Number of years lead (−) or lag (+) of saving at reference turning points
(blank = no lead or lag; × = turning point missed)

Reference turning point	National saving ratio	Nonfederal saving ratio	Personal saving ratio				Corporate saving ratio	Government saving ratio	
			Total	Non-agricultural individuals	Agriculture	Unincorporated business		State and local	Federal
	1	2	3	4	5	6	7	8	9
Peak 1899				×	−1	×		×	×
Trough 1900	+1	+1	+1		+1	+1	+2	−2	−2
Peak 1903	−1	−1	−1	−1	−1	−1		−1	−2
Trough 1904				−1	−1			−1	
Peak 1907	−2	−2	−2	−2	−2	−2	−2	¹)−3	−1
Trough 1908			−1	−1	−1		+1		
Peak 1910				−1	−1			−1	
Trough 1911							+1	−1	
Peak 1913	−1	−1	−1	−1	−1		×		−1
Trough 1914			−1		+2	+1	×	+1	
Peak 1918	−2	−1	−3		²)	−2	−2	−2	−2
Trough 1919	−1	×	−3	×	×	−2	−1	−1	−1
Peak 1920		×	−2	×	×			−1	
Trough 1921					+1		+1	−1	
Peak 1923						−1		−1	
Trough 1924					×	−1		−1	
Peak 1926	−1	−1	−1	−1	×			−2	+1
Trough 1927	+1	+1	+1	+1		+1			+1
Peak 1929							−1	−1	4
Trough 1932			+1	+1	³)+2		+2		+
Peak 1937					−2	−3		⁴)−3	5
Trough 1938					−2			+1	+)4
Peak 1944	−3	⁷)−1	−2	⁸)−1	−2	−2	⁶)	⁹)	−1
Trough 1946	¹⁰)−1	+1	+1	+1	+1	+1		+2	−2
Peak 1948						×	×	×	−1

¹ Additional trough in 1906 and peak in 1907.
² Additional peak in 1914 and trough in 1916.
³ Additional trough in 1930 and peak in 1932.
⁴ Additional trough in 1935 and peak in 1936.
⁵ Additional peak in 1935 and trough in 1936.
⁶ Additional peak in 1940 and trough in 1941, but difference between them is small (0.9).
⁷ Value for 1943 is negligibly (0.1) lower than that for 1942.
⁸ An apparent peak in 1939 has been disregarded as it is only 0.1 higher than value for 1940.
⁹ Additional peaks in 1938 and 1940 and troughs in 1939 and 1941.
¹⁰ Value for 1944 same as for 1945.

Source: See notes to Appendix Table Z-7.

Reference turning point	Missing	Simultaneous	Leading	Lagging
Peak 1899	F	H, U	A	C, S
Trough 1900		H	F	A, U, C, S
Peak 1903		C	H, A, U, S, F	
Trough 1904		H, U, C, F	A, S	
Peak 1907		C	H, A, U, S, F	
Trough 1908		U, C, S, F	H, A	
Peak 1910		U, C, F	H, A, S	
Trough 1911		H, U, F	S	A, C
Peak 1913		U, C, S	H, F	A
Trough 1914		H, C, F		A, U, S
Peak 1918		H, A	U, C, S, F	
Trough 1919	H	A	U, C, S, F	
Peak 1920	H	A, U, C, F	S	
Trough 1921		H, A, U, F	S	C
Peak 1923		H, C, F	U, S	A
Trough 1924	A	H, C, F	U, S	
Peak 1926	A	U, C, F	H, S	
Trough 1927		A, C, S		H, U, F
Peak 1929		H, A, U, C, F	S	
Trough 1932		C, S	U	H, A, F
Peak 1937		H, A, C, F	U	S
Trough 1938		H, A, U, C		S, F
Peak 1944		H, C, S	A, U, F	
Trough 1946	S	H, C	F	A, U
Peak 1948	U, C, S	H, A	F	
Total number of cases	9	70	45	26

H = Nonagricultural households.
A = Agriculture.
U = Unincorporated business.
C = Corporations.
S = State and local governments.
F = Federal government.

Source: Table T-1.

251

COMPARISON OF TURNING POINTS IN SAVING-INCOME RATIOS OF MAIN SAVER GROUPS AND IN REFERENCE CYCLE CHRONOLOGY: 1899 to 1948

Reference turning point	Missing	Simultaneous	Leading	Lagging
Peak 1899	H, U, S, F	C	A	
Trough 1900		H	S, F	A, U, C
Peak 1903		C	H, A, U, S, F	
Trough 1904		U, C, F,	H, A, S	
Peak 1907			H, A, U, C, S, F	
Trough 1908		U, S, F	H, A	C
Peak 1910		U, C, F	H, A, S	
Trough 1911		H, A, U, F	S	C
Peak 1913	C	U, S	H, A, F	
Trough 1914	C	H, F		A, U, S
Peak 1918		H, A	U, C, S, F	
Trough 1919	H, A		U, C, S, F	
Peak 1920	H, A	U, C, F	S	
Trough 1921		H, A, U, F	S	C
Peak 1923		H, C, F	U, S	A
Trough 1924	A	H, C, F	U, S	
Peak 1926	A	U, C	H, S	F
Trough 1927		A, C, S		H, U, F
Peak 1929		H, A, U, F	C, S	
Trough 1932		U, S		H, A, C, F
Peak 1937		H, C, F	A, U, S	
Trough 1938		H, U, C	A	S, F
Peak 1944		C, S	H, A, U, F	
Trough 1946		C	F	H, A, U, S
Peak 1948	U, C, S	H, A	F	
Total number of cases	15	57	54	24

H = Nonagricultural households.
A = Agriculture.
U = Unincorporated business.
C = Corporations.
S = State and local governments.
F = Federal government.

Source: See notes to Table Z-7.

TIMING OF TURNING POINTS IN MAIN FORMS OF PERSONAL SAVING
1899 to 1948
(Part 1)

Number of years lead (−) or lag (+) of saving at reference turning points
(blank = no lead or lag; × = turning point missed)

Reference turning point	Currency	Commercial bank deposits	Savings bank deposits	Savings and loan associations	Mortgage holdings	Insurance and pension funds	U.S. Government bonds	State and local government bonds
Peak 1899			+1	−1		×		
Trough 1900	+1		+1	−1		×		
Peak 1903	−1	−2	−1	+1		−1	−1	−2
Trough 1904			−1	+1		−1		−2
Peak 1907	−2	−2	−2	×	−2	−1	−1	+1
Trough 1908		−1		×	−2	−1	−1	+1
Peak 1910	−1	−1	−1	×	−2	−1	−2	
Trough 1911		−1	−1	×	−2	−1	−2	
Peak 1913	−1	−2	−1	−1		−2	−2	−1
Trough 1914					+1		+2	−1
Peak 1918		−2	−2	−1	−1	−1		
Trough 1919		−1	−2	−1	−1	−1	+1	
Peak 1920		−1		×		×	+1	+2
Trough 1921				×	+1	×	+1	+3
Peak 1923	−1	−1	+1	+1		×		+2
Trough 1924	+1	+2	+1	+1		×		+2
Peak 1926		+1	+1	+1	×	×	−1	+1
Trough 1927	+1	+1	+2	×	×	×		+1
Peak 1929	+2		+2	×		−1	+2	+2
Trough 1932	+2	−1	+1		+1			+1
Peak 1937	−1	−1	+2	+4	−1		−4	
Trough 1938			+3	+4	+1		−3	+4
Peak 1944	−1	+1	+1	×	−3	+1		
Trough 1946	×	×	×	×	−3			−1
Peak 1948	×	×	×	×	−1	−1	−1	
Average difference								
Regarding sign	−0.04	−0.48	0.22	0.57	−0.61	−0.65	−0.44	0.52
Disregarding sign	0.65	0.91	1.17	1.29	0.96	0.76	1.00	1.08

Source: Table T-6.

Z-18
(Part 2)

TIMING OF TURNING POINTS IN MAIN FORMS OF PERSONAL SAVING
1899 to 1948

Number of years lead (−) or lag (+) of saving at reference turning points
(blank = no lead or lag; × = turning point missed)

Reference turning point	Corporate and foreign bonds	Corporate stock	Nonfarm		Farm real estate	Consumer durables	Producer durables
			Residential real estate	Non-residential real estate			
Peak 1899		×		×	−1		×
Trough 1900		−2		−1	−1		×
Peak 1903	−1	−1		−1	−1		−1
Trough 1904	−1	+1			+1		
Peak 1907	−2	−1			−1	−1	
Trough 1908	−1				−1		
Peak 1910	−2			−1			
Trough 1911	−1						
Peak 1913	−1	−1			−1	−1	
Trough 1914	−1			+1			+1
Peak 1918	−3	−2	−2	−2	−1	−2	−1
Trough 1919		−1	−1	−1	−1	−1	
Peak 1920		−1	−1	×	−1		
Trough 1921	+1		−1	×			
Peak 1923		−1	×	×			
Trough 1924		−1	×	×			
Peak 1926	−1	−1	−1		−1		
Trough 1927	+2	−1	×	×	−1	+1	+1
Peak 1929	+1		×	×	−2		
Trough 1932		+3	+1	+3			
Peak 1937	−3		×				
Trough 1938	−1		×				
Peak 1944	−2	−3	−3	−3	−3	−3	−3
Trough 1946	−1	−4	−2	−3	−1	−2	−3
Peak 1948		−1		−1		−1	
Average difference							
Regarding sign	−0.68	−0.71	−0.53	−0.50	−0.64	−0.40	−0.26
Disregarding sign	1.00	1.04	0.63	0.94	0.72	0.48	0.43

Source Table T-6.

254

BALANCE SHEET STRUCTURE OF HOUSEHOLDS OF DIFFERENT INCOME Z-19
Early 1950

Money income (1949) before taxes	Total assets	Liquid assets	Car	House	Farm	Live-stock and crops	Life insur-ance	Other real estate	Stock	Busi-ness[1]	Retire-ment fund	Debt	Net worth
	$ bill.	Percent of total assets											
Under $ 1,000	39	14	3	27	31	7	5	9	1	3	2)	12	88
$ 1,000 to 1,999	47	17	5	34	16	5	6	13	1	3	2)	9	91
$ 2,000 to 2,999	72	19	6	35	11	3	8	11	2	4	1	15	85
$ 3,000 to 3,999	84	15	7	38	7	2	8	12	4	4	3	16	84
$ 4,000 to 4,999	66	15	7	41	3	2	9	9	3	7	4	15	85
$ 5,000 to 7,499	107	15	6	31	10	2	8	13	2	11	2	12	88
$ 7,500 and over	188	12	3	15	6	1	6	11	17	28	1	5	95
All households[3]	4)613	14	5	28	9	3	7	12	7	13	2	11	89

[1] Includes closely held corporations.
[2] No cases reported or less than 0.5 percent.
[3] As in Appendix Tables Z-20 to Z-24, includes unattached individuals but excludes residents in hotels, large boarding houses, tourist camps, and hospitals or other institutions (penal, educational, religious, etc.) and members of the armed forces and other persons living on military reservations.
[4] Includes unascertained item of $10 billion.

Source: Derived from Table W-46 in Volume III.

BALANCE SHEET STRUCTURE OF HOUSEHOLDS BY OCCUPATION OF HEAD Z-20
Early 1950

Occupation	Total assets	Liquid assets	Car	House	Farm[1]	Live-stock and crops	Life insur-ance	Other real estate	Stock	Busi-ness[2]	Retire-ment fund	Debt	Net worth
	$ bill.	Percent of total assets											
Professional and semiprofessional	61	18	5	29	3)	9	14	13	7	5	10	90	
Managerial	40	15	5	37	3)	9	12	6	13	3	12	88	
Self-employed	155	10	3	18	3)	6	11	9	43	3)	6	94	
Clerical and sales	49	20	8	43	3)	10	10	4	2	4	18	82	
Skilled and semi-skilled	87	15	9	54	3)	9	8	1	1	3	18	82	
Unskilled and service	23	17	7	48	3)	11	12	2	3)	3	14	86	
Farm operator	97	10	4	59	16	3	7	1	3)	3)	12	88	
Retired	55	25	2	28	3)	6	21	18	3)	3)	2	98	
All other	46	19	5	43	3)	7	15	8	1	2	8	92	
All households	613	14	5	37	3	7	12	7	13	2	11	89	

[1] House for all except farm operator.
[2] Includes closely held corporations.
[3] No cases reported or less than 0.5 percent.

Source: Derived from Table W-47 in Volume III.

Z-21   BALANCE SHEET STRUCTURE OF HOUSEHOLDS OF DIFFERENT NET WORTH
Early 1950

Net worth	Total assets	Liquid assets	Car	House	Farm	Live-stock and crops	Life insur-ance	Other real estate	Stock	Busi-ness [1]	Retire-ment fund	Debt	Net worth
	$ bill.	Percent of total assets											
Negative	2	6	22	26	[3])	8	19	11	1	1	6	490	−390
$−50 to +50	[2])	6	34	25	[3])	1	30	[3])	[3])	[3])	4	100	−
$100 to 400	2	16	20	17	[3])	4	40	1	[3])	[3])	2	39	61
$500 to 900	4	16	30	16	1	4	27	1	[3])	1	4	32	68
$1 000 to 1 900	11	20	23	27	2	2	18	2	[3])	1	5	32	68
$2 000 to 4 900	38	17	12	39	5	2	12	5	1	2	5	24	76
$5 000 to 9 900	79	16	7	52	4	3	8	4	1	2	3	18	82
$10 000 to 24 900	162	15	5	41	7	2	7	11	2	8	2	9	91
$25 000 to 59 900	135	16	4	22	15	3	5	18	4	12	1	6	94
$60 000 and over	180	11	1	10	11	2	6	14	18	27	[3])	3	97
All households	613	14	5	28	9	3	7	12	7	13	2	11	89

[1] Includes closely held corporations.
[2] Less than $0.5 bill.
[3] No cases reported or less than 0.5 percent.

Source: Derived from Table W-49 in Volume III.

Z-22   BALANCE SHEET STRUCTURE OF HOUSEHOLDS BY AGE OF HEAD
Early 1950

Age of head	Total assets	Liquid assets	Car	House	Farm	Live-stock and crops	Life insur-ance	Other real estate	Stock	Busi-ness [1]	Retire-ment fund	Debt	Net worth
	$ bill.	Percent of total assets											
18 to 24	9	18	21	26	6	8	3	10	1	5	2	20	80
25 to 34	69	14	11	34	7	3	5	9	1	13	3	27	73
35 to 44	130	13	6	32	10	3	6	10	5	13	2	15	85
45 to 54	155	15	4	28	9	3	9	9	7	14	2	9	91
55 to 64	145	12	3	25	9	2	8	15	7	18	1	4	96
65 or more	99	19	2	28	11	1	8	15	13	3	[3])	4	96
All households	613 [2]	14	5	28	9	3	7	12	7	13	2	11	89

[1] Includes closely held corporations.
[2] Includes unascertained item of $6 billion.
[3] No cases reported or less than 0.5 percent.

Source: Derived from Table W-48 in Volume III.

Early 1950

Percent of total assets

Saver groups	Proportion of households	Price-insensitive assets (claims)			Price-sensitive assets (equities)				Debt
		Total	Liquid assets [1]	Other claims [2]	Total	Stock and interest in unincorporated business	Real estate [3]	Other [4]	
	1	2	3	4	5	6	7	8	9
I. By net worth									
Negative	5	31	6	25	69	2	37	30	490
$−50 to +50	6	40	6	34	60	0	25	35	100
$100 to 400	9	58	16	42	41	0	17	24	39
$500 to 900	8	47	16	31	52	1	17	34	32
$1 000 to 1 900	10	43	20	23	57	1	31	25	32
$2 000 to 4 900	17	34	17	17	60	3	49	14	24
$5 000 to 9 900	17	27	16	11	73	3	66	10	18
$10 000 to 24 900	18	24	15	9	76	10	59	7	9
$25 000 to 59 900	7	22	16	6	77	16	55	6	6
$60 000 and over	3	17	11	6	83	45	35	3	3
II. By income									
Under $1 000	14	19	14	5	81	4	67	10	12
$1 000 to 1 999	19	23	17	6	77	4	63	10	9
$2 000 to 2 999	21	28	19	9	72	6	57	9	15
$3 000 to 3 999	18	26	15	11	74	8	57	9	16
$4 000 to 4 999	11	28	15	13	72	10	53	9	15
$5 000 to 7 499	11	25	15	10	75	13	54	8	12
$7 500 and over	5	19	12	7	81	45	32	4	5
III. By occupation									
Professional and semiprofessional	7	32	18	14	68	20	43	5	10
Managerial	4	27	15	12	73	19	49	5	12
Self-employed	8	16	10	6	84	52	29	3	6
Clerical and sales	13	34	20	14	67	6	53	8	18
Skilled and semi-skilled	28	27	15	12	73	2	62	9	18
Unskilled and service	12	31	17	14	69	2	60	7	14
Farm operator	9	13	10	3	87	1	66	20	12
Retired	5	31	25	6	69	18	49	2	2
All other	14	28	19	9	72	9	58	5	8
IV. By age									
18 to 24	10	23	18	5	77	6	42	29	20
25 to 34	23	22	14	8	78	14	50	14	27
35 to 44	22	21	13	8	79	18	52	9	15
45 to 54	18	26	15	11	74	21	46	7	9
55 to 64	14	21	12	9	79	25	49	5	4
65 and over	12	27	19	8	73	16	54	3	4
All households	100	22	11	11	78	20	50	8	11

[1] Deposits in financial institutions and U.S. Government securities. (Currency not included.)
[2] Life insurance reserves, and pension and retirement funds (excluding Social Security funds).
[3] Home, farm, and other real estate.
[4] Car, livestock, and crop inventories.

Source: Derived from Appendix Tables Z-19 to Z-22, and Z-24.

DISTRIBUTION OF AGGREGATE NUMBER, INCOME, ASSETS, AND NET WORTH OF SPENDING UNITS BY NET WORTH, INCOME, OCCUPATION, AND AGE

Early 1950

Percent of all spending units

	Number	Income before taxes	Income after taxes	Net saving	Total assets	Net worth
	1	2	3	4	5	6
I. By net worth						
1. Negative	5	3	3	−13	0	−1
2. Zero	6	3	3	−1	0	0
3. $100 to 400	9	5	6	−1	0	0
4. $500 to 900	8	6	6	−4	1	1
5. $1 000 to 1 900	10	8	8	−16	2	1
6. $2 000 to 4 900	17	15	16	10	6	5
7. $5 000 to 9 900	17	17	17	13	13	12
8. $10 000 to 24 900	18	21	21	40	26	27
9. $25 000 to 59 900	7	12	11	27	22	23
10. $60 000 and over	3	10	9	45	30	32
II. By money income before taxes						
1. Under $1 000	14	2	2	−37	6	6
2. $1 000 to 1 999	19	9	9	−15	8	8
3. $2 000 to 2 999	21	16	17	3	12	11
4. $3 000 to 3 999	18	19	20	9	14	13
5. $4 000 to 4 999	11	15	15	20	11	11
6. $5 000 to 7 499	11	19	19	35	17	17
7. $7 500 and over	5	20	18	85	31	33
8. Not ascertained	1	0	0	0	1	1
III. By occupation of head of spending unit						
1. Professional and semiprofessional	7	11	.	12	10	10
2. Managerial	4	} 21	.	} 54	7	6
3. Self-employed	8		.		25	27
4. Clerical and sales	13	13	.	14	8	7
5. Skilled and semiskilled	28	28	.	21	14	13
6. Unskilled and service	12	10	.	3	4	4
7. Farm operator	9	7	.	7	16	15
8. Retired	5	} 10	.	} −11	9	10
9. All other	14		.		7	8
IV. By age of head of spending unit						
1. 18 to 24	10	7	.	−4	2	1
2. 25 to 34	23	23	.	9	11	9
3. 35 to 44	22	26	.	25	21	20
4. 45 to 54	18	22	.	33	25	26
5. 55 to 64	14	15	.	31	24	25
6. 65 and over	12	7	.	4	16	18
7. Not ascertained	1	0	.	2	1	1

Source: From Volume III, Tables W-58, W-60, and W-61; also see text.

Period Averages: 1897 to 1949

$ mill.

Period	Social accounting concept			Business accounting concept		Cash flow concept	
	Standard	Excluding consumer durables	Broad	Standard	Excluding consumer durables	Standard	Excluding consumer durables
	1	2	3	4	5	6	7
A. Economic periods							
1897–1908	2 712	2 451	2 864	3 324	2 989	5 696	4 376
1909–1914	4 016	3 618	4 325	4 848	4 271	8 666	6 344
1915–1921	6 597	6 298	6 800	9 372	7 595	16 599	11 680
1922–1929	13 200	11 250	13 756	15 212	12 846	27 304	18 774
1930–1933	−4 207	−3 016	−3 704	−8 925	−6 569	6 286	1 078
1934–1938	1 334	587	1 606	1 377	1 626	14 305	8 086
1939–1945	2 343	2 140	11 511	7 332	6 343	17 834	9 855
1946–1949	32 680	24 482	26 815	48 306	36 666	63 580	41 407
1897–1949	6 517	5 452	7 529	8 906	7 365	17 562	11 356
Normal period [1])	8 475	6 939	8 318	10 878	8 846	18 924	12 648
B. Quadrennial periods							
1898–1901	2 190	2 000	2 382	2 785	2 601	4 833	3 811
1902–1905	3 267	2 975	3 348	3 696	3 274	6 096	4 699
1906–1909	3 368	2 993	3 497	4 572	4 056	7 579	5 757
1910–1913	4 224	3 781	4 568	5 033	4 399	8 849	6 477
1914–1917	7 322	6 851	7 644	10 822	9 889	15 837	12 529
1918–1921	5 101	5 008	5 217	6 426	4 140	15 161	9 235
1922–1925	12 286	10 399	12 698	15 246	12 610	25 600	17 845
1926–1929	14 114	12 100	14 814	15 180	13 082	29 008	19 703
1930–1933	−4 207	−3 016	−3 704	−8 925	−6 569	6 286	1 078
1934–1937	1 166	259	1 408	1 590	1 792	14 435	8 191
1938–1941	8 034	6 346	9 712	9 267	7 860	20 870	12 755
1942–1945	−3 433	−2 126	11 033	3 694	3 481	13 786	6 408
1946–1949	32 680	24 482	26 815	48 306	36 666	63 580	41 407
1898–1949	6 624	5 542	7 649	9 053	7 483	17 840	11 530

[1]) 1897–1949 excluding 1917–1918, 1930–1933, 1942–1945.

General note: The figures shown in the S tables do not always reflect minor revisions made in the T tables.

Column 1 – Table T-1, col. 1.

Column 2 – Table T-1, col. 1 minus Table T-6, col. 5.

Column 3 – Table T-4, col. 1.

Column 4 – Table T-2, col. 1.

Column 5 – Table T-2, col. 1 minus Table T-7, col. 5.

Column 6 – Table T-3, col. 1.

Column 7 – Table T-3, col. 1 minus the sum of Table T-10, col. 4 and Table A-66, col. 3.

PERSONAL SAVING; CURRENT VALUES; SOCIAL ACCOUNTING, BUSINESS
ACCOUNTING, AND CASH FLOW CONCEPTS

Period Averages: 1897 to 1949

$ mill.

Period	Social accounting concept			Business accounting concept		Cash flow concept	
	Standard	Excluding consumer durables	Broad	Standard	Excluding consumer durables	Standard	Excluding consumer durables
	1	2	3	4	5	6	7
A. Economic periods							
1897–1908	1 943	1 683	2 096	2 390	2 055	4 181	2 861
1909–1914	2 965	2 569	3 276	3 612	3 035	6 374	4 052
1915–1921	7 232	6 932	7 435	9 558	7 781	14 128	9 210
1922–1929	9 152	7 209	9 716	10 802	8 436	18 564	10 034
1930–1933	251	1 442	754	−2 031	324	7 394	2 186
1934–1938	3 541	2 795	3 814	3 600	3 849	11 432	5 213
1939–1945	24 925	24 723	25 638	28 316	27 327	35 230	27 251
1946–1949	22 973	14 774	23 858	32 328	20 688	40 535	18 362
1897–1949	8 491	7 429	8 897	10 209	8 668	15 685	9 479
Normal period	6 539	5 005	6 933	8 221	6 190	13 353	7 078
B. Quadrennial periods							
1898–1901	1 529	1 338	1 720	1 962	1 778	3 558	2 536
1902–1905	2 331	2 039	2 413	2 625	2 203	4 421	3 023
1906–1909	2 584	2 208	2 713	3 447	2 930	5 626	3 804
1910–1913	3 061	2 622	3 410	3 714	3 080	6 452	4 080
1914–1917	5 716	5 244	6 036	8 145	7 212	11 964	8 656
1918–1921	7 576	7 483	7 692	9 221	6 936	14 228	8 302
1922–1925	8 885	6 998	9 297	11 136	8 502	17 727	9 972
1926–1929	9 419	7 420	10 134	10 468	8 370	19 400	10 096
1930–1933	251	1 442	754	−2 031	324	7 394	2 186
1934–1937	3 498	2 590	3 739	3 684	3 885	11 746	5 502
1938–1941	8 270	6 585	9 100	9 536	8 128	17 602	9 487
1942–1945	36 278	37 585	36 794	40 833	40 620	46 594	39 216
1946–1949	22 973	14 774	23 858	32 328	20 688	40 535	18 362
1898–1949	8 644	7 564	9 051	10 390	8 820	15 942	9 632

Column 1 – Table T-6, col. 1.

Column 2 – Table T-6, col. 1 minus col. 5.

Column 3 – Table T-4, col. 4.

Column 4 – Table T-7, col. 1.

Column 5 – Table T-7, col. 1 minus col. 5.

Column 6 – Sum of Table T-10, col. 1, Table A-66, col. 1, and Table U-11, col. 1.

Column 7 – Column 6 minus the sum of Table T-10, col. 4 and Table A-66, col. 3.

Variant Deflators and Divisors; Period Averages: 1897 to 1949

Period	Aggregate national saving			National saving per unit (Deflated by general price level)			
	Deflated by			Divided by			
	General price level	Wage level	Group purchasing power	Number of inhabitants	Number of households	Number of consuming units	Labor force
	$ mill.			$			
	1	2	3	4	5	6	7
A. Economic periods							
1897–1908	5 244	7 893	5 567	65.0	306.2	92.4	165.3
1909–1914	6 561	9 453	7 181	69.4	314.8	97.6	169.4
1915–1921	7 443	10 649	8 293	72.0	318.5	101.1	182.4
1922–1929	13 041	13 872	13 137	111.8	472.3	156.1	283.7
1930–1933	−5 746	−5 437	−5 552	−45.8	−183.6	−62.8	−111.0
1934–1938	1 534	1 135	2 001	11.7	44.6	15.8	27.5
1939–1945	3 470	2 481	8 969	26.8	101.0	36.4	65.6
1946–1949	23 043	14 733	22 759	158.6	575.5	219.5	370.4
1897–1949	6 790	7 494	7 824	62.1	265.4	87.0	154.4
Normal period	8 841	9 452	9 186	79.6	337.7	88.5	196.7
B. Quadrennial periods							
1898–1901	4 550	7 001	4 876	60.2	287.9	86.0	158.1
1902–1905	6 338	9 421	6 625	77.8	365.4	110.4	196.7
1906–1909	5 963	8 823	6 412	68.0	313.6	95.8	165.8
1910–1913	6 822	9 862	7 514	72.1	326.7	101.3	175.7
1914–1917	9 964	14 583	11 049	98.0	436.4	137.8	247.2
1918–1921	4 434	6 006	4 959	41.8	183.0	58.7	106.5
1922–1925	12 130	13 428	12 288	107.0	457.4	149.7	274.4
1926–1929	13 953	14 315	13 986	116.6	487.3	162.4	293.0
1930–1933	−5 746	−5 437	−5 552	−45.8	−183.6	−62.8	−111.0
1934–1937	1 303	964	1 726	10.0	37.5	13.4	23.2
1938–1941	9 278	6 694	9 852	70.2	264.0	95.5	164.4
1942–1945	−2 591	−1 897	6 620	−18.5	−69.0	−25.4	−38.4
1946–1949	23 043	14 733	22 759	158.6	575.5	219.5	370.4
1898–1949	6 880	7 577	7 932	62.8	267.8	87.9	155.8

Column 1 – Table T-12, col. 1.

Column 2 – Table T-13, col. 1.

Column 3 – Table T-14, col. 1.

Column 4 – Table T-12, col. 1 divided by total population (1900–1945 *Historical Statistics*, p. 26; 1946–1949 *Statistical Abstract*, various issues).

Column 5 – Table T-12, col. 1 divided by number of households estimated as follows: 1896–1940 census-year data from *Statistical Abstract*, 1950, p. 23 [figures for intercensal years obtained by multiplying total population (see col. 4) by ratio of families to total population interpolated linearly between census-year ratios]; 1941–1949 data from *Statistical Abstract*, 1950, p. 23 (figures are for July 1 for 1941–1945, June 15 for 1946, and April 15 for 1947–1949).

Column 6 – Table T-12, col. 1 divided by number of consuming units obtained as follows: (a) For 1896 to 1930, total population (see col. 4) multiplied by ratio of consuming units to total population, annual ratios being derived by linear interpolation between census-year ratios. Number of consuming units in census years was obtained by multiplying each sex-age group by appropriate weights from Thompson and Whelpton, *Population Trends in the United States*, p. 169. For 1890 and 1900, the average of weights for men and women was applied to each age group, since the age breakdown was not available by sex. Population-by-age figures were taken from *Historical Statistics*, p. 28 and *Statistical Abstract*, various issues. (b) For 1931 to 1938, from Kuznets, *National Income and Its Composition*, p. 151. The method used for 1896 to 1930 was designed to correspond to this series. The results are very close to Kuznets' figures for the overlapping period. (c) For 1939 to 1949, estimated by multiplying age-sex group weights from Thompson and Whelpton, *op. cit.* by population figures.

Column 7 – Table T-12, col. 1 divided by labor force obtained for 1896 to 1899 from straight line interpolation between June 1890 and June 1900 values given in Durand, *Labor Force in the United States*, p. 209; for 1900 to 1928, from National Industrial Conference Board annual average estimates (see *Historical Statistics*, p. 65); and for 1929 to 1949, from Council of Economic Advisers, *Annual Economic Review*, Jan. 1951, Table A-11.

Variant Deflators and Divisors; Period Averages: 1897 to 1949

Period	Aggregate personal saving			Personal saving per unit (Deflated by general price level)			
	Deflated by			Divided by			
	General price level	Wage level	Group purchasing power	Number of inhabitants	Number of households	Number of consuming units	Labor force
	$ mill.			$			
	1	2	3	4	5	6	7
A. Economic periods							
1897–1908	3 756	5 646	3 962	46.5	218.7	66.0	118.0
1909–1914	4 852	6 996	5 298	51.4	233.1	72.2	125.4
1915–1921	7 830	11 267	8 662	75.5	333.4	106.0	191.5
1922–1929	9 050	9 644	9 094	77.7	328.4	108.4	197.2
1930–1933	−146	−132	−190	−0.9	−2.2	−1.0	−1.8
1934–1938	4 270	3 391	4 251	33.2	128.7	45.1	88.0
1939–1945	21 901	16 269	24 925	161.0	598.9	219.8	352.9
1946–1949	16 322	10 450	17 288	112.5	408.6	155.6	262.6
1897–1949	8 316	8 261	8 997	70.9	291.4	98.4	170.6
Normal period	6 915	7 262	7 232	61.7	260.0	86.0	152.9
B. Quadrennial periods							
1898–1901	3 191	4 899	3 412	42.4	202.4	60.4	111.2
1902–1905	4 524	6 719	4 684	55.4	260.1	78.6	140.0
1906–1909	4 582	6 770	4 916	52.2	240.6	73.6	127.2
1910–1913	4 944	7 157	5 444	52.3	236.9	73.4	127.4
1914–1917	7 622	11 238	8 534	74.9	333.1	105.2	188.9
1918–1921	7 075	9 893	7 689	67.2	295.4	94.4	171.3
1922–1925	8 775	9 729	8 869	77.5	331.2	108.4	198.7
1926–1929	9 326	9 559	9 320	77.9	325.6	108.5	195.8
1930–1933	−146	−132	−190	−0.9	−2.2	−1.0	−1.8
1934–1937	4 208	3 400	4 135	32.8	127.4	44.6	89.4
1938–1941	9 583	6 936	9 896	72.6	273.5	98.8	170.1
1942–1945	29 874	22 372	34 901	217.8	808.0	297.7	468.0
1946–1949	16 322	10 450	17 288	112.5	408.6	155.6	262.6
1898–1949	8 452	8 384	9 146	71.9	295.4	99.9	173.0

Columns 1 to 3 – Tables T-12, T-13, and T-14, col. 2, respectively.

Columns 4 to 7 – Same procedures as for Table S-3 except that numerator is Table T-12, col. 2.

NATIONAL SAVING BY MAJOR SAVER GROUPS; SOCIAL ACCOUNTING CONCEPT

Current Values; Period Averages: 1897 to 1949

$ mill.

Period	National saving	Personal saving			Corporate saving	Government saving	
		Nonagricultural individuals	Agriculture	Unincorporated business		State and local	Federal
	1	2	3	4	5	6	7
A. *Economic periods*							
1897–1908	2 712	1 813	31	99	609	127	32
1909–1914	4 016	2 908	–93	150	720	255	76
1915–1921	6 597	7 104	–487	615	2 092	95	–2 822
1922–1929	13 200	8 844	108	200	2 016	1 104	928
1930–1933	–4 207	2 473	10	–2 232	–3 398	59	–1 119
1934–1938	1 334	2 741	356	444	–1 307	1 240	–2 140
1939–1945	2 343	19 271	3 112	2 542	2 517	2 095	–27 194
1946–1949	32 680	20 013	2 628	332	6 201	1 528	1 978
1897–1949	6 517	7 514	592	385	1 221	750	–3 945
Normal period	8 475	5 978	264	297	1 417	675	–156
B. *Quadrennial periods*							
1898–1901	2 190	1 348	–10	190	559	95	8
1902–1905	3 267	2 064	130	137	716	181	38
1906–1909	3 368	2 632	–14	–35	584	144	56
1910–1913	4 224	3 075	–264	250	790	277	96
1914–1917	7 322	5 260	181	274	1 926	193	–513
1918–1921	5 101	7 688	–933	821	1 920	24	–4 419
1922–1925	12 286	8 506	195	184	1 782	875	744
1926–1929	14 114	9 183	20	216	2 251	1 333	1 112
1930–1933	–4 207	2 473	10	–2 232	–3 398	59	–1 119
1934–1937	1 166	2 438	347	713	–1 491	1 174	–2 015
1938–1941	8 034	6 779	1 226	266	663	1 468	–2 368
1942–1945	–3 433	27 935	4 318	4 026	3 598	2 572	–45 881
1946–1949	32 680	20 013	2 628	332	6 201	1 528	1 978
1898–1949	6 624	7 646	603	396	1 238	763	–4 022

Source: Table T-1.

264

NATIONAL SAVING BY MAJOR SAVER GROUPS
BUSINESS ACCOUNTING CONCEPT
Current Values; Period Averages: 1897 to 1949

$ mill.

Period	National saving	Personal saving			Corporate saving	Government saving	
		Nonagricultural individuals	Agriculture	Unincorporated business		State and local	Federal
	1	2	3	4	5	6	7
A. Economic periods							
1897–1908	3 324	1 909	307	173	765	135	33
1909–1914	4 848	3 137	274	200	877	280	79
1915–1921	9 372	8 825	−229	962	2 328	279	−2 793
1922–1929	15 212	9 800	730	273	2 159	1 287	964
1930–1933	−8 925	1 719	−1 158	−2 592	−5 812	18	−1 100
1934–1938	1 377	2 177	957	467	−1 386	1 274	−2 111
1939–1945	7 332	20 933	4 423	2 960	3 719	2 423	−27 126
1946–1949	48 306	25 702	4 987	1 639	11 170	2 620	2 188
1897–1949	8 906	8 472	1 144	593	1 671	933	−3 907
Normal period	10 878	6 924	801	495	1 930	847	−120
B. Quadrennial periods							
1898–1901	2 785	1 356	312	295	718	97	8
1902–1905	3 696	2 211	222	192	844	188	39
1906–1909	4 572	2 824	516	106	902	164	59
1910–1913	5 033	3 320	126	268	916	304	100
1914–1917	10 822	5 803	1 372	970	2 921	257	−502
1918–1921	6 426	10 232	−1 720	710	1 295	288	−4 378
1922–1925	15 244	9 738	982	416	2 234	1 092	782
1926–1929	15 180	9 861	477	129	2 084	1 483	1 145
1930–1933	−8 925	1 719	−1 158	−2 592	−5 812	18	−1 100
1934–1937	1 590	1 731	1 174	779	−1 320	1 214	−1 988
1938–1941	9 267	7 146	1 828	561	542	1 517	−2 328
1942–1945	3 694	30 477	5 933	4 423	5 552	3 103	−45 793
1946–1949	48 306	25 702	4 987	1 639	11 170	2 620	2 188
1898–1949	9 053	8 625	1 158	607	1 696	950	−3 982

Source: Table T-2.

NATIONAL SAVING BY MAJOR SAVER GROUPS; CASH FLOW CONCEPT
Current Values; Period Averages: 1897 to 1949

$ mill.

| Period | National saving | Personal saving | | | Corporate saving | Government saving | |
		Nonagricultural individuals	Agriculture	Unincorporated business		State and local	Federal
	1	2	3	4	5	6	7

A. Economic periods

Period							
1897–1908	5 696	3 059	757	366	1 287	181	46
1909–1914	8 666	4 934	992	448	1 860	349	83
1915–1921	16 599	11 824	964	1 340	5 091	331	−2 952
1922–1929	27 304	15 316	2 169	1 078	6 200	1 643	898
1930–1933	6 286	8 268	357	−1 232	−1 625	1 235	−717
1934–1938	14 305	7 545	2 290	1 597	2 767	2 321	−2 215
1939–1945	17 834	25 438	5 821	3 972	7 935	3 638	−28 970
1946–1949	63 580	30 636	7 098	2 801	17 312	3 464	2 269
1897–1949	17 562	12 132	2 286	1 267	4 603	1 426	−4 153
Normal period	18 924	10 379	1 881	1 093	4 639	1 226	−294

B. Quadrennial periods

Period							
1898–1901	4 833	2 372	704	481	1 125	132	18
1902–1905	6 096	3 362	678	380	1 392	232	52
1906–1909	7 579	4 234	1 076	316	1 641	242	70
1910–1913	8 849	5 091	845	517	1 901	390	106
1914–1917	15 837	8 405	2 300	1 260	4 874	270	−1 272
1918–1921	15 161	13 433	−356	1 151	4 461	357	−3 886
1922–1925	25 600	14 335	2 362	1 030	5 811	1 330	732
1926–1929	29 008	16 297	1 976	1 127	6 588	1 955	1 064
1930–1933	6 286	8 268	357	−1 232	−1 625	1 235	−717
1934–1937	14 435	7 300	2 519	1 926	2 841	2 215	−2 367
1938–1941	20 870	12 846	3 136	1 621	4 964	2 730	−4 426
1942–1945	13 786	33 801	7 394	5 400	9 541	4 324	−46 674
1946–1949	63 580	30 636	7 098	2 801	17 312	3 464	2 269
1898–1949	17 840	12 337	2 315	1 290	4 679	1 452	−4 233

Source: Table T-3.

266

SHARE OF MAJOR SAVER GROUPS IN NATIONAL SAVING
SOCIAL ACCOUNTING CONCEPT

Current Values; Selected Periods: 1897 to 1949

Percent

Period	Combination of groups			Individual groups					
	Non-federal	Private	Personal	Nonagri-cultural individuals	Agricul-ture	Unincor-porated business	Corpo-rations	State and local governments	Federal government
	1	2	3	4	5	6	7	8	9
A. Economic periods									
1897–1908	98.9	94.2	71.7	66.9	1.1	3.7	22.5	4.7	1.2
1909–1914	98.2	91.8	73.9	72.5	−2.3	3.7	17.9	6.4	1.9
1915–1921	142.7	141.3	109.6	107.7	−7.4	9.3	31.7	1.4	−42.8
1922–1929	93.0	84.6	69.4	67.0	0.8	1.6	15.2	8.4	7.0
1930–1933	73.4	74.8	−6.0	−58.8	−0.2	53.1	80.8	−1.4	26.6
1934–1938	259.5	167.1	264.6	204.4	27.1	33.1	−97.5	92.4	−159.6
1939–1945	1 259.3	1 170.0	1 062.8	821.8	132.7	108.4	107.2	89.3	−1 159.4
1946–1949	94.0	89.3	70.3	61.2	8.0	1.0	19.0	4.7	6.1
1897–1949	160.5	149.0	130.3	115.3	9.1	5.9	18.7	11.5	−60.6
Normal period	101.9	93.9	77.2	70.6	3.1	3.5	16.7	8.0	−1.8
B. Quadrennial periods									
1898–1901	99.6	95.3	69.8	61.5	−0.4	8.7	25.5	4.3	0.3
1902–1905	98.8	93.3	71.4	63.2	4.0	4.2	21.9	5.5	1.2
1906–1909	98.3	94.0	76.7	78.1	−0.4	−1.0	17.3	4.3	1.7
1910–1913	97.7	91.1	72.5	72.9	−6.3	5.9	18.6	6.6	2.3
1914–1917	107.0	104.4	78.1	71.8	2.5	3.7	26.3	2.6	−7.0
1918–1921	186.6	186.1	148.5	150.7	−18.3	16.1	37.6	0.5	−86.6
1922–1925	93.9	86.8	72.3	69.3	1.5	1.5	14.5	7.1	6.1
1926–1929	92.2	82.7	66.8	65.1	0.1	1.5	15.9	9.5	7.9
1930–1933	73.4	74.8	−6.0	−58.8	−0.2	53.1	80.8	−1.4	26.6
1934–1937	272.8	172.1	299.9	209.0	29.7	61.1	−127.8	100.7	−172.7
1938–1941	129.4	111.2	103.0	84.3	15.4	3.3	8.2	18.2	−29.4
1942–1945	−1 236.4	−1 161.5	−1 056.7	−813.7	−125.8	−117.3	−104.8	−74.9	1 336.4
1946–1949	94.0	89.3	70.3	61.2	8.0	1.0	19.0	4.7	6.1
1898–1949	160.7	149.2	130.5	115.4	9.1	6.0	18.7	11.5	−60.7

Source: Table S-5.

267

SHARE OF MAJOR SAVER GROUPS IN NATIONAL SAVING; BUSINESS ACCOUNTING CONCEPT

Current Values; Selected Periods: 1897 to 1949

Percent

Period	Combination of groups			Individual groups					
	Non-federal	Private	Personal	Nonagri-cultural individuals	Agricul-ture	Unincor-porated business	Corpor-ations	State and local governments	Federal government
	1	2	3	4	5	6	7	8	9
A. Economic periods									
1897–1908	99.0	94.9	71.9	57.4	9.3	5.2	23.0	4.1	1.0
1909–1914	98.4	92.6	74.5	64.7	5.7	4.1	18.1	5.8	1.7
1915–1921	129.8	126.8	102.0	94.2	−2.4	10.3	24.8	3.0	−29.8
1922–1929	93.7	85.2	71.0	64.4	4.8	1.8	14.2	8.5	6.3
1930–1933	87.7	87.9	22.8	−19.3	13.0	29.0	65.1	−0.2	12.3
1934–1938	253.3	160.8	261.5	158.1	69.5	33.9	−100.7	92.5	−153.3
1939–1945	469.7	436.7	386.0	285.4	60.3	40.3	50.7	33.0	−369.8
1946–1949	95.4	90.0	66.9	53.2	10.3	3.4	23.1	5.4	4.5
1897–1949	143.9	133.4	114.6	95.1	12.8	6.7	18.8	10.5	−43.9
Normal period	101.1	93.3	75.6	63.7	7.4	4.6	17.7	7.8	−1.1
B. Quadrennial periods									
1898–1901	99.8	96.3	70.5	48.7	11.2	10.6	25.8	3.5	0.3
1902–1905	98.9	93.8	71.0	59.8	6.0	5.2	22.8	5.1	1.1
1906–1909	98.7	95.1	75.4	61.8	11.3	2.3	19.7	3.6	1.3
1910–1913	98.0	92.0	73.8	66.0	2.5	5.3	18.2	6.0	2.0
1914–1917	104.7	102.3	75.3	53.6	12.7	9.0	27.0	2.4	−4.6
1918–1921	168.2	163.7	143.5	159.2	−26.8	11.0	20.2	4.5	−68.1
1922–1925	95.0	87.8	73.1	63.9	6.4	2.7	14.7	7.2	5.1
1926–1929	92.5	82.7	69.0	65.0	3.1	0.9	13.7	9.8	7.5
1930–1933	87.7	87.9	22.8	−19.3	13.0	29.0	65.1	−0.2	12.3
1934–1937	224.9	148.6	231.6	108.8	73.8	49.0	−83.0	76.3	−125.0
1938–1941	125.1	108.7	102.9	77.1	19.7	6.0	5.8	16.4	−25.1
1942–1945	1 339.6	1 255.6	1 105.3	825.0	160.6	119.7	150.3	84.0	−1 239.6
1946–1949	95.4	90.0	66.9	53.2	10.3	3.4	23.1	5.4	4.5
1898–1949	144.0	133.5	114.8	95.3	12.8	6.7	18.7	10.5	−44.0

Source: Table S-6.

Current Values; Selected Periods: 1897 to 1949

Percent

Period	Combination of groups			Individual groups					
	Non-federal	Private	Personal	Nonagri-cultural individuals	Agricul-ture	Unincor-porated business	Corpo-rations	State and local governments	Federal government
	1	2	3	4	5	6	7	8	9
A. Economic periods									
1897–1908	99.2	96.0	73.4	53.7	13.3	6.4	22.6	3.2	0.8
1909–1914	99.1	95.1	73.6	56.9	11.5	5.2	21.5	4.0	1.0
1915–1921	117.8	115.8	85.1	71.2	5.8	8.1	30.7	2.0	−17.8
1922–1929	96.6	90.6	67.9	56.1	7.9	3.9	22.7	6.0	3.3
1930–1933	111.4	91.7	117.6	131.6	5.7	−19.6	−25.9	19.7	−11.4
1934–1938	115.4	99.2	79.9	52.7	16.0	11.2	19.3	16.2	−15.5
1939–1945	262.4	242.0	197.5	142.6	32.6	22.3	44.5	20.4	−162.4
1946–1949	96.4	91.0	63.8	48.2	11.2	4.4	27.2	5.4	3.6
1897–1949	123.6	115.5	89.3	69.1	13.0	7.2	26.2	8.1	−23.6
Normal period	101.6	95.1	70.6	54.9	9.9	5.8	24.5	6.5	−1.6
B. Quadrennial periods									
1898–1901	99.6	96.9	73.6	49.1	14.6	9.9	23.3	2.7	0.4
1902–1905	99.1	95.3	72.5	55.2	11.1	6.2	22.8	3.8	0.8
1906–1909	99.2	96.0	74.3	55.9	14.2	4.2	21.7	3.2	0.9
1910–1913	98.7	94.3	72.8	57.5	9.5	5.8	21.5	4.4	1.2
1914–1917	108.1	106.4	75.6	53.1	14.5	8.0	30.8	1.7	−8.0
1918–1921	125.7	123.3	93.9	88.6	−2.3	7.6	29.4	2.4	−25.6
1922–1925	97.1	91.9	69.2	56.0	9.2	4.0	22.7	5.2	2.9
1926–1929	96.3	89.6	66.9	56.2	6.8	3.9	22.7	6.7	3.7
1930–1933	111.4	91.7	117.6	131.6	5.7	−19.6	−25.9	19.7	−11.4
1934–1937	116.4	101.1	81.4	50.6	17.5	13.3	19.7	15.3	−16.4
1938–1941	121.3	108.2	84.4	61.6	15.0	7.8	23.8	13.1	−21.2
1942–1945	438.6	407.2	338.0	245.2	53.6	39.2	69.2	31.4	−338.6
1946–1949	96.4	91.0	63.8	48.2	11.2	4.4	27.2	5.4	3.6
1898–1949	123.7	115.6	89.4	69.2	13.0	7.2	26.2	8.1	−23.7

Source: Table S-7.

NONAGRICULTURAL AND AGRICULTURAL SAVING EXCLUDING CONSUMER
DURABLES; SOCIAL ACCOUNTING, BUSINESS ACCOUNTING,
AND CASH FLOW CONCEPTS

Period Averages: 1897 to 1949

$ mill.

Period	Social accounting		Business accounting		Cash flow	
	Nonagricultural individuals	Agriculture	Nonagricultural individuals	Agriculture	Nonagricultural individuals	Agriculture
	1	2	3	4	5	6
A. Economic periods						
1897–1908	1 585	−1	1 617	265	1 913	580
1909–1914	2 582	−163	2 645	190	2 960	645
1915–1921	6 811	−494	7 253	−434	7 646	224
1922–1929	6 942	67	7 542	621	7 567	1 388
1930–1933	3 448	226	3 758	−842	3 427	−10
1934–1938	2 068	283	2 425	957	1 890	1 726
1939–1945	19 092	3 090	20 050	4 317	18 175	5 104
1946–1949	12 679	1 764	15 218	3 832	10 574	4 988
1897–1949	6 532	511	7 071	1 004	6 556	1 656
Normal period	4 562	146	5 072	623	4 740	1 245
B. Quadrennial periods						
1898–1901	1 183	−35	1 196	287	1 489	566
1902–1905	1 801	101	1 838	174	2 146	497
1906–1909	2 317	−74	2 384	440	2 670	818
1910–1913	2 706	−334	2 772	40	3 067	496
1914–1917	4 931	38	5 057	1 185	5 681	1 715
1918–1921	7 476	−814	8 136	−1 910	8 316	−1 164
1922–1925	6 635	180	7 231	855	7 319	1 623
1926–1929	7 250	−46	7 854	387	7 815	1 154
1930–1933	3 448	226	3 758	−842	3 427	−10
1934–1937	1 641	237	1 952	1 154	1 640	1 936
1938–1941	5 190	1 129	5 830	1 738	5 395	2 471
1942–1945	29 164	4 395	30 337	5 860	27 135	6 682
1946–1949	12 679	1 764	15 218	3 832	10 574	4 988
1898–1949	6 648	521	7 197	1 015	6 667	1 675

Column 1 – Table T-8, col. 1 minus col. 5.

Column 2 – Table A-3, col. 1 minus col. 5.

Column 3 – Table T-9, col. 1 minus col. 4.

Column 4 – Table A-1, col. 1 minus col. 5.

Column 5 – Table T-10, col. 1 minus col. 4.

Column 6 – Table A-66, col. 1 minus col. 3.

Selected Periods: 1897 to 1949

Percent

Period	Combination of groups			Individual groups					
	Non-federal	Private	Personal	Nonagri-cultural individuals	Agricul-ture	Unincor-porated business	Corpo-rations	State and local governments	Federal government
	1	2	3	4	5	6	7	8	9
A. Economic periods									
1897–1908	98.8	93.6	68.7	64.7	–0.1	4.0	24.9	5.2	1.3
1909–1914	97.9	90.9	71.0	71.4	–4.5	4.2	19.8	7.0	2.1
1915–1921	144.8	143.3	110.1	108.2	–7.8	9.8	33.2	1.5	–44.8
1922–1929	91.8	82.0	64.1	61.7	0.6	1.8	17.9	9.8	8.3
1930–1933	62.9	64.9	–47.8	–114.3	–7.5	74.0	112.7	–2.0	37.1
1934–1938	464.3	253.3	475.9	352.1	48.2	75.6	–222.6	211.0	–364.3
1939–1945	1 370.9	1 273.0	1 155.5	892.2	144.4	118.8	117.6	97.9	–1 270.9
1946–1949	91.9	85.7	60.3	51.8	7.2	1.4	25.3	6.2	8.1
1897–1949	172.4	158.6	136.2	119.8	9.4	7.1	22.4	13.8	–72.4
Normal period	102.2	92.5	72.1	65.7	2.1	4.3	20.4	9.7	–2.3
B. Quadrennial periods									
1898–1901	99.6	94.9	66.9	59.2	–1.8	9.5	28.0	4.8	0.4
1902–1905	98.7	92.6	68.5	60.5	3.4	4.6	24.1	6.1	1.3
1906–1909	98.1	93.3	73.8	77.4	–2.5	–1.2	19.5	4.8	1.9
1910–1913	97.5	90.1	69.4	71.6	–8.8	6.6	20.8	7.3	2.5
1914–1917	107.5	104.7	76.5	72.0	0.6	4.0	28.1	2.8	–7.5
1918–1921	188.2	187.8	149.4	149.3	–16.2	16.4	38.3	0.5	–88.2
1922–1925	92.8	84.4	67.3	63.8	1.7	1.8	17.1	8.4	7.2
1926–1929	90.8	79.8	61.3	59.9	–0.4	1.8	18.5	11.0	9.2
1930–1933	62.9	64.9	–47.8	–114.3	–7.5	74.0	112.7	–2.0	37.1
1934–1937	878.0	424.6	1 000.2	633.5	91.4	275.3	–575.6	453.4	–778.0
1938–1941	137.3	114.2	103.8	81.8	17.8	4.2	10.4	23.1	–37.3
1942–1945	–2 057.6	–1 936.6	–1 767.4	–1 371.5	–206.7	–189.3	–169.2	–121.0	2 157.6
1946–1949	91.9	85.7	60.3	51.8	7.2	1.4	25.3	6.2	8.1
1898–1949	172.6	158.8	136.5	119.9	9.4	7.1	22.3	13.8	–72.6

Columns 1 to 3, 6 to 9 – Table T-1.

Column 4 – Table T-1, col. 3 minus Table T-8, col. 5.

Column 5 – Table T-1, col. 4 minus Table A-3, col. 5.

SHARE OF MAJOR SAVER GROUPS IN NATIONAL SAVING EXCLUDING
CONSUMER DURABLES; BUSINESS ACCOUNTING CONCEPT; CURRENT VALUES
Selected Periods: 1897 to 1949

Percent

Period	Combination of groups			Individual groups					
	Non-federal	Private	Personal	Nonagri-cultural individuals	Agricul-ture	Unincor-porated business	Corpo-rations	State and local governments	Federal government
	1	2	3	4	5	6	7	8	9
A. Economic periods									
1897–1908	98.9	94.4	68.8	54.1	8.9	5.8	25.6	4.5	1.1
1909–1914	98.2	91.6	71.1	61.9	4.4	4.7	20.5	6.6	1.8
1915–1921	136.7	133.0	102.4	95.5	−5.7	12.7	30.6	3.7	−36.8
1922–1929	92.5	82.5	65.7	58.7	4.8	2.1	16.8	10.0	7.5
1930–1933	83.3	83.6	−4.9	−57.2	12.8	39.5	88.5	−0.3	16.7
1934–1938	229.9	151.5	236.8	149.2	58.9	28.7	−85.3	78.4	−129.9
1939–1945	527.6	489.4	430.8	316.1	68.1	46.7	58.6	38.2	−427.7
1946-1949	94.0	86.9	56.4	41.5	10.5	4.5	30.5	7.1	6.0
1897–1949	153.1	140.4	117.7	96.0	13.6	8.1	22.7	12.7	−53.0
Normal period	101.4	91.8	70.0	57.3	7.0	5.6	21.8	9.6	−1.4
B. Quadrennial periods									
1898–1901	99.7	96.0	68.4	46.0	11.0	11.4	27.6	3.7	0.3
1902–1905	98.8	93.1	67.3	56.1	5.3	5.9	25.8	5.7	1.2
1906–1909	98.6	94.5	72.3	58.8	10.8	2.6	22.2	4.1	1.4
1910–1913	97.7	90.8	70.0	63.0	0.9	6.1	20.8	6.9	2.3
1914–1917	105.0	102.4	72.9	51.1	12.0	9.8	29.5	2.6	−5.1
1918–1921	205.7	198.8	167.5	196.5	−46.1	17.1	31.3	6.9	−105.8
1922–1925	93.8	85.1	67.4	57.3	6.8	3.3	17.7	8.7	6.2
1926–1929	91.2	79.9	64.0	60.0	3.0	1.0	15.9	11.3	8.8
1930–1933	83.3	83.6	−4.9	−57.2	12.8	39.5	88.5	−0.3	16.7
1934–1937	211.0	143.2	216.9	108.9	64.4	43.5	−73.7	67.8	−111.0
1938–1941	129.6	110.3	103.4	74.2	22.1	7.1	6.9	19.3	−29.6
1942–1945	1 415.4	1 326.3	1 166.8	871.4	168.3	127.1	159.5	89.1	−1 315.4
1946–1949	94.0	86.9	56.4	41.5	10.5	4.5	30.5	7.1	6.0
1898–1949	153.3	140.6	117.9	96.2	13.6	8.1	22.7	12.7	−53.2

Columns 1 to 3, 6 to 9 – Table T-2.

Column 4 – Table T-2, col. 3 minus Table T-9, col. 4.

Column 5 – Table T-2, col. 4 minus Table A-1, col. 5.

SHARE OF MAJOR SAVER GROUPS IN NATIONAL SAVING EXCLUDING CONSUMER DURABLES; CASH FLOW CONCEPT; CURRENT VALUES

Selected Periods: 1897 to 1949

Percent

Period	Combination of groups			Individual groups					
	Non-federal	Private	Personal	Nonagricultural individuals	Agriculture	Unincorporated business	Corporations	State and local governments	Federal government
	1	2	3	4	5	6	7	8	9
A. Economic periods									
1897–1908	99.0	94.8	65.4	43.8	13.2	8.4	29.5	4.2	1.0
1909–1914	98.7	93.2	63.9	46.7	10.2	7.1	29.3	5.5	1.3
1915–1921	125.2	122.4	78.8	65.5	1.9	11.5	43.6	2.8	−25.3
1922–1929	95.2	86.4	53.4	40.3	7.4	5.7	33.0	8.8	4.8
1930–1933	166.5	52.0	202.6	317.8	−0.9	−114.2	−150.7	114.5	−66.5
1934–1938	127.4	98.6	64.5	23.4	21.3	19.7	34.2	28.7	−27.4
1939–1945	393.9	357.0	276.5	184.4	51.8	40.3	80.5	36.9	−294.0
1946–1949	94.5	86.1	44.3	25.5	12.0	6.8	41.8	8.4	5.5
1897–1949	136.6	124.0	83.5	57.7	14.6	11.2	40.5	12.6	−36.6
Normal period	102.3	92.7	56.0	37.5	9.8	8.6	36.7	9.7	−2.3
B. Quadrennial periods									
1898–1901	99.5	96.0	66.5	39.1	14.8	12.6	29.5	3.5	0.5
1902–1905	98.9	93.9	64.3	45.7	10.6	8.1	29.6	5.0	1.1
1906–1909	98.8	94.6	66.1	46.4	14.2	5.5	28.5	4.2	1.2
1910–1913	98.3	92.3	63.0	47.4	7.7	8.0	29.3	6.0	1.6
1914–1917	110.2	108.0	69.1	45.3	13.7	10.1	38.9	2.2	−10.1
1918–1921	142.1	138.2	89.9	90.0	−12.6	12.5	48.3	3.9	−42.2
1922–1925	96.0	88.5	55.9	41.0	9.1	5.8	32.6	7.5	4.1
1926–1929	94.6	84.6	51.2	39.7	5.9	5.7	33.4	9.9	5.4
1930–1933	166.5	52.0	202.6	317.8	−0.9	−114.2	−150.7	114.5	−66.5
1934–1937	128.9	101.9	67.2	20.0	23.6	23.5	34.7	27.0	−28.9
1938–1941	134.7	113.3	74.4	42.3	19.4	12.7	38.9	21.4	−34.7
1942–1945	828.4	760.9	612.0	423.5	104.3	84.3	148.9	67.5	−728.4
1946–1949	94.5	86.1	44.3	25.5	12.0	6.8	41.8	8.4	5.5
1898–1949	136.7	124.1	83.5	57.8	14.5	11.2	40.6	12.6	−36.7

Columns 1 to 3, 6 to 9 – Table T-3.

Column 4 – Table T-3, col. 3 minus Table T-10, col. 4.

Column 5 – Table T-3, col. 4 minus Table A-66, col. 3.

NATIONAL SAVING BY MAJOR SAVER GROUPS; SOCIAL ACCOUNTING CONCEPT
DEFLATED BY GROSS NATIONAL PRODUCT DEFLATOR (1929 = 100)

Period Averages: 1897 to 1949

$ mill.

Period	National saving	Personal saving			Corporate saving	Government saving	
		Nonagricultural individuals	Agriculture	Unincorporated business		State and local	Federal
	1	2	3	4	5	6	7
A. Economic periods							
1897–1908	5 244	3 487	72	197	1 184	248	56
1909–1914	6 561	4 768	−153	238	1 171	414	124
1915–1921	7 443	7 649	−420	601	2 281	129	−2 797
1922–1929	13 041	8 751	102	198	1 982	1 092	917
1930–1933	−5 746	2 448	23	−2 617	−4 274	48	−1 374
1934–1938	1 534	3 280	425	565	−1 622	1 515	−2 631
1939–1945	3 470	16 931	2 785	2 185	2 215	1 925	−22 570
1946–1949	23 043	14 206	1 878	237	4 268	1 110	1 344
1897–1949	6 790	7 463	510	343	1 140	769	−3 436
Normal period	8 841	6 346	225	344	1 450	742	−266
B. Quadrennial periods							
1898–1901	4 550	2 788	−1	404	1 155	197	8
1902–1905	6 338	4 004	255	264	1 388	352	74
1906–1909	5 963	4 667	−18	−68	1 028	255	98
1910–1913	6 822	4 969	−429	405	1 279	443	155
1914–1917	9 964	7 045	204	373	2 604	274	−536
1918–1921	4 434	7 149	−782	708	1 678	29	−4 348
1922–1925	12 130	8 404	185	185	1 758	864	733
1926–1929	13 953	9 098	18	211	2 206	1 320	1 101
1930–1933	−5 746	2 448	23	−2 617	−4 274	48	−1 374
1934–1937	1 303	2 910	401	897	−1 854	1 442	−2 493
1938–1941	9 278	7 873	1 412	298	746	1 717	−2 768
1942–1945	−2 591	22 947	3 591	3 336	2 958	2 103	−37 525
1946–1949	23 043	14 206	1 878	237	4 268	1 110	1 344
1898–1949	6 880	7 578	518	356	1 149	781	−3 502

Source: Table T-12.

274

Selected Periods: 1897 to 1949

Percent

Period	Combination of groups			Individual groups					
	Non-federal	Private	Personal	Nonagricultural individuals	Agriculture	Unincorporated business	Corporations	State and local governments	Federal government
	1	2	3	4	5	6	7	8	9
A. Economic periods									
1897–1908	98.9	94.2	71.6	66.5	1.4	3.8	22.6	4.7	1.1
1909–1914	98.2	91.9	74.0	72.7	−2.3	3.6	17.9	6.3	1.9
1915–1921	137.5	135.8	105.2	102.8	−5.6	8.1	30.6	1.7	−37.6
1922–1929	93.0	84.6	69.4	67.1	0.8	1.5	15.2	8.4	7.0
1930–1933	76.1	76.9	2.5	−42.6	−0.4	45.5	74.4	−0.8	23.9
1934–1938	271.5	172.7	278.4	213.9	27.7	36.9	−105.7	98.8	−171.5
1939–1945	750.4	694.9	631.1	487.9	80.2	63.0	63.8	55.5	−650.4
1946–1949	94.1	89.3	70.8	61.6	8.2	1.0	18.5	4.8	5.8
1897–1949	150.6	139.3	122.5	109.9	7.5	5.1	16.8	11.3	−50.6
Normal period	103.0	94.6	78.2	71.8	2.5	3.9	16.4	8.4	−3.0
B. Quadrennial periods									
1898–1901	99.8	95.5	70.1	61.3	0	8.9	25.4	4.3	0.2
1902–1905	98.9	93.3	71.4	63.2	4.0	4.2	21.9	5.6	1.2
1906–1909	98.3	94.0	76.8	78.3	−0.3	−1.1	17.2	4.3	1.6
1910–1913	97.7	91.2	72.5	72.8	−6.3	5.9	18.7	6.5	2.3
1914–1917	105.4	102.6	76.5	70.7	2.0	3.7	26.1	2.8	−5.4
1918–1921	198.1	197.4	159.6	161.2	−17.6	16.0	37.8	0.7	−98.0
1922–1925	93.9	86.8	72.3	69.3	1.5	1.5	14.5	7.1	6.0
1926–1929	92.1	82.6	66.8	65.2	0.1	1.5	15.8	9.5	7.9
1930–1933	76.1	76.9	2.5	−42.6	−0.4	45.5	74.4	−0.8	23.9
1934–1937	291.4	180.7	323.0	223.3	30.8	68.9	−142.3	110.7	−191.4
1938–1941	129.8	111.3	103.3	84.9	15.2	3.2	8.0	18.5	−29.8
1942–1945	−1 348.5	−1 267.3	−1 153.1	−885.7	−138.6	−128.8	−114.2	−81.2	1 448.4
1946–1949	94.1	89.3	70.8	61.6	8.2	1.0	18.5	4.8	5.8
1898–1949	151.0	139.6	122.9	110.1	7.5	5.2	16.7	11.4	−50.9

Source: Table S-15.

NATIONAL SAVING BY MAJOR SAVER GROUPS; SOCIAL ACCOUNTING CONCEPT
DEFLATED BY GROUP PURCHASING POWER INDICES (1929 = 100)

Period Averages: 1897 to 1949

$ mill.

Period	National saving	Personal saving			Corporate saving	Government saving	
		Nonagri-cultural individuals	Agriculture	Unincor-porated business		State and local	Federal
	1	2	3	4	5	6	7
A. Economic periods							
1897–1908	5 567	3 682	71	209	1 258	282	64
1909–1914	7 181	5 174	−136	260	1 270	472	141
1915–1921	8 293	8 476	−419	605	2 333	142	−2 844
1922–1929	13 137	8 788	104	203	2 009	1 106	928
1930–1933	−5 552	2 372	30	−2 593	−4 166	42	−1 237
1934–1938	2 002	3 307	429	516	−1 442	1 364	−2 172
1939–1945	8 969	19 784	3 060	2 081	2 085	1 953	−19 994
1946–1949	22 759	15 365	1 725	198	3 462	992	1 017
1897–1949	7 824	8 129	538	330	1 126	768	−3 067
Normal period	9 186	6 667	230	336	1 430	726	−202
B. Quadrennial periods							
1898–1901	4 876	2 984	0	428	1 226	228	10
1902–1905	6 625	4 158	249	278	1 462	394	84
1906–1909	6 412	5 002	−20	−66	1 101	284	111
1910–1913	7 514	5 404	−398	438	1 384	508	178
1914–1917	11 049	7 940	204	390	2 737	307	−529
1918–1921	4 959	7 770	−783	702	1 674	33	−4 436
1922–1925	12 288	8 487	190	192	1 791	882	746
1926–1929	13 986	9 088	18	214	2 228	1 330	1 109
1930–1933	−5 552	2 372	30	−2 593	−4 166	42	−1 237
1934–1937	1 726	2 928	401	806	−1 656	1 301	−2 054
1938–1941	9 852	8 148	1 501	246	622	1 558	−2 224
1942–1945	6 620	27 679	3 988	3 234	2 881	2 263	−33 425
1946–1949	22 759	15 365	1 725	198	3 462	992	1 017
1898–1949	7 932	8 256	547	344	1 134	779	−3 127

Source: Table T-14.

CONCEPT; DEFLATED BY GROUP PURCHASING POWER INDICES (1929 = 100)

Selected Periods: 1897 to 1949

Percent

Period	Combination of groups			Individual groups					
	Non-federal	Private	Personal	Nonagri-cultural individuals	Agricul-ture	Unincor-porated business	Corpo-rations	State and local governments	Federal government
	1	2	3	4	5	6	7	8	9
A. Economic periods									
1897–1908	98.9	93.8	71.2	66.2	1.3	3.7	22.6	5.1	1.2
1909–1914	98.1	91.5	73.8	72.0	−1.9	3.6	17.7	6.6	2.0
1915–1921	134.3	132.6	104.5	102.2	−5.1	7.3	28.1	1.7	−34.3
1922–1929	92.9	84.5	69.2	66.9	0.8	1.5	15.3	8.4	7.1
1930–1933	77.7	78.4	3.4	−42.7	−0.5	46.7	75.0	−0.7	22.3
1934–1938	208.5	140.4	212.4	165.2	21.4	25.8	−72.0	68.1	−108.5
1939–1945	323.0	301.2	277.9	220.6	34.1	23.2	23.3	21.8	−222.9
1946–1949	95.6	91.2	76.0	67.5	7.6	0.9	15.2	4.4	4.5
1897–1949	139.2	129.4	115.0	103.9	6.9	4.2	14.4	9.8	−39.2
Normal period	102.2	94.3	78.7	72.6	2.5	3.7	15.6	7.9	−2.2
B. Quadrennial periods									
1898–1901	99.8	95.1	70.0	61.2	0	8.8	25.1	4.7	0.2
1902–1905	98.8	92.8	70.7	62.8	3.8	4.2	22.1	6.0	1.3
1906–1909	98.3	93.9	76.7	78.0	−0.3	−1.0	17.2	4.4	1.7
1910–1913	97.6	90.8	72.4	71.9	−5.3	5.8	18.4	6.8	2.4
1914–1917	104.8	102.0	77.2	71.9	1.9	3.5	24.8	2.8	−4.8
1918–1921	189.5	188.8	155.1	156.7	−15.8	14.2	33.7	0.7	−89.5
1922–1925	94.0	86.8	72.2	69.1	1.5	1.6	14.6	7.2	6.1
1926–1929	92.0	82.5	66.6	65.0	0.1	1.5	15.9	9.5	7.9
1930–1933	77.7	78.4	3.4	−42.7	−0.5	46.7	75.0	−0.7	22.3
1934–1937	219.0	143.6	239.5	169.6	23.2	46.7	−95.9	75.4	−119.0
1938–1941	122.5	106.7	100.4	82.7	15.2	2.5	6.3	15.8	−22.6
1942–1945	604.9	570.7	527.2	418.1	60.2	48.8	43.5	34.2	−504.9
1946–1949	95.6	91.2	76.0	67.5	7.6	0.9	15.2	4.4	4.5
1898–1949	139.4	129.6	115.3	104.1	6.9	4.3	14.3	9.8	−39.4

Source: Table S-17.

SHARE OF MAJOR SAVER GROUPS IN NONFEDERAL SAVING
SOCIAL ACCOUNTING CONCEPT; CURRENT VALUES

Selected Periods: 1897 to 1949

Percent

Period	Combination of groups		Individual groups				
	Private	Personal	Non-agricultural individuals	Agriculture	Unincorporated business	Corporations	State and local governments
	1	2	3	4	5	6	7
A. Economic periods							
1897–1908	95.2	72.5	67.7	1.2	3.7	22.7	4.8
1909–1914	93.5	75.3	73.8	−2.4	3.8	18.2	6.5
1915–1921	99.0	76.8	75.4	−5.2	6.5	22.2	1.0
1922–1929	91.0	74.6	72.1	0.8	1.6	16.4	9.0
1930–1933	102.0	−8.1	−80.1	−0.3	72.3	110.1	−1.9
1934–1938	64.3	101.9	78.7	10.5	12.8	−37.6	35.6
1939–1945	92.9	84.4	65.3	10.5	8.6	8.5	7.1
1946–1949	95.1	74.8	65.2	8.6	1.1	20.2	5.0
1897–1949	92.9	81.2	71.8	5.7	3.7	11.7	7.2
Normal period	92.2	75.8	69.3	3.1	3.4	16.4	7.8
B. Quadrennial periods							
1898–1901	95.6	70.0	61.8	−0.4	8.7	25.6	4.4
1902–1905	94.4	72.2	63.9	4.0	4.3	22.2	5.6
1906–1909	95.6	78.0	79.5	−0.4	−1.0	17.6	4.4
1910–1913	93.3	74.2	74.6	−6.4	6.1	19.1	6.7
1914–1917	97.5	72.9	67.1	2.3	3.5	24.6	2.5
1918–1921	99.8	79.6	80.8	−9.8	8.6	20.2	0.2
1922–1925	92.4	77.0	73.7	1.6	1.6	15.4	7.6
1926–1929	89.7	72.5	70.7	0.1	1.7	17.2	10.3
1930–1933	102.0	−8.1	−80.1	−0.3	72.3	110.1	−1.9
1934–1937	63.0	109.9	76.6	10.9	22.4	−46.9	36.9
1938–1941	85.9	79.6	65.1	11.9	2.5	6.3	14.1
1942–1945	94.0	85.5	65.8	10.2	9.5	8.5	6.1
1946–1949	95.1	74.8	65.2	8.6	1.1	20.2	5.0
1898–1949	92.8	81.2	71.8	5.7	3.7	11.6	7.2

Source: Table T-1.

278

SOCIAL ACCOUNTING CONCEPT; CURRENT VALUES

Economic Period Averages: 1897 to 1949

$ mill.

	1897 to 1908	1909 to 1914	1915 to 1921	1922 to 1929	1930 to 1933	1934 to 1938	1939 to 1945	1946 to 1949	1897 to 1949
1. Buildings	369	750	559	3 196	−881	−640	−168	3 749	859
2. Net purchase of farm land	77	115	52	146	10	−3	−66	110	59
3. Producer durables	3	0	−13	27	−10	−29	−9	69	4
4. Consumer durables	228	326	292	1 902	−974	673	184	7 334	982
5. Currency	27	11	199	−6	271	153	2 424	−278	367
6. Commercial bank deposits	210	395	1 071	750	−1 368	1 175	4 166	1 697	1 033
7. Savings bank deposits	127	167	297	470	521	264	1 080	1 196	455
8. Savings and loan associations	10	74	166	573	−202	−162	530	1 382	263
9. Other deposits	−	−	1	4	−2	22	40	97	15
10. Life insurance reserves (net)	131	197	381	927	594	1 401	2 372	3 382	988
11. Private pension reserves	−	−	1	55	50	60	271	988	128
12. Government insurance reserves	1	1	23	151	19	692	2 916	3 288	726
13. U.S. Government securities	−1	−1	1 709	−1 053	622	123	6 865	498	1 069
14. State and local govt. securities	54	106	376	409	396	−235	−159	571	165
15. Other bonds	310	374	1 120	1 550	181	−584	−767	−313	329
16. Preferred stock	84	96	280	597	72	−58	−55	149	161
17. Common stock	384	523	971	1 647	563	378	642	1 590	806
18. Mortgage holdings	57	299	752	783	−113	−64	−38	1 263	340
19. Other claims	1	4	9	28	30	30	40	56	21
20. Mortgage debt	115	299	577	2 115	−579	−37	224	4 568	783
21. Consumer debt	60	114	168	492	−862	596	−77	2 858	320
22. Borrowing on securities	72	60	175	564	−1 283	−208	437	−764	15
23. Tax accruals	14	56	224	140	29	104	412	151	138
24. Total net saving	1 813	2 908	7 104	8 844	2 473	2 741	19 271	20 013	7 514

Source: Table T-8.

NONAGRICULTURAL INDIVIDUALS' SAVING BY MAJOR COMPONENTS
SOCIAL ACCOUNTING CONCEPT; CURRENT VALUES
Quadrennial Period Averages: 1898 to 1949

$ mill.

	1898 to 1901	1902 to 1905	1906 to 1909	1910 to 1913	1914 to 1917	1918 to 1921	1922 to 1925
1. Buildings	116	448	708	770	607	532	3 406
2. Net purchase of farm land	62	82	102	116	129	−8	−14
3. Producer durables	2	3	4	0	−8	−16	22
4. Consumer durables	165	263	315	369	329	213	1 874
5. Currency	50	52	−12	32	200	122	6
6. Commercial bank deposits	220	299	219	438	1 388	500	1 638
7. Savings bank deposits	140	145	117	174	201	351	453
8. Savings and loan associations	−7	13	43	76	101	210	500
9. Other deposits	–	–	–	0	0	2	3
10. Life insurance reserves (net)	100	148	172	204	274	438	753
11. Private pension reserves	–	–	–	–	–	2	22
12. Government insurance reserves	1	1	1	1	5	35	109
13. U.S. Government securities	36	−18	−24	8	618	2 372	−1 006
14. State and local government securities	33	20	103	100	239	476	447
15. Other bonds	259	378	409	312	928	1 149	1 550
16. Preferred stock	144	46	68	98	210	315	464
17. Common stock	221	428	657	532	660	1 118	1 017
18. Mortgage holdings	51	61	59	320	543	888	155
19. Other claims	1	2	2	4	6	11	20
20. Mortgage debt	63	147	192	290	418	689	1 767
21. Consumer debt	57	70	80	112	115	200	360
22. Borrowing on securities	110	80	34	37	232	102	718
23. Tax accruals	18	11	7	40	406	30	67
24. Total net saving	1 348	2 064	2 632	3 075	5 260	7 688	8 506

Source: Table T-8.

280

NONAGRICULTURAL INDIVIDUALS' SAVING BY MAJOR COMPONENTS
SOCIAL ACCOUNTING CONCEPT; CURRENT VALUES
Quadrennial Period Averages: 1898 to 1949

$ mill.

	1926 to 1929	1930 to 1933	1934 to 1937	1938 to 1941	1942 to 1945	1946 to 1949	1898 to 1949
1. Buildings	2 986	−881	−816	964	−1 242	3 749	873
2. Net purchase of farm land	306	10	−3	−49	−68	110	60
3. Producer durables	32	−10	−32	−9	−11	69	4
4. Consumer durables	1 931	−974	797	1 595	−1 229	7 334	999
5. Currency	−18	271	186	734	3 514	−278	374
6. Commercial bank deposits	−138	−1 368	1 434	1 155	6 170	1 697	1 050
7. Savings bank deposits	486	521	282	207	1 730	1 196	462
8. Savings and loan associations	646	−202	−202	214	712	1 382	268
9. Other deposits	5	−2	20	51	27	97	16
10. Life insurance reserves (net)	1 101	594	1 379	1 714	2 810	3 382	1 005
11. Private pension reserves	88	50	60	59	431	988	131
12. Government insurance reserves	192	19	586	1 404	3 978	3 288	740
13. U.S. Government securities	−1 099	622	166	678	11 323	498	1 090
14. State and local government securities	370	396	−282	−111	−179	571	168
15. Other bonds	1 550	181	−718	−524	−828	−313	334
16. Preferred stock	731	72	−56	−27	−86	149	164
17. Common stock	2 277	563	398	506	692	1 590	820
18. Mortgage holdings	1 410	−113	−31	−169	53	1 263	345
19. Other claims	37	30	30	35	43	56	21
20. Mortgage debt	2 463	−579	−87	594	−162	4 568	797
21. Consumer debt	625	−862	826	566	−782	2 858	325
22. Borrowing on securities	410	−1 283	−236	−154	894	−764	14
23. Tax accruals	213	29	258	640	−46	151	140
24. Total net saving	9 183	2 473	2 438	6 779	27 935	20 013	7 646

Source: Table T-8.

NONAGRICULTURAL INDIVIDUALS' SAVING BY MAJOR COMPONENTS
SOCIAL ACCOUNTING CONCEPT; CURRENT VALUES
Economic Periods: 1897 to 1949

Percent

	1897 to 1908	1909 to 1914	1915 to 1921	1922 to 1929	1930 to 1933	1934 to 1938	1939 to 1945	1946 to 1949	1897 to 1949
1. Buildings	20.3	25.8	7.9	36.1	−35.4	−23.3	−0.9	18.7	11.5
2. Net purchase of farm land	4.3	4.0	0.7	1.6	0.4	−0.1	−0.3	0.5	0.8
3. Producer durables	0.2	0	−0.2	0.3	−0.4	−1.1	0	0.3	0
4. Consumer durables	12.6	11.2	4.1	21.5	−39.4	24.6	1.0	36.6	13.1
5. Currency	1.5	0.4	2.8	0.1	11.0	5.6	12.6	−1.4	4.9
6. Commercial bank deposits	11.6	13.6	15.1	8.5	−55.3	42.9	21.6	8.5	13.7
7. Savings bank deposits	7.0	5.8	4.2	5.3	21.1	9.6	5.6	6.0	6.1
8. Savings and loan associations	0.6	2.5	2.3	6.5	−8.2	−5.9	2.7	6.9	3.5
9. Other deposits	−	0	0	0	−0.1	0.8	0.2	0.5	0.2
10. Life insurance reserves (net)	7.2	6.8	5.4	10.5	24.0	51.1	12.3	16.9	13.1
11. Private pension reserves	−	−	0	0.6	2.0	2.2	1.4	4.9	1.7
12. Government insurance reserves	0.1	0	0.3	1.7	0.8	25.2	15.1	16.4	9.7
13. U.S. Government securities	−0.1	0	24.1	−11.9	25.2	4.5	35.6	2.5	14.2
14. State and local govt. securities	3.0	3.6	5.3	4.6	16.0	−8.6	−0.8	2.9	2.2
15. Other bonds	17.1	12.9	15.8	17.5	7.3	−21.3	−4.0	−1.6	4.4
16. Preferred stock	4.7	3.3	3.9	6.8	2.9	−2.1	−0.3	0.7	2.1
17. Common stock	21.2	18.0	13.7	18.6	22.8	13.8	3.3	7.9	10.7
18. Mortgage holdings	3.2	10.3	10.6	8.8	−4.6	−2.3	−0.2	6.3	4.5
19. Other claims	0.1	0.1	0.1	0.3	1.2	1.1	0.2	0.3	0.3
20. Mortgage debt	6.3	10.3	8.2	23.9	−23.4	−1.3	1.1	22.8	10.4
21. Consumer debt	3.3	3.9	2.4	5.6	−34.8	21.7	−0.4	14.3	4.3
22. Borrowing on securities	4.0	2.1	2.5	6.4	−51.9	−7.6	2.3	−3.8	0.2
23. Tax accruals	0.7	1.9	3.1	1.6	1.2	3.8	2.1	0.8	1.8
24. Total net saving	100.0	100.0	100.0	100.0	100.0	100.0	100.0	100.0	100.0

Source: Table T-8.

Quadrennial Periods: 1898 to 1949

Percent

	1898 to 1901	1902 to 1905	1906 to 1909	1910 to 1913	1914 to 1917	1918 to 1921	1922 to 1925
1. Buildings	8.6	21.7	26.9	25.1	11.6	7.0	40.1
2. Net purchase of farm land	4.6	3.9	3.9	3.8	2.5	−0.1	−0.2
3. Producer durables	0.2	0.1	0.2	0	−0.1	−0.2	0.3
4. Consumer durables	12.3	12.7	12.0	12.0	6.3	2.8	22.0
5. Currency	3.7	2.5	−0.5	1.1	3.8	1.6	0.1
6. Commercial bank deposits	16.3	14.5	8.3	14.3	26.4	6.5	19.2
7. Savings bank deposits	10.4	7.0	4.4	5.7	3.8	4.6	5.3
8. Savings and loan associations	−0.5	0.6	1.6	2.5	1.9	2.7	5.9
9. Other deposits	–	–	–	0	0	0	0
10. Life insurance reserves (net)	7.5	7.2	6.5	6.6	5.2	5.7	8.8
11. Private pension reserves	–	–	–	–	–	0	0.3
12. Government insurance reserves	0.1	0	0	0	0.1	0.5	1.3
13. U.S. Government securities	2.7	−0.9	−0.9	0.2	11.8	30.9	−11.8
14. State and local government securities	2.4	1.0	3.9	3.2	4.5	6.2	5.3
15. Other bonds	19.2	18.3	15.6	10.1	17.6	14.9	18.2
16. Preferred stock	10.7	2.2	2.6	3.2	4.0	4.1	5.4
17. Common stock	16.4	20.8	25.0	17.3	12.5	14.5	12.0
18. Mortgage holdings	3.8	3.0	2.2	10.4	10.3	11.5	1.8
19. Other claims	0.1	0.1	0.1	0.1	0.1	0.1	0.2
20. Mortgage debt	4.7	7.2	7.3	9.5	8.0	9.0	20.7
21. Consumer debt	4.2	3.4	3.0	3.6	2.2	2.6	4.2
22. Borrowing on securities	8.2	3.9	1.3	1.2	4.4	1.3	8.4
23. Tax accruals	1.4	0.5	0.3	1.3	7.7	0.4	0.8
24. Total net saving	100.0	100.0	100.0	100.0	100.0	100.0	100.0

Source: Table T-8.

283

SHARE OF MAJOR COMPONENTS IN NONAGRICULTURAL INDIVIDUALS' SAVING
SOCIAL ACCOUNTING CONCEPT; CURRENT VALUES
Quadrennial Periods: 1898 to 1949

Percent

	1926 to 1929	1930 to 1933	1934 to 1937	1938 to 1941	1942 to 1945	1946 to 1949	1898 to 1949
1. Buildings	32.5	−35.4	−33.5	14.2	−4.5	18.7	11.5
2. Net purchase of farm land	3.3	0.4	−0.1	−0.7	−0.2	0.5	0.8
3. Producer durables	0.4	−0.4	−1.3	−0.1	0	0.3	0
4. Consumer durables	21.0	−39.4	32.7	23.5	−4.4	36.6	13.1
5. Currency	−0.2	11.0	7.6	10.8	12.6	−1.4	4.9
6. Commercial bank deposits	−1.5	−55.3	58.8	17.0	22.1	8.5	13.7
7. Savings bank deposits	5.3	21.1	11.6	3.0	6.2	6.0	6.0
8. Savings and loan associations	7.0	−8.2	−8.3	3.2	2.5	6.9	3.5
9. Other deposits	0.1	−0.1	0.8	0.8	0.1	0.5	0.2
10. Life insurance reserves (net)	12.0	24.0	56.6	25.3	10.1	16.9	13.1
11. Private pension reserves	1.0	2.0	2.5	0.9	1.5	4.9	1.7
12. Government insurance reserves	2.1	0.8	24.0	20.7	14.2	16.4	9.7
13. U.S. Government securities	−12.0	25.2	6.8	10.0	40.5	2.5	14.3
14. State and local government securities	4.0	16.0	−11.7	−1.6	−0.6	2.9	2.2
15. Other bonds	16.9	7.3	−29.5	−7.6	−3.0	−1.6	4.4
16. Preferred stock	8.0	2.9	−2.3	−0.4	−0.3	0.7	2.1
17. Common stock	24.8	22.8	16.3	7.4	2.5	7.9	10.7
18. Mortgage holdings	15.4	−4.6	−1.3	−2.5	0.2	6.3	4.5
19. Other claims	0.4	1.2	1.2	0.5	0.2	0.3	0.3
20. Mortgage debt	26.8	−23.4	−3.6	8.8	−0.5	22.8	10.4
21. Consumer debt	6.8	−34.8	33.9	8.3	−2.8	14.3	4.3
22. Borrowing on securities	4.5	−51.9	−9.7	−2.3	3.2	−3.8	0.2
23. Tax accruals	2.3	1.2	10.6	9.4	−0.2	0.8	1.8
24. Total net saving	100.0	100.0	100.0	100.0	100.0	100.0	100.0

Source: Table T-8.

284

AGRICULTURAL SAVING BY MAJOR COMPONENTS
SOCIAL ACCOUNTING CONCEPT; CURRENT VALUES
Economic Period Averages: 1897 to 1949

$ mill.

	1897 to 1908	1909 to 1914	1915 to 1921	1922 to 1929	1930 to 1933	1934 to 1938	1939 to 1945	1946 to 1949	1897 to 1949
1. Buildings	107	168	327	80	−226	−126	−40	1 040	143
2. Producer durables	57	71	34	−8	−220	127	308	1 161	148
3. Consumer durables	32	70	7	41	−216	81	22	865	82
4. Inventories	47	103	−8	−119	−29	−215	164	−396	−27
5. Currency	10	−5	32	−3	42	24	403	−73	59
6. Bank deposits	56	55	194	41	−325	220	971	275	196
7. Life insurance (net)	15	25	42	84	50	111	156	212	75
8. U.S. Government securities	−	−	143	−106	0	33	619	188	102
9. Equity in cooperatives	6	11	26	28	0	38	92	192	40
10. Mortgage holdings	4	14	118	−94	−20	−18	−4	7	0
11. Equity in veterans' funds	−	−	1	10	−14	12	59	98	17
12. Land costs	95	185	94	230	140	300	746	180	241
13. Real estate mortgage debt	91	316	816	−134	−486	−181	−300	183	64
14. Consumer debt	6	9	−6	29	−47	27	−5	142	15
15. Other short-term debt	124	150	482	−246	−535	14	12	445	68
16. Debt write-down	2	3	16	37	93	90	9	4	25
17. Net sales of farm land	77	115	52	146	10	−3	−66	110	59
18. Tax accruals	3	12	41	15	−2	−15	−10	56	11
19. Total net saving									
a. Excluding land costs	31	−93	−487	108	10	356	3 112	2 628	592
b. Including land costs	126	92	−393	338	150	656	3 857	2 808	833

Source: Tables A-3, A-54 and Volume II, Table B-61.

AGRICULTURAL SAVING BY MAJOR COMPONENTS
SOCIAL ACCOUNTING CONCEPT; CURRENT VALUES
Quadrennial Period Averages: 1898 to 1949

$ mill.

	1898 to 1901	1902 to 1905	1906 to 1909	1910 to 1913	1914 to 1917	1918 to 1921	1922 to 1925
1. Buildings	93	117	132	172	264	349	70
2. Producer durables	41	72	79	74	24	46	−84
3. Consumer durables	26	29	60	70	143	−120	15
4. Inventories	2	154	7	−5	280	−168	−163
5. Currency	15	14	3	−5	74	−24	14
6. Bank deposits	67	55	68	53	212	135	82
7. Life insurance (net)	12	16	20	26	32	47	72
8. U.S. Government securities	−	−	−	−	125	125	−200
9. Equity in cooperatives	6	6	7	10	21	29	30
10. Mortgage holdings	4	4	3	17	56	153	−164
11. Equity in veterans' funds	−	−	−	−	−	2	9
12. Land costs	180	10	10	220	220	0	−40
13. Real estate mortgage debt	81	94	109	375	458	1 041	−247
14. Consumer debt	4	5	12	4	29	−34	39
15. Other short-term debt	126	150	158	163	413	428	−345
16. Debt write-down	1	2	2	2	4	26	43
17. Net sales of farm land	62	82	102	116	129	−8	−14
18. Tax accruals	0	5	9	14	18	54	10
19. Total net saving							
a. Excluding land costs	−10	130	−14	−264	181	−933	195
b. Including land costs	170	140	−4	−44	401	−933	155

Source: Tables A-3, A-54 and Volume II, Table B-61.

AGRICULTURAL SAVING BY MAJOR COMPONENTS
SOCIAL ACCOUNTING CONCEPT; CURRENT VALUES
Quadrennial Period Averages: 1898 to 1949

$ mill.

	1926 to 1929	1930 to 1933	1934 to 1937	1938 to 1941	1942 to 1945	1946 to 1949	1898 to 1949
1. Buildings	89	−226	−134	−1	−91	1 040	144
2. Producer durables	68	−220	116	258	323	1 161	151
3. Consumer durables	66	−216	110	107	−78	865	83
4. Inventories	−74	−29	−300	218	100	−396	−29
5. Currency	−19	42	38	132	568	−73	60
6. Bank deposits	0	−325	275	225	1 475	275	200
7. Life insurance (net)	97	50	110	128	174	212	76
8. U.S. Government securities	−12	0	27	100	997	188	104
9. Equity in cooperatives	25	0	39	50	121	192	41
10. Mortgage holdings	−25	−20	−21	−4	−4	7	0
11. Equity in veterans' funds	12	−14	14	1	103	98	17
12. Land costs	500	140	290	640	750	180	238
13. Real estate mortgage debt	−20	−486	−182	−146	−422	183	64
14. Consumer debt	18	−47	54	22	−51	142	15
15. Other short-term debt	−148	−535	−34	160	−88	445	69
16. Debt write-down	30	93	105	21	2	4	26
17. Net sales of farm land	306	10	−3	−49	−68	110	60
18. Tax accruals	20	−2	−12	−21	−2	56	11
19. Total net saving							
a. Excluding land costs	20	10	347	1 226	4 318	2 628	603
b. Including land costs	520	150	637	1 866	5 068	2 808	841

Source: Tables A-3, A-54 and Volume II, Table B-61.

CHANGE IN NET WORTH OF UNINCORPORATED BUSINESS BY MAJOR COMPONENTS; SOCIAL ACCOUNTING CONCEPT; CURRENT VALUES

Economic Period Averages: 1897 to 1949

$ mill.

	1897 to 1908	1909 to 1914	1915 to 1921	1922 to 1929	1930 to 1933	1934 to 1938	1939 to 1945	1946 to 1949	1897 to 1949
1. Buildings	105	80	118	468	−68	−203	−158	155	86
2. Producer durables	10	38	105	159	−197	20	76	1 204	132
3. Inventories	4	25	342	57	−550	154	315	248	91
4. Cash	70	117	256	100	−400	220	1 586	−125	268
5. U.S. Government securities	−	−	121	19	−50	20	871	−375	104
6. Net receivables	56	54	123	−130	−1 676	213	−37	404	−66
7. Real estate debt	28	74	137	420	−7	−42	−54	433	117
8. Bank loans	118	89	312	53	−702	21	166	746	113
9. Undistributed profit and net investment	99	150	615	200	−2 232	444	2 542	332	385

Source: See notes to Table U-3, col. 3.

CHANGE IN NET WORTH OF UNINCORPORATED BUSINESS BY MAJOR COMPONENTS; SOCIAL ACCOUNTING CONCEPT; CURRENT VALUES

Quadrennial Period Averages: 1898 to 1949

$ mill.

	1898 to 1901	1902 to 1905	1906 to 1909	1910 to 1913	1914 to 1917	1918 to 1921	1922 to 1925
1. Buildings	104	98	108	86	74	146	392
2. Producer durables	-17	22	40	50	99	88	156
3. Inventories	23	7	-28	88	39	558	105
4. Cash	170	130	-95	138	328	150	125
5. U.S. Government securities	–	–	–	–	75	138	12
6. Net receivables	64	66	61	55	117	96	-92
7. Real estate debt	14	37	48	72	101	163	436
8. Bank loans	139	150	73	94	356	191	78
9. Undistributed profit and net investment	190	137	-35	250	274	821	184

	1926 to 1929	1930 to 1933	1934 to 1937	1938 to 1941	1942 to 1945	1946 to 1949	1898 to 1949
1. Buildings	545	-68	-220	-89	-220	155	85
2. Producer durables	163	-197	41	154	-36	1 204	136
3. Inventories	8	-550	230	145	369	248	96
4. Cash	75	-400	225	450	2 375	-125	273
5. U.S. Government securities	25	-50	25	125	1 400	-375	106
6. Net receivables	-167	-1 676	458	-351	94	404	-67
7. Real estate debt	405	-7	-46	-44	-57	433	120
8. Bank loans	28	-702	92	212	13	746	113
9. Undistributed profit and net investment	216	-2 232	713	266	4 026	332	396

Source: See notes to Table U-3, col. 3.

289

SAVING OF STATE GOVERNMENTS BY MAJOR COMPONENTS
SOCIAL ACCOUNTING CONCEPT; CURRENT VALUES

Economic Period Averages: 1897 to 1949

$ mill.

	1897 to 1908	1909 to 1914	1915 to 1921	1922 to 1929	1930 to 1933	1934 to 1938	1939 to 1945	1946 to 1949	1897 to 1949
1. Public construction	2	38	93	410	556	381	−37	466	187
2. Land purchases	0	1	3	8	12	10	8	32	7
3. Investment in real property	0	2	−5	20	−5	−16	22	25	5
4. Cash	4	8	39	41	−13	34	251	352	75
5. U.S. Government securities	0	0	4	6	8	9	500	482	105
6. State and local govt. securities	6	12	25	54	47	77	−88	45	17
7. Other liquid assets	4	2	9	19	17	28	−18	0	7
8. Unemployment compensation funds	–	–	–	–	–	193	800	214	140
9. Net tax accruals	3	16	39	32	−26	39	73	144	35
10. Liabilities	5	41	73	164	184	43	−133	570	84
11. Total net saving	15	37	133	425	410	712	1 645	1 188	495

Period averages derived from annual figures obtained as follows (all lines except 8, 9, and 11 converted from fiscal to calendar year by arithmetic averaging):

Line 1 – 1897–1949: Table G-15, cols. 2 and 3 minus Table G-13, col. 5.

Line 2 – 1897–1949: Table G-15, col. 4.

Line 3 – 1897–1949: First differences of Table G-16, col. 8.

Lines 4 to 7 – 1897–1949: First differences of Table G-17.

Line 8 – 1897–1949: Table G-13, col. 9 minus col. 10.

Line 9 – 1897–1928: First differences of Table G-20, cols. 2, 3, and 4.
1929–1949: First differences of Table G-20, cols. 2 and 3.

Line 10 – 1897–1949: First differences of Table G-21, col. 1.

Line 11 – 1897–1949: See notes to Table T-1, col. 7.

SAVING OF STATE GOVERNMENTS BY MAJOR COMPONENTS
SOCIAL ACCOUNTING CONCEPT; CURRENT VALUES
Quadrennial Period Averages: 1898 to 1949

$ mill.

	1898 to 1901	1902 to 1905	1906 to 1909	1910 to 1913	1914 to 1917	1918 to 1921	1922 to 1925
1. Public construction	1	4	6	34	67	114	354
2. Land purchases	0	0	0	2	4	2	7
3. Investment in real property	0	0	0	0	5	−10	29
4. Cash	4	4	4	11	16	53	28
5. U.S. Government securities	0	0	0	0	2	5	5
6. State and local government securities	4	2	17	14	8	32	53
7. Other liquid assets	4	4	6	3	2	13	18
8. Unemployment compensation funds	–	–	–	–	–	–	–
9. Net tax accruals	1	5	5	10	35	46	26
10. Liabilities	5	3	8	38	54	94	186
11. Total net saving	9	16	30	36	84	162	332

	1926 to 1929	1930 to 1933	1934 to 1937	1938 to 1941	1942 to 1945	1946 to 1949	1898 to 1949
1. Public construction	467	556	382	305	−276	466	191
2. Land purchases	9	12	9	11	6	32	7
3. Investment in real property	10	−5	−8	2	25	25	6
4. Cash	54	−13	40	182	260	352	77
5. U.S. Government securities	8	8	10	51	826	482	107
6. State and local government securities	55	47	68	36	−161	45	17
7. Other liquid assets	20	17	24	−14	−6	0	7
8. Unemployment compensation funds	–	–	140	473	1 027	214	143
9. Net tax accruals	38	−26	49	60	68	144	35
10. Liabilities	142	184	46	5	−230	570	85
11. Total net saving	519	410	669	1 101	1 998	1 188	504

Source: Same as for Table S-28

SAVING OF LOCAL GOVERNMENTS BY MAJOR COMPONENTS
SOCIAL ACCOUNTING CONCEPT; CURRENT VALUES
Economic Period Averages: 1897 to 1949

$ mill.

	1897 to 1908	1909 to 1914	1915 to 1921	1922 to 1929	1930 to 1933	1934 to 1938	1939 to 1945	1946 to 1949	1897 to 1949
1. Public construction and equipment	160	255	87	847	600	−73	−293	29	206
2. Land purchases	16	21	10	66	63	46	47	84	39
3. Investment in real property	4	30	31	56	−86	101	38	50	29
4. Cash	13	24	61	116	−80	285	64	461	95
5. U.S. Government securities	0	0	17	7	−6	9	302	33	46
6. State and local govt. securities	20	56	99	194	−136	9	−118	24	30
7. Other liquid assets	1	4	8	15	−18	5	16	112	14
8. Net tax accruals	26	76	171	173	−212	78	81	477	101
9. Liabilities	129	249	522	794	472	−68	−313	931	304
10. Total net saving	112	217	−38	678	−350	527	450	340	256

Period averages derived from annual figures obtained as follows:

Line 1 – 1897–1949: Table G-6, cols. 2, 5, and 6 minus Table G-1, col. 5.

Lines 2 and 3 – 1897–1949: First differences of Table G-7, cols. 6 and 8 respectively.

Lines 4 to 7 – 1897–1949: First differences of Table G-8.

Line 8 – 1897–1928: First differences of Table G-20, col. 5.
1929–1949: First differences of Table G-20, col. 4.

Line 9 – 1897–1949: First differences of Table G-7, col. 10.

Line 10 – 1897–1949: Sum of lines 1 through 8 minus line 9.

292

SAVING OF LOCAL GOVERNMENTS BY MAJOR COMPONENTS
SOCIAL ACCOUNTING CONCEPT; CURRENT VALUES
Quadrennial Period Averages: 1898 to 1949

$ mill.

	1898 to 1901	1902 to 1905	1906 to 1909	1910 to 1913	1914 to 1917	1918 to 1921	1922 to 1925
1. Public construction and equipment	116	168	230	258	192	25	736
2. Land purchases	18	12	18	22	16	6	56
3. Investment in real property	1	1	12	36	38	25	24
4. Cash	3	38	7	30	14	92	113
5. U.S. Government securities	0	0	0	0	0	30	4
6. State and local government securities	6	30	36	51	70	124	178
7. Other liquid assets	0	3	2	4	4	12	14
8. Net tax accruals	21	29	29	64	170	170	170
9. Liabilities	78	117	219	224	395	623	752
10. Total net saving	86	165	114	241	109	−138	543

	1926 to 1929	1930 to 1933	1934 to 1937	1938 to 1941	1942 to 1945	1946 to 1949	1898 to 1949
1. Public construction and equipment	958	600	−116	280	−768	29	208
2. Land purchases	76	63	44	70	27	84	39
3. Investment in real property	89	−86	97	45	50	50	29
4. Cash	118	−80	292	57	118	461	97
5. U.S. Government securities	10	−6	−4	70	474	33	47
6. State and local government securities	210	−136	27	−62	−160	24	30
7. Other liquid assets	16	−18	5	4	25	112	14
8. Net tax accruals	175	−212	95	31	113	477	103
9. Liabilities	837	472	−65	129	−696	931	309
10. Total net saving	814	−350	505	368	574	340	259

Source: Same as for Table S-30.

Period averages derived from annual figures obtained as follows:

Line 1 – 1897–1928: Table F-2, col. 3 minus replacement cost depreciation (see notes to Table F-11, col. 10).
1929–1949: Table F-16, col. 2 minus replacement cost depreciation (see notes to Table F-22, col. 12).

Line 2 – 1897–1928: See notes to Table F-2, col. 5 and Table F-11, col. 10.
1929–1949: See notes to Table F-16, col. 9 and Table F-22, col. 12.

Line 3 – 1897–1928: See notes to Table F-2, col. 5.
1929–1949: Table F-16, col. 1.

Line 4 – 1897–1928: First differences of Table F-4, col. 7.
1929–1949: First differences of Table F-14, col. 10.

Line 5 – 1897–1928: First differences of Table F-4, col. 9.
1929–1949: First differences of Table F-14, col. 12.

Line 6 – 1897–1928: First differences of Table F-3, cols. 1, 6 to 8.
1929–1949: First differences of Table F-13, cols. 1, 6 to 8.

Line 7 – 1897–1928: First differences of Table F-3, cols. 9 and 10.
1929–1949: First differences of Table F-13, cols. 9 and 10.

Line 8 – 1897–1928: First differences of Table F-4, cols. 1 to 4 and 6.
1929–1949: First differences of Table F-14, cols. 6, 7, and 9.

Line 9 – 1897–1928: First differences of Table F-4, cols. 5 and 10.
1929–1949: Table F-15, col. 5; Table F-17, col. 6; and first differences of Table F-14, cols. 8 and 13.

Line 10 – 1897–1928: First differences of Tables F-26, col. 1.
1929–1949: First differences of Table F-26, cols. 2 and 4.

Line 11 – 1939–1949: Table F-31, col. 8.

Line 12 – 1897–1928: Table F-7, col. 4.
1929–1949: Table F-19, col. 5.

Line 13 – 1897–1928: First differences of Table F-5, cols. 1 to 5.
1929–1949: First differences of Table F-18, cols. 1 to 5.

Line 14 – 1897–1928: Included in line 15.
1929–1949: First differences of Table F-20, col. 1.

Line 15 – 1897–1928: First differences of Table F-6, col. 1.
1929–1949: First differences of Table F-20, col. 2.

Line 16 – 1897–1928: Sum of Table F-8, col. 5 and first differences of Table F-5, cols. 6 to 8 and of Table F-6, cols. 2 to 4.
1929–1949: Sum of Table F-21, col. 5; Table F-15, col. 7; and first differences of Table F-18, cols. 6 to 8 and of Table F-20, cols. 3 to 5.

Line 17 – 1917–1949: First differences of Table F-27, col. 4.

Line 18 – 1897–1949: Sum of lines 1 to 10 minus lines 12 to 17; line 11 added in line 18b.

SAVING OF FEDERAL GOVERNMENT BY MAJOR COMPONENTS
SOCIAL ACCOUNTING CONCEPT; CURRENT VALUES
Economic Period Averages: 1897 to 1949

$ mill.

	1897 to 1908	1909 to 1914	1915 to 1921	1922 to 1929	1930 to 1933	1934 to 1938	1939 to 1945	1946 to 1949	1897 to 1949
1. Public construction	34	77	19	19	190	306	196	367	119
2. Equipment	0	2	0	3	14	28	34	−115	0
3. Land purchases	4	0	4	4	27	54	89	179	34
4. Inventories	0	0	10	−8	0	139	270	288	71
5. Fixed assets of govt. corporations	0	1	5	4	14	202	812	−196	114
6. Gold, silver, coin, etc.	61	30	204	49	−16	1 880	726	1 036	402
7. Bank deposits	9	−8	55	−32	240	162	3 424	−5 544	71
8. Loans and investments	0	0	163	48	660	904	−233	1 438	242
9. Miscellaneous assets	0	0	1	15	−152	137	2 418	−206	308
10. Personal tax accruals	0	18	227	81	−134	131	402	−158	88
11. Military assets	−	−	−	−	−	−	8 457	−6 750	608
12. Direct debt	4	3	3 155	−878	1 882	3 001	33 956	−5 361	4 791
13. Gold and silver certificates	70	43	219	65	−42	1 989	928	1 390	471
14. Guaranteed obligs. held by public	−	−	−	−	45	933	−613	−132	1
15. Other bonds, notes, and debentures	−	−	62	98	24	−6	−24	94	28
16. Miscellaneous liabilities	3	0	36	−15	41	154	945	−909	77
17. Interest accruals	−	−	37	−14	12	10	139	26	25
18. Total net saving									
a. Excluding military assets	32	76	−2 822	928	−1 119	−2 140	−27 194	1 978	−3 945
b. Including military assets	32	76	−2 822	928	−1 119	−2 140	−18 737	−4 772	−3 338

SAVING OF FEDERAL GOVERNMENT BY MAJOR COMPONENTS
SOCIAL ACCOUNTING CONCEPT; CURRENT VALUES
Quadrennial Period Averages: 1898 to 1949

$ mill.

	1898 to 1901	1902 to 1905	1906 to 1909	1910 to 1913	1914 to 1917	1918 to 1921	1922 to 1925
1. Public construction	16	29	72	77	48	4	7
2. Equipment	0	0	0	2	0	1	0
3. Land purchases	0	12	0	0	6	0	0
4. Inventories	–	0	0	0	18	0	–16
5. Fixed assets of government corporations	0	0	1	1	1	8	1
6. Gold, silver, coin, etc.	60	51	72	66	234	108	184
7. Bank deposits	17	–12	–4	12	188	–96	–26
8. Loans and investments	–	0	0	0	0	284	45
9. Miscellaneous assets	–	0	0	0	19	–16	13
10. Personal tax accruals	–	–	6	16	839	–436	72
11. Military assets	–	–	–	–	–	–	–
12. Direct debt	12	–12	3	11	1 536	3 985	–775
13. Gold and silver certificates	73	52	85	70	266	114	208
14. Guaranteed obligations held by public	–	–	–	–	–	–	–
15. Other bonds, notes, and debentures	0	1	–1	0	0	109	154
16. Miscellaneous liabilities	1	2	5	–2	20	47	–33
17. Interest accruals	–	–	–	–	44	21	–18
18. Total net saving							
a. Excluding military assets	8	38	56	96	–513	–4 419	744
b. Including military assets	8	38	56	96	–513	–4 419	744

Source: Same as for Table S-32.

SAVING OF FEDERAL GOVERNMENT BY MAJOR COMPONENTS
SOCIAL ACCOUNTING CONCEPT; CURRENT VALUES
Quadrennial Period Averages: 1898 to 1949

$ mill.

	1926 to 1929	1930 to 1933	1934 to 1937	1938 to 1941	1942 to 1945	1946 to 1949	1898 to 1949
1. Public construction	31	190	312	281	131	367	121
2. Equipment	6	14	26	21	47	−115	0
3. Land purchases	8	27	57	61	104	179	35
4. Inventories	0	0	82	364	199	288	72
5. Fixed assets of government corporations	7	14	197	152	1 324	−196	116
6. Gold, silver, coin, etc.	−86	−16	1 862	2 586	−827	1 036	410
7. Bank deposits	−37	240	−25	449	5 770	−5 544	72
8. Loans and investments	52	660	1 152	196	−625	1 438	246
9. Miscellaneous assets	16	−152	277	1 784	2 340	−206	314
10. Personal tax accruals	90	−134	262	722	−118	−158	89
11. Military assets	–	–	–	850	13 950	−6 750	619
12. Direct debt	−981	1 882	3 236	5 098	54 840	−5 361	4 883
13. Gold and silver certificates	−78	−42	1 773	2 974	−637	1 390	481
14. Guaranteed obligations held by public	–	45	1 071	436	−1 414	−132	1
15. Other bonds, notes, and debentures	43	24	4	4	−58	94	29
16. Miscellaneous liabilities	2	41	122	446	1 277	−909	78
17. Interest accruals	−10	12	10	26	219	26	25
18. Total net saving							
a. Excluding military assets	1 112	−1 119	−2 015	−2 368	−45 881	1 978	−4 022
b. Including military assets	1 112	−1 119	−2 015	−1 518	−31 931	−4 772	−3 402

Source: Same as for Table S-32.

Period averages derived from annual figures obtained as follows:

Lines 1, 4, 5, 7, 8, 13, 14, 18 to 20, 22, 23, 26, 27, 30, 31, 33, 36, 37, 40, 44, 46 — From Table T-6.

Line   2 – Table R-6, cols. 1 to 4 minus cols. 5   and 7.

Line   3 – Table R-9, col. 1 minus cols. 2 and 5.

Line   6 – Sum of lines 1, 4, and 5.

Line   9 – Sum of Table P-19, col. 12 and Table A-32, col. 9.

Line 10 – Table A-32, col. 8.

Line 11 – Sum of lines 7 to 10.

Line 12 – Sum of lines 6 and 11.

Line 15 – Table L-1, col. 3 minus first differences of Table U-1, col. 1.

Line 16 – Table L-1, col. 6.

Line 17 – Line 14 minus sum of lines 15 and 16.

Line 21 – Sum of Table I-1, col. 1 minus col. 7, Table I-14, col. 10, and Table I-9, col. 1 minus col. 3, minus Table I-13, col. 1.

Line 24 – Table V-2, cols. 8 and 10.

Line 25 – Table V-2, col. 11.

Line 28 – Table V-1, col. 5.

Line 29 – Table V-1, cols. 6 to 8.

Line 32 – Sum of lines 13 to 31.

Line 34 – Table R-4, cols. 6 and 8.

Line 35 – Table R-7, sum of cols. 3, 4, and 6.

Line 38 – Sum of first differences of Table D-1, col. 6 minus col. 8, and first differences of Table U-6, col. 3 minus first differences of Table D-1, col. 4.

Line 39 – Table I-1, col. 1 minus cols. 7 and 10 plus Table I-9, col. 2.

Line 41 – Table D-10, cols. 3 and 10.

Line 42 – Table D-8, col. 11 minus Table D-10, cols. 3 and 10.

Line 43 – Table T-6, cols. 26 and 28 minus line 38 of this table.

Line 45 – Sum of lines 33, 36 to 40, 43 and 44.

SOCIAL ACCOUNTING CONCEPT; CURRENT VALUES
Economic Period Averages: 1897 to 1949

$ mill.

	1897 to 1908	1909 to 1914	1915 to 1921	1922 to 1929	1930 to 1933	1934 to 1938	1939 to 1945	1946 to 1949	1897 to 1949
1. Residential real estate	311	694	544	3 028	−909	−544	−30	3 570	823
2. One- to four-family	286	630	489	2 647	−842	−464	6	3 533	760
3. Multi-family	26	63	55	381	−67	−80	−36	36	63
4. Other nonfarm real estate	162	136	133	636	−40	−299	−295	334	121
5. Farm real estate	107	168	327	80	−226	−126	−40	1 040	143
6. Real estate	581	998	1 004	3 744	−1 174	−969	−365	4 944	1 087
7. Producer durables	70	109	125	178	−426	125	375	2 434	285
8. Consumer durables	260	395	299	1 939	−1 190	754	206	8 199	1 063
9. Inventories	3	43	318	−10	−626	27	374	58	55
10. Livestock	48	84	16	−52	47	−88	105	−207	8
11. Tangible assets other than real estate	382	632	758	2 055	−2 196	818	1 060	10 484	1 411
12. Total tangible assets	963	1 630	1 763	5 799	−3 370	−151	695	15 428	2 498
13. Currency	38	6	232	−8	313	177	2 828	−351	426
14. Commercial bank deposits	337	567	1 521	891	−2 094	1 615	6 723	1 847	1 498
15. Demand deposits ⎱ of nonagricultur-	67	150	294	−93	−7	625	2 285	510	456
16. Time deposits ⎰ al individuals	144	245	777	842	−1 362	550	1 881	1 188	577
17. Deposits of agric. and uninc. business	126	172	450	141	−725	440	2 557	150	465
18. Savings bank deposits	127	167	297	470	521	264	1 080	1 196	455
19. Savings and loan associations	10	74	166	573	−202	−162	530	1 382	263
20. Other deposits	6	11	27	32	−2	60	133	289	56
21. Life insurance reserves (gross)	175	277	471	1 176	986	1 446	2 327	3 662	1 105
22. Private pension reserves	−	−	1	55	50	60	271	988	128
23. Government insurance reserves	1	1	24	161	4	704	2 975	3 386	743
24. U.S. savings bonds	−	−	143	−106	0	247	6 006	1 584	939
25. Other U.S. Government securities	−1	−1	1 831	−1 034	572	−72	2 350	−1 272	336
26. State and local govt. securities	54	106	376	409	396	−235	−159	571	165
27. Other bonds	310	374	1 120	1 550	181	−584	−763	−313	329
28. Preferred stock	84	96	280	597	72	−58	−55	149	161
29. Common stock	384	523	971	1 647	563	378	642	1 590	806
30. Mortgage holdings	61	313	870	688	−133	−82	−43	1 270	340
31. Other claims	1	4	9	28	30	30	40	56	21
32. Intangible assets	1 586	2 519	8 337	7 129	1 258	3 789	24 885	16 032	7 771
33. Residential mortgage debt	95	275	543	2 007	−601	−22	259	4 499	754
34. One- to four-family	74	216	417	1 386	−613	99	292	4 285	630
35. Multi-family	21	59	127	621	12	−121	−34	214	123
36. Nonresidential mortgage debt	48	98	171	528	15	−57	−89	502	146
37. Farm mortgage debt	91	316	817	−124	−453	−122	−295	183	75
38. Consumer debt	46	100	153	469	−800	565	−77	2 701	299
39. Policy loans	29	55	48	165	342	−66	−201	69	42
40. Borrowing on securities	72	60	175	564	−1 283	−208	437	−764	15
41. Borrowing on bonds	−	−	−	−	−	−	271	−369	8
42. Borrowing on stocks	72	60	175	564	−1 283	−208	166	−396	7
43. Other short-term liabilities	208	211	696	15	390	−89	215	1 091	297
44. Tax accruals	17	68	265	155	26	89	402	207	149
45. Liabilities	606	1 185	2 868	3 780	−2 363	89	650	8 487	1 777
46. Total net saving	1 943	2 965	7 232	9 152	251	3 541	24 925	22 973	8 491

PERSONAL SAVING BY MAJOR COMPONENTS
SOCIAL ACCOUNTING CONCEPT; CURRENT VALUES
Quadrennial Period Averages: 1898 to 1949

$ mill.

	1898 to 1901	1902 to 1905	1906 to 1909	1910 to 1913	1914 to 1917	1918 to 1921	1922 to 1925
1. Residential real estate	63	394	642	709	567	534	3 273
2. One- to four-family	55	358	595	646	501	487	2 951
3. Multi-family	8	36	47	63	66	47	322
4. Other nonfarm real estate	157	152	175	146	114	143	525
5. Farm real estate	93	117	132	172	264	349	70
6. Real estate	313	663	949	1 027	945	1 026	3 868
7. Producer durables	27	98	123	124	116	117	93
8. Consumer durables	191	292	375	439	472	93	1 883
9. Inventories	-50	123	-27	8	126	494	64
10. Livestock	76	38	6	74	193	-104	-122
11. Tangible assets other than real estate	243	550	477	645	907	601	1 918
12. Total tangible assets	556	1 213	1 426	1 672	1 852	1 627	5 786
13. Currency	66	66	-9	28	274	98	20
14. Commercial bank deposits	458	484	192	629	1 928	786	1 845
15. Demand deposits ⎱ of nonagricultural	108	114	-16	164	612	-54	422
16. Time deposits ⎰ individuals	112	184	235	274	776	555	1 216
17. Deposits of agric. and uninc. business	237	185	-27	190	540	285	208
18. Savings bank deposits	140	145	117	174	201	352	453
19. Savings and loan associations	-7	13	43	76	101	210	500
20. Other deposits	6	6	7	10	22	30	33
21. Life insurance reserves (gross)	126	192	248	283	344	550	924
22. Private pension reserves	0	0	0	0	0	2	22
23. Government insurance reserves	1	1	1	1	5	37	118
24. U.S. savings bonds	–	–	–	–	125	125	-200
25. Other U.S. Government securities	36	-18	-24	8	693	2 510	-994
26. State and local government securities	33	20	103	100	239	476	447
27. Other bonds	259	378	409	312	929	1 149	1 550
28. Preferred stock	144	46	68	98	210	315	464
29. Common stock	221	428	657	532	660	1 118	1 017
30. Mortgage holdings	55	65	62	337	600	1 040	-10
31. Other claims	1	2	2	4	6	11	20
32. Intangible assets	1 538	1 828	1 876	2 591	6 336	8 808	6 210
33. Residential mortgage debt	43	127	171	267	388	652	1 653
34. One- to four-family	32	100	135	209	304	496	1 171
35. Multi-family	10	26	36	58	84	156	482
36. Nonresidential mortgage debt	34	57	69	95	132	200	550
37. Farm mortgage debt	81	94	109	375	458	1 042	-238
38. Consumer debt	39	53	68	97	122	169	360
39. Policy loans	13	26	56	54	39	64	99
40. Borrowing on securities	110	80	34	37	232	102	715
41. Borrowing on bonds	–	–	–	–	–	–	–
42. Borrowing on stocks	110	80	34	37	232	102	715
43. Other short-term liabilities	225	258	196	224	678	545	-101
44. Tax accruals	19	16	16	54	424	84	77
45. Liabilities	565	711	718	1 202	2 472	2 858	3 115
46. Total net saving	1 529	2 331	2 584	3 061	5 716	7 576	8 885

Source: Same as for Table S-34.

PERSONAL SAVING BY MAJOR COMPONENTS
SOCIAL ACCOUNTING CONCEPT; CURRENT VALUES
Quadrennial Period Averages: 1898 to 1949

$ mill.

	1926 to 1929	1930 to 1933	1934 to 1937	1938 to 1941	1942 to 1945	1946 to 1949	1898 to 1949
1. Residential real estate	2 783	−909	−716	1 039	−1 056	3 570	838
2. One- to four-family	2 344	−842	−627	1 051	−993	3 533	774
3. Multi-family	440	−67	−89	−12	−63	36	64
4. Other nonfarm real estate	748	−40	−320	−164	−406	334	120
5. Farm real estate	89	−226	−134	−1	−91	1 040	144
6. Real estate	3 620	−1 174	−1 171	874	−1 553	4 944	1 102
7. Producer durables	264	−426	126	412	276	2 434	291
8. Consumer durables	1 995	−1 190	908	1 702	−1 307	8 199	1 081
9. Inventories	−84	−626	58	196	434	58	60
10. Livestock	18	47	−128	167	36	−207	7
11. Tangible assets other than real estate	2 193	−2 196	963	2 477	−562	10 484	1 438
12. Total tangible assets	5 812	−3 370	−208	3 350	−2 115	15 428	2 541
13. Currency	−36	313	224	866	4 081	−351	434
14. Commercial bank deposits	−63	−2 094	1 934	1 830	10 020	1 847	1 523
15. Demand deposits ⎱ of nonagricultural	−608	−7	696	1 035	3 050	510	463
16. Time deposits ⎰ individuals	469	−1 362	739	120	3 121	1 188	587
17. Deposits of agric. and uninc. business	75	−725	500	675	3 850	150	473
18. Savings bank deposits	486	521	282	207	1 730	1 196	462
19. Savings and loan associations	646	−202	−202	214	712	1 382	268
20. Other deposits	30	−2	58	100	148	289	57
21. Life insurance reserves (gross)	1 429	986	1 406	1 728	2 745	3 662	1 125
22. Private pension reserves	88	50	60	59	431	988	131
23. Government insurance reserves	204	4	600	1 405	4 081	3 386	757
24. U.S. savings bonds	−12	0	207	1 167	9 445	1 584	957
25. Other U.S. Government securities	−1 074	572	11	−264	4 275	−1 272	343
26. State and local government securities	370	396	−282	−111	−179	571	168
27. Other bonds	1 550	181	−718	−518	−828	−313	334
28. Preferred stock	·731	72	−56	−27	−86	149	164
29. Common stock	2 277	563	398	506	692	1 590	820
30. Mortgage holdings	1 386	−133	−52	174	48	1 270	346
31. Other claims	37	30	30	35	43	56	21
32. Intangible assets	8 048	1 258	3 901	7 023	37 359	16 032	7 908
33. Residential mortgage debt	2 361	−601	−77	624	−122	4 499	768
34. One- to four-family	1 601	−613	60	621	−46	4 285	643
35. Multi-family	760	12	−137	4	−77	214	125
36. Nonresidential mortgage debt	507	15	−56	−74	−96	502	149
37. Farm mortgage debt	−10	−453	−114	−133	−422	183	75
38. Consumer debt	579	−800	790	551	−770	2 701	305
39. Policy loans	231	342	−82	−114	−239	69	43
40. Borrowing on securities	413	−1 283	−236	−154	894	−764	14
41. Borrowing on bonds	–	–	–	–	474	−369	8
42. Borrowing on stocks	413	−1 283	−236	−154	421	−396	6
43. Other short-term liabilities	132	390	−274	769	−230	1 091	300
44. Tax accruals	233	26	245	618	−48	207	152
45. Liabilities	4 445	−2 363	195	2 087	−1 034	8 487	1 805
46. Total net saving	9 419	251	3 498	8 270	36 278	22 973	8 644

Source: Same as for Table S-34.

PERSONAL SAVING BY MAJOR COMPONENTS
BUSINESS ACCOUNTING CONCEPT; CURRENT VALUES
Economic Period Averages: 1897 to 1949

$ mill.

	1897 to 1908	1909 to 1914	1915 to 1921	1922 to 1929	1930 to 1933	1934 to 1938	1939 to 1945	1946 to 1949	1897 to 1949
1. Residential real estate	340	748	928	3 564	−630	−233	836	5 902	1 308
2. Other nonfarm real estate	169	156	261	793	10	−212	−105	825	239
3. Farm real estate	118	199	481	222	−167	−63	124	1 525	259
4. Real estate	628	1 104	1 670	4 578	−787	−509	855	8 252	1 807
5. Producer durables	91	142	392	255	−541	88	478	2 932	379
6. Consumer durables	334	577	1 777	2 366	−2 356	−249	993	11 640	1 541
7. Inventories	162	125	425	74	−1 132	186	1 095	1 096	277
8. Livestock	195	329	−175	180	−836	385	664	860	211
9. Tang. assets other than real estate	781	1 173	2 420	2 875	−4 866	410	3 230	16 530	2 409
10. Total tangible assets	1 409	2 277	4 089	7 453	−5 653	3 −99	4 085	24 783	4 216
11. Intangible assets	1 557	2 464	8 289	6 964	916	855	25 086	15 964	7 728
12. Liabilities	577	1 130	2 820	3 615	−2 706	155	851	8 418	1 735
13. Total net saving	2 390	3 612	9 558	10 802	−2 031	3 600	28 316	32 328	10 209

Period averages derived from annual figures obtained as follows:

Lines 1 to 3, 5, 6, 13 – From Table T-7.

Line 4 – Sum of lines 1–3.

Line 7 – Table A-32, col. 3 plus first differences of Table P-19, col. 3.

Line 8 – Table A-32, col. 2.

Line 9 – Sum of lines 5 to 8.

Line 10 – Sum of lines 4 and 9.

Lines 11 and 12 – See notes to Table T-7, col. 8.

PERSONAL SAVING BY MAJOR COMPONENTS
BUSINESS ACCOUNTING CONCEPT; CURRENT VALUES
Quadrennial Period Averages: 1898 to 1949
$ mill.

	1898 to 1901	1902 to 1905	1906 to 1909	1910 to 1913	1914 to 1917	1918 to 1921	1922 to 1925
1. Residential real estate	75	427	703	765	672	1 113	3 803
2. Other nonfarm real estate	159	160	193	168	155	329	686
3. Farm real estate	96	128	160	204	325	566	220
4. Real estate	330	715	1 055	1 136	1 152	2 008	4 710
5. Producer durables	42	123	159	161	207	498	185
6. Consumer durables	184	422	516	634	933	2 286	2 637
7. Inventories	220	113	267	85	1 388	−648	432
8. Livestock	214	134	292	308	601	−871	79
9. Tangible assets other than real estate	660	792	1 234	1 189	3 130	1 264	3 333
10. Total tangible assets	990	1 507	2 289	2 325	4 281	3 272	8 044
11. Intangible assets	1 524	1 802	1 820	2 537	6 296	8 743	6 111
12. Liabilities	552	684	662	1 148	2 432	2 794	3 016
13. Total net saving	1 962	2 625	3 447	3 714	8 145	9 221	11 136

	1926 to 1929	1930 to 1933	1934 to 1937	1938 to 1941	1942 to 1945	1946 to 1949	1898 to 1949
1. Residential real estate	3 325	−630	−446	1 606	11	5 902	1 333
2. Other nonfarm real estate	899	10	−241	−31	−177	825	241
3. Farm real estate	223	−167	−72	69	142	1 525	263
4. Real estate	4 447	−787	−759	1 644	−24	8 252	1 837
5. Producer durables	325	−541	80	440	427	2 934	387
6. Consumer durables	2 095	−2 356	−201	1 414	213	11 640	1 571
7. Inventories	−285	−1 132	392	599	1 157	1 096	283
8. Livestock	282	−836	466	510	667	860	208
9. Tangible assets other than real estate	2 416	−4 866	737	2 963	2 464	16 530	2 450
10. Total tangible assets	6 863	−5 653	−22	4 606	2 440	24 783	4 287
11. Intangible assets	7 816	916	3 984	7 137	37 598	15 964	7 865
12. Liabilities	4 214	−2 706	278	2 201	−795	8 418	1 761
13. Total net saving	10 468	−2 031	3 684	9 536	40 833	32 328	10 390

Source: Same as for Table S-36.

Period averages derived from annual figures obtained as follows:

Line 1 – Sum of lines 2 and 3. Table R-4, sum of cols. 1–4 minus col. 7 plus Table R-7, col. 1 minus col. 5.

Line 2 – Sum of Table T-10, col. 3 and Table U-11, col. 2.

Line 3 – Table A-66, cols. 2 and 16.

Line 4 – Sum of lines 1 to 3.

Line 5 – Sum of Table T-10, col. 5, Table U-11, col. 3, and Table A-66, col. 4.

Line 6 – Sum of Table T-10, col. 4 and Table A-66, col. 3.

Line 7 – Table A-32, col. 3 plus first differences of Table P-19, col. 3.

Line 8 – Table A-32, col. 2.

Line 9 – Sum of lines 5 to 8.

Line 10 – Sum of lines 4 and 9.

Line 11 – Sum of Table T-10, col. 7 plus Table A-66, col. 6.

Line 12 – Sum of Table T-10, col. 8, Table U-11, col. 5, and Table A-66, col. 7.

Line 13 – Table T-10, col. 9.

Line 14 – Table T-10, col. 12.

Line 15 – Sum of Table T-10, cols. 10 and 11, and Table A-66, col. 10.

Line 16 – Sum of Table T-10, cols. 14 and 15, and Table A-66, col. 8.

Line 17 – Table T-10, col. 18.

Line 18 – Sum of Table T-10, cols. 16 and 17, and Table A-66, col. 12.

Line 19 – Sum of Table T-10, col. 19, Table U-11, col. 6, and Table A-66, col. 9.

Lines 20 and 21 – Table T-10, cols. 20 and 21, respectively.

Line 22 – Table V-1, col. 5.

Line 23 – Table V-1, cols. 6 to 8.

Line 24 – Sum of Table T-10, col. 13 and Table A-66, col. 11.

Line 25 – Sum of lines 11 to 24.

Line 26 – Table R-4, col. 6 plus Table R-7, cols. 3 and 4.

Line 27 – Sum of Table T-10, col. 26 and Table U-11, col. 11.

Line 28 – Table A-66, col. 13.

Line 29 – Table T-10, col. 24 plus first differences of Table D-1, col. 5 minus Table U-11, col. 7.

Line 30 – Table T-10, col. 23.

Line 31 – Sum of Table A-66, col. 14 and Table U-11, cols. 7 and 10 minus sum of Table U-11, cols. 8 and 9, and first differences of Table D-1, col. 5.

Line 32 – Sum of lines 26 to 31.

Line 33 – Sum of lines 10 and 25 minus line 32.

304

PERSONAL SAVING BY MAJOR COMPONENTS
CASH FLOW CONCEPT; CURRENT VALUES
Economic Period Averages: 1897 to 1949

$ mill.

	1897 to 1908	1909 to 1914	1915 to 1921	1922 to 1929	1930 to 1933	1934 to 1938	1939 to 1945	1946 to 1949	1897 to 1949
1. Residential real estate	741	1 291	1 619	4 699	842	1 279	2 580	8 053	2 370
2. Other nonfarm real estate	282	306	433	1 070	474	161	266	1 181	492
3. Farm real estate	236	357	691	511	162	249	460	1 952	506
4. Real estate	1 260	1 954	2 743	6 281	1 478	1 689	3 306	11 186	3 368
5. Producer durables	439	646	1 156	1 374	750	1 150	1 671	4 752	1 277
6. Consumer durables	1 320	2 321	4 919	8 531	5 204	6 219	7 983	22 172	6 206
7. Inventories	162	125	425	74	-1 132	186	1 095	1 096	277
8. Livestock	195	329	-175	180	-836	385	664	860	211
9. Tang. assets other than real estate	2 115	3 422	6 325	10 160	3 984	7 940	11 412	28 880	7 972
10. Total tangible assets	3 375	5 377	9 068	16 441	5 462	9 629	14 718	40 066	11 340
11. Currency	38	6	232	-8	313	177	2 828	-351	426
12. Commercial bank deposits	256	385	1 148	279	-2 558	1 393	6 544	1 561	1 216
13. Savings bank deposits	26	7	69	95	-208	-82	523	690	128
14. Savings and loan associations	-14	27	79	293	-572	-380	311	1 032	94
15. Other deposits	6	21	39	32	258	64	363	331	112
16. Life insurance reserves (net)	161	195	434	1 056	476	1 282	2 095	2 926	930
17. Private pension reserves	–	–	0	0	0	0	21	125	12
18. Government insurance reserves	–	–	-3	-25	-396	-103	313	-866	-68
19. U.S. Government securities	-1	-1	1 973	-1 140	572	-197	8 208	-214	1 181
20. State and local govt. securities	54	106	376	409	396	-235	-159	571	165
21. Other bonds	310	374	1 120	1 550	181	-584	-763	-313	329
22. Preferred stock	84	96	280	597	72	-58	-55	149	161
23. Common stock	384	523	971	1 647	563	378	642	1 590	806
24. Mortgage holdings	61	313	868	647	-357	-270	-74	1 263	295
25. Intangible assets	1 363	2 054	7 586	5 433	-1 258	1 385	20 798	8 492	5 787
26. Residential mortgage debt	95	275	543	2 007	-676	-94	253	4 499	740
27. Nonresidential mortgage debt	48	98	171	528	54	-90	-91	502	146
28. Farm mortgage debt	91	316	816	-134	-486	-181	-300	183	64
29. Consumer debt	48	101	150	457	-774	560	-68	2 622	294
30. Borrowing on securities	72	60	175	564	-1 283	-208	437	-764	15
31. Other short-term liabilities	204	206	669	-114	-20	-404	51	982	182
32. Liabilities	557	1 057	2 525	3 308	-3 185	-419	282	8 024	1 442
33. Total net saving	4 181	6 374	14 128	18 564	7 394	11 432	35 230	40 535	15 685

PERSONAL SAVING BY MAJOR COMPONENTS
CASH FLOW CONCEPT; CURRENT VALUES
Quadrennial Period Averages: 1898 to 1949

$ mill.

	1898 to 1901	1902 to 1905	1906 to 1909	1910 to 1913	1914 to 1917	1918 to 1921	1922 to 1925
1. Residential real estate	434	827	1 186	1 308	1 293	1 850	4 775
2. Other nonfarm real estate	257	276	330	316	316	509	921
3. Farm real estate	203	249	297	361	505	797	495
4. Real estate	893	1 352	1 813	1 986	2 114	3 156	6 191
5. Producer durables	358	470	569	665	818	1 368	1 218
6. Consumer durables	1 022	1 398	1 822	2 372	3 308	5 926	7 758
7. Inventories	220	113	267	85	1 388	−648	432
8. Livestock	214	134	292	308	601	−871	79
9. Tangible assets other than real estate	1 816	2 114	2 949	3 430	6 115	5 775	9 486
10. Total tangible assets	2 709	3 467	4 762	5 416	8 230	8 932	15 678
11. Currency	66	66	−9	28	274	98	20
12. Commercial bank deposits	406	396	61	446	1 670	339	1 296
13. Savings bank deposits	53	40	−8	14	−8	114	136
14. Savings and loan associations	−28	−9	10	31	35	109	297
15. Other deposits	6	6	7	20	47	31	29
16. Life insurance reserves (net)	129	198	174	202	277	531	882
17. Private pension reserves	−	−	−	−	−	0	0
18. Government insurance reserves	−	−	−	−	−12·	7	7
19. U.S. Government securities	36	−18	−24	8	818	2 635	−1 194
20. State and local government securities	33	20	103	100	239	476	447
21. Other bonds	259	378	409	312	928	1 149	1 550
22. Preferred stock	144	46	68	98	210	315	464
23. Common stock	221	428	657	532	660	1 118	1 017
24. Mortgage holdings	55	65	62	337	600	1 038	−30
25. Intangible assets	1 378	1 618	1 508	2 125	5 738	7 959	4 920
26. Residential mortgage debt	43	127	171	267	388	652	1 653
27. Nonresidential mortgage debt	34	57	69	95	132	200	550
28. Farm mortgage debt	81	94	109	375	458	1 041	−247
29. Consumer debt	40	54	71	97	127	160	356
30. Borrowing on securities	110	80	34	37	232	102	715
31. Other short-term liabilities	220	252	191	218	668	508	−159
32. Liabilities	529	664	644	1 089	2 002	2 662	2 868
33. Total net saving	3 558	4 421	5 626	6 452	11 964	14 228	17 727

Source: Same as for Table S-38.

PERSONAL SAVING BY MAJOR COMPONENTS
CASH FLOW CONCEPT; CURRENT VALUES
Quadrennial Period Averages: 1898 to 1949

$ mill.

	1926 to 1929	1930 to 1933	1934 to 1937	1938 to 1941	1942 to 1945	1946 to 1949	1898 to 1949
1. Residential real estate	4 624	842	1 053	3 242	1 818	8 053	2 408
2. Other nonfarm real estate	1 219	474	134	340	194	1 181	497
3. Farm real estate	528	162	239	392	487	1 952	513
4. Real estate	6 370	1 478	1 425	3 973	2 498	11 186	3 418
5. Producer durables	1 532	750	1 136	1 554	1 670	4 752	1 297
6. Consumer durables	9 305	5 204	6 244	8 122	7 378	22 172	6 310
7. Inventories	−285	−1 132	392	599	1 157	1 096	283
8. Livestock	282	−836	466	510	667	860	208
9. Tangible assets other than real estate	10 833	3 984	8 238	10 785	10 872	28 880	8 098
10. Total tangible assets	17 204	5 462	9 664	14 758	13 371	40 066	11 517
11. Currency	−36	313	224	866	4 081	−351	434
12. Commercial bank deposits	−737	−2 558	1 708	1 642	9 842	1 561	1 236
13. Savings bank deposits	55	−208	−76	−116	1 003	690	130
14. Savings and loan associations	288	−572	−425	6	489	1 032	97
15. Other deposits	36	258	70	112	534	331	114
16. Life insurance reserves (net)	1 231	476	1 278	1 504	2 487	2 926	946
17. Private pension reserves	0	0	0	−12	50	125	12
18. Government insurance reserves	−57	−396	−60	−291	770	−866	−69
19. U.S. Government securities	−1 087	572	−240	858	13 500	−214	1 204
20. State and local government securities	370	396	−282	−111	−179	571	168
21. Other bonds	1 550	181	−718	−518	−828	−313	334
22. Preferred stock	731	72	−56	−27	−86	149	164
23. Common stock	2 277	563	398	506	692	1 590	820
24. Mortgage holdings	1 324	−357	−259	−242	35	1 263	299
25. Intangible assets	5 946	−1 258	1 561	4 174	32 392	8 492	5 889
26. Residential mortgage debt	2 361	−676	−157	604	−122	4 499	755
27. Nonresidential mortgage debt	507	54	−95	−79	−96	502	148
28. Farm mortgage debt	−20	−486	−182	−146	−422	183	64
29. Consumer debt	558	−774	767	546	−733	2 622	299
30. Borrowing on securities	413	−1 283	−236	−154	894	−764	14
31. Other short-term liabilities	−70	−20	−617	552	−352	982	183
32. Liabilities	3 749	−3 185	−521	1 324	−832	8 024	1 463
33. Total net saving	19 400	7 394	11 746	17 602	46 594	40 535	15 942

Source: Same as for Table S-38.

SHARE OF MAJOR COMPONENTS IN PERSONAL SAVING
SOCIAL ACCOUNTING CONCEPT; CURRENT VALUES
Economic Periods: 1897 to 1949

Percent

	1897 to 1908	1909 to 1914	1915 to 1921	1922 to 1929	1930 to 1933	1934 to 1938	1939 to 1945	1946 to 1949	1897 to 1949
1. Residential real estate	16.0	23.4	7.5	33.1	−361.5	−15.3	−0.1	15.5	9.7
2. Other nonfarm real estate	8.4	4.6	1.8	7.0	−15.7	−8.4	−1.2	1.5	1.4
3. Farm real estate	5.5	5.7	4.5	0.9	−89.8	−3.5	−0.2	4.5	1.7
4. Real estate	29.9	33.7	13.9	40.9	−467.0	−27.3	−1.5	21.5	12.8
5. Producer durables	3.6	3.7	1.7	1.9	−169.6	3.5	1.5	10.6	3.4
6. Consumer durables	13.4	13.3	4.1	21.2	−473.3	21.2	0.8	35.7	12.5
7. Inventories	0.2	1.5	4.4	−0.1	−248.9	0.8	1.5	0.3	0.6
8. Livestock	2.5	2.8	0.2	−0.6	18.8	−2.5	0.4	−0.9	0.1
9. Tangible assets other than real estate	19.7	21.3	10.5	22.5	−873.0	23.0	4.3	45.6	16.6
10. Total tangible assets	49.6	55.0	24.4	63.4	−1340.0	−4.2	2.9	67.2	29.4
11. Currency	1.9	0.2	3.2	−0.1	124.6	5.0	11.3	−1.5	5.0
12. Commercial bank deposits	17.3	19.1	21.0	9.7	−832.4	45.5	27.0	8.0	17.6
13. Savings bank deposits	6.5	5.6	4.1	5.1	207.1	7.4	4.3	5.2	5.4
14. Savings and loan associations	0.5	2.5	2.3	6.3	−80.4	−4.6	2.1	6.0	3.1
15. Other deposits	0.3	0.4	0.4	0.3	−0.6	1.7	0.5	1.3	0.7
16. Life insurance reserves (net)	7.5	7.5	5.9	11.1	256.0	42.6	10.1	15.6	12.5
17. Private pension reserves	−	−	0	0.6	19.9	1.7	1.1	4.3	1.5
18. Government insurance reserves	0.1	0	0.4	1.8	1.8	19.8	11.9	14.7	8.8
19. U.S. Government securities	−0.1	0	27.3	−12.5	227.6	4.9	33.5	1.4	15.0
20. State and local govt. securities	2.8	3.6	5.2	4.5	157.3	−6.6	−0.6	2.5	1.9
21. Other bonds	15.9	12.6	15.5	16.9	72.0	−16.4	−3.1	−1.4	3.9
22. Preferred stock	4.3	3.3	3.9	6.5	28.6	−1.6	−0.2	0.6	1.9
23. Common stock	19.7	17.7	13.4	18.0	224.0	10.6	2.6	6.9	9.5
24. Mortgage holdings	3.1	10.6	12.0	7.5	−53.0	−2.3	−.2	5.5	4.0
25. Other claims	0.1	0.1	0.1	0.3	11.9	0.9	0.2	0.2	0.2
26. Intangible assets	80.1	83.1	114.6	76.1	364.2	108.6	100.6	69.5	91.0
27. Residential mortgage debt	4.9	9.3	7.5	21.9	−239.0	−0.6	1.0	19.6	8.9
28. Nonresidential mortgage debt	2.5	3.3	2.4	5.8	5.9	−1.6	−0.4	2.2	1.7
29. Farm mortgage debt	4.7	10.7	11.3	−1.4	−180.0	−3.4	−1.2	0.8	0.9
30. Consumer debt	2.4	3.4	2.1	5.1	−318.3	15.9	0.3	11.8	3.5
31. Borrowing on securities	3.7	2.0	2.4	6.2	−510.1	−5.9	1.8	−3.3	0.2
32. Other short-term liabilities	10.7	7.1	9.6	0.2	155.3	−2.5	0.9	4.7	3.5
33. Tax accruals	0.9	2.3	3.7	1.7	10.5	2.5	1.6	0.9	1.8
34. Liabilities	29.7	38.1	39.0	39.5	−1075.7	4.4	3.4	36.6	20.4
35. Total net saving	100.0	100.0	100.0	100.0	100.0	100.0	100.0	100.0	100.0

Source: Same as for Table S-34.

SHARE OF MAJOR COMPONENTS IN PERSONAL SAVING
SOCIAL ACCOUNTING CONCEPT; CURRENT VALUES
Quadrennial Periods: 1898 to 1949

Percent

	1898 to 1901	1902 to 1905	1906 to 1909	1910 to 1913	1914 to 1917	1918 to 1921	1922 to 1925
1. Residential real estate	4.1	16.9	24.9	23.2	9.9	7.1	36.8
2. Other nonfarm real estate	10.3	6.5	6.8	4.8	2.0	1.9	5.9
3. Farm real estate	6.1	5.0	5.1	5.6	4.6	4.6	0.8
4. Real estate	20.5	28.4	36.8	33.6	16.5	13.6	43.5
5. Producer durables	1.8	4.2	4.8	4.0	2.0	1.5	1.0
6. Consumer durables	12.5	12.5	14.5	14.3	8.3	1.2	21.2
7. Inventories	−3.3	5.3	−1.1	0.3	2.2	6.5	0.7
8. Livestock	5.0	1.6	0.2	2.4	3.4	−1.4	−1.4
9. Tangible assets other than real estate	16.0	23.6	18.5	21.0	15.9	7.8	21.7
10. Total tangible assets	36.4	52.0	55.2	54.6	32.4	21.5	65.1
11. Currency	4.3	2.8	−0.4	0.9	4.8	1.3	0.2
12. Commercial bank deposits	29.9	20.8	7.4	20.5	33.7	10.4	20.7
13. Savings bank deposits	9.2	6.2	4.5	5.7	3.5	4.6	5.1
14. Savings and loan associations	−0.5	0.6	1.7	2.5	1.8	2.8	5.6
15. Other deposits	0.4	0.3	0.3	0.3	0.4	0.4	0.4
16. Life insurance reserves (net)	7.4	7.1	7.4	7.5	5.3	6.4	9.3
17. Private pension reserves	0	0	0	0	0	0	0.3
18. Government insurance reserves	0.1	0	0	0	0.1	0.5	1.3
19. U.S. Government securities	2.3	−0.8	−0.9	0.2	14.3	34.8	−13.4
20. State and local government securities	2.1	0.9	4.0	3.3	4.2	6.3	5.0
21. Other bonds	17.0	16.3	15.8	10.2	16.2	15.2	17.4
22. Preferred stock	9.4	2.0	2.6	3.2	3.7	4.2	5.2
23. Common stock	14.5	18.4	25.4	17.4	11.5	14.8	11.4
24. Mortgage holdings	3.6	2.8	2.4	11.0	10.5	13.7	−0.1
25. Other claims	0.1	0.1	0.1	0.1	0.1	0.1	0.2
26. Intangible assets	99.8	77.5	70.3	82.8	110.1	115.5	68.6
27. Residential mortgage debt	2.8	5.5	6.6	8.7	6.8	8.6	18.6
28. Nonresidential mortgage debt	2.3	2.4	2.7	3.1	2.3	2.6	6.2
29. Farm mortgage debt	5.3	4.0	4.2	12.2	8.0	13.8	−2.7
30. Consumer debt	2.6	2.3	2.7	3.2	2.1	2.2	4.0
31. Borrowing on securities	7.2	3.4	1.3	1.2	4.1	1.3	8.0
32. Other short-term liabilities	14.7	11.1	7.6	7.3	11.9	7.2	−1.1
33. Tax accruals	1.2	0.7	0.6	1.7	7.4	1.1	0.9
34. Liabilities	36.1	29.4	25.7	37.4	42.6	36.8	33.9
35. Total net saving	100.0	100.0	100.0	100.0	100.0	100.0	100.0

Source: Same as for Table S-34.

SHARE OF MAJOR COMPONENTS IN PERSONAL SAVING
SOCIAL ACCOUNTING CONCEPT; CURRENT VALUES
Quadrennial Periods: 1898 to 1949

Percent

	1926 to 1929	1930 to 1933	1934 to 1937	1938 to 1941	1942 to 1945	1946 to 1949	1898 to 1949
1. Residential real estate	29.6	−361.5	−20.5	12.5	−2.9	15.5	9.7
2. Other nonfarm real estate	7.9	−15.7	−9.2	−2.0	−1.1	1.5	1.4
3. Farm real estate	0.9	−89.8	−3.8	0	−0.3	4.5	1.7
4. Real estate	38.4	−467.0	−33.5	10.5	−4.3	21.5	12.8
5. Producer durables	2.8	−169.6	3.6	5.0	0.8	10.6	3.4
6. Consumer durables	21.2	−473.3	25.9	20.5	−3.6	35.7	12.5
7. Inventories	−0.9	−248.9	1.7	2.4	1.2	0.3	0.7
8. Livestock	0.2	18.8	−3.7	2.0	0.1	−0.9	0.1
9. Tangible assets other than real estate	23.3	−873.0	27.5	29.9	−1.5	45.6	16.6
10. Total tangible assets	61.7	−1 340.0	−5.9	40.4	−5.8	67.2	29.4
11. Currency	−0.4	124.6	6.4	10.4	11.2	−1.5	5.0
12. Commercial bank deposits	−0.7	−832.4	55.3	22.1	27.6	8.0	17.6
13. Savings bank deposits	5.2	207.1	8.1	2.5	4.8	5.2	5.3
14. Savings and loan associations	6.9	−80.4	−5.8	2.6	2.0	6.0	3.1
15. Other deposits	0.3	−0.6	1.7	1.2	0.4	1.3	0.7
16. Life insurance reserves (net)	12.7	256.0	42.6	22.2	8.2	15.6	12.5
17. Private pension reserves	0.9	19.9	1.7	0.7	1.2	4.3	1.5
18. Government insurance reserves	2.2	1.8	17.2	17.0	11.2	14.7	8.8
19. U.S. Government securities	−11.5	227.6	6.2	10.9	37.8	1.4	15.0
20. State and local government securities	3.9	157.3	−8.1	−1.3	−0.5	2.5	1.9
21. Other bonds	16.5	72.0	−20.5	−6.2	−2.3	−1.4	3.9
22. Preferred stock	7.8	28.6	−1.6	−0.3	−0.2	0.6	1.9
23. Common stock	24.2	224.0	11.4	6.1	1.9	6.9	9.5
24. Mortgage holdings	14.7	−53.0	−1.5	−2.1	0.1	5.5	4.0
25. Other claims	0.4	11.9	0.9	0.4	0.1	0.2	0.2
26. Intangible assets	83.1	364.2	114.0	86.2	103.5	69.5	91.0
27. Residential mortgage debt	25.1	−239.0	−2.2	7.5	−0.3	19.6	8.9
28. Nonresidential mortgage debt	5.4	5.9	−1.6	−0.9	−0.3	2.2	1.7
29. Farm mortgage debt	−0.1	−180.0	−3.3	−1.6	−1.2	0.8	0.9
30. Consumer debt	6.1	−318.3	22.6	6.6	−2.1	11.8	3.5
31. Borrowing on securities	4.4	−510.1	−6.8	−1.9	2.5	−3.3	0.2
32. Other short-term liabilities	1.4	155.3	−7.8	9.3	−0.6	4.7	3.5
33. Tax accruals	2.5	10.5	7.0	7.5	−0.1	0.9	1.8
34. Liabilities	44.8	−1 075.7	7.9	26.5	−2.1	36.6	20.4
35. Total net saving	100.0	100.0	100.0	100.0	100.0	100.0	100.0

Source: Same as for Table S-34.

SHARE OF MAJOR COMPONENTS IN PERSONAL SAVING
BUSINESS ACCOUNTING CONCEPT; CURRENT VALUES
Economic Periods: 1897 to 1949

Percent

	1897 to 1908	1909 to 1914	1915 to 1921	1922 to 1929	1930 to 1933	1934 to 1938	1939 to 1945	1946 to 1949	1897 to 1949
1. Residential real estate	14.2	20.7	9.7	33.0	31.0	−6.5	3.0	18.3	12.8
2. Other nonfarm real estate	7.1	4.3	2.7	7.3	−0.5	−5.9	−0.4	2.6	2.3
3. Farm real estate	5.0	5.5	5.0	2.1	8.2	−1.8	0.4	4.7	2.5
4. Real estate	26.3	30.5	17.4	42.4	38.7	−14.2	3.0	25.6	17.7
5. Producer durables	3.8	3.9	4.1	2.4	26.6	2.4	1.7	9.1	3.7
6. Consumer durables	14.0	16.0	18.6	21.9	116.0	−6.9	3.5	36.0	15.1
7. Inventories	6.8	3.5	4.4	0.7	55.8	5.2	3.9	3.4	2.7
8. Livestock	8.1	9.1	−1.8	1.7	41.2	10.7	2.3	2.7	2.1
9. Tangible assets other than real estate	32.7	32.5	25.3	26.6	239.5	11.4	11.4	51.1	23.6
10. Total tangible assets	59.0	63.1	42.8	69.0	278.3	−2.8	14.4	76.7	41.3
11. Currency	1.6	0.2	2.4	−0.1	−15.4	4.9	10.0	−1.1	4.2
12. Commercial bank deposits	14.1	15.7	15.9	8.2	103.1	44.9	23.7	5.7	14.7
13. Savings bank deposits	5.3	4.6	3.1	4.3	−25.6	7.3	3.8	3.7	4.5
14. Savings and loan associations	0.4	2.0	1.7	5.3	10.0	−4.5	1.9	4.3	2.6
15. Other deposits	0.3	0.3	0.3	0.3	0.1	1.7	0.5	0.9	0.5
16. Life insurance reserves (net)	6.1	6.1	4.4	9.4	−31.7	42.0	8.9	11.1	10.4
17. Private pension reserves	−	−	0	0.5	−2.5	1.7	1.0	3.1	1.3
18. Government insurance reserves	0	0	0.2	1.5	−0.2	19.6	10.5	10.5	7.3
19. U.S. Government securities	−0.1	0	20.6	−10.6	−28.2	4.9	29.5	1.0	12.5
20. State and local govt. securities	2.2	2.9	3.9	3.8	−19.5	−6.5	−0.6	1.8	1.6
21. Other bonds	13.0	10.4	11.7	14.4	−8.9	−16.2	−2.7	−1.0	3.2
22. Preferred stock	3.5	2.7	2.9	5.5	−3.5	−1.6	−0.2	0.5	1.6
23. Common stock	16.1	14.5	10.2	15.2	−27.7	10.5	2.3	4.9	7.9
24. Mortgage holdings	2.5	8.7	9.1	6.4	6.6	−2.3	−0.2	3.9	3.3
25. Other claims	0.1	0.1	0.1	0.3	−1.5	0.8	0.1	0.2	0.2
26. Intangible assets	65.2	68.2	86.7	64.5	−45.1	107.1	88.6	49.4	75.7
27. Residential mortgage debt	4.0	7.6	5.7	18.6	29.6	−0.6	0.9	13.9	7.4
28. Nonresidential mortgage debt	2.0	2.7	1.8	4.9	−0.7	−1.6	−0.3	1.6	1.4
29. Farm mortgage debt	3.8	8.8	8.5	−1.2	22.3	−3.4	−1.0	0.6	0.7
30. Consumer debt	1.9	2.8	1.6	4.3	39.4	15.7	−0.3	8.4	2.9
31. Borrowing on securities	3.0	1.7	1.8	5.2	63.2	−5.8	1.5	−2.4	0.1
32. Other short-term liabilities	8.7	5.9	7.3	0.1	−19.2	−2.5	0.8	3.4	2.9
33. Tax accruals	0.7	1.9	2.8	1.4	−1.3	2.5	1.4	0.6	1.5
34. Liabilities	24.1	31.3	29.5	33.5	133.2	4.3	3.0	26.0	17.0
35. Total net saving	100.0	100.0	100.0	100.0	100.0	100.0	100.0	100.0	100.0

Sources: Same as for Tables S-34 and S-36.

311

SHARE OF MAJOR COMPONENTS IN PERSONAL SAVING
BUSINESS ACCOUNTING CONCEPT; CURRENT VALUES

Quadrennial Periods: 1898 to 1949

Percent

	1898 to 1901	1902 to 1905	1906 to 1909	1910 to 1913	1914 to 1917	1918 to 1921	1922 to 1925
1. Residential real estate	3.8	16.3	20.4	20.6	8.2	12.1	34.1
2. Other nonfarm real estate	8.1	6.1	5.6	4.5	1.9	3.6	6.2
3. Farm real estate	4.9	4.9	4.6	5.5	4.0	6.1	2.0
4. Real estate	16.8	27.3	30.6	30.6	14.1	21.8	42.3
5. Producer durables	2.1	4.7	4.6	4.3	2.5	5.4	1.7
6. Consumer durables	9.4	16.1	15.0	17.1	11.5	24.8	23.7
7. Inventories	11.2	4.3	7.8	2.3	17.0	−7.0	3.9
8. Livestock	10.9	5.1	8.5	8.3	7.4	−9.4	0.7
9. Tangible assets other than real estate	33.6	30.2	35.8	32.0	38.4	13.7	29.9
10. Total tangible assets	50.4	57.4	66.4	62.6	52.6	35.5	72.2
11. Currency	3.3	2.5	−0.3	0.7	3.4	1.1	0.2
12. Commercial bank deposits	23.3	18.4	5.6	16.9	23.7	8.5	16.6
13. Savings bank deposits	7.1	5.5	3.4	4.7	2.5	3.8	4.1
14. Savings and loan associations	−0.4	0.5	1.2	2.1	1.2	2.3	4.5
15. Other deposits	0.3	0.2	0.2	0.3	0.3	0.3	0.3
16. Life insurance reserves (net)	5.8	6.3	5.6	6.2	3.7	5.3	7.4
17. Private pension reserves	0	0	0	0	0	0	0.2
18. Government insurance reserves	0.1	0	0	0	0.1	0.4	1.1
19. U.S. Government securities	1.8	−0.7	−0.7	0.2	10.0	28.6	−10.7
20. State and local government securities	1.7	0.8	3.0	2.7	2.9	5.2	4.0
21. Other bonds	13.2	14.4	11.9	8.4	11.4	12.5	13.9
22. Preferred stock	7.4	1.8	2.0	2.6	2.6	3.4	4.2
23. Common stock	11.3	16.3	19.1	14.3	8.1	12.1	9.1
24. Mortgage holdings	2.8	2.5	1.8	9.1	7.4	11.3	−0.1
25. Other claims	0.1	0.1	0.1	0.1	0.1	0.1	0.2
26. Intangible assets	77.8	68.6	52.9	68.3	77.4	94.9	55.0
27. Residential mortgage debt	2.2	4.8	5.0	7.2	4.8	7.1	14.8
28. Nonresidential mortgage debt	1.8	2.2	2.0	2.6	1.6	2.2	4.9
29. Farm mortgage debt	4.1	3.6	3.2	10.1	5.6	11.3	−2.1
30. Consumer debt	2.0	2.0	2.0	2.6	1.5	1.8	3.2
31. Borrowing on securities	5.6	3.0	1.0	1.0	2.8	1.1	6.4
32. Other short-term liabilities	11.5	9.8	5.7	6.0	8.3	5.9	−0.9
33. Tax accruals	1.0	0.6	0.5	1.4	5.2	0.9	0.7
34. Liabilities	28.2	26.0	19.4	30.9	29.8	30.3	27.0
35. Total net saving	100.0	100.0	100.0	100.0	100.0	100.0	100.0

Sources: Same as for Tables S-34 and S-36.

Quadrennial Periods: 1898 to 1949

Percent

	1926 to 1929	1930 to 1933	1934 to 1937	1938 to 1941	1942 to 1945	1946 to 1949	1898 to 1949
1. Residential real estate	31.8	31.0	−12.1	16.8	0	18.3	12.8
2. Other nonfarm real estate	8.6	−0.5	−6.5	−0.3	−0.4	2.6	2.3
3. Farm real estate	2.1	8.2	−2.0	0.7	0.3	4.7	2.5
4. Real estate	42.5	38.7	−20.6	17.2	−0.1	25.6	17.7
5. Producer durables	3.1	26.6	2.2	4.6	1.0	9.1	3.7
6. Consumer durables	20.0	116.0	−5.5	14.8	0.5	36.0	15.1
7. Inventories	−2.7	55.8	10.7	6.3	2.8	3.4	2.7
8. Livestock	2.7	41.2	12.6	5.3	1.6	2.7	2.0
9. Tangible assets other than real estate	23.1	239.5	20.0	31.0	6.0	51.1	23.6
10. Total tangible assets	65.6	278.3	−0.6	48.3	6.0	76.7	41.3
11. Currency	−0.3	−15.4	6.1	9.1	10.0	−1.1	4.2
12. Commercial bank deposits	−0.6	103.1	52.5	19.2	24.5	5.7	14.7
13. Savings bank deposits	4.6	−25.6	7.7	2.2	4.2	3.7	4.4
14. Savings and loan associations	6.2	10.0	−5.5	2.2	1.7	4.3	2.6
15. Other deposits	0.3	0.1	1.6	1.1	0.4	0.9	0.5
16. Life insurance reserves (net)	11.4	−31.7	40.4	19.3	7.3	11.1	10.4
17. Private pension reserves	0.8	−2.5	1.6	0.6	1.1	3.1	1.3
18. Government insurance reserves	2.0	−0.2	16.3	14.7	10.0	10.5	7.3
19. U.S. Government securities	−10.4	−28.2	5.9	9.5	33.6	1.0	12.5
20. State and local government securities	3.5	−19.5	−7.7	−1.2	−0.4	1.8	1.6
21. Other bonds	14.8	−8.9	−19.5	−5.4	−2.0	−1.0	3.2
22. Preferred stock	7.0	−3.5	−1.5	−0.3	−0.2	0.5	1.6
23. Common stock	21.8	−27.7	10.8	5.3	1.7	4.9	7.9
24. Mortgage holdings	13.2	6.6	−1.4	−1.8	0.1	3.9	3.3
25. Other claims	0.4	−1.5	0.8	0.4	0.1	0.2	0.2
26. Intangible assets	74.7	−45.1	108.1	74.9	92.1	49.4	75.7
27. Residential mortgage debt	22.6	29.6	−2.1	6.5	−0.3	13.9	7.4
28. Nonresidential mortgage debt	4.8	−0.7	−1.5	−0.8	−0.2	1.6	1.4
29. Farm mortgage debt	−0.1	22.3	−3.1	−1.4	−1.0	0.6	0.7
30. Consumer debt	5.5	39.4	21.4	5.8	−1.9	8.4	2.9
31. Borrowing on securities	3.9	63.2	−6.4	−1.6	2.2	−2.4	0.1
32. Other short-term liabilities	1.3	−19.2	−7.4	8.1	−0.6	3.4	2.9
33. Tax accruals	2.2	−1.3	6.6	6.5	−0.1	0.6	1.5
34. Liabilities	40.2	133.2	7.5	23.1	−1.9	26.0	17.0
35. Total net saving	100.0	100.0	100.0	100.0	100.0	100.0	100.0

Sources: Same as for Tables S-34 and S-36.

SHARE OF MAJOR COMPONENTS IN PERSONAL SAVING
CASH FLOW CONCEPT; CURRENT VALUES
Economic Periods: 1897 to 1949

Percent

	1897 to 1908	1909 to 1914	1915 to 1921	1922 to 1929	1930 to 1933	1934 to 1938	1939 to 1945	1946 to 1949	1897 to 1949
1. Residential real estate	17.7	20.3	11.5	25.3	11.4	11.2	7.3	19.9	15.1
2. Other nonfarm real estate	6.7	4.8	3.1	5.8	6.4	1.4	0.8	2.9	3.1
3. Farm real estate	5.6	5.6	4.9	2.8	2.2	2.2	1.3	4.8	3.2
4. Real estate	30.1	30.7	19.4	33.8	20.0	14.8	9.4	27.6	21.5
5. Producer durables	10.5	10.1	8.2	7.4	10.1	10.1	4.7	11.7	8.1
6. Consumer durables	31.6	36.4	34.8	46.0	70.4	54.4	22.7	54.7	39.6
7. Inventories	3.9	2.0	3.0	0.4	−15.3	1.6	3.1	2.7	1.8
8. Livestock	4.7	5.2	−1.2	1.0	−11.3	3.4	1.9	2.1	1.3
9. Tangible assets other than real estate	50.6	53.7	44.8	54.7	53.9	69.5	32.4	71.2	50.8
10. Total tangible assets	80.7	84.4	64.2	88.6	73.9	84.2	41.8	98.8	72.3
11. Currency	0.9	0.1	1.6	0	4.2	1.5	8.0	−0.9	2.7
12. Commercial bank deposits	6.1	6.0	8.1	1.5	−34.6	12.2	18.6	3.9	7.8
13. Savings bank deposits	0.6	0.1	0.5	0.5	−2.8	−0.7	1.5	1.7	0.8
14. Savings and loan associations	−0.3	0.4	0.6	1.6	−7.7	−3.3	0.9	2.5	0.6
15. Other deposits	0.1	0.3	0.3	0.2	3.5	0.6	1.0	0.8	0.7
16. Life insurance reserves (net)	3.8	3.1	3.1	5.7	6.4	11.2	5.9	7.2	5.9
17. Private pension reserves	–	–	–	0	0	0	0.1	0.3	0.1
18. Government insurance reserves	–	–	0	−0.1	−5.4	−0.9	0.9	−2.1	−0.4
19. U.S. Government securities	0	0	14.0	−6.1	7.7	−1.7	23.3	−0.5	7.5
20. State and local govt. securities	1.3	1.7	2.7	2.2	5.4	−2.1	−0.5	1.4	1.1
21. Other bonds	7.4	5.9	7.9	8.4	2.4	−5.1	−2.2	−0.8	2.1
22. Preferred stock	2.0	1.5	2.0	3.2	1.0	−0.5	−0.2	0.4	1.0
23. Common stock	9.2	8.2	6.9	8.9	7.6	3.3	1.8	3.9	5.1
24. Mortgage holdings	1.5	4.9	6.1	3.5	−4.8	−2.4	−0.2	3.1	1.9
25. Intangible assets	32.6	32.2	53.7	29.3	−17.0	12.1	59.0	21.0	36.9
26. Residential mortgage debt	2.3	4.3	3.8	10.8	−9.1	−0.8	0.7	11.1	4.7
27. Nonresidential mortgage debt	1.2	1.5	1.2	2.8	0.7	−0.8	−0.3	1.2	0.9
28. Farm mortgage debt	2.2	5.0	5.8	−0.7	−6.6	−1.6	−0.9	0.5	0.4
29. Consumer debt	1.1	1.6	1.1	2.5	−10.5	4.9	−0.2	6.5	1.9
30. Borrowing on securities	1.7	0.9	1.2	3.0	−17.4	−1.8	1.2	−1.9	0.1
31. Other short-term liabilities	4.9	3.2	4.7	−0.6	−0.3	−3.5	0.1	2.4	1.2
32. Liabilities	13.3	16.6	17.9	17.8	−43.1	−3.7	0.8	19.8	9.2
33. Total net saving	100.0	100.0	100.0	100.0	100.0	100.0	100.0	100.0	100.0

Source: Same as for Table S-38.

SHARE OF MAJOR COMPONENTS IN PERSONAL SAVING
CASH FLOW CONCEPT; CURRENT VALUES
Quadrennial Periods: 1898 to 1949

Percent

	1898 to 1901	1902 to 1905	1906 to 1909	1910 to 1913	1914 to 1917	1918 to 1921	1922 to 1925
1. Residential real estate	12.1	18.7	21.1	20.3	10.8	13.0	26.9
2. Other nonfarm real estate	7.2	6.2	5.9	4.9	2.6	3.6	5.2
3. Farm real estate	5.7	5.6	5.3	5.6	4.2	5.6	2.8
4. Real estate	25.1	30.6	32.2	30.8	17.7	22.2	34.9
5. Producer durables	10.1	10.6	10.1	10.3	6.8	9.6	6.9
6. Consumer durables	28.7	31.6	32.4	36.8	27.7	41.7	43.8
7. Inventories	6.2	2.6	4.8	1.3	11.6	-4.6	2.4
8. Livestock	6.0	3.0	5.2	4.8	5.0	-6.1	0.4
9. Tangible assets other than real estate	51.0	47.8	52.4	53.2	51.1	40.6	53.5
10. Total tangible assets	76.1	78.4	84.7	83.9	68.8	62.8	88.4
11. Currency	1.8	1.5	-0.2	0.4	2.3	0.7	0.1
12. Commercial bank deposits	11.4	9.0	1.1	6.9	14.0	2.4	7.3
13. Savings bank deposits	1.5	0.9	-0.1	0.2	-0.1	0.8	0.8
14. Savings and loan associations	-0.8	-0.2	0.2	0.5	0.3	0.8	1.7
15. Other deposits	0.2	0.1	0.1	0.3	0.4	0.2	0.2
16. Life insurance reserves (net)	3.6	4.5	3.1	3.1	2.3	3.7	5.0
17. Private pension reserves	–	–	–	–	–	0	0
18. Government insurance reserves	–	–	–	–	-0.1	0	0
19. U.S. Government securities	1.0	-0.4	-0.4	0.1	6.8	18.5	-6.7
20. State and local government securities	0.9	0.5	1.8	1.5	2.0	3.3	2.5
21. Other bonds	7.3	8.6	7.3	4.8	7.8	8.1	8.7
22. Preferred stock	4.1	1.0	1.2	1.5	1.8	2.2	2.6
23. Common stock	6.2	9.7	11.7	8.2	5.5	7.9	5.7
24. Mortgage holdings	1.5	1.5	1.1	5.2	5.0	7.3	-0.2
25. Intangible assets	38.7	36.6	26.8	32.9	48.0	55.9	27.8
26. Residential mortgage debt	1.2	2.9	3.0	4.1	3.2	4.6	9.3
27. Nonresidential mortgage debt	1.0	1.3	1.2	1.5	1.1	1.4	3.1
28. Farm mortgage debt	2.3	2.1	1.9	5.8	3.8	7.3	-1.4
29. Consumer debt	1.1	1.2	1.3	1.5	1.1	1.1	2.0
30. Borrowing on securities	3.1	1.8	0.6	0.6	1.9	0.7	4.0
31. Other short-term liabilities	6.2	5.7	3.4	3.4	5.6	3.6	-0.9
32. Liabilities	14.9	15.0	11.5	16.9	16.7	18.7	16.2
33. Total net saving	100.0	100.0	100.0	100.0	100.0	100.0	100.0

Source: Same as for Table S-38.

SHARE OF MAJOR COMPONENTS IN PERSONAL SAVING
CASH FLOW CONCEPT; CURRENT VALUES
Quadrennial Periods: 1898 to 1949

Percent

	1926 to 1929	1930 to 1933	1934 to 1937	1938 to 1941	1942 to 1945	1946 to 1949	1898 to 1949
1. Residential real estate	23.8	11.4	9.0	18.4	3.9	19.9	15.1
2. Other nonfarm real estate	6.3	6.4	1.1	1.9	0.4	2.9	3.1
3. Farm real estate	2.7	2.2	2.0	2.2	1.0	4.8	3.2
4. Real estate	32.8	20.0	12.1	22.6	5.4	27.6	21.4
5. Producer durables	7.9	10.1	9.7	8.8	3.6	11.7	8.1
6. Consumer durables	48.0	70.4	53.2	46.1	15.8	54.7	39.6
7. Inventories	−1.5	−15.3	3.3	3.4	2.5	2.7	1.8
8. Livestock	1.5	−11.3	4.0	2.9	1.4	2.1	1.3
9. Tangible assets other than real estate	55.8	53.9	70.1	61.2	23.3	71.2	50.8
10. Total tangible assets	88.7	73.9	82.3	83.8	28.7	98.8	72.2
11. Currency	−0.2	4.2	1.9	4.9	8.8	−0.9	2.7
12. Commercial bank deposits	−3.8	−34.6	14.5	9.3	21.1	3.9	7.8
13. Savings bank deposits	0.3	−2.8	−0.6	−0.7	2.2	1.7	0.8
14. Savings and loan associations	1.5	−7.7	−3.6	0	1.0	2.5	0.6
15. Other deposits	0.2	3.5	0.6	0.6	1.1	0.8	0.7
16. Life insurance reserves (net)	6.3	6.4	10.9	8.5	5.3	7.2	5.9
17. Private pension reserves	0	0	0	−0.1	0.1	0.3	0.1
18. Government insurance reserves	−0.3	−5.4	−0.5	−1.7	1.7	−2.1	−0.4
19. U.S. Government securities	−5.6	7.7	−2.0	4.9	29.0	−0.5	7.6
20. State and local government securities	1.9	5.4	−2.4	−0.6	−0.4	1.4	1.1
21. Other bonds	8.0	2.4	−6.1	−2.9	−1.8	−0.8	2.1
22. Preferred stock	3.8	1.0	−0.5	0.2	−0.2	0.4	1.0
23. Common stock	11.7	7.6	3.4	2.9	1.5	3.9	5.1
24. Mortgage holdings	6.8	−4.8	−2.2	−1.4	0.1	3.1	1.9
25. Intangible assets	30.6	−17.0	13.3	23.7	69.5	21.0	36.9
26. Residential mortgage debt	12.2	−9.1	−1.3	3.4	−0.3	11.1	4.7
27. Nonresidential mortgage debt	2.6	0.7	−0.8	−0.4	−0.2	1.2	0.9
28. Farm mortgage debt	−0.1	−6.6	−1.6	−0.8	−0.9	0.5	0.4
29. Consumer debt	2.9	−10.5	6.5	3.1	−1.6	6.5	1.9
30. Borrowing on securities	2.1	−17.4	−2.0	−0.9	1.9	−1.9	0.1
31. Other short-term liabilities	−0.4	−0.3	−5.3	3.1	−0.8	2.4	1.1
32. Liabilities	19.3	−43.1	−4.4	7.5	−1.8	19.8	9.2
33. Total net saving	100.0	100.0	100.0	100.0	100.0	100.0	100.0

Source: Same as for Table S-38.

DISTRIBUTION OF PERSONAL SAVING BY MAJOR FORMS, GROSS OF LIABILITIES; SOCIAL ACCOUNTING CONCEPT; CURRENT VALUES

Economic Periods: 1897 to 1949

Percent

Forms of saving	1897 to 1908	1909 to 1914	1915 to 1921	1922 to 1929	1930 to 1933	1934 to 1939	1940 to 1945	1946 to 1949	1897 to 1949
I. By liquidity									
1. Class A	20.3	19.9	41.7	6.3	42.2	58.5	76.8	14.9	38.7
2. Class B	39.5	33.2	31.9	41.6	−104.1	26.0	7.8	18.0	25.0
3. Class C	25.2	31.7	18.6	34.5	60.5	−28.0	−1.4	19.9	14.1
4. Class D	15.0	15.3	7.8	17.6	101.4	43.5	16.8	47.2	22.2
II. By use									
5. For self-use	37.8	39.2	17.5	44.9	159.6	−4.1	2.7	49.0	24.3
6. For use by borrowers themselves	35.0	34.1	55.4	29.2	−79.6	−10.3	31.3	11.6	30.2
7. For use by intermediaries	27.2	26.6	27.1	25.9	20.0	114.5	65.9	39.4	45.5
III. Claims and equities									
8. Short-term claims	20.3	19.9	22.2	15.1	69.3	53.7	44.1	13.9	26.3
9. Long-term claims	23.5	25.8	47.9	22.4	−97.4	40.8	50.7	31.4	39.8
10. Equities	56.2	54.3	29.9	62.4	128.1	5.5	5.2	54.7	33.9
IV. By contract status									
11. Contractual	6.9	6.7	4.9	10.8	−49.3	60.7	21.8	25.5	19.2
12. Noncontractual	93.1	93.3	95.1	89.2	149.3	39.3	78.2	74.5	80.8

All figures taken from same sources as Table S-34.

Line 1 – Sum of currency, deposits, and U.S. Government securities.

Line 2 – Sum of other securities and life insurance.

Line 3 – Sum of real estate, mortgages, and other claims.

Line 4 – Sum of producer durables, consumer durables, pension and retirement funds, inventories, and livestock.

Line 5 – Tangible assets.

Line 6 – Sum of securities and mortgages and other claims.

Line 7 – Sum of currency, deposits, life insurance reserves, and pension reserves.

Line 8 – Currency and deposits.

Line 9 – Sum of insurance and pension reserves, mortgages, and bonds.

Line 10 – Sum of real estate, producer durables, consumer durables, inventories, livestock, stocks, and other claims.

Line 11 – Sum of insurance and pension reserves.

Line 12 – Sum of real estate, other tangible assets, currency, deposits, securities, mortgages, and other claims.

317

DISTRIBUTION OF NET PERSONAL SAVING BY MAJOR FORMS
SOCIAL ACCOUNTING CONCEPT; CURRENT VALUES
Economic Periods: 1897 to 1949

Percent

Forms of saving	1897 to 1908	1909 to 1914	1915 to 1921	1922 to 1929	1930 to 1933	1934 to 1938	1939 to 1945	1946 to 1949	1897 to 1949
I. By use									
1. For self-use	24.4	21.2	−8.5	31.7	−763.8	−12.0	2.7	28.1	10.9
2. For use by borrowers themselves	41.4	43.4	71.3	33.5	1168.0	−7.2	28.8	18.2	34.5
3. For use by intermediaries	34.2	35.3	37.2	34.8	−304.2	119.2	68.5	53.7	54.5
II. Claims and equities									
4. Short-term claims	25.8	25.5	27.3	19.7	−592.3	52.6	43.7	18.1	30.0
5. Long-term claims	29.3	34.2	66.2	29.9	681.5	43.7	51.7	44.3	47.5
6. Equities	44.9	40.2	6.5	50.4	10.8	3.7	4.6	37.6	22.5
III. By contract status									
7. Contractual	7.6	7.5	6.2	13.4	277.6	64.1	23.2	34.7	22.8
8. Noncontractual	92.4	92.5	93.8	86.6	−177.6	35.9	76.8	65.3	77.2

All figures taken from same sources as Table S-34.

Gross saving (Table S-46) less:

Line 1 – Mortgage debt, consumer debt, and other short-term liabilities.

Line 2 – Borrowing on securities and tax accruals.

Line 3 – Policy loans.

Line 4 – Tax accruals.

Line 5 – Borrowing on bonds and policy loans.

Line 6 – Mortgage debt, consumer debt, other short-term liabilities, and borrowing on stocks.

Line 7 – Policy loans.

Line 8 – All other liabilities.

DISTRIBUTION OF NONAGRICULTURAL INDIVIDUALS' SAVING
BY MAJOR FORMS, GROSS OF LIABILITIES
SOCIAL ACCOUNTING CONCEPT; CURRENT VALUES

Economic Periods: 1897 to 1949

Percent

Forms of saving	1897 to 1908	1909 to 1914	1915 to 1921	1922 to 1929	1930 to 1933	1934 to 1938	1939 to 1945	1946 to 1949	1897 to 1949
I. By liquidity									
1. Class A	17.8	18.5	41.5	6.0	−169.2	50.2	75.2	17.1	36.4
2. Class B	47.1	38.6	38.2	42.9	2 273.2	26.9	9.2	20.2	28.2
3. Class C	24.1	33.5	16.6	33.7	−1 022.5	−21.6	−1.2	19.3	14.5
4. Class D	11.1	9.4	3.7	17.3	−981.5	44.5	16.7	43.4	20.9
II. By use									
5. For self-use	32.3	34.2	10.7	42.8	−1 989.0	0	−0.3	41.9	21.6
6. For use by borrowers themselves	42.3	40.2	62.9	32.2	1 878.0	−13.1	32.5	14.2	32.8
7. For use by intermediaries	25.4	25.6	26.3	25.0	211.0	113.1	67.8	43.9	45.6
III. Claims and equities									
8. Short-term claims	17.9	18.5	20.9	14.5	−836.7	46.3	41.0	15.2	24.2
9. Long-term claims	27.5	29.4	53.1	24.2	2 212.3	42.5	56.1	36.2	43.0
10. Equities	54.7	52.1	25.9	61.3	−1 275.6	11.2	2.8	48.6	32.8
IV. By contract status									
11. Contractual	7.5	7.1	5.4	10.4	1 047.7	66.8	26.7	28.7	21.3
12. Noncontractual	92.5	92.9	94.6	89.6	−947.7	33.2	73.3	71.3	78.7

Assets included in each group are similar to those in Table S-46.
Figures taken from same sources as Table S-20.

S-49 DISTRIBUTION OF NET NONAGRICULTURAL INDIVIDUALS' SAVING BY MAJOR FORMS; SOCIAL ACCOUNTING CONCEPT; CURRENT VALUES

Economic Periods: 1897 to 1949

Percent

Forms of saving	1897 to 1908	1909 to 1914	1915 to 1921	1922 to 1929	1930 to 1933	1934 to 1938	1939 to 1945	1946 to 1949	1897 to 1949
I. By use									
1. For self-use	27.7	26.7	2.0	30.1	−16.7	−20.4	−1.1	19.2	10.7
2. For use by borrowers themselves	44.3	44.2	67.8	36.8	121.5	−11.1	29.5	22.1	36.4
3. For use by intermediaries	28.0	29.0	30.1	33.0	−4.8	131.5	71.6	58.7	52.9
II. Claims and equities									
4. Short-term claims	19.9	20.3	21.3	18.7	−32.7	49.2	40.6	19.7	26.5
5. Long-term claims	30.4	33.6	61.4	31.9	70.7	50.8	58.1	50.2	49.7
6. Equities	49.7	46.1	17.3	49.4	62.0	0	1.3	30.1	23.7
III. By contract status									
7. Contractual	7.3	6.8	5.7	12.8	26.8	78.5	28.8	38.3	24.5
8. Noncontractual	92.7	93.2	94.3	87.2	73.2	21.5	71.2	61.7	75.5

Assets and liabilities included in each group are similar to those in Table S-47.
Figures taken from same sources as Table S-20.

320

MAJOR COMPONENTS OF PERSONAL SAVING AS PERCENT OF TOTAL PERSONAL DISPOSABLE INCOME; SOCIAL ACCOUNTING CONCEPT; CURRENT VALUES

Economic Period Averages: 1897 to 1949

	1897 to 1908	1909 to 1914	1915 to 1921	1922 to 1929	1930 to 1933	1934 to 1938	1939 to 1945	1946 to 1949	1897 to 1949 Weighted averages	1897 to 1949 Unweighted averages
	1	2	3	4	5	6	7	8	9	10
1. Residential real estate	1.75	2.43	1.00	4.23	−1.59	−0.88	−0.03	2.08	1.31	1.37
2. Other nonfarm real estate	0.91	0.48	0.24	0.89	−0.07	−0.48	−0.27	0.19	0.19	0.35
3. Farm real estate	0.60	0.59	0.60	0.11	−0.40	−0.20	−0.04	0.60	0.23	0.29
4. Producer durables	0.40	0.38	0.23	0.25	−0.75	0.20	0.34	1.42	0.45	0.29
5. Consumer durables	1.46	1.39	0.55	2.71	−2.08	1.21	0.19	4.77	1.69	1.34
6. Inventories	0.29	0.45	0.61	−0.08	−1.02	−0.10	0.44	−0.09	0.10	0.14
7. Currency	0.21	0.02	0.43	−0.01	0.55	0.29	2.55	−0.20	0.68	0.48
8. Commercial bank deposits	1.89	1.99	2.79	1.24	−3.66	2.60	6.07	1.07	2.38	2.13
9. Savings bank deposits	0.71	0.59	0.55	0.66	0.91	0.42	0.97	0.70	0.72	0.68
10. Savings and loan associations	0.06	0.26	0.31	0.80	−0.35	−0.26	0.48	0.80	0.42	0.26
11. Other deposits	0.03	0.04	0.05	0.04	0	0.10	0.12	0.17	0.09	0.06
12. Life insurance reserves (net)	0.82	0.78	0.78	1.41	1.13	2.44	2.28	2.09	1.68	1.35
13. Private pension reserves	−	−	0	0.08	0.09	0.10	0.25	0.57	0.20	0.10
14. Government insurance reserves	0.01	0	0.04	0.23	0.01	1.13	2.69	1.97	1.18	0.61
15. U.S. Government securities	−0.01	0	3.62	−1.59	1.00	0.28	7.54	0.18	2.02	1.15
16. State and local government securities	0.30	0.37	0.69	0.57	0.69	−0.38	−0.14	0.33	0.26	0.29
17. Other bonds	1.74	1.31	2.06	2.17	0.32	−0.94	−0.69	−0.18	0.52	0.99
18. Stock	2.62	2.17	2.29	3.13	1.12	0.52	0.53	1.01	1.54	1.87
19. Mortgage holdings	0.34	1.10	1.60	0.96	−0.23	−0.13	−0.04	0.74	0.54	0.53
20. Other claims	0.01	0.01	0.02	0.04	0.05	0.05	0.04	0.03	0.03	0.03
21. Residential mortgage debt	0.53	0.96	1.00	2.80	−1.05	−0.04	0.23	2.62	1.20	0.91
22. Nonresidential mortgage debt	0.29	0.34	0.31	0.74	0.03	−0.09	−0.08	0.29	0.23	0.25
23. Farm mortgage debt	0.51	1.11	1.50	−0.17	−0.79	−0.20	−0.27	0.11	0.12	0.29
24. Consumer debt	0.26	0.35	0.28	0.66	−1.40	0.91	−0.07	1.57	0.47	0.35
25. Borrowing on securities	0.40	0.21	0.32	0.79	−2.25	−0.34	0.39	−0.44	0.02	0.12
26. Other short-term liabilities	1.17	0.74	1.28	0.02	0.68	−0.14	0.19	0.63	0.47	0.64
27. Tax accruals	0.10	0.23	0.49	0.22	0.05	0.14	0.36	0.12	0.24	0.26
28. Total net saving	10.91	10.39	13.29	12.77	0.44	5.71	22.50	13.36	13.47	11.50

Columns 1 to 9 – Period total figures of Table S-34 divided by period total figures for personal disposable income as given in Volume III, Table N-1, col. 9.

Column 10 – Annual saving figures of Table T-6 divided by personal disposable income as given in Volume III, Table N-1, col. 9.

SOURCES OF CHARTS

Chart I
    Personal saving: Table T-6, col. 1.
    Personal disposable income: Table N-1, col. 9.
    Regression lines: Constants from Appendix Table Z-2.

Chart II
    Table II, col. 1.

Chart III
    National saving, three concepts: Table II, col. 1.
    Inventory valuation adjustment: Table P-19, col. 7.
    Depreciation: See notes to Tables T-7, C-41, F-11, F-22, G-6, and G-15.

Chart IV
    Table II, col. 1.

Chart V
    Derived from figures in Table T-1, col. 1.

Chart VI
    Derived from figures in Table T-1, col. 2.

Chart VII
    Current aggregate: Table S-1, col. 1.
    Deflated aggregate: Table S-3, col. 1.
    Deflated per head: Table S-3, col. 4.

Chart VIII
    Current aggregate: Table S-2, col. 1.
    Deflated aggregate: Table S-4, col. 1.
    Deflated per head: Table S-4, col. 4.

Chart IX
    Derived from figures given in following sources:
    National saving, broad: Table T-4, col. 1.
    National saving, excluding consumer durables: Table T-1, col. 1 minus Table T-6, col. 5.
    National saving, standard: Table T-1, col. 1.
    Personal saving, broad: Table T-4, col. 4.
    Personal saving, excluding consumer durables: Table T-6, col. 1 minus col. 5.
    Personal saving, standard: Table T-6, col. 1.

Chart X
    Derived from figures given in following sources:
    National saving, cash flow: Table T-3, col. 1.
    National saving, business accounting: Table T-2, col. 1.
    National saving, social accounting: Table T-1, col. 1.
    Personal saving, cash flow: Table T-3, col. 2.
    Personal saving, business accounting: Table T-2, col. 2.
    Personal saving, social accounting: Table T-1, col. 2.

Chart XI
    Derived from figures given in following sources:
    National saving, deflated per head: Table T-12, col. 1 divided by total population (1900-1945,
        Historical Statistics, p. 26; 1946-1949, *Statistical Abstract*, various issues).
    National saving, deflated aggregate: Table T-12, col. 1.
    National saving, current aggregate: Table T-1, col. 1.
    Personal saving, deflated per head: Table T-12, col. 2 divided by total population.
    Personal saving, deflated aggregate: Table T-12, col. 2.
    Personal saving, current aggregate: Table T-1, col. 2.

Chart XII

Deflated per head: Table T-12, col. 1 divided by total population.

Deflated aggregate: Table T-12, col. 1.

Current aggregate: Table T-1, col. 1.

Straight line and parabolic trend lines: Constants given in Appendix Table Z-1.

Chart XIII

Deflated per head: Table T-12, col. 2 divided by total population.

Deflated aggregate: Table T-12, col. 2.

Current aggregate: Table T-1, col. 2.

Straight line and parabolic trend lines: Constants given in Appendix Table Z-2.

Chart XIV

Derived from the same sources as were the averages shown in Table VI.

Chart XV

Population: 1805-1945 from *Historical Statistics*, p. 26; 1946-1951 from *Statistical Abstract*, various issues.

Net national product: 1869-1896, Kuznets' preliminary unpublished estimates; 1897-1949, Table N-2, col. 2; 1950-1951 based on Department of Commerce figures for gross national product as given in *Survey of Current Business*, July 1952, p. 28.

Industrial production: 1869-1898, Frickey's index of production for manufacture (*Production in the United States 1860-1914*, p. 54) linked to 1899 value; 1899-1918, index of manufacturing production of the National Bureau of Economic Research (*Historical Statistics*, p. 179) linked to 1919 value; 1919-1951, Federal Reserve Board's index before 1953 revision (*Federal Reserve Bulletin*, e.g. 1951, p. 1,563).

Agricultural production: 1869-1909, Strauss and Bean, *Gross Farm Income and Indices of Farm Production and Prices in the United States 1869-1937*, Table 61, p. 126 (the ideal index); 1910-1951, Cooper, Barton, and Brodell, *Progress of Farm Mechanization*, Department of Agriculture Misc. Publication 630, p. 81 as revised and brought up to date by the Bureau of Agricultural Economics.

Reproducible tangible wealth: 1805-1895, Goldsmith, "The Growth of Reproducible Wealth of the United States of America from 1805 to 1950," *Income and Wealth*, Series II, pp. 307, 315-323; 1896-1949, Volume III, Table W-3, col. 3; 1950, 1951, rough preliminary estimates.

National saving: 1805-1896, figures given on page 83; 1897-1949, Table T-12, col. 1; 1950-1951 extrapolated from 1949 figure on basis of Department of Commerce figures (see *Survey of Current Business*, July 1952).

Chart XVI

Table S-5.

Chart XVII

Appendix Table Z-7.

Chart XVIII

Saving-income ratio: Appendix Table Z-7, col. 2.

Deflated per head: Table T-12, col. 3 divided by nonfarm population (see sources of data shown for Charts XI and XIX).

Deflated aggregate: Table S-15, col. 2.

Current aggregate: Table S-5, col. 2.

Chart XIX

Saving-income ratio: Appendix Table Z-7, col. 3.

Deflated per head: Table T-12, col. 4 divided by farm population (1896-1908 figures linearly interpolated between estimates for 1890, 1900, and 1910 from Cooper, Bartin, and Brodell, *Progress of Farm Mechanization*, Department of Agriculture Misc. Publication 630, p. 5; 1909-1915, *Agricultural Statistics*, 1942, p. 663; 1916-1949, Bureau of the Census, Bureau of Agricultural Economics *Release No. 16-A*, July 18, 1951).

324

Deflated aggregate: Table S-15, col. 3.

Current aggregate: Table S-5, col. 3.

Chart XX

Net worth change-income ratio: Table xv, col. 5.

Deflated per head, deflated aggregate, and current aggregate: Table xiv, cols. 1, 2, and 3 respectively.

Chart XXI

Saving-income ratio: Appendix Table Z-7, col. 5.

Deflated per head: Table T-12, col. 6 divided by total population (1900-1945, *Historical Statistics*, p. 26; 1946-1949, *Statistical Abstract*, various issues).

Deflated aggregate: Table S-15, col. 5.

Current aggregate: Table S-5, col. 5.

Chart XXII

Saving-income ratio: Appendix Table Z-7, col. 6.

Deflated per head: Deflated aggregate figures divided by total population (see sources of Chart xxi).

Deflated aggregate: Current aggregate figures divided by gross national product deflator (Table T-16, col. 1).

Current aggregate: Sum of Table G-13, col. 4 minus col. 5 ,converted to calendar-year basis by averaging of adjacent fiscal years, Table G-12, col. 5, and first differences of Table G-20, cols. 2, 3, and 4.

Chart XXIII

Saving-income ratio: Appendix Table Z-7, col. 7.

Deflated per head: Deflated aggregate figures divided by total population (see sources of Chart xxi).

Deflated aggregate: Current aggregate figures divided by gross national product deflator (Table T-16, col. 1).

Current aggregate: Sum of Table G-1, col. 4 minus col. 5, Table G-12, col. 2, and first differences of Table G-20, col. 5.

Chart XXIV

Saving-income ratio: Appendix Table Z-7, col. 8.

Deflated per head: Table T-12, col. 8 divided by total population (see sources of Chart xxi).

Deflated aggregate: Table S-15, col. 7.

Current aggregate: Table S-5, col. 7.

Military assets: Table F-31.

Chart XXV

Table S-8.

Chart XXVI

Nonfederal saving: Table S-8, col. 1.

Federal saving: Table S-8, col. 9.

Chart XXVII

Including consumer durables: Table S-19.

Excluding consumer durables: Derived from Tables S-5 and S-11.

Chart XXVIII

Table xix, col. 4 and Table xx, col. 4.

Charts XXIX and XXX

Table S-40.

Chart XXXI

Table xxii.

Charts XXXII and XXXIII
    Tables S-46 and S-47.

Chart XXXIV
    Table S-46, section III (for gross) and Table S-47, section II (for net).

Charts XXXV to XXXVII
    Saving series: Tables T-1 and T-6.
    Reference cycles: 1896-1949, Moore, *Statistical Indicators of Cyclical Revivals and Recessions*, National Bureau of Economic Research, Occasional Paper 31, p. 6 and chart readings.

Chart XXXVIII
    Table XXXII, cols. 4 and 5.

Chart XXXIX
    Table XXXVI.

Chart XL
    Table XLI.

Chart XLI
    Table XLIV.

Chart XLII
    Total population: From Table XLII, col. 1.
    Estate tax population: *Statistics of Income*, 1948, Part I.
    Population with estates of less than $60,000: Derived from data in Volume III, Table W-65.

Chart XLIII
    Statistics of Income, 1948, Part I.

Chart XLIV
    Statistics of Income, 1922, 1944, 1946, and 1949.

826

PART II
TABLES OF ANNUAL ESTIMATES OF SAVING

TABLES OF ANNUAL ESTIMATES OF SAVING

338

T-1   TABLE T–1

Column 1 – Sum of cols. 2, 6, 7, and 8.

Column 2 – Sum of cols. 3–5.

Column 3 – From Table T-8, col. 1.

Column 4 – From Table A-3, col. 1.

Column 5 – From Table U-3, col. 3.

Column 6 – From Table C-1, col. 12.

Column 7 – Sum of Table G-1, col. 4 minus col. 5; Table G-12, col. 2; Table G-13, col. 4 minus col. 5 converted to calendar year basis by simple arithmetic averaging; Table G-12, col. 5; and first differences of Table G-20, col. 1.

Column 8 – From Table F-1, col. 8.

T-2   TABLE T–2

Column 1 – Sum of cols. 2, 6, 7, and 8.

Column 2 – Sum of cols. 3–5.

Column 3 – From Table T-9, col. 1.

Column 4 – From Table A-1, col. 1.

Column 5 – From Table U-3, col. 1.

Column 6 – Table C-1, col. 8 plus Table C-51.

Column 7 – Table G-12, cols. 2 and 5 plus first differences of Table G-20, col. 1.

Column 8 – From Table F-1, col. 6.

T-3   TABLE T–3

Column 1 – 1897–1949: Sum of cols. 2, 6, 7, and 8.

Column 2 – 1897–1949: Sum of cols. 3–5.

Column 3 – 1897–1949: From Table T-10, col. 1.

Column 4 – 1897–1949: Table A-66, col. 1 plus Table A-32, col. 1 minus Table A-32, col. 7 (i.e. substituting A-32, col. 1 for col. 7 in Table A-66, col. 5 in order to conform the treatment of agricultural to that of corporate inventories).

Column 5 – 1897–1949: Table U-11, col. 1 minus col. 4 plus first differences of Table P-19, col. 3 (same reason as in col. 4).

Column 6 – 1897–1949: Sum of Table C-1, col. 1, Table C-2, cols. 3 and 4, Table C-41, col. 1, and Table C-46, col. 5 minus Table C-2, col. 2.

Column 7 – 1897–1949: Sum of Table G-12, cols. 2 and 5, Table G-6, cols. 7–9, and Table G-15, cols. 5 and 6 converted to calendar-year basis by arithmetic averaging.

Column 8 – 1897–1928: Sum of Table F-2, col. 11 minus col. 12 and Table F-11, col. 9.
1929–1949: Table F-12, col. 12 plus Table F-22, col. 11 minus sum of Table F-17, cols. 1 and 3.

344

NATIONAL SAVING BY MAJOR SAVER GROUPS

Social Accounting Concept; Current Values: 1897 to 1949

$ mill.

Year	National saving	Personal saving				Corporate Saving	Government saving	
		Total	Nonagri-cultural individuals	Agriculture	Unincor-porated business		State and local	Federal
	1	2	3	4	5	6	7	8
1897	934	547	659	42	−154	294	69	24
1898	1 620	1 288	823	233	232	370	68	−106
1899	2 820	2 190	1 724	107	359	546	71	13
1900	2 102	1 274	1 068	−29	235	672	124	32
1901	2 220	1 363	1 778	−350	−65	648	118	91
1902	3 946	2 942	2 214	478	250	724	216	64
1903	2 766	1 501	1 608	−139	32	1 067	143	55
1904	2 043	1 424	1 564	83	−223	396	226	−3
1905	4 313	3 458	2 870	98	490	678	139	38
1906	4 206	3 240	2 897	96	247	730	115	121
1907	3 128	2 098	2 249	−272	121	773	158	99
1908	2 451	1 996	2 303	27	−334	413	81	−39
1909	3 687	3 000	3 078	95	−173	418	224	45
1910	4 597	3 244	2 793	−9	460	1 104	161	88
1911	2 934	2 094	2 782	−653	−35	577	199	64
1912	5 230	4 239	3 878	268	93	565	296	130
1913	4 137	2 667	2 846	−661	482	916	451	103
1914	3 511	2 545	2 070	401	74	741	199	26
1915	6 272	4 684	4 466	207	11	1 246	197	145
1916	9 579	5 563	5 853	−1 102	812	3 192	215	609
1917	9 926	10 072	8 652	1 219	201	2 525	160	−2 831
1918	1 607	12 686	10 916	1 501	269	422	61	−11 562
1919	6 566	9 764	10 331	−1 758	1 191	2 484	132	−5 814
1920	9 969	6 568	6 497	−1 634	1 705	3 437	−187	151
1921	2 261	1 286	3 010	−1 842	118	1 338	88	−451
1922	7 949	6 300	5 956	−198	542	948	500	201
1923	13 607	9 880	9 808	331	−259	2 354	412	961
1924	12 134	8 616	7 738	581	297	1 455	1 267	796
1925	15 453	10 744	10 523	66	155	2 369	1 321	1 019
1926	15 891	10 103	9 295	−42	850	3 394	1 222	1 172
1927	13 692	10 074	10 173	−114	15	1 368	1 108	1 142
1928	10 907	6 014	6 284	109	−379	2 105	1 753	1 035
1929	15 968	11 485	10 979	127	379	2 136	1 248	1 099
1930	5 820	5 617	7 989	−177	−2 195	−514	903	−186
1931	−3 305	2 466	6 005	9	−3 548	−3 360	−478	−1 933
1932	−10 491	−3 273	−719	192	−2 746	−5 032	−953	−1 233
1933	−8 851	−3 805	−3 383	16	−438	−4 687	765	−1 124
1934	−4 417	−954	−1 451	−1 129	1 626	−2 718	1 411	−2 156
1935	237	2 349	623	1 248	478	−1 287	750	−1 575
1936	1 560	5 275	4 261	−22	1 036	−1 405	1 227	−3 537
1937	7 286	7 322	6 319	1 291	−288	−553	1 309	−792
1938	2 002	3 715	3 954	393	−632	−574	1 501	−2 640
1939	4 842	6 852	6 082	827	−57	−89	804	−2 725
1940	10 983	8 543	6 535	947	1 061	1 618	1 845	−1 023
1941	14 309	13 971	10 544	2 737	690	1 697	1 724	−3 083
1942	4 500	33 237	23 801	5 044	4 392	2 863	1 816	−33 416
1943	−3 642	36 167	27 846	4 399	3 922	4 234	2 720	−46 763
1944	−7 280	39 299	30 778	4 216	4 305	4 787	3 166	−54 532
1945	−7 311	36 409	29 314	3 612	3 483	2 507	2 587	−48 814
1946	25 035	22 527	18 520	3 327	680	2 103	2 145	−1 740
1947	32 358	20 186	19 284	1 419	−517	4 254	1 603	6 315
1948	42 165	26 723	22 659	3 969	95	8 974	1 095	5 373
1949	31 164	22 457	19 589	1 799	1 069	9 473	1 271	−2 037

NATIONAL SAVING BY MAJOR SAVER GROUPS
Business Accounting Concept; Current Values: 1897 to 1949
$ mill.

Year	National saving	Personal saving				Corporate saving	Government saving	
		Total	Nonagricultural individuals	Agriculture	Unincorporated business		State and local	Federal
	1	2	3	4	5	6	7	8
1897	1 240	793	521	423	−151	359	65	23
1898	1 683	1 289	741	317	231	433	67	−106
1899	3 960	2 941	1 691	531	719	933	73	13
1900	2 404	1 527	1 113	194	220	715	128	34
1901	3 094	2 092	1 877	204	11	789	121	92
1902	4 522	3 209	2 339	385	485	1 027	222	64
1903	2 782	1 604	1 764	−55	−105	972	150	56
1904	2 554	1 719	1 708	122	−111	604	232	−1
1905	4 928	3 968	3 034	436	498	774	149	37
1906	5 510	4 226	3 099	704	423	1 027	134	123
1907	4 189	2 921	2 518	195	208	982	183	103
1908	3 018	2 385	2 501	234	−350	571	98	−36
1909	5 572	4 255	3 179	933	143	1 029	243	45
1910	4 669	3 351	2 923	114	314	1 042	185	91
1911	3 569	2 560	3 020	−397	−63	717	224	68
1912	6 486	4 983	4 161	493	329	1 049	321	133
1913	5 408	3 962	3 176	294	492	855	484	107
1914	3 383	2 558	2 363	210	−15	572	224	29
1915	7 258	5 202	4 760	182	260	1 681	225	150
1916	14 920	9 227	6 364	846	2 017	4 787	285	621
1917	17 726	15 593	9 724	4 252	1 617	4 645	294	−2 806
1918	7 461	16 769	12 746	2 821	1 202	1 961	261	−11 530
1919	12 482	13 587	12 700	−1 235	2 122	4 295	376	−5 776
1920	8 179	6 354	10 194	−4 807	967	1 437	182	206
1921	−2 419	175	5 287	−3 661	−1 451	−2 512	331	−413
1922	11 845	9 146	7 223	990	933	1 781	688	230
1923	16 190	11 990	11 303	740	−53	2 540	660	1 000
1924	15 090	11 124	8 963	1 758	403	1 636	1 497	833
1925	17 852	12 286	11 465	440	381	2 980	1 521	1 065
1926	15 521	10 513	9 949	14	550	2 400	1 401	1 207
1927	15 184	11 523	10 758	831	−66	1 210	1 276	1 175
1928	12 935	7 491	6 949	835	−293	2 485	1 889	1 070
1929	17 078	12 344	11 789	229	326	2 239	1 367	1 128
1930	−264	2 984	8 272	−2 330	−2 958	−4 061	974	−161
1931	−10 341	−846	5 524	−2 160	−4 210	−7 085	−499	−1 911
1932	−16 428	−6 330	−2 043	−1 114	−3 173	−7 771	−1 107	−1 220
1933	−8 667	−3 934	−4 877	970	−27	−4 330	705	−1 108
1934	−3 202	−116	−2 424	660	1 648	−2 401	1 449	−2 134
1935	399	2 387	−348	2 225	510	−1 204	767	−1 551
1936	2 951	5 954	3 553	1 250	1 151	−761	1 270	−3 512
1937	6 214	6 512	6 142	562	−192	−912	1 369	−755
1938	522	3 265	3 961	86	−782	−1 654	1 515	−2 604
1939	5 725	7 400	6 125	1 101	174	210	806	−2 691
1940	10 805	9 204	6 881	1 112	1 211	722	1 863	−984
1941	20 016	18 274	11 618	5 015	1 641	2 891	1 884	−3 033
1942	13 078	38 623	25 917	7 724	4 982	5 545	2 252	−33 342
1943	3 562	40 442	30 078	6 067	4 297	6 478	3 318	−46 676
1944	−2 329	42 786	33 485	4 711	4 590	5 615	3 712	−54 442
1945	466	41 480	32 427	5 230	3 823	4 570	3 129	−48 713
1946	43 298	32 942	22 574	7 528	2 840	9 081	2 881	−1 606
1947	56 126	34 644	25 130	7 944	1 570	12 320	2 645	6 517
1948	55 888	34 363	29 449	3 776	1 138	13 519	2 382	5 624
1949	37 912	27 363	25 655	700	1 008	9 758	2 574	−1 783

NATIONAL SAVING BY MAJOR SAVER GROUPS

Cash Flow Concept; Current Values: 1897 to 1949

$ mill.

| Year | National saving | Personal saving | | | | Corporate saving | Government saving | |
| | | Total | Nonagricultural individuals | Agriculture | Unincorporated business | | State and local | Federal |
	1	2	3	4	5	6	7	8
1897	3 114	2 321	1 489	794	38	671	89	33
1898	3 606	2 831	1 720	691	420	776	95	−96
1899	5 985	4 513	2 693	914	906	1 344	105	23
1900	4 497	3 150	2 150	598	402	1 139	164	44
1901	5 247	3 737	2 927	615	195	1 242	162	103
1902	6 777	4 912	3 417	819	676	1 533	256	76
1903	5 110	3 347	2 876	391	80	1 506	189	68
1904	5 012	3 570	2 900	591	79	1 151	280	11
1905	7 487	5 854	4 257	911	686	1 376	205	52
1906	8 340	6 308	4 468	1 206	634	1 698	197	137
1907	7 109	5 037	3 889	739	409	1 699	255	118
1908	6 066	4 595	3 921	812	−138	1 311	180	−20
1909	8 800	6 562	4 656	1 548	358	1 857	338	43
1910	8 154	5 832	4 530	757	545	1 934	291	97
1911	7 264	5 175	4 686	304	185	1 652	343	94
1912	10 411	7 764	5 955	1 232	577	2 071	455	121
1913	9 565	7 038	5 192	1 086	760	1 946	470	111
1914	7 800	5 872	4 583	1 027	262	1 700	195	33
1915	11 864	8 649	7 034	1 064	551	2 924	238	53
1916	21 047	13 351	9 245	1 794	2 312	7 348	312	36
1917	22 637	19 986	12 758	5 313	1 915	7 523	336	−5 208
1918	14 148	21 178	15 660	3 962	1 556	5 316	319	−12 665
1919	21 404	18 128	15 503	133	2 492	7 400	426	−4 550
1920	17 698	11 464	13 356	−3 340	1 448	4 823	252	1 159
1921	7 394	6 143	9 214	−2 178	−893	306	431	514
1922	21 206	14 901	11 027	2 392	1 482	5 098	845	362
1923	26 219	18 395	15 729	2 127	539	6 138	878	808
1924	25 922	17 954	13 792	3 116	1 046	5 235	1 769	964
1925	29 054	19 658	16 791	1 814	1 053	6 774	1 830	792
1926	28 033	18 515	15 777	1 443	1 295	6 636	1 766	1 116
1927	28 650	20 456	17 169	2 319	968	5 393	1 718	1 083
1928	27 161	16 929	13 796	2 362	771	7 078	2 309	845
1929	32 186	21 701	18 446	1 782	1 473	7 244	2 028	1 213
1930	15 709	12 170	14 601	−747	−1 684	602	2 112	825
1931	4 852	8 262	11 752	−668	−2 822	−2 810	635	−1 235
1932	−1 201	3 415	4 780	384	−1 749	−3 891	413	−1 138
1933	5 786	5 727	1 941	2 458	1 328	−401	1 780	−1 320
1934	10 587	9 117	4 070	2 102	2 945	1 625	2 350	−2 505
1935	13 859	11 102	5 890	3 555	1 657	2 945	1 778	−1 966
1936	14 005	12 765	7 982	2 535	2 248	3 372	2 264	−4 396
1937	19 288	13 998	11 260	1 884	854	3 421	2 469	−600
1938	13 788	10 177	8 524	1 374	279	2 473	2 746	−1 608
1939	18 430	14 851	11 233	2 393	1 225	4 656	1 911	−2 988
1940	22 495	17 154	12 498	2 408	2 248	5 129	3 048	−2 836
1941	28 767	28 227	19 127	6 368	2 732	7 596	3 214	−10 270
1942	17 318	44 552	29 378	9 110	6 064	9 326	3 394	−39 954
1943	10 343	47 559	34 710	7 545	5 304	10 496	4 599	−52 311
1944	13 024	48 987	37 252	6 222	5 513	9 812	4 993	−50 768
1945	14 460	45 280	33 865	6 698	4 717	8 531	4 310	−43 661
1946	55 611	39 318	26 451	9 099	3 768	13 571	3 513	−791
1947	66 950	41 879	29 398	9 866	2 615	18 192	3 302	3 577
1948	72 316	42 204	33 776	6 076	2 352	20 550	3 370	6 192
1949	59 442	38 739	32 919	3 352	2 468	16 935	3 670	98

Column 1 – Sum of Table T-1, col. 1, Table R-3, col. 6, Table F-31, col. 8, adjustment for the understatement of individuals' bank deposits on account of call loans by nonfinancial corporations derived according to procedure described in notes to col. 7, and net soil improvement costs from col. 8.

Column 2 – Sum of Table T-1, col. 1 and Table F-31, col. 8.

Columns 3 and 4 – Table T-1, cols. 1 and 2 respectively, plus Table R-3, col. 6, call loan adjustment and net soil improvement.

Column 5 – Table T-1, col. 3 plus Table R-3, col. 6 and call loan adjustment.

Column 6 – Sum of Table T-6, col. 2 and Table R-3, col. 6.

Column 7 – Table T-8, col. 6 plus call loan adjustment obtained by taking successive differences of Table D-8, col. 5 minus col. 9 for the period 1920–1942.

Column 8 – Table A-3, col. 1 plus net soil improvement obtained by equally distributing within the period totals given in Volume II, Table B-61, col. 1 plus col. 2 minus col. 3.

Column 9 – Sum of Table T-1, col. 8 and Table F-31, col. 8.

ALTERNATIVE ESTIMATE OF SAVING

(Including Military Assets, Net Soil Improvement, Alternative Estimate of Real Estate, and Adjustment for Call Loans of Nonfinancial Corporations); Social Accounting Concept: 1897 to 1949

$ mill.

Year	National saving			Personal saving adjusted	Nonagricultural saving			Agricultural saving adjusted	Federal government saving including military assets
	Total adjusted	Including military assets	Including other adjustments		Total adjusted	Real estate adjusted	Bank deposits adjusted		
	1	2	3	4	5	6	7	8	9
1897	1 297	934	1 297	910	672	83	137	392	24
1898	1 977	1 620	1 977	1 645	830	48	173	583	−106
1899	3 183	2 820	3 183	2 553	1 737	84	317	457	13
1900	2 112	2 102	2 112	1 284	1 068	3	232	−19	32
1901	2 254	2 220	2 254	1 397	1 802	162	361	−340	91
1902	4 006	3 946	4 006	3 002	2 264	320	306	488	64
1903	2 849	2 766	2 849	1 584	1 681	475	205	−129	55
1904	2 117	2 043	2 117	1 498	1 628	422	101	93	−3
1905	4 423	4 313	4 423	3 568	2 970	646	793	108	38
1906	4 330	4 206	4 330	3 364	3 011	725	307	106	121
1907	3 265	3 128	3 265	2 235	2 376	807	36	−262	99
1908	2 563	2 451	2 563	2 108	2 405	650	−116	37	−39
1909	3 831	3 687	3 831	3 144	3 212	863	600	105	45
1910	4 950	4 597	4 950	3 597	2 926	864	360	211	88
1911	3 272	2 934	3 272	2 432	2 900	769	620	−433	64
1912	5 581	5 230	5 581	4 590	4 009	852	582	488	130
1913	4 491	4 137	4 491	3 021	2 980	867	321	−441	103
1914	3 837	3 511	3 837	2 871	2 176	703	−49	621	26
1915	6 598	6 272	6 598	5 010	4 572	713	1 392	427	145
1916	9 922	9 579	9 922	5 906	5 976	811	1 991	−882	609
1917	10 212	9 926	10 212	10 358	8 718	442	3 018	1 439	−2 831
1918	1 816	1 607	1 816	12 895	10 905	−69	1 577	1 721	−11 562
1919	6 923	6 566	6 923	10 121	10 468	889	3 231	−1 538	−5 814
1920	9 902	9 969	9 902	6 501	6 650	637	−992	−1 854	151
1921	2 228	2 261	2 228	1 253	3 197	1 071	−1 251	−2 062	−451
1922	8 029	7 949	8 029	6 380	6 256	2 586	1 960	−418	201
1923	14 001	13 607	14 001	10 274	10 422	3 728	1 330	111	961
1924	12 514	12 134	12 514	8 996	8 338	4 428	1 878	361	796
1925	16 263	15 453	16 263	11 554	10 833	4 710	871	566	1 019
1926	16 849	15 891	16 849	11 061	9 753	4 446	−853	458	1 172
1927	14 299	13 692	14 299	10 681	10 280	3 697	2 286	386	1 142
1928	10 234	10 907	10 234	5 341	5 111	3 196	−3 541	609	1 035
1929	17 953	15 968	17 953	13 470	12 464	1 717	439	627	1 099
1930	7 354	5 820	7 354	7 151	9 383	−60	1 101	−37	−186
1931	−2 823	−3 305	−2 823	2 948	6 347	−550	−1 115	149	−1 933
1932	−10 451	−10 491	−10 451	−3 233	−819	−1 598	−1 256	332	−1 233
1933	−8 895	−8 851	−8 895	−3 849	−3 567	−1 788	−1 308	156	−1 124
1934	−4 443	−4 417	−4 443	−980	−1 617	−1 675	1 141	−989	−2 156
1935	523	237	523	2 635	569	−1 081	2 326	1 588	−1 575
1936	1 890	1 560	1 890	5 605	4 251	−311	2 423	318	−3 537
1937	7 660	7 286	7 660	7 696	6 353	−37	637	1 631	−792
1938	2 363	2 002	2 363	4 076	3 975	174	148	733	−2 640
1939	5 435	4 942	5 335	7 345	6 235	1 105	2 506	1 167	−2 625
1940	12 433	11 283	12 133	9 693	6 745	1 495	1 790	1 887	−723
1941	18 561	17 309	15 561	15 223	10 856	2 068	3 122	3 677	−83
1942	17 770	16 900	5 370	34 107	23 731	−352	6 792	5 984	−21 016
1943	15 614	14 958	−2 986	36 823	27 562	−1 477	9 903	5 339	−28 163
1944	10 244	9 620	−6 656	39 923	30 462	−1 758	11 181	5 156	−37 632
1945	503	589	−7 397	36 323	29 048	−1 593	10 879	3 792	−40 914
1946	21 470	20 935	25 570	23 062	18 875	2 119	6 780	3 507	−5 840
1947	26 096	25 258	33 196	21 024	19 942	3 952	618	1 599	−785
1948	35 308	34 165	43 308	27 866	23 622	5 843	−1 264	4 149	−2 627
1949	24 386	23 364	32 186	23 479	20 431	5 183	−458	1 979	−9 837

TABLE T–5

Column 1 – Sum of Table T-2, col. 1, Table R-3, col. 4, Table F-31, col. 6, call loan adjustment and net soil improvement as derived in notes to Table T-4, cols. 7 and 8.

Column 2 – Sum of Table T-2, col. 1 and Table F-31, col. 6

Columns 3 and 4 – Table T-2, cols. 1 and 2 respectively plus Table R-3, col. 4, call loan adjustment, and net soil improvement.

Column 5 – Sum of Table T-2, col. 3, Table R-3, col. 4, and call loan adjustment.

Column 6 – Sum of Table T-7, col. 2 and Table R-3, col. 4.

Column 7 – Table T-2, col. 4 plus net soil improvement.

Column 8 – Sum of Table T-2, col. 8 and Table F-31, col. 6.

ALTERNATIVE ESTIMATE OF SAVING

(Including Military Assets, Net Soil Improvement, Alternative Estimate of Real Estate, and Adjustment for Call Loans of Nonfinancial Corporations); Business Accounting Concept: 1897 to 1949

$ mill.

Year	National saving			Personal saving adjusted	Nonagricultural saving		Agricultural saving adjusted	Federal government saving including military assets
	Total adjusted	Including military assets	Including other adjustments		Total adjusted	Real estate adjusted		
	1	2	3	4	5	6	7	8
1897	1 599	1 240	1 599	1 152	530	60	773	23
1898	2 038	1 683	2 038	1 644	746	38	667	−106
1899	4 325	3 960	4 325	3 306	1 706	96	881	13
1900	2 419	2 404	2 419	1 542	1 118	34	204	34
1901	3 132	3 094	3 132	2 130	1 905	184	214	92
1902	4 586	4 522	4 586	3 273	2 393	348	395	64
1903	2 872	2 782	2 872	1 694	1 844	517	−45	56
1904	2 635	2 554	2 635	1 800	1 779	460	132	−1
1905	5 046	4 928	5 046	4 086	3 142	696	446	37
1906	5 645	5 510	5 645	4 361	3 224	793	714	123
1907	4 339	4 189	4 339	3 071	2 658	883	205	103
1908	3 143	3 018	3 143	2 510	2 616	730	244	−36
1909	5 727	5 572	5 727	4 410	3 324	930	943	45
1910	5 034	4 669	5 034	3 716	3 068	938	334	91
1911	3 918	3 569	3 918	2 909	3 149	834	−177	68
1912	6 850	6 486	6 850	5 347	4 305	930	713	133
1913	5 771	5 408	5 771	4 325	3 319	919	514	107
1914	3 718	3 383	3 718	2 893	2 478	757	430	29
1915	7 596	7 258	7 596	5 540	4 878	786	402	150
1916	15 283	14 920	15 283	9 590	6 507	934	1 066	621
1917	18 052	17 726	18 052	15 919	9 830	692	4 472	−2 806
1918	7 742	7 461	7 742	17 050	12 807	375	3 041	−11 530
1919	12 940	12 482	12 940	14 045	12 938	1 517	−1 015	−5 776
1920	8 278	8 179	8 278	6 453	10 513	1 668	−5 027	206
1921	−2 346	−2 419	−2 346	248	5 580	1 727	−3 881	−413
1922	12 010	11 845	12 010	9 311	7 608	3 114	770	230
1923	16 696	16 190	16 696	12 496	12 029	4 422	520	1 000
1924	15 578	15 090	15 578	11 612	9 671	5 093	1 538	833
1925	18 766	17 852	18 766	13 200	11 879	5 353	940	1 065
1926	16 583	15 521	16 583	11 575	10 511	5 093	514	1 207
1927	15 891	15 184	15 891	12 230	10 965	4 312	1 331	1 175
1928	12 362	12 935	12 362	6 918	5 876	3 814	1 335	1 070
1929	19 177	17 078	19 177	14 443	13 388	2 421	729	1 128
1930	1 374	−264	1 374	4 622	9 770	581	−2 190	−161
1931	−9 785	−10 341	−9 785	−290	5 940	−96	−2 020	−1 911
1932	−16 367	−16 428	−16 367	−6 269	−2 122	−1 476	−974	−1 220
1933	−8 691	−8 667	−8 691	−3 958	−5 041	−1 671	1 110	−1 108
1934	−3 183	−3 202	−3 183	−97	−2 545	−1 400	800	−2 134
1935	720	399	720	2 708	−367	−870	2 565	−1 551
1936	3 329	2 951	3 329	6 332	3 591	−18	1 590	−3 512
1937	6 671	6 214	6 671	6 969	6 259	475	902	−755
1938	975	522	975	3 718	4 074	740	426	−2 604
1939	6 315	5 725	6 315	7 990	6 375	1 704	1 441	−2 691
1940	12 265	11 005	12 065	10 464	7 201	2 172	2 052	−784
1941	24 307	22 916	21 407	19 665	12 069	2 930	5 955	−133
1942	26 310	25 278	14 110	39 655	26 009	651	8 664	−21 142
1943	22 600	21 762	4 400	41 280	29 976	−353	7 007	−28 476
1944	14 918	14 071	−1 482	43 633	33 392	−378	5 651	−38 042
1945	8 136	7 966	636	41 650	32 417	−9	5 410	−41 213
1946	40 347	39 498	44 147	33 791	23 243	4 062	7 708	−5 406
1947	52 514	51 226	57 414	35 932	26 238	6 734	8 124	1 617
1948	52 966	51 288	57 566	36 041	30 947	9 155	3 956	1 024
1949	35 433	33 912	39 433	28 884	26 996	8 274	880	−5 783

Column 1 – 1897–1949: Sum of cols. 2–22 less sum of cols. 23–29.

Column 2 – 1897–1949: Sum of Table R-6, cols. 1–4 less cols. 5 and 7, and Table R-9, col. 1 less cols. 2 and 5.

Column 3 – 1897–1949: Sum of Table R-12, col. 1 less cols. 2 and 5; Table R-13, col. 1 less col. 5; Table R-19, col. 1 less col. 2; Table R-14, col. 11; and Table R-15, col. 11.

Column 4 – 1897–1949: Table A-3, cols. 3 and 12.

Column 5 – 1897–1949: Sum of Table Q-1, col. 7 and Table A-3, col. 5.

Column 6 – 1897–1949: Sum of Table A-3, col. 4 and Table P-1, cols. 11 and 12.

Column 7 – 1897–1949: Sum of Table P-19, col. 12 and Table A-3, col. 6.

Column 8 – 1897–1949: Sum of Table L-1, col. 2 and first differences of Table A-53, col. 2.

Column 9 – 1897–1949: Sum of Table L-1, cols. 3 and 6 and first differences of Table A-53, col. 3.

Column 10 – 1897–1949: Sum of Table L-27, col. 1 and first differences of Table L-44, cols. 2, 3, and 5.

Column 11 – 1897–1949: Table L-39, col. 1 and first differences of Table A-53, col. 6.

Column 12 – 1897–1928: Table J-1, col. 8.
1929–1949: Table J-1, col. 9.

Column 13 – 1897–1920: Sum of Table M-2, col. 1 and first differences of Table A-53, col. 7.
1921–1949: Sum of Table M-1, col. 1 and first differences of Table A-53, col. 7.

Column 14 – 1897–1949: Sum of Table I-1, col. 10, Table I-9, cols. 4 (to 1929) or 5 (from 1930) and Table I-14, col. 10.

Column 15 – 1918–1928: Table F-9, col. 11.
1929–1949: Table F-23, col. 11.

Column 16 – 1897–1914: First differences of Table G-19, cols. 6 and 11.
1915–1949: Table G-19, cols. 5 and 10.

Column 17 – 1921–1949: Table I-15, col. 2.

Column 18 – 1897–1949: Sum of Table V-1, col. 2 and Table V-2, col. 8.

Column 19 – 1897–1949: Table V-1, col. 3.

Column 20 – 1897–1949: Table V-1, col. 4.

Column 21 – 1897–1949: Table V-1, sum of cols. 5–8.

Column 22 – 1897–1949: Table K-5, col. 2.

Column 23 – 1897–1949: Sum of Table R-6, cols. 6 and 8 and Table R-9, cols. 3, 4, and 6.

Column 24 – 1897–1949: Sum of Table R-12, cols. 3, 4, and 6, Table R-13, col. 6, and Table R-19, cols. 3 and 4.

Column 25 – 1897–1949: First differences of Table A-54, col. 2 plus Table A-65, col. 2.

Column 26 – 1897–1949: Sum of Table U-5, col. 6, Table A-65, col. 3, and first differences of Table A-54, col. 3.

Column 27 – 1897–1949: First differences of Table D-8, col. 11.

Column 28 – 1897–1926: Sum of first differences of Table D-1, col. 6 less col. 8, Table A-65, col. 4, the first differences of Table A-54, col. 4, less the sum of first differences of Table U-6, col. 7, Table A-57, col. 6, and first differences of Table D-1, col. 4.
1927–1949: Same procedure as for 1897–1926 except Table U-4, col. 9 used instead of Table D-1, col. 4.

Column 29 – 1897–1949: First differences of sum of Table F-29, col. 1 and Table A-64, col. 4.

PERSONAL SAVING BY MAJOR COMPONENTS
Social Accounting Concept; Current Values: 1897 to 1949

$ mill.

Year	Total	Nonfarm construction		Farm construc-tion	Consumer durables	Producer durables	Inven-tories	Cur-rency	Commer-cial bank deposits	Savings bank deposits
		Resi-dential	Nonres-idential							
	1	2	3	4	5	6	7	8	9	10
1897	547	70	152	74	147	−43	−105	27	184	91
1898	1 288	41	125	86	124	−9	271	40	325	118
1899	2 190	71	118	82	237	24	207	116	588	119
1900	1 274	3	198	95	182	34	193	63	292	193
1901	1 363	138	188	108	220	58	−569	43	625	131
1902	2 942	270	227	121	273	136	543	60	453	145
1903	1 501	402	149	116	283	94	−38	56	223	121
1904	1 424	358	106	116	238	65	−133	−72	136	130
1905	3 458	546	126	116	374	95	270	219	1 123	183
1906	3 240	611	181	122	516	165	247	63	474	168
1907	2 098	680	242	119	430	177	−238	116	−279	71
1908	1 996	548	137	128	101	49	−30	−280	−101	55
1909	3 000	729	140	159	453	101	−63	64	674	174
1910	3 244	731	134	179	485	110	472	42	464	148
1911	2 094	651	98	155	352	74	−446	−71	785	163
1912	4 239	721	150	181	476	153	511	88	764	201
1913	2 667	733	204	171	442	158	−207	51	502	186
1914	2 545	597	93	165	165	57	499	−136	212	132
1915	4 684	607	60	171	211	−2	409	299	1 726	168
1916	5 563	688	169	287	839	131	−817	326	2 923	352
1917	10 072	376	133	435	673	277	1 185	605	2 853	152
1918	12 686	−58	−8	413	−301	246	−168	962	1 462	176
1919	9 764	752	67	635	461	233	556	−21	4 061	441
1920	6 568	540	240	385	514	359	1 970	365	−1 017	506
1921	1 286	904	272	−37	−301	−370	−796	−914	−1 364	283
1922	6 300	2 186	400	44	896	−116	107	129	2 471	403
1923	9 880	3 158	471	93	2 184	183	471	85	1 254	435
1924	8 616	3 748	509	63	1 841	71	−915	−31	2 075	508
1925	10 744	4 000	720	82	2 634	234	104	−104	1 581	465
1926	10 103	3 788	818	59	2 697	314	30	−38	−355	538
1927	10 074	3 166	806	148	1 680	202	−227	−53	2 642	664
1928	6 014	2 725	691	98	1 661	182	−263	−55	−1 745	586
1929	11 485	1 454	645	50	1 951	357	196	0	−795	158
1930	5 617	−74	451	−127	−66	25	−729	−2	−899	761
1931	2 466	−512	40	−230	−1 096	−438	−228	752	−3 663	1 028
1932	−3 273	−1 447	−243	−291	−2 099	−704	−539	312	−1 979	313
1933	−3 805	−1 604	−406	−255	−1 500	−589	−819	191	−1 833	−19
1934	−954	−1 499	−435	−256	−662	−345	−1 311	−12	2 139	337
1935	2 349	−992	−435	−141	560	1	800	178	2 483	211
1936	5 275	−311	−247	−99	1 768	329	−671	528	2 767	350
1937	7 322	−61	−165	−42	1 964	518	900	200	349	232
1938	3 715	143	−214	−90	139	86	−24	−9	339	189
1939	6 852	952	−188	−24	1 353	201	134	448	2 440	364
1940	8 543	1 285	−158	16	2 234	489	555	894	2 004	248
1941	13 971	1 776	−97	93	3 081	833	789	2 129	2 537	26
1942	33 237	−262	−386	−39	−1 314	150	1 643	4 214	6 256	284
1943	36 167	−1 193	−495	−50	−1 505	−184	−170	4 665	9 979	1 566
1944	39 299	−1 442	−440	−108	−1 660	464	354	4 578	10 588	2 322
1945	36 409	−1 327	−303	−167	−748	672	50	2 867	13 258	2 747
1946	22 527	1 764	269	713	6 401	1 536	120	77	8 677	1 986
1947	20 186	3 294	90	1 135	9 079	2 514	−2 191	−323	1 477	1 209
1948	26 723	4 880	448	1 234	8 529	3 023	2 850	−435	−2 131	703
1949	22 457	4 341	530	1 076	8 786	2 665	−1 374	−723	−634	888

PERSONAL SAVING BY MAJOR COMPONENTS
Social Accounting Concept; Current Values: 1897 to 1949

$ mill.

Year	Credit unions and coops.	Savings and loan associations	Mortgage holdings	Life insurance reserves	Pension and retirement funds			Securities			
					U.S. Government	State and local	Private	U.S. Government	State and local	Corporate and foreign bonds	Stocks
	11	12	13	14	15	16	17	18	19	20	21
1897	5	−20	62	83	−	0	−	−24	31	58	105
1898	5	1	57	96	−	1	−	92	26	121	99
1899	5	−20	61	103	−	1	−	129	56	287	543
1900	5	−5	49	113	−	1	−	−45	18	235	259
1901	7	−5	53	140	−	1	−	−33	31	393	561
1902	6	6	55	151	−	1	−	−16	2	465	715
1903	7	14	71	148	−	1	−	−24	15	82	475
1904	7	17	65	170	−	1	−	−24	20	302	356
1905	6	16	68	191	−	1	−	−7	45	664	353
1906	7	31	42	208	−	1	−	7	67	417	805
1907	7	43	69	170	−	1	−	−75	122	81	692
1908	6	43	78	178	−	2	−	3	212	610	656
1909	7	55	58	213	−	1	−	−32	10	529	745
1910	7	60	216	205	−	1	−	8	138	−26	804
1911	6	75	253	245	−	0	−	19	109	407	250
1912	7	89	259	233	−	1	−	4	143	667	929
1913	20	82	621	234	−	3	−	−1	8	198	536
1914	20	81	472	200	−	0	−	−2	226	471	456
1915	20	102	267	272	−	5	−	−3	299	1 459	688
1916	21	90	548	354	−	7	−	−123	218	1 089	1 380
1917	26	131	1 111	394	−	8	−	3 401	213	692	956
1918	26	105	506	367	6	14	−	8 670	497	1 005	956
1919	31	172	1 144	529	9	14	−	3 148	28	524	1 999
1920	32	280	2 236	520	21	22	−	−668	682	1 668	1 818
1921	32	283	276	526	34	27	10	−611	696	1 400	956
1922	33	348	−180	664	35	29	30	−2 686	745	1 262	1 347
1923	34	450	180	791	35	39	10	−277	624	1 567	1 228
1924	33	602	−463	821	90	43	20	−1 516	195	1 436	1 254
1925	33	599	426	1 021	160	41	30	−295	225	1 937	2 093
1926	29	630	684	1 136	161	46	40	−639	149	1 895	1 761
1927	31	741	1 318	1 249	130	60	70	−2 260	446	2 019	2 075
1928	33	685	1 650	1 290	127	66	80	−975	379	1 628	3 406
1929	27	526	1 891	1 115	157	70	160	−473	508	660	4 789
1930	−4	198	781	1 006	125	71	50	−227	585	666	1 278
1931	−1	−229	−183	766	−401	72	50	720	1 781	556	599
1932	−2	−421	−232	268	−38	73	50	689	128	−398	227
1933	1	−358	−899	535	29	87	50	1 108	−912	−100	437
1934	47	−242	−533	1 127	53	106	50	−233	−857	39	420
1935	55	−300	133	1 510	137	120	50	−898	−8	−938	−67
1936	63	−175	100	1 693	452	130	80	978	−360	−915	185
1937	67	−90	−92	1 624	1 245	157	60	1 026	97	−1 059	831
1938	66	−3	−202	1 606	961	159	60	4	−45	−45	228
1939	81	170	−292	1 722	1 108	178	50	−80	−118	−674	568
1940	106	287	−280	1 842	1 138	189	50	289	−129	−416	491
1941	149	401	80	2 197	1 684	204	75	3 401	−151	−963	627
1942	109	297	−232	2 496	2 424	223	125	10 574	−183	61	189
1943	111	612	−238	2 871	3 710	240	200	14 666	−150	−653	470
1944	165	833	18	3 188	4 413	259	600	17 797	−76	−1 141	519
1945	207	1 107	646	3 381	4 801	253	800	11 843	−306	−1 580	1 246
1946	248	1 267	1 582	3 382	3 354	335	800	−2 273	−218	−1 226	1 818
1947	348	1 304	1 680	3 568	3 494	392	1 050	1 259	411	−694	2 074
1948	271	1 327	1 203	3 632	2 935	528	1 050	1 171	1 184	574	1 441
1949	288	1 629	615	3 790	1 929	578	1 050	1 089	906	94	1 620

Social Accounting Concept; Current Values: 1897 to 1949

$ mill.

Year	Share in saving of foreign corporations other than U.S. subsidiaries	Liabilities						
		Nonfarm mortgage debt on		Farm mortgage debt	Debt to banks and other institutions	Borrowing on securities	Consumer and other debt	Tax liabilities
		Residental structures	Non-residential structures					
	22	23	24	25	26	27	28	29
1897	1	−1	22	74	135	71	32	18
1898	1	19	28	77	68	71	50	19
1899	1	26	30	80	219	109	55	19
1900	1	64	40	83	233	111	60	19
1901	1	63	40	85	301	149	72	18
1902	1	97	49	89	266	76	79	16
1903	2	110	53	92	281	71	74	15
1904	2	132	59	96	40	30	62	17
1905	2	169	66	99	332	143	109	15
1906	2	187	73	103	343	42	130	16
1907	2	135	58	107	−29	−49	93	17
1908	3	134	60	110	34	36	13	15
1909	3	228	84	115	299	105	173	16
1910	4	236	85	314	157	8	122	16
1911	4	204	78	408	142	52	135	16
1912	4	217	79	418	317	104	163	44
1913	4	411	137	359	111	−15	137	138
1914	4	356	125	284	14	108	99	181
1915	5	249	99	265	644	397	190	235
1916	7	328	117	570	628	284	323	676
1917	9	617	186	711	1 038	137	264	605
1918	10	271	103	600	408	367	152	299
1919	10	362	150	1 312	1 776	792	652	−15
1920	11	1 166	349	1 772	916	−669	574	−192
1921	12	811	196	486	−1 477	−84	−145	245
1922	14	996	297	89	−210	655	129	−95
1923	18	1 700	546	−111	644	−104	301	177
1924	22	1 737	553	−742	−828	842	147	81
1925	26	2 179	804	−190	209	1 478	643	145
1926	30	2 603	544	−45	−40	−2	453	187
1927	34	2 393	540	109	−231	1 327	353	376
1928	39	2 500	554	10	189	1 645	981	395
1929	44	1 949	389	−116	46	−1 329	1 091	−25
1930	30	566	212	−223	−990	−2 051	1 281	−513
1931	30	−563	71	−284	−1 223	−2 010	1 144	−188
1932	30	−1 147	−144	−598	−879	−1 026	435	329
1933	30	−1 260	−80	−706	−953	−45	−455	478
1934	30	14	−90	−26	−231	−284	−851	385
1935	30	−225	−100	−86	171	−114	230	264
1936	30	−203	23	−194	146	−27	1 102	553
1937	30	106	−59	−149	281	−520	1 216	−222
1938	32	196	−58	−156	−102	−97	419	−537
1939	34	566	−108	−183	276	−153	1 100	77
1940	36	781	−75	−85	490	−277	1 303	490
1941	38	955	−55	−109	815	−90	978	2 444
1942	40	−231	−144	−421	−545	64	−4 199	−1 092
1943	42	−545	−186	−562	−41	563	−1 509	607
1944	44	−108	−90	−456	54	1 567	307	702
1945	47	394	35	−251	475	1 384	1 459	−411
1946	50	4 241	445	95	1 690	−2 662	3 115	1 211
1947	55	4 940	548	105	1 654	−477	3 703	566
1948	60	4 901	518	226	971	−116	2 550	−1 296
1949	60	3 914	498	305	−156	197	1 642	346

Column 1 – Sum of cols. 2–8.

Column 2 – Sum of Table R-4, cols. 1–4 minus cols. 5 and 7, and Table R-7, col. 1 minus cols. 2 and 5.

Column 3 – Sum of Table R-10, col. 1 less cols. 2 and 5; Table R-13, col. 1 less col. 3; Table R-17, col. 1 less col. 2; Table R-14, col. 9 and Table R-15, col. 9.

Column 4 – Table A-1, cols. 3 and 12.

Column 5 – Sum of Table Q-1, col. 1 and Table A-1, col. 5.

Column 6 – Sum of Table A-1, col. 4 and Table P-1, cols. 3 and 4.

Column 7 – Table A-32, col. 1 plus first differences of Table P-19, col. 3.

Column 8 – Table T-6, cols. 8–22 less cols. 23–29.

PERSONAL SAVING BY MAJOR COMPONENTS

Business Accounting Concept; Current Values: 1897 to 1949

$ mill.

| Year | Total | Nonfarm real estate | | Farm real estate | Consumer durables | Producer durables | Inventories | All other components[1] |
		Residential	Nonresidential					
	1	2	3	4	5	6	7	8
1897	793	51	143	71	12	−80	344	252
1898	1 289	33	121	85	39	−25	386	650
1899	2 941	81	119	87	186	40	977	1 451
1900	1 527	29	206	97	199	69	358	569
1901	2 092	156	191	113	312	82	18	1 220
1902	3 209	294	232	130	390	162	629	1 372
1903	1 604	437	157	128	421	118	−152	495
1904	1 719	389	113	126	365	86	−34	674
1905	3 968	588	137	130	511	127	544	1 931
1906	4 226	668	197	148	677	209	929	1 398
1907	2 921	743	262	152	657	232	187	688
1908	2 385	615	155	153	241	68	90	1 063
1909	4 255	785	158	185	490	127	1 029	1 481
1910	3 351	793	154	210	546	150	365	1 133
1911	2 560	705	118	186	542	117	−318	1 210
1912	4 983	786	172	212	700	188	878	2 047
1913	3 962	776	226	207	749	190	648	1 166
1914	2 558	642	111	197	434	78	127	969
1915	5 202	668	81	209	453	47	516	3 228
1916	9 227	791	215	349	1 263	225	2 118	4 266
1917	15 593	586	213	544	1 582	479	5 196	6 993
1918	16 769	314	111	578	1 309	641	1 254	12 562
1919	13 587	1 279	250	854	2 511	653	980	7 060
1920	6 354	1 405	518	705	3 715	793	−3 342	2 560
1921	175	1 454	436	127	1 608	−96	−4 968	1 614
1922	9 146	2 629	544	184	1 796	−43	1 253	2 783
1923	11 990	3 740	640	255	3 173	280	582	3 320
1924	11 124	4 305	675	214	2 541	177	−87	3 299
1925	12 286	4 539	887	229	3 038	325	298	2 970
1926	10 513	4 331	1 010	202	2 777	383	−557	2 367
1927	11 523	3 681	958	280	1 714	258	333	4 299
1928	7 491	3 243	843	228	1 769	250	238	920
1929	12 344	2 044	786	181	2 120	408	−27	6 832
1930	2 984	463	560	−13	−412	−33	−3 718	6 137
1931	−846	−132	113	−166	−2 083	−529	−2 979	4 930
1932	−6 330	−1 346	−248	−259	−3 676	−852	−1 999	2 050
1933	−3 934	−1 507	−385	−229	−3 251	−751	821	1 368
1934	−116	−1 269	−375	−195	−2 014	−424	607	3 554
1935	2 387	−816	−367	−89	−720	−69	1 892	2 556
1936	5 954	−66	−174	−42	688	282	760	4 506
1937	6 512	368	−47	36	1 242	530	175	4 208
1938	3 265	617	−99	−27	−441	121	−581	3 675
1939	7 400	1 454	−64	32	786	210	558	4 424
1940	9 204	1 852	−25	79	1 926	519	731	4 122
1941	18 274	2 499	65	191	3 385	910	3 728	7 496
1942	38 623	579	−190	116	−22	295	4 400	33 445
1943	40 442	−251	−284	159	−171	−37	1 262	39 764
1944	42 786	−285	−202	154	−45	625	408	42 131
1945	41 480	1	−32	140	1 090	824	1 225	38 232
1946	32 942	3 393	625	1 049	8 871	1 728	5 552	11 724
1947	34 644	5 626	574	1 652	12 696	2 940	4 891	6 265
1948	34 363	7 657	1 015	1 801	12 654	3 644	1 833	5 759
1949	27 363	6 933	1 086	1 599	12 338	3 425	−4 451	6 433

[1] Shown separately in Table T–6.

Column 1 – 1897–1949: Sum of cols. 2–19 less cols. 20–24 plus cols. 25 and 26 less col. 27.

Column 2 – 1897–1949: Table R-6, cols. 1–4 less cols. 5 and 7.

Column 3 – 1897–1949: Table R-9, col. 1 less cols. 2 and 5.

Column 4 – 1897–1949: Sum of Table A-3, cols. 10 and 11. Figures include Table A-13, col. 5 but, since the overstatement is small, the adjustment was not made.

Column 5 – 1897–1949: Table Q-1, col. 7.

Column 6 – 1897–1949: Table L-1, col. 1 less first differences of Table U-1, col. 1.

Column 7 – 1897–1949: Sum of Table L-27, col. 1, first differences of Table L-44, cols. 2, 3, and 5, and Table L-39, col. 1.

Column 8 – 1897–1928: Table J-1, col. 8.
    1929–1949: Table J-1, col. 9.

Column 9 – 1897–1920: Table M-2, col. 7.
    1921–1949: Table M-1, col. 7.

Column 10 – 1897–1920: Table M-2, col. 2.
    1921–1949: Table M-1, col. 2.

Column 11 – 1897–1949: Sum of Table I-1, col. 10, Table I-9, col. 4 (to 1929) or 5 (from 1930), and Table I-14, col. 10 less first differences of Table A-53, col. 4.

Column 12 – 1918–1928: Table F-9, col. 11 less Table F-28, col. 4.
    1929–1949: Table F-23, col. 11 less Table F-28, col. 4.

Column 13 – 1897–1914: First differences of Table G-19, cols. 6 and 11.
    1915–1949: Table G-19, sum of cols. 5 and 10.

Column 14 – 1921–1949: Table I-15, col. 2.

Column 15 – 1897–1949: Table V-1, col. 2 less first differences of Table U-1, col. 2.

Column 16 – 1897–1949: Table V-1, col. 3.

Column 17 – 1897–1949: Table V-1, col. 4.

Column 18 – 1897–1949: Table V-1, cols. 5–8.

Column 19 – 1897–1949: Table K-5, col. 2.

Column 20 – 1897–1949: Table R-4, sum of cols. 6 and 8.

Column 21 – 1897–1949: Table R-7, sum of cols. 3, 4, and 6.

Column 22 – 1897–1949: First differences of Table D-8, col. 11.

Column 23 – 1897–1949: First differences of Table D-1, col. 6 less col. 8.

Column 24 – 1897–1949: First differences of Table F-29, col. 1.

Column 25 – 1897–1949: Table R-19, col. 1 less col. 2.

Column 26 – 1897–1949: Table P-1, col. 12.

Column 27 – 1897–1949: Table R-19, col. 3 plus col. 4.

NONAGRICULTURAL INDIVIDUALS' SAVING BY MAJOR COMPONENTS

Social Accounting Concept; Current Values: 1897 to 1949

$ mill.

Year	Total	Real estate 1- to 4- family homes	Real estate Multi-family homes	Farm land and subdivisions	Consumer durables	Currency and commercial bank deposits	Savings bank and other deposits	Savings and loan associations	Mortgage holdings Farm	Mortgage holdings Non-farm
	1	2	3	4	5	6	7	8	9	10
1897	659	63	7	57	122	137	91	−20	54	3
1898	823	35	6	57	102	173	118	1	53	0
1899	1 724	66	5	58	206	317	119	−20	48	8
1900	1 068	−1	4	63	157	232	193	−5	39	7
1901	1 778	120	18	69	196	361	131	−5	39	11
1902	2 214	248	22	74	246	306	145	6	42	10
1903	1 608	365	37	79	259	205	121	14	46	21
1904	1 564	322	36	84	209	101	130	17	45	16
1905	2 870	499	47	89	337	793	183	16	37	28
1906	2 897	568	43	94	455	307	168	31	17	23
1907	2 249	633	47	100	383	36	71	43	45	21
1908	2 303	509	39	105	64	−116	55	43	56	17
1909	3 078	669	60	110	358	600	174	55	20	36
1910	2 793	664	67	113	387	360	148	60	172	30
1911	2 782	592	59	115	287	620	163	75	205	30
1912	3 878	657	64	117	396	582	201	89	211	30
1913	2 846	671	62	119	405	321	186	82	218	385
1914	2 070	528	69	118	122	−49	132	81	157	302
1915	4 466	531	76	125	127	1 392	168	102	115	142
1916	5 853	614	74	132	716	1 991	353	90	204	258
1917	8 652	331	45	142	352	3 018	153	131	341	654
1918	10 916	−54	−4	153	−376	1 577	177	105	128	261
1919	10 331	683	69	181	252	3 231	442	172	793	141
1920	6 497	485	55	−201	728	−1 048	508	280	834	1 126
1921	3 010	835	69	−166	248	−1 271	285	283	50	218
1922	5 956	1 999	187	−154	1 067	2 060	406	348	−164	147
1923	9 808	2 851	307	−135	2 142	1 286	439	450	−345	704
1924	7 738	3 402	346	−114	1 854	1 958	511	602	−611	339
1925	10 523	3 551	449	345	2 432	1 271	468	599	−263	812
1926	9 295	3 265	523	326	2 603	−653	542	630	135	916
1927	10 173	2 624	542	314	1 738	2 710	670	741	−6	1 326
1928	6 284	2 286	439	297	1 566	−1 897	594	685	74	1 572
1929	10 979	1 199	255	288	1 816	−783	160	526	−24	1 919
1930	7 989	−81	7	17	66	−279	757	198	−74	864
1931	6 005	−478	−34	16	−848	−1 495	1 027	−229	−123	−46
1932	−719	−1 329	−118	4	−1 796	−1 307	311	−421	−207	−3
1933	−3 383	−1 481	−123	5	−1 320	−1 308	−18	−358	−358	−505
1934	−1 451	−1 353	−146	5	−653	1 131	344	−242	−274	−208
1935	623	−857	−135	−5	439	2 291	226	−300	−2	148
1936	4 261	−253	−58	−6	1 587	2 433	373	−175	−103	215
1937	6 319	−45	−16	−6	1 816	627	264	−90	−56	155
1938	3 954	188	−45	−5	177	158	220	−3	−44	−153
1939	6 082	947	5	−5	1 219	2 506	409	170	−34	−254
1940	6 535	1 292	−7	−92	2 149	1 790	305	287	−37	−239
1941	10 544	1 776	0	−93	2 835	3 102	97	401	−36	120
1942	23 801	−199	−63	−103	−1 351	6 772	302	297	−71	−155
1943	27 846	−1 144	−49	−121	−1 525	9 903	1 581	612	−56	−177
1944	30 778	−1 386	−56	−136	−1 435	11 181	2 363	833	−67	91
1945	29 314	−1 244	−83	86	−606	10 879	2 781	1 107	7	639
1946	18 520	1 807	−43	101	5 634	6 780	2 046	1 267	95	1 479
1947	19 284	3 311	−17	108	8 076	618	1 302	1 304	59	1 617
1948	22 659	4 816	64	116	7 644	−1 264	813	1 327	102	1 092
1949	19 589	4 199	142	113	7 982	−458	1 012	1 629	93	514

NONAGRICULTURAL INDIVIDUALS' SAVING BY MAJOR COMPONENTS
Social Accounting Concept; Current Values: 1897 to 1949

$ mill.

| Year | Life insurance reserves | Pension and retirement funds | | | Securities | | | |
		U.S. Government	State and local	Private	U.S. Government	State and local	Corporate and foreign bonds	Stocks
	11	12	13	14	15	16	17	18
1897	74	–	0	–	–24	31	58	105
1898	85	–	1	–	92	26	121	99
1899	91	–	1	–	129	56	287	543
1900	101	–	1	–	–45	18	235	259
1901	125	–	1	–	–33	31	393	561
1902	136	–	1	–	–16	2	465	715
1903	134	–	1	–	–24	15	82	475
1904	152	–	1	–	–24	20	302	356
1905	172	–	1	–	–7	45	664	353
1906	188	–	1	–	7	67	417	805
1907	154	–	1	–	–75	122	81	692
1908	159	–	2	–	3	212	610	656
1909	188	–	1	–	–32	10	529	745
1910	182	–	1	–	8	138	–26	804
1911	218	–	0	–	19	109	407	250
1912	207	–	1	–	4	143	667	929
1913	208	–	3	–	–1	8	198	536
1914	177	–	0	–	–2	226	471	456
1915	243	–	5	–	–3	299	1 459	688
1916	319	–	7	–	–123	218	1 089	1 380
1917	355	–	8	–	2 601	213	692	956
1918	330	6	14	–	7 120	497	1 005	956
1919	477	9	14	–	2 698	28	524	1 999
1920	469	18	22	–	–218	682	1 668	1 818
1921	477	30	27	10	–111	696	1 400	956
1922	604	31	29	30	–2 336	745	1 262	1 347
1923	721	32	39	10	–27	624	1 567	1 228
1924	751	79	43	20	–1 466	195	1 436	1 254
1925	935	142	41	30	–195	225	1 937	2 093
1926	1 043	143	46	40	–589	149	1 895	1 761
1927	1 149	115	60	70	–2 360	446	2 019	2 075
1928	1 184	124	66	80	–1 075	379	1 628	3 406
1929	1 027	146	70	160	–373	508	660	4 789
1930	926	117	71	50	–77	585	666	1 278
1931	706	–344	72	50	770	1 781	556	599
1932	248	–28	73	50	689	128	–398	227
1933	494	28	87	50	1 108	–912	–100	437
1934	1 041	48	106	50	–183	–857	39	420
1935	1 398	125	120	50	–864	–8	–938	–67
1936	1 569	413	130	80	841	–360	–915	185
1937	1 507	1 243	157	60	870	97	–1 059	831
1938	1 491	958	159	60	–50	–45	–45	228
1939	1 601	1 108	178	50	–166	–118	–674	568
1940	1 713	1 138	189	50	186	–129	–416	491
1941	2 050	1 682	204	75	2 742	–151	–963	627
1942	2 347	2 398	223	125	8 924	–183	61	189
1943	2 710	3 651	240	200	11 992	–150	–653	470
1944	3 006	4 298	259	600	14 618	–76	–1 141	519
1945	3 179	4 589	253	800	9 759	–306	–1 580	1 246
1946	3 179	3 164	335	800	–2 579	–218	–1 226	1 818
1947	3 358	3 397	392	1 050	982	411	–694	2 074
1948	3 420	2 897	528	1 050	2 528	1 184	574	1 441
1949	3 569	1 862	578	1 050	1 063	906	94	1 620

Social Accounting Concept; Current Values: 1897 to 1949

$ mill.

Year	Share in saving of foreign corporations other than U.S. subsidiaries	Mortgage debt		Borrowing on securities	Consumer debt	Net tax liabilities	Nonprofit institutions		
		1- to 4-family homes	Multi-family homes				Real estate	Equipment	Mortgage debt
	19	20	21	22	23	24	25	26	27
1897	1	−6	5	71	45	17	50	2	20
1898	1	12	7	71	61	19	42	1	20
1899	1	19	7	109	57	18	39	0	20
1900	1	54	10	111	49	19	67	5	20
1901	1	45	18	149	61	17	65	4	20
1902	1	74	23	76	74	7	78	7	20
1903	2	86	24	71	72	6	52	3	20
1904	2	105	27	30	44	17	38	0	20
1905	2	137	32	143	91	14	47	1	20
1906	2	151	36	42	104	15	65	7	20
1907	2	104	31	−49	90	8	88	9	20
1908	3	102	32	36	−24	6	58	1	21
1909	3	183	45	105	150	0	55	1	21
1910	4	186	50	8	95	14	55	0	21
1911	4	155	49	52	134	−1	42	−3	21
1912	4	164	53	104	113	36	66	0	20
1913	4	330	81	−15	106	111	81	4	31
1914	4	280	76	108	87	177	41	−4	31
1915	5	186	63	397	131	214	24	−10	31
1916	7	252	76	284	219	659	52	−7	31
1917	9	496	121	137	24	573	43	−10	31
1918	10	198	73	367	30	280	11	−21	31
1919	10	253	109	792	310	−97	25	−15	35
1920	11	930	236	−669	409	−282	−58	−22	36
1921	12	603	208	−84	52	218	10	−8	43
1922	14	700	296	655	163	−105	85	12	54
1923	18	1 241	459	−104	351	162	109	18	121
1924	22	1 236	501	842	271	76	145	23	125
1925	26	1 507	672	1 478	655	135	194	35	157
1926	30	1 811	792	−2	557	172	204	36	150
1927	34	1 644	749	1 327	192	351	223	38	92
1928	39	1 673	827	1 645	775	375	199	31	98
1929	44	1 275	674	−1 329	976	−45	184	25	66
1930	30	137	429	−2 051	−699	−543	171	22	52
1931	30	−537	−26	−2 010	−1 195	−188	78	1	40
1932	30	−1 029	−118	−1 026	−1 349	349	−24	−23	−2
1933	30	−1 023	−237	−45	−203	498	−112	−39	−2
1934	30	254	−240	−284	463	385	−131	−42	−2
1935	30	−61	−164	−114	933	284	−116	−36	−2
1936	30	−108	−95	−27	1 284	573	−73	−27	−2
1937	30	155	−49	−520	622	−212	−81	−23	−34
1938	32	254	−58	−97	−323	−512	−80	−18	−35
1939	34	518	48	−153	877	92	−92	−13	−25
1940	36	762	19	−277	1 099	515	−71	−7	−25
1941	38	950	5	−90	612	2 464	−57	1	−35
1942	40	−172	−59	64	−3 144	−1 062	−149	−13	−37
1943	42	−416	−129	563	−1 161	627	−216	−20	−40
1944	44	−3	−105	1 567	399	702	−206	−11	−40
1945	47	408	−14	1 384	778	−451	−173	−1	−40
1946	50	4 143	98	−2 662	3 259	1 161	−9	32	−7
1947	55	4 751	189	−477	3 230	491	62	48	45
1948	60	4 637	264	−116	2 519	−1 347	237	82	95
1949	60	3 610	304	197	2 425	298	427	113	145

Column 1 – Sum of cols. 2–7.

Column 2 – Table R-4, cols. 1-4 less cols. 5 and 7.

Column 3 – Table R-7, col. 1 less cols. 2 and 5.

Column 4 – Table Q-1, col. 1.

Column 5 – Table R-17, col. 1 less col. 2.

Column 6 – Table P-1, col. 4.

Column 7 – Table T-8, cols. 4, 6–19 less cols. 20–24, 27.

Business Accounting Concept; Current Values: 1897 to 1949

$ mill.

Year	Total	Real estate		Consumer durables	Institutional		All other components [1]
		1- to 4- family homes	Multi- family homes		Real estate	Equip- ment	
	1	2	3	4	5	6	7
1897	521	44	7	6	48	1	415
1898	741	27	6	29	41	1	637
1899	1 691	74	7	162	40	0	1 408
1900	1 113	25	4	173	69	6	836
1901	1 877	138	18	275	66	5	1 375
1902	2 339	271	23	345	80	7	1 613
1903	1 764	399	38	377	55	3	892
1904	1 708	353	36	318	41	1	959
1905	3 034	539	49	454	50	3	1 939
1906	3 099	624	44	594	70	8	1 759
1907	2 518	702	41	581	94	11	1 089
1908	2 501	573	42	188	64	2	1 632
1909	3 179	725	60	396	60	3	1 935
1910	2 923	724	69	448	60	2	1 620
1911	3 020	644	61	462	48	0	1 805
1912	4 161	721	65	604	73	3	2 695
1913	3 176	713	63	680	89	8	1 623
1914	2 363	573	69	362	46	−1	1 314
1915	4 760	590	78	348	31	−5	3 718
1916	6 364	713	78	1 101	67	1	4 404
1917	9 724	532	54	1 171	73	3	7 891
1918	12 746	305	9	1 018	54	0	11 360
1919	12 700	1 191	88	2 016	82	6	9 317
1920	10 194	1 317	88	3 448	34	−2	5 309
1921	5 287	1 365	89	1 901	70	6	1 856
1922	7 223	2 426	203	1 833	137	18	2 606
1923	11 303	3 412	328	2 984	174	24	4 381
1924	8 963	3 938	367	2 454	208	28	1 968
1925	11 465	4 072	467	2 768	258	38	3 862
1926	9 949	3 789	542	2 648	268	38	2 664
1927	10 758	3 122	559	1 748	284	37	5 008
1928	6 949	2 783	460	1 653	261	29	1 763
1929	11 789	1 769	275	1 971	250	24	7 500
1930	8 272	439	24	−247	234	18	7 804
1931	5 524	−108	−24	−1 750	125	−5	7 286
1932	−2 043	−1 225	−121	−3 232	−4	−32	2 571
1933	−4 877	−1 382	−125	−2 925	−88	−49	−308
1934	−2 424	−1 128	−141	−1 891	−92	−46	874
1935	−348	−683	−133	−738	−81	−41	1 328
1936	3 553	−12	−54	597	−32	−31	3 085
1937	6 142	371	−3	1 149	−21	−22	4 668
1938	3 961	647	−30	−358	−14	−16	3 732
1939	6 125	1 433	21	692	−24	−13	4 016
1940	6 881	1 841	11	1 856	−1	−5	3 179
1941	11 618	2 474	25	3 104	22	4	5 989
1942	25 917	612	−33	−169	−61	−8	25 576
1943	30 078	−235	−16	−332	−123	−16	30 800
1944	33 485	−268	−17	4	−98	−8	33 872
1945	32 427	36	−35	1 056	−52	1	31 421
1946	22 574	3 378	15	7 910	135	37	11 099
1947	25 130	5 561	65	11 390	253	57	7 804
1948	29 449	7 495	162	11 418	465	93	9 816
1949	25 655	6 695	238	11 220	653	123	6 726

[1] Shown separately in Table T-8.

Column 1 – 1897–1949: Sum of cols. 2–22 less sum of cols. 23–26.

Column 2 – 1897–1949: Table R-4, sum of cols. 1 to 4 less col. 7 plus Table R-7, col. 1 less col. 5.

Column 3 – 1897–1949: Nonprofit institutions' expenditures on new construction from Table R-17, col. 1.

Column 4 – 1897–1949: Sum of Table Q-5, col. 1. Table Q-14, col. 4, and Table P-16, col. 4.

Column 5 – 1897–1949: Nonprofit institutions' expenditures on producer durables taken as about 20 percent of their expenditures on new construction (cf. notes to Table P-1, col. 4).

Column 6 – 1897–1949: Table A-3, sum of cols. 10 and 11.

Column 7 – 1897–1949: Table L-1, col. 2.

Column 8 – 1897–1949: Table L-1, cols. 3 and 6 less first differences of Table U-1, col. 1 less Table L-23, cols. 6 and 9.

Column 9 – 1897–1949: Table L-38, col. 6.

Column 10 – 1911–1949: First differences of Table L-44, col. 2.

Column 11 – 1911–1949: Table L-42, col. 3.

Column 12 – 1897–1949: Table J-11, col. 5.

Column 13 – 1897–1949: Table M-2, col. 1.

Column 14 – 1897–1949: Table I-8, col. 11.

Column 15 – 1897–1949: Sum of Table I-9, col. 7, Table I-14, col. 10, and Table I-4, col. 9.

Column 16 – 1920–1949: Table F-30, col. 1.

Column 17 – 1915–1949: Table G-19, col. 1 less sum of cols. 4 and 9.

Column 18 – 1921–1939: Taken as equal to zero on assumption that employee contributions equaled employee benefits for this period.
1940–1949: Employee contributions less employee benefits roughly estimated on basis described in notes to Table I-15, col. 1.

Column 19 – 1897–1949: Table V-1, col. 2 less accrued interest on savings bonds from Table V-3, col. 3 less col. 6; issues of Adjusted Service Bonds from Bureau of Public Debt; and change in holdings of U.S. Government bonds by unincorporated business, from first differences in Table U-1, col. 2.

Column 20 – 1897–1949: Table V-1, col. 3.

Column 21 – 1897–1949: Table V-1, col. 4.

Column 22 – 1897–1949: Table V-1, sum of cols. 5–8.

Column 23 – 1897–1949: First differences of Table D-8, col. 11. Possible small amounts of accrued interest included in loans outstanding are not treated here.

Column 24 – 1897–1923: First differences of Table D-1, cols. 8–10 minus col. 3.
1924–1949: First differences of Table D-1, cols. 8–10 minus col. 3 less first differences from Table D-7, col. 6.

Column 25 – 1897–1949: Table R-4, col. 6 plus Table R-7, sum of cols. 3 and 4.

Column 26 – 1897–1949: Table R-17, sum of cols. 3 and 4.

$ mill.

Year	Total	Real estate		Consumer durables	Producer durables	Farm land and subdivisions	Currency	Commer-cial bank deposits	Savings bank deposits
		Resi-dential	Nonresi-dential						
	1	2	3	4	5	6	7	8	9
1897	1 489	387	73	694	13	57	11	104	18
1898	1 720	378	68	726	13	57	32	116	39
1899	2 693	436	69	873	13	58	88	201	34
1900	2 150	393	99	906	19	63	47	152	104
1901	2 927	527	98	1 029	19	69	35	287	35
1902	3 417	673	114	1 124	22	74	48	213	47
1903	2 876	824	91	1 193	18	79	50	104	18
1904	2 900	806	80	1 180	16	84	−67	111	22
1905	4 257	1 005	89	1 369	18	89	178	547	73
1906	4 468	1 173	120	1 601	24	94	47	181	51
1907	3 889	1 207	139	1 664	28	100	93	−141	−53
1908	3 921	1 089	102	1 353	20	105	−235	29	−72
1909	4 656	1 274	108	1 634	22	110	46	450	43
1910	4 530	1 306	110	1 775	22	113	42	203	11
1911	4 686	1 238	100	1 875	20	115	−43	535	6
1912	5 955	1 339	118	2 113	24	117	72	366	29
1913	5 192	1 350	145	2 331	29	119	59	110	10
1914	4 583	1 240	104	2 116	21	118	−110	−93	−59
1915	7 034	1 269	90	2 202	17	125	237	986	−25
1916	9 245	1 421	120	3 131	23	132	262	1 538	128
1917	12 758	1 242	137	3 447	26	142	409	2 364	−75
1918	15 660	998	122	3 529	23	153	725	568	−54
1919	15 503	1 981	151	4 813	29	181	6	2 896	225
1920	13 356	2 165	107	6 654	21	−201	375	−1 789	256
1921	9 214	2 257	147	5 473	29	−166	−619	−1 016	29
1922	11 027	3 479	217	5 671	43	−154	80	1 607	132
1923	15 729	4 665	257	7 216	51	−135	71	799	125
1924	13 792	5 315	284	7 182	57	−114	−17	1 523	174
1925	16 791	5 642	352	8 004	70	345	−110	894	112
1926	15 777	5 519	368	8 452	74	326	2	−1 164	151
1927	17 169	4 942	391	8 038	78	314	−32	2 194	246
1928	13 796	4 583	375	8 355	75	297	−52	−2 407	138
1929	18 446	3 450	371	9 083	74	288	12	−1 354	−326
1930	14 601	1 921	362	7 050	72	17	20	−828	191
1931	11 752	1 348	258	5 384	52	16	668	−2 580	174
1932	4 780	138	132	3 542	26	4	272	−1 929	−448
1933	1 941	−41	47	3 372	9	5	125	−1 690	−731
1934	4 070	204	44	4 054	9	5	−8	916	−40
1935	5 890	665	55	5 052	11	−5	108	1 976	−120
1936	7 982	1 439	91	6 409	18	−6	466	1 777	−37
1937	11 260	1 903	117	7 129	23	−6	178	260	−107
1938	8 524	2 182	126	5 632	25	−5	19	−46	−108
1939	11 233	3 061	118	6 644	24	−5	366	1 968	31
1940	12 498	3 508	142	7 970	28	−92	786	842	−73
1941	19 127	4 216	166	9 582	33	−93	1 765	1 185	−313
1942	29 378	2 343	84	6 459	17	−103	3 616	3 014	−77
1943	34 710	1 543	23	6 164	5	−121	4 024	5 745	884
1944	37 252	1 535	48	6 439	10	−136	4 093	6 932	1 428
1945	33 865	1 852	94	7 604	19	86	2 321	8 361	1 778
1946	26 451	5 318	284	15 108	57	101	−197	6 752	1 232
1947	29 398	7 690	410	19 977	82	108	−259	625	649
1948	33 776	9 882	630	21 741	126	116	−233	−1 298	342
1949	32 919	9 322	831	23 423	166	113	−424	−306	538

NONAGRICULTURAL INDIVIDUALS' SAVING BY MAJOR COMPONENTS
Cash Flow Concept; Current Values: 1897 to 1949

$ mill.

Year	Postal Savings	Credit unions	Savings and loan associations	Mort-gage holdings	Life insurance		Pension and retirement funds		
					Stock and mutual	Frater-nal orders	U.S. Govern-ment	State and local	Private
	10	11	12	13	14	15	16	17	18
1897	–	–	–44	57	79	5	–	–	–
1898	–	–	–23	53	87	6	–	–	–
1899	–	–	–42	56	100	4	–	–	–
1900	–	–	–24	46	113	9	–	–	–
1901	–	–	–25	50	130	13	–	–	–
1902	–	–	–15	52	153	13	–	–	–
1903	–	–	–7	67	145	19	–	–	–
1904	–	–	–6	61	172	12	–	–	–
1905	–	–	–8	65	179	21	–	–	–
1906	–	–	7	40	170	17	–	–	–
1907	–	–	13	66	129	19	–	–	–
1908	–	–	4	73	118	21	–	–	–
1909	–	–	14	56	152	–3	–	–	–
1910	•	–	22	202	137	23	–	–	–
1911	11	0	30	235	153	37	–	–	–
1912	17	0	41	241	160	29	–	–	–
1913	12	0	30	603	155	31	–	–	–
1914	19	0	23	459	147	28	–	–	–
1915	15	0	40	257	178	23	–	–14	–
1916	38	0	21	462	253	29	–	–16	–
1917	31	0	57	995	296	47	–	–18	–
1918	25	1	31	389	267	22	–	–20	–
1919	–7	1	79	934	462	25	–	–23	–
1920	2	2	170	1 960	554	58	41	–24	–
1921	–17	2	155	259	464	68	64	–27	0
1922	–14	2	197	–32	552	83	42	–31	0
1923	–1	3	274	338	707	28	40	–34	0
1924	2	2	380	–296	737	105	41	–40	0
1925	1	2	336	525	932	77	33	–46	0
1926	5	3	327	732	1 003	73	28	–53	0
1927	10	4	387	1 260	1 101	87	32	–62	0
1928	5	6	294	1 580	1 142	98	27	–64	0
1929	10	0	146	1 824	951	80	–62	–73	0
1930	81	–6	–217	685	789	75	–93	–75	0
1931	361	–3	–626	–379	462	65	–823	–79	0
1932	296	–3	–764	–517	–5	39	–131	–83	0
1933	307	0	–681	–1 136	301	41	–52	–89	0
1934	–2	5	–497	–731	832	58	–31	–97	0
1935	–6	12	–533	–103	1 160	58	–23	–105	0
1936	59	20	–379	–70	1 284	55	–74	–115	0
1937	10	26	–291	–50	1 223	72	328	–118	0
1938	–18	26	–201	–308	1 132	77	–160	–118	0
1939	27	36	–46	–364	1 246	76	–206	–113	0
1940	25	46	83	–338	1 357	59	–292	–114	–20
1941	49	57	186	58	1 570	85	–28	–133	–30
1942	65	8	66	–250	1 808	103	284	–150	–20
1943	370	9	•406	–246	2 160	131	1 116	–166	10
1944	554	34	613	15	2 395	140	1 356	–173	90
1945	591	23	870	639	2 461	185	767	–180	120
1946	351	49	991	1 568	2 653	152	–610	–130	110
1947	133	76	984	1 670	2 633	175	–319	–126	160
1948	–87	82	955	1 187	2 650	148	–429	–98	120
1949	–141	93	1 199	599	2 475	143	–1 678	–119	110

$ mill.

| Year | Securities | | | | Borrowing on securities | Consumer debt | Residential real estate debt | Real estate debt of nonprofit institutions |
	U.S. Government bonds	State and local bonds	Corporate and foreign bonds	Stocks				
	19	20	21	22	23	24	25	26
1897	−24	31	58	105	71	45	−1	20
1898	92	26	121	99	71	60	19	20
1899	129	56	287	543	109	57	26	20
1900	−45	18	235	259	111	49	64	20
1901	−33	31	393	561	149	60	63	20
1902	−16	2	465	715	76	74	97	20
1903	−24	15	82	475	71	72	110	20
1904	−24	20	302	356	30	43	132	20
1905	−7	45	664	353	143	91	169	20
1906	7	67	417	805	42	104	187	20
1907	−75	122	81	692	−49	89	135	20
1908	3	212	610	656	36	−24	134	21
1909	−32	10	529	745	105	148	228	21
1910	8	138	−26	804	8	95	236	21
1911	19	109	407	250	52	134	204	21
1912	4	143	667	929	104	112	217	21
1913	−1	8	198	536	−15	106	411	31
1914	−2	226	471	456	108	86	356	31
1915	−3	299	1 459	688	397	132	249	31
1916	−123	218	1 089	1 380	284	218	328	31
1917	2 601	213	692	956	137	19	617	31
1918	7 120	497	1 005	956	367	28	271	31
1919	2 698	28	524	1 999	792	310	362	35
1920	−218	682	1 668	1 818	−669	412	1 166	36
1921	−111	696	1 400	956	−84	59	811	43
1922	−2 336	745	1 262	1 347	655	160	996	54
1923	−27	624	1 567	1 228	−104	350	1 700	121
1924	−1 466	195	1 436	1 254	842	258	1 737	125
1925	−195	225	1 937	2 093	1 478	624	2179	157
1926	−589	149	1 895	1 761	−2	531	2 603	150
1927	−2 360	446	2 019	2 075	1 327	189	2 393	92
1928	−1 075	379	1 628	3 406	1 645	751	2 500	98
1929	−373	508	660	4 789	−1 329	926	1 949	66
1930	−77	585	666	1 278	−2 051	−652	546	52
1931	770	1 781	556	599	−2 010	−1 145	−633	40
1932	689	128	−398	227	−1 026	−1 280	−1 257	−2
1933	1 108	−912	−100	437	−45	−214	−1 360	−2
1934	−183	−857	39	420	−284	442	−86	−2
1935	−864	−8	−938	−67	−114	876	−325	−2
1936	−955	−360	−915	185	−27	1 212	−273	−2
1937	836	97	−1 059	831	−520	640	56	−34
1938	−77	−45	−45	228	−97	−232	156	−35
1939	−200	−118	−674	568	−153	838	546	−25
1940	145	−129	−416	491	−277	1 051	761	−25
1941	2 677	−151	−963	627	−90	588	955	−35
1942	8 842	−183	61	189	64	−2 998	−231	−37
1943	11 854	−150	−653	470	563	−1 110	−545	−40
1944	14 392	−76	−1 141	519	1 567	396	−108	−40
1945	9 418	−306	−1 580	1 246	1 384	766	394	−40
1946	−2 961	−218	−1 226	1 818	−2 662	3 179	4 241	−7
1947	559	411	−694	2 074	−477	3 112	4 940	45
1948	2 038	1 184	574	1 441	−116	2 415	4 901	95
1949	520	906	94	1 620	197	2 309	3 914	145

TABLE T–11

Column 1 – Table T-1, col. 4 minus the following: sum of Table A-3, cols. 3, 4, and 6 and Table A-3, col. 12 minus Table A-54, first differences of cols. 2 and 5, Table A-65, col. 2, and Table A-3, col. 11, allocated to farm operators and nonfarm owners on basis of Table A-14, col. 6 linearly interpolating between the percentages.

Column 2 – Table T-1, col. 3 plus the proportion of agricultural saving allocated to nonfarm owners (see notes to col. 1).

Column 3 – Col. 2 plus alternative estimate of nonagricultural individuals' saving through residential construction as given in Table R-3, col. 6.

Column 4 – Table T-2, col. 4 minus the following: sum of Table A-1, cols. 3, 4, and 6 and Table A-1, col. 12 minus Table A-54, first differences of cols. 2 and 5, Table A-65, col. 2 and Table A-3, col. 11, allocated on basis of Table A-14, col. 6.

Column 5 – Table T-3, col. 3 plus the proportion of col. 4 allocated to nonfarmers.

Column 6 – Col. 5 plus Table R-3, col. 4.

General note: These figures do not reflect slight revisions made in the underlying tables after Table T-11 was prepared.

TABLE T–12

Columns 1 to 8 – Table T-1, cols. 1–8, respectively, divided by Table T-16, col. 1.

TABLE T–13

Columns 1 to 8 – Table T-1, cols. 1–8, respectively, divided by Table T-16, col. 2.

Social and Business Accounting Concepts: 1897 to 1949

$ mill.

Year	Social accounting concept			Business accounting concept		
	Farm operators	Other individuals		Farm operators	Other individuals	
		Estimate A	Estimate B		Estimate A	Estimate B
	1	2	3	4	5	6
1897	32	669	682	286	658	667
1898	156	900	907	209	849	854
1899	75	1 756	1 769	362	1 860	1 875
1900	−45	1 081	1 081	107	1 197	1 202
1901	−272	1 700	1 724	107	1 974	2 002
1902	291	2 401	2 451	232	2 492	2 546
1903	−122	1 590	1 663	−59	1 767	1 847
1904	21	1 612	1 676	54	1 762	1 833
1905	29	2 939	3 039	262	3 208	3 316
1906	17	2 976	3 090	427	3 376	3 501
1907	−192	2 169	2 296	125	2 588	2 728
1908	−11	2 341	2 443	131	2 604	2 719
1909	15	3 158	3 292	561	3 551	3 696
1910	−31	2 815	2 948	50	2 987	3 132
1911	−437	2 566	2 684	−265	2 888	3 017
1912	119	4 027	4 158	271	4 383	4 527
1913	−460	2 645	2 779	163	3 307	3 450
1914	257	2 214	2 320	145	2 428	2 543
1915	122	4 551	4 657	113	4 829	4 947
1916	−710	5 461	5 584	541	6 669	6 812
1917	957	8 914	8 980	2 905	11 071	11 177
1918	1 619	10 798	10 787	2 529	13 038	13 099
1919	−1 413	9 986	10 123	−979	12 444	12 682
1920	−1 387	6 250	6 347	−3 209	8 596	8 859
1921	−1 233	2 401	2 568	−2 295	3 921	4 194
1922	−127	5 885	6 285	682	7 531	8 016
1923	329	9 792	10 362	664	11 379	12 061
1924	590	7 729	8 409	1 387	9 334	10 122
1925	−38	10 630	11 340	234	11 680	12 494
1926	−23	9 258	9 916	34	9 920	10 082
1927	−94	10 153	10 684	507	11 082	11 713
1928	60	6 333	6 804	519	7 265	7 836
1929	76	11 030	11 293	143	11 875	12 252
1930	−125	7 937	7 951	−1 457	7 399	7 517
1931	−30	6 044	6 006	−1 393	4 757	4 793
1932	152	−678	−829	−702	−2 454	−2 584
1933	81	−3 448	−3 632	608	−4 515	−4 679
1934	−473	−2 107	−2 283	578	−2 342	−2 473
1935	998	873	784	1 556	321	267
1936	311	4 128	4 128	1 055	3 948	3 996
1937	849	6 561	6 585	381	6 123	6 230
1938	268	4 117	4 148	40	4 007	4 130
1939	679	6 257	6 410	833	6 420	6 670
1940	737	6 745	6 955	833	7 160	7 480
1941	2 280	11 001	11 293	3 707	12 926	13 357
1942	4 253	24 592	24 502	5 964	27 677	27 749
1943	4 226	28 019	27 735	5 324	30 821	30 719
1944	4 078	30 916	30 600	4 455	33 741	33 648
1945	3 585	29 341	29 075	4 667	32 990	32 980
1946	2 967	18 880	19 235	5 673	24 429	25 098
1947	1 468	19 235	19 893	5 660	27 414	28 522
1948	2 489	24 139	25 102	2 501	30 724	32 222
1949	1 263	20 125	20 967	699	25 656	26 997

NATIONAL SAVING BY MAJOR SAVER GROUPS

Social Accounting Concept; Deflated by Gross National Product Deflator (1929 = 100)
1897 to 1949

$ mill.

Year	National saving	Personal saving				Corporate saving	Government saving	
		Total	Nonagricultural individuals	Agriculture	Unincorporated business		State and local	Federal
	1	2	3	4	5	6	7	8
1897	2 123	1 243	1 498	95	−350	668	157	55
1898	3 682	2 927	1 870	530	527	841	155	−241
1899	5 875	4 562	3 592	223	748	1 138	148	27
1900	4 204	2 548	2 136	−58	470	1 344	248	64
1901	4 440	2 726	3 556	−700	−300	1 296	236	182
1902	7 737	5 769	4 341	937	490	1 420	424	125
1903	5 319	2 887	3 092	−267	62	2 052	275	106
1904	4 006	2 792	3 067	163	−437	776	443	−6
1905	8 294	6 650	5 519	188	942	1 304	267	73
1906	7 511	5 786	5 173	171	441	1 304	205	216
1907	5 302	3 556	3 812	−461	205	1 310	268	168
1908	4 456	3 629	4 187	49	−607	751	147	−71
1909	6 584	5 357	5 496	170	−309	746	400	80
1910	7 792	5 498	4 734	−15	780	1 871	273	149
1911	4 890	3 490	4 637	−1 088	−58	962	332	107
1912	8 172	6 623	6 059	419	145	883	463	203
1913	6 464	4 167	4 447	−1 033	753	1 431	705	161
1914	5 486	3 977	3 234	627	116	1 158	311	41
1915	9 649	7 206	6 871	318	17	1 917	303	223
1916	13 304	7 726	8 129	−1 531	1 128	4 433	299	846
1917	11 409	11 577	9 945	1 401	231	2 902	184	−3 254
1918	1 640	12 945	11 139	1 532	274	431	62	−11 798
1919	5 969	8 876	9 392	−1 598	1 083	2 258	120	−5 285
1920	7 975	5 254	5 198	−1 307	1 364	2 750	−150	121
1921	2 153	1 225	2 867	−1 754	112	1 274	84	−430
1922	8 029	6 364	6 016	−200	547	958	505	203
1923	13 340	9 686	9 616	324	−254	2 308	404	942
1924	12 014	8 531	7 661	575	294	1 441	1 254	788
1925	15 150	10 533	10 317	65	152	2 323	1 295	999
1926	15 428	9 809	9 024	−41	825	3 295	1 186	1 138
1927	13 692	10 074	10 173	−114	15	1 368	1 108	1 142
1928	10 799	5 954	6 222	108	−375	2 084	1 736	1 025
1929	15 968	11 485	10 979	127	379	2 136	1 248	1 099
1930	6 063	5 851	8 322	−184	−2 286	−535	941	−194
1931	−3 799	2 834	6 902	10	−4 078	−3 862	−549	−2 222
1932	−13 450	−4 196	−922	246	−3 521	−6 451	−1 222	−1 581
1933	−11 801	−5 073	−4 511	21	−584	−6 249	1 020	−1 499
1934	−5 591	−1 208	−1 837	−1 429	2 058	−3 441	1 786	−2 729
1935	293	2 900	769	1 541	590	−1 589	926	−1 944
1936	1 926	6 512	5 260	−27	1 279	−1 735	1 515	−4 367
1937	8 572	8 614	7 434	1 519	−339	−651	1 540	−932
1938	2 412	4 476	4 764	473	−761	−692	1 808	−3 181
1939	5 834	8 255	7 328	996	−69	−107	969	−3 283
1940	13 075	10 170	7 780	1 127	1 263	1 926	2 196	−1 218
1941	15 724	15 353	11 587	3 008	758	1 865	1 895	−3 388
1942	4 091	30 215	21 637	4 585	3 993	2 603	1 651	−30 378
1943	−3 010	29 890	23 013	3 636	3 241	3 499	2 248	−38 647
1944	−5 732	30 944	24 235	3 320	3 390	3 769	2 493	−42 939
1945	−5 712	28 445	22 902	2 822	2 721	1 959	2 021	−38 136
1946	19 869	17 879	14 698	2 640	540	1 669	1 702	−1 381
1947	23 279	14 522	13 873	1 021	−372	3 060	1 153	4 543
1948	28 110	17 815	15 106	2 646	63	5 983	730	3 582
1949	20 915	15 072	13 147	1 207	717	6 358	853	−1 367

Social Accounting Concept; Deflated by Index of Wage Level (1929 = 100)
1897 to 1949

$ mill.

| Year | National saving | Personal saving | | | | Corporate saving | Government saving | |
| | | Total | Nonagricultural individuals | Agriculture | Unincorporated business | | State and local | Federal |
	1	2	3	4	5	6	7	8
1897	3 221	1 886	2 272	145	−531	1 014	238	83
1898	5 400	4 293	2 743	777	773	1 233	227	−353
1899	9 097	7 065	5 561	345	1 158	1 761	229	42
1900	6 569	3 981	3 338	−91	734	2 100	388	100
1901	6 938	4 259	5 556	−1 094	−203	2 025	369	284
1902	11 958	8 915	6 709	1 448	758	2 194	654	194
1903	7 903	4 289	4 594	−397	91	3 048	408	157
1904	5 837	4 069	4 469	237	−637	1 131	646	−8
1905	11 981	9 606	7 972	272	1 361	1 883	386	106
1906	11 368	8 757	7 830	259	668	1 973	311	327
1907	8 021	5 379	5 767	−697	310	1 982	405	254
1908	6 450	5 253	6 060	71	−879	1 087	213	−103
1909	9 454	7 692	7 892	244	−444	1 072	574	115
1910	10 945	7 724	6 650	−21	1 095	2 628	383	210
1911	6 986	4 986	6 624	−1 555	−83	1 374	474	152
1912	12 163	9 858	9 019	623	216	1 314	688	302
1913	9 402	6 061	6 468	−1 502	1 095	2 082	1 025	234
1914	7 802	5 656	4 600	891	164	1 647	442	58
1915	13 635	10 183	9 709	450	24	2 709	428	315
1916	19 158	11 126	11 706	−2 204	1 624	6 384	430	1 218
1917	17 725	17 986	15 450	2 177	359	4 509	286	−5 055
1918	2 363	18 656	16 053	2 207	396	620	90	−17 003
1919	8 311	12 359	13 077	−2 225	1 508	3 144	167	−7 359
1920	10 719	7 062	6 986	−1 757	1 833	3 696	−201	162
1921	2 629	1 495	3 500	−2 142	137	1 556	102	−524
1922	9 463	7 500	7 090	−236	645	1 128	595	239
1923	14 953	10 857	10 778	364	−285	2 587	453	1 056
1924	13 047	9 265	8 320	625	319	1 564	1 362	856
1925	16 266	11 309	11 077	69	163	2 494	1 390	1 073
1926	16 383	10 415	9 582	−43	876	3 499	1 260	1 208
1927	13 971	10 280	10 381	−116	15	1 396	1 131	1 165
1928	11 017	6 075	6 347	110	−383	2 126	1 771	1 045
1929	15 968	11 485	10 979	127	379	2 136	1 248	1 099
1930	5 820	5 617	7 989	−177	−2 195	−514	903	−186
1931	−3 554	2 652	6 457	10	−3 815	−3 613	−514	−2 078
1932	−12 952	−4 041	−888	237	−3 390	−6 212	−1 176	−1 522
1933	−11 064	−4 756	−4 229	20	−548	−5 859	956	−1 405
1934	−4 749	−1 026	−1 560	−1 214	1 748	−2 923	1 517	−2 318
1935	247	2 447	649	1 300	498	−1 341	781	−1 641
1936	1 592	5 383	4 348	−22	1 057	−1 434	1 252	−3 609
1937	6 746	6 780	5 851	1 195	−267	−512	1 212	−733
1938	1 788	3 317	3 530	351	−564	−512	1 340	−2 357
1939	4 285	6 065	5 382	732	−50	−79	712	−2 412
1940	9 387	7 302	5 585	809	907	1 383	1 577	−874
1941	11 267	11 001	8 302	2 155	543	1 336	1 357	−2 428
1942	3 125	23 081	16 528	3 503	3 050	1 988	1 261	−23 206
1943	−2 276	22 604	17 404	2 749	2 451	2 646	1 700	−29 227
1944	−4 282	23 117	18 105	2 480	2 532	2 816	1 862	−32 078
1945	−4 154	20 687	16 656	2 052	1 979	1 424	1 470	−27 735
1946	13 176	11 856	9 747	1 751	358	1 107	1 129	−916
1947	15 121	9 433	9 011	663	−242	1 988	749	2 951
1948	18 019	11 420	9 683	1 696	41	3 835	468	2 296
1949	12 617	9 092	7 931	728	433	3 835	514	−825

Column 1   – Sum of cols. 2, 6, 7, and 8.

Column 2   – Sum of cols. 3–5.

Columns 3 and 4 – Table T-1, cols. 3 and 4 divided by Table T-16, cols. 3 and 4, respectively.

Columns 5 and 6 – Table T-1, cols. 5 and 6 divided by Table T-16, col. 5.

Columns 7 and 8 – Table T-1, cols. 7 and 8 divided by Table T-16, cols. 6 and 7, respectively.

Social Accounting Concept; Deflated by Indices of Group Purchasing Power (1929 = 100)
1897 to 1949

$ mill.

Year	National saving	Personal saving				Corporate saving	Government saving	
		Total	Nonagricultural individuals	Agriculture	Unincorporated business		State and local	Federal
	1	2	3	4	5	6	7	8
1897	2 225	1 257	1 533	100	−376	717	186	65
1898	3 777	2 996	1 914	530	552	881	179	−279
1899	6 362	4 944	3 918	228	798	1 213	173	32
1900	4 556	2 764	2 322	−58	500	1 430	288	74
1901	4 810	2 945	3 783	−700	−138	1 379	274	212
1902	8 182	6 052	4 612	919	521	1 508	480	142
1903	5 565	2 956	3 153	−262	65	2 178	311	120
1904	4 122	2 830	3 128	157	−455	808	491	−7
1905	8 634	6 901	5 740	181	980	1 356	296	81
1906	8 107	6 221	5 571	175	475	1 404	235	247
1907	5 777	3 852	4 089	−461	224	1 431	304	190
1908	4 713	3 834	4 429	47	−642	794	165	−80
1909	7 049	5 757	5 919	158	−320	774	431	87
1910	8 317	5 885	5 078	−14	821	1 971	298	163
1911	5 543	4 007	5 058	−989	−62	1 030	383	123
1912	8 928	7 148	6 573	412	163	991	548	241
1913	7 304	4 736	4 907	−1 002	831	1 579	805	184
1914	5 971	4 255	3 508	617	130	1 300	368	48
1915	10 579	7 891	7 569	304	18	2 077	352	259
1916	14 818	8 962	9 145	−1 360	1 177	4 626	321	909
1917	12 820	13 027	11 536	1 257	234	2 936	188	−3 331
1918	2 549	13 988	12 405	1 317	266	418	63	−11 920
1919	6 868	9 970	10 229	−1 342	1 083	2 258	125	−5 485
1920	8 327	5 649	5 553	−1 247	1 343	2 706	−147	119
1921	2 091	1 149	2 894	−1 861	116	1 312	90	−460
1922	8 221	6 451	6 078	−204	577	1 009	543	218
1923	13 610	9 883	9 808	334	−259	2 354	412	961
1924	12 140	8 622	7 738	587	297	1 455	1 267	796
1925	15 198	10 535	10 317	65	153	2 346	1 308	1 009
1926	15 554	9 824	9 024	−42	842	3 360	1 210	1 160
1927	13 590	9 972	10 072	−115	15	1 368	1 108	1 142
1928	10 906	6 013	6 284	108	−379	2 105	1 753	1 035
1929	15 968	11 485	10 979	127	379	2 136	1 248	1 099
1930	5 835	5 655	8 152	−186	−2 311	−541	921	−200
1931	−3 679	2 726	6 747	11	−4 032	−3 818	−531	−2 056
1932	−13 007	−4 101	−899	274	−3 476	−6 370	−1 135	−1 401
1933	−11 356	−5 042	−4 511	23	−554	−5 933	911	−1 292
1934	−5 168	−1 441	−1 860	−1 429	1 848	−3 089	1 585	−2 223
1935	630	2 851	779	1 541	531	−1 430	833	−1 624
1936	2 597	6 371	5 260	−27	1 138	−1 544	1 379	−3 609
1937	8 838	8 751	7 523	1 519	−291	−559	1 408	−762
1938	3 056	4 668	4 822	491	−645	−586	1 614	−2 640
1939	6 556	8 498	7 509	1 047	−58	−91	874	−2 725
1940	12 801	10 219	7 970	1 199	1 050	1 602	1 983	−1 003
1941	16 922	16 119	12 260	3 220	639	1 571	1 759	−2 527
1942	13 456	33 871	25 054	5 095	3 722	2 426	1 730	−24 571
1943	7 269	34 806	27 570	4 073	3 163	3 415	2 450	−33 402
1944	3 688	37 263	30 175	3 698	3 390	3 769	2 753	−40 097
1945	2 067	33 664	27 918	3 087	2 659	1 914	2 120	−35 631
1946	21 214	19 252	16 246	2 540	466	1 440	1 589	−1 067
1947	22 343	15 419	14 834	887	−302	2 488	1 041	3 395
1948	26 781	18 557	16 185	2 321	51	4 825	629	2 770
1949	20 697	15 923	14 195	1 153	575	5 093	710	−1 029

Columns 1 and 2 – Table T-2, col. 1 divided by Table T-16, cols. 1 and 2, respectively.

Column 3   – Sum of col. 6, Table T-2, col. 6 divided by Table T-16, col. 5 and Table T-2, cols. 7 and 8 divided by Table T-16, cols. 6 and 7, respectively.

Columns 4 and 5 – Table T-2, col. 2 divided by Table T-16, cols. 1 and 2, respectively.

Column 6   – Sum of Table T-2, cols. 3–5, divided by Table T-16, cols. 3–5, respectively.

Columns 7 and 8 – Table T-3, col. 1 divided by Table T-16, cols. 1 and 2, respectively.

Column 9   – Sum of col. 12, Table T-3, col. 6 divided by Table T-16, col. 5 and Table T-3, cols. 7 and 8 divided by Table T-16, cols. 6 and 7 respectively.

Columns 10 and 11 – Table T-3, col. 2 divided by Table T-16, cols. 1 and 2, respectively.

Column 12   – Sum of Table T-3, cols. 3–5 divided by Table T-16, cols. 3–5, respectively.

Business Accounting and Cash Flow Concepts; Deflated by Various Deflators (1929 = 100) 1897 to 1949

$ mill.

Year	Business accounting concept						Cash flow concept					
	National saving			Personal saving			National saving			Personal saving		
	Gross national product	Wage level	Purchasing power	Gross national product	Wage level	Purchasing power	Gross national product	Wage level	Purchasing power	Gross national product	Wage level	Purchasing power
	1	2	3	4	5	6	7	8	9	10	11	12
1897	2 818	4 276	2 965	1 802	2 734	1 851	7 077	10 738	7 413	5 275	8 003	5 446
1898	3 825	5 610	3 921	2 930	4 297	2 993	8 195	12 020	8 415	6 434	9 437	6 570
1899	8 250	12 774	8 845	6 127	9 487	6 571	12 469	19 306	13 377	9 402	14 558	10 078
1900	4 808	7 513	5 174	3 054	4 772	3 276	8 994	14 053	9 419	6 300	9 844	6 513
1901	6 188	9 669	6 599	4 184	6 538	4 425	10 488	16 388	11 133	7 474	11 678	7 873
1902	8 867	13 703	9 398	6 292	9 724	6 623	13 288	20 536	14 034	9 631	14 885	10 102
1903	5 350	7 949	5 573	3 085	4 583	3 141	9 827	14 600	10 172	6 437	9 563	6 540
1904	5 008	7 297	5 154	3 371	4 911	3 419	9 827	14 320	10 058	7 000	10 200	7 076
1905	9 477	13 689	9 815	7 631	11 022	7 871	14 398	20 797	14 872	11 258	16 261	11 573
1906	9 839	14 892	10 552	7 546	11 422	8 053	14 893	22 541	15 951	11 264	17 049	12 004
1907	7 100	10 741	7 663	4 951	7 490	5 294	12 049	18 228	12 944	8 537	12 915	9 081
1908	5 487	7 942	5 773	4 336	6 276	4 548	11 029	15 963	11 547	8 355	12 092	8 700
1909	9 950	14 287	10 393	7 598	10 910	7 933	15 714	22 564	16 369	11 718	16 826	12 197
1910	7 914	11 117	8 427	5 680	7 979	6 054	13 820	19 414	14 565	9 885	13 886	10 392
1911	5 948	8 498	6 618	4 267	6 095	4 776	12 107	17 295	13 102	8 625	12 321	9 311
1912	10 134	15 084	11 068	7 786	11 588	8 388	16 267	24 212	17 700	12 131	18 056	13 000
1913	8 450	12 291	9 298	6 191	9 005	6 769	14 945	21 739	16 299	10 997	15 995	11 907
1914	5 286	7 518	5 775	3 997	5 684	4 302	12 188	17 333	13 212	9 175	13 049	9 808
1915	11 166	15 778	12 241	8 003	11 309	8 769	18 252	25 791	19 798	13 306	18 802	14 405
1916	20 722	29 840	22 201	12 815	18 454	13 911	29 232	42 094	31 180	18 543	26 702	20 011
1917	20 375	31 654	21 675	17 923	27 845	19 229	26 020	40 423	27 731	22 972	35 689	24 715
1918	7 613	10 972	8 473	17 111	24 660	18 149	14 437	20 806	15 346	21 610	31 144	22 811
1919	11 347	15 800	12 371	12 352	17 199	13 560	19 458	27 094	20 554	16 480	22 947	17 717
1920	6 543	8 795	7 241	5 083	6 832	5 805	14 138	19 030	14 914	9 171	12 327	10 005
1921	-2 304	-2 813	-2 583	167	203	-37	7 042	8 598	7 049	5 850	7 143	5 785
1922	11 965	14 101	12 277	9 238	10 888	9 384	21 420	25 245	22 029	15 052	17 739	15 295
1923	15 873	17 791	16 197	11 755	13 176	11 997	25 705	28 812	26 240	18 034	20 214	18 416
1924	14 941	16 226	15 108	11 014	11 961	11 142	25 665	27 873	25 953	17 776	19 305	17 985
1925	17 502	18 792	17 563	12 045	12 933	12 053	28 484	30 583	28 604	19 273	20 693	19 301
1926	15 069	16 001	15 176	10 207	10 838	10 218	27 216	28 900	27 452	17 976	19 088	18 028
1927	15 184	15 494	15 085	11 523	11 758	11 424	28 650	29 235	28 503	20 456	20 873	20 309
1928	12 807	13 066	12 997	7 417	7 567	7 483	26 892	27 435	27 138	16 761	17 100	16 906
1929	17 078	17 078	17 078	12 344	12 344	12 344	32 186	32 186	32 186	21 701	21 701	21 701
1930	-275	-264	-580	3 108	2 984	2 874	16 364	15 709	16 016	12 677	12 170	12 340
1931	-11 886	-11 119	-11 849	-972	-910	-1 211	5 577	5 217	5 381	9 497	8 884	9 182
1932	-21 062	-20 281	-20 702	-8 115	-7 815	-8 161	-1 540	-1 483	-1 416	43 782	4 216	4 310
1933	-11 556	-10 834	-11 067	-5 245	-4 918	-5 151	7 715	7 233	7 874	7 636	7 159	7 780
1934	-4 053	-3 443	-3 700	-147	-125	-400	13 401	11 384	13 131	11 541	9 803	11 226
1935	493	416	794	2 947	2 486	2 879	17 110	14 436	16 814	13 706	11 565	13 593
1936	3 643	3 011	4 201	7 351	6 076	7 194	17 290	14 291	17 217	15 759	13 026	15 454
1937	7 311	5 754	7 604	7 661	6 030	7 779	22 692	17 859	22 018	16 468	12 961	16 484
1938	629	466	1 477	3 934	2 915	4 140	16 612	12 311	16 266	12 261	9 087	12 398
1939	6 898	5 066	7 533	8 916	6 549	9 134	22 205	16 310	21 987	17 893	13 142	18 147
1940	12 863	4 235	12 751	10 957	7 867	10 998	26 780	19 226	26 090	20 421	14 662	20 515
1941	21 996	15 761	23 041	20 081	14 389	20 928	31 612	22 651	34 158	31 019	22 226	32 263
1942	11 889	9 082	21 633	35 112	26 822	39 305	15 744	12 026	27 022	40 502	30 939	45 265
1943	2 944	2 226	13 736	33 423	25 276	38 863	8 548	6 464	20 872	39 305	29 724	45 629
1944	-1 834	-1 370	8 192	33 690	25 168	40 574	10 255	7 661	21 060	38 572	28 816	46 321
1945	364	265	8 768	32 406	23 568	38 271	11 297	8 216	19 754	35 375	25 727	41 578
1946	34 363	22 788	34 863	26 144	17 338	27 494	44 136	29 269	44 142	31 205	20 694	32 730
1947	40 378	26 227	37 641	24 924	16 189	25 214	48 165	31 285	45 015	30 129	19 570	30 309
1948	37 259	23 884	35 391	22 909	14 685	23 855	48 211	30 904	45 121	28 136	18 036	28 944
1949	25 444	15 349	25 365	18 364	11 078	19 582	39 894	24 066	38 534	25 999	15 684	27 330

Column 1 – 1896–1928: Gross national product in current prices divided by gross national product in 1929 prices, based on preliminary version of estimates made by S. Kuznets (unpublished).

1929–1941: Gross national product in current prices divided by gross national product in 1939 prices, shifted to 1929 base, derived from data in Department of Commerce, *Survey of Current Business*, July 1950, p. 9, Jan. 1951, p. 9, and Feb. 1951, pp. 4, 9.

1942–1945: The 1941 figure linked to Kuznets' gross national product deflator ("Long-Term Changes in the National Income of the United States of America since 1870," *Income and Wealth*, Series II, p. 40), in order to adjust the Department of Commerce series for the probable overpricing of certain types of war expenditures.

1946–1949: Same procedure as for 1929–1941.

Column 2 – 1896–1924: Snyder's index of money wages as shown in Tucker, "Statistics of Gold and Prices, 1791–1932," *Review of Economic Statistics*, 1934, pp. 25–27, shifted to 1929 base. The 1925 figure in this series differs from Clark's figure by only a fraction of one percent.

1925–1947: Index of hourly wages based on average of quarterly data in Clark, "A System of Equations Explaining the U.S. Trade Cycle," *Econometrica*, 1949, pp. 110–114.

1948–1949: Index of hourly wages based on continuation of Clark's method.

Column 3 – 1896–1912: Snyder's cost of living index (from Tucker, *op. cit.*, p. 27) linked in 1913 to the Bureau of Labor Statistics cost of living index.

1913–1949: Bureau of Labor Statistics cost of living index (*Historical Statistics*, p. 236, and *Survey of Current Business*, various issues).

Column 4 – 1896–1909: Average of (a) wholesale prices of all commodities (*Statistical Abstract* and *Survey of Current Business*, various issues, shifted to 1929 base) and (b) wages (col. 2) with weights of two and one, respectively. This average continued beyond 1909 approximates index of Bureau of Agricultural Economics reasonably well for the period 1910–1930.

1910–1949: Prices paid by farmers for production and family maintenance (*Agricultural Statistics*, 1929, p. 622 and *Survey of Current Business*, various issues), converted to 1929 base.

Column 5 – 1896–1949: Unweighted average of indices of wages; cost of commercial, industrial, and public utility construction; wholesale prices of nonagricultural commodities; and prices of producer durables. Wage index from col. 2; commodities index from *Survey of Current Business, Statistical Supplement*, 1942, 1947, 1949, and current issues, shifted to 1929 base; producer durables index derived from expenditures in original cost and 1929 prices from Tables P-5, P-6, P-13, and P-14; construction cost index from construction expenditures in original cost (from Table R-27, cols. 1 and 8, and Table R-28, cols. 6 and 7) and expenditures in 1929 prices (obtained by using price indices from Table R-20, cols. 3 and 4). Equal weights were used as there are no satisfactory data for determining weights accurately, but for the year 1929 equal weights are in good accord with figures in Table I in Goldsmith, R. W., "A Perpetual Inventory of National Wealth" (*Studies in Income and Wealth*, vol. XIV), provided bulk of wages are reflected in structures.

Columns 6 and 7 – 1896–1928: Unweighted average of indices of nonagricultural wholesale prices (see notes to col. 5); wage rates (col. 2) and cost of public construction (Table R-20, col. 8).

1929–1949: Derived from *Survey of Current Business*, July 1950, p. 9, and Jan. 1951, p. 9, as ratio of purchases of goods and services in current prices to purchases in 1939 prices, the quotient being then shifted to 1929 base.

DEFLATORS OF NATIONAL SAVING AND ITS MAJOR FORMS

Annual Averages (1929 = 100): 1896 to 1949

Percent

Year	Gross national product	Wage level	Group purchasing power				
			Nonagri-cultural individuals	Agriculture	Business	Government	
						State and local	Federal
	1	2	3	4	5	6	7
1896	45	29	43	42	41	37	37
1897	44	29	43	42	41	37	37
1898	44	30	43	44	42	38	38
1899	48	31	44	47	45	41	41
1900	50	32	46	50	47	43	43
1901	50	32	47	50	47	43	43
1902	51	33	48	52	48	45	45
1903	52	35	51	53	49	46	46
1904	51	35	50	53	49	46	46
1905	52	36	50	54	50	47	47
1906	56	37	52	55	52	49	49
1907	59	39	55	59	54	52	52
1908	55	38	52	57	52	49	49
1909	56	39	52	60	54	52	52
1910	59	42	55	64	56	54	54
1911	60	42	55	66	56	52	52
1912	64	43	59	65	57	54	54
1913	64	44	58	66	58	56	56
1914	64	45	59	65	57	54	54
1915	65	46	59	68	60	56	56
1916	72	50	64	81	69	67	67
1917	87	56	75	97	86	85	85
1918	98	68	88	114	101	97	97
1919	110	79	101	131	110	106	106
1920	125	93	117	131	127	127	127
1921	105	86	104	99	102	98	98
1922	99	84	98	97	94	92	92
1923	102	91	100	99	100	100	100
1924	101	93	100	99	100	100	100
1925	102	95	102	101	101	101	101
1926	103	97	103	101	101	101	101
1927	100	98	101	99	100	100	100
1928	101	99	100	101	100	100	100
1929	100	100	100	100	100	100	100
1930	96	100	98	95	95	98	93
1931	87	93	89	82	88	90	94
1932	78	81	80	70	79	84	88
1933	75	80	75	70	79	84	87
1934	79	93	78	79	88	89	97
1935	81	96	80	81	90	90	97
1936	81	98	81	81	91	89	98
1937	85	108	84	85	99	93	104
1938	83	112	82	80	98	93	100
1939	83	113	81	79	98	92	100
1940	84	117	82	79	101	93	102
1941	91	127	86	85	108	98	122
1942	110	144	95	99	118	105	136
1943	121	160	101	108	124	111	140
1944	127	170	102	114	127	115	136
1945	128	176	105	117	131	122	137
1946	126	190	114	131	146	135	163
1947	139	214	130	160	171	154	186
1948	150	234	140	171	186	174	194
1949	149	247	138	156	186	179	198

Column 1 – 1897–1949: Sum of cols. 2, 3, and 6.

Column 2 – 1897–1949: First differences of Table L-3, col. 7.

Column 3 – 1897–1949: Sum of cols. 4 and 5.

Column 4 – 1897–1949: First differences of Table L-5, col. 9.

Column 5 – 1921–1943: First differences of Table L-9, col. 6.

Column 6 – 1897–1949: Sum of cols. 7 and 8.

Column 7 – 1897–1949: First differences of Table L-6, col. 8.

Column 8 – 1921–1943: First differences of Table L-9, col. 10.

NONFARM INDIVIDUALS' CASH SAVING: 1897 to 1949

(Currency and Deposits in Commercial Banks)

$ mill.

Year	Total cash saving	Currency	Demand deposits			Time deposits		
			Total	In operating banks	In closed banks	Total	In operating banks	In closed banks
	1	2	3	4	5	6	7	8
1897	187	11	95	95	–	81	81	–
1898	303	32	204	204	–	67	67	–
1899	607	88	454	454	–	65	65	–
1900	272	47	91	91	–	134	134	–
1901	581	35	363	363	–	183	183	–
1902	446	48	241	241	–	157	157	–
1903	245	50	98	98	–	97	97	–
1904	21	–67	–84	–84	–	172	172	–
1905	1 213	178	723	723	–	312	312	–
1906	407	47	206	206	–	154	154	–
1907	–224	93	–367	–367	–	50	50	–
1908	–366	–235	–384	–384	–	253	253	–
1909	630	46	101	101	–	483	483	–
1910	460	42	213	213	–	205	205	–
1911	700	–43	206	206	–	537	537	–
1912	762	72	362	362	–	328	328	–
1913	511	59	425	425	–	27	27	–
1914	71	–110	292	292	–	–111	–111	–
1915	1 812	237	758	758	–	817	817	–
1916	2 861	262	1 676	1 676	–	923	923	–
1917	2 918	409	1 032	1 032	–	1 477	1 477	–
1918	1 777	725	1 084	1 084	–	–32	–32	–
1919	3 631	6	1 773	1 773	–	1 852	1 852	–
1920	–548	375	–1 562	–1 562	–	639	639	–
1921	–1 771	–619	–913	–937	24	–239	–275	36
1922	2 460	80	1 005	997	8	1 375	1 364	11
1923	1 186	71	–159	–171	12	1 274	1 256	18
1924	1 958	–17	889	862	27	1 086	1 046	40
1925	1 471	–110	453	445	8	1 128	1 112	16
1926	–353	2	–1 160	–1 172	12	805	775	30
1927	2 510	–32	1 352	1 318	34	1 190	1 148	42
1928	–1 897	–52	–2 416	–2 390	–26	571	576	–5
1929	–583	12	94	69	25	–689	–734	45
1930	–579	20	–732	–756	24	133	77	56
1931	–2 395	668	–510	–738	228	–2 553	–2 938	385
1932	–1 407	272	–400	–484	84	–1 279	–1 438	159
1933	–1 608	125	14	–390	404	–1 747	–2 415	668
1934	1 731	–8	672	829	–157	1 067	1 256	–189
1935	2 291	108	1 440	1 555	–115	743	962	–219
1936	2 933	466	1 770	1 775	–5	697	766	–69
1937	427	178	–200	–198	–2	449	477	–28
1938	358	19	545	605	–60	–206	–116	–90
1939	2 706	366	2 000	2 001	–1	340	371	–31
1940	2 590	786	1 403	1 440	–37	401	424	–23
1941	3 702	1 765	1 991	2 032	–41	–54	40	–94
1942	8 772	3 616	4 832	4 852	–20	324	372	–48
1943	12 703	4 024	6 001	6 002	–1	2 678	2 679	–1
1944	13 181	4 093	4 778	4 778	–	4 310	4 310	–
1945	13 579	2 321	6 087	6 087	–	5 171	5 171	–
1946	7 080	–197	4 096	4 096	–	3 181	3 181	–
1947	718	–259	–111	–111	–	1 088	1 088	–
1948	–1 964	–233	–2 015	–2 015	–	284	284	–
1949	–658	–424	–431	–431	–	197	197	–

MONEY IN CIRCULATION OUTSIDE TREASURY AND BANKING SYSTEM
1896 to 1949

$ mill.

End of year	Money outside Treasury and Federal Reserve banks	Vault cash of banks	Money outside banks	End of year	Money outside Treasury and Federal Reserve banks	Vault cash of banks	Money outside banks
	1	2	3		1	2	3
1896	1 669	532	1 137	1923	4 897	975	3 922
1897	1 742	557	1 185	1924	4 903	1 004	3 899
1898	1 920	695	1 225	1925	4 941	1 133	3 808
1899	2 005	653	1 352	1926	4 920	1 131	3 789
1900	2 200	774	1 426	1927	4 856	1 139	3 717
1901	2 280	804	1 476	1928	4 732	1 029	3 703
1902	2 380	840	1 540	1929	4 649	940	3 709
1903	2 499	902	1 597	1930	4 660	958	3 702
1904	2 604	1 040	1 564	1931	5 388	1 020	4 368
1905	2 708	933	1 775	1932	5 428	813	4 615
1906	2 924	1 075	1 849	1933	5 518	782	4 736
1907	3 120	1 154	1 966	1934	5 534	815	4 719
1908	3 134	1 400	1 734	1935	5 882	954	4 928
1909	3 167	1 358	1 809	1936	6 550	1 023	5 527
1910	3 240	1 399	1 841	1937	6 571	905	5 666
1911	3 318	1 518	1 800	1938	6 912	1 159	5 753
1912	3 404	1 536	1 868	1939	7 581	1 193	6 388
1913	3 503	1 604	1 899	1940	8 732	1 403	7 329
1914	3 319	1 549	1 770	1941	11 160	1 545	9 615
1915	3 574	1 472	2 102	1942	15 407	1 464	13 943
1916	3 937	1 495	2 442	1943	20 428	1 612	18 816
1917	4 329	1 276	3 053	1944	25 326	1 801	23 525
1918	5 180	1 133	4 047	1945	28 515	2 025	26 490
1919	5 306	1 239	4 067	1946	28 952	2 222	26 730
1920	5 525	1 029	4 496	1947	28 868	2 392	26 476
1921	4 589	1 006	3 583	1948	28 224	2 145	26 079
1922	4 693	929	3 764	1949	27 600	2 185	25 415

Column 1 – 1896–1913: From *Daily Statement of the U.S. Treasury*, plus minor coin, estimated as average of succeeding June figures, which increase from $20 million in June 1902 to $55 million in June 1913 (Federal Reserve Board, *Banking and Monetary Statistics*, table 109, p. 408). 1896–1899 figures based on assumption of $2 million increase per year.

    1914–1916: *Banking and Monetary Statistics*, table 110, p. 409. Figures from 1914 to 1934 increased to account for gold coin eliminated from reported series from 1914 to 1934 (cf. *Banking and Monetary Statistics*, p. 407). On the assumption that the unrecorded disappearance of U.S. gold coins discovered in 1934 was due exclusively to exports and occurred gradually from 1914 on, the adjustment was reduced linearly from $287 million in 1914 to zero in 1934.

    1917–1944: Schwartz, Anna and Oliver, Elma, *Currency Held by the Public, the Banks and the Treasury* (National Bureau of Economic Research Technical Paper 4, 1947), table 2. Figures refer to end-of-year dates, 1917–1921, and to last Wednesday-of-year dates, 1922–1944 (cf. note to 1914–1916 for adjustment for gold coins).

    1945–1949: *Federal Reserve Bulletin*, 1950, p. 1355. Figures refer to end of December.

Column 2 – 1896–1914: Currency holdings of all banks obtained by linear interpolation between estimates for call dates. Latter are derived as (a) sum of specie, legal tender notes, bank notes of other banks on hand, and circulating bank notes of issuing banks on hand for national banks multiplied by (b) value at each call date of ratios of linear trend fitted to ratios of vault cash of all banks to vault cash of all national banks as of June 30, as reported in *Annual Report of the Comptroller of the Currency*, 1931.

    1915–1916: Obtained by linear interpolation between preceding and succeeding June figures for vault cash, estimated as difference between currency in circulation (*Banking and Monetary Statistics*, table 110, p. 409) and currency outside banks (*ibid.*, table 9, p. 34).

    1917–1944: Schwartz and Oliver, *loc. cit.*

    1945–1949: Col. 1 minus col. 3.

Column 3 – 1896–1944: Col. 1 minus col. 2.

    1945–1949: *Federal Reserve Bulletin*, 1950, p. 1356.

TABLE L–3   L-3

Column 1 – 1896–1949: From Table L-2, col. 3. Excludes amounts held by Treasury and by banks.

Column 2 – 1896–1949: From Table L-12, col. 2.

Column 3 – 1896–1949: Estimated as 1 percent of col. 1 to cover nonindividual holders such as state and local governments, savings and loan associations, fraternal life insurance, and credit unions, but not of unincorporated business, which are included in col. 7. (Currency holdings of state and local governments at end of 1946 were estimated by Reeve and Associates in "Government Component in the National Wealth," *Studies in Income and Wealth*, vol. XII, table 2, p. 466, at \$175 million and by the Federal Reserve Board, in memorandum Research & Statistics 1147, at \$100 million, compared with an estimate in col. 3 of \$267 million for state and local governments plus other domestic nonindividual holders excluding corporations.)

Column 4 – 1918–1949: Obtained by cumulation from 1918 on of changes in foreign holdings of currency (cf. Table K-2, col. 14). Resulting figures probably understate actual foreign holdings (cf. Table K-6, line 14).

Column 5 – 1896–1949: Col. 1 minus the sum of cols. 2–4.

Column 6 – 1896–1949: From Table A-55, col. 5.

Column 7 – 1896–1949: Col. 5 minus col. 6.

TABLE L–4   L-4

Column 1 – 1896–1915A, 1917: Derived from revised banking statistics of Federal Reserve Board for June 30 dates. December figures were estimated for total deposits (i.e. time and demand deposits excluding interbank and U.S. Government deposits) by multiplying the average of successive June figures by the ratio of Dec. figures to average of June figures for total deposits of national banks (derived from *Annual Reports of the Comptroller of the Currency*). Dec. estimates for demand deposits are obtained by multiplying total deposits by the average of the ratios of demand deposits to demand plus time deposits on preceding and succeeding June dates.

    1915B–1916, 1918–1923A: Same method as above except separate ratios of Dec. to June average figures were derived for time deposits and demand deposits from data for member banks of Federal Reserve System as shown in *Banking and Monetary Statistics*, p. 72.

    1923B–1949: Not shown since demand deposits adjusted for items in process of collection are available directly (see col. 3).

Column 2 – 1896–1917: Same source and method as col. 1, 1896–1915A, using "cash items," "clearing house exchanges," "checks on banks in same place," or "outside checks" as items representing "items in process of collection" of national banks (from *Annual Report of the Comptroller of the Currency*).

    1918–1923A: Same source as col. 1, 1915B–1923A. Because of the rough nature of this estimate of float, no further refinement for reserve float has been made in this column. Reserve float, as included in this column for the years 1939B to 1949, is the difference between "uncollected items" and "deferred availability items" from the balance sheets of the Federal Reserve banks as shown in *Banking and Monetary Statistics*, p. 330, and *Federal Reserve Bulletin*, various issues. For year-ends from 1918 to 1923, the reserve float amounted to 199, 201, 118, 40, 84, and 27 millions of dollars respectively.

    1923B–1939A: From estimates of Federal Reserve Board as used in deriving "adjusted demand deposits" in *Banking and Monetary Statistics*, table 9.

    1939B–1949: From *Derivation of Liquid Asset Distribution Estimates*, table I, line 11 (memorandum of Federal Reserve Board, Research & Statistics 1147, Aug. 1950).

Column 3 – 1896–1923A: Col. 1 minus col. 2.

    1923B–1941: *Banking and Monetary Statistics*, table 9. Year-end data are given from 1923 on.

    1942–1949: *Federal Reserve Bulletin*, various issues.

Column 4 – 1896–1939: Estimated as one-half of bank float in col. 2 (cf. Friend and Natrella, *Individuals' Saving*, part II, pp. 6–9).

    1940–1949: *Ibid.*, table 1, line 4.

Column 5 – 1942–1949: *Ibid.*, table 1, line 13. (Part of employees withholding tax deposits and special funds for retirement of maturing securities not reported in corporate cash.) Also added to this column are government advances to manufacturing corporations in 1942, 1943, and 1944 (cf. *ibid.*, p. 16).

Column 6 – 1896–1949: Col. 3 minus sum of cols. 4 and 5.

DISTRIBUTION OF CURRENCY OUTSIDE BANKS AND TREASURY
1896 to 1949

$ mill.

End of year	Total currency outstanding	Corporations	Other nonindividual holders	Foreigners	Individuals and miscellaneous		
					Total	Farmers	Other
	1	2	3	4	5	6	7
1896	1 137	110	11	–	1 016	306	710
1897	1 185	130	12	–	1 043	322	721
1898	1 225	130	12	–	1 083	330	753
1899	1 352	140	13	–	1 199	358	841
1900	1 426	150	14	–	1 262	374	888
1901	1 476	157	14	–	1 305	382	923
1902	1 540	160	15	–	1 365	394	971
1903	1 597	160	16	–	1 421	400	1 021
1904	1 564	200	15	–	1 349	395	954
1905	1 775	190	17	–	1 568	436	1 132
1906	1 849	200	18	–	1 631	452	1 179
1907	1 966	200	19	–	1 747	475	1 272
1908	1 734	250	17	–	1 467	430	1 037
1909	1 809	260	18	–	1 531	448	1 083
1910	1 841	250	18	–	1 573	448	1 125
1911	1 800	280	18	–	1 502	420	1 082
1912	1 868	260	18	–	1 590	436	1 154
1913	1 899	240	18	–	1 641	428	1 213
1914	1 770	250	15	–	1 505	402	1 103
1915	2 102	280	18	–	1 804	464	1 340
1916	2 442	290	22	–	2 130	528	1 602
1917	3 053	290	28	–	2 735	724	2 011
1918	4 047	290	38	22	3 697	961	2 736
1919	4 067	300	39	52	3 676	934	2 742
1920	4 496	330	43	82	4 041	924	3 117
1921	3 583	310	34	112	3 127	629	2 498
1922	3 764	330	36	142	3 256	678	2 578
1923	3 922	340	38	203	3 341	692	2 649
1924	3 899	360	38	191	3 310	678	2 632
1925	3 808	390	37	175	3 206	684	2 522
1926	3 789	400	37	184	3 168	644	2 524
1927	3 717	400	36	166	3 115	623	2 492
1928	3 703	450	36	157	3 060	620	2 440
1929	3 709	450	36	163	3 060	608	2 452
1930	3 702	440	36	168	3 058	586	2 472
1931	4 368	340	43	175	3 810	670	3 140
1932	4 615	350	46	97	4 122	710	3 412
1933	4 736	350	47	26	4 313	776	3 537
1934	4 719	370	47	1	4 301	772	3 529
1935	4 928	400	49	0	4 479	842	3 637
1936	5 527	440	55	25	5 007	904	4 103
1937	5 666	380	57	22	5 207	926	4 281
1938	5 753	460	58	37	5 198	898	4 300
1939A	6 388	510	64	168	5 646	980	4 666
1939B	6 388	800	64	168	5 356	980	4 376
1940	7 329	800	73	206	6 250	1 088	5 162
1941	9 615	900	96	240	8 379	1 452	6 927
1942	13 943	900	139	311	12 593	2 050	10 543
1943	18 816	1 000	188	370	17 258	2 691	14 567
1944	23 525	1 000	235	454	21 836	3 176	18 660
1945	26 490	1 000	265	522	24 703	3 722	20 981
1946	26 730	1 100	267	583	24 780	3 996	20 784
1947	26 476	1 100	265	654	24 457	3 932	20 525
1948	26 079	1 100	261	696	24 022	3 730	20 202
1949	25 415	1 100	254	762	23 299	3 431	19 868

DERIVATION OF ADJUSTED DEMAND DEPOSITS
IN OPERATING COMMERCIAL BANKS: 1896 to 1949

$ mill.

End of year	Reported demand deposits	Bank float	Demand deposits less interbank and bank float	Deductible mail float	Special adjustments	Adjusted demand deposits
	1	2	3	4	5	6
1896	2 857	147	2 710	74	–	2 636
1897	3 307	185	3 122	92	–	3 030
1898	3 818	300	3 518	150	–	3 368
1899	4 211	167	4 044	84	–	3 960
1900	4 828	320	4 508	160	–	4 348
1901	5 477	417	5 060	208	–	4 852
1902	5 813	359	5 454	180	–	5 274
1903	5 878	308	5 570	154	–	5 416
1904	6 735	472	6 263	236	–	6 027
1905	7 636	681	6 955	340	–	6 615
1906	7 554	244	7 310	122	–	7 188
1907	7 354	431	6 923	216	–	6 707
1908	7 947	595	7 352	298	–	7 054
1909	8 497	730	7 767	365	–	7 402
1910	8 160	327	7 833	164	–	7 669
1911	9 065	494	8 571	247	–	8 324
1912	9 315	518	8 797	259	–	8 538
1913	9 703	497	9 206	248	–	8 958
1914	10 345	550	9 795	275	–	9 520
1915A	12 263	832	11 431	416	–	11 015
1915B	12 542	832	11 710	416	–	11 294
1916	14 262	689	13 573	344	–	13 229
1917	16 742	1 387	15 355	694	–	14 661
1918	18 900	1 776	17 124	888	–	16 236
1919	22 034	2 302	19 732	1 151	–	18 581
1920	19 946	1 630	18 316	815	–	17 501
1921	18 403	1 385	17 018	692	–	16 326
1922	21 245	2 205	19 040	1 102	–	17 938
1923A	21 932	2 570	19 362	1 285	–	18 077
1923B	–	2 654	19 144	1 327	–	17 817
1924	–	2 964	20 898	1 482	–	19 416
1925	–	3 371	22 288	1 686	–	20 602
1926	–	3 235	21 721	1 618	–	20 103
1927	–	2 680	22 730	1 340	–	21 390
1928	–	4 817	23 081	2 408	–	20 673
1929	–	4 049	22 809	2 024	–	20 785
1930	–	3 045	20 967	1 522	–	19 445
1931	–	2 186	17 412	1 093	–	16 319
1932	–	1 193	15 728	596	–	15 132
1933	–	1 191	15 035	596	–	14 439
1934	–	1 953	18 459	976	–	17 483
1935	–	2 323	22 115	1 162	–	20 953
1936	–	2 642	25 483	1 321	–	24 162
1937	–	2 344	23 959	1 172	–	22 787
1938	–	1 838	25 986	919	–	25 067
1939A	–	1 959	29 793	980	–	28 813
1939B	–	1 800	29 793	900	–	28 893
1940	–	2 800	34 945	1 429	–	33 516
1941	–	3 300	38 992	1 734	–	37 258
1942	–	4 100	48 922	2 067	100	46 755
1943	–	4 600	60 803	2 228	500	58 075
1944	–	4 200	66 930	2 032	775	64 123
1945	–	5 300	75 851	2 888	335	72 628
1946	–	6 400	83 314	3 077	265	79 972
1947	–	7 400	87 121	3 640	250	83 231
1948	–	7 000	85 520	3 415	250	81 855
1949	–	7 400	85 750	3 674	250	81 826

TABLE L-5

Column 1 – 1896–1949: From Table L-4, col. 6.

Column 2 – 1904–1928: From Table F-4, col. 5.
1929–1949: From Table F-14, col. 8.

Column 3 – 1896–1928A: Estimated as 75 percent of combined local and state government deposits as given in Tables G-8, col. 2, and G-17, col. 2 (in the latter case fiscal-year dates averaged).
1928B–1933: State and local government deposits in member banks (Federal Reserve Board, *Banking and Monetary Statistics*, p. 78) increased by ratio of 1934 Federal Deposit Insurance Corporation figure, adjusted for uninsured banks, to 1934 member bank figure.
1934–1946: Deposits of state and local governments in all operating insured commercial banks from *Annual Report of the Federal Deposit Insurance Corporation* increased by ratio of adjusted demand deposits in all commercial banks (*Banking and Monetary Statistics*, table 9, and *Federal Reserve Bulletin*) to adjusted demand deposits in insured commercial banks (derived from *Banking and Monetary Statistics*, pp. 108, 110, and *Federal Reserve Bulletin*).
1947–1949: From *Annual Report of the Comptroller of the Currency*.

Column 4 – 1896–1949: From Table L-12, col. 4.

Column 5 – 1896–1949: Deposits of savings and loan associations, credit unions, fraternal orders, and mutual accident and sick benefit funds from Tables J-2, L-41, I-10, and I-14.

Column 6 – 1896–1949: From Table L-7, col. 5.

Column 7 – 1896–1949: Col. 1 minus sum of cols. 2–6.

Column 8 – 1896–1922: Estimated as same percentage of total farmers' deposits in Table A-56, col. 1 as demand deposits are of total deposits excluding interbank, government, corporation, foreign, and financial institution deposits.
1923–1949: From Table A-56, col. 5.

Column 9 – 1896–1949: Col. 7 minus col. 8.

TABLE L-6

Column 1 – 1896–1923A: Same sources and methods as Table L-4, col. 1. Includes Postal Savings deposits re-deposited in commercial banks.
1923B–1941: From *Banking and Monetary Statistics*, table 9. Excludes Postal Savings redeposited in banks.
1942–1949: From *Federal Reserve Bulletin*. Same coverage as 1923B to 1941.

Column 2 – 1896–1910: Not applicable.
1911–1923A: From *Banking and Monetary Statistics*, table 154.
1923B–1949: Not shown; already deducted from col. 1.

Column 3 – 1896–1928: Estimated as 25 percent of combined local and state government deposits, the former from Table G-8, col. 2 and the latter from averaging fiscal-year figures in Table G-17, col. 2.
1929–1933: State and local government deposits in member banks (*Banking and Monetary Statistics*, p. 78) increased by ratio of 1934 Federal Deposit Insurance Corporation figure, adjusted for uninsured banks, to 1934 member bank figure.
1934–1946: Figures for all insured banks from *Annual Report of the Federal Deposit Insurance Corporation* increased by 5 percent to account for deposits in uninsured banks. Ratio based on 1947–1949 relationship.
1947–1949: From *Annual Report of the Comptroller of the Currency*.

Column 4 – 1896–1949: From Table L-12, col. 3.

Column 5 – 1896–1949: From Table L-7, col. 4.

Column 6 – 1896–1949: Col. 1 minus cols. 2–5.

Column 7 – 1896–1922: Estimated as the same percentage of total farmers' deposits as time deposits are of total deposits excluding government, corporate, and foreign deposits.
1923–1949: From Table A-56, col. 6.

Column 8 – 1896–1949: Col. 6 minus col. 7.

DISTRIBUTION OF DEMAND DEPOSITS
IN OPERATING COMMERCIAL BANKS: 1896 to 1949

$ mill.

End of year	Total adjusted demand deposits	Federal corporations	State and local governments	Corporations	Other financial institutions	Foreigners	Individuals and miscellaneous		
							Total	Farmers	Non-farmers
	1	2	3	4	5	6	7	8	9
1896	2 636	–	98	1 254	23	25	1 236	142	1 094
1897	3 030	–	100	1 539	29	28	1 334	145	1 189
1898	3 368	–	103	1 624	32	32	1 577	184	1 393
1899	3 960	–	105	1 693	34	36	2 092	245	1 847
1900	4 348	–	104	1 945	36	42	2 221	283	1 938
1901	4 852	–	123	2 008	37	48	2 636	335	2 301
1902	5 274	–	199	2 080	33	51	2 911	369	2 542
1903	5 416	–	199	2 109	33	52	3 023	383	2 640
1904	6 027	1	248	2 736	32	61	2 949	393	2 556
1905	6 615	0	249	2 523	37	69	3 737	458	3 279
1906	7 188	0	250	2 809	46	70	4 013	528	3 485
1907	6 707	1	245	2 707	41	69	3 644	526	3 118
1908	7 054	1	258	3 457	38	76	3 224	490	2 734
1909	7 402	2	281	3 654	45	85	3 335	500	2 835
1910	7 669	2	315	3 648	48	84	3 572	524	3 048
1911	8 324	3	359	4 047	49	95	3 771	517	3 254
1912	8 538	3	380	3 831	52	99	4 173	557	3 616
1913	8 958	3	403	3 744	52	103	4 653	612	4 041
1914	9 520	3	404	3 837	53	231	4 992	659	4 333
1915A	11 015	2	398	4 372	66	359	5 818	727	5 091
1915B	11 294	2	398	4 372	67	359	6 096	775	5 321
1916	13 229	3	433	4 621	84	103	7 985	988	6 997
1917	14 661	2	491	4 706	89	217	9 156	1 127	8 029
1918	16 236	5	499	4 773	81	331	10 547	1 434	9 113
1919	18 581	3	544	5 199	96	217	12 522	1 636	10 886
1920	17 501	6	734	5 791	91	130	10 749	1 425	9 324
1921	16 326	10	927	5 504	102	128	9 655	1 268	8 387
1922	17 938	8	1 096	5 925	108	127	10 674	1 290	9 384
1923A	18 077	16	1 106	6 181	128	133	10 513	1 300	9 213
1923B	17 817	16	1 106	6 181	128	133	10 253	1 300	8 953
1924	19 416	22	1 246	6 631	141	261	11 115	1 300	9 815
1925	20 602	20	1 350	7 327	157	188	11 560	1 300	10 260
1926	20 103	24	1 502	7 754	177	258	10 388	1 300	9 088
1927	21 390	28	1 462	7 626	198	370	11 706	1 300	10 406
1928A	20 673	23	1 672	9 072	231	359	9 316	1 300	8 016
1928B	20 673	23	1 688	9 072	231	359	9 300	1 300	8 000
1929	20 785	23	1 733	9 212	201	347	9 269	1 200	8 069
1930	19 445	28	1 769	8 810	239	286	8 313	1 000	7 313
1931	16 319	21	1 692	6 911	199	221	7 275	700	6 575
1932	15 132	28	1 453	6 624	172	164	6 691	600	6 091
1933	14 439	49	1 714	6 094	170	111	6 301	600	5 701
1934	17 483	77	2 336	7 266	197	177	7 430	900	6 530
1935	20 953	55	2 768	8 505	224	216	9 185	1 100	8 085
1936	24 162	86	3 011	9 271	251	383	11 160	1 300	9 860
1937	22 787	60	2 747	8 456	249	313	10 962	1 300	9 662
1938	25 067	69	3 034	9 590	270	537	11 567	1 300	10 267
1939A	28 813	96	2 982	10 849	341	877	13 668	1 400	12 268
1939B	28 893	96	2 982	10 579	341	877	14 018	1 400	12 618
1940	33 516	97	3 408	13 140	392	921	15 558	1 500	14 058
1941	37 258	89	3 788	13 867	454	970	18 090	2 000	16 090
1942	46 755	137	4 054	17 290	529	903	23 842	2 900	20 942
1943	58 075	137	4 416	21 175	575	828	30 944	4 000	26 944
1944	64 123	128	4 584	21 177	518	994	36 722	5 000	31 722
1945	72 628	202	5 175	21 395	564	1 283	44 009	6 200	37 809
1946	79 972	232	6 057	22 370	645	1 463	49 205	7 300	41 905
1947	83 231	165	6 800	25 007	669	1 196	49 394	7 600	41 794
1948	81 855	114	7 299	25 500	779	1 184	46 979	7 200	39 779
1949	81 826	118	7 545	25 900	969	1 146	46 148	6 800	39 348

DISTRIBUTION OF TIME DEPOSITS
IN OPERATING COMMERCIAL BANKS: 1896 to 1949

$ mill.

End of year	Total	Postal Savings System	State and local governments	Corporations	Foreigners	Individuals and miscellaneous		
						Total	Farmers	Other
	1	2	3	4	5	6	7	8
1896	602	—	32	70	1	499	58	441
1897	701	—	34	80	2	585	63	522
1898	793	—	34	90	2	667	78	589
1899	887	—	35	110	2	740	86	654
1900	1 060	—	35	120	2	903	115	788
19 01	1 276	—	41	120	2	1 113	142	971
1902	1 490	—	66	130	3	1 291	163	1 128
1903	1 601	—	66	130	3	1 402	177	1 225
1904	1 878	—	83	180	3	1 612	215	1 397
1905	2 204	—	83	170	4	1 947	238	1 709
1906	2 412	—	83	180	4	2 145	282	1 863
1907	2 531	—	82	210	4	2 235	322	1 913
1908	2 924	—	86	280	4	2 554	388	2 166
1909	3 505	—	94	290	4	3 117	468	2 649
1910	3 753	—	105	300	4	3 344	490	2 854
1911	4 425	10	120	360	5	3 930	539	3 391
1912	4 799	26	126	350	5	4 292	573	3 719
1913	4 800	37	134	310	5	4 314	568	3 746
1914	4 779	56	134	390	12	4 187	552	3 635
1915A	5 798	69	133	490	19	5 087	635	4 452
1915B	5 325	69	133	490	19	4 614	587	4 027
1916	6 404	107	144	500	5	5 648	698	4 950
1917	8 164	139	164	520	11	7 330	903	6 427
1918	8 250	146	166	520	17	7 401	1 006	6 395
1919	10 409	130	181	600	11	9 487	1 240	8 247
1920	11 230	55	244	680	8	10 243	1 357	8 886
1921	10 926	44	309	650	10	9913	1 302	8 611
1922	12 478	56	365	700	11	11 346	1 371	9 975
1923A	13 926	63	369	750	13	12 731	1 500	11 231
1923B	13 871		369	750	13	12 739	1 500	11 239
1924	15 280	—	416	950	29	13 885	1 600	12 285
1925	16 570	—	450	1 100	23	14 997	1 600	13 397
1926	17 508	—	501	1 200	35	15 772	1 600	14 172
1927	18 962	—	487	1 400	55	17 020	1 700	15 320
1928A	19 761	—	557	1 450	58	17 696	1 800	15 896
1928B	19 761	—	500	1 450	58	17 753	1 800	15 953
1929	19 192	—	712	1 500	61	16 919	1 700	15 219
1930	19 012	—	609	1 460	47	16 896	1 600	15 296
1931	15 366	—	465	1 210	33	13 658	1 300	12 358
1932	13 631	—	409	1 180	22	12 020	1 100	10 920
1933	11 019	—	360	1 140	14	9 505	1 000	8 505
1934	12 213	—	352	980	20	10 861	1 100	9 761
1935	13 170	—	425	800	22	11 923	1 200	10 723
1936	14 046	—	364	860	33	12 789	1 300	11 489
1937	14 779	—	617	770	26	13 366	1 400	11 966
1938	14 776	—	604	880	42	13 250	1 400	11 850
1939A	15 258	—	553	1 020	64	13 621	1 400	12 221
1939B	15 258	—	553	1 000	64	13 641	1 400	12 241
1940	15 777	—	549	1 000	63	14 165	1 500	12 665
1941	15 884	—	517	1 000	62	14 305	1 600	12 705
1942	16 352	—	417	1 000	58	14 877	1 800	13 077
1943	19 224	—	415	1 000	53	17 756	2 000	15 756
1944	24 074	—	444	1 000	64	22 566	2 500	20 066
1945	30 135	—	521	1 000	77	28 537	3 300	25 237
1946	33 808	—	697	1 000	93	32 018	3 600	28 418
1947	35 249	—	867	1 000	76	33 306	3 800	29 506
1948	35 804	—	1 138	1 000	76	33 590	3 800	29 790
1949	36 146	—	1 286	1 000	73	33 787	3 800	29 987

TABLE L–7   L–7

Column 1 – 1928–1949: From Table K-4, col. 7.

Column 2 – 1928–1949: Estimated at 8 percent of col. 1 on basis of Department of the Treasury, *Census of Foreign-Owned Assets in the United States,* which showed an excess of about 8 percent over figures for regularly reporting banks which underlie col. 1.

Column 3 – 1896–1912: Estimated at 0.74 percent of total deposits (excluding interbank and U.S. Government deposits), the ratio prevailing in 1913.

1913–1927: Obtained by cumulating backwards from 1928 value one-half of changes in all foreign deposits in American banks (including both those of foreign banks and other foreigners) as estimated in Table K-2, cols. 10 and 11. Ratio of one-half was based on average prevailing during the five years 1928–1932.

1928–1949: Sum of cols. 1 and 2.

From a comparison of the estimates of col. 3 with those of the Securities and Exchange Commission available since 1932, it will become evident that two adjustments made by the Securities and Exchange Commission (cf. Friend and Natrella, *Individuals' Saving,* part II, pp. 22–23 and 25–26 of preliminary mimeographed version) have not been accepted. The first (relating to the deposits of foreign government agencies and commissions with domestic commercial banks) has been omitted because it appeared on investigation that the assumption used to justify the deduction, viz. that these deposits had been classified by the American banks reporting them with interbank deposits, was very doubtful. The second adjustment (an allowance for the change in unrecorded deposits for the years 1933–1941, estimated as generally one-third of the residual item in the balance of payments statistics) has not been adopted because of its arbitrariness and because of doubts that cumulated total unreported foreign deposits amounted to as much as $1,110 million from 1941 on as estimated by the Securities and Exchange Commission.

Column 4 – 1896–1949: Estimated on basis of: (a) proportion of open account time deposits to all other deposits (excluding interbank and U.S. Government deposits) with member banks in New York City since it is known that most foreign deposits are held with New York banks and cannot generally have been in the form of savings deposits evidenced by pass book; and (b) ratio of foreign time to demand deposits disclosed in the *Census of Foreign-Owned Assets in the United States.* Resulting ratio is 5 percent through 1919, rises gradually to 15 percent in 1929, and then declines to 6 percent in 1941 and later years.

Column 5 – 1896–1949: Col. 3 minus col. 4.

DISTRIBUTION OF FOREIGN DEPOSITS IN COMMERCIAL BANKS
1896 to 1949

$ mill.

End of year	Reported deposits of foreigners (excluding foreign banks)	Foreign deposits in nonreporting banks	Foreign deposits in commercial banks			End of year	Reported deposits of foreigners (excluding foreign banks)	Foreign deposits in nonreporting banks	Foreign deposits in commercial banks		
			Total	Time deposits	Demand deposits				Total	Time deposits	Demand deposits
	1	2	3	4	5		1	2	3	4	5
1896	.	.	26	1	25	1923	.	.	146	13	133
1897	.	.	30	2	28	1924	.	.	290	29	261
1898	.	.	34	2	32	1925	.	.	211	23	188
1899	.	.	38	2	36	1926	.	.	293	35	258
1900	.	.	44	2	42	1927	.	.	425	55	370
1901	.	.	50	2	48	1928	386	31	417	58	359
1902	.	.	54	3	51	1929	377	31	408	61	347
1903	.	.	55	3	52	1930	308	25	333	47	286
1904	.	.	64	3	61	1931	235	19	254	33	221
1905	.	.	73	4	69	1932	172	14	186	22	164
1906	.	.	74	4	70	1933	116	9	125	14	111
1907	.	.	73	4	69	1934	182	15	197	20	177
1908	.	.	80	4	76	1935	220	18	238	22	216
1909	.	.	89	4	85	1936	385	31	416	33	383
1910	.	.	88	4	84	1937	314	25	339	26	313
1911	.	.	100	5	95	1938	536	43	579	42	537
1912	.	.	104	5	99	1939	871	70	941	64	877
1913	.	.	108	5	103	1940	911	73	984	63	921
1914	.	.	243	12	231	1941	956	76	1 032	62	970
1915	.	.	378	19	359	1942	890	71	961	58	903
1916	.	.	108	5	103	1943	816	65	881	53	828
1917	.	.	228	11	217	1944	979	79	1 058	64	994
1918	.	.	348	17	331	1945	1 195	95	1 290	77	1 213
1919	.	.	228	11	217	1946	1 441	115	1 556	93	1 463
1920	.	.	138	8	130	1947	1 178	94	1 272	76	1 196
1921	.	.	138	10	128	1948	1 167	93	1 260	76	1 184
1922	.	.	138	11	127	1949	1 129	90	1 219	73	1 146

$ mill.

End of year	Deposits in banks closed during year	Deposits in closed banks repaid during year	Difference between deposits in banks closing and repayments		End of year	Deposits in banks closed during year	Deposits in closed banks repaid during year	Difference between deposits in banks closing and repayments	
			Annually	Cumulative				Annually	Cumulative
	1	2	3	4		1	2	3	4
1921	108	10	98	98	1936	11	188	−177	2 703
1922	41	15	26	124	1937	20	110	−90	2 613
1923	76	25	51	175	1938	11	224	−213	2 400
1924	158	50	108	283	1939	35	104	−69	2 331
1925	119	80	39	322	1940	6	65	−59	2 272
1926	181	100	81	403	1941	4	243	−239	2 033
1927	202	89	113	516	1942	2	114	−112	1 921
1928	77	90	−13	503	1943	6	44	−38	1 883
1929	256	131	125	628	1944	0	–	–	1 883
1930	243	100	143	771	1945	0	–	–	1 883
1931	1 390	361	1 029	1 800	1946	0	–	–	1 883
1932	825	389	436	2 236	1947	0	–	–	1 883
1933	4 600	2 660	1 940	4 176	1948	0	–	–	1 883
1934	37	675	−638	3 538	1949	2	–	2	1 885
1935	10	668	−658	2 880					

Column 1 – 1921–1932: Deposits of national banks placed in receivership, as given in the *Annual Reports of the Comptroller of the Currency*, multiplied by the ratio of deposits in all suspended banks to deposits in suspended national banks as given in *Banking and Monetary Statistics*, pp. 285, 287.

1933: Up to March 4: banks placed in receivership or conservatorship as reported in the *Annual Report of the Comptroller of the Currency*. March 16 to Dec. 31: national banks suspended during the banking holiday but licensed between March 16 and Dec. 31; banks remaining unlicensed (but not placed in receivership) on Dec. 31; and banks otherwise liquidated (cf. *Annual Report of the Comptroller of the Currency*, 1933, pp. 3, 401). Total deposits for national banks multiplied by ratio of deposits in all suspended banks to deposits in suspended national banks as for years 1921–1932.

1934–1940: *Banking and Monetary Statistics*, p. 283.

1941–1949: *Federal Reserve Bulletin*, various issues.

Column 2 – 1921–1925: Estimated on the basis of relationship for the following years.

1926–1932: Deposits paid out by receivers for closed national banks as reported in *Annual Reports of the Comptroller of the Currency* multiplied by ratio between book value of not yet liquidated assets of all closed banks to not yet liquidated assets of national banks.

1933: Deposits paid out by national banks placed in conservatorships and receiverships; plus deposits paid out by national banks licensed between March 16 and Dec. 31, by national banks unlicensed by Dec. 31, and by national banks placed in other types of liquidations; plus other releases of deposits (cf. *Annual Report of the Comptroller of the Currency*, 1933, pp. 3, 401). Totals multiplied by ratio between total unliquidated assets of all banks to the same for national banks.

1934: Deposits paid out by national banks closed prior to 1933 plus national banks closed in 1933 less amount paid out in prior year (*Annual Report of the Comptroller of the Currency*, 1934, pp. 448, 503) multiplied as above to obtain estimates for all banks; plus deposits paid out by Federal Deposit Insurance Corporation on account of banks failing in 1934 (cf. *Annual Reports of the Federal Deposit Insurance Corporation*).

1935–1943: Deposits paid out by national banks in receivership or conservatorship (cf. *Annual Reports of the Comptroller of the Currency*) multiplied by ratio as above, plus deposits paid out for banks failing after 1934, assumed to be equal to deposits in banks suspended in each year (*Banking and Monetary Statistics*, p. 283).

1944–1949: Assumed to be negligible.

Column 3 – 1921–1949: Col. 1 minus col. 2.

Column 4 – 1921–1949: Cumulation of figures in col. 3.

Column 1 – From Table L-8, col. 4. No account taken of small changes after 1943.

Column 2 – Col. 1 reduced by 10 percent to account for deposits of governments, banks, and foreigners. This ratio is below that prevailing for operating commercial banks from 1930 to 1933—about 14 percent—because it was assumed that a considerable portion of the interbank and government deposits ordinarily held by banks which had to close were withdrawn before the date of insolvency or were secured by collateral and segregated.

Column 3 – Estimated as one-half of col. 2.

Columns 4 to 6 – Estimated as same percentage distribution for each year as in operating banks, derived from Table L-5.

Column 7 – See col. 3. This ratio is slightly higher than the proportion of time deposits for operating banks as closed banks were concentrated in localities where the proportion of time deposits tended to be above the national average.

Columns 8 to 10 – Same as cols. 4, 5, and 6, derived from Table L-6.

Column 1 – Rough estimates based on estimates of total corporate deposits in closed banks shown in Table L-9, cols. 4 and 8. It has been assumed that about two-thirds of corporate deposits in closed banks was written off or carried in accounts other than cash in their balance sheets until the middle thirties (cf. Friend and Natrella, *Individuals' Saving*, part II, p. 25) but that thereafter remaining claims to deposits in closed banks were eliminated rapidly altogether from corporate cash accounts. Deposits in closed banks carried as cash before 1930 and after 1940 are regarded as so small that a separate estimation is not warranted.

Column 2 – Estimated at about 15 percent of total deposits, approximately the ratio of corporate time to total corporate deposits shown in Table L-12.

Column 3 – Col. 1 minus col. 2.

DISTRIBUTION OF DEPOSITS IN CLOSED COMMERCIAL BANKS
1921 to 1943
$ mill.

End of year	All deposits in closed banks	Deposits less those of governments, banks, and foreigners	Demand deposits				Time deposits			
			Total	Corporations	Farm	Nonfarm	Total	Corporations	Farm	Nonfarm
	1	2	3	4	5	6	7	8	9	10
1921	98	88	44	16	4	24	44	3	5	36
1922	124	112	56	20	4	32	56	3	6	47
1923	175	157	79	29	6	44	78	4	9	65
1924	283	255	128	48	9	71	127	8	14	105
1925	322	290	145	56	10	79	145	10	14	121
1926	403	363	182	78	13	91	181	13	17	151
1927	516	464	232	91	16	125	232	18	21	193
1928	503	453	227	112	16	99	226	17	21	188
1929	628	565	283	141	18	124	282	23	26	233
1930	771	694	347	179	20	148	347	28	30	289
1931	1 800	1 620	810	394	40	376	810	66	70	674
1932	2 236	2 012	1 006	501	45	460	1 006	90	83	833
1933	4 176	3 758	1 879	925	90	864	1 879	201	177	1 501
1934	3 538	3 184	1 592	788	97	707	1 592	132	148	1 312
1935	2 880	2 592	1 296	624	80	592	1 296	81	122	1 093
1936	2 703	2 433	1 217	552	78	587	1 216	77	115	1 024
1937	2 613	2 352	1 176	512	79	585	1 176	64	116	996
1938	2 400	2 160	1 080	489	66	525	1 080	67	107	906
1939A	2 331	2 098	1 049	465	60	524	1 049	73	101	875
1939B	2 331	2 098	1 049	451	60	538	1 049	71	101	877
1940	2 272	2 045	1 023	469	53	501	1 022	67	101	854
1941	2 033	1 830	915	397	58	460	915	59	96	760
1942	1 921	1 729	865	364	61	440	864	54	98	712
1943	1 883	1 695	848	344	65	439	847	45	91	711

DEPOSITS IN CLOSED COMMERCIAL BANKS INCLUDED IN CORPORATE CASH
1930 to 1940
$ mill.

End of year	Total	Time deposits	Demand deposits	End of year	Total	Time deposits	Demand deposits
	1	2	3		1	2	3
1930	100	15	85	1936	150	20	130
1931	150	25	125	1937	100	15	85
1932	200	30	170	1938	75	10	65
1933	400	60	340	1939	50	5	45
1934	300	45	255	1940	25	–	25
1935	200	30	170				

CORPORATE CASH BY MAJOR INDUSTRIAL GROUPS
1896 to 1926
$ mill.

End of year	All taxable corporations (excluding banks)		Manufacturing	Trade	Transportation and other public utilities	Finance (excluding banks)	All other
	Adjusted	Unadjusted					
	1	2	3	4	5	6	7
1896	1 434	1 384	.	.	199	187	.
1897	1 749	1 688	.	.	237	234	.
1898	1 844	1 779	.	.	273	223	.
1899	1 943	1 875	881	294	296	227	177
1900	2 215	2 137	996	332	340	267	202
1901	2 285	2 205	944	315	414	313	219
1902	2 370	2 287	944	315	457	339	232
1903	2 399	2 315	916	305	499	354	241
1904	3 116	3 007	1 218	406	693	360	330
1905	2 883	2 782	1 090	363	668	352	309
1906	3 189	3 077	1 181	394	740	422	340
1907	3 117	3 008	1 177	392	733	368	338
1908	3 987	3 847	1 479	493	1 042	373	460
1909	4 204	4 057	1 451	484	1 179	444	499
1910	4 198	4 051	1 545	515	1 063	455	473
1911	4 687	4 523	1 736	579	1 182	498	528
1912	4 441	4 285	1 742	581	1 013	471	478
1913	4 294	4 143	1 701	567	920	509	446
1914	4 477	4 320	1 711	570	965	614	460
1915	5 142	4 962	1 955	652	1 120	703	532
1916	5 411	5 221	1 921	535	1 362	834	569
1917	5 516	5 323	2 115	607	1 086	1 007	508
1918	5 583	5 387	2 472	562	924	983	446
1919	6 099	5 885	2 469	850	834	1 227	505
1920	6 801	6 563	2 626	803	1 242	1 278	614
1921	6 464	6 237	2 286	877	1 296	1 126	652
1922	6 955	6 711	2 497	899	1 466	1 139	710
1923	7 271	7 016	2 916	715	1 464	1 267	654
1924	7 941	7 663	3 045	894	1 659	1 299	766
1925	8 817	8 508	3 267	1 017	1 879	1 476	869
1926	9 354	9 026	3 578	1 195	1 812	1 539	902

Column 1 – 1896–1926: Col. 2 multiplied by 1.036, the 1926 ratio between col. 2 and Table L-13, col. 1.

Column 2 – 1896–1898: Sum of cols. 5 and 6 and estimated sum of cols. 3, 4, and 7 extrapolated from 1899 on basis of cols. 5 plus 6.
1899–1926: Sum of cols. 3–7.

Column 3 – 1899–1926: Table L-14, col. 6.

Column 4 – 1899–1915: Estimated as one-third of col. 3.
1916–1926: Table L-16, col. 7.

Column 5 – 1896–1926: From Table L-17, col. 1.

Column 6 – 1896–1926: From Table L-21, col. 1.

Column 7 – 1899–1926: Estimated at 30 percent of col. 4 plus col. 5. This proportion was derived from an average of the ratios from 1926–1941 of cash holdings of all other corporations (agriculture, mining, construction, service, miscellaneous) to cash holdings of trade corporations and transportation and public utilities corporations combined (cf. Table L-13).

CORPORATE CASH BY TYPE
(Excluding Deposits in Closed Banks): 1896 to 1949

$ mill.

End of year	Total	Currency	Time deposits	Demand deposits	End of year	Total	Currency	Time deposits	Demand deposits
	1	2	3	4		1	2	3	4
1896	1 434	110	70	1 254	1924	7 941	360	950	6 631
1897	1 749	130	80	1 539	1925	8 817	390	1 100	7 327
1898	1 844	130	90	1 624	1926	9 354	400	1 200	7 754
1899	1 943	140	110	1 693	1927	9 426	400	1 400	7 626
1900	2 215	150	120	1 945	1928	10 972	450	1 450	9 072
1901	2 285	157	120	2 008	1929	11 162	450	1 500	9 212
1902	2 370	160	130	2 080	1930	10 710	440	1 460	8 810
1903	2 399	160	130	2 109	1931	8 461	340	1 210	6 911
1904	3 116	200	180	2 736	1932	8 154	350	1 180	6 624
1905	2 883	190	170	2 523	1933	7584	350	1 140	6 094
1906	3 189	200	180	2 809	1934	8 616	370	980	7 266
1907	3 117	200	210	2 707	1935	9 705	400	800	8 505
1908	3 987	250	280	3 457	1936	10 571	440	860	9 271
1909	4 204	260	290	3 654	1937	9 606	380	770	8 456
1910	4 198	250	300	3 648	1938	10 930	460	880	9 590
1911	4 687	280	360	4 047	1939A	12 379	510	1 020	10 849
1912	4 441	260	350	3 831	1939B	12 379	800	1 000	10 579
1913	4 294	240	310	3 744	1940	14 940	800	1 000	13 140
1914	4 477	250	390	3 837	1941	15 767	900	1 000	13 867
1915	5 142	280	490	4 372	1942	19 190	900	1 000	17 290
1916	5 411	290	500	4 621	1943	23 175	1 000	1 000	21 175
1917	5 516	290	520	4 706	1944	23 177	1 000	1 000	21 177
1918	5 583	290	520	4 773	1945	23 395	1 000	1 000	21 395
1919	6 099	300	600	5 199	1946	24 470	1 100	1 000	22 370
1920	6 801	330	680	5 791	1947	27 107	1 100	1 000	25 007
1921	6 464	310	650	5 504	1948	27 600	1 100	1 000	25 500
1922	6 955	330	700	5 925	1949	28 000	1 100	1 000	25 900
1923	7 271	340	750	6 181					

Column 1 – 1896–1926: From Table L-11, col. 1.

    1927–1947: From Table L-13, col. 1 minus estimate of corporate deposits in closed banks from Table L-10, col. 1.

    1948–1949: Estimated at 1947 level plus change in cash holdings of corporations and of insurance companies from *Derivation of Liquid Asset Distribution Estimates* (memorandum of Federal Reserve Board, Research & Statistics 1147, Aug. 1950).

Column 2 – 1896–1928: Estimated on the basis of a relative increase in the importance of corporations in total business as measured by the percentage of total cash held by corporations; a relative decrease in the importance of currency as measured by the percentage of total cash in currency form; and the ratio of currency to total corporate cash in 1929.

    1929–1939A: From Shapiro, S., "The Distribution of Deposits and Currency in the United States, 1929–1939," *Journal of the American Statistical Association*, Dec. 1943, tables i and iii.

    1939B–1949: Federal Reserve Board estimates (Research & Statistics 1147, table iii, lines 3 and 10).

Column 3 – 1896–1928: Estimated on the basis of proportion of time deposits in corporate cash in later years; a relative increase in the importance of time deposits as measured by proportion of time deposits in total cash; and a relative increase in the importance of corporations in total business.

    1929–1939A: Shapiro, *op. cit.*, table iv.

    1939B–1949: Federal Reserve Board estimates (Research & Statistics 1147, table iv, lines 3 and 10).

Column 4 – 1896–1949: Col. 1 minus sum of cols. 2 and 3.

CASH OF ALL CORPORATIONS REPORTING TO BUREAU OF INTERNAL REVENUE
BY MAJOR INDUSTRIAL GROUPS

Corrected for Nonreporting and Limitation of Consolidated Reporting: 1926 to 1947

$ mill.

End of year	Corrected total (excluding banks)	Manufacturing	Trade	Transportation and other public utilities	Railroad special deposits	Agriculture	Mining and quarrying	Construction	Service	Miscellaneous	Finance (excluding banks)
	1	2	3	4	5	6	7	8	9	10	11
1926	9 354	3 578	1 195	1 370	295	50	418	224	317	6	1 901
1927	9 426	3 575	1 230	1 563	276	60	368	201	253	10	1 890
1928	10 972	3 951	1 328	1 585	380	54	422	207	263	6	2 776
1929	11 162	3 902	1 317	1 649	296	63	430	219	465	7	2 814
1930	10 810	4 017	1 303	1 709	293	43	338	226	308	5	2 568
1931	8 611	3 504	1 070	1 346	185	70	247	164	223	6	1 796
1932	8 354	3 365	1 066	1 363	164	53	239	138	242	3	1 721
1933	7 984	3 109	1 013	1 356	181	61	259	105	216	2	1 682
1934	8 916	3 419	1 165	1 528	152	73	304	110	259	6	1 900
1935	9 905	3 840	1 179	1 458	136	81	342	124	302	7	2 436
1936	10 721	4 066	1 272	1 860	197	88	373	125	394	7	2 339
1937	9 706	3 738	1 201	1 387	180	83	388	140	377	4	2 208
1938	11 005	4 549	1 354	1 682	127	62	368	134	253	15	2 461
1939	12 429	5 189	1 391	1 849	189	52	439	146	275	19	2 880
1940	14 965	6 516	1 566	2 159	230	67	526	155	287	31	3 428
1941	15 767	7 036	1 781	2 369	267	75	533	193	328	41	3 144
1942	19 190	9 194	2 751	2 503	196	89	538	323	426	50	3 120
1943	23 175	11 901	3 221	3 158	286	124	523	327	551	43	3 041
1944	23 177	12 088	3 581	2 727	269	123	534	273	578	42	2 962
1945	23 395	11 431	4 032	2 779	219	125	564	266	686	51	3 242
1946	24 470	11 230	4 381	2 882	188	143	650	326	779	44	3 847
1947	27 107	12 027	5 150	3 014	153	152	805	418	834	50	4 504

Column 1 – 1926–1947: Sum of cols. 2–11.

Column 2 – 1926–1947: *Statistics of Income* data on "cash" increased to take account of corporations not reporting balance sheets by ratio of receipts of all corporations to receipts of corporations reporting balance sheet data. Adjustment was made in this column as well as cols. 3, 4, and 6–9 for the years 1934–1941 for changes due to reporting by corporations that previously filed consolidated returns as follows: from data in *Statistics of Income*, 1934, the 1934 ratios of cash of corporations industrially classified on 1934 basis to cash of corporations classified on 1933 basis were computed for each industry group, and used as divisors on the cash reported by these groups from 1934–1941. (Col. 1 is not affected by these corrections between industry groups.)

Columns 3 and 4 – 1926–1947: Same source and method as col. 2.

Column 5 – 1926–1940: Special deposits, demand loans and deposits, time drafts and deposits, and deposits in lieu of mortgaged property sold of Class I railroads and Class I switching and terminal companies, increased to account for Class II and III railroads and switching and terminal companies, by a ratio derived from the relative holdings of cash (account 708 in *Statistics of Railways*).
1941–1947: As above, excepting demand loans and deposits, time drafts and deposits, which were indistinguishable in these years.

Columns 6 to 9 – 1926–1947: Same source and method as col. 2.

Column 10 – 1926–1947: From *Statistics of Income*, various issues.

Column 11 – 1926–1947: From Table L-22, col. 6.

CASH OF MANUFACTURING CORPORATIONS   L-14
1899 to 1926

End of year	New sample	National Bureau of Economic Research Sample of:		Weighted average of National Bureau of Economic Research samples	Linked index	Estimate for all manufacturing corporations
		Large manufacturing corporations	Medium and small manufacturing corporations			
	1916 = 100.00	1926 = 100.00				$ mill.
	1	2	3	4	5	6
1899	45.84	–	–	–	24.6	881
1900	51.84	–	–	–	27.8	996
1901	49.19	–	–	–	26.4	944
1902	49.10	–	–	–	26.4	944
1903	47.64	–	–	–	25.6	916
1904	63.37	–	–	–	34.0	1 218
1905	56.77	–	–	–	30.5	1 090
1906	61.43	–	–	–	33.0	1 181
1907	61.23	–	–	–	32.9	1 177
1908	77.00	–	–	–	41.3	1 479
1909	75.52	–	–	–	40.6	1 451
1910	80.43	–	–	–	43.2	1 545
1911	90.35	–	–	–	48.5	1 736
1912	90.69	–	–	–	48.7	1 742
1913	88.56	–	–	–	47.6	1 701
1914	89.03	–	–	–	47.8	1 711
1915	101.79	–	–	–	54.7	1 955
1916	100.00	60.22	40.66	53.7	53.7	1 921
1917	–	74.48	28.33	59.1	59.1	2 115
1918	–	77.79	51.81	69.1	69.1	2 472
1919	–	77.02	52.99	69.0	69.0	2 469
1920	–	69.39	81.32	73.4	73.4	2 626
1921	–	67.40	56.75	63.9	63.9	2 286
1922	–	70.28	68.71	69.8	69.8	2 497
1923	–	77.68	89.27	81.5	81.5	2 916
1924	–	86.85	81.46	85.1	85.1	3 045
1925	–	95.80	82.35	91.3	91.3	3 267
1926	–	100.00	100.00	100.0	100.0	3 578

Column 1 – 1899–1916: Table L-15, col. 7.

Column 2 – 1916–1926: From Lutz, Friedrich A., *Corporate Cash Balances, 1914–43*, p. 114, table D-2, col. 1.

Column 3 – 1916–1926: *Ibid.*, p. 119, table D-3, col. 1.

Column 4 – 1916–1926: Arithmetic average of cols. 2 and 3, col. 2 being given a weight of 2 and col. 3 a weight of 1.

Column 5 – 1899–1915: Col. 1 for 1899–1915 linked to col. 4 at 1916, i.e., multiplied by 53.7/100.0.
1916–1926: Same as col. 4.

Column 6 – 1899–1925: 1926 value multiplied by index (col. 5) of cash of manufacturing corporations.
1926: From Table L-13, col. 2.

Column 1 – 1899–1916: All large manufacturing corporations (excluding U.S. Steel Corporation) reporting cash at least back to 1908 in the annual volumes of *Moody's Industrials*.

Column 2 – 1899–1916: Cash of corporations in col. 1.

Column 3 – 1900–1908: Cash of corporations reporting in previous year.
1909–1916: Same as col. 2.

Column 4 – 1900–1916: Median value of the set of ratios of cash in given year to cash in previous year of each corporation reporting in both years.

Column 5 – 1899–1916: Col. 4 chained, 1916 value being taken as 100.

Column 6 – 1899–1916: Derived from percentage of total value of product accounted for by establishments producing $1 million and over, as reported in the *Census of Manufactures* from 1904 to 1939. This group of establishments averaged 65 percent of the total value of manufacturing product for the census years 1919–1925, corresponding to the 2 to 1 weight given the sample of large corporations for 1916–1926. The adjustment ratio was applied to the index derived from the *Moody* sample for 1899–1916 to take account of the fact that for those years only data for the larger rapidly growing corporations were available, which accounted for an increasing percentage of total manufacturing. The annual ratios were derived by interpolating geometrically between the *Census of Manufactures* percentages and then calculating the ratio of the 1916 value to each given year's value.

Column 7 – 1899–1916: Col. 5 multiplied by col. 6. The adjusted index based on medians avoids the wide fluctuations caused by large absolute changes in cash holdings of a few companies.

Column 1 – 1916–1922: Cash holdings of eight trade corporations in National Bureau of Economic Research sample (*Corporate Financial Data for Studies in Business Finance*, Financial Research Program, National Bureau of Economic Research, table A-71).

Column 2 – 1916–1919: Estimated cash holdings for twenty-seven corporations based on 1922 ratio of cash holdings of the 27 corporations (col. 2) and the 8 corporations (col. 1).
1920–1926: Cash holdings of 27 corporations in the National Bureau of Economic Research samples (*ibid.*, table A-38).

Column 3 – 1916–1926: Col. 2 divided by 1926 holdings of 27 corporations.

Column 4 – 1916–1926: Based on sample of medium and small trade corporations by National Bureau of Economic Research (*ibid.*, table B-39).

Column 5 – 1916–1926: Col. 4 divided by 1926 value of col. 4.

Column 6 – 1916–1926: Average of cols. 3 and 5. The 1 to 1 weighting of the indices is based on the relative holdings of cash of trade corporations with total assets greater than $1 million and those with less than $1 million as reported in *Statistics of Income*.

Column 7 – 1916–1925: 1926 value times col. 6.
1926: Obtained by increasing the cash holdings of trade corporations as reported in *Statistics of Income* by 2.68 percent, the step-up being based on the average of 1931–1935 ratios of receipts of all trade corporations to receipts of trade corporations submitting balance sheets. (Earlier figures unavailable.)

CONSTRUCTION OF INDEX OF CASH OF MANUFACTURING CORPORATIONS L-15

(Excluding United States Steel Corporation): 1899 to 1916

End of year	Corporations reporting	Cash of all corporations (excluding U.S. Steel)	Cash of link corporations	Median of link relatives	Chain index of medians	Adjustment ratio	Adjusted index
	number	$ thous.	$ thous.	prev. yr. = 1	1916 = 100.0	1916 = 1	1916 = 100.00
	1	2	3	4	5	6	7
1899	4	5 888	.	.	29.5	1.554	45.84
1900	9	11 305	5 860	1.168	34.4	1.507	51.84
1901	12	15 044	12 152	0.978	33.6	1.464	49.19
1902	18	24 333	17 975	1.031	34.6	1.419	49.10
1903	27	32 734	23 512	1.001	34.6	1.377	47.64
1904	34	57 750	41 759	1.368	47.4	1.337	63.37
1905	38	56 179	54 345	0.921	43.7	1.299	56.77
1906	43	54 641	52 186	1.113	48.6	1.264	61.43
1907	44	77 114	72 097	1.027	49.9	1.227	61.23
1908	50	129 727	111 518	1.295	64.6	1.192	77.00
1909	50	131 985		1.007	65.1	1.160	75.52
1910	50	133 603		1.087	70.8	1.136	80.43
1911	50	165 636		1.145	81.1	1.114	90.35
1912	50	152 936		1.026	83.2	1.090	90.69
1913	50	136 250		0.997	83.0	1.067	88.56
1914	50	166 643		1.027	85.2	1.045	89.03
1915	50	209 894		1.169	99.6	1.022	101.79
1916	50	178 721		1.004	100.0	1.000	100.00

CASH HOLDINGS OF TRADE CORPORATIONS L-16

1916 to 1926

End of year	National Bureau of Economic Research sample		Index, large trade corporations	Sample medium and small corporations	Index, medium and small trade corporations	Index, all trade corporations	Cash of all trade corporations adjusted
	8 corporations	27 corporations					
	$ mill.	$ mill.	1926 = 100.0	$ thous.	1926 = 100.0	1926 = 100.0	$ mill.
	1	2	3	4	5	6	7
1916	12.2	15.1	16.3	191	73.2	44.8	535
1917	14.1	17.5	18.9	216	82.8	50.8	607
1918	17.5	21.7	23.5	184	70.5	47.0	562
1919	32.3	40.0	43.3	258	98.9	71.1	850
1920	20.2	30.7	33.2	264	101.1	67.2	803
1921	38.1	46.7	50.5	251	96.2	73.4	877
1922	33.4	41.4	44.8	276	105.7	75.2	899
1923	–	40.0	43.3	199	76.2	59.8	715
1924	–	59.2	64.1	223	85.4	74.8	894
1925	–	65.2	70.6	260	99.6	85.1	1 017
1926	–	92.4	100.0	261	100.0	100.0	1 195

Column 1 – 1896–1931: Col. 2 times 1.186 to cover subgroups not included in col. 2. The step-up ratio is based on the proportion in 1932 of cash of all transportation and public utility corporations to that of the groups covered in col. 2.

1932: From *Statistics of Income,* except steam railroad cash from col. 3.

Column 2 – 1896–1932: Sum of cols. 3–8.

Column 3 – 1896–1932: From Table L-19, col. 3.

Column 4 – 1896–1932: From Table L-20, col. 1.

Column 5 – 1896–1915: Extrapolated from 1916 value, using index of railroad cash (Table L-18, col. 6).

1916–1932: Cash of Class I companies and their lessors from *Statistics of Railways,* increased to include the cash of Class II and Class III companies. The step-up ratio was based on cash reported in account 708 by Class I and by Class II and III companies.

Column 6 – 1896: Extrapolated from 1897 using 1897–1902 slope.

1897: Extrapolated geometrically on basis of 1902, 1907, and 1912 values.

1898–1901: Linear interpolations.

1902, 1907, 1912, 1917, 1922, 1927: Estimated as percentage of 1932 value on basis of data on current assets and on value of plant and equipment in *Census of Electrical Industries.*

1903–1919: Linear interpolations between census years.

1920–1931: Interpolated between census years on basis of electric light and power company kwh capacity from Gould, J. M., *Output and Productivity in the Electric and Gas Utilities 1844–1942,* table 19.

1932: As reported in *Statistics of Income.*

Column 7 – 1896–1928: Extrapolated from cash reported in *Statistics of Income* for 1932 using assets of manufacturing gas companies as index. The index was interpolated linearly between 1904 and 1929 values given in Gould, *op. cit.,* and was extrapolated to 1896 using same slope.

1929–1931: Assumed equal to reported 1932 cash.

1932: From *Statistics of Income.*

Column 8 – 1896–1931: Extrapolated on basis of 1932 value using an index derived from cash holdings of Bell System and of Western Union Company obtained from *Moody's Manual.*

1932: From *Statistics of Income.*

CASH OF TRANSPORTATION AND PUBLIC UTILITY CORPORATIONS
BY INDUSTRIAL SUBGROUPS: 1896 to 1932

L-17

$ mill.

End of year	Total trans. and public utilities	Total columns 3 to 8	Steam railroads	Electric railways	Switching and terminal	Electric light and power	Gas	Telephone and telegraph
	1	2	3	4	5	6	7	3
1896	199	168	100	42	11	5	4	6
1897	237	200	114	48	12	6	6	14
1898	273	230	136	54	15	7	8	10
1899	296	250	147	58	16	9	10	10
1900	340	287	164	64	18	10	12	19
1901	414	349	213	74	23	11	14	14
1902	457	385	212	78	23	13	16	43
1903	499	421	210	76	23	16	18	78
1904	693	584	349	88	38	19	20	70
1905	668	563	355	90	39	22	22	35
1906	740	624	412	96	45	25	24	22
1907	733	618	375	92	41	28	26	56
1908	1 042	879	540	108	59	33	28	111
1909	1 179	994	663	120	72	38	31	70
1910	1 063	896	586	112	64	44	33	57
1911	1 182	997	644	118	70	49	35	81
1912	1 013	854	523	106	57	55	37	76
1913	920	776	458	100	50	62	39	67
1914	965	814	451	100	49	70	41	103
1915	1 120	944	553	108	60	78	43	102
1916	1 362	1 148	661	118	72	85	45	167
1917	1 086	916	533	98	59	93	47	86
1918	924	779	390	84	60	107	49	89
1919	834	703	221	108	44	122	51	157
1920	1 242	1 047	598	146	21	137	53	92
1921	1 296	1 093	591	138	37	151	55	121
1922	1 466	1 236	757	114	39	166	57	103
1923	1 464	1 234	653	160	34	209	60	118
1924	1 659	1 399	792	164	31	253	62	97
1925	1 879	1 584	865	228	28	297	64	102
1926	1 812	1 528	832	138	44	340	66	108
1927	1 783	1 503	769	146	41	384	68	95
1928	1 963	1 655	876	176	50	381	70	102
1929	1 856	1 565	802	148	60	378	72	105
1930	1 816	1 531	709	186	51	375	72	138
1931	1 459	1 230	496	148	39	372	72	103
1932	1 403	1 183	447	150	29	369	72	116

399

Column 1 – Number of railroads among 47 included in sample (all roads with assets of over $100 million in 1916) reporting cash in *Moody's Railroads* for each year.

Column 2 – Sum of cash reported by all railroads in sample for which information was available. (From 1910 on, col. 2 equals col. 3 equals col. 4.)

Column 3 – Cash in given year of those railroads which also reported in previous year.

Column 4 – Cash in given year of those railroads which also reported in succeeding year.

Column 5 – Col. 3 divided by col. 4 value of previous year.

Column 6 – Col. 5 chained, 1916 taken as 100. The effect of this procedure is to base movements of cash holdings of all railroads on the holdings of those railroads reporting in consecutive years.

Column 7 – Col. 6 multiplied by $ 660.9 million, the value for cash holdings of all railroads in 1916 as shown in Table L-19, col. 3.

Column 1 – 1896–1916: From Table L-18, col. 6.

Column 2 – 1916–1932: Sum of cash items (cash, deposits in lieu of mortgaged property sold, demand loans and deposits, time drafts and deposits, and special deposits) reported in annual volumes of *Statistics of Railways.*

Column 3 – 1896–1915: Col. 1 multiplied by 1916 value of col. 3.
1916–1932: Col. 2 increased by annual ratio of cash of all railroads to cash of Class I railroads. (*Statistics of Railways*, account 708.)

CONSTRUCTION OF INDEX OF CASH OF STEAM RAILROADS

1896 to 1916

End of year	Roads reporting	Total cash reporting	Cash of railroads reporting in		Link relatives	Chain index	Estimate of total cash of steam railroads
			Previous year	Succeeding year			
	number	$ thous.	$ thous.	$ thous.	Prev. yr. = 100	1916 = 100	$ mill.
	1	2	3	4	5	6	7
1896	32	52 293	.	52 293	.	15.14	100.1
1897	36	71 902	59 624	71 172	114.02	17.26	114.1
1898	37	95 717	84 655	95 211	118.94	20.53	135.7
1899	36	102 908	102 908	96 243	108.08	22.19	146.7
1900	36	109 266	107 580	103 908	111.78	24.80	163.9
1901	35	137 755	135 115	136 142	130.03	32.25	213.1
1902	37	146 456	135 400	143 158	99.45	32.07	212.0
1903	38	145 983	141 879	141 879	99.11	31.78	210.0
1904	39	240 798	235 846	240 798	166.23	52.83	349.2
1905	43	255 651	244 493	254 853	101.53	53.64	354.5
1906	43	297 512	296 142	297 512	116.20	62.33	411.9
1907	44	273 413	270 591	273 413	90.95	56.69	374.7
1908	45	404 259	394 089	404 259	144.14	81.71	540.0
1909	47	504 081	496 455	504 081	122.81	100.35	663.2
1910	47		445 387		88.36	88.66	586.0
1911	47		489 195		109.84	97.38	643.6
1912	47		397 428		81.24	79.12	522.9
1913	47		347 888		87.53	69.25	457.7
1914	47		342 752		98.52	68.23	450.9
1915	47		420 553		122.70	83.72	553.3
1916	47		502 341		119.45	100.00	660.9

CASH OF ALL STEAM RAILROADS

(Including Special Deposits): 1896 to 1932

End of year	Index of cash	Cash of Class I railroads	Estimate for all steam railroads	End of year	Index of cash	Cash of Class I railroads	Estimate for all steam railroads	End of year	Index of cash	Cash of Class I railroads	Estimate for all steam railroads
	1916=100	$ mill.	$ mill.		1916=100	$ mill.	$ mill.		1916=100	$ mill.	$ mill.
	1	2	3		1	2	3		1	2	3
1896	15.14	.	100	1909	100.35	.	663	1921	.	575	591
1897	17.26	.	114	1910	88.66	.	586	1922	.	737	757
1898	20.53	.	136	1911	97.38	.	644	1923	.	635	653
1899	22.19	.	147	1912	79.12	.	523	1924	.	764	792
1900	24.80	.	164	1913	69.25	.	458	1925	.	832	865
1901	32.25	.	213	1914	68.23	.	451	1926	.	799	832
1902	32.07	.	212	1915	83.72	.	553	1927	.	739	769
1903	31.78	.	210	1916	100.00	643	661	1928	.	845	876
1904	52.83	.	349	1917	.		519	533	1929	.	772	802
1905	53.64	.	355	1918	.	380	390	1930	.	688	709
1906	62.33	.	412	1919	.	215	221	1931	.	476	496
1907	56.69	.	375	1920	.	582	598	1932	.	432	447
1908	81.71	.	540								

Column 1 – 1896–1931: Estimated as twice col. 2, on basis of relationship between reported cash of the group in Bureau of Internal Revenue, *Statistics of Income*, 1932 ($150 million) and 1932 value of col. 2 ($77 million).

　　　　　　1932: From *Statistics of Income*.

Column 2 – 1896–1932: Sum of cols. 3–5.

Column 3 – 1896–1901: Rough estimates.

　　　　　　1902, 1907: From *Census of Electrical Industries*.

　　　　　　1912, 1917, 1922, 1927: Estimates based on "cash and current assets" or "cash, notes, and accounts receivable" as reported in *Census of Electrical Industries* and 1907 cash.

　　　　　　1903–1906, 1908–1911, 1913–1916, 1918–1921: Linear interpolations between census years.

　　　　　　1923–1932: Estimates based on 1927 cash and cash of electric railways reporting to Interstate Commerce Commission published in *Statistics of Railways*.

Column 4 – 1896–1915: Sum of 1916 estimates for cols. 4 and 5 multiplied by railroad cash index (Table L-18, col. 6).

　　　　　　1916: Estimated as same proportion of 1917 value as 1916 steam railroad cash, is of 1917 steam railroad cash (Table L-19, col. 3).

　　　　　　1917–1921, 1928–1929, 1931: *Moody's Manual*.

　　　　　　1922–1927, 1930, 1932: *Statistics of Railways*.

Column 5 – 1896–1915: Combined with col. 4.

　　　　　　1916–1932: All cash items and special deposits of nonoperating subsidiaries to Class I carriers from annual volumes of *Statistics of Railways*.

L-21

TABLE L–21

Column 1 – 1896–1926: Sum of cols. 2–5.

Column 2 – 1896–1926: From Table I–5, col. 10.

Column 3 – 1896–1926: From Table V-55, col. 2.

Column 4 – 1896–1926: From Table V-56, col. 2.

Column 5 – 1896–1925: Extrapolated from 1926 value using the sum of cols. 3 and 4 as index.

　　　　　　1926: Estimated on basis of separate estimates for constituent groups as slightly more than half the 1930 cash holdings of financial corporations, excluding banks and insurance companies, as reported in *Statistics of Income*, 1930.

1896 to 1932

$ mill.

End of year	Total industrial group		Electric railways	Pullman Company	Car lessors	End of year	Total industrial group		Electric railways	Pullman Company	Car lessors
	Adjusted	Unadjusted					Adjusted	Unadjusted			
	1	2	3	4	5		1	2	3	4	5
1896	42	21	16	5	—	1915	108	54	26	28	
1897	48	24	18	6	—	1916	118	59	26	10	23
1898	54	27	20	7	—	1917	98	49	26	8	15
1899	58	29	22	7	—	1918	84	42	28	0	14
1900	64	32	24	8	—	1919	108	54	30	9	15
1901	74	37	26	11	—	1920	146	73	32	26	15
1902	78	39	28	11	—	1921	138	69	34	20	15
1903	76	38	28	10	—	1922	114	57	36	6	15
1904	88	44	27	17	—	1923	160	80	38	12	30
1905	90	45	27	18	—	1924	164	82	47	3	32
1906	96	48	27	21	—	1925	228	114	77	4	33
1907	92	46	27	19	—	1926	138	69	43	4	22
1908	108	54	27	27	—	1927	146	73	43	6	24
1909	120	60	27	33	—	1928	176	88	56	6	26
1910	112	56	27	29	—	1929	148	74	38	5	31
1911	118	59	27	32	—	1930	186	93	43	4	46
1912	106	53	27	26	—	1931	148	74	27	11	36
1913	100	50	27	23	—	1932	150	77	25	13	39
1914	100	50	27	23	—						

CASH OF FINANCIAL CORPORATIONS EXCLUDING BANKS

1896 to 1926

$ mill.

End of year	All financial corporations excluding banks	Life insurance companies	Fire and marine insurance companies	Casualty and other insurance companies	Other financial corporations	End of year	All financial corporations excluding banks	Life insurance companies	Fire and marine insurance companies	Casualty and other insurance companies	Other financial corporations
	1	2	3	4	5		1	2	3	4	5
1896	187	46	19	3	119	1912	471	67	48	15	341
1897	234	61	24	3	146	1913	509	73	52	16	368
1898	223	69	20	4	130	1914	614	95	60	21	438
1899	227	67	21	4	135	1915	703	114	70	22	497
1900	267	75	25	5	162	1916	834	110	86	27	611
1901	313	89	30	5	189	1917	1 007	104	111	30	762
1902	339	96	32	6	205	1918	983	86	107	33	757
1903	354	111	31	7	205	1919	1 227	112	133	41	941
1904	360	104	33	7	216	1920	1 278	125	136	44	973
1905	352	77	35	8	232	1921	1 125	120	118	38	849
1906	422	70	46	9	297	1922	1 139	127	116	42	854
1907	368	67	39	8	254	1923	1 267	120	132	47	968
1908	373	72	37	10	254	1924	1 299	127	125	58	989
1909	444	72	47	11	314	1925	1 476	124	145	66	1 141
1910	455	71	46	14	324	1926	1 539	117	153	69	1 200
1911	498	75	52	14	357						

Column 1 – 1926–1947: Cash holdings of financial corporations submitting balance sheets from annual volumes of *Statistics of Income.*

Column 2 – 1926–1929: Estimated as same proportion of col. 1 as in 1930.
            1930–1947: *Statistics of Income, Source Book.*

Column 3 – 1926–1947: Col. 1 minus col. 2.

Column 4 – 1926–1930: Estimated as same as 1931.
            1931–1937: Ratio of receipts of all financial corporations except banks to receipts of financial corporations except banks submitting balance sheets with income tax returns. All data are reported in *Statistics of Income* except receipts of banks which submitted balance sheets. The latter were estimated on basis of relationship to total bank receipts in 1938 and to number of banks not filing balance sheets.
            1938–1947: As above, except all data taken from *Statistics of Income.*

Column 5 – 1926–1947: Adjustment ratio for lack of consolidated reporting 1934–1941. The ratio was taken as 1 for other years and the 1934 ratio of cash of nonbank financial corporations, classified on 1934 basis, to cash of nonbank financial corporations, classified on 1933 basis, was used for the period 1934–1941. Data are from *Statistics of Income,* 1934.

Column 6 – 1926–1947: Col. 3 multiplied by col. 4 divided by col. 5.

CASH OF FINANCIAL CORPORATIONS EXCLUDING BANKS
1926 to 1947

$ mill. (except cols. 4 and 5)

End of year	Cash holdings of			Adjustment ratio for coverage	Adjustment ratio for consolidation	Adjusted cash holdings of financial corporations excluding banks
	All financial corporations	Banks	Financial less banks			
	1	2	3	4	5	6
1926	9 777	8 015	1 762	1.0789	1.000	1 901
1927	9 721	7 969	1 752	1.0789	1.000	1 890
1928	14 278	11 705	2 573	1.0789	1.000	2 776
1929	14 471	11 863	2 608	1.0789	1.000	2 814
1930	13 207	10 827	2 380	1.0789	1.000	2 568
1931	9 375	7 710	1 665	1.0789	1.000	1 796
1932	9 581	7 967	1 614	1.0661	1.000	1 721
1933	9 252	7 690	1 562	1.0770	1.000	1 682
1934	13 702	11 446	2 256	1.0645	1.264	1 900
1935	16 985	14 091	2 894	1.0639	1.264	2 436
1936	18 872	16 104	2 768	1.0680	1.264	2 339
1937	17 685	15 060	2 625	1.0630	1.264	2 208
1938	20 314	17 409	2 905	1.0710	1.264	2 461
1939	25 518	22 091	3 427	1.0621	1.264	2 880
1940	31 103	27 009	4 094	1.0585	1.264	3 428
1941	30 434	26 683	3 751	1.0595	1.264	3 144
1942	30 837	27 918	2 919	1.0689	1.000	3 120
1943	30 714	27 751	2 963	1.0263	1.000	3 041
1944	33 152	30 267	2 885	1.0267	1.000	2 962
1945	38 105	34 941	3 164	1.0246	1.000	3 242
1946	38 404	34 660	3 744	1.0274	1.000	3 847
1947	42 318	37 911	4 407	1.0221	1.000	4 504

Column 1 – 1897–1920: Estimated at 1.25 percent throughout the period. The assumption that the rate on demand deposits was about the same as the average for the years 1921–1929 was necessitated by the absence of specific information. A rate of 1.25 percent, however, is compatible with the information available for all banks in the U.S. for the years 1908–1909 (cf. National Monetary Commission, *Special Report from the Banks of the United States*, April 28, 1909, part II) and 1909–1910 (cf. *Annual Report of the Comptroller of the Currency*, 1910, pp. 782–785); and with that for banks in New York State in 1917 (cf. *Hearings before the Joint Commission of Agricultural Inquiry*, 67th Congress, 1st Session, 1922, vol. II, pp. 605–607).

    1921–1926: Estimated on basis of data for national banks regarding total interest paid, interest paid on savings and interbank deposits and deposits as of June 30th, as given in the *Annual Reports of the Comptroller of the Currency*. The estimates so obtained were then linked to those derived for later periods.

    1927–1935: The ratio of interest paid during each year to deposits (excluding interbank deposits) on June 30 of the same year in member banks of the Federal Reserve System (cf. *Banking and Monetary Statistics*, pp. 73–75, 263–263).

    1936–1949: No interest paid on demand deposits.

Column 2 – 1897–1909: Assumed equal to the average interest rate paid by mutual savings banks, derived from Tables L-38, col. 4 and L-28, col. 2, as the average rate paid on all time deposits by commercial banks in 1909 and 1910 was virtually identical with the rate paid on savings deposits by mutual savings banks (cf. National Monetary Commission. *Special Report from the Banks of the United States*, April 28, 1909, p. 59; *Annual Report of the Comptroller of the Currency*, 1910, pp. 767–768).

    1910–1920: Estimated as falling from 100 percent of the average rate paid by mutual savings banks in 1909 to 88 percent in 1921, the latter figure representing the ratio between the average rate paid by mutual savings banks and the average rate paid by commercial banks on time deposits, as shown in this column.

    1921–1926: Estimated at 10 percent below the average rate on savings deposits for national banks, as shown in the *Annual Report of the Comptroller of the Currency*, the relationship prevailing in later years when both series were available.

    1927–1933: The ratio of interest paid during each year to deposits (excluding interbank) on June 30 of the same year in member banks of the Federal Reserve System (cf. *Banking and Monetary Statistics*, pp. 73–75, 262–263).

    1934–1949: Same procedure, but based on figures for all insured commercial banks (cf. *Annual Report of the Federal Deposit Insurance Corporation*, various issues).

Column 3 – 1897–1949: Sum of cols. 4–6.

Column 4 – 1897–1949: The rate of col. 1 applied to average of year-end demand deposits in farmers' accounts, as given in Table L-5, col. 8.

Column 5 – 1897–1949: The rate of col. 1 applied to average of year-end demand deposits in unincorporated business accounts as given in Table U-1, col. 1.

Column 6 – 1897–1949: The rate of col. 1 applied to average of year-end demand deposits in nonfarm individuals' accounts (excluding unincorporated business accounts), taken as Table L-5, col. 9 less Table U-1, col. 1.

Column 7 – 1897–1949: Sum of cols. 8 and 9.

Columns 8 and 9 – 1897–1949: Rate of col. 2 applied to average of year-end time deposits of individuals, as given in Table L-6, cols. 7 and 8, respectively.

1897 to 1949

$ mill. (except cols. 1 and 2)

Year	Average rate of interest, percent		Interest paid on individual accounts						
	Demand deposits	Time deposits	Demand deposits				Time deposits		
			Total	To farmers	To unincorporated business	To others	Total	To farmers	To others
	1	2	3	4	5	6	7	8	9
1897	1.25	3.64	16	2	10	4	20	2	18
1898	1.25	3.62	18	2	11	5	23	3	20
1899	1.25	3.57	23	3	14	6	25	3	22
1900	1.25	3.48	27	3	16	8	28	3	25
1901	1.25	3.46	30	4	17	9	34	4	30
1902	1.25	3.37	34	4	20	10	40	5	35
1903	1.25	3.41	37	5	21	11	46	6	40
1904	1.25	3.46	37	5	20	12	52	7	45
1905	1.25	3.47	41	5	22	14	62	8	54
1906	1.25	3.52	48	6	26	16	72	9	63
1907	1.25	3.62	48	7	25	16	79	11	68
1908	1.25	3.69	43	6	22	15	88	13	75
1909	1.25	3.70	41	6	20	15	105	16	89
1910	1.25	3.60	43	6	21	16	116	17	99
1911	1.25	3.57	45	6	22	17	129	18	111
1912	1.25	3.52	50	7	24	19	145	20	125
1913	1.25	3.49	55	7	26	22	150	20	130
1914	1.25	3.51	60	8	28	24	150	20	130
1915	1.25	3.50	68	9	32	27	163	21	142
1916	1.25	3.44	88	11	40	37	176	22	154
1917	1.25	3.43	107	13	44	50	222	27	195
1918	1.25	3.46	123	16	45	62	255	33	222
1919	1.25	3.46	144	19	49	76	292	39	253
1920	1.25	3.43	145	19	54	72	339	45	294
1921	1.35	3.46	138	18	59	61	349	46	303
1922	1.20	3.42	122	15	52	55	364	46	318
1923	1.19	3.38	126	15	53	58	407	49	358
1924	1.19	3.33	127	15	52	60	444	52	392
1925	1.10	3.28	134	15	53	66	473	52	421
1926	1.18	3.27	129	15	56	58	503	52	451
1927	1.18	3.32	130	15	57	58	545	55	490
1928	1.25	3.24	131	16	59	56	563	57	506
1929	1.30	3.32	120	16	62	42	575	58	517
1930	1.13	3.25	99	12	54	33	550	54	496
1931	0.78	2.86	61	7	32	22	436	41	395
1932	0.69	2.84	48	4	25	19	365	34	331
1933	0.30	2.57	20	2	11	7	277	27	250
1934	0.07	2.42	5	1	2	2	246	25	221
1935	0.05	2.00	5	1	2	2	228	23	205
1936	–	1.71	–	–	–	–	211	21	190
1937	–	1.61	–	–	–	–	211	22	189
1938	–	1.55	–	–	–	–	207	22	185
1939	–	1.43	–	–	–	–	192	20	172
1940	–	1.30	–	–	–	–	181	19	162
1941	–	1.20	–	–	–	–	171	19	152
1942	–	1.10	–	–	–	–	161	19	142
1943	–	0.93	–	–	–	–	152	18	134
1944	–	0.87	–	–	–	–	176	20	156
1945	–	0.87	–	–	–	–	222	25	197
1946	–	0.84	–	–	–	–	254	29	225
1947	–	0.87	–	–	–	–	284	32	252
1948	–	0.90	–	–	–	–	301	34	267
1949	–	0.91	–	–	–	–	307	35	272

Column 1 – 1896–1915A, 1917: Estimated as average of preceding and following June figures (derived from revised banking statistics of Federal Reserve Board) multiplied by ratio of December to average of preceding and following June figures for national banks (derived from *Annual Report of the Comptroller of the Currency*). Where data were not given for June 30 or Dec. 31, those for nearest call dates were used.

         1915B–1916, 1918–1932: Same as above except that multiplier is based on figures for member banks of the Federal Reserve System (derived from *Banking and Monetary Statistics*, p. 72).

         1933: Total assets of member banks multiplied by ratio of deposits of all commercial banks to deposits of member banks (derived from *Banking and Monetary Statistics*, pp. 19 and 72). This method yields figures for 1932 and 1934 about one-half percent below the figures shown.

         1934–1949: Total assets of insured commercial banks from *Annual Report of the Federal Deposit Insurance Corporation* multiplied by ratio of deposits of all commercial banks (*Banking and Monetary Statistics*, p. 19, and *Federal Reserve Bulletin*, various issues) to deposits of insured commercial banks.

Column 2 – 1896–1923A: Same sources and method as col. 1.

         1923B–1938: *Banking and Monetary Statistics*, table 3, p. 19.

         1939–1949: *Federal Reserve Bulletin*, various issues.

Column 3 – 1896–1932: Average of preceding and succeeding June figures from revised banking statistics of Federal Reserve Board.

         1933: Estimated as declining from June 1933 figure (from above source) by approximately one-half decline in total loans of nonmember banks plus decline in real estate loans of member banks, since decline in total loans of member banks was very small in June-Dec. 1933 period and proportion of real estate loans to total loans of nonmember banks is near 50 percent. Shift in source from 1932 to 1934 results in an overstatement of decline in real estate loans in 1933 or 1934, but since sources do not overlap, size of error, though probably under $100 million, is unknown.

         1934–1949: Real estate loans of insured commercial banks (from *Annual Report of the Federal Deposit Insurance Corporation*) plus real estate loans of uninsured banks, estimated as 50 percent of their total loans, the latter taken as the difference between total loans of insured commercial banks (*ibid.*) and total loans of all commercial banks (cf. col. 2). Percentage of real estate loans to total loans for uninsured banks was assumed to be slightly higher than that for insured banks not members of the Federal Reserve System, which was about 40 percent (derived from *Annual Report of the Federal Deposit Insurance Corporation* and *Federal Reserve Bulletin*, various issues).

Column 4 – 1896–1949: From Table A-61, col. 9.

Column 5 – 1896–1949: Col. 3 minus col. 4.

Column 6 – 1896–1949: Col. 2 minus col. 3.

Column 7 – 1896–1915A and 1917: Sum of Dec. estimates for U.S. Government securities and for all other investments. Estimates made separately for U.S. Government and for other securities by multiplying average of June figures for all commercial banks (derived from revised banking statistics of Federal Reserve Board) by ratio of December figures to average of preceding and following June figures for national banks (derived from *Annual Report of the Comptroller of the Currency*). Where data were not given for June 30 or Dec. 31, data for nearest call date were used.

         1915B–1916, 1918–1923A: Average of June figures (as above) multiplied by ratio of Dec. to June averages for member banks (derived from *Banking and Monetary Statistics*, p. 72).

         1923B–1938: *Banking and Monetary Statistics*, p. 19.

         1939–1949: *Federal Reserve Bulletin*, various issues.

Column 8 – 1896–1949: Col. 1 minus sum of cols. 2 and 7. Consists mostly of cash but also contains real estate and minor miscellaneous assets. In 1948 and 1949, the derived figures come within 0.1 percent of total assets for commercial banks less banks in possessions as reported in *Annual Report of the Comptroller of the Currency.*

ASSETS OF COMMERCIAL BANKS
1896 to 1949
$ mill.

End of year	Total assets	Loans					Investments	Cash and other assets
		Total	On real estate			Other		
			Total	Farm	Nonfarm			
	1	2	3	4	5	6	7	8
1896	6 126	3 561	420	85	335	3 141	834	1 731
1897	6 896	3 922	420	88	332	3 502	924	2 050
1898	7 703	4 149	440	98	342	3 709	1 130	2 424
1899	8 085	4 712	464	112	352	4 248	1 263	2 110
1900	10 011	5 310	510	134	376	4 800	1 489	3 212
1901	10 780	6 100	572	160	412	5 528	1 737	2 943
1902	11 730	6 784	646	182	464	6 138	1 928	3 018
1903	12 286	7 539	722	197	525	6 817	2 099	2 648
1904	14 052	7 737	812	216	596	6 925	2 354	3 961
1905	15 529	8 690	944	247	697	7 746	2 509	4 330
1906	16 316	9 537	1 064	286	778	8 473	2 721	4 058
1907	16 432	9 479	1 100	299	801	8 379	3 081	3 872
1908	17 643	9 707	1 152	305	847	8 555	2 978	4 958
1909	18 864	10 578	1 312	344	968	9 266	3 084	5 202
1910	19 226	11 076	1 469	412	1 057	9 607	3 182	4 968
1911	20 574	11 643	1 606	510	1 096	10 037	3 593	5 338
1912	21 822	12 580	1 752	599	1 153	10 828	3 647	5 595
1913	22 683	12 901	1 816	645	1 171	11 085	3 733	6 049
1914	23 058	13 225	1 894	658	1 236	11 331	4 364	5 469
1915A	27 388	15 420	2 044	699	1 345	13 376	4 576	7 392
1915B	27 527	15 507	2 044	699	1 345	13 463	4 602	7 418
1916	30 972	17 383	2 244	867	1 377	15 139	5 064	8 525
1917	36 747	19 963	2 420	946	1 474	17 543	6 917	9 867
1918	40 988	21 467	2 519	973	1 546	18 948	9 001	10 520
1919	47 843	26 584	2 888	1 147	1 741	23 696	9 321	11 938
1920	46 644	28 473	3 290	1 390	1 900	25 183	8 378	9 793
1921	42 208	25 338	3 522	1 487	2 035	21 816	8 293	8 577
1922	47 267	26 176	3 954	1 455	2 499	22 222	10 187	10 904
1923A	49 203	27 619	4 460	1 331	3 129	23 159	10 222	11 362
1923B	49 203	27 216	4 460	1 331	3 129	22 756	10 080	11 907
1924	54 224	28 356	4 964	1 136	3 828	23 392	11 480	14 388
1925	57 475	31 284	5 490	1 107	4 383	25 794	11 727	14 464
1926	58 105	31 962	5 850	1 066	4 784	26 112	11 965	14 178
1927	61 433	33 196	6 058	1 012	5 046	27 138	13 584	14 653
1928	66 429	35 123	6 202	955	5 247	28 921	14 216	17 090
1929	65 621	35 966	6 170	904	5 266	29 796	13 501	16 154
1930	61 985	32 034	5 903	850	5 053	26 131	14 666	15 285
1931	51 420	25 226	5 326	839	4 487	19 900	14 427	11 767
1932	45 738	20 081	4 562	789	3 773	15 519	15 002	10 655
1933	40 640	16 246	4 150	617	3 533	12 096	14 543	9 851
1934	47 586	14 988	3 523	525	2 998	11 465	18 747	13 851
1935	52 338	15 119	3 523	515	3 008	11 596	20 863	16 356
1936	57 672	16 358	3 643	512	3 131	12 715	23 114	18 200
1937	55 475	17 100	3 816	523	3 293	13 284	21 233	17 142
1938	58 243	16 364	4 029	541	3 488	12 335	22 305	19 574
1939	64 997	17 238	4 323	558	3 765	12 915	23 430	24 329
1940	72 799	18 800	4 671	568	4 103	14 129	25 129	28 870
1941	78 886	21 714	5 002	558	4 444	16 712	29 032	28 140
1942	96 891	19 221	4 804	493	4 311	14 417	48 172	29 498
1943	114 199	19 117	4 574	462	4 112	14 543	65 978	29 104
1944	137 090	21 644	4 488	462	4 026	17 156	83 886	31 560
1945	160 151	26 083	4 836	519	4 317	21 247	97 936	36 132
1946	149 517	31 122	7 297	701	6 596	23 825	82 871	35 524
1947	155 156	38 057	9 503	814	8 689	28 554	78 226	38 873
1948	154 506	42 488	10 926	869	10 057	31 562	71 811	40 207
1949	157 462	42 965	11 646	905	10 741	31 319	77 232	37 265

NON-REAL ESTATE LOANS OF COMMERCIAL BANKS
1896 to 1949

$ mill.

End of year	Total	Farm	Nonfarm Total	Nonfarm For purchasing or carrying securities	Nonfarm Consumer loans	Nonfarm Other	End of year	Total	Farm	Nonfarm Total	Nonfarm For purchasing or carrying securities	Nonfarm Consumer loans	Nonfarm Other
	1	2	3	4	5	6		1	2	3	4	5	6
1896	3 141	310	2 831	445		2 386	1923A	23 159	2 944	20 215	3 511	974	15 730
1897	3 502	318	3 184	519		2 665	1923B	22 756	2 944	19 812	3 511	974	15 327
1898	3 709	355	3 354	594		2 760	1924	23 392	2 674	20 718	4 469	1 063	15 186
1899	4 248	407	3 841	708		3 133							
							1925	25 794	2 699	23 095	5 878	1 287	15 930
1900	4 800	488	4 312	825		3 487	1926	26 112	2 568	23 544	5 727	1 432	16 385
1901	5 528	583	4 945	983		3 962	1927	27 138	2 552	24 586	7 110	1 561	15 915
1902	6 138	662	5 476	1 065		4 411	1928A	28 921	2 596	26 325	7 924	1 814	16 587
1903	6 817	716	6 101	1 142		4 959	1928B	28 921	2 596	26 325	8 234	1 814	16 277
1904	6 925	783	6 142	1 177		4 965	1929	29 796	2 491	27 305	8 278	2 049	16 978
1905	7 746	898	6 848	1 330		5 518	1930	26 131	2 109	24 022	7 251	1 869	14 902
1906	8 473	1 038	7 435	1 378		6 057	1931	19 900	1 650	18 250	4 739	1 324	12 187
1907	8 379	1 086	7 293	1 329		5 964	1932	15 519	1 272	14 247	3 324	894	10 029
1908	8 555	1 110	7 445	1 372		6 073	1933	12 096	913	11 183	3 078	718	7 387
1909	9 266	1 250	8 016	1 470		6 546	1934A	11 465	628	10 837	2 696	837	7 304
							1934B	11 465	628	10 837	2 684	837	7 316
1910	9 607	1 338	8 269	1 455		6 814	1935	11 596	735	10 861	2 664	1 051	7 146
1911	10 037	1 380	8 657	1 489		7 168	1936	12 715	621	12 094	2 695	1 407	7 992
1912	10 828	1 520	9 308	1 578		7 730	1937	13 284	683	12 601	2 044	1 668	8 889
1913	11 085	1 597	9 488	1 547		7 941	1938	12 335	789	11 546	1 879	1 669	7 998
1914	11 331	1 606	9 725	1 642		8 083	1939	12 915	900	12 015	1 635	1 911	8 469
1915A	13 376	1 748	11 628	2 054		9 574	1940	14 129	984	13 145	1 412	2 105	9 628
1915B	13 463	1 748	11 715	2 068		9 647	1941	16 712	1 073	15 639	1 296	2 315	12 028
1916	15 139	2 034	13 105	2 357		10 748	1942	14 417	924	13 493	1 567	1 730	10 196
1917	17 543	2 489	15 054	2 465		12 589	1943	14 543	936	13 607	2 366	1 448	9 793
1918	18 948	2 662	16 286	2 797		13 489	1944	17 156	949	16 207	4 602	1 557	10 048
1919A	23 696	3 454	20 242	3 579		16 663							
1919B	23 696	3 454	20 242	3 624		16 618	1945	21 247	1 034	20 213	6 876	1 947	11 390
							1946	23 825	1 289	22 536	3 174	3 164	16 198
1920	25 183	3 870	21 313	2 969		18 344	1947	28 554	1 593	26 961	2 047	4 077	20 837
1921	21 816	3 281	18 535	2 894		15 641	1948	31 562	1 946	29 616	2 305	4 536	22 775
1922	22 222	3 088	19 134	3 567		15 567	1949	31 319	2 049	29 270	2 634	4 858	21 778

Column 1 – 1896–1949: Table L-24, col. 6.

Column 2 – 1896–1949: Table A-62, col. 2.

Column 3 – 1896–1949: Col. 1 minus col. 2.

Column 4 – 1896–1949: From Table D-8, sum of cols. 3 and 4.

Column 5 – 1896–1922: Included in col. 6.
1923–1949: Sum of installment loans and single-payment loans of commercial banks, Table D-4, cols. 2 and 10.

Column 6 – 1896–1949: Col. 3 minus cols. 4 and 5.

1934 to 1949

$ mill. (except cols. 3 and 6)

End of year	Loans			Securities other than U.S. Government		
	All banks	Insured banks	Ratio	All banks	Insured banks	Ratio
	1	2	3	4	5	6
1934	14 988	14 614	1.0256	6 709	6 322	1.0612
1935	15 119	14 719	1.0272	7 171	6 841	1.0482
1936	16 358	15 965	1.0246	7 780	7 558	1.0294
1937	17 100	16 750	1.0209	7 077	6 807	1.0397
1938	16 364	16 024	1.0212	7 234	6 944	1.0418
1939	17 238	16 866	1.0221	7 114	6 860	1.0370
1940	18 800	18 397	1.0219	7 372	7 099	1.0385
1941	21 714	21 262	1.0213	7 225	6 985	1.0344
1942	19 221	18 907	1.0166	6 793	6 633	1.0241
1943	19 117	18 844	1.0145	6 136	5 983	1.0256
1944	21 644	21 355	1.0135	6 329	6 157	1.0279
1945	26 083	25 769	1.0122	7 331	7 133	1.0278
1946	31 122	30 740	1.0124	8 091	7 893	1.0251
1947	38 057	37 592	1.0124	9 006	8 753	1.0289
1948	42 488	41 979	1.0121	9 189	8 932	1.0288
1949	42 965	42 499	1.0110	10 227	9 977	1.0251

Column 1 – 1934–1938: From *Banking and Monetary Statistics*, p. 19.
    1939–1949: From *Federal Reserve Bulletin*, various issues.

Column 2 – 1934–1948: From *Annual Report of the Federal Deposit Insurance Corporation*, 1938 and following issues.
    1949: From Federal Deposit Insurance Corporation, *Assets and Liabilities of Operating Insured Commercial and Savings Banks*, no. 32, Dec. 31, 1949.

Column 3 – 1934–1949: Col. 1 divided by col. 2.

Column 4 – 1934–1935: Total investments of commercial banks from *Banking and Monetary Statistics*, p. 19, minus estimated U.S. Government bonds held. Latter were estimated (as in Table V-74) as the product of average of preceding and following June figures in *Banking and Monetary Statistics* multiplied by ratio of U.S. Government bonds held at end of year by insured commercial banks to average of June holdings, from *Annual Report of the Federal Deposit Insurance Corporation*, 1938.
    1936–1949: Same source as col. 1.

Column 5 – 1934–1949: Same source as col. 2.

Column 6 – 1934–1949: Col. 4 divided by col. 5.

INDIVIDUALS' SAVING THROUGH MUTUAL SAVINGS BANKS

1897 to 1949

$ mill.

Year	Total	Operating banks			Closed banks	Year	Total	Operating banks			Closed banks
		Change in deposits	Change in surplus		Change in deposits			Change in deposits	Change in surplus		Change in deposits
			Unadjusted	Adjusted					Unadjusted	Adjusted	
	1	2	3	4	5		1	2	3	4	5
1897	91	85	10	8	-2	1924	506	442	72	64	0
1898	118	108	6	11	-1	1925	464	399	87	65	0
1899	119	109	8	14	-4	1926	533	464	85	70	-1
1900	193	180	11	15	-2	1927	654	582	84	72	0
1901	131	114	6	17	0	1928	581	505	26	76	0
1902	145	129	2	17	-1	1929	148	68	27	80	0
1903	121	104	-2	17	0	1930	674	586	81	79	9
1904	130	113	8	17	0	1931	664	583	-6	83	-2
1905	183	169	7	14	0	1932	10	-83	33	90	3
1906	168	154	-3	14	0	1933	-334	-441	87	94	13
1907	71	58	-12	14	-1	1934	335	250	-41	92	-7
1908	55	42	28	13	0	1935	214	133	32	87	-6
1909	174	158	5	13	3	1936	288	185	161	107	-4
1910	148	127	50	16	5	1937	220	114	-142	110	-4
1911	152	134	12	20	-2	1938	206	108	-28	100	-2
1912	184	161	20	24	-1	1939	335	245	-1	90	0
1913	174	146	10	27	1	1940	222	135	-20	87	0
1914	112	86	15	28	-2	1941	-24	-125	14	101	0
1915	152	125	. 9	29	-2	1942	216	108	-13	108	0
1916	313	283	-39	30	0	1943	1 188	1 076	57	112	0
1917	120	90	60	32	-2	1944	1 752	1 634	104	118	0
1918	151	116	8	35	0	1945	2 138	2 003	204	135	0
1919	446	407	21	39	0	1946	1 620	1 481	177	139	0
1920	503	455	23	48	0	1947	1 065	928	104	137	0
1921	301	247	73	54	0	1948	784	642	112	142	0
1922	419	360	80	57	2	1949	1 027	888	112	139	0
1923	436	376	49	61	-1						

Column 1 – Sum of cols. 2, 4, and 5.

Column 2 – Annual change in Table L-28, col. 2.

Column 3 – Annual change in Table L-28, col. 3.

Column 4 – From Table L-31, col. 3.

Column 5 – From Table L-37, col. 4.

LIABILITIES AND SURPLUS OF MUTUAL SAVINGS BANKS
1896 to 1949

$ mill.

End of year	Total surplus and liabilities	Deposits	Surplus	Other liabilities	End of year	Total surplus and liabilities	Deposits	Surplus	Other liabilities
	1	2	3	4		1	2	3	4
1896	1 911	1 742	167	2	1923	7 023	6 378	632	13
1897	2 008	1 827	177	4	1924	7 538	6 820	704	14
1898	2 122	1 935	183	4	1925	8 025	7 219	791	15
1899	2 241	2 044	191	6	1926	8 572	7 683	876	13
1900	2 430	2 224	202	4	1927	9 240	8 265	960	15
1901	2 548	2 338	208	2	1928	9 780	8 770	986	24
1902	2 679	2 467	210	2	1929	9 873	8 838	1 013	22
1903	2 785	2 571	208	6	1930	10 535	9 424	1 094	17
1904	2 912	2 684	216	12	1931	11 137	10 012	1 088	37
1905	3 085	2 853	223	9	1932	11 103	9 929	1 121	53
1906	3 231	3 007	220	4	1933	10 758	9 488	1 208	62
1907	3 277	3 065	208	4	1934	11 008	9 738	1 167	103
1908	3 345	3 107	236	2	1935	11 173	9 871	1 199	103
1909	3 508	3 265	241	2	1936	11 485	10 056	1 360	69
1910	3 690	3 392	291	7	1937	11 562	10 170	1 218	174
1911	3 837	3 526	303	8	1938	11 611	10 278	1 190	143
1912	4 015	3 687	323	5	1939	11 852	10 523	1 189	140
1913	4 170	3 833	333	4	1940	11 981	10 658	1 169	154
1914	4 273	3 919	348	6	1941	11 808	10 533	1 183	92
1915	4 408	4 044	357	7	1942	11 907	10 641	1 170	96
1916	4 651	4 327	318	6	1943	13 024	11 717	1 227	80
1917	4 810	4 417	378	15	1944	14 761	13 351	1 331	79
1918	4 940	4 533	386	21	1945	16 987	15 354	1 535	98
1919	5 363	4 940	407	16	1946	18 665	16 835	1 712	118
1920	5 840	5 395	430	15	1947	19 714	17 763	1 816	135
1921	6 160	5 642	503	15	1948	20 474	18 405	1 928	141
1922	6 597	6 002	583	12	1949	21 493	19 293	2 040	160

Column 1 – 1896–1949: Sum of cols. 2–4.

Column 2 – 1896–1908: Obtained by adding year-end figures from *Annual Reports, New York State Superintendent of Banks* to figures for Massachusetts and Connecticut, interpolated between reporting dates, and to figures for all other states, interpolated between midyear dates, as shown in the *Annual Report of the Comptroller of the Currency.*
> 1909: *Annual Report of the Comptroller of the Currency*, linear interpolation from April 28, 1909 (special call report for National Monetary Commission) to June 30, 1910.
> 1910–1922: Same as for 1896–1908.
> 1923–1937: *Banking and Monetary Statistics*, table 1, p. 17.
> 1938–1949: *Annual Report of the Comptroller of the Currency* (December 31, 1938 figure for deposits is identical with the *Banking and Monetary Statistics* figure).

Columns 3 and 4 – 1896–1922: Same source as col. 2.
> 1923–1935: *Annual Report of the Comptroller of the Currency*, average of June 30 figures, various issues.
> 1936–1949: *Annual Report of the Comptroller of the Currency*, various issues.

Column 1 – 1896–1949: From Table L-28, col. 1.

Columns 2 to 10 – 1896–1937: Obtained by multiplying col. 1 with average of relevant percentages on preceding and following June 30, derived from tabulation of assets and liabilities of mutual savings banks by the Federal Reserve Board.

    Total assets as tabulated by the Board agree closely with June figures of the Comptroller of the Currency, but latter figures were used as controlling totals since they were available by states at time computations were made, facilitating development of Dec. 31 figures (cf. notes to Table L-28).

    1938–1949: *Annual Report of the Comptroller of the Currency*, various issues.

ASSETS OF MUTUAL SAVINGS BANKS
1896 to 1949
$ mill.

End of year	Total assets	Cash	Loans			Securities				Other assets
			Total	Real estate	Other	Total	U.S. Government	State and local government	Other	
	1	2	3	4	5	6	7	8	9	10
1896	1 911	96	883	738	145	886	158	488	240	46
1897	2 008	104	907	764	143	949	159	524	266	48
1898	2 122	117	940	791	149	1 012	153	562	297	53
1899	2 241	116	986	825	161	1 067	134	563	370	72
1900	2 430	122	1 052	877	175	1 169	102	580	487	87
1901	2 548	127	1 099	913	186	1 238	76	596	566	84
1902	2 679	123	1 164	963	201	1 304	59	632	613	88
1903	2 785	128	1 214	1 008	206	1 351	45	660	646	92
1904	2 912	134	1 267	1 066	201	1 412	38	670	704	99
1905	3 085	133	1 357	1 141	216	1 496	31	691	774	99
1906	3 231	136	1 457	1 228	229	1 544	19	698	827	94
1907	3 277	144	1 497	1 284	213	1 534	20	675	839	102
1908	3 345	157	1 543	1 352	191	1 565	13	682	870	80
1909	3 508	161	1 642	1 446	196	1 642	14	723	905	63
1910	3 690	166	1 749	1 542	207	1 701	11	756	934	74
1911	3 837	169	1 849	1 642	207	1 758	12	766	980	61
1912	4 015	169	1 971	1 754	217	1 807	12	787	1 008	68
1913	4 170	183	2 068	1 847	221	1 844	13	832	999	75
1914	4 273	205	2 119	1 897	222	1 868	13	855	1 000	81
1915	4 408	220	2 178	1 958	220	1 922	9	846	1 067	88
1916	4 651	242	2 275	2 061	214	2 046	23	865	1 158	88
1917	4 810	236	2 338	2 126	212	2 140	139	837	1 164	96
1918	4 940	227	2 302	2 095	207	2 312	415	728	1 169	99
1919	5 363	225	2 473	2 199	274	2 574	686	676	1 212	91
1920	5 840	222	2 768	2 423	345	2 757	856	688	1 213	93
1921	6 160	222	2 932	2 636	296	2 907	973	702	1 232	99
1922	6 597	224	3 180	2 929	251	3 087	1 088	699	1 300	106
1923	7 023	232	3 533	3 294	239	3 146	1 131	674	1 341	112
1924	7 538	241	3 950	3 724	226	3 226	1 100	709	1 417	121
1925	8 025	241	4 342	4 101	241	3 298	1 019	754	1 525	144
1926	8 572	249	4 775	4 518	257	3 394	891	823	1 680	154
1927	9 240	249	5 240	4 970	270	3 585	776	887	1 922	166
1928	9 780	235	5 672	5 359	313	3 677	665	919	2 093	196
1929	9 873	257	5 786	5 460	326	3 613	533	908	2 172	217
1930	10 540	337	5 987	5 713	274	3 963	569	970	2 424	253
1931	11 137	423	6 148	5 948	200	4 254	668	1 006	2 580	312
1932	11 103	444	6 073	5 918	155	4 153	711	955	2 487	433
1933	10 758	463	5 669	5 551	118	4 067	839	904	2 324	559
1934	11 008	517	5 449	5 350	99	4 315	1 255	880	2 180	727
1935	11 173	536	5 174	5 085	89	4 614	1 787	827	2 000	849
1936	11 485	540	5 042	4 950	92	4 984	2 222	804	1 958	919
1937	11 562	555	4 949	4 857	92	5 145	2 521	763	1 861	913
1938	11 611	578	4 895	4 816	79	5 267	2 883	674	1 710	871
1939	11 852	814	4 925	4 836	89	5 293	3 102	620	1 571	820
1940	11 981	968	4 958	4 859	99	5 289	3 224	608	1 457	766
1941	11 808	795	4 905	4 812	93	5 473	3 700	439	1 334	635
1942	11 907	661	4 694	4 627	67	6 032	4 551	313	1 168	520
1943	13 024	796	4 474	4 420	54	7 376	6 088	201	1 087	378
1944	14 761	582	4 362	4 305	57	9 544	8 321	130	1 093	273
1945	16 987	608	4 272	4 208	64	11 905	10 662	93	1 150	202
1946	18 665	816	4 515	4 441	74	13 159	11 759	63	1 337	175
1947	19 714	886	4 944	4 855	89	13 696	11 978	65	1 653	188
1948	20 474	878	5 686	5 583	103	13 709	11 476	71	2 162	201
1949	21 493	873	6 578	6 472	106	13 822	11 428	86	2 308	220

Column 1 – 1896–1949: From Table L-29, col. 4.

Column 2 – 1896–1913: Estimated by applying average ratio of farm to total mortgages as reported in
    Annual Report of the Comptroller of the Currency, 1914 and 1915, to total mortgages, 1896–1913.
  1914–1915: See 1896–1913.
  1916–1918: Linear interpolation between 1915 and 1919 values.
  1919–1922: Estimated from examination of state data in *Annual Report of the Comptroller of the
    Currency*.
  1923–1933: Estimated as declining from 1.74 percent of total mortgages in 1923 to 1.69 percent
    of total mortgages in 1933. Ratios are obtained by linear interpolation between 1922 and
    1934 values.
  1934: From Horton, D. C., *Regional Variations in the Sources and in the Tenure Distribution of
    Farm Mortgage Credit Outstanding, January 1, 1935* (Bureau of Agricultural Economics process-
    ed report, Feb. 1938).
  1935–1946: Estimated on basis of 1934 and 1947 ratios as declining from 1.55 percent of total
    mortgages in 1935 to 0.66 percent in 1946.
  1947–1949: *Annual Report of the Comptroller of the Currency*.

Column 3 – 1896–1949: Col. 1 minus col. 2.

Column 4 – 1896–1949: From Table L-29, col. 9.

Column 5 – 1896–1949: Col. 4 minus col. 6.

Column 6 – 1896–1908: Estimated as sum of: (a) bank stocks held as reported in *Annual Report of the
    Comptroller of the Currency*; and (b) other stocks, estimated as same percentage of nongovern-
    ment securities as in 1909, i.e., ratio of 1909 stocks less bank stocks (assumed equal to 1908)
    to total nongovernment securities.
  1909: Estimated on basis of average percentage of stocks to total nongovernment securities as
    reported in *Annual Report of the Comptroller of Currency*, 1909 and 1910.
  1910–1928: Estimated as a declining percentage of total nongovernment securities, linearly
    interpolated between June 1910 (4.16 percent) and June 1929 (3.47 percent) values.
  1929–1935: Estimated as average percentage of nongovernment securities on June 30 preceding
    and succeeding as calculated from *Annual Report of the Comptroller of the Currency*.
  1936–1949: From *Annual Report of the Comptroller of the Currency*.

Column 7 – 1896–1949: From Table L-29, col. 10.

Columns 8 and 9 – 1896–1908: Total of cols. 8 and 9 interpolated between reported June figures in *Annual
    Report the Comptroller of the Currency* and split in same proportion as average of 1909–1913
    ratio.
  1909–1935: Average of preceding and succeeding June figures as reported in *Annual Report of
    the Comptroller of the Currency*.
  1936–1949: From *Annual Report of the Comptroller of the Currency*.

Column 10 – 1896–1949: Col. 7 minus sum of cols. 8 and 9.

1896 to 1949

$ mill.

End of year	Real estate loans			Corporate securities			Miscellaneous assets			
	Total	Farm	Nonfarm	Total	Bonds	Stocks	Total	Bank premises	Other real estate	Other assets
	1	2	3	4	5	6	7	8	9	10
1896	738	32	706	240	192	48	46	24	11	11
1897	764	33	731	266	221	45	48	24	11	13
1898	791	34	757	297	249	48	53	26	12	15
1899	825	35	790	370	327	43	72	29	13	30
1900	877	38	839	487	444	43	87	29	13	45
1901	913	39	874	566	518	48	84	29	13	42
1902	963	41	922	613	565	48	88	29	13	46
1903	1 008	43	965	646	600	46	92	29	13	50
1904	1 066	46	1 020	704	660	44	99	29	13	57
1905	1 141	49	1 092	774	731	43	99	29	13	57
1906	1 228	53	1 175	827	785	42	94	29	12	53
1907	1 284	55	1 229	839	798	41	102	29	13	60
1908	1 352	58	1 294	870	830	40	80	30	13	37
1909	1 446	62	1 384	905	865	40	63	33	11	19
1910	1 542	66	1 476	934	895	39	74	35	9	30
1911	1 642	70	1 572	980	940	40	61	36	10	15
1912	1 754	75	1 679	1 008	967	41	68	38	11	19
1913	1 847	79	1 768	999	959	40	75	40	12	23
1914	1 897	88	1 809	1 000	960	40	81	40	16	25
1915	1 958	77	1 881	1 067	1 025	42	88	40	19	29
1916	2 061	67	1 994	1 158	1 113	45	88	40	21	27
1917	2 126	62	2 064	1 164	1 119	45	96	40	23	33
1918	2 095	57	2 038	1 169	1 124	45	99	42	21	36
1919	2 199	57	2 142	1 212	1 166	46	91	42	14	35
1920	2 423	57	2 366	1 213	1 167	46	93	44	11	38
1921	2 636	53	2 583	1 232	1 186	46	99	48	12	39
1922	2 929	51	2 878	1 300	1 252	48	106	52	9	45
1923	3 294	57	3 237	1 341	1 292	49	112	61	6	45
1924	3 724	64	3 660	1 417	1 365	52	121	71	6	44
1925	4 101	71	4 030	1 525	1 470	55	144	79	8	57
1926	4 518	78	4 440	1 680	1 620	60	154	88	12	54
1927	4 970	85	4 885	1 922	1 854	68	166	97	14	55
1928	5 359	92	5 267	2 093	2 020	73	196	106	19	71
1929	5 460	93	5 367	2 172	2 095	77	217	112	34	71
1930	5 713	97	5 616	2 424	2 333	91	253	118	54	81
1931	5 948	101	5 847	2 580	2 457	123	312	128	96	88
1932	5 918	100	5 818	2 487	2 353	134	433	136	191	106
1933	5 551	94	5 457	2 324	2 188	136	559	138	316	105
1934	5 350	90	5 260	2 180	2 053	127	727	137	458	132
1935	5 085	81	5 004	2 000	1 874	126	849	135	602	112
1936	4 950	75	4 875	1 958	1 816	142	919	133	699	87
1937	4 857	69	4 788	1 861	1 724	137	913	133	691	89
1938	4 816	65	4 751	1 710	1 556	154	871	129	656	86
1939	4 836	61	4 775	1 571	1 435	136	820	126	602	92
1940	4 859	57	4 802	1 457	1 261	196	766	122	554	90
1941	4 812	52	4 760	1 334	1 162	172	635	118	424	93
1942	4 627	46	4 581	1 168	1 005	163	520	115	317	88
1943	4 420	41	4 379	1 087	929	158	378	107	197	74
1944	4 305	36	4 269	1 093	934	159	273	102	96	75
1945	4 208	31	4 177	1 150	984	166	202	95	35	72
1946	4 441	29	4 412	1 337	1 157	180	175	92	18	65
1947	4 855	28	4 827	1 653	1 507	146	188	93	11	84
1948	5 583	34	5 549	2 162	2 005	157	201	100	8	93
1949	6 472	36	6 436	2 308	2 151	157	220	103	7	110

RETAINED EARNINGS AND CAPITAL GAINS OR LOSSES OF MUTUAL SAVINGS BANKS: 1897 to 1949

$ mill.

Year	Retained earnings			Change in reported surplus	Inferred net capital gain or loss	Year	Retained earnings			Change in reported surplus	Inferred net capital gain or loss
	New York	Massa-chusetts	U.S.				New York	Massa-chusetts	U.S.		
	1	2	3	4	5		1	2	3	4	5
1897	3.6	.	8	10	2	1924	37.5	12.0	64	72	8
1898	5.0	.	11	6	−5	1925	38.5	11.8	65	87	22
1899	6.1	.	14	8	−6	1926	41.5	12.2	70	85	15
1900	7.1	.	15	11	−4	1927	43.2	12.4	72	84	12
1901	8.0	.	17	6	−11	1928	45.2	13.4	76	26	−50
1902	8.1	.	17	2	−15	1929	47.7	14.0	80	27	−53
1903	8.0	.	17	−2	−19	1930	50.5	10.8	79	81	2
1904	8.0	.	17	8	−9	1931	53.0	12.2	83	−6	−89
1905	7.1	.	14	7	−7	1932	55.3	15.4	90	33	−57
1906	6.5	3.7	14	−3	−17	1933	54.0	20.4	94	87	−7
1907	6.1	4.4	14	−12	−26	1934	51.5	21.0	92	−41	−133
1908	6.0	3.8	13	28	15	1935	47.1	21.2	87	32	−55
1909	6.2	3.3	13	5	−8	1936	62.8	21.2	107	161	54
1910	8.0	3.8	16	50	34	1937	62.6	22.8	110	−142	−252
1911	10.5	4.1	20	12	−8	1938	55.2	23.5	100	−28	−128
1912	13.3	4.1	24	20	−4	1939	48.5	22.8	90	−1	−91
1913	14.5	5.0	27	10	−17	1940	46.3	22.8	87	−20	−107
1914	15.2	4.9	28	15	−13	1941	55.6	23.8	101	14	−87
1915	16.0	5.4	29	9	−20	1942	59.3	25.3	108	−13	−121
1916	16.5	5.3	30	−39	−69	1943	60.0	25.5	112	57	−55
1917	17.7	5.5	32	60	28	1944	66.9	25.3	118	104	−14
1918	20.0	5.4	35	8	−27	1945	83.3	22.3	135	204	69
1919	23.0	5.5	39	21	−18	1946	84.5	24.6	139	177	38
1920	26.3	9.1	48	23	−25	1947	80.5	25.5	137	104	−33
1921	29.5	10.8	54	73	19	1948	85.0	25.8	142	112	−30
1922	32.1	11.2	57	80	23	1949	74.8	24.2	139	112	−27
1923	35.2	11.2	61	49	−12						

Column 1 – 1897–1934: Unpublished estimates of Savings Banks Trust Co. made from samples taken at five-year intervals from *Annual Reports, New York State Superintendent of Banks*, representing 20 percent of total assets of all banks in the state. Retained income was defined as total operating income less operating expenses and dividends paid. The sample was then raised on the rates of sample assets to assets of all banks. Estimates for intervening years were made from a curve plotted for sample years. Estimates were checked against complete tabulations made for 1908, 1909, and 1932, and tied to reported figures for 1935.
1935–1949: *Annual Reports, New York State Superintendent of Banks.*

Column 2 – 1906–1949: Retained earnings equals: total ordinary income; minus total ordinary charges; plus transfers to guaranty fund; minus ordinary dividends; minus extra dividends; minus banking houses written down; minus assessments. From *Annual Reports, Massachusetts Commissioner of Banks.*

Column 3 – 1897–1944: Estimated by dividing New York bank earnings (1897–1905), or sum of New York and Massachusetts earnings (1906–1947), by annual percentages of New York and Massachusetts deposits to total U.S. deposits, as shown in *Annual Report of the Comptroller of the Currency*, reduced by multiplying them by 0.931, the ratio between computed and reported earnings figures for 1945–1947.
1945–1949: From *Mutual Savings Bank Earnings*, annual releases of the National Association of Mutual Savings Banks, New York, N.Y. Amounts added to surplus and guarantee accounts less capital gains and losses.

Column 4 – 1897–1949: Annual change of Table L-28, col. 3.

Column 5 – 1897–1949: Col. 4 minus col. 3.

1935 to 1949

$ mill.

Year	New York	Massachusetts	Other states		United States	
			Estimate A	Estimate B	Estimate A	Estimate B
	1	2	3	4	5	6
1935	−46.2	−14.6	−22.1	.	−82.9	.
1936	−41.8	−9.7	−19.1	.	−70.6	.
1937	−37.8	−13.2	−19.2	.	−70.2	.
1938	−108.2	−18.2	−46.0	.	−172.4	.
1939	−56.8	−21.1	−28.1	.	−106.0	.
1940	−66.6	−22.7	−31.9	.	−121.2	.
1941	−131.0	−22.1	−55.5	.	−208.6	.
1942	−81.8	−26.7	−40.3	.	−148.8	.
1943	−36.1	−23.9	−22.5	.	−82.5	.
1944	−22.5	−9.9	−12.2	.	−44.6	.
1945	36.3	10.9	17.8	25.0	65.0	72.2
1946	31.8	13.4	17.0	16.3	62.2	61.5
1947	−13.9	−1.7	−5.8	1.1	−21.4	−14.5
1948	−11.0	−5.7	−6.0	−4.1	−22.7	−20.8
1949	−8.8	−4.6	−4.6	−12.0	−18.0	−25.4

Column 1 – 1935–1949: *Annual Report, New York State Superintendent of Banks.*

Column 2 – 1935–1949: *Annual Report, Massachusetts Commissioner of Banks.* Includes profits from securities sold and matured, real estate by foreclosure, recoveries on loans, transfers from reserve, and miscellaneous; less charges on securities sold, depreciation of securities charged off, premiums charged off, losses and depreciation on real estate by foreclosure, loans, transfer to reserve, and miscellaneous.

Column 3 – 1935–1949: Col. 5 minus sum of cols. 1 and 2.

Column 4 – 1945–1949: *Mutual Savings Bank Earnings,* annual release of National Association of Mutual Savings Banks. Figures for "other states" obtained by subtracting figures for New York and Massachusetts (adjusted for "transfers from or to reserves") from total.

Column 5 – 1935–1949: Sum of cols. 1 and 2 multiplied by proportion of total U.S. deposits to sum of New York and Massachusetts deposits.

Column 6 – 1945–1949: Same source as col. 4.

Column 1 – 1934–1942: Ratio of midyear deposits of banks reporting to Federal Deposit Insurance Corporation (cf. *Assets and Liabilities of Operating Insured Banks*, various issues) to midyear deposits of all mutual savings banks as shown in Table L-28, col. 2.

1943–1949: Same method, but based on average deposits of banks reporting to Federal Deposit Insurance Corporation (cf. *Annual Report of Federal Deposit Insurance Corporation*, 1947, p. 155).

Columns 2 to 11 – 1934–1949: *Annual Report of Federal Deposit Insurance Corporation*, various issues, e.g. 1947, pp. 154–155.

Column 1 – 1935–1949: Table L-32, col. 5.

Column 2 – 1943–1949: Based on Table L-33, col. 2 minus col. 8 and ratio of total deposits of insured mutual savings banks to those of all mutual savings banks (from Table L-33, col. 1). The ratios are too small before 1943 (less than 0.20) to justify a blow-up estimate.

Column 3 – 1945–1949: From *Mutual Savings Bank Earnings* (annual release of National Association of Mutual Savings Banks), cf. Table L-32, col. 6.

Column 4 – 1935–1949: Table L-31, col. 5.

Column 5 – 1935–1949: Average of cols. 1 and 4.

CAPITAL GAINS AND LOSSES OF INSURED MUTUAL SAVINGS BANKS
1934 to 1949

$ mill. (except col. 1)

Year	Proportion of deposits in insured mutual savings banks	Recoveries and profits						Losses and charge-offs			
		Total	On securities			On loans	Other	Total	On securities	On loans	Other
			Total	Recoveries	Profits						
	1	2	3	4	5	6	7	8	9	10	11
1934	0.11	5	2	1	1	1	2	11	5	3	3
1935	0.11	7	3	1	2	2	2	9	3	3	3
1936	0.10	12	4	0	4	1	7	12	3	2	7
1937	0.10	10	3	0	3	1	6	15	7	5	3
1938	0.10	8	4	0	4	1	3	28	13	1	14
1939	0.12	14	9	1	8	0	5	26	10	2	14
1940	0.13	12	9	2	7	0	3	47	14	18	15
1941	0.17	23	17	3	14	1	5	35	17	6	12
1942	0.18	19	12	5	7	1	6	33	10	9	14
1943	0.64	129	72	41	31	11	46	169	33	74	62
1944	0.66	102	62	31	31	15	25	114	18	68	28
1945	0.67	182	127	48	79	4	51	136	37	29	70
1946	0.68	187	125	35	90	2	60	142	72	3	67
1947	0.68	99	60	32	28	1	38	112	59	4	49
1948	0.68	60	22	15	7	0	38	77	24	7	46
1949	0.68	78	54	20	34	0	24	88	31	8	49

COMPARISON OF FOUR ESTIMATES OF NET CAPITAL GAINS AND LOSSES OF MUTUAL SAVINGS BANKS: 1935 to 1949

$ mill.

Year	Estimates based on				Average of estimates shown in cols. 1 and 4	Year	Estimates based on				Average of estimates shown in cols. 1 and 4
	Reported capital gains and losses			Comparison of estimated retained net earnings and reported surplus change			Reported capital gains and losses			Comparison of estimated retained net earnings and reported surplus change	
	A	B	C				A	B	C		
	1	2	3	4	5		1	2	3	4	5
1935	−83	−	−	−55	−69	1943	−83	−63	−	−55	−69
1936	−71	−	−	54	−8	1944	−45	−18	−	−14	−30
1937	−70	−	−	−252	−161						
1938	−172	−	−	−128	−150	1945	65	69	72	69	67
1939	−106	−	−	−91	−98	1946	62	66	62	38	50
						1947	−21	−19	−15	−33	−27
1940	−121	−	−	−107	−114	1948	−23	−25	−21	−30	−26
1941	−209	−	−	−87	−148	1949	−18	−15	−25	−27	−22
1942	−149	−	−	−121	−135						

Column 1 – 1897–1934: Table L-31, col. 5.
 1935–1942: Table L-34, col. 5.
 1943–1949: Table L-34, col. 2.

Columns 2 to 4 – 1897–1905: Allocation is very arbitrary, guided by experience in later period. Generally rough estimate was first made (as in following period until 1929) of losses on mortgages and real estate and gains or losses on securities obtained as residual. Capital losses throughout intended to include write-offs of bond premiums.
 1906–1934: Allocation guided mostly by the results of Massachusetts savings banks as shown in *Annual Reports, Massachusetts Commissioner of Banks.*
 1935–1942: Allocation estimated on basis of reported results for Massachusetts and New York savings banks.
 1943–1949: Based on mutual savings banks included in the statistics of the Federal Deposit Insurance Corporation (cf. Table L-33). Profits or losses on "other assets" have been allocated to real estate.

Column 1 – From Table L-35, col. 2.

Column 2 – Very rough estimates based on such indicators as total profits on securities (col. 1); trend of U.S. Government bond prices; volume of holdings of U.S. Government securities; and profits or losses on U.S. Government securities by life insurance companies. Estimates have been expressed in round figures and have been kept on the conservative side, i.e., they have been entered only when it appeared fairly certain that in a given year substantial profits or losses on U.S. Government securities were made.

Column 3 – Very rough guesses based on considerations similar to those applying for col. 2.

Column 4 – Col. 1 minus cols. 2 and 3.

DISTRIBUTION OF TOTAL NET CAPITAL GAINS OR LOSSES OF MUTUAL SAVINGS BANKS: 1897 to 1949

$ mill.

Year	Total estimated net capital gain or loss	Allocated to:			Year	Total estimated net capital gain or loss	Allocated to:		
		Securities	Mortgages, loans and real estate	Other assets			Securities	Mortgages, loans and real estate	Other assets
	1	2	3	4		1	2	3	4
1897	2	0	2	–	1924	8	12	–2	–2
1898	–5	–3	–2	–	1925	22	26	–2	–2
1899	–6	–4	–2	–	1926	15	20	–3	–2
1900	–4	–2	–2	–	1927	12	19	–5	–2
1901	–11	–9	–2	–	1928	–50	–38	–10	–2
1902	–15	–12	–3	–	1929	–53	–41	–10	–2
1903	–19	–16	–3	–	1930	2	10	–10	2
1904	–9	–6	–3	–	1931	–89	–67	–20	–2
1905	–7	–4	–3	–	1932	–57	–25	–30	–2
1906	–17	–13	–4	–	1933	–7	25	–30	–2
1907	–26	–21	–5	–	1934	–133	–101	–30	–2
1908	15	20	–5	–	1935	–69	–27	–40	–2
1909	–8	–3	–5	–	1936	–8	34	–40	–2
1910	34	39	–5	–	1937	–161	–99	–60	–2
1911	–8	–4	–4	–	1938	–150	–57	–90	–3
1912	–4	0	–4	–	1939	–98	–2	–90	–6
1913	–17	–13	–4	–	1940	–114	–16	–90	–8
1914	–13	–10	–3	–	1941	–148	8	–150	–6
1915	–20	–17	–3	–	1942	–135	15	–150	0
1916	–69	–66	–3	–	1943	–63	60	–123	0
1917	28	32	–4	–	1944	–18	66	–84	0
1918	–27	–23	–4	–	1945	69	119	–50	0
1919	–18	–14	–4	–	1946	66	78	–12	0
1920	–25	–21	–4	–	1947	–19	1	–20	0
1921	19	23	–4	–	1948	–25	–3	–22	0
1922	23	27	–2	–2	1949	–15	34	–49	0
1923	–12	–8	–2	–2					

DISTRIBUTION OF MUTUAL SAVINGS BANKS' PROFITS OR LOSSES ON SECURITIES: 1929 to 1949

$ mill.

Year	Total	On U.S. Government securities	On state and municipal securities	On other securities	Year	Total	On U.S. Government securities	On state and municipal securities	On other securities
	1	2	3	4		1	2	3	4
1929	–41	0	0	–41	1940	–16	0	0	–16
1930	10	0	0	10	1941	8	10	0	–2
1931	–67	0	0	–67	1942	15	10	0	5
1932	–25	0	0	–25	1943	60	45	5	10
1933	25	0	0	25	1944	66	56	10	0
1934	–101	0	0	–101	1945	119	90	10	19
1935	–27	0	0	–27	1946	78	50	10	18
1936	34	0	0	34	1947	1	1	0	0
1937	–99	0	0	–99	1948	–3	–3	0	0
1938	–57	0	0	–57	1949	34	24	5	5
1939	–2	0	0	–2					

DEPOSITS AND PAYMENTS TO DEPOSITORS
OF MUTUAL SAVINGS BANKS IN LIQUIDATION: 1896 to 1938

$ mill.

Year	Deposits in banks suspended during year	Estimated deposits in banks in liquidation at year's end	Change in deposits in closed banks		Year	Deposits in banks suspended during year	Estimated deposits in banks in liquidation at year's end	Change in deposits in closed banks	
			Unadjusted	Adjusted for depositors' losses				Unadjusted	Adjusted for depositors' losses
	1	2	3	4		1	2	3	4
1896	6	13	.	.	1918	–	0	–1	0
1897	2	11	–2	–2	1919	0	0	0	0
1898	3	10	–1	–1	1920	0	0	0	0
1899	0	6	–4	–4	1921	–	0	0	0
1900	0	3	–3	–2	1922	2	2	2	2
1901	1	2	–1	0	1923	–	1	–1	–1
1902	–	1	–1	–1	1924	–	1	0	0
1903	–	1	0	0	1925	–	1	0	0
1904	1	1	0	0	1926	–	0	–1	–1
1905	–	1	0	0	1927	–	0	0	0
1906	–	1	0	0	1928	0	0	0	0
1907	0	0	–1	–1	1929	–	0	0	0
1908	0	0	0	0	1930	16	14	14	9
1909	3	3	3	3	1931	0	11	–3	–2
1910	8	9	6	5	1932	9	16	5	3
1911	0	7	–2	–2	1933	25	34	18	13
1912	1	6	–1	–1	1934	–	24	–10	–7
1913	3	6	0	1	1935	–	15	–9	–6
1914	1	4	–2	–2	1936	–	8	–7	–4
1915	–	2	–2	–2	1937	–	2	–6	–4
1916	–	2	0	0	1938	–	0	–2	–2
1917	–	1	–1	–2					

Column 1 – 1896–1933: *Annual Report of the Federal Deposit Insurance Corporation,* 1934, pp. 112–113.

Column 2 – 1896–1938: Estimated on basis of average five-year liquidation period.

Column 3 – 1897–1938: Annual change in col. 2.

Column 4 – 1897–1938: Deposits minus losses during year, from *Annual Report of the Federal Deposit Insurance Corporation,* 1934, pp. 111–113, adjusted as for col. 2 on basis of average liquidation period of five years.

TABLE L-38

Column 1 – *Annual Reports, New York State Superintendent of Banks.*

Column 2 – *Annual Reports, Massachusetts Commissioner of Banks.*

Column 3 – Computed from *Annual Reports of the Comptroller of the Currency.*

Column 4 – Sum of cols. 1 and 2 divided by col. 3. For the year 1908, a check is provided by the interest payments by mutual savings banks shown in the National Monetary Commission, *Special Report from the Banks of the United States,* April 28, 1909, p. 44. Figure of $115 million for the twelve months ending April 28, 1909 is virtually identical with estimate of $114 million for 1908 shown in Table L-38.

For the years 1945 to 1949, payments to depositors of interest and dividends as reported in the National Association of Mutual Savings Banks, *Mutual Savings Bank Earnings,* annual issues, are also virtually identical to figures shown in Table L-38.

Column 5 – From Table L-27, sum of cols. 2 and 5.

Column 6 – Col. 5 minus col. 4.

ANNUAL IN- OR OUTPAYMENTS BY OR TO DEPOSITORS
IN MUTUAL SAVINGS BANKS: 1897 to 1949

$ mill. (except col. 3)

Year	Dividends paid		Ratio of N.Y. and Mass. deposits to U.S. total	Estimated U.S. dividends	Annual change in U.S. deposits	Estimated annual in- or out- payments
	New York	Massachusetts				
	1	2	3	4	5	6
1897	26.6	17.5	0.675	65	83	18
1898	27.9	18.2	0.680	68	107	39
1899	29.5	18.6	0.676	71	105	34
1900	31.3	19.1	0.682	74	178	104
1901	33.6	19.5	0.676	79	114	35
1902	34.9	20.2	0.677	81	128	47
1903	36.8	21.0	0.676	86	104	18
1904	39.9	22.0	0.682	91	113	22
1905	43.2	22.8	0.689	96	169	73
1906	47.0	23.7	0.687	103	154	51
1907	50.0	25.4	0.684	110	57	−53
1908	50.9	26.8	0.680	114	42	−72
1909	53.2	27.1	0.679	118	161	43
1910	54.6	27.9	0.681	121	132	11
1911	56.7	29.2	0.680	126	132	6
1912	58.6	30.6	0.681	131	160	29
1913	60.6	32.4	0.680	137	147	10
1914	63.2	34.1	0.681	143	84	−59
1915	65.1	35.4	0.681	148	123	−25
1916	68.8	36.8	0.683	155	283	128
1917	72.2	39.1	0.682	163	88	−75
1918	73.8	42.2	0.682	170	116	−54
1919	79.7	45.3	0.688	182	407	225
1920	88.0	49.7	0.692	199	455	256
1921	97.9	54.2	0.697	218	247	29
1922	105.8	56.3	0.704	230	362	132
1923	117.1	60.0	0.709	250	375	125
1924	126.6	65.0	0.715	268	442	174
1925	136.8	69.4	0.719	287	399	112
1926	149.4	74.4	0.718	312	463	151
1927	163.5	79.8	0.724	336	582	246
1928	178.5	86.0	0.721	367	505	138
1929	191.9	93.1	0.723	394	68	−326
1930	197.1	98.5	0.723	409	595	186
1931	200.6	96.4	0.730	407	581	174
1932	184.0	86.8	0.735	368	−80	−448
1933	152.8	71.4	0.740	303	−428	−731
1934	142.9	65.4	0.735	283	243	−40
1935	119.9	60.8	0.733	247	127	−120
1936	101.6	56.8	0.727	218	181	−37
1937	102.8	54.8	0.725	217	110	−107
1938	104.2	52.3	0.733	214	106	−108
1939	107.5	49.8	0.736	214	245	31
1940	106.3	46.9	0.736	208	135	−73
1941	93.6	44.5	0.734	188	−125	−313
1942	91.2	43.6	0.727	185	108	−77
1943	95.7	43.6	0.727	192	1 076	884
1944	105.6	44.1	0.726	206	1 634	1 428
1945	116.0	47.5	0.726	225	2 003	1 778
1946	129.3	52.0	0.727	249	1 481	1 232
1947	146.6	56.9	0.730	279	928	649
1948	160.7	60 1	0.735	300	642	342
1949	197.3	62.5	0.742	350	888	538

Column 1 – Sum of cols. 2 and 3.

Column 2 – Sum of annual changes in Table L-40, cols. 2 and 4.

Column 3 – Sum of annual changes in Table L-40, cols. 5 and 6.

Column 1 – 1911–1949: Same as Table L-41, col. 1.

Columns 2 to 6 – 1911–1935: Allocated for all years from distribution by type of liability in sources for col. 1, above.

        1936–1947: Col. 1 allocated by distribution of liabilities in *Annual Report of Operations of Federal Credit Unions*, published annually by Farm Credit Administration and Federal Deposit Insurance Corporation; and in State Banking Reports from Iowa, Minnesota, Wisconsin, Ohio, Michigan, Illinois, Massachusetts, Indiana, New York, and Rhode Island.

        1948–1949: Share capital and reserves from same source as col. 1; remaining columns distributed on basis of previous years.

Note: Details may not add to total because of rounding.

INDIVIDUALS' SAVING THROUGH CREDIT UNIONS: 1912 to 1949

$ mill.

Year	Saving	Change in shares and deposits	Change in reserves and undivided earnings	Year	Saving	Change in shares and deposits	Change in reserves and undivided earnings
	1	2	3		1	2	3
1912	0.1	0.1	0	1931	−1.0	−1.5	0.5
1913	0.1	0.1	0	1932	−1.5	−1.6	0.1
1914	0.1	0.1	0	1933	1.3	1.0	0.3
				1934	7.4	6.4	1.0
1915	0.2	0.2	0				
1916	0.5	0.5	0	1935	15.2	13.1	2.1
1917	0.6	0.5	0.1	1936	22.9	22.4	0.5
1918	0.9	0.8	0.1	1937	32.2	28.8	3.4
1919	1.3	1.3	0	1938	31.2	29.4	1.8
				1939	44.8	41.4	3.4
1920	2.3	2.1	0.2	1940	57.4	53.8	3.6
1921	2.3	2.0	0.3	1941	71.1	66.0	5.1
1922	2.7	2.4	0.3	1942	18.2	16.2	2.0
1923	3.7	3.3	0.4	1943	14.6	14.7	−0.1
1924	3.3	2.9	0.4	1944	40.7	39.8	0.9
1925	2.7	2.5	0.2	1945	34.5	29.1	5.4
1926	4.5	4.0	0.5	1946	60.5	56.6	3.9
1927	5.7	5.2	0.5	1947	93.3	86.5	6.8
1928	7.9	7.3	0.6	1948	109.9	93.8	16.1
1929	2.2	1.7	0.5	1949	123.5	106.9	16.6
1930	−4.3	−4.5	0.2				

LIABILITIES AND EQUITY OF CREDIT UNIONS: 1911 to 1949

$ mill.

End of year	Total	Deposits	Other liabilities	Share capital	Reserves	Undivided earnings and surplus	End of year	Total	Deposits	Other liabilities	Share capital	Reserves	Undivided earnings and surplus
	1	2	3	4	5	6		1	2	3	4	5	6
1911	0	0	0	0	0	0	1931	36.6	7.7	0.8	23.3	3.5	1.3
1912	0.1	0	0	0.1	0	0	1932	35.6	7.9	1.3	21.5	3.6	1.3
1913	0.2	0.1	0	0.1	0	0	1933	37.0	8.1	1.4	22.3	3.8	1.4
1914	0.3	0.1	0	0.2	0	0	1934	44.4	9.7	1.4	27.1	4.4	1.8
1915	0.5	0.2	0	0.3	0	0	1935	59.5	12.0	1.3	37.9	5.6	2.7
1916	1.0	0.4	0	0.6	0	0	1936	83.1	11.6	2.0	60.7	5.9	2.9
1917	1.7	0.6	0.1	0.9	0	0.1	1937	115.4	15.7	2.1	85.4	8.2	4.0
1918	2.5	1.0	0	1.3	0.1	0.1	1938	147.2	14.4	2.7	116.1	8.8	5.2
1919	3.9	1.3	0.1	2.3	0.1	0.1	1939	192.7	15.4	3.4	156.5	10.6	6.8
1920	6.3	2.0	0.2	3.7	0.2	0.2	1940	252.3	13.6	5.6	212.1	12.4	8.6
1921	8.6	2.1	0.2	5.6	0.3	0.4	1941	322.5	15.4	4.7	276.3	15.5	10.6
1922	11.3	2.6	0.2	7.5	0.5	0.5	1942	340.3	16.8	4.3	291.1	18.4	9.7
1923	15.0	3.3	0.2	10 1	0.7	0.7	1943	355.3	19.2	4.7	303.4	19.2	8.8
1924	18.3	3.7	0.2	12.6	0.9	0.9	1944	397.9	22.9	6.6	339.5	20.5	8.4
1925	21.2	3.9	0.4	14.9	1.1	0.9	1945	434.6	25.3	8.8	366.2	24.5	9.8
1926	25.9	4.3	0.6	18.5	1.5	1.0	1946	495.2	17.8	8.9	430.3	27.6	10.6
1927	31.8	5.3	0.8	22.7	1.8	1.2	1947	591.1	24.9	11.5	509.7	30.0	15.0
1928	39.8	8.1	0.9	27.2	2.2	1.4	1948	701.5	25.0	12.0	603.4	43.9	17.2
1929	42.4	8.7	1.3	28.3	2 6	1.5	1949	828.0	35.0	17.0	700.3	43.3	34.4
1930	37.7	7.6	0.9	24.9	2.9	1.4							

Column 1 – 1911–1916: *Annual Report, Massachusetts Commissioner of Banks*, part II, *Credit Unions*.
  1917–1928: Estimated from State Banking Reports for Massachusetts and New York.
  1929–1932: Estimated from State Banking Reports for Massachusetts, New York, and Rhode Island.
  1933–1935: Estimated from reports of above states and Indiana.
  1936–1946: Department of Labor, Bureau of Labor Statistics, *Consumers' Cooperatives and Credit Unions: Operations in 1946*, Bulletin 922, p. 18.
  1947–1949: Department of Labor, "Operations of Credit Unions in 194." *Monthly Labor Review*, Oct. 1948, Sept. 1949, and Sept. 1950 issues.

Columns 2, 8, and 10 – 1911–1947: Allocated for all years from data on distribution by type of assets in sources listed in col. 1 and in additional State Banking Reports for later years from Iowa, Minnesota, Wisconsin, Ohio, Michigan, and Illinois.
  1948–1949: Estimated on basis of change in total assets and relation of these items to the total in previous years.

Column 3 – 1939–1949: Farm Credit Administration and Federal Deposit Insurance Corporation, *Annual Report of Operations of Federal Credit Unions*, 1939–1949. Assumed zero for years before 1939.

Column 4 – 1911–1949: Same as for col. 2, but includes "loans to other credit unions" by Federal Credit Unions from 1939–1948, from Farm Credit Administration and Federal Deposit Insurance Corporation *Reports*.

Column 5 – 1911–1928: Estimated by applying ratio of "personal" to "total" loans for each year to "total" loans for the period 1929–1934.
  1929–1949: *Federal Reserve Bulletin*, various issues.

Column 6 – 1911–1949: Col. 4 minus col. 5.

Column 7 – 1911–1947: Same as for col. 2, but excluding "loans to other credit unions" by Federal Credit Unions for 1939–1948, from Farm Credit Administration and Federal Deposit Insurance Corporation *Reports*.
  1948–1949: Same source as col. 2.

Column 9 – 1911–1949: Col. 7 minus col. 8.

Note: Details may not add to totals because of rounding.

ASSETS OF CREDIT UNIONS
1911 to 1949

$ mill.

End of year	Total	Cash	Federal savings and loan shares	Loans			Investments			Other assets
				Total	Personal	Other	Total	U.S. Government securities	Other	
	1	2	3	4	5	6	7	8	9	10
1911	0	0	—	0	0	0	0	0	0	0
1912	0.1	0	—	0.1	0.1	0	0	0	0	0
1913	0.2	0	—	0.2	0.1	0.1	0	0	0	0
1914	0.3	0	—	0.2	0.1	0.1	0	0	0	0
1915	0.5	0.1	—	0.4	0.3	0.1	0	0	0	0
1916	1.0	0.2	—	0.8	0.6	0.2	0	0	0	0
1917	1.7	0.2	—	1.3	1.0	0.3	0.1	0	0.1	0
1918	2.5	0.4	—	2.0	1.5	0.5	0.2	0	0.2	0
1919	3.9	0.4	—	3.3	2.5	0.8	0.3	0	0.3	0
1920	6.3	0.5	—	5.3	4.1	1.2	0.5	0	0.5	0.1
1921	8.6	0.5	—	7.3	5.6	1.7	0.7	0	0.7	0.1
1922	11.3	0.7	—	9.5	7.3	2.2	1.0	0	1.0	0.1
1923	15.0	1.0	—	12.5	9.6	2.9	1.4	0	1.4	0.1
1924	18.3	1.3	—	15.2	11.7	3.5	1.6	0	1.6	0.2
1925	21.2	2.1	—	17.3	13.3	4.0	1.6	0	1.6	0.2
1926	25.9	2.2	—	21.7	16.6	5 1	1.8	0	1.8	0.2
1927	31.8	2.6	—	26.4	20.2	6.2	2.5	0	2.5	0.3
1928	39.8	3.2	—	32.8	25.2	7.6	3.2	0	3.2	0.6
1929	42.4	2.6	—	35.2	23.0	12.2	3.7	0	3.7	0.9
1930	37.7	2.8	—	31.0	23.0	8.0	2.8	0.5	2.3	1.1
1931	36.6	3.0	—	28.7	21.0	7.7	3.5	1.0	2.5	1.4
1932	35.6	3.4	—	26.6	19.0	7.6	4.2	2.0	2.2	1.4
1933	37.0	3.3	—	26.5	20.0	6.5	5.4	2.5	2.9	1.8
1934	44.4	4.6	—	30.7	25.0	5.7	6.9	2.7	4.2	2.2
1935	59.5	7.7	—	40.4	37.0	3.4	8.4	3.0	5.4	3.0
1936	83.1	11.0	—	58.7	58.0	0.7	10.2	3.8	6.4	3.2
1937	115.4	13.9	—	84.5	83.0	1.5	12.9	4.0	8.9	4.1
1938	147.2	20.8	—	109.6	103.0	6.6	13.2	4.4	8.8	3.6
1939	192.7	28.1	2.0	142.3	135.0	7.3	16.7	6.5	10.2	3.6
1940	252.3	36.2	4.0	188.2	174.0	14.2	19.6	9.5	10.1	3.4
1941	322.5	57.6	9.7	216.0	200.0	16.0	35.7	17.0	18.7	3.5
1942	340.3	78.7	17.5	149.9	130.0	19.9	90.7	77.0	13.7	3.5
1943	355.3	61.3	20.1	125.1	104.0	21.1	146.4	130.0	16.4	2.4
1944	397.9	59.4	19.7	122.3	100.0	22.3	194.3	175.0	19.3	2.2
1945	434.6	60.7	18.1	126.9	103.0	23.9	226.4	210.0	16.4	2.5
1946	495.2	55.1	17.9	188.2	153.0	35.2	231.9	220.0	11.9	2.1
1947	591.1	61.1	18.2	281.4	225.0	56.4	228.3	215.0	13.3	2.1
1948	701.5	65.0	18.3	398.4	312.0	86.4	218.0	208.0	10.0	2.2
1949	828.0	65.0	22.7	508.2	402.0	106.2	230.1	215.0	15.1	2.0

L-42   TABLE L-42

Column 1 – 1911–1949: Table L-39, col. 2.

Column 2 – 1911–1934: Estimated by applying dividend rate of mutual savings banks (computed from
           Annual Reports of the Comptroller of the Currency, and New York and Massachusetts annual
           banking reports) to total shares and deposits of credit unions as given in Table L-41.
           1935–1949: Estimated by applying to shares and deposits dividend rates computed from Farm
           Credit Administration and Federal Deposit Insurance Corporation, *Annual Report of Operations
           of Federal Credit Unions,* and Department of Labor, Bureau of Labor Statistics, *Consumers'
           Cooperatives and Credit Unions: Operations in 1946.*

Column 3 – 1911–1949: Col. 1 minus col. 2.

L-43   TABLE L-43

Columns 1 to 5 – 1911–1940: *Banking and Monetary Statistics,* p. 519.
              1941–1949: *Federal Reserve Bulletin,* various issues (e.g. 1950, p. 695).

Column 6 – 1911–1949: Same as cols. 1–5. Includes working cash with postmasters; 5 percent reserve fund
           and miscellaneous working funds with Treasury; accrued interest on bond investments; and
           accounts due from late postmasters.

           Note: Details may not add to totals because of rounding.

ANNUAL IN- OR OUTPAYMENTS OF CREDIT UNIONS: 1911 to 1949

$ mill.

Year	Annual change in shares and deposits	Dividends and interest paid	Estimated annual in- or out- payments	Year	Annual change in shares and deposits	Dividends and interest paid	Estimated annual in- or out- payments
	1	2	3		1	2	3
1911	–	0	0	1931	−1.5	1.3	−2.8
1912	0.1	0	0.1	1932	−1.6	1.1	−2.7
1913	0.1	0	0.1	1933	1.0	1.0	0
1914	0.1	0	0.1	1934	6.4	1.0	5.4
1915	0.2	0	0.2	1935	13.1	1.2	11.9
1916	0.5	0	0.5	1936	22.4	1.9	20.5
1917	0.5	0.1	0.4	1937	28.8	2.8	26.0
1918	0.8	0.1	0.7	1938	29.4	3.7	25.7
1919	1.3	0.1	1.2	1939	41.4	5.0	36.4
1920	2.1	0.2	1.9	1940	53.8	7.4	46.4
1921	2.0	0.3	1.7	1941	66.0	9.3	56.7
1922	2.4	0.4	2.0	1942	16.2	7.7	8.5
1923	3.3	0.5	2.8	1943	14.7	5.7	9.0
1924	2.9	0.7	2.2	1944	39.8	5.5	34.3
1925	2.5	0.8	1.7	1945	29.1	6.3	22.8
1926	4.0	0.9	3.1	1946	56.6	7.4	49.2
1927	5.2	1.2	4.0	1947	86.5	10.2	76.3
1928	7.3	1.5	5.8	1948	93.8	12.2	81.6
1929	1.7	1.6	0.1	1949	106.9	14.3	92.6
1930	−4.5	1.4	−5.9				

ASSETS OF POSTAL SAVINGS SYSTEM: 1911 to 1949

$ mill.

End of year	Total	Cash in banks	U.S. Government securities Total	Direct obli- gations	Guaran- teed ob- ligations	Other assets	End of year	Total	Cash in banks	U.S. Government securities Total	Direct obli- gations	Guaran- teed ob- ligations	Other assets
	1	2	3	4	5	6		1	2	3	4	5	6
1911	11	10	0	0	–	1	1931	616	511	70	70	–	35
1912	28	26	0	0	–	2	1932	920	793	71	71	–	56
1913	40	37	0	0	–	2	1933	1 235	914	200	200	–	120
1914	60	56	1	1	–	3	1934	1 237	540	597	467	130	100
1915	76	69	1	1	–	6	1935	1 237	287	853	706	147	98
1916	115	107	2	2	–	6	1936	1 296	145	1 058	892	167	93
1917	148	139	3	3	–	6	1937	1 308	130	1 097	931	167	80
1918	172	146	18	18	–	8	1938	1 291	86	1 132	965	166	73
1919	168	130	30	30	–	8	1939	1 319	53	1 192	1 046	146	74
1920	171	55	105	105	–	10	1940	1 348	36	1 224	1 078	146	88
1921	154	44	103	103	–	8	1941	1 396	26	1 274	1 128	146	95
1922	141	56	77	77	–	8	1942	1 464	16	1 345	1 219	126	102
1923	142	63	72	72	–	8	1943	1 843	10	1 716	1 716	–	118
1924	139	98	33	33	–	8	1944	2 411	8	2 252	2 252	–	152
1925	141	100	33	33	–	8	1945	3 022	6	2 837	2 837	–	179
1926	148	106	33	33	–	8	1946	3 387	6	3 182	3 182	–	200
1927	158	116	34	34	–	8	1947	3 525	6	3 308	3 308	–	212
1928	163	129	25	25	–	9	1948	3 449	7	3 244	3 244	–	198
1929	174	138	26	26	–	10	1949	3 312	7	3 118	3 118	–	187
1930	253	209	27	27	–	17							

TABLE L–44

Columns 1 to 5 – From Post Office Department, Division of Postal Savings, Bureau of Operations.

Note: Details may not add to total because of rounding.

LIABILITIES AND SURPLUS OF POSTAL SAVINGS SYSTEM
1911 to 1949

L-44

$ mill.

End of year	Total liabilities and surplus	Due depositors		Accounts payable	Surplus	End of year	Total liabilities and surplus	Due depositors		Accounts payable	Surplus
		Certificates outstanding	Accrued interest					Certificates outstanding	Accrued interest		
	1	2	3	4	5		1	2	3	4	5
1911	11	11	0	0	0	1930	253	245	5	2	0
1912	28	28	0	0	0	1931	616	606	8	3	0
1913	40	40	0	0	0	1932	920	902	14	3	1
1914	60	59	1	0	0	1933	1 235	1 209	21	4	2
						1934	1 237	1 207	25	3	2
1915	76	74	1	0	1						
1916	115	112	1	0	2	1935	1 237	1 201	28	6	2
1917	148	143	2	0	2	1936	1 296	1 260	31	2	2
1918	172	168	2	0	2	1937	1 308	1 270	33	3	2
1919	168	161	3	0	3	1938	1 291	1 252	34	3	2
						1939	1 319	1 279	36	3	2
1920	171	163	3	0	4						
1921	154	146	3	3	3	1940	1 348	1 304	37	5	2
1922	141	132	3	4	1	1941	1 396	1 353	38	2	2
1923	142	131	3	6	1	1942	1 464	1 418	41	2	2
1924	139	133	4	2	0	1943	1 843	1 788	49	4	2
						1944	2 411	2 342	63	3	4
1925	141	134	4	3	0						
1926	148	139	4	4	0	1945	3 022	2 933	81	4	4
1927	158	149	4	5	0	1946	3 387	3 284	95	3	5
1928	163	154	4	5	0	1947	3 525	3 417	106	-3	5
1929	174	164	4	5	0	1948	3 449	3 330	112	2	5
						1949	3 312	3 189	114	4	5

433

J-1

TABLE J–1

Column 1 – First differences of Table J-5, col. 2.

Column 2 – First differences of Table J-5, col. 6.

Column 3 – First differences of Table J-2, col. 3.

Column 4 – Col. 1 plus col. 2 minus col. 3.

Column 5 – First differences of Table J-6, col. 1.

Column 6 – First differences of Table J-6, col. 4.

Column 7 – Col. 5 minus col. 6.

Column 8 – Col. 4 plus col. 7.

Column 9 – Col. 8 minus Table J-9, col. 5 (net capital gains of operating associations) plus Table J-7, col. 4 (loss on deposits and shares of closed associations).

J-2

TABLE J–2

Column 1 – 1896–1921: United States Building and Loan League, *Building and Loan Annals*, various volumes. Excludes (as for 1922–1949) mortgage loans offset by mortgage pledged shares.
1922–1947: Home Loan Bank Board, *Trends in the Savings and Loan Field*, 1948, table 1, col. 2 minus col. 4.
1948–1949: Home Loan Bank Board, *Statistical Summary*, 1950, table 4 minus mortgage loans offset (col. 10).

Column 2 – 1896–1921: Obtained by applying the appropriate percentages of Table J-3, to total net assets (col. 1 of this table).
1922–1949: Same sources as col. 1.

Column 3 – 1896–1931: Obtained by applying the appropriate percentages of Table J-3 to total net assets (col. 1 of this table).
1932–1946: From Friend and Natrella, *Individuals' Saving*, part II, table 5, line 2.
1947–1949: Same method as 1896–1931.

Column 4 – 1896–1949: Same sources as col. 1.

Columns 5 and 6 – 1896–1921: Same method as col. 2.
1922–1949: Same sources as col. 1.

Column 7 – 1896–1916: Assumed to be zero.
1917–1919: Estimated on assumption that change in total security holdings (col. 6) is entirely attributable to U.S. Government securities.
1920–1924: Estimated on assumption of gradual liquidation of U.S. Government securities held at end of 1919.
1925–1928: Assumed to be zero.
1929–1935: Same method as 1917–1919.
1936–1949: Home Loan Bank Board, *Statistical Summary*, 1950, table 4.

Column 8 – 1932–1948: From *Statistical Abstract*, 1949, p. 452.
1949: From Home Loan Bank Board, *Report of Home Loan Bank Board for the Year Ending December 31, 1949*, p. 40.

Column 9 – 1896–1949: Col. 1 minus sum of cols. 2–6 and 8.

Column 10 – 1896–1949: From Table J-4, col. 2. Excluded from cols. 1 and 2.

INDIVIDUALS' SAVING THROUGH SAVINGS AND LOAN ASSOCIATIONS
1897 to 1949

$ mill.

Year	Operating associations				Closed associations			All associations	
	Change in			Total saving	Change in			Total saving	
								Including	Excluding
	Shares	Surplus	Share loans		Gross assets	Share loans	Net assets	Capital gains and losses	
	1	2	3	4	5	6	7	8	9
1897	8	−2	26	−20	−	−	−	−20	.
1898	−1	−2	−4	1	−	−	−	1	.
1899	−15	−3	2	−20	−	−	−	−20	.
1900	−6	−4	−5	−5	−	−	−	−5	.
1901	−3	−2	0	−5	−	−	−	−5	.
1902	10	−1	3	6	−	−	−	6	.
1903	10	−1	−5	14	−	−	−	14	.
1904	11	1	−5	17	−	−	−	17	.
1905	12	1	−3	16	−	−	−	16	.
1906	32	0	1	31	−	−	−	31	.
1907	43	4	4	43	−	−	−	43	.
1908	34	11	2	43	−	−	−	43	.
1909	46	11	2	55	−	−	−	55	.
1910	57	5	2	60	−	−	−	60	.
1911	70	8	3	75	−	−	−	75	.
1912	80	8	−1	89	−	−	−	89	.
1913	80	8	6	82	−	−	−	82	.
1914	77	9	5	81	−	−	−	81	.
1915	98	8	4	102	−	−	−	102	.
1916	83	10	3	90	−	−	−	90	.
1917	126	9	4	131	−	−	−	131	.
1918	103	3	1	105	−	−	−	105	.
1919	159	16	3	172	−	−	−	172	.
1920	270	22	12	280	−	−	−	280	.
1921	274	23	14	283	−	−	−	283	.
1922	335	27	14	348	−	−	−	348	.
1923	437	31	18	450	−	−	−	450	.
1924	600	47	45	602	−	−	−	602	.
1925	518	55	4	599	−	−	−	599	.
1926	601	61	32	630	−	−	−	630	.
1927	693	75	27	741	−	−	−	741	.
1928	646	74	35	685	−	−	−	685	.
1929	543	50	48	545	−	−	−	545	526
1930	86	25	14	97	77	3	74	171	198
1931	−368	−15	−41	−342	49	1	48	−294	−229
1932	−609	−54	−106	−557	32	0	32	−525	−421
1933	−659	−36	−32	−663	176	3	173	−490	−358
1934	−312	2	−35	−275	−27	−2	−25	−300	−242
1935	−329	−35	−24	−340	−54	−2	−52	−392	−300
1936	−175	−19	−14	−180	−58	−2	−56	−236	−175
1937	−116	−3	−6	−113	−26	−1	−25	−138	−90
1938	−10	10	−8	8	−46	0	−46	−38	−3
1939	55	−16	−2	41	49	0	49	90	170
1940	212	−13	−2	201	20	0	20	221	287
1941	380	12	−3	395	−38	0	−38	357	401
1942	258	27	−17	302	−42	0	−42	260	297
1943	584	38	−8	630	−41	0	−41	589	612
1944	811	38	−12	861	−51	0	−51	810	833
1945	1 060	73	4	1 129	−16	0	−16	1 113	1 107
1946	1 183	106	−1	1 290	−3	0	−3	1 287	1 267
1947	1 205	104	3	1 306	0	0	0	1 306	1 304
1948	1 211	114	3	1 322	0	0	0	1 322	1 327
1949	1 496	131	3	1 624	0	0	0	1 624	1 629

ASSETS OF OPERATING SAVINGS AND LOAN ASSOCIATIONS
1896 to 1949

$ mill.

End of year	Total assets	Mortgage loans	Share loans	Real estate owned	Cash	Bonds Total	U.S. Government	Federal Home Loan Bank stock	Other assets	Mortgage loans offset
	1	2	3	4	5	6	7	8	9	10
1896	504	429	16	23	20	1	0	0	15	94
1897	513	403	42	27	25	0	0	0	16	89
1898	513	396	38	31	27	0	0	0	21	87
1899	500	376	40	33	29	0	0	0	22	83
1900	490	371	35	31	30	0	0	0	23	82
1901	484	367	35	31	29	0	0	0	22	81
1902	494	378	38	27	24	0	0	0	27	83
1903	494	394	33	24	22	1	0	0	20	87
1904	507	423	28	21	19	1	0	0	15	93
1905	531	448	25	20	21	2	0	0	15	98
1906	566	487	26	16	22	2	0	0	13	107
1907	614	538	30	11	18	2	0	0	15	118
1908	658	575	32	11	20	2	0	0	18	126
1909	718	628	34	11	24	2	0	0	19	138
1910	781	690	36	10	25	2	0	0	18	152
1911	863	768	39	12	28	3	0	0	13	169
1912	952	847	38	14	32	3	0	0	18	186
1913	1 045	930	44	16	31	3	0	0	21	204
1914	1 136	1 013	49	18	34	4	0	0	18	222
1915	1 243	1 098	53	24	45	3	0	0	20	241
1916	1 341	1 175	56	29	58	3	0	0	20	258
1917	1 485	1 293	60	30	64	8	5	0	30	284
1918	1 594	1 387	61	29	55	31	28	0	31	304
1919	1 786	1 552	64	21	66	54	51	0	29	341
1920	2 112	1 860	76	15	63	51	47	0	47	408
1921	2 413	2 179	90	9	72	53	46	0	10	478
1922	2 802	2 468	104	10	80	36	27	0	104	541
1923	3 311	2 917	122	12	99	24	13	0	137	632
1924	3 996	3 519	167	10	110	13	0	0	177	770
1925	4 628	4 204	171	11	127	12	0	0	103	881
1926	5 302	4 810	203	19	146	16	0	0	108	1 032
1927	6 081	5 488	230	36	165	21	0	0	141	1 098
1928	6 809	6 060	265	88	200	31	0	0	165	1 207
1929	7 411	6 507	313	174	174	50	19	0	193	1 284
1930	7 471	6 402	327	238	203	44	13	0	257	1 358
1931	7 093	5 890	286	370	168	51	20	0	328	1 324
1932	6 478	5 148	180	642	147	54	23	0	307	1 259
1933	5 896	4 437	148	828	143	85	54	15	240	1 122
1934	5 523	3 710	113	1 012	166	286	255	22	214	883
1935	5 220	3 292	89	1 163	185	235	204	24	232	655
1936	5 165	3 237	75	1 150	210	188	150	28	277	523
1937	5 178	3 410	69	1 014	199	152	130	35	299	422
1938	5 190	3 555	61	890	215	134	120	38	297	353
1939	5 204	3 757	59	681	267	111	100	41	288	320
1940	5 382	4 084	57	492	301	105	100	45	298	290
1941	5 765	4 552	54	328	340	136	120	49	306	246
1942	5 882	4 556	37	203	405	344	320	52	285	227
1943	6 395	4 584	29	117	465	887	853	58	255	209
1944	7 275	4 800	17	60	413	1 703	1 671	64	218	183
1945	8 602	5 376	21	33	450	2 456	2 420	74	192	145
1946	10 067	7 141	20	26	536	2 047	2 009	86	211	135
1947	11 572	8 856	23	13	560	1 787	1 740	103	230	115
1948	12 924	10 305	26	12	663	1 500	1 454	121	297	104
1949	14 550	11 600	29	15	850	1 540	1 497	136	380	100

DISTRIBUTION OF ASSETS
OF OPERATING SAVINGS AND LOAN ASSOCIATIONS: 1896 to 1949

Percent

End of year	Mortgage loans	Share loans	Real estate owned	Cash	Securities	Other assets	End of year	Mortgage loans	Share loans	Real estate owned	Cash	Securities	Other assets
	1	2	3	4	5	6		1	2	3	4	5	6
1896	85.2	3.2	4.5	3.9	0.1	3.1	1923	88.1	3.7	0.4	3.0	0.7	4.1
1897	78.8	8.1	5.3	4.9	0	2.9	1924	88.1	4.2	0.2	2.7	0.3	4.5
1898	77.2	7.5	6.1	5.3	0	3.9	1925	90.8	3.7	0.2	2.7	0.3	2.3
1899	75.3	8.1	6.5	5.7	0	4.4	1926	90.7	3.8	0.4	2.7	0.3	2.1
1900	75.9	7.2	6.4	6.1	0	4.4	1927	90.2	3.8	0.7	2.7	0.3	2.3
1901	75.9	7.1	6.3	5.9	0	4.8	1928	89.0	3.9	1.3	2.9	0.5	2.4
1902	76.5	7.7	5.5	4.9	0.1	5.3	1929	87.9	4.2	2.3	2.3	0.7	2.6
1903	79.9	6.7	4.8	4.4	0.1	4.1	1930	85.7	4.4	3.2	2.7	0.6	3.4
1904	83.4	5.6	4.1	3.8	0.3	2.8	1931	83.0	4.1	5.2	2.4	0.7	4.6
1905	84.4	4.7	3.8	3.9	0.3	2.9	1932	79.5	2.8	9.9	2.3	0.8	4.7
1906	86.1	4.6	2.9	3.8	0.4	2.2	1933	75.3	2.5	14.0	2.5	1.4	4.3
1907	87.7	4.9	1.8	2.9	0.4	2.3	1934	67.2	2.0	18.3	3.0	5.2	4.3
1908	87.4	4.9	1.7	3.1	0.3	2.6	1935	63.0	1.7	22.3	3.6	4.5	4.9
1909	87.5	4.8	1.5	3.3	0.3	2.6	1936	62.7	1.4	22.3	4.1	3.6	5.9
1910	88.4	4.7	1 3	3.2	0.3	2.1	1937	65.9	1.3	19.6	3.8	2.9	6.5
1911	89.0	4.6	1.4	3.2	0.3	1.5	1938	68.5	1.2	17.1	4.1	2.6	6.5
1912	89.0	3.9	1.4	3.4	0.3	2.0	1939	72.3	1.1	13.1	5.1	2.1	6.3
1913	89.0	4.2	1.5	3.0	0.3	2.0	1940	75.8	1.1	9.1	5.6	2.0	6.4
1914	89.2	4.3	1.6	3.0	0.3	1.6	1941	79.0	0.9	5.7	5.9	2.4	6.1
1915	88.3	4.3	1.9	3.6	0.2	1.7	1942	77.5	0.6	3.5	6.9	5.8	5.7
1916	87.6	4.2	2.1	4.3	0.2	1.6	1943	71.7	0.4	1.8	7.3	13.9	4.9
1917	87.0	4.0	2.0	4.3	0.5	2.2	1944	66.0	0.2	0.8	5.7	23.4	3.9
1918	87.0	3.8	1.8	3.5	1.9	2.0	1945	62.5	0.2	0.4	5.2	28.6	3.1
1919	86.9	3.6	1.2	3.7	3.0	1.6	1946	70.9	0.2	0.3	5.3	20.3	3.0
1920	88.0	3.6	0.7	3.0	2.5	2.2	1947	76.5	0.2	0.1	4.8	15.4	3.0
1921	90.3	3.7	0.4	3.0	2.2	0.4	1948	79.7	0.2	0.1	5.1	11.6	3.3
1922	88.1	3.7	0.4	2.8	1.3	3.7	1949	79.7	0.2	0.1	5.8	10.6	3.6

Column 1 – 1896–1921: Built up from data for Massachusetts, New Jersey, Ohio, and Pennsylvania. These four states during this period held between 60 and 64 percent of the assets of all savings and loan associations in the country.
1922–1947: Based on reports from most or all states, taken from Home Loan Bank Board, *Trends in the Savings and Loan Field*, 1947, table 1.
1948–1949: Derived from Home Loan Bank Board, *Statistical Summary*, 1950, table 4.

Column 2 – 1896–1931: Built up from state data like col. 1.
1932–1946: Derived from data in Friend and Natrella, *Individuals' Saving*, part ii, table 5, line 2.
1947–1949: Assumed unchanged from 1946.

Column 3 – 1896–1929: Built up from state data like col. 1.
1930–1947: From Home Loan Bank Board, *Trends in the Savings and Loan Field*, 1947, table 1.
1948–1949: Same source as col. 1.

Column 4 – 1896–1932: Built up from state data like col. 1.
1933–1935: Federal Home Loan Bank Board estimates, published in Hart, A. G., *Debts and Recovery, A Study of Changes in the Internal Debt Structure from 1929 to 1937 and a Program for the Future*, p. 303.
1936–1947: From Home Loan Bank Board, *Trends in the Savings and Loan Field*, 1947, table 1.
1948–1949: Same source as col. 1.

Column 5 – 1896–1932: Built up from state data like col. 1.
1933–1935: Same source as col. 4.
1936–1947: From Home Loan Bank Board, *Trends in the Savings and Loan Field*, 1947, table 1.
1948–1949: Same source as col. 1.

Column 6 – 1896–1932: Built up from state data like col. 1.
1933–1935: 100.0 minus sum of cols. 1–5.
1936–1947: From Home Loan Bank Board, *Trends in the Savings and Loan Field*, 1947, table 1. Includes such items as furniture and fixtures, loans to other savings and loan associations, delinquent dues, fines, and rents due from borrowers, fire insurance and taxes advanced, stationery and supplies, and other miscellaneous assets; also, since 1933, stock of Federal Home Loan Banks.
1948–1949: 100.0 minus sum of cols. 1–5.

GROSS AND NET MORTGAGE LOANS OF OPERATING SAVINGS AND LOAN ASSOCIATIONS: 1896 to 1949

J. 4

$ mill.

End of year	Gross loans	Mortgage pledged shares	Percent of mortgage pledged shares to gross loans	Net loans	End of year	Gross loans	Mortgage pledged shares	Percent of mortgage pledged shares to gross loans	Net loans
	1	2	3	4		1	2	3	4
1896	523	94	18	429	1923	3 549	632	18	2 917
1897	492	89	18	403	1924	4 289	770	18	3 519
1898	483	87	18	396	1925	5 085	881	17	4 204
1899	459	83	18	376	1926	5 842	1 032	18	4 810
1900	453	82	18	371	1927	6 586	1 098	17	5 488
1901	448	81	18	367	1928	7 267	1 207	17	6 060
1902	461	83	18	378	1929	7 791	1 284	16	6 507
1903	481	87	18	394	1930	7 760	1 358	18	6 402
1904	516	93	18	423	1931	7 214	1 324	18	5 890
1905	546	98	18	448	1932	6 407	1 259	20	5 148
1906	594	107	18	487	1933	5 559	1 122	20	4 437
1907	657	118	18	539	1934	4 593	883	19	3 710
1908	702	126	18	576	1935	3 947	655	17	3 292
1909	766	138	18	628	1936	3 760	523	14	3 237
1910	842	152	18	690	1937	3 832	422	11	3 410
1911	936	169	18	767	1938	3 908	353	9	3 555
1912	1 033	186	18	847	1939	4 077	320	8	3 757
1913	1 134	204	18	930	1940	4 374	290	7	4 084
1914	1 236	222	18	1 014	1941	4 798	246	5	4 552
1915	1 339	241	18	1 098	1942	4 783	227	5	4 556
1916	1 433	258	18	1 175	1943	4 793	209	4	4 584
1917	1 576	284	18	1 292	1944	4 983	183	4	4 800
1918	1 691	304	18	1 387	1945	5 521	145	3	5 376
1919	1 893	341	18	1 552	1946	7 276	135	2	7 141
1920	2 268	408	18	1 860	1947	8 971	115	1	8 856
1921	2 657	478	18	2 179	1948	10 409	104	1	10 305
1922	3 009	541	18	2 468	1949	11 700	100	1	11 600

Column 1 – 1896–1921: Obtained by applying the average percentage for four states (Ohio, Massachusetts, New Jersey, and Pennsylvania) to total gross assets as reported in *Savings and Loan Annals,*
1922–1945: Home Loan Bank Board, *Home Loan Bank Review, Statistical Supplement,* 1947. table 7.
1946–1949: Home Loan Bank Board, *Statistical Summary,* 1950, table 4.

Column 2 – 1896–1921: Assumed at 18 percent of gross mortgage loans, the average for the period 1922–1935.
1922–1945: Home Loan Bank Board, *Home Loan Bank Review, Statistical Supplement,* 1947, table 7.
1946–1949: Home Loan Bank Board, *Trends in the Savings and Loan Field,* 1949, table 1.

Column 3 – 1896–1949: Col. 2 divided by col. 1.

Column 4 – 1896–1949: Col. 1 minus col. 2.

439

Column 1 – 1896–1921: United States Building and Loan League, *Building and Loan Annals,* various issues. Excludes, as for 1922–1949, mortgage pledged shares.

        1922–1947: Home Loan Bank Board, *Trends in the Savings and Loan Field,* 1948, table 1, col. 2 minus col. 8 of this table.

        1948–1949: Home Loan Bank Board, *Statistical Summary,* 1950, table 4 minus col. 8 of this table.

Column 2 – 1896–1935: Col. 1 minus sum of cols. 3–7.

        1936–1947: Home Loan Bank Board, *Trends in the Savings and Loan Field,* 1948, table 1.

        1948–1949: Same source as col. 1.

Column 3 – 1934–1945: Home Loan Bank Board, *Home Loan Bank Review, Statistical Supplement,* 1947, tables 5 and 7.

        1946–1947: Home Loan Bank Board, *Trends in the Savings and Loan Field,* 1947, 1948, table 2.

        1948–1949: Home Loan Bank Board, *Combined Financial Statements,* 1948, 1949.

Column 4 – 1932–1935: Hart, Albert, *Debts and Recovery,* p. 318.

        1936–1947: Same source as col. 3.

        1948–1949: *Report of the Home Loan Bank Board For the Year Ending December 31, 1949,* p. 39.

Columns 5 and 6 – 1896–1935: Obtained by multiplying 1936 value by an index derived from the movements shown in the combined balance sheets of the savings and loan associations in seven states (Massachusetts, New Jersey, New York, Pennsylvania, Ohio, California, and Illinois). The figures for the individual states are taken from the annual reports of the commissioner of banks, or other state officers supervising the savings and loan associations.

        1936–1946: Home Loan Bank Board, *Home Loan Bank Review, Statistical Supplement,* 1947, table 7 minus Federal Home Loan Bank advances (col. 4 of this table).

        1947–1949: Obtained by subtracting col. 4 from total borrowings as given in Home Loan Bank Board, *Statistical Summary,* 1950, table 4.

Column 7 – 1896–1935: Same source as col. 5. Includes such items as advance payments, incomplete loans, unearned premiums, interest paid in advance, deposits from other financial institutions, and other liabilities.

        1936–1949: Col. 1 minus sum of cols. 2–6.

Column 8 – 1896–1949: Same as Table J-2, col. 10. Figures are not included in cols. 1 and 2.

1896 to 1949

$ mill.

End of year	Total liabilities and surplus	Private repurchasable shares	Government share capital	Federal Home Loan Bank advances	Borrowed money	Surplus reserves and undivided profits	Other liabilities	Mortgage pledged shares
	1	2	3	4	5	6	7	8
1896	504	436	–	–	5	49	14	94
1897	513	444	–	–	4	47	18	89
1898	513	443	–	–	4	45	21	87
1899	500	428	–	–	4	42	26	83
1900	490	422	–	–	3	38	27	82
1901	484	419	–	–	4	36	25	81
1902	494	429	–	–	5	35	25	83
1903	494	439	–	–	6	34	15	87
1904	507	450	–	–	7	35	15	93
1905	531	462	–	–	8	36	25	98
1906	566	494	–	–	9	36	27	107
1907	614	537	–	–	10	40	27	118
1908	658	571	–	–	10	51	26	126
1909	718	617	–	–	10	62	29	138
1910	781	674	–	–	10	67	30	152
1911	863	744	–	–	13	75	31	169
1912	952	824	–	–	14	83	31	186
1913	1 045	904	–	–	15	91	35	204
1914	1 136	981	–	–	18	100	37	222
1915	1 243	1 079	–	–	19	108	37	241
1916	1 341	1 162	–	–	19	118	42	258
1917	1 485	1 288	–	–	19	127	51	284
1918	1 594	1 391	–	–	24	130	49	304
1919	1 786	1 550	–	–	39	146	51	341
1920	2 112	1 820	–	–	55	168	69	408
1921	2 413	2 094	–	–	60	191	68	478
1922	2 802	2 429	–	–	74	218	81	541
1923	3 311	2 866	–	–	91	249	105	632
1924	3 996	3 466	–	–	107	296	127	770
1925	4 628	4 014	–	–	117	351	146	881
1926	5 302	4 615	–	–	122	412	153	1 032
1927	6 081	5 308	–	–	121	487	165	1 098
1928	6 809	5 954	–	–	113	561	181	1 207
1929	7 411	6 497	–	–	125	611	178	1 284
1930	7 471	6 583	–	–	123	636	129	1 358
1931	7 093	6 215	–	–	119	621	138	1 324
1932	6 478	5 606	–	1	111	567	193	1 259
1933	5 896	4 947	–	85	95	531	238	1 122
1934	5 523	4 635	16	87	80	533	172	883
1935	5 220	4 306	71	103	65	498	177	655
1936	5 165	4 131	171	144	50	479	190	523
1937	5 178	4 015	253	198	49	476	187	422
1938	5 190	4 005	259	198	45	486	197	353
1939	5 204	4 060	250	182	43	470	199	320
1940	5 382	4 272	220	200	33	457	200	290
1941	5 765	4 652	196	218	38	469	192	246
1942	5 882	4 910	168	131	22	496	155	227
1943	6 395	5 494	69	108	26	534	164	209
1944	7 275	6 305	36	127	72	572	163	183
1945	8 602	7 365	21	190	146	645	235	145
1946	10 067	8 548	15	284	118	751	351	135
1947	11 572	9 753	7	426	115	855	416	115
1948	12 924	10 964	5	515	75	969	396	104
1949	14 550	12 460	2	433	107	1100	448	100

Column 1 – Sum of cols. 2–6.

Columns 2 to 5 – Obtained by: (a) applying to estimated total assets of closed associations (Table J-7, col. 3) the respective asset's percentage share of total assets of operating associations in the year of closing (Table J-3); and (b) reducing the value so obtained by 20 percent for the year of closing and for each of the following four years. This procedure is based on the assumption of an average liquidation period of 4.5 years; an approximately even liquidation over the entire period; and the absence of losses on these types of assets.

Column 6 – Obtained by: (a) applying to estimated total assets of closed associations (Table J-7, col. 3) the percentage of mortgage loans and real estate owned among operating associations (Table J-3, cols. 1 plus 3); and (b) reducing the difference between the value so obtained and the estimated total loss (Table J-7, col. 5) by 20 percent during the year of closing and during each of the following four years. This procedure assigns total loss to mortgages and real estate owned.

Column 1 – *Savings and Loan Annals,* 1946, p. 187.

Column 2 – Based on the assumption that the surplus of closed associations bore the same ratio to their liabilities as prevailed, in the same year, for operating associations. The ratio is, therefore, derived by dividing Table J-5, col. 6 by the sum of cols. 2–5, and 7.

Column 3 – Col. 1 plus col. 2.

Column 4 – *Savings and Loan Annals,* 1946, p. 187. Refers to loss estimated at time of closing.

Column 5 – Col. 2 plus col. 4. This assumes the loss of entire estimated surplus.

Note: No estimates are made for years before 1930 and after 1942 because amounts included are insignificant (for liabilities of associations closed from 1920 to 1929 and 1943 to 1947 see *Savings and Loan Annals,* 1946, p. 187).

442

COMPOSITION OF ASSETS OF CLOSED SAVINGS AND LOAN ASSOCIATIONS   J-6
1930 to 1946

$ mill.

End of year	Total	Cash	Securities	Share loans	Other assets	Mortgage loans and real estate owned	End of year	Total	Cash	Securities	Share loans	Other assets	Mortgage loans and real estate owned
	1	2	3	4	5	6		1	2	3	4	5	6
1930	77.3	1.9	0.4	3.1	2.4	69.5	1939	173.3	5.7	2.9	1.4	7.4	155.9
1931	126.6	2.7	0.7	4.5	4.5	114.2							
1932	158.6	3.0	0.9	4.6	5.2	144.9	1940	193.8	7.2	3.0	1.5	9.1	173.0
1933	334.7	6.6	2.8	7.6	12.1	305.6	1941	156.0	5.2	2.1	1.1	5.9	141.7
1934	308.0	5.1	3.0	5.3	10.2	284.4	1942	114.1	3.6	1.6	0.7	3.5	104.7
							1943	72.7	1.5	0.8	0.3	1.4	68.7
1935	253.7	4.3	2.9	3.7	7.9	234.9	1944	22.0	0.4	0.2	0	0.4	21.0
1936	196.1	3.0	2.4	2.1	5.6	183.0							
1937	170.0	2.7	2.3	1.1	4.8	159.1	1945	6.0	0.1	0.1	0	0.2	5.6
1938	124.2	3.0	2.1	1.0	5.2	112.9	1946	2.6	0	0	0	0	2.6

TOTAL LIABILITIES, ASSETS, AND LOSSES OF CLOSED SAVINGS AND   J-7
LOAN ASSOCIATIONS: 1930 to 1942

$ mill.

Year	Liabilities	Surplus	Total assets	Loss on deposits and shares	Total loss	Year	Liabilities	Surplus	Total assets	Loss on deposits and shares	Total loss
	Of associations closing during year						Of associations closing during year				
	1	2	3	4	5		1	2	3	4	5
1930	80.4	8.1	88.5	24.7	32.8	1937	44.7	4.5	49.2	15.8	20.3
1931	61.9	6.4	68.3	22.3	28.7	1938	36.0	3.7	39.7	11.3	15.0
1932	52.8	4.7	57.5	20.3	25.0	1939	81.9	8.1	90.0	27.0	35.1
1933	215.5	20.5	236.0	44.0	64.5	1940	69.6	6.5	76.1	6.7	13.2
1934	34.7	3.4	38.1	10.2	13.6	1941	8.6	0.8	9.4	1.1	1.9
1935	31.9	3.4	35.3	15.8	19.2	1942	8.9	0.8	9.7	1.8	2.6
1936	20.3	2.1	22.4	9.1	11.2						

$ mill. (except col. 1)

End of year	Number of associations	Total assets	Gross operating income	Operating expense	Net operating income	Non-operating income
	1	2	3	4	5	6
1938	3 094	3 548	163	57	106	5
1939	3 110	4 048	183	62	121	5
1940	3 508	4 411	213	70	143	5
1941	3 536	4 655	236	77	159	6
1942	3 722	5 020	255	79	176	6
1943	3 681	5 502	255	72	183	6
1944	3 652	6 399	270	78	192	6
1945	3 655	7 654	297	89	208	17
1946	3 660	8 985	354	110	244	22
1947	3 670	10 427	416	129	287	10
1948	3 733	11 733	487	150	336	4
1949	3 822	13 278	558	166	392	5

End of year	Non-operating charges	Net income	Dividends	Retained net operating income	Change in reserves and undivided profits	Indicated net capital gain or loss
	7	8	9	10	11	12
1938	6	105	83	23	28	5
1939	5	122	92	29	17	−12
1940	5	142	105	38	19	−19
1941	5	160	114	45	24	−21
1942	4	177	123	53	29	−24
1943	3	186	131	52	42	−10
1944	2	196	138	54	51	−3
1945	2	223	148	60	72	12
1946	2	263	167	77	90	13
1947	2	295	195	92	105	13
1948	2	338	228	108	109	1
1949	2	395	268	124	132	8

Columns 1 and 2 – Home Loan Bank Board, *Combined Financial Statements of Members of the Federal Home Loan Bank System,* various years (generally tables 1 and 14).

Column 3 – Same source as col. 1. Net income from real estate owned is included.

Column 4 – Same source as col. 1. Operating expense includes interest charges.

Columns 5 to 9 – Same source as col. 1.

Column 10 – Col. 5 minus col. 9.

Column 11 – Derived from *Combined Financial Statements,* table 1.

Column 12 – Col. 11 minus col. 10.

444

$ mill. (except col. 2)

Year	Retained net operating income of reporting associations	Share of reporting associations in assets of all associations	Retained net operating income of all associations	Change in reported surplus of all associations	Indicated capital gain or loss		
					All associations	Associations reporting to FHLBB	Other associations
	1	2	3	4	5	6	7
1929	.	.	31	50	19	.	.
1930	.	.	27	25	−2	.	.
1931	.	.	28	−15	−43	.	.
1932	.	.	30	−54	−84	.	.
1933	.	.	52	−36	−88	.	.
1934	.	.	50	2	−48	.	.
1935	.	.	41	−35	−76	.	.
1936	.	.	33	−19	−52	.	.
1937	.	.	29	−3	−32	.	.
1938	23	68	34	10	−24	5	−29
1939	29	78	37	−16	−53	−12	−41
1940	38	82	46	−13	−59	−19	−40
1941	45	81	55	12	−43	−21	−22
1942	53	85	62	27	−35	−24	−11
1943	52	86	61	38	−23	−10	−13
1944	54	88	61	38	−23	−3	−20
1945	60	89	67	73	6	12	−6
1946	77	89	86	106	20	13	7
1947	92	90	102	104	2	13	−11
1948	108	91	119	114	−5	1	−6
1949	124	91	136	131	−5	8	−13

Column 1 – 1938–1949: Table J-8, col. 10.

Column 2 – 1938–1949: Table J-8, col. 2 divided by Table J-2, col. 1.

Column 3 – 1929–1937: Rate of retained operating income to average assets of Massachusetts associations (calculated from Massachusetts Commissioner of Banks, *Annual Report*, part III) applied to average assets of all operating associations (Table J-2, col. 1). This procedure appeared justified as the same method applied to 1939–1946 data yielded figures practically identical with those of Table J-9, col. 3.
1938–1949: Col. 1 divided by col. 2.

Column 4 – 1929–1949: Derived from Table J-5, col. 6.

Column 5 – 1929–1949: Col. 4 minus col. 3.

Column 6 – 1938–1949: Table J-8, col. 12.

Column 7 – 1938–1949: Col. 5 minus col. 6.

TWO ESTIMATES OF NET CAPITAL LOSSES OF SAVINGS AND LOAN ASSOCIATIONS

Period Total: 1930 to 1945

$ mill.

	Operating associations	Closed association	All associations
Method I			
1. Retained net operating income	713	0	713
2. Change in surplus	109	−75	34
3. Losses to shareholders and depositors	–	210	210
4. Estimated total capital loss	604	285	889
Method II			
1. Reduction in book value of real estate holdings	1 130	–	1 130
2. Estimated sales of real estate (book value)	1 300	500	1 800
3. Average loss ratio on book value of real estate sales	.25	.40	–
4. Estimated loss on real estate sales	325	} 200	} 770
5. Write-offs on real estate before sale	245		
6. Loss on exchange of mortgages for Home Owners' Loan Corporation bonds	80	–	80
7. Estimated total capital loss	650	200	850

Method I

Line 1 – From estimated combined income accounts for all operating associations (Table J-9, col. 3).

Line 2 – For operating associations from combined balance sheets, after addition of $75 million representing surplus of closed associations, as shown in Table J-7, col. 2, which may be supposed to have been gradually eliminated from statistics. For closed associations rough estimate from Table J-7, col. 2.

Line 3 – Table J-7, col. 4. Probably minimum figure as it is based on loss estimates made at time of closing.

Line 4 – Sum of lines 1 and 3 minus line 2.

Method II

Line 1 – From combined balance sheet of all operating associations (Table J-2, col. 4).

Line 2 – Rough estimate.

Line 3 – For operating associations, based on Federal Home Loan Bank Board, *IX Annual Report*, 1941, p. 254; for closed associations, rough estimate.

Line 4 – Line 2 multiplied by line 3.

Line 5 – Assumed to bear same relation to loss on sale as reported by Massachusetts savings banks (Lintner, John, *Mutual Savings Banks in the Savings and Mortgage Markets*, pp. 279, 290), i.e. 75 percent.

Line 6 – Rough estimate, based on fact that associations received about $900 million of Home Owners' Loan Corporation bonds (Home Loan Bank Board, *Safeguarding the Nation's Homes*, 1936, p. 11) and average reduction of mortgage loan principal in exchange for Home Owners' Loan Corporation bonds was a little under 10 percent.

Line 7 – Sum of lines 4–6.

Cash Flow Concept: 1897 to 1949

$ mill. (except col. 2)

Year	Private re-purchasable shares, operating associations	Dividend rate (percent)	Divi-dends	Increase in private re-purchasable shares, all associations	Cash saving	Year	Private re-purchasable shares, operating associations	Dividend rate (percent)	Divi-dends	Increase in private re-purchasable shares, all associations	Cash saving
	1	2	3	4	5		1	2	3	4	5
1897	440	5.95	26	−18	−44	1924	3 166	5.52	175	555	380
1898	444	5.89	26	3	−23	1925	3 740	5.55	208	544	336
1899	436	5.62	25	−17	−42	1926	4 314	5.61	242	569	327
1900	425	5.41	23	−1	−24	1927	4 962	5.63	279	666	387
1901	420	5.26	22	−3	−25	1928	5 631	5.63	317	611	294
1902	424	5.08	22	7	−15	1929	6 226	5.61	349	495	146
1903	434	5.12	22	15	−7	1930	6 540	5.55	363	146	−217
1904	444	5.05	22	16	−6	1931	6 399	5.42	347	−279	−626
1905	456	5.05	23	15	−8	1932	5 910	4.95	293	−471	−764
1906	478	5.01	24	31	7	1933	5 276	4.30	227	−454	−681
1907	516	5.02	26	39	13	1934	4 791	4.07	195	−302	−497
1908	554	5.07	28	32	4	1935	4 470	3.93	176	−357	−533
1909	594	5.08	30	44	14	1936	4 218	3.84	162	−217	−379
1910	646	5.09	33	55	22	1937	4 073	3.84	156	−135	−291
1911	709	5.17	37	67	30	1938	4 010	3.81	153	−48	−201
1912	784	5.13	40	81	41	1939	4 032	3.78	152	106	−46
1913	864	5.10	44	74	30	1940	4 166	3.63	151	234	83
1914	942	5.20	49	72	23	1941	4 462	3.56	159	345	186
1915	1 030	5.24	54	94	40	1942	4 781	3.49	167	233	66
1916	1 120	5.26	59	80	21	1943	5 202	2.78	145	551	406
1917	1 225	5.32	65	122	57	1944	5 900	2.69	159	772	613
1918	1 340	5.31	71	102	31	1945	6 835	2.48	170	1 040	870
1919	1 470	5.27	77	156	79	1946	7 956	2.39	190	1 181	991
1920	1 685	5.20	88	258	170	1947	9 150	2.38	218	1 202	984
1921	1 957	5.39	105	260	155	1948	10 358	2.44	253	1 208	955
1922	2 262	5.47	124	321	197	1949	11 712	2.51	294	1 493	1 199
1923	2 648	5.49	145	419	274						

Column 1 – 1897–1949: Average of year-end private repurchasable shares outstanding in operating associations, from Table J-5, col. 2.

Column 2 – 1897–1939: Average dividend rate paid by Massachusetts building and loan associations, from *Annual Report, Massachusetts Commissioner of Banks*, part III, various years.
      1940–1946: Average dividend rate paid by federal savings and loan associations derived from figures in *Annual Report of Federal Home Loan Bank Administration*.
      1947–1949: Average dividend rate paid by member associations of the Federal Home Loan Bank System, from data in Home Loan Bank Board, *Combined Financial Statements*.

Column 3 – 1897–1949: Col. 1 multiplied by col. 2.

Column 4 – 1897–1949: Change in shares outstanding in operating associations and assets of closed associations less increase in share loans for all associations from Table J-1, cols. 1 and 5 less cols. 3 and 6.

Column 5 – 1897–1949: Col. 4 less col. 3.

I-1 TABLE I–1

Column 1 – 1897–1949: Col. 3 minus col. 2.

Column 2 – 1897–1949: Table I-3, col. 10.

Column 3 – 1897–1949: Table I-2, annual change in col. 6. In 1926 the reported increase has been reduced by $79 million because of the *Spectator Life Insurance Yearbook* change in the basis of Travelers Insurance Company from admitted assets of the life department (used for 1925 and prior years) to admitted assets of the entire company (used for 1926 and later years).

Column 4 – 1897–1949: Col. 6 minus col. 5.

Columns 5 and 8 – 1897–1949: Same percentage of cols. 6 and 9, respectively, as col. 2 is of col. 3.

Column 6 – 1897–1949: Table I-2, annual change in col. 8.

Column 7 – 1897–1949: Col. 9 minus col. 8.

Column 9 – 1897–1904: From *The Brown Book of Life Insurance Economics, 1910–11*, table D, p. 71 (this tabulation does not cover all companies but should account for about 90 percent of the total).
1905–1922: Obtained by totaling figures for individual companies as given in *Spectator Life Insurance Yearbook*, various issues.
1923–1948: From "Gain and Loss Exhibit Summary," *Spectator Life Insurance Yearbook*: (a) subtracting gains and losses of Canadian companies for the years in which they were included in summaries; and (b) adjusting, from 1939 on, for changes in special investment reserves.
1949: Preliminary estimate based on Table I-7, col. 14 minus col. 13.

Column 10 – 1897–1949: Col. 4 minus col. 7.

Column 11 – 1897–1949: Col. 5 minus col. 8.

Column 12 – 1897–1949: Col. 6 minus col. 9.

I-2 TABLE I–2

Column 1 – 1896–1948: From *Spectator Life Insurance Yearbook*, various issues.
1949: From Institute of Life Insurance, *Life Insurance Fact Book*, 1950.

Columns 2 and 3 – 1896–1948: Same source as col. 1.

Column 4 – 1930–1946: Change in assets of companies omitted from yearbook "aggregate" table, derived from examination of individual companies reports in *Spectator Life Insurance Yearbook* or *Best's Life Insurance Reports*.

Column 5 – 1918, 1945: Borrowings on U.S. Government securities. Obtained from examination of reports of individual companies as summarized in *Spectator Life Insurance Yearbook*.
1932–1936: Borrowings from Reconstruction Finance Corporation. Obtained from examination of reports of individual companies as summarized in *Spectator Life Insurance Yearbook*.

Column 6 – 1896–1948: Col. 1 plus col. 4 minus cols. 2, 3, and 5.
1949: Rough estimate.

Column 7 – 1896–1947: Same source as col. 1.
1948–1949: From Table I-5, col. 9.

Column 8 – 1896–1949: Col. 6 minus col. 7.

448

1897 to 1949

$ mill.

Year	Saving including capital gains						Adjustment for capital gains			Saving excluding capital gains		
	Before change in policy loans			After change in policy loans			Attributable to		Total			
	U.S. policy-holders	Foreign policy-holders	Total	U.S. policy-holders	Foreign policy-holders	Total	U.S. policy-holders	Foreign policy-holders		U.S. policy-holders	Foreign policy-holders	Total
	1	2	3	4	5	6	7	8	9	10	11	12
1897	96	7	103	89	7	96	10	1	11	79	6	85
1898	106	8	114	101	8	109	10	1	11	91	7	98
1899	123	6	129	110	5	115	9	0	9	101	5	106
1900	131	11	142	114	10	124	7	1	8	107	9	116
1901	157	10	167	139	9	148	8	1	9	131	8	139
1902	162	14	176	144	12	156	2	0	2	142	12	154
1903	142	25	167	116	20	136	−22	−4	−26	138	24	162
1904	211	19	230	182	17	199	21	2	23	161	15	176
1905	188	15	203	155	12	167	−22	−2	−24	177	14	191
1906	206	10	216	168	8	176	−27	−1	−28	195	9	204
1907	128	−3	125	44	−1	43	−116	3	−113	160	−4	156
1908	308	16	324	245	13	258	85	4	89	160	9	169
1909	254	4	258	222	4	226	24	0	24	198	4	202
1910	220	2	222	171	2	173	−22	0	−22	193	2	195
1911	276	2	278	229	2	231	3	0	3	226	2	228
1912	238	0	238	192	0	192	−25	0	−25	217	0	217
1913	240	4	244	171	3	174	−44	−1	−45	215	4	219
1914	269	−1	268	192	−1	191	−3	0	−3	195	−1	194
1915	255	−3	252	210	−2	208	−43	1	−42	253	−3	250
1916	340	−1	339	332	−1	331	4	0	4	328	−1	327
1917	401	−6	395	378	−6	372	8	0	8	370	−6	364
1918	376	−10	366	369	−10	359	8	0	8	361	−10	351
1919	477	−23	454	490	−24	466	0	0	0	490	−24	466
1920	525	−21	504	469	−19	450	−19	1	−18	488	−20	468
1921	596	−10	586	394	−7	387	−77	1	−76	471	−8	463
1922	700	−11	689	616	−10	606	24	0	24	592	−10	582
1923	773	−5	768	716	−5	711	−13	0	−13	729	−5	724
1924	911	2	913	786	2	788	32	0	32	754	2	756
1925	1 088	14	1 102	966	13	979	12	0	12	954	13	967
1926	1 241	28	1 269	1 091	25	1 116	14	0	14	1 077	25	1 102
1927	1 400	17	1 417	1 216	15	1 231	31	0	31	1 185	15	1 200
1928	1 479	31	1 510	1 268	27	1 295	18	0	18	1 250	27	1 277
1929	1 431	33	1 464	1 060	25	1 085	−8	0	−8	1 068	25	1 093
1930	1 335	30	1 365	916	21	937	−56	−1	−57	972	22	994
1931	1 221	28	1 249	672	15	687	−55	−1	−56	727	16	743
1932	598	13	611	170	4	174	−71	−2	−73	241	6	247
1933	260	6	266	296	7	303	−213	−5	−218	509	12	521
1934	846	18	864	955	20	975	−132	−3	−135	1 087	23	1 110
1935	1 334	26	1 360	1 450	28	1 478	−26	0	−26	1 476	28	1 504
1936	1 605	32	1 637	1 731	35	1 766	69	1	70	1 662	34	1 696
1937	1 329	28	1 357	1 340	29	1 369	−237	−5	−242	1 577	34	1 611
1938	1 466	28	1 494	1 475	29	1 504	−74	−1	−75	1 549	30	1 579
1939	1 439	28	1 467	1 577	31	1 608	−79	−2	−81	1 656	33	1 689
1940	1 518	30	1 548	1 672	33	1 705	−104	−2	−106	1 776	35	1 811
1941	1 871	36	1 907	2 039	40	2 079	−58	−1	−59	2 097	41	2 138
1942	2 151	41	2 192	2 382	46	2 428	−24	0	−24	2 406	46	2 452
1943	2 744	53	2 797	3 048	59	3 107	273	5	278	2 775	54	2 829
1944	3 187	61	3 248	3 421	66	3 487	341	7	348	3 080	59	3 139
1945	3 560	69	3 629	3 729	72	3 801	463	9	472	3 266	63	3 329
1946	3 275	60	3 335	3 345	61	3 406	67	1	68	3 278	60	3 338
1947	3 392	63	3 455	3 347	62	3 409	−100	−2	−102	3 447	64	3 511
1948	3 671	67	3 738	3 556	65	3 621	26	0	26	3 530	65	3 595
1949	3 891	71	3 962	3 709	68	3 777	18	0	18	3 691	68	3 759

I-2　　POLICYHOLDERS' EQUITY IN U.S. LIFE INSURANCE COMPANIES

1896 to 1949

$ mill.

End of year	Admitted assets	Capital stock	Deferred and uncollected net premiums	Assets of companies omitted	Borrowings	Adjusted admitted assets	Policy loans	Policy-holders' equity
	1	2	3	4	5	6	7	8
1896	1 244	12	24	–	–	1 208	45	1 163
1897	1 345	12	22	–	–	1 311	52	1 259
1898	1 463	12	26	–	–	1 425	57	1 368
1899	1 595	12	29	–	–	1 554	71	1 483
1900	1 742	13	33	–	–	1 696	89	1 607
1901	1 911	14	34	–	–	1 863	108	1 755
1902	2 092	14	39	–	–	2 039	128	1 911
1903	2 265	16	43	–	–	2 206	159	2 047
1904	2 499	17	46	–	–	2 436	190	2 246
1905	2 706	19	48	–	–	2 639	226	2 413
1906	2 924	23	46	–	–	2 855	266	2 589
1907	3 053	26	47	–	–	2 980	348	2 632
1908	3 380	29	47	–	–	3 304	414	2 890
1909	3 644	34	48	–	–	3 562	446	3 116
1910	3 876	41	51	–	–	3 784	495	3 289
1911	4 164	47	55	–	–	4 062	542	3 520
1912	4 409	51	58	–	–	4 300	588	3 712
1913	4 659	52	63	–	–	4 544	658	3 886
1914	4 935	54	69	–	–	4 812	735	4 077
1915	5 190	53	73	–	–	5 064	779	4 285
1916	5 537	55	79	–	–	5 403	787	4 616
1917	5 941	56	87	–	–	5 798	810	4 988
1918	6 475	59	98	–	154	6 164	817	5 347
1919	6 791	62	111	–	–	6 618	805	5 813
1920	7 320	67	131	–	–	7 122	859	6 263
1921	7 936	75	153	–	–	7 708	1 058	6 650
1922	8 652	77	178	–	–	8 397	1 141	7 256
1923	9 455	94	196	–	–	9 165	1 198	7 967
1924	1 0394	95	221	–	–	1 0078	1 323	8 755
1925	11 538	106	252	–	–	11 180	1 446	9 734
1926	12 940	128	284	–	–	12 528	1 599	10 929
1927	14 392	132	315	–	–	13 945	1 785	12 160
1928	15 961	149	357	–	–	15 455	2 000	13 455
1929	17 482	164	399	–	–	16 919	2 379	14 540
1930	18 880	177	440	21	–	18 284	2 807	15 477
1931	20 160	170	467	10	–	19 533	3 369	16 164
1932	20 754	162	462	44	30	20 144	3 806	16 338
1933	20 896	149	449	133	21	20 410	3 769	16 641
1934	21 844	148	456	41	7	21 274	3 658	17 616
1935	23 216	149	460	29	2	22 634	3 540	19 094
1936	24 874	143	464	5	1	24 271	3 411	20 860
1937	26 249	151	475	5	–	25 628	3 399	22 229
1938	27 755	147	486	0	–	27 122	3 389	23 733
1939	29 243	159	500	5	–	28 589	3 248	25 341
1940	30 802	158	508	1	–	30 137	3 091	27 046
1941	32 731	168	521	2	–	32 044	2 919	29 125
1942	34 931	169	527	1	–	34 236	2 683	31 553
1943	37 766	191	543	1	–	37 033	2 373	34 660
1944	41 054	204	576	7	–	40 281	2 134	38 147
1945	44 797	224	638	5	30	43 910	1 962	41 948
1946	48 191	248	703	5	–	47 245	1 891	45 354
1947	51 743	259	784	–	–	50 700	1 937	48 763
1948	55 512	252	822	–	–	54 438	2 054	52 384
1949	59 555	.	.	–	–	58 400	2 239	56 161

450

Year	Canadian policyholders				Foreign policyholders other than Canadian					Total foreign share in change in admitted assets
	Premium income			Change in admitted assets	Insurance in force			Foreign share in admitted assets		
	Canadian	Total	Canadian share		Foreign	Total	Foreign share	Total	Annual change	
	$ mill.		ratio		$ mill.		ratio	$ mill.		
	1	2	3	4	5	6	7	8	9	10
1896	3	228	.014	.	638	5 943	.107	129	.	.
1897	3	243	.012	1	651	6 326	.103	135	6	7
1898	4	258	.016	2	674	6 825	.099	141	6	8
1899	4	292	.014	2	722	7 774	.093	145	4	6
1900	4	325	.012	2	781	8 562	.091	154	9	11
1901	5	366	.014	2	833	9 594	.087	162	8	10
1902	6	407	.015	3	916	10 775	.085	173	11	14
1903	6	448	.013	2	1 024	11 547	.089	196	23	25
1904	7	488	.014	3	1 086	12 548	.087	212	16	19
1905	7	516	.014	3	1 142	13 364	.085	224	12	15
1906	7	526	.013	3	1 107	13 707	.081	231	7	10
1907	7	533	.013	2	1 065	14 063	.076	226	−5	−3
1908	7	546	.013	4	1 039	14 519	.072	238	12	16
1909	7	565	.012	3	1 029	15 420	.067	239	1	4
1910	8	593	.013	3	1 026	16 404	.063	238	−1	2
1911	9	632	.014	4	1 038	18 003	.058	236	−2	2
1912	10	673	.015	4	1 044	19 265	.054	232	−4	0
1913	12	715	.017	4	1 049	20 564	.051	232	0	4
1914	13	746	.017	5	1 024	21 589	.047	226	−6	−1
1915	14	784	.018	5	982	22 777	.043	218	−8	−3
1916	16	848	.019	6	951	24 679	.039	211	−7	−1
1917	18	929	.019	8	923	27 189	.034	197	−14	−6
1918	21	994	.021	8	881	29 870	.029	179	−18	−10
1919	25	1 207	.021	10	771	35 840	.022	146	−33	−23
1920	30	1 385	.022	11	664	42 281	.016	114	−32	−21
1921	33	1 537	.021	12	556	45 943	.012	92	−22	−10
1922	36	1 686	.021	14	397	50 291	.008	67	−25	−11
1923	40	1 900	.021	16	304	56 804	.005	46	−21	−5
1924	43	2 122	.020	18	172	63 780	.003	30	−16	2
1925	48	2 384	.020	22	150	67 343	.002	22	−8	14
1926	53	2 624	.020	25	110	73 066	.002	25	3	28
1927	58	2 874	.020	28	111	80 592	.001	14	−11	17
1928	64	3 146	.020	30	107	87 172	.001	15	1	31
1929	70	3 350	.021	31	111	94 025	.001	17	2	33
1930	74	3 524	.021	29	115	98 062	.001	18	1	30
1931	76	3 661	.021	26	112	98 932	.001	20	2	28
1932	74	3 504	.021	13	104	91 046	.001	20	0	13
1933	71	3 322	.021	6	96	89 073	.001	20	0	6
1934	69	3 521	.020	17	92	88 949	.001	21	1	18
1935	68	3 692	.018	24	91	90 261	.001	23	2	26
1936	69	3 683	.019	31	.	93 201	.001	24	1	32
1937	70	3 762	.019	26	.	96 662	.001	26	2	28
1938	70	3 800	.018	27	.	98 251	.001	27	1	28
1939	70	3 825	.018	26	.	99 954	.001	29	2	28
1940	70	3 944	.019	29	.	102 413	.001	30	1	30
1941	72	4 080	.018	34	.	106 644	.001	32	2	36
1942	77	4 181	.018	39	.	110 471	.001	34	2	41
1943	80	4 421	.018	50	.	117 348	.001	37	3	53
1944	86	4 869	.018	58	.	124 625	.001	40	3	61
1945	92	5 249	.018	65	.	132 953	.001	44	4	69
1946	97	5 727	.017	57	.	146 357	.001	47	3	60
1947	104	6 197	.017	59	.	157 699	.001	51	4	63
1948	.	6 597	.017	64	.	167 368	.001	54	3	67
1949	.	6 818	.017	67	.	177 123	.001	58	4	71

TABLE I-3

Column 1 – 1896–1947: Superintendent of Insurance of Canada, *Abstract of Statements of Insurance Companies in Canada,* 1947, p. 16A. Figures represent the sum of "Ordinary and industrial" and "Group" columns in "Premium income and annuity consideration in Canada" table.

Column 2 – 1896–1949: From "Total premium income" line in "Combined aggregates" table, *Spectator Life Insurance Yearbook,* various issues.

Column 3 – 1896–1947: Col. 1 divided by col. 2.
1948–1949: Estimated as equal to 1947.

Column 4 – 1897–1949: Col. 3 multiplied by change in adjusted admitted assets as shown in Table I-1, col. 3.

Column 5 – 1896–1935: From Stalson, J. Owen, *Marketing Life Insurance: Its History in America,* appendix 28.

Column 6 – 1896–1946: "Ordinary business" and "Industrial business" columns from *Spectator Life Insurance Yearbook,* various issues, "Aggregates" table; group insurance is excluded.
1947–1949: Institute of Life Insurance, *Life Insurance Fact Book,* 1950.

Column 7 – 1896–1935: Col. 5 divided by col. 6.
1936–1949: Estimated at 1927–1935 value.

Column 8 – 1896–1949: Col. 7 multiplied by adjusted admitted assets as shown in Table I-2, col. 6.

Column 9 – 1897–1949: Annual change in col. 8 adjusted in 1926 for inclusion of part of assets of Travelers Insurance Company not previously included (cf. note to Table I-1, col. 3).

Column 10 – 1897–1949: Sum of cols. 4 and 9.

TABLE I-4

Columns 1 and 2 – 1910, 1915, 1920–1947: From Superintendent of Insurance of Canada, *Annual Report,* part II, various issues.

Column 3 – 1910, 1915, 1920–1947: Col. 1 minus col. 2.

Column 4 – 1921–1947: Annual change in col. 3.

Column 5 – 1926–1949: Reserve of U.S. residents in five Canadian insurance companies doing the largest business in U.S., obtained from the reports of these companies or through correspondence with them.

Column 6 – 1910, 1915, 1920–1925: Col. 1 multiplied by ratio of col. 6 to col. 1 in 1926.
1926–1935: Col. 5 multiplied by ratio of col. 6 to col. 5 in 1936.
1936: Col. 5 multiplied by ratio of total foreign liabilities of all Canadian companies to total foreign liabilities of five largest companies derived from *Canada Yearbook,* 1938, p. 968.
1937–1946: Col. 5 multiplied by ratio linearly interpolated between 1936 and 1947 values.
1947: From Canada, Bureau of Statistics, *Canada Yearbook,* 1948, p. 1115.
1948–1949: Col. 5 multiplied by 1947 ratio of col. 6 to col. 5.

Column 7 – 1910, 1915, 1920–1947: Same percentage of col. 6 as for all foreign policyholders (col. 2 divided by col. 1).
1948–1949: Estimated on basis of same percentage of col. 6 as in 1947.

Column 8 – 1910, 1915, 1920–1949: Col. 6 minus col. 7.

Column 9 – 1911–1920: Obtained by linear interpolation between 1910, 1915, and 1920 values of col. 8.
1921–1949: First differences in col. 8.

U.S. POLICYHOLDERS' SAVING
THROUGH CANADIAN LIFE INSURANCE COMPANIES: 1910 to 1949

$ mill.

Year	All foreign policyholders in Canadian companies				U.S. policyholders				
	Reserves	Policy loans	Equity in reserves		Reserves		Policy loans	Equity in reserves	
			End of year	Annual change	5 largest companies	All companies		End of year	Annual change
	1	2	3	4	5	6	7	8	9
1910	30	3	27	.	.	9	1	8	.
1911	.	.	.	.	.	.	.	.	1
1912	.	.	.	.	.	.	.	.	1
1913	.	.	.	.	.	.	.	.	2
1914	.	.	.	.	.	.	.	.	2
1915	60	8	52	.	.	18	2	16	2
1916	.	.	.	.	.	.	.	.	2
1917	.	.	.	.	.	.	.	.	2
1918	.	.	.	.	.	.	.	.	2
1919	.	.	.	.	.	.	.	.	2
1920	100	11	89	.	.	30	3	27	3
1921	112	15	97	8	.	34	4	30	3
1922	148	25	123	26	.	44	7	37	7
1923	178	31	147	24	.	53	9	44	7
1924	234	40	194	47	.	70	12	58	14
1925	259	40	219	25	.	78	12	66	8
1926	303	47	256	37	88	91	14	77	11
1927	350	52	298	42	109	113	17	96	19
1928	430	64	366	68	164	170	25	145	49
1929	500	77	423	57	203	210	32	178	33
1930	559	88	471	48	242	250	39	211	33
1931	614	105	509	38	283	293	50	243	32
1932	612	114	498	−11	285	295	55	240	−3
1933	636	112	524	26	290	300	53	247	7
1934	693	105	588	64	309	319	48	271	24
1935	740	98	642	54	330	341	45	296	25
1936	792	92	700	58	359	371	43	328	32
1937	855	92	763	63	389	403	44	359	31
1938	911	92	819	56	419	435	44	391	32
1939	946	90	856	37	443	462	44	418	27
1940	985	93	892	36	464	485	46	439	21
1941	1 031	91	940	48	494	518	46	472	33
1942	1 081	86	995	55	526	553	44	509	37
1943	1 140	77	1 063	68	564	594	40	554	45
1944	1 209	70	1 139	76	608	642	37	605	51
1945	1 284	68	1 216	77	662	700	37	663	58
1946	1 347	65	1 282	66	723	767	37	730	67
1947	1 441	67	1 374	92	783	833	38	795	65
1948	.	.	.	.	837	891	41	850	55
1949	.	.	.	.	891	948	44	904	54

I-5

TABLE I-5

Columns 1, 2, 5, 8, 9 and 10 – 1896–1948: From tables of "Aggregates" in *Spectator Life Insurance Year-books.* Statement (or "admitted assets") values as shown in these tables were considered to be not materially different from book values for practical purposes except in case of 1946 and 1947 mortgage totals, which were adjusted for a substantial nonadmitted item.

1949: From Life Insurance Association of America, release dated May 24, 1950.

Columns 3 and 4 – 1896–1940: Breakdown of col. 2 based on ratios for forty-nine large companies (1906, 1911, 1916, 1920–1940 actual ratios; 1896–1905 ratios extrapolated from 1906, 1911, and 1916 ratios; 1907–1910, 1912–1915, 1917–1919 ratios interpolated). Figures may not add to col. 2 due to rounding.

1941–1948: Breakdown based on data for almost all U.S. companies as shown in table "Classification of mortgages" in Spectator Company, *Compendium of Official Life Insurance Reports.* Figures may not add to col. 2 due to rounding.

1949: Same source as col. 1.

Columns 6 and 7 – 1896, 1901: Estimated from partial book value data as follows: expansion of sixteen-company data (compiled from *State Insurance Reports*) by ratios, computed from *Spectator Life Insurance Yearbooks,* of total bonds and stocks of sixteen companies to total bonds and stocks of all companies.

1906, 1911, 1916: Expansion of forty-nine-company data by ratio, computed from *Spectator Life Insurance Yearbooks,* of bonds of forty-nine companies to bonds of all companies.

1897–1900, 1902–1905, 1907–1910, 1912–1915, 1917–1919: Ratios of total bonds to total admitted assets were estimated by interpolating corresponding ratios for sixteen or forty-nine companies for the various years from 1896 to 1920 as indicated above, and such estimated ratios were applied to total admitted assets of all companies as shown in *Spectator Life Insurance Yearbooks.*

1920–1948: Same method as 1906.

1949: Same source as col. 1.

Column 11 – 1896–1949: Col. 1 less sums of cols. 2 and 5–10.

I-6

TABLE I-6

Column 1 – 1896–1901: Actual totals for all companies compiled from *Spectator Life Insurance Yearbooks* and State Insurance Reports.

1902–1942: Expansion of forty-nine-company data by ratios, computed from *Spectator Life Insurance Yearbooks,* of total bonds of forty-nine companies to total bonds of all companies.

1943–1948: All-company aggregates from *Spectator Life Insurance Yearbooks* converted to book value basis by ratios obtaining in the case of forty-nine companies.

1949: Life Insurance Association of America, release dated May 24, 1950.

Column 2 – 1896–1901: Expansion of sixteen-company data by ratios of total bonds (excluding U.S. government) and stocks of sixteen to all companies.

1906, 1911, 1916, 1920–1942: Expansion of forty-nine-company data by ratios of total bond holdings (excluding U.S. Government) of forty-nine to all companies.

1897–1900, 1902–1905, 1907–1910, 1912–1915, 1917–1919: Obtained by applying interpolated ratios of state and local government bonds to total bonds (less U.S. Government) derived from data for sixteen or forty-nine companies to bond holdings of all companies as shown in *Spectator Life Insurance Yearbooks.*

1943–1948: Expansion of forty-nine-company data by ratios of total bond holdings (excluding U.S. Government) of forty-nine to all companies.

1949: Same source as col. 1.

Column 3 – 1896, 1901: Expansion of sixteen company data by ratios of total bonds (excluding U.S. Government) and stocks of sixteen to all companies.

1906, 1911, 1916, 1920–1942: Expansion of forty-nine-company data by similarly derived ratios.

1897–1900, 1902–1905, 1907–1910, 1912–1915, 1917–1919, 1943–1948: Same method as col. 2.

1949: Same source as col. 1.

Columns 4 and 5 – 1896, 1901: Totals from State Insurance Reports.

1897–1900, 1902–1948: Same method as col. 2.

1949: Same method as col. 1.

Column 6 – 1896–1905: Total stock holdings (from Table I-5, col. 7) multiplied by percentage of preferred stock to total stock in 1906.

1906, 1911, 1916, 1920–1949: Total stock holdings (from Table I-5, col. 7) multiplied by percentage of preferred stock to total stock for forty-nine U.S. legal reserve life insurance companies (holding approximately 90 percent of all life insurance company assets) derived from Life Insurance Association of America, *1949 Record of Life Insurance Investments.*

1907–1910, 1912–1915, 1917–1919: Same as above, but percentages obtained by linear interpolation between benchmark years, 1906, 1911, 1916, and 1920.

Column 7 – 1896–1949: Table I-5, col. 7 minus Table I-6, col. 6.

454

ASSETS OF ALL UNITED STATES LEGAL RESERVE
LIFE INSURANCE COMPANIES (BOOK VALUES): 1896 to 1949

$ mill.

End of year	Total admitted assets	Mortgage loans			Real estate	Bonds	Stocks	Col-lateral loans	Policy loans and premium notes	Cash	Other admitted assets
		Total	Farm	Other							
	1	2	3	4	5	6	7	8	9	10	11
1896	1 244	442	120	322	135	421	47	38	45	46	70
1897	1 345	452	124	328	138	471	50	44	52	61	77
1898	1 463	455	127	328	145	530	53	44	57	69	110
1899	1 595	468	133	335	154	596	57	50	71	67	132
1900	1 742	501	144	357	158	672	62	64	89	75	121
1901	1 911	532	155	377	166	759	66	65	108	89	126
1902	2 092	573	171	402	170	854	77	61	128	96	133
1903	2 265	624	190	434	178	950	89	67	159	111	87
1904	2 499	672	209	463	181	1 077	104	44	190	104	127
1905	2 706	724	230	494	171	1 196	118	46	226	77	148
1906	2 924	826	268	559	170	1 325	134	53	266	70	80
1907	3 053	921	307	614	170	1 374	125	46	348	67	2
1908	3 380	989	340	650	167	1 511	121	31	414	72	75
1909	3 644	1 087	384	703	167	1 618	112	20	446	72	122
1910	3 876	1 230	446	784	173	1 708	100	19	495	71	80
1911	4 164	1 361	507	854	171	1 823	86	15	542	75	91
1912	4 409	1 488	576	913	176	1 897	84	19	588	67	90
1913	4 659	1 622	651	971	166	1 969	82	21	658	73	68
1914	4 935	1 771	737	1 034	171	2 048	81	20	735	95	14
1915	5 190	1 784	768	1 016	173	2 197	81	17	780	114	44
1916	5 537	1 897	844	1 053	174	2 390	83	15	787	110	81
1917	5 941	2 026	931	1 095	179	2 616	85	18	810	104	103
1918	6 475	2 138	1 014	1 124	179	2 907	88	18	817	86	242
1919	6 791	2 089	1 021	1 068	168	3 093	88	28	805	112	408
1920	7 320	2 183	1 098	1 085	172	3 415	89	41	859	125	436
1921	7 936	2 803	1 445	1 358	186	3 520	78	30	1 058	120	141
1922	8 652	3 133	1 599	1 534	197	3 747	75	26	1 141	127	206
1923	9 455	3 674	1 834	1 840	243	3 879	80	24	1 198	120	237
1924	10 394	4 187	1 984	2 203	239	4 112	82	18	1 323	127	306
1925	11 538	4 814	2 075	2 739	266	4 419	98	20	1 446	124	351
1926	12 940	5 580	2 142	3 438	303	4 670	104	26	1 599	117	541
1927	14 392	6 200	2 167	4 033	350	5 155	102	27	1 785	133	640
1928	15 961	6 778	2 130	4 648	403	5 687	191	33	2 000	141	728
1929	17 482	7 316	2 097	5 219	464	6 011	352	32	2 379	147	781
1930	18 880	7 598	2 047	5 551	548	6 450	497	31	2 807	152	797
1931	20 160	7 673	1 990	5 684	683	6 846	568	31	3 369	179	811
1932	20 754	7 336	1 844	5 492	934	6 911	551	24	3 806	324	868
1933	20 896	6 702	1 616	5 086	1 264	7 328	535	20	3 769	451	827
1934	21 844	5 877	1 274	4 603	1 689	8 757	537	15	3 658	613	698
1935	23 216	5 358	1 070	4 288	1 986	10 332	560	13	3 540	829	598
1936	24 874	5 128	947	4 182	2 144	12 119	560	10	3 411	842	660
1937	26 249	5 244	897	4 347	2 190	13 621	574	9	3 399	726	486
1938	27 755	5 459	884	4 574	2 177	14 781	566	7	3 389	770	606
1939	29 243	5 683	877	4 806	2 134	16 007	568	6	3 248	929	668
1940	30 802	5 972	883	5 089	2 060	17 330	582	7	3 091	1 048	712
1941	32 731	6 442	913	5 529	1 873	19 199	607	9	2 919	877	805
1942	34 931	6 726	896	5 830	1 659	21 653	622	6	2 683	725	857
1943	37 766	6 714	841	5 873	1 350	24 879	635	5	2 373	875	935
1944	41 054	6 686	799	5 886	1 061	28 642	702	4	2 134	711	1 114
1945	44 797	6 636	776	5 860	857	32 489	873	3	1 962	780	1 197
1946	48 191	7 179	795	6 384	735	35 324	1 144	7	1 891	774	1 137
1947	51 743	8 694	895	7 799	860	36 753	1 379	9	1 937	1 020	1 091
1948	55 512	10 823	987	9 835	1 054	37 965	1 427	0	2 054	909	1 280
1949	59 555	12 894	1 136	11 758	1 245	39 232	1 730	0	2 239	906	1 309

SECURITIES HELD BY ALL UNITED STATES LEGAL RESERVE LIFE INSURANCE COMPANIES (BOOK VALUES): 1896 to 1949

$ mill.

End of year	Bonds					Stocks	
	Domestic			Foreign		Preferred	Common
	U.S. Government	State and local government	Corporate	Canadian	Other		
	1	2	3	4	5	6	7
1896	21	84	297	8	11	6	41
1897	14	84	349	9	16	7	43
1898	12	82	404	10	21	7	46
1899	9	78	471	10	28	8	49
1900	6	71	547	11	36	8	54
1901	5	61	635	12	45	9	57
1902	4	70	719	12	49	10	67
1903	3	79	802	13	53	12	77
1904	4	91	910	13	58	14	90
1905	4	102	1 016	13	62	16	102
1906	3	115	1 128	12	66	18	116
1907	3	122	1 169	14	67	17	108
1908	2	136	1 283	16	73	16	105
1909	2	148	1 373	18	76	15	97
1910	2	160	1 447	20	79	13	87
1911	1	173	1 543	23	83	12	74
1912	1	183	1 591	30	91	12	72
1913	1	194	1 635	38	100	11	71
1914	1	205	1 685	47	110	12	69
1915	1	223	1 790	58	125	12	69
1916	1	247	1 928	71	142	12	71
1917	72	270	2 040	94	139	13	72
1918	529	260	1 895	104	119	14	74
1919	773	261	1 836	118	105	14	74
1920	825	299	2 038	150	105	15	74
1921	831	361	2 050	163	115	16	62
1922	878	363	2 219	199	88	16	59
1923	826	346	2 419	227	63	17	63
1924	722	360	2 749	236	45	15	67
1925	663	372	3 085	259	39	16	82
1926	515	361	3 482	279	32	17	87
1927	464	375	3 962	320	34	25	77
1928	414	436	4 442	356	38	132	59
1929	336	574	4 666	396	39	255	97
1930	324	625	5 036	431	35	391	106
1931	380	741	5 220	471	34	457	111
1932	451	790	5 164	480	26	445	106
1933	860	864	5 117	470	18	431	104
1934	1 856	1 085	5 331	470	16	434	103
1935	2 906	1 249	5 663	501	14	455	105
1936	3 934	1 385	6 280	508	11	447	113
1937	4 645	1 494	6 961	515	7	464	110
1938	4 951	1 595	7 695	532	7	443	123
1939	5 396	1 758	8 277	569	7	435	133
1940	5 848	1 892	8 985	599	6	438	144
1941	6 827	1 805	9 895	666	6	466	141
1942	9 337	1 572	9 980	758	6	472	150
1943	12 547	1 301	10 079	946	6	485	150
1944	16 541	966	10 063	1 067	6	538	164
1945	20 581	619	10 074	1 208	7	693	180
1946	21 637	496	11 882	1 300	10	867	277
1947	20 019	478	14 862	1 376	19	1 098	281
1948	16 741	875	18 883	1 446	20	1 142	285
1949	15 259	1 052	21 451	1 449	20	1 384	346

CAPITAL GAINS AND LOSSES
OF UNITED STATES LIFE INSURANCE COMPANIES: 1929 to 1949

I-7

$ mill.

Year	On real estate			On mortgage loans			On bonds		
	Total	Realized	Revalu-ation	Total	Realized	Revalu-ation	Total	Realized	Revalu-ation
	1	2	3	4	5	6	7	8	9
1929	−6	1	−7	0	0	0	4	2	2
1930	−12	0	−12	0	0	0	1	6	−5
1931	−16	0	−16	0	0	0	11	11	0
1932	−27	−1	−26	0	0	0	−8	0	−8
1933	−26	−1	−25	0	0	0	−24	3	−27
1934	−23	2	−25	−2	−1	−1	−21	10	−31
1935	−26	6	−32	−2	−1	−1	−15	26	−41
1936	−61	11	−72	0	0	0	40	47	−7
1937	−9	17	−26	0	0	0	−101	14	−115
1938	−47	9	−56	0	0	0	−124	41	−165
1939	−68	8	−76	0	0	0	−94	43	−137
1940	−71	8	−79	−32	1	−33	−78	54	−132
1941	−63	14	−77	−14	0	−14	−75	51	−126
1942	−42	21	−63	−8	0	−8	0	59	−59
1943	−34	20	−54	−6	−2	−4	187	150	37
1944	−7	23	−30	−1	−1	0	249	168	81
1945	9	30	−21	4	2	2	380	315	65
1946	13	30	−17	2	1	1	129	146	−17
1947	−4	11	−15	0	0	0	43	68	−25
1948	−9	8	−17	0	1	−1	30	27	3
1949	−17	4	−21	−6	1	−7	24	34	−10

Year	On stocks			Amortization of bond premium or discount	Total
	Total	Realized	Revaluation		
	10	11	12	13	14
1929	5	5	0	3	6
1930	2	2	0	4	−5
1931	−2	0	−2	3	−4
1932	−8	−1	−7	3	−40
1933	−11	0	−11	1	−60
1934	−4	−1	−3	−1	−51
1935	−1	−1	0	−5	−49
1936	7	1	6	−12	−26
1937	−2	0	−2	−17	−129
1938	−5	0	−5	−18	−194
1939	14	3	11	−21	−169
1940	4	1	3	−24	−201
1941	−5	−1	−4	−27	−184
1942	−10	0	−10	−28	−88
1943	10	0	10	−23	134
1944	18	3	15	−18	241
1945	21	4	17	−14	400
1946	−7	4	−11	−17	120
1947	−15	1	−16	−21	3
1948	−10	1	−11	−21	−10
1949	17	−	17	−18	0

TABLE I–7

Column 1 – Sum of cols. 2 and 3.

Column 2 – Difference between items "gross profit on sale or maturity" of real estate and of other assets and "gross loss on sale or maturity" of real estate and other assets, as shown in statements of each of eighteen largest life insurance companies, increased by 25 percent to take account of smaller life insurance companies. This ratio approximates relation between total assets of eighteen largest and of all other life insurance companies for average of the period. Amounts attributable to "other assets" are very small—less than 0.2 percent of those for real estate—and have been included because they are more likely to result from transactions connected with real estate than with mortgage loans or securities.

Column 3 – Difference between items "gross increase, by adjustment, in book value" of real estate and of other assets, and "gross decrease, by adjustment, in book value" of real estate and other assets, obtained by same procedure as described under col. 2.

Column 4 – Sum of cols. 5 and 6.

Columns 5 and 6 – Derived by same procedure as described under cols. 2 and 3, respectively.

Column 7 – Sum of cols. 8 and 9.

Columns 8 and 9 – Derived by same procedure described under cols. 2 and 3, respectively.

Column 10 – Sum of cols. 11 and 12.

Columns 11 and 12 – Derived by same procedure as described under cols. 2 and 3, respectively.

Column 13 – Difference between items "accrual of discount" and "amortization of premium," derived by same method as described under col. 2.

Column 14 – Sum of cols. 1, 4, 7, 10, and 13.

TABLE I–8

Columns 1 and 2 – 1897–1949: From *Spectator Life Insurance Yearbook,* various issues. Figures exclude accident and health insurance business.

Column 3 – 1911: Assumed equal to 1912.
1912–1949: Same source as cols. 1 and 2.

Column 4 – 1897–1949: First differences in Table I-2, col. 7 (derived from *Spectator* data).

Column 5 – 1911–1949: Same source as col. 1.

Column 6 – 1911–1949: Same source as col. 1.

Column 7 – 1920: Estimated as zero on the basis of small figure for total annuity premiums from *Statistical Abstract.*
1921–1928: Roughly interpolated between 1920 and 1929.
1929, 1934–1939: Roughly estimated as one-fourth of annuity premiums, from *Statistical Abstract,* various issues, on basis of relationship in later years.
1930–1933: Roughly interpolated between 1929 and 1934 figures.
1940–1948: Figure for 1949 extrapolated on basis of group annuities in force from *Life Insurance Fact Book,* 1950.
1949: Estimated as three-quarters of total premiums on group annuities (from Institute of Life Insurance, *Tally,* August 1950) based on evidence that approximately one-half of the pension plans were noncontributory and that the employees paid half the cost of contributory plans.

Column 8 – 1946–1949: Estimated at one-third of employers' contributions to group insurance, from *Survey of Current Business,* July 1950, table 34, based on unpublished Federal Security Agency estimate that $200 million out of $600 million of survey was for group life.

Column 9 - 1897–1949: Cols. 1, 3, and 5 minus cols. 2, 4, and 6–8. This combination does not account for accrued interest included in stockholders' dividends on deposit or for the accrued interest included in policyholders' loans.

Column 10 – 1897–1949: Col. 9 multiplied by ratio of domestic policyholders' saving to saving of all policyholders, derived as ratio of Table I-1, col. 1 to Table I-1, col. 3.

Column 11 – 1897–1949: Col. 10 less farmers' share derived as col. 10 multiplied by farmers' percentage of accrued reserves of life insurance companies from Table A-57, col. 4.

NET CASH FLOW BETWEEN POLICYHOLDERS
AND UNITED STATES LIFE INSURANCE COMPANIES: 1897 to 1949

I-8

$ mill.

Year	Premiums	Benefits	Increase in dividends on deposit	Increase in policy loans	Premiums on supplementary contracts not involving life contingencies	Benefits paid on supplementary contracts not involving life contingencies	Employers' contributions for group insurance		Net cash payments by policyholders		
							Annuities	Life	Total	U.S.	Non-farm
	1	2	3	4	5	6	7	8	9	10	11
1897	243	139	–	7	–	–	–	–	97	90	79
1898	258	147	–	5	–	–	–	–	106	99	87
1899	292	160	–	14	–	–	–	–	118	113	100
1900	325	169	–	18	–	–	–	–	138	127	113
1901	366	192	–	19	–	–	–	–	155	146	130
1902	407	200	–	20	–	–	–	–	187	172	153
1903	448	226	–	31	–	–	–	–	191	162	145
1904	488	247	–	31	–	–	–	–	210	193	172
1905	516	265	–	36	–	–	–	–	215	199	179
1906	526	287	–	40	–	–	–	–	199	190	170
1907	533	310	–	82	–	–	–	–	141	144	129
1908	546	336	–	66	–	–	–	–	144	134	118
1909	565	361	–	32	–	–	–	–	172	173	152
1910	593	387	–	49	–	–	–	–	157	156	137
1911	632	414	2	47	5	3	–	–	175	174	153
1912	673	449	2	46	5	3	–	–	182	182	160
1913	715	470	2	70	5	3	–	–	179	176	155
1914	746	509	4	77	6	4	–	–	166	167	147
1915	784	545	2	44	7	5	–	–	199	201	178
1916	848	566	4	8	9	5	–	–	282	283	253
1917	929	590	4	23	12	7	–	–	325	330	296
1918	994	710	7	7	13	8	–	–	289	297	267
1919	1 207	740	2	–12	13	10	–	–	484	516	462
1920	1 385	745	14	54	15	12	0	–	603	620	554
1921	1 537	840	8	199	14	11	0	–	509	518	464
1922	1 686	1 006	6	83	17	12	5	–	603	613	552
1923	1 900	1 089	22	57	21	14	5	–	778	783	707
1924	2 122	1 205	23	125	25	15	10	–	815	813	737
1925	2 384	1 246	23	123	30	21	10	–	1 037	1 024	932
1926	2 624	1 373	25	153	39	25	15	–	1 122	1 097	1 003
1927	2 874	1 500	26	186	48	29	15	–	1 218	1 203	1 101
1928	3 146	1 699	34	215	65	37	20	–	1 274	1 248	1 142
1929	3 350	1 962	48	379	75	46	25	–	1 061	1 037	951
1930	3 524	2 247	36	428	86	52	40	–	879	860	789
1931	3 661	2 607	13	562	128	63	55	–	515	503	462
1932	3 504	3 087	6	437	158	79	70	–	–5	–5	–5
1933	3 322	3 016	14	–37	159	96	85	–	335	327	301
1934	3 521	2 705	7	–111	194	106	100	–	922	903	832
1935	3 692	2 535	22	–118	227	120	125	–	1 279	1 255	1 160
1936	3 683	2 429	35	–129	245	132	115	–	1 416	1 388	1 284
1937	3 762	2 437	30	–12	249	167	100	–	1 349	1 321	1 223
1938	3 800	2 578	31	–10	268	176	110	–	1 245	1 222	1 132
1939	3 825	2 642	35	–141	295	184	100	–	1 370	1 344	1 246
1940	3 944	2 681	72	–157	323	213	110	–	1 492	1 464	1 357
1941	4 080	2 550	49	–172	330	233	127	–	1 721	1 688	1 570
1942	4 181	2 443	53	–236	321	241	143	–	1 964	1 927	1 808
1943	4 421	2 407	71	–310	353	248	163	–	2 337	2 293	2 160
1944	4 869	2 528	81	–239	399	274	192	–	2 594	2 545	2 395
1945	5 249	2 719	37	–172	455	301	218	–	2 675	2 624	2 461
1946	5 727	2 848	153	–71	477	346	254	100	2 880	2 828	2 653
1947	6 197	3 045	65	46	499	386	298	130	2 856	2 804	2 633
1948	6 597	3 308	105	117	532	427	352	160	2 870	2 819	2 650
1949	6 818	3 545	131	184	539	478	400	200	2 681	2 633	2 475

459

TABLE I-9

Column 1 – 1897–1949: First differences of Table I-10, col. 1.

Column 2 – 1897–1949: First differences of Table I-10, col. 12.

Column 3 – 1897–1949: First differences of estimates of current liabilities obtained by multiplying Table I-10, col. 1 by annual ratio of current liabilities to total assets, for all fraternal orders, as reported in the *Fraternal Monitor*.

Column 4 – 1897–1949: Col. 1 minus sum of cols. 2 and 3.

Column 5 – 1930–1949: Col. 4 minus net capital gains, or plus net capital losses from Table I-13, col. 1.

Column 6 – 1897–1900: Extrapolated on basis of orders operating in New York State (cf. *Annual Report, New York State Superintendent of Insurance*).
1901–1948: From *Spectator Life Insurance Yearbook*, various issues.
1949: Assumed same as 1948.

Column 7 – 1897–1949: Col. 6 minus col. 2.

TABLE I-10

Column 1 – 1896–1900: Estimated from data in *New York Insurance Report* and *Spectator Life Insurance Yearbook*. Total assets include other assets not shown separately (cf. Table I-11, col. 12).
1901–1915A: *Spectator Life Insurance Yearbook*.
1915B–1949: *Fraternal Monitor* (total minus assets of Canadian orders).

Columns 2 to 4, 6 to 12 – 1896–1949: Obtained by applying to col. 1 appropriate percentages from Table I-11.

Column 5 – 1925–1949: Estimated at between 10 and 8 percent of total mortgage loans on basis of information for 1948, 1939, and 1929 obtained by correspondence from sixteen large orders. (For these three years the average percentages were 8.2, 8.6, and 9.7, respectively.)

Note: Details may not add to totals because of rounding.

INDIVIDUALS' SAVING THROUGH FRATERNAL ORDERS
1897 to 1949

$ mill.

Year	Change in			Saving		Excess of policyholders' payments over claims	Policy-holders' net payments
	Total assets	Policy loans	Current liabilities	Unadjusted	Adjusted		
	1	2	3	4	5	6	7
1897	2	0	0	2	.	3	3
1898	3	0	0	3	.	4	4
1899	2	0	0	2	.	4	4
1900	4	0	0	4	.	7	7
1901	4	0	0	4	.	8	8
1902	7	0	1	6	.	10	10
1903	8	0	1	7	.	16	16
1904	9	0	1	8	.	11	11
1905	12	0	1	11	.	18	18
1906	12	0	1	11	.	15	15
1907	9	0	1	8	.	17	17
1908	19	1	1	17	.	21	20
1909	13	1	1	11	.	−7	−7
1910	12	0	1	11	.	22	22
1911	19	1	2	16	.	34	33
1912	16	1	1	14	.	27	26
1913	20	1	1	18	.	29	28
1914	6	0	0	6	.	27	27
1915	23	1	2	20	.	23	22
1916	22	1	−2	23	.	25	24
1917	24	1	2	21	.	43	42
1918	30	1	23	6	.	21	20
1919	16	1	−19	34	.	19	18
1920	32	1	0	31	.	55	54
1921	56	2	3	51	.	63	61
1922	62	3	4	55	.	62	59
1923	54	2	−5	57	.	18	16
1924	48	2	2	44	.	70	68
1925	66	2	1	63	.	67	65
1926	58	3	0	55	.	61	58
1927	62	2	3	57	.	63	61
1928	50	2	2	46	.	57	55
1929	45	2	−1	44	.	46	44
1930	37	1	−4	40	43	52	51
1931	29	2	0	27	57	53	51
1932	14	0	1	13	32	47	47
1933	29	6	3	20	27	41	35
1934	36	5	−7	38	36	35	30
1935	55	13	1	41	29	41	28
1936	43	7	−1	37	35	34	27
1937	39	8	4	27	40	42	34
1938	48	7	0	41	49	44	37
1939	49	4	2	43	55	42	38
1940	41	0	1	40	68	40	40
1941	67	2	3	62	91	45	43
1942	73	−2	5	70	78	52	54
1943	73	−7	7	73	73	56	63
1944	92	−3	8	87	84	62	65
1945	100	−5	9	96	74	81	86
1946	74	−2	5	71	87	66	68
1947	86	0	8	78	81	70	70
1948	67	2	3	62	83	76	74
1949	83	3	7	73	83	76	73

ASSETS OF FRATERNAL ORDERS
1896 to 1949
$ mill.

End of year	Total	Cash	Real estate	Mortgage loans		Securities						Policy loans
				Total	Farm mort-gages	Total	U.S. Govern-ment	State and local govern-ment	Foreign bonds	Corporate bonds	Stocks	
	1	2	3	4	5	6	7	8	9	10	11	12
1896	12	2	0	1	—	7	1	6	—	0	—	1
1897	14	3	0	1	—	8	1	8	—	0	—	1
1898	18	3	1	2	—	10	1	9	—	1	—	1
1899	20	4	1	2	—	12	1	11	—	1	—	1
1900	25	4	1	2	—	15	1	13	—	1	—	1
1901	29	5	1	3	—	18	1	15	—	1	—	1
1902	38	6	1	4	—	22	1	19	—	2	—	1
1903	44	8	1	4	—	26	1	23	—	2	—	2
1904	52	9	2	5	—	32	2	27	—	3	—	2
1905	64	12	2	6	—	39	2	34	—	3	—	3
1906	76	19	2	8	—	40	2	34	—	4	—	3
1907	86	18	2	9	—	47	2	41	—	5	—	3
1908	104	15	3	11	—	66	2	57	0	7	—	4
1909	117	17	4	11	—	76	2	66	1	8	—	5
1910	129	19	4	13	—	84	2	72	1	9	—	5
1911	148	19	5	15	—	100	2	85	2	10	—	6
1912	164	18	6	17	—	112	2	96	2	12	—	6
1913	184	19	7	20	—	126	2	110	2	16	—	7
1914	190	18	7	21	—	132	1	117	1	12	—	8
1915A	213	20	7	24	—	149	1	135	1	13	—	8
1915B	223	20	8	25	—	156	1	142	1	13	—	9
1916	245	24	9	28	—	169	0	156	0	13	—	10
1917	269	23	9	31	—	184	7	163	1	14	—	11
1918	299	23	9	34	—	209	17	175	2	16	—	12
1919	315	27	10	31	—	219	26	175	2	16	—	13
1920	347	25	12	38	—	244	23	200	5	16	—	14
1921	403	27	12	43	—	286	20	239	10	17	—	16
1922	465	25	14	56	—	339	16	290	16	18	—	19
1923	519	25	16	61	—	388	16	329	19	24	—	21
1924	567	26	18	80	—	414	14	348	22	30	—	23
1925	633	25	22	98	10	457	13	381	26	37	—	25
1926	691	26	27	107	11	500	11	413	30	46	—	28
1927	753	27	27	124	12	543	9	444	35	55	—	30
1928	803	25	27	139	14	578	6	467	40	65	—	32
1929	848	22	24	154	15	605	3	485	44	73	—	34
1930	885	30	26	172	17	610	4	486	44	76	—	35
1931	914	26	30	179	17	623	5	494	46	78	—	37
1932	928	20	35	186	17	613	5	484	45	79	—	37
1933	957	22	49	177	16	624	2	455	46	120	1	43
1934	933	25	62	159	15	662	4	525	47	87	1	48
1935	1 048	29	85	140	13	702	50	519	48	84	1	61
1936	1 091	28	96	136	12	732	63	477	49	139	4	68
1937	1 130	34	99	149	13	746	102	441	48	149	6	76
1938	1 178	32	100	152	13	783	78	476	49	170	10	83
1939	1 227	42	101	157	14	812	81	480	49	190	12	87
1940	1 268	51	93	162	14	848	87	474	52	221	14	87
1941	1 335	52	83	172	15	912	93	502	55	246	16	89
1942	1 408	41	73	183	15	997	147	573	59	194	24	87
1943	1 481	43	62	181	15	1 087	221	533	65	238	30	80
1944	1 573	39	47	184	15	1 202	378	398	71	316	39	77
1945	1 673	44	40	182	15	1 313	396	437	77	358	45	72
1946	1 747	42	38	189	16	1 384	412	455	80	388	49	70
1947	1 833	37	38	205	17	1 461	444	462	84	418	53	70
1948	1 900	38	40	256	21	1 471	445	464	87	420	55	72
1949	1 983	40	38	293	24	1 513	442	484	91	438	58	75

DISTRIBUTION OF ASSETS OF FRATERNAL ORDERS
1896 to 1949

Percent

End of year	Total	Cash	Real estate	Mortgage loans	Securities						Policy loans	Other assets
					Total	U.S. Government	State and local government	Foreign bonds	Corporate bonds	Stocks		
	1	2	3	4	5	6	7	8	9	10	11	12
1896	100.0	17.9	3.0	10.1	59.9	4.2	53.1	–	2.6	–	4.0	5.1
1897	100.0	17.9	3.0	10.1	59.9	4.1	52.9	–	2.9	–	4.0	5.1
1898	100.0	17.9	3.0	10.1	59.9	3.9	52.8	–	3.2	–	4.0	5.1
1899	100.0	17.9	3.0	10.1	59.9	3.7	52.7	–	3.5	–	4.0	5.1
1900	100.0	17.9	3.0	10.1	59.9	3.5	52.6	–	3.8	–	4.0	5.1
1901	100.0	17.9	3.0	10.1	59.9	3.4	52.5	–	4.1	–	4.0	5.1
1902	100.0	17.9	3.0	10.1	59.9	3.2	52.3	–	4.4	–	4.0	5.1
1903	100.0	17.9	3.0	10.1	59.9	3.0	52.2	–	4.7	–	4.0	5.1
1904	100.0	17.9	3.0	10.1	59.9	2.8	52.1	–	5.0	–	4.0	5.1
1905	100.0	17.9	3.0	10.1	59.9	2.6	52.0	–	5.3	–	4.0	5.1
1906	100.0	25.0	3.1	10.1	51.7	2.1	44.8	–	4.8	–	4.0	6.1
1907	100.0	21.1	2.9	10.1	55.0	2.1	47.5	–	5.4	–	4.0	6.9
1908	100.0	14.4	2.8	10.3	63.4	2.2	54.7	0.2	6.3	–	4.0	5.1
1909	100.0	14.4	3.2	9.6	65.0	2.0	55.9	0.5	6.6	–	4.0	3.8
1910	100.0	14.6	2.8	10.2	64.5	1.7	55.4	0.8	6.6	–	4.0	3.9
1911	100.0	12.6	3.2	10.3	67.3	1.5	57.6	1.1	7.1	–	4.0	2.6
1912	100.0	10.8	3.8	10.4	68.6	1.4	58.5	1.4	7.3	–	4.0	2.4
1913	100.0	10.4	3.8	10.7	68.8	1.0	59.9	1.0	6.8	–	4.0	2.3
1914	100.0	9.3	3.5	10.9	69.4	0.7	61.6	0.7	6.4	–	4.0	2.9
1915	100.0	9.2	3.5	11.2	70.2	0.4	63.5	0.4	5.9	–	4.0	1.9
1916	100.0	9.8	3.5	11.6	69.0	0.1	63.6	0.0	5.3	–	4.0	2.1
1917	100.0	8.4	3.2	11.5	68.6	2.7	60.5	0.2	5.2	–	4.0	4.3
1918	100.0	7.8	3.1	11.2	69.9	5.6	58.6	0.5	5.2	–	4.0	3.8
1919	100.0	8.6	3.1	9.8	69.5	8.3	55.3	0.8	5.1	–	4.0	5.0
1920	100.0	7.2	3.3	11.0	70.4	6.6	57.5	1.6	4.7	–	4.0	4.1
1921	100.0	6.7	3.1	10.6	71.0	5.0	59.3	2.4	4.3	–	4.0	4.6
1922	100.0	5.3	3.0	12.1	73.0	3.4	62.4	3.4	3.8	–	4.0	2.6
1923	100.0	4.9	3.1	11.8	74.7	3.0	63.7	3.7	4.6	–	4.0	1.5
1924	100.0	4.5	3.1	14.2	73.1	2.5	61.4	3.9	5.3	–	4.0	1.1
1925	100.0	3.9	3.4	15.5	72.2	2.0	60.2	4.1	5.9	–	4.0	1.0
1926	100.0	3.7	4.0	15.5	72.3	1.6	59.7	4.4	6.6	–	4.0	0.5
1927	100.0	3.6	3.6	16.5	72.0	1.2	58.9	4.6	7.3	–	4.0	0.3
1928	100.0	3.1	3.4	17.3	72.0	0.7	58.2	5.0	8.1	–	4.0	0.2
1929	100.0	2.6	2.8	18.2	71.3	0.4	57.2	5.1	8.6	–	4.0	1.1
1930	100.0	3.4	3.0	19.4	68.9	0.4	54.9	5.0	8.6	–	4.0	1.3
1931	100.0	2.8	3.3	19.6	68.1	0.5	54.1	5.0	8.5	–	4.0	2.2
1932	100.0	2.1	3.8	20.0	66.1	0.5	52.2	4.9	8.5	–	4.0	4.1
1933	100.0	2.3	5.1	18.5	65.2	0.2	47.6	4.8	12.5	0.1	4.5	4.4
1934	100.0	2.5	6.3	16.0	66.7	0.4	52.7	4.7	8.8	0.1	4.8	3.7
1935	100.0	2.8	8.1	13.3	67.0	4.8	49.5	4.6	8.0	0.1	5.8	3.0
1936	100.0	2.6	8.8	12.5	67.1	5.8	43.7	4.5	12.7	0.4	6.2	2.8
1937	100.0	3.0	8.8	13.2	66.0	9.0	39.0	4.3	13.2	0.5	6.7	2.3
1938	100.0	2.7	8.5	12.9	66.5	6.6	40.4	4.2	14.4	0.9	7.0	2.4
1939	100.0	3.4	8.2	12.8	66.2	6.6	39.1	4.0	15.5	1.0	7.1	2.3
1940	100.0	4.0	7.3	12.8	66.9	6.9	37.4	4.1	17.4	1.1	6.9	2.1
1941	100.0	3.9	6.2	12.9	68.3	7.0	37.6	4.1	18.4	1.2	6.7	2.0
1942	100.0	2.9	5.2	13.0	70.8	10.4	40.7	4.2	13.8	1.7	6.2	1.9
1943	100.0	2.9	4.2	12.2	73.4	14.9	36.0	4.4	16.1	2.0	5.4	1.9
1944	100.0	2.5	3.0	11.7	76.4	24.0	25.3	4.5	20.1	2.5	4.9	1.5
1945	100.0	2.6	2.4	10.9	78.5	23.7	26.1	4.6	21.4	2.7	4.3	1.3
1946	100.0	2.4	2.2	10.8	79.2	23.6	26.0	4.6	22.2	2.8	4.0	1.4
1947	100.0	2.0	2.1	11.2	79.7	24.2	25.2	4.6	22.8	2.9	3.8	1.2
1948	100.0	2.0	2.1	13.5	77.4	23.4	24.4	4.6	22.1	2.9	3.8	1.2
1949	100.0	2.0	1.9	14.8	76.3	22.3	24.4	4.6	22.1	2.9	3.8	1.2

Column 2 – 1896–1905: Five-year average, 1906–1910, for all orders operating in New York State.
1906–1947: Computed from *Annual Report, New York State Superintendent of Insurance,* various issues.
1948–1949: Assumed equal to 1947.

Column 3 – 1896–1947: Same source as col. 2.
1948–1949: Percentage of real estate owned to total assets of all fraternal orders, as reported in various issues of *Fraternal Monitor.*

Column 4 – 1896–1949: Same source as col. 3.

Column 5 – 1896–1947: Same source as col. 2.
1948–1949: Col. 1 minus sum of cols. 2–4, 11, and 12.

Column 6 – 1896–1906: Extrapolated on basis of relevant percentage for aggregate of twelve large orders reported individually in *Annual Report, New York State Superintendent of Insurance.* (Orders included are: Aid Association for Lutherans, Catholic Order of Foresters, Knights of Columbus, Knights of Pythias, Maccabees, Modern Woodmen of America, Royal Arcanum, Royal Neighbors of America, Women's Benefit Association, Woodmen's Circle, Woodmen of the World, Polish National Alliance of America.)
1907, 1912, 1916, 1922, 1929: Computed from aggregate of twelve large orders (as above) reported individually in *Annual Report, New York State Superintendent of Insurance.*
1908–1928: Linearly interpolated between percentages computed for 1907, 1912, 1916, 1922, and 1929.
1930–1931: Linearly interpolated between 1929 and 1932 percentages.
1932–1938: Percentage of government bonds held by fraternal orders from Friend and Natrella, *Individuals' Saving,* part II, table 17, line 8, adjusted for Canadian government bonds held, to total assets of fraternal orders from *Fraternal Monitor.* Friend and Natrella estimated holdings of government bonds on basis of holdings of ten largest orders operating in New York State (as above, excluding Royal Arcanum and Knights of Pythias). Adjustment for Canadian government bonds was made on basis of their share in total assets (around 2 percent) of eleven largest orders (includes Royal Arcanum).
1939–1949: Same as for 1932–1938 except that government bonds held taken from *Fraternal Monitor.* Same adjustment made for Canadian government bonds.

Column 7 – 1896–1929: Same as col. 6.
1930–1931: Col. 5 minus sum of cols. 6, 8–10, all of which are linearly interpolated between 1929 and 1932 percentages.
1932–1947: Percentage of state and local government bonds held by fraternal orders from Friend and Natrella, *op. cit.,* table 18, line 5, to total assets of fraternal orders.
1948–1949: Same proportion of state and local government and corporate bonds as in 1947.

Column 8 – 1896–1907: Assumed negligible as in 1907 New York sample (see notes to col. 6).
1908–1947: Obtained by linear interpolation between percentages computed for 1907, 1912, 1916, 1922, 1929, 1932, 1939, and 1947 from aggregates for twelve large orders (cf. col. 6).
1948–1949: Assumed same as 1947.

Column 9 – 1896–1931: Same method as col. 6.
1932–1947: Estimated as part of corporate securities (col. 5 minus cols. 6–8) on the basis of the relative holdings of corporate bonds and stocks in 1932, 1939, and 1947 by twelve large orders. (The percentage ranges from 100 in 1932 to 94 in 1939 to 89 in 1947.)
1948–1949: Same method as col. 7.

Column 10 – 1896–1947: Same method as col. 9.
1948–1949: Assumed same as 1947.

Column 11 – 1896–1932: Estimated at 4.0 percent of total assets on basis of later figures.
1933–1947: Computed from data for twelve large orders reported individually in *Annual Report, New York State Superintendent of Insurance.*
1948–1949: Assumed same as 1947.

Column 12 – 1896–1947: Col. 1 minus sum of cols. 2–5 and 11.
1948–1949: Assumed same as 1947.

Note: Details may not add to totals because of rounding.

CAPITAL GAINS AND LOSSES OF FRATERNAL ORDERS
1897 to 1949

I-12

$ mill.

Year	Net current income	Increase in net assets	Inferred capital gain or loss	Reported capital gain or loss	Year	Net current income	Increase in net assets	Inferred capital gain or loss	Reported capital gain or loss
	1	2	3	4		1	2	3	4
1897	2	2	0	–	1924	73	46	–27	–
1898	3	3	0	–	1925	54	65	11	–
1899	2	2	0	–	1926	62	58	–4	–
1900	4	4	0	–	1927	55	59	4	–
1901	4	4	0	–	1928	54	48	–6	–
1902	6	6	0	–	1929	42	46	4	–
1903	7	7	0	–	1930	44	41	–3	–
1904	6	8	2	–	1931	59	29	–30	–
1905	12	11	–1	–	1932	32	13	–19	–
1906	14	11	–3	–	1933	33	26	–7	–
1907	13	8	–5	–	1934	41	43	2	–
1908	16	17	1	–	1935	42	54	12	–
1909	15	12	–3	–	1936	42	44	2	–
1910	14	11	–3	–	1937	48	35	–13	–
1911	15	17	2	–	1938	52	48	–4	–8
1912	16	14	–2	–	1939	55	47	–8	–12
1913	17	18	1	–	1940	49	40	–9	–28
1914	17	6	–11	–	1941	55	64	9	–29
1915	26	21	–5	–	1942	63	68	5	–8
1916	34	24	–10	–	1943	72	66	–6	0
1917	20	22	2	–	1944	82	84	2	3
1918	16	7	–9	–	1945	95	91	–4	22
1919	7	35	28	–	1946	85	69	–16	–
1920	36	32	–4	–	1947	81	78	–3	–
1921	46	53	7	–	1948	85	64	–21	–
1922	40	58	18	–	1949	86	76	–10	–
1923	46	59	13	–					

Column 1 – 1897–1904: Estimated by applying the ratio for 1905 of income as published in *Annual Report, New York State Superintendent of Insurance* to that as given in *Fraternal Monitor*, adjusted to exclude foreign orders.

1905–1949: Net income of all orders as reported by *Fraternal Monitor*, various issues, adjusted to exclude foreign orders on the basis of the ratio of total assets of foreign to all reported orders (see Table I-10, col. 1).

Column 2 – 1897–1949: From Table I-9, col. 1 minus col. 3.

Column 3 – 1897–1949: Col. 2 minus col. 1.

Column 4 – 1938–1945: Obtained by raising New York State figures on the basis of ratio of total assets of orders reported in New York to those of all U.S. orders as given in Table I-10. Figures from the New York reports are the difference between columns headed "profit on sale, maturity, and increase in book value of ledger assets" and "loss on sale, maturity, and decrease in book value of ledger assets."

DISTRIBUTION OF CAPITAL GAINS AND LOSSES OF FRATERNAL ORDERS
BY TYPE OF ASSET: 1930 to 1949

$ mill.

Year	Total	On mortgages and real estate	On securities	On other assets	Year	Total	On mortgages and real estate	On securities	On other assets
	1	2	3	4		1	2	3	4
1930	−3	−3	0	0	1940	−28	−15	−10	−3
1931	−30	−8	−19	−3	1941	−29	−15	−11	−3
1932	−19	−4	−13	−2	1942	−8	−8	2	−2
1933	−7	−2	−4	−1	1943	0	−5	5	0
1934	2	0	2	0	1944	3	0	3	0
1935	12	0	12	0	1945	22	0	22	0
1936	2	0	2	0	1946	−16	0	−16	0
1937	−13	−3	−8	−2	1947	−3	0	−3	0
1938	−8	−4	−2	−2	1948	−21	0	−21	0
1939	−12	−6	−4	−2	1949	−10	0	−10	0

Column 1 – 1930–1937: Table I-12, col. 3.
   1938–1945: Table I-12, col. 4.
   1946–1949: Table I-12, col. 3.

Columns 2, 3 and 4 – 1930–1943: Roughly allocated on the basis of holdings of each type of asset in 1930 and
   estimates for losses of mutual savings banks and savings and loan associations.
   1944–1949: Profits and losses assumed concentrated on securities.

TABLE I-14

Column 1 – 1896–1902: Extrapolated, from 1903 value, on basis of reported excess of income over disbursements from *Spectator Insurance Yearbook, Life* and *Casualty Volumes*.
   1903–1947: *Spectator Life Insurance Yearbook*, various issues. Declines shown between 1905 and
   1906 and between 1910 and 1911 are accounted for largely by a shift in classification of two
   stipulated-premium companies to legal-reserve companies. (Northwestern National Life Company with assets of $ 4.2 million in 1905 was included with the life companies beginning in
   1906. Bankers' Life Association, with assets of $ 15.4 million in 1910, was reorganized in 1911
   and included in the legal-reserve statistics beginning with 1911).
   1948–1949: Sum of total assets of accident and sick benefit companies except Mutual Benefit
   Health and Accident Association (assumed as equal to 1947); assessment life companies (from
   Spectator Life Insurance Yearbook for 1948 and estimated for 1949) and Mutual Benefit Health
   and Accident Association (from annual statements).

Columns 2 to 9 – 1896–1938: Col. 1 multiplied by percentages computed for fraternal order life insurance
   (cf. Table I-11).
   1939–1949: Total assets of the largest individual company (Mutual Benefit Health and Accident
   Association, accounting for about 11 percent of the group total for 1939 and 30 percent in
   1947) for which information by type of asset was available were subtracted from col. 1. Remaining total assets were distributed as for 1896–1938. Reported assets by type of Mutual
   Benefit Health and Accident Association were added back to give totals and distributions for
   1939–1949.

Column 10 – 1897–1949: Annual change in col. 1, adjusted in 1906 and 1911 for change in classification of
   two companies (cf. note to col. 1).

Note: Details may not add to totals because of rounding.

ASSETS OF MUTUAL ACCIDENT, SICK BENEFIT, AND ASSESSMENT LIFE ASSOCIATIONS: 1896 to 1949

$ mill.

End of year	Total assets	Cash	Mort-gages	Securities					Other	Change in assets
				Total	U.S. Government	State and local government	Other bonds	Stocks		
	1	2	3	4	5	6	7	8	9	10
1896	3.2	0.6	0.3	1.9	0.1	1.7	0.1	0	0.4	.
1897	5.5	1.0	0.6	3.3	0.2	2.9	0.2	0	0.7	2.3
1898	7.1	1.3	0.7	4.3	0.3	3.7	0.2	0	0.9	1.6
1899	7.3	1.3	0.7	4.4	0.3	3.8	0.3	0	0.9	0.2
1900	9.0	1.6	0.9	5.4	0.3	4.7	0.3	0	1.1	1.7
1901	13.7	2.5	1.4	8.2	0.4	7.2	0.6	0	1.6	4.7
1902	16.4	2.9	1.7	9.8	0.5	8.6	0.7	0	2.0	2.7
1903	19.0	3.4	1.9	11.4	0.6	9.9	0.9	0	2.3	2.6
1904	20.0	3.6	2.0	12.0	0.6	10.4	1.0	0	2.4	1.0
1905	22.5	4.0	2.3	13.5	0.6	11.7	1.2	0	2.7	2.5
1906	20.7	5.2	2.1	10.7	0.4	9.3	1.0	0	2.7	−1.8
1907	22.7	4.8	2.3	12.5	0.5	10.8	1.2	0	3.1	2.0
1908	23.8	3.4	2.5	15.1	0.5	13.0	1.6	0	2.8	1.1
1909	27.4	3.9	2.6	17.8	0.6	15.3	1.9	0	3.1	3.6
1910	28.7	4.2	2.9	18.5	0.5	15.9	2.1	0	3.1	1.3
1911	16.2	2.0	1.7	10.9	0.3	9.3	1.3	0	1.6	3.0
1912	18.0	1.9	1.9	12.3	0.2	10.5	1.6	0	1.9	1.8
1913	19.0	2.0	2.0	13.1	0.2	11.4	1.5	0	1.9	1.0
1914	18.1	1.7	2.0	12.6	0.1	11.2	1.3	0	1.8	−0.9
1915	16.8	1.5	1.9	11.8	0.1	10.7	1.0	0	1.6	−1.3
1916	19.8	1.9	2.3	13.7	0	12.6	1.1	0	1.9	3.0
1917	22.4	1.9	2.6	15.4	0.6	13.6	1.2	0	2.5	2.6
1918	22.8	1.8	2.6	15.9	1.3	13.3	1.3	0	2.5	0.4
1919	27.5	2.4	2.7	19.1	2.3	15.2	1.6	0	3.3	4.7
1920	28.7	2.1	3.2	20.2	1.9	16.5	1.8	0	3.2	1.2
1921	32.4	2.2	3.4	23.0	1.6	19.2	2.2	0	3.8	3.7
1922	48.9	2.6	5.9	35.7	1.7	30.5	3.5	0	4.7	16.5
1923	54.0	2.6	6.4	40.3	1.6	34.2	4.5	0	4.7	5.1
1924	76.8	3.5	10.9	56.1	1.9	47.1	7.1	0	6.3	22.8
1925	80.4	3.1	12.5	58.0	1.6	48.4	8.0	0	6.8	3.6
1926	84.1	3.1	13.0	60.8	1.3	50.2	9.3	0	7.2	3.7
1927	90.7	3.3	15.0	65.3	1.1	53.4	10.8	0	7.1	6.6
1928	84.7	2.6	14.7	61.0	0.6	49.3	11.1	0	6.4	−6.0
1929	88.1	2.3	16.0	62.8	0.4	50.4	12.1	0	7.0	3.4
1930	79.5	2.7	15.4	54.8	0.3	43.6	10.9	0	6.6	−8.6
1931	61.4	1.7	12.0	41.8	0.3	33.2	8.3	0	5.9	−18.1
1932	56.9	1.2	11.4	37.6	0.3	29.7	7.6	0	6.7	−4.5
1933	56.2	1.3	10.4	36.6	0.1	26.8	9.6	0.1	7.9	−0.7
1934	60.2	1.5	9.6	40.2	0.2	31.7	8.2	0.1	8.9	4.0
1935	64.9	1.8	8.6	43.5	3.1	32.1	8.2	0.1	11.0	4.7
1936	60.8	1.6	7.6	40.8	3.5	26.6	10.5	0.2	10.8	−4.1
1937	67.5	2.0	8.9	44.6	6.1	26.3	11.9	0.3	12.0	6.7
1938	75.3	2.0	9.7	50.1	5.0	30.4	14.0	0.7	13.5	7.8
1939	86.1	3.6	9.9	58.9	6.8	33.3	17.8	1.0	13.7	10.8
1940	83.9	3.9	9.6	58.4	6.7	31.3	19.3	1.1	12.0	−2.2
1941	93.3	4.5	9.9	66.8	7.6	35.3	22.7	1.2	12.1	9.4
1942	104.9	4.5	10.8	78.2	12.0	43.4	20.9	1.9	11.4	11.6
1943	127.9	5.7	11.9	98.5	21.9	47.4	26.6	2.6	11.8	23.0
1944	152.2	6.9	13.3	120.9	39.1	43.2	35.1	3.5	11.1	24.3
1945	192.7	9.1	15.5	155.5	51.3	53.0	46.1	5.1	12.6	40.5
1946	209.9	11.5	16.0	169.8	55.2	57.3	51.3	6.0	12.6	17.2
1947	249.4	10.8	19.6	205.1	65.3	69.0	62.5	8.3	13.9	39.5
1948	268.5	13.2	24.3	216.4	65.0	75.3	66.4	9.7	14.6	19.1
1949	284.2	14.2	27.2	228.3	63.9	81.8	71.0	11.6	14.5	15.7

INDIVIDUALS' SAVING THROUGH PRIVATE INDEPENDENT
(SELF-INSURED) PENSION FUNDS: 1920 to 1949

$ mill.

| Year | Assets end of year | Increase in assets during year | | Year | Assets end of year | Increase in assets during year | | Year | Assets end of year | Increase in assets during year | |
| | | Total | Excluding fund income | | | Total | Excluding fund income | | | Total | Excluding fund income |
	1	2	3		1	2	3		1	2	3
1920	50	.	.	1930	550	50	25	1940	1 100	50	20
1921	60	10	5	1931	600	50	20	1941	1 175	75	45
1922	90	30	25	1932	650	50	20	1942	1 300	125	90
1923	100	10	5	1933	700	50	20	1943	1 500	200	165
1924	120	20	15	1934	750	50	20	1944	2 100	600	560
1925	150	30	20	1935	800	50	20	1945	2 900	800	740
1926	190	40	30	1936	880	80	45	1946	3 700	800	710
1927	260	70	55	1937	940	60	25	1947	4 750	1 050	950
1928	340	80	60	1938	1 000	60	25	1948	5 800	1 050	920
1929	500	160	135	1939	1 050	50	15	1949	6 850	1 050	890

Column 1 – 1920–1929: Extrapolated on basis of assets of seventeen noncontributory funds as given in Latimer, M.W., *Industrial Pension Systems in the United States and Canada,* Industrial Relations Councilors, Inc., 1932, p. 593.

1930–1931: Extrapolated on basis of trend in 1930's.

1932–1934: Extrapolated on basis of assets of ninety-one to ninety-three funds (*Industrial Pension Systems...*, p. 3).

1935–1938: Extrapolated on basis of assets of sixty-four to sixty-six funds (Latimer, M.W., and Tufel, Karl, *Trends in Industrial Pensions,* 1940, p. 79).

1939: Federal Reserve Board estimates, slightly modified, particularly on basis of pension trust of Bell System.

1940–1949: 1939 value plus annual increase from col. 2.

Column 2 – 1920–1939: Derived from col. 1.

1940–1949: Estimates based on: (1) Department of Commerce estimates for employers' contributions to pension funds, minus Saving Study estimates for adjustment for contributions to group annuities; (2) employees' contributions, estimated as one-third of employers' contributions; (3) estimated income from investments of funds; and (4) estimated benefit payments. Results are obviously rough. (Consideration of additional, though incomplete, evidence makes it likely that figures in cols. 1 to 3 after 1943 are slightly too high.)

Column 3 – 1920–1949: Obtained by deducting from col. 2 an estimate of interest and dividend income of funds, based on yields (on book values) of assets held (cf. Table I-16).

1920 to 1949

$ mill.

End of year	Total	U.S. Government securities	Other outside bonds	Outside stocks		Sponsoring companies				
				Preferred	Common	Bonds	Preferred stock	Common stock	Book debt	Total
	1	2	3	4	5	6	7	8	9	10
1920	50	10	11	0	0	4	3	5	17	29
1921	60	11	14	0	0	5	4	6	20	35
1922	90	18	19	0	0	7	5	8	33	53
1923	100	21	21	0	0	7	6	9	36	58
1924	120	27	24	0	0	9	7	11	42	69
1925	150	35	30	0	0	11	9	13	52	85
1926	190	48	38	0	0	14	11	16	63	104
1927	260	74	54	0	0	19	16	23	74	132
1928	340	100	67	0	0	24	19	29	101	173
1929	500	156	99	0	0	36	29	42	138	245
1930	550	175	105	0	0	37	30	45	158	270
1931	600	196	110	0	0	39	31	47	177	294
1932	650	217	115	0	0	41	33	49	195	318
1933	700	244	120	0	0	51	34	51	199	335
1934	750	269	125	0	0	61	35	53	206	355
1935	800	294	130	0	0	68	36	54	216	374
1936	880	330	140	2	1	82	39	59	227	407
1937	940	359	145	5	3	86	40	60	241	427
1938	1 000	399	162	7	5	92	42	62	225	421
1939	1 050	437	175	10	7	97	42	63	214	416
1940	1 100	469	186	13	9	98	42	63	209	412
1941	1 175	516	201	17	11	103	42	64	205	414
1942	1 300	608	218	21	14	109	45	68	195	417
1943	1 500	764	245	28	19	115	50	76	193	434
1944	2 100	1 152	340	47	31	141	72	107	206	526
1945	2 900	1 629	472	74	49	169	98	147	251	665
1946	3 700	2 042	633	95	64	216	127	191	318	852
1947	4 749	2 573	857	117	78	325	157	235	392	1 109
1948	5 800	3 063	1 104	145	97	408	194	291	484	1 377
1949	6 850	3 551	1 387	172	116	460	230	346	576	1 612

Columns 1 to 10 – Sum of respective cols. of Table I-17 and Table I-18. Col. 1 includes small amounts of cash and accrued interest.

DISTRIBUTION OF ASSETS OF PRIVATE INDEPENDENT PENSION FUNDS OF COMPANIES OTHER THAN BELL SYSTEM: 1920 to 1949

$ mill.

End of year	Total	U.S. Government securities	Other outside bonds	Outside stocks		Sponsoring companies				
				Preferred	Common	Bonds	Preferred stock	Common stock	Book debt	Total
	1	2	3	4	5	6	7	8	9	10
1920	41	10	11	0	0	4	3	5	8	20
1921	50	11	14	0	0	5	4	6	10	25
1922	71	18	19	0	0	7	5	8	14	34
1923	79	21	21	0	0	7	6	9	15	37
1924	96	27	24	0	0	9	7	11	18	45
1925	120	35	30	0	0	11	9	13	22	55
1926	154	48	38	0	0	14	11	16	27	68
1927	225	74	54	0	0	19	16	23	39	97
1928	287	100	67	0	0	24	19	29	48	120
1929	433	156	99	0	0	36	29	42	71	178
1930	467	175	105	0	0	37	30	45	75	187
1931	501	196	110	0	0	39	31	47	78	195
1932	536	217	115	0	0	41	33	49	81	204
1933	573	241	120	0	0	42	34	51	85	212
1934	611	266	125	0	0	44	35	53	88	220
1935	648	292	130	0	0	45	36	54	91	226
1936	717	330	140	2	1	49	39	59	97	244
1937	763	359	145	5	3	50	40	60	101	251
1938	809	388	150	7	5	51	42	62	104	259
1939	845	414	152	10	7	52	42	63	105	262
1940	875	438	153	13	9	52	42	63	105	262
1941	920	470	156	17	11	53	42	64	107	266
1942	1 011	526	167	21	14	57	45	68	113	283
1943	1 172	621	188	28	19	63	50	76	127	316
1944	1 725	932	267	47	31	90	72	107	179	448
1945	2 457	1 351	369	74	49	123	98	147	246	614
1946	3 182	1 751	477	95	64	159	127	191	318	795
1947	3 923	2 158	589	117	78	197	157	235	392	981
1948	4 844	2 664	727	145	97	242	194	291	484	1 211
1949	5 760	3 168	864	172	116	288	230	346	576	1 440

Column 1 – Table I-15, col. 1 minus Table I-18, col. 1.

Columns 2 to 9 – Obtained by applying to col. 1 an estimated percentage distribution, based for recent years on distribution of assets of about two dozen funds with over $1 billion total assets, but representing little more than guesses for earlier years. In determining these percentages it has been assumed that proportion of securities of and claims against the sponsoring companies as well as of outside bonds has declined over time, while share of U.S. Government securities has increased, and that no investments were made in outside stocks before 1936. (Later evidence indicates that proportions allocated to cols. 3–5 and 7–9 may be somewhat too high and that of col. 2 too low.)

Column 10 – Sum of cols. 6–9.

PENSION TRUST FUNDS OF BELL SYSTEM
1913 to 1949

$ mill.

End of year	Total	Bell companies' notes	Bell companies' bonds	Cash and accrued interest	U.S. Government securities	Other bonds	End of year	Total	Bell companies' notes	Bell companies' bonds	Cash and accrued interest	U.S. Government securities	Other bonds
	1	2	3	4	5	6		1	2	3	4	5	6
1913	2	2	–	–	–	–	1932	114	–	–	–	–	–
1914	2	2	–	–	–	–	1933	127	114	9	1	3	–
1915	2	2	–	–	–	–	1934	139	118	17	2	3	–
1916	2	2	–	–	–	–	1935	152	125	23	2	2	–
1917	9	9	–	–	–	–	1936	163	130	33	1	–	–
1918	9	9	–	–	–	–	1937	177	140	36	1	–	–
1919	9	9	–	–	–	–	1938	191	121	41	6	11	12
1920	9	9	–	–	–	–	1939	205	109	45	6	23	22
1921	10	10	–	–	–	–	1940	225	104	46	12	31	32
1922	19	19	–	–	–	–	1941	255	98	50	17	46	44
1923	21	21	–	–	–	–	1942	289	82	52	22	82	51
1924	24	24	–	–	–	–	1943	328	66	52	10	143	57
1925	30	30	–	–	–	–	1944	375	27	51	6	220	73
1926	36	36	–	–	–	–	1945	443	5	46	12	278	103
1927	35	35	–	–	–	–	1946	518	–	57	15	291	156
1928	53	53	–	–	–	–	1947	827	–	128	16	415	268
1929	67	67	–	–	–	–	1948	956	–	166	15	399	377
1930	83	83	–	–	–	–	1949	1090	–	172	11	383	523
1931	99	99	–	–	–	–							

Column 1 – 1913–1927: From consolidated balance sheet of Bell System as shown in *Moody's Public Utilities*, various issues.

1928–1935: Report of the Federal Trade Commission, *Investigation of the Telephone Industry in the United States*, 1939, p. 465. (Fund was transferred to the Bankers Trust Company as trustee on July 1, 1928 when it contained $34.8 million.)

1936–1948: From *Moody's Public Utilities*, various issues. Figures given for years prior to 1946 represent pension trust fund holdings of American Telephone and Telegraph and its telephone subsidiaries, while those for 1947 and 1948 also include Western Electric and Bell laboratories. If comparable data were available for the earlier years the figures would be about one-third higher.

1949: From *Annual Report to the Stockholders*, American Telephone and Telegraph Company.

Columns 2 to 6 – 1913–1932: No information; assets may be presumed to have consisted entirely of Bell companies' notes.

1933–1949: Same sources as col. 1.

Note: Details may not add to total due to rounding.

Column 1 – 1897–1949: Sum of cols. 2–8

Column 2 – 1897–1949: Table V-2, col. 9.

Column 3 – 1897–1949: Table V-7, col. 3.

Column 4 – 1897–1949: Table V-8, col. 3.

Column 5 – 1897–1949: Table V-9, col. 3.

Column 6 – 1897–1949: Table V-10, col. 3.

Column 7 – 1897–1949: Table V-44, col. 12.

Column 8 – 1905–1949: Table V-47, col. 5.

NONFARM INDIVIDUALS' SAVING THROUGH SECURITIES,[1] BY MAJOR TYPES V-1
1897 to 1949
$ mill.

Year	Total	U.S. Government bonds	State and local government bonds	Corporate and foreign bonds	Preferred stock	Common stock	Commisssions	Taxes
	1	2	3	4	5	6	7	8
1897	170	−24	31	58	27	58	20	−
1898	338	92	26	121	74	−4	29	−
1899	1 015	129	56	287	277	220	46	−
1900	467	−45	18	235	78	144	37	−
1901	952	−33	31	393	148	343	70	−
1902	1 166	−16	2	465	33	633	49	−
1903	548	−24	15	82	26	407	42	−
1904	654	−24	20	302	62	245	49	−
1905	1 055	−7	45	664	64	218	69	2
1906	1 296	7	67	417	74	649	75	7
1907	820	−75	122	81	92	543	52	5
1908	1 481	3	212	610	59	541	52	4
1909	1 252	−32	10	529	45	639	56	5
1910	924	8	138	−26	54	701	44	5
1911	785	19	109	407	99	114	33	4
1912	1 743	4	143	667	146	745	34	4
1913	741	−1	8	198	94	414	25	3
1914	1 151	−2	226	471	141	300	13	2
1915	2 443	−3	299	1 459	125	509	50	4
1916	2 564	−123	218	1 089	385	919	70	6
1917	4 762	2 901	213	692	189	703	56	8
1918	9 728	7 270	497	1 005	97	806	43	10
1919	5 699	3 148	28	524	696	1 177	107	19
1920	3 900	−268	682	1 668	444	1 271	84	19
1921	2 941	−111	696	1 400	22	855	64	15
1922	1 068	−2 286	745	1 262	318	914	98	17
1923	3 342	−77	624	1 567	359	765	88	16
1924	1 469	−1 416	195	1 436	383	748	104	19
1925	4 060	−195	225	1 937	794	1 096	176	27
1926	3 216	−589	140	1 805	581	971	179	30
1927	2 280	−2 260	446	2 019	945	852	244	34
1928	4 438	−975	379	1 628	647	2 294	414	51
1929	5 484	−473	508	660	750	3 424	541	74
1930	2 302	−227	585	666	194	695	337	52
1931	3 656	720	1 781	556	138	218	209	34
1932	642	689	128	−398	0	52	130	41
1933	533	1 108	−912	−100	−44	210	202	69
1934	−631	−233	−857	39	6	276	101	37
1935	−1 927	−914	−8	−938	−215	−16	120	44
1936	−149	941	−360	−915	−210	170	166	59
1937	839	970	97	−1 059	195	433	145	58
1938	88	−50	−45	−45	−67	146	115	34
1939	−390	−166	−118	−674	11	422	104	31
1940	132	186	−129	−416	−11	392	85	25
1941	2 755	3 242	−151	−963	−41	571	73	24
1942	10 091	10 024	−183	61	−38	153	55	19
1943	13 059	13 392	−150	−653	−154	439	153	32
1944	15 720	16 418	−76	−1 141	−103	430	158	34
1945	10 419	11 059	−306	−1 580	−47	989	256	48
1946	−1 905	−2 279	−218	−1 226	14	1 496	259	49
1947	2 773	982	411	−694	345	1 522	175	32
1948	4 127	928	1 184	574	135	1 038	234	34
1949	3 483	863	906	94	101	1 293	194	32

[1] Changes in individuals' borrowing on securities are disregarded here as in Tables V-2, V-3, and V-6 to V-10.

Column   1 – 1897–1916: First differences of residual of gross public debt as given in Table F-7, col. 1, and non-interest-bearing debt, derived by averaging June 30 figures given in *Historical Statistics*, p. 305.

    1917–1939: First differences of sum of interest-bearing debt (*Banking and Monetary Statistics*, p. 509) and matured debt, derived by averaging June 30 figures given in *Historical Statistics*, p. 305. Figures for 1933–1937 adjusted to exclude not fully guaranteed issues of Home Owners' Loan Corporation (Table V-5, col. 8) and Tennessee Valley Authority bonds based on credit of U.S. (Table V-5, col. 6).

    1940–1948: First differences of sum of long-term debt, matured debt (both series obtained from *Statistical Abstract*, various issues), and U.S. guaranteed debt (Table F-20, col. 1). Figures for certain periods were adjusted as follows: (1) 1940–1943: Tennessee Valley Authority bonds (Table V-5, col. 6) subtracted; (2) 1941–1948: U.S. savings stamps added (June 30 figures as given in *Statistical Abstract*, 1949, p. 447, and *Annual Report of the Secretary of the Treasury*, 1949, pp. 400–401, converted to year-end by simple arithmetic averaging), (3) 1946–1948: special U.S. notes issued to International Bank and Monetary Fund added (*Annual Report of the Secretary of the Treasury*, 1947, 1948, 1949).

    1949: From Department of the Treasury, *Treasury Bulletin*, Feb. 1950, same items as 1940–1948.

Column   2 – 1935–1949: Table V-6, sum of cols. 1 and 8.

Column   3 – 1897–1949: Col. 1 minus col. 2.

Column   4 – 1917–1939: First differences of sum of U.S. interest-bearing debts held by U.S. agencies and trust funds (National Bureau of Economic Research) and matured debt (*Statistical Abstract*) minus direct and guaranteed obligations held by Postal Savings System (Table L-43, cols. 4 and 5).

    1940–1949: First differences of sum of U.S. Government securities held by U.S. Government agencies and trusts as estimated by Friend and Natrella, *Individuals' Saving*, part II, table 17, lines 1 and 2, and total matured debt outstanding (*Statistical Abstract* and *Treasury Bulletin*) minus direct and guaranteed obligations held by Postal Savings System (Table L-43, cols. 4 and 5).

Column   5 – 1897–1949: Table V-48, col. 1 minus cols. 18, 24, and 25.

Column   6 – 1935–1949: From Table V-6, col. 8.

Column   7 – 1897–1949: Col. 5 minus col. 6.

Column   8 – 1917–1934: From Table V-4, col. 2.
    1935–1949: From Table V-3, col. 2.

Column   9 – 1897–1949: Sum of cols. 10 and 11.

Column 10 – 1935–1949: Col. 2 minus cols. 6 and 8.

Column 11 – 1897–1949: Col. 1 minus sum of cols. 4, 5, 8, and 10 except for 1933–1936, which was adjusted to exclude Home Owners' Loan Corporation and Federal Farm Mortgage Corporation bonds received by individuals in exchange for mortgages (see Table M-21, cols. 6 and 7 and note to Table M-1, col. 4).

BY INDIVIDUALS: 1897 to 1949

$ mill.

Year	Net issues			Holdings of federal agencies	Nonindividuals' holdings			Change in farmers' holdings	Change in holdings of other individuals		
	Total	Savings bonds	Other securities		Total	Savings bonds	Other securities		Total	Savings bonds	Other securities
	1	2	3	4	5	6	7	8	9	10	11
1897	9	–	9	–	33	–	33	–	–24	–	–24
1898	183	–	183	–	91	–	91	–	92	–	92
1899	67	–	67	–	–62	–	–62	–	129	–	129
1900	–1	–	–1	–	44	–	44	–	–45	–	–45
1901	–59	–	–59	–	–26	–	–26	–	–33	–	–33
1902	–27	–	–27	–	–11	–	–11	–	–16	–	–16
1903	–14	–	–14	–	10	–	10	–	–24	–	–24
1904	–8	–	–8	–	16	–	16	–	–24	–	–24
1905	–1	–	–1	–	6	–	6	–	–7	–	–7
1906	31	–	31	–	24	–	24	–	7	–	7
1907	–35	–	–35	–	40	–	40	–	–75	–	–75
1908	23	–	23	–	20	–	20	–	3	–	3
1909	1	–	1	–	33	–	33	–	–32	–	–32
1910	5	–	5	–	–3	–	–3	–	8	–	8
1911	43	–	43	–	24	–	24	–	19	–	19
1912	2	–	2	–	–2	–	–2	–	4	–	4
1913	3	–	3	–	4	–	4	–	–1	–	–1
1914	1	–	1	–	3	–	3	–	–2	–	–2
1915	–3	–	–3	–	0	–	0	–	–3	–	–3
1916	12	–	12	–	135	–	135	–	–123	–	–123
1917	6 156	–	6 156	27	2 728	–	2 728	500	2 901	–	2 901
1918	13 704	–	13 704	146	4 888	–	4 888	1 400	7 270	–	7 270
1919	4 776	–	4 776	386	1 242	–	1 242	0	3 148	–	3 148
1920	–1 854	–	–1 854	–466	–720	–	–720	–400	–268	–	–268
1921	–552	–	–552	57	2	–	2	–500	–111	–	–111
1922	–669	–	–669	55	1 962	–	1 962	–400	–2 286	–	–2 286
1923	–832	–	–832	56	–611	–	–611	–200	–77	–	–77
1924	–964	–	–964	–28	580	–	580	–100	–1 416	–	–1 416
1925	–737	–	–737	83	–525	–	–525	–100	–195	–	–195
1926	–1 168	–	–1 168	96	–625	–	–625	–50	–589	–	–589
1927	–1 121	–	–1 121	134	1 005	–	1 005	0	–2 260	–	–2 260
1928	–677	–	–677	161	137	–	137	0	–975	–	–975
1929	–969	–	–969	117	–613	–	–613	0	–473	–	–473
1930	–254	–	–254	111	–138	–	–138	0	–227	–	–227
1931	1 768	–	1 768	–326	1 374	–	1 374	0	720	–	720
1932	2 927	–	2 927	–13	2 251	–	2 251	0	689	–	689
1933	3 791	–	3 791	37	2 593	–	2 593	0	1 108	–	1 108
1934	7 171	–	7 171	739	5 885	–	5 885	0	–233	–	–233
1935	2 861	154	2 707	198	3 262	28	3 234	16	–914	110	–1 024
1936	4 183	321	3 862	–76	3 228	40	3 188	37	941	244	697
1937	2 936	489	2 447	1 795	115	67	48	56	970	366	604
1938	2 541	478	2 063	944	1 593	72	1 521	54	–50	352	–402
1939	3 177	767	2 410	1 156	2 101	112	1 989	86	–166	569	–735
1940	3 288	986	2 302	1 213	1 786	130	1 656	103	186	753	–567
1941	13 502	2 945	10 557	1 797	8 304	193	8 111	159	3 242	2 593	649
1942	47 825	8 910	38 915	2 670	34 581	927	33 654	550	10 024	7 433	2 591
1943	56 928	12 313	44 615	4 379	37 883	1 169	36 714	1 274	13 392	9 870	3 522
1944	62 088	12 998	49 090	4 170	40 121	1 196	38 925	1 379	16 418	10 423	5 995
1945	45 927	7 863	38 064	4 911	29 173	1 012	28 161	784	11 059	6 067	4 992
1946	–18 093	1 639	–19 732	3 591	–19 411	741	–20 152	6	–2 279	892	–3 171
1947	–2 350	2 312	–4 662	3 411	–7 020	530	–7 550	277	982	1 505	–523
1948	–4 085	3 022	–7 107	2 996	–8 252	895	–9 147	243	928	1 884	–956
1949	4 373	1 713	2 660	2 021	1 263	184	1 079	226	863	1 303	–440

Column 1 – From Table V-6, col. 1.

Column 2 – First differences in Table A-53, col. 5.

Column 3 – Col. 1 minus col. 2.

Column 4 – From Table V-6, col. 3.

Column 5 – Col. 2 minus net interest accruals, derived for 1940–1947 from data given in *Balance Sheet of Agriculture*, 1948, p. 28 and for 1935–1939, 1948, and 1949 on basis of holdings of savings bonds by farmers.

Column 6 – Col. 4 minus col. 5.

V-4 TABLE V-4

Column 1 – 1917–1934: Estimated at 17 percent of changes in holdings of U.S. Government securities by all individuals as calculated in Table V-2, col. 1 minus sum of cols. 4 and 5. This proportion is based on average share of farmers in total national income for years 1917 to 1919, as shown in Table A-5, col. 3.

Column 2 – 1917–1918: Assumed to be about same as estimates for col. 1.

1919–1934: Rough estimates based on assumption that all Liberty and Victory bonds bought by farmers between 1917 and middle of 1919 were liquidated by mid-1920's; and that amount of sales during any given year depended largely on farmers' financial situation.

Total of net sales for years 1920–1926 is $150 million below net purchases for 1917–1919 because it can be estimated on basis of assumed timing of sales and average price of U.S. Government securities (cf. *Banking and Monetary Statistics*, p. 475) that farmers' receipts from sales fell short by this amount of the par value paid for Liberty and Victory bonds.

SAVING THROUGH U.S. SAVINGS BONDS BY FARMERS AND NONFARMERS V-3
1935 to 1949
$ mill.

Year	Change in accrual value of holdings			Net cash purchases		
	Total	Farmers	Nonfarmers	Total	Farmers	Nonfarmers
	1	2	3	4	5	6
1935	126	16	110	126	16	110
1936	281	37	244	276	36	240
1937	422	56	366	412	55	357
1938	406	54	352	386	52	334
1939	655	86	569	625	83	542
1940	856	103	753	816	98	718
1941	2 752	159	2 593	2 682	152	2 530
1942	7 983	550	7 433	7 893	541	7 352
1943	11 144	1 274	9 870	10 994	1 261	9 733
1944	11 802	1 379	10 423	11 552	1 353	10 199
1945	6 851	784	6 067	6 471	740	5 731
1946	898	6	892	458	−52	510
1947	1 782	277	1 505	1 292	210	1 082
1948	2 127	243	1 884	1 567	173	1 394
1949	1 529	226	1 303	916	156	760

HOLDINGS OF U.S. GOVERNMENT SECURITIES BY FARMERS V-4
Alternative Estimates of Changes: 1917 to 1934
$ mill.

Year	Mechanical estimate	Freehand estimate	Year	Mechanical estimate	Freehand estimate
	1	2		1	2
1917	578	500	1926	−109	−50
1918	1 474	1 400	1927	−382	0
1919	535	0	1928	−165	0
			1929	−80	0
1920	−114	−400			
1921	−104	−500	1930	−37	0
1922	−457	−400	1931	114	0
1923	−46	−200	1932	118	0
1924	−258	−100	1933	202	0
			1934	93	0
1925	−48	−100			

OBLIGATIONS OF U.S. CORPORATIONS AND AGENCIES
NOT FULLY GUARANTEED BY U.S. TREASURY
(Excluding Federal Land Banks and Obligations Held by U.S. Treasury or Agencies)
1923 to 1949

$ mill.

End of year	Total	Federal Home Loan Bank Board	Federal Farm Mortgage Corporation	Federal Intermediate Credit Banks	Federal Housing Administration	Tennessee Valley Authority	Banks for cooperatives	Home Owners' Loan Corporation	Commodity Credit Corporation	Other
	1	2	3	4	5	6	7	8	9	10
1923	31	–	–	31	–	–	–	–	–	–
1924	50	–	–	50	–	–	–	–	–	–
1925	59	–	–	59	–	–	–	–	–	–
1926	69	–	–	69	–	–	–	–	–	–
1927	51	–	–	51	–	–	–	–	–	–
1928	45	–	–	45	–	–	–	–	–	–
1929	50	–	–	50	–	–	–	–	–	–
1930	102	–	–	102	–	–	–	–	–	–
1931	77	–	–	77	–	–	–	–	–	–
1932	72	–	–	72	–	–	–	–	–	–
1933	740	–	–	128	–	–	–	612	–	–
1934	577	–	–	164	–	–	–	324	–	89
1935	151	–	–	131	–	–	–	20	–	–
1936	147	–	–	144	–	–	–	2	–	1
1937	258	78	–	175	–	–	–	1	–	4
1938	297	90	–	169	–	2	–	–	–	36
1939	359	49	85	207	1	8	–	–	–	9
1940	401	91	85	201	4	8	–	–	–	12
1941	440	91	85	236	2	8	–	–	–	18
1942	465	70	85	301	1	8	–	–	–	–
1943	413	64	–	325	–	6	18	–	–	–
1944	577	67	–	274	–	–	24	–	212	–
1945	322	69	–	245	–	–	8	–	–	–
1946	495	169	–	293	–	–	33	–	–	–
1947	689	262	–	358	–	–	69	–	–	–
1948	965	415	–	480	–	–	70	–	–	–
1949	772	204	–	490	–	–	78	–	–	–

Column 1 – 1923–1949: Sum of cols. 2–10.

Columns 2 and 3, 5 to 10 – 1933–1949: *Daily Treasury Statements.*

Column 4 – 1923–1932: *Statistical Abstract*, 1931, p. 286.
1933–1949: *Daily Treasury Statements.*

478

SAVING THROUGH U.S. SAVINGS BONDS
BY INDIVIDUALS AND NONINDIVIDUALS
1935 to 1949

$ mill.

Year	Increase in savings bonds held by individuals	Estimated net interest accruals on bonds held by individuals	Increase in savings bonds held by individuals excluding interest accruals	Increase in holdings of Series E bonds		Increase in individuals' holdings of other series		Change in nonindividuals' holdings of savings bonds
				Including	Excluding	Including	Excluding	
				Interest accruals		Interest accruals		
	1	2	3	4	5	6	7	8
1935	126	0	126	–	–	126	126	28
1936	281	5	276	–	–	281	276	40
1937	422	10	412	–	–	422	412	67
1938	406	20	386	–	–	406	386	72
1939	655	30	625	–	–	655	625	112
1940	856	40	816	–	–	856	816	130
1941	2 752	70	2 682	1 134	1 134	1 618	1 548	193
1942	7 983	90	7 893	5 789	5 780	2 194	2 113	927
1943	11 144	150	10 994	9 034	8 966	2 110	2 028	1 169
1944	11 802	250	11 552	9 558	9 387	2 244	2 165	1 196
1945	6 851	380	6 471	5 212	4 897	1 639	1 574	1 012
1946	898	440	458	−464	−864	1 362	1 322	741
1947	1 782	490	1 292	734	272	1 048	1 020	530
1948	2 127	560	1 567	1 191	649	936	918	895
1949	1 529	613	916	1 577	932	−48	−16	184

Column 1 – Friend and Natrella, *Individuals' Saving*, part II, table 10, col. 6A.

Column 2 – Accruals on E bonds, as reported in the *Treasury Bulletin*, plus accruals on other series estimated from reported totals on basis of assumed proportion of individuals' holdings.

Column 3 – Col. 1 minus col. 2.

Columns 4 and 5 – Department of the Treasury, *Treasury Bulletin*, various issues.

Column 6 – Col. 1 minus col. 4.

Column 7 – Col. 3 minus col. 5.

Column 8 – Difference in total amount of savings bonds outstanding (including interest accruals) as reported in Department of the Treasury, *Treasury Bulletin*, minus col. 1.

SAVING THROUGH STATE AND LOCAL GOVERNMENT SECURITIES BY INDIVIDUALS: 1897 to 1949

$ mill.

Year	Net issues	Change in holdings of		Year	Net issues	Change in holdings of	
		Nonindividuals	Individuals			Nonindividuals	Individuals
	1	2	3		1	2	3
1897	84	53	31	1923	974	350	624
1898	85	59	26	1924	850	655	195
1899	82	26	56	1925	746	521	225
1900	81	63	18	1926	810	661	149
1901	88	57	31	1927	1 080	634	446
1902	92	90	2	1928	967	588	379
1903	126	111	15	1929	1 062	554	508
1904	132	112	20	1930	1 261	676	585
1905	130	85	45	1931	1 229	−552	1 781
1906	163	96	67	1932	274	146	128
1907	225	103	122	1933	−809	103	−912
1908	324	112	212	1934	−449	408	−857
1909	197	187	10	1935	201	209	−8
1910	312	174	138	1936	−346	14	−360
1911	328	219	109	1937	−112	−209	97
1912	299	156	143	1938	395	440	−45
1913	107	'99	8	1939	287	405	−118
1914	495	269	226	1940	274	403	−129
1915	483	184	299	1941	−370	−219	−151
1916	406	188	218	1942	−727	−544	−183
1917	412	199	213	1943	−852	−702	−150
1918	415	−82	497	1944	−572	−496	−76
1919	354	326	28	1945	−281	25	−306
1920	1 013	331	682	1946	30	248	−218
1921	1 087	391	696	1947	1 398	987	411
1922	1 182	437	745	1948	2 024	840	1 184
				1949	2 285	1 379	906

Column 1 – 1897–1932: First differences of Table G-21, col. 1, converted to year-end figures by arithmetic averaging, plus col. 2.
    1933–1949: First differences of Table V-11, col. 3 minus Table V-49, sum of cols. 13–15.

Column 2 – 1897–1932: From Table V-49, col. 1.
    1933–1949: From Table V-49, col. 1 minus sum of cols. 13–15.

Column 3 – 1897–1949: Col. 1 minus col. 2.

SAVING THROUGH CORPORATE AND FOREIGN BONDS
BY INDIVIDUALS 1897 to 1949:

$ mill.

| Year | Net issues | Change in holdings of | | Year | Net issues | Change in holdings of | |
| | | Nonindividuals | Individuals | | | Nonindividuals | Individuals |
	1	2	3		1	2	3
1897	190	132	58	1923	2 112	545	1 567
1898	262	141	121	1924	2 708	1 272	1 436
1899	525	238	287	1925	2 799	862	1 937
1900	500	265	235	1926	3 039	1 144	1 895
1901	757	364	393	1927	3 550	1 531	2 019
1902	734	269	465	1928	2 457	829	1 628
1903	352	270	82	1929	665	5	660
1904	703	401	302	1930	1 955	1 289	666
1905	970	306	664	1931	221	−335	556
1906	802	385	417	1932	−898	−500	−398
1907	526	445	81	1933	−497	−397	−100
1908	778	168	610	1934	203	164	39
1909	874	345	529	1935	−597	341	−938
1910	502	528	−26	1936	−94	821	−915
1911	988	581	407	1937	−955	104	−1 059
1912	986	319	667	1938	445	490	−45
1913	543	345	198	1939	−610	64	−674
1914	681	210	471	1940	−55	361	−416
1915	1 232	−227	1 459	1941	−391	572	−963
1916	1 445	356	1 089	1942	−415	−476	61
1917	1 047	355	692	1943	−1 112	−459	−653
1918	793	−212	1 005	1944	−1 125	16	−1 141
1919	777	253	524	1945	−1 343	237	−1 580
1920	1 881	213	1 668	1946	1 157	2 383	−1 226
1921	1 635	235	1 400	1947	3 294	3 988	−694
1922	1 826	564	1 262	1948	5 199	4 625	574
				1949	3 293	3 199	94

Column 1 – From Table V-14, col. 1.

Column 2 – From Table V-50, col. 1.

Column 3 – Col. 1 minus col. 2.

INDIVIDUALS' SAVING THROUGH PREFERRED STOCK [1]
1897 to 1949

$ mill.

Year	Net issues	Change in holdings of		Year	Net issues	Change in holdings of	
		Nonindividuals	Individuals			Nonindividuals	Individuals
	1	2	3		1	2	3
1897	33	6	27	1923	465	106	359
1898	76	2	74	1924	449	66	383
1899	284	7	277	1925	897	103	794
1900	76	−2	78	1926	637	56	581
1901	148	0	148	1927	1 028	83	945
1902	32	−1	33	1928	974	327	647
1903	27	1	26	1929	1 118	368	750
1904	72	10	62	1930	290	96	194
1905	96	32	64	1931	103	−35	138
1906	84	10	74	1932	−99	−99	0
1907	83	−9	92	1933	−90	−46	−44
1908	60	1	59	1934	23	17	6
1909	48	3	45	1935	−118	97	−215
1910	61	7	54	1936	−151	59	−210
1911	114	15	99	1937	187	−8	195
1912	189	43	146	1938	−49	18	−67
1913	109	15	94	1939	−19	−30	11
1914	63	−78	141	1940	−9	2	−11
1915	57	−68	125	1941	−40	1	−41
1916	352	−33	385	1942	15	53	−38
1917	187	−2	189	1943	−86	68	−154
1918	97	0	97	1944	27	130	−103
1919	693	−3	696	1945	225	272	−47
1920	444	0	444	1946	289	275	14
1921	25	3	22	1947	590	245	345
1922	336	18	318	1948	286	151	135
				1949	379	278	101

[1] Disregarding changes in individuals' borrowing on securities and individuals' payments of commissions, etc. to brokers and dealers.

Column 1 – 1897–1918: From Table V-17, col. 1.
1919–1949: From Table V-18, col. 8.

Column 2 – 1897–1949: From Table V-51, col. 1.

Column 3 – 1897–1949: Col. 1 minus col. 2.

$ mill.

Year	Net issues	Change in holdings of		Year	Net issues	Change in holdings of	
		Nonindividuals	Individuals			Nonindividuals	Individuals
	1	2	3		1	2	3
1897	76	18	58	1923	1 023	258	765
1898	21	25	−4	1924	979	231	748
1899	253	33	220	1925	1 409	313	1 096
1900	162	18	144	1926	1 210	239	971
1901	376	33	343	1927	1 232	380	852
1902	661	28	633	1928	3 369	1 075	2 294
1903	438	31	407	1929	6 368	2 944	3 424
1904	293	48	245	1930	1 625	930	695
1905	306	88	218	1931	511	293	218
1906	698	49	649	1932	135	83	52
1907	555	12	543	1933	494	284	210
1908	530	−11	541	1934	109	−167	276
1909	673	34	639	1935	245	261	−16
1910	721	20	701	1936	663	493	170
1911	165	51	114	1937	555	122	433
1912	768	23	745	1938	157	11	146
1913	435	21	414	1939	264	−158	422
1914	289	−11	300	1940	299	−93	392
1915	404	−105	509	1941	366	−205	571
1916	893	−26	919	1942	137	−16	153
1917	718	15	703	1943	237	−202	439
1918	778	−28	806	1944	395	−35	430
1919	1 195	18	1 177	1945	902	−87	989
1920	1 244	−27	1 271	1946	1 775	279	1 496
1921	855	0	855	1947	1 613	91	1 522
1922	951	37	914	1948	1 208	170	1 038
				1949	1 741	448	1 293

[1] Disregarding changes in individuals' borrowing on securities and individuals' payments of commissions, etc. to brokers and dealers.

Column 1 – From Table V-19, col. 1.

Column 2 – From Table V-52, col. 1.

Column 3 – Col. 1 minus col. 2.

TABLE V–11

Column 1 – 1932–1949: Figures underlying Securities and Exchange Commission estimates (cf. Friend and Natrella, *Individuals' Saving*, part II, table 10, line 7).

Column 2 – 1932–1947: Obtained by averaging June 30 data as given in *Annual Report of the Secretary of the Treasury*, 1946, p. 667, and 1949, p. 591.
1948–1949: Holdings of state and local government sinking funds obtained by same method and from same source as for 1932–1947, using preliminary information from Treasury for June 1950; plus Dec. 31 holdings of U.S. Government investment accounts from *Daily Treasury Statements*, March 15, 1949 and March 15, 1950 (cf. Table V-49, col. 15).

Column 3 – 1932–1949: Col. 1 plus col. 2.

TABLE V–12

Column 1 – Col. 2 linked in 1900 to National Bureau of Economic Research series (Table V-15, col. 3).

Column 2 – Sum of cols. 3 and 7.

Column 3 – Col. 4 minus sum of cols. 5 and 6.

Columns 4 and 5 – Derived from figures given in Interstate Commerce Commission, *Statistics of Railways*, various issues. Table 155.

Column 6 – Same procedure as Table V-27, col. 3.

Column 7 – Col. 8 reduced by 12 percent, the 1900–1909 average ratio of cash offerings to extinguishments in National Bureau of Economic Research data (Table V-15).

Column 8 – Tabulation of Saving Study cards for each issue derived from "General Investment News," *Commerical and Financial Chronicle*. Larger issues were checked in security manuals to eliminate noncash issues.

STATE AND LOCAL GOVERNMENT SECURITIES OUTSTANDING
1932 to 1949

$ mill.

End of year	Amount outstanding			End of year	Amount outstanding		
	Excluding fund holdings	Holdings of sinking funds and federal agencies and trust funds	Including fund holdings		Excluding fund holdings	Holdings of sinking funds and federal agencies and trust funds	Including fund holdings
	1	2	3		1	2	3
1932	18 012	1 666	19 678	1941	17 489	2 379	19 868
1933	17 298	1 786	19 084	1942	16 751	2 318	19 069
1934	17 031	1 971	19 002	1943	15 795	2 118	17 913
				1944	14 978	1 810	16 788
1935	17 313	2 114	19 427				
1936	17 027	2 231	19 258	1945	14 357	1 556	15 913
1937	16 884	2 318	19 202	1946	14 224	1 472	15 696
1938	17 318	2 277	19 595	1947	15 677	1 490	17 167
1939	17 549	2 216	19 765	1948	17 844	1 517	19 361
1940	17 818	2 298	20 116	1949	20 321	1 536	21 857

CASH ISSUES OF STRAIGHT DOMESTIC CORPORATE BONDS
1897 to 1900

$ mill.

Year	All industries		Railroads				Public utilities and industrials	
	Adjusted	Unadjusted	Total	Change in bonds outstanding	Change in intercorporate holdings	Change due to reorganization	Adjusted	Unadjusted
	1	2	3	4	5	6	7	8
1897	205	184	60	45	−15	0	124	141
1898	249	223	80	125	−5	50	143	162
1899	488	437	47	107	52	8	390	443
1900	410	367	117	162	37	8	250	284

RETIREMENT OF CORPORATE SECURITIES: 1933 to 1949
(Securities and Exchange Commission Data)

$ mill.

| Year | Total | Bonds | Stocks | | Common | |
| | | | Total | Preferred | Total | Investment companies |
	1	2	3	4	5	6
1933	683	601	82	40	42	42
1934	713	635	78	32	46	45
1935	2 740	2 444	296	245	51	50
1936	3 939	3 429	510	449	61	60
1937	2 403	2 085	318	247	71	70
1938	1 670	1 504	166	125	41	40
1939	2 721	2 550	171	130	41	40
1940	3 074	2 814	260	204	56	50
1941	2 817	2 516	301	235	66	50
1942	1 464	1 327	137	92	45	36
1943	2 129	1 800	329	238	91	70
1944	3 899	3 391	508	391	117	83
1945	6 905	5 995	910	751	159	138
1946	4 798	3 625	1 173	970	203	190
1947	2 523	2 011	512	381	131	106
1948	1 684	1 284	400	216	184	157
1949	1 875	1 583	292	142	150	113

Column 1 – Sum of cols. 2 and 3.

Columns 2, 3, and 6 – From Securities and Exchange Commission worksheets (see also Friend and Natrella, *Individuals' Saving*, part II, table 11).

Columns 4 and 5 – Derived from col. 3 by assuming:(a) that the figures for retirements of stocks of investment companies, which were available in Securities and Exchange Commission worksheets, applied exclusively to common stock; and (b) that repurchases by public tender or in the open market could be divided for each year in the proportion prevailing during the years 1943 and 1945, the years in which such repurchases were heaviest. (For these two years the proportions were determined on the basis of information on individual issues in the Securities and Exchange Commission files, separately for railroad, public utility, and other stocks, and the proportions so obtained were applied to total stock retirements in each of the three industry groups as estimated in the Securities and Exchange Commission worksheets.) Col. 4 also includes stock calls for which separate estimates were available in Securities and Exchange Commission worksheets.

NET ISSUES OF CORPORATE AND FOREIGN BONDS
1897 to 1949
$ mill.

Year	Total	Corporate straight	Railroad equipment	Real estate	Income, railroad	Income, serial and equipment	Investment company	Customer ownership sales	Direct sales to pension funds	Federal land banks	Joint stock land banks	U.S. instrumentalities	Foreign
	1	2	3	4	5	6	7	8	9	10	11	12	13
1897	190	205	−5	5	−26	6	–	–	–	–	–	–	5
1898	262	249	1	5	0	7	–	–	–	–	–	–	–
1899	525	488	10	5	−21	20	–	–	–	–	–	–	23
1900	500	410	13	5	−21	6	–	–	–	–	–	–	87
1901	757	569	15	5	12	33	–	–	–	–	–	–	123
1902	734	623	37	5	7	22	–	–	–	–	–	–	40
1903	352	340	42	5	−6	11	–	–	–	–	–	–	−40
1904	703	663	22	5	9	15	–	–	–	–	–	–	−11
1905	970	789	26	5	37	20	–	–	–	–	–	–	93
1906	802	708	71	5	26	38	–	–	–	–	–	–	−46
1907	526	473	60	5	−22	34	–	–	–	–	–	–	−24
1908	778	654	−11	10	−10	48	–	–	–	–	–	–	87
1909	874	770	5	10	16	49	–	–	–	–	–	–	24
1910	502	458	5	10	−12	75	–	–	–	–	–	–	−34
1911	988	847	−18	15	−11	127	–	–	–	–	–	–	28
1912	986	762	25	15	−6	120	–	–	–	–	–	–	70
1913	543	417	51	20	−7	35	–	–	–	–	–	–	27
1914	681	648	19	20	−1	−19	–	–	–	–	–	–	14
1915	1 232	519	−21	21	15	−5	–	–	–	–	–	–	703
1916	1 445	434	−41	20	77	8	–	–	–	–	–	–	947
1917	1 047	459	3	21	−9	17	–	–	–	27	–	–	529
1918	793	159	−29	20	0	167	–	–	–	115	8	–	353
1919	777	338	−41	106	1	115	–	1	–	144	48	–	65
1920	1 881	779	375	117	3	192	–	2	3	48	19	–	343
1921	1 635	1 000	18	59	5	14	–	4	1	99	7	–	428
1922	1 826	610	48	273	21	−66	–	6	1	210	126	–	597
1923	2 112	863	206	417	56	19	–	9	0	164	146	31	201
1924	2 708	1 276	131	514	−51	14	–	13	1	108	81	19	602
1925	2 799	853	22	1 148	−32	120	–	15	1	67	81	9	515
1926	3 039	1 447	18	997	−23	9	–	12	2	77	89	10	401
1927	3 550	2 070	−35	842	−14	43	46	12	3	81	−23	−18	543
1928	2 457	743	−84	1 074	79	−118	74	8	3	35	7	−6	642
1929	665	184	14	420	−13	−60	75	7	8	13	−17	5	29
1930	1 955	1 607	−10	231	−20	58	0	7	1	−3	−28	52	60
1931	221	565	−104	189	3	−21	−25	8	1	−15	−4	−25	−351
1932	−898	−264	−118	−50	−1	−34	−23	1	1	−23	−115	−5	−267
1933	−497	−394	−111	−50	−16	−57	−2	–	10	45	−58	56	80
1934	203	−96	−32	−50	−12	−31	−2	–	8	592	−97	125	−202
1935	−597	−437	−82	−50	−9	91	−3	–	7	155	−65	−122	−82
1936	−94	172	−33	−50	1	−7	5	–	13	33	−40	14	−202
1937	−955	−593	55	−75	1	−11	−10	–	4	−165	−32	112	−241
1938	445	646	−116	−100	0	60	−5	–	6	−40	−22	40	−24
1939	−610	−413	−15	−100	0	−5	−5	–	5	−21	−14	62	−104
1940	−55	−111	54	−100	0	157	−5	–	1	−24	−33	42	−36
1941	−391	−471	144	−100	0	58	−5	–	5	−15	−27	39	−19
1942	−415	−151	−15	−150	0	−20	−5	–	5	−172	−16	25	84
1943	−1 112	−713	−3	−160	0	−47	−10	–	4	−171	−17	−52	57
1944	−1 125	−698	–	−160	–	–	–	–	17	−512	−3	164	67
1945	−1 343	−1 071	–	−140	–	–	–	–	17	−209	−1	−255	316
1946	1 157	1 096	–	−90	–	–	–	–	35	72	–	173	−129
1947	3 294	3 004	–	−50	–	–	–	–	96	−51	–	194	101
1948	5 199	4 830	–	−60	–	–	–	–	68	−16	–	276	101
1949	3 293	3 456	–	−60	–	–	–	–	37	69	–	−193	−16

Column 1 – 1897–1949: Sum of cols. 2–13.

Column 2 – 1897–1899: From Table V-12, col. 1.
           1900–1943: From Table V-15, col. 3.
           1944–1949: Friend and Natrella, *Individuals' Saving,* part II, table 11, line 1c. For 1948 and
               1949 American Telephone and Telegraph Company bonds converted (from Table V-30, col. 2)
               were added to Friend and Natrella figures, which treated bond conversions as cash retire-
               ments of bonds.

Column 3 – 1897–1915: First differences of Table V-26, col. 4.
           1916–1943: First differences of Table V-26, col. 3.
           1944–1949: Included in col. 2.

Column 4 – 1897–1909: First differences of Table R-41, col. 1.
           1910–1942: From Table R-43, col. 5.
           1943–1949: Figures from Table R-43, col. 5, adjusted for small amounts of real estate bonds
               included in col. 2.

Column 5 – 1897–1915: First differences of Table V-26, col. 2.
           1916–1943: First differences of Table V-26, col. 1.
           1944–1949: Included in col. 2.

Column 6 – 1897–1899: Estimated by National Bureau of Economic Research on basis of a special tabula-
               tion to be 5 percent of Table V-12, col. 7.
           1900–1943: Serial equipment, and income bonds of public utility and industrial corporations
               (from National Bureau of Economic Research, Corporate Bond Study) including an undeter-
               mined amount of income bonds, issued in exchange, and so overstating net cash issues.
           1944–1949: Included in col. 2.

Column 7 – 1927–1943: From Table V-39, col. 9.
           1944–1949: Included in col. 2.

Column 8 – 1919–1932: From Table V-41, col. 2.

Column 9 – 1920–1949: Estimated at change in bonds of Bell companies held by pension funds of system
               (Table I-18, col. 3) plus two-thirds of change in holdings of sponsoring companies' bonds in
               other pension funds (Table I-17, col. 6).

Column 10 – 1917–1949: First differences of Table V-78, col. 11.

Column 11 – 1918–1949: First differences of Table V-77, col. 8.

Column 12 – 1923–1949: First differences of Table V-5, col. 1 minus col. 8.

Column 13 – 1897–1949: From Table K-3, col. 4.

Columns 1 to 12 – From tabulations of the National Bureau of Economic Research, Corporate Bond Study.
        These figures are given with slight revisions in Hickman, W. Braddock, *The Volume of Corporate
        Bond Financing since 1900,* pp. 360–363.

Note: Details may not add to totals because of rounding.

CASH OFFERINGS AND EXTINGUISHMENTS OF STRAIGHT DOMESTIC
CORPORATE BONDS: 1900 to 1943
(National Bureau of Economic Research Data)

$ mill.

Year	All industries			Railroads			Utilities			Other industries		
	Offer-ings	Extin-guish-ments	Net issues	Offer-ings	Extin-guish-ments	Net issues	Offer-ings	Extin-guish-ments	Net issues	Offer-ings	Extin-guish-ments	Net issues
	1	2	3	4	5	6	7	8	9	10	11	12
1900	497	88	410	196	88	108	258	0	258	43	0	43
1901	629	60	569	401	60	342	179	0	179	48	0	48
1902	699	76	623	346	44	302	280	32	248	73	0	73
1903	465	125	340	266	114	152	142	11	131	57	0	57
1904	773	110	663	477	72	406	223	39	184	73	0	73
1905	1 070	281	789	694	243	451	269	38	230	107	0	107
1906	847	139	708	390	72	318	332	40	292	124	26	98
1907	676	202	473	458	165	293	147	38	109	71	0	71
1908	811	157	654	469	102	366	255	21	234	87	34	54
1909	1 107	337	770	612	221	392	319	33	286	176	83	93
1910	917	459	458	393	303	90	326	48	279	197	108	89
1911	1 113	266	847	495	145	350	451	99	352	167	22	145
1912	1 177	415	762	436	137	299	528	120	408	213	157	55
1913	937	520	417	459	270	189	368	166	202	110	83	27
1914	1 040	392	648	500	215	285	392	109	284	148	69	79
1915	1 015	496	519	591	302	290	306	87	219	117	107	10
1916	1 039	605	434	310	205	105	444	232	212	285	167	118
1917	886	427	459	318	154	164	280	109	170	289	164	125
1918	638	480	159	162	137	26	362	205	157	114	138	−24
1919	878	540	338	176	136	40	499	200	300	203	205	−2
1920	1 289	510	779	189	163	26	419	231	188	681	116	565
1921	1 745	746	1 000	382	403	−21	585	184	401	778	159	619
1922	1 900	1 289	610	287	281	6	802	545	257	811	464	347
1923	1 777	914	863	211	95	116	912	335	577	654	484	170
1924	1 996	720	1 276	553	79	474	939	418	521	503	222	281
1925	2 043	1 190	853	344	308	37	1 022	374	648	677	509	168
1926	2 481	1 034	1 447	244	133	111	1 315	532	783	922	368	553
1927	3 714	1 644	2 070	595	268	328	1 948	933	1 014	1 171	443	728
1928	2 654	1 911	743	460	342	117	1 382	915	467	812	654	159
1929	1 848	1 664	184	328	240	89	945	415	529	575	1 009	−434
1930	2 793	1 186	1 607	711	304	407	1 480	486	994	602	395	207
1931	1 826	1 262	565	382	236	145	1 194	782	413	250	243	7
1932	499	763	−264	0	123	−123	486	433	53	13	206	−193
1933	72	465	−394	15	59	−44	57	238	−182	0	168	−168
1934	379	475	−96	217	117	99	135	142	−7	27	215	−188
1935	1 954	2 392	−437	126	226	−100	1 223	1 215	8	605	951	−345
1936	3 529	3 357	172	622	643	−22	2 058	1 992	66	850	722	128
1937	1 420	2 013	−593	168	253	−86	807	1 296	−489	445	464	−19
1938	1 884	1 238	646	60	82	−22	1 153	833	320	671	323	348
1939	1 721	2 134	−413	27	99	−72	1 106	1 368	−262	588	667	−78
1940	2 074	2 185	−111	244	327	−83	1 168	959	209	662	899	−237
1941	1 884	2 355	−471	52	184	−132	1 342	1 580	− 238	490	591	−100
1942	762	913	−151	17	224	−208	464	463	1	281	226	56
1943	726	1 439	−713	61	441	−380	384	660	−276	281	338	−57

Columns 1, 5, 9, 13, 17, 21, and 25 – 1934–1949: From Friend and Natrella, *Individuals' Saving,* part II, table 12.

Columns 2, 3, 4, 6, 10, 14, 18, 22, and 26 – 1934–1949: Total issues are divided into stocks and bonds on basis of Securities and Exchange Commission worksheets, and into preferred and common for new stocks.

Columns 7 and 8 – 1934–1949: Total stock from above source split into preferred and common in ratio of 1 to 4 on basis of information in Securities and Exchange Commission worksheets.

Columns 11, 12, 15, and 16 – 1934–1949: Assumed to be all common stock.

Columns 19, 20, 23, and 24 – 1934–1949: Total stock from above source split on basis of information in Securities and Exchange Commission worksheets.

Columns 27 and 28 – 1934–1948: Same source as columns 19, 20, 23, and 24.
        1949: Roughly estimated on basis of split in earlier years.

(Securities and Exchange Commission Data)

$ mill.

Year	New securities offered for cash				Investment company issues			
	Total	Bonds	Preferred	Common	Total	Bonds	Preferred	Common
	1	2	3	4	5	6	7	8
1934	397	372	6	19	152	21	26	105
1935	2 331	2 223	86	22	171	33	28	110
1936	4 573	4 030	271	272	201	33	34	134
1937	2 309	1 618	406	285	200	33	33	134
1938	2 154	2 043	86	25	60	10	10	40
1939	2 164	1 979	98	87	60	10	10	40
1940	2 677	2 386	183	108	50	5	9	36
1941	2 667	2 390	167	110	50	0	10	40
1942	1 063	917	112	34	69	1	14	54
1943	1 169	989	124	56	118	6	22	90
1944	3 169	3 124	31	14	224	55	34	135
1945	6 010	4 855	758	397	312	16	59	237
1946	6 900	4 882	1 127	891	384	19	73	292
1947	6 577	5 036	762	779	282	7	55	220
1948	7 113	6 007	492	614	297	2	59	236
1949	5 410	4 256	422	732	378	0	76	302

Year	Securities held by affiliated companies				Securities held by Reconstruction Finance Corporation			
	Total	Bonds	Preferred	Common	Total	Bonds	Preferred	Common
	9	10	11	12	13	14	15	16
1934	0	0	0	0	0	0	0	0
1935	13	10	0	3	0	0	0	0
1936	8	5	0	3	0	0	0	0
1937	9	8	0	1	0	0	0	0
1938	43	37	0	6	0	0	0	0
1939	31	6	0	25	0	0	0	0
1940	21	1	0	20	73	73	0	0
1941	86	1	0	85	0	0	0	0
1942	17	3	0	14	0	0	0	0
1943	55	5	0	50	2	2	0	0
1944	44	11	0	33	17	16	0	1
1945	143	2	0	141	104	104	0	0
1946	187	0	0	187	16	16	0	0
1947	132	2	0	130	0	0	0	0
1948	29	0	0	29	0	0	0	0
1949	112	2	0	110	0	0	0	0

Year	Private sales to foreigners				Foreign issues offered in U.S.				Amounts offered but not sold			
	Total	Bonds	Preferred	Common	Total	Bonds	Preferred	Common	Total	Bonds	Preferred	Common
	17	18	19	20	21	22	23	24	25	26	27	28
1934	0	0	0	0	0	0	0	0	4	1	1	2
1935	12	12	0	0	10	10	0	0	19	13	5	1
1936	1	1	0	0	53	38	7	8	34	4	15	15
1937	3	3	0	0	4	3	1	0	42	3	23	16
1938	7	7	0	0	4	3	1	0	21	3	14	4
1939	17	17	0	0	74	73	1	0	16	1	8	7
1940	14	14	0	0	1	0	1	0	33	2	20	11
1941	5	5	0	0	1	0	1	0	14	4	6	4
1942	9	9	0	0	1	0	1	0	6	1	4	1
1943	11	11	0	0	18	18	0	0	4	0	3	1
1944	14	4	7	3	27	27	0	0	17	1	11	5
1945	15	15	0	0	64	55	6	3	63	7	37	19
1946	14	14	0	0	203	192	6	5	118	16	57	45
1947	12	12	0	0	53	34	9	10	68	10	28	30
1948	31	31	0	0	64	55	4	5	139	12	56	71
1949	24	24	0	0	13	9	2	2	104	8	48	48

Column 1 – 1897–1949: Sum of cols. 2–13. For definition see Volume II, pp. 284–285.

Column 2 – 1897–1920: From Table V-20, col. 1.
    1921–1933: From Table V-21, col. 1.
    1934–1948: Same procedure as described in notes to Table V-21 except that classification of issues of over $1 million was based on comparison with Securities and Exchange Commission file of cash offerings and figures for total of issues of under $1 million were taken from Securities and Exchange Commission worksheets. From the figures so obtained Securities and Exchange Commission estimates for unsold offerings were deducted.
    1949: Derived from Securities and Exchange Commission worksheets (same as used in Table V-16) in which industrial breakdown was available. Rough breakdown of unsold offerings was deducted.

Column 3 – 1897–1932: Assumed equal to one-third of col. 2, roughly on basis of relative proportions of total preferred stock outstanding of industrial, etc., corporations with assets more than and less than $5 million as reported in *Statistics of Income*, 1931.
    1933–1949: Assumed to be included in col. 2.

Column 4 – 1897–1904: Derived from analysis of issues of electric light and power companies reported in General Investment News columns of weekly issues of the *Commercial and Financial Chronicle* excluding all ascertainable issues or parts of issues not sold for cash, sold to other corporations or foreigners, or used to acquire outstanding securities from domestic individuals. All issues of $3 million or more were individually examined. Cash issues representing individuals' saving in issues of $1 to $3 million were taken as 50 percent of issues of this size.
    1905–1949: Same procedure as for issues included in col. 2.

Column 5 – 1897–1948: Same procedure as for issues included in col. 2 except that up to 1933 all issues of $1 million or more were individually examined ($3 million or over for 1925–1929).
    1949: Assumed included in col. 4.

Column 6 – 1914–1932: From Table V-41, col. 3.

Column 7 – 1897–1949: From Table V-27, col. 4.

Column 8 – 1897–1907: From Table V-32, col. 4.
    1908–1912: Assumed equal to $5 million a year.
    1913–1949: Assumed negligible on basis of outstanding stock of street railways reported in *Census of Electric Railways*, quinquennial issues, until 1932. After 1933 assumed negligible except for possible few issues included in col. 4.

Column 9 – 1922–1949: From Table V-30, col. 4.

Column 10 – 1916–1932: Cash issues roughly estimated as one-half of Table V-42, col. 3. Assumed negligible for other years.

Column 11 – 1897–1920: Assumed negligible.
    1921–1949: Estimated at two-thirds of changes in preferred stock of sponsoring companies held by pension funds as shown in Table I-17, col. 7.

Column 12 – 1897–1926: Assumed negligible.
    1927–1949: From Table V-40, col. 8.

Column 13 – 1897–1949: From Table V-43, col. 5.

PREFERRED STOCK ISSUES REPRESENTING INDIVIDUALS' SAVING BY INDUSTRY: 1897 to 1949

$ mill.

Year	Total	Industrial		Electric light and power			Rail-roads	Street rail-ways	Bell system	Em-ployee owner-ship sales	Pension fund sales	Invest-ment com-panies	New incor-pora-tions
		Re-ported	Adjust-ment for small issues	Oper-ating com-panies	Hold-ing com-panies	Customer owner-ship sales							
	1	2	3	4	5	6	7	8	9	10	11	12	13
1897	33	13	4	4	0	—	6	1	—	—	—	—	5
1898	76	44	15	1	0	—	10	1	—	—	—	—	5
1899	284	138	46	0	0	—	80	13	—	—	—	—	7
1900	76	29	10	0	0	—	28	1	—	—	—	—	8
1901	148	117	39	0	0	—	-18	1	—	—	—	—	9
1902	32	37	12	0	0	—	-28	1	—	—	—	—	10
1903	27	15	5	1	0	—	-12	6	—	—	—	—	12
1904	72	12	4	0	0	—	39	6	—	—	—	—	11
1905	96	23	8	0	0	—	46	6	—	—	—	—	13
1906	84	27	9	5	0	—	17	11	—	—	—	—	15
1907	83	27	9	1	0	—	25	6	—	—	—	—	15
1908	60	21	7	0	0	—	14	5	—	—	—	—	13
1909	48	42	14	2	1	—	-33	5	—	—	—	—	17
1910	61	50	17	4	3	—	-35	5	—	—	—	—	17
1911	114	91	30	2	2	—	-31	5	—	—	—	—	15
1912	189	102	34	22	13	—	-5	5	—	—	—	—	18
1913	109	44	15	7	10	—	13	—	—	—	—	—	20
1914	63	24	8	25	2	8	-21	—	—	—	—	—	17
1915	57	22	7	10	6	5	-13	—	—	—	—	—	20
1916	352	195	65	4	15	4	39	—	—	2	—	—	28
1917	187	116	39	5	2	7	-21	—	—	5	—	—	34
1918	97	58	19	2	0	4	-18	—	—	5	—	—	27
1919	890	531	177	4	10	16	92	—	—	8	—	—	52
1920	580	333	111	22	10	37	-9	—	—	10	—	—	66
1921	142	41	14	19	2	68	-47	—	—	10	1	—	34
1922	488	154	51	44	12	111	24	—	39	15	1	—	37
1923	638	217	72	76	57	149	-7	—	15	20	1	—	38
1924	594	81	27	88	77	215	17	—	29	25	1	—	34
1925	1 095	353	118	109	197	251	-4	—	2	30	1	—	38
1926	865	322	107	108	71	198	-18	—	4	35	1	—	37
1927	1 308	368	123	257	192	192	28	—	1	40	3	68	36
1928	1 483	496	165	91	206	128	55	—	0	40	2	261	39
1929	1 928	642	214	41	268	109	29	—	0	40	7	540	38
1930	420	124	41	28	153	115	-15	—	-1	20	1	-77	31
1931	247	23	8	51	54	135	-19	—	-12	10	1	-29	25
1932	10	4	1	4	0	15	-16	—	0	0	1	-21	22
1933	42	25	—	0	0	—	-1	—	0	—	1	-4	21
1934	50	13	—	2	C	—	-12	—	0	—	1	26	20
1935	126	72	—	21	0	—	-18	—	0	—	1	28	22
1936	297	169	—	63	0	—	7	—	0	—	2	34	22
1937	429	305	—	106	0	—	-6	—	-32	—	1	33	22
1938	75	52	—	28	0	—	-12	—	-22	—	1	10	18
1939	110	20	—	31	40	—	-9	—	0	—	0	10	18
1940	195	82	—	75	4	—	13	—	-5	—	0	9	17
1941	192	101	—	90	0	—	-6	—	-20	—	0	10	17
1942	104	60	—	47	0	—	-33	—	2	—	2	14	12
1943	136	109	—	20	0	—	-30	—	0	—	3	22	12
1944	419	254	—	103	0	—	1	—	-3	—	15	34	15
1945	967	764	—	117	0	—	-15	—	0	—	17	59	25
1946	1 258	827	—	306	2	—	-27	—	0	—	19	73	58
1947	971	556	—	230	8	—	40	—	0	—	20	55	62
1948	489	192	—	188	0	—	-33	—	0	—	25	59	58
1949	520	103	—	263	—	—	5	—	0	—	24	76	49

NET ISSUES OF PREFERRED STOCK
1919 to 1949
$ mill.

Year	Industrials			Public utilities			Other net	Total net
	Issues	Retirements	Net	Issues	Retirements	Net		
	1	2	3	4	5	6	7	8
1919	708	186	522	30	11	19	152	693
1920	444	120	324	69	16	53	67	444
1921	55	96	−41	89	21	68	−2	25
1922	205	109	96	167	43	124	116	336
1923	289	150	139	282	23	259	67	465
1924·	108	105	3	380	40	340	106	449
1925	471	154	317	557	44	513	67	897
1926	429	190	239	377	38	339	59	637
1927	491	188	303	641	92	549	176	1 028
1928	661	305	356	425	204	221	397	974
1929	856	552	304	418	258	160	654	1 118
1930	165	104	61	296	26	270	−41	290
1931	31	96	−65	240	48	192	−24	103
1932	5	97	−92	19	12	7	−14	−99
1933	25	120	−95	0	12	−12	17	−90
1934	13	22	−9	2	5	−3	35	23
1935	72	213	−141	21	31	−10	33	−118
1936	169	377	−208	63	71	−8	65	−151
1937	305	93	212	106	149	−43	18	187
1938	52	45	7	28	79	−51	−5	−49
1939	20	48	−28	71	81	−10	19	−19
1940	82	124	−42	79	80	−1	34	−9
1941	101	158	−57	90	74	16	1	−40
1942	60	70	−10	47	19	28	−3	15
1943	109	172	−63	20	50	−30	7	−86
1944	254	204	50	103	188	−85	62	27
1945	764	515	249	117	227	−110	86	225
1946	827	446	381	308	523	−215	123	289
1947	556	223	333	238	158	80	177	590
1948	192	111	81	188	92	96	109	286
1949	103	80	23	263	61	202	154	379

Column 1 - Table V-17, cols. 2 plus 3.

Column 2 – Table V-25, col. 4.

Column 3 – Col. 1 minus col. 2.

Column 4 – Table V-17, sum of cols. 4–6.

Column 5 – Table V-25, col. 2.

Column 6 - Col. 4 minus col. 5.

Column 7 – Table V-17, sum of cols. 7–13.

Column 8 – Sum of cols. 3, 6, and 7.

TABLE V–19   V-19

Column 1 – 1897–1949: Sum of cols. 2–20.

Column 2 – 1897–1920: From Table V-20, col. 7.
  1921–1949: Same procedure as for Table V-17, col. 2.

Column 3 – 1897–1932: Roughly estimated as 40 percent of col. 2 on basis of procedure described for Table V-17, col. 3.
  1933–1949: Roughly estimated as 20 percent of col. 2 on assumption that statistics are substantially more complete than for 1897–1932.

Column 4 – 1897–1949: Same procedure as for Table V-17, col. 4.

Column 5 – 1897–1917: Estimated for period as a whole at 75 percent of col. 4, but distributed more evenly over individual years, based on comparison of reported net issues and reported change in outstanding stock (cf. Table V-34).
  1918–1949: Assumed to be negligible.

Column 6 – 1897–1949: Same procedure as for Table V-17, col. 5.

Column 7 – 1914–1932: From Table V-41, col. 4. Assumed negligible for other years.

Column 8 – 1897–1949: From Table V-28, col. 7.

Column 9 – 1897–1907: From Table V-32, col. 1.
  1908–1912: Assumed equal to $20 million a year.
  1913–1949: Assumed negligible (cf. note to Table V-17, col. 8).

Column 10 – 1897–1921: From Table V-29, col. 3.
  1922–1949: From Table V-30, col. 3 plus col. 5.

Column 11 – 1897–1949: From Table V-35, col. 8.

Column 12 – 1918–1949: First differences of Table V-77, col. 11.

Column 13 – 1901–1934: Derived from information on stock issues by all larger title and guarantee companies in *Moody's Manuals*.

Column 14 – 1917–1949: From Table V-40, col. 1.

Column 15 – 1897–1949: From Table V-36, col. 5.

Column 16 – 1897–1949: From Table V-37, col. 8.

Column 17 – 1897–1949: From Table V–43, col. 6.

Column 18 – 1897–1920: Assumed negligible.
  1921–1949: Estimated at two-thirds of changes in common stock of sponsoring companies held by pension funds as shown in Table I-17, col. 8, assuming other increasing in holdings were not publicly offered.

Column 19 – 1916–1931: Cash issues roughly estimated as one-half of Table V-42, col. 2. Assumed negligible for other years.

Column 20 – 1915–1949: From Table K-3, col. 5.

COMMON STOCK ISSUES REPRESENTING INDIVIDUALS' SAVING
BY INDUSTRY: 1897 to 1949

$ mill.

Year	Total	Industrial		Electric light and power				Railroads	Street railways
		Reported	Adjustment for small issues	Operating compan'es	Adjustment for under-coverage	Holding companies	Customer ownership sales		
	1	2	3	4	5	6	7	8	9
1897	76	15	6	7	5	0	–	–18	14
1898	21	28	11	18	13	0	–	–112	19
1899	253	83	33	14	10	4	–	–22	38
1900	162	58	23	24	18	0	–	–168	46
1901	376	88	35	13	10	0	–	–18	43
1902	661	52	21	16	12	0	–	153	88
1903	438	48	19	30	15	5	–	28	33
1904	293	37	15	6	7	0	–	–11	25
1905	306	32	13	2	5	7	–	–15	25
1906	698	65	26	3	6	12	–	221	56
1907	555	68	27	7	7	0	–	124	25
1908	530	51	20	11	7	0	–	194	20
1909	673	58	23	6	5	13	–	306	20
1910	721	48	19	17	9	3	–	356	20
1911	165	38	15	12	7	0	–	–181	20
1912	768	93	37	20	10	7	–	309	20
1913	435	47	19	11	9	2		90	–
1914	289	17	7	7	8	0	1	51	–
1915	404	34	14	5	7	0	1	12	–
1916	893	226	90	12	10	0	0	111	–
1917	718	114	46	19	13	0	1	9	–
1918	778	117	47	10	–	0	0	175	–
1919	1 195	349	140	21	–	0	2	–51	–
1920	1 244	258	103	13	–	0	4	–85	–
1921	855	125	50	8	–	10	8	12	–
1922	951	80	32	59	–	3	13	30	–
1923	1 023	209	84	89	–	2	17	37	–
1924	979	163	65	75	–	12	26	–85	–
1925	1 409	297	119	93	–	40	30	77	–
1926	1 210	236	94	61	–	14	37	–38	–
1927	1 232	184	74	150	–	37	36	–118	–
1928	3 369	846	338	79	–	92	34	244	–
1929	6 368	1 688	675	221	–	407	29	119	–
1930	1 625	188	75	79	–	19	13	–32	–
1931	511	11	4	48	–	2	16	–40	–
1932	135	8	3	2	–	2	2	–38	–
1933	494	121	24	0	–	0	–	133	–
1934	109	18	4	0	–	0	–	–134	–
1935	245	13	3	12	–	0	–	–20	–
1936	663	257	51	1	–	0	–	82	–
1937	555	261	52	0	–	0	–	–26	–
1938	157	20	4	0	–	0	–	–35	–
1939	264	79	16	0	–	0	–	–21	–
1940	299	83	17	7	–	0	–	18	–
1941	366	71	14	8	–	0	–	123	–
1942	137	13	3	1	–	0	–	–7	–
1943	237	39	8	3	–	0	–	10	–
1944	395	76	15	6	–	0	–	–69	–
1945	902	232	46	56	–	0	–	–21	–
1946	1 775	730	146	77	–	0	–	–54	–
1947	1 613	413	83	142	–	41	–	68	–
1948	1 208	230	46	171	–	19		140	–
1949	1 741	212	42	555	–	0	–	1	–

COMMON STOCK ISSUES REPRESENTING INDIVIDUALS' SAVING BY INDUSTRY: 1897 to 1949

$ mill.

Year	Bell system	Commercial banks	Joint stock land banks	Title and guarantee companies	Investment companies	Insurance cos.		New incorporations	Pension fund sales	Employee owner-ship sales	Foreign companies
						Life	Casualty, surety, fire and marine				
	10	11	12	13	14	15	16	17	18	19	20
1897	4	0	–	–	–	0	1	42	–	–	–
1898	2	0	–	–	–	0	0	42	–	–	–
1899	9	22	–	–	–	0	3	59	–	–	–
1900	27	63	–	–	–	1	1	69	–	–	–
1901	12	102	–	2	–	1	5	83	–	–	–
1902	44	169	–	4	–	0	8	94	–	–	–
1903	32	116	–	3	–	2	3	104	–	–	–
1904	11	97	–	1	–	1	1	103	–	–	–
1905	6	100	–	1	–	2	8	120	–	–	–
1906	25	132	–	1	–	4	12	135	–	–	–
1907	35	110	–	1	–	3	13	135	–	–	–
1908	14	81	–	0	–	3	8	121	–	–	–
1909	0	78	–	2	–	5	2	155	–	–	–
1910	–13	94	–	0	–	7	10	151	–	–	–
1911	26	78	–	0	–	6	5	139	–	–	–
1912	11	86	–	2	–	4	3	166	–	–	–
1913	–5	71	–	4	–	1	7	179	–	–	–
1914	–2	41	–	0	–	2	1	156	–	–	–
1915	18	44	–	0	–	0	5	177	–	–	87
1916	11	61	–	3	–	0	2	248	–	2	117
1917	41	90	–	0	1	1	7	309	–	2	65
1918	1	108	2	0	1	3	26	243	–	2	43
1919	–1	199	7	1	1	3	35	471	–	5	10
1920	–1	274	–1	0	2	5	20	590	–	5	57
1921	108	147	0	0	2	7	13	310	1	5	49
1922	144	125	18	1	2	2	31	330	1	8	72
1923	35	114	9	5	3	12	20	342	1	10	34
1924	166	95	1	5	3	0	35	304	1	12	101
1925	44	153	7	24	5	11	61	344	1	15	88
1926	165	127	4	20	5	22	41	331	2	20	69
1927	42	185	1	12	101	4	76	325	5	25	93
1928	219	363	–5	21	495	16	136	347	4	30	110
1929	50	1 139	0	6	1 561	12	78	339	9	30	5
1930	498	132	0	0	319	12	15	280	2	15	10
1931	39	0	4	0	197	0	0	223	1	5	1
1932	–61	0	–9	0	26	0	0	199	1	–	0
1933	–1	0	0	0	27	0	4	185	1	–	0
1934	–3	0	0	0	40	0	6	177	1	–	0
1935	–6	0	0	–	46	1	0	195	1	–	0
1936	0	0	–1	–	59	0	5	193	3	–	13
1937	0	0	–1	–	61	8	0	199	1	–	0
1938	0	0	–2	–	5	0	4	160	1	–	0
1939	0	0	0	–	6	12	10	161	1	–	0
1940	0	5	–3	–	1	0	14	157	0	–	0
1941	1	3	–5	–	–15	10	0	155	1	–	0
1942	2	0	–7	–	21	1	0	107	3	–	0
1943	6	30	–11	–	6	22	10	108	5	–	1
1944	22	84	–2	–	64	13	38	131	21	–	–4
1945	31	111	–1	–	115	20	25	223	27	–	38
1946	21	152	–2	–	115	24	15	517	29	–	5
1947	53	62	–2	–	131	12	41	555	29	–	–15
1948	165	50	0	–	87	0	18	519	37	–	15
1949	168	36	0	–	188	32	46	442	37	–	–18

Column 1 – 1897–1920: Sum of cols. 2–6. In all columns, issues of financial institutions, public utilities, and railroads were excluded.

Column 2 – 1897–1904: Based on examination of all individual issues of this size mentioned in the General Investment News columns of *Commercial and Financial Chronicle*. All issues and parts of issues not purchased for cash by individuals were excluded.

    1905–1920: Same as for 1897–1904 except that examination was made of all issues of this size included in the semiannual or monthly lists of capital flotations in the *Journal of Commerce*.

Column 3 – 1897–1904: Same source and method as col. 2.

    1905–1920: Same as col. 2 except that figures are based on individual examination of only about one-half of the issues of this size, while estimates for issues not individually examined were obtained by applying to their aggregate offering price, as derived from the *Journal of Commerce* lists, a ratio of 0.60, approximately the period's proportion between aggregate offering price and cash offerings representing individuals' saving found for the examined issues.

Column 4 – 1897–1904: Same source and method as col. 2.

    1905–1920: Combined with col. 5.

Column 5 – 1897–1904: Estimated at 35 percent of total issues of this size mentioned in the General Investment News columns of the *Commercial and Financial Chronicle*, the ratio being based on, but slightly above, that found to exist for larger issues on assumption that proportion of noncash issues generally decreased with size of issue.

    1905–1920: Same as col. 3 except that only about 20 percent of issues of this size were individually examined and ratio of cash to total was put at 70 percent.

Column 6 – 1897–1908: Same source as col. 2, 1897–1904. Annual totals were based on totals for three or six month periods. All issues were assumed to be sold for cash. Figures are rounded to nearest $5 million.

    1909–1920: Estimated, on basis of relation for issues of $1 to $10 million, at 80 percent of aggregate offering price of issues of this size. Latter were derived from annual totals of all issues other than railroads, street railways, and public utilities compiled from the *Journal of Commerce* lists by: (a) multiplying the annual totals by the percentage of industrial issues based on classification of issues for a two-months sample (March and October) for each year; and (b) assuming, on basis of distribution for issues of $1 to $5 million, that 45 percent of total industrial issues consisted of preferred stock.

Column 7 – 1897–1920: Sum of cols. 8–12.

Column 8 – 1897–1920: Same method as col. 2.

Column 9 – 1897–1920: Same method as col. 3.

Column 10 – 1897–1920: Same method as col. 4.

Column 11 – 1897–1920: Same method as col. 5 except cash issues of this size were estimated at 25 percent of total issues for 1897–1904 and at 50 percent for 1905–1920.

Column 12 – 1897–1920: Same method as col. 6 except that for 1909–1920 ratio of cash to total offerings was assumed at 50 percent and of common stock at 55 percent of total stock issues of this size and industry group.

STOCK ISSUES OF INDUSTRIAL AND MISCELLANEOUS CORPORATIONS
REPRESENTING INDIVIDUALS' SAVING: 1897 to 1920

$ mill.

Year	Preferred stock (size of issue)[1]						Common stock (size of issue)[1]					
	All issues	$10 million and over	$5–10 million	$3–5 million	$1–3 million	Under $1 million	All issues	$10 million and over	$5–10 million	$3–5 million	$1–3 million	Under $1 million
	1	2	3	4	5	6	7	8	9	10	11	12
1897	13	2	2	0	4	5	15	0	0	0	5	10
1898	44	22	10	0	7	5	28	10	1	0	7	10
1899	138	66	16	17	29	10	83	17	11	16	24	15
1900	29	5	1	0	13	10	58	12	0	4	22	20
1901	117	65	28	0	9	15	88	26	18	6	18	20
1902	37	11	10	0	6	10	52	15	5	0	17	15
1903	15	0	0	0	5	10	48	7	7	6	13	15
1904	12	0	6	0	1	5	37	10	0	7	5	15
1905	23	2	5	6		10	32	0	17	0		15
1906	27	10	0	7		10	65	11	22	12		20
1907	27	0	0	12		15	68	0	2	36		30
1908	21	0	0	11		10	51	0	13	18		20
1909	42	14	6	14		8	58	27	6	19		6
1910	50	2	3	37		8	48	0	8	34		6
1911	91	34	17	25		15	38	15	0	12		11
1912	102	32	24	35		11	93	20	38	27		8
1913	44	0	17	23		4	47	0	11	33		3
1914	24	0	8	9		7	17	0	3	8		6
1915	22	0	5	14		3	34	14	0	18		2
1916	195	82	31	71		11	226	119	41	58		8
1917	116	40	17	43		16	114	15	35	51		13
1918	58	15	0	18		25	117	58	23	17		19
1919	531	236	83	168		44	349	166	56	94		33
1920	333	164	28	87		54	258	75	43	99		41

[1] Size as reported for entire issue in source, not size of proportion representing individuals' saving.

CASH ISSUES OF PREFERRED AND COMMON STOCK
OF INDUSTRIAL AND MISCELLANEOUS CORPORATIONS REPRESENTING
INDIVIDUALS' SAVING: 1921 to 1933

$ mill.

Year	All issues	Issues of total size of:					All issues listed in *Commercial and Financial Chronicle*	Difference
		$10 million and over	$5–10 million	$3–5 million	$1–3 million	Under $1 million		
	1	2	3	4	5	6	7	8
I. Preferred stock								
1921	41	13	0	7	12	9	44	−3
1922	154	62	27	10	35	20	173	−19
1923	217	80	27	39	43	28	220	−3
1924	81	10	0	10	37	24	83	−2
1925	353	153	31	53	87	29	365	−12
1926	322	136	36	27	86	37	357	−35
1927	368	156	26	44	105	37	376	−8
1928	496	96	99	86	170	45	553	−57
1929	642	281	77	59	165	60	694	−52
1930	124	96	0	4	19	5	235	−111
1931	23	0	15	0	7	1	17	6
1932	4	0	0	0	4	0	5	−1
1933	25	0	7	3	6	9	15	10
II. Common stock								
1921	125	102	0	10	9	4	99	26
1922	80	8	20	18	27	7	103	−23
1923	209	76	45	19	54	15	241	−32
1924	163	31	58	18	38	18	173	−10
1925	297	81	69	40	72	35	323	−26
1926	236	118	28	31	46	13	257	−21
1927	184	15	32	58	56	23	188	−4
1928	846	325	123	104	229	65	1 010	−164
1929	1 688	987	254	136	230	81	1 786	−98
1930	188	118	13	8	31	18	266	−78
1931	11	0	0	0	8	3	12	−1
1932	8	0	0	0	6	2	8	0
1933	121	38	11	10	17	45	127	−6

Column 1 – Sum of cols. 2–6. In all columns, issues of financial institutions, public utilities, and railroads were excluded.

Column 2 – Based on examination of all individual issues of this size in monthly lists of *Commerical and Financial Chronicle*.

Columns 3 and 4 – Obtained by applying to year's total unexamined issues of this size group, ratio between total and cash issues representing individuals' saving prevailing in sample of issues of same size group (sample included about 60 percent of both preferred and common issues of $5–10 million and 10 percent of preferred and 20 percent of common stock issues of $3–5 million).

Column 5 – For 1921–1924 and 1930–1933 same procedure as for col. 4; for 1925–1929 obtained by applying a ratio slightly higher than that prevailing for issues of $3–5 million.

Column 6 – Obtained by assuming 100 percent of all preferred and common stock issues of under $1 million included in *Chronicle* lists to consist of cash issues representing individuals' saving. (For method of determining share of industrial issues in totals see note to Table V-20, col. 6. Class of stock is available from lists in *Chronicle*.)

Column 7 – Based on tabulation of all issues of $1 million or more listed in *Chronicle*, and estimate for issues of under $1 million (cf. col. 6) for which ratio of cash to total offerings was taken at 50 percent, based on ratio for issues of $1 to $5 million.

Column 8 – Col. 1 minus col. 7.

Year	Reported issues			Cash issues representing individuals' saving			Cash issues as percent of reported issues		
	Total	Preferred	Common	Total	Preferred	Common	Total	Preferred	Common
	$ mill.						Percent		
	1	2	3	4	5	6	7	8	9
1905	285	120	165	55	23	32	19	19	19
1906	272	79	193	92	27	65	34	34	34
1907	158	32	126	95	27	68	60	84	54
1908	180	29	151	72	21	51	40	72	34
1909	208	67	141	100	42	58	48	63	41
1910	254	80	174	98	50	48	38	62	28
1911	214	126	88	129	91	38	60	72	43
1912	500	219	281	195	102	93	39	46	33
1913	214	79	135	91	44	47	42	56	35
1914	82	37	45	41	24	17	50	65	38
1915	255	111	144	56	22	34	22	20	24
1916	613	267	346	421	195	226	69	73	65
1917	364	164	200	230	116	114	63	71	57
1918	261	72	189	175	58	117	67	80	62
1919	1 354	733	621	880	531	349	65	72	56
1920	980	428	552	591	333	258	60	78	47
1921	143	44	99	166	41	125	116	93	126
1922	276	173	103	234	154	80	85	89	78
1923	461	220	241	426	217	209	92	99	87
1924	256	83	173	244	81	163	95	98	94
1925	688	365	323	650	353	297	94	97	92
1926	614	357	257	558	322	236	91	90	92
1927	564	376	188	552	368	184	98	98	98
1928	1 563	553	1 010	1 342	496	846	86	90	84
1929	2 480	694	1 786	2 330	642	1 688	94	92	95
1930	501	235	266	312	124	188	62	53	71
1931	29	17	12	34	23	11	117	135	92
1932	13	5	8	12	4	8	92	80	100
1933	142	15	127	146	25	121	103	167	95

Columns 1 to 3 – 1905–1920: All stock issues of industrial, etc., corporations from monthly lists of capital flotations in the *Journal of Commerce*. Each issue over $1 million was classified as preferred or common by reference to *Moody's Industrials* or news items in the *Commercial and Financial Chronicle*. Industrial, etc., issues under $1 million were estimated on the basis of an industry classification of issues in two months of each year except for 1905–1908, for which an estimate of issues of this size was made on the basis of data in the *Commercial and Financial Chronicle* (cf. notes to Table V-20, col. 6).

1921–1933: All stock issues of industrial, etc., corporations from monthly lists of capital flotations in the *Commercial and Financial Chronicle*. Issues under $1 million (under $3 million, 1925–1929) were classified according to industry on basis of classification of small issues for four months of each year.

Column 4 – 1905–1933: Col. 5 plus col. 6.

Column 5 – 1905–1933: From Table V-17, col. 2.

Column 6 – 1905–1933: From Table V-19, col. 2.

Columns 7 to 9 – 1905–1933: Cols. 4, 5, and 6 as a percentage of cols. 1, 2, and 3 respectively. Percentage of 126 in 1921 results from shifting of certain issues which were listed in 1920 but sold in 1921. Percentages from 1931–1933 in preferred stock are affected by treatment of a large issue listed in 1930 which was sold gradually over the period 1930–1935.

Column 1 – Based on amounts of issue or offerings as given from 1897 to 1904 in General Investment News column of weekly issues of *Commercial and Financial Chronicle*; for 1905 to 1920 in semiannual or monthly lists of new issues in *Journal of Commerce*; and from 1921 to 1933 in monthly lists of new issues of *Commercial and Financial Chronicle*; or obtained by multiplication of par value or given offering price and number of shares. Includes all issues of originally indicated amount of $3 million and over for 1897–1904, but only issues of $10 million and over from 1905 to 1933.

Columns 2 and 3 – Includes all issues offered for cash except those in cols. 4–8, i.e. issues the proceeds of which were to be used for capital expenditures, working capital, repayment of debt evidenced by securities, acquisition of existing tangible and intangible assets other than securities, and miscellaneous and unascertainable purposes.

Columns 4 and 5 – In principle based on redemption price of own securities retired; when this was not known retirement was assumed to have occurred at par. For period in which separate comprehensive estimates of retirements are not available these two columns have to be treated as cash issues not representing individuals' saving.

Column 6 – Includes acquisition of (a) securities issued during the same year and not included in year's statistics of offerings, and (b) outstanding securities from other nonindividual holders.

Column 7 – Covers all acquisitions of securities except those included in col. 6.

Column 8 – Includes sales to other domestic corporations and to foreigners. Also offerings the proceeds of which do not accrue to the issuer, but to other holders, which for preferred issues amount to $15 million in 1912 and $14 million in 1922.

Column 9 – Includes securities issued in reorganization but excludes securities of predecessor companies.

Column 10 – Includes both tangible and intangible property and securities of other companies, including predecessor companies.

Column 11 – Includes stock issued in split-up.

Column 12 – Includes offerings for which no evidence exists that the stock was issued.

Note: Figures may not add to total due to rounding.

DISTRIBUTION OF PREFERRED STOCK ISSUES
OF INDUSTRIAL CORPORATIONS OF OVER $3 MILLION, 1897 to 1904,
OR OVER $10 MILLION, 1905 to 1933,
BY CHARACTER OF ISSUE AND USE OF PROCEEDS

$ mill.

Year	All issues	Cash issues representing individuals' saving						Other cash issues	Issues not offered for cash			Unissued, unsold, unknown
		For new money		For retirement of		For acquisition of			Exchanged for		Stock dividends, bonus shares	
		To general public	To share-holders	Bonds, notes	Preferred stock	New	Out-standing		Securi-ties of issuer	Other assets		
						Securities						
	1	2	3	4	5	6	7	8	9	10	11	12
1897	14	4	0	0	0	0	0	0	0	10	0	0
1898	216	33	0	0	0	0	0	0	0	163	0	19
1899	776	81	0	0	0	0	23	0	38	370	0	264
1900	161	6	0	0	0	0	10	0	0	91	8	45
1901	691	81	11	0	0	0	5	9	0	531	0	53
1902	115	16	5	0	0	0	0	0	0	70	0	24
1903	15	0	0	0	0	0	0	0	0	1	0	14
1904	6	0	6	0	0	0	0	0	0	0	0	0
1905	87	0	2	0	0	0	26	8	0	49	0	2
1906	53	10	0	0	0	0	0	0	0	43	0	0
1907	0	0	0	0	0	0	0	0	0	0	0	0
1908	0	0	0	0	0	0	0	0	0	0	0	0
1909	24	14	0	0	0	0	0	0	0	10	0	0
1910	10	0	2	0	0	0	0	0	0	0	2	6
1911	46	34	0	0	0	0	0	0	0	12	0	0
1912	119	22	10	0	0	0	6	15	8	34	10	14
1913	0	0	0	0	0	0	0	0	0	0	0	0
1914	0	0	0	0	0	0	0	0	0	0	0	0
1915	85	0	0	0	0	0	0	0	60	0	0	25
1916	95	73	10	0	6	0	0	0	0	6	0	0
1917	55	0	30	0	0	10	0	15	0	0	0	0
1918	15	15	0	0	0	0	0	0	0	0	0	0
1919	328	62	133	21	40	20	15	0	0	35	0	2
1920	203	28	135	0	4	0	0	0	12	0	0	23
1921	15	0	13	0	0	0	0	0	0	0	0	2
1922	76	30	18	0	2	0	12	14	0	0	0	0
1923	80	8	10	62	0	0	0	0	0	0	0	0
1924	10	0	5	0	0	0	5	0	0	0	0	0
1925	153	108	33	12	0	0	0	0	0	0	0	0
1926	152	36	14	0	19	68	15	0	0	0	0	0
1927	158	119	0	17	12	0	9	0	0	0	0	0
1928	120	34	22	0	15	25	19	5	0	0	0	0
1929	292	196	0	1	45	40	10	0	0	0	0	0
1930	199	49	36	0	11	0	0	0	56	0	0	47
1931	0	0	0	0	0	0	0	0	0	0	0	0
1932	0	0	0	0	0	0	0	0	0	0	0	0
1933	0	0	0	0	0	0	0	0	0	0	0	0

Column 1 – Based on amounts of issue or offerings as given from 1897 to 1904 in General Investment News column of weekly issues of *Commercial and Financial Chronicle*; for 1905 to 1920 in semiannual or monthly lists of new issues in *Journal of Commerce*; and from 1921 to 1933 in monthly lists of new issues of *Commercial and Financial Chronicle*; or obtained by multiplication of par value or given offering price and number of shares. Includes all issues of originally indicated amount of $3 million and over for 1897–1904, but only issues of $10 million and over from 1905 to 1933.

Columns 2 and 3 – Includes all issues offered for cash except those in cols. 4–8, i.e. issues the proceeds of which were to be used for capital expenditures, working capital, repayment of debt not evidenced by securities, acquisition of existing tangible and intangible assets other than securities, and miscellaneous and unascertainable purposes.

Columns 4 and 5 – In principle based on redemption price of own securities retired; when this was not known retirement was assumed to have occurred at par. For period in which separate comprehensive estimates of retirements are not available these two columns have to be treated as cash issues not representing individuals' saving.

Column 6 – Includes acquisition of (a) securities issued during the same year and not included in year's statistics of offerings, and (b) outstanding securities from other nonindividual holders.

Column 7 – Covers all acquisitions of securities except those included in col. 6.

Column 8 – Includes sales to other domestic corporations and to foreigners. Also offerings the proceeds of which do not accrue to the issuer, but to other holders, which for common issues amount to $12 million in 1923 and $17 million in 1929.

Column 9 – Includes securities issued in reorganization but excludes securities of predecessor companies.

Column 10 – Includes both tangible and intangible property and securities of other companies, including predecessor companies.

Column 11 – Includes stock issued in split-up.

Column 12 – Includes offerings for which no evidence exists that the stock was issued.

Note: Figures may not add to total due to rounding.

DISTRIBUTION OF COMMON STOCK ISSUES OF INDUSTRIAL CORPORATIONS OF OVER $3 MILLION, 1897 to 1904, OR OVER $10 MILLION, 1905 to 1933, BY CHARACTER OF ISSUE AND USE OF PROCEEDS

$ mill.

Year	All issues	Cash issues representing individuals' saving						Other cash issues	Issues not offered for cash			Unissued, unsold, unknown
		For new money		For retirement of		For acquisition of			Exchanged for		Stock dividends, bonus shares	
		To general public	To shareholders	Bonds, notes	Preferred stock	New	Out-standing		Securities of issuer	Other assets		
						Securities						
	1	2	3	4	5	6	7	8	9	10	11	12
1897	124	0	0	0	0	0	0	0	0	52	5	67
1898	321	10	16	0	0	0	3	0	13	154	56	68
1899	2 020	35	19	0	0	0	75	0	11	635	150	1 095
1900	661	12	0	0	0	0	10	0	0	167	12	459
1901	1 023	71	11	0	0	0	0	54	17	684	19	167
1902	419	15	5	0	0	0	0	0	0	261	0	139
1903	105	0	14	0	0	0	0	10	0	50	0	32
1904	10	0	10	0	0	0	0	0	0	0	0	0
1905	86	0	0	0	0	0	0	0	19	68	0	0
1906	85	0	11	0	0	0	0	0	0	74	0	0
1907	0	0	0	0	0	0	0	0	0	0	0	0
1908	40	0	0	0	0	0	0	0	0	0	16	24
1909	59	2	26	0	0	0	0	0	0	31	0	0
1910	68	0	0	0	0	0	0	0	0	18	40	10
1911	38	0	15	0	0	0	0	0	0	23	0	0
1912	138	0	20	0	0	0	0	0	0	94	5	20
1913	40	0	0	0	0	0	0	0	12	18	0	10
1914	15	0	0	0	0	0	0	0	0	0	0	15
1915	100	14	0	0	0	0	40	0	0	20	25	0
1916	141	19	40	0	0	15	25	0	0	36	0	6
1917	40	15	0	0	0	0	0	0	0	8	15	2
1918	68	0	58	0	0	0	0	10	0	0	0	0
1919	275	21	124	15	0	5	51	12	0	33	0	14
1920	184	22	59	0	0	0	0	56	0	0	30	17
1921	102	32	49	0	0	20	0	0	0	0	0	0
1922	25	0	0	8	0	0	17	0	0	0	0	0
1923	94	0	76	0	0	0	0	18	0	0	0	0
1924	31	0	31	0	0	0	0	0	0	0	0	0
1925	92	12	51	3	15	0	12	0	0	0	0	0
1926	118	13	105	0	0	0	0	0	0	0	0	0
1927	15	0	15	0	0	0	0	0	0	0	0	0
1928	397	17	248	30	28	0	63	10	0	0	0	0
1929	1 067	55	484	380	52	4	25	67	0	0	0	0
1930	191	40	78	0	0	0	42	30	0	0	0	0
1931	0	0	0	0	0	0	0	0	0	0	0	0
1932	0	0	0	0	0	0	0	0	0	0	0	0
1933	40	0	40	0	0	0	0	0	0	0	0	0

RETIREMENT OF PREFERRED STOCK
1919 to 1949

$ mill.

Year	Public utilities		Other domestic		Total retire-ments	Year	Public utilities		Other domestic		Total retire-ments
	Refund-ing issues	Retire-ments	Refund-ing issues	Retire-ments			Refund-ing issues	Retire-ments	Refund-ing issues	Retire-ments	
	1	2	3	4	5		1	2	3	4	5
1919	1	11	109	186	197	1934	0	5	0	22	27
1920	5	16	30	120	136	1935	33	31	48	213	244
1921	9	21	1	96	117	1936	43	71	155	377	448
1922	27	43	16	109	152	1937	86	149	266	93	242
1923	11	23	66	150	173	1938	17	79	14	45	124
1924	25	40	12	105	145	1939	133	81	4	48	129
1925	28	44	71	154	198	1940	126	80	67	124	204
1926	23	38	114	190	228	1941	109	74	18	158	232
1927	68	92	112	188	280	1942	4	19	7	70	89
1928	160	204	252	305	509	1943	18	50	64	172	222
1929	205	258	550	552	810	1944	99	188	189	204	392
1930	13	26	10	104	130	1945	156	227	500	515	742
1931	31	48	1	96	144	1946	322	523	276	446	969
1932	2	12	2	97	109	1947	215	158	62	223	381
1933	2	12	30	120	132	1948	18	92	8	111	203
						1949	–	61	–	80	141

Columns 1 and 3 – 1919–1948: From *Commercial and Financial Chronicle*, annual summaries of security issues. Col. 1 shows the *Chronicle* figures for all stock issued by public utilities for purpose of refunding; col. 3, all stock issued by domestic corporations except railroads, utilities, real estate, and financial corporations for purpose of refunding.

Column 2 – 1919–1933: Estimated on basis of relationship existing between col. 2 and col. 1 for 1934–1948. (Retirements equal $10.0 million plus 1.21 multiplied by refunding issues.)
1934–1949: Estimates of preferred stock retirements by call, public tender, and repurchase in the open market of public utility securities. (For sources and methods cf. Table V-13.)

Column 4 – 1919–1933: Same method as col. 2. (Retirements equal $95.5 million plus 0.83 multiplied by refunding issues.)
1934–1949: Same source as col. 2.

Column 5 – 1919–1949: Col. 2 plus col. 4.

RAILROAD INCOME BONDS AND EQUIPMENT TRUST OBLIGATIONS OUTSTANDING: 1896 to 1949

$ mill.

End of year	Income bonds		Equipment trust obligations		End of year	Income bonds		Equipment trust obligations	
	Actually outstanding	Total outstanding	Actually outstanding	Total outstanding		Actually outstanding	Total outstanding	Actually outstanding	Total outstanding
	1	2	3	4		1	2	3	4
1896	.	287	.	45	1923	420	425	931	969
1897	.	261	.	40	1924	369	377	1 062	1 107
1898	.	261	.	41	1925	337	343	1 084	1 138
1899	.	240	.	51	1926	314	321	1 102	1 153
1900	.	219	.	64	1927	300	306	1 067	1 115
1901	.	231	.	79	1928	379	388	983	1 028
1902	.	238	.	116	1929	366	375	997	1 047
1903	.	232	.	158	1930	346	378	987	1 027
1904	.	241	.	180	1931	349	380	883	924
1905	.	278	.	206	1932	348	379	765	806
1906	.	304	.	277	1933	332	363	654	695
1907	.	282	.	337	1934	320	361	622	663
1908	.	272	.	326	1935	311	358	540	592
1909	.	288	.	331	1936	312	360	507	558
1910	.	276	.	336	1937	313	365	362	643
1911	.	265	.	318	1938	313	365	446	500
1912	.	259	.	343	1939	313	363	431	487
1913	.	252	.	394	1940	.	.	485	521
1914	.	251	.	413	1941	.	.	629	633
1915	.	266	.	392	1942	.	.	614	614
1916	343	361	351	373	1943	.	.	611	612
1917	334	352	354	396	1944	.	.	603	603
1918	334	353	325	376	1945	.	.	596	596
1919	335	354	284	313	1946	.	.	629	630
1920	338	357	659	691	1947	.	.	783	786
1921	343	360	677	720	1948	.	.	1 050	1 050
1922	364	381	725	759	1949	.	.	1 343	1 343

General Note: All data are given in Interstate Commerce Commission, *Statistics of Railways*, as of June 30 prior to 1916 and as of Dec. 31 from 1916 to the present. Hence, the data given in this table as of Dec. 31 prior to 1916 are a result of linear interpolation of June 30 data.

Column 1 – 1916–1937: *Statistics of Railways*, 1916–1937, statement 16.
1938–1939: *Statistics of Railways*, 1938–1939, table 141.

Column 2 – 1896–1897: *Statistics of Railways*, 1898, p. 55.
1898–1907: *Statistics of Railways*, 1908, p. 62.
1908–1912: *Statistics of Railways*, 1912, statement 26.
1913–1914: *Statistics of Railways*, 1913–1914, statement 26. Figures cover only Class I and II railroads and their nonoperating subsidiaries.
1915–1939: Col. 1 plus income bonds nominally outstanding as given in *Statistics of Railways*, 1915–1938, statement 16, or 1939, table 141.

Column 3 – 1916–1939: Same source as col. 1, 1916–1939.
1940–1949: *Statistics of Railways*, 1940–1949, table 141.

Column 4 – 1896–1914: Same source as col. 2, 1896–1914.
1915–1949: Col. 3 plus equipment trust obligations nominally outstanding as given in *Statistics of Railways*, 1915–1938, statement 16, or 1939–1949, table 141.

Column 1 – 1897–1907: Derived from *Statistics of Railways*, 1940, table 155. Dec. 31 figures are obtained by linear interpolation between June 30 dates.

    1908–1914: Same source as for 1897–1907. Stock of switching and terminal companies being omitted from the statistics, the reported figures were increased in the ratio of all steam railway stock to stock of Class I, II, and III railroads. Dec. 31 figures were obtained by interpolation between June 30 reporting dates. 1914 figure is reduced by $21 million to account for distribution of Baltimore and Ohio stock to Union Pacific stockholders. (Correction for this noncash transaction is made to avoid overstatement of net cash issues of preferred stock.)

    1915–1949: *Statistics of Railways*, 1949, table 155 (for Class I, II, and III railroads and their lessors) and table 141 in annual volumes (for switching and terminal companies). From Dec. 31, 1916 on, reported figures are on year-end basis. Figures for 1917, 1944, and 1945 adjusted for reclassification in table 155 of Great Northern stock from common to preferred.

Column 2 – 1897–1949: Total railway stock held by railways was derived from *Statistics of Railways*, 1940 and 1949, table 155, for 1897–1905 and for 1910–1949, and obtained by linear interpolation for 1906–1909. Since the 1910–1949 figures did not include switching and terminal companies, an estimate was made on the basis of switching and terminal company stock held by Class I, II, and III railroads, as given in table 143, for 1929–1949.

    The percentage of preferred stock held was estimated from a sample of railroads holding $50 million or more of railroad stock in 1900, 1912, 1922, 1929, 1939, and 1946. The reports of these railroads to the Interstate Commerce Commission were examined in these six years, and the percentage of holdings of preferred to total railroad stockholding was computed and interpolated linearly for the intervening years. Percentages for 1900 were used before 1900, and 1946 percentages were used after 1946.

Column 3 – 1897–1948: Derived from examination in *Moody's Railroads*, *Poor's Manual Railroad*, and *Statistics of Railways* of changes in capitalization due to reorganizations. Reorganizations examined were those of Class I railroads of over 1,000 miles of track selected from almost a thousand cases listed in Interstate Commerce Commission, Bureau of Statistics, *Receivership and Trusteeships, 1894–1942*; those additional reorganizations covered by Locklin's *Statistical Analysis of 31 Reorganizations of Class I Railways, 1914–1933*; and those listed in annual volumes of *Statistics of Railways*, 1934–1948. These changes, not involving cash, must be deducted to obtain col. 4. The presumably small amounts attributable to other railroads (and included in col. 2) have in effect been deducted twice.

    1949: All reorganizations (3) completed in this year were examined as above.

Column 4 – 1897–1949: Col. 1 minus cols. 2 and 3.

Columns 1 to 3 – See notes to Table V-27, cols. 1, 2, and 3.

Column 4 – From Stevens, W. H. S., and Hobbs, E. S., *Analysis of Steam Railway Dividends, 1890–1941*, Interstate Commerce Commission, 1943, table 14, p. 38, and *Statistics of Railways*, 1948, table 123. The $46 million in 1914 represent dividends on Union Pacific Railroad stock, paid in stock of Baltimore and Ohio (see notes to Table V-21, col. 1) and the $19 million in 1947, distribution of New York, Chicago, and St. Louis Railroad stock to stockholders of Chesapeake and Ohio.

Column 5 – Derived from examination in *Moody's Railroads* and *Poor's Manual Railroad* of the reports on convertible bond issues of various railroads. A number of these issues were listed in Rollins, Montgomery, *Convertible Securities*, 1913, and several other large issues were noted in Ripley, W. Z., *Railroads: Finance and Organization*. In all cases total amount converted was available, but for some issues amount converted in any year was estimated as equally distributed between all years, within the allowable period for reconversion, in which stock price was above conversion price.

Column 6 – Adjustment for stock dividends paid to railroads in 1921 and 1923, counted both in col. 2 and col. 4, and for change in railroad holdings in certain large reorganizations counted both in col. 2 and col. 3. Only major cases of such duplications could be taken into account.

Column 7 – Col. 1 minus cols. 2–5 plus col. 6.

1897 to 1949

$ mill.: par value

Year	Change in outstanding stock	Change in inter-corporate holdings	Change due to reorgani-zation	Net cash issues	Year	Change in outstanding stock	Change in inter-corporate holdings	Change due to reorgani-zation	Net cash issues
	1	2	3	4		1	2	3	4
1897	74	2	66	6	1923	18	7	18	−7
1898	98	5	83	10	1924	83	25	41	17
1899	102	10	12	80	1925	2	6	0	−4
1900	69	16	25	28	1926	−11	7	0	−18
1901	−11	7	0	−18	1927	54	26	0	28
1902	−26	2	0	−28	1928	54	−4	3	55
1903	−6	6	0	−12	1929	31	2	0	29
1904	47	8	0	39	1930	9	24	0	−15
1905	56	10	0	46	1931	−25	14	−20	−19
1906	25	8	0	17	1932	−1	15	0	−16
1907	32	7	0	25	1933	−4	−3	0	−1
1908	21	7	0	14	1934	3	15	0	−12
1909	−30	3	0	−33	1935	−8	10	0	−18
1910	−35	4	−4	−35	1936	7	0	0	7
1911	−16	7	8	−31	1937	14	20	0	−6
1912	−1	4	0	−5	1938	−2	10	0	−12
1913	9	−4	0	13	1939	1	10	0	−9
1914	−17	4	0	−21	1940	14	1	0	13
1915	37	4	46	−13	1941	−87	−21	−60	−6
1916	30	−9	0	39	1942	−21	12	0	−33
1917	143	7	157	−21	1943	−29	1	0	−30
1918	−42	−24	0	−18	1944	78	4	73	1
1919	93	1	0	92	1945	−28	−9	−4	−15
1920	−1	8	0	−9	1946	−24	8	−5	−27
1921	−96	1	−50	−47	1947	23	−23	6	40
1922	34	0	10	24	1948	13	13	33	−33
					1949	−4	−4	−5	5

NET CASH ISSUES OF COMMON STOCK OF RAILROADS

1897 to 1949

$ mill.: par value

Year	Change in outstanding stock	Change in intercorporate holdings	Change due to reorgani- zation	Change due to stock dividends	Change due to conversion of bonds	Adjustment for dupli- cation	Net cash issues
	1	2	3	4	5	6	7
1897	7	24	1	0	0	0	−18
1898	−24	67	21	0	0	0	−112
1899	127	149	0	0	0	0	−22
1900	77	248	−3	0	0	0	−168
1901	100	113	0	0	5	0	−18
1902	201	29	0	0	19	0	153
1903	164	110	0	0	26	0	28
1904	152	128	0	0	35	0	−11
1905	176	148	0	0	43	0	−15
1906	376	135	0	0	20	0	221
1907	253	120	2	0	7	0	124
1908	314	109	0	2	9	0	194
1909	408	64	−5	0	43	0	306
1910	438	58	−13	5	32	0	356
1911	−33	119	−8	0	37	0	−181
1912	416	79	0	0	28	0	309
1913	22	−89	0	0	21	0	90
1914	156	39	0	46	20	0	51
1915	85	43	4	8	18	0	12
1916	−7	−153	12	2	21	0	111
1917	126	79	27	0	11	0	9
1918	−206	−381	0	0	0	0	175
1919	−52	−9	−13	0	21	0	−51
1920	45	106	20	0	4	0	−85
1921	56	−11	9	102	4	60	12
1922	27	−17	5	0	9	0	30
1923	92	5	14	50	9	23	37
1924	146	246	−17	0	2	0	−85
1925	67	−12	0	2	0	0	77
1926	−42	−10	0	6	0	0	−38
1927	119	221	6	10	0	0	−118
1928	128	−136	20	0	0	0	244
1929	54	−65	0	0	0	0	119
1930	157	172	7	10	0	0	−32
1931	22	56	6	0	0	0	−40
1932	35	71	0	2	0	0	−38
1933	−6	−127	−12	0	0	0	133
1934	−71	63	0	0	0	0	−134
1935	−7	16	−3	0	0	0	−20
1936	12	−85	0	15	0	0	82
1937	66	92	0	0	0	0	−26
1938	−23	12	0	0	0	0	−35
1939	−15	6	0	0	0	0	−21
1940	−23	−35	−6	0	0	0	18
1941	−172	−213	−114	0	0	−32	123
1942	50	57	0	0	0	0	−7
1943	−34	−27	−18	1	0	0	10
1944	−46	−8	14	0	17	0	−69
1945	−38	−102	78	0	7	0	−21
1946	−12	24	18	0	0	0	−54
1947	−193	−209	−128	19	0	−57	68
1948	12	08	63	0	0	0	−149
1949	−24	−28	−6	0	0	−9	1

CASH ISSUES OF BELL SYSTEM CAPITAL STOCK
1897 to 1921

$ mill.

Year	Changes in total stock outstanding	Stock issued for conversion purposes	Cash issues of capital stock	Year	Changes in total stock outstanding	Stock issued for conversion purposes	Cash issues of capital stock
	1	2	3		1	2	3
1897	4	0	4	1910	−6	7	−13
1898	2	0	2	1911	40	14	26
1899	9	0	9	1912	14	3	11
				1913	5	10	−5
1900	27	0	27	1914	−2	0	−2
1901	12	0	12				
1902	44	0	44	1915	54	36	18
1903	32	0	32	1916	26	15	11
1904	11	0	11	1917	42	1	41
				1918	1	0	1
1905	6	0	6	1919	−1	0	−1
1906	25	0	25				
1907	35	0	35	1920	0	1	−1
1908	14	0	14	1921	123	15	108
1909	76	76	0				

Column 1 – 1897–1899: Federal Communications Commission, *Report on the American Telephone and Telegraph Co., Corporate Financial History*, 1935, exhibit 1360A, table 18. This column is the sum of first differences of par value of capital stock outstanding and the additional premium on that stock.

1900–1921: *Annual Report to the Stockholders, American Telephone and Telegraph Co.*, 1900–1921. Col. 1 was constructed in the same manner for this period as for 1896–1899. Prior to 1922 capital stock represents, along with common stock outstanding, about $20 million of preferred stock outstanding of American Telephone and Telegraph Co. subsidiaries. Basic 1900 figure was decreased by $26 million to account for exchange of $52 million American Telephone and Telegraph Co. stock for $26 million of American Bell Telephone Co. stock. Basic 1918 figure was decreased by $8 million to account for exchange of 60,000 shares of American Telephone and Telegraph Co. stock at $125 for stock of Bell Telephone Co. of Pennsylvania, acquired from New York Telephone Co.

Column 2 – 1897–1899: Estimated at less than $1 million.

1900–1921: Federal Communications Commission, *Report of the American Telephone and Telegraph Co., Corporate Financial History*, 1935, exhibit 1360B, schedule 27A and 27B.

Column 3 – 1897–1921: Col. 1 minus col. 2.

Column 1 – 1922–1941: *Annual Report to the Stockholders, American Telephone and Telegraph Co., 1922–1941.*
This column is the sum of the first differences of the par of the common stock outstanding and of the premiums thereon.

 From 1936 on, two companies (Southern New England Telephone Co. and Cincinnati and Suburban Bell Telephone Co.), of which American Telephone and Telegraph Co. owned less than half of the outstanding stock, were eliminated from the totals. Hence, amount of stock of these companies not held by American Telephone and Telegraph Co. was added back to the change in reported totals between 1935 and 1936.

 In 1930 $30 million has been deducted from reported change to take account of the exchange of $15 million par value American Telephone and Telegraph Co. stock at a premium of $15 million for common stock of Teletype Corporation.

1942–1947: Federal Communications Commission, *Statistics of the Communications Industries in the U.S.*, 1942–1947, table 25. This column was constructed in the same way for this period as for 1922–1941.

1948–1949: Derived from data in *Moody's Public Utilities*, 1948, 1949, 1950.

Column 2 – 1922–1935: Federal Communications Commission, *Report on the American Telephone and Telegraph Co., Corporate Financial History*, 1935, exhibit 1360B, schedule 27A and 27B. All of this stock was issued at a premium but, since total par value of stock issued in conversion is substantially equal to par value of bonds converted, premium was evidently paid in cash and is included in col. 1.

1936–1947: All positive changes in American Telephone and Telegraph Co. stock outstanding were considered to be for conversion purposes. (These changes were obtained from same source as col. 1 and treated in the same manner.) Thus, only increases in capital stock of Bell system operating subsidiaries and premiums on conversions were considered to represent a public cash investment in capital stock during this period.

1948–1949: Estimated as total of decline in outstanding convertible debentures as reported in *Moody's Public Utilities*, 1948, 1949, 1950.

Column 3 – 1922–1949: Col. 1 minus col. 2.

Column 4 – 1922–1949: Same sources and treatment as col. 1.

Column 5 – 1922–1949: Same sources and treatment as col. 1.

Column 6 – 1922–1949: Sum of cols. 3–5.

V-31

TABLE V–31

Column 1 – 1890: Result of applying 1922 ratio of stock of operating to total electric railways to the 1890 figure (cf. *Census of Electric Railways*, 1902) for all electric railways.

1902–1932: Sum of cols. 2 and 3.

Columns 2 and 3 – 1890: Col. 1 split in same ratio as in 1902.

1902, 1907, 1912, 1917: The 1922 ratio between operating railways (cf. *Census of Electric Railways*) was applied to the figure for total electric railways to obtain a value for operating electric railways.

1922, 1927, 1932: *Census of Electric Railways*, 1932, p. 63.

Column 4 – 1890: Same procedure as col. 1.

1902–1932: Same procedure as col. 2.

CASH ISSUES OF BELL SYSTEM CAPITAL STOCK
1922 to 1949

V-30

$ mill.

Year	Change in common stock outstanding	Stock issued for conversion purposes	Cash issues of common stock	Change in preferred stock outstanding	Change in installment on capital stock	Cash issues of capital stock
	1	2	3	4	5	6
1922	155	24	131	39	13	183
1923	39	6	33	15	2	50
1924	163	8	155	29	11	195
1925	51	6	45	2	–1	46
1926	144	0	144	4	21	169
1927	52	0	52	1	–10	43
1928	200	0	200	0	19	219
1929	36	0	36	0	14	50
1930	665	206	459	–1	39	497
1931	78	0	78	–12	–39	27
1932	–3	0	–3	0	–58	–61
1933	0	0	0	0	–1	–1
1934	0	0	0	0	–3	–3
1935	–1	0	–1	0	–5	–6
1936	4	0	4	0	–4	0
1937	0	0	0	–32	0	–32
1938	0	0	0	–22	0	–22
1939	0	0	0	0	0	0
1940	0	0	0	–5	0	–5
1941	1	0	1	–20	0	–19
1942	2	0	2	2	0	4
1943	17	11	6	0	0	6
1944	81	59	22	–3	0	19
1945	109	78	31	0	0	31
1946	65	44	21	0	0	21
1947	133	88	45	0	8	53
1948	265	176	89	0	76	165
1949	253	172	81	0	87	168

CAPITALIZATION OF OPERATING ELECTRIC RAILWAYS
Selected Years: 1890 to 1932

V-31

$ mill.

End of year	Total capital stock	Common stock	Preferred stock	Funded debt	End of year	Total capital stock	Common stock	Preferred stock	Funded debt
	1	2	3	4		1	2	3	4
1890	226	207	19	122	1917	1 585	1 352	233	2 098
1902	872	798	74	683	1922	1 520	1 238	282	2 134
1907	1 380	1 194	186	1 153	1927	1 452	1 132	320	2 078
1912	1 560	1 323	237	1 601	1932	1 315	974	341	1 953

TABLE V-32

V-32

Column 1 – Sum of cols. 2 and 3.

Column 2 – Obtained from analysis, mostly based on information in security manuals, of changes in the amount of stock outstanding of all (about fifty) electric railway companies having a capitalization of $10 million or more in 1902 according to *Census of Electric Railways*.

Column 3 – Derived by allocating equally through periods 1897–1902 and 1903–1907, 40 percent of period totals of change in amount of stock outstanding of smaller companies. Estimates for change in capitalization of smaller companies were obtained by subtracting from changes in the figures for all companies as given in *Census of Electric Railways* (cf. Table V-31), the amounts of changes in capital stock outstanding of large companies obtained from the special analysis. Percentage is based on relation of cash to total issues for large companies.

Columns 4 to 6: Same procedure as for cols. 1, 2, and 3, respectively, except that in col. 6 a ratio of 50 percent is used.

V-33

TABLE V-33

Column 1 – 1902: *Census of Electric Light & Power Companies*, 1902, p. 16.
1907, 1912, 1917: *Census of Electric Light & Power Companies*, 1917, p. 103.
1922: *Census of Electric Light & Power Companies*, 1922, p. 115.
1927: *Census of Electric Light & Power Companies*, 1927, p. 37.
1932: *Census of Electric Light & Power Companies*, 1932, p. 23.
1937: *Census of Electric Light & Power Companies*, 1937, p. 14.
1938: *Statistics of Electric Utilities in the U.S.*, 1948.

Columns 2 and 3 – 1902, 1907, 1912, 1917, 1922: Same source as col. 1.
1927, 1932, 1937: Estimated as percentage of col. 1, the percentage linearly interpolated between 1922 and 1938 percentages.
1938: Same source as col. 1.

Column 4 – 1902–1938: Same source as col. 1.

V-34

TABLE V-34

Column 1 – 1903–1904: Stock issues of $1 million and over of public utility operating companies from General Investment News columns in weekly issues of the *Commercial and Financial Chronicle*.
1905–1937: Same as above from monthly lists of capital flotations in *New York Journal of Commerce and Financial Bulletin*, 1905–1920 and in *Commercial and Financial Chronicle*, 1921–1937 (each issue examined to separate operating company issues from holding company issues); plus stock issues sold directly under customer ownership plans from *Moody's Public Utilities* and from *Electrical World* (cf. Table V-41, cols. 3 and 4).

Columns 2 and 3 – 1903–1937: Same sources as col. 1. From 1905–1920, each issue had to be classified as preferred or common by reference to *Moody's* or *Poor's Manuals, Public Utilities*.

Column 4 – 1918–1937: From Table V-25, col. 2.

Columns 5 and 6 – 1903–1937: Cols. 1 and 2, respectively, minus col. 4.

Column 7 – 1903–1937: Same as col. 3.

Column 8 – 1903–1937: Differences between stock outstanding in successive quinquennial reports of *Census of Electrical Industries-Electric Light and Power* (cf. Table V-33).

Columns 9 and 10 – 1903–1922: Same source as col. 8.
1923–1937: Distribution of col. 8 between preferred and common stock based on interpolation of ratios for 1922 (above) and 1937 (from *Statistics of Electrical Utilities in the United States*, 1948).

514

CASH ISSUES OF ELECTRIC RAILWAYS: 1897 to 1907

$ mill.

Year	Common stock			Preferred stock			Year	Common stock			Preferred stock		
	Total issues	Large issues	Small issues	Total issues	Large issues	Small issues		Total issues	Large issues	Small issues	Total issues	Large issues	Small issues
	1	2	3	4	5	6		1	2	3	4	5	6
1897	14	0	14	1	0	1	1903	33	8	25	6	0	6
1898	19	5	14	1	0	1	1904	25	0	25	6	0	6
1899	38	24	14	13	12	1							
							1905	25	0	25	6	0	6
1900	46	32	14	1	0	1	1906	56	31	25	11	5	6
1901	43	29	14	1	0	1	1907	25	0	25	6	0	6
1902	88	74	14	1	0	1							

CAPITALIZATION OF PRIVATELY OWNED ELECTRIC LIGHT AND POWER COMPANIES; SELECTED YEARS: 1902 to 1938

$ mill.

End of year	Total capital stock	Common stock	Preferred stock	Funded debt	End of year	Total capital stock	Common stock	Preferred stock	Funded debt
	1	2	3	4		1	2	3	4
1902	373	349	24	255	1927	5 095	3 698	1397	5 310
1907	741	666	75	601	1932	6 936	4 847	2 089	6 888
1912	1 155	978	177	898	1937	6 572	4 416	2 156	7 381
1917	1 550	1 279	271	1 297	1938	6 376	4 284	2 092	7 060
1922	2 111	1 589	522	2 249					

COMPARISON OF NET STOCK ISSUES OF OPERATING ELECTRIC LIGHT AND POWER COMPANIES WITH CHANGES IN STOCK OUTSTANDING

Selected Period Totals: 1903 to 1937

$ mill.

Year	Issues			Preferred stock retirements	Net issues			Change in outstanding		
	Total	Preferred	Common		Total	Preferred	Common	Total	Preferred	Common
	1	2	3	4	5	6	7	8	9	10
1903–07	153	31	122	–	153	31	122	368	51	317
1908–12	215	42	173	–	215	42	173	414	102	312
1913–17	148	90	58	–	148	90	58	395	94	301
1918–22	490	346	144	91	399	255	144	561	310	251
1923–27	2 076	1 487	589	237	1 839	1 250	589	2 984	1 123	1 861
1928–32	1 276	681	595	548	728	133	595	1 841	655	1 186
1933–37	164	145	19	268	–104	–123	19	–364	–128	–236
1903–17	516	163	353	–	516	163	353	1 177	247	930
1918–37	4 006	2 659	1 347	1 144	2 862	1 515	1 347	5 022	1 960	3 062
1903–37	4 522	2 822	1 700	1 144	3 378	1 678	1 700	6 199	2 207	3 992

Column 1 – 1897–1949: Derived from common stock outstanding at year-end from *Annual Reports of the Comptroller of the Currency*, 1896–1948, e.g. 1948 volume, p. 129. June data were interpolated to obtain the estimates for Dec. 31 for all years to 1940, except 1926–1930 and 1931–1934. For former period extrapolation was based on data for the 150 largest banks. For 1931–1934 period, linear interpolation also proved to be inadequate and freehand interpolation was applied.
        Figures cover changes in common stock of all active banks in continental United States since almost all bank preferred stock has been held by Reconstruction Finance Corporation.

Column 2 – 1897–1920: *Federal Reserve Bulletin*, Sept. 1937, p. 897, extrapolated on basis of data from the *Annual Report of the Comptroller of the Currency* on national banks going into receivership.
        1921–1938: *Federal Reserve Bulletin*, various issues, e.g. Sept. 1937, p. 897.

Column 3 – 1897–1925: Ignored because of absence of information.
        1926–1941: *Statistics of Income, Source Book.*
        1942–1949: Figures for national banks from the *Annual Report of the Comptroller of the Currency,* supplemented by Federal Reserve Board estimates.

Column 4 – 1897–1948: Figures derived from the 150 largest banks as reported in *Moody's Manual.*
        1949: Not estimated, but assumed to be negligible.

Column 5 – 1897–1949: The sum of cols. 1, 2, and 4 minus col. 3.

Column 6 – 1897–1948: Same source as col. 4.
        1949: Not estimated, but assumed to be negligible.

Column 7 – 1897–1948: Col. 6 plus 10 percent of that part of col. 5 not accounted for in col. 6.
        1949: Not estimated, but assumed to be negligible.

Column 8 – 1897–1949: Col. 5 plus col. 7. For the years 1897, 1898, 1931–1939, and 1942 where col. 8 would be negative it was assumed that cols. 2 and especially 4 were understated sufficiently to balance the negative entry in col. 5 plus col. 7 as it unlikely that substantial amounts of stock have been retired for cash.

Column 1 – 1897–1949: *Spectator Life Insurance Yearbook*, 1896–1949.

Column 2 – 1931–1938: *Spectator Life Insurance Yearbook*, 1931–1939.

Column 3 – 1897–1925: Derived from a sample of large companies (over $100 million assets in 1948) examined in *Moody's Manuals.*
        1926–1946: *Statistics of Income, Source Book.*
        1947–1949: Assumed same as 1946.

Column 4 – 1897–1949: Col. 1 plus col. 2 minus col. 3.

Column 5 – 1897–1949: Same as col. 4 except that where negative values appear in col. 4 it was assumed that col. 2 was understated sufficiently to balance the negative entry in col. 4 as it is unlikely that substantial amounts of stock have been redeemed for cash. Premiums are ignored because of insufficient information.

CASH ISSUES OF COMMON STOCK OF COMMERCIAL BANKS
1897 to 1949

$ mill.

Year	Change in stock outstanding (par value)	Common stock eliminated through receivership	Stock dividends	Write-downs of common stock outstanding (sample)	Inferred new issues	Premiums		Cash issues
						Sample	Estimated total	
	1	2	3	4	5	6	7	8
1897	−30	9	−	0	−21	0	0	0
1898	−19	4	−	0	−15	0	0	0
1899	16	4	−	0	20	0	2	22
1900	51	4	−	0	55	3	8	63
1901	89	4	−	0	93	.0	9	102
1902	123	4	−	0	127	30	42	169
1903	95	2	−	0	97	10	19	116
1904	71	9	−	0	80	9	17	97
1905	86	5	−	0	91	0	9	100
1906	114	5	−	0	119	0	13	132
1907	96	4	−	0	100	0	10	110
1908	55	19	−	0	74	0	7	81
1909	61	7	−	0	68	4	10	78
1910	76	7	−	0	83	4	11	94
1911	66	5	−	0	71	0	7	78
1912	72	4	−	0	76	4	10	86
1913	60	5	−	0	65	0	6	71
1914	25	9	−	3	37	0	4	41
1915	31	9	−	0	40	0	4	44
1916	54	2	−	0	56	1	5	61
1917	75	2	−	0	77	6	13	90
1918	77	2	−	0	79	21	29	108
1919	174	4	−	0	178	6	21	199
1920	225	12	−	0	237	17	37	274
1921	105	24	−	0	129	6	18	147
1922	82	14	−	0	96	22	29	125
1923	82	22	−	0	104	0	10	114
1924	58	28	−	0	86	1	9	95
1925	89	25	−	0	114	30	39	153
1926	90	34	28	0	96	19	31	127
1927	163	25	103	0	85	94	100	185
1928	171	20	23	0	168	175	195	363
1929	386	33	103	9	325	790	814	1 139
1930	6	112	14	0	104	17	28	132
1931	−200	208	38	0	−30	0	0	0
1932	−450	108	2	0	−344	0	0	0
1933	−450	427	1	2	−22	1	2	0
1934	−76	4	5	70	−7	0	0	0
1935	−76	2	3	20	−57	0	0	0
1936	−13	2	14	5	−20	6	0	0
1937	26	1	49	1	−21	0	0	0
1938	−3	2	4	0	−5	0	0	0
1939	−7	−	5	0	−12	0	0	0
1940	3	−	3	4	4	1	1	5
1941	15	−	13	0	2	1	1	3
1942	16	−	17	0	−1	2	0	0
1943	62	−	43	0	19	9	11	30
1944	90	−	46	1	45	36	39	84
1945	173	−	98	0	75	29	36	111
1946	160	−	35	0	125	17	27	152
1947	96	−	42	0	54	3	8	62
1948	83	−	42	0	41	5	9	50
1949	135	−	99	−	36	−	−	36

CASH ISSUES OF STOCK OF LIFE INSURANCE COMPANIES
1897 to 1949

$ mill.

Year	Change in stock outstanding (par value)	Receivership losses	Stock dividends	Inferred new issues	Cash offerings	Year	Change in stock outstanding (par value)	Receivership losses	Stock dividends	Inferred new issues	Cash offerings
	1	2	3	4	5		1	2	3	4	5
1897	0	–	0	0	0	1923	17	–	5	12	12
1898	0	–	0	0	0	1924	1	–	1	0	0
1899	0	–	0	0	0	1925	11	–	0	11	11
1900	1	–	0	1	1	1926	22	–	0	22	22
1901	1	–	0	1	1	1927	4	–	0	4	4
1902	0	–	0	0	0	1928	17	–	1	16	16
1903	2	–	0	2	2	1929	14	–	2	12	12
1904	1	–	0	1	1	1930	13	–	1	12	12
1905	2	–	0	2	2	1931	–7	2	1	–6	0
1906	4	–	0	4	4	1932	–8	1	0	–7	0
1907	3	–	0	3	3	1933	–12	6	0	–6	0
1908	3	–	0	3	3	1934	–1	1	1	–1	0
1909	5	–	0	5	5	1935	1	0	0	1	1
1910	7	–	0	7	7	1936	–6	1	0	–5	0
1911	6	–	0	6	6	1937	8	0	0	8	8
1912	4	–	0	4	4	1938	–4	1	0	–3	0
1913	1	–	0	1	1	1939	12	–	0	12	12
1914	2	–	0	2	2	1940	–1	–	0	–1	0
1915	–1	–	0	–1	0	1941	10	–	0	10	10
1916	2	–	2	0	0	1942	1	–	0	1	1
1917	1	–	0	1	1	1943	22	–	0	22	22
1918	3	–	0	3	3	1944	13	–	0	13	13
1919	3	–	0	3	3	1945	20	–	0	20	20
1920	5	–	0	5	5	1946	24	–	0	24	24
1921	8	–	1	7	7	1947	12	–	0	12	12
1922	2	–	0	2	2	1948	–7	–	0	–7	0
						1949	32	–	0	32	32

TABLE V–37

Column 1 – 1897–1949: *Spectator Insurance Yearbook, Fire and Marine Volume* and *Casualty and Surety Volume,* 1896–1949.

Column 2 – 1897–1925: Derived from a sample of large insurance companies (over $25 million assets) examined in *Moody's Manual,* 1948, 1930.
1926–1949: *Statistics of Income, Source Book.*

Column 3 – 1897–1949: Same sources as col. 2.

Column 4 – 1897–1949: Same sources as col. 2.

Column 5 – 1897–1949: Col. 1 minus col. 2 plus col. 3 minus col. 4.

Column 6 – 1897–1949: Same sources as col. 2.

Column 7 – 1897–1949: Col. 6 plus 10 percent of the part of col. 5 not taken into account by col. 6.

Column 8 – 1897–1949: Col. 5 plus col. 7. For the years 1931, 1932, 1935, 1937, 1941, and 1942, where a negative entry would appear in col. 8, the figures for write-down and receivership were considered to be understated to an extent sufficient to offset the excess of col. 1 over col. 3 minus col. 2.

CASH ISSUES OF STOCK
OF CASUALTY, SURETY, FIRE, AND MARINE INSURANCE COMPANIES: 1897 to 1949

$ mill.

Year	Change in outstanding (par value)	Stock dividends	Write-downs	Write-ups	Inferred new issues	Premiums		Net cash issues
						Sample	Estimated total	
	1	2	3	4	5	6	7	8
1897	1	0	0	0	1	0	0	1
1898	0	0	0	0	0	0	0	0
1899	3	0	0	0	3	0	0	3
1900	1	0	0	0	1	0	0	1
1901	5	0	0	0	5	0	0	5
1902	7	0	0	0	7	0	1	8
1903	3	0	0	0	3	0	0	3
1904	1	0	0	0	1	0	0	1
1905	7	0	0	0	7	0	1	8
1906	11	1	1	0	11	0	1	12
1907	12	0	0	0	12	0	1	13
1908	7	0	0	0	7	0	1	8
1909	2	0	0	0	2	0	0	2
1910	9	1	0	0	8	1	2	10
1911	4	0	0	0	4	1	1	5
1912	3	0	0	0	3	0	0	3
1913	11	4	0	0	7	0	0	7
1914	2	1	0	0	1	0	0	1
1915	5	1	0	0	4	1	1	5
1916	8	7	0	0	1	1	1	2
1917	7	1	0	0	6	1	1	7
1918	22	0	0	0	22	2	4	26
1919	29	0	0	0	29	4	6	35
1920	18	0	0	0	18	1	2	20
1921	13	1	0	0	12	0	1	13
1922	43	16	0	0	27	2	4	31
1923	23	6	0	0	17	2	3	20
1924	33	2	0	0	31	1	4	35
1925	47	3	0	0	44	14	17	61
1926	36	14	0	0	22	18	19	41
1927	62	10	0	0	52	20	24	76
1928	112	15	0	0	97	31	39	136
1929	68	20	0	0	48	26	30	78
1930	8	1	0	0	7	8	8	15
1931	−57	4	14	0	−47	5	5	0
1932	−187	0	93	0	−94	4	4	0
1933	−7	0	4	0	−3	7	7	4
1934	6	1	0	0	5	1	1	6
1935	1	4	0	0	−3	0	0	0
1936	13	7	0	1	5	0	0	5
1937	−3	8	0	0	−11	0	0	0
1938	6	2	0	0	4	0	0	4
1939	12	1	0	6	5	4	5	10
1940	9	0	1	0	10	3	4	14
1941	5	9	0	0	−4	0	0	0
1942	0	2	0	2	−4	0	0	0
1943	24	7	0	8	9	0	1	10
1944	37	0	0	2	35	0	3	38
1945	47	6	0	26	15	9	10	25
1946	17	0	0	3	14	0	1	15
1947	25	0	0	1	24	16	17	41
1948	18	–	–	–	18	–	–	18
1949	46	–	–	–	46	–	–	46

V-38   TABLE V-38

Columns 1 and 4 – 1927–1936: *Investment Trusts and Investment Companies, Part II, Statistical Survey of Investment Trusts and Investment Companies*, p. 190.
 1937–1941: Friend and Natrella, *Individuals' Saving*, part II, table 12. All sales attributed to open-end companies. Figures for 1937 may contain sales of face-amount installment certificates, which may be estimated at about $40 million; their repurchases are estimated at about $13 million.
 1942–1949: Securities and Exchange Commission, *Statistical Bulletin*, various issues. Data for closed-end companies in col. 4 excludes transactions of investment-holding companies, obtained from Securities and Exchange Commission files.

Column 2 – 1927–1936: *Investment Trusts and Investment Companies, Part II*, p. 265. Covers 40 open-end companies which accounted for 96 percent of sales by all open-end companies during the period.
 1937–1941: Friend and Natrella, *op. cit.*, table 13, less col. 5.
 1942–1949: Securities and Exchange Commission, *Statistical Bulletin*, various issues.

Column 3 – 1927–1949: Col. 1 minus col. 2.

Column 5 – 1927–1935: *Investment Trusts and Investment Companies, Part II*, pp. 258–261 (excluding investment-holding companies).
 1936–1941: Same source and procedure as col. 6.
 1942–1949: Securities and Exchange Commission, *Statistical Bulletin*, various issues. Excludes data for investment-holding companies obtained from Securities and Exchange Commission files.

Column 6 – 1927–1949: Col. 4 minus col. 5. For 1936–1941 obtained on basis of data for 1933–1935 and 1942.

V-39   TABLE V-39

Column 1 – 1927–1936: *Investment Trusts and Investment Companies, Part II, Statistical Survey of Investment Trusts and Investment Companies*, p. 190, table 60, col. 1.
 1937–1941: Table V-38, col. 4.
 1942–1949: Securities and Exchange Commission, *Statistical Bulletin*, various issues; transactions of investment-holding companies, obtained from Securities and Exchange Commission files, excluded.

Column 2 – 1927–1935: Estimated from data in *Investment Trusts and Investment Companies, Part II*, p. 190, table 60, and p. 195, table 61. Sales of "bonds and units of bonds and stocks" from table 61 for 1931 through 1935 were considered as entirely by closed-end investment companies. For each year from 1927 through 1930, totals shown in the same table were multiplied by 0.644, the ratio of total sales of bonds of these companies for 1927–1935 (given in the same table as $220.8 million) reduced by sales of bonds for 1931–1935 ($8.6 million) to bond sales by both closed-end and holding companies ($338.0 million) reduced by sales for 1931–1935 ($8.6 million).
 1936–1941: For 1936, estimated in same proportion of total sales as for 1935. No bond sales, 1937–1941.
 1942–1949: Same source as col. 1.

Column 3 – 1927–1935: Col. 1 minus col. 2.
 1936–1941: For 1936, estimated as same proportion of total sales as in 1935. No stock sales 1937–1941.
 1942–1949: Same source as col. 1.

Column 4 – 1927–1935: *Investment Trusts and Investment Companies, Part II*, pp. 258–261, tables 74–77 (excluding transactions of investment-holding companies).
 1936–1941: Table V-38, col. 5.
 1942–1949: Same source as col. 1.

Columns 5, 6 and 7 – 1927–1935: Same source as col. 4.
 1936–1941: Estimated as same proportion of total bond and stock purchases as in 1935.
 1942–1949: Same source as col. 1.

Column 8 – 1927–1949: Col. 1 minus col. 4.

Column 9 – 1927–1949: Col. 2 minus col. 5.

Column 10 – 1927–1949: Col. 3 minus sum of cols. 6 and 7.

ISSUE AND RETIREMENT OF OWN SECURITIES
BY MANAGEMENT INVESTMENT COMPANIES: 1927 to 1949

$ mill.

Year	Open-end companies			Closed-end companies			Year	Open-end companies			Closed-end companies		
	Sales	Repur-chases	Net sales	Sales	Repur-chases	Net sales		Sales	Repur-chases	Net sales	Sales	Repur-chases	Net sales
	1	2	3	4	5	6		1	2	3	4	5	6
1927	20	2	18	168	3	165	1939	60	25	35	0	15	−15
1928	40	8	32	540	3	537	1940	50	35	15	0	15	−15
1929	89	21	68	1 567	63	1 504	1941	50	35	15	0	15	−15
1930	29	15	14	27	138	−111	1942	66	25	41	1	16	−15
1931	22	12	10	5	75	−70	1943	113	52	61	6	25	−19
1932	26	8	18	2	44	−42	1944	168	73	95	21	25	−4
1933	82	12	70	2	17	−15	1945	290	111	179	22	69	−47
1934	69	19	50	1	13	−12	1946	362	140	222	22	69	−47
1935	86	17	69	10	27	−17	1947	264	89	175	9	18	−9
1936	123	29	94	15	15	0	1948	273	128	145	1	22	−21
1937	200	50	150	0	30	−30	1949	376	105	271	2	6	−4
1938	60	25	35	0	15	−15							

TRANSACTIONS IN OWN SECURITIES
BY CLOSED-END MANAGEMENT INVESTMENT COMPANIES
1927 to 1949

$ mill.

Year	Sales			Purchases				Net sales		
	Total	Bonds	Stocks	Total	Bonds	Preferred stock	Common stock	Total	Bonds	Stocks
	1	2	3	4	5	6	7	8	9	10
1927	168	49	119	3	3	0	0	165	46	119
1928	540	75	465	3	1	1	1	537	74	463
1929	1 567	77	1 490	63	2	52	9	1 504	75	1 429
1930	27	11	16	138	11	102	25	−111	0	−111
1931	5	0	5	75	25	37	13	−70	−25	−45
1932	2	0	2	44	23	13	8	−42	−23	−19
1933	2	2	0	17	4	8	5	−15	−2	−13
1934	1	0	1	13	2	9	2	−12	−2	−10
1935	10	6	4	27	9	16	2	−17	−3	−14
1936	15	10	5	15	5	10	0	0	5	−5
1937	0	0	0	30	10	20	0	−30	−10	−20
1938	0	0	0	15	5	10	0	−15	−5	−10
1939	0	0	0	15	5	10	0	−15	−5	−10
1940	0	0	0	15	5	10	0	−15	−5	−10
1941	0	0	0	15	5	10	0	−15	−5	−10
1942	1	1	0	16	6	10	0	−15	−5	−10
1943	6	6	0	25	16	9	0	−19	−10	−9
1944	21	19	2	25	19	6	0	−4	0	−4
1945	22	16	6	69	50	19	0	−47	−34	−13
1946	22	19	3	69	33	36	0	−47	−14	−33
1947	9	7	2	18	7	11	0	−9	0	−9
1948	1	1	0	22	2	20	0	−21	−1	−20
1949	2	0	2	6	1	5	0	−4	−1	−3

Column 1 – 1917–1949: Sum of cols. 2, 3, 5–7 minus col. 4.

Column 2 – 1927–1933: Issues of common stock excluding intercompany transactions. Data given in Securities and Exchange Commission, *Investment Trusts and Investment Companies, Part II, Statistical Survey of Investment Trusts and Investment Companies*, p. 195. Units of common and preferred stocks were divided by applying percentages obtained from a tabulation of Saving Study cards covering, by amount, about one-half of such issues by investment companies. From the Securities and Exchange Commission series for bonds and units of bonds and stocks, figures for bond sales as estimated in Table V–39 were subtracted and the remainder was assumed to consist of common stock. Data for intercompany transactions were split between common and preferred stock on basis of a percentage distribution of cumulated amounts of common and preferred stock issues.
    1934–1949: From Table V-16, col. 8.

Column 3 – 1927–1933: From Table V-38, col. 3.
    1934–1949: Included in col. 2.

Column 4 – 1927–1933: *Investment Trusts . . .*, p. 233.
    1934–1949: From Table V-13, col. 6.

Column 5 – 1927–1930: *Investment Trusts . . .*, Roughly same percentage of table 60, col. 3 as col. 1 of table 61 is of table 60, cols. 1 and 2.
    1931–1936: *Investment Trusts . . .*, Assumed as one-half of table 60, col. 3.
    1937–1942: Negligible.
    1943–1949: From Securities and Exchange Commission file of quarterly reports.

Column 6 – 1927–1949: Net proceeds minus redemptions (Table V-70, col. 1 minus col. 2).

Column 7 – 1917–1949: Change in total assets minus change in certificate loans (Table V-72, change in col. 1 minus change in col. 10).

Column 8 – 1927–1933: See note to col. 2.
    1934–1949: From Table V-16, col. 7.

CASH ISSUES BY INVESTMENT COMPANIES
OF STOCK REPRESENTING INDIVIDUALS' SAVING: 1917 to 1949

$ mill.

Year	Common stock							Preferred stock
	Total	Closed-end and management investment companies	Open-end investment companies	Repurchases by closed-end and management investment companies	Unclassified companies	Fixed and semifixed investment trusts	Face amount certificates	
	1	2	3	4	5	6	7	8
1917	1	–	–	–	–	–	1	–
1918	1	–	–	–	–	–	1	–
1919	1	–	–	–	–	–	1	–
1920	2	–	–	–	–	–	2	–
1921	2	–	–	–	–	–	2	–
1922	2	–	–	–	–	–	2	–
1923	3	–	–	–	–	–	3	–
1924	3	–	–	–	–	–	3	–
1925	5	–	–	–	–	–	5	–
1926	5	–	–	–	–	–	5	–
1927	101	56	18	0	4	18	5	68
1928	495	390	32	1	32	34	8	261
1929	1 561	1 219	68	19	224	61	8	540
1930	319	8	14	35	68	256	8	–77
1931	197	–9	10	16	7	196	9	–29
1932	26	–6	18	9	2	19	2	–21
1933	27	–7	70	5	3	–39	5	–4
1934	40	105	–	45	12	–39	7	26
1935	46	110	–	50	1	–28	13	28
1936	59	134	–	60	–	–36	21	34
1937	61	134	–	70	–	–25	22	33
1938	5	40	–	40	–	–18	23	10
1939	6	40	–	40	–	–5	11	10
1940	1	36	–	50	–	–7	22	9
1941	–15	40	–	50	–	–5	0	10
1942	21	54	–	36	–	–2	5	14
1943	6	90	–	70	3	–4	–13	22
1944	64	135	–	83	2	–5	15	34
1945	115	237	–	138	1	–8	23	59
1946	115	292	–	190	–3	–10	26	73
1947	131	220	–	106	4	–5	18	55
1948	87	236	–	157	0	–3	11	59
1949	188	302	–	113	0	–5	4	76

CUSTOMER OWNERSHIP SALES BY ELECTRIC LIGHT AND POWER COMPANIES
1914 to 1932

$ mill.

Year	All securities	Bonds and notes	Preferred stock	Common stock	Year	All securities	Bonds and notes	Preferred stock	Common stock
	1	2	3	4		1	2	3	4
1914	9	0	8	1	1924	254	13	215	26
1915	6	0	5	1	1925	296	15	251	30
1916	4	0	4	0	1926	247	12	198	37
1917	8	0	7	1	1927	240	12	192	36
1918	4	0	4	0	1928	170	8	128	34
1919	19	1	16	2	1929	145	7	109	29
1920	43	2	37	4	1930	135	7	115	13
1921	80	4	68	8	1931	159	8	135	16
1922	130	6	111	13	1932	18	1	15	2
1923	175	9	149	17					

Column 1 – From statistics of *Electrical World* as summarized in *Moody's Public Utilities*, 1925, p. xlv; 1930, p. xxvi; 1935, p. a25; and 1940, p. a27. Where figures for same year differ, that found in the latest manual has been used except for 1924, in which figure shown in col. 1 was regarded as most trustworthy of several ones shown.

For period before 1920 only number of shares sold is given, and values in col. 1 have been derived on assumption of an average price per share of slightly under $100, which corresponds to average of the years 1920–1924.

Columns 2 to 4 – Derived from col. 1 on assumption that proportion of bonds amounted to 5 percent; that of common stock to 10 percent (with exception of 1926–1929 when it was assumed to be 15–20 percent) and that of preferred stock to 85 percent (except from 1926–1929 when it was assumed to decline to 75–80 percent). Percentages are based on distribution for 1924, only year for which figures for three types of securities are given by the *Electrical World*.

SALE OF STOCK TO EMPLOYEES
(Treasury Stock or Newly Issued Stock): 1916 to 1932

$ mill.

Year	Total	Common	Preferred	Year	Total	Common	Preferred
	1	2	3		1	2	3
1916	10	5	5	1925	90	30	60
1917	15	5	10	1926	110	40	70
1918	15	5	10	1927	130	50	80
1919	25	10	15	1928	140	60	80
				1929	140	60	80
1920	30	10	20				
1921	30	10	20	1930	70	30	40
1922	45	15	30	1931	30	10	20
1923	60	20	40	1932	0	0	0
1924	75	25	50				

Columns 1 to 3 – Annual figures are rough estimates based on data for total sales in National Industrial Conference Board, *Employee Stock Purchase Plans in the United States*. Total figures were considerably reduced to account for probable inclusion in source of issues already in statistics of public offerings, and were slightly reduced to place totals on basis of cost to purchaser rather than market value as shown in source.

Year	Index of incorporations	Whole-sale prices	Com-bined index	Cash sales to individuals of stock of new corporations			Year	Index of incorporations	Whole-sale prices	Com-bined index	Cash sales to individuals of stock of new corporations		
				Total	Pre-ferred	Com-mon					Total	Pre-ferred	Com-mon
	1946–1948 = 100			$ mill.				1946–1948 = 100			$ mill.		
	1	2	3	4	5	6		1	2	3	4	5	6
1897	23.9	32.9	7.9	47	5	42	1923	88.0	72.1	63.4	380	38	342
1898	22.7	34.2	7.8	47	5	42	1924	81.2	69.4	56.4	338	34	304
1899	29.8	36.9	11.0	66	7	59	1925	88.0	72.4	63.7	382	38	344
1900	32.7	39.6	12.9	77	8	69	1926	85.8	71.4	61.3	368	37	331
1901	39.3	39.1	15.4	92	9	83	1927	89.1	67.6	60.2	361	36	325
1902	41.9	41.6	17.4	104	10	94	1928	95.0	67.7	64.3	386	39	347
1903	46.0	42.1	19.4	116	12	104	1929	94.5	66.6	62.9	377	38	339
1904	45.2	42.1	19.0	114	11	103	1930	84.6	61.4	51.9	311	31	280
1905	52.2	42.4	22.1	133	13	120	1931	77.4	53.3	41.3	248	25	223
1906	57.3	43.6	25.0	150	15	135	1932	75.6	48.8	36.9	221	22	199
1907	54.3	46.1	25.0	150	15	135	1933	69.5	49.3	34.3	206	21	185
1908	50.5	44.4	22.4	134	13	121	1934	59.9	54.9	32.9	197	20	177
1909	60.1	47.7	28.7	172	17	155	1935	63.2	57.3	36.2	217	22	195
1910	56.3	49.7	28.0	168	17	151	1936	62.4	57.6	35.9	215	22	193
1911	55.9	45.9	25.7	154	15	139	1937	59.8	61.6	36.8	221	22	199
1912	63.0	48.8	30.7	184	18	166	1938	51.4	57.6	29.6	178	18	160
1913	67.2	49.3	33.1	199	20	179	1939	52.5	56.8	29.8	179	18	161
1914	60.5	47.7	28.9	173	17	156	1940	50.2	57.7	29.0	174	17	157
1915	67.0	48.9	32.8	197	20	177	1941	45.4	63.1	28.6	172	17	155
1916	75.6	60.9	46.0	276	28	248	1942	28.6	69.3	19.8	119	12	107
1917	70.7	80.8	57.1	343	34	309	1943	28.3	70.5	20.0	120	12	108
1918	50.3	89.4	45.0	270	27	243	1944	34.3	71.1	24.4	146	15	131
1919	92.8	94.0	87.2	523	52	471	1945	57.4	72.0	41.3	248	25	223
1920	98.9	110.6	109.4	656	66	590	1946	116.7	82.1	95.8	575	58	517
1921	80.3	71.5	57.4	344	34	310	1947	98.9	103.9	102.8	617	62	555
1922	88.1	69.5	61.2	367	37	330	1948	84.4	114.0	96.2	577	58	519
							1949	75.1	108.9	81.8	491	49	442

Column 1 – 1897–1943: Annual median index of incorporations (Evans, G. H., *Business Incorporations in the United States, 1800–1943*) converted to 1946–1948 basis.

    1944–1945: Linked to 1943 figure and extrapolated by the number of business incorporations in New York, Illinois, Delaware, and Maine (*Survey of Current Business, Statistical Supplement,* 1949, p. 25).

    1946–1948: Linked to 1945 figure and extrapolated by number of incorporations in forty-eight states as given in Dun and Bradstreet, *Statistical Review.*

    1949: Extrapolated on basis of revised Department of Commerce figures in *Survey of Current Business,* Feb. 1950, p. S–4.

Column 2 – 1897–1912: Linked to 1913 figure and extrapolated by the index of wholesale prices of all commodities (Bureau of Labor Statistics, *Release 4924*).

    1913–1948: Wholesale price index of all commodities other than farm products (Bureau of Labor Statistics, *Release 5812*), converted to 1946–1948 basis.

    1949: Same as 1913–1948 using figures in *Survey of Current Business.*

Column 3 – 1897–1949: Col. 1 multiplied by col. 2.

Column 4 – 1897–1949: Col. 3 multiplied by $600 million, the average purchase of stock in new corporations by individuals in 1945 to 1948 as estimated on basis of data in Bridge L., "The Financing of Investment by New Firms," *Conference on Research in Business Finance.*

Column 5 – 1897–1949: Estimated at 10 percent of col. 4 on basis of relation between preferred and common stock of small corporations in period from 1931–1946, as reported in *Statistics of Income.*

Column 6 – 1897–1949: Col. 4 minus col. 5.

Column 1 – 1897: Derived from reported sales in *Commercial and Financial Chronicle*.
1898–1949: Derived from reported sales in *New York Stock Exchange Yearbook*, various issues.

Column 2 – 1897–1924: Estimated by applying commission rates (from *Important Changes in Commissions, 1856 to 1942*, multilithed release of the New York Stock Exchange) to an average of stock prices constructed by extrapolating backward, by means of Cowles Commission index of stock prices, 1871–1937 (*Historical Statistics*, p. 281), the series for the New York Stock Clearing Corporation average price of settled share published monthly in *The Exchange*, 1925–1941.
1925–1941: Commission rates applied to New York Stock Clearing Corporation average price of settled shares.
1942–1948: Commission rates applied to an extrapolation of the New York Stock Clearing Corporation series by means of Standard and Poor's index of 402 stocks (*Survey of Current Business, Statistical Supplement*, 1947, and subsequent issues).
1949: Not estimated.

Column 3 – 1897–1948: Col. 1 multiplied by col. 2.
1949: Not estimated.

Column 4 – 1897–1942: Col. 3 divided by 1.055 to adjust to stock commissions on New York Stock Exchange as computed in Table V-45, col. 3 for 1943.
1943–1949: From Table V-45, col. 3.

Column 5 – 1897–1913: Relationship assumed unchanged at 1914 value.
1914–1924: Reduced 1 percent per year from 1925 basis.
1925–1927: Assumed equal to 1928 value.
1928–1932: Estimated on basis of number of shares traded in 1928, 1929, and 1932 on the New York Stock Exchange and thirty-three other exchanges as reported in U.S. Congress, Senate, *Stock Exchange Practices*, pp. 7852–7855. (Hearings before Committee on Banking and Currency, Part 17, United States Senate, 73rd Congress, 2nd Session) and ratio of average traded value of stocks on other exchanges and on New York Stock Exchange, approximating 40 percent for the years 1935–1948. Figures for 1930 and 1931 obtained by interpolation between 1929 and 1932 values.
1933–1934: Estimated by interpolating between 1932 and 1935 values.
1935–1949: Based on ratio of average annual market value of shares sold on all exchanges and on New York Stock Exchange (*Survey of Current Business, Statistical Supplement*, 1947, and subsequent issues).

Column 6 – 1897–1949: Col. 4 multiplied by col. 5.

BROKERS' AND DEALERS' COMMISSIONS AND SPREAD ON TRANSACTIONS IN STOCKS BY DOMESTIC INDIVIDUALS: 1897 to 1949

V-44
(Part 1)

Year	Twice NYSE reported stock sales	Average commission rate	Total commissions, NYSE		Share all exchanges, NYSE	Commissions, all exchanges
			Unadjusted	Adjusted		
	Mill. shares	Cents per share	$ mill.		Percent	$ mill.
	1	2	3	4	5	6
1897	154.6	12.5	19.3	18.3	110	20
1898	225.4	12.5	28.2	26.7	110	29
1899	352.8	12.5	44.1	41.8	110	46
1900	276.8	12.5	34.6	32.8	110	36
1901	529.8	12.5	66.2	62.7	110	69
1902	373.4	12.5	46.7	44.3	110	49
1903	317.0	12.5	39.6	37.5	110	41
1904	373.8	12.5	46.7	44.3	110	49
1905	521.2	12.5	65.2	61.8	110	68
1906	564.4	12.5	70.6	66.9	110	74
1907	389.2	12.5	48.6	46.1	110	51
1908	389.0	12.5	48.6	46.1	110	51
1909	424.8	12.5	53.1	50.3	110	55
1910	327.4	12.5	40.9	38.8	110	43
1911	251.8	12.5	31.5	29.9	110	33
1912	263.0	12.5	32.9	31.2	110	34
1913	165.8	12.5	20.7	19.6	110	22
1914	94.8	12.5	11.8	11.2	110	12
1915	345.0	12.5	43.1	40.9	110	45
1916	465.2	12.5	58.2	55.2	111	62
1917	369.2	12.5	46.2	43.8	112	49
1918	286.6	12.5	35.8	33.9	113	38
1919	636.6	14.0	89.1	84.5	114	96
1920	455.2	15.0	68.3	64.7	115	74
1921	345.6	15.0	51.8	49.1	116	57
1922	521.8	15.0	78.3	74.2	117	87
1923	473.0	15.0	71.0	67.3	118	79
1924	568.0	15.0	85.2	80.8	119	96
1925	919.4	16.0	147.1	139.4	120	167
1926	903.8	17.0	153.6	145.6	120	175
1927	1 163.4	18.0	209.4	198.5	120	238
1928	1 861.8	19.0	353.7	335.3	120	402
1929	2 249.6	20.0	449.9	426.4	120	512
1930	1 621.2	17.5	283.7	268.9	117	315
1931	1 153.6	15.0	173.0	164.0	115	189
1932	850.4	12.5	106.3	100.8	113	114
1933	1 309.6	12.5	163.7	155.2	114	177
1934	647.6	12.5	81.0	76.8	115	88
1935	763.2	12.5	95.4	90.4	115	104
1936	992.0	12.5	124.0	117.5	115	135
1937	819.0	12.5	102.4	97.1	113	110
1938	595.0	14.0	83.3	79.0	111	88
1939	524.0	14.0	73.4	69.6	114	79
1940	415.2	14.0	58.1	55.1	117	64
1941	341.2	14.0	47.8	45.3	118	53
1942	251.4	14.0	35.2	33.4	116	39
1943	557.5	18.0	100.4	95.2	117	111
1944	526.2	19.0	100.0	94.4	118	111
1945	755.2	20.5	154.8	148.7	120	178
1946	733.4	21.5	157.7	150.2	115	173
1947	507.2	21.5	109.0	99.7	118	118
1948	604.4	26.0	157.1	137.0	118	162
1949	544.4	.	.	116.0	119	138

527

Column 7 – 1897–1912: Volume of odd-lot trading assumed to be of such small magnitude as not to affect total commissions on stocks significantly.

1913–1920: Estimated on basis of ratio (approximately 28 percent) of total odd-lot trading on New York Stock Exchange in 1921 to once reported round-lot trading. This ratio is assumed to have declined 1 percent per year to 20 percent in 1913.

1921–1938: Sum of purchases and sales of odd lots on New York Stock Exchange through three leading odd-lot houses (Hardy, C. H., *Odd Lot Trading on the New York Stock Exchange*, p. 118).

1939–1948: Summation of weekly data from Securities and Exchange Commission, *Annual Report*, various issues.

1949: Securities and Exchange Commission, *Statistical Bulletin*.

Column 8 – 1897–1949: Col. 7 multiplied by 12.5¢ per share.

Column 9 – 1897–1926: Estimated at 7 percent of commissions paid on stock trading on all exchanges including odd-lot differential. Figure is equal to ratio of over-the-counter and exchange sales of outstanding corporate stock for fiscal year ending June 30, 1920 and for the calendar year 1926 as estimated by Friend, Irwin (*Activity on Over-the-Counter Markets*, 1951, p. 9). This ratio has been used throughout the period as there are no other reasonably reliable data on which an estimate for other years can be based.

It should be noted, however, that the only other estimate which has been found points to a substantially higher ratio for over-the-counter trading. Professor Hollander's estimates for 1910 ("Bank Loans and Stock Exchange Speculation," *Publications of the National Monetary Commission*, vol. xx, part v, 1911, p. 23) lead to the conclusion that stock trading on exchanges other than New York Stock Exchange and on the over-the-counter market amounted to at least 37 percent of the volume and 42 percent of the value of trading on New York Stock Exchange. Allowing 10 percent of New York Stock Exchange total for other exchanges (cf. col. 5), these estimates indicate a ratio of over-the-counter to exchange trading of slightly less than 30 percent. Since it is most unlikely that the ratio of over-the-counter trading would have declined so sharply between 1910 and 1920 it has been felt advisable to disregard Professor Hollander's admittedly rough data.

1927–1949: Assumed to be equal to the ratios of over-the-counter to exchange sales of outstanding corporate stock as estimated by Friend for the years 1929, 1935, 1937, 1939, 1946, 1948, and 1949 and to values obtained by linear interpolation for intervening years. The ratio of over-the-counter spreads to stock exchange commissions (including odd-lot differential), it is true, should be somewhat larger than these figures because the proportion of the over-the-counter spread to value of transactions is higher than the corresponding rate on stock exchange transactions and the proportion of over-the-counter transactions is higher for bonds than for stocks. On the other hand the proportion of transactions between dealers is higher in the over-the-counter market and the volume of stock exchange trading on which Friend's ratios are based include customers' odd-lot transactions twice (*op. cit.*, p. 12). In the absence of quantitative information on these four factors it has been assumed that they would approximately cancel in their effect on the ratio.

Column 10 – 1897–1949: Col. 9 multiplied by sum of cols. 6 and 8.

Column 11 – 1897–1949: Sum of cols. 6, 8, and 10.

Column 12 – 1897–1923: Estimated at 95 percent of col. 11.

1924–1928: Estimated to have declined from 95 in 1923 to 85 percent in 1928 to reflect increasing importance of trading by foreign customers and investment companies.

1929–1935: Estimated to have risen from 85 in 1929 and 1930 to 90 percent in 1935 of col. 11.

1936–1949: Estimated at 90 percent of col. 11.

Year	Odd-lot differential		Over-the-counter trading spread		Commissions and spread	
	NYSE odd-lot volume	Differential			Total	Individuals
	Mill. shares	$ mill.	Percent	\$ mill.	\$ mill.	
	7	8	9	10	11	12
1897	–	–	7	1	21	20
1898	–	–	7	2	31	29
1899	–	–	7	3	49	46
1900	–	–	7	3	39	37
1901	–	–	7	5	74	70
1902	–	–	7	3	52	49
1903	–	–	7	3	44	42
1904	–	–	7	3	52	49
1905	–	–	7	5	73	69
1906	–	–	7	5	79	75
1907	–	–	7	4	55	52
1908	–	–	7	4	55	52
1909	–	–	7	4	59	56
1910	–	–	7	3	46	44
1911	–	–	7	2	35	33
1912	–	–	7	2	36	34
1913	16.6	2.1	7	2	26	25
1914	10.0	1.2	7	1	14	13
1915	38.0	4.8	7	3	53	50
1916	53.5	6.7	7	5	74	70
1917	44.3	5.5	7	4	59	56
1918	35.8	4.5	7	3	45	43
1919	82.8	10.4	7	7	113	107
1920	61.5	7.7	7	6	88	84
1921	47.9	6.0	7	4	67	64
1922	75.0	9.4	7	7	103	98
1923	62.0	7.8	7	6	93	88
1924	69.2	8.6	7	7	112	104
1925	103.8	13.0	7	13	193	176
1926	103.7	13.0	7	13	201	179
1927	133.5	16.7	10	26	281	244
1928	229.2	28.6	13	56	487	414
1929	296.8	37.1	16	88	637	541
1930	216.4	27.1	16	55	397	337
1931	176.3	22.0	15	32	243	209
1932	127.5	15.9	15	19	149	130
1933	186.7	23.3	15	30	230	202
1934	95.3	11.9	14	14	114	101
1935	105.8	13.2	14	16	133	120
1936	139.8	17.5	21	32	185	166
1937	132.8	16.6	27	34	161	145
1938	95.1	11.9	28	28	128	115
1939	76.4	9.6	30	27	116	104
1940	56.6	7.1	34	24	95	85
1941	44.5	5.6	37	22	81	73
1942	31.6	4.0	41	18	61	55
1943	54.3	6.8	44	52	170	153
1944	55.0	6.9	48	57	175	158
1945	82.9	10.4	51	96	284	256
1946	100.7	12.6	55	102	288	259
1947	64.7	8.1	54	68	194	175
1948	70.6	8.8	52	89	260	234
1949	57.9	7.2	48	70	215	194

TABLE V–45

Column 1 – New York Stock Exchange 1 percent "charge on commissions of member firms" as reported in the New York Stock Exchange, *Annual Reports of the President,* multiplied by 100 and adjusted to annual basis by means of reported market value of stock trading (*Survey of Current Business, Statistical Supplement,* 1947, and subsequent issues) on assumption that Jan.-Dec. "charge on commissions" is collected on Dec.-Nov. business of member firms.

Column 2 – Twice bond sales on the New York Stock Exchange (*Commercial and Financial Chronicle*) multiplied by $2 per bond commission. This ratio was obtained by relating bond commissions (from *Important Changes in Commissions, 1856 to 1942,* multilithed release of the New York Stock Exchange) to average prices for bonds, computed by dividing market value by face value of bond sales (*Survey of Current Business, Statistical Supplement,* 1947, and subsequent issues) and estimated size of individual bond transaction.

Column 3 – Col. 1 minus col. 2.

Column 4 – Reported stock sales on the New York Stock Exchange (*New York Stock Exchange Yearbook,* various issues), doubled to reflect both purchases and sales.

Column 5 – See note to Table V-44, col. 2.

Column 6 – Col. 4 multiplied by col. 5.

Column 7 – Col. 6 divided by col. 3.

V-46 TABLE V–46

Line 1 – From U.S. Congress, Senate, *Stock Exchange Practices* (Hearings before the Committee on Banking and Currency, U.S. Senate, 73rd Congress. 2nd Session), part 17, pp. 7869, 7875, 7881, 7885, and 7899.

Line 2a – Obtained by blowing-up figures of line 1 on the basis of proportion of the number of reporting and nonreporting firms.

Line 2b – Rough guesses based on assumption that most of the nonreporting firms and members are of relatively small size.

Line 3 – Obtained by multiplying twice bond sales on New York Stock Exchange by commission rate of $2 per bond.

Line 4 – Rough estimates.

Line 5a – Line 2a minus line 3 minus line 4.

Line 5b – Line 2b minus line 3 minus line 4.

Line 6 – From Table V-44, col. 6.

COMPUTATION OF ADJUSTMENT FACTOR
FOR COMMISSIONS ON STOCK: 1943 to 1949

Year	Commissions on N.Y. Stock Exchange			Twice reported stock sales	Average commission per share	Estimated commission on stock sales	Adjustment factor
	Total	On bond sales	On stock sales				
	$ mill.			mill. shares	cents	$ mill.	
	1	2	3	4	5	6	7
1943	108.2	13.0	95.2	557.5	18.0	100.4	105.5
1944	105.2	10.8	94.4	526.2	19.0	100.0	105.9
1945	157.7	9.0	148.7	755.2	20.5	154.8	104.1
1946	155.6	5.4	150.2	733.4	21.5	157.7	105.0
1947	104.0	4.3	99.7	507.2	21.5	109.0	109.3
1948	141.0	4.0	137.0	604.4	26.0	157.1	114.7
1949	119.3	3.3	116.0	544.4	.	.	.

COMPARISON OF TWO ESTIMATES OF BROKERS' COMMISSIONS
ON TRADING IN STOCKS: 1928 to 1932

$ mill.

	1928	1929	1930	1931	1932
1. Net commissions, reporting exchange member firms and individual members	355	473	289	202	149
2. Estimated commissions including nonreporting firms					
(a) Maximum	500	655	380	235	160
(b) Minimum	400	525	320	215	155
3. Estimated bond commissions	18	18	12	14	14
4. Estimated commodity futures commissions	50	60	50	30	30
5. Estimated stock commissions					
(a) Maximum	432	577	318	191	116
(b) Minimum	332	447	258	171	111
6. Estimate of Table V–44	402	512	315	189	114

INDIVIDUALS' PAYMENTS OF STOCK TRANSFER TAX
1905 to 1949

$ mill.

Year	Stock transfer tax receipts			Estimated individuals' payments	Year	Stock transfer tax receipts			Estimated individuals' payments
	Federal	New York	U.S. total	U.S. total			Federal	New York	U.S. total	U.S. total	
	Reported year			Calendar year			Reported year			Calendar year	
	1	2	3	4	5		1	2	3	4	5
1905	0	2	2	2	2	1928	24	28	52	59	51
1906	0	7	7	7	7	1929	47	40	87	87	74
1907	0	5	5	5	5	1930	34	27	61	61	52
1908	0	4	4	4	4	1931	22	18	40	40	34
1909	0	5	5	5	5	1932	25	22	47	47	41
1910	0	5	5	5	5	1933	40	38	78	78	69
1911	0	4	4	4	4	1934	21	21	42	42	37
1912	0	4	4	4	4	1935	24	25	49	49	44
1913	0	3	3	3	3	1936	32	34	66	66	59
1914	0	2	2	2	2	1937	35	30	65	65	58
1915	0	4	4	4	4	1938	18	20	38	38	34
1916	0	5	5	6	6	1939	16	18	34	34	31
1917	0	8	8	8	8	1940	13	15	28	28	25
1918	2	5	7	11	10	1941	13	14	27	27	24
1919	8	7	15	20	19	1942	12	9	21	21	19
1920	13	11	24	20	19	1943	18	18	36	36	32
1921	9	7	16	16	15	1944	20	18	38	38	34
1922	9	8	17	18	17	1945	28	25	53	53	48
1923	10	9	19	17	16	1946	28	26	54	54	49
1924	8	7	15	20	19	1947	20	16	36	36	32
1925	13	12	25	29	27	1948	20	18	38	38	34
1926	17	16	33	33	30	1949	18	17	35	35	32
1927	17	17	34	38	34						

Column 1 – 1905–1928: Receipts during fiscal year ending June 30 of year indicated, as reported in the *Annual Report of the Secretary of the Treasury,* various issues.
1929–1949: Receipts during calendar year compiled from data of the Bureau of Internal Revenue.

Column 2 – 1905–1926: Receipts during fiscal year ending Sept. 30 of year indicated for 1905–1915 and June 30 for 1916–1926, from *New York Stock Exchange Yearbook,* various issues.
1927–1949: Receipts during calendar year from *New York Stock Exchange Yearbook,* 1950.

Column 3 – 1905–1949: Sum of cols. 1 and 2.

Column 4 – 1905–1915: Calendar year totals estimated as equal to col. 3.
1916–1925: Calendar year totals estimated as average of fiscal years overlapping indicated year.
1926–1928: Total of calendar year receipts of federal government and New York State government, estimated as average of overlapping fiscal year receipts where calendar year receipts are not given.
1929–1949: Sum of calendar year receipts, equal to col. 3.

Column 5 – 1905–1949: Obtained by applying to col. 4 shares of individuals in stock trading shown in notes to Table V-44, col. 12. Receipts of states other than New York are not available separately and are assumed to be only a small percentage of the New York receipts.

TABLE V–48   V-48

Column 1 – 1897–1949: Sum of cols. 2–29.

Column 2 – 1897–1928: First differences of Table I-6, col. 1.
 1929–1949: From Table V-53, col. 2.

Column 3 – 1910–1949: First differences of Table V-54, col. 6.

Column 4 – 1897–1949: First differences of Table I-10, col. 7.

Column 5 – 1920–1949: First differences of Table I-16, col. 2.

Column 6 – 1897–1949: First differences of Table I-14, col. 5.

Column 7 – 1897–1949: First differences of Table V-55, col. 6.

Column 8 – 1897–1949: First differences of Table V-56, col. 6.

Column 9 – 1927–1949: First differences of Table V-60, col. 3.

Column 10 – 1921–1949: First differences of Table V-62, col. 3.

Column 11 – 1927–1949: From Table V-66, col. 1.

Column 12 – 1927–1949: From Table V-68, col. 3.

Column 13 – 1924–1949: First differences of Table V-72, col. 6.

Column 14 – 1897–1949: First differences of Tables V-74, col. 3, minus Table V-75, col. 2.

Column 15 – 1926–1935: First differences of Table V-76, col. 2.

Column 16 – 1897–1949: First differences of Table L-29, col. 7, minus Table L-36, col. 2.

Column 17 – 1915–1949: First differences of figures given in *Banking and Monetary Statistics*, table **91** pp. 343, 344, and *Federal Reserve Bulletin*.

Column 18 – 1917–1949: First differences of Table V-78, col. 3.

Column 19 – 1918–1949: First differences of Table V-77, col. 3.

Column 20 – 1897–1949: First differences of Table J-2, col. 7.

Column 21 – 1931–1944: First differences of Table J-6, col. 3, minus small amounts arbitrarily assumed to be holdings of state and local government bonds, included in Table V-49, col. 11.

Column 22 – 1912–1949: First differences of Table L-41, col. 8.

Column 23 – 1912–1949: First differences of Table L-43, col. 3 (includes both direct and guaranteed obligations).

Column 24 – 1918–1928: First differences of year-end holdings from Table F-9, col. 10.
 1929–1949: First differences of Table F-23, cols. 3 and 6.

Column 25 – 1918–1927: Sum of first differences of year-end holdings (derived as average of June holdings from Table F-9, cols. 8 and 9).
 1928: Difference of Table F-24, col. 8, for year-end of 1928 and year-end 1927 derived as above.
 1929–1940: First differences of Table F-24, col. 8.

Column 26 – 1915–1949: First differences of Table G-17, col. 5, converted to calendar-year basis by simple arithmetic interpolation.

Column 27 – 1918–1949: First differences of Table G-8, col. 5.

Column 28 – 1917–1949: First differences of Table V-73, col. 2, minus cols. 9–13 of this table.

Column 29 – 1936–1949: Sum of Table K-2, col. 12, and Friend and Natrella, *Individuals' Saving*, part II, table 14, line 2. Includes special U.S. notes issued to International Bank for Reconstruction and Development and to International Monetary Fund since these are included in U.S. Government securities outstanding (cf. Table V-2, col. 1).

ANNUAL CHANGES IN INSTITUTIONAL HOLDINGS OF U.S. GOVERNMENT (DIRECT AND GUARANTEED) SECURITIES
(Adjusted for Capital Gains and Losses): 1897 to 1949

$ mill.

Year	Total	Life insurance companies	Savings bank insurance departments	Fraternal order life insurance companies	Pension funds	Insurance companies		
						Mutual accident	Fire and marine	Casualty and miscellaneous
	1	2	3	4	5	6	7	8
1897	33	−7	—	0	—	0	14	0
1898	91	−2	—	0	—	0	−1	0
1899	−62	−3	—	0	—	0	8	0
1900	44	−3	—	0	—	0	−2	0
1901	−26	−1	—	0	—	0	−6	0
1902	−11	−1	—	0	—	0	2	0
1903	10	−1	—	0	—	0	−1	0
1904	16	1	—	1	—	0	0	0
1905	6	0	—	—	—	0	0	0
1906	24	−1	—	0	—	0	−5	1
1907	40	0	—	0	—	0	−4	0
1908	20	−1	—	0	—	0	−1	0
1909	33	0	—	0	—	0	−3	0
1910	−3	0	0	0	—	0	−4	0
1911	24	−1	0	0	—	0	−5	0
1912	−2	0	0	0	—	0	−5	0
1913	4	0	0	0	—	0	0	0
1914	3	0	0	−1	—	0	0	0
1915	0	0	0	0	—	0	1	0
1916	135	0	0	−1	—	0	1	1
1917	2 737	71	0	7	—	1	44	12
1918	4 963	457	0	10	—	1	43	19
1919	1 326	244	0	9	—	1	55	26
1920	−692	52	0	−3	10	0	64	33
1921	68	6	0	−3	1	0	58	35
1922	2 010	47	0	−4	7	0	48	43
1923	−567	−52	0	0	3	0	5	0
1924	656	−104	0	−2	6	0	−1	7
1925	−364	−59	0	−1	8	0	−15	1
1926	−457	−148	0	−2	13	0	−1	12
1927	1 172	−51	0	−2	26	0	13	13
1928	229	−50	0	−3	26	0	−14	3
1929	−540	−136	0	−3	56	0	−35	−14
1930	−50	−48	0	1	19	0	−15	−19
1931	938	36	0	1	21	0	−12	−18
1932	2 296	73	0	0	21	0	−16	−23
1933	2 581	450	0	−3	27	0	39	32
1934	5 966	1 056	1	2	25	0	58	62
1935	3 379	1 045	1	46	25	3	67	60
1936	3 712	1 078	2	13	36	0	48	92
1937	1 341	743	1	39	29	3	74	68
1938	2 546	265	2	−24	40	−1	57	104
1939	3 221	450	2	3	38	2	8	31
1940	2 901	469	2	6	32	0	38	64
1941	10 058	977	4	6	47	1	108	125
1942	37.055	2 466	5	54	92	4	170	312
1943	41 732	3 012	7	74	156	10	203	232
1944	44 385	3 813	6	157	388	17	173	249
1945	33 808	3 839	7	18	477	12	196	192
1946	−16 062	994	6	16	413	4	117	103
1947	−3 552	−1 904	4	32	531	10	306	242
1948	−5 395	−3 371	4	1	490	0	279	265
1949	3 230	−1 636	−5	−3	488	−1	309	229

ANNUAL CHANGES IN INSTITUTIONAL HOLDINGS OF U.S. GOVERNMENT (DIRECT AND GUARANTEED) SECURITIES
(Adjusted for Capital Gains and Losses): 1897 to 1949

$ mill.

Year	Management investment companies				Face amount investment companies	Commercial banks		Mutual savings banks	Federal Reserve banks	Federal land banks	Joint stock land banks
	Open-end	Closed-end	Holding	Unclas-sified		Oper-ating	Closed				
	9	10	11	12	13	14	15	16	17	18	19
1897	–	–	–	–	–	25	–	1	–	–	–
1898	–	–	–	–	–	100	–	–6	–	–	–
1899	–	–	–	–	–	–48	–	–19	–	–	–
1900	–	–	–	–	–	81	–	–32	–	–	–
1901	–	–	–	–	–	7	–	–26	–	–	–
1902	–	–	–	–	–	5	–	–17	–	–	–
1903	–	–	–	–	–	26	–	–14	–	–	–
1904	–	–	–	–	–	21	–	–7	–	–	–
1905	–	–	–	–	–	13	–	–7	–	–	–
1906	–	–	–	–	–	41	–	–12	–	–	–
1907	–	–	–	–	–	43	–	1	–	–	–
1908	–	–	–	–	–	29	–	–7	–	–	–
1909	–	–	–	–	–	35	–	1	–	–	–
1910	–	–	–	–	–	4	–	–3	–	–	–
1911	–	–	–	–	–	29	–	1	–	–	–
1912	–	–	–	–	–	3	–	0	–	–	–
1913	–	–	–	–	–	3	–	1	–	–	–
1914	–	–	–	–	–	3	–	0	–	–	–
1915	–	–	–	–	–	–13	–	–4	16	–	–
1916	–	–	–	–	–	78	–	14	39	–	–
1917	–	–	–	–	–	1 498	–	116	67	9	–
1918	–	–	–	–	–	2 221	–	276	117	–1	2
1919	–	–	–	–	–	–146	–	271	61	17	10
1920	–	–	–	–	–	–928	–	170	–13	–22	–10
1921	–	1	–	–	–	–182	–	117	–53	28	0
1922	–	0	–	–	–	1 329	–	115	202	5	26
1923	–	0	–	–	–	–217	–	43	–302	8	–13
1924	–	0	–	–	0	332	–	–31	406	–15	0
1925	–	0	–	–	0	–223	–	–81	–165	–6	–1
1926	–	1	–	–	0	–442	16	–128	–60	5	–2
1927	1	2	2	2	0	728	–7	–115	302	1	–8
1928	19	–1	4	4	0	362	8	–111	–389	–1	2
1929	–18	20	17	15	0	–536	–10	–132	283	–6	–4
1930	0	15	7	7	0	134	–4	36	218	2	–1
1931	4	38	0	1	0	1 158	82	99	88	–12	4
1932	0	–30	0	0	0	1 225	–85	43	1 038	89	–4
1933	–5	–41	0	0	0	735	417	128	582	–37	1
1934	5	4	0	1	7	4 073	–291	416	–7	28	14
1935	–4	–3	0	0	4	1 604	–126	532	1	–51	–7
1936	1	0	–	0	–6	1 542	–	435	–1	2	0
1937	14	–2	–	0	–1	–1 178	–	299	134	8	–3
1938	–16	3	–	0	–2	890	–	362	0	15	0
1939	3	2	–	0	1	1 220	–	219	–80	23	5
1940	–2	5	–	0	0	1 418	–	122	–300	–6	–3
1941	2	3	–	0	1	4 024	–	466	70	84	–7
1942	11	7	0	0	1	19 546	–	841	3 935	91	–1
1943	10	7	0	–2	0	18 398	–	1 492	5 354	140	–2
1944	6	23	0	–1	9	17 655	–	2 177	7 303	–178	0
1945	6	4	0	–1	15	12 899	–	2 251	5 416	–75	–1
1946	–6	–16	0	0	–6	~15 926	–	1 047	–912	–9	0
1947	12	–1	0	0	–11	–5 584	–	218	–791	–32	0
1948	22	7	0	0	–12	–6 599	–	–499	774	–3	0
1949	39	1	0	0	3	4 383	–	–72	–4 448	5	0

ANNUAL CHANGES IN INSTITUTIONAL HOLDINGS OF U.S. GOVERNMENT (DIRECT AND GUARANTEED) SECURITIES
(Adjusted for Capital Gains and Losses): 1897 to 1949

$ mill.

Year	Savings and loan associations Operating	Closed	Credit unions	Postal Savings System	Federal personal sector trust funds	Alien Property Custodian and German special deposits	State governments	Local governments	Non-financial corporations	For-eigners
	20	21	22	23	24	25	26	27	28	29
1897	0	—	—	—	—	—	—	—	—	—
1898	0	—	—	—	—	—	—	—	—	—
1899	0	—	—	—	—	—	—	—	—	—
1900	0	—	—	—	—	—	—	—	—	—
1901	0	—	—	—	—	—	—	—	—	—
1902	0	—	—	—	—	—	—	—	—	—
1903	0	—	—	—	—	—	—	—	—	—
1904	0	—	—	—	—	—	—	—	—	—
1905	0	—	—	—	—	—	—	—	—	—
1906	0	—	—	—	—	—	—	—	—	—
1907	0	—	—	—	—	—	—	—	—	—
1908	0	—	—	—	—	—	—	—	—	—
1909	0	—	—	—	—	—	—	—	—	—
1910	0	—	—	—	—	—	—	—	—	—
1911	0	—	—	—	—	—	—	—	—	—
1912	0	—	0	0	—	—	—	—	—	—
1913	0	—	0	0	—	—	—	—	—	—
1914	0	—	0	1	—	—	—	—	—	—
1915	0	—	0	0	—	—	0	—	—	—
1916	0	—	0	1	—	—	2	—	—	—
1917	5	—	0	1	—	—	6	—	900	—
1918	23	—	0	15	6	70	4	200	1 500	—
1919	23	—	0	12	9	58	6	−130	800	—
1920	−4	—	0	75	21	29	4	30	−200	—
1921	−1	—	0	−2	34	4	6	20	−1	—
1922	−19	—	0	−26	35	8	4	80	110	—
1923	−14	—	0	−5	35	1	6	−15	−50	—
1924	−13	—	0	−39	90	1	4	−25	40	—
1925	0	—	0	0	160	7	6	−25	30	—
1926	0	—	0	0	161	2	7	30	79	—
1927	0	—	0	1	130	36	10	−15	103	—
1928	0	—	0	−9	127	−34	7	25	254	—
1929	19	—	0	1	157	−78	8	0	−144	—
1930	−6	—	1	1	125	−39	10	−5	−489	—
1931	7	1	1	43	−401	−23	8	65	−253	—
1932	3	0	1	1	−38	−6	4	−95	95	—
1933	31	1	1	129	29	−4	8	10	51	—
1934	201	0	0	397	53	0	8	20	−167	—
1935	−51	0	0	256	167	1	7	−20	−178	—
1936	−54	0	1	205	481	1	10	−5	−171	2
1937	−20	0	0	39	1 218	0	13	−11	−213	87
1938	−10	0	0	35	937	1	10	62	−95	−89
1939	−20	0	2	60	1 118	−21	9	54	82	10
1940	0	0	3	32	1 135	−14	63	56	−215	−4
1941	20	0	8	50	1 670	—	122	110	1 991	176
1942	200	0	60	71	2 383	—	278	−9	6 129	409
1943	533	−1	53	371	3 709	—	728	452	6 171	625
1944	818	−1	45	536	4 442	—	1 130	962	4 441	215
1945	749	—	35	585	4 710	—	1 168	491	65	750
1946	−411	—	10	345	3 358	—	864	64	−5 742	−375
1947	−269	—	−5	126	3 500	—	702	−39	−1 213	614
1948	−286	—	−7	−64	2 860	—	369	57	198	120
1949	43	—	7	−126	1 962	—	−9	50	1 985	26

536

TABLE V–49   V-49

Column 1 – 1897–1949: Sum of cols. 2–15.

Column 2 – 1897–1928: First differences of Table I-6, col. 2.
1929–1949: From Table V-53, col. 3.

Column 3 – 1897–1949: First differences of Table I-10, col. 8.

Column 4 – 1897–1949: First differences of Table I-14, col. 6.

Column 5 – 1897–1949: First differences of Table V-55, col. 7.

Column 6 – 1897–1949: First differences of Table V-56, col. 7.

Column 7 – 1915–1949: First differences of Table V-72, col. 7.

Column 8 – 1897–1919: First differences of Table V-74, col. 4.
1920–1949: First differences of Table V-74, col. 4, minus Table V-75, col. 3.

Column 9 – 1926–1942: First differences of Table V-76, col. 3.

Column 10 – 1897–1949: First differences of Table L-29, col. 8, minus Table L-36, col. 3.

Column 11 – 1897–1949: First differences of residual of Table J-2, col. 6 minus col. 7, plus residual of first differences of Table J-6, col. 3 and Table V-48, col. 21.

Column 12 – 1897–1949: First differences of Table V-73, col. 3.

Column 13 – 1897–1949: First differences of Table G-17, cols. 3 and 4, converted to year-end by simple arithmetic averaging.

Column 14 – 1897–1949: First differences of Table G-8, cols. 3 and 4.

Column 15 – 1930–1949: First differences of year-end figures derived by simple arithmetic averaging of June 30 figures given in *Annual Report of the Secretary of the Treasury*, 1946, p. 667, and later editions, and year-end figures from *Daily Treasury Statement*, Mar. 15, 1949 and Mar. 15, 1950.

ANNUAL CHANGES IN INSTITUTIONAL HOLDINGS OF STATE AND LOCAL GOVERNMENT SECURITIES

(Adjusted for Capital Gains and Losses): 1897 to 1949

$ mill.

Year	Total	Insurance companies					Face amount investment companies
		Life	Fraternal order	Mutual accident	Fire and marine	Casualty and miscellaneous	
	1	2	3	4	5	6	7
1897	53	0	2	1	0	0	—
1898	59	−2	1	1	−3	0	—
1899	26	−4	2	0	1	2	—
1900	63	−7	2	1	0	1	—
1901	57	−10	2	2	6	0	—
1902	90	9	4	1	2	1	—
1903	111	9	4	1	4	2	—
1904	112	12	4	0	4	1	—
1905	85	11	7	1	6	1	—
1906	96	13	0	−2	−2	2	—
1907	103	7	7	2	2	−1	—
1908	112	14	16	2	7	5	—
1909	187	12	9	2	6	3	—
1910	174	12	6	1	5	3	—
1911	219	13	13	−7	4	5	—
1912	156	10	11	1	5	4	—
1913	99	11	14	1	3	−2	—
1914	269	11	7	0	−1	0	—
1915	184	18	18	0	2	1	0
1916	188	24	14	2	4	5	0
1917	199	23	7	1	6	6	0
1918	−82	−10	12	0	13	12	0
1919	326	1	0	2	12	11	0
1920	331	38	25	1	8	9	0
1921	391	62	39	3	−1	3	0
1922	437	2	51	11	−6	4	0
1923	350	−17	39	4	15	5	0
1924	655	14	19	13	13	8	0
1925	521	12	33	1	10	10	0
1926	661	−11	32	2	17	14	0
1927	634	14	31	3	30	19	0
1928	588	61	23	−4	16	15	0
1929	554	189	18	1	3	4	0
1930	676	81	1	−7	−15	−14	0
1931	−552	158	8	−10	−12	−10	0
1932	146	69	−10	−4	−14	−17	0
1933	318	95	−29	−3	−5	4	0
1934	775	204	68	5	−10	−6	1
1935	433	158	−4	0	−9	6	1
1936	191	103	−42	−6	23	−1	0
1937	−153	107	−36	0	−4	−4	0
1938	438	102	35	4	−6	−1	1
1939	288	188	4	3	−6	7	0
1940	480	140	−6	−2	8	9	0
1941	−97	−88	28	4	−4	4	−1
1942	−616	−267	71	8	−14	−5	−2
1943	−1 006	−268	−40	4	−10	−9	−3
1944	−1 049	−365	−135	−4	−8	−5	0
1945	−569	−378	39	10	−15	−13	0
1946	1	−127	18	4	−1	−4	−1
1947	1 060	−11	7	12	31	34	0
1948	1 010	188	2	6	103	99	0
1949	1 590	100	20	7	116	182	0

ANNUAL CHANGES IN INSTITUTIONAL HOLDINGS OF STATE AND LOCAL GOVERNMENT SECURITIES
(Adjusted for Capital Gains and Losses): 1897 to 1949

$ mill.

Year	Commercial banks Operating	Commercial banks Closed	Mutual savings banks	Savings and loan associations	Non-financial corporations	State governments	Local governments	Federal agencies and trust funds
	8	9	10	11	12	13	14	15
1897	11	—	36	−1	0	4	0	—
1898	20	—	38	0	0	4	0	—
1899	34	—	1	0	5	−15	0	—
1900	12	—	17	0	0	13	24	—
1901	21	—	16	0	5	16	−1	—
1902	11	—	36	0	0	−16	42	—
1903	28	—	28	1	5	5	24	—
1904	33	—	10	0	5	8	35	—
1905	5	—	21	1	0	11	21	—
1906	26	—	7	0	5	12	35	—
1907	59	—	−23	0	5	12	33	—
1908	7	—	7	0	10	19	25	—
1909	31	—	41	0	10	24	49	—
1910	13	—	33	0	5	23	73	—
1911	82	—	10	1	10	18	70	—
1912	29	—	21	0	10	12	53	—
1913	18	—	45	0	0	0	9	—
1914	137	—	23	1	15	−6	82	—
1915	58	—	−9	−1	10	4	83	—
1916	23	—	19	0	20	15	62	—
1917	97	—	−28	0	10	24	53	—
1918	23	—	−109	0	10	25	−58	—
1919	74	—	−52	0	10	31	237	—
1920	16	—	12	1	25	38	158	—
1921	40	—	14	3	35	35	158	—
1922	114	—	−3	2	30	39	193	—
1923	68	—	−25	2	50	53	156	—
1924	239	—	35	2	60	69	183	—
1925	112	—	45	−1	70	51	178	—
1926	174	5	69	4	70	44	241	—
1927	156	4	64	5	40	64	204	—
1928	120	3	32	10	70	60	182	—
1929	93	−5	−11	0	0	51	211	—
1930	332	10	62	0	−70	55	240	1
1931	−122	80	36	0	−20	38	−698	0
1932	207	46	−51	0	38	36	−167	13
1933	−112	212	−51	1	−9	60	79	76
1934	279	−85	−24	0	−24	59	148	160
1935	227	−77	−53	0	−40	59	31	134
1936	26	−35	−23	6	−37	52	34	91
1937	−147	−26	−41	−16	−42	103	−105	58
1938	447	−24	−89	−8	−21	111	−62	−51
1939	270	−18	−54	−2	13	−27	−61	−29
1940	340	−19	−12	−6	−49	1	−59	135
1941	30	−29	−169	10	−4	58	−64	128
1942	−159	−42	−126	8	−16	−54	13	−31
1943	−247	—	−117	10	−22	−99	−128	−77
1944	121	—	−81	−2	−17	−198	−283	−72
1945	439	—	−47	4	−14	−293	−244	−57
1946	400	—	−40	2	−3	−122	−114	−11
1947	871	—	2	9	32	49	4	20
1948	391	—	6	−1	46	83	69	18
1949	893	—	10	−3	54	170	138	−97

Column 1 – 1897–1949: Sum of cols. 2–20.

Column 2 – 1897–1928: First differences of Table I-6, cols. 3–5.
1929–1949: From Table V-53, col. 4.

Column 3 – 1912–1949: First differences of Table V-54, col. 8.

Column 4 – 1897–1949: First differences of Table I-10, cols. 9 and 10.

Column 5 – 1920–1949: First differences of Table I-16, cols. 3 and 6.

Column 6 – 1897–1949: First differences of Table I-14, col. 7.

Column 7 – 1897–1949: First differences of Table V-55, col. 8.

Column 8 – 1897–1949: First differences of Table V-56, col. 8.

Column 9 – 1926–1949: First differences of Table V-60, col. 4.

Column 10 – 1921–1949: First differences of Table V-62, col. 4.

Column 11 – 1932–1949: First differences of Table V-69, col. 3.

Column 12 – 1915–1949: First differences of Table V-72, col. 3.

ANNUAL CHANGES IN INSTITUTIONAL HOLDINGS OF CORPORATE AND FOREIGN BONDS (Adjusted for Capital Gains and Losses): 1897 to 1949

V-50
(Part 1)

$ mill.

Year	Total	Insurance companies			Pension funds	Insurance companies			Management investment companies		Fixed and semifixed investment trusts	Face amount investment companies
		Life	Savings bank	Fraternal order		Mutual accident	Fire and marine	Casualty and miscellaneous	Open-end	Closed-end		
	1	2	3	4	5	6	7	8	9	10	11	12
1897	132	58	–	0	–	0	–2	0	–	–	–	–
1898	141	61	–	1	–	0	–11	1	–	–	–	–
1899	238	74	–	0	–	0	3	2	–	–	–	–
1900	265	85	–	0	–	0	0	3	–	–	–	–
1901	364	98	–	0	–	1	25	0	–	–	–	–
1902	269	88	–	1	–	0	9	2	–	–	–	–
1903	270	88	–	0	–	0	13	3	–	–	–	–
1904	401	113	–	1	–	0	18	0	–	–	–	–
1905	306	110	–	0	–	0	20	4	–	–	–	–
1906	385	115	–	1	–	0	–4	2	–	–	–	–
1907	445	44	–	1	–	0	8	–1	–	–	–	–
1908	168	122	–	2	–	1	28	7	–	–	–	–
1909	345	95	–	2	–	0	23	7	–	–	–	–
1910	528	79	–	1	–	0	16	4	–	–	–	–
1911	581	103	–	2	–	–1	20	9	–	–	–	–
1912	319	63	0	2	–	1	17	7	–	–	–	–
1913	345	61	0	4	–	–1	24	1	–	–	–	–
1914	210	69	0	–5	–	0	11	3	–	–	–	–
1915	–227	131	0	1	–	0	24	8	–	–	–	1
1916	356	168	0	–1	–	0	33	15	–	–	–	0
1917	355	132	0	2	–	0	6	10	–	–	–	0
1918	–212	–155	0	3	–	0	61	21	–	–	–	1
1919	253	–59	0	0	–	1	51	20	–	–	–	0
1920	213	234	0	3	15	0	35	12	–	–	–	1
1921	235	35	0	6	4	0	–7	1	–	17	–	0
1922	564	178	0	7	7	2	–33	–3	–	0	–	0
1923	545	203	0	9	2	0	54	23	–	–2	–	1
1924	1 272	321	0	9	5	3	45	30	–	2	–	0
1925	862	353	0	11	8	1	27	36	–	7	–	2
1926	1 144	410	0	13	11	1	56	49	1	19	–	2
1927	1 531	523	1	14	21	2	101	66	0	52	–	1
1928	829	520	0	15	18	0	45	61	–1	21	–	1
1929	5	222	0	12	44	1	–7	34	4	52	–	1
1930	1 289	349	0	3	7	–1	–60	–10	–1	–3	–	2
1931	–335	171	1	4	7	–3	–48	–7	–2	–61	–	3
1932	–500	–34	0	0	7	0	–57	–28	1	–7	1	–1
1933	–397	–9	0	42	15	2	–49	–33	0	–12	3	3
1934	164	185	1	–32	15	–2	–21	–20	0	5	2	5
1935	341	361	0	–2	12	0	–21	–17	2	–3	3	2
1936	821	570	1	56	24	2	–45	7	4	–12	0	5
1937	104	741	0	9	9	2	–35	–8	–1	–19	–2	7
1938	490	852	0	22	23	2	–39	–14	4	18	–2	4
1939	64	670	0	20	18	4	–45	–22	7	4	–1	–1
1940	361	775	1	34	12	1	–38	–27	10	–17	–1	0
1941	572	977	0	28	20	4	–13	–8	12	–14	–1	–6
1942	–476	146	0	–48	23	–2	–16	–18	24	–5	0	0
1943	–459	–76	–1	50	33	6	–13	–31	27	–1	0	–6
1944	16	–222	0	84	121	8	–27	–15	24	–4	–1	11
1945	237	–363	0	48	160	11	–31	–13	23	1	0	6
1946	2 383	1 774	1	33	208	5	–4	5	–16	–12	0	–7
1947	3 988	3 201	2	34	333	11	8	29	9	–5	0	–12
1948	4 625	3 892	1	5	330	4	53	101	4	0	0	0
1949	3 199	2 447	8	22	335	5	54	122	19	3	0	–1

Column 13 – 1914–1934: First differences of figures given in *Banking and Monetary Statistics*, table 85, pp. 330–333.

Column 14 – 1897–1919: First differences of Table V-74, col. 5.
1920–1949: First differences of Table V-74, col. 5, minus Table V-75, col. 4.

Column 15 – 1921–1932: First differences of bond holdings of closed banks, estimated as a percentage of Table V-76, col. 4. Annual percentages estimated on basis of relationship between other bonds and stock holdings of operating commercial banks (Table V-74, cols. 5–7).
1933–1945: Same as 1921–1932, using 1930–1932 percentage (84 percent).

Column 16 – 1897–1949: First differences of Table L-30, col. 5, minus Table L-36, col. 4.

Column 17 – 1917–1949: First differences of Table V-78, col. 4.

Column 18 – 1928–1949: First differences of Table F-25, col. 6.

Column 19 – 1912–1949: First differences of Table L-41, col. 9.

Column 20 – 1897–1949: Table K-2, col. 3 minus Friend and Natrella, *Individuals' Saving*, part II, table 14, line 2.

ANNUAL CHANGES IN INSTITUTIONAL HOLDINGS OF CORPORATE AND FOREIGN BONDS (Adjusted for Capital Gains and Losses): 1897 to 1949

$ mill.

Year	Federal Reserve banks	Commercial banks		Mutual savings banks	Federal land banks	Federal land bank bonds held by federal agencies and trust funds	Credit unions	Foreigners
		Operating	Closed					
	13	14	15	16	17	18	19	20
1897	–	47	–	29	–	–	–	0
1898	–	74	–	28	–	–	–	–13
1899	–	128	–	78	–	–	–	–47
1900	–	116	–	117	–	–	–	–56
1901	–	191	–	74	–	–	–	–25
1902	–	153	–	47	–	–	–	–31
1903	–	101	–	35	–	–	–	30
1904	–	175	–	60	–	–	–	34
1905	–	120	–	71	–	–	–	–19
1906	–	126	–	54	–	–	–	91
1907	–	224	–	13	–	–	–	156
1908	–	–121	–	32	–	–	–	97
1909	–	35	–	35	–	–	–	148
1910	–	77	–	30	–	–	–	321
1911	–	268	–	45	–	–	–	135
1912	–	27	–	27	–	–	0	175
1913	–	64	–	–8	–	–	0	200
1914	1	426	–	1	–	–	0	–296
1915	11	124	–	65	–	–	0	–592
1916	–3	330	–	88	–	–	0	–274
1917	–4	227	–	6	1	–	0	–25
1918	–5	–142	–	5	–1	–	0	0
1919	0	358	–	42	0	–	0	–160
1920	0	119	–	1	2	–	1	–210
1921	0	142	22	19	0	–	0	–4
1922	0	324	9	66	0	–	0	7
1923	0	174	9	40	–2	–	0	34
1924	2	734	28	73	0	–	1	19
1925	1	277	4	105	0	–	0	30
1926	0	398	24	150	0	–	0	10
1927	–2	533	–11	234	0	–	1	–5
1928	9	–69	–3	166	0	0	0	46
1929	2	–523	–3	116	13	0	1	36
1930	–5	742	34	228	1	0	–2	5
1931	24	–843	233	191	–11	0	1	5
1932	–26	–403	128	–79	1	0	–1	–2
1933	–4	–660	485	–190	–3	0	1	12
1934	–1	186	–124	–34	–1	0	1	–1
1935	–	232	–69	–152	0	–30	1	22
1936	–	372	–84	–92	0	–30	1	42
1937	–	–540	–87	7	1	0	3	17
1938	–	–197	–75	–111	–1	0	0	4
1939	–	–407	–59	–119	0	0	1	–6
1940	–	–91	–95	–158	1	0	0	–46
1941	–	–171	–132	–97	9	0	9	–45
1942	–	–221	–218	–162	0	0	–5	26
1943	–	–360	–3	–86	7	–28	2	21
1944	–	25	–6	5	–11	0	3	21
1945	–	478	–7	31	–6	–14	–3	–84
1946	–	345	–	155	0	0	–4	–100
1947	–	36	–	350	0	0	1	–9
1948	–	–206	–	498	2	0	–3	–56
1949	–	94	–	141	–2	0	5	–53

Column 1 – 1897–1949: Sum of cols. 2–12.

Column 2 – 1897–1928: First differences of Table I-6, col. 6.
1929–1949: From Table V-53, col. 6.

Column 3 – 1933–1949: First differences of Table I-10, col. 11, divided between common and preferred stocks according to percentage distribution of total stock holdings of legal reserve life insurance companies. (See Table I-6, cols. 6 and 7.)

Column 4 – 1920–1949: First differences of Table I-16, cols. 4 and 7.

Column 5 – 1897–1949: First differences of Table I-14, col. 8, split by same procedure as for col. **3**.

Column 6 – 1897–1922: First differences of Table V-55, col. 9.
1923–1949 From Table V-57, col. 2.

Column 7 – 1897–1922: First differences of Table V-56, col. 9.
1923–1949: From Table V-57, col. 5 (figures for period 1933–1939 assumed to be negligible).

Column 8 – 1928–1949: First differences of Table V-60, col. 5.

Column 9 – 1921–1949: First differences of Table V-62, col. 5.

Column 10 – 1927–1949: Sum of Table V-66, col. 2 and Table V-68, col. 2.

Column 11 – 1924–1949: First differences of Table V-72, col. 9. (All stocks of face amount installment investment companies assumed to be preferred in accordance with Securities and Exchange Commission docket, which shows 99 percent to be preferred.)

Column 12 – 1897–1949: From Table K-2, col. 4.

ANNUAL CHANGES IN INSTITUTIONAL HOLDINGS OF PREFERRED STOCK V-51
(Adjusted for Capital Gains and Losses): 1897 to 1949

$ mill.

Year	Total	Insurance companies		Pension funds	Insurance companies			Management investment companies			Face amount investment companies	Foreigners
		Life	Fraternal order		Mutual accident	Fire and marine	Casualty and miscellaneous	Open-end	Closed-end	Holding and unclassified		
	1	2	3	4	5	6	7	8	9	10	11	12
1897	6	1	–	–	0	4	1	–	–	–	–	0
1898	2	0	–	–	0	0	0	–	–	–	–	2
1899	7	1	–	–	0	4	1	–	–	–	–	1
1900	–2	0	–	–	0	3	0	–	–	–	–	–5
1901	0	1	–	–	0	0	1	–	–	–	–	–2
1902	–1	1	–	–	0	–2	0	–	–	–	–	0
1903	1	2	–	–	0	2	0	–	–	–	–	–3
1904	10	2	–	–	0	–1	1	–	–	–	–	8
1905	32	2	–	–	0	4	1	–	–	–	–	25
1906	10	2	–	–	0	0	1	–	–	–	–	7
1907	–9	–1	–	–	0	–1	0	–	–	–	–	–7
1908	1	–1	–	–	0	4	1	–	–	–	–	–3
1909	3	–1	–	–	0	–2	–1	–	–	–	–	7
1910	7	–2	–	–	0	1	0	–	–	–	–	8
1911	15	–1	–	–	0	3	1	–	–	–	–	12
1912	43	0	–	–	0	3	0	–	–	–	–	40
1913	15	–1	–	–	0	–2	1	–	–	–	–	17
1914	–78	1	–	–	0	1	0	–	–-	–	–	–80
1915	–68	0	–	–	0	2	0	–	–	–	–	–70
1916	–33	0	–	–	0	6	1	–	–	–	–	–40
1917	–2	1	–	–	0	0	1	–	–	–	–	–4
1918	0	1	–	–	0	–3	2	–	–	–	–	0
1919	–3	0	–	–	0	13	4	–	–	–	–	–20
1920	0	1	–	3	0	13	5	–	–	–	–	–22
1921	3	1	–	1	0	–8	–3	–	12	–	–	0
1922	18	0	–	1	0	13	4	–	0	–	–	0
1923	106	1	–	1	0	10	5	–	–1	–	–	90
1924	66	–2	–	1	0	10	5	–	1	–	1	50
1925	103	1	–	2	0	10	5	–	5	–	0	80
1926	56	1	–	2	0	10	5	–	13	–	0	25
1927	83	8	–	5	0	30	10	–	38	7	0	–15
1928	327	107	–	3	0	30	10	1	36	14	1	125
1929	368	90	–	10	0	30	10	1	70	57	0	100
1930	96	109	–	1	0	10	15	1	–16	26	0	–50
1931	–35	65	–	1	0	10	15	–2	–74	0	0	–50
1932	–99	3	–	2	0	10	15	0	–28	–1	0	–100
1933	–46	4	1	1	0	–	–	0	–4	–2	4	–50
1934	17	6	0	1	0	–	–	1	7	2	0	0
1935	97	15	0	1	0	–	–	7	43	0	1	30
1936	59	–16	2	5	0	–	–	–4	10	0	2	60
1937	–8	22	2	4	0	–	–	–1	–53	0	–2	20
1938	18	–5	3	4	0	–	–	7	1	0	3	5
1939	–30	–20	1	3	0	–	–	3	–11	0	2	–8
1940	2	–2	2	3	0	–	10	1	6	0	1	–19
1941	1	5	1	4	0	–	10	0	5	0	–2	–22
1942	53	10	6	7	1	–	10	6	15	0	–4	2
1943	68	–9	5	12	1	25	15	21	1	–4	5	–4
1944	130	25	7	41	1	25	15	21	–5	–2	6	–4
1945	272	102	6	53	1	25	15	51	8	–1	22	–10
1946	275	198	1	50	1	25	20	8	–23	–1	3	–7
1947	245	189	5	52	2	0	5	18	5	–1	–14	–16
1948	151	82	2	65	1	0	5	–3	15	–1	0	–15
1949	278	177	2	63	2	0	10	19	11	–1	–2	–3

ANNUAL CHANGES IN INSTITUTIONAL HOLDINGS OF COMMON STOCK
(Adjusted for Capital Gains and Losses): 1897 to 1949

$ mill.

Year	Total	Insurance companies		Pension funds	Insurance companies		
		Life	Fraternal order		Mutual accident	Fire and marine	Casualty and miscellaneous
	1	2	3	4	5	6	7
1897	18	2	—	—	0	11	1
1898	25	3	—	—	0	2	2
1899	33	3	—	—	0	14	1
1900	18	5	—	—	0	8	2
1901	33	3	—	—	0	1	1
1902	28	10	—	—	0	–7	2
1903	31	10	—	—	0	12	2
1904	48	13	—	—	0	–7	1
1905	88	12	—	—	0	9	1
1906	49	14	—	—	0	0	1
1907	12	–8	—	—	0	–2	2
1908	–11	–3	—	—	0	15	1
1909	34	–8	—	—	0	18	3
1910	20	–10	—	—	0	19	2
1911	51	–13	—	—	0	5	2
1912	23	–2	—	—	0	11	1
1913	21	–1	—	—	0	–14	1
1914	–11	–2	—	—	0	0	0
1915	–105	0	—	—	0	13	1
1916	–26	2	—	—	0	16	0
1917	15	1	—	—	0	4	1
1918	–28	2	—	—	0	–10	8
1919	18	0	—	—	0	19	5
1920	–27	0	—	5	0	23	2
1921	0	–12	—	1	0	10	5
1922	37	–3	—	2	0	7	–2
1923	258	4	—	1	0	25	15
1924	231	4	—	2	0	25	15
1925	313	15	—	2	0	25	15
1926	239	5	—	3	0	25	15
1927	380	–10	—	7	0	75	20
1928	1 075	–18	—	6	0	75	20
1929	2 944	34	—	13	0	75	20
1930	930	29	—	3	0	50	10
1931	293	16	—	2	0	50	10
1932	83	1	—	2	0	50	10
1933	284	1	0	2	0	15	—
1934	–167	1	0	2	0	15	—
1935	261	3	0	1	0	15	—
1936	493	–4	1	6	0	15	—
1937	122	5	0	3	0	–15	—
1938	11	–1	1	4	0	–15	—
1939	–158	–6	1	3	0	–15	—
1940	–93	0	0	2	0	70	15
1941	–205	1	1	3	0	70	15
1942	–16	3	2	7	0	70	15
1943	–202	–3	1	13	0	10	5
1944	–35	7	2	43	0	10	5
1945	–87	26	0	58	1	10	5
1946	279	63	3	59	0	50	45
1947	91	48	–1	58	0	45	45
1948	170	21	0	75	0	75	40
1949	448	44	1	74	0	160	60

ANNUAL CHANGES IN INSTITUTIONAL HOLDINGS OF COMMON STOCK
(Adjusted for Capital Gains and Losses): 1897 to 1949

$ mill.

Year	Management investment companies				Fixed and semifixed investment trusts	Commercial banks		Mutual savings banks	For-eigners
	Open-end	Closed-end	Holding	Unclas-sified		Oper-ating	Closed		
	8	9	10	11	12	13	14	15	16
1897	–	–	–	–	–	7	–	–3	0
1898	–	–	–	–	–	12	–	3	3
1899	–	–	–	–	–	19	–	–5	1
1900	–	–	–	–	–	17	–	0	–14
1901	–	–	–	–	–	29	–	5	–6
1902	–	–	–	–	–	22	–	0	1
1903	–	–	–	–	–	16	–	–2	–7
1904	–	–	–	–	–	26	–	–2	17
1905	–	–	–	–	–	17	–	–1	50
1906	–	–	–	–	–	19	–	–1	16
1907	–	–	–	–	–	34	–	–1	–13
1908	–	–	–	–	–	–18	–	–1	–5
1909	–	–	–	–	–	5	–	0	16
1910	–	–	–	–	–	–6	–	–1	16
1911	–	–	–	–	–	32	–	1	24
1912	–	–	–	–	–	–5	–	1	17
1913	–	–	–	–	–	1	–	–1	35
1914	–	–	–	–	–	47	–	0	–56
1915	–	–	–	–	–	6	–	2	–127
1916	–	–	–	–	–	30	–	3	–77
1917	–	–	–	–	–	16	–	0	–7
1918	–	–	–	–	–	–28	–	0	0
1919	–	–	–	–	–	28	–	1	–35
1920	–	–	–	–	–	–11	–	0	–46
1921	–	–	–	–	–	–7	3	0	0
1922	–	1	–	–	–	29	1	2	0
1923	–	–6	–	–	–	3	1	1	214
1924	2	5	–	–	–	57	2	3	116
1925	3	23	–	–	–	35	1	3	191
1926	7	60	–	–	–	55	4	5	60
1927	13	67	93	30	17	92	–2	8	–30
1928	24	269	177	61	32	130	2	5	292
1929	51	1 198	779	242	63	239	4	4	222
1930	16	–13	346	106	247	6	5	14	111
1931	9	11	–26	10	186	–163	45	32	111
1932	15	15	–25	3	3	–102	24	11	76
1933	70	63	–32	5	–68	–70	93	2	203
1934	22	–30	12	18	–15	–145	–24	–9	–14
1935	55	–60	2	2	–1	–10	–13	–1	268
1936	82	–111	–	0	–6	12	–16	16	498
1937	45	–63	–	–	–21	–18	–17	–5	208
1938	54	18	–	–	–15	–86	–14	17	48
1939	14	–19	–	–	–4	–32	–10	–18	–72
1940	–8	–6	–	–	–6	–32	–18	60	–170
1941	–3	3	–	–	–3	–42	–25	–24	–201
1942	–5	–40	–3	0	–2	–31	–42	–9	19
1943	8	–50	–33	–30	–5	–74	0	–5	–39
1944	20	–33	–28	–9	–4	–16	–2	1	–31
1945	36	–80	–1	–10	–8	–43	–1	7	–87
1946	179	–21	–11	1	–10	–33	--	14	–60
1947	122	–27	–16	4	–4	–4	–	–34	–145
1948	127	–35	–7	–1	–3	–1	–	11	–132
1949	184	–33	–7	–3	–5	–4	–	0	–23

Column 1 – 1897–1949: Sum of cols. 2–16.

Column 2 – 1897–1928: First differences of Table I-6, col. 7.
   1929–1949: From Table V-53, col. 7.

Column 3 – 1933–1949: First differences of Table I-10, col. 11, minus Table V-51, col. 3.

Column 4 – 1920–1949: First differences of Table I-16, sum of cols. 5 and 8.

Column 5 – 1897–1949: First differences of Table I-14, col. 8, minus Table V-51, col. 5.

Column 6 – 1897–1922: First differences of Table V-55, col. 10.
   1923–1949: From Table V-57, col. 3.

Column 7 – 1897–1922: First differences of Table V-56, col. 10.
   1923–1949: From Table V-57, col. 6 (figures for period 1933–1939 assumed to be negligible).

Column 8 – 1924–1926: First differences of Table V-60, col. 6.
   1927–1949: Table V-61, col. 7, minus sum of Table V-50, col. 9, and Table V-51, col. 8. For years in which no reported figures (Table V-61, col. 7) were given, average of Table V-61, cols. 5 and 6 was used.

Column 9 – 1922–1926: First differences of Table V-62, col. 6.
   1927–1949: Table V-63, col. 7, minus sum of Table V-50, col. 10, and Table V-51, col. 9. For years in which no reported figures (Table V-63, col. 7) were given, average of Table V-63, cols. 5 and 6, was used.

Column 10 – 1927–1949: From Table V-66, col. 3.

Column 11 – 1927–1949: From Table V-68, col. 1 (figures for 1937–1941 assumed to be negligible).

Column 12 – 1927–1949: From Table V-70, col. 9.

Column 13 – 1897–1949: First differences of Table V-74, col. 7. All stock holdings assumed to be common.

Column 14 - 1921–1945: First differences of Table V-76, col. 4, minus Table V-50, col. 15.

Column 15 – 1897–1949: First differences of Table L-30, col. 6. All stock holdings assumed to be common.

Column 16 – 1897–1949: From Table K-2, col. 5.

1929 to 1949

$ mill.

Year	Bonds				Stocks		
	Total	U.S. Government	State and local government	Other	Total	Preferred	Common
	1	2	3	4	5	6	7
1929	275	−136	189	222	124	90	34
1930	382	−48	81	349	138	109	29
1931	365	36	158	171	81	65	16
1932	108	73	69	−34	4	3	1
1933	536	450	95	−9	5	4	1
1934	1 445	1 056	204	185	7	6	1
1935	1 564	1 045	158	361	18	15	3
1936	1 751	1 078	103	570	−20	−16	−4
1937	1 591	743	107	741	27	22	5
1938	1 219	265	102	852	−6	−5	−1
1939	1 308	450	188	670	−26	−20	−6
1940	1 384	469	140	775	−2	−2	0
1941	1 866	977	−88	977	6	5	1
1942	2 345	2 466	−267	146	13	10	3
1943	2 668	3 012	−268	−76	−12	−9	−3
1944	3 226	3 813	−365	− 222	32	25	7
1945	3 098	3 839	−378	−363	128	102	26
1946	2 641	994	−127	1 774	261	198	63
1947	1 286	−1 904	−11	3 201	237	189	48
1948	709	−3 371	188	3 892	103	82	21
1949	911	−1 636	100	2 447	221	177	44

Column 1 – 1929–1949: Sum of cols. 2–4.

Column 2 – 1929–1939: Obtained by multiplying net figure of acquisitions minus liquidations and gains as given by Hart, *A Study of the Investment Performance of the Eighteen Largest Domestic Life Insurance Companies in Bonds and Stocks, 1929–1944* (appendix B, tables 3, 4, 8) by step-up ratio, which was derived by averaging successive ratios of Hart's figures of bond holdings (appendix B, table 1) and bond holdings of all legal reserve life insurance companies as given in Table I-6. From blown-up net figure, annual changes in reported holdings of foreign government bonds were subtracted. (Figures from Table I-6, sum of first differences of cols. 4 and 5.)
    1940–1949: Same procedure as for 1929–1939, except basic figures obtained from American Life Convention and Life Insurance Association of America, *Investment Bulletin* No. 26, and No. 28.

Column 3 – 1929–1949: Net figure of acquisitions minus liquidations and gains blown up by same ratio as for col. 2.

Column 4 – 1929–1949: Sum of net purchases of railroad, public utility, and other miscellaneous bonds. Net figures obtained by same procedure as col. 3, using separate ratios for each industry, derived from same source as Table I-6.

Column 5 – 1929–1949: Net figure blown up by ratio of Hart's figures of stock holdings (appendix B, table 13) and stock holdings of all life insurance companies (Table I-6, cols. 6 and 7).

Columns 6 and 7 – 1929–1949: Derived by applying to col. 5 percentage distribution of stock holdings of all life insurance companies (Table I-6, cols. 6 and 7).

Column 1 – 1909–1937: Massachusetts, *Annual Report of the Commissioner of Insurance*, various issues.
       1938–1943: New York, *Annual Report of the Superintendent of Banks*, and Massachusetts insurance report (cited above), various issues.
       1944–1947: Connecticut, *Annual Report of the Superintendent of Banks*, and Massachusetts and New York reports, various issues.
       1948–1949: Massachusetts and New York annual reports and estimates for Connecticut.

Column 2 – 1919–1939: Col. 1 multiplied by 1940 ratio of cash to all other assets for Massachusetts.
       1940–1949: Col. 1 multiplied by annual ratios of cash to total assets computed from Massachusetts reports.

Column 3 – 1909–1923: Col. 1 multiplied by average ratio to total assets for 1924–1928, from Berman, Edward, *Massachusetts System of Savings Bank Life Insurance*, Department of Labor, Bureau of Labor Statistics, Bulletin 615, table 9.
       1924–1949: Col. 1 multiplied by annual ratios to total assets for Massachusetts from Bureau of Labor Statistics Bulletins 615 and 688 and letter of Massachusetts Commissioner of Insurance (1940–1948).

Column 4 – 1918–1949: Same procedure as col. 3 for 1924–1949, and extrapolated for earlier years.

Column 5 – 1911–1949: Same procedure as col. 3.

Columns 6 and 7 – 1911–1949: Col. 5 multiplied by annual ratio of U.S. Government and state and local government bonds, respectively, to total holdings of securities by mutual savings banks (cf. *Annual Reports of the Comptroller of the Currency*).

Column 8 – 1913–1949: Col. 5 minus sum of cols. 6, 7, and 9.

Column 9 – 1925–1948: Col. 1 multiplied by annual ratios to total assets for Massachusetts (cf. Department of Labor, *Operation of Savings Bank Life Insurance in Massachusetts and New York*, Bureau of Labor Statistics Bulletin 688 (and Bulletin 615) for 1924–1939 and letter of Massachusetts Commissioner of Insurance for 1940–1948).
       1949: Rough estimate based on 1948 figure and on increase in assets.

Column 10 – 1915–1949: Same procedure as for col. 4.

Note: Details may not add to totals because of rounding.

1909 to 1949

$ mill.

End of year	Total	Cash	Mort-gages	Policy loans	Securities					Other securities
					Total	U.S. Government bonds	State and local government bonds	Corporate securities		
								Bonds	Stocks	
	1	2	3	4	5	6	7	8	9	10
1909	0.1	—	0.1	—	—	—	—	—	—	—
1910	0.1	—	0.1	—	—	—	—	—	—	—
1911	0.2	—	0.1	—	0.1	0	0.1	—	—	—
1912	0.3	—	0.2	—	0.1	0	0.1	—	—	—
1913	0.4	—	0.2	—	0.2	0	0.1	0.1	—	—
1914	0.5	—	0.3	—	0.2	0	0.1	0.1	—	—
1915	0.7	—	0.4	—	0.2	0	0.1	0.1	—	0.1
1916	0.8	—	0.5	—	0.2	0	0.1	0.1	—	0.1
1917	1.0	—	0.6	—	0.3	0.1	0.1	0.1	—	0.1
1918	1.2	—	0.7	0.1	0.3	0.1	0.1	0.1	—	0.1
1919	1.4	0.1	0.8	0.1	0.3	0.1	0.1	0.1	—	0.1
1920	1.7	0.1	1.0	0.1	0.3	0.1	0.1	0.1	—	0.2
1921	2.0	0.1	1.2	0.1	0.4	0.1	0.1	0.2	—	0.2
1922	2.3	0.1	1.3	0.1	0.5	0.2	0.1	0.2	—	0.3
1923	2.8	0.1	1.6	0.2	0.6	0.2	0.1	0.3	—	0.3
1924	3.4	0.1	2.0	0.2	0.7	0.3	0.1	0.3	—	0.4
1925	4.2	0.1	2.5	0.3	0.9	0.3	0.2	0.3	0.1	0.4
1926	5.2	0.2	3.1	0.4	1.1	0.3	0.2	0.5	0.1	0.4
1927	6.2	0.2	3.6	0.4	1.5	0.3	0.4	0.6	0.2	0.5
1928	7.6	0.3	4.3	0.5	1.9	0.3	0.5	0.8	0.3	0.6
1929	9.1	0.4	5.0	0.6	2.2	0.3	0.6	0.9	0.4	0.9
1930	10.6	0.5	5.7	0.8	2.5	0.2	0.7	1.2	0.4	1.1
1931	12.3	0.5	6.5	1.1	3.3	0.3	0.9	1.6	0.5	0.9
1932	13.7	0.6	6.8	1.4	4.0	0.5	1.1	2.0	0.4	0.9
1933	15.2	0.7	7.1	1.6	4.6	0.6	1.2	2.5	0.3	1.1
1934	17.6	0.9	7.4	1.8	6.2	1.5	1.3	3.2	0.2	1.3
1935	20.2	1.0	7.4	2.0	8.2	2.9	1.6	3.3	0.4	1.6
1936	23.1	0.9	7.7	2.2	10.7	5.0	1.7	3.6	0.4	1.6
1937	26.1	1.0	7.7	2.4	13.2	6.3	2.0	4.5	0.4	1.8
1938	28.9	1.2	7.9	2.8	15.2	8.3	1.9	4.5	0.5	1.8
1939	32.1	1.6	8.2	3.1	17.1	10.0	2.0	4.5	0.6	2.1
1940	35.5	2.2	8.3	3.4	19.3	11.8	2.2	4.8	0.5	2.4
1941	39.6	1.4	8.6	3.7	23.9	16.2	1.9	5.3	0.5	2.0
1942	43.7	1.3	8.7	3.8	28.1	21.2	1.5	5.0	0.4	1.8
1943	48.6	1.0	8.4	3.7	33.8	27.9	1.1	4.4	0.4	1.7
1944	54.2	1.5	7.9	3.7	39.3	34.2	0.6	4.0	0.5	1.9
1945	60.9	1.5	7.7	3.7	46.1	41.3	0.4	3.9	0.5	2.0
1946	68.7	1.5	8.3	3.9	52.8	47.2	0.3	4.8	0.5	2.3
1947	77.1	1.5	10.4	4.3	58.5	51.1	0.3	6.6	0.5	2.4
1948	86.0	1.4	13.7	4.9	63.3	54.7	0.3	7.9	0.4	2.7
1949	96.0	2.0	18.0	6.0	67.0	50.2	0.3	16.0	0.5	3.0

Column 1 – 1896–1949: *Spectator Insurance Yearbook, Fire and Marine Volume,* for indicated years. Totals for 1932–1935 adjusted to include assets of small mutual companies omitted from main tables in those years and amounting to less than 2 percent of total assets shown for 1932.

Columns 2–5 and 11 – 1896–1931: Col. 1 multiplied by percentage for each type of asset computed from New York State Superintendent of Insurance, *Annual Report.*
    1932–1949: *Spectator Insurance Yearbook.*

Column 6 – 1896–1901: Col. 5 minus sum of cols. 9 and 10, multiplied by percentage of U.S. Government to total bonds computed from New York State *Insurance Reports.*
    1902–1911: Col. 5 minus sum of cols. 9 and 10, multiplied by percentages interpolated linearly between 1901 and 1912 percentages.
    1912–1928: Col. 5 minus sum of cols. 9 and 10, multiplied by percentages interpolated linearly between percentages obtained from samples of twenty large companies, from New York State *Insurance Reports* for 1912, 1917, 1922, and 1929. For 1912–1916, however, 1912 ratio was used. Samples accounted for 35 to 40 percent of total securities for all companies in the various years.
    1929–1931: Col. 5 minus sum of cols. 9 and 10, multiplied by percentages interpolated linearly between 1932 percentage obtained from *Spectator Insurance Yearbook* and percentage from twenty-company sample for 1929, adjusted on ratio of percentages obtained from similar sample in 1932 to *Spectator Insurance Yearbook* percentage.
    1932–1949: *Spectator Insurance Yearbook.*

Column 7 – 1896–1912: Col. 5 minus sum of cols. 6, 9, and 10 multiplied by percentage of state and local government bonds obtained from twenty-company sample for 1912.
    1913–1928: Col. 5 minus sum of cols. 9 and 10, multiplied by percentages interpolated linearly between samples for 1912, 1917, 1922, and 1929.
    1929–1931: Same procedure as for col. 6.
    1932–1949: *Spectator Insurance Yearbook.* Totals for 1932–1935 adjusted to exclude foreign government bonds estimated at $30 million annually.

Column 8 – 1896–1912: Same procedure as for col. 6.
    1913–1916: Col. 5 minus sum of cols. 6, 7, 9, and 10.
    1917–1931: Same procedure as for col. 7, 1913–1928.
    1932–1949: Same procedure as for col. 7. Totals for 1932–1935 adjusted to include foreign government bonds estimated at $30 million annually.

Columns 9 and 10 – 1896–1901: Total stocks estimated by multiplying col. 5 by percentages computed from New York State samples for 1896 and 1900, with linear interpolation for intervening years. 1901 percentage interpolated between 1900 sample and computed figures for 1902. Col. 9 estimated at 23.4 percent of total stocks, average for 1902–1906. Col. 10 estimated as total stocks minus preferred stock.
    1902–1931: Computed from percentages shown in Rose, D. C., *A Scientific Approach to Investment Management,* table IX, pp. 351–353, adjusted to include holdings of common stock of other (subsidiary) insurance companies, excluded by Rose, and estimated by him to amount to about 25 percent of all stocks held in more recent years (assumed 25 percent, 1927–1931, and decreased by 1 percent annually, 1926–1902). Rose's proportions for 1931 were also adjusted to link to 1932 *Spectator* proportions on ratio of preferred and common stocks to total securities in each. Percentages agree closely with those computed from New York State sample for 1906.
    1932–1948: Total stocks from *Insurance Yearbook* separated into preferred and common by application of percentages obtained from samples of 20 large companies for 1932, 1936, 1939, 1942, 1946, and 1948. Intervening years estimated by interpolation between absolutes computed for sample years.
    1949: Same method as 1932–1948, using 1948 percentage.

Data taken from *Spectator Yearbooks* used in Table V-55 and Table V-56 probably should have been adjusted for a few companies which are included in both the casualty and surety volume and the fire and marine volume. But because of the large amount of work involved, the problem of deciding the proper classification of each company and because of the fact that the consolidated series of total admitted assets would be only 5 to 10 percent below the sum of the assets series of the two groups used here, the adjustment was not made.

Note: Details may not add to totals because of rounding.

ASSETS OF FIRE AND MARINE INSURANCE COMPANIES
1896 to 1949
$ mill.

| End of year | Total | Cash | Mort- gages | Real estate | Securities | | | | | | Other assets |
					Total	U.S. Government	State and local government	Other bonds	Preferred stock	Common stock	
	1	2	3	4	5	6	7	8	9	10	11
1896	360	19	64	33	209	19	26	103	14	46	35
1897	388	24	58	35	234	33	26	101	18	57	37
1898	360	20	53	32	223	32	23	90	18	59	33
1899	401	21	54	35	251	40	24	93	22	73	40
1900	413	25	51	36	260	38	24	93	25	81	42
1901	451	30	51	36	287	32	30	118	25	82	46
1902	451	32	47	30	292	34	32	127	23	75	50
1903	479	31	48	31	320	33	36	140	25	87	49
1904	497	33	48	32	336	33	40	158	24	80	48
1905	544	35	51	32	374	33	46	178	28	89	52
1906	548	46	46	34	363	28	44	174	28	89	60
1907	558	39	53	33	367	24	46	182	27	87	66
1908	604	37	54	33	419	23	53	210	31	102	61
1909	660	47	56	33	461	20	59	233	29	120	63
1910	705	46	61	33	498	16	64	249	30	139	67
1911	745	52	64	31	526	11	68	269	33	144	71
1912	775	48	65	32	556	6	73	286	36	155	74
1913	792	52	66	32	567	6	76	310	34	141	74
1914	816	60	68	33	578	6	75	321	35	141	76
1915	874	70	68	33	620	7	77	345	37	154	83
1916	966	86	71	32	679	8	81	378	43	170	98
1917	1 078	111	71	31	739	52	87	384	43	174	126
1918	1 190	107	74	29	844	95	100	445	40	164	136
1919	1 391	133	75	28	993	150	112	496	53	183	160
1920	1 569	136	87	27	1 137	214	120	531	66	206	182
1921	1 592	118	84	35	1 189	272	119	524	58	216	166
1922	1 627	116	82	40	1 217	320	113	491	71	223	171
1923	1 782	132	86	47	1 327	325	128	545	77	252	190
1924	1 913	125	88	45	1 458	324	141	590	88	315	196
1925	2 092	145	87	46	1 605	309	151	617	112	416	209
1926	2 248	153	93	48	1 743	308	168	673	117	478	212
1927	2 503	171	92	49	1 983	321	198	774	137	553	208
1928	2 868	195	93	53	2 280	307	214	819	166	773	246
1929	3 084	213	97	54	2 493	272	217	812	202	990	226
1930	2 835	163	95	59	2 303	257	202	752	221	870	216
1931	2 641	153	85	63	2 155	245	190	704	241	774	185
1932	2 484	160	93	75	1 988	229	176	647	223	713	167
1933	2 230	156	85	83	1 750	268	171	598	224	489	157
1934	2 274	189	74	86	1 777	326	161	577	226	487	147
1935	2 556	195	65	87	2 061	393	152	556	229	731	149
1936	2 815	212	58	85	2 310	441	175	511	232	951	150
1937	2 631	240	56	86	2 100	515	171	476	229	709	149
1938	2 751	246	51	89	2 215	572	165	437	225	816	150
1939	2 840	329	49	86	2 219	580	159	392	221	867	157
1940	2 934	409	47	84	2 224	618	167	354	221	864	170
1941	3 052	430	46	83	2 302	726	163	341	221	851	190
1942	3 124	387	44	77	2 424	896	149	325	221	833	193
1943	3 447	366	42	72	2 772	1 099	139	312	247	975	195
1944	3 750	361	39	66	3 087	1 272	131	285	273	1 126	197
1945	4 237	357	33	63	3 569	1 468	116	254	300	1 431	215
1946	4 490	470	32	64	3 634	1 585	115	250	327	1 357	291
1947	4 971	532	29	66	3 986	1 891	146	258	321	1 370	357
1948	5 515	543	32	69	4 482	2 170	249	311	315	1 437	389
1949	6 558	625	48	85	5 357	2 479	365	365	387	1 761	443

Column 1 – 1896–1931: *Spectator Insurance Yearbook, Casualty and Surety Volume,* various issues. Spectator totals were adjusted to exclude life insurance assets of companies with both life and health-and-accident departments, Lloyd's and reciprocal companies, and title and mortgage guarantee companies. Assets of such companies were subtracted from published totals in a company-by-company examination for 1896, 1902, 1907, 1912, 1917, 1922, and 1927. Totals, excluding noncasualty companies, were estimated for intervening years by linear interpolation on ratio of revised *Spectator* totals to totals for same years obtained from *Annual Reports* of the Superintendent of Insurance for New York State.

    1932–1949: *Spectator Insurance Yearbook, Casualty and Surety Volume,* for indicated years.

*Columns 2–5 and 11–*1896–1905: Col. 1 multiplied by ratios of specified assets to total assets computed from New York State *Insurance Report,* 1906.

    1906–1931: Col. 1 multiplied by ratios of specified assets to total assets computed for each year from New York State *Insurance Reports.*

    1932–1949: *Spectator Insurance Yearbook.*

*Columns 6 to 8–*1896–1911: Col. 5 minus sum of cols. 9 and 10, multiplied by ratios of each type of bond to total bonds computed from sample of twelve large companies for 1912.

    1912–1928: Col. 5 minus sum of cols. 9 and 10, multiplied by percentages calculated for each type of bond (except for U.S. Government, which were calculated at 1912 ratio for 1913–1917) by linear interpolation between twelve-company sample ratios for 1912, 1917, 1922, and 1929. The twelve companies accounted for 40–55 percent of total securities held by all companies in the various years.

    1929: Col. 5 minus sum of cols. 9 and 10, multiplied by percentage of each type of bond shown as computed by adjusting twelve-company sample percentages by ratio for each type of security of sample to *Spectator Insurance Yearbook* percentage in 1932.

    1930–1931: Col. 5 minus sum of cols. 9 and 10, multiplied by percentages computed by linear interpolation for each type of bond between 1929 and 1932 percentages.

    1932–1949: *Spectator Insurance Yearbook.*

*Columns 9 and 10–*1896–1901: Total stocks, estimated as for cols. 6–8, divided into preferred and common by applying average percentages for 1902–1906.

    1902–1931: Total stocks, estimated from twelve-company sample for 1912, 1917, and 1929, and by linear interpolation for intervening years, divided into preferred and common in proportions applicable to fire insurance companies (Rose, D. C., *A Scientific Approach to Investment Management,* table IX, pp. 351–353) as proportions of common and preferred stock shown in Rose's sample of twenty-five fire insurance companies agree closely with those computed from twelve-casualty-company sample for 1932.

    1932–1948: Divided into preferred and common by linear interpolation between percentages derived from twelve-company sample for 1932, 1936, 1939, 1942, 1946, and 1948.

    1949: Same method as 1932–1948, using 1948 percentage.

Note: Details may not add to totals because of rounding.

$ mill.

End of year	Total	Cash	Mort-gages	Real estate	Securities						Other assets
					Total	U.S. Government	State and local government	Other bonds	Preferred stock	Common stock	
	1	2	3	4	5	6	7	8	9	10	11
1896	39	3	2	3	27	0	7	12	2	6	4
1897	43	3	2	3	30	0	7	12	3	7	4
1898	46	4	2	4	32	0	7	13	3	9	5
1899	55	4	3	4	38	0	9	15	4	10	6
1900	62	5	3	5	43	0	10	18	4	12	6
1901	67	5	3	5	46	0	10	18	5	13	7
1902	74	6	4	6	51	0	11	20	5	15	7
1903	84	7	4	7	58	0	13	23	5	17	8
1904	88	7	4	7	61	0	14	23	6	18	9
1905	98	8	5	8	68	0	15	27	7	19	10
1906	108	9	5	8	75	1	17	29	8	20	11
1907	111	8	6	9	75	1	16	28	8	22	14
1908	130	10	8	9	89	1	21	35	9	23	14
1909	147	11	10	9	101	1	24	42	8	26	16
1910	163	14	10	10	110	1	27	46	8	28	19
1911	184	14	11	12	126	1	32	55	9	30	22
1912	208	15	12	13	140	1	36	62	9	31	28
1913	212	16	14	13	140	1	34	63	10	32	29
1914	226	21	15	12	144	1	34	66	10	32	34
1915	240	22	16	12	154	1	35	74	10	33	35
1916	268	27	14	12	175	2	40	89	11	33	40
1917	314	30	14	11	205	14	46	99	12	34	53
1918	389	33	14	11	267	33	58	120	14	42	64
1919	478	41	15	14	333	59	69	140	18	47	76
1920	579	44	23	21	393	92	78	152	23	49	99
1921	621	38	27	29	436	127	81	153	20	54	91
1922	682	42	31	30	481	170	85	150	24	52	98
1923	751	47	36	30	525	170	90	173	28	64	113
1924	847	58	38	34	592	177	98	203	33	82	125
1925	953	66	47	36	666	178	108	239	41	101	139
1926	1 096	69	55	38	779	190	122	288	48	131	156
1927	1 268	79	63	39	928	203	141	354	62	169	158
1928	1 460	95	74	45	1 061	206	156	415	69	214	184
1929	1 544	104	76	51	1 121	192	160	449	74	245	193
1930	1 491	91	78	54	1 082	173	146	439	90	233	186
1931	1 440	70	79	53	1 053	155	136	432	107	222	184
1932	1 338	70	74	58	977	132	119	404	122	199	160
1933	1 248	72	70	57	897	164	123	371	119	120	151
1934	1 289	98	62	60	918	226	117	351	117	107	151
1935	1 442	121	56	63	1 033	286	123	334	115	174	169
1936	1 636	150	52	63	1 199	378	122	341	112	245	172
1937	1 661	184	36	62	1 198	446	118	333	111	190	181
1938	1 824	219	34	65	1 321	550	117	319	110	224	186
1939	1 945	294	33	63	1 371	581	124	297	109	260	185
1940	2 067	347	32	61	1 430	645	133	270	116	267	196
1941	2 234	370	35	60	1 551	770	137	262	123	259	218
1942	2 473	310	33	57	1 856	1 082	132	244	130	267	218
1943	2 750	328	30	57	2 113	1 314	123	213	147	316	223
1944	3 027	301	26	53	2 420	1 563	118	198	165	375	226
1945	3 351	298	24	51	2 728	1 755	105	185	183	501	250
1946	3 606	368	32	52	2 835	1 858	101	190	200	486	320
1947	4 122	480	38	56	3 162	2 100	135	219	204	504	386
1948	4 724	508	44	71	3 657	2 365	234	320	205	532	444
1949	5 447	522	45	82	4 328	2 594	416	442	244	633	469

Columns 1 and 4–From respective parts of Table V-58, col. 5. Period estimates were also checked against estimates derived by deflating reported values of stockholdings by means of stock price indices (cf. Table V-59, col. 7).

Columns 2 and 5 – Based on change in market value of preferred stock held as estimated in Tables V-55 and V-56, respectively. (Cost figures do not permit a distinction between common and preferred stocks without an issue-by-issue computation which was ruled out because of the amount of effort required.)

Columns 3 and 6 – Col. 1 minus col. 2 and col. 4 minus col. 5, respectively.

Column 1 – 1923–1949: From respective parts of Table V-59, col. 8.

Column 2 – 1923–1948: Difference between realized capital gains and capital losses as shown in *Annual Reports* of the New York Superintendent of Insurance. Since these reports cover a very large proportion, measured by volume of assets, of all companies – generally more than 90 percent – it has been regarded as unnecessary to adjust for the omission of smaller companies.
1949: Not estimated.

Column 3 – 1923–1948: Col. 2 adjusted for arbitrary allowance for presumed losses on bonds.
1949: Net profit on sale of stock by large companies (cf. note to Table V-59, col. 1) multiplied by ratios of market value of stock held by all companies to those of large companies (from Table V-59, col. 3 divided by col. 2).

Column 4 – 1923–1949: Col. 1 minus col. 3.

Column 5 – 1923–1949: Derived roughly as col. 4 divided by number of years in period.

NET PURCHASES OR SALES OF STOCKS BY FIRE, CASUALTY, AND MISCELLANEOUS INSURANCE COMPANIES: 1923 to 1949

$ mill.

Year	Fire insurance companies			Casualty and miscellaneous insurance companies			Year	Fire insurance companies			Casualty and miscellaneous insurance companies		
	Total stock	Preferred stock	Common stock	Total stock	Preferred stock	Common stock		Total stock	Preferred stock	Common stock	Total stock	Preferred stock	Common stock
	1	2	3	4	5	6		1	2	3	4	5	6
1923	35	10	25	20	5	15	1937	–15	–	–15	15	.	.
1924	35	10	25	20	5	15	1938	–15	–	–15	15	.	.
1925	35	10	25	20	5	15	1939	–15	–	–15	15	.	.
1926	35	10	25	20	5	15	1940	70	–	70	25	10	15
1927	105	30	75	30	10	20	1941	70	–	70	25	10	15
1928	105	30	75	30	10	20	1942	70	–	70	25	10	15
1929	105	30	75	30	10	20	1943	35	25	10	20	15	5
1930	60	10	50	25	15	10	1944	35	25	10	20	15	5
1931	60	10	50	25	15	10	1945	35	25	10	20	15	5
1932	60	10	50	25	15	10	1946	75	25	50	65	20	45
1933	15	–	15	–10	.	.	1947	45	–	45	50	5	45
1934	15	–	15	–10	.	.	1948	75	–	75	45	5	40
1935	15	–	15	–10	.	.	1949	160	–	160	70	10	60
1936	15	–	15	–10	.	.							

DERIVATION OF NET PURCHASES OR SALES OF STOCKS BY FIRE AND CASUALTY INSURANCE COMPANIES; SELECTED PERIODS: 1923 to 1949

$ mill.

Period	Change in cost of stocks held	Realized capital gains		Inferred net purchases or sales	Annual net purchases or sales	Period	Change in cost of stocks held	Realized capital gains		Inferred net purchases or sales	Annual net purchases or sales
		Total	On stocks					Total	On stocks		
	Fire insurance companies						Casualty insurance companies				
	1	2	3	4	5		1	2	3	4	5
1923–26	180	45	45	135	35	1923–26	80	10	10	70	20
1927–29	400	85	85	315	105	1927–29	120	25	25	95	30
1930–32	80	–135	–100	180	60	1930–32	60	–30	–20	80	25
1933–36	0	–90	–70	70	15	1933–36	–40	–15	–10	–30	–10
1937–39	–70	–40	–30	–40	–15	1937–39	30	–20	–15	45	15
1940–42	140	–80	–60	200	70	1940–42	30	–50	–40	70	25
1943–45	130	45	30	100	35	1943–45	70	20	10	60	20
1946	100	28	25	75	75	1946	80	15	15	65	65
1947	50	7	5	45	45	1947	50	0	0	50	50
1948	70	–5	–5	75	75	1948	40	–5	–5	45	45
1949	160		0	160	160	1949	70		0	70	70

DATA USED IN DERIVATION OF NET PURCHASES OR SALES OF STOCKS BY FIRE AND CASUALTY INSURANCE COMPANIES; SELECTED YEARS: 1922 to 1949

$ mill.

Year	Large companies		All companies					
	Cost	Market	Market	Deflated market (1929 prices)	Change in			
					Market	Deflated market	Deflated market adjusted	Cost
	1	2	3	4	5	6	7	8
Fire and marine insurance companies								
1922	137	160	294	569				
1926	222	289	595	832	301	263	156	180
1929	418	577	1 192	1 192	597	360	443	400
1932	462	500	936	2 542	−256	1 350	864	80
1936	464	609	1 183	1 375	247	−1 167	−497	0
1939	425	581	1 088	1 639	−95	264	164	−70
1942	498	560	1 054	1 933	−34	294	169	140
1945	561	865	1 731	1 856	677	−77	−37	130
1946	612	836	1 684	2 011	−47	155	149	100
1947	635	837	1 691	2 114	7	103	88	50
1948	669	868	1 752	2 217	61	103	76	70
1949	747	1 080	2 148	.	.	.	.	160
Casualty and miscellaneous insurance companies								
1922	34	37	76	142				
1926	65	67	179	246	103	104	65	80
1929	120	145	319	320	140	74	85	120
1932	147	146	321	779	2	459	399	60
1936	133	143	357	399	36	−380	−172	−40
1939	146	153	369	526	12	127	−77	30
1942	159	154	397	668	28	142	89	30
1945	184	241	684	704	287	36	36	70
1946	211	246	686	782	2	78	77	80
1947	228	253	708	848	22	66	59	50
1948	241	261	737	894	29	46	36	40
1949	264	312	877	.	.	.	.	70

Columns 1 and 2 – 1922–1948: From company statements as summarized in *Annual Reports* of the New York Superintendent of Insurance.

1949: From company statements filed with District of Columbia Insurance Department.

Column 3 – 1922–1949: Table V-55, sum of cols. 9 and 10 for fire insurance companies, and Table V-56, sum of cols. 9 and 10, for casualty insurance companies.

Column 4 – 1922–1949: Table V-55, col. 10, divided by *Standard Statistics* common stock price index for Dec. (from *Banking and Monetary Statistics*, pp. 480–481, and *Federal Reserve Bulletin*, various issues, converted to Dec. 1929 = 100) plus Table V-55, col. 9, divided by preferred stock index (from same source adjusted to Dec. 1929 = 100). For casualty insurance companies, same indices were used with Table V-56, cols. 10 and 9, respectively.

Column 5 – 1926–1949: Derived from col. 3.

Column 6 – 1926–1949: Derived from col. 4.

Column 7 – 1926–1949: Change in deflated market value of preferred and common stock multiplied by average of appropriate price index, on 1929 basis, for period of change.

Column 8 – 1926–1949: First differences of col. 1 blown up in accordance with ratio between cols. 3 and 2, rounded to nearest $10 million.

ASSETS OF OPEN-END MANAGEMENT INVESTMENT COMPANIES
1924 to 1949
$ mill.

End of year	Total	Cash	U.S. Government securities	Other bonds	Preferred stock	Common stock	Other assets
	1	2	3	4	5	6	7
1924	2	–	–	–	–	2	–
1925	6	1	–	–	–	5	–
1926	17	4	–	1	–	12	–
1927	46	10	1	1	–	34	–
1928	123	21	20	–	1	81	–
1929	134	19	2	4	2	107	–
1930	102	8	2	3	3	86	–
1931	64	5	6	1	1	50	1
1932	74	7	6	2	1	58	–
1933	170	7	1	2	1	159	–
1934	211	22	6	2	2	179	–
1935	356	23	2	4	9	318	–
1936	506	39	3	8	5	451	–
1937	405	56	17	7	4	319	2
1938	530	49	1	11	11	455	3
1939	532	37	4	18	14	456	3
1940	476	40	2	28	15	388	3
1941	428	40	4	40	15	326	3
1942	515	39	15	64	21	375	1
1943	660	28	25	91	42	474	–
1944	872	43	31	115	63	620	–
1945	1 266	69	37	138	114	908	–
1946	1 297	69	31	122	122	953	–
1947	1 412	71	43	131	140	1 027	–
1948	1 515	69	65	135	137	1 109	–
1949	1 939	82	104	154	156	1 443	–

Column 1 – 1924–1926: Assets of three large companies (Massachusetts Investors Trust, Incorporated Investors, and State Street Investment Corporation) obtained from *Moody's Manual* linked to 1927 total for all companies included in Securities and Exchange Commission report, *Investment Trusts and Investment Companies, Part II*, p. 136.

1927–1936: *Investment Trusts and Investment Companies, Part II, Statistical Survey of Investment Trusts and Investment Companies.*

1937–1941: Based on assets of large companies (eight companies 1936–1939; ten companies 1940–1948) from *Moody's Manual*. These companies accounted for 64 percent of the assets of all reporting operating companies in 1936 and for 55 percent in 1942. Annual blow-up ratios were obtained by linear interpolation between proportions of these companies to totals for 1936 and 1942 shown in col. 1.

1942–1949: Securities and Exchange Commission, *Statistical Bulletin*, various issues.

Column 2 – 1924–1926: Col. 1 multiplied by percentage of cash to total assets in 1927.

1927–1936: Same source as for col. 1. Figures are "liquid assets" less U.S. Government securities shown in col. 3.

1937–1941: Col. 1 multiplied by percentage of cash to total assets from sample of eight to ten companies.

1942–1949: Same source as for col. 1.

Column 3 – 1924–1926: Total assets multiplied by percentage of U.S. Government securities in 1927.

1927–1936: Same source as for col. 1. U.S. Government securities, shown in *Investment Trusts...* only for open- and closed-end companies combined, were estimated for open-end companies as same percentage of total assets as for all investment companies (*op cit.*, p. 133). For 1928, however, $20 million was added to the computed figure for U.S. securities temporarily held by one open-end company (*op. cit.*, p. 56, table 6, note b).

1937–1941: Same source as col. 1, except for Keystone Custodian Funds, which had been classified as fixed investment trust before 1936. Total securities held in these funds, for which data by type of security were obtained from *Moody's Manual*, were deducted from total securities estimated for open-end companies; and smaller total distributed according to sample distribution. U.S. Government securities and "other bonds," "common stocks," and "preferred stocks" held by Keystone were then added to make up total for all open-end companies.

1942–1949: Same source as col. 1.

Columns 4, 5 and 6 – 1924–1936: Same source as col. 2, using percentages for relevant type of securities.

1937–1941: See col. 3.

1942–1948: Total of nongovernment securities, as published in Securities and Exchange Commission, *Statistical Bulletin*, distributed annually according to percentages computed from eight to ten sample companies for 1942–1948, after adjustment for Keystone Custodian Funds as above. All securities of other investment companies and miscellaneous securities reported are included with common stock.

1949: Other bonds and preferred stock estimated as average of 1948 figure and figure estimated as same proportion of col. 1 minus sum of cols. 2, 3, and 7 as in 1948. This extrapolation is based on assumption that a large part of the increase in market value of securities held resulted from relatively greater increase in common stock prices than in prices of other securities. Hence other bonds and preferred stock are assumed to have increased less than proportionately to all securities, and common stock is taken as col. 1 minus sum of cols. 2–5 and 7.

Column 7 – 1924–1949: Same source and method as col. 2.

NET PURCHASES OF SECURITIES (OTHER THAN U.S. GOVERNMENT SECURITIES) BY OPEN-END INVESTMENT COMPANIES: 1927 to 1949

$ mill.

Year	Net proceeds from sales of own securities	Annual change, assets other than non-U.S. Government securities	Annual change, liabilities	Retained ordinary earnings	Net purchases of securities (other than U.S. Government securities)		
					Estimated from		Reported
					Cash flow	Deflation of reported holdings	
	1	2	3	4	5	6	7
1927	16	7	–	0	9	17	–
1928	29	30	20	0	19	30	–
1929	61	–20	–18	0	63	50	–
1930	12	–11	–3	0	20	12	–
1931	8	2	0	–1	5	5	–
1932	16	1	0	–1	14	18	–
1933	63	–5	2	–2	68	61	70
1934	44	20	1	–3	22	30	23
1935	62	–3	3	–5	63	58	64
1936	84	17	1	–28	40	44	82
1937	134	33	–	–	101	29	43
1938	30	–22	–	–	52	99	65
1939	30	–9	–	–	39	10	–
1940	11	1	–	–	10	–1	3
1941	11	2	–	–	9	10	9
1942	36	8	–	–	28	49	25
1943	52	–2	–	–	54	71	56
1944	82	21	–	–	61	115	65
1945	156	32	–	–	124	134	110
1946	193	–6	–	–	199	169	171
1947	154	14	–	–	140	156	149
1948	123	20	–	–	103	93	128
1949	241	52	–	–	189	206	222

Column 1 – 1927–1949: Gross proceeds, as given in Table V-38, col. 3, reduced by assumed load of 8 percent on sales (Table V-38, col. 1) from Securities and Exchange Commission, *Investment Trusts and Investment Companies, Part II, Statistical Survey of Investment Trusts and Investment Companies*, p. 220.

Column 2 – 1927–1949: Table V-60, sum of first differences of cols. 2, 3, and 7.

Column 3 - 1927–1936: *Ibid.*, p. 137.

Column 4 – 1927–1936: *Ibid.*, p. 151. Figures are "Balance to surplus" less "Profit or loss on sale of securities."

Column 5 – 1927–1949: Col. 1 minus col. 2 plus cols. 3 and 4.

Column 6 – 1927–1949: "Other bonds," "preferred stocks," and "common stocks" from Table V-60, cols. 4 to 6, deflated for each year by appropriate year-end price indices; annual changes in deflated totals for each type of security were then multiplied by appropriate indexes of average prices for year and combined for the three types of securities.

Column 7 – 1933–1935: *Ibid.*, p. 630.
 1936–1938: *Ibid.*, p. 640. Published figures, which accounted for 54 percent of total for all companies, were raised to cover 100 percent.
 1939: Assumed to be negligible.
 1940–1941: National Association of Investment Companies (release of Sept. 1949). Figures include practically all open-end companies covered by Securities and Exchange Commission statistics.
 1942–1949: Securities and Exchange Commission, *Statistical Bulletin*, various issues.

Column 1 – 1921–1922: Total assets of Adams Express Company, American International Corporation, and Railway and Light Securities Company.

  1923: Total for same companies as for 1921–1922 slightly increased by estimated assets of new companies formed during year for which balance sheets were not published.

  1924: Same procedure as for 1923, with total assets of U.S. and Foreign Securities Corporation and International Securities Trust added.

  1925: Same procedure as for 1924, with total assets of American Founders Trust added.

  1926: Same procedure as for 1925, with total assets of Continental Securities Corporation, North American Investment Corporation, Overseas Securities Corporation, and General Public Service Corporation added.

  1927–1936: Securities and Exchange Commission, *Investment Trusts and Investment Companies, Part II, Statistical Survey of Investment Trusts and Investment Companies,* pp. 138, 140, 152.

  1937–1941: Estimated on basis of total assets of fifteen largest closed-end investment companies from *Moody's Manual,* which accounted for 63 percent of total assets reported to Securities and Exchange Commission for 1936, and about 60 and 74 percent for 1937 and 1942, respectively, of totals in Securities and Exchange Commission monthly *Statistical Bulletin.* (Figures published adjusted to exclude holding and unclassified investment companies and investment trusts for 1942 and 1948. Companies excluded are those classified in the Securities and Exchange Commission *Report,* pp. 733–745, as holding or unclassified companies, insofar as they were included in *Statistical Bulletin* totals.)

  Figures in col. 1 obtained by dividing totals for fifteen companies by annual ratios derived by straight line interpolation between 0.60 in 1937 and 0.74 in 1942.

  1942–1949: Total assets as reported in Securities and Exchange Commission monthly *Statistical Bulletin,* excluding holding and unclassified companies on basis of Securities and Exchange Commission's file of quarterly reports.

Column 2 – 1921–1926: Estimated as same percentage of total assets as in 1927.

  1927–1936: Same source as col. 1.

  1937–1941: Col. 1 multiplied by percentages computed from fifteen-company Moody's sample, for which complete asset distributions were obtained for 1936, 1939, 1942, 1946, and 1948. Linear interpolations were used to obtain percentage distribution by type of assets for intervening years. 1940 and 1941 percentages were interpolated between 1939 sample percentage and 1942 percentage derived from this table.

  1942–1949: Same source as col. 1.

Column 3 – 1921–1926: Same procedure as col. 2.

  1927–1936: Holdings of U.S. Government securities, shown only for all investment companies combined in Securities and Exchange Commission, *Report, op. cit.,* were estimated at percentage of total assets for all companies, except for 1928, when allowance was made for $20 million of U.S. securities temporarily held by one open-end company (cf. Securities and Exchange Commission, *Report,* p. 56, table 6, note b).

  1937–1941: Same method as col. 2.

  1942–1949: Same source as col. 1.

Columns 4 to 6 – 1921–1936: Same procedure as col. 2.

  1937–1948: Col. 1 minus sum of cols. 2, 3, and 7 multiplied by percentages derived from samples as described in col. 2. For 1942–1948, securities of other investment companies derived from same source as col. 1 are attributed entirely to common stock.

  1949: Other bonds estimated as average of 1948 figure and figure equal to col. 1 minus sum of cols. 2, 3, and 7 multiplied by percentage of col. 4 to sum of cols. 4–6 in 1948. Same method is used for preferred stock, and common stock is taken as a residual.

Column 7 – 1921–1949: Same sources and methods as col. 2.

Note: Details may not add to totals because of rounding.

$ mill.; market value

End of year	Total	Cash	U.S. Government securities	Other bonds	Preferred stock	Common stock	Other assets
	1	2	3	4	5	6	7
1921	100	11	1	17	12	56	3
1922	100	11	1	17	12	57	2
1923	90	10	1	15	11	51	2
1924	100	11	1	17	12	56	3
1925	140	15	1	24	17	79	4
1926	250	27	2	43	30	139	9
1927	555	60	4	95	68	309	19
1928	1 445	325	3	116	104	853	45
1929	2 638	444	23	168	174	1 753	76
1930	1 800	222	38	165	158	1 152	64
1931	953	116	76	104	84	524	47
1932	766	98	46	97	56	428	40
1933	830	58	5	85	52	593	37
1934	818	57	9	90	59	579	24
1935	1 044	75	6	87	102	752	22
1936	1 261	102	6	75	112	932	33
1937	738	47	4	56	59	556	15
1938	842	49	7	74	60	639	14
1939	784	41	9	78	49	599	9
1940	692	38	14	61	55	517	7
1941	616	34	17	47	60	452	5
1942	654	40	24	42	75	468	4
1943	759	44	31	41	76	551	16
1944	835	49	54	37	71	606	18
1945	1 050	59	58	38	79	797	19
1946	904	52	42	26	56	709	20
1947	773	45	41	21	61	587	17
1948	784	47	48	21	76	566	25
1949	976	39	49	24	87	769	8

NET PURCHASES OF SECURITIES (OTHER THAN U.S. GOVERNMENT
SECURITIES) BY CLOSED-END INVESTMENT COMPANIES: 1927 to 1949

$ mill.

Year	Net proceeds from sales of own securities	Annual change, assets other than corporate and foreign securities	Annual change, liabilities	Retained ordinary earnings	Net purchases of securities (other than U.S. Government securities)		
					Estimated from		Reported
					Cash flow	Deflation of reported holdings	
	1	2	3	4	5	6	7
1927	156	45	–	0	111	203	–
1928	507	290	14	–4	227	426	–
1929	1 418	170	29	–3	1 274	1 366	–
1930	–112	–219	–4	–1	102	–165	–
1931	–70	–85	–22	2	–5	–242	–
1932	–42	–55	–13	3	3	–44	–
1933	–15	–84	10	–4	75	–63	47
1934	–12	–10	–22	–5	–29	7	–18
1935	–18	13	8	–7	–30	–32	–20
1936	–1	38	33	–20	–26	–26	–113
1937	–30	–75	–	–	45	–142	–135
1938	–15	4	–	–	–19	27	37
1939	–15	–11	–	–	–4	–47	–
1940	–15	0	–	–	–15	–17	–
1941	–15	–3	–	–	–12	5	–
1942	–15	12	–	–	–27	–10	–30
1943	–19	23	–	–	–42	–12	–50
1944	–5	30	–	–	–35	–35	–42
1945	–48	15	–	–	–63	–8	–71
1946	–48	–22	–	–	–26	–24	–56
1947	–9	–11	–	–	2	–92	–27
1948	–21	17	–	–	–38	–2	–20
1949	–3	–24	–	–	21	131	–19

Column 1 – 1927–1949: Gross proceeds, as given in Table V-38, col. 6 reduced by assumed load of sales
(from Table V-38, col. 4) of 5.5 percent, based on Securities and Exchange Commission,
*Investment Trusts and Investment Companies, Part II, Statistical Survey of Investment Trusts
and Investment Companies*, p. 205.

Column 2 – 1927–1949: Table V-62, sum of the first differences of cols. 2, 3, and 7.

Column 3 – 1927–1936: Securities and Exchange Commission, *Investment Trusts and Investment Companies,
Part II, Statistical Survey of Investment Trusts and Investment Companies*, pp. 139–141.
Excludes funded debt and capital stock outstanding.

Column 4 – 1927–1936: Securities and Exchange Commission, *Investment Trusts and Investment Companies,
Part II, Statistical Survey of Investment Trusts and Investment Companies*, pp. 149–150.
Figures are "Balance to surplus" minus "Profit or loss on sale of securities." Excludes Atlas
and Equity companies.

Column 5 – 1927–1949: Col. 1 minus col. 2 plus cols. 3 and 4.

Column 6 – 1927–1949: Same procedure as Table V-61, col. 6.

Column 7 – 1933–1949: Same source as Table V-61, col. 7 minus net purchases by management investment
holding companies from Table V-65, col. 5, and by unclassified management investment
companies from Table V-67, col. 4.

COMPARISON OF NET PURCHASES OF SECURITIES (OTHER THAN U.S. GOVERNMENT SECURITIES) BY OPEN- AND CLOSED-END MANAGEMENT INVESTMENT COMPANIES ESTIMATED BY DIFFERENT METHODS: 1927 to 1949

$ mill.

Year	Open-end companies				Closed-end companies			
	Reported by S.E.C.	Deflated by security price indices	Cash flow method	Change in reported portfolios	Reported by S.E.C.	Deflated by security price indices	Cash flow method	Change in reported portfolios
	1	2	3	4	5	6	7	8
1927	–	17	9	22	–	203	111	260
1928	–	30	19	47	–	426	227	601
1929	–	50	63	31	–	1 366	1 274	1 022
1930	–	12	20	–21	–	–165	102	–620
1931	–	5	5	–40	–	–242	–5	–763
1932	–	18	14	9	–	–44	3	–131
1933	70	61	68	101	47	–63	75	149
1934	23	30	22	21	–18	7	–29	–2
1935	64	58	63	148	–20	–32	–30	213
1936	82	44	40	133	–113	–26	–26	178
1937	43	29	101	–134	–135	–142	45	–448
1938	65	99	52	147	37	27	–19	102
1939	–	10	39	11	–	–47	–4	–47
1940	3	–1	10	–57	–	–17	–15	–93
1941	9	10	9	–50	–	5	–12	–74
1942	25	49	28	79	–30	–10	–27	26
1943	56	71	54	147	–50	–12	–42	83
1944	65	115	61	191	–42	–35	–35	46
1945	110	134	124	362	–71	–8	–63	200
1946	171	169	199	37	–56	–24	–26	–123
1947	149	156	140	101	–27	–92	2	–122
1948	128	93	103	83	–20	–2	–38	–6
1949	222	206	189	372	–19	131	21	217
1927–32	–	132	130	48	–	1 544	1 706	369
1933–38	347	321	346	416	–202	–229	16	192
1939–41	12	19	58	–96	–	–59	–31	–214
1942–49	926	993	898	1 372	–315	–52	–208	321
1927–49	1 285	1 465	1 432	1 740	–517	1 204	1 483	668

Column 1 – Table V-61, col. 7.

Column 2 – Table V-61, col. 6.

Column 3 – Table V-61, col. 5.

Column 4 – Table V-60, sum of annual changes in cols. 4–6.

Column 5 – Table V-63, col. 7.

Column 6 – Table V-63, col. 6.

Column 7 – Table V-63, col. 5.

Column 8 – Table V-62, sum of annual changes in cols. 4–6.

Column 1 – 1927–1935: Sales from Securities and Exchange Commission, *Investment Trusts and Investment Companies, Part II, Statistical Survey of Investment Trusts and Investment Companies*, p. 190, minus 5.5 percent loading charges (cf. *ibid.*, p. 205) minus purchases (cf. *ibid.*, pp. 258–261). Covers twenty to forty-four companies with total assets of $868 million in 1927 and $1906 million in 1936 and an unspecified number of other companies for which data were obtained by the Securities and Exchange Commission from various published sources (cf. *ibid.*, p. 190).
1936–1941: Not estimated but assumed to be negligible.
1942–1949: From Securities and Exchange Commission file of quarterly reports, minus loading charges on sales. Covers twelve to fourteen companies registered under 1940 Investment Company Act with total assets of $671 million in 1942 and $759 million in 1948.

Column 2 – 1928–1936: Securities and Exchange Commission, *Investment Trusts and Investment Companies, Part II, Statistical Survey of Investment Trusts and Investment Companies*, p. 158, raised to cover all holding companies (cf. *ibid.*, p. 112). U.S. Government securities estimated as same proportion as for all management investment companies (*ibid.*, p. 133).
1937–1943: Not estimated but assumed to be negligible.
1944–1949: Securities and Exchange Commission file of quarterly reports.

Column 3 – 1928–1936: Securities and Exchange Commission, *Investment Trusts and Investment Companies, Part II, Statistical Survey of Investment Trusts and Investment Companies*, p. 159, raised to cover all holding companies (cf. col. 2).

Column 4 – 1927–1935, 1942–1949: Col. 1 minus col. 2 plus col. 3. 1927 estimated.

Column 5 – 1942–1949: Securities and Exchange Commission file of quarterly reports.

V-66   TABLE V-66

Columns 1, 2, and 3 – Estimated roughly to be 2, 5, and 93 percent, respectively, of Table V-65, col. 4.

NET PORTFOLIO PURCHASES
BY MANAGEMENT INVESTMENT HOLDING COMPANIES: 1927 to 1949

$ mill.

Year	Net proceeds from sales of own securities	Annual change in assets excluding corporate and foreign securities	Annual change in liabilities (excluding capital)	Estimated net portfolio purchases	Net portfolio purchases reported to S.E.C.
	1	2	3	4	5
1927	118	.	.	100	—
1928	234	74	31	191	—
1929	876	132	94	838	—
1930	249	−124	−1	372	—
1931	−8	−31	−50	−27	—
1932	−19	4	−3	−26	—
1933	−5	−19	−48	−34	—
1934	12	−6	−5	13	—
1935	10	13	5	2	—
1936	—	−4	0	—	—
1937	—	—	—	—	—
1938	—	—	—	—	—
1939	—	—	—	—	—
1940	—	—	—	—	—
1941	—	—	—	—	—
1942	−3	—	—	−3	−2
1943	−35	—	—	−35	−19
1944	−16	13	—	−29	−35
1945	−4	−3	—	−1	10
1946	−16	−4	—	−12	−13
1947	−6	11	—	−17	3
1948	−4	4	—	−8	−5
1949	−3	5	—	−8	−7

NET PURCHASES OF SECURITIES, BY TYPE,
BY MANAGEMENT INVESTMENT HOLDING COMPANIES: 1927 to 1949

$ mill.

Year	U.S. Government bonds	Preferred stock	Common stock	Year	U.S. Government bonds	Preferred stock	Common stock
	1	2	3		1	2	3
1927	2	5	93	1938	—	—	—
1928	4	10	177	1939	—	—	—
1929	17	42	779	1940	—	—	—
1930	7	19	346	1941	—	—	—
1931	0	−1	−26	1942	0	0	−3
1932	0	−1	−25	1943	0	−2	−33
1933	0	−2	−32	1944	0	−1	−28
1934	0	1	12	1945	0	0	−1
1935	0	0	2	1946	0	−1	−11
1936	—	—	—	1947	0	−1	−16
1937	—	—	—	1948	0	−1	−7
				1949	0	−1	−7

TABLE V-67

Column 1 – 1927–1936: Securities and Exchange Commission, *Investment Trusts and Investment Companies, Part II, Statistical Survey of Investment Trusts and Investment Companies*, p. 190, minus 5.5 percent loading charge. Redemptions not available. Covers twelve to twenty-one companies with total assets of $233 million in 1927 and $310 million in 1936 and an unspecified number of other companies for which data were obtained by the Securities and Exchange Commission from various published sources (cf. *ibid.*, p. 190, note d).

    1942–1949: Securities and Exchange Commission file of quarterly reports; sales minus loading charges and redemptions for four to eight companies registered under 1940 Investment Company Act, with total assets of $147 million in 1942 and $99 million in 1948.

Columns 2 and 4 – 1943–1949: Securities and Exchange Commission file of quarterly reports.

Column 3 – 1942–1949: Col. 1 minus col. 2.

TABLE V-68

Column 1 – 1927–1936: 80 percent of Table V-67, col. 1.
    1937–1941: Not estimated but assumed to be negligible.
    1942–1949: 90 percent of Table V-67, col. 3.

Columns 2 and 3 – 1927–1936: 5 percent of Table V-67, col. 1.
    1937–1941: Not estimated but assumed to be negligible.
    1942–1949: 5 percent of Table V-67, col. 3.

NET PORTFOLIO PURCHASES
BY UNCLASSIFIED MANAGEMENT INVESTMENT COMPANIES: 1927 to 1949

$ mill.

| Year | Net proceeds from sales of own securities | Annual change, assets excluding corporate and foreign securities | Portfolio purchases | | Year | Net proceeds from sales of own securities | Annual change, assets excluding corporate and foreign securities | Portfolio purchases | |
| | | | Estimated | Net reported to S.E.C. | | | | Estimated | Net reported to S.E.C. |
	1	2	3	4		1	2	3	4
1927	38	.	.	.	1938	.	.	.	.
1928	76	.	.	.	1939	.	.	.	.
1929	302	.	.	.	1940	.	.	.	.
1930	132	.	.	.	1941	.	.	.	.
1931	13	.	.	.	1942	0	.	.	−5
1932	4	.	.	.	1943	3	37	−34	−40
1933	6	.	.	.	1944	2	13	−11	−10
1934	23	.	.	.	1945	1	13	−12	10
1935	2	.	.	.	1946	−3	−4	1	0
1936	0	.	.	.	1947	4	0	4	−5
1937	.	.	.	.	1948	0	1	−1	1
					1949	0	3	−3	−2

NET PURCHASES OF SECURITIES, BY TYPE,
BY UNCLASSIFIED MANAGEMENT INVESTMENT COMPANIES: 1927 to 1949

$ mill.

| Year | Common stock | Preferred stock | U.S. Government bonds | Year | Common stock | Preferred stock | U.S. Government bonds |
	1	2	3		1	2	3
1927	30	2	2	1938	−	−	−
1928	61	4	4	1939	−	−	−
1929	242	15	15	1940	−	−	−
1930	106	7	7	1941	−	−	−
1931	10	1	1	1942	−	−	−
1932	3	−	−	1943	−30	−2	−2
1933	5	−	−	1944	−9	−1	−1
1934	18	1	1	1945	−10	−1	−1
1935	2	0	0	1946	1	0	0
1936	0	0	0	1947	4	0	0
1937	−	−	−	1948	−1	0	0
				1949	−3	0	0

TABLE V-69

Column 1 – 1927–1936: Securities and Exchange Commission, *Investment Trusts and Investment Companies,* *Part II, Statistical Survey of Investment Trusts and Investment Companies,* p. 114. Published figures, which accounted for 80 percent of all trusts in 1927 and 90 percent in 1936, were adjusted for assets not included in Securities and Exchange Commission totals; annual adjustment ratios obtained by linear interpolation between 1927 and 1936. Figures for years before 1927 may be assumed negligible, as sales of fixed-trust certificates during 1927 are estimated at $25 million (*ibid.,* p. 190) and thus account for practically all assets at end of 1927 if allowance is made for increase in market value during year.

   1937–1948: Estimated from data obtained from sample of fourteen trusts accounting for 68 percent of 1936 Securities and Exchange Commission total assets.

   1949: Rough estimate based on Table V-70, col. 5.

Column 2 – 1927–1936: Col. 1 multiplied by percentage of each type of asset shown (*ibid.,* p. 168).

   1937–1949: Estimated as same percentage of total assets as in 1936.

Column 3 – 1927–1936: Same source as col. 2.

   1937–1949: Estimated from North American Bond Trust data.

Column 4 – 1927–1936: Same source as col. 2.

   1937–1949: Col. 1 minus sum of cols. 2 and 3. Stocks are assumed all common. (See U.S. Congress, *Investment Trusts and Investment Companies, House Document No. 567,* 76th Congress, 3rd Session.)

TABLE V-70

Column 1 – 1927–1936: Securities and Exchange Commission, *Investment Trusts and Investment Companies,* *Part II, Statistical Survey of Investment Trusts and Investment Companies,* p. 190, divided by 1.08 to eliminate loading charges.

Columns 2 and 3 – 1927–1936: Estimated distribution of total of $340 million for 1927–1935 (*ibid.,* p. 245).

Columns 4 and 5 – 1927–1936: Col. 1 minus col. 2 or 3, respectively.

   1937–1948: Estimated from sample of fourteen large trusts accounting for 68 percent of 1936 assets of Securities and Exchange Commission.

   1949: Rough estimate based on preceding years.

Columns 6 and 7 – 1927–1949: First differences from Table V-69, cols. 2 and 3, respectively. Figures for 1927 estimated.

Column 8 – 1927–1949: Col. 4 minus sum of cols. 6 and 7.

Column 9 – 1927–1949: Col. 5 minus sum of cols. 6 and 7.

Column 10 – 1927–1949: Annual common stock portfolio (from Table V-69, col. 4) divided by year-end price index; resulting annual changes multiplied by annual average price index.

ASSETS OF FIXED AND SEMIFIXED INVESTMENT TRUSTS
1927 to 1949

$ mill.

End of year	Total	Cash	Bonds	Stocks	End of year	Total	Cash	Bonds	Stocks
	1	2	3	4		1	2	3	4
1927	31	1	0	30	1938	94	2	5	87
1928	84	3	0	81	1939	92	2	4	86
1929	164	11	0	153	1940	73	2	3	68
1930	358	45	0	313	1941	56	1	2	53
1931	278	25	0	253	1942	56	1	2	53
1932	216	10	1	205	1943	66	2	2	62
1933	204	6	4	194	1944	70	2	1	67
1934	159	5	6	148	1945	82	2	1	79
1935	190	5	9	176	1946	62	2	1	59
1936	189	5	9	175	1947	47	1	1	45
1937	106	3	7	96	1948	36	1	1	34
					1949	32	1	1	30

NET PURCHASES OF SECURITIES
(OTHER THAN U.S. GOVERNMENT SECURITIES) BY FIXED AND SEMIFIXED INVESTMENT TRUSTS: 1927 to 1949

$ mill.

Year	Net proceeds from sales	Estimated redemptions		Net cash receipts from sales of own securities		Annual change in cash held	Annual change in bonds	Net purchases of securities (other than U.S. Government securities) estimated on basis of		
								Sales of own securities		Deflation of reported holdings
		A	B	A	B			A	B	
	1	2	3	4	5	6	7	8	9	10
1927	23	5	5	18	18	1	0	17	17	–
1928	44	10	10	34	34	2	0	32	32	34
1929	81	20	10	61	71	8	0	53	63	101
1930	311	55	30	256	281	34	0	222	247	275
1931	246	50	80	196	166	−20	0	216	186	145
1932	69	50	80	19	−11	−15	1	33	3	−6
1933	11	50	80	−39	−69	−4	3	−38	−68	−100
1934	11	50	25	−39	−14	−1	2	−40	−15	−38
1935	22	50	20	−28	2	0	3	−31	−1	−27
1936	14	50	20	−36	−6	0	0	−36	−6	−42
1937	–	–	–	−25		−2	−2	−21		−26
1938	–	–	–	−18		−1	−2	−15		−19
1939	–	–	–	−5		0	−1	−4		−1
1940	–	–	–	−7		0	−1	−6		−7
1941	–	–	–	−5		−1	−1	−3		−6
1942	–	–	–	−2		0	0	−2		−4
1943	–	–	–	−4		1	0	−5		−1
1944	–	–	–	−5		0	−1	−4		−4
1945	–	–	–	−8		0	0	−8		−11
1946	–	–	–	−10		0	0	−10		−12
1947	–	–	–	−5		−1	0	−4		−12
1948	–	–	–	−3		0	0	−3		−11
1949	–	–	–	−5		0	0	−5		−7

COMPARISON OF NET PURCHASES OF SECURITIES (OTHER THAN U.S. GOVERNMENT SECURITIES) BY FIXED AND SEMIFIXED INVESTMENT TRUSTS ESTIMATED BY DIFFERENT METHODS: 1927 to 1949

$ mill.

Year	Deflated by securities price indices	Cash flow method	Change in reported portfolio value	Year	Deflated by securities price indices	Cash flow method	Chance in reported portfolio value
	1	2	3		1	2	3
1927	–	17	–	1940	–7	–6	–19
1928	34	32	51	1941	–6	–3	–16
1929	101	63	72	1942	–4	–2	0
1930	275	247	160	1943	–1	–5	9
1931	145	186	–60	1944	–4	–4	4
1932	–6	3	–47	1945	–11	–8	12
1933	–100	–68	–8	1946	–12	–10	–20
1934	–38	–15	–44	1947	–12	–4	–14
1935	–27	–1	–31	1948	–11	–3	–11
1936	–42	–6	–1	1949	–7	–5	–4
1937	–26	–21	–81				
1938	–19	–15	–11	1927–36	359 [1]	458	154 [2]
1939	–1	–4	–2	1927–35	401 [1]	464	155 [2]

[1] Includes $17 million estimated for 1927.

[2] Includes $62 million estimated for 1927.

Column 1 – 1928–1949: Table V-70, col. 10.

Column 2 – 1927–1949: Table V-70, col. 9.

Column 3 – 1928–1949: Table V-69, sum of annual changes in cols. 3 and 4.

TABLE V–72

Data cover assets of Investors Syndicate (since June 1949 known as Investors Diversified Services Inc.) and Fidelity Investment Association, which together accounted for 98 percent in 1927 and 94 percent in 1936 of total assets of all face amount installment certificate companies included in Securities and Exchange Commission, *Investment Trusts and Investment Companies, Part II, Statistical Survey of Investment Trusts and Investment Companies*, Washington, 1939, and *Companies Issuing Face Amount Installment Certificates*, Washington, 1940. Fidelity suspended operations in 1938 and was liquidated, except for $2 million of assets, by the end of 1943. All securities are at market values. Mortgages are almost entirely on urban properties, at least until 1936, as indicated by the Securities and Exchange Commission report on face amount companies, pp. 39–42. A quantitative breakdown is not feasible as Investors Syndicate did not furnish the necessary data.

Column 1 – 1914–1926: Annual financial report of Investors Syndicate and of Fidelity Investment Association on file at Securities and Exchange Commission or summaries in *Moody's Manual;* Minnesota State Banking *Report*, 1920, for Investors Syndicate.

1927–1936: Securities and Exchange Commission, *Investment Trusts and Investment Companies, Companies Issuing Face Amount Installment Certificates*, pp. 37, 97, 98, 137–139.

1937–1949: Annual financial reports on file at Securities and Exchange Commission, or summaries in *Moody's Manual.*

Columns 2 to 12 – 1914–1919: Extrapolated on basis of 1920 ratios for Investors Syndicate.

1920: Minnesota State Banking *Report* for Investors Syndicate, adjusted to total assets of both companies.

1921–1926: Based on ratios obtained by linear interpolation between 1920 and 1927.

1927–1949: Same sources as for col. 1.

Note: Details may not add to totals because of rounding.

ASSETS OF FACE AMOUNT INSTALLMENT INVESTMENT COMPANIES
1914 to 1949
$ mill.

End of year	Total	Cash	Mortgages		Securities					Certificate loans	Real estate	Other
			Guaranteed by Federal Housing Authority	Other	Total	U.S. Government bonds	State and local government bonds	Other bonds	Stocks			
	1	2	3	4	5	6	7	8	9	10	11	12
1914	0.5	—	—	—	0.4	—	0.1	0.3	—	—	—	0.1
1915	0.7	—	—	—	0.6	—	0.1	0.5	—	—	—	0.1
1916	1.1	—	0.1		0.9	—	0.1	0.8	—	—	—	0.1
1917	1.7	—	0.3		1.3	0.1	0.2	1.1	—	—	—	0.1
1918	2.6	0.1	0.5		1.9	0.2	0.2	1.5	—	—	—	0.1
1919	3.8	0.1	0.8		2.6	0.2	0.3	2.1	—	0.2	—	0.1
1920	5.7	0.2	1.8		3.3	0.2	0.4	2.7	—	0.3	—	0.1
1921	7.6	0.3	2.8		3.8	0.3	0.6	2.9	0.1	0.5	0.1	0.1
1922	10.0	0.3	4.0		4.4	0.4	0.8	3.2	0.2	0.9	0.2	0.2
1923	13.3	0.4	5.9		5.3	0.4	1.0	3.5	0.4	1.2	0.3	0.3
1924	17.3	0.4	7.6		6.3	0.6	1.2	3.9	0.6	2.0	0.4	0.6
1925	23.0	0.5	10.0		8.9	0.7	1.4	6.0	0.8	2.5	0.5	0.6
1926	28.6	0.5	12.4		11.1	0.8	1.6	7.7	1.0	2.9	0.7	1.0
1927	34.0	0.9	15.5		13.0	0.9	1.8	9.1	1.2	3.2	0.4	1.2
1928	42.0	0.7	21.5		14.6	1.2	2.0	9.9	1.5	3.6	0.5	1.1
1929	52.4	0.5	27.1		16.2	1.4	2.2	11.0	1.6	5.9	0.7	2.0
1930	63.9	1.5	31.4		19.0	1.5	2.4	13.3	1.8	9.1	0.9	2.0
1931	75.7	1.5	34.3		22.6	1.7	2.6	16.3	2.0	12.0	2.5	2.8
1932	75.8	3.4	33.6		21.8	2.1	2.8	14.8	2.1	10.2	5.1	1.7
1933	78.8	6.5	30.1		29.8	2.3	3.0	18.0	6.5	8.1	2.4	1.9
1934	83.9	4.1	23.4		43.4	9.7	3.9	23.3	6.5	6.1	5.0	1.9
1935	96.8	4.7	26.9		50.5	13.3	5.1	24.7	7.4	5.9	6.9	1.9
1936	118.0	3.5	14.8	34.1	50.1	6.9	4.7	29.9	8.7	6.2	5.5	3.6
1937	141.2	4.4	28.1	37.1	55.0	6.3	4.6	36.8	7.3	7.2	6.6	2.8
1938	164.7	5.8	47.4	32.8	61.1	4.8	5.8	41.0	9.5	7.8	5.5	4.3
1939	176.3	5.1	62.8	28.4	63.8	5.5	6.3	40.4	11.6	8.8	4.6	2.8
1940	194.0	9.5	78.9	25.6	64.9	5.1	6.1	40.4	13.3	9.0	2.4	3.7
1941	190.4	5.4	90.5	23.7	56.0	6.5	5.2	34.0	11.2	10.1	1.0	2.8
1942	202.3	6.2	113.8	18.1	51.6	7.4	3.0	34.1	7.1	8.4	0.6	3.6
1943	186.7	7.7	105.1	18.2	48.2	7.4	0.4	28.5	11.9	6.0	0.3	1.2
1944	201.7	6.5	95.7	18.3	74.4	16.7	0.3	39.4	18.0	5.6	0.2	1.0
1945	223.5	7.9	70.1	22.5	117.4	32.1	0.7	45.1	39.5	4.6	0.1	0.9
1946	250.9	6.8	48.4	79.7	106.8	26.2	0.1	37.9	42.6	5.6	0.1	3.5
1947	270.8	10.9	66.2	109.1	70.9	15.4	0.1	26.4	29.0	7.3	0.2	6.2
1948	283.6	8.9	96.1	104.6	58.6	3.9	0.1	25.5	29.1	9.5	0.4	5.5
1949	289.5	4.9	72.8	136.0	59.0	6.9	0.1	24.6	27.3	11.4	0.3	5.1

Column 1 – 1896–1921: Sum of cols. 2 and 3.

        1922–1926: Obtained by roughly extrapolating 1927 value by means of: (a) tax exempt interest receipts reported by nonfinancial corporations in *Statistics of Income*, tentatively adjusted for changes in rate of yield on book value; and (b) holdings of U.S. Government securities by sample of about fifty large nonfinancial corporations as shown in their balance sheets as reproduced in security manuals. The 1922 value so obtained ($3,400 million) falls about midway between the estimate of the Federal Trade Commission for end of 1922 ($2,932 million), consisting of $2,591 million of U.S. Government securities, $93 million of Federal Farm Loan and War Finance bonds, and $248 million of state and local government securities (Senate Document 148, *Taxation and Tax Exempt Income*, p. 32); and Hardy's estimate for June 30, 1923 ($3,999 million), consisting of $3,534 million of U.S Government securities, $126 million of Federal Farm Loan Bonds, and $338 million of state and local government securities (Hardy, C. O.,*Tax Exempt Securities and the Surtax*, p. 50).

        1927–1932: Obtained by multiplying holdings of tax exempt securities from *Statistics of Income* by 1.285, the 1932 ratio between the Bureau of Internal Revenue and Securities and Exchange Commission figures (see cols. 2 and 3). Bureau of Internal Revenue figures are averages of year-end holdings adjusted for corporations not reporting balance sheets by ratio of interest on government obligations received by all corporations to interest received by corporations reporting balance sheets. Difference between the two figures is due chiefly to the fact that the Securities and Exchange Commission estimate includes holdings by financial corporations other than banks and insurance companies, which cannot be segregated in the Bureau of Internal Revenue statistics before 1938. (In that year holdings of financial corporations other than banks and insurance companies amounted to approximately 40 percent of those of all nonfinancial corporations, as reported to the Bureau of Internal Revenue.)

        1933–1949: Sum of cols. 2 and 3.

Column 2 – 1896–1916: Assumed negligible as total amount of U.S. Government securities outstanding at end of 1916 not held by banks and insurance companies amounted to only about $139 million.

        1917–1921: Roughly interpolated between 1916 and 1922 values on basis of holdings of about 50 large nonfinancial corporations (see col. 1).

        1922–1931: Col. 1 minus col. 3.

        1932–1949: Estimates of Securities and Exchange Commission (Friend and Natrella, *Individuals' Saving*, part II, table 17, line 10).

Column 3 – 1896–1921: Assumed roughly at 2.8 percent of total state and local government securities outstanding (excluding holdings of state and local sinking, trust, and investment funds, as given in Table G-21, col. 1, converted to year-end basis, and col. 2), the ratio obtaining in 1922.

        1922: Estimated at 8.5 percent of total of col. 1 on basis of Federal Trade Commission breakdown (*Taxation and Tax Exempt Income*, p. 32).

        1923–1925: Estimated to rise regularly from 8.5 percent of col. 1 in 1922 to 14.4 percent in 1926.

        1926: Figures obtained from *Statistics of Income*, 1926, pp. 360, 398, increased by 28.5 percent to compensate for omission in the Bureau of Internal Revenue figures of financial institutions other than banks and insurance companies.

        1927–1931: Estimated to rise regularly from 14.4 percent of col. 1 in 1926 to 17.0 percent in 1932.

        1932–1949: Securities and Exchange Commission (Friend and Natrella, *Individuals' Saving*, part II, table 18, line 6).

Column 4 – 1897–1949: First differences of col. 1.

Column 5 – 1924–1949: First differences of Table V-60, col. 3, Table V-62, col. 3 and Table V-72, col. 6 plus Table V-66, col. 1 and Table V-68, col. 3.

Column 6 – 1897–1949: Col. 4 minus col. 5.

1896 to 1949

$ mill.

	All corporations other than banks and insurance companies			Change in holdings		
Year	All tax exempt securities	U.S. Government	State and local government	Total	Investment companies	Total excluding investment companies
	1	2	3	4	5	6
1896	50	0	50	0	–	0
1897	50	0	50	0	–	0
1898	50	0	50	0	–	0
1899	55	0	55	5	–	5
1900	55	0	55	0	–	0
1901	60	0	60	5	–	5
1902	60	0	60	0	–	0
1903	65	0	65	5	–	5
1904	70	0	70	5	–	5
1905	70	0	70	0	–	0
1906	75	0	75	5	–	5
1907	80	0	80	5	–	5
1908	90	0	90	10	–	10
1909	100	0	100	10	–	10
1910	105	0	105	5	–	5
1911	115	0	115	10	–	10
1912	125	0	125	10	–	10
1913	125	0	125	0	–	0
1914	140	0	140	15	–	15
1915	150	0	150	10	–	10
1916	170	0	170	20	–	20
1917	1 080	900	180	910	–	910
1918	2 590	2 400	190	1 510	–	1 510
1919	3 400	3 200	200	810	–	810
1920	3 225	3 000	225	–175	–	–175
1921	3 260	3 000	260	35	–	35
1922	3 400	3 110	290	140	–	140
1923	3 400	3 060	340	0	–	0
1924	3 500	3 100	400	100	1	99
1925	3 600	3 130	470	100	0	100
1926	3 750	3 210	540	150	1	149
1927	3 900	3 320	580	150	7	143
1928	4 250	3 600	650	350	26	324
1929	4 140	3 490	650	–110	34	–144
1930	3 610	3 030	580	–530	29	–559
1931	3 380	2 820	560	–230	44	–274
1932	3 483	2 885	598	103	–30	133
1933	3 479	2 890	589	–4	–46	42
1934	3 305	2 740	565	–174	17	–191
1935	3 084	2 559	525	–221	–4	–217
1936	2 871	2 383	488	–213	–5	–208
1937	2 627	2 181	446	–244	11	–255
1938	2 496	2 071	425	–131	–14	–117
1939	2 597	2 159	438	101	6	95
1940	2 336	1 947	389	–261	3	–264
1941	4 329	3 944	385	1 993	6	1 987
1942	10 461	10 092	369	6 132	19	6 113
1943	16 625	16 278	347	6 164	15	6 149
1944	21 086	20 756	330	4 461	37	4 424
1945	21 161	20 845	316	75	24	51
1946	15 444	15 131	313	–5 717	–28	–5 689
1947	14 263	13 918	345	–1 181	0	–1 181
1948	14 524	14 133	391	261	17	244
1949	16 606	16 161	445	2 082	43	2 039

Column 1 – 1896–1949: Table L-24, col. 7.

Column 2 – 1896–1949: Sum of cols. 3–5.

Column 3 – 1896–1915A, 1917: Estimated as average of preceding and following June figures (from revised banking statistics of Federal Reserve Board) multiplied by ratio of Dec. figure to average of preceding and following June figures for national banks (derived from *Annual Report of the Comptroller of the Currency*).

    1915B–1916, 1918–1923A: Estimated as average of June figures (as for 1896 to 1915) multiplied by ratio of Dec. figures to average of preceding and following June figures for member banks (from *Banking and Monetary Statistics*, p. 72).

    1923B–1933: Estimated as average of June figures (from *Banking and Monetary Statistics*, p. 19) multiplied by ratios computed as for 1915 to 1923.

    1934–1935: Averages of June figures (from *Banking and Monetary Statistics*, p. 19) multiplied by ratio of Dec. to June averages for insured commercial banks, derived from *Annual Report of the Federal Deposit Insurance Corporation*.

    1936–1938: *Banking and Monetary Statistics*, p. 19.

    1939–1949: *Federal Reserve Bulletin*, various issues.

Column 4 – 1896–1932: Estimated as non-U.S. Government securities (col. 1 minus col. 3) multiplied by average percentage of state and local government securities in preceding and following June, derived from revised Federal Reserve Board banking statistics.

    1933: Non-U.S. Government securities multiplied by average of 1932 and 1934 percentages.

    1934–1949: State and local government bonds held by insured commercial banks (from *Annual Report of the Federal Deposit Insurance Corporation*) multiplied by ratio of non-U.S. Government securities of all commercial banks (from *Banking and Monetary Statistics* and from *Federal Reserve Bulletin*, various issues) to non-U.S. Government securities of insured commercial banks (cf. Table L-26).

Column 5 – 1896–1949: Col. 1 minus sum of cols. 3, 4, 6, and 7.

Column 6 – 1914–1933: Total paid-in capital of Federal Reserve banks (*Banking and Monetary Statistics*, pp. 330–332).

    1934–1941: *Banking and Monetary Statistics*, p. 109.

    1942–1948: *Federal Reserve Bulletin*, various issues.

    1949: Federal Deposit Insurance Corporation, *Assets and Liabilities of Operating Insured Banks*, Dec. 1949, no. 32, p. 10.

Column 7 – 1896–1909: Estimated at 13 percent of all securities less government bonds, the ratio on April 28, 1909 (National Monetary Commission, *Special Report from the Banks of the United States*).

    1910–1924: Estimated as all securities minus government bonds and Federal Reserve bank stock multiplied by a percentage linearly interpolated between 13 percent in 1909 and 8.6 percent in 1925.

    1925–1927: Same as for 1910–1924 except that percentage is estimated as average for preceding and following June for member banks (derived from *Banking and Monetary Statistics*, p. 79).

    1928–1933: Same as above except percentage is estimated from Dec. figures for member banks (from *Banking and Monetary Statistics*, p. 77).

    1934–1949: Estimated by same method as col. 4.

SECURITIES HELD BY OPERATING COMMERCIAL BANKS

1896 to 1949

V-74

$ mill.

End of year	Total	Bonds				Stocks	
		Total	U.S. Government	State and local government	Other	Federal Reserve bank	Other
	1	2	3	4	5	6	7
1896	834	786	358	104	324	–	48
1897	924	869	383	115	371	–	55
1898	1 130	1 063	483	135	445	–	67
1899	1 263	1 177	435	169	573	–	86
1900	1 489	1 386	516	181	689	–	103
1901	1 737	1 605	523	202	880	–	132
1902	1 928	1 774	528	213	1 033	–	154
1903	2 099	1 929	554	241	1 134	–	170
1904	2 354	2 158	575	274	1 309	–	196
1905	2 509	2 296	588	279	1 429	–	213
1906	2 721	2 489	629	305	1 555	–	232
1907	3 081	2 815	672	364	1 779	–	266
1908	2 978	2 730	701	371	1 658	–	248
1909	3 084	2 831	736	402	1 693	–	253
1910	3 182	2 925	740	415	1 770	–	257
1911	3 593	3 304	769	497	2 038	–	289
1912	3 647	3 363	772	526	2 065	–	284
1913	3 733	3 448	775	544	2 129	–	285
1914	4 364	4 014	778	681	2 555	18	332
1915A	4 576	4 183	765	739	2 679	55	338
1915B	4 602	4 207	764	745	2 698	55	340
1916	5 064	4 638	842	768	3 028	56	370
1917	6 917	6 460	2 340	865	3 255	71	386
1918	9 001	8 562	4 561	888	3 113	81	358
1919	9 321	8 848	4 415	962	3 471	87	386
1920	8 378	7 903	3 437	978	3 488	100	375
1921	8 293	7 822	3 255	1 018	3 549	103	368
1922	10 187	9 683	4 584	1 132	3 967	107	397
1923A	10 222	9 712	4 367	1 200	4 145	110	400
1923B	10 080	9 585	4 442	1 156	3 987	110	385
1924	11 480	10 926	4 774	1 395	4 757	112	442
1925	11 727	11 133	4 551	1 507	5 075	117	477
1926	11 965	11 308	4 109	1 681	5 518	125	532
1927	13 584	12 828	4 837	1 837	6 154	132	624
1928	14 216	13 315	5 199	1 957	6 159	147	754
1929	13 501	12 337	4 663	2 050	5 624	171	993
1930	14 666	13 497	4 822	2 382	6 293	170	999
1931	14 427	13 430	5 930	2 235	5 265	161	836
1932	15 002	14 117	7 155	2 417	4 545	151	734
1933	14 543	13 734	7 915	2 280	3 539	145	664
1934	18 747	18 081	12 038	2 559	3 484	147	519
1935	20 863	20 224	13 692	2 786	3 746	130	509
1936	23 114	22 462	15 334	2 837	4 291	131	521
1937	21 233	20 597	14 156	2 690	3 751	133	503
1938	22 305	21 754	15 071	3 137	3 546	134	417
1939	23 430	22 909	16 316	3 407	3 186	136	385
1940	25 129	24 637	17 759	3 747	3 131	139	353
1941	29 032	28 579	21 808	3 777	2 994	142	311
1942	48 172	47 746	41 379	3 618	2 749	146	280
1943	65 978	65 618	59 852	3 371	2 395	154	206
1944	83 886	83 533	77 557	3 517	2 459	163	190
1945	97 936	97 612	90 606	3 981	3 025	177	147
1946	82 871	82 570	74 780	4 406	3 384	187	114
1947	78 226	77 921	69 221	5 277	3 423	195	110
1948	71 811	71 501	62 622	5 668	3 211	201	109
1949	77 232	76 916	67 005	6 561	3 350	211	105

577

TABLE V-75

Column 1 – From Table R-55, col. 2. (Figures are essentially derived by blow-up of data for member banks of insured commercial banks, procedures being explained in detail in notes to Table R-55. Estimate for 1920 obtained by same procedure as was used with estimates for 1921–1926.)

Column 2 – Very rough estimates based on such indicators as total gains from sale of securities (Table R-55, col. 3), assuming that valuation adjustments, recoveries, and realized losses (Table R-55, cols. 4 and 5) were relatively small in the case of U.S. Government securities; the trend of U.S. Government bond prices; the volume of holdings of U.S. Government securities; and the profits or losses on U.S. Government securities by life insurance companies. Estimates have been expressed in round figures and have been kept on the conservative side, i.e., they have been entered only when it appeared fairly certain that in a given year substantial profits or losses on U.S. Government securities were taken.

Column 3 – Very rough guesses based on considerations similar to those applying for col. 2.

Column 4 – Col. 1 minus cols. 2 and 3.

TABLE V-76

Column 1 – Figures represent estimated original book value of all remaining assets plus cash in hand of receivers of all closed banks (i.e., all banks suspended from active operations but not yet fully liquidated, absorbed by other banks, or reopened; for the years 1933 and 1934 unlicensed banks were included with banks in the process of liquidation). Estimates for total assets are the sum of those for main types of assets shown in cols. 2–12.

Columns 2 to 12 – Estimates for all banks in receivership are based upon those for national banks in receivership expanded in the ratio of loans and investments of the two groups. Estimates for national banks were prepared as follows, utilizing data in the *Annual Reports of the Comptroller of the Currency* on the remaining assets of banks classified by the year in which receivership was instituted:

1. Book value of different types of assets at time of suspension was estimated on assumption that total assets at that time had same composition as assets of all "country member banks." This assumption was based on similarity in size of average capital of national banks put into receivership and all country member banks, a similarity which applied to all years which underlie the final estimates;

2. Liquidation of assets was assumed to follow a pattern under which best assets are liquidated first, and assets with the smallest liquidation value last; the reports of the Comptroller divide assets into three quality classes, good (A), doubtful (B), and worthless (C);

3. In classification of each type of assets as to quality (which was required for the calculation though not given in the Comptroller's reports) distribution of losses shown in the income and loss statement of active banks was used as a basis of determining distribution of losses for closed banks between total security holdings and total loans. For this purpose total losses of banks placed into receivership were tentatively estimated by assuming a recovery ratio of 100 percent for A assets, 50 percent for B assets, and zero for C assets. Securities of the federal government were always regarded as A assets, and wherever it was necessary to classify securities it was assumed that the percentage of C assets would be greater among "other securities" than among securities issued by local governments. Among loans, grade A assets were assumed to be most prevalent among loans on securities, including open market paper, while grade C assets were assumed to consist mostly of "other loans." Of other assets, cash and due from banks were always classified as A; and buildings, furniture, other real estate, and "all other" assets as B.

4. As between securities and loans, the speed of liquidation within each grade of assets (A, B, and C) was assumed to be equal, regardless of type of asset involved;

5. In order to distribute for any one year the total remaining assets of banks closed in a given previous year and still in process of liquidation among A, B, and C grades, as a first step assets of those banks, whose liquidation was completed during the year, had to be deducted from original assets of the banks in process of liquidation at the beginning of the year. (Total of these original assets, was, of course, larger than book value of remaining assets of the same banks, the difference representing book value of assets which have been liquidated.) As a second step, in order to determine kind of assets still unsold, it was assumed that all A assets are liquidated first, then all B assets, and C assets last. By thus assuming that remaining assets consist of the lowest grade of assets at time of receivership it is possible to estimate for the banks put into receivership in a specific year the composition of their assets in each of the following years until completion of liquidation.

DISTRIBUTION OF NET PROFITS OR LOSSES
ON SECURITIES OF OPERATING COMMERCIAL BANKS: 1920 to 1949

$ mill.

Year	Total	U.S. Government	State and local government	Other	Year	Total	U.S. Government	State and local government	Other
	1	2	3	4		1	2	3	4
1920	−152	−50	0	−102	1935	80	50	0	30
1921	−81	0	0	−81	1936	298	100	25	173
1922	94	0	0	94	1937	0	0	0	0
1923	4	0	0	4	1938	17	25	0	−8
1924	36	0	0	36	1939	72	25	0	47
1925	41	0	0	41	1940	61	25	0	36
1926	45	0	0	45	1941	59	25	0	34
1927	103	0	0	103	1942	1	25	0	−24
1928	74	0	0	74	1943	81	75	0	6
1929	−12	0	0	−12	1944	114	50	25	39
1930	−48	25	0	−73	1945	263	150	25	88
1931	−260	−50	−25	−185	1946	139	100	25	14
1932	−342	0	−25	−317	1947	28	25	0	3
1933	−346	25	−25	−346	1948	−6	0	0	−6
1934	−191	50	0	−241	1949	45	0	0	45

BOOK VALUE OF ASSETS OF CLOSED COMMERCIAL BANKS
AFTER WRITE-DOWNS ON LIQUIDATED ASSETS
(EXCLUDING BANKS CLOSED AFTER 1933): 1921 to 1945

V-76

$ mill.

End of year	Total assets	Securities			Loans			Cash	Due from banks	Real estate	Other assets	Undisbursed cash
		U.S. Government	State and local government	Other	On real estate	On securities	Other					
	1	2	3	4	5	6	7	8	9	10	11	12
1921	150	−	−	25	15	10	80	−	−	5	−	15
1922	200	−	−	35	20	10	110	−	−	5	−	20
1923	300	−	−	45	30	15	170	−	−	10	−	30
1924	450	−	−	75	40	25	250	−	−	15	−	45
1925	525	−	−	80	45	25	300	−	−	20	−	55
1926	658	16	5	108	52	31	341	−	22	22	4	57
1927	650	9	9	95	48	22	371	−	9	27	3	57
1928	647	17	12	94	42	41	356	−	9	21	1	54
1929	614	7	7	95	40	35	339	2	10	20	2	57
1930	735	3	17	134	63	49	357	−	−	31	3	78
1931	2 082	85	97	412	157	175	737	17	93	96	19	194
1932	2 388	−	143	564	224	217	900	−	−	139	25	176
1933	5 487	417	355	1 142	607	554	1 531	62	351	313	54	101
1934	3 948	126	270	994	484	348	1 248	2	11	251	44	170
1935	3 039	−	193	912	362	202	1 004	−	−	190	32	144
1936	2 427	−	158	812	262	147	762	−	−	136	22	128
1937	1 942	−	132	708	185	105	571	−	−	98	17	126
1938	1 540	−	108	619	135	75	439	−	−	69	12	83
1939	1 309	−	90	549	100	55	345	−	−	51	7	112
1940	1 059	−	71	436	70	36	246	−	−	33	5	162
1941	592	−	42	279	33	17	129	−	−	15	2	75
1942	101	−	−	19	5	−	17	−	−	3	−	57
1943	47	−	−	16	−	−	8	−	−	−	−	23
1944	24	−	−	8	−	−	4	−	−	−	−	12
1945	−	−	−	−	−	−	−	−	−	−	−	−

ASSETS AND LIABILITIES OF JOINT STOCK LAND BANKS
1918 to 1949
$ mill.

End of year	Assets							Liabilities and net worth				
	Total	Cash	U.S. Government securities	Mortgage loans	Purchase money mortgages, contracts etc.	Real estate, sheriffs' certificates, etc.	Other assets	Bonds	Notes and interest payable	Other liabilities	Capital stock and paid-in surplus	Earned surplus and reserves
	1	2	3	4	5	6	7	8	9	10	11	12
1918	11.8	1.7	2.4	7.4	0	0	0.3	7.7	1.9	0.1	2.1	0
1919	74.7	2.4	12.7	54.7	0	0	4.9	56.1	7.0	2.3	8.8	0.5
1920	99.4	1.3	3.1	78.0	0	0	17.0	75.3	14.3	1.4	8.1	0.3
1921	95.8	2.9	3.0	81.7	0	·0	8.2	81.5	5.1	0.6	8.0	0.6
1922	268.8	9.5	28.7	218.8	0	0	11.8	208.0	18.6	13.5	26.2	2.5
1923	428.7	9.2	15.7	392.6	0.8		10.4	354.1	28.3	7.5	35.0	3.8
1924	491.5	12.5	15.7	446.4	2.3		14.6	435.1	8.1	7.9	35.7	4.7
1925	591.7	11.6	15.2	545.6	4.3		15.0	516.1	12.8	11.7	43.0	8.1
1926	683.5	11.8	13.7	632.5	7.0		18.5	605.3	8.5	13.3	46.5	9.9
1927	653.8	9.3	6.0	609.5	13.0		16.0	582.0	4.3	10.7	47.5	9.3
1928	656.7	7.9	8.1	605.2	5.6	14.1	15.8	589.0	10.2	5.0	43.3	9.2
1929	640.1	9.6	4.5	584.2	8.9	18.8	14.1	572.4	8.4	5.7	43.3	10.3
1930	611.6	9.2	3.3	552.6	12.4	21.4	12.7	544.0	9.7	5.8	43.2	8.9
1931	606.2	6.8	7.0	529.6	13.2	35.2	14.4	540.0	7.5	4.8	46.9	7.0
1932	485.9	6.6	3.5	409.5	11.0	42.6	12.7	425.3	8.9	6.1	38.4	7.2
1933	441.8	8.0	4.2	353.7	13.2	50.3	12.4	367.1	16.2	10.2	38.2	10.2
1934	336.6	15.0	18.3	232.9	14.0	49.1	7.4	270.2	9.2	8.7	38.1	10.4
1935	264.6	9.5	11.7	165.4	18.0	54.0	6.0	205.2	7.3	6.5	37.7	7.9
1936	226.1	9.8	11.9	126.5	22.6	51.0	4.3	165.0	9.4	7.4	37.1	7.2
1937	194.4	7.7	9.4	99.3	25.2	49.2	3.5	133.2	7.2	5.9	35.8	12.3
1938	168.5	7.5	9.2	83.5	24.0	41.5	2.8	111.4	8.3	5.4	34.1	9.3
1939	149.5	11.4	14.0	62.9	22.2	36.9	2.1	96.9	7.6	3.8	33.9	7.4
1940	118.2	9.4	11.4	45.9	21.1	28.5	1.8	64.1	16.1	4.0	31.1	2.9
1941	79.0	3.4	4.1	31.4	19.5	19.5	1.1	37.4	10.8	2.4	25.8	2.5
1942	53.5	2.8	3.4	19.7	13.2	13.7	0.6	21.2	8.3	1.6	19.4	3.0
1943	13.7	1.0	1.3	2.8	4.5	4.1	0.1	3.7	3.5	0.9	8.0	−2.4
1944	8.2	0.9	1.1	0.9	2.5	2.7	0	1.4	2.1	0.6	5.9	−1.7
1945	4.3	0.3	0.3	0.3	1.7	1.6	0	0.2	0.4	0.2	4.7	−1.2
1946	2.5	0.2	0.2	0.1	1.5	0.5	0	0	0.1	0.2	2.7	−0.5
1947	1.0	0.1	0.1	0	0.6	0.2	0	0	0.1	0.1	0.9	−0.1
1948	0.8	0.3	0	0	0.5	0	0	–	–	–	0.8	–
1949	0.5	0.2	0	0	0.3	0	0	–	–	–	0.5	–

Columns 1, 4 to 12 – 1918–1949: From *Annual Reports*, Federal Farm Loan Board and Farm Credit Administration. Figures are for years ending Dec. 31, except for 1918, 1919, and 1921, which are for Nov. 30. Col. 7 includes unsold farm loan bonds amounting to $4.3 million in 1919, $14.9 million in 1920, $5.5 million in 1921, and $5.0 million in 1922.

Columns 2 and 3 – 1918–1933: Same source as col. 1. Figures for U.S. Government securities include negligible amounts of other securities for some years.
1934–1949: Same source as col. 1 but published figures combine cash and securities which were split by average ratio of each to total of cash and securities for 1918–1933.

Note: Details may not add to total because of rounding.

ASSETS AND LIABILITIES OF FEDERAL LAND BANKS
1917 to 1949

$ mill.

End of year	Total	Cash	Securities		Loans		Real estate owned	Other assets	Capital stock and paid-in surplus	Earned surplus and reserves	Bonds	Other liabilities
			U.S. Government	Other	Mortgage	Other						
	1	2	3	4	5	6	7	8	9	10	11	12
1917	43	3	9	1	30	0	0	0	10	0	27	6
1918	162	3	8	0	149	0	0	2	16	0	142	4
1919	312	2	25	0	284	0	0	1	22	1	286	3
1920	366	4	3	2	356	0	0	1	26	2	334	4
1921	468	11	31	2	423	0	0	1	27	4	433	4
1922	697	6	36	2	651	0	0	2	37	7	643	10
1923	876	11	44	0	814	0	0	7	43	9	807	17
1924	992	12	29	0	944	0	0	7	49	11	915	17
1925	1 071	13	23	0	1 023	0	0	12	54	13	982	22
1926	1 155	16	28	0	1 097	0	0	14	58	13	1 059	25
1927	1 244	20	29	0	1 176	0	0	19	62	16	1 140	26
1928	1 285	16	28	0	1 196	0	12	33	65	18	1 175	27
1929	1 301	14	22	13	1 200	0	15	37	65	18	1 188	30
1930	1 298	16	24	14	1 191	0	20	33	66	17	1 185	30
1931	1 283	11	12	3	1 171	0	38	48	66	16	1 170	31
1932	1 380	12	101	4	1 149	0	60	54	189	16	1 147	28
1933	1 447	26	64	1	1 245	0	78	33	206	18	1 192	31
1934	2 330	30	92	0	1 977	0	82	149	377	18	1 784	151
1935	2 392	26	41	0	2 154	0	92	79	330	28	1 939	95
1936	2 457	51	43	0	2 156	24	100	83	367	49	1 972	69
1937	2 390	29	51	1	2 134	14	87	74	398	63	1 807	122
1938	2 341	20	66	0	2 117	20	78	40	421	79	1 767	74
1939	2 300	37	89	0	2 043	13	80	38	424	92	1 746	38
1940	2 220	35	83	1	1 987	8	68	38	324	105	1 722	69
1941	2 193	37	167	10	1 889	14	46	30	320	117	1 707	49
1942	2 086	43	258	10	1 698	8	28	41	383	128	1 535	40
1943	1 901	31	398	17	1 404	5	13	33	330	129	1 364	78
1944	1 442	40	220	6	1 159	3	5	9	319	142	852	129
1945	1 232	48	145	0	1 029	1	2	7	236	162	643	191
1946	1 114	37	136	0	931	2	0	8	138	179	715	82
1947	990	25	104	0	852	2	0	7	56	196	664	74
1948	970	22	101	2	834	4	0	7	56	201	648	65
1949	1 011	20	106	0	874	5	0	6	58	206	717	30

Columns 1 to 3, 5, 9 to 11 – 1917–1949: Data obtained from the Department of Agriculture, Farm Credit Administration, *Combined Statements of the Federal Land Banks.* All figures given are less reserves.

Column 4 – 1917–1922: Same source as col. 1. Consists wholly of Farm Loan Bonds on hand.
1923–1949: Same source as col. 1.

Column 6 – 1917–1949: Same source as col. 1. Includes loans in suspense, loans called for foreclosures, judgments, etc., and loans in process of closing.

Column 7 – 1917–1949: Same source as col. 1. Includes sheriffs' certificates, judgments, etc.

Column 8 – 1917–1949: Same source as col. 1. Includes notes and accounts receivable, accrued interest, banking house, furniture, fixtures, and equipment, due from and deposits with Secretary of Treasury, deferred expense, and other assets.

Column 12 – 1917–1949: Same source as col. 1. Includes interest accrued and matured coupons on farm loan bonds, notes, accounts, and bills payable, and other liabilities.

Column 1 – Sum of cols. 2–5.

Column 2 – From Table R-4, col. 9.

Column 3 – From Table R-7, col. 7.

Column 4 – From Table R-10, col. 7.

Column 5 – From Table R-13, col. 8.

Column 6 – Sum of cols. 7–10.

Column 7 – From Table R-6, col. 9.

Column 8 – From Table R-9, col. 7.

Column 9 – From Table R-12, col. 7.

Column 10 – From Table R-13, col. 10.

Original and Replacement Cost Depreciation: 1897 to 1949

$ mill.

Year	Original cost depreciation					Replacement cost depreciation				
	Total	1- to 4-family dwellings	Multi-family dwellings	Commercial buildings	Industrial buildings	Total	1- to 4-family dwellings	Multi-family dwellings	Commercial buildings	Industrial buildings
	1	2	3	4	5	6	7	8	9	10
1897	143	50	2	64	27	169	69	2	69	29
1898	84	15	−1	49	21	95	23	−1	51	22
1899	120	55	0	45	20	110	47	−2	45	20
1900	77	−29	−6	77	35	46	−55	−6	74	33
1901	194	93	0	70	31	174	75	0	69	30
1902	315	197	0	82	36	288	174	−1	80	35
1903	390	313	14	41	22	350	279	13	38	20
1904	285	248	9	15	13	250	217	9	12	12
1905	455	402	17	20	16	406	362	15	15	14
1906	549	473	8	45	23	482	417	7	37	21
1907	731	598	10	90	33	654	529	16	79	30
1908	528	471	10	31	16	449	407	7	22	13
1909	586	542	15	14	15	518	486	15	5	12
1910	581	538	19	11	13	506	478	17	1	10
1911	509	489	12	0	8	442	437	10	−11	6
1912	602	557	12	19	14	523	493	11	8	11
1913	387	383	−18	6	16	330	341	−19	−6	14
1914	250	293	−7	−41	5	193	248	−7	−51	3
1915	395	404	15	−25	1	322	345	13	−35	−1
1916	513	461	2	44	6	381	362	−2	20	1
1917	−65	36	−67	−46	12	−323	−165	−76	−86	4
1918	5	107	−64	−60	22	−440	−252	−77	−122	11
1919	948	938	−21	−6	37	302	430	−40	−107	19
1920	371	387	−148	67	65	−671	−445	−181	−85	40
1921	838	762	−119	172	23	188	232	−139	86	9
1922	1 778	1 726	−93	136	9	1 247	1 299	−109	60	−3
1923	2 060	2 171	−131	12	8	1 379	1 610	−152	−74	−5
1924	2 588	2 702	−134	19	1	1 933	2 166	−155	−66	−12
1925	2 318	2 565	−205	−43	1	1 681	2 044	−223	−128	−12
1926	2 050	1 978	−250	298	24	1 414	1 454	−269	216	13
1927	1 499	1 478	−190	195	16	897	980	−207	119	5
1928	860	1 110	−367	92	25	256	613	−388	17	14
1929	293	494	−399	171	27	−369	−76	−419	107	19
1930	55	302	−405	152	6	−527	−218	−422	113	0
1931	396	429	2	−28	−7	−11	59	−8	−51	−11
1932	−297	−196	−3	−88	−10	−378	−300	0	−68	−10
1933	−455	−359	112	−203	−5	−553	−458	114	−202	−7
1934	−1 474	−1 382	99	−187	−4	−1 727	−1 607	94	−206	−8
1935	−781	−622	31	−184	−6	−990	−796	29	−212	−11
1936	−38	96	41	−170	−5	−316	−145	37	−199	−9
1937	238	216	46	−32	8	−247	−200	33	−82	2
1938	344	393	28	−71	−6	−178	−66	13	−114	−11
1939	916	915	−27	30	−2	360	429	−43	−18	−8
1940	1 077	1 079	−8	2	4	450	530	−26	−52	−2
1941	1 582	1 524	20	17	21	782	826	−5	−53	14
1942	778	784	26	−32	0	−161	−27	−4	−122	−8
1943	262	181	113	−24	−8	−787	−728	80	−122	−17
1944	−273	−265	88	−86	−10	−1 547	−1 383	49	−193	−20
1945	−499	−372	−21	−113	7	−1 962	−1 652	−69	−236	−5
1946	−868	−765	−83	−63	43	−2 687	−2 336	−141	−238	28
1947	426	810	−124	−300	40	−2 166	−1 440	−206	−539	19
1948	2 766	2 858	−102	−17	27	−312	179	−200	−293	2
1949	2 985	3 085	−66	−42	8	100	589	−162	−311	−16

PERSONAL SAVING THROUGH NONFARM REAL ESTATE
1929 Prices: 1897 to 1949

$ mill.

Year	Total	1- to 4-family dwellings	Multi-family dwellings	Commercial buildings	Industrial buildings	Year	Total	1- to 4-family dwellings	Multi-family dwellings	Commercial buildings	Industrial buildings
	1	2	3	4	5		1	2	3	4	5
1897	407	170	7	162	68	1924	2 042	2 273	−145	−74	−12
1898	213	54	−3	113	49						
1899	237	99	0	95	43	1925	1 888	2 219	−189	−130	−12
						1926	1 608	1 615	−227	208	12
1900	84	−121	−12	148	69	1927	1 065	1 118	−174	116	5
1901	367	160	−3	145	65	1928	363	712	−367	4	14
1902	595	360	−1	164	72	1929	−369	−76	−419	107	19
1903	709	568	25	75	41						
1904	504	442	16	23	23	1930	−523	−224	−432	132	1
						1931	−6	72	−7	−58	−13
1905	789	705	31	25	28	1932	−587	−455	−7	−110	−15
1906	893	779	10	65	39	1933	−689	−586	154	−248	−9
1907	1 217	984	29	148	56	1934	−2 052	−1 955	134	−224	−7
1908	830	758	11	37	24						
1909	957	904	25	6	22	1935	−1 174	−988	41	−216	−11
						1936	−349	−168	48	−220	−9
1910	961	904	34	4	19	1937	−267	−235	42	−76	2
1911	862	844	23	−16	11	1938	−212	−115	24	−110	−11
1912	988	929	24	15	20	1939	270	327	−54	4	−7
1913	721	721	−22	−4	26						
1914	460	533	3	−81	5	1940	273	340	−30	−36	−1
						1941	480	514	−6	−41	13
1915	658	679	39	−57	−3	1942	−66	8	8	−76	−6
1916	728	681	11	35	1	1943	−525	−531	87	−68	−13
1917	−360	−161	−96	−109	6	1944	−1 140	−1 046	58	−137	−15
1918	−512	−294	−88	−143	13						
1919	367	489	−34	−106	18	1945	−1 512	−1 272	−47	−188	−5
						1946	−2 846	−2 488	−113	−258	13
1920	−604	−386	−155	−92	29	1947	−2 458	−1 907	−155	−401	5
1921	272	296	−126	93	9	1948	−1 428	−1 032	−159	−234	−3
1922	1 538	1 562	−89	67	−2	1949	−949	−560	−149	−229	−11
1923	1 410	1 647	−148	−83	−6						

Column 1 – Sum of cols. 2–5.

Column 2 – From Table R-5, col. 9.

Column 3 – From Table R-8, col. 7.

Column 4 – From Table R-11, col. 7.

Column 5 – From Table R-13, col. 9.

TABLE R-3

Column 1 – Sum of Table R-4, col. 9 and Table R-7, col. 7.

Column 2 – Sum of Table R-5, col. 9 and Table R-8, col. 7.

Column 3 – Sum of Table R-6, col. 9 and Table R-9, col. 7.

Columns 4, 5, and 6 – Twenty percent of Tables R-4, R-5, and R-6 respectively, cols. 1–4 minus col. 5 to bring estimates in line with census-type benchmark figures.

Column 7 – Col. 1 plus col. 4.

Column 8 – Col. 2 plus col. 5.

Column 9 – Col. 3 plus col. 6.

Alternative Estimate: 1897 to 1949

$ mill.

Year	Unadjusted saving			Saving through additional construction expenditures			Saving adjusted for possible understatement		
	Original cost	1929 prices	Replace-ment cost	Original cost	1929 prices	Replace-ment cost	Original cost	1929 prices	Replace-ment cost
	1	2	3	4	5	6	7	8	9
1897	52	177	71	9	31	13	61	208	84
1898	14	51	22	5	16	7	19	67	29
1899	55	99	45	15	29	13	70	128	58
1900	−35	−133	−61	5	0	0	−30	−133	−61
1901	93	157	75	28	52	24	121	209	99
1902	197	359	173	54	104	50	251	463	223
1903	327	593	292	80	149	73	407	742	365
1904	257	458	226	71	132	64	328	590	290
1905	419	736	377	108	198	100	527	934	477
1906	481	789	424	125	216	114	606	1 005	538
1907	608	1 013	545	140	236	127	748	1 249	672
1908	481	769	414	115	192	102	596	961	516
1909	557	929	501	145	253	134	702	1 182	635
1910	557	938	495	145	250	133	702	1 188	628
1911	501	867	447	129	225	118	630	1 092	565
1912	569	953	504	144	244	131	713	1 197	635
1913	365	699	322	143	259	134	508	958	456
1914	286	536	241	115	202	106	401	738	347
1915	419	718	358	118	199	106	537	917	464
1916	463	692	360	143	215	123	606	907	483
1917	−31	−257	−241	106	100	66	75	−157	−175
1918	43	−382	−329	61	−14	−11	104	−396	−340
1919	917	455	390	238	148	137	1 155	603	527
1920	239	−541	−626	263	82	97	502	−459	−529
1921	643	170	93	273	175	167	916	345	260
1922	1 633	1 473	1 190	485	456	400	2 118	1 929	1 590
1923	2 040	1 499	1 458	682	579	570	2 722	2 078	2 028
1924	2 568	2 128	2 011	788	702	680	3 356	2 830	2 691
1925	2 360	2 030	1 821	814	738	710	3 174	2 768	2 531
1926	1 728	1 388	1 185	762	679	658	2 490	2 067	1 843
1927	1 288	944	773	631	555	531	1 919	1 499	1 304
1928	743	345	225	571	491	471	1 314	836	696
1929	95	−495	−495	377	263	263	472	−232	−232
1930	−103	−656	−640	118	14	14	15	−642	−626
1931	431	65	51	36	−43	−38	467	22	13
1932	−199	−462	−300	−130	−199	−151	−329	−661	−451
1933	−247	−432	−344	−164	−241	−184	−411	−673	−528
1934	−1 283	−1 821	−1 513	−131	−212	−176	−1 414	−2 033	−1 689
1935	−591	−947	−767	−54	−111	−89	−645	−1 058	−856
1936	137	−120	−108	48	0	0	185	−120	−108
1937	262	−193	−167	107	25	24	369	−168	−143
1938	421	−91	−53	123	32	31	544	−59	−22
1939	888	273	386	250	156	153	1 138	429	539
1940	1 071	310	504	320	207	210	1 391	517	714
1941	1 544	508	821	431	266	292	1 975	774	1 113
1942	810	16	−31	72	−78	−90	882	−62	−121
1943	294	−444	−648	−102	−234	−284	192	−678	−932
1944	−177	−988	−1 334	−93	−239	−316	−270	−1 227	−1 650
1945	−393	−1 319	−1 721	−10	−189	−266	−403	−1 508	−1 987
1946	−848	−2 601	−2 477	669	227	355	−179	−2 374	−2 122
1947	686	−2 062	−1 646	1 108	347	658	1 794	−1 715	−988
1948	2 756	−1 191	−21	1 498	457	963	4 254	−734	942
1949	3 019	−709	427	1 341	412	842	4 360	−297	1 269

TABLE R-4

Column 1 – 1897–1919: Total private nonfarm residential expenditures on one- to four-family homes as estimated in Table R-25, col. 11 allocated to corporations and individuals on basis of Table R-29, col. 1, interpolating between decadal percentages.

1920–1949: Same method as for 1897–1919 except expenditure estimates of Table R-28, col. 3 used.

Column 2 – 1897–1949: From Table R-30, col. 5.

Column 3 – 1897–1914: From Table R-31, col. 3. Figures for this column and for col. 2 include small amounts, varying between 1 and 5 percent, attributable to investment by corporations.

1915–1949: Department of Commerce, *Construction and Construction Materials, Statistical Supplement*, May 1950, p. 6.

Column 4 – 1897–1949: From Table R-32, col. 5.

Column 5 – 1897–1949: Sum of: (a) the depreciation of cols. 1–4 – depreciation calculated on a linear basis assuming average life of sixty years for new structures and builders' profits and thirty years for alterations and additions and dealers' commissions; (b) fire losses estimated from Table R-72, col. 6. Ninety-two percent of fire losses on residential dwellings were attributed to individually owned buildings and divided between one- to four-family dwellings and multi-family dwellings on basis of cumulated depreciated original cost.

Column 6 – 1897–1949: Change in total of mortgage debt on one- to four-family dwellings (cf. Tables M-5, col. 1 and M-9, col. 1) allocated to corporations and individuals on basis of Table R-29, col. 1, interpolating between decadal percentages.

Column 7 – 1926–1949: From Table R-45, col. 6.

Column 8 – 1930–1940: From Table M-26, col. 3.

Column 9 – 1897–1949: The sum of cols. 1–4 minus sum of cols. 5–8.

TABLE R-5

Columns 1 to 4 – Table R-4, cols. 1–4 divided by construction cost index shown in Table R-20, col. 1.

Column 5 – Depreciation calculated from annual totals for cols. 1–4 and corresponding figures for preceding years (shown in Tables R-27 and R-26) plus fire loss adjustment from Table R-72, col. 7 allocated to one- to four-family dwellings according to method described in notes to Table R-4, col. 5.

Column 6 – Table R-4, col. 6 divided by index of cost of living (1897–1913, Douglas, P. H., *Real Wages in the U.S., 1890–1946*, pp. 38, 60; 1914–1949, Bureau of Labor Statistics) shifted to 1929 base.

Column 7 – Table R-4, col. 7 divided by index of construction cost (cf. Table R-20, col. 1).

Column 8 – Table M-26, col. 3 divided by cost of living index.

Column 9 – Sum of cols. 1–4 minus sum of cols. 5–8.

TABLE R-6

Columns 1 to 4 – Same as Table R-4, cols. 1–4 respectively.

Column 5 – Depreciation in 1929 prices of new construction expenditures, builders' profits, expenditures on alterations and additions, and dealers' commissions on sale of old structures (components of Table R-5, col. 5) multiplied by appropriate price indices (cf. notes to Table R-5, cols. 1–4); plus adjustment for fire losses from Table R-72, col. 8 allocated to one- to four-family dwellings according to method described in notes to Table R-4, col. 5.

Columns 6 to 8 – Same as Table R-4, cols. 6-8.

Column 9 – Sum of cols. 1–4 minus sum of cols. 5–8.

INDIVIDUALS' SAVING THROUGH ONE- TO FOUR-FAMILY NONFARM DWELLINGS; ORIGINAL COST DEPRECIATION: 1897 to 1949

$ mill.

Year	Expenditures on new structures	Builders' additional profit	Expenditures on alterations and additions	Dealers' commissions on sales of old structures	Depreciation (including adjustment for fire losses)	Change in gross mortgage debt	Net purchases by institutions	Write-downs	Net saving including write-downs
	1	2	3	4	5	6	7	8	9
1897	295	21	24	31	327	−6	–	–	50
1898	286	21	26	30	336	12	–	–	15
1899	333	25	26	35	345	19	–	–	55
1900	276	21	43	38	353	54	–	–	−29
1901	378	29	48	43	360	45	–	–	93
1902	460	37	90	52	368	74	–	–	197
1903	570	47	102	56	376	86	–	–	313
1904	589	49	65	54	404	105	–	–	248
1905	749	63	62	69	404	137	–	–	402
1906	857	74	98	81	486	151	–	–	473
1907	865	76	122	80	441	104	–	–	598
1908	794	71	96	70	458	102	–	–	471
1909	954	87	75	80	471	183	–	–	542
1910	952	88	95	84	495	186	–	–	538
1911	882	83	112	81	514	155	–	–	489
1912	960	91	121	81	532	164	–	–	557
1913	960	91	138	76	552	330	–	–	383
1914	871	84	119	73	574	280	–	–	293
1915	872	85	140	70	577	186	–	–	404
1916	994	97	145	81	604	252	–	–	461
1917	859	85	125	92	629	496	–	–	36
1918	683	68	110	99	655	198	–	–	107
1919	1 428	144	130	162	673	253	–	–	938
1920	1 488	152	175	230	728	930	–	–	387
1921	1 565	160	185	224	769	603	–	–	762
1922	2 517	260	200	263	814	700	–	–	1 726
1923	3 295	456	210	335	884	1 241	–	–	2 171
1924	3 804	531	230	337	964	1 236	–	–	2 702
1925	3 946	554	250	370	1 048	1 507	–	–	2 565
1926	3 773	540	270	355	1 126	1 811	23	–	1 978
1927	3 350	363	290	344	1 192	1 644	33	–	1 478
1928	3 135	343	315	325	1 264	1 673	71	–	1 110
1929	2 316	254	340	300	1 325	1 275	116	–	494
1930	1 312	97	305	249	1 375	127	149	10	302
1931	1 124	83	175	196	1 397	−572	289	35	429
1932	460	34	105	152	1 403	−1 084	573	55	−196
1933	277	21	145	127	1 389	−1 073	563	50	−359
1934	376	29	200	139	1 397	204	475	50	−1 382
1935	669	51	250	165	1 406	−111	412	50	−622
1936	1 073	124	295	180	1 430	−143	254	35	96
1937	1 296	150	320	230	1 461	130	164	25	216
1938	1 449	169	295	194	1 492	234	−32	20	393
1939	2 004	236	320	224	1 533	508	−182	10	915
1940	2 321	274	335	251	1 582	752	−242	10	1 079
1941	2 776	330	375	319	1 644	950	−318	–	1 524
1942	1 304	209	225	313	1 690	−172	−251	–	784
1943	604	97	160	348	1 720	−416	−276	–	181
1944	517	84	220	462	1 746	−3	−195	–	−265
1945	676	110	340	602	1 777	408	−85	–	−372
1946	3 062	503	570	1 062	1 852	4 143	−33	–	−765
1947	4 940	816	735	1 034	1 987	4 751	−23	–	810
1948	6 653	1 106	925	955	2 147	4 637	−3	–	2 858
1949	6 273	1 050	825	865	2 308	3 610	10	–	3 085

R-5   INDIVIDUALS' SAVING THROUGH ONE- TO FOUR-FAMILY NONFARM
DWELLINGS; 1929 PRICES: 1897 to 1949

$ mill.

Year	Expenditures on new structures	Builders' additional profit	Expenditures on alterations and additions	Dealers' commissions on sales of old structures	Depreciation (including adjustment for fire losses)	Change in gross mortgage debt	Net purchases by institutions	Write-downs	Net saving including write-downs
	1	2	3	4	5	6	7	8	9
1897	710	50	58	75	737	−14	–	–	170
1898	660	48	60	69	755	28	–	–	54
1899	727	55	57	76	772	44	–	–	99
1900	573	44	89	79	785	121	–	–	−121
1901	805	62	102	91	801	99	–	–	160
1902	959	77	188	109	815	158	–	–	360
1903	1 159	96	207	114	832	176	–	–	568
1904	1 204	100	133	110	888	217	–	–	442
1905	1 486	125	123	137	883	283	–	–	705
1906	1 632	141	187	154	1 034	301	–	–	779
1907	1 611	142	227	149	949	196	–	–	984
1908	1 493	133	180	132	980	200	–	–	758
1909	1 806	165	142	152	1 001	360	–	–	904
1910	1 789	165	179	158	1 042	345	–	–	904
1911	1 679	158	213	154	1 081	279	–	–	844
1912	1 785	169	225	151	1 108	293	–	–	929
1913	1 851	175	266	146	1 145	572	–	–	721
1914	1 668	161	228	140	1 186	478	–	–	533
1915	1 629	159	262	131	1 188	314	–	–	679
1916	1 742	170	254	142	1 231	396	–	–	681
1917	1 302	129	189	139	1 257	663	–	–	−161
1918	860	86	139	125	1 278	226	–	–	−294
1919	1 549	156	141	176	1 283	250	–	–	489
1920	1 254	128	147	194	1 314	795	–	–	−386
1921	1 640	168	194	235	1 362	579	–	–	296
1922	2 867	296	228	300	1 413	716	–	–	1 562
1923	3 348	463	213	340	1 470	1 247	–	–	1 647
1924	3 925	548	237	348	1 547	1 238	–	–	2 273
1925	4 101	576	260	385	1 631	1 472	–	–	2 219
1926	3 894	557	279	366	1 702	1 755	24	–	1 615
1927	3 501	379	303	359	1 765	1 625	34	–	1 118
1928	3 269	358	328	339	1 837	1 671	74	–	712
1929	2 316	254	340	300	1 895	1 275	116	–	−76
1930	1 343	99	313	255	1 941	130	153	10	−224
1931	1 249	92	195	218	1 967	−645	321	39	72
1932	604	45	138	200	1 980	−1 360	753	69	−455
1933	364	28	190	167	1 953	−1 423	739	66	−586
1934	453	35	241	167	1 954	261	572	64	−1 955
1935	830	63	311	205	1 962	−139	512	62	−988
1936	1 273	147	350	214	1 984	−177	302	43	−168
1937	1 382	160	342	245	2 004	155	175	30	−235
1938	1 504	175	306	201	2 026	284	−33	24	−115
1939	2 042	241	326	228	2 058	626	−186	12	327
1940	2 282	269	329	247	2 094	919	−238	12	340
1941	2 533	301	342	291	2 137	1 106	−290	–	514
1942	1 127	180	194	270	2 161	−181	−217	–	8
1943	499	80	132	287	2 169	−412	−228	–	−531
1944	391	64	167	350	2 169	−3	−148	–	−1 046
1945	480	78	241	427	2 169	389	−60	–	−1 272
1946	1 960	322	365	680	2 192	3 644	−21	–	−2 488
1947	2 610	431	388	546	2 239	3 655	−12	–	−1 907
1948	3 159	525	439	453	2 292	3 317	−1	–	−1 032
1949	3 072	514	404	424	2 353	2 616	5	–	−560

$ mill.

Year	Expenditures on new structures	Builders' additional profit	Expenditures on alterations and additions	Dealers' commissions on sales of old structures	Depreciation (including adjustment for fire losses)	Change in gross mortgage debt	Net purchases by institutions	Write-downs	Net saving including write-downs
	1	2	3	4	5	6	7	8	9
1897	295	21	24	31	308	−6	–	–	69
1898	286	21	26	30	328	12	–	–	23
1899	333	25	26	35	353	19	–	–	47
1900	276	21	43	38	379	54	–	–	−55
1901	378	29	48	43	378	45	–	–	75
1902	460	37	90	52	391	74	–	–	174
1903	570	47	102	56	410	86	–	–	279
1904	589	49	65	54	435	105	–	–	217
1905	749	63	62	69	444	137	–	–	362
1906	857	74	98	81	542	151	–	–	417
1907	865	76	122	80	510	104	–	–	529
1908	794	71	96	70	522	102	–	–	407
1909	954	87	75	80	527	183	–	–	486
1910	952	88	95	84	555	186	–	–	478
1911	882	83	112	81	566	155	–	–	437
1912	960	91	121	81	596	164	–	–	493
1913	960	91	138	76	594	330	–	–	341
1914	871	84	119	73	619	280	–	–	248
1915	872	85	140	70	636	186	–	–	345
1916	994	97	145	81	703	252	–	–	362
1917	859	85	125	92	830	496	–	–	−165
1918	683	68	110	99	1 014	198	–	–	−252
1919	1 428	144	130	162	1 181	253	–	–	430
1920	1 488	152	175	230	1 560	930	–	–	−445
1921	1 565	160	185	224	1 299	603	–	–	232
1922	2 517	260	200	263	1 241	700	–	–	1 299
1923	3 295	456	210	335	1 445	1 241	–	–	1 610
1924	3 804	531	230	337	1 500	1 236	–	–	2 166
1925	3 946	554	250	370	1 569	1 507	–	–	2 044
1926	3 773	540	270	355	1 650	1 811	23	–	1 454
1927	3 350	363	290	344	1 690	1 644	33	–	980
1928	3 135	343	315	325	1 761	1 673	71	–	613
1929	2 316	254	340	300	1 895	1 275	116	–	−76
1930	1 312	97	305	249	1 895	127	149	10	−218
1931	1 124	83	175	196	1 767	−572	289	35	59
1932	460	34	105	152	1 507	−1 084	573	55	−300
1933	277	21	145	127	1 488	−1 073	563	50	−458
1934	376	29	200	139	1 622	204	475	50	−1 607
1935	669	51	250	165	1 580	−111	412	50	−796
1936	1 073	124	295	180	1 671	−143	254	35	−145
1937	1 296	150	320	230	1 877	130	164	25	−200
1938	1 449	169	295	194	1 951	234	−32	20	−66
1939	2 004	236	320	224	2 019	508	−182	10	429
1940	2 321	274	335	251	2 131	752	−242	10	530
1941	2 776	330	375	319	2 342	950	−318	–	826
1942	1 304	209	225	313	2 501	−172	−251	–	−27
1943	604	97	160	348	2 629	−416	−276	–	−728
1944	517	84	220	462	2 864	−3	−195	–	−1 383
1945	676	110	340	602	3 057	408	−85	–	−1 652
1946	3 062	503	570	1 062	3 423	4 143	−33	–	−2 336
1947	4 940	816	735	1 034	4 237	4 751	−23	–	−1 440
1948	6 653	1 106	925	955	4 826	4 637	−3	–	179
1949	6 273	1 050	825	865	4 804	3 610	10	–	589

TABLE R-7

Column 1 – 1897–1914: From Table R-25, col. 10 multiplied by percentages shown in Table R-29, col. 2 (linear interpolation between decadal percentages).

1915–1949: Same method as for 1897–1914, except expenditure figures from Table R-28, col. 4.

Column 2 – 1897–1949: Total expenditures on multi-family dwellings, original cost, depreciated on linear basis assuming average life expectancy of fifty years; plus adjustment for fire losses (cf. notes to Table R-4, col. 5); depreciation allocated to individuals on basis of Table R-29, col. 2.

Column 3 – 1897–1924: First differences of Table M-6, col. 1 multiplied by Table R-29, col. 2.

1925–1949: First differences of Table M-10, col. 1 multiplied by Table R-29, col. 2.

Column 4 – 1897–1949: Table R-43, col. 6 (very small values for 1896–1909 disregarded) multiplied by Table R-29, col. 2.

Column 5 – 1926–1949: Table R-45, col. 7.

Column 6 – 1930–1940: Table M-26, col. 4.

Column 7 – 1897–1949: Col. 1 minus sum of cols. 2–6.

TABLE R–8

Column 1 – Values in Table R-7, col. 1, deflated by construction cost index as given in Table R-20, col. 2 except for minor differences due to rounding.

Column 2 – Derived by depreciating total expenditures on multi-family dwellings, deflated values, and allocating a proportion to individuals on basis of Table R-29, col. 2; also includes fire loss adjustment (cf. notes to Table R-5, col. 5).

Columns 3 and 4 – Table R-7, cols. 3 and 4, divided by index of cost of living (1897–1913, Douglas, *op. cit.*, pp. 38, 60; 1914–1949, Bureau of Labor Statistics) shifted to 1929 base.

Column 5 – Table R-7, col. 5 divided by index of construction cost (Table R-20, col. 2).

Column 6 – Table M-26, col. 4 divided by cost of living index.

Column 7 – Col. 1 minus sum of cols. 2–6.

TABLE R–9

Column 1 – From Table R-7, col. 1.

Column 2 – Depreciation allowances in 1929 prices (cf. Table R-8, col. 2) multiplied by construction cost index (Table R-20, col. 2) plus adjustment for fire losses (cf. Table R-6, col. 5).

Columns 3 and 4 – Table R-7, cols. 3 and 4 respectively.

Column 5 – From Table R-45, col. 7.

Column 6 – From Table M-26, col. 4.

Column 7 – Col. 1 minus sum of cols. 2–6.

INDIVIDUALS' SAVING THROUGH MULTI-FAMILY DWELLINGS
Original Cost Depreciation: 1897 to 1949

$ mill.

Year	Expenditures on new structures	Depreciation (including adjustment for fire losses)	Change in gross mortgage debt	Change in real estate bonds	Net purchases by institutions	Write-downs	Net saving including write-downs
	1	2	3	4	5	6	7
1897	16	9	5	0	–	–	2
1898	15	9	7	0	–	–	–1
1899	17	10	7	0	–	–	0
1900	15	11	10	0	–	–	–6
1901	29	11	18	0	–	–	0
1902	34	11	23	0	–	–	0
1903	49	11	24	0	–	–	14
1904	49	13	27	0	–	–	9
1905	62	13	32	0	–	–	17
1906	63	19	36	0	–	–	8
1907	64	23	31	0	–	–	10
1908	58	16	32	0	–	–	10
1909	78	18	45	0	–	–	15
1910	87	18	47	3	–	–	19
1911	80	19	44	5	–	–	12
1912	86	21	48	5	–	–	12
1913	85	22	75	6	–	–	–18
1914	93	24	70	6	–	–	–7
1915	102	24	57	6	–	–	15
1916	104	26	70	6	–	–	2
1917	81	27	115	6	–	–	–67
1918	38	29	67	6	–	–	–64
1919	117	29	78	31	–	–	–21
1920	120	32	203	33	–	–	–148
1921	123	34	192	16	–	–	–119
1922	239	36	223	73	–	–	–93
1923	369	41	349	110	–	–	–131
1924	413	46	369	132	–	–	–134
1925	522	55	387	285	–	–	–205
1926	606	62	549	243	2	–	–250
1927	632	69	547	202	4	–	–190
1928	540	76	578	249	4	–	–367
1929	363	81	580	94	7	–	–399
1930	124	83	368	51	17	10	–405
1931	87	83	–102	41	28	35	2
1932	14	81	–162	–11	54	55	–3
1933	13	77	–277	–10	61	50	112
1934	11	76	–280	–10	76	50	99
1935	22	75	–204	–10	80	50	31
1936	62	75	–120	–10	41	35	41
1937	81	74	–60	–14	10	25	46
1938	71	73	–59	–19	28	20	28
1939	108	74	56	–18	13	10	–27
1940	83	74	27	–18	–2	10	–8
1941	82	73	23	–18	–16	–	20
1942	45	74	–33	–26	4	–	26
1943	37	74	–95	–34	–21	–	113
1944	20	74	–71	–34	–37	–	88
1945	16	74	20	–34	–23	–	–21
1946	70	73	123	–25	–18	–	–83
1947	136	77	205	–16	–6	–	–124
1948	244	78	280	–16	4	–	–102
1949	326	81	320	–16	7	–	–66

INDIVIDUALS' SAVING THROUGH MULTI-FAMILY DWELLINGS
1929 Prices: 1897 to 1949

$ mill.

Year	Expenditures on new structures	Depreciation (including adjustment for fire losses)	Change in gross mortgage debt	Change in real estate bonds	Net purchases by institutions	Write-downs	Net saving including write-downs
	1	2	3	4	5	6	7
1897	40	21	12	0	–	–	7
1898	36	22	17	0	–	–	–3
1899	38	22	16	0	–	–	0
1900	32	22	22	0	–	–	–12
1901	61	24	40	0	–	–	–3
1902	72	24	49	0	–	–	–1
1903	99	25	49	0	–	–	25
1904	100	28	56	0	–	–	16
1905	125	28	66	0	–	–	31
1906	121	39	72	0	–	–	10
1907	120	33	58	0	–	–	29
1908	109	35	63	0	–	–	11
1909	148	35	88	0	–	–	25
1910	165	38	87	6	–	–	34
1911	152	41	79	9	–	–	23
1912	161	42	86	9	–	–	24
1913	163	45	130	10	–	–	–22
1914	179	47	119	10	–	–	3
1915	192	47	96	10	–	–	39
1916	181	51	110	9	–	–	11
1917	119	53	154	8	–	–	–96
1918	48	53	76	7	–	–	–88
1919	127	53	77	31	–	–	–34
1920	102	55	174	28	–	–	–155
1921	129	56	184	15	–	–	–126
1922	273	59	228	75	–	–	–89
1923	376	63	351	110	–	–	–148
1924	425	68	370	132	–	–	–145
1925	542	75	378	278	–	–	–189
1926	625	83	532	235	2	–	–227
1927	661	91	540	200	4	–	–174
1928	560	97	577	249	4	–	–367
1929	363	101	580	94	7	–	–419
1930	127	103	377	52	17	10	–432
1931	97	103	–115	46	31	39	–7
1932	18	102	–203	–14	71	69	–7
1933	17	98	–367	–13	79	66	154
1934	13	96	–358	–13	90	64	134
1935	28	94	–255	–12	98	62	41
1936	73	93	–148	–12	49	43	48
1937	86	92	–72	–17	11	30	42
1938	73	91	–72	–23	29	24	24
1939	109	91	69	–22	13	12	–54
1940	81	90	33	–22	–2	12	–30
1941	75	90	27	–21	–15	–	–6
1942	40	91	–35	–27	3	–	8
1943	31	89	–94	–34	–17	–	87
1944	15	87	–69	–33	–28	–	58
1945	11	87	19	–32	–16	–	–47
1946	46	85	108	–22	–12	–	–113
1947	74	86	158	–12	–3	–	–155
1948	117	85	200	–11	2	–	–159
1949	160	86	232	–12	3	–	–149

Replacement Cost Depreciation: 1897 to 1949

$ mill.

Year	Expenditures on new structures	Depreciation (including adjustment for fire losses)	Change in gross mortgage debt	Change in real estate bonds	Net purchases by institutions	Write-downs	Net saving including write-downs
	1	2	3	4	5	6	7
1897	16	9	5	0	–	–	2
1898	15	9	7	0	–	–	–1
1899	17	12	7	0	–	–	–2
1900	15	11	10	0	–	–	–6
1901	29	11	18	0	–	–	0
1902	34	12	23	0	–	–	–1
1903	49	12	24	0	–	–	13
1904	49	13	27	0	–	–	9
1905	62	15	32	0	–	–	15
1906	63	20	36	0	–	–	7
1907	64	17	31	0	–	–	16
1908	58	19	32	0	–	–	7
1909	78	18	45	0	–	–	15
1910	87	20	47	3	–	–	17
1911	80	21	44	5	–	–	10
1912	86	22	48	5	–	–	11
1913	85	23	75	6	–	–	–19
1914	93	24	70	6	–	–	–7
1915	102	26	57	6	–	–	13
1916	104	30	70	6	–	–	–2
1917	81	36	115	6	–	–	–76
1918	38	42	67	6	–	–	–77
1919	117	48	78	31	–	–	–40
1920	120	65	203	33	–	–	–181
1921	123	54	192	16	–	–	–139
1922	239	52	223	73	–	–	–109
1923	369	62	349	110	–	–	–152
1924	413	67	369	132	–	–	–155
1925	522	73	387	285	–	–	–223
1926	606	81	549	243	2	–	–269
1927	632	86	547	202	4	–	–207
1928	540	97	578	249	4	–	–388
1929	363	101	580	94	7	–	–419
1930	124	100	368	51	17	10	–422
1931	87	93	–102	41	28	35	–8
1932	14	78	–162	–11	54	55	0
1933	13	75	–277	–10	61	50	114
1934	11	81	–280	–10	76	50	94
1935	22	77	–204	–10	80	50	29
1936	62	79	–120	–10	41	35	37
1937	81	87	–60	–14	10	25	33
1938	71	88	–59	–19	28	20	13
1939	108	90	56	–18	13	10	–43
1940	83	92	27	–18	–2	10	–26
1941	82	98	23	–18	–16	–	–5
1942	45	104	–33	–26	4	–	–4
1943	37	107	–95	–34	–21	–	80
1944	20	113	–71	–34	–37	–	49
1945	16	122	20	–34	–23	–	–69
1946	70	131	123	–25	–18	–	–141
1947	136	159	205	–16	–6	–	–206
1948	244	176	280	–16	4	–	–200
1949	326	177	320	–16	7	–	–162

R-10

Column 1 – 1897–1914: Total expenditures on commercial construction, estimated at 20 percent of total commercial, industrial, and public utility construction (cf. Table R-27) on basis of data for net expenditures on construction by type, derived from changes in value of real estate improvements at census dates as estimated by Kuznets, Simon, *National Product since 1869*, table iv, 5a, and allocated to corporations and unincorporated business on basis of Table R-29, col. 3, linear interpolation between decadal percentages.

1915–1949: Total nonresidential building minus industrial and institutional construction as given by Department of Commerce, *Construction and Construction Materials, Statistical Supplement*, May 1950, p. 6, plus estimates of hotel construction derived according to the procedure described in Table R-28, col. 2, allocated according to Table R-29, col. 3.

Column 2 – 1897–1949: Depreciation calculated from total expenditures on commercial construction (cf. col. 1 and similarly derived values for 1857–1896 shown in Tables R-27 and R-26) on assumption of forty year life, including allowances for fire losses derived from Table R-73, col. 6 allocated to unincorporated business according to Table R-29, col. 3.

Column 3 – 1897–1949: Seventy-five percent of change in total nonresidential mortgage debt as given in Tables M-7, col. 1, M-11, col. 1 and M-12, col. 3 allocated to unincorporated business according to Table R-29, col. 3.

Column 4 – 1897–1909: Fifty-five percent of net receipts on payments on account of real estate bonds as shown in Table R-41, col. 1 allocated to unincorporated business according to Table R-29, col. 3.

1910–1949: Table R-43, col. 7 multiplied by Table R-29, col. 3.

Column 5 – 1897–1925: Assumed to be negligible.

1926–1949: From Table R-45, col. 8.

Column 6 – 1930–1940: From Table M-26, col. 5.

Column 7 – 1897–1949: Col. 1 minus sum of cols. 2–6.

R-11

Column 1 – Table R-10, col. 1 divided by index of construction cost (Table R-20, col. 3) except for minor differences due to rounding.

Column 2 – Derived from col. 1 (and similarly derived values for 1857–1896) on assumption of forty-year life; includes allowances for fire losses derived from Table R-73, col. 7.

Columns 3 and 4 – Table R-10, col. 3 and 4, divided by index of cost of living (1897–1913, Douglas, *op. cit.*, pp. 38, 60; 1914–1949, Bureau of Labor Statistics shifted to 1929 base).

Column 5 – Table R-10, col. 5 divided by index of cost of construction (Table R-20, col. 3).

Column 6 – Table M-26, col. 5 deflated by index of cost of living.

Column 7 – Col. 1 minus sum of cols. 2–6.

R-12

Column 1 – From Table R-10, col. 1.

Column 2 – Depreciation of col. 1 in 1929 prices (see Table R-11, col. 2) multiplied by appropriate price index (Table R-20, col. 3); includes allowances for fire losses derived from Table R-73, col. 8.

Columns 3 to 6 – From Table R-10, cols. 3, 4, 5, and 6 respectively.

Column 7 – Col. 1 minus sum of cols. 2–6.

SAVING THROUGH COMMERCIAL STRUCTURES BY UNINCORPORATED BUSINESS; ORIGINAL COST DEPRECIATION: 1897 to 1949

$ mill.

Year	Expenditures on new structures	Depreciation (including adjustment for fire losses)	Change in gross mortgage debt	Change in real estate bonds	Net purchases by institutions	Write-downs	Net saving including write-downs
	1	2	3	4	5	6	7
1897	112	46	0	2	–	–	64
1898	104	48	5	2	–	–	49
1899	105	51	7	2	–	–	45
1900	148	53	16	2	–	–	77
1901	144	56	16	2	–	–	70
1902	167	59	24	2	–	–	82
1903	134	63	28	2	–	–	41
1904	116	66	33	2	–	–	15
1905	128	66	40	2	–	–	20
1906	171	78	46	2	–	–	45
1907	198	73	33	2	–	–	90
1908	143	76	32	4	–	–	31
1909	149	77	54	4	–	–	14
1910	151	81	56	3	–	–	11
1911	137	84	48	5	–	–	0
1912	160	86	50	5	–	–	19
1913	193	88	93	6	–	–	6
1914	138	91	82	6	–	–	–41
1915	132	93	58	6	–	–	–25
1916	221	96	75	6	–	–	44
1917	200	100	139	7	–	–	–46
1918	113	105	62	6	–	–	–60
1919	212	108	78	32	–	–	–6
1920	482	116	264	35	–	–	67
1921	444	126	129	17	–	–	172
1922	506	135	155	80	–	–	136
1923	567	145	291	119	–	–	12
1924	588	155	270	144	–	–	19
1925	754	167	314	316	–	–	–43
1926	874	184	119	269	4	–	298
1927	834	197	215	222	5	–	195
1928	761	211	170	278	10	–	92
1929	724	223	208	106	16	–	171
1930	573	233	94	57	32	5	152
1931	293	235	–42	45	53	30	–28
1932	137	237	–163	–12	123	40	–88
1933	84	235	–111	–12	125	50	–203
1934	98	230	–120	–12	137	50	–187
1935	113	226	–130	–12	163	50	–184
1936	156	228	7	–12	73	30	–170
1937	209	231	–32	–17	34	25	–32
1938	174	228	–10	–23	40	10	–71
1939	172	226	–63	–22	–4	5	30
1940	186	229	–32	–22	4	5	2
1941	217	232	2	–22	–12	–	17
1942	88	234	–71	–33	–10	–	–32
1943	22	235	–98	–44	–47	–	–24
1944	40	235	–6	–44	–59	–	–86
1945	118	236	114	–44	–75	–	–113
1946	568	244	466	–33	–46	–	–63
1947	429	256	504	–22	–9	–	–300
1948	655	267	427	–22	0	–	–17
1949	588	279	360	–22	13	–	–42

SAVING THROUGH COMMERCIAL STRUCTURES BY UNINCORPORATED
BUSINESS; 1929 PRICES: 1897 to 1949

$ mill.

Year	Expenditures on new structures	Depreciation (including adjustment for fire losses)	Change in gross mortgage debt	Change in real estate bonds	Net purchases by institutions	Write-downs	Net saving including write-downs
	1	2	3	4	5	6	7
1897	266	99	0	5	–	–	162
1898	236	106	12	5	–	–	113
1899	227	111	16	5	–	–	95
1900	304	116	36	4	–	–	148
1901	304	120	35	4	–	–	145
1902	346	127	51	4	–	–	164
1903	269	133	57	4	–	–	75
1904	235	140	68	4	–	–	23
1905	252	140	83	4	–	–	25
1906	324	163	92	4	–	–	65
1907	368	154	62	4	–	–	148
1908	267	159	63	8	–	–	37
1909	281	161	106	8	–	–	6
1910	282	168	104	6	–	–	4
1911	253	174	86	9	–	–	–16
1912	289	176	89	9	–	–	15
1913	347	180	161	10	–	–	–4
1914	255	186	140	10	–	–	–81
1915	240	189	98	10	–	–	–57
1916	355	193	118	9	–	–	35
1917	282	196	186	9	–	–	–109
1918	136	201	71	7	–	–	–143
1919	205	202	77	32	–	–	–106
1920	370	206	226	30	–	–	–92
1921	446	213	124	16	–	–	93
1922	528	220	159	82	–	–	67
1923	556	227	292	120	–	–	–83
1924	574	234	270	144	–	–	–74
1925	729	244	307	308	–	–	–130
1926	845	257	115	261	4	–	208
1927	819	267	212	219	5	–	116
1928	740	278	170	278	10	–	4
1929	724	287	208	106	16	–	107
1930	622	296	96	58	35	5	132
1931	337	296	–47	51	61	34	–58
1932	188	298	–204	–15	169	50	–110
1933	105	293	–147	–16	157	66	–248
1934	113	285	–154	–15	157	64	–224
1935	124	277	–162	–15	178	62	–216
1936	168	278	9	–15	79	37	–220
1937	208	278	–38	–20	34	30	–76
1938	175	273	–12	–28	40	12	–110
1939	168	267	–78	–27	–4	6	4
1940	176	268	–39	–27	4	6	–36
1941	192	268	2	–26	–11	–	–41
1942	72	266	–75	–35	–8	–	–76
1943	18	264	–97	–44	–37	–	–68
1944	30	261	–6	–43	–45	–	–137
1945	85	260	109	–42	–54	–	–188
1946	354	260	410	–29	–29	–	–258
1947	228	263	388	–17	–5	–	–401
1948	319	264	305	–16	0	–	–294
1949	289	267	261	–16	6	–	–229

SAVING THROUGH COMMERCIAL STRUCTURES BY UNINCORPORATED BUSINESS; REPLACEMENT COST DEPRECIATION: 1897 to 1949

$ mill.

Year	Expenditures on new structures	Depreciation (including adjustment for fire losses)	Change in gross mortgage debt	Change in real estate bonds	Net purchases by institutions	Write-downs	Net saving including write-downs
	1	2	3	4	5	6	7
1897	112	41	0	2	–	–	69
1898	104	46	5	2	–	–	51
1899	105	51	7	2	–	–	45
1900	148	56	16	2	–	–	74
1901	144	57	16	2	–	–	69
1902	167	61	24	2	–	–	80
1903	134	66	28	2	–	–	38
1904	116	69	33	2	–	–	12
1905	128	71	40	2	–	–	15
1906	171	86	46	2	–	–	37
1907	198	84	33	2	–	–	79
1908	143	85	32	4	–	–	22
1909	149	86	54	4	–	–	5
1910	151	91	56	3	–	–	1
1911	137	95	48	5	–	–	–11
1912	160	97	50	5	–	–	8
1913	193	100	93	6	–	–	–6
1914	138	101	82	6	–	–	–51
1915	132	103	58	6	–	–	–35
1916	221	120	75	6	–	–	20
1917	200	140	139	7	–	–	–86
1918	113	167	62	6	–	–	–122
1919	212	209	78	32	–	–	–107
1920	482	268	264	35	–	–	–85
1921	444	212	129	17	–	–	86
1922	506	211	155	80	–	–	60
1923	567	231	291	119	–	–	–74
1924	588	240	270	144	–	–	–66
1925	754	252	314	316	–	–	–128
1926	874	266	119	269	4	–	216
1927	834	273	215	222	5	–	119
1928	761	286	170	278	10	–	17
1929	724	287	208	106	16	–	107
1930	573	272	94	57	32	5	113
1931	293	258	–42	45	53	30	–51
1932	137	217	–163	–12	123	40	–68
1933	84	234	–111	–12	125	50	–202
1934	98	249	–120	–12	137	50	–206
1935	113	254	–130	–12	163	50	–212
1936	156	257	7	–12	73	30	–199
1937	209	281	–32	–17	34	25	–82
1938	174	271	–10	–23	40	10	–114
1939	172	274	–63	–22	–4	5	–18
1940	186	283	–32	–22	4	5	–52
1941	217	302	2	–22	–12	–	–53
1942	88	324	–71	–33	–10	–	–122
1943	22	333	–98	–44	–47	–	–122
1944	40	342	–6	–44	–59	–	–193
1945	118	359	114	–44	–75	–	–236
1946	568	419	466	–33	–46	–	–238
1947	429	495	504	–22	–9	–	–539
1948	655	543	427	–22	0	–	–293
1949	588	548	360	–22	13	–	–311

TABLE R-13

Column 1 – 1897–1914: Total expenditures on industrial construction estimated at 20 percent of total commercial, industrial, and public utility construction (cf. Table R-27) on basis of data for net expenditures on construction by type derived from changes in value of real estate improvements at census dates as estimated by Kuznets, Simon, *National Product since 1869*, Table IV, 5A, and allocated to corporations and unincorporated business on basis of Table R-29, col. 4, linear interpolation between decadal percentages.

1915–1949: From *Construction and Construction Materials, Statistical Supplement*, May 1950, table 3 multiplied by Table R-29, col. 4.

Column 2 – 1897–1949: Col. 1 divided by index of construction cost (Table R-20, col. 3).

Column 3 – 1897–1949: Derived from col. 1 (and figures for 1857–1896 similarly derived) on basis of forty-year life and allowing for fire losses.

Column 4 – 1897–1949: Same procedure as for col. 3 except expenditure series given in col. 2 used.

Column 5 – 1897–1949: Col. 4 multiplied by appropriate price index (Table R-20, col. 3).

Column 6 – 1897–1949: Twenty-five percent of total nonresidential mortgage debt (cf. Tables M-7, col. 1, M-11, col. 1 and M-12, col. 3) allocated to unincorporated business according to Table R-29, col. 4.

Column 7 – 1897–1949: Col. 6 divided by index of cost of living (see Table R-10, col. 3).

Column 8 – 1897–1949: Col. 1 minus sum of cols. 3 and 6.

Column 9 – 1897–1949: Col. 2 minus sum of cols. 4 and 7.

Column 10 – 1897–1949: Col. 1 minus sum of cols. 5 and 6.

TABLE R-14

Column 1 – From Table R-33, col. 4.

Column 2 – Col. 1 deflated by index for commercial and industrial construction (Table R-20, col. 3).

Column 3 – Derived from col. 1 assuming twenty-year life for period 1897–1929 and twenty-five-year life for period 1930–1949. Estimates of development expenditures for years 1877–1896 required for this calculation were obtained according to procedure described in Table R-33.

Column 4 – Same method as col. 3 but based on expenditure figures of col. 2.

Column 5 – Col. 4 multiplied by Table R-20, col. 3.

Column 6 – Col. 1 minus col. 3.

Column 7 – Col. 2 minus col. 4.

Column 8 – Col. 1 minus col. 5.

Columns 9, 10, and 11 – Cols. 6–8 allocated to unincorporated business according to complements of percentages given in Table C-16, col. 3. Percentages for missing years obtained by linear interpolation. Percentage 1897–1908 assumed to be unchanged from 1909 value.

$ mill.

Year	Expenditures on new structures		Depreciation (including fire loss adjustment)			Change in gross mortgage debt		Net saving		
	Original cost	1929 prices	Original cost	1929 prices	Replacement cost	Original cost	1929 prices	Origina cost	1929 prices	Replacement cost
	1	2	3	4	5	6	7	8	9	10
1897	46	109	19	41	17	0	0	27	68	29
1898	41	93	19	42	18	1	2	21	49	22
1899	41	89	20	44	20	1	2	20	43	20
1900	57	117	20	44	22	2	4	35	69	33
1901	54	114	21	45	22	2	4	31	65	30
1902	60	124	21	46	22	3	6	36	72	35
1903	46	93	21	46	23	3	6	22	41	20
1904	39	78	22	47	23	4	8	13	23	12
1905	41	81	21	45	23	4	8	16	28	14
1906	52	99	24	50	26	5	10	23	39	21
1907	57	107	21	45	24	3	6	33	56	30
1908	40	74	21	44	24	3	6	16	24	13
1909	40	75	20	43	23	5	10	15	22	12
1910	38	70	20	42	23	5	9	13	19	10
1911	32	59	20	41	22	4	7	8	11	6
1912	38	69	20	42	23	4	7	14	20	11
1913	43	78	20	40	22	7	12	16	26	14
1914	31	57	20	42	22	6	10	5	5	3
1915	24	43	19	39	21	4	7	1	−3	−1
1916	29	46	18	37	23	5	8	6	1	1
1917	40	56	19	38	27	9	12	12	6	4
1918	45	54	19	36	30	4	5	22	13	11
1919	62	60	20	37	38	5	5	37	18	19
1920	99	76	20	35	45	14	12	65	29	40
1921	52	52	22	36	36	7	7	23	9	9
1922	37	39	20	33	32	8	8	9	−2	−3
1923	44	43	21	34	34	15	15	8	−6	−5
1924	37	36	22	34	35	14	14	1	−12	−12
1925	41	40	23	35	36	17	17	1	−12	−12
1926	51	49	21	31	32	6	6	24	12	13
1927	49	48	22	32	33	11	11	16	5	5
1928	56	55	23	33	34	8	8	25	14	14
1929	57	57	21	29	29	9	9	27	19	19
1930	32	35	22	30	28	4	4	6	1	0
1931	13	15	22	30	26	−2	−2	−7	−13	−11
1932	4	6	21	30	21	−7	−9	−10	−15	−10
1933	11	13	21	29	23	−5	−7	−5	−9	−7
1934	11	13	21	28	25	−6	−8	−4	−7	−8
1935	9	10	21	28	26	−6	−7	−6	−11	−11
1936	13	14	18	23	22	0	0	−5	−9	−9
1937	25	24	18	23	24	−1	−1	8	2	2
1938	12	12	18	23	23	0	0	−6	−11	−11
1939	13	12	18	23	24	−3	−4	−2	−7	−8
1940	22	21	19	23	25	−1	−1	4	−1	−2
1941	40	36	19	23	26	0	0	21	13	14
1942	17	14	20	23	28	−3	−3	0	−6	−8
1943	8	6	20	23	29	−4	−4	−8	−13	−17
1944	10	8	20	23	30	0	0	−10	−15	−20
1945	32	23	20	23	32	5	5	7	−5	−5
1946	84	53	22	23	37	19	17	43	13	28
1947	85	45	24	24	45	21	16	40	5	19
1948	70	34	25	24	50	18	13	27	−3	2
1949	49	24	26	24	50	15	11	8	−11	−16

SAVING THROUGH CAPITAL EXPENDITURES
FOR OIL AND GAS WELL DRILLING: 1897 to 1949

$ mill.

Year	Expenditures		Depreciation			Saving					
						Total			By unincorporated business		
	Original cost	1929 prices	Original cost	1929 prices	Replace-ment cost	Original cost	1929 prices	Replace-ment cost	Original cost	1929 prices	Replace-ment cost
	1	2	3	4	5	6	7	8	9	10	11
1897	13	31	9	20	8	4	11	5	1	2	1
1898	14	32	9	21	9	5	11	5	1	2	1
1899	20	43	10	22	10	10	21	10	2	4	2
1900	24	49	11	24	12	13	25	12	3	5	2
1901	22	46	11	25	12	11	21	10	2	4	2
1902	24	50	12	27	13	12	23	11	2	4	2
1903	31	63	13	29	14	18	34	17	3	7	3
1904	32	65	14	31	15	18	34	17	3	7	3
1905	28	55	16	33	17	12	22	11	2	4	2
1906	31	59	17	36	19	14	23	12	3	4	2
1907	40	74	18	38	21	22	36	19	4	7	4
1908	42	78	20	41	22	22	37	20	4	7	4
1909	43	81	22	44	23	21	37	20	4	7	4
1910	44	82	23	48	26	21	34	18	4	6	3
1911	46	85	25	51	28	21	34	18	4	6	3
1912	56	101	27	54	30	29	47	26	5	8	4
1913	76	136	30	59	33	46	77	43	7	12	7
1914	71	131	33	65	35	38	66	36	6	10	5
1915	62	113	36	69	38	26	44	24	4	6	3
1916	106	170	39	74	46	67	96	60	9	13	8
1917	163	229	45	82	58	118	147	105	15	19	13
1918	215	259	54	93	77	161	166	138	19	20	16
1919	231	224	64	103	106	167	121	125	19	13	14
1920	392	301	79	114	149	313	187	243	35	21	27
1921	235	236	93	125	124	142	111	111	16	13	13
1922	251	262	104	135	129	147	127	122	17	15	14
1923	269	264	116	145	148	153	119	121	18	14	14
1924	272	266	128	155	159	144	111	113	17	13	13
1925	326	315	141	167	173	185	148	153	22	17	18
1926	355	343	157	180	186	198	163	169	24	19	20
1927	283	278	171	193	197	112	85	86	14	10	10
1928	251	245	182	202	208	69	43	43	8	5	5
1929	302	302	194	212	212	108	90	90	13	11	11
1930	260	282	204	221	204	56	61	56	7	8	7
1931	145	167	210	226	197	−65	−59	−52	−8	−7	−6
1932	186	255	214	229	167	−28	26	19	−3	3	2
1933	137	172	217	232	185	−80	−60	−48	−10	−7	−6
1934	199	228	221	234	205	−22	−6	−6	−3	−1	−1
1935	242	264	226	237	217	16	27	25	2	3	3
1936	297	321	233	241	223	64	80	74	8	10	9
1937	413	410	240	246	248	173	164	165	22	20	21
1938	368	369	246	249	248	122	120	120	15	15	15
1939	368	359	251	252	259	117	107	109	15	13	14
1940	398	377	250	254	268	148	123	130	19	16	17
1941	423	375	250	256	289	173	119	134	23	16	18
1942	306	251	253	255	310	53	−4	−4	7	−1	−1
1943	347	275	253	253	320	94	22	27	13	3	4
1944	526	402	257	253	331	269	149	195	38	21	27
1945	598	433	264	255	352	334	178	246	48	26	35
1946	653	406	272	256	411	381	150	242	56	22	36
1947	773	410	285	256	482	488	154	291	73	23	44
1948	1 051	511	308	201	530	743	250	515	111	38	77
1949	1 064	522	336	269	548	728	253	516	109	38	77

1897 to 1949

$ mill.

Year	Expenditures		Depreciation			Saving					
						Total			By unincorporated business		
	Original cost	1929 prices	Original cost	1929 prices	Replacement cost	Original cost	1929 prices	Replacement cost	Original cost	1929 prices	Replacement cost
	1	2	3	4	5	6	7	8	9	10	11
1897	14	33	7	16	7	7	17	7	1	2	1
1898	15	34	8	17	7	7	17	8	1	2	1
1899	22	48	8	18	8	14	30	14	2	4	2
1900	25	51	9	19	9	16	32	16	2	5	2
1901	25	53	9	20	9	16	33	16	2	5	2
1902	29	60	10	21	10	19	39	19	3	5	3
1903	33	67	11	23	11	22	44	22	3	6	3
1904	28	57	11	24	12	17	33	16	2	4	2
1905	35	69	12	26	13	23	43	22	3	5	2
1906	42	79	13	27	14	29	52	28	3	5	3
1907	46	85	14	29	16	32	56	30	3	5	3
1908	32	60	15	31	17	17	29	15	1	2	1
1909	39	73	16	32	17	23	41	22	2	3	1
1910	41	76	16	34	18	25	42	23	2	3	1
1911	39	72	17	36	20	22	36	19	1	2	1
1912	47	85	18	37	20	29	48	27	2	3	2
1913	49	88	19	39	22	30	49	27	2	3	2
1914	41	76	20	41	22	21	35	19	1	2	1
1915	50	91	21	43	24	29	48	26	2	3	1
1916	75	120	23	45	28	52	75	47	3	4	2
1917	109	153	25	48	34	84	105	75	4	5	4
1918	120	145	28	51	42	92	94	78	4	4	4
1919	87	84	30	54	56	57	30	31	3	1	1
1920	130	100	32	56	73	98	44	57	4	2	3
1921	69	69	35	57	57	34	12	12	2	1	1
1922	76	79	36	59	57	40	20	19	2	1	1
1923	106	104	38	60	61	68	44	45	3	2	2
1924	83	81	40	62	63	43	19	20	2	1	1
1925	83	80	42	64	66	41	16	17	2	1	1
1926	92	89	44	65	67	48	24	25	2	1	1
1927	80	79	46	67	68	34	12	12	1	1	1
1928	78	76	48	68	70	30	8	8	1	0	0
1929	85	85	50	70	70	35	15	15	2	1	1
1930	64	69	51	71	65	13	−2	−1	1	0	0
1931	44	51	52	72	63	−8	−21	−19	0	−1	−1
1932	27	37	53	71	52	−26	−34	−25	−1	−2	−1
1933	32	40	53	72	57	−21	−32	−25	−1	−2	−1
1934	43	49	54	72	63	−11	−23	−20	−1	−1	−1
1935	48	52	54	73	67	−6	−21	−19	0	−1	−1
1936	62	67	56	74	68	6	−7	−6	0	0	0
1937	76	75	57	75	76	19	0	0	1	0	0
1938	53	53	58	75	75	−5	−22	−22	0	−1	−1
1939	66	65	59	76	78	7	−11	−12	0	−1	−1
1940	83	79	60	76	80	23	3	3	1	0	0
1941	105	93	62	77	87	43	16	18	2	1	1
1942	120	99	64	78	95	56	21	25	3	1	1
1943	131	104	67	79	100	64	25	31	4	1	2
1944	135	103	69	80	105	66	23	30	4	1	2
1945	122	88	72	81	112	50	7	10	3	0	1
1946	122	76	74	81	130	48	−5	−8	2	0	0
1947	178	94	76	81	153	102	13	25	5	1	1
1948	209	102	80	82	169	129	20	40	6	1	2
1949	176	86	84	83	169	92	3	7	5	0	0

Column 1 – Estimated at 3 percent of value of output. This ratio is based on relation between development expenditures reported in the censuses of mines and quarries for 1919 and 1929 (*XIVth Census*, p. 51; *XVth Census*, p. 9)—the only years for which the information is available—and value of output. Figures for value of output are sum of those for metallic minerals, bituminous coal, and anthracite (*Historical Statistics*, pp. 141–142, until 1944; *Statistical Abstract*, 1949, pp. 759ff. for 1945–1948; preliminary estimate for 1949).

Column 2 – Col. 1 divided by index of cost of industrial and commercial construction (cf. Table R-20, col. 3).

Column 3 – Derived from col. 1 on assumption of forty-year life. Estimates of development expenditures for years 1857–1896 required for this calculation were obtained in same way as those of col. 1.

Column 4 – Same method as col. 3 but based on expenditure figures of col. 2.

Column 5 – Col. 4 multiplied by index of cost of commercial and industrial construction (cf. Table R-20, col. 3).

Column 6 – Col. 1 minus col. 3.

Column 7 – Col. 2 minus col. 4.

Column 8 – Col. 1 minus col. 5.

Columns 9 to 11 – Cols. 6–8 allocated to unincorporated business according to complements of the percentages given in Table C-16, col. 4. Percentages for missing years obtained by linear interpolation. Percentage for 1897–1901 assumed to be unchanged from 1902 value.

Column 1 – 1897–1914: Estimated to be 60 percent of total commercial, industrial, and public utility construction (cf. note to Table R-10, col. 1).
1915–1949: *Construction and Construction Materials, Statistical Supplement*, May 1950, table 3. Sum of public utility and "all other private" construction.

Column 2 – 1897–1949: Col. 1 divided by price index given in Table R-20, col. 4.

Column 3 – 1897–1949: Depreciation calculated from col. 1 (and similarly derived values for earlier period) on assumption of fifty-year life; includes allowances for fire losses (cf. Table R-73).

Column 4 – 1897–1949: Same procedure as for col. 3 except depreciation calculated from col. 2.

Column 5 – 1897–1949: Depreciation allowances in 1929 prices (cf. col. 4) multiplied by price index from Table R-20, col. 4 plus fire loss adjustment.

Column 6 – 1897–1949: Col. 1 minus col. 3.

Column 7 – 1897–1949: Col. 2 minus col. 4.

Column 8 – 1897–1949: Col. 1 minus col. 5.

SAVING THROUGH PUBLIC UTILITY CONSTRUCTION
1897 to 1949

$ mill.

Year	Expenditures on new structures		Depreciation (including adjustments for fire losses)			Net saving		
	Original cost	1929 prices	Original cost	1929 prices	Replacement cost	Original cost	1929 prices	Replacement cost
	1	2	3	4	5	6	7	8
1897	506	1 127	171	355	160	335	772	346
1898	471	1 006	182	376	176	289	630	295
1899	477	966	193	398	197	284	568	280
1900	682	1 312	205	418	218	477	894	464
1901	675	1 331	218	445	225	457	886	450
1902	784	1 516	231	469	242	553	1 047	542
1903	626	1 177	242	489	261	384	688	365
1904	551	1 044	263	528	278	288	516	273
1905	617	1 134	265	530	288	352	604	329
1906	829	1 462	319	630	354	510	832	475
1907	955	1 649	291	586	339	664	1 063	616
1908	705	1 228	314	613	352	391	615	353
1909	746	1 311	325	629	358	421	682	388
1910	757	1 319	341	658	377	416	661	380
1911	687	1 182	355	681	395	332	501	292
1912	814	1 373	367	700	416	447	673	398
1913	999	1 673	384	728	434	615	945	565
1914	714	1 231	402	758	440	312	473	274
1915	616	1 049	406	766	449	210	283	167
1916	726	1 097	422	787	521	304	310	205
1917	851	1 020	439	805	672	412	215	179
1918	756	776	459	822	802	297	−46	−46
1919	735	724	468	820	833	267	−96	−98
1920	852	761	494	837	936	358	−76	−84
1921	678	627	509	864	934	169	−237	−256
1922	877	982	522	879	785	355	103	92
1923	1 296	1 354	541	896	858	755	458	438
1924	1 473	1 506	566	918	899	907	588	574
1925	1 415	1 465	593	945	913	822	520	502
1926	1 528	1 569	618	971	946	910	598	582
1927	1 576	1 643	637	994	953	939	649	623
1928	1 482	1 531	663	1 020	986	819	511	496
1929	1 681	1 681	692	1 049	1 048	989	632	633
1930	1 612	1 684	724	1 083	1 037	888	601	575
1931	1 007	1 120	742	1 101	991	265	19	16
1932	507	617	748	1 111	914	−241	−494	−407
1933	306	374	739	1 096	896	−433	−722	−590
1934	362	414	742	1 091	954	−380	−677	−592
1935	391	445	743	1 088	956	−352	−643	−565
1936	542	606	748	1 091	974	−206	−485	−432
1937	736	772	754	1 092	1 040	−18	−320	−304
1938	635	674	761	1 093	1 029	−126	−419	−394
1939	711	755	770	1 094	1 029	−59	−339	−318
1940	804	838	779	1 093	1 048	25	−255	−244
1941	904	892	788	1 092	1 105	116	−200	−201
1942	805	740	797	1 086	1 181	8	−346	−376
1943	577	498	806	1 079	1 249	−229	−581	−672
1944	737	651	803	1 076	1 216	−66	−425	−479
1945	848	735	827	1 073	1 237	21	−338	−389
1946	1 426	1 105	850	1 074	1 387	576	31	39
1947	2 407	1 605	890	1 084	1 628	1 517	521	779
1948	3 067	1 890	936	1 095	1 780	2 131	795	1 287
1949	3 394	2 083	986	1 114	1 830	2 408	969	1 564

SAVING THROUGH INSTITUTIONAL (NONPROFIT) CONSTRUCTION

Original Cost Depreciation: 1897 to 1949

$ mill.

| Year | Expenditures | Depreciation (including fire loss adjustment) | Change in | | Saving | Year | Expenditures | Depreciation (including fire loss adjustment) | Change in | | Saving |
			Gross mortgage debt	Real estate bonds outstanding					Gross mortgage debt	Real estate bonds outstanding	
	1	2	3	4	5		1	2	3	4	5
1897	73	25	20	0	28	1924	284	76	100	25	83
1898	68	27	20	0	21						
1899	69	29	20	0	20	1925	352	94	100	57	101
						1926	368	100	100	50	118
1900	99	30	20	0	49	1927	391	107	50	42	192
1901	98	32	20	0	46	1928	375	114	45	53	163
1902	114	34	20	0	60	1929	371	121	45	21	184
1903	91	36	20	0	35						
1904	80	39	20	0	21	1930	362	128	40	12	182
						1931	258	133	30	10	85
1905	89	39	20	0	30	1932	132	136	0	−2	−2
1906	120	50	20	0	50	1933	47	135	0	−2	−86
1907	139	45	20	0	74	1934	44	136	0	−2	−90
1908	102	38	20	1	43						
1909	108	48	20	1	39	1935	55	136	0	−2	−79
						1936	91	123	0	−2	−30
1910	110	50	20	1	39	1937	117	138	−30	−4	13
1911	100	52	20	1	27	1938	126	140	−30	−5	21
1912	118	45	20	1	52	1939	118	142	−20	−5	1
1913	145	56	30	1	58						
1914	104	58	30	1	15	1940	142	143	−20	−5	24
						1941	166	144	−30	−5	57
1915	90	59	30	1	0	1942	84	145	−30	−7	−24
1916	120	53	30	1	36	1943	23	146	−30	−10	−83
1917	137	64	30	1	42	1944	48	146	−30	−10	−58
1918	122	68	30	1	23						
1919	151	69	30	5	47	1945	94	146	−30	−10	−12
						1946	284	149	0	−7	142
1920	107	73	30	6	−2	1947	410	157	50	−5	208
1921	147	77	40	3	27	1948	630	165	100	−5	370
1922	217	80	40	14	83	1949	831	178	150	−5	508
1923	257	83	100	21	53						

Column 1 – 1897–1949: From Tables R-28, col. 8 and R-27, col. 9.

Column 2 – 1897–1949: Depreciation calculated from col. 1 (and similarly derived values for earlier period) on basis of fifty-year life, including adjustment for fire losses.

Column 3 – 1897–1946: Derived from Table R-44, col. 1 using linear interpolations between benchmark dates with occasional modifications (particularly for 1930–1936).
1947–1949: Rough estimates based on volume of construction.

Column 4 – 1897–1909: Derived by same procedure as for later period.
1910–1949: From Table R-43, col. 8.

Column 5 – 1897–1949: Col. 1 minus sum of cols. 2–4.

1929 Prices: 1897 to 1949

$ mill.

Year	Expenditures	Depreciation (including fire loss adjustment)	Change in		Saving	Year	Expenditures	Depreciation (including fire loss adjustment)	Change in		Saving
			Gross mortgage debt	Real estate bonds outstanding					Gross mortgage debt	Real estate bonds outstanding	
	1	2	3	4	5		1	2	3	4	5
1897	179	58	48	0	73	1924	292	170	100	25	-3
1898	160	61	48	0	51	1925	360	159	98	56	47
1899	154	65	47	0	42	1926	373	164	97	48	64
1900	209	69	45	0	95	1927	402	170	49	42	141
1901	212	73	44	0	95	1928	384	178	45	53	108
1902	243	76	43	0	124	1929	371	185	45	21	120
1903	188	79	41	0	68	1930	368	193	41	12	122
1904	167	88	41	0	38	1931	284	197	34	11	42
1905	180	86	41	0	53	1932	170	200	0	-3	-27
1906	233	109	40	0	84	1933	59	200	0	-3	-138
1907	264	95	38	0	131	1934	50	198	0	-3	-145
1908	196	78	39	2	77	1935	64	198	0	-2	-132
1909	209	101	39	2	67	1936	102	184	0	-2	-80
1910	196	90	37	2	67	1937	118	199	-36	-5	-40
1911	189	108	36	2	43	1938	122	199	-36	-6	-35
1912	219	91	36	2	90	1939	113	201	-25	-6	-57
1913	268	115	52	2	99	1940	134	199	-24	-6	-35
1914	197	120	51	2	24	1941	149	200	-35	-6	-10
1915	169	122	51	2	-6	1942	72	198	-32	-7	-87
1916	201	105	47	2	47	1943	19	195	-30	-10	-136
1917	191	128	40	1	22	1944	37	194	-29	-10	-118
1918	150	131	34	1	-16	1945	68	192	-29	-10	-85
1919	163	132	30	5	-4	1946	186	191	0	-6	1
1920	90	135	26	5	-76	1947	228	192	38	-4	2
1921	154	141	38	3	-28	1948	313	194	72	-4	51
1922	242	143	41	14	44	1949	410	198	109	-4	107
1923	260	147	101	21	-9						

Column 1 – Derived by dividing original expenditures (see Tables R-28, col. 8 and R-27, col. 9) by index of construction cost shown in Table R-20, col. 5.

Column 2 – Depreciation calculated from col. 1 (and similarly derived values for earlier period) on basis of fifty-year life, including adjustment for fire losses.

Columns 3 and 4 – Table R-17, cols. 3 and 4 divided by cost of living index (1897–1913, Douglas, *op. cit.*, pp. 38, 60; 1914–1949, Bureau of Labor Statistics shifted to 1929 base).

Column 5 – Col. 1 minus sum of cols. 2–4.

SAVING THROUGH INSTITUTIONAL (NONPROFIT) CONSTRUCTION
Replacement Cost Depreciation: 1897 to 1949

$ mill.

Year	Ex-pendi-tures	Depre-ciation (including fire loss adjustment)	Change in Gross mortgage debt	Change in Real estate bonds out-standing	Saving	Year	Ex-pendi-tures	Depre-ciation (including fire loss adjustment)	Change in Gross mortgage debt	Change in Real estate bonds out-standing	Saving
	1	2	3	4	5		1	2	3	4	5
1897	73	23	20	0	30	1924	284	139	100	25	20
1898	68	26	20	0	22						
1899	69	30	20	0	19	1925	352	158	100	57	37
						1926	368	164	100	50	54
1900	99	32	20	0	47	1927	391	168	50	42	131
1901	98	33	20	0	45	1928	375	176	45	53	101
1902	114	36	20	0	58	1929	371	187	45	21	118
1903	91	39	20	0	32						
1904	80	42	20	0	18	1930	362	191	40	12	119
						1931	258	180	30	10	38
1905	89	42	20	0	27	1932	132	156	0	−2	−22
1906	120	55	20	0	45	1933	47	159	0	−2	−110
1907	139	51	20	0	68	1934	44	175	0	−2	−129
1908	102	44	20	1	37						
1909	108	53	20	1	34	1935	55	171	0	−2	−114
						1936	91	164	0	−2	−71
1910	110	55	20	1	34	1937	117	198	−30	−4	−47
1911	100	58	20	1	21	1938	126	206	−30	−5	−45
1912	118	52	20	0	46	1939	118	210	−20	−5	−67
1913	145	64	30	1	50						
1914	104	63	30	1	10	1940	142	213	−20	−5	−46
						1941	166	223	−30	−5	−22
1915	90	66	30	1	−7	1942	84	233	−30	−7	−112
1916	120	68	30	1	21	1943	23	239	−30	−10	−176
1917	137	94	30	1	12	1944	48	254	−30	−10	−166
1918	122	111	30	1	−20						
1919	151	126	30	5	−10	1945	94	267	−30	−10	−133
						1946	284	293	0	−7	−2
1920	107	165	30	6	−94	1947	410	348	50	−5	17
1921	147	137	40	3	−33	1948	630	393	100	−5	142
1922	217	132	40	14	31	1949	831	404	150	−5	282
1923	257	148	100	21	−12						

Column 1 – From Tables R-28, col. 8 and R-27, col. 9.

Column 2 – Derived from col. 1 (and similarly derived values for earlier period shown in Table R-27, col. 9) on basis of fifty-year life, including adjustment for fire losses.

Columns 3 and 4 – Same as for Table R-17, cols. 3 and 4.

Column 5 – Col. 1 minus sum of cols. 2–4.

Column 1 – 1837–1900: Value for 1901 extrapolated back by average of index of wholesale prices of building materials and index of wages (see Warren, G. F. and Pearson, F. H., *Gold and Prices*, pp. 31, 317).

           1901–1909: Value for 1910 extrapolated by Marshall and Stevens' index of building cost (see *Stevens' Valuation Quarterly*, Jan. 1949, pp. 57–58).

           1910–1915: Value for 1915 extrapolated by Boeckh's unweighted building cost index of residences (see Boeckh, E. H. and Associates, *Building Costs*, June 1948, p. 6).

           1915–1949: Boeckh's building cost index for residences as weighted by the National Housing Authority index (see Table R-32) shifted to 1929 base.

Column 2 – 1837–1909: Same method as col. 1.

           1910–1949: Boeckh's construction cost index for brick and wood apartments, hotels, and office buildings shifted to 1929 base (Boeckh, E. H. and Associates, *Building Costs*, Dec. 1949 and Oct. 1950).

Column 3 – 1847–1900: Same method as col. 1.

           1901–1949: Marshall and Stevens' index of building cost.

Column 4 – 1847–1900: Same method as col. 1.

           1901–1914: Value for 1915 extrapolated by Marshall and Stevens' index of building cost (cf. col. 1).

           1915–1949: Obtained by dividing the Department of Commerce estimates (cf. *Construction and Construction Materials, Statistical Supplement*, May 1950) of public utility expenditures in current values by expenditures in 1939 prices and setting the 1929 value equal to 100.

Column 5 – 1847–1900: Same method as col. 1.

           1901–1914: Same method as col. 4.

           1915–1949: Boeckh's unweighted index of building cost for apartments, hotels, and office buildings.

Column 6 – 1870–1914: Value for 1905 extrapolated back by average of index of wholesale prices of building materials and index of wages (cf. note to col. 1, 1837–1900).

           1915–1949: Public Roads Administration index of highway construction cost extrapolated prior to 1922 by a weighted average of the Interstate Commerce Commission indices for account numbers 3, 5, 6, and 11. (See *Construction and Construction Materials, Statistical Supplement*, May 1950, pp. 45, 58).

Column 7 – 1877–1914: Same method as col. 6.

           1915–1949: Simple average of the George A. Fuller Company Index, the American Appraisal Company Index, and the Turner Construction Company Index (see *Construction and Construction Materials, Statistical Supplement*, May 1950) and col. 6, each shifted to 1929 base before averaging.

Column 8 – 1847–1900: Same method as col. 1.

           1901–1914: Same method as col. 6.

           1915–1949: Simple average of Engineering News-Record Construction Cost Index and Associated General Contractors Index, each shifted to 1929 base before averaging (see *Construction and Construction Materials, Statistical Supplement*, May 1950).

CONSTRUCTION COST INDICES: 1837 to 1949

1929 = 100.0

Year	Private residential		Commercial and industrial	Public utility	Institutional	Highway	Military and naval	Public
	1- to 4-family	Multi-family						
	1	2	3	4	5	6	7	8
1837	33.7	33.6	–	–	–	–	–	–
1838	33.7	33.6	–	–	–	–	–	–
1839	33.7	33.6	–	–	–	–	–	–
1840	31.3	31.2	–	–	–	–	–	–
1841	32.5	32.4	–	–	–	–	–	–
1842	30.1	30.0	–	–	–	–	–	–
1843	28.9	28.8	–	–	–	–	–	–
1844	28.9	28.8	–	–	–	–	–	–
1845	30.7	30.6	–	–	–	–	–	–
1846	31.3	31.2	–	–	–	–	–	–
1847	30.1	30.0	30.4	32.5	29.5	–	–	23.8
1848	30.1	30.0	30.4	32.5	29.5	–	–	23.8
1849	29.5	29.4	29.8	31.8	28.9	–	–	23.3
1850	30.1	30.0	30.4	32.5	29.5	–	–	23.8
1851	30.1	30.0	30.4	32.5	29.5	–	–	23.8
1852	31.3	31.2	31.6	33.8	30.7	–	–	24.7
1853	32.5	32.4	32.8	35.1	31.9	–	–	25.7
1854	33.7	33.6	34.0	36.4	33.1	–	–	26.6
1855	34.3	34.2	46.8	37.0	33.6	–	–	27.1
1856	35.6	35.4	35.9	38.4	34.9	–	–	28.0
1857	35.6	35.4	35.9	38.4	34.9	–	–	28.0
1858	33.7	33.6	34.0	36.4	33.1	–	–	26.6
1859	32.5	32.4	32.8	35.1	31.9	–	–	25.7
1860	33.1	33.0	33.4	35.7	32.5	–	–	26.1
1861	31.9	31.8	32.2	34.4	31.3	–	–	25.2
1862	34.9	34.8	35.2	37.6	34.2	–	–	27.6
1863	42.2	42.0	42.5	45.5	41.4	–	–	33.3
1864	52.4	52.2	52.9	56.5	51.4	–	–	41.3
1865	56.0	55.8	56.5	60.4	45.9	–	–	44.2
1866	60.3	60.0	60.8	65.0	59.1	–	–	47.5
1867	57.8	57.6	58.3	62.4	56.7	–	–	45.6
1868	57.2	57.0	57.7	61.7	56.1	–	–	45.1
1869	55.4	55.2	55.9	59.8	54.3	–	–	43.7
1870	52.4	52.2	52.9	56.5	51.4	62.6	–	41.3
1871	53.0	52.8	53.5	57.2	52.0	63.3	–	41.8
1872	55.4	55.2	55.9	59.8	54.3	66.1	–	43.7
1873	54.8	54.6	55.3	59.1	53.8	65.4	–	43.2
1874	52.4	52.2	52.9	56.5	51.4	62.6	–	41.3
1875	48.8	48.6	49.2	52.6	47.9	58.2	–	38.5
1876	46.4	46.2	46.8	50.1	45.5	55.4	–	36.6
1877	43.4	43.2	43.8	46.8	42.6	51.8	43.0	34.2
1878	41.0	40.8	41.3	44.2	40.2	48.9	40.6	32.3
1879	41.6	41.4	41.9	44.9	40.8	49.6	41.2	32.8
1880	44.0	43.8	44.4	47.5	43.2	52.5	43.6	34.7
1881	45.2	45.0	45.6	48.8	44.3	53.9	44.8	35.6
1882	47.0	46.8	47.4	50.7	46.1	56.1	46.6	37.1
1883	46.4	46.2	46.8	50.1	45.5	55.4	46.0	36.6
1884	46.4	46.2	46.8	50.1	45.5	55.4	46.0	36.6
1885	45.2	45.0	45.6	48.8	44.3	53.9	44.8	35.6
1886	45.2	45.0	45.6	48.8	44.3	53.9	44.8	35.6
1887	45.8	45.6	46.2	49.4	44.9	54.6	45.4	36.1
1888	45.2	45.0	45.6	48.8	44.3	53.9	44.8	35.6
1889	45.8	45.6	46.2	49.4	44.9	54.6	45.4	36.1
1890	47.6	47.4	48.0	51.3	46.7	56.8	47.2	37.5
1891	45.8	45.6	46.2	49.4	44.9	54.6	45.4	36.1
1892	44.6	44.4	45.0	48.1	43.7	53.2	44.2	35.2

1929 = 100.0

Year	Private residential		Commercial and industrial	Public utility	Institutional	Highway	Military and naval	Public
	1- to 4-family	Multi-family						
	1	2	3	4	5	6	7	8
1893	44.0	43.8	44.4	47.5	43.2	52.5	43.6	34.7
1894	42.8	42.6	43.1	46.2	42.0	51.0	42.4	33.7
1895	41.6	41.4	41.9	44.9	40.8	49.6	41.2	32.8
1896	42.8	42.6	43.1	46.2	42.0	51.0	42.4	33.7
1897	41.6	41.4	41.9	44.9	40.8	49.6	41.2	32.8
1898	43.4	43.2	43.8	46.8	42.6	51.8	43.0	34.2
1899	45.8	45.6	46.2	49.4	44.9	54.6	45.4	36.1
1900	48.2	48.0	48.6	52.0	47.3	57.5	47.8	38.0
1901	47.0	46.8	47.4	50.7	46.1	56.1	46.6	37.1
1902	47.9	47.7	48.3	51.7	47.0	57.5	47.8	38.0
1903	49.2	49.0	49.6	53.2	48.3	59.7	49.6	39.4
1904	48.9	48.7	49.3	52.8	48.0	58.2	48.4	38.5
1905	50.4	50.1	50.8	54.4	49.4	61.1	50.7	40.4
1906	52.5	52.3	52.9	56.7	51.5	66.9	55.5	44.2
1907	53.7	53.4	54.1	57.9	52.6	70.5	58.5	46.6
1908	53.2	52.9	53.6	57.4	52.1	66.1	54.9	43.7
1909	52.8	52.5	53.2	56.9	51.7	67.6	56.1	44.7
1910	53.2	52.9	53.6	57.4	56.1	70.5	58.5	46.6
1911	52.5	52.2	54.3	58.1	52.8	71.2	59.1	47.0
1912	53.8	53.3	55.3	59.3	53.8	71.9	59.7	47.5
1913	51.9	51.9	55.7	59.7	54.2	74.1	61.5	48.9
1914	52.2	51.9	54.2	58.0	52.7	71.2	59.1	47.0
1915	53.5	53.1	54.8	58.7	53.3	71.9	59.7	47.5
1916	57.0	57.5	62.4	66.2	59.8	76.1	66.4	60.7
1917	66.0	68.0	71.2	83.4	71.8	87.6	77.9	77.2
1918	79.3	79.7	83.0	97.4	81.6	105.9	89.2	89.0
1919	92.1	92.1	103.2	101.5	92.8	117.2	103.1	96.7
1920	118.7	118.7	130.3	112.0	118.6	152.4	130.8	122.4
1921	95.4	95.4	99.5	108.2	95.3	126.1	104.5	97.1
1922	87.8	87.8	95.8	89.3	89.5	114.9	97.2	88.5
1923	98.4	98.2	101.9	95.7	98.9	128.0	108.7	101.8
1924	96.9	97.2	102.4	97.8	97.1	122.8	106.6	101.9
1925	96.2	96.3	103.4	96.6	97.8	116.7	104.5	98.9
1926	96.9	97.0	103.4	97.4	98.6	112.3	104.6	99.0
1927	95.7	95.6	101.9	95.9	97.2	110.6	102.9	99.2
1928	95.9	96.4	102.9	96.8	97.7	103.5	101.0	99.1
1929	100.0	100.0	100.0	100.0	100.0	100.0	100.0	100.0
1930	97.6	97.3	92.1	95.7	98.4	93.1	93.4	98.3
1931	89.9	90.1	87.0	89.9	90.8	83.4	83.3	91.3
1932	76.1	76.4	72.8	82.2	77.5	66.2	72.3	80.0
1933	76.2	76.9	79.8	81.8	79.5	83.3	76.3	82.1
1934	83.0	84.0	87.4	87.4	87.8	91.2	84.3	92.0
1935	80.5	81.8	91.6	87.9	86.0	87.5	83.2	91.0
1936	84.2	84.5	92.5	89.4	89.5	90.0	85.9	94.3
1937	93.7	94.3	100.7	95.3	99.5	86.2	93.6	103.4
1938	96.3	97.0	99.6	94.2	103.2	79.0	92.0	103.4
1939	98.1	98.8	102.3	94.2	104.4	78.8	91.7	103.3
1940	101.7	101.8	105.7	95.9	106.3	77.7	93.5	105.2
1941	109.6	109.3	112.9	101.4	111.3	88.8	102.0	111.4
1942	115.8	114.9	121.7	108.8	117.4	119.3	119.2	118.7
1943	121.2	120.2	126.3	115.8	121.9	137.8	127.8	123.6
1944	132.1	130.1	130.9	113.2	130.5	125.4	124.3	127.5
1945	140.9	139.7	138.2	115.3	138.5	121.3	126.4	131.0
1946	156.2	153.4	160.7	129.1	152.7	133.4	149.4	148.2
1947	189.3	184.6	188.4	150.0	179.9	152.4	183.0	173.9
1948	210.6	207.7	205.5	162.3	201.1	171.7	203.6	193.7
1949	204.2	204.0	203.7	162.9	202.8	165.9	201.0	199.6

R-21

TABLE R-21

Lines 1 and 2 – Thompson, W. S. and Whelpton, P. K., *Population Trends in the United States*, 1933, p. 26.

Line 3 – Martin, Robert F., *National Income in the United States, 1799–1938*, pp. 6–7, table 1.

Line 4 – Sum of 0.5 multiplied by line 1c plus 0.2 multiplied by line 2c plus 0.3 multiplied by line 3c.

Line 5 – Current price estimate (cf. R–27, col. 1) deflated by average of industrial and residential construction cost indices on 1929 basis. These indices were computed by linking the average of wholesale price index of building materials and index of average hourly earnings to index of building costs by Marshall and Stevens and to Boeckh's index of residential construction respectively.

Line 6 – Derived by following steps:

$$1860 \text{ volume} - \frac{1870 \text{ volume}}{1 + \text{change in volume } 1860-1870} = \frac{965}{1 + 0.29} = 745$$

(Same procedure for 1850 and 1840).

R-22

TABLE R-22

Column 1 – 1837–1868: Rough linear interpolation between estimates for 1840, 1850, 1860, and 1870 from Table R–21.

Column 2 – 1837–1839: Estimate for 1840 extrapolated by index of wholesale prices of building materials (see Warren, G. F. and Pearson, F. H., *Gold and Prices*, p. 30).
1840–1868: Average of indices of residential and industrial construction costs. Industrial construction cost index is index of building cost by Marshall and Stevens shifted to 1929 base and extrapolated prior to 1901 by an average of index of wholesale prices of building materials and index of wages (see *Stevens' Valuation Quarterly* and *Gold and Prices*, pp. 30, 31, 317). Residential construction cost index is consolidated Boeckh index of construction cost shifted to 1929 base and extrapolated prior to 1915 as for industrial construction.

Column 3 – 1837–1868: Col. 1 multiplied by col. 2.

Column 4 – 1837–1868: 41 percent of col. 3, average percentage during 1869–1874, based on ratio of indices of values of total residential to total new building as given by Long, C. D., Jr. (*Building Cycles and the Theory of Investment*, appendix B, section 2) and assuming that during the period 1901–1912 residential construction accounted for 30 percent of total new construction.

610

DERIVATION OF CONSTRUCTION ACTIVITY
Selected Dates: 1840 to 1870

	1840	1850	1860	1870
1. U.S. population in places of 2500 and over (000):				
(a) Total	1 973	3 901	6 531	10 095
(b) Net change from previous decade (000)	+888	+1 928	+2 630	+3 564
(c) Percentage change	+82.0	+97.7	+67.4	+54.6
2. U.S. population in places under 2500 (000):				
(a) Total	15 096	19 291	24 912	28 464
(b) Net change from previous decade (000)	+3 315	+4 195	+5 621	+3 552
(c) Percentage change	+27.9	+27.8	+29.1	+14.3
3. National income:				
(a) In constant prices ($ mill.)	3 282	5 450	9 212	8 843
(b) Net change from previous decade ($ mill.)	+1 199	+2 168	+3 762	−369
(c) Percentage change	+57.6	+66.1	+69.0	−4.0
4. Average net percentage change from previous decade	63.8	74.2	60.2	29.0
5. Kuznets' new construction, 1929 prices ($ mill.)	–	–	–	965
6. Derived construction expenditure, 1929 prices ($ mill.)	265	465	745	.

EXPENDITURES ON TOTAL AND RESIDENTIAL CONSTRUCTION
1837 to 1868

$ mill.

Year	Value of construction, 1929 prices	Construction cost index, 1929 = 100	Value of construction, current prices		Year	Value of construction, 1929 prices	Construction cost index, 1929 = 100	Value of construction, current prices	
			Total	Residential				Total	Residential
	1	2	3	4		1	2	3	4
1837	235	32	75	31	1853	549	31	170	70
1838	245	32	78	32	1854	577	32	185	76
1839	255	32	82	34	1855	605	33	200	82
1840	265	30	80	33	1856	633	34	215	88
1841	285	31	88	36	1857	661	34	225	92
1842	305	29	88	36	1858	689	32	220	90
1843	325	27	88	36	1859	717	31	222	91
1844	345	27	93	38	1860	745	31	231	95
1845	365	29	106	43	1861	767	30	230	94
1846	385	30	116	48	1862	789	33	260	107
1847	405	29	117	48	1863	811	40	324	133
1848	425	29	123	50	1864	833	50	417	171
1849	445	28	125	51	1865	855	53	453	186
1850	465	29	135	55	1866	877	57	500	205
1851	493	29	143	59	1867	899	55	494	203
1852	521	30	156	64	1868	921	54	497	204

Columns 1 and 2 – Housing and Home Finance Agency, *Housing Statistics Handbook*, table 1, p. 5.

Columns 3 to 6 – Derived from data in the 1940 Census of Housing, *Characteristics by Type of Structure*, table A-4, p. 6.

Column 7 – Sum of cols. 3–5.

Column 8 – Same source as cols. 1 and 2.

Column 9 – Total single-family units as shown in *Housing Statistics Handbook*, table 2, p. 6, minus rural nonfarm units from col. 3.

Column 10 – Total two-family units as shown in source cited for col. 9 minus rural nonfarm units from col. 4.

Column 11 – Total three- and four-family units minus rural nonfarm from col. 5, applying 1940 *Census of Housing* ratios of three- and four-family housing to total over-two-family housing to figures on over-two-family units started as shown in *Housing Statistics Handbook*, table 2, p. 6.

Column 12 – Total of over-four-family units derived as described under col. 11, minus rural nonfarm units from col. 1.

Columns 13 and 14 – Derived from average permit valuation figures shown in *Housing Statistics Handbook*, table 12, p.15.

Column 15 – Col. 10 multiplied by col. 13.

Column 16 – Col. 11 multiplied by col. 14.

Column 17 – Col. 12 multiplied by col. 14.

Column 18 – Sum of cols. 9, 15, 16, and 17.

Column 19 – Sum of cols. 9, 15, and 16.

Column 20 – Sum of cols. 2 and 18. Rural nonfarm units started have not been weighted by col. 13 since amounts involved are so small.

Column 21 – Sum of cols. 7 and 19.

Column 22 – Ratio of col. 21 to col. 20.

SHARE OF ONE- TO FOUR-FAMILY HOMES IN TOTAL EXPENDITURES FOR NEW PRIVATELY FINANCED NONFARM DWELLING UNITS: 1920 to 1939

Year	Total units started, urban and rural nonfarm	Rural nonfarm units started						Urban nonfarm units started				
		Total	One-family	Two-family	Three-and four-family	Over-four-family	Total one-to four-family	Total	One-family	Two-family	Three-and four-family	Over-four-family
	Thousands											
	1	2	3	4	5	6	7	8	9	10	11	12
1920	247	51	45	4	1	1	50	196	157	20	6	13
1921	449	90	82	6	1	1	89	359	234	64	19	42
1922	716	142	130	9	2	1	141	574	307	137	40	90
1923	871	173	158	12	2	1	172	698	355	163	56	124
1924	893	177	162	12	2	1	176	716	372	161	57	126
1925	937	185	172	10	2	1	184	752	400	147	42	163
1926	849	168	156	9	2	1	167	681	335	108	49	189
1927	810	167	155	9	2	1	166	643	299	90	53	201
1928	753	159	147	9	2	1	158	594	289	69	49	187
1929	509	109	101	6	1	1	108	400	215	45	29	111
1930	330	94	88	4	1	1	93	236	139	25	16	56
1931	254	80	75	3	1	1	79	174	112	19	6	37
1932	134	70	66	2	1	1	69	64	52	5	1	6
1933	93	48	45	1	1	1	47	45	31	4	3	7
1934	126	77	73	2	1	1	76	49	36	3	3	7
1935	216	103	97	4	1	1	102	113	85	4	8	16
1936	304	106	100	3	2	1	105	198	140	12	12	34
1937	332	118	112	3	2	1	117	214	151	14	11	38
1938	399	144	135	4	4	1	143	255	177	15	18	45
1939	458	155	146	5	3	1	154	303	224	16	14	49

Year	Average permit valuation: two-family and over to single-family		Number weighted by ratio of average valuations					Urban and rural nonfarm		Total expenditures on one- to four-family units
	Two-family	Over-two-family	Two-family	Three-and four-family	Over-four-family	Total all types	Total one-to four-family	Total all types	Total one-to four-family	
	Ratio		Thousands							Percent
	13	14	15	16	17	18	19	20	21	22
1920	–	–	–	–	–	–	–	–	–	–
1921	0.95	1.01	61	19	42	356	314	446	403	90
1922	0.84	0.93	115	37	84	543	459	685	600	88
1923	1.00	0.96	163	54	119	691	572	864	744	86
1924	1.00	1.01	161	58	127	718	591	895	767	86
1925	0.96	0.93	141	39	152	732	580	917	764	83
1926	0.94	0.86	102	42	163	642	479	810	646	80
1927	0.90	0.86	81	46	173	599	426	766	592	77
1928	0.82	0.84	57	41	157	544	387	703	545	78
1929	0.82	0.89	37	26	99	377	278	486	386	79
1930	0.79	0.77	20	12	43	214	171	308	264	86
1931	0.75	0.75	14	5	28	159	131	239	210	88
1932	0.82	0.76	4	1	5	62	57	132	126	95
1933	0.81	0.79	3	2	6	42	36	90	83	92
1934	0.82	0.67	2	2	5	45	40	122	116	95
1935	0.70	0.77	3	6	12	106	94	209	196	94
1936	0.70	0.84	8	10	29	187	158	293	263	90
1937	0.71	0.84	10	9	32	202	170	320	287	90
1938	0.70	0.78	11	14	35	237	202	381	345	91
1939	0.72	0.85	12	12	42	290	248	445	402	90

TABLE R–24

Columns 1 to 3 – 1940–1947: *The Housing Situation—The Factual Background*, Housing and Home Finance
   Agency, June 1948, table XXXI. Basic source of data: Bureau of Labor Statistics.
   1948–1949: *Survey of Current Business*, Sept. 1950, p. 9.

Columns 4 and 5 – 1940–1944: Arbitrary ratio of 0.2 applied to total over-four-family units (same source as
   for cols. 1–3) to obtain number of three- and four-family units started.
   1945–1947: From special tabulation supplied by the Bureau of Labor Statistics.
   1948–1949: Same procedure as for 1940–1944.

Columns 6 and 7 – 1940–1946: Derived from average permit valuation figures shown in *Housing Statistics
   Handbook*, 1948, table 13, p. 16. Basic source of data: Bureau of Labor Statistics.
   1947–1949: Assumed same as for 1946.

Column 8 – 1940–1949: Col. 3 multiplied by col. 6.

Column 9 – 1940–1949: Col. 4 multiplied by col. 7.

Column 10 – 1940–1949: Col. 5 multiplied by col. 7.

Column 11 – 1940–1949: Sum of cols. 2, 8, 9, and 10.

Column 12 – 1940–1949: Col. 11 minus col. 10.

Column 13 – 1940–1949: Ratio of col. 12 to col. 11 multiplied by 100.

TABLE R–25

Column 1 – 1900–1907: Colean, Miles L., *American Housing Problems and Prospects*, Twentieth Century
   Fund, table 10, p. 364.
   1908–1909: Twentieth Century Fund figures slightly reduced to bring them in line with Bureau
   of Labor Statistics series.
   1910–1919: Schumm, G. A., *Construction Industry in the United States*, Bureau of Labor
   Statistics Bulletin 786. The Bureau of Labor Statistics 1910–1919 decade total of 3,980,000
   units compares with decade total of 3,993,000 units estimated by Wickens, D. L., in *Residential
   Real Estate*, although annual distribution of his totals shown in *American Housing Problems
   and Prospects, op. cit.*, differs somewhat from the Bureau of Labor Statistics annual data.

Columns 2 and 3 – 1900–1909: *American Housing Problems and Prospects, op. cit.*
   1910–1919: Derived by applying annual percentages of urban nonfarm and rural nonfarm units
   to total nonfarm units shown in *American Housing Problems and Prospects* to col. 1.

Columns 4 and 5 – 1900–1919: Estimates for percentages of single-family, two-family and over-two-family
   dwelling units taken from Chawner, Lowell, *Residential Building, Housing Monograph
   Series No. 1*, National Resources Committee, 1939, fig. 7, p. 14.

Columns 6 and 7 – 1900–1919: Estimates for three- and four-family and over-four-family units calculated
   by using Bureau of the Census, *Census of Housing*, 1940, data on ratio of three- and four-
   family units built in 1900–1909 and 1910–1919 decades to over-two-family units built in
   these periods. (For 1900–1909, 41.5 percent of over-two-family units remaining in 1940 were
   three- and four-family structures; for 1910–1919, 38.8 percent.)

Column 8 – 1900–1914: Derived by dividing annual expenditures for new nonfarm residential construction
   shown in *Residential Building, op. cit.*, table V, p. 13, by annual number of units started as
   shown in table IV, p. 13 of the same source.

Column 9 – 1897–1899: Extrapolated from 1900 value on basis of index of total residential buildings from
   Long, C. D., Jr., *Building Cycles and the Theory of Investment*, p. 226.
   1900–1914: Col. 1 multiplied by col. 8 rounded to nearest ten million.
   1915–1919: *Construction and Construction Materials, Statistical Supplement*, May 1950, p. 6.

Column 10 – 1897–1899: Extrapolated on basis of 1900 value as in col. 9.
   1900–1919: Col. 9 multiplied by col. 7.

Column 11 – 1897–1919: Col. 9 minus col. 10.

SHARE OF ONE- TO FOUR-FAMILY DWELLING UNITS IN TOTAL EXPENDITURES FOR NEW PRIVATELY FINANCED NONFARM DWELLING UNITS
1940 to 1949

Year	New privately financed dwelling units started (thousands)					Ratio of average permit valuation two-family and over to single-family	
	Total	Single-family	Two-family	Three- and four-family	Over-four-family	Two-family	Over-two-family
	1	2	3	4	5	6	7
1940	530	448	26	11	45	.67	.80
1941	619	533	28	12	46	.67	.75
1942	301	252	17	6	26	.82	.78
1943	184	136	18	6	24	.92	.91
1944	139	114	11	3	11	1.14	1.03
1945	208	184	9	4	11	.90	.91
1946	662	590	24	10	38	.94	.85
1947	846	740	34	14	58	.94	.85
1948	914	763	46	21	83	.94	.85
1949	989	792	35	32	130	.94	.85

Year	Number of dwelling units weighted by ratio of average valuation (thousands)					Percent of total expenditures on one- to four-family
	Two-family	Three- and four-family	Over-four-family	Total all types	One-to four-family	
	8	9	10	11	12	13
1940	17	9	36	510	474	93
1941	19	9	34	595	561	94
1942	14	5	20	291	271	93
1943	17	5	22	180	158	88
1944	13	3	11	141	130	92
1945	8	4	10	206	196	95
1946	23	9	32	654	622	95
1947	32	12	49	833	784	94
1948	43	18	71	895	824	92
1949	33	27	110	962	852	89

R-25　EXPENDITURES ON NEW PRIVATE NONFARM RESIDENTIAL CONSTRUCTION,
BY TYPE; ORIGINAL COST
1897 to 1919

Year	Total nonfarm dwelling	Urban nonfarm	Rural nonfarm	Single-family	Two-family	Three- and four-family	Over-four-family	Average expenditure per dwelling unit	Private nonfarm residential expenditures		
									Total	Over-four-family	1- to 4-family
	000 units			Percent of total				$	$ mill.		
	1	2	3	4	5	6	7	8	9	10	11
1897	.	.	.	.	.	.	.	.	320	19	301
1898	.	.	.	.	.	.	.	.	310	18	292
1899	.	.	.	.	.	.	.	.	360	20	340
1900	204	149	55	79	11	4	6	1 460	300	18	282
1901	303	191	112	74	13	5	8	1 380	420	34	386
1902	327	176	151	72	14	6	8	1 560	510	41	469
1903	411	191	220	72	13	6	9	1 550	640	58	582
1904	416	256	160	70	14	7	9	1 590	660	59	601
1905	459	288	171	72	13	6	9	1 830	840	76	764
1906	464	302	162	74	13	5	8	2 060	960	77	883
1907	433	284	149	72	14	6	8	2 230	970	78	892
1908	425	269	156	67	20	5	8	2 090	890	71	819
1909	555	368	187	64	20	7	9	1 950	1 080	97	983
1910	475	361	114	66	18	6	10	2 300	1 090	109	981
1911	480	360	120	65	19	6	10	2 110	1 010	101	909
1912	490	360	130	64	20	6	10	2 240	1 100	110	990
1913	455	333	122	62	22	6	10	2 420	1 100	110	990
1914	445	345	100	60	21	7	12	2 300	1 020	122	898
1915	475	418	57	61	19	7	13	.	1 044	136	908
1916	480	443	37	60	21	7	12	.	1 176	141	1 035
1917	230	149	81	62	20	7	11	.	1 006	111	895
1918	120	54	66	72	17	4	7	.	764	53	711
1919	330	247	83	71	13	6	10	.	1 652	165	1 487

616

EXPENDITURES ON NEW CONSTRUCTION, BY TYPE; ORIGINAL COST
1837 to 1868

$ mill.

Year	Total	Private residential	Farm	All other private		Public		
				Total	Institutional	Total	U.S. Government	State and local government
	1	2	3	4	5	6	7	8
1837	75	31	14	25	2	5	4	1
1838	78	32	14	28	2	4	3	1
1839	82	34	14	31	2	3	2	1
1840	80	33	14	30	2	3	2	1
1841	88	36	17	32	3	3	2	1
1842	88	36	17	33	3	2	1	1
1843	88	36	20	30	2	2	1	1
1844	93	38	20	31	2	4	2	2
1845	106	43	23	36	3	4	2	2
1846	116	48	23	41	3	4	2	2
1847	117	48	28	37	3	4	2	2
1848	123	50	28	41	3	4	2	2
1849	125	51	31	39	3	4	2	2
1850	135	55	31	44	4	5	2	3
1851	143	59	33	46	4	5	2	3
1852	156	64	34	53	4	5	2	3
1853	170	70	36	57	5	7	4	3
1854	185	76	37	62	5	10	6	4
1855	200	82	39	69	6	10	6	4
1856	215	88	42	74	6	11	7	4
1857	225	92	43	77	6	13	8	5
1858	220	90	48	70	6	12	7	5
1859	222	91	51	70	6	10	5	5
1860	231	95	51	75	6	10	4	6
1861	230	94	56	71	6	9	3	6
1862	260	107	59	83	7	11	4	7
1863	324	133	62	115	9	14	6	8
1864	417	171	65	166	13	15	7	8
1865	453	186	68	184	15	15	6	9
1866	500	205	74	205	16	16	6	10
1867	494	203	82	189	15	20	9	11
1868	497	204	88	183	15	22	10	12

Column 1 – From Table R-22, col. 3.

Column 2 – From Table R-22, col. 4.

Column 3 – Same procedure as for Table R-27, col. 5.

Column 4 – Col. 1 minus sum of cols. 2, 3, and 6.

Column 5 – Roughly estimated as 8 percent of col. 4.

Column 6 – Sum of cols. 7 and 8.

Column 7 – Same source as Table R-27, col. 11.

Column 8 – Same procedure as for Table R-27, col. 12.

Column 1 – 1869–1914: Kuznets' unpublished annual estimates decreased by 10 percent to approximate level of Department of Commerce estimates. (For decadal estimates cf. Kuznets, S., *National Product since 1869*, table II, 5, p. 99, col. 9.)

Column 2 – 1869–1896: Derived from col. 1 by estimating share of residential construction as follows: (1) ratios of indices of value of total residential building to total new building were computed from estimates by Long, C. D., Jr. (cf. *Building Cycles and the Theory of Investment*, appendix B, section 2), thus obtaining indices of share of residential building; (2) estimated that share of residential construction during 1901–1912 period was roughly 30 percent of total new construction, thus deriving a base value for indices.
1897–1914: From Table R-25, col. 9.

Column 3 – 1869–1896: Derived by estimating share of detached and multi-family dwellings from Long's figures (cf. *op. cit.*, appendix B, section 1).
1897–1914: From Table R-25, col. 11.

Column 4 – 1869–1914: Col. 2 minus col. 3.

Column 5 – 1869–1896: Series described in notes to Table A-8, col. 4 increased by 55 percent in order to bring estimates into line with Census figures. (See notes to Table A-1, col. 3.)
1897–1914: Table A-7, col. 1 increased by 55 percent.

Column 6 – 1869–1914: Col. 1 minus sum of cols. 2, 5, and 10.

Columns 7 and 8 – 1869–1914: Col. 6 minus col. 9 split among commercial, industrial, and public utility construction in the ratio 20:20:60 on basis of data for net expenditures on construction by type derived from changes in value of real estate improvements at census dates as estimated by Kuznets, S., *National Product since 1869*, table IV, 5A. Expenditures allocated to corporate and unincorporated businesses by same procedure as for Table R-28, cols. 6 and 7.

Column 9 – 1869–1914: Roughly estimated at 8 percent of col. 6 (cf. notes to Table R-28, col. 8).

Column 10 – 1869–1914: Col. 11 plus col. 12.

Column 11 – 1869–1914: From Series H 27–32 "Federal expenditures for public works: 1791 to 1919" (excluding expenditures for "Outside continental United States" and "All other"), *Historical Statistics of the United States*, p. 169 adjusted to calendar-year basis by a two-year moving average.

Column 12 – 1869–1896: See notes to Table G-6, cols. 7 and 8.
1897–1914: Sum of Table G-6, cols. 2 and 6 and calendar-year estimates, obtained by linear interpolation, of Table G-15, col. 1.

Column 1 – 1915–1949: Sum of cols. 2 and 5.

Column 2 – 1915–1949: *Construction and Construction Materials, Statistical Supplement*, May 1950, p. 6. Sum of new dwelling units and nonhousekeeping units after deducting expenditures on construction of hotels, latter series obtained as follows:
1915–1919: Extrapolated on basis of relationship in 1920 of construction expenditures on total nonhousekeeping buildings to expenditures on hotels.
1920–1948: *Construction and Construction Materials, Statistical Supplement*, May 1949, p. 7.
1949: Roughly estimated on basis of relationship in 1946–1948 at 25 percent of construction of nonhousekeeping buildings.

Column 3 – 1915–1919: From Table R-25, col. 11.
1920–1949: Obtained by multiplying col. 2 by share of total of one- to four-family dwellings taken from Table R-23, col. 22 for 1921–1939 and from Table R-24, col. 13 for 1940–1949. 1920 assumed to be same as 1921.

Column 4 – 1915–1949: Col. 2 minus col. 3.

Column 5 – 1915–1949: *Construction and Construction Materials, Statistical Supplement*, May 1950, pp. 6–8. Sum of new private construction on nonresidential buildings, public utility, and "all other private"; also hotels (derived according to procedure stated in col. 2).

Columns 6 and 7 – 1915–1949: Private nonfarm nonresidential building expenditures, excluding institutions, as given in *Construction and Construction Materials, Statistical Supplement*, May 1950, allocated to corporate and unincorporated businesses on basis of Table R-29, cols. 4 and 5, linearly interpolating between decadal percentages. Public utility and "All other private" construction assumed to be entirely corporate.

Column 8 – 1915–1919: Roughly estimated as 8 percent of col. 5 on basis of the post-1920 relationship.
1920–1949: *Construction and Construction Materials, Statistical Supplement*, May 1950, p. 7. Sum of religious, educational, hospital, and institutional construction.

EXPENDITURES ON NEW CONSTRUCTION, BY TYPE; ORIGINAL COST
1869 to 1914

$ mill.

Year	Total	Private residential			Farm	All other private				Public		
		Total	1- to 4-family	Multi-family		Total	Corporate business	Unincorporated business	Institutions	Total	U.S. Government	State and local government
	1	2	3	4	5	6	7	8	9	10	11	12
1869	541	222	220	2	96	201	134	51	16	22	9	13
1870	479	201	199	2	112	141	94	36	11	25	11	14
1871	462	208	204	4	121	104	70	26	8	29	14	15
1872	776	349	339	10	133	261	175	65	21	33	17	16
1873	807	274	260	14	146	350	236	86	28	37	19	18
1874	699	294	282	12	157	210	141	52	17	38	19	19
1875	693	277	266	11	163	215	146	52	17	38	17	21
1876	658	276	270	6	157	188	129	44	15	37	14	23
1877	615	277	266	11	146	156	108	36	12	36	11	25
1878	595	315	309	6	138	103	71	24	8	39	12	27
1879	651	326	319	7	129	152	106	34	12	44	14	30
1880	749	367	349	18	113	222	155	49	18	47	15	32
1881	981	432	415	17	104	394	277	85	32	51	16	35
1882	1 015	477	439	38	96	385	272	82	31	57	19	38
1883	1 057	455	419	36	87	456	323	97	36	59	18	41
1884	1 155	543	500	43	78	473	337	98	38	61	16	45
1885	1 075	538	511	27	73	401	286	83	32	63	14	49
1886	1 289	632	607	25	90	502	362	100	40	65	12	53
1887	1 353	568	540	28	105	608	438	121	49	72	14	58
1888	1 280	461	429	32	122	617	448	120	49	80	17	63
1889	1 354	515	479	36	138	611	445	117	49	90	21	69
1890	1 973	671	637	34	157	1 049	768	197	84	96	21	75
1891	1 741	644	612	32	169	823	605	152	66	105	23	82
1892	2 166	758	728	30	155	1 137	838	208	91	116	27	89
1893	1 738	521	500	21	160	930	688	168	74	127	30	97
1894	1 624	552	524	28	141	795	589	142	64	136	31	105
1895	1 671	585	544	41	147	795	590	141	64	144	29	115
1896	1 421	426	392	34	138	705	529	120	56	152	27	125
1897	1 557	320	301	19	158	916	685	158	73	163	31	132
1898	1 516	310	292	18	175	853	640	145	68	178	36	142
1899	1 593	360	340	20	181	864	650	145	69	188	37	151
1900	1 946	300	282	18	202	1 236	932	205	99	208	43	165
1901	2 081	420	386	34	214	1 223	926	199	98	224	42	182
1902	2 387	510	469	41	229	1 420	1 079	227	114	228	44	184
1903	2 309	640	582	58	229	1 134	864	179	91	306	55	251
1904	2 224	660	601	59	239	999	764	155	80	326	63	263
1905	2 522	840	764	76	240	1 117	858	170	89	325	61	264
1906	3 062	960	883	77	262	1 501	1 158	223	120	339	67	272
1907	3 388	970	892	78	270	1 732	1 340	253	139	416	74	342
1908	2 915	890	819	71	277	1 277	992	183	102	471	85	386
1909	3 196	1 080	983	97	307	1 351	1 052	191	108	458	86	372
1910	3 287	1 090	981	109	336	1 372	1 073	189	110	489	84	405
1911	3 116	1 010	909	101	319	1 245	976	169	100	542	84	458
1912	3 452	1 100	990	110	346	1 474	1 159	197	118	532	81	451
1913	3 819	1 100	990	110	346	1 810	1 426	239	145	563	83	480
1914	3 277	1 020	898	122	346	1 294	1 022	168	104	617	94	523

EXPENDITURES ON NEW PRIVATE NONFARM CONSTRUCTION, BY TYPE

Original Cost: 1915 to 1949

$ mill.

Year	Total	Residential			All other private			
		Total	1- to 4-family	Multi-family	Total	Corporate business	Unincorporated business	Institutions
	1	2	3	4	5	6	7	8
1915	2 174	1 044	908	136	1 130	885	155	90
1916	2 672	1 176	1 035	141	1 496	1 125	251	120
1917	2 716	1 006	895	111	1 710	1 332	241	137
1918	2 292	764	711	53	1 528	1 247	159	122
1919	3 537	1 652	1 487	165	1 885	1 464	270	151
1920	4 656	1 722	1 550	172	2 934	2 246	581	107
1921	4 032	1 811	1 630	181	2 221	1 580	494	147
1922	5 494	2 979	2 622	357	2 515	1 753	545	217
1923	7 183	3 991	3 432	559	3 192	2 324	611	257
1924	7 978	4 608	3 963	645	3 370	2 462	624	284
1925	8 740	4 952	4 110	842	3 788	2 644	792	352
1926	9 371	4 965	3 972	993	4 406	3 112	926	368
1927	8 980	4 579	3 526	1 053	4 401	3 128	882	391
1928	8 510	4 231	3 300	931	4 279	3 090	814	375
1929	7 660	3 086	2 438	648	4 574	3 419	784	371
1930	5 385	1 606	1 381	225	3 779	2 812	605	362
1931	3 496	1 344	1 183	161	2 152	1 585	309	258
1932	1 534	510	484	26	1 024	750	142	132
1933	1 037	317	292	25	720	580	93	47
1934	1 243	417	396	21	826	673	109	44
1935	1 623	749	704	45	874	695	124	55
1936	2 525	1 255	1 129	126	1 270	1 009	170	91
1937	3 376	1 533	1 364	169	1 843	1 493	233	117
1938	3 094	1 676	1 525	151	1 418	1 106	186	126
1939	3 857	2 343	2 109	234	1 514	1 208	188	118
1940	4 479	2 627	2 443	184	1 852	1 502	208	142
1941	5 521	3 108	2 922	186	2 413	1 990	257	166
1942	2 930	1 476	1 373	103	1 454	1 265	105	84
1943	1 535	723	636	87	812	759	30	23
1944	1 683	591	544	47	1 092	994	50	48
1945	2 628	749	712	37	1 879	1 635	150	94
1946	8 212	3 393	3 223	170	4 819	3 883	652	284
1947	11 124	5 532	5 200	332	5 592	4 668	514	410
1948	14 343	7 612	7 003	609	6 731	5 376	725	630
1949	14 087	7 419	6 603	816	6 668	5 200	637	831

SHARE OF INDIVIDUALS (INCLUDING UNINCORPORATED BUSINESS ENTERPRISES) IN NONFARM PRIVATE STRUCTURES
Selected Dates: 1870 to 1948

Percent

Year	1- to 4-family dwellings	Multi-family dwellings	Commercial structures	Industrial structures (factories)	Year	1- to 4-family dwellings	Multi-family dwellings	Commercial structures	Industrial structures (factories)
	1	2	3	4		1	2	3	4
1870	100	95	90	50	1920	96	70	55	9
1880	100	95	80	40	1930	95	55	45	6
1890	99	90	70	32	1940	95	45	40	5
1900	98	85	65	25	1948	95	40	40	5
1910	97	80	60	15					

Column 1 – 1870–1920: Rough estimates based on 1930 value.

1930–1948: Share of individuals in mortgage debt on one- to four-family dwellings as estimated by Department of Commerce (*Survey of Current Business*, Sept. 1946, p. 17).

Columns 2 and 3 – 1870–1920: Same as col. 1.

1930–1948: Estimated on basis of distribution of mortgagors of one large insurance company and other collateral data.

Column 4 – 1870–1890: Rough estimates based on extrapolation of later values.

1900–1940: Assumed slightly below percentage of value of output in manufacturing and mining accounted for by partnerships and sole proprietorships, as reported by Bureau of the Census for adjacent years.

1948: Assumed equal to 1940.

ADDITIONAL BUILDERS' PROFITS ON NEW CONSTRUCTION
OF ONE- TO FOUR-FAMILY NONFARM HOMES
Original Cost: 1890 to 1949

Year	1- to 4-family home construction expenditures	Percent of homes built for sale	Builders' profits			Year	1- to 4-family home construction expenditures	Percent of homes built for sale	Builders' profits		
			As percent of expenditures on		Amount				As percent of expenditures on		Amount
			Homes built for sale	All 1- to 4-family home construction					Homes built for sale	All 1- to 4-family home construction	
	$ mill.				$ mill.		$ mill.				$ mill.
	1	2	3	4	5		1	2	3	4	5
1890	637	40.0	15	6.0	38	1920	1 550	65.0	15	9.8	152
1891	612	41.0	15	6.2	38	1921	1 630	65.5	15	9.8	160
1892	728	42.0	15	6.3	46	1922	2 622	66.0	15	9.9	260
1893	500	43.0	15	6.4	32	1923	3 432	66.5	20	13.3	456
1894	524	44.0	15	6.6	35	1924	3 963	67.0	20	13.4	531
1895	544	45.0	15	6.8	37	1925	4 110	67.5	20	13.5	554
1896	392	46.0	15	6.9	27	1926	3 972	68.0	20	13.6	540
1897	301	47.0	15	7.0	21	1927	3 526	68.5	15	10.3	363
1898	292	48.0	15	7.2	21	1928	3 300	69.0	15	10.4	343
1899	340	49.0	15	7.4	25	1929	2 438	69.5	15	10.4	254
1900	282	50.0	15	7.5	21	1930	1 381	70.0	10	7.0	97
1901	386	51.0	15	7.6	29	1931	1 183	70.5	10	7.0	83
1902	469	52.0	15	7.8	37	1932	484	71.0	10	7.1	34
1903	582	53.0	15	8.0	47	1933	292	71.5	10	7.2	21
1904	601	54.0	15	8.1	49	1934	396	72.0	10	7.2	29
1905	764	55.0	15	8.2	63	1935	704	72.5	10	7.2	51
1906	883	56.0	15	8.4	74	1936	1 129	73.0	15	11.0	124
1907	892	57.0	15	8.5	76	1937	1 364	73.5	15	11.0	150
1908	819	58.0	15	8.7	71	1938	1 525	74.0	15	11.1	169
1909	983	59.0	15	8.8	87	1939	2 109	74.5	15	11.2	236
1910	981	60.0	15	9.0	88	1940	2 443	75.0	15	11.2	274
1911	909	60.5	15	9.1	83	1941	2 922	75.5	15	11.3	330
1912	990	61.0	15	9.2	91	1942	1 373	76.0	20	15.2	209
1913	990	61.5	15	9.2	91	1943	636	76.5	20	15.3	97
1914	898	62.0	15	9.3	84	1944	544	77.0	20	15.4	84
1915	908	62.5	15	9.4	85	1945	712	77.5	20	15.5	110
1916	1 035	63.0	15	9.4	97	1946	3 223	78.0	20	15.6	503
1917	895	63.5	15	9.5	85	1947	5 200	78.5	20	15.7	816
1918	711	64.0	15	9.6	68	1948	7 003	79.0	20	15.8	1 106
1919	1 487	64.5	15	9.7	144	1949	6 603	79.5	20	15.9	1 050

Column 1 - 1890–1914: From Table R-27, col. 3.
1915–1949: From Table R-28, col. 3.

Column 2 – 1890–1949: Rough estimate. Since these estimates were prepared some evidence has become available which indicates that share of homes built for sale of 75–80 percent applied to recent years should not be substantially in error (cf. Bureau of Labor Statistics sales price survey for New York, Philadelphia, and Pittsburgh in *New Housing in Metropolitan Areas, 1949–1951*, and Maisel, S. J., *Journal of Political Economy*, vol. LIX, p. 169, for San Francisco Bay area). An originally neglected source (*Monthly Labor Review*, May 1941, pp. 1283–1285), however, suggests that estimated ratios for the thirties, and by inference those for preceding decades, are too high. In 1938, e.g., the Bureau of Labor Statistics investigation showed only a little less than one-half of one-family homes built for sale while rough estimates used here assume a ratio of 74 percent for one- to four-family homes. Provided assumed rate of builders' profit is correct, estimates, therefore, may overstate aggregate builders' profits by 50 percent; this, however, would imply an overstatement of total home construction expenditures by only about 5 percent.

Column 3 – 1890–1949: Rough estimates.

Column 4 – 1890–1949: Col. 2 multiplied by col. 3.

Column 5 – 1890–1949: Col. 1 multiplied by col. 4.

1867 to 1914

Year	New construction expenditures on 1- to 4- family homes	Alterations and additions		Year	New construction expenditures on 1- to 4- family homes	Alterations and additions	
		Ratio to new expenditures	Amount			Ratio to new expenditures	Amount
	$ mill.	1920–1930 = 100	$ mill.		$ mill.	1920–1930 = 100	$ mill.
	1	2	3		1	2	3
1867	201	43	9	1891	612	94	58
1868	202	43	9	1892	728	81	59
1869	220	80	18	1893	500	100	50
1870	199	57	11	1894	524	81	42
1871	204	67	14	1895	544	78	42
1872	339	67	23	1896	392	94	37
1873	260	125	32	1897	301	81	24
1874	282	143	40	1898	292	88	26
1875	266	162	43	1899	340	76	26
1876	270	143	39	1900	282	154	43
1877	266	150	40	1901	386	125	48
1878	309	100	31	1902	469	192	90
1879	319	90	29	1903	582	175	102
1880	349	77	27	1904	601	108	65
1881	415	69	29	1905	764	81	62
1882	439	63	28	1906	883	111	98
1883	419	65	27	1907	892	138	122
1884	500	71	36	1908	819	117	96
1885	511	95	49	1909	983	76	75
1886	607	58	35	1910	981	97	95
1887	540	71	38	1911	909	123	112
1888	429	94	40	1912	990	122	121
1889	479	71	34	1913	990	139	138
1890	637	71	45	1914	898	133	119

Column 1 – 1867–1868: From Table R-26, col. 2 minus small adjustment for multi-family construction.
1869–1914: From Table R-27, col. 3.

Column 2 – 1867: Assumed to be same as value for 1868.
1868–1914: Ratio of alteration expenditures to total new residential building expenditures as estimated by Long, C. D., Jr., (cf. *Building Cycles and the Theory of Investment*, appendix B, section 2).

Column 3 – 1867–1914: Obtained by applying index to base value of 10 percent, which is roughly 1920–1930 average relationship of the Department of Commerce estimates of expenditures for alterations and additions to new residential construction expenditures, and multiplying by col. 1.

Column 1 – 1857–1897: Value for 1898 extrapolated by expenditures on private residential construction in 1929 prices (Tables R-26 and R-27 deflated by construction cost index).

1898–1909: Value for 1910 extrapolated by number of deeds recorded in eight counties and Washington, D.C. (see Fisher, E., *Urban Real Estate Markets: Characteristics and Financing*, table A-1, p. 159).

1910–1949: Index of real estate activity, not corrected for growth of population or for long-term trend. Values were approximated from charts prepared by Roy Wenzlick & Co. and shifted to 1929 base (see *Real Estate Analyst*, July 27, 1948, no. 33, p. 283 and current issues. Later revised figures, extended back to 1900, show a less pronounced rise over the period).

Column 2 – 1857–1917: Value for 1918 extrapolated by index of construction cost of one- to four-family dwellings, shown in Table R-20.

1918–1921: Value for 1922 extrapolated by index of asking prices for single family houses in Washington, D.C. based on newspaper advertisements, as compiled by the National Housing Agency and its successor, the Housing and Home Finance Agency (unpublished data).

1922–1938: Average of indices, on 1929 base, of prices of houses in Washington, D.C. (as above) and of single-family houses, new and old, in Toledo, approximated from chart 4 (p. 84) in Hoad, W. M., *Real Estate Prices* (unpublished thesis, University of Michigan).

1939–1947: Same as for 1922–1938, except that the index prepared by Hoad was extrapolated by the Housing Price Index prepared by United Industrial Associates (cf. U.S. Congress, House of Representatives, *High Cost of Housing*, House Document 647, 80th Congress, 2nd Session, p. 37).

1948–1949: Estimated on the basis of 1947 in absence of specific data.

Column 3 – 1857–1949: Col. 1 multiplied by col. 2.

Column 4 – 1857–1949: Indices of col. 3 applied to base value of $350 million derived as follows:

(1) An average was computed, on basis of average value in current prices, for one- to four-family homes (including builders' profits and alterations and additions) for the period 1922–1930.

(2) An estimate of value of land involved was added by assuming it to be one-fifth of total value including cost and builders' profit, but excluding alterations and additions.

(3) It was assumed that average value of real estate activity during period 1922–1930 giving rise to dealers' commissions was equal to 10 percent of average value of all one- to four-family homes.

This estimate was based on Toledo data given by Hoad (*op. cit.*, p. 51) according to which transfers excluding gifts, inheritances, foreclosures, and surrenders averaged slightly less than 14 percent of which about three-tenths or 4 percent involved newly built homes, many of which would not give rise to dealers' commission.

Assumption of an average market turnover period of ten years is corroborated by other scattered evidence. The Federal Reserve Board, Survey of Consumer Finances, e.g., found in January 1949 that about one-half of homeowners sampled had acquired their houses since Pearl Harbor, indicating a median turnover period of a little over seven years (*Federal Reserve Bulletin*, 1949, p. 1041). This figure may be assumed to be somewhat lower than average market turnover as it includes acquisition by means other than purchase and refers to a period of particularly high real estate activity. Fisher tentatively concludes (*Urban Real Estate Markets...*, p. 43) that "the average term of ownership is less than ten years."

(4) Average index of value of real estate activity in col. 3 for the same period—1922–1930— was found to be 106.6 (1929 = 100).

(5) Value of real estate activity obtained in (3) was divided by the corresponding index of value of real estate activity to yield the base value of real estate activity.

(6) Finally, it was assumed that dealers' profits were roughly 5 percent of the total value of real estate activity for any given year.

Column 5 – 1857–1949: Indices in col. 3 applied to base value of $300 million derived the same way as base value for col. 4 except that estimated share of land in total real estate activity was excluded since land is not considered a depreciable asset.

Year	Index of real estate activity	Index of real estate prices	Index of value of real estate activity	Dealers' commissions		Year	Index of real estate activity	Index of real estate prices	Index of value of real estate activity	Dealers' commissions	
				Total	Depreciable					Total	Depreciable
	1929 = 100			$ mill.			1929 = 100			$ mill.	
	1	2	3	4	5		1	2	3	4	5
1857	10	28.1	2.8	10	8	1904	47	38.5	18.1	63	54
1858	11	26.6	2.9	10	9	1905	58	39.7	23.0	80	69
1859	11	25.6	2.8	10	8	1906	65	41.4	26.9	94	81
1860	12	26.1	3.1	11	9	1907	63	42.3	26.6	93	80
1861	12	25.1	3.0	10	9	1908	56	41.9	23.5	82	70
1862	12	27.5	3.3	12	10	1909	64	41.6	26.6	93	80
1863	13	33.3	4.3	15	13	1910	67	41.9	28.1	98	84
1864	13	41.3	5.4	19	16	1911	65	41.4	26.9	94	81
1865	13	44.1	5.7	20	17	1912	64	42.4	27.1	95	81
1866	14	47.5	6.6	23	20	1913	62	40.9	25.4	89	76
1867	14	45.6	6.4	22	19	1914	59	41.1	24.2	85	73
1868	14	45.1	6.3	22	19	1915	55	42.2	23.2	81	70
1869	16	43.7	7.0	24	21	1916	60	44.9	26.9	94	81
1870	16	41.3	6.6	23	20	1917	59	52.0	30.7	107	92
1871	16	41.8	6.7	23	20	1918	53	62.5	33.1	116	99
1872	26	43.7	11.4	40	34	1919	74	73.0	54.0	189	162
1873	20	43.2	8.6	30	26	1920	94	81.7	76.8	269	230
1874	23	41.3	9.5	33	28	1921	82	91.1	74.7	261	224
1875	23	38.5	8.9	31	27	1922	94	93.4	87.8	307	263
1876	24	36.6	8.8	31	26	1923	115	97.1	111.7	391	335
1877	26	34.2	8.9	31	27	1924	112	100.3	112.3	393	337
1878	31	32.3	10.0	35	30	1925	121	101.8	123.2	431	370
1879	32	32.8	10.5	37	32	1926	118	100.2	118.2	414	355
1880	34	34.7	11.8	41	35	1927	113	101.3	114.5	401	344
1881	39	35.6	13.9	49	42	1928	109	99.4	108.3	379	325
1882	41	37.0	15.2	53	46	1929	100	100.0	100.0	350	300
1883	40	36.6	14.6	51	44	1930	88	94.4	83.1	291	249
1884	48	36.6	17.6	62	53	1931	76	85.8	65.2	228	196
1885	48	35.6	17.1	60	51	1932	65	78.0	50.7	177	152
1886	57	35.6	20.3	71	61	1933	53	79.9	42.3	148	127
1887	50	36.1	18.0	63	54	1934	58	79.6	46.2	162	139
1888	41	35.6	14.6	51	44	1935	67	82.0	54.9	192	165
1889	46	36.1	16.6	58	50	1936	76	79.0	60.0	210	180
1890	57	37.5	21.4	75	64	1937	92	83.2	76.5	268	230
1891	57	36.1	20.6	72	62	1938	80	80.8	64.6	226	194
1892	69	35.2	24.3	85	73	1939	92	81.0	74.5	261	224
1893	48	34.7	16.7	58	50	1940	100	83.7	83.7	293	251
1894	52	33.7	17.5	61	52	1941	118	90.1	106.3	372	319
1895	57	32.8	18.7	65	56	1942	115	90.7	104.3	365	313
1896	40	33.7	13.5	47	40	1943	118	98.4	116.1	406	348
1897	31	32.8	10.2	36	31	1944	141	109.2	154.0	539	462
1898	29	34.2	9.9	35	30	1945	159	126.3	200.8	703	602
1899	32	36.1	11.6	41	35	1946	206	171.9	354.1	1 239	1 062
1900	33	38.0	12.5	44	38	1947	185	186.2	344.5	1 206	1 034
1901	39	37.0	14.4	50	43	1948	171	186.2	318.4	1 114	955
1902	46	37.8	17.4	61	52	1949	154	187.2	288.3	1 009	865
1903	48	38.8	18.6	65	56						

EXPENDITURES ON OIL AND GAS WELL DRILLING
1897 to 1949
$ mill.

Year	Value of output (at well)			Estimated expenditures	Expenditure ratio	Year	Value of output (at well)			Estimated expenditures	Expenditure ratio
	Total	Crude oil	Natural gas				Total	Crude oil	Natural gas		
	1	2	3	4	5		1	2	3	4	5
1897	47	41	6	13	0.280	1924	1 129	1 023	106	272	0.241
1898	50	44	6	14	0.280	1925	1 397	1 285	112	326	0.233
1899	73	65	8	20	0.280	1926	1 573	1 448	125	355	0.226
1900	86	76	10	24	0.280	1927	1 300	1 173	127	283	0.218
1901	77	66	11	22	0.280	1928	1 195	1 055	140	251	0.210
1902	84	71	13	24	0.280	1929	1 438	1 280	158	302	0.210
1903	109	95	14	31	0.280	1930	1 217	1 070	147	260	0.214
1904	116	101	15	32	0.280	1931	669	551	118	145	0.217
1905	101	84	17	28	0.280	1932	779	680	99	186	0.239
1906	111	92	19	31	0.280	1933	705	608	97	137	0.194
1907	142	120	22	40	0.280	1934	1 011	905	106	199	0.197
1908	151	129	22	42	0.280	1935	1 071	961	110	242	0.226
1909	154	128	26	43	0.280	1936	1 217	1 098	119	297	0.244
1910	157	128	29	44	0.280	1937	1 636	1 513	123	413	0.252
1911	165	134	31	46	0.280	1938	1 487	1 373	114	368	0.247
1912	199	164	35	56	0.280	1939	1 414	1 294	120	368	0.260
1913	273	237	36	76	0.280	1940	1 513	1 385	128	398	0.263
1914	252	214	38	71	0.280	1941	1 741	1 602	139	423	0.243
1915	220	179	41	62	0.280	1942	1 797	1 643	154	306	0.170
1916	380	331	49	106	0.280	1943	1 986	1 809	177	347	0.175
1917	581	523	58	163	0.280	1944	2 223	2 033	190	526	0.237
1918	767	704	63	215	0.280	1945	2 285	2 094	191	598	0.262
1919	826	760	66	231	0.280	1946	2 655	2 443	212	653	0.246
1920	1 441	1 361	80	392	0.272	1947	3 853	3 578	275	773	0.201
1921	887	815	72	235	0.264	1948	5 529	5 196	333	1 051	0.190
1922	980	895	85	251	0.257	1949	5 250	4 900	350	1 064	0.203
1923	1 079	978	101	269	0.249						

Column 1 – 1897–1949: Sum of cols. 2 and 3.

Column 2 – 1897–1943: *Historical Statistics*, p. 146.

    1944–1948: Department of Interior, Bureau of Mines, *Minerals Yearbook*, 1948, p. 903.

    1949: Estimated on basis of index of crude petroleum output (*Federal Reserve Bulletin*) and average price (Kansas-Oklahoma) at well (*Survey of Current Business*) adjusted for small difference (as determined for 1947) from national average (cf. *Statistical Abstract*, 1949, p. 792).

Column 3 – 1897–1902: *Census of Mines and Quarries*, 1902, p. 770. Figures referring to sales value at point of consumption multiplied by 0.41 (the 1922–1926 ratio) to obtain value at well.

    1903–1905: Interpolated on basis of output of natural gas (Burns, A. F., *Production Trends in the United States since 1870*, pp. 292–293).

    1906–1921: *Historical Statistics*, p. 146. Figures referring to values at points of consumption multiplied by 0.41 (the 1922–1926 ratio) to obtain value at wells.

    1922–1928: Department of Interior, Bureau of Mines, *Mineral Resources of the U.S.*, various issues.

    1929–1948: Department of Interior, Bureau of Mines, *Minerals Yearbook*, various issues.

    1949: Rough estimate.

Column 4 – 1897–1928: Col. 1 multiplied by col. 5.

    1929–1938: Difference between expenditures for new private construction including and excluding crude petroleum and natural gas drilling, as given in *Survey of Current Business*, *National Income Supplement*, July 1947, tables 2 and 31, respectively.

    1939–1949: *Construction and Construction Materials, Statistical Supplement*, May 1950, p. 70.

Column 5 – 1897–1928: Assumed to decrease from 28 percent in 1919 (calculated on basis of development expenditures of $231 million in 1919 as given in *XIVth Census*, vol. XI, p. 305) to 21 percent in 1928 (the 1929–1930 ratio); ratio for earlier years assumed to be same as for 1919.

    1929–1947: Col. 4 divided by col. 1.

    1948–1949: Based on ratio of col. 1 to col. 4, assuming relation between cols. 1 and 3 prevailing in preceding years.

$ mill. (except cols. 6 and 7)

End of year	Total nonfarm mortgage debt	Residential			Non-residential	Share of	
		Total	One- to four-family	Multi-family		Residential in total	Multi-family in total residential
	1	2	3	4	5	6	7
1890	3 430	2 293	2 110	183	1 137	0.669	0.080
1896	4 239	2 840	2 579	261	1 399	0.670	0.092
1897	4 239	2 840	2 573	267	1 399	0.670	0.094
1898	4 269	2 860	2 585	275	1 409	0.670	0.096
1899	4 309	2 887	2 604	283	1 422	0.670	0.098
1900	4 409	2 954	2 659	295	1 455	0.670	0.100
1901	4 510	3 022	2 705	317	1 488	0.670	0.105
1902	4 662	3 124	2 780	344	1 538	0.670	0.110
1903	4 838	3 241	2 868	373	1 597	0.670	0.115
1904	5 047	3 381	2 975	406	1 666	0.670	0.120
1905	5 313	3 560	3 115	445	1 753	0.670	0.125
1906	5 612	3 760	3 271	489	1 852	0.670	0.130
1907	5 829	3 905	3 378	527	1 924	0.670	0.135
1908	6 045	4 050	3 483	567	1 995	0.670	0.140
1909	6 410	4 295	3 672	623	2 115	0.670	0.145
1910	6 785	4 546	3 864	682	2 239	0.670	0.150
1911	7 108	4 762	4 024	738	2 346	0.670	0.155
1912	7 451	4 992	4 193	799	2 459	0.670	0.160
1913	8 103	5 429	4 533	896	2 674	0.670	0.165
1914	8 672	5 810	4 822	988	2 862	0.670	0.170
1915	9 075	6 080	5 016	1 064	2 995	0.670	0.175
1916	9 606	6 436	5 278	1 158	3 170	0.670	0.180
1917	10 612	7 110	5 795	1 315	3 502	0.670	0.185
1918	11 058	7 409	6 001	1 408	3 649	0.670	0.190
1919	11 617	7 783	6 265	1 518	3 834	0.670	0.195
1920	13 516	9 042	7 234	1 808	4 474	0.670	0.200
1921	14 744	9 952	7 862	2 090	4 792	0.675	0.210
1922	16 197	11 014	8 591	2 423	5 183	0.680	0.220
1923	18 766	12 836	9 884	2 952	5 930	0.684	0.230
1924	21 335	14 700	11 172	3 528	6 635	0.689	0.240
1925	24 462	16 989	12 742	4 247	7 473	0.694	0.250
1926	27 590	19 795	14 648	5 147	7 795	0.718	0.260
1927	30 829	22 436	16 378	6 058	8 393	0.728	0.270
1928	34 069	25 193	18 139	7 054	8 876	0.740	0.280
1929	35 849	27 570	19 481	8 089	8 279	0.769	0.290

Column 1 – 1890: Estimated on assumption that amount of nonfarm mortgages reported outstanding in the Census of 1890 (cf. *Report on Real Estate Mortgages in the United States*, p. 92) was overstated by 10 percent (cf. Carroll D. Wright's opinion that the result may have been off by 5 to 10 percent, as quoted by Frederiksen, D. M., "Mortgage Banking in America," *Journal of Political Economy*, 1894, p. 203).

1896: Rough estimate derived on assumption of a constant rate of increase between 1890 and 1912.

1897–1911: Interpolated between values for 1896 and 1912 on basis of changes in nonfarm mortgages held by institutions (including insurance companies, banks, and savings and loan associations) as given in or estimated from their balance sheets (cf. Table M-3, col. 3).

1912: Estimated at 46 percent of 1922 value on basis of Horton, D. C., *Long-Term Debts in the United States*, p. 139.

1913–1915: Interpolated between 1912 and 1916 values on basis of annual estimates in Kuvin, L., *Private Long-Term Debt and Interest in the United States*, p. 36.

1916–1928: Estimated at 111.7 percent of series of urban real estate mortgage debt (excluding debt of corporations) of Department of Commerce (*Survey of Current Business*, Sept. 1946, p. 13), the 1929 ratio between total nonfarm mortgage debt as estimated in Table R-35, col. 1, and the Department of Commerce estimate.

1929: From R-35, col. 1.

Column 2 – 1890: From Table R-40, col. 4 reduced for overstatement (see Table R-39, col. 7).

1896–1919: Col. 1 multiplied by col. 6.

1920: Same source as 1890.

1921–1924: Col. 1 multiplied by col. 6.

1925–1928: Col. 3 divided by 1.00 minus col. 7.

1929: From Table R-35, col. 2.

Column 3 – 1890, 1896–1924: Col. 2 minus col. 4.

1925–1929: Estimates of Home Loan Bank Board (*Statistical Summary*, 1949, p. 18).

Column 4 – 1890, 1896–1928: Col. 2 multiplied by col. 7.

1929: From Table R-35, col. 4.

Column 5 – 1890, 1896–1928: Col. 1 minus col. 2.

1929: From Table R-35, col. 5.

Column 6 – 1890: Col. 2 divided by col. 1.

1896–1919: Obtained by linear interpolation between 1890 and 1920 values.

1920: Col. 2 divided by col. 1 rounded to the nearest hundred.

1921–1924: Obtained by linear interpolation between 1920 and 1925 values.

1925–1929: Col. 2 divided by col. 1.

Column 7 – 1890, 1896-1929: Increased gradually to its 1929 value on basis of statistics of construction of one- to four- and multi-family dwellings given in Table R-28.

1929 to 1949

$ mill.

End of year	Total	Residential			Nonres- idential	End of year	Total	Residential			Nonres- idential
		Total	One- to four- family	Multi- family				Total	One- to four- family	Multi- family	
	1	2	3	4	5		1	2	3	4	5
1929	35 849	27 570	19 481	8 089	8 279	1940	30 552	24 864	18 400	6 464	5 688
1930	36 930	28 373	19 615	8 758	8 557	1941	31 712	25 917	19 400	6 517	5 795
1931	36 111	27 582	19 013	8 569	8 529	1942	31 218	25 660	19 219	6 441	5 558
1932	34 270	26 135	17 872	8 263	8 135	1943	30 233	25 002	18 781	6 221	5 231
1933	30 672	24 474	16 743	7 731	6 198	1944	30 042	24 831	18 778	6 053	5 211
1934	30 066	24 139	16 958	7 181	5 927	1945	30 901	25 308	19 208	6 100	5 593
1935	29 230	23 615	16 841	6 774	5 615	1946	37 116	29 969	23 569	6 400	7 147
1936	28 958	23 220	16 690	6 530	5 738	1947	44 297	35 470	28 570	6 900	8 827
1937	28 971	23 233	16 827	6 406	5 738	1948	51 301	41 051	33 451	7 600	10 250
1938	29 160	23 354	17 073	6 281	5 806	1949	57 101	45 651	37 251	8 400	11 450
1939	29 706	24 011	17 608	6 403	5 695						

Column 1 – 1929–1949: Sum of cols. 2 and 5.

Column 2 – 1929–1949: Sum of cols. 3 and 4.

Column 3 – 1929–1949: *Survey of Current Business*, Oct. 1950, p. 15.

Column 4 – 1929–1944: *Survey of Current Business*, Sept. 1946, p. 17.
1945–1949: Rough estimates, based partly on construction expenditures for multi-family dwellings as shown in Table R-28.

Column 5 – 1929–1944: *Survey of Current Business*, Sept. 1946, p. 17.
1945–1947: Figures for multi-family residential and commercial mortgage debt from *Survey of Current Business*, Oct. 1948, minus col. 4.
1948–1949: Rough estimates.

Columns 1 and 2 – 1890–1945: *Historical Statistics*, p. 174; exclude unoccupied units.
    1948: Derived from *Federal Reserve Bulletin*, 1949, p. 1038.

Column 3 – 1890, 1920: *Abstract of XIVth Census*, p. 47; figures refer to mortgaged owner-occupied homes only.
    1930: Wickens, D. L., *Residential Real Estate*, pp. 80, 82.
    1940: *Bureau of Census Release*, Series 1943-H, No. 1.
    1948: *Federal Reserve Bulletin*, Sept. 1949, p. 1045.

Column 4 – 1930: Wickens, *op. cit.*
    1940: Same source as col. 3.

Columns 5 and 6 – 1930: Wickens, *op. cit.*, p. 3.
    1940: *Bureau of Census Release*, Series 1943-H, No. 1. (Value of vacant units divided equally between owner-occupied and rented properties.)
    1948: *Federal Reserve Bulletin*, 1949, p. 1045, for owner-occupied units ($180 billion); rough estimate for rented units (cf. Table R-39, cols. 2 and 3).

Column 7 – 1890–1930: Bureau of the Census, *XVIth Census, Housing*, vol. IV, part I, p. 3.
    1920b, 1930b, 1933: Wickens, *op. cit.*, pp. 203–204; figures refer to fifty or fifty-two cities only, excluding largest ones.
    1940: Bureau of the Census, *XVIth Census, Housing*, vol. IV, p. 7.
    1948: *Federal Reserve Bulletin*, 1949, p. 1038.

Column 8 – 1933: Wickens, *op. cit.*, p. 209; figure refers to forty-four cities, excluding largest ones.
    1948: Derived from *Federal Reserve Bulletin*, Oct. 1949, p. 1195 (table 15).

Column 9 – 1890, 1920a, 1920b, 1930, 1933: *Abstract of XIVth Census*, pp. 45, 51. Wickens, *op. cit.*, pp. 203–204; figures refer to fifty or fifty-two cities only, excluding largest ones.
    1940: *XVIth Census, Housing*, vol. IV, p. 7.
    1948: *Federal Reserve Bulletin*, Sept. 1949, p. 1044; figure is median determined from table 6, average probably slightly higher.

Column 10 – 1930, 1933: Wickens, *op. cit.*, p. 204; figures refer to forty-four cities only, excluding largest ones.

Column 11 – 1890, 1920: Same source as col. 9.
    1933: Wickens, *op. cit.*, p. 205.
    1940: Same source as col. 9.
    1948: *Federal Reserve Bulletin*, Sept. 1949, p. 1045.

Column 12 – 1933: Wickens, *op. cit.*, p. 205.

R-37   TABLE R-37

Column 1 – Bureau of the Census, *XVIth Census, Housing*, vol. IV, p. 12.

Column 2 – Col. 1 stepped up by 7.4 percent, proportion of homes for which distribution of mortgages by type of holder was not reported.

Column 3 – Home Loan Bank Board, *Statistical Summary*, 1948, p. 18.

Column 4 – Col. 3 minus col. 2.

BASIC DATA ON OWNER-OCCUPIED AND RENTED NONFARM RESIDENTIAL REAL ESTATE; SELECTED DATES: 1890 to 1948

End of year	Number of dwelling units		Average value per dwelling unit		Aggregate value of dwelling units		Ratio of mortgaged dwelling units		Debt ratio for mortgaged dwelling units		Aggregate mortgage debt	
	Owner-occupied	Rented	Owner-occupied	Rented	Owner-occupied	Rented	Owner-occupied	Rented	Owner-occupied	Rented	Owner-occupied	Rented
	mill.		$ thous.		$ bill.		Percent				$ bill.	
	1	2	3	4	5	6	7	8	9	10	11	12
1890	2.9	5.0	3.3	.	.	.	27.7	.	37.5	.	1.0	.
1900	3.6	6.2	.	.	.	.	32.0	.	.	.	.	.
1910	5.2	8.4	.	.	.	.	33.3	.	.	.	.	.
1920	7.0	10.2	4.9	.	.	.	a) 39.8	.	a) 34.7	.	6.0	.
							b) 48.9		b) 41.5			
1930	10.5	12.4	5.8	4.3	64.7	57.9	a) 45.3	.	50.8	51.9	.	.
							b) 50.8					
1933	.	.	.	.	.	.	55.3	39.8	55.6	60.0	13.2	12.9
1940	11.4	16.3	3.6	2.4	44.2	43.2	45.3	.	52.3	.	11.0	.
1945	15.9	15.4	.	.	.	.	.	.	.	.	.	.
1948	20.0	13.3	9.1	.	180.0	70.0	45.0	24.0	37.0	.	32.0	.

MORTGAGES ON OWNER-OCCUPIED AND RENTED ONE- TO FOUR-FAMILY NONFARM HOMES

1939 and 1940

$ mill.

Type of mortgagee	Mortgages on owner-occupied homes 4/1/1940		Mortgages on all homes 12/31/1939	Mortgages on rented homes
	Reported	Adjusted		
	1	2	3	4
1. Commercial bank	1 398	1 501	1 754	253
2. Savings bank	1 733	1 861	2 128	267
3. Savings and loan association	1 778	1 910	3 758	1 848
4. Life insurance company	768	825	1 490	665
5. Other insurance company	[1])	[1])	[1])	[1])
6. Home Owners' Loan Corporation	1 463	1 571	2 038	467
7. Mortgage company	609	654		
8. Individual	2 203	2 366	6 440	2 294
9. Other	836	898		
10. Not reporting	212	228		
11. Total	11 000	11 814	17 608	5 794

[1] Not shown separately; probably small.

R-38   TABLE R–38

Columns 1 and 3 – Based on Wickens, D. L., *Residential Real Estate*, p. 234. Largest cities (New York, Chicago, Philadelphia, Los Angeles, Detroit, and Boston) not included. Covers all owner-occupied dwellings.

Columns 2 and 4 – Bureau of the Census, *XVIth Census, Housing*, vol. IV, part 1, p. 73.

R-39   TABLE R–39

Column 1 – From Table R-40, col. 1.

Column 2 – Derived from Table R-36, cols. 1 and 2. Values in this column, as well as in cols. 3–6, represent the magnitude indicated in the heading for rented structures divided by that for owner-occupied structures.

Column 3 – Estimated on basis of data shown in Table R-36, cols. 3 and 4.

Column 4 – Estimated on basis of data shown in Table R-36, cols. 7 and 8.

Column 5 – Estimated on the basis of data shown in Table R-36, cols. 9 and 10. Value for 1890 is particularly uncertain.

Column 6 – Product of cols. 2–5.

Column 7 – Col. 1 multiplied by col. 6.

    This procedure leads to an overstatement of total mortgage debt on nonfarm residential real estate because the mortgage debt on multi-family structures in which the owner occupies one dwelling unit is included both in col. 1 and in col. 7. The extent of this duplication is not exactly known. For 1940, however, it can be estimated, on the basis of Bureau of the Census data in *XVIth Census, Housing*, vol. 1, as leading to an overstatement equal to about 30 percent of col. 7.

DISTRIBUTION OF MORTGAGES
ON OWNER-OCCUPIED NONFARM HOMES: 1933 and 1940

Percent

Holder	Total debt		Debt excluding Home Owners' Loan Corporation holdings	
	12/31/1933 52 cities	4/1/1940 All U.S.	12/31/1933 52 cities	4/1/1940 All U.S.
	1	2	3	4
1. Commercial bank	15.4	13.0	15.9	15.1
2. Savings bank	15.9	16.0	16.4	18.5
3. Savings and loan association	13.1	16.5	13.5	19.1
4. Life insurance company	13.7	7.1	14.1	8.2
5. Home Owners' Loan Corporation	3.0	13.6	–	–
6. Mortgage company	6.9	5.6	7.1	6.5
7. Individual	23.9	20.4	24.6	23.6
8. Other	8.1	7.8	8.3	9.1
a. Title and trust corporation	3.1	.	3.2	.
b. Construction corporation	0.6	.	0.6	.
c. Other	4.4	.	4.5	.
Total	100.0	100.0	100.0	100.0

DERIVATION OF MORTGAGE DEBT
ON RENTED NONFARM RESIDENTIAL REAL ESTATE

Selected Dates: 1890 to 1948

End of year	Mortgage debt on owner-occupied homes	Number of dwelling units	Average value per dwelling unit	Proportion of mortgaged structures	Debt ratio	Aggregate mortgage debt	Estimated mortgage debt on rented structures
	$ mill.	Ratio of rented to owner-occupied nonfarm residential real estate					$ mill.
	1	2	3	4	5	6	7
1890	1 047	1.72	0.90	0.80	1.30	1.61	1 686
1920	6 000	1.46	0.75	0.65	1.05	0.75	4 500
1940	12 600	1.43	0.67	0.65	1.20	0.75	9 450
1948	32 000	0.67	0.65	0.53	1.35	0.31	9 920

Column 1 – 1890, 1920: *Abstract of XIVth Census*, p. 51.
        1933: Wickens, D. L., *Residential Real Estate*, p. 205.
        1940: Bureau of the Census, *XVIth Census, Housing*, vol. IV, p. 7. Figure increased proportionately for nonreporting and for unoccupied units.
        1948: *Federal Reserve Bulletin*, Sept. 1949, p. 1045.

Column 2 – 1890, 1920, 1940, 1948: From Table R-39, col. 7.
        1933: Wickens, D. L., *Residential Real Estate*, p. 205.

Column 3 – 1890-1948: Sum of cols. 1 and 2. There is some doubt whether estimates of col. 2 include all mortgages on basis of which real estate bonds were issued as the sources make no specific mention of this type of indebtedness. The matter is of substantial quantitative importance chiefly for 1933.

Column 4 – 1890–1948: Col. 3 minus estimates for real estate bonds secured by mortgages on apartments and apartment hotels as shown in Table R-43, col. 2.

Column 5 – 1890–1948: From Tables R-34, col. 2 and R-35, col. 2.

Column 6 – 1890–1948: Col. 4 minus col. 5.

Column 1 – 1896–1912: Extrapolated on basis of 1913 value to take account of fact that real estate bonds began to be issued in small quantities in 1893 (cf. Fisher, E., *Urban Real Estate Markets: Characteristics and Financing*, p. 29).
        1913: Clark, Evans (Editor), *The Internal Debts of the United States*, p. 74.
        1914–1917: Interpolated between 1913 and 1918 values.
        1918–1919: From Table R-42, col. 5.
        1920: Persons, C. E., "Credit Expansion, 1920 to 1929 and Its Lessons," *Quarterly Journal of Economics*, Nov. 1930, vol. 45, 1930–1931, p. 100.
        1921–1929, 1931: From Table R-42, col. 5.
        1930, 1933, 1934: Horton, D. C., *Long-Term Debts in the U.S.*, 1937, pp. 133, 136.
        1932: Rough estimate.
        1935–1947: Freehand interpolation between 1934 and 1948 values, based on assumptions that reorganizations of real estate bonds were started in 1933 and were completed by 1941, most of the write-downs (exchange of new bonds of lower par value or of stock for old bonds) occurring from 1933 to 1937.
        1948–1949: Rough estimate based on information obtained from dealers in real estate bonds. There is apparently no statistical information available as to present volume of real estate bonds outstanding.

Column 2 – 1919–1931: From Table R-42, col. 2.
        1932–1949: Assumed negligible.

Column 3 – 1919–1931: From Table R-42, col. 3.
        1932–1949: Rough estimates intended to include both amortization and open market repurchases and based on assumptions that about two-fifths of total reduction between 1931 and 1948 of $5,000 million in face value of amount outstanding was due to write-downs in reorganization (including exchange for securities other than mortgage bonds) involving a total write-down of about $2 billion (cf. estimate of bond houses, cited in *Wall Street Journal*, Oct. 26, 1949, p. 8, that 25 to 30 percent of bondholders' original investment, which should be about equal total amounts issued of between $7 and $8 billion, was wiped out in reorganization); and another two-fifths to repurchases, on the average at 50 percent of face value.

BENCHMARK DATA ON MORTGAGE DEBT
ON NONFARM RESIDENTIAL REAL ESTATE; SELECTED DATES: 1890 to 1948

$ mill.

End of year	On owner-occupied structures	On rented structures	Total debt		Time series (excluding real estate bonds)	Difference
			Benchmark data			
			Including	Excluding		
			Real estate bonds			
	1	2	3	4	5	6
1890	1 047	1 686	2 733	2 733	2 293	440
1920	6 000	4 500	10 500	10 310	9 042	1 268
1933	13 219	12 860	26 079	23 698	24 474	−776
1940	12 600	9 450	22 050	20 930	24 864	−3 934
1948	32 000	9 920	41 920	41 320	41 051	269

REAL ESTATE BONDS

1896 to 1949

$ mill.

Year	Amount outstanding (end of year)	New issues	Cash retirements or repurchases	Year	Amount outstanding (end of year)	New issues	Cash retirements or repurchases
	1	2	3		1	2	3
1896	15	.	.	1923	1 224	497	80
1897	20	.	.	1924	1 738	664	150
1898	25	.	.	1925	2 886	1 448	300
1899	30	.	.	1926	3 883	1 347	350
1900	35	.	.	1927	4 725	1 102	350
1901	40	.	.	1928	5 799	1 424	350
1902	45	.	.	1929	6 219	695	275
1903	50	.	.	1930	6 450	356	125
1904	55	.	.	1931	6 639	239	50
1905	60	.	.	1932	6 300	−	50
1906	65	.	.	1933	5 952	−	50
1907	70	.	.	1934	5 000	−	50
1908	80	.	.	1935	4 200	−	50
1909	90	.	.	1936	3 800	−	50
1910	100	.	.	1937	3 400	−	75
1911	115	.	.	1938	3 200	−	100
1912	130	.	.	1939	3 000	−	100
1913	150	.	.	1940	2 800	−	100
1914	170	.	.	1941	2 600	−	100
1915	191	.	.	1942	2 450	−	150
1916	211	.	.	1943	2 250	−	200
1917	232	.	.	1944	2 050	−	200
1918	252	.	.	1945	1 850	−	200
1919	358	121	15	1946	1 700	−	150
1920	475	142	25	1947	1 600	−	100
1921	534	94	35	1948	1 500	−	100
1922	807	333	60	1949	1 400	−	100

ISSUE AND RETIREMENT OF REAL ESTATE BONDS: 1918 to 1931

$ mill.

Year	New issues		Retirements	Increase in outstanding	Total outstanding (end of year)
	Commercial and Financial Chronicle	Estimated total			
	1	2	3	4	5
1918	.	.	.	.	252
1919	58	121	15	106	358
1920	68	142	25	117	475
1921	45	94	35	59	534
1922	160	333	60	273	807
1923	239	497	80	417	1 224
1924	319	664	150	514	1 738
1925	696	1 448	300	1 148	2 886
1926	647	1 347	350	997	3 883
1927	573	1 192	350	842	4 725
1928	684	1 424	350	1 074	5 799
1929	334	695	275	420	6 219
1930	171	356	125	231	6 450
1931	115	239	50	189	6 639
1919–31	4 109	8 552	2 165	6 387	–

Column 1 – 1919–1931: *Commercial and Financial Chronicle,* various issues.

Column 2 – 1919–1931: Col. 1 multiplied by ratio obtained by assuming that increase in real estate bonds outstanding between end of 1920 and end of 1930 amounted to $6,387 million (cf. Table R-41, col. 1), and that retirements for same period totaled 25.32 percent of new issues (cf. col. 3).

Column 3 – 1919–1931: Estimate of total retirements is based on the fact that for 1,090 issues between 1919 and 1931, aggregating $2,684 million, 13.6 percent were called and an additional 12.5 percent matured within the period (cf. Johnson, E. A. and Laird, J., "Long-Term Real Estate Securities," *Journal of Land and Public Utility Economics,* vol. XII, 1936, p. 46). Distribution of this total among the thirteen years of the period was arbitrary, taking into account amount of real estate bonds outstanding and amount of new issues during the year, and allowing for the fact from 1930 on calls were negligible and an increasing proportion of amortization and maturities were defaulted.

Column 4 – 1919–1931: Col. 2 minus col. 3.

Column 5 – 1918–1929, 1931: Cumulation of col. 4 from 1930 value.
1930: From Table R-41, col. 1.

TABLE R–43

Column 1 – 1910–1949: From Table R-41, col. 1.

Column 2 – 1910–1949: Estimated at 40 percent of col. 1 on basis of distribution of Chicago real estate bonds (Koester, G., *Journal of Land and Public Utility Economics,* 1939, p. 51) and of real estate bonds issued by American Bond and Mortgage Company from Jan. to Nov. 1927 (Gray, J. and Terborgh, G. W., *First Mortgages in Urban Real Estate Finance,* p. 24).

Column 3 – 1910–1949: Estimated at 55 percent of col. 1 on basis of same sources as for col. 2.

Column 4 – 1910–1949: Estimated at 5 percent of col. 1 on basis of same sources as for col. 2.

Column 5 – 1910: Rough estimate.
1911–1931: Change in col. 1.
1932–1949: Assumed equal to Table R-41, col. 3.

Column 6 – 1910–1949: Estimated at 40 percent of col. 5.

Column 7 – 1910–1949: Estimated at 55 percent of col. 5.

Column 8 – 1910–1949: Estimated at 5 percent of col. 5.

ALLOCATION OF REAL ESTATE BONDS OUTSTANDING
BY TYPE OF UNDERLYING STRUCTURE: 1910 to 1949

$ mill.

Year	Outstanding (end of year)				Net change excluding write-downs			
	Total	Apartment houses and apartment hotels	Commercial properties	Non-profit and institutional properties	Total	Apartment houses and apartment hotels	Commercial properties	Non-profit and institutional properties
	1	2	3	4	5	6	7	8
1910	100	40	55	5	10	4	5	1
1911	115	46	63	6	15	6	8	1
1912	130	52	72	6	15	6	8	1
1913	150	60	82	8	20	8	11	1
1914	170	68	94	8	20	8	11	1
1915	191	76	105	10	21	8	12	1
1916	211	84	116	11	20	8	11	1
1917	232	93	127	12	21	8	12	1
1918	252	101	138	13	20	8	11	1
1919	358	143	197	18	106	43	58	5
1920	475	190	261	24	117	47	64	6
1921	534	214	293	27	59	24	32	3
1922	807	323	444	40	273	109	150	14
1923	1 224	490	673	61	417	167	229	21
1924	1 738	695	956	87	514	206	283	25
1925	2 886	1 155	1 587	144	1 148	460	631	57
1926	3 883	1 553	2 136	194	997	399	548	50
1927	4 725	1 890	2 599	236	842	337	463	42
1928	5 799	2 320	3 189	290	1 074	430	591	53
1929	6 219	2 488	3 420	311	420	168	231	21
1930	6 450	2 580	3 548	322	231	92	127	12
1931	6 639	2 656	3 651	332	189	76	103	10
1932	6 300	2 520	3 465	315	−50	−20	−28	−2
1933	5 952	2 381	3 273	298	−50	−20	−28	−2
1934	5 000	2 000	2 750	250	−50	−20	−28	−2
1935	4 200	1 680	2 310	210	−50	−20	−28	−2
1936	3 800	1 520	2 090	190	−50	−20	−28	−2
1937	3 400	1 360	1 870	170	−75	−30	−41	−4
1938	3 200	1 280	1 760	160	−100	−40	−55	−5
1939	3 000	1 200	1 650	150	−100	−40	−55	−5
1940	2 800	1 120	1 540	140	−100	−40	−55	−5
1941	2 600	1 040	1 430	130	−100	−40	−55	−5
1942	2 450	980	1 348	122	−150	−60	−83	−7
1943	2 250	900	1 238	112	−200	−80	−110	−10
1944	2 050	820	1 128	102	−200	−80	−110	−10
1945	1 850	740	1 018	92	−200	−80	−110	−10
1946	1 700	680	935	85	−150	−60	−83	−7
1947	1 600	640	880	80	−100	−40	−55	−5
1948	1 500	600	825	75	−100	−40	−55	−5
1949	1 400	560	770	70	−100	−40	−55	−5

Column 1 – 1900–1946: Sum of cols. 2–4.

Column 2 – 1900–1912: Rough estimates based on 1922 value.

          1922: 1926 value reduced in proportion to value of land and buildings as estimated in Keller, E. A., *A Study of the Physical Assets Sometimes Called Wealth of the United States, 1922–33*, p. 128.

          1926, 1936: Bureau of the Census, *Census of Religious Bodies*, plus an allowance of 10 percent for debt on parsonages.

          1929–1946: Obtained by capitalizing estimated interest payments by religious organizations (cf. *Survey of Current Business, National Income Supplement*, July 1947, table 23, incorporating some additional revisions) at the rate of 6.5 percent in 1929, 5.6 percent in 1939, and 5.0 percent in 1946. (Rate of 5.9 percent for 1936 is obtained by division of estimated interest, $33 million, by Census figure plus 10 percent for debt outstanding. Rates for other years based on 1936 value and movements of urban mortgage interest rates indicated by other sources.)

Column 3 – 1900–1912: Rough estimates based on 1922 value and value of land and buildings of private colleges and universities as reported in Bureau of Education, *Biennial Survey of Education*, various issues.

          1922–1926: Estimate based on 1929 value reduced in proportion to estimated value of land and buildings of private educational institutions (cf. Keller, *op. cit.*, p. 125).

          1929–1946: Obtained by capitalizing estimated interest payments by "Educational Services" (*Survey of Current Business, National Income Supplement*, July 1947, table 23) at the rate of 6.5 percent in 1926 and 1929, 5.9 percent in 1936, 5.6 percent in 1939, and 5.0 percent in 1946.

Column 4 – 1900–1926: Rough estimates based on 1929 value and movement of cols. 2 and 3.

          1929–1946: Obtained by capitalizing interest payments of "Nonprofit organizations not elsewhere classified" (cf. *Survey of Current Business, National Income Supplement*, July 1947, table 23), at same rates as applied in col. 3.

Column 1 – Sum of cols. 2–4.

Column 2 – Assumed equal to 95 percent of change in institutional holdings (Table R-47, col. 1) corresponding to assumed share of individuals in one- to four-family dwellings.

Column 3 – Estimated at 50 percent of change in institutional holdings (Table R-48, col. 1).

Column 4 – Estimated at between 60 and 50 percent of change in institutional holdings (Table R-49, col. 1).

Column 5 – Sum of cols. 6-8.

Column 6 – Assumed equal to 95 percent of change in institutional holdings (Table R-51, col. 1).

Column 7 – Estimated at 50 percent of change in institutional holdings (Table R-52, col. 1).

Column 8 – Estimated at between 60 and 50 percent of change in institutional holdings (Table R-53, col. 1).

MORTGAGE DEBT OF NONPROFIT INSTITUTIONS
Selected Years: 1900 to 1946

$ bill.

End of year	Total	Churches	Educational institutions	Other	End of year	Total	Churches	Educational institutions	Other
	1	2	3	4		1	2	3	4
1900	0.27	0.15	0.10	0.02	1929	1.36	0.50	0.75	0.11
1912	0.51	0.25	0.22	0.04	1936	1.51	0.56	0.83	0.12
1922	0.83	0.38	0.38	0.07	1939	1.43	0.52	0.80	0.11
1926	1.23	0.48	0.65	0.10	1946	1.26	0.58	0.58	0.10

INDIVIDUALS' SAVING IN CONNECTION WITH CHANGE OF OWNERSHIP THROUGH FORECLOSURE OF NONFARM REAL ESTATE: 1926 to 1949

$ mill.

Year	Book value basis				Cash basis			
	Total	1- to 4-family dwellings	Multi-family dwellings	Non-residential properties	Total	1- to 4-family dwellings	Multi-family dwellings	Non-residential properties
	1	2	3	4	5	6	7	8
1926	28	22	2	4	29	23	2	4
1927	39	32	3	4	42	33	4	5
1928	78	68	3	7	85	71	4	10
1929	137	121	5	11	139	116	7	16
1930	149	118	12	19	198	149	17	32
1931	251	207	16	28	370	289	28	53
1932	557	443	34	80	750	573	54	123
1933	530	412	40	78	749	563	61	125
1934	527	377	56	94	688	475	76	137
1935	490	287	68	135	655	412	80	163
1936	258	183	29	46	368	254	41	73
1937	117	104	−1	14	208	164	10	34
1938	−107	−121	10	4	36	−32	28	40
1939	−400	−351	−7	−42	−173	−182	13	−4
1940	−489	−433	−22	−34	−240	−242	−2	4
1941	−542	−433	−44	−65	−346	−318	−16	−12
1942	−413	−335	−22	−56	−257	−251	4	−10
1943	−491	−368	−42	−81	−344	−276	−21	−47
1944	−393	−263	−50	−80	−291	−195	−37	−59
1945	−209	−93	−30	−86	−183	−85	−23	−75
1946	−99	−34	−19	−46	−97	−33	−18	−46
1947	−52	−27	−10	−15	−38	−23	−6	−9
1948	−17	−8	−1	−8	1	−3	4	0
1949	−5	−1	−1	−3	30	10	7	13

HOLDINGS OF NONFARM REAL ESTATE BY INSTITUTIONS
(Excluding Own Premises): 1925 to 1949

$ mill.

End of year	Total institutional holdings	Commercial banks		Mutual savings banks	Insurance companies			Mortgage companies	Savings and loan associations		Home Owners' Loan Corporation
		Operating	Closed		Life	Fraternal	Fire, marine and other		Operating	Closed	
	1	2	3	4	5	6	7	8	9	10	11
1925	406	284	4	8	67	6	26	–	11	–	–
1926	438	289	3	12	79	8	28	–	19	–	–
1927	484	290	6	14	97	9	32	–	36	–	–
1928	573	296	3	19	119	9	39	–	88	–	–
1929	728	306	3	34	145	9	45	12	174	–	–
1930	910	317	10	54	203	11	57	17	238	3	–
1931	1 211	345	38	96	252	15	63	25	370	7	–
1932	1 894	450	71	191	386	20	85	33	642	16	–
1933A	2 556	469	158	316	562	32	101	42	828	48	–
1933B	2 448	469	158	316	454	32	101	42	828	48	–
1934	3 134	531	137	458	729	43	113	50	1 012	61	–
1935	3 826	630	103	602	1 015	63	124	59	1 163	61	6
1936	4 163	640	67	699	1 128	72	124	68	1 150	48	167
1937	4 298	600	44	691	1 207	75	125	69	1 014	36	437
1938	4 201	572	27	656	1 216	76	131	68	890	23	542
1939	3 734	491	16	602	1 141	76	125	68	681	24	510
1940	3 164	404	6	554	1 075	70	120	67	492	19	357
1941	2 489	309	–	424	902	60	114	54	328	10	288
1942	1 979	207	–	317	817	52	105	46	203	5	227
1943	1 345	119	–	197	643	41	95	34	117	2	97
1944	808	58	–	96	446	28	78	30	60	–	12
1945	479	34	–	35	270	19	61	25	33	–	2
1946	313	27	–	18	160	13	47	22	26	–	–
1947	235	24	–	11	116	10	38	23	13	–	–
1948	210	22	–	8	100	9	35	24	12	–	–
1949	200	22	–	7	89	7	36	24	15	–	–

Column 1 – Sum of cols. 2–11.

Column 2 – From Table R-54, col. 2.

Column 3 – From Table R-58, col. 3.

Column 4 – From Table R-61, sum of cols. 2 and 7.

Column 5 – From Table R-63, sum of cols. 4, 6, and 10.

Column 6 – From Table R-65, sum of cols. 3 and 8.

Column 7 – From Table R-66, sum of cols. 3 and 8.

Column 8 – From Table R-69, col. 2.

Column 9 – From Table J-2, col. 4.

Column 10 – From Table J-6, col. 6 minus Table M-9, col. 12.

Column 11 – From Table R-68, col. 1.

HOLDINGS OF ONE- TO FOUR-FAMILY NONFARM DWELLINGS BY INSTITUTIONS: 1925 to 1949

$ mill.

End of year	Total institutional holdings	Commercial banks		Mutual savings banks	Insurance companies			Mortgage companies	Savings and loan associations		Home Owners' Loan Corporation
		Operating	Closed		Life	Fraternal	Fire, marine and other		Operating	Closed	
	1	2	3	4	5	6	7	8	9	10	11
1925	189	125	2	5	31	3	12	–	11	–	–
1926	212	130	2	7	37	4	13	–	19	–	–
1927	246	135	3	8	45	4	15	–	36	–	–
1928	318	140	2	11	55	4	18	–	88	–	–
1929	445	150	2	20	67	4	21	7	174	–	–
1930	569	155	5	32	94	5	27	10	238	3	–
1931	787	165	17	58	117	7	29	17	370	7	–
1932	1 253	200	32	115	178	9	39	22	642	16	–
1933A	1 687	200	71	190	260	15	47	28	828	48	–
1933B	1 637	200	71	190	210	15	47	28	828	48	–
1934	2 034	225	62	275	302	18	47	32	1 012	61	–
1935	2 336	263	47	361	337	21	41	36	1 163	61	6
1936	2 529	263	30	419	350	22	39	41	1 150	48	167
1937	2 638	225	20	415	385	24	40	42	1 014	36	437
1938	2 511	218	12	392	336	21	36	41	890	23	542
1939	2 142	176	7	342	308	21	34	39	681	24	510
1940	1 686	140	3	298	290	19	32	36	492	19	357
1941	1 230	95	–	212	226	15	29	27	328	10	288
1942	877	64	–	142	181	12	23	20	203	5	227
1943	490	37	–	81	119	8	17	12	117	2	97
1944	213	18	–	36	64	4	11	8	60	–	12
1945	115	11	–	12	39	3	9	6	33	–	2
1946	79	8	–	6	24	2	7	6	26	–	–
1947	51	8	–	5	14	1	5	5	13	–	–
1948	43	7	–	4	10	1	4	5	12	–	–
1949	42	7	–	4	7	1	3	5	15	–	–

Column 1 – Sum of cols. 2–11.

Column 2 – From Table R-54, col. 4.

Column 3 – From Table R-58, col. 5.

Column 4 – From Table R-61, col. 3.

Column 5 – From Table R-63, col. 4.

Column 6 – From Table R-65, col. 4.

Column 7 – From Table R-66, col. 4.

Column 8 – From Table R-69, col. 4.

Columns 9 to 11 – Same as Table R-46, cols. 9, 10, and 11 respectively.

HOLDINGS OF MULTI-FAMILY DWELLINGS BY INSTITUTIONS
1925 to 1949

$ mill.

End of year	Total institutional holdings	Commercial banks		Mutual savings banks	Insurance companies			Mortgage companies
		Operating	Closed		Life	Fraternal	Fire, marine, and other	
	1	2	3	4	5	6	7	8
1925	40	20	—	2	12	1	5	—
1926	43	20	—	3	14	1	5	—
1927	49	20	—	3	18	2	6	—
1928	55	20	—	4	22	2	7	—
1929	65	20	—	7	27	2	8	1
1930	88	25	1	11	37	2	10	2
1931	121	35	4	19	46	3	12	2
1932	189	50	7	38	71	4	16	3
1933A	270	60	16	63	103	6	18	4
1933B	250	60	16	63	83	6	18	4
1934	362	75	14	92	145	8	22	6
1935	497	87	10	120	230	14	28	8
1936	555	87	7	140	266	17	29	9
1937	553	75	4	138	281	17	29	9
1938	574	72	3	132	306	19	33	9
1939	560	59	2	130	306	20	33	10
1940	515	47	1	128	279	18	31	11
1941	426	32	—	106	234	16	29	9
1942	382	21	—	87	222	14	29	9
1943	297	12	—	58	181	11	27	8
1944	198	6	—	30	125	8	22	7
1945	139	3	—	11	91	6	21	7
1946	101	3	—	6	62	5	18	7
1947	81	2	—	3	48	4	16	8
1948	79	2	—	2	46	4	16	9
1949	75	2	—	2	42	3	17	9

Column 1 – Sum of cols. 2–8.

Column 2 – From Table R-54, col. 5.

Column 3 – From Table R-58, col. 6.

Column 4 – From Table R-61, col. 4.

Column 5 – From Table R-63, col. 6.

Column 6 – From Table R-65, col. 5.

Column 7 – From Table R-66, col. 5.

Column 8 – From Table R-69, col. 5.

HOLDINGS OF NONRESIDENTIAL PROPERTIES BY INSTITUTIONS (EXCLUDING OWN PREMISES): 1925 to 1949

R-49

$ mill.

End of year	Total institutional holdings	Commercial banks		Mutual savings banks	Insurance companies			Mortgage companies
		Operating	Closed		Life	Fraternal	Fire, marine, and other	
	1	2	3	4	5	6	7	8
1925	177	139	2	1	24	2	9	–
1926	183	139	1	2	28	3	10	–
1927	189	135	3	3	34	3	11	–
1928	200	136	1	4	42	3	14	–
1929	218	136	1	7	51	3	16	4
1930	253	137	4	11	72	4	20	5
1931	303	145	17	19	89	5	22	6
1932	452	200	32	38	137	7	30	8
1933A	599	209	71	63	199	11	36	10
1933B	561	209	71	63	161	11	36	10
1934	738	231	61	91	282	17	44	12
1935	993	280	46	121	448	28	55	15
1936	1 079	290	30	140	512	33	56	18
1937	1 107	300	20	138	541	34	56	18
1938	1 116	282	12	132	574	36	62	18
1939	1 032	256	7	130	527	35	58	19
1940	963	217	2	128	506	33	57	20
1941	833	182	–	106	442	29	56	18
1942	720	122	–	88	414	26	53	17
1943	558	70	–	58	343	22	51	14
1944	397	34	–	30	257	16	45	15
1945	225	20	–	12	140	10	31	12
1946	133	16	–	6	74	6	22	9
1947	103	14	–	3	54	5	17	10
1948	88	13	–	2	44	4	15	10
1949	83	13	–	1	40	3	16	10

Column 1 – Sum of cols. 2–8.

Column 2 – From Table R-54, col. 6.

Column 3 – From Table R-58, col. 7.

Column 4 – From Table R-61, col. 7.

Column 5 – From Table R-63, col. 10.

Column 6 – From Table R-65, col. 8.

Column 7 – From Table R-66, col. 8.

Column 8 – From Table R-69, col. 6.

643

NET CHANGE (CASH BASIS) IN INSTITUTIONAL HOLDINGS
OF NONFARM REAL ESTATE (EXCLUDING OWN PREMISES): 1926 to 1949

$ mill.

Year	Total institutional holdings	Commercial banks		Mutual savings banks	Insurance companies			Mortgage companies	Savings and loan associations		Home Owners' Loan Corporation
		Operating	Closed		Life	Fraternal	Fire, marine, and other		Operating	Closed	
	1	2	3	4	5	6	7	8	9	10	11
1926	35	5	−1	7	12	2	2	−	8	−	−
1927	51	1	3	7	18	1	4	−	17	−	−
1928	101	6	−1	15	22	0	7	−	52	−	−
1929	162	10	2	25	30	0	6	12	67	10	−
1930	250	36	8	30	66	2	12	5	66	25	−
1931	458	88	30	62	60	4	6	8	175	25	−
1932	939	205	40	125	153	5	22	8	356	25	−
1933	950	125	105	155	194	12	16	9	274	60	−
1934	912	169	−13	172	291	11	12	8	232	30	−
1935	901	126	−16	184	304	20	11	9	227	30	6
1936	487	10	−24	137	156	9	0	9	39	−10	161
1937	260	−40	−9	52	85	3	1	1	−104	0	271
1938	103	−28	−5	55	42	1	6	−1	−100	0	133
1939	−174	−81	−6	36	−27	0	−6	0	−156	30	36
1940	−252	−87	−5	42	−16	−6	−5	−1	−130	30	−74
1941	−392	−95	2	20	−129	−10	−6	−13	−121	−10	−30
1942	−276	−102	−	43	−56	−8	−9	−8	−90	−10	−36
1943	−419	−88	−	3	−150	−11	−10	−12	−63	−10	−78
1944	−394	−61	−	−17	−192	−13	−17	−4	−34	−10	−46
1945	−285	−24	−	−11	−182	−9	−17	−5	−27	−5	−5
1946	−163	−7	−	−5	−119	−6	−14	−3	−7	−	−2
1947	−55	−3	−	13	−41	−3	−9	1	−13	−	−
1948	3	−2	−	19	−10	−1	−3	1	−1	−	−
1949	51	0	−	48	1	−2	1	0	3	−	−

Column 1 – Sum of cols. 2–11.

Column 2 - From Table R-56, col. 3.

Column 3 – From Table R-60, col. 3.

Column 4 – From Table R-62, col. 3.

Column 5 – From Table R-64, col. 3.

Column 6 – First differences of Table R-65, col. 3 plus col. 8.

Column 7 – First differences of Table R-66, col. 3 plus col. 8.

Column 8 – First differences of Table R-46, col. 8.

Column 9 – From Table R-67, col. 3.

Column 10 – From Table R-67, col. 6.

Column 11 – From Table R-68, col. 4.

NET CHANGE (CASH BASIS) IN INSTITUTIONAL HOLDINGS
OF ONE- TO FOUR-FAMILY NONFARM DWELLINGS: 1926 to 1949

$ mill.

| Year | Total insti-tutional holdings | Commercial banks | | Mutual savings banks | Insurance companies | | | Mortgage com-panies | Savings and loan associations | | Home Owners' Loan Corpo-ration |
| | | Oper-ating | Closed | | Life | Fraternal | Fire, marine, and other | | Oper-ating | Closed | |
	1	2	3	4	5	6	7	8	9	10	11
1926	24	5	0	3	6	1	1	0	8	–	–
1927	35	5	1	2	8	0	2	0	17	–	–
1928	75	5	0	5	10	0	3	0	52	–	–
1929	122	10	1	11	13	0	3	7	67	10	–
1930	157	11	3	14	28	1	6	3	66	25	–
1931	304	25	13	30	25	2	2	7	175	25	–
1932	603	60	18	63	64	2	10	5	356	25	–
1933	593	26	47	81	85	6	8	6	274	60	–
1934	500	52	–6	91	94	3	0	4	232	30	–
1935	434	45	–7	94	38	3	–6	4	227	30	6
1936	267	0	–12	66	19	1	–2	5	39	–10	161
1937	173	–38	–4	8	36	2	1	1	–104	0	271
1938	–34	–7	–3	–5	–44	–3	–4	–1	–100	0	133
1939	–192	–42	–3	–32	–21	0	–2	–2	–156	30	36
1940	–255	–36	–2	–26	–10	–2	–2	–3	–130	30	–74
1941	–335	–45	0	–56	–57	–4	–3	–9	–121	–10	–30
1942	–264	–31	–	–40	–41	–3	–6	–7	–90	–10	–36
1943	–290	–27	–	–36	–58	–4	–6	–8	–63	–10	–78
1944	–205	–19	–	–28	–54	–4	–6	–4	–34	–10	–46
1945	–89	–7	–	–14	–26	–1	–2	–2	–27	–5	–5
1946	–35	–3	–	–4	–16	–1	–2	0	–7	–	–2
1947	–24	0	–	3	–10	–1	–2	–1	–13	–	–
1948	–3	–1	–	3	–3	0	–1	0	–1	–	–
1949	11	0	–	10	–1	0	–1	0	3	–	–

Column 1 – Sum of cols. 2–11.

Column 2 – From Table R-56, col. 6.

Column 3 – From Table R-60, col. 6.

Column 4 – From Table R-62, col. 6.

Column 5 – From Table R-64, col. 6.

Column 6 – First differences of Table R-65, col. 4.

Column 7 – First differences of Table R-66, col. 4.

Column 8 – First differences of Table R-47, col. 8.

Column 9 – From Table R-67, col. 3.

Column 10 – From Table R-67, col. 6.

Column 11 – From Table R-68, col. 5.

NET CHANGE (CASH BASIS) IN INSTITUTIONAL HOLDINGS OF MULTI-FAMILY DWELLINGS: 1926 to 1949

$ mill.

Year	Total institutional holdings	Commercial banks		Mutual savings banks	Insurance companies			Mortgage companies
		Operating	Closed		Life	Fraternal	Fire, marine and other	
	1	2	3	4	5	6	7	8
1926	4	0	–	2	2	0	0	–
1927	7	0	–	1	4	1	1	–
1928	9	0	–	4	4	0	1	–
1929	14	0	–	6	6	0	1	1
1930	34	11	1	7	12	0	2	1
1931	57	25	3	14	12	1	2	0
1932	108	40	4	28	30	1	4	1
1933	122	36	11	34	36	2	2	1
1934	153	42	–1	38	66	2	4	2
1935	160	19	–2	40	89	6	6	2
1936	82	0	–2	32	47	3	1	1
1937	19	–12	–2	16	17	0	0	0
1938	57	–3	0	21	33	2	4	0
1939	26	–13	0	25	12	1	0	1
1940	–5	–12	0	25	–15	–2	–2	1
1941	–32	–15	0	23	–34	–2	–2	–2
1942	8	–11	–	26	–5	–2	0	0
1943	–42	–9	–	8	–35	–3	–2	–1
1944	–73	–6	–	–3	–55	–3	–5	–1
1945	–46	–3	–	–4	–36	–2	–1	0
1946	–36	0	–	–1	–31	–1	–3	0
1947	–13	–1	–	3	–13	–1	–2	1
1948	7	0	–	6	0	0	0	1
1949	14	0	–	15	–1	–1	1	0

Column 1 – Sum of cols. 2–8.

Column 2 – From Table R-56, col. 9.

Column 3 – From Table R-60, col. 9.

Column 4 – From Table R-62, col. 9.

Column 5 – From Table R-64, col. 9.

Column 6 – First differences of Table R-65, col. 5.

Column 7 – First differences of Table R-66, col. 5.

Column 8 – First differences of Table R-48, col. 8.

NET CHANGE (CASH BASIS) IN INSTITUTIONAL HOLDINGS
OF NONFARM NONRESIDENTIAL REAL ESTATE
(EXCLUDING OWN PREMISES): 1926 to 1949

$ mill.

Year	Total institutional holdings	Commercial banks		Mutual savings banks	Insurance companies			Mortgage companies
		Operating	Closed		Life	Fraternal	Fire, marine and other	
	1	2	3	4	5	6	7	8
1926	7	0	−1	2	4	1	1	−
1927	9	−4	2	4	6	0	1	−
1928	17	1	−1	6	8	0	3	−
1929	26	0	1	8	11	0	2	4
1930	59	14	4	9	26	1	4	1
1931	97	38	14	18	23	1	2	1
1932	228	105	18	34	59	2	8	2
1933	235	63	47	40	73	4	6	2
1934	259	75	−6	43	131	6	8	2
1935	307	62	−7	50	177	11	11	3
1936	138	10	−10	39	90	5	1	3
1937	68	10	−3	28	32	1	0	0
1938	80	−18	−2	39	53	2	6	0
1939	−8	−26	−3	43	−18	−1	−4	1
1940	8	−39	−3	43	9	−2	−1	1
1941	−25	−35	2	53	−38	−4	−1	−2
1942	−20	−60	−	57	−10	−3	−3	−1
1943	−86	−52	−	32	−57	−4	−2	−3
1944	−116	−36	−	14	−83	−6	−6	1
1945	−150	−14	−	7	−120	−6	−14	−3
1946	−92	−4	−	0	−72	−4	−9	−3
1947	−18	−2	−	7	−18	−1	−5	1
1948	−1	−1	−	10	−7	−1	−2	0
1949	26	0	−	23	3	−1	1	0

Column 1 – Sum of cols. 2–8.

Column 2 – From Table R-56, col. 12.

Column 3 – From Table R-60, col. 12.

Column 4 – From Table R-62, col. 12.

Column 5 – From Table R-64, col. 12.

Column 6 – First differences of Table R-65, col. 8.

Column 7 – First differences of Table R-66, col. 8.

Column 8 – First differences of Table R-69, col. 6.

Column 1 – 1925–1937: Extrapolated on basis of holdings of real estate other than bank premises by member banks (*Banking and Monetary Statistics*, pp. 72, 74).
1938–1949: Sum of cols. 2 and 7.

Column 2 – 1925–1937: Col. 1 minus col. 7.
1938–1949: Sum of cols. 3 and 6.

Column 3 – 1925–1933: Sum of cols. 4 and 5.
1934–1937: Estimated at 1.30 times holdings of residential real estate by insured banks (cf. Federal Deposit Insurance Corporation, *Assets and Liabilities of Operating Insured Banks*), the 1938–1941 ratio between similarly reported figure for holdings of residential real estate and estimate of the Home Loan Bank Board used in col. 3. Step-up is intended to take account of indirect holdings of real estate which were reported only in one aggregate figure for both bank premises and all other types of real estate.
1938–1948: Home Loan Bank Board, *Statistical Summary*, 1949, p. 18.
1949: Estimated unchanged from 1948.

Column 4 – 1925–1928: Assumed slightly below 1929.
1929: Home Loan Bank Board, *Sixth Annual Report*, p. 100.
1930–1933: Roughly interpolated between 1929 and 1934 values.
1934–1936: Estimated at 75 percent of col. 3, the 1937 ratio.
1937: Home Loan Bank Board, *Sixth Annual Report*, p. 100.
1938–1949: Estimated at three-fourths of col. 3, the 1937 ratio.

Column 5 – 1925–1933: Rough estimates.
1934–1949: Col. 3 minus col. 4.

Column 6 – 1925–1937: Col. 2 minus col. 3.
1938–1941: Same method as col. 3, 1934–1937.
1942–1949: Estimated at 1.43 times holdings of residential real estate, the 1941 ratio.

Column 7 – 1925–1949: From Table A-10, col. 8.

DISTRIBUTION OF HOLDINGS OF REAL ESTATE
BY OPERATING COMMERCIAL BANKS: 1925 to 1949
(Excluding Bank Premises)

$ mill.

End of year	Total	Nonfarm					Farm
		Total	Residential			Non-residential	
			Total	1- to 4-family	Multi-family		
	1	2	3	4	5	6	7
1925	330	284	145	125	20	139	46
1926	335	289	150	130	20	139	46
1927	335	290	155	135	20	135	45
1928	340	296	160	140	20	136	44
1929	350	306	170	150	20	136	44
1930	360	317	180	155	25	137	43
1931	390	345	200	165	35	145	45
1932	505	450	250	200	50	200	55
1933	520	469	260	200	60	209	51
1934	590	531	300	225	75	231	59
1935	700	630	350	263	87	280	70
1936	710	640	350	263	87	290	70
1937	656	600	300	225	75	300	56
1938	621	572	290	218	72	282	49
1939	533	491	235	176	59	256	42
1940	437	404	187	140	47	217	33
1941	332	309	127	95	32	182	23
1942	227	207	85	64	21	122	20
1943	136	119	49	37	12	70	17
1944	72	58	24	18	6	34	14
1945	45	34	14	11	3	20	11
1946	35	27	11	8	3	16	8
1947	29	24	10	8	2	14	5
1948	24	22	9	7	2	13	2
1949	22	22	9	7	2	13	0

Column 1 – 1921–1949: Sum of cols. 2, 6, and 9.

Column 2 – 1921–1949: Sum of cols. 3 and 4 minus col. 5.

Column 3 – 1921–1926: Included in "Other current earnings" of member banks (*Banking and Monetary Statistics* p. 262). Estimated by deducting other items combined in this figure by extrapolating backwards from later years when these items were shown separately. Residual thus obtained was compared for plausibility with movement of bond prices during same period. To obtain estimates for all banks estimates for member banks were multiplied by ratio of security assets of all banks to those of member banks on June 30 of same year (*Banking and Monetary Statistics*, pp. 19, 72).

    1927–1931: Data for member banks (*Banking and Monetary Statistics*, pp. 262–263) raised by ratio of security assets of all banks to those of member banks on June 30 of same year.

    1932–1935: Combined with profits from revaluation of securities. For 1932–1933 data available for member banks (*Banking and Monetary Statistics* p. 263) and for 1934–1935 for all insured banks (*ibid.*, p. 277) raised by ratio of security assets of all banks to securities held by member banks on June 30, 1932 and 1933 and to securities held by all insured banks on June 30, 1934 and 1935 (*Banking and Monetary Statistics*, pp. 19, 72, 108). Separation of total into estimates for profits from sale and profits from revaluation of securities represents interpolation between data for years 1927–1931 and 1936 and following years.

    1936–1941: Data for all insured banks (*Banking and Monetary Statistics*, p. 277) raised by ratio of securities held by all banks to securities held by insured banks on June 30 of same year (*Banking and Monetary Statistics*, pp. 19, 108).

    1942–1949: Data for insured banks (*Annual Reports of the Federal Deposit Insurance Corporation*, various issues) increased to take account of noninsured banks by ratio indicated in Table L-26, col. 6.

Column 4 – 1921–1926: For member banks combined with profits from revaluation of other assets (*Banking and Monetary Statistics*, p. 262); because of greater stability of profits from revaluation of loans and "Other assets," the latter two items (cols. 5 and 6) were estimated independently. Estimates of profits from revaluation of securities represent residuals. Estimates raised to include all banks by ratio used in col. 3.

    1927–1949: Same method and sources as in col. 3.

Column 5 – 1921–1933: Data for member banks raised to cover all commercial banks by ratio of securities held by all commercial banks to securities held by member banks on June 30 of the same year (*Banking and Monetary Statistics*, p. 262 for losses on securities by member banks, p. 19 for securities held by all banks, and p. 72 for securities held by member banks).

    1934–1941: Data for insured commercial banks raised to cover all commercial banks by ratio of securities held by all commercial banks to insured commercial banks on June 30 of same year (*Banking and Monetary Statistics*, p. 277 for losses of insured banks, p. 19 for securities held by all banks, and p. 108 for securities held by insured banks).

    1942–1949: Data for insured banks (*Annual Report of the Federal Deposit Insurance Corporation*, various issues) increased slightly to take account of noninsured banks.

Column 6 – 1921–1949: Col. 7 minus col. 8.

Column 7 – 1921–1926: Based upon relationship between profits from revaluation of loans to losses from revaluation of loans during a three-year period two to five years earlier as it appeared that this relationship was relatively stable during the years 1927 to 1940 (e.g., the profits from revaluation of loans for 1930 were compared to the losses during the years 1926 to 1928).

    Estimates for all banks obtained by raising estimates for member banks by ratio of loan assets of all banks to loan assets of member banks on June 30 of same year (*Banking and Monetary Statistics*, p. 262 for profits and losses on loans, p. 19 for loan assets of all commercial banks, and p. 72 for loans of all member banks).

    1927–1933: Data for member banks raised to cover all banks by ratio of loans of all commercial banks to loans of member banks on June 30 of same year.

    1934–1941: Data for insured banks raised to cover all banks by ratio of loans of all insured commercial banks to loans of all commercial banks on June 30 of same year (*Banking and Monetary Statistics*, p. 277 for earnings of insured banks, p. 19 for loans of all commercial banks, and p. 109 for loans of all insured commercial banks).

    1942–1949: Same method and sources as described in col. 3.

Column 8 – 1921–1949: Same method and sources as for col. 5. Figures for 1947 and particularly for 1948 and 1949 reflect introduction of regular reserves for losses on bad debts irrespective of the year's actual experience, resulting from a change in Treasury regulation (*Daily Treasury Statement*, Dec. 8, 1947).

CAPITAL GAINS AND LOSSES OF OPERATING COMMERCIAL BANKS
1921 to 1949

$ mill.

Year	Net total	On securities				On loans			Other		
		Net	Gains		Losses	Net	Increase in valuation	Losses	Net	Gains	Losses
			From sale	Increase in valuation							
	1	2	3	4	5	6	7	8	9	10	11
1921	−316	−81	20	23	124	−218	22	240	−17	17	34
1922	−132	94	84	47	37	−215	29	244	−11	21	32
1923	−175	4	26	30	52	−176	29	205	−3	23	26
1924	−128	36	66	18	48	−155	37	192	−9	21	30
1925	−104	41	66	25	50	−144	40	184	−1	25	26
1926	−126	45	80	17	52	−140	38	178	−31	21	52
1927	−63	103	142	14	53	−138	36	174	−28	23	51
1928	−92	74	124	16	66	−130	37	167	−36	21	57
1929	−212	−12	102	27	141	−159	35	194	−41	27	68
1930	−332	−48	98	17	163	−235	32	267	−49	19	68
1931	−658	−260	94	18	372	−357	38	395	−41	23	64
1932	−867	−342	53	20	415	−498	32	530	−27	43	70
1933	−925	−346	63	30	439	−515	26	541	−64	23	87
1934	−768	−191	128	85	404	−516	55	571	−61	34	95
1935	−201	80	197	130	247	−243	84	327	−38	36	74
1936	85	298	277	181	160	−143	114	257	−70	32	102
1937	−91	0	122	60	182	−53	92	145	−38	45	83
1938	−126	17	180	64	227	−95	58	153	−48	40	88
1939	−57	72	224	69	221	−72	67	139	−57	35	92
1940	−39	61	184	76	199	−49	67	116	−51	33	84
1941	−10	59	150	76	167	−34	72	106	−35	36	71
1942	−50	1	68	57	124	−12	70	82	−39	33	72
1943	64	81	106	94	119	11	87	76	−28	74	102
1944	96	114	133	95	114	14	85	71	−32	56	88
1945	251	263	274	126	137	11	68	57	−23	55	78
1946	128	139	214	61	136	3	75	72	−14	68	82
1947	−32	28	103	47	122	−53	69	122	−7	50	57
1948	−222	−6	62	55	123	−225	90	315	9	66	57
1949	−168	45	75	44	74	−201	52	253	−12	47	59

Column 9 – 1921–1949: Col. 10 minus col. 11. Cols. 9–11 do not include depreciation on bank premises and fixtures.

Column 10 – 1921–1941: Estimates for member banks based upon ratio to bank premises and other real estate assets during the years 1927 to 1930, raised to cover all banks by ratio of total loans and securities held by all commercial banks to total loans and securities held by member banks (sources as for col. 7).
1942–1949: Same method and sources as in col. 3.

Column 11 – 1921–1949: Same method and sources as in col. 5.

Column 1 – First differences of Table R-54, col. 2.

Column 2 – Sum of cols. 5, 8, and 11.

Column 3 – Sum of cols. 1 and 2.

Column 4 – First differences of Table R-54, col. 4.

Column 5 – From Table R-57, col. 4.

Column 6 – Sum of cols. 4 and 5.

Column 7 – First differences of Table R-54, col. 5.

Column 8 – From Table R-57, col. 5.

Column 9 – Sum of cols. 7 and 8.

Column 10 – First differences of Table R-54, col. 6.

Column 11 – From Table R-57, col. 6.

Column 12 – Sum of cols. 10 and 11.

Column 1 – Difference between total net losses on loans, for given year, as shown in Table R-55, col. 6, and 1923–1929 average of about $150 million. This procedure assumes that during base period net losses on real estate loans were negligible. If, on the other hand, it is assumed that share of real estate loans in total net losses on loans in base period was equal to their proportion in total loans outstanding, approximately one-quarter of total net losses on loans, i.e. somewhat less than $40 million a year, would have to be added to estimates of col. 1. A similar allowance would then have to be made for the years before 1930 and after 1935. From 1936 on net losses on loans were below base period level, hence no allowance was necessary for excess losses.

Column 2 – Total of $500 million for period 1930–1935 was estimated on assumption of an average loss on real estate loans outstanding at end of 1929 of about 10 percent. This ratio was derived from rates of loss suffered by mutual savings banks, savings and loan associations, and life insurance companies on different types of real estate loans. Figure implies that 34 percent of excess of total net losses on loans above those of base period 1923–1929 are attributable to real estate loans, which appears to be a reasonable relationship somewhat, but not very much, exceeding proportion of real estate loans in total loans. Estimates for individual years were obtained by taking 34 percent of the respective values in col. 1.

Column 3 – Estimated at 15 percent of col. 2 on assumption that rate of losses for farm mortgages was same as that for all mortgage loans.

Columns 4 to 6 – Estimated at 25 percent, 25 percent, and 50 percent, respectively, of losses of nonfarm mortgage loans (col. 2 minus col. 3). These ratios were derived from estimates of distribution of nonfarm mortgage loans by operating commercial banks, as shown in Table M-13 and differential rates of loss for the three types of loans for mutual savings banks, savings and loan associations, and life insurance associations.

CHANGES IN NONFARM REAL ESTATE HOLDINGS
OF OPERATING COMMERCIAL BANKS: 1926 to 1949

$ mill.

Year	All foreclosed real estate			1- to 4- family dwellings			Multi-family dwellings			Nonresidential properties		
	Change in holdings	Capital loss	Net	Change in holdings	Capital loss	Net	Change in holdings	Capital loss	Net	Change in holdings	Capital loss	Net
	1	2	3	4	5	6	7	8	9	10	11	12
1926	5	–	5	5	–	5	0	–	0	0	–	0
1927	1	–	1	5	–	5	0	–	0	–4	–	–4
1928	6	–	6	5	–	5	0	–	0	1	–	1
1929	10	–	10	10	–	10	0	–	0	0	–	0
1930	11	25	36	5	6	11	5	6	11	1	13	14
1931	28	60	88	10	15	25	10	15	25	8	30	38
1932	105	100	205	35	25	60	15	25	40	55	50	105
1933	19	106	125	0	26	26	10	26	36	9	54	63
1934	62	107	169	25	27	52	15	27	42	22	53	75
1935	99	27	126	38	7	45	12	7	19	49	13	62
1936	10	–	10	0	–	0	0	–	0	10	–	10
1937	–40	–	–40	–38	–	–38	–12	–	–12	10	–	10
1938	–28	–	–28	–7	–	–7	–3	–	–3	–18	–	–18
1939	–81	–	–81	–42	–	–42	–13	–	–13	–26	–	–26
1940	–87	–	–87	–36	–	–36	–12	–	–12	–39	–	–39
1941	–95	–	–95	–45	–	–45	–15	–	–15	–35	–	–35
1942	–102	–	–102	–31	–	–31	–11	–	–11	–60	–	–60
1943	–88	–	–88	–27	–	–27	–9	–	–9	–52	–	–52
1944	–61	–	–61	–19	–	–19	–6	–	–6	–36	–	–36
1945	–24	–	–24	–7	–	–7	–3	–	–3	–14	–	–14
1946	–7	–	–7	–3	–	–3	0	–	0	–4	–	–4
1947	–3	–	–3	0	–	0	–1	–	–1	–2	–	–2
1948	–2	–	–2	–1	–	–1	0	–	0	–1	–	–1
1949	0	–	0	0	–	0	0	–	0	0	–	0

LOSSES ON REAL ESTATE LOANS BY OPERATING COMMERCIAL BANKS
1930 to 1935

R-57

$ mill.

Year	Total net losses on loans in excess of 1923–1929 average	Losses allocated to				
		All real estate loans	Loans on			
			Farm real estate	1- to 4-family homes	Multi-family dwellings	Nonresidential real estate
	1	2	3	4	5	6
1930	85	29	4	6	6	13
1931	207	70	10	15	15	30
1932	348	118	18	25	25	50
1933	365	125	19	26	26	54
1934	366	126	19	27	27	53
1935	93	32	5	7	7	13
1930–35	1 464	500	75	106	106	213

Column 1 – 1921–1942: From Table V-76, col. 10. Figures represent book value of assets not yet liquidated, i.e., they are net of losses on liquidated assets.

Column 2 – 1921–1942: Estimated at 2.5 percent of total assets of closed banks, approximately the ratio for operating banks (Table V-76, col. 1).

Column 3 – 1921–1942: Col. 1 minus sum of cols. 2 and 8.

Column 4 – 1921–1942: Sum of cols. 5 and 6.

Columns 5 to 7 – 1921–1942: Estimated at 45, 10, and 45 percent, respectively, of col. 3. These ratios are based on the distribution of nonfarm real estate (excluding bank premises) in operating banks around 1930 (cf. Table R-55).

Column 8 – 1921–1929: Estimated at about one-half of all real estate holdings other than bank premises up to 1929 because of large share of closed banks in farm areas.
1930–1931: Interpolated between 1929 and 1932 values.
1932–1942: Estimated at 10 percent of total real estate holdings (excluding bank premises), approximately the ratio in operating banks in 1932.

TABLE R-59

R-59

Columns 1 to 8 – Rough estimates based on total holdings and changes in holdings of different types of real estate, as shown in Table R-58, and rate of loss on such loans by operating commercial banks (Table R-57) and other mortgagees. It was assumed, however, that the loss experience of closed banks was more unfavorable than that of operating lenders.

DISTRIBUTION OF HOLDINGS OF REAL ESTATE
BY CLOSED COMMERCIAL BANKS: 1921 to 1942

$ mill.

End of year	Total	Bank premises	Other nonfarm real estate					Farm real estate
			Total	Residential			Non-residential	
				Total	1- to 4-family	Multi-family		
1	2	3	4	5	6	7	8
1921	5	5	–	–	–	–	–	–
1922	5	5	–	–	–	–	–	–
1923	10	8	1	1	1	–	–	1
1924	15	11	2	1	1	–	1	2
1925	20	13	4	2	2	–	2	3
1926	22	16	3	2	2	–	1	3
1927	27	16	6	3	3	–	3	5
1928	21	16	3	2	2	–	1	2
1929	20	15	3	2	2	–	1	2
1930	31	18	10	6	5	1	4	3
1931	96	52	38	21	17	4	17	6
1932	139	60	71	39	32	7	32	8
1933	313	137	158	87	71	16	71	18
1934	251	99	137	76	62	14	61	15
1935	190	76	103	57	47	10	46	11
1936	136	61	67	37	30	7	30	8
1937	98	49	44	24	20	4	20	5
1938	69	39	27	15	12	3	12	3
1939	51	33	16	9	7	2	7	2
1940	33	26	6	4	3	1	2	1
1941	15	15	–	–	–	–	–	–
1942	3	3	–	–	–	–	–	–

LOSSES SUFFERED IN LIQUIDATION OF REAL ESTATE
BY CLOSED COMMERCIAL BANKS: 1926 to 1943

R-59

$ mill.

Year	Total	Bank premises	Other nonfarm real estate					Farm real estate
			Total	Residential			Non-residential	
				Total	1- to 4-family	Multi-family		
1	2	3	4	5	6	7	8
1926	4	3	–	–	–	–	–	1
1927	3	2	–	–	–	–	–	1
1928	7	3	2	1	1	–	1	2
1929	5	2	2	1	1	–	1	1
1930	3	1	1	–	–	–	1	1
1931	5	2	2	1	1	–	1	1
1932	10	2	7	4	3	1	3	1
1933	25	5	18	10	8	2	8	2
1934	11	2	8	4	3	1	4	1
1935	24	5	18	10	8	2	8	1
1936	16	3	12	6	5	1	6	1
1937	19	4	14	7	6	1	7	1
1938	15	2	12	6	5	1	6	1
1939	8	2	5	3	2	1	2	1
1940	8	2	5	3	2	1	2	1
1941	13	5	8	4	3	1	4	–
1942	7	7	–	–	–	–	–	–
1943	2	2	–	–	–	–	–	–

655

TABLE R–60

Column 1 – First differences of Table R-58, col. 3.

Column 2 - From Table R-59, col. 3.

Column 3 – Sum of cols. 1 and 2.

Column 4 – First differences of Table R-58, col. 5.

Column 5 – From Table R-59, col. 5.

Column 6 – Sum of cols. 4 and 5.

Column 7 – First differences of Table R-58, col. 6.

Column 8 - From Table R-59, col. 6.

Column 9 – Sum of cols. 7 and 8.

Column 10 – First differences of Table R-58, col. 7.

Column 11 – From Table R-59, col. 7.

Column 12 – Sum of cols. 10 and 11.

TABLE R–61

Column 1 – 1925–1949: Sum of Table L-30, cols. 8 and 9.

Column 2 – 1925–1949: Sum of cols. 3 and 4.

Column 3 – 1925–1937: Estimated at 60 percent of all real estate excluding bank premises, the ratio prevailing in 1938.
1938–1948: Home Loan Bank Board, *Statistical Summary*, 1949, p. 18.
1949: Rough estimate.

Column 4 – 1925–1949: Estimated at 50 percent of all real estate other than one- to four-family dwellings and bank premises, on basis of ratio of foreclosures in a sample of mortgage loans made by Massachusetts Savings Banks (cf. Lintner, John, *Mutual Savings Banks in the Savings and Mortgage Markets*, pp. 362, 378).

Column 5 – 1925–1949: Sum of cols. 6 and 7.

Column 6 – 1925–1949: From Table L-30, col. 8.

Column 7 – 1925–1949: Estimated at 50 percent of all real estate other than one- to four-family dwellings and bank premises, as indicated under col. 4.

CHANGES IN NONFARM REAL ESTATE HOLDINGS, BY MAIN TYPES, OF CLOSED COMMERCIAL BANKS: 1926 to 1941

$ mill.

Year	All foreclosed real estate			1- to 4- family dwellings			Multi-family dwellings			Nonresidential properties		
	Change in holdings	Capital loss	Net	Change in holdings	Capital loss	Net	Change in holdings	Capital loss	Net	Change in holdings	Capital loss	Net
	1	2	3	4	5	6	7	8	9	10	11	12
1926	−1	−	−1	0	−	0	−	−	−	−1	−	−1
1927	3	−	3	1	−	1	−	−	−	2	−	2
1928	−3	2	−1	−1	1	0	−	−	−	−2	1	−1
1929	0	2	2	0	1	1	−	−	−	0	1	1
1930	7	1	8	3	−	3	1	−	1	3	1	4
1931	28	2	30	12	1	13	3	−	3	13	1	14
1932	33	7	40	15	3	18	3	1	4	15	3	18
1933	87	18	105	39	8	47	9	2	11	39	8	47
1934	−21	8	−13	−9	3	−6	−2	1	−1	−10	4	−6
1935	−34	18	−16	−15	8	−7	−4	2	−2	−15	8	−7
1936	−36	12	−24	−17	5	−12	−3	1	−2	−16	6	−10
1937	−23	14	−9	−10	6	−4	−3	1	−2	−10	7	−3
1938	−17	12	−5	−8	5	−3	−1	1	0	−8	6	−2
1939	−11	5	−6	−5	2	−3	−1	1	0	−5	2	−3
1940	−10	5	−5	−4	2	−2	−1	1	0	−5	2	−3
1941	−6	8	2	−3	3	0	−1	1	0	−2	4	2

DISTRIBUTION OF HOLDINGS OF REAL ESTATE BY MUTUAL SAVINGS BANKS: 1925 to 1949

$ mill.

End of year	Total	Residential			Nonresidential		
		Total	1- to 4-family	Multi-family	Total	Bank premises	Other
	1	2	3	4	5	6	7
1925	87	7	5	2	80	79	1
1926	100	10	7	3	90	88	2
1927	111	11	8	3	100	97	3
1928	125	15	11	4	110	106	4
1929	146	27	20	7	119	112	7
1930	172	43	32	11	129	118	11
1931	224	77	58	19	147	128	19
1932	327	153	115	38	174	136	38
1933	454	253	190	63	201	138	63
1934	595	367	275	92	228	137	91
1935	737	481	361	120	256	135	121
1936	832	559	419	140	273	133	140
1937	824	553	415	138	271	133	138
1938	785	524	392	132	261	129	132
1939	728	472	342	130	256	126	130
1940	676	426	298	128	250	122	128
1941	542	318	212	106	224	118	106
1942	432	229	142	87	203	115	88
1943	304	139	81	58	165	107	58
1944	198	66	36	30	132	102	30
1945	130	23	12	11	107	95	12
1946	110	12	6	6	98	92	6
1947	104	8	5	3	96	93	3
1948	108	6	4	2	102	100	2
1949	110	6	4	2	104	103	1

R-62

CHANGES IN REAL ESTATE HOLDINGS OF MUTUAL SAVINGS BANKS
1926 to 1949

$ mill.

Year	All foreclosed real estate			1- to 4- family dwellings			Multi family dwellings			Nonresidential properties		
	Change in holdings	Capital loss	Net	Change in holdings	Capital loss	Net	Change in holdings	Capital loss	Net	Change in holdings	Capital loss	Net
	1	2	3	4	5	6	7	8	9	10	11	12
1926	4	3	7	2	1	3	1	1	2	1	1	2
1927	2	5	7	1	1	2	0	1	1	1	3	4
1928	5	10	15	3	2	5	1	3	4	1	5	6
1929	15	10	25	9	2	11	3	3	6	3	5	8
1930	20	10	30	12	2	14	4	3	7	4	5	9
1931	42	20	62	26	4	30	8	6	14	8	10	18
1932	95	30	125	57	6	63	19	9	28	19	15	34
1933	125	30	155	75	6	81	25	9	34	25	15	40
1934	142	30	172	85	6	91	29	9	38	28	15	43
1935	144	40	184	86	8	94	28	12	40	30	20	50
1936	97	40	137	58	8	66	20	12	32	19	20	39
1937	−8	60	52	−4	12	8	−2	18	16	−2	30	28
1938	−35	90	55	−23	18	−5	−6	27	21	−6	45	39
1939	−54	90	36	−50	18	−32	−2	27	25	−2	45	43
1940	−48	90	42	−44	18	−26	−2	27	25	−2	45	43
1941	−130	150	20	−86	30	−56	−22	45	23	−22	75	53
1942	−107	150	43	−70	30	−40	−19	45	26	−18	75	57
1943	−120	123	3	−61	25	−36	−29	37	8	−30	62	32
1944	−101	84	−17	−45	17	−28	−28	25	−3	−28	42	14
1945	−61	50	−11	−24	10	−14	−19	15	−4	−18	25	7
1946	−17	12	−5	−6	2	−4	−5	4	−1	−6	6	0
1947	−7	20	13	−1	4	3	−3	6	3	−3	10	7
1948	−3	22	19	−1	4	3	−1	7	6	−1	11	10
1949	−1	49	48	0	10	10	0	15	15	−1	24	23

Column 1 – First differences of Table R-61, cols. 2 plus 7.

Column 2 – From Table L-35, col. 3.

Column 3 – Sum of cols. 1 and 2.

Column 4 – First differences of Table R-61, col. 3.

Column 5 – Estimated at 20 percent of col. 2. Ratio is based on distribution of total losses in a sample of mortgage loans made by Massachusetts savings banks between 1918 and 1931 (cf. Lintner, John, *Mutual Savings Banks in the Savings and Mortgage Markets*, pp. 362, 378). However, the proportion of losses allocated to one- to four-family dwellings has been somewhat reduced and that allocated to losses on multi-family dwellings correspondingly increased, to take account of probability that a higher proportion of mortgage loans, and hence of losses, made by New York savings banks was on multi-family dwellings than is the case in Massachusetts.

Column 6 – Sum of cols. 4 and 5.

Column 7 – First differences of Table R-61, col. 4.

Column 8 – Estimated at 30 percent of col. 2 by procedure indicated under col. 5.

Column 9 – Sum of cols. 7 and 8.

Column 10 – First differences of Table R-61, col. 7. This column excludes bank premises which obviously would not be affected by foreclosures.

Column 11 – Estimated at 50 percent of col. 2 on basis of procedure indicated under col. 5.

Column 12 – Sum of cols. 10 and 11.

658

DISTRIBUTION OF HOLDINGS OF REAL ESTATE
BY LIFE INSURANCE COMPANIES: 1925 to 1949

$ mill

End of year	Total	Nonfarm									Farm
		Total	Residential				Nonresidential				
			Total	1- to 4- family	Multi-family		Total	For own occupancy	For investment	Other	
					For investment	Other					
	1	2	3	4	5	6	7	8	9	10	11
1925	262	227	53	31	10	12	174	150	—	24	35
1926	298	249	61	37	10	14	188	160	—	28	49
1927	343	277	73	45	10	18	204	170	—	34	66
1928	394	309	87	55	10	22	222	180	—	42	85
1929	453	346	104	67	10	27	242	191	—	51	107
1930	535	412	141	94	10	37	271	199	—	72	123
1931	663	472	173	117	10	46	299	210	—	89	191
1932	904	616	259	178	10	71	357	220	—	137	288
1933A	1 219	791	373	260	10	103	418	219	—	199	428
1933B	1 111	683	303	210	10	83	380	219	—	161	428
1934	1 513	955	457	302	10	145	498	216	—	282	558
1935	1 830	1 241	577	337	10	230	664	216	—	448	589
1936	1 991	1 357	626	350	10	266	731	219	—	512	634
1937	2 045	1 433	676	385	10	281	757	216	—	541	612
1938	2 048	1 441	652	336	10	306	789	215	—	574	607
1939	2 001	1 401	654	308	40	306	747	220	—	527	600
1940	1 918	1 370	644	290	75	279	726	220	—	506	548
1941	1 654	1 212	545	226	85	234	667	225	—	442	442
1942	1 483	1 147	508	181	105	222	639	225	—	414	336
1943	1 207	1 002	429	119	129	181	573	230	—	343	205
1944	930	811	324	64	135	125	487	230	—	257	119
1945	727	645	270	39	140	91	375	235	—	140	82
1946	668	634	236	24	150	62	398	235	89	74	34
1947	814	800	269	14	207	48	531	258	219	54	14
1948	1 028	1 022	296	10	240	46	726	299	383	44	6
1949	1 241	1 238	350	7	301	42	888	333	515	40	3

Column 1 – 1925–1949: Sum of cols. 2 and 11.

Column 2 – 1925–1933A: Total real estate owned, as reported in *Life Insurance Fact Book*, 1950, p. 67, minus farm holdings which were extrapolated on basis of the relationship in 1933 of the Institute of Life Insurance estimates, derived from individual company reports, of farm holdings and the Bureau of Agricultural Economics series (Table A-10, col. 6).
1933B–1949: Sum of cols. 3 and 7.

Column 3 – 1925–1949: Sum of cols. 4–6.

Column 4 – 1925–1933A: Extrapolated on basis of relationship of one- to four-family to total nonfarm holdings excluding properties held for investment and for own occupancy, in 1933B.
1933B–1937: Home Loan Bank Board, *Mortgage and Real Estate Investments of Life Insurance Companies*, 1947. Sum of real estate sold under contract and real estate owned (excluding investment properties).
1938–1949: Same procedure as for 1933–1937 except data taken from Home Loan Bank Board, *Mortgage Investments of Life Insurance Companies*, 1949, p. 9.

Column 5 – 1925–1945: Rough estimates based on unpublished data prepared by Life Insurance Association of America.
1946: Unpublished estimate of Life Insurance Association of America.
1947–1949: *Life Insurance Fact Book*, 1950, p. 67.

Column 6 – 1925–1933A: Extrapolated on the basis of the relationship of multi-family to total nonfarm holdings, excluding properties held for investment and for own occupancy, in 1933B.
1933B–1937: Figures for real estate sold under contract and real estate owned other than one- to four-family nonfarm properties as estimated by Home Loan Bank Board (Federal Savings and Loan Insurance Corporation, *Mortgage and Real Estate Investments of Life Insurance Companies, 1947*) split between multi-family and nonresidential according to 1938 proportion.
1938–1949: Same procedure as for col. 4.

Column 7 – 1925–1949: Sum of cols. 8–10.

Column 8 – 1925–1928: Rough estimates.
1929–1938: Estimated at 120 percent of "Home and branch office real estate owned" of 26 large companies (*Temporary National Economic Committee Hearings*, part 10A, p. 255).
1939–1945: Rough extrapolation.
1946–1949: Same source as for col. 5.

Column 9 – 1946–1949: Same source as for col. 5.

Column 10 – 1925–1933A: Extrapolated on basis of relationship of nonresidential to total nonfarm holdings, excluding properties held for investment and for own occupancy, in 1933B.
1933B–1949: Same procedure as for col. 6.

Column 11 – 1925–1949: From Table A-10, col. 6. Bureau of Agricultural Economics rather than Institute of Life Insurance figures for farm holdings were accepted since the latter include sales contracts which have been treated in mortgage debt series.

CHANGES IN NONFARM REAL ESTATE HOLDINGS OF LIFE INSURANCE COMPANIES: 1926 to 1949

$ mill.

Year	All foreclosed real estate			1- to 4- family dwellings			Multi-family dwellings			Nonresidential properties		
	Change in holdings	Capital loss	Net	Change in holdings	Capital loss	Net	Change in holdings	Capital loss	Net	Change in holdings	Capital loss	Net
	1	2	3	4	5	6	7	8	9	10	11	12
1926	12	–	12	6	–	6	2	–	2	4	–	4
1927	18	–	18	8	–	8	4	–	4	6	–	6
1928	22	–	22	10	–	10	4	–	4	8	–	8
1929	26	4	30	12	1	13	5	1	6	9	2	11
1930	58	8	66	27	1	28	10	2	12	21	5	26
1931	49	11	60	23	2	25	9	3	12	17	6	23
1932	134	19	153	61	3	64	25	5	30	48	11	59
1933	176	18	194	82	3	85	32	4	36	62	11	73
1934	275	16	291	92	2	94	62	4	66	121	10	131
1935	286	18	304	35	3	38	85	4	89	166	11	177
1936	113	43	156	13	6	19	36	11	47	64	26	90
1937	79	6	85	35	1	36	15	2	17	29	3	32
1938	9	33	42	–49	5	–44	25	8	33	33	20	53
1939	–75	48	–27	–28	7	–21	0	12	12	–47	29	–18
1940	–66	50	–16	–18	8	–10	–27	12	–15	–21	30	9
1941	–173	44	–129	–64	7	–57	–45	11	–34	–64	26	–38
1942	–85	29	–56	–45	4	–41	–12	7	–5	–28	18	–10
1943	–174	24	–150	–62	4	–58	–41	6	–35	–71	14	–57
1944	–197	5	–192	–55	1	–54	–56	1	–55	–86	3	–83
1945	–176	–6	–182	–25	–1	–26	–34	–2	–36	–117	–3	–120
1946	–110	–9	–119	–15	–1	–16	–29	–2	–31	–66	–6	–72
1947	–44	3	–41	–10	0	–10	–14	1	–13	–20	2	–18
1948	–16	6	–10	–4	1	–3	–2	2	0	–10	3	–7
1949	–11	12	1	–3	2	–1	–4	3	–1	–4	7	3

Column 1 – Sum of first differences of Table R-63, cols. 4, 6, and 10.

Column 2 – Losses on nonfarm real estate are assumed to be about 70 percent of total real estate losses as given in Table I-7, col. 1. Percentage estimated on basis of data on mortgage holdings and foreclosures of the largest life insurance companies.

Column 3 – Sum of cols. 1 and 2.

Column 4 – First differences of Table R-63, col. 4.

Column 5 – Assumed to be 15 percent of col. 2.

Column 6 – Sum of cols. 4 and 5.

Column 7 – First differences of Table R-63, col. 6.

Column 8 – Assumed to be 25 percent of col. 2.

Column 9 – Sum of cols. 7 and 8.

Column 10 – First differences of Table R-63, col. 10.

Column 11 – Assumed to be 60 percent of col. 2.

Column 12 – Sum of cols. 10 and 11.

DISTRIBUTION OF HOLDINGS OF REAL ESTATE
BY FRATERNAL LIFE INSURANCE COMPANIES
1925 to 1949

$ mill.

End of year	Total	Nonfarm							Farm
		Total	Residential			Nonresidential			
			Total	1- to 4- family	Multi-family	Total	For own occupancy	Other	
1	2	3	4	5	6	7	8	9
1925	22	20	4	3	1	16	14	2	2
1926	27	24	5	4	1	19	16	3	3
1927	27	24	6	4	2	18	15	3	3
1928	27	24	6	4	2	18	15	3	3
1929	24	21	6	4	2	15	12	3	3
1930	26	23	7	5	2	16	12	4	3
1931	30	27	10	7	3	17	12	5	3
1932	35	31	13	9	4	18	11	7	4
1933	49	44	21	15	6	23	12	11	5
1934	62	56	26	18	8	30	13	17	6
1935	85	76	35	21	14	41	13	28	9
1936	96	86	39	22	17	47	14	33	10
1937	99	89	41	24	17	48	14	34	10
1938	100	90	40	21	19	50	14	36	10
1939	101	91	41	21	20	50	15	35	10
1940	93	84	37	19	18	47	14	33	9
1941	83	75	31	15	16	44	15	29	8
1942	73	66	26	12	14	40	14	26	7
1943	62	56	19	8	11	37	15	22	6
1944	47	42	12	4	8	30	14	16	5
1945	40	36	9	3	6	27	17	10	4
1946	38	34	7	2	5	27	21	6	4
1947	38	34	5	1	4	29	24	5	4
1948	40	36	5	1	4	31	27	4	4
1949	38	34	4	1	3	30	27	3	4

Column 1 – From Table I-10, col. 3.

Column 2 – Column 1 minus col. 9.

Columns 3 to 8 – Col. 2 distributed on the basis of Table R-63.

Column 9 – Assumed to be 10 percent of col. 1.

DISTRIBUTION OF HOLDINGS OF REAL ESTATE BY FIRE, MARINE, CASUALTY, AND MISCELLANEOUS INSURANCE COMPANIES
1925 to 1949

$ mill.

End of year	Total	Nonfarm							Farm
		Total	Residential			Nonresidential			
			Total	1- to 4- family	Multi-family	Total	For own occupancy	Other	
	1	2	3	4	5	6	7	8	9
1925	82	82	17	12	5	65	56	9	—
1926	86	86	18	13	5	68	58	10	—
1927	88	88	21	15	6	67	56	11	—
1928	98	98	25	18	7	73	59	14	—
1929	105	105	29	21	8	76	60	16	—
1930	113	113	37	27	10	76	56	20	—
1931	116	116	41	29	12	75	53	22	—
1932	133	133	55	39	16	78	48	30	—
1933	140	140	65	47	18	75	39	36	—
1934	146	146	69	47	22	77	33	44	—
1935	150	150	69	41	28	81	26	55	—
1936	148	148	68	39	29	80	24	56	—
1937	148	148	69	40	29	79	23	56	—
1938	154	154	69	36	33	85	23	62	—
1939	149	149	67	34	33	82	24	58	—
1940	145	145	63	32	31	82	25	57	—
1941	143	143	58	29	29	85	29	56	—
1942	134	134	52	23	29	82	29	53	—
1943	129	129	44	17	27	85	34	51	—
1944	119	119	33	11	22	86	41	45	—
1945	114	114	30	9	21	84	53	31	—
1946	116	116	25	7	18	91	69	22	—
1947	122	122	21	5	16	101	84	17	—
1948	140	140	20	4	16	120	105	15	—
1949	167	167	20	3	17	147	131	16	—

Column 1 – Sum of Tables V-55, col. 4 and V-56, col. 4.

Column 2 – Assumed equal to col. 1.

Column 3 – Sum of cols. 4 and 5.

Columns 4, 5, 7, and 8 – Col. 2 distributed on basis of Table R-63.

Column 6 – Sum of cols. 7 and 8.

Column 9 – Assumed to be negligible.

Column 1 – First differences of Table J-2, col. 4.

Column 2 – From Table J-9, col. 5. It has been assumed that net capital gains and losses indicated for years 1945–1949 are applicable to sales of securities rather than to those of real estate. For other years entire capital loss has been allocated to real estate although part probably was debited to mortgage account to reflect write-downs on loans adjusted without foreclosure.

Column 3 – Col. 1 plus col. 2.

Column 4 – Very rough estimates guided by total mortgage and real estate holdings of closed institutions as calculated in Table J-6, col. 6, but differing from those shown in Table R-46, col. 10.

Column 5 – Very rough distribution of total capital loss of $200 million, as estimated in Table J-10, Method II, line 4, assuming that sales were concentrated in the latter part of the period.

Column 6 – Col. 4 plus col. 5.

Column 7 – Col. 3 plus col. 6.

Column 1 – Unpublished data supplied by Home Owners' Loan Corporation. Includes real estate owned and in process of acquisition. Figures represent cost, i.e. principal of mortgages foreclosed plus arrears plus acquisition cost.

Column 2 – First differences of col. 1.

Column 3 – Unpublished data supplied by Home Owners' Loan Corporation. Figures include commissions and selling expenses.

Column 4 – Col. 2 plus col. 3.

CHANGES IN HOLDINGS OF REAL ESTATE
BY SAVINGS AND LOAN ASSOCIATIONS: 1926 to 1949

$ mill.

Year	Operating associations			Closed associations			All associations
	Change in real estate holdings	Capital loss	Net	Change in real estate holdings	Capital loss	Net	Net
	1	2	3	4	5	6	7
1926	8	–	8	–	–	–	8
1927	17	–	17	–	–	–	17
1928	52	–	52	–	–	–	52
1929	86	–19	67	10	–	10	77
1930	64	2	66	20	5	25	91
1931	132	43	175	20	5	25	200
1932	272	84	356	20	5	25	381
1933	186	88	274	50	10	60	334
1934	184	48	232	20	10	30	262
1935	151	76	227	20	10	30	257
1936	–13	52	39	–20	10	–10	29
1937	–136	32	–104	–20	20	0	–104
1938	–124	24	–100	–20	20	0	–100
1939	–209	53	–156	20	10	30	–126
1940	–189	59	–130	20	10	30	–100
1941	–164	43	–121	–30	20	–10	–131
1942	–125	35	–90	–30	20	–10	–100
1943	–86	23	–63	–30	20	–10	–73
1944	–57	23	–34	–30	20	–10	–44
1945	–27	–	–27	–10	5	–5	–32
1946	–7	–	–7	–	–	–	–7
1947	–13	–	–13	–	–	–	–13
1948	–1	–	–1	–	–	–	–1
1949	3	–	3	–	–	–	3

HOLDINGS OF REAL ESTATE
BY HOME OWNERS' LOAN CORPORATION: 1935 to 1949

R-68

$ mill.

Year	Holdings of real estate	Change in real estate holdings			Year	Holdings of real estate	Change in real estate holdings		
		Cost	Capital loss on sale	Net change			Cost	Capital loss on sale	Net change
	1	2	3	4		1	2	3	4
1935	6	6	–	6	1943	97	–130	52	–78
1936	167	161	–	161	1944	12	–85	39	–46
1937	437	270	1	271	1945	2	–10	5	–5
1938	542	105	28	133	1946	–	–2	–	–2
1939	510	–32	68	36	1947	–	–	–	–
1940	357	–153	79	–74	1948	–	–	–	–
1941	288	–69	39	–30	1949	–	–	–	–
1942	227	–61	25	–36					

Column 1 – 1929–1937: Estimated on the assumption that real estate holdings of mortgage companies moved in the same way as those of other institutional holders.

1938–1949: Rough estimates based until 1947 on balance sheets of mortgage companies as tabulated by Bureau of Internal Revenue (*Statistics of Income*, part II, various issues).

Column 2 – 1929–1949: Sum of cols. 3 and 6.

Column 3 – 1929–1949: Sum of cols. 4 and 5.

Columns 4 to 7 – 1929–1949: Col. 1 divided among one- to four-family, multi-family, nonresidential, and farm properties according to the percentage distribution of the holdings of these four types of properties by other institutions.

Column 1 – 1897–1899: *Spectator Insurance Yearbook, Fire and Marine Volume*, 1949, p. 284.

1900–1915: National Board of Fire Underwriters, "Report of Committee of Statistics and Origin of Fires," *Statistical Abstract*, 1948, p. 460. In these years, estimates of U.S. fire losses were taken from reports published by *New York Journal of Commerce*. All estimates from 1897–1915 were stepped up by ratio (1.2044) between National Board of Fire Underwriters and *Journal of Commerce* estimates for 1916. The $350 million loss in San Francisco earthquake in 1906 was not included in step-up.

1916–1945: National Board of Fire Underwriters report (see above). Estimates are obtained by adding 25 percent (after 1935, 30 percent) of all fire losses reported to Actuarial Bureau Committee to account for unreported and uninsured losses.

1946–1948: *Spectator Insurance Yearbook, Fire and Marine Volume*, 1949, p. 284. Data are taken from National Board of Fire Underwriters reports and are comparable to those for 1916–1945.

1949: *Spectator Insurance Yearbook, Fire and Marine Volume*, 1950.

Column 2 – 1897–1913: Estimated at 18 percent of col. 1 except for 1906, when estimated at 18 percent of difference between total U.S. loss and San Francisco earthquake fire loss, all of latter being attributed to nonfarm fire losses. The 18 percent ratio was based upon ratio between farm and total fire losses in 1914–1916.

1914–1936: Obtained by same method as 1937–1945 figures, except that in carrying estimate back multiplier was stepped up gradually from 3.50 in 1936 to 4.60 in 1914 to account for decreasing importance of farm mutual fire insurance. Data on farm mutual fire insurance in force and loss ratios were taken from *Historical Statistics*, p. 98.

1937–1945: From Botts, Ralph R. and Houseman, Earl, *Method of Estimating Farm Fire Losses in the United States*, Bureau of Agricultural Economics, July 1948, p. 8. In this report farm fire losses are computed as a multiple (3.476) of losses of farm mutual fire insurance companies, latter being product of insurance in force and loss per $100 of insurance, multiplier being based on 1945 farm fire loss experience.

1946–1947: Botts and Houseman, *op. cit.* Computed from a sample of farm mutual fire insurance companies.

1948–1949: *Agricultural Finance Review, Supplement*, May 1950, p. 30. Figures given for farm fire losses in U.S. 1937–1949 in *Agricultural Finance Review, Supplement*, May 1950, differ from estimates for these years given in this table, but since differences are very small it was decided not to revise the series.

Column 3 – 1897–1949: Col. 1 less col. 2.

DISTRIBUTION OF HOLDINGS OF REAL ESTATE
BY MORTGAGE COMPANIES: 1929 to 1949

$ mill.

End of year	Total	Nonfarm real estate					Farm
		Total	Residential			Non-residential	
			Total	1- to 4-family	Multi-family		
	1	2	3	4	5	6	7
1929	15	12	8	7	1	4	3
1930	20	17	12	10	2	5	3
1931	30	25	19	17	2	6	5
1932	40	33	25	22	3	8	7
1933	50	42	32	28	4	10	8
1934	60	50	38	32	6	12	10
1935	70	59	44	36	8	15	11
1936	80	68	50	41	9	18	12
1937	80	69	51	42	9	18	11
1938	80	68	50	41	9	18	12
1939	80	68	49	39	10	19	12
1940	80	67	47	36	11	20	13
1941	65	54	36	27	9	18	11
1942	55	46	29	20	9	17	9
1943	40	34	20	12	8	14	6
1944	35	30	15	8	7	15	5
1945	30	25	13	6	7	12	5
1946	25	22	13	6	7	9	3
1947	25	23	13	5	8	10	2
1948	25	24	14	5	9	10	1
1949	25	24	14	5	9	10	1

FARM AND NONFARM FIRE LOSSES IN THE UNITED STATES: 1897 to 1949

$ mill.

Year	Total	Farm	Nonfarm	Year	Total	Farm	Nonfarm
	1	2	3		1	2	3
1897	140.4	25.3	115.1	1924	549.1	77.6	471.5
1898	157.3	28.3	129.0	1925	559.4	81.0	478.4
1899	185.0	33.3	151.7	1926	562.0	75.5	486.5
1900	193.8	34.9	158.9	1927	472.9	76.3	396.6
1901	199.7	35.9	163.8	1928	464.6	84.4	380.2
1902	194.0	34.9	159.1	1929	459.5	91.9	367.6
1903	175.0	31.5	143.5	1930	502.0	106.0	396.0
1904	276.1	49.7	226.4	1931	451.6	102.4	349.2
1905	199.0	35.8	163.2	1932	400.9	102.6	298.3
1906	553.1	36.6	516.5	1933	271.4	82.9	188.5
1907	259.0	46.6	212.4	1934	271.2	74.6	196.6
1908	262.4	47.2	215.2	1935	235.3	60.4	174.9
1909	227.3	40.9	186.4	1936	266.7	80.7	186.0
1910	257.7	46.4	211.3	1937	255.0	65.7	189.3
1911	261.4	47.1	214.3	1938	258.5	73.3	185.2
1912	248.6	44.7	203.9	1939	275.1	76.8	198.3
1913	245.4	44.2	201.2	1940	285.9	72.6	213.3
1914	266.7	49.4	217.3	1941	303.9	69.9	234.0
1915	207.2	38.0	169.2	1942	314.3	64.7	249.6
1916	258.4	48.5	209.9	1943	373.0	75.4	297.6
1917	289.5	46.6	242.9	1944	437.3	77.4	359.9
1918	353.9	50.7	303.2	1945	484.3	80.3	404.0
1919	320.5	50.1	270.4	1946	561.5	82.0	479.5
1920	447.9	55.4	392.5	1947	692.6	99.0	593.6
1921	495.4	67.1	428.3	1948	711.1	99.0	612.1
1922	506.5	75.4	431.1	1949	667.5	95.0	572.5
1923	535.4	73.3	462.1				

R-71 TABLE R–71

Column 1 – From Table R-70, col. 3.

Columns 2 to 11 – Distribution of nonfarm farm losses estimated with the help of four sources:

Division of fire losses by type of structure was based on tables giving fire losses by occupancy groups available from 1936 on in *Quarterly of the National Fire Protection Association.* These were aggregated into public buildings, dwellings, and commercial buildings.

For all types of structures, losses were divided equally between buildings and contents according to National Board of Fire Underwriters, *Statistics of Fires in American Cities Having a Population of 20,000 and Upward—1928, Report of the Committee on Statistics and Origins of Fires,* 1929.

Building and contents losses by occupancy groups were estimated from reports in Simon, Herbert A., Shepherd, Ronald W., and Sharp, Frederick W., *Fire Losses and Fire Risks* (Bureau of Public Administration, University of California, Berkeley, 1943) on fire losses in Oakland and Berkeley, 1935–1939. Corroborative evidence was obtained from "Buildings and Contents Losses," *Quarterly of the National Fire Protection Association,* 1938, p. 249.

As a result, the following percentages were obtained:

	Percentage of total nonfarm fire losses
Dwellings:	
Building	22
Contents (household goods)	8
Public buildings:	
Building	7
Contents (equipment)	3
Commercial:	
Buildings	20
Equipment	20
Inventories	20
	100

Fire losses on commercial property (manufacturing and mercantile) were divided 4 : 1 between corporate and unincorporated business.

668

NONFARM FIRE LOSSES BY TYPE OF PROPERTY
1897 to 1949

$ mill.

Year	Total	Public		Private							
		Buildings	Equip-ment	Dwellings	House-hold goods	Corporate			Noncorporate		
						Buildings	Equip-ment	Inven-tory	Buildings	Equip-ment	Inven-tory
	1	2	3	4	5	6	7	8	9	10	11
1897	115.1	8.1	3.5	25.3	9.2	18.4	18.4	18.4	4.6	4.6	4.6
1898	129.0	9.0	3.9	28.4	10.3	20.6	20.6	20.6	5.2	5.2	5.2
1899	151.7	10.6	4.5	33.3	12.1	24.3	24.3	24.3	6.1	6.1	6.1
1900	158.9	11.1	4.8	34.9	12.7	25.4	25.4	25.4	6.4	6.4	6.4
1901	163.8	11.4	4.9	36.0	13.1	26.2	26.2	26.2	6.6	6.6	6.6
1902	159.1	11.1	4.8	35.1	12.7	25.4	25.4	25.4	6.4	6.4	6.4
1903	143.5	10.0	4.3	31.6	11.5	23.0	23.0	23.0	5.7	5.7	5.7
1904	226.4	15.8	6.8	49.8	18.1	36.2	36.2	36.2	9.1	9.1	9.1
1905	163.2	11.5	4.9	35.9	13.1	26.1	26.1	26.1	6.5	6.5	6.5
1906	516.5	36.2	15.5	113.6	41.3	82.6	82.6	82.6	20.7	20.7	20.7
1907	212.4	14.8	6.4	46.7	17.0	34.0	34.0	34.0	8.5	8.5	8.5
1908	215.2	15.1	6.5	47.4	17.2	34.4	34.4	34.4	8.6	8.6	8.6
1909	186.4	13.0	5.6	41.0	14.9	29.8	29.8	29.8	7.5	7.5	7.5
1910	211.3	14.8	6.3	46.4	16.9	33.8	33.8	33.8	8.5	8.5	8.5
1911	214.3	15.0	6.4	47.1	17.1	34.3	34.3	34.3	8.6	8.6	8.6
1912	203.9	14.3	6.1	44.8	16.3	32.6	32.6	32.6	8.2	8.2	8.2
1913	201.2	14.1	6.1	44.3	16.1	32.2	32.2	32.2	8.0	8.0	8.0
1914	217.3	15.2	6.5	47.8	17.4	34.7	34.8	34.8	8.7	8.7	8.7
1915	169.2	11.8	5.1	37.1	13.5	27.1	27.1	27.1	6.8	6.8	6.8
1916	209.9	14.7	6.3	46.1	16.8	33.6	33.6	33.6	8.4	8.4	8.4
1917	242.9	17.0	7.3	53.4	19.4	38.9	38.9	38.9	9.7	9.7	9.7
1918	303.2	21.3	9.1	66.7	24.3	48.5	48.5	48.5	12.1	12.1	12.1
1919	270.4	18.9	8.1	59.5	21.6	43.3	43.3	43.3	10.8	10.8	10.8
1920	392.5	27.5	11.8	86.3	31.4	62.8	62.8	62.8	15.7	15.7	15.7
1921	428.3	30.0	12.9	94.3	34.3	68.5	68.5	68.5	17.1	17.1	17.1
1922	431.1	30.2	12.9	94.9	34.5	69.0	69.0	69.0	17.2	17.2	17.2
1923	462.1	32.3	13.9	101.7	37.0	73.9	73.9	73.9	18.5	18.5	18.5
1924	471.5	33.0	14.2	103.7	37.7	75.4	75.4	75.4	18.9	18.9	18.9
1925	478.4	33.5	14.3	105.2	38.3	76.6	76.6	76.6	19.1	19.1	19.1
1926	486.5	34.1	14.6	107.0	38.9	77.8	77.8	77.8	19.5	19.5	19.5
1927	396.6	27.8	11.9	87.3	31.7	63.4	63.4	63.4	15.9	15.9	15.9
1928	380.2	26.6	11.4	83.7	30.5	60.8	60.8	60.8	15.2	15.2	15.2
1929	367.6	25.7	11.1	80.9	29.4	58.8	58.8	58.8	14.7	14.7	147.
1930	396.0	27.7	11.9	87.1	31.7	63.4	63.4	63.4	15.8	15.8	15.8
1931	349.2	24.4	10.5	76.7	27.9	55.9	55.9	55.9	14.0	14.0	14.0
1932	298.3	20.9	9.0	65.7	23.9	47.7	47.7	47.7	11.9	11.9	11.9
1933	188.5	13.2	5.6	41.5	15.1	30.2	30.2	30.2	7.5	7.5	7.5
1934	196.6	13.8	5.9	43.3	15.7	31.4	31.4	31.4	7.9	7.9	7.9
1935	174.9	12.2	5.2	38.5	14.0	28.0	28.0	28.0	7.0	7.0	7.0
1936	186.0	13.0	5.6	40.9	14.9	29.8	29.8	29.8	7.4	7.4	7.4
1937	189.3	13.2	5.7	41.6	15.1	30.3	30.3	30.3	7.6	7.6	7.6
1938	185.2	13.0	5.6	40.8	14.8	29.6	29.6	29.6	7.4	7.4	7.4
1939	198.3	13.9	6.0	43.7	15.9	31.7	31.7	31.7	7.9	7.9	7.9
1940	213.3	15.0	6.4	47.0	17.1	34.1	34.1	34.1	8.5	8.5	8.5
1941	234.0	16.4	7.0	51.5	18.7	37.4	37.4	37.4	9.4	9.4	9.4
1942	249.6	17.5	7.5	54.9	20.0	39.9	39.9	39.9	10.0	10.0	10.0
1943	297.6	20.8	8.9	65.5	23.8	47.7	47.6	47.6	11.9	11.9	11.9
1944	359.9	25.2	10.8	79.1	28.8	57.6	57.6	57.6	14.4	14.4	14.4
1945	404.0	28.3	12.1	88.9	32.3	64.6	64.6	64.6	16.2	16.2	16.2
1946	479.5	33.6	14.4	105.4	38.4	76.7	76.7	76.7	19.2	19.2	19.2
1947	593.6	41.6	17.8	130.6	47.5	95.0	95.0	95.0	23.7	23.7	23.7
1948	612.1	42.8	18.4	134.7	49.0	97.9	97.9	97.9	24.5	24.5	24.5
1949	572.5	40.1	17.2	125.9	45.8	91.6	91.6	91.6	22.9	22.9	22.9

Column 1 – From Table R-71, col. 4.

Column 2 – Col. 1 divided by Table R-20, col. 1.

Column 3 – Sum of depreciation on fire losses on residential buildings during thirty years preceding year indicated on assumption that buildings are destroyed after existence of half their expected life of sixty years. Absolute figures from 1897 on are from col. 1. Fire losses from 1867 to 1896 are estimated from data in *Statistical Abstract*, 1947, p. 447 (extrapolating backwards from 1876) by method described in notes to Table R-70 for total fire losses and in notes to Table R-71 for percentage of fire losses in dwellings.

Column 4 – Same procedure as for col. 3 except expenditure series given in col. 2 used.

Column 5 – Col. 2 multiplied by Table R-20, col. 1.

Column 6 – Col. 1 minus col. 3.

Column 7 – Col. 2 minus col. 4.

Column 8 – Col. 1 minus col. 5.

1897 to 1949

$ mill.

Year	Fire losses		Depreciation			Net adjustment		
	Original cost	1929 prices	Original cost	1929 prices	Replacement cost	Original cost	1929 prices	Replacement cost
	1	2	3	4	5	6	7	8
1897	25	60	21	46	19	4	14	6
1898	28	65	22	47	20	6	18	8
1899	33	72	22	49	22	11	23	11
1900	35	73	23	50	24	12	23	11
1901	36	77	23	52	24	13	25	12
1902	35	73	24	53	25	11	20	10
1903	32	65	25	54	27	7	11	5
1904	50	102	25	56	27	25	46	23
1905	36	71	26	58	29	10	13	7
1906	114	217	28	62	33	86	155	81
1907	47	88	31	66	35	16	22	12
1908	47	88	32	67	36	15	21	11
1909	41	78	33	69	36	8	9	5
1910	46	86	34	71	38	12	15	8
1911	47	90	34	72	38	13	18	9
1912	45	84	35	74	40	10	10	5
1913	44	85	36	75	39	8	10	5
1914	48	92	37	76	40	11	16	8
1915	37	69	38	77	41	−1	−8	−4
1916	46	81	38	78	44	8	3	2
1917	53	80	39	79	52	14	1	1
1918	67	84	40	80	63	27	4	4
1919	60	65	42	81	75	18	−16	−15
1920	86	72	43	81	96	43	−9	−10
1921	94	99	45	82	78	49	17	16
1922	95	108	47	83	73	48	25	22
1923	102	104	49	84	83	53	20	19
1924	104	107	52	85	82	52	22	22
1925	105	109	54	86	83	51	23	22
1926	107	110	57	88	85	50	22	22
1927	87	91	59	89	85	28	2	2
1928	84	88	61	90	86	23	−2	−2
1929	81	81	63	90	90	18	−9	−9
1930	87	89	65	91	89	22	−2	−2
1931	77	86	66	91	82	11	−5	−5
1932	66	87	67	92	70	−1	−5	−4
1933	42	55	68	92	70	−26	−37	−28
1934	43	52	68	91	76	−25	−39	−33
1935	38	47	68	89	72	−30	−42	−34
1936	41	49	67	86	72	−26	−37	−31
1937	42	45	65	83	78	−23	−38	−36
1938	41	43	65	81	78	−24	−38	−37
1939	44	45	65	80	78	−21	−35	−34
1940	47	46	65	79	80	−18	−33	−33
1941	52	47	65	77	84	−13	−30	−32
1942	55	47	66	76	88	−11	−29	−33
1943	66	54	66	75	91	0	−21	−25
1944	79	60	67	74	98	12	−14	−19
1945	89	63	68	73	103	21	−10	−14
1946	105	67	70	73	114	35	−6	−9
1947	131	69	73	72	136	58	−3	−5
1948	135	64	75	72	152	60	−8	−17
1949	126	62	77	72	147	49	−10	−21

Column 1 – Sum of Table R-71, cols. 6 and 9.

Column 2 – Col. 1 divided by Table R-20, col. 3.

Column 3 – See note to Table R-72, col. 3. Losses are accumulated for twenty years since life expectancy of these buildings is estimated at forty years.

Column 4 – Same procedure as for col. 3 except expenditure series of col. 2 used.

Column 5 – Col. 4 multiplied by Table R-20, col. 3.

Column 6 – Col. 1 minus col. 3.

Column 7 – Col. 2 minus col. 4.

Column 8 – Col. 1 minus col. 5.

ADJUSTMENT FOR FIRE LOSSES ON NONRESIDENTIAL BUILDINGS
1897 to 1949

$ mill.

Year	Fire losses		Depreciation			Net adjustment		
	Original cost	1929 prices	Original cost	1929 prices	Replacement cost	Original cost	1929 prices	Replacement cost
	1	2	3	4	5	6	7	8
1897	23	55	22	49	21	1	6	2
1898	26	59	22	50	22	4	9	4
1899	30	65	23	51	24	7	14	6
1900	32	66	24	53	26	8	13	6
1901	33	70	25	55	26	8	15	7
1902	32	66	26	56	27	6	10	5
1903	29	58	26	57	28	3	1	1
1904	45	91	27	59	29	18	32	16
1905	33	65	28	61	31	5	4	2
1906	103	195	30	65	34	73	130	69
1907	42	78	33	69	37	9	9	5
1908	43	80	34	71	38	9	9	5
1909	37	70	35	72	38	2	−2	−1
1910	42	78	36	73	39	6	5	3
1911	43	79	36	74	40	7	5	3
1912	41	74	37	75	41	4	−1	0
1913	40	72	37	75	42	3	−3	−2
1914	44	81	38	76	41	6	5	3
1915	34	62	39	76	42	−5	−14	−8
1916	42	67	39	76	47	3	−9	−5
1917	49	69	40	77	55	9	−8	−6
1918	61	73	42	78	65	19	−5	−4
1919	54	52	43	78	80	11	−26	−26
1920	78	60	45	77	100	33	−17	−22
1921	86	86	48	77	77	38	9	9
1922	86	90	50	78	75	36	12	11
1923	92	90	53	80	82	39	10	10
1924	94	92	56	81	83	38	11	11
1925	96	93	59	81	84	37	12	12
1926	97	94	60	80	83	37	14	14
1927	79	78	61	77	78	18	1	1
1928	76	74	63	77	79	13	−3	−3
1929	74	74	64	77	77	10	−3	−3
1930	79	86	66	77	71	13	9	8
1931	70	80	68	77	67	2	3	3
1932	60	82	69	78	57	−9	4	3
1933	38	48	70	77	61	−32	−29	−23
1934	39	45	69	76	66	−30	−31	−27
1935	35	38	69	74	68	−34	−36	−33
1936	37	40	69	73	68	−32	−33	−31
1937	38	38	69	71	71	−31	−33	−33
1938	37	37	68	70	70	−31	−33	−33
1939	40	39	67	69	71	−27	−30	−31
1940	43	41	66	68	72	−23	−27	−29
1941	47	42	64	66	75	−17	−24	−28
1942	50	41	62	64	78	−12	−23	−28
1943	60	48	60	62	78	0	−14	−18
1944	72	55	59	60	79	13	−5	−7
1945	81	59	58	58	80	23	1	1
1946	96	60	58	56	90	38	4	6
1947	119	63	59	55	104	60	8	15
1948	122	59	61	54	111	61	5	11
1949	114	56	63	53	108	51	3	6

Q-1   TABLE Q–1

Column 1 – Sum of cols. 2 and 3.

Column 2 – Table Q-2, col. 1 minus Table Q-15, col. 6.

Column 3 – Table Q-14, col. 6 plus Table P-16, col. 8.

Column 4 – Sum of cols. 5 and 6.

Column 5 – Table Q-3, col. 1 minus Table Q-15, col. 7.

Column 6 – Table Q-14, col. 9 plus Table P-17, col. 6.

Column 7 – Sum of cols. 8 and 9.

Column 8 – Table Q-4, col. 1 minus Table Q-15, col. 8.

Column 9 – Table Q-14, col. 11 plus Table P-17, col. 10.

Q-2   TABLE Q–2

Column 1 – Sum of cols. 2–11.

Columns 2 to 11 – Table Q-5, cols. 2–11 minus Table Q-7, cols. 2–11. For content of cols. 5 and 11 see Table Q–10.

Q-3   TABLE Q–3

Column 1 – Sum of cols. 2–11.

Columns 2 to 11 – Table Q-6, cols. 2–11 minus Table Q-8, cols. 2–11.

$ mill.

Year	Original cost depreciation			1929 prices			Replacement cost depreciation		
	Total	New goods	Used goods	Total	New goods	Used goods	Total	New goods	Used goods
	1	2	3	4	5	6	7	8	9
1897	6	6	0	424	420	4	122	121	1
1898	29	29	0	325	323	2	102	102	0
1899	162	162	0	617	616	1	206	206	0
1900	173	173	0	435	437	-2	157	158	-1
1901	275	275	0	503	506	-3	196	197	-1
1902	345	344	1	618	618	0	246	246	0
1903	377	375	2	625	623	2	259	258	1
1904	318	315	3	454	451	3	209	207	2
1905	454	452	2	778	774	4	337	335	2
1906	594	590	4	1 025	1 023	2	455	454	1
1907	581	577	4	768	766	2	383	382	1
1908	188	185	3	35	32	3	64	62	2
1909	396	393	3	701	696	5	358	355	3
1910	448	446	2	729	725	4	387	384	3
1911	462	457	5	525	524	1	287	285	2
1912	604	600	4	601	601	0	396	394	2
1913	680	676	4	580	582	-2	405	406	-1
1914	362	356	6	77	74	3	122	118	4
1915	348	344	4	57	56	1	127	126	1
1916	1 101	1 100	1	915	916	-1	716	717	-1
1917	1 171	1 166	5	423	421	2	352	350	2
1918	1 018	973	45	-370	-402	32	-376	-414	38
1919	2 016	1 980	36	276	261	15	252	229	23
1920	3 448	3 386	62	588	566	22	728	694	34
1921	1 901	1 890	11	188	186	2	248	245	3
1922	1 833	1 798	35	1 036	998	38	1 067	1 024	43
1923	2 984	2 923	61	2 092	2 026	66	2 142	2 071	71
1924	2 454	2 390	64	1 829	1 760	69	1 854	1 780	74
1925	2 768	2 688	80	2 443	2 359	84	2 432	2 345	87
1926	2 648	2 610	38	2 695	2 646	49	2 603	2 555	48
1927	1 748	1 722	26	1 745	1 704	41	1 738	1 698	40
1928	1 653	1 581	72	1 911	1 830	81	1 566	1 487	79
1929	1 971	1 851	120	1 816	1 699	117	1 816	1 699	117
1930	-247	-256	9	210	186	24	66	44	22
1931	-1 750	-1 691	-59	-847	-809	-38	-848	-813	-35
1932	-3 232	-3 137	-95	-2 185	-2 110	-75	-1 796	-1 729	-67
1933	-2 925	-2 884	-41	-1 902	-1 882	-20	-1 320	-1 304	-16
1934	-1 891	-1 900	9	-984	-1 000	16	-653	-668	15
1935	-738	-802	64	417	327	90	439	361	78
1936	597	462	135	1 992	1 821	171	1 587	1 441	146
1937	1 149	919	230	2 213	1 969	244	1 816	1 593	223
1938	-358	-368	10	220	232	-12	177	186	-9
1939	692	629	63	1 593	1 539	54	1 219	1 167	52
1940	1 856	1 724	132	2 813	2 701	112	2 149	2 038	111
1941	3 104	2 964	140	3 585	3 496	89	2 835	2 740	95
1942	-169	-157	-12	-583	-506	-77	-1 351	-1 263	-88
1943	-332	-356	24	-1 387	-1 358	-29	-1 525	-1 493	-32
1944	4	-83	87	-1 488	-1 524	36	-1 435	-1 477	42
1945	1 056	928	128	-668	-747	79	-606	-699	93
1946	7 910	7 671	239	5 404	5 306	98	5 634	5 499	135
1947	11 390	11 088	302	6 609	6 522	87	8 076	7 938	138
1948	11 418	11 061	357	5 652	5 556	96	7 644	7 477	167
1949	11 220	11 080	140	5 707	5 743	-36	7 982	8 045	-63

NONFARM INDIVIDUALS' SAVING THROUGH MAIN TYPES OF CONSUMER
DURABLE GOODS; ORIGINAL COST DEPRECIATION: 1897 to 1949

$ mill.

Year	Total	Fur-niture	Household appliances	House furnishings	China etc.	Musical instruments	Books	Pas-senger cars	Passenger car accessories	Medical appliances	Miscel-laneous
	1	2	3	4	5	6	7	8	9	10	11
1897	4	5	12	−8	−10	2	−1	0	0	1	3
1898	29	4	7	−8	5	6	8	0	0	2	5
1899	163	26	21	21	46	15	12	3	0	3	16
1900	175	28	21	33	57	26	10	4	0	1	−5
1901	277	51	31	43	74	40	14	3	0	2	19
1902	345	65	36	67	93	51	14	4	0	2	13
1903	375	77	33	69	105	61	15	4	0	2	9
1904	318	74	24	48	89	44	15	11	0	1	12
1905	452	100	35	56	130	64	17	19	1	4	26
1906	605	140	50	87	168	76	12	35	1	5	31
1907	576	123	43	74	148	83	11	44	1	7	42
1908	183	59	15	1	9	34	4	62	2	4	−7
1909	390	114	24	46	70	53	11	57	2	6	7
1910	444	123	28	50	83	51	6	74	2	4	23
1911	455	137	38	45	93	65	12	34	2	3	26
1912	599	154	64	53	86	84	19	122	3	1	13
1913	676	174	53	65	93	96	31	131	3	6	24
1914	356	133	26	23	6	64	14	94	3	11	−18
1915	342	108	37	10	−13	57	19	129	4	21	−30
1916	1 100	198	74	101	145	97	21	417	9	25	13
1917	1 167	200	122	153	177	108	28	318	8	46	7
1918	977	220	137	203	81	111	32	43	0	115	35
1919	1 982	430	172	242	355	259	55	353	58	17	41
1920	3 393	680	344	486	437	341	83	829	65	31	97
1921	1 897	554	157	241	204	200	84	427	16	−6	20
1922	1 803	436	140	251	154	186	47	614	20	−27	−18
1923	2 928	508	230	381	394	244	42	1 045	38	−3	49
1924	2 394	587	238	287	159	343	63	687	24	−12	18
1925	2 691	539	255	295	216	339	54	929	50	−14	28
1926	2 612	523	280	212	232	402	50	854	35	−9	33
1927	1 719	514	247	191	151	322	73	173	20	5	23
1928	1 577	414	146	164	135	407	55	245	0	−3	14
1929	1 847	343	200	159	126	429	66	431	52	8	33
1930	−257	82	86	−46	−79	290	19	−615	19	10	−23
1931	−1 693	−59	−28	−179	−250	−175	8	−943	−13	−6	−48
1932	−3 141	−333	−232	−375	−327	−399	−86	−1 212	−50	−26	−101
1933	−2 891	−387	−171	−435	−418	−484	−86	−721	−47	−23	−119
1934	−1 905	−341	−73	−299	−313	−464	−69	−265	−4	10	−87
1935	−808	−220	−2	−231	−253	−448	−50	416	26	14	−60
1936	459	−60	106	−1	−131	−355	−22	845	61	23	−7
1937	918	−12	193	66	15	−303	13	806	61	37	42
1938	−368	−103	73	22	6	−332	2	−102	−1	20	47
1939	630	2	130	147	71	−238	13	401	18	23	63
1940	1 725	112	227	240	180	−102	25	902	29	28	84
1941	2 966	322	447	410	385	68	42	1 131	77	48	36
1942	−155	263	3	401	509	159	95	−1 760	−2	55	122
1943	−353	216	−393	404	584	−53	162	−1 452	15	75	89
1944	−78	293	−463	370	617	−96	248	−1 228	−5	73	113
1945	934	507	−300	399	834	−47	307	−1 065	81	61	157
1946	7 679	1 145	795	913	1 284	724	360	1 500	454	68	436
1947	11 100	1 431	1 751	1 074	1 136	977	292	3 449	472	43	475
1948	11 070	1 575	1 727	1 023	1 001	897	209	3 768	378	51	441
1949	11 084	1 414	1 130	659	694	982	125	5 420	310	47	303

NONFARM INDIVIDUALS' SAVING THROUGH MAIN TYPES OF CONSUMER DURABLE GOODS; 1929 PRICES: 1897 to 1949

$ mill.

Year	Total	Fur-niture	Household appliances	House furnishings	China etc.	Musical instruments	Books	Pas-senger cars	Passenger car accessories	Medical appliances	Miscel-laneous
	1	2	3	4	5	6	7	8	9	10	11
1897	417	150	69	28	56	17	20	0	0	6	71
1898	322	86	37	13	69	29	34	0	0	4	50
1899	617	139	75	99	159	42	40	2	0	5	56
1900	439	82	60	81	168	57	20	2	0	0	-31
1901	507	135	76	102	85	73	22	2	0	2	10
1902	618	151	86	159	130	78	20	2	0	3	-11
1903	620	166	69	133	161	96	18	2	0	2	-27
1904	456	157	37	55	135	68	15	8	0	0	-19
1905	772	229	65	92	253	92	18	6	0	7	10
1906	1 056	292	94	138	376	115	5	10	1	8	17
1907	760	163	54	81	315	110	-8	11	1	9	24
1908	26	25	-8	-31	66	37	-19	17	1	5	-67
1909	689	175	29	89	277	73	11	44	1	10	-20
1910	719	141	29	84	320	72	-4	57	2	5	13
1911	517	58	35	39	268	76	-8	34	1	4	10
1912	597	32	73	55	214	130	-1	114	3	-3	-20
1913	579	1	42	63	177	144	17	134	4	2	-5
1914	72	-48	-2	-3	-51	107	-6	130	3	13	-71
1915	52	-74	26	-12	-89	78	4	175	5	28	-89
1916	914	61	82	24	99	171	-1	486	11	28	-47
1917	419	69	121	-101	-145	178	-9	342	10	40	-86
1918	-403	-37	77	-158	-379	114	-18	-4	0	97	-95
1919	258	38	93	-96	-77	233	-6	150	45	-12	-110
1920	566	-50	182	-30	-117	213	-7	416	38	-14	-65
1921	189	58	35	-27	-213	107	21	304	10	-22	-84
1922	1 002	73	48	111	-74	142	21	755	28	-18	-84
1923	2 031	132	104	206	55	154	20	1 275	53	7	25
1924	1 765	293	136	202	-91	238	51	888	39	0	9
1925	2 364	313	178	218	83	283	53	1 145	63	-4	32
1926	2 651	355	228	193	204	337	63	1 162	49	0	60
1927	1 702	399	210	213	171	244	88	295	26	10	46
1928	1 827	327	138	228	170	328	68	545	-4	-2	29
1929	1 695	290	196	234	175	363	76	262	43	7	49
1930	186	90	119	37	13	557	32	-680	23	8	-13
1931	-808	103	44	-14	-145	166	23	-961	14	-7	-31
1932	-2 110	-96	-132	-162	-162	-103	-72	-1 266	-26	-22	-69
1933	-1 888	-169	-21	-296	-288	-298	-64	-615	-25	-17	-95
1934	-1 004	-157	109	-211	-202	-289	-49	-169	14	16	-66
1935	321	78	188	-152	-160	-282	-28	642	49	19	-33
1936	1 817	310	325	86	-57	-75	0	1 077	87	25	39
1937	1 967	296	404	87	67	-25	34	902	80	37	85
1938	231	200	190	52	71	-149	13	-252	8	20	78
1939	1 541	366	276	186	116	82	19	344	28	24	100
1940	2 702	468	428	239	191	345	30	841	27	27	106
1941	3 497	541	668	349	335	596	43	819	71	48	27
1942	-504	270	-89	234	274	566	103	-1 942	-60	52	88
1943	-1 357	182	-588	225	328	-135	157	-1 597	-30	63	38
1944	-1 521	114	-685	120	275	-336	244	-1 335	-37	58	61
1945	-744	207	-516	92	384	-270	296	-1 141	60	46	98
1946	5 311	657	505	408	609	1 390	302	714	358	50	318
1947	6 528	715	1 119	340	311	1 561	166	1 722	297	22	275
1948	5 558	645	1 012	263	188	1 229	68	1 735	182	21	215
1949	5 743	605	651	134	108	1 464	16	2 511	104	14	136

TABLE Q-4

Column 1 – Sum of cols. 2–11.

Columns 2 to 11 – Table Q-5, cols. 2-11 minus Table Q-9, cols. 2–11.

TABLE Q-5

Column 1 – 1897–1949: Sum of cols. 2–11.

Columns 2 to 7 – 1897–1928: Figures for total consumers' expenditures on durable goods at retail prices obtained by: (1) increasing W. H. Shaw's estimates of expenditures at manufactures' prices (*Value of Commodity Output since 1869*, pp. 40–51, 68) by an estimated retail markup ratio for the different commodities (cf. Table Q-10); (2) adjusting for inventory changes; for years prior to 1919 this adjustment was assumed to be negligible; for years 1919–1929 following percentage changes were derived from estimates by Simon Kuznets (cf. *Commodity Flow and Capital Formation*, p. 307, line 10 as percentage of line 9):

1919	–6.0 percent		1924	–0.6 percent	
1920	–3.3	,,	1925	–0.7	,,
1921	11.4	,,	1926	–2.1	,,
1922	–3.3	,,	1927	2.6	,,
1923	–6.0	,,	1928	–2.7	,,
			1929	–1.2	,,

(3) linking resulting series to Department of Commerce estimate for 1929. This procedure was extended backwards for years prior to 1897 whenever it was required for calculation of depreciation. Annual estimates for years 1870–1878 and 1880–1888 were derived by linear interpolation between Shaw's figures. Estimates of expenditures on durable goods by nonfarmers obtained by applying to figures for total expenditures the ratio of farm income to total national income given in Table A-4, col. 4 and Table A-5, col. 3.

1929–1949: Expenditures at retail prices obtained from *Survey of Current Business, National Income Supplement*, various issues, split between nonfarmers and farmers according to ratio given in Table A-5, col. 3.

Column 8 – 1897–1949: Total consumers' expenditures on passenger cars as estimated in Table P-13, col. 1 minus farmers' expenditures (cf. Table A-24, col. 8).

Column 9 – 1897–1940: Same method as for cols. 2–7, except that figures are further adjusted to include only amounts spent by consumers (cf. Table Q-11).

1941–1949: Table Q-13, col. 8 multiplied by the complement of the farmers' share (cf. Table A-5, col. 3).

Columns 10 and 11 – 1897–1949: Same procedure as for cols. 2–7.

TABLE Q-6

Column 1 – Sum of cols 2–11.

Columns 2 to 11 – Table Q-5, cols. 2–11 deflated by appropriate price index as given in Table Q-16.

NONFARM INDIVIDUALS' SAVING THROUGH MAIN TYPES OF CONSUMER DURABLE GOODS; REPLACEMENT COST DEPRECIATION: 1897 to 1949

$ mill.

Year	Total	Fur-niture	Household appliances	House furnishings	China etc.	Musical instruments	Books	Pas-senger cars	Passenger car accessories	Medical appliances	Miscel-laneous
	1	2	3	4	5	6	7	8	9	10	11
1897	120	36	18	8	19	7	6	0	0	2	24
1898	102	23	10	3	24	11	11	0	0	2	18
1899	206	39	22	30	58	17	13	4	0	2	21
1900	159	26	19	27	63	25	7	4	0	0	−12
1901	197	44	26	35	39	35	9	4	0	1	4
1902	246	52	30	55	59	42	8	4	0	1	−5
1903	257	58	25	48	74	52	7	4	0	1	−12
1904	209	56	14	21	61	37	6	12	0	0	2
1905	334	81	25	34	111	52	8	14	1	3	5
1906	469	110	37	55	161	65	2	27	0	4	8
1907	379	68	23	35	137	67	−3	35	1	5	11
1908	59	10	−3	−11	27	22	−9	54	2	2	−35
1909	352	71	12	35	105	42	5	83	3	6	−10
1910	381	62	13	34	121	41	−2	99	3	3	7
1911	281	30	17	17	107	48	−4	57	2	2	5
1912	392	19	37	24	89	75	0	157	4	−2	−11
1913	404	0	22	29	77	85	10	178	4	2	−3
1914	117	−31	−1	−1	−22	60	−5	146	4	8	−41
1915	123	−48	14	−5	−39	46	2	182	5	18	−52
1916	716	41	46	14	51	95	−1	471	10	20	−31
1917	349	47	78	−81	−104	103	−7	340	9	34	−70
1918	−415	−32	60	−165	−333	79	−17	−4	0	95	−98
1919	226	41	80	−104	−73	195	−6	192	54	−14	−139
1920	694	−87	196	−44	−135	224	−10	603	56	−19	−90
1921	248	77	36	−32	−237	105	24	394	14	−27	−106
1922	1 029	86	48	113	−71	126	22	793	30	−19	−99
1923	2 076	161	114	228	63	153	22	1 250	52	7	26
1924	1 785	329	145	213	−106	245	52	861	37	0	9
1925	2 350	337	186	238	88	272	54	1 087	60	−4	32
1926	2 559	372	233	207	206	330	61	1 049	44	0	57
1927	1 696	407	213	224	172	245	86	273	23	9	44
1928	1 484	331	136	223	172	331	67	201	−4	−2	29
1929	1 695	290	196	234	175	363	76	262	43	7	49
1930	44	86	114	36	12	397	31	−648	21	8	−13
1931	−812	83	40	−11	−130	82	21	−873	11	−6	−29
1932	−1 729	−61	−101	−117	−130	−37	−63	−1 126	−19	−21	−54
1933	−1 308	−108	−15	−219	−226	−96	−54	−484	−18	−16	−72
1934	−671	−109	76	−172	−160	−100	−40	−139	10	15	−52
1935	357	50	131	−122	−126	−98	−23	520	34	17	−26
1936	1 438	204	226	71	−46	−26	0	894	63	23	29
1937	1 591	209	287	76	56	−10	28	785	59	35	66
1938	185	137	139	44	57	−54	11	−236	6	19	62
1939	1 168	245	195	155	95	27	17	316	20	22	76
1940	2 039	320	293	207	162	112	25	790	20	26	84
1941	2 741	417	475	325	308	203	37	850	57	46	23
1942	−1 262	236	−72	242	297	214	90	−2 346	−57	51	83
1943	−1 492	162	−494	239	366	−54	145	−1 930	−29	65	38
1944	−1 474	114	−624	138	333	−137	229	−1 615	−35	61	62
1945	−696	226	−503	114	497	−112	284	−1 411	59	48	102
1946	5 505	774	537	549	861	626	314	1 024	405	54	361
1947	7 946	931	1 377	529	509	804	198	2 834	384	24	356
1948	7 480	931	1 323	435	328	681	87	3 112	259	24	300
1949	8 045	846	822	213	182	801	20	4 786	170	17	188

NONFARM INDIVIDUALS' EXPENDITURES ON MAIN TYPES
OF CONSUMER DURABLE GOODS; ORIGINAL COST: 1897 to 1949

$ mill.

Year	Total	Fur-niture	Household appliances	House furnishings	China etc.	Musical instruments	Books	Pas-senger cars	Passenger car accessories	Medical appliances	Miscel-laneous
	1	2	3	4	5	6	7	8	9	10	11
1897	689	134	49	132	152	38	39	0	0	11	134
1898	721	135	45	132	167	43	48	0	0	12	139
1899	868	159	60	162	211	53	53	4	0	14	152
1900	901	164	63	177	227	66	52	6	0	13	133
1901	1 024	191	75	190	249	82	58	7	0	15	157
1902	1 118	209	84	218	275	96	60	9	0	16	151
1903	1 186	226	85	228	299	110	63	11	0	17	147
1904	1 172	229	79	216	298	97	65	21	0	16	151
1905	1 360	261	94	233	358	120	70	35	1	20	168
1906	1 590	309	115	276	420	137	68	62	1	23	179
1907	1 652	300	115	278	427	149	70	88	2	27	196
1908	1 340	243	93	216	309	105	65	129	3	26	151
1909	1 621	305	106	271	386	127	75	151	4	30	166
1910	1 761	322	115	286	417	129	72	199	5	30	186
1911	1 858	346	131	291	447	148	80	186	5	31	193
1912	2 095	372	164	309	459	172	89	310	7	30	183
1913	2 312	403	161	330	484	191	105	395	8	36	199
1914	2 092	375	140	298	412	166	91	397	9	44	160
1915	2 179	362	157	292	401	165	99	487	11	58	147
1916	3 110	465	202	391	569	213	104	889	18	69	190
1917	3 421	484	262	458	618	233	115	948	20	100	183
1918	3 454	523	291	533	543	246	125	773	14	192	214
1919	4 728	757	343	604	852	408	155	1 187	79	117	226
1920	6 520	1 044	543	896	986	515	193	1 803	103	147	290
1921	5 378	960	387	702	799	400	206	1 512	68	124	220
1922	5 551	877	393	754	782	409	180	1 780	83	110	183
1923	7 051	985	511	937	1 068	492	183	2 375	118	129	253
1924	6 989	1 105	550	904	886	623	214	2 248	118	113	228
1925	7 771	1 100	602	976	996	656	217	2 719	153	106	246
1926	8 231	1 125	667	955	1 067	760	225	2 915	151	106	260
1927	7 807	1 158	678	989	1 031	722	262	2 440	151	119	257
1928	8 056	1 101	616	1 013	1 062	853	258	2 649	140	110	254
1929	8 705	1 071	705	1 054	1 091	929	282	2 973	203	120	277
1930	6 764	842	624	871	888	857	243	1 913	182	124	220
1931	5 177	723	532	738	713	450	236	1 332	153	110	190
1932	3 405	461	326	533	624	254	142	732	112	88	133
1933	3 237	409	378	437	496	181	138	900	108	85	105
1934	3 893	457	479	529	556	212	149	1 129	141	115	126
1935	4 806	586	555	558	579	224	162	1 719	163	118	142
1936	6 069	759	670	757	659	304	186	2 219	201	128	186
1937	6 668	823	769	805	772	350	217	2 335	217	150	230
1938	5 359	746	656	738	733	313	200	1 425	171	145	232
1939	6 290	859	714	838	766	388	205	1 912	203	159	246
1940	7 504	970	821	923	857	471	211	2 583	226	174	268
1941	9 061	1 184	1 065	1 114	1 079	581	226	3 092	289	207	224
1942	6 063	1 137	636	1 155	1 253	649	286	176	220	230	321
1943	5 730	1 099	228	1 229	1 404	416	372	160	244	271	307
1944	5 924	1 181	137	1 272	1 532	332	486	101	235	295	353
1945	7 008	1 404	289	1 379	1 862	363	583	61	335	310	422
1946	14 358	2 073	1 419	1 996	2 466	1 185	682	2 684	766	344	743
1947	19 112	2 414	2 495	2 293	2 494	1 541	661	5 129	900	345	840
1948	20 742	2 628	2 634	2 400	2 536	1 584	621	6 153	944	374	868
1949	22 555	2 542	2 177	2 186	2 401	1 804	577	8 665	1 024	390	789

NONFARM INDIVIDUALS' EXPENDITURES ON MAIN TYPES OF CONSUMER DURABLE GOODS; 1929 PRICES: 1897 to 1949

$ mill.

Year	Total	Fur-niture	Household appliances	House furnishings	China etc.	Musical instruments	Books	Pas-senger cars	Passenger car accessories	Medical appliances	Miscel-laneous
	1	2	3	4	5	6	7	8	9	10	11
1897	2 289	554	186	445	448	97	131	0	0	31	397
1898	2 256	502	160	439	473	112	149	0	0	32	389
1899	2 623	567	205	536	581	129	160	2	0	35	408
1900	2 516	521	198	531	611	148	145	3	0	31	328
1901	2 645	586	222	563	544	169	152	4	0	34	371
1902	2 820	615	242	634	603	180	154	5	0	36	351
1903	2 897	643	236	628	655	204	157	6	0	36	332
1904	2 819	648	213	571	658	183	159	14	0	34	339
1905	3 229	736	251	624	811	213	167	15	0	42	370
1906	3 641	823	294	691	983	243	157	23	1	45	381
1907	3 481	717	268	658	978	246	146	28	1	49	390
1908	2 837	591	214	563	771	180	135	41	1	47	294
1909	3 581	754	256	697	1 018	221	165	80	2	55	333
1910	3 726	735	263	709	1 108	226	150	114	3	54	364
1911	3 641	664	276	678	1 109	236	146	112	3	55	362
1912	3 841	646	323	704	1 109	297	153	225	5	49	330
1913	3 957	620	300	720	1 120	322	171	297	7	55	345
1914	3 581	578	260	663	929	297	148	353	8	68	277
1915	3 669	556	291	661	910	278	157	468	11	87	250
1916	4 704	695	355	699	1 109	382	151	917	20	95	281
1917	4 422	711	407	570	866	404	143	953	22	118	228
1918	3 721	611	373	506	618	354	134	709	14	195	207
1919	4 461	692	397	558	907	488	145	924	66	104	180
1920	4 839	609	504	612	849	489	142	1 245	71	108	210
1921	4 497	723	374	606	720	405	171	1 169	52	103	174
1922	5 377	745	397	743	825	460	173	1 694	79	106	155
1923	6 641	811	467	846	931	495	174	2 423	120	123	251
1924	6 717	985	515	858	767	606	208	2 319	122	109	228
1925	7 706	1 020	576	896	934	684	216	2 865	161	106	248
1926	8 468	1 076	654	892	1 054	775	233	3 231	167	110	276
1927	7 947	1 137	668	940	1 026	719	268	2 640	164	122	263
1928	8 460	1 088	623	998	1 055	845	261	3 084	145	111	250
1929	8 705	1 071	705	1 054	1 091	929	282	2 973	203	120	277
1930	7 373	882	652	897	943	1 203	250	2 007	194	124	221
1931	6 303	905	597	873	793	906	255	1 467	191	111	205
1932	4 756	714	426	738	778	704	160	822	152	93	169
1933	4 659	643	540	591	634	557	166	1 144	153	93	138
1934	5 337	658	689	652	702	608	180	1 375	191	124	158
1935	6 627	903	794	691	731	648	198	2 122	228	128	184
1936	8 302	1 155	964	920	812	885	225	2 673	279	137	252
1937	8 759	1 164	1 082	921	918	979	258	2 684	295	159	299
1938	7 132	1 092	900	880	909	898	235	1 521	246	154	297
1939	8 513	1 284	1 010	1 005	940	1 175	238	2 085	285	169	322
1940	9 964	1 422	1 201	1 064	1 010	1 454	246	2 748	301	182	336
1941	11 200	1 535	1 498	1 199	1 177	1 710	259	2 979	360	217	266
1942	7 351	1 298	779	1 119	1 154	1 721	328	146	231	236	339
1943	6 327	1 235	272	1 158	1 258	1 043	402	132	256	266	305
1944	5 995	1 182	150	1 104	1 264	818	518	84	246	283	346
1945	6 713	1 287	297	1 120	1 437	875	607	49	343	294	404
1946	13 137	1 761	1 335	1 485	1 743	2 633	655	1 873	677	320	655
1947	15 191	1 854	2 027	1 473	1 522	2 992	555	3 116	694	309	649
1948	15 128	1 820	2 015	1 452	1 457	2 859	485	3 430	666	321	623
1949	16 210	1 817	1 725	1 370	1 429	3 298	456	4 546	672	324	573

Q-7   TABLE Q–7

Column 1 – Sum of cols. 2–11.

Columns 2 to 11 – Table Q-5, cols. 2–11 depreciated on basis of rates given in Table Q-12.

Q-8   TABLE Q–8

Column 1 – Sum of cols. 2–11.

Columns 2 to 11 – Table Q-6, cols. 2–11 depreciated on basis of rates given in Table Q-12.

Q-9   TABLE Q–9

Column 1 – Sum of cols. 2–11.

Columns 2 to 11 – Table Q-8, cols. 2-11 multiplied by appropriate price index from Table Q-16.

682

DEPRECIATION ON NONFARM INDIVIDUALS' HOLDINGS OF MAIN TYPES OF CONSUMER DURABLE GOODS; ORIGINAL COST: 1897 to 1949

$ mill.

Year	Total	Fur- niture	Household appliances	House furnishings	China etc.	Musical instruments	Books	Pas- senger cars	Passenger car accessories	Medical appliances	Miscel- laneous
	1	2	3	4	5	6	7	8	9	10	11
1897	685	129	37	140	162	36	40	0	0	10	131
1898	692	131	38	140	162	37	40	0	0	10	134
1899	705	133	39	141	165	38	41	1	0	11	136
1900	726	136	42	144	170	40	42	2	0	12	138
1901	747	140	44	147	175	42	44	4	0	13	138
1902	773	144	48	151	182	45	46	5	0	14	138
1903	811	149	52	159	194	49	48	7	0	15	138
1904	854	155	55	168	209	53	50	10	0	15	139
1905	908	161	59	177	228	56	53	16	0	16	142
1906	985	169	65	189	252	61	56	27	0	18	148
1907	1 076	177	72	204	279	66	59	44	1	20	154
1908	1 157	184	78	215	300	71	61	67	1	22	158
1909	1 231	191	82	225	316	74	64	94	2	24	159
1910	1 317	199	87	236	334	78	66	125	3	26	163
1911	1 403	209	93	246	354	83	68	152	3	28	167
1912	1 496	218	100	256	373	88	70	188	4	29	170
1913	1 636	229	108	265	391	95	74	264	5	30	175
1914	1 736	242	114	275	406	102	77	303	6	33	178
1915	1 837	254	120	282	414	108	80	358	7	37	177
1916	2 010	267	128	290	424	116	83	472	9	44	177
1917	2 254	284	140	305	441	125	87	630	12	54	176
1918	2 477	303	154	330	462	135	93	730	14	77	179
1919	2 746	327	171	362	497	149	100	834	21	100	185
1920	3 127	364	199	410	549	174	110	974	38	116	193
1921	3 481	406	230	461	595	200	122	1 085	52	130	200
1922	3 748	441	253	503	628	223	133	1 166	63	137	201
1923	4 123	477	281	556	674	248	141	1 330	80	132	204
1924	4 595	518	312	617	727	280	151	1 561	94	125	210
1925	5 080	561	347	681	780	317	163	1 790	103	120	218
1926	5 619	002	387	743	835	358	175	2 061	110	115	227
1927	6 088	644	431	798	880	400	189	2 267	131	114	234
1928	6 479	687	470	849	927	446	203	2 404	140	113	240
1929	6 858	728	505	895	965	500	216	2 542	151	112	244
1930	7 021	760	538	917	967	567	224	2 528	163	114	243
1931	6 870	782	560	917	963	625	228	2 275	166	116	238
1932	6 546	794	558	908	951	653	228	1 944	162	114	234
1933	6 128	796	549	872	914	665	224	1 621	155	108	224
1934	5 798	798	552	828	869	676	218	1 394	145	105	213
1935	5 614	806	557	789	832	672	212	1 303	137	104	202
1936	5 610	819	564	758	790	659	208	1 374	140	105	193
1937	5 750	835	576	739	757	653	204	1 529	156	113	188
1938	5 727	849	583	716	727	645	198	1 527	172	125	185
1939	5 660	857	584	691	695	626	192	1 511	185	136	183
1940	5 779	858	594	683	677	573	186	1 681	197	146	184
1941	6 095	862	618	704	694	513	184	1 961	212	159	188
1942	6 218	874	633	754	744	490	191	1 936	222	175	199
1943	6 083	883	621	825	820	469	210	1 612	229	196	218
1944	6 002	888	600	902	915	428	238	1 329	240	222	240
1945	6 074	897	589	980	1 028	410	276	1 126	254	249	265
1946	6 679	928	624	1 083	1 182	461	322	1 184	312	276	307
1947	8 012	983	744	1 219	1 358	564	369	1 680	428	302	365
1948	9 672	1 053	907	1 377	1 535	687	412	2 385	566	323	427
1949	11 471	1 128	1 047	1 527	1 707	822	452	3 245	714	343	486

DEPRECIATION ON NONFARM INDIVIDUALS' HOLDINGS OF MAIN TYPES
OF CONSUMER DURABLE GOODS; 1929 PRICES: 1897 to 1949

$ mill.

Year	Total	Furniture	Household appliances	House furnishings	China etc.	Musical instruments	Books	Passenger cars	Passenger car accessories	Medical appliances	Miscellaneous
	1	2	3	4	5	6	7	8	9	10	11
1897	1 872	404	117	417	392	80	111	0	0	25	326
1898	1 934	416	123	426	404	83	115	0	0	28	339
1899	2 006	428	130	437	422	87	120	0	0	30	352
1900	2 077	439	138	450	443	91	125	1	0	31	359
1901	2 138	451	146	461	459	96	130	2	0	32	361
1902	2 202	464	156	475 .	473	102	134	3	0	33	362
1903	2 277	477	167	495	494	108	139	4	0	34	359
1904	2 363	491	176	516	523	115	144	6	0	34	358
1905	2 457	507	186	532	558	121	149	9	0	35	360
1906	2 585	531	200	553	607	128	152	13	0	37	364
1907	2 721	554	214	577	663	136	154	17	0	40	366
1908	2 811	566	222	594	705	143	154	24	0	42	361
1909	2 892	579	227	608	741	148	154	36	1	45	353
1910	3 007	594	234	625	788	154	154	57	1	49	351
1911	3 124	606	241	639	841	160	154	78	2	51	352
1912	3 244	614	250	649	895	167	154	111	2	52	350
1913	3 378	619	258	657	943	178	154	163	3	53	350
1914	3 509	626	262	666	980	190	154	223	5	55	348
1915	3 617	630	265	673	999	200	153	293	6	59	339
1916	3 790	634	273	675	1 010	211	152	431	9	67	328
1917	4 003	642	286	671	1 011	226	152	611	12	78	314
1918	4 124	648	296	664	997	240	152	713	14	98	302
1919	4 203	654	304	654	984	255	151	774	21	116	290
1920	4 273	659	322	642	966	276	149	829	33	122	275
1921	4 308	665	339	633	933	298	150	865	42	125	258
1922	4 375	672	349	632	899	318	152	939	51	124	239
1923	4 610	679	363	640	876	341	154	1 148	67	116	226
1924	4 952	692	379	656	858	368	157	1 431	83	109	219
1925	5 342	707	398	678	851	401	163	1 720	98	110	216
1926	5 817	721	426	699	850	438	170	2 069	118	110	216
1927	6 245	738	458	727	855	475	180	2 345	138	112	217
1928	6 633	761	485	770	885	517	193	2 539	149	113	221
1929	7 010	781	509	820	916	566	206	2 711	160	113	228
1930	7 187	792	533	860	930	646	218	2 687	171	116	234
1931	7 111	802	553	887	938	740	232	2 428	177	118	236
1932	6 866	810	558	900	940	807	232	2 088	178	115	238
1933	6 547	812	561	887	922	855	230	1 759	178	110	233
1934	6 341	815	580	863	904	897	229	1 544	177	108	224
1935	6 306	825	606	843	891	930	226	1 480	179	109	217
1936	6 485	845	639	834	869	960	225	1 596	192	112	213
1937	6 792	868	678	834	851	1 004	224	1 782	215	122	214
1938	6 901	892	710	828	838	1 047	222	1 773	238	134	219
1939	6 972	918	734	819	824	1 093	219	1 741	257	145	222
1940	7 262	954	773	825	819	1 109	216	1 907	274	155	230
1941	7 703	994	830	850	842	1 114	216	2 160	289	169	239
1942	7 855	1 028	868	885	880	1 155	225	2 088	291	184	251
1943	7 684	1 053	860	933	930	1 178	245	1 729	286	203	267
1944	7 516	1 068	835	984	989	1 154	274	1 419	283	225	285
1945	7 457	1 080	813	1 028	1 053	1 145	311	1 190	283	248	306
1946	7 826	1 104	830	1 077	1 134	1 243	353	1 159	319	270	337
1947	8 663	1 139	908	1 133	1 211	1 431	389	1 394	397	287	374
1948	9 570	1 175	1 003	1 189	1 269	1 630	417	1 695	484	300	408
1949	10 467	1 212	1 074	1 236	1 321	1 834	440	2 035	568	310	437

DEPRECIATION ON NONFARM INDIVIDUALS' HOLDINGS OF MAIN TYPES OF CONSUMER DURABLE GOODS; REPLACEMENT COST: 1897 to 1949

$ mill.

Year	Total	Fur-niture	Household appliances	House furnishings	China etc.	Musical instruments	Books	Pas-senger cars	Passenger car accessories	Medical appliances	Miscel-laneous
	1	2	3	4	5	6	7	8	9	10	11
1897	569	98	31	124	133	31	33	0	0	9	110
1898	619	112	35	129	143	32	37	0	0	10	121
1899	662	120	38	132	153	36	40	0	0	12	131
1900	742	138	44	150	164	41	45	2	0	13	145
1901	827	147	49	155	210	47	49	3	0	14	153
1902	872	157	54	163	216	54	52	5	0	15	156
1903	929	168	60	180	225	58	56	7	0	16	159
1904	963	173	65	195	237	60	59	9	0	16	149
1905	1 026	180	69	199	247	68	62	21	0	17	163
1906	1 121	199	78	221	259	72	66	35	1	19	171
1907	1 273	232	92	243	290	82	73	53	1	22	185
1908	1 281	233	96	227	282	83	74	75	1	24	186
1909	1 269	234	94	236	281	85	70	68	1	24	176
1910	1 380	260	102	252	296	88	74	100	2	27	179
1911	1 577	316	114	274	340	100	84	129	3	29	188
1912	1 703	353	127	285	370	97	89	153	3	32	194
1913	1 908	403	139	301	407	106	95	217	4	34	202
1914	1 975	406	141	299	434	106	96	251	5	36	201
1915	2 056	410	143	297	440	119	97	305	6	40	199
1916	2 394	424	156	377	518	118	105	418	8	49	221
1917	3 072	437	184	539	722	130	122	608	11	66	253
1918	3 869	555	231	698	876	167	142	777	14	97	312
1919	4 502	716	263	708	925	213	161	995	25	131	365
1920	5 826	1 131	347	940	1 121	291	203	1 200	47	166	380
1921	5 130	883	351	734	1 036	295	182	1 118	54	151	326
1922	4 522	791	345	641	853	283	158	987	53	129	282
1923	4 975	824	397	709	1 005	339	161	1 125	66	122	227
1924	5 204	776	405	691	992	378	162	1 387	81	113	219
1925	5 421	763	416	738	908	384	163	1 632	93	110	214
1926	5 672	753	434	748	861	430	164	1 866	107	100	203
1927	6 111	751	465	765	859	477	176	2 167	128	110	213
1928	6 572	770	480	790	890	522	191	2 448	144	112	225
1929	7 010	781	509	820	916	566	206	2 711	160	113	228
1930	6 720	756	510	835	876	460	212	2 561	161	116	233
1931	5 989	640	492	749	843	368	215	2 205	142	116	219
1932	5 134	522	427	650	754	291	205	1 858	131	109	187
1933	4 545	517	393	656	722	277	192	1 384	126	101	177
1934	4 564	566	403	701	716	312	189	1 268	131	100	178
1935	4 449	536	424	680	705	322	185	1 199	129	101	168
1936	4 631	555	444	686	705	330	186	1 325	138	105	157
1937	5 077	614	482	729	716	360	189	1 550	158	115	164
1938	5 174	609	517	694	676	367	189	1 661	165	126	170
1939	5 122	614	519	683	671	361	188	1 596	183	137	170
1940	5 465	650	528	716	695	359	186	1 793	206	148	184
1941	6 320	767	590	789	771	378	189	2 242	232	161	201
1942	7 325	901	708	913	956	435	196	2 522	277	179	238
1943	7 222	937	722	990	1 038	470	227	2 090	273	206	269
1944	7 398	1 067	761	1 134	1 199	469	257	1 716	270	234	291
1945	7 704	1 178	792	1 265	1 365	475	299	1 472	276	262	320
1946	8 853	1 299	882	1 447	1 605	559	368	1 660	361	290	382
1947	11 166	1 483	1 118	1 764	1 985	737	463	2 295	516	321	484
1948	13 262	1 697	1 311	1 965	2 208	903	534	3 041	685	350	568
1949	14 510	1 696	1 355	1 973	2 219	1 003	557	3 879	854	373	601

TABLE Q–10

Lines 1, 2, 6, 7, and 8 – Unpublished preliminary estimates by National Bureau of Economic Research for years 1899, 1909, 1919, and 1929; linked to estimates based on data of Department of Commerce for year 1929 and applied to periods 1867–1900, 1901–1910, 1911–1919, and 1920–1929, respectively.

Line 3 – Estimate for 1929 based on data of Department of Commerce extrapolated back by line 1.

Line 4 – Estimate for 1929 based on data of Department of Commerce extrapolated back on basis of unpublished estimates by National Bureau of Economic Research for jewelry stores for years 1899, 1909, 1919, and 1929.

Line 5 – Estimate for 1929 based on data of Department of Commerce extrapolated back by line 1.

Line 9 – Estimate for 1929 based on data of Department of Commerce held constant for all periods.

Line 10 – Weighted average of lines 10a, b, and c.

Line 10a – Estimate for 1929 based on data of Department of Commerce extrapolated back by line 4.

Line 10b – Estimate for 1929 based on data of Department of Commerce extrapolated back by line 8.

Line 10c – Estimate for 1929 based on data of Department of Commerce held constant for all periods.

TABLE Q–11

Estimates are based on data of Department of Commerce showing amounts spent on consumers' durables by consumers and nonconsumers in years 1929, 1935, and 1939. As ratios based on these data for individual categories were fairly constant, showing no trend but a slight cyclical fluctuation, an average of the three years was taken and applied to all years prior to 1929. However, estimates for wheel goods were modified on basis of data in Lough, W. M., *High-Level Consumption*, pp. 253–257. Low values for passenger car accessories are due to fact that they cover only accessories bought directly by consumers but exclude those installed by garages, service stations, etc., which figure as part of repair bills classified as current expenditures. As no data were available upon which to base a satisfactory consumer allocation for musical instruments, it was arbitrarily assumed to be 90 percent.

MARKUP[1] ON CONSUMER DURABLE GOODS
Selected Periods: 1867 to 1929

Percent

Commodity	1867–1900	1901–1910	1911–1919	1920–1929
1. Furniture	45	52	59	66
2. Household appliances	62	69	79	88
3. House furnishings	48	55	63	70
4. China, tableware, utensils, jewelry and watches	77	85	93	100
5. Musical instruments, radios	82	95	108	121
6. Books	56	60	76	86
7. Passenger cars	45	45	45	45
8. Passenger car accessories	123	123	123	140
9. Ophthalmic and orthopedic products	274	274	274	274
10. Miscellaneous	71	73	82	89
(a) Luggage	82	91	100	109
(b) Wheel goods, durable toys, and sports equipment	70	70	70	90
(c) Pleasure craft	20	20	20	20

[1] Excess of retail over producers' prices.

CONSUMER ALLOCATION OF CONSUMER DURABLE GOODS
Selected Periods: 1867 to 1929

Percent

Commodity	1867–1919	1920–1928	1929
1. Furniture	97	97	97
2. Household appliances	92	92	92
3. House furnishings	70	70	70
4. China, tableware, utensils, jewelry and watches	90	90	90
5. Musical instruments, radios	90	90	90
6. Books	74	74	74
7. Passenger cars	70	70	70
8. Passenger car accessories	10	30	40
9. Ophthalmic and orthopedic products	100	100	100
10. Miscellaneous:			
(a) Luggage	92	92	92
(b) Wheel goods, durable toys. and sports equipment	70	99.5	99.5
(c) Pleasure craft	100	100	100

Lines 1 to 4 – Based on Dewhurst, J. F. and Associates, *America's Needs and Resources*, p. 198.

Lines 5 and 9 – Based on Epstein, Lenore A., "Consumers' Tangible Assets," *Studies in Income and Wealth*, vol. XII, p. 442. Life expectancy of musical instruments was allowed to decrease over time because of increase in expenditures, first on phonographs and then on radios, both of which depreciate faster than pianos, which predominated in the earlier years; that for ophthalmic and orthopedic products was rounded from four to five years.

Line 6 – Rough estimate.

Line 7 – Depreciation calculated assuming an average life of six years for cars purchased in 1890–1919, nine years for 1920–1929, and twelve years for 1930–1949. New passenger cars because of better information on pattern of depreciation were not subject to linear depreciation used for all other commodities but were assumed to follow the pattern of depreciation outlined by Keller, E. A., *A Study of the Physical Assets Sometimes Called Wealth of the United States, 1922–1933*, p. 135, table 62.

ANNUAL DEPRECIATION RATES (percent)

Year of life	6-year life	9-year life	12-year life
1st	15.5	10.5	9
2nd	28	21	17
3rd	22	17.5	14.5
4th	16	14	11
5th	10.5	12	10
6th	6	9	9
7th	2	6	8
8th		4	7
9th		4	4.5
10th		2	3
11th			3
12th			3
13th			1

These rates probably understate somewhat depreciation during first year, if it be regarded as measured by changes in resale and trade-in value, and correspondingly overstate it for later years. The difference, however, would not seem to be significant except for the 1930's.

Lines 8 and 10 – Based on Department of the Treasury, Bureau of Internal Revenue, *Bulletin F*.

Q-13   TABLE Q-13

Column 1 – 1941–1949: From reports of Rubber Manufacturers Association.

Column 2 – 1941–1942: Estimated by applying to total automotive inner tubes the proportion of passenger car to total automotive casings, derived from figures given in reports of Rubber Manufacturers Association.
1943: Based on figures given by War Production Board in *Facts for Industry*, Series Release 26-2-4, table 2.
1944–1949: Same source as col. 1.

Column 3 – 1941–1949: Weighted average of cols. 1 and 2, weights being respectively 6 and 1, based roughly on relative importance in wholesale price index.

Column 4 – 1941–1949: Bureau of Labor Statistics index of wholesale prices of tires and tubes shifted to 1941 basis.

Column 5 – 1941–1949: Col. 3 multiplied by col. 4.

Column 6 – 1941–1949: Department of Commerce estimates (see *Survey of Current Business, National Income Supplement*, July 1947, p. 43, and *Survey of Current Business*, July 1950, p. 25).

Column 7 – 1941: Based on Department of Commerce estimate.
1942–1949: Index of col. 5 applied to 1941 estimate.

Column 8 – 1941–1949: Col. 6 minus col. 7. This column reflects slight revisions not incorporated in further calculations based on these figures, e.g. Table Q–5.

LIFE EXPECTANCIES AND DEPRECIATION
RATES OF CONSUMER DURABLE GOODS

Commodity	Expected life (no. of years)	Annual depreciation rate (percent) [1]
1. Furniture	20	5.00
2. Household appliances	12	8.33
3. House furnishings	10	10.00
4. China, tableware, utensils, jewelry and watches	10	10.00
5. Musical instruments, radios 1897–1919	20	5.00
1920–1929	15	6.66
1930–1949	10	10.00
6. Books	10	10.00
7. Passenger cars 1899–1919	6	([2])
1920–1929	9	([2])
1930–1949	12	([2])
8. Passenger car accessories	5	20.00
9. Ophthalmic and orthopedic products	5	20.00
10. Miscellaneous consumer durable goods [3]	10	10.00

[1] Assumes linear depreciation.

[2] Passenger cars not subjected to linear depreciation. For rates, see note to line 7.

[3] Includes luggage, wheel goods, and pleasure craft.

EXPENDITURES FOR TIRES, TUBES, PARTS, AND ACCESSORIES

1941 to 1949

Year	Domestic replacement shipments of passenger car		Combination casings and inner tubes			Consumption expenditures		
	Casings	Inner tubes	Index of production	Index of prices	Index of value	Tires, tubes, parts, and accessories	Tires and tubes	Parts and accessories
	000		1941 = 100.0			$ mill.		
	1	2	3	4	5	6	7	8
1941	34 118	28 663	100.0	100.0	100.0	634	318	316
1942	2 734	2 223	8.0	121.5	9.7	265	31	234
1943	10 605	5 954	29.8	125.8	37.5	334	119	215
1944	18 330	14 138	53.2	123.8	65.9	418	210	208
1945	25 462	23 386	75.5	119.1	89.9	603	286	317
1946	54 792	49 854	162.2	119.5	193.8	1 414	616	798
1947	52 890	39 862	153.1	114.8	175.8	1 626	559	1 067
1948	41 450	34 918	121.5	117.0	142.2	1 590	452	1 138
1949	36 503	27 342	105.6	113.5	119.9	1 626	381	1 245

MARKUP, DEPRECIATION, AND SAVING OF SECOND HAND FURNITURE AND ANTIQUES: 1883 to 1949

$ mill. (except col. 3)

Year	Consumer expenditures on new furniture		Markup per-centage	Markup of second hand furniture and antiques							
				Original cost			1929 prices			Replacement cost	
	Un-adjusted	Adjusted		Amount	Depre-ciation	Saving	Amount	Depre-ciation	Saving	Depre-ciation	Saving
	1	2	3	4	5	6	7	8	9	10	11
1883	135	–	–	–	–	–	–	–	–	–	–
1884	140	–	–	–	–	–	–	–	–	–	–
1885	145	–	–	–	–	–	–	–	–	–	–
1886	150	–	–	–	–	–	–	–	–	–	–
1887	155	145	3.0	4	–	–	12	–	–	–	–
1888	160	150	3.0	4	–	–	12	–	–	–	–
1889	165	155	3.0	5	–	–	15	–	–	–	–
1890	168	160	3.0	5	–	–	15	–	–	–	–
1891	178	165	3.0	5	–	–	15	–	–	–	–
1892	203	175	3.0	5	–	–	15	–	–	–	–
1893	177	178	3.0	5	–	–	17	–	–	–	–
1894	146	174	3.0	5	–	–	17	–	–	–	–
1895	166	174	3.0	5	–	–	18	–	–	–	–
1896	160	170	3.0	5	–	–	20	–	–	–	–
1897	156	161	3.0	5	5	0	21	17	4	4	1
1898	158	157	3.0	5	5	0	19	17	2	5	0
1899	184	165	3.0	5	5	0	18	17	1	5	0
1900	189	169	3.0	5	5	0	16	18	–2	6	–1
1901	220	181	3.0	5	5	0	15	18	–3	6	–1
1902	240	198	3.0	6	5	1	18	18	0	6	0
1903	258	218	3.0	7	5	2	20	18	2	6	1
1904	264	234	3.0	7	5	2	20	18	2	6	1
1905	298	256	3.0	8	6	2	23	19	4	7	1
1906	353	283	3.0	8	6	2	21	19	2	7	1
1907	343	303	3.0	9	6	3	21	19	2	8	1
1908	283	308	3.0	9	7	2	22	19	3	8	1
1909	356	327	3.0	10	7	3	25	20	5	8	2
1910	375	342	3.0	10	8	2	23	20	3	9	1
1911	396	351	3.0	11	8	3	21	21	0	11	0
1912	428	368	3.0	11	9	2	19	21	–2	12	–1
1913	459	403	3.0	12	9	3	18	21	–3	14	–2
1914	431	418	3.0	13	10	3	20	21	–1	14	–1
1915	412	425	3.0	13	10	3	20	21	–1	14	–1
1916	527	451	3.0	14	11	3	21	21	0	14	0

MARKUP, DEPRECIATION, AND SAVING OF SECOND HAND FURNITURE AND ANTIQUES: 1883 to 1949

$ mill. (except col. 3)

Year	Consumer expenditures on new furniture		Markup percentage	Markup of second hand furniture and antiques							
				Original cost			1929 prices			Replacement cost	
	Un-adjusted	Adjusted		Amount	Depreciation	Saving	Amount	Depreciation	Saving	Depreciation	Saving
	1	2	3	4	5	6	7	8	9	10	11
1917	583	482	3.0	14	11	3	21	21	0	14	0
1918	638	518	3.0	16	12	4	19	21	−2	18	−2
1919	902	612	3.0	18	13	5	16	20	−4	22	−4
1920	1 181	766	3.0	23	14	9	13	19	−6	33	−10
1921	1 023	865	3.0	26	15	11	20	19	1	25	1
1922	953	939	3.0	28	17	11	24	19	5	22	6
1923	1 071	1 026	3.0	31	19	12	26	20	6	24	7
1924	1 201	1 086	3.0	33	21	12	29	20	9	22	11
1925	1 217	1 093	3.0	33	23	10	31	21	10	23	10
1926	1 229	1 134	3.0	34	25	9	33	23	10	24	10
1927	1 263	1 196	3.0	36	27	9	35	24	11	24	12
1928	1 205	1 223	3.0	37	29	8	37	26	11	26	11
1929	1 167	1 216	2.8	34	29	5	34	27	7	27	7
1930	905	1 154	2.8	32	32	0	34	29	5	28	4
1931	767	1 061	2.7	29	33	−4	36	31	5	25	4
1932	486	906	2.5	23	32	−9	36	32	4	21	2
1933	442	753	2.7	20	32	−12	31	33	−2	21	−1
1934	495	619	3.1	19	30	−11	27	34	−7	24	−5
1935	648	568	3.2	18	29	−11	28	33	−5	21	−3
1936	830	580	3.1	18	27	−9	27	33	−6	22	−4
1937	904	664	2.9	19	26	−7	27	32	−5	23	−4
1938	809	737	2.4	18	24	−6	26	31	−5	21	−3
1939	931	824	2.2	18	22	−4	27	30	−3	20	−2
1940	1 044	904	2.0	18	21	−3	26	30	−4	20	−2
1941	1 295	997	1.9	19	20	−1	25	29	−4	22	−3
1942	1 260	1 068	1.8	19	19	0	22	27	−5	24	−5
1943	1 222	1 150	1.7	19	19	0	21	26	−5	23	−4
1944	1 295	1 223	1.6	20	19	1	20	25	−5	25	−5
1945	1 541	1 323	1.5	20	19	1	18	24	−0	26	−6
1946	2 319	1 527	1.3	20	19	1	17	23	−6	27	−7
1947	2 700	1 815	1.2	21	19	2	16	22	−6	29	−8
1948	2 920	2 155	1.1	23	19	4	16	21	−5	30	−7
1949	2 803	2 457	0.9	23	20	3	16	20	−4	28	−5

TABLE Q–14

Column 1 – 1883–1949: See notes to Table Q-5, cols. 2–7.

Column 2 – 1887–1949: Five-year moving average of col. 1 centered at last year.

Column 3 – 1887–1928: Assumed at 3 percent, roughly the 1929–1937 average relationship.
1929–1949: Ratio of col. 4 to col. 2.

Column 4 – 1887–1928: Col. 2 multiplied by col. 3.
1929–1949: Department of Commerce estimates (cf. *Survey of Current Business, National Income Supplement,* July 1947).

Column 5 – 1897–1949: Based on assumed ten-year depreciation period.

Column 6 – 1897–1949: Col. 4 minus col. 5.

Column 7 – 1887–1949: Col. 4 deflated by Table Q-16, col. 1, thus implying a price movement similar to new furniture.

Column 8 – 1897–1949: Col. 7 depreciated, assuming ten-year period.

Column 9 – 1897–1949: Col. 7 minus col. 8.

Column 10 – 1897–1949: Col. 8 multiplied by Table Q-16, col. 1.

Column 11 – 1897–1949: Col. 4 minus col. 10.

TABLE Q–15

Column 1 - Losses on durable goods roughly estimated at 60 percent of total fire losses on household goods (Table R-71, col. 5). Computations based on unrounded figures.

Column 2 - Col. 1 deflated by index derived by dividing nonfarm expenditures on new consumer durable goods, original cost, by expenditures in 1929 prices. (Index used was obtained from aggregates which included expenditures on monuments and tombstones. When this category was eliminated from the estimates, it was decided not to rework the series in 1929 and current prices, particularly since the absolute amounts of fire losses are relatively small.) For the years prior to 1897, this index was extrapolated by Warren and Pearson's index of wholesale prices (*Gold and Prices,* p. 31).

Column 3 - Sum of depreciation on fire losses during six years preceding year indicated. Absolute figures from 1897 on are from col. 1 (see notes to Table R-72, col. 2).

Column 4 - Same procedure as col. 3 except that absolute figures are taken from col. 2.

Column 5 - Col. 4 multiplied by index described in col. 2.

Column 6 - Col. 1 minus col. 3.

Column 7 - Col. 2 minus col. 4.

Column 8 - Col. 1 minus col. 5.

ADJUSTMENT TO INDIVIDUALS' SAVING THROUGH CONSUMER DURABLE GOODS DUE TO FIRE LOSSES: 1897 to 1949

$ mill.

Year	Fire losses		Depreciation			Net adjustment		
	Original cost	1929 prices	Original cost	1929 prices	Replacement cost	Original cost	1929 prices	Replacement cost
	1	2	3	4	5	6	7	8
1897	5	17	7	20	6	−2	−3	−1
1898	6	19	6	20	6	0	−1	0
1899	7	21	6	20	7	1	1	0
1900	8	22	6	20	7	2	2	1
1901	8	21	6	20	8	2	1	0
1902	8	20	7	20	8	1	0	0
1903	7	17	7	20	8	0	−3	−1
1904	11	26	8	21	9	3	5	2
1905	8	19	8	21	9	0	−2	−1
1906	25	57	10	24	10	15	33	15
1907	10	21	11	27	13	−1	−6	−3
1908	10	21	12	27	13	−2	−6	−3
1909	9	20	12	27	12	−3	−7	−3
1910	10	21	12	27	13	−2	−6	−3
1911	10	20	12	27	14	−2	−7	−4
1912	10	19	11	23	12	−1	−4	−2
1913	10	17	10	20	12	0	−3	−2
1914	10	17	10	19	11	0	−2	−1
1915	8	14	10	18	11	−2	−4	−3
1916	10	15	10	17	11	0	−2	−1
1917	11	14	10	16	12	1	−2	−1
1918	14	15	10	16	15	4	−1	−1
1919	13	12	11	15	16	2	−3	−3
1920	19	14	12	14	19	7	0	0
1921	20	17	13	14	17	7	3	3
1922	20	19	15	15	15	5	4	5
1923	22	21	17	16	17	5	5	5
1924	23	22	19	17	18	4	5	5
1925	23	23	20	18	18	3	5	5
1926	24	25	22	20	20	2	5	4
1927	19	19	22	21	21	−3	−2	−2
1928	18	18	22	21	21	−4	−3	−3
1929	17	17	21	21	21	−4	−4	−4
1930	19	21	20	21	19	−1	0	0
1931	17	21	19	20	16	−2	1	1
1932	14	20	18	20	14	−4	0	0
1933	9	13	16	19	13	−7	−6	−4
1934	10	14	15	18	13	−5	−4	−3
1935	8	11	14	17	12	−6	−6	−4
1936	9	12	12	16	12	−3	−4	−3
1937	9	12	10	14	11	−1	−2	−2
1938	9	12	9	13	10	0	−1	−1
1939	10	14	9	12	9	1	2	1
1940	10	13	9	12	9	1	1	1
1941	11	14	9	13	10	2	1	1
1942	12	15	10	13	11	2	2	1
1943	14	15	11	14	13	3	1	1
1944	17	17	12	14	14	5	3	3
1945	19	18	13	15	16	6	3	3
1946	23	21	15	16	17	8	5	6
1947	29	23	17	17	21	12	6	8
1948	29	21	20	19	26	9	2	3
1949	27	20	23	20	27	4	0	0

INDICES OF PRICES OF CONSUMER DURABLE GOODS
1877 to 1949
1929 = 100.0

Year	Furniture	Household appliances	House furnishings	China etc.	Musical instruments	Books	Medical appliances	Passenger cars	Passenger car accessories	Miscellaneous
	1	2	3	4	5	6	7	8	9	10
1877	35.4	–	–	–	46.7	–	–	–	–	–
1878	33.7	–	–	–	46.7	–	–	–	–	–
1879	32.1	–	–	–	46.7	–	–	–	–	–
1880	32.2	–	–	–	46.7	–	–	–	–	–
1881	32.3	–	–	–	46.6	–	–	–	–	–
1882	32.4	–	–	–	46.5	–	–	–	–	–
1883	32.5	–	–	–	46.4	–	–	–	–	–
1884	32.6	–	–	–	46.4	–	–	–	–	–
1885	32.7	35.0	–	–	46.3	–	–	–	–	–
1886	32.8	34.0	–	–	46.2	–	–	–	–	–
1887	32.9	32.7	36.3	45.3	46.1	37.4	–	–	–	42.5
1888	33.0	32.8	35.8	45.2	46.1	37.5	–	–	–	42.6
1889	33 2	34.1	35.5	45.2	46.0	39.0	–	–	–	44.3
1890	32.6	34.0	35.2	45.1	44.9	38.9	–	–	–	43.9
1891	32.6	34.0	35.8	45.0	43.9	38.9	–	–	–	43.7
1892	32.6	33.0	34.3	42.0	47.8	37.7	44.9	–	–	42.1
1893	30.2	31.3	34.8	39.2	46.6	35.7	42.6	–	–	40.2
1894	29.7	30.1	32.5	37.7	43.1	34.4	41.0	–	–	38.7
1895	27.2	28.1	29.7	37.2	38.6	32.1	38.3	–	–	36.2
1896	24.4	26.9	29.7	37.2	38.6	30.7	36.6	–	–	34.4
1897	24.2	26.4	29.6	33.9	39.0	30.1	35.9	–	–	33.6
1898	27.0	28.0	30.2	35.3	38.4	32.0	38.1	–	–	35.8
1899	28.0	29.1	30.2	36.3	41.4	33.1	39.5	171.6	159.4	37.2
1900	31.4	31.7	33.3	37.1	44.7	36.1	43.0	171.6	159.4	40.5
1901	32.6	33.8	33.7	45.7	48.6	37.8	43.9	171.6	159.4	42.4
1902	33.9	34.7	34.4	45.6	53.4	38.8	45.1	169.4	157.4	43.0
1903	35.1	36.0	36.3	45.6	53.8	40.2	46.7	169.7	157.7	44.2
1904	35.3	36.8	37.8	45.3	52.7	40.9	47.6	154.8	143.8	44.7
1905	35.5	37.3	37.4	44.2	56.5	41.6	48.4	233.9	217.3	45.4
1906	37.5	39.1	40.0	42.7	56.4	43.5	50.6	271.5	252.3	46.9
1907	41.9	43.0	42.2	43.7	60.3	47.7	55.5	312.6	290.5	50.4
1908	41.1	43.4	38.3	40.0	58.0	48.0	55.8	312.5	290.4	51.4
1909	40.4	41.4	38.8	37.9	57.4	45.8	53.2	189.1	175.7	50.0
1910	43.8	43.7	40.3	37.6	56.9	48.2	56.0	174.6	162.2	51.1
1911	52.1	47.4	42.9	40.3	62.7	54.4	57.5	165.7	154.0	53.3
1912	57.5	50.8	43.9	41.4	58.0	57.9	61.2	138.0	128.2	55.3
1913	65.1	53.9	45.8	43.2	59.4	61.7	65.2	133.0	123.6	57.8
1914	64.9	53.9	44.9	44.3	55.9	61.7	65.2·	112.6	104.6	57.8

694

INDICES OF PRICES OF CONSUMER DURABLE GOODS
1877 to 1949
1929 = 100.0

Year	Furniture	Household appliances	House furnishings	China etc.	Musical instruments	Books	Medical appliances	Passenger cars	Passenger car accessories	Miscellaneous
	1	2	3	4	5	6	7	8	9	10
1915	65.1	54.1	44.1	44.1	59.4	63.4	67.0	104.1	96.7	58.8
1916	66.8	56.9	55.9	51.3	55.9	69.1	73.0	96.9	90.0	67.5
1917	68.1	64.5	80.4	71.4	57.7	80.1	84.6	99.5	92.5	80.5
1918	85.6	78.1	105.2	87.8	69.5	93.2	98.5	109.0	101.3	103.3
1919	109.5	86.3	108.3	94.0	83.7	106.8	112.9	128.5	119.4	125.7
1920	171.5	107.8	146.4	116.1	105.3	136.0	136.0	144.8	144.8	138.4
1921	132.8	103.7	115.8	111.0	98.8	120.8	120.8	129.3	129.3	126.4
1922	117.7	98.9	101.4	94.8	88.9	103.6	103.6	105.1	105.1	118.0
1923	121.4	109.5	110.7	114.7	99.3	104.9	104.9	98.0	98.0	100.6
1924	112.2	106.9	105.3	115.6	102.8	103.2	103.2	96.9	96.9	100.3
1925	107.9	104.6	108.9	106.6	95.9	100.4	100.4	94.9	94.9	99.2
1926	104.5	101.9	107.0	101.3	98.1	96.4	96.4	90.2	90.2	94.0
1927	101.8	101.5	105.2	100.5	100.4	97.5	97.5	92.4	92.4	97.8
1928	101.2	98.9	102.5	100.6	100.9	98.8	98.8	96.4	96.4	101.7
1929	100.0	100.0	100.0	100.0	100.0	100.0	100.0	100.0	100.0	100.0
1930	95.4	95.7	97.1	94.2	71.2	97.0	100.0	95.3	93.9	99.6
1931	79.8	89.1	84.5	89.9	49.7	92.3	99.0	90.8	80.1	92.7
1932	64.5	76.6	72.2	80.2	36.1	88.7	95.2	89.0	73.6	78.7
1933	63.7	70.0	74.0	78.3	32.4	83.3	91.8	78.7	71.0	75.8
1934	69.5	69.5	81.2	79.2	34.8	82.6	92.5	82.1	74.1	79.5
1935	64.9	69.9	80.7	79.1	34.6	81.9	92.5	81.0	71.9	77.3
1936	65.7	69.5	82.3	81.2	34.4	82.7	93.1	83.0	72.1	73.6
1937	70.7	71.1	87.4	84.1	35.8	84.3	94.2	87.0	73.4	76.9
1938	68.3	72.8	83.8	80.6	34.8	85.2	93.8	93.7	69.4	78.3
1939	66.9	70.7	83.4	81.5	33.0	86.1	94.2	91.7	71.3	76.5
1940	68.2	68.4	86.8	84.9	32.4	85.8	95.4	94.0	75.1	79.6
1941	77.1	71.1	92.9	91.6	34.0	87.2	95.4	103.8	80.3	83.9
1942	87.6	81.6	103.2	108.6	37.7	87.2	97.5	120.8	95.3	94.8
1943	89.0	83.9	106.1	111.6	39.9	92.5	101.7	120.9	95.4	100.6
1944	99.9	91.1	115.2	121.2	40.6	93.9	104.2	120.9	95.4	102.1
1945	109.1	97.4	123.1	129.6	41.5	96.1	105.6	123.7	97.6	104.5
1946	117.7	106.3	134.4	141.5	45.0	104.2	107.5	143.3	113.1	113.4
1947	130.2	123.1	155.7	163.9	51.5	119.1	111.8	164.6	129.9	129.5
1948	144.4	130.7	165.3	174.0	55.4	128.1	116.5	179.4	141.5	139.3
1949	139.9	126.2	159.6	168.0	54.7	126.6	120.3	190.6	150.4	137.6

Column 1 – 1877–1929: Index of prices for household furniture (group 12) as estimated by W. H. Shaw (cf. *Value of Commodity Output since 1869*, pp. 292, 293) shifted to 1929 base and adjusted by ratio of current retail price markup to that of 1929 (cf. Table Q-5). For 1877, 1878, and 1880–1888 figures were obtained by linear interpolation between estimates for 1869, 1879, and 1889.

1930–1942: Index of retail prices for household furniture (group 20) as estimated by Henry Shavell (cf. *Survey of Current Business*, May 1943, p. 17) shifted to 1929 base.

1943–1949: Value for 1942 extrapolated by Bureau of Labor Statistics retail price index for furniture.

Column 2 – 1885–1929: Weighted harmonic mean of Shaw's price index for heating and cooking apparatus and household appliances, except electrical, and for electrical household appliances and supplies, weights being corresponding estimates of expenditures, adjusted by retail price markup ratio of current year to 1929. Price index for nonelectrical appliances group is index estimated by Shaw for group 13a and extrapolated prior to 1913 by the implicit index of prices of all consumer durable goods as recomputed to 1929 base by National Bureau of Economic Research. Price index for electrical appliances group was assumed to be same as recomputed implicit price index for entire period.

1930–1942: Weighted harmonic mean of Shavell's retail price indices, shifted to 1929 base, for heating and cooking apparatus (group 23), refrigerators, washing machines, and sewing machines (group 24), and miscellaneous electrical household appliances (group 25), weights being Department of Commerce estimates of expenditures for these groups (cf. *Survey of Current Business*, April 1942, p. 16, and May 1943, p. 17).

1943–1949: Value for 1942 extrapolated by Bureau of Labor Statistics index of retail prices of house furnishings.

Column 3 – 1887–1929: Weighted harmonic mean of Shaw's price indices (on 1929 base) for floor coverings (group 14a), miscellaneous house furnishings (group 14b), and carpenters' and mechanics' tools (group 35), weights being corresponding estimates of expenditures, adjusted by ratio of current retail price markup to that of 1929.

1930–1942: Weighted harmonic mean of Shavell's retail price indices (on 1929 base) of floor coverings (group 21), miscellaneous durable house furnishings and equipment (group 22), writing equipment (group 33), and tools (group 56), using as weights corresponding Department of Commerce estimates of expenditures (*Survey of Current Business, National Income Supplement*, July 1947, pp. 42–43).

1943–1949: Value for 1942 extrapolated by Bureau of Labor Statistics index of retail prices of house furnishings.

Column 4 – 1887–1929: Weighted harmonic mean of Shaw's price indices (on 1929 base) for china and household utensils (group 15) and jewelry, silverware, clocks, and watches (group 17), the weights being corresponding estimated expenditures, adjusted by ratio of current retail price markup to that of 1929. For group 15, values for 1887–1888 are linear interpolations of price indices for 1879 and 1889. For group 17, values for 1887–1890 are assumed to be same as for 1891.

1930–1942: Weighted harmonic mean of Shavell's retail price indices (on 1929 base) of china, glassware, tableware, and household utensils (group 26), clocks and watches (group 30), and jewelry and sterling silverware (group 31), the weights being Department of Commerce corresponding estimates of expenditures (*Survey of Current Business*, April 1942 and May 1943).

1943–1949: Value for 1942 extrapolated by Bureau of Labor Statistics index of retail prices of house furnishings.

Column 5 – 1877–1879: Value for 1889 extrapolated by implicit price index of consumer durable goods.

1880–1888: Linear interpolation between 1879 and 1889 price indices.

1889–1929: Shaw's price index for musical instruments (group 16) shifted to 1929 base, adjusted by ratio of current retail price markup to that of 1929.

1930–1942: Weighted harmonic mean of Shavell's retail price indices (on 1929 base) for radio apparatus and phonographs (group 27), pianos (group 28), and other musical instruments (group 29), weights being corresponding Department of Commerce estimates.

1943–1947: Value for 1942 extrapolated by Bureau of Labor Statistics consumer price index.

Column 6 – 1887–1929: Shaw's implicit price index of consumer durable goods as recomputed to 1929 base by National Bureau of Economic Research, adjusted by ratio of current retail price markup to that of 1929.

1930–1942: Shavell's retail price index for books and other durable printed matter (group 32) shifted to 1929 base.

1943–1949: Index for 1942 extrapolated by Bureau of Labor Statistics consumer price index.

Column 7 – 1892–1929: Shaw's recomputed implicit price index of consumer durable goods.

      1930–1942: Shavell's retail price index for ophthalmic products and surgical and orthopedic appliances (group 34) shifted to 1929 base.

      1943–1949: Index for 1942 extrapolated by Bureau of Labor Statistics retail price index of eyeglasses.

Column 8 – 1899–1929: Shaw's price index for motor vehicles (group 20a) shifted to 1929 base.

      1930–1942: Shavell's retail price index for passenger cars (group 38) shifted to 1929 base.

      1943–1949: Value for 1942 extrapolated by Bureau of Labor Statistics wholesale price index for automobiles.

Column 9 – 1899–1929: Same as col. 8, adjusted by ratio of current retail price markup to that of 1929.

      1930–1942: Shavell's retail price index for passenger car replacement parts and accessories (group 40) shifted to 1929 base.

      1943–1949: Value for 1942 extrapolated by Bureau of Labor Statistics index of wholesale prices of automobiles.

Column 10 – 1887–1929: Weighted harmonic mean of Shaw's price indices (on 1929 base) for luggage (group 19), carriages and wagons (group 20c), motorcycles and bicycles (group 21), and pleasure craft (group 22), weights being corresponding estimates of expenditures, adjusted by ratio of combined current retail price markup to that of 1929. Price index for luggage was estimated by Shaw from 1913 onward and extrapolated back by his recomputed implicit price index for all consumer durable goods. Latter index was used throughout for motorcycles and bicycles and was used to extrapolate price index for carriages and wagons back of 1907. Price index for pleasure craft was taken to be same as for ships and boats.

      1930–1942: Weighted harmonic mean of Shavell's retail price indices (on 1929 base) for luggage (group 36), wheel goods, durable toys, and sport equipment (group 37), and pleasure craft (group 41), weights being corresponding Department of Commerce estimates of expenditures.

      1943–1949: Value for 1942 extrapolated by Bureau of Labor Statistics consumer price index.

General note: The Department of Commerce deflators for 1929–1949 (*Survey of Current Business, 1951 National Income Supplement*, p. 146) were not available at the time the estimates were made. For a discussion of the differences see Volume II, Chapter X, Section 2g.

Column 1 – 1896–1908: Table D-2, col. 3.
           1909–1922: Table D-3, col. 2.
           1923–1949: Table D-4, col. 1.

Column 2 – 1896–1922: Estimated to increase by one percentage point a year from 23 percent of total consumer credit outstanding in 1923 (proportion indicated for that year by relationship between cols. 1 and 2) to 50 percent in 1896. This increase, to be regarded as a very rough estimate only, is based on rise in share of unincorporated business in volume of retail trade and in retail inventories (see Table P-26, col. 3), and presumably in consumer credit granted by retail trade establishments.
           1923–1949: Table D-6, col. 10.

Column 3 – 1896–1922: Estimated at 6 percent of col. 1, the relationship prevailing in 1923–1925.
           1923–1949: From Table D-6, col. 6.

Column 4 – 1896–1949: Col. 2 minus col. 3.

Column 5 – 1896–1949: From Table D-5, col. 3.

Column 6 – 1896–1949: Col. 1 minus col. 5.

Column 7 – 1896–1949: Col. 6 reduced in proportion of ratio of credit extended by unincorporated lenders (col. 2) to total consumer credit outstanding (col. 1). This procedure implies that farmers draw their consumer credit in the same proportion from corporate and unincorporated lenders as all consumers.

Columns 8 and 9 – 1896–1949: Same procedure as col. 7, but on the basis of the ratio of cols. 3 and 4, respectively, to col. 1.

Column 10 – 1896–1949: Col. 6 minus col. 7.

SHORT-TERM CONSUMER DEBT:[1] 1896 to 1949

$ mill.

End of year	Total short term consumer debt outstanding	Debt to unincorporated creditors			Farmers' debt	Nonfarm consumer debt				
		Total	Medical practitioners	Others		Total	To unincorporated creditors			To corporate creditors
							Total	Medical practitioners	Others	
	1	2	3	4	5	6	7	8	9	10
1896	413	206	25	181	33	380	190	23	167	190
1897	468	229	28	201	40	428	210	26	184	218
1898	538	258	32	226	46	492	236	29	207	256
1899	602	283	36	247	49	553	260	33	227	293
1900	659	303	40	263	53	606	279	37	242	327
1901	728	328	44	284	58	670	302	40	262	368
1902	812	357	49	308	63	749	330	45	285	419
1903	894	384	54	330	68	826	355	50	305	471
1904	948	398	57	341	76	872	366	52	314	506
1905	1 046	429	63	366	77	969	397	58	339	572
1906	1 168	467	70	397	88	1 080	432	65	367	648
1907	1 269	495	76	419	94	1 175	458	70	388	717
1908	1 257	478	75	403	107	1 150	437	69	368	713
1909	1 432	530	86	444	123	1 309	484	78	406	825
1910	1 542	555	93	462	131	1 411	508	85	423	903
1911	1 679	588	101	487	126	1 553	544	93	451	1 009
1912	1 817	618	109	509	144	1 673	569	100	469	1 104
1913	1 927	636	116	520	141	1 786	589	107	482	1 197
1914	2 037	652	122	530	159	1 878	601	112	489	1 277
1915	2 175	674	130	544	157	2 018	626	121	505	1 392
1916	2 423	727	145	582	172	2 251	675	135	540	1 576
1917	2 533	735	152	583	256	2 277	661	137	524	1 616
1918	2 588	725	155	570	280	2 308	646	138	508	1 662
1919	2 918	788	175	613	280	2 638	712	158	554	1 926
1920	3 304	859	198	661	231	3 073	799	184	615	2 274
1921	3 249	812	195	617	120	3 129	782	188	594	2 347
1922	3 469	833	208	625	167	3 302	793	198	595	2 509
1923	3 860	878	232	646	184	3 676	836	221	615	2 840
1924	4 159	917	250	667	195	3 964	874	238	636	3 090
1925	4 928	1 032	287	745	276	4 652	974	271	703	3 678
1926	5 510	1 120	315	805	272	5 238	1 065	300	765	4 173
1927	5 714	1 117	336	781	263	5 451	1 066	321	745	4 385
1928	6 567	1 228	368	860	311	6 256	1 170	351	819	5 086
1929	7 628	1 413	416	997	350	7 278	1 348	397	951	5 930
1930	6 821	1 317	399	918	255	6 566	1 268	384	884	5 298
1931	5 518	1 210	370	840	173	5 345	1 172	358	814	4 173
1932	4 085	1 066	346	720	110	3 975	1 037	337	700	2 938
1933	3 912	921	328	593	163	3 749	883	314	569	2 866
1934	4 389	957	313	644	192	4 197	915	299	616	3 282
1935	5 434	1 060	324	736	297	5 137	1 002	306	696	4 135
1936	6 788	1 212	358	854	332	6 456	1 153	341	812	5 303
1937	7 480	1 308	383	925	379	7 101	1 242	364	878	5 859
1938	7 047	1 219	352	867	296	6 751	1 168	337	831	5 583
1939	7 969	1 270	359	911	334	7 635	1 217	344	873	6 418
1940	9 115	1 384	378	1 006	362	8 753	1 329	363	966	7 424
1941	9 862	1 482	411	1 071	468	9 394	1 412	392	1 020	7 982
1942	6 578	1 217	436	781	304	6 274	1 161	416	745	5 113
1943	5 378	1 159	463	696	238	5 140	1 108	443	665	4 032
1944	5 803	1 256	491	765	236	5 567	1 205	471	734	4 362
1945	6 637	1 353	521	832	263	6 374	1 299	500	799	5 075
1946	10 191	1 800	589	1 211	498	9 693	1 712	560	1 152	7 981
1947	13 673	2 143	620	1 523	723	12 950	2 030	587	1 443	10 920
1948	16 319	2 408	649	1 759	821	15 498	2 287	616	1 671	13 211
1949	18 778	2 635	669	1 966	832	17 946	2 518	639	1 879	15 428

[1] Excluding borrowing on securities and life insurance policy loans.

TABLE D–2

Column 1 – 1896–1898: Roughly extrapolated from 1899 by a combined index of wholesale prices (*Statistical Abstract*, 1947, p. 287), cost of living (Snyder, C., *Business Cycles and Business Measurements*, p. 290), and volume of production (Persons, W., *Forecasting Business Cycles*, p. 170).
1899–1908: Realized national income as estimated by Martin, Robert F., *National Income in the U.S., 1799–1938*, p. 6.

Column 2 – 1896–1908: Computed from the linear trend equation $y = 5.52 + 0.16x$ for the period 1909–1916, where y is the ratio of short-term consumer debt (Table D-3) to realized national income (Martin, *op. cit.*) and x is realized national income.

Column 3 – 1896–1908: Col. 2 multiplied by col. 1. Computed from unrounded figures.

TABLE D–3

Column 1 – 1909–1922: Values read off from chart in Nugent, R., *Consumer Credit and Economic Stability*, p. 120.
1923: *Ibid.*, p. 116.

Column 2 – 1909–1922: Obtained by multiplying col. 1 by $ 55.06 million, quotient of the 1923 value of col. 1 and estimate of total consumer debt outstanding at end of 1923 of Table D-4, col. 1.
1923: From Table D-4, col. 1.

DERIVATION OF SHORT-TERM CONSUMER DEBT

1896 to 1908

End of year	National income	Ratio of consumer debt to national income	Consumer debt	End of year	National income	Ratio of consumer debt to national income	Consumer debt
	$ bill.	Percent	$ mill.		$ bill.	Percent	$ mill.
	1	2	3		1	2	3
1896	12.0	3.44	413	1903	19.6	4.56	894
1897	13.0	3.60	468	1904	20.1	4.72	948
1898	14.3	3.76	538	1905	21.4	4.88	1 046
1899	15.4	3.92	602	1906	23.2	5.04	1 168
1900	16.2	4.08	659	1907	24.4	5.20	1 269
1901	17.2	4.24	728	1908	23.5	5.36	1 257
1902	18.4	4.40	812				

DERIVATION OF SHORT-TERM CONSUMER DEBT

1909 to 1923

End of year	Index of consumer debt	Estimated amount of consumer debt	End of year	Index of consumer debt	Estimated amount of consumer debt
	1923-1937 = 100.0	$ mill.		1923-1937 = 100.0	$ mill.
	1	2		1	2
1909	26.0	1 432	1917	46.0	2 533
1910	28.0	1 542	1918	47.0	2 588
1911	30.5	1 679	1919	53.0	2 918
1912	33.0	1 817	1920	60.0	3 304
1913	35.0	1 927	1921	59.0	3 249
1914	37.0	2 037	1922	63.0	3 469
1915	39.5	2 175	1923	70.1	3 860
1916	44.0	2 423			

Column 1 – 1923–1949: Sum of cols. 2–12.

Column 2 – 1923–1928: Nugent, R., *Consumer Credit and Economic Stability*, p. 115.
           1929–1949: Federal Reserve Board figures as given in *Statistical Abstract*, 1947, p. 420, and
           Federal Reserve Bulletin, various issues, e.g. 1950, p. 736. Federal Reserve figures for cols.
           2–8 for year 1929 are almost identical with Nugent's.

Column 3 – 1923–1928: Nugent, *op. cit.*, p. 388–389.
           1929–1949: Same source as col. 2.

Column 4 – 1923–1928: Nugent, *op. cit.*, p. 372–373.
           1929–1949: Same source as col. 2.

Column 5 – 1923–1928: Nugent, *op. cit.*, p. 360–361.
           1929–1949: Same source as col. 2.

Column 6 – 1923–1928: Nugent, *op. cit.*, p. 113.
           1929–1949: Same source as col. 2. Series covers unregulated lenders and miscellaneous personal
           loan agencies.

Column 7 – 1923–1933: Inapplicable.
           1934–1949: Same source as col. 2.

Column 8 – 1923–1927: Estimated together with col. 9 on basis of movement of total for receivables of
           retail merchants and intermediary financing agencies (mostly installment finance companies)
           given in Nugent, *op. cit.*, p. 116, linked at end of 1928 to Federal Reserve Board series.
           1928–1949: Same source as col. 2 (1928 figure is that estimated by Federal Reserve Board for
           end of January 1929).

Column 9 – 1923–1927: See col. 8.
           1928–1949: Same source as col. 2 (1928 figure is that estimated by Federal Reserve Board for
           end of Jan. 1929).

Column 10 – 1923–1928: Estimated at 2.28 times nondepartmentalized consumer loans of commercial banks
           as given in Nugent, *op. cit.*, p. 115, the ratio for each of the years 1929–1936 between Nugent's
           series and the Federal Reserve Board estimates. Does not include loans to farmers.
           1929–1949: Single-payment loans (from same source as col. 2) minus col. 11.

Column 11 – 1923–1937: Nugent, *op. cit.*, 115.
           1938–1949: From Table D-6, col. 3.

Column 12 – 1923–1928: Nugent, *op. cit.*, p. 113.
           1929–1949: Same source as col. 2. Series covers consumers' debts to medical practitioners,
           funeral directors, laundries, correspondence schools, and public utilities.

COMPONENTS OF SHORT-TERM CONSUMER DEBT
1923 to 1949

D-4

$ mill.

End of year	Grand total	Installment loans						Install-ment sale credit	Charge ac-counts	Single-payment loans		Service credit
		Commer-cial banks	Small loan com-panies	Indus-trial banks and loan companies	Credit unions	Miscel-laneous lenders	Insured repair and moderni-zation loans			Commer-cial banks	Pawn-brokers	
	1	2	3	4	5	6	7	8	9	10	11	12
1923	3 860	1	45	62	14	45	–	2 303		973	80	337
1924	4 159	1	56	80	17	53	–	2 442		1 062	87	361
1925	4 928	2	75	105	20	61	–	2 877		1 285	94	409
1926	5 510	3	98	136	23	67	–	3 204		1 429	100	450
1927	5 714	6	137	163	27	70	–	3 168		1 555	107	481
1928	6 567	18	193	193	29	79	–	2 087	1 531	1 796	111	530
1929	7 628	43	263	219	23	95	–	2 515	1 749	2 006	119	596
1930	6 821	45	277	218	23	93	–	2 032	1 611	1 824	125	573
1931	5 518	39	287	184	21	78	–	1 595	1 381	1 285	117	531
1932	4 085	31	268	143	19	58	–	999	1 114	863	99	491
1933	3 912	29	246	121	20	50	–	1 122	1 081	689	87	467
1934	4 389	44	264	125	25	60	25	1 317	1 203	793	82	451
1935	5 434	88	287	156	37	79	170	1 805	1 292	963	85	472
1936	6 788	161	326	191	58	102	244	2 436	1 419	1 246	85	520
1937	7 480	258	374	221	83	125	147	2 752	1 459	1 410	94	557
1938	7 047	312	380	224	103	117	146	2 313	1 487	1 357	85	523
1939	7 969	523	448	230	135	96	200	2 792	1 544	1 388	80	533
1940	9 115	692	498	236	174	99	268	3 450	1 650	1 413	75	560
1941	9 862	784	531	241	200	102	285	3 744	1 764	1 531	70	610
1942	6 578	426	417	161	130	91	206	1 617	1 513	1 304	65	648
1943	5 378	316	364	126	104	86	123	882	1 498	1 132	60	687
1944	5 803	357	384	128	100	88	113	891	1 758	1 200	55	729
1945	6 637	477	439	146	103	93	164	942	1 981	1 470	50	772
1946	10 191	956	597	215	153	109	322	1 648	3 054	2 208	55	874
1947	13 673	1 435	701	300	225	119	568	3 086	3 612	2 642	65	920
1948	16 319	1 709	817	364	312	131	739	4 528	3 854	2 827	75	963
1949	18 778	1 951	929	425	402	142	801	6 240	3 909	2 907	80	992

CONSUMER DEBT OF FARMERS

1896 to 1949

End of year	Farmers' share		Estimated consumer debt of farmers	End of year	Farmers' share		Estimated consumer debt of farmers	End of year	Farmers' share		Estimated consumer debt of farmers
	In national income	In total consumer debt			In national income	In total consumer debt			In national income	In total consumer debt	
	Percent	Percent	$ mill.		Percent	Percent	$ mill.		Percent	Percent	$ mill.
	1	2	3		1	2	3		1	2	3
1896	13.5	8.1	33	1914	13.0	7.8	159	1932	5.2	2.7	110
1897	14 3	8.6	40	1915	12.0	7.2	157	1933	7.4	4.2	163
1898	14.3	8.6	46	1916	11.8	7.1	172	1934	7.6	4.4	192
1899	13.7	8.2	49	1917	16.9	10.1	256	1935	9.6	5.5	297
1900	13.5	8.1	53	1918	18.0	10.8	280	1936	8.6	4.9	332
1901	13.2	7.9	58	1919	16.0	9.6	280	1937	9.0	5.1	379
1902	13.0	7.8	63	1920	11.6	7.0	231	1938	7.8	4.2	296
1903	12.6	7.6	68	1921	6.1	3.7	120	1939	7.7	4.2	334
1904	13.3	8.0	76	1922	8.0	4.8	167	1940	7.1	4.0	362
1905	12.3	7.4	77	1923	8.0	4.8	184	1941	8.5	4.7	468
1906	12.5	7.5	88	1924	8.0	4.7	195	1942	9.7	4.6	304
1907	12.4	7.4	94	1925	9.6	5.6	276	1943	10.0	4.4	238
1908	14.1	8.5	107	1926	8.5	4.9	272	1944	8.9	4.1	236
1909	14 4	8.6	123	1927	8.3	4.6	263	1945	9.0	4.0	263
1910	14.2	8.5	131	1928	8.6	4.7	311	1946	10.6	4.9	498
1911	12.5	7.5	126	1929	8.2	4.6	350	1947	10.8	5.3	723
1912	13.1	7.9	144	1930	7.0	3.7	255	1948	9.8	5.0	821
1913	12.1	7.3	141	1931	5.8	3.1	173	1949	8.2	4.4	832

Column 1 – 1896–1909: Table A-4, col. 4.
　　　　　　1910–1949: Table A-5, col. 3.

Column 2 – 1896–1922: The 1923 ratio extrapolated on the basis of farmers' share in national income as given in col. 1.
　　　　　　1923–1949: Obtained by dividing col. 3 by total consumer debt, as given in Table D-1, col. 1.

Column 3 – 1896–1922: Col. 2 applied to total consumer debt (Table D-1, col. 1).
　　　　　　1923–1949: Col. 1 applied to sum of installment sale credit to, and charge accounts of, consumers (Table D-4, cols. 8 and 9). This estimate is based on the assumption that farmers' share in other components of consumer debt (viz. cols. 2–7, 10, and 12 of Table D-4) is very small, and that the omission is compensated by the fact that their share in installment sale and charge account credit is probably somewhat smaller than their share in national income.

1923 to 1949

$ mill.

End of year	Miscel- laneous small loan companies	Unincor- porated money- lenders	Pawn- brokers	Charge accounts	Install- ment sale credit	Service creditors				Total
						Medical practi- tioners	Funeral directors	Laun- dries	Hospi- tals	
	1	2	3	4	5	6	7	8	9	10
1923	7	36	80		485	232	14	13	11	878
1924	8	42	87		490	250	14	14	12	917
1925	12	49	94		545	287	15	16	14	1 032
1926	15	54	100		585	315	17	18	16	1 120
1927	21	56	107		540	336	18	21	18	1 117
1928	29	63	111	383	209	368	21	24	20	1 228
1929	40	76	119	437	252	416	22	28	23	1 413
1930	43	74	125	403	203	399	21	27	22	1 317
1931	43	62	117	395	160	370	18	24	21	1 210
1932	39	46	99	379	100	346	16	21	20	1 066
1933	30	40	87	270	112	328	14	19	21	921
1934	27	48	82	301	132	313	14	19	21	957
1935	24	63	85	323	181	324	16	20	24	1 060
1936	21	82	85	355	244	358	18	22	27	1 212
1937	19	100	94	365	275	383	19	24	29	1 308
1938	19	94	85	372	231	352	18	22	26	1 219
1939	22	77	80	386	279	359	18	22	27	1 270
1940	25	79	75	412	345	378	19	23	28	1 384
1941	27	82	70	441	374	411	21	25	31	1 482
1942	21	73	65	378	162	436	22	27	33	1 217
1943	18	69	60	374	88	463	23	29	35	1 159
1944	19	70	55	440	89	491	25	30	37	1 256
1945	22	74	50	495	94	521	26	32	39	1 353
1946	30	87	55	764	165	589	29	37	44	1 800
1947	35	95	65	903	309	620	31	38	47	2 143
1948	41	105	75	964	453	649	32	40	49	2 408
1949	46	114	80	977	624	669	33	42	50	2 635

Column 1 – 1923–1928: Fifteen percent of loans by small loan companies as estimated by Nugent, R., *Consumer Credit and Economic Stability*, p. 115.
                1929–1949: Fifteen percent (1929–1932); 13, 11, 9, and 7 percent (1933–1936); and 5 percent (1937–1949) of loans by small loan companies as estimated by Federal Reserve Board. The percentages for 1932 and later years are those suggested by Friend, I. and Natrella, V., *Individuals' Saving*, part II, p. 90, of preliminary mimeographed memorandum.

Column 2 – 1923–1949: Eighty percent of loans by unregulated lenders and miscellaneous agencies as estimated by Nugent, *op. cit.*, p. 115 (1923–1928) and Federal Reserve Board (1929–1949). The percentage is that used by Friend and Natrella for 1932 and later years.

Column 3 – 1923–1928: Nugent, *op. cit.*, p. 115.
                1929–1949: Federal Reserve Board estimates. Based on Nugent until 1941, and on small sample thereafter.

Column 4 – 1923–1928: Estimated together with col. 5 to decline from 21 percent to 17 percent of total charge accounts plus installment sale credit. These percentages are based on 1928 ratio of 16 percent, and consideration that ratio must have been declining over this period since proportion of installment sale credit in which share of corporations is larger than in charge account credit has been increasing over the period.
                1929–1949: Estimated at 25 percent of total charge accounts. There is no quantitative basis for a close estimate. Share of corporations in total retail sales can be estimated from data in *Census of Business* and *Statistics of Income* at a little less than one-half. There is, however, little doubt that share of corporations in total charge accounts is considerably higher than that in total sales since they dominate some of the branches of retail trade in which most of the charge accounts are concentrated, particularly the department store field.

Column 5 – 1923–1928: See col. 4.
                1929–1949: Estimated at 10 percent of total installment sale credit as estimated by the Federal Reserve Board.

Column 6 – 1923–1937: Nugent, *op. cit.*, p. 113.
                1938–1949: Total of cols. 6–9 estimated at 80 percent of total credit extended by all service creditors, approximately the ratio obtaining in 1937. (It has been assumed that all public utility companies and correspondence schools are incorporated.) Division between cols. 6–9 based on 1935–1937 average.

Columns 7 and 8 – 1923–1937: Estimated at one-half of total receivables of funeral directors and laundries respectively, as estimated by Nugent, *op. cit.*, p. 113.
                1938–1949: See col. 6.

Column 9 – 1923–1937: Nugent, *op. cit.*, p. 113.
                1938–1949: See col. 6.

Column 10 – 1923–1949: Sum of cols. 1–9.

706

1923 to 1949

$ mill.

End of year	Debt reported with finance charge		Finance charges				
	All lenders	Unincorporated lenders		Lenders		Borrowers	
			Total	Unincorporated	Incorporated	Nonfarm	Farm
	1	2	3	4	5	6	7
1923	1 570	287	157	29	128	149	8
1924	1 686	302	169	30	139	161	8
1925	1 988	335	199	34	165	188	11
1926	2 228	361	223	36	187	212	11
1927	2 247	354	225	35	190	215	10
1928	2 488	383	249	38	211	237	12
1929	2 991	447	299	45	254	285	14
1930	2 513	402	251	40	211	242	9
1931	2 013	339	201	34	167	195	6
1932	1 330	245	133	24	109	129	4
1933	1 409	239	141	24	117	135	6
1934	1 628	262	163	26	137	156	7
1935	2 213	329	221	33	188	209	12
1936	2 975	411	297	41	256	282	15
1937	3 450	469	276	38	238	262	14
1938	3 051	410	183	25	158	175	8
1939	3 721	436	223	26	197	214	9
1940	4 552	499	273	30	243	262	11
1941	4 941	526	296	32	264	282	14
1942	2 360	300	142	18	124	135	7
1943	1 470	217	88	13	75	84	4
1944	1 519	214	91	13	78	87	4
1945	1 708	218	102	13	89	98	4
1946	2 983	307	179	18	161	170	9
1947	5 005	469	300	28	272	284	16
1948	6 807	633	408	38	370	388	20
1949	8 838	818	530	49	481	507	23

Column 1 – 1923–1949: Table D-4, sum of cols. 2, 4, 6, 8, and 11. For 1923 to 1927, Table D-4, col. 8 is segregated from Table D-4, col. 9 on basis of their relationship in 1928.

Column 2 – 1923–1949: Table D-6, sum of cols. 2, 3, and 5. From 1923 to 1927, Table D-6, col. 4 is segregated from Table D-6, col. 5 on basis of their relationship in 1928.

Columns 3 and 4 – 1923–1936: Estimated as 10 percent of cols. 1 and 2 respectively. Figures represent finance charges included in outstanding at end of year.
1937: Estimated as 8 percent of cols. 1 and 2 respectively.
1938–1949: Estimated as 6 percent of cols. 1 and 2 respectively.

Column 5 – 1923–1949: Col. 3 minus col. 4.

Column 6 – 1923–1949: Estimated as same percentage of total finance charges as nonfarm consumer debt is of total consumer debt, the ratios being derived by dividing Table D-1, col. 6 by Table D-1, col. 1.

Column 7 – 1923–1949: Col. 3 minus col. 6.

Column 1 – 1896–1915A: Estimated as 70 percent of loans on collateral, approximately the 1915–1919 percentage for national banks, derived from *Annual Report of the Comptroller of the Currency,* various issues. Loans on collateral were estimated by multiplying non-real estate loans of commercial banks (cf. Table L-24, col. 6) by average percentage of collateral loans to total non-real estate loans for preceding and succeeding June dates, derived from Federal Reserve Board revised banking statistics.

        1915B–1919A: Same as 1896–1915A, except that average of ratios of loans on stocks and bonds to loans on collateral for preceding and following June dates for national banks was used instead of a constant proportion of 70 percent.

        1919B–1938: Table D-9, col. 1.

        1939–1949: Not available.

Column 2 – 1896–1938: Col. 1 minus col. 4.

        1939–1949: Not available.

Column 3 – 1896–1920: Estimated as 40 percent of col. 2.

        1921–1937: Estimated as a varying percentage of col. 2; ratio is assumed to rise regularly from 0.40 in 1920 to 0.48 in 1925 and to 0.65 in 1929, to fall to 0.60 in 1930 and to decline regularly to 0.30 in 1938. The 1938 ratio is based on actual reports (see below) while that for 1930 is derived from data for a group of large banks in U.S. Congress, Senate Committee on Banking and Currency, *Operation of National and Federal Reserve Banking Systems,* pp. 1011–1012.

        1938–1949: Bank loans to other than brokers and dealers for all insured commercial banks from *Federal Reserve Bulletin,* 1945, p. 1220; 1949, p. 958; 1950, p. 1208, increased by 2.5 percent to account for loans of uninsured banks. Step-up ratio is based on 1948 and 1949 data in the *Annual Report of the Federal Deposit Insurance Corporation,* and *Annual Report of the Comptroller of the Currency,* from which separate figures were derived for all insured commercial banks in the U.S., excluding possessions and all commercial banks in the U.S. excluding possessions.

Column 4 – 1896–1916: Estimated from regression equation $y = 16.32 + 0.2418x$ (where y is percentage of loans to brokers and dealers to total bank loans on securities, and x estimated value of reported stock trading on the New York Stock Exchange in $ billions from Table D-16, col. 3) derived from relation obtaining from 1917 to 1933. While the regression equation was derived using earlier estimates of bank loans on securities, it was retained as the figures obtained from the revised regression equation would differ only very little from those shown here.

        1917–1918: Estimated at 110 percent of street loans by daily reporting banks in New York City (from *Banking and Monetary Statistics,* p. 495). End-of-year data were computed by averaging last figure for each year with first figure for the following year. (For derivation of percentage used, see notes to Table D-9, col. 2.)

        1919–1938: Table D-9, col. 2.

        1939–1949: From *Federal Reserve Bulletin,* various issues, adjusted as for 1934–1938 (see note to Table D-9, col. 2).

Column 5 – 1896–1908: Regarded as insignificant.

        1909–1917: Roughly estimated on basis of trend from 1918 to 1924.

        1918–1938: *Banking and Monetary Statistics,* p. 494.

        1939–1941: Rough estimates.

        1942–1949: Assumed negligible.

Column 6 – 1896–1949: Sum of cols. 3–5.

Column 7 – 1896–1919: Estimated as 5 percent of col. 3.

        1920–1949: Estimated as varying percentage of col. 3, increasing linearly from 0.05 in 1919 to 0.10 in 1924, to 0.20 in 1929, and declining linearly to 0.10 from 1934 on.

Column 8 – 1896–1917: Estimated to rise linearly from zero in 1896 to 13 percent of col. 4 in 1917, the average ratio for 1918 to 1922.

        1918–1928: Col. 4 minus 110 percent of estimated borrowing from banks by members of New York Stock Exchange. This ratio is suggested by a comparison of data in *Banking and Monetary Statistics,* p. 494, with figures of col. 4 for early part of period.

        1929–1934A: Col. 4 minus 110 percent of borrowing from banks by members of New York Stock Exchange, estimated as total borrowing of New York Stock Exchange members (from *Banking and Monetary Statistics,* p. 500) minus borrowing from other than banks *(ibid.,* p. 494).

        1934B–1940: Sum of cols. 4 and 5 minus 110 percent of total borrowing of New York Stock Exchange members *(Banking and Monetary Statistics,* p. 500).

        1941–1949: From Table D-10, col. 12.

$ mill.

End of year	Bank loans on securities				Other loans to brokers and dealers	Total loans for purchasing or carrying securities	Bank loans on securities to		Other loans by individuals or partnerships	Net foreign debit balance in brokerage accounts	Individuals' net borrowing on securities
	Total	To customers except brokers and dealers		To brokers and dealers			Nonindividual customers	Incorporated brokers and dealers			
		Total	For purchasing or carrying securities								
	1	2	3	4	5	6	7	8	9	10	11
1896	882	728	291	154	–	445	15	0	–	–	430
1897	1 023	840	336	183	–	519	17	1	–	–	501
1898	1 156	936	374	220	–	594	19	3	–	–	572
1899	1 376	1 113	445	263	–	708	22	5	–	–	681
1900	1 586	1 269	508	317	–	825	25	8	–	–	792
1901	1 877	1 490	596	387	–	983	30	12	–	–	941
1902	2 062	1 662	665	400	–	1 065	33	15	–	–	1 017
1903	2 218	1 794	718	424	–	1 142	36	18	–	–	1 088
1904	2 253	1 793	717	460	–	1 177	36	23	–	–	1 118
1905	2 506	1 960	784	546	–	1 330	39	30	–	–	1 261
1906	2 619	2 069	828	550	–	1 378	41	34	–	–	1 303
1907	2 540	2 019	808	521	–	1 329	40	35	–	–	1 254
1908	2 624	2 086	834	538	–	1 372	42	40	–	–	1 290
1909	2 813	2 239	896	574	20	1 490	45	46	4	–	1 395
1910	2 818	2 271	908	547	50	1 505	45	47	10	–	1 403
1911	2 897	2 347	939	550	80	1 569	47	51	16	–	1 455
1912	3 085	2 511	1 004	574	110	1 688	50	57	22	–	1 559
1913	3 056	2 515	1 006	541	130	1 677	50	57	26	–	1 544
1914	3 217	2 625	1 050	592	160	1 802	52	66	32	–	1 652
1915A	3 942	3 146	1 258	796	190	2 244	63	94	38	–	2 049
1915B	3 968	3 166	1 266	802	190	2 258	63	94	38	–	2 063
1916	4 506	3 582	1 433	924	220	2 577	72	114	44	–	2 347
1917	5 092	4 378	1 751	714	250	2 715	88	93	50	–	2 484
1918	5 695	4 830	1 932	865	280	3 077	97	73	56	–	2 851
1919A	6 759	5 300	2 120	1 459	475	4 054	106	210	95	–	3 643
1919B	6 872	5 413	2 165	1 459	475	4 099	108	210	95	–	3 686
1920	6 080	5 185	2 074	895	405	3 374	124	152	81	–	3 017
1921	5 490	4 476	1 880	1 014	380	3 274	132	123	76	10	2 933
1922	6 051	4 358	1 874	1 693	505	4 072	150	202	101	31	3 588

Column 9 – 1896–1908: Assumed negligible.

1909–1928: Estimated as 20 percent of col. 5, based on percentage on July 31, 1929–1932, in U.S. Congress, Senate, *Stock Exchange Practices*, p. 7923, for street loans placed by thirty-three large banks for nonbank lenders.

1929, 1930, and 1931: Estimated as 23, 17, and 10 percent of col. 5, respectively, on basis of *Stock Exchange Practices*, p. 7923.

1932–1949: Assumed negligible.

Column 10 – 1896–1920: Assumed negligible.

1921–1949: From Table D-11, col. 1.

Column 11 – 1896–1949: Col. 6 minus sum of cols. 7-10. Three corrections are omitted because of lack of information and because of a presupposition that corrections are small in size and of opposite effect on total borrowing on securities by individuals. These are loans to incorporated brokers and dealers by others than banks (particularly as data used in col. 5 seem to be based on borrowing by New York Stock Exchange members only); incorporated brokers' and dealers' loans to individual customers; and unincorporated brokers' and dealers' loans to nonindividual customers.

INDIVIDUALS' NET BORROWING ON SECURITIES
1896 to 1949

$ mill.

End of year	Bank loans on securities				Other loans to brokers and dealers	Total loans for purchasing or carrying securities	Bank loans on securities to		Other loans by individuals or partnerships	Net foreign debit balance in brokerage accounts	Individuals' net borrowing on securities
	Total	To customers except brokers and dealers		To brokers and dealers			Nonindividual customers	Incorporated brokers and dealers			
		Total	For purchasing or carrying securities								
	1	2	3	4	5	6	7	8	9	10	11
1923	6 087	4 684	2 108	1 403	450	3 961	190	160	90	37	3 484
1924	7 221	5 096	2 344	2 125	550	5 019	234	277	110	72	4 326
1925	8 781	5 582	2 679	3 199	1 050	6 928	321	449	210	144	5 804
1926	8 658	6 106	3 175	2 552	1 300	7 027	444	363	260	158	5 802
1927	9 857	6 389	3 642	3 468	1 830	8 940	583	608	366	254	7 129
1928A	10 484	6 565	4 005	3 919	3 885	11 809	721	1 108	777	429	8 774
1928B	10 993	7 074	4 315	3 919	3 885	12 119	777	1 108	777	429	9 028
1929	11 264	8 530	5 544	2 734	2 450	10 728	1 109	1 040	564	316	7 699
1930	10 477	8 065	4 839	2 412	610	7 861	871	1 033	104	205	5 648
1931	7 620	6 548	3 667	1 072	140	4 879	587	558	14	82	3 638
1932	5 779	5 115	2 660	664	75	3 399	372	365	–	50	2 612
1933	5 120	4 003	1 961	1 117	75	3 153	235	270	–	81	2 567
1934A	4 595	3 452	1 553	1 143	65	2 761	155	246	–	77	2 283
1934B	4 652	3 579	1 611	1 073	65	2 749	161	168	–	77	2 343
1935	4 583	3 309	1 390	1 274	30	2 694	139	255	–	71	2 229
1936	4 635	3 181	1 241	1 454	40	2 735	124	345	–	64	2 202
1937	4 118	3 142	1 068	976	30	2 074	107	255	–	30	1 682
1938	4 005	2 998	872	1 007	40	1 919	87	217	–	30	1 585
1939	.	.	814	821	40	1 675	81	161	–	1	1 432
1940	.	.	745	667	40	1 452	74	247	–	−24	1 155
1941	.	.	679	617	20	1 316	68	207	–	−24	1 065
1942	.	.	612	955	–	1 567	61	405	–	−28	1 129
1943	.	.	945	1 421	–	2 366	94	621	–	−41	1 692
1944	.	.	2 322	2 280	–	4 602	232	1 160	–	−49	3 259
1945	.	.	3 696	3 180	–	6 876	370	1 930	–	−67	4 643
1946	.	.	1 649	1 525	–	3 174	165	1 105	–	−77	1 981
1947	.	.	1 220	827	–	2 047	122	487	–	−66	1 504
1948	.	.	962	1 343	–	2 305	96	863	–	−46	1 392
1949	.	.	876	1 758	–	2 634	88	1 008	–	−47	1 585

1919 to 1938

$ mill.

End of year	Loans by banks			Loans to brokers and dealers		Total loans on securities	End of year	Loans by banks			Loans to brokers and dealers		Total loans on securities
	Total	To brokers and dealers	To others	By others than banks	Total			Total	To brokers and dealers	To others	By others than banks	Total	
	1	2	3	4	5	6		1	2	3	4	5	6
1919	6 872	1 459	5 413	475	1 934	7 347	1929	11 264	2 734	8 530	2 450	5 184	13 714
1920	6 080	895	5 185	405	1 300	6 485	1930	10 477	2 412	8 065	610	3 022	11 087
1921	5 490	1 014	4 476	380	1 394	5 870	1931	7 620	1 072	6 548	140	1 212	7 760
1922	6 051	1 693	4 358	505	2 198	6 556	1932	5 779	664	5 115	75	739	5 854
1923	6 087	1 403	4 684	450	1 853	6 537	1933	5 120	1 117	4 003	75	1 192	5 195
1924	7 221	2 125	5 096	550	2 675	7 771	1934A	4 595	1 143	3 452	65	1 208	4 660
1925	8 781	3 199	5 582	1 050	4 249	9 831	1934B	4 652	1 073	3 579	65	1 138	4 717
1926	8 658	2 552	6 106	1 300	3 852	9 958	1935	4 583	1 274	3 309	30	1 304	4 613
1927	9 857	3 468	6 389	1 830	5 298	11 687	1936	4 635	1 454	3 181	40	1 494	4 675
1928A	10 484	3 919	6 565	3 885	7 804	14 369	1937	4 118	976	3 142	30	1 006	4 148
1928B	10 993	3 919	7 074	3 885	7 804	14 878	1938	4 005	1 007	2 998	40	1 047	4 045

Column 1 – 1919–1928A: Estimated at 145 percent of total loans on securities by weekly reporting member banks on last Wednesday (for 1919–1930, Friday) of years as shown in *Banking and Monetary Statistics*, pp. 132–141. Ratio is based on estimate of Livermore, Shaw, "Loans on Securities, 1921–1932," *Review of Economic Statistics*, vol. XIV, p. 191, that loans on securities by weekly reporting member banks amounted to about 68.8 percent of total loans by banks on securities. Loans to banks cannot be eliminated from these data but do not appear to have constituted a significant part of the total.

1928B–1934A: Estimated at 111 percent of loans on securities to other than banks by all member banks (*Banking and Monetary Statistics*, p. 76) based on Livermore's estimate (*op. cit.*) that loans on securities by all member banks amounted to about 90 percent of those by all banks.

1934B–1938: Sum of cols. 2 and 3.

Column 2 – 1919–1925: Estimated at 110 percent of street loans by daily reporting banks in New York City from the weekly data in *Banking and Monetary Statistics*, table 140, pp. 495–497.

For all years except 1924, 1925, and 1928 the last Dec. figure was averaged with the first figure for Jan. of the following year to obtain a year end figure. For 1924, 1925, and 1928 year-end figures were given.

1926–1927: Estimated at 124 percent of loans to brokers and dealers in New York City for own account and for out-of-town banks, as shown in *Banking and Monetary Statistics*, p. 497.

1928A: Estimated at 111 percent of all member bank loans to brokers and dealers (*Banking and Monetary Statistics*, p. 76) on the basis of Livermore's computations (*op. cit.*). Overlapping data in 1925–1928 permitted linking to make a continuous series.

1928B–1934A: Same procedure as for col. 1.

1934B–1938: Loans by all insured commercial banks to brokers and dealers for purchasing or carrying securities (*Banking and Monetary Statistics*, p. 109) increased by 0.5 percent to account for loans of uninsured banks. Step-up ratio is based on 1948 and 1949 data in the *Annual Report of the Federal Deposit Insurance Corporation* and *Annual Report of the Comptroller of the Currency* (see note to Table D-8, col. 3).

Column 3 – 1919–1928A: Col. 1 minus col. 2.

1928B–1934A: Same procedure as for col. 1.

1934B–1937: Same source and method as col. 2, step-up ratio for this item being 2.5 percent.

1938: Estimated on basis that total loans on securities for all member banks, regardless of purpose, declined by 4.6 percent from Dec. 1937 to Dec. 1938 (cf. *Federal Reserve Bulletin*, April 1939, p. 322).

Column 4 – 1919–1938: *Banking and Monetary Statistics*, table 139, p. 494.

Column 5 – 1919–1938: Sum of cols. 2 and 4.

Column 6 – 1919–1938: Sum of cols. 1 and 4.

Column 1 – 1941–1949: From Table D–8, col. 3.

Column 2 – 1941–1949: Sum of cols. 3 and 4.

Column 3 – 1941–1949: Friend, I. and Natrella, V., *Individuals' Saving*, part II, table 15, line 2a, adjusted for coverage by ratio of col. 1 to corresponding figure to table 15, line 2.

Column 4 – 1941–1949: From Friend and Natrella, *op. cit.*, line 2c; adjusted for coverage by ratio of col. 1 to corresponding figure in line 2; and reduced by 10 percent, assumed share of nonindividual borrowers.

Column 5 – 1941–1949: Col. 1 minus col. 2.

Column 6 – 1941–1949: Same source and method as col. 3.

Column 7 – 1941–1949: Col. 5 minus col. 6.

Column 8 – 1941–1949: From Table D–8, sum of cols. 4 and 5.

Column 9 – 1941: Estimated at about 10 percent above borrowing by members of the New York Stock Exchange (*Banking and Monetary Statistics*, p. 500).
1942–1949: Sum of cols. 10 and 11.

Column 10 – 1941: Assumed to be negligible.
1942: Rough estimate.
1943–1949: Estimated at between 20 and 30 percent in excess of borrowing by members of the New York Stock Exchange on U.S. Government securities (*The Exchange*, Jan. issues).

Column 11 – 1941: Equal to col. 9.
1942–1949: Assumed to be about 10 percent in excess of borrowing by members of the New York Stock Exchange on securities other than U.S. Government securities (*The Exchange*, Jan. issues).

Column 12 – 1941–1949: Col. 8 minus col. 9. Reasonableness of resulting figures was checked by comparison with borrowing reported to Bureau of Internal Revenue by incorporated security brokers and dealers (cf. Table D–13, cols. 8–10). While resulting figures are generally in excess of notes, etc., payable within less than one year reported by incorporated security brokers and dealers, and constitute a varying proportion of their total borrowing, figures shown in col. 12 remain in all years below total reported borrowing, and generally, also, below total notes, etc., payable alone. For 1946–1947 an additional check is possible against difference between money borrowed by all brokers and dealers registered with Securities and Exchange Commission and by registered members of the New York Stock Exchange (cf. Table D–14). Results of this comparison are satisfactory for 1947 but rather poor for 1946, which may be due to the fact that neither Securities and Exchange Commission nor Bureau of Internal Revenue figures refer consistently to the end of the year and changes in borrowing were apparently very substantial in the course of 1946.

Column 13 – 1941: Rough estimate.
1942–1949: Obtained by subtracting col. 10 from total loans to brokers and dealers on U.S. Government securities, as estimated by Friend and Natrella on basis of data for weekly reporting member banks (*Individuals' Saving*, part II, table 15, line 1a).

Column 14 – 1941–1949: Col. 12 minus col. 13. It may be assumed that a substantial part of this column reflects borrowing on incorporated dealers' inventories of state and local government securities, particularly from 1945 on.

D-11   TABLE D–11

Column 1 – 1920–1933: Estimated as a percentage of total borrowing by brokers and dealers, Table D–8, col. 4 plus col. 5, rising linearly from 0 percent in 1920 to 6.8 percent in 1930–1933, the 1934 percentage.
1934–1949: Foreign debit balances minus foreign credit balances in brokerage accounts, from "Statistics of International Capital Movements" in Department of the Treasury, *Treasury Bulletin*, various issues or supplements.

Column 2 – 1921–1949: First differences of col. 1.

1941 to 1949

$ mill.

End of year	Loans by banks to customers						
	Total	To individuals			To nonindividuals		
		Total	On U.S Government securities	On other securities	Total	On U.S. Government securities	On other securities
	1	2	3	4	5	6	7
1941	679	611	–	611	68	–	68
1942	612	555	36	519	57	–	57
1943	945	689	286	403	256	211	45
1944	2 322	1 230	762	468	1 092	1 039	53
1945	3 696	1 838	1 295	543	1 858	1 798	60
1946	1 649	1 093	510	583	556	491	65
1947	1 220	989	395	594	231	165	66
1948	962	898	320	578	64	0	64
1949	876	815	270	545	61	0	61

End of year	Loans to brokers and dealers						
	Total	To unincorporated firms			To corporations		
		Total	On U.S. Government securities	On other securities	Total	On U.S. Government securities	On other securities
	8	9	10	11	12	13	14
1941	637	430	–	430	207	50	157
1942	955	550	150	400	405	315	90
1943	1 421	800	300	500	621	502	119
1944	2 280	1 120	500	620	1 160	972	188
1945	3 180	1 250	600	650	1 930	1 549	381
1946	1 525	420	200	220	1 105	839	266
1947	827	340	70	270	487	237	250
1948	1 343	480	200	280	863	620	243
1949	1 758	750	150	600	1 008	637	371

FOREIGN CUSTOMERS' NET DEBIT BALANCES
WITH BROKERS AND DEALERS: 1920 to 1949

$ mill.

Year	Amount	Annual change	Year	Amount	Annual change	Year	Amount	Annual change
	1	2		1	2		1	2
1920	0	.	1930	205	–111	1940	–24	–25
1921	10	10	1931	82	–123	1941	–24	0
1922	31	21	1932	50	–32	1942	–28	–4
1923	37	6	1933	81	31	1943	–41	–13
1924	72	35	1934	77	–4	1944	–49	–8
1925	144	72	1935	71	–6	1945	–67	–18
1926	158	14	1936	64	–7	1946	–77	–10
1927	254	96	1937	30	–34	1947	–66	11
1928	429	175	1938	30	0	1948	–46	20
1929	316	–113	1939	1	–29	1949	–47	–1

D-12   TABLE D-12

Columns 1, 6, and 9 – 1935–1941: *Banking and Monetary Statistics*, p. 503.
    1942–1949: *Federal Reserve Bulletin*, 1950, p. 1367.

Columns 2 to 5, 7, 8, 10, 11 – 1935–1941: *Banking and Monetary Statistics*, p. 503.
    1942–1949: Federal Reserve Board estimates.

D-13   TABLE D-13

Column 1 – 1935–1937: *Statistics of Income Source Book*. Group is designated as "Stock and bond brokers, investment brokers, investment bankers."
    Figures for a similarly described group are available in the *Source Book* back to 1930. Number of corporations included and figures reported under individual balance sheet headings, however, indicate that classification must have been changed substantially after 1933 and possibly again after 1934 with result that figures for years 1930 to 1934 are not comparable to those for the later period.
    1938–1945: From *Statistics of Income*, part II, various issues. Group is designated as "Security and commodity exchange brokers and dealers."
    1946–1947: From *Treasury Department Releases*, S-1057 and S-2449.

Columns 2 to 5, 9 – 1935–1947: Same source as col. 1.

Column 6 – 1935–1947: Same source as col. 1. Includes gross capital assets minus reserves and land.

Column 7 – 1935–1947: Same source as col. 1. Includes for 1935 $15 million designated as "Inventories" which probably represent additional holdings of securities.

Column 8 – 1935–1947: Same source as col. 1. In 1935 and 1936 included under "Notes and accounts payable," which have been regarded as equivalent to sum of cols. 8 and 9 from 1937 on.

Column 10 – 1935–1947: Same source as col. 1. Figures for 1935 and 1936 are those reported under "Bonded debt and mortgages."

Column 11 – 1935–1947: Same source as col. 1. "Surplus reserves" (amounting to $20 million in 1938) included in 1935 to 1937.

Column 12 – 1935–1947: Same source as col. 1. Includes capital stock, net surplus, and undivided profits and, from 1938 on, surplus reserves.

    Note: Details may not add to totals because of rounding.

714

DEBIT AND CREDIT BALANCES AND RELATED ITEMS OF MEMBER FIRMS OF THE NEW YORK STOCK EXCHANGE CARRYING MARGIN ACCOUNTS 1935 to 1949

D-12

$ mill.

End of year	Assets					Liabilities					
		Net debit balances due from			Commodity margins and other debit balances	Money borrowed	Net credit balances due to				Pending delivery, net
	Cash	Member firms of security exchanges	Customers and partners	Firm investment and trading accounts			Member firms of national exchanges	Customers, free	Customers and partners, other	Firm account and all other	
	1	2	3	4	5	6	7	8	9	10	11
1935	179	122	1 333	135	111	929	100	286	103	41	10
1936	249	109	1 459	164	120	1 048	91	342	133	49	14
1937	232	78	1 019	108	109	688	68	278	111	35	10
1938	190	105	1 023	106	92	755	84	247	82	31	12
1939	207	91	922	78	93	638	77	266	92	29	13
1940	204	56	689	99	71	427	52	281	76	26	11
1941	211	52	608	86	73	368	46	289	80	29	4
1942	160	43	550	154	56	378	39	270	69	24	3
1943	181	55	800	188	59	558	55	354	79	34	6
1944	209	69	1 048	260	60	726	60	472	114	38	9
1945	313	77	1 150	413	96	795	72	654	141	63	26
1946	456	39	545	312	107	218	41	694	150	52	14
1947	393	47	585	315	121	240	45	612	199	65	25
1948	349	39	560	312	103	257	40	586	140	46	15
1949	306	57	886	400	108	524	53	633	185	56	36

PRINCIPAL ASSETS AND LIABILITIES OF INCORPORATED SECURITY AND COMMODITY BROKERS AND DEALERS: 1935 to 1947

D-13

$ mill.

End of year	Total assets	Cash	Notes and accounts receivable	Investments		Net capital assets	Other assets	Accounts payable	Notes, mortgages, etc. payable		Other liabilities	Net capital
				Government	Other				Less 1 year	1 year and over		
	1	2	3	4	5	6	7	8	9	10	11	12
1935	1 320	113	271	197	642	20	77	584		48	147	540
1936	1 242	114	285	176	593	15	58	616		28	148	450
1937	922	93	164	180	405	12	68	150	217	40	110	405
1938	950	119	220	161	350	18	82	197	139	69	160	385
1939	818	135	150	145	320	23	45	180	134	43	110	352
1940	724	108	151	86	324	14	41	160	106	54	92	312
1941	714	97	121	159	273	14	49	147	119	68	109	271
1942	893	73	169	290	315	28	18	218	178	172	94	231
1943	1 125	87	139	421	418	33	27	237	369	225	63	231
1944	1 529	87	191	509	655	35	52	352	549	317	77	234
1945	2 175	139	284	680	982	33	57	541	786	463	103	282
1946	1 833	140	288	710	568	39	88	373	504	443	198	315
1947	1 420	170	303	396	357	39	155	333	276	217	278	316

TABLE D–14

Columns 1 to 4 – Securities and Exchange Commission Release, Survey Series 141, Nov. 26, 1948. Figures are taken from last report of firms during year. They thus do not refer uniformly to one date but are distributed over the entire calendar year. It is understood, however, that about two-thirds of the reports reflect the firms' situation at a date in December.

Columns 5 and 6 – Federal Reserve Bulletin, Aug. 1950, p. 1039. All figures refer to end of Dec.

Columns 7 and 8 – Treasury Department Releases, S-1051, Apr. 21, 1949 and S-2449, Sept. 22, 1950. "Notes and accounts receivable" have been regarded as equivalent to customers' debit balances; "Accounts payable" to customers' credit balances; and "Bonds, notes, mortgages, maturity less than one year" to money borrowed. Figures refer to end of corporations' fiscal year.

TABLE D–15

Column 1 – Securities and Exchange Commission Release, Survey Series 141, Nov. 26, 1948. Figures are taken from latest report of firm during 1946, most of which refer to a date in December.

Column 2 – Col. 1 minus col. 3.

Column 3 – Estimated at three-fourths of differences between figures for all registered brokers and dealers and those which are members of New York Stock Exchange.

Column 4 – Col. 3 divided by col. 1.

Column 5 – Sum of cols. 6 and 7.

Column 6 – Securities and Exchange Commission figures for members of New York Stock Exchange increased by 20 percent to take account of other brokers and dealers.

Column 7 – From *Treasury Department Release*, S-1051, Apr. 21, 1949.

Column 8 – Col. 7 divided by col. 5.

Column 9 – Sum of cols. 10 and 11.

Column 10 – Figures for New York Stock Exchange members carrying margin accounts as given in *Federal Reserve Bulletin*, Aug. 1950, increased by 20 percent to take account of other unincorporated brokers and dealers.

Column 11 – Same source and procedure as col. 7.

Column 12 – Col. 11 divided by col. 9.

MAIN BALANCE SHEET ITEMS OF SECURITY BROKERS AND DEALERS: 1946 and 1947

D-14

$ mill.

	All registered brokers and dealers		Registered member firms of New York Stock Exchange		New York Stock Exchange member firms carrying margin accounts		Incorporated brokers and dealers	
	1946	1947	1946	1947	1946	1947	1946	1947
	1	2	3	4	5	6	7	8
Number of firms	3 284	3 284	528	528	.	.	1 261	1 326
Cash	622	577	430	407	456	393	140	170
Customers' debit balances	1 038	754	823	573	540	578	288	303
Debit balances in firms and partners' account (net)	.	.	.	.	277	284	.	.
Inventory of securities, total	1 609	1 145	762	565	.	.	1 278	753
Inventory of securities, government	810	535	393	302	.	.	711	396
Inventory of securities, other	798	610	369	263	.	.	568	357
Customers' free credit balances	713	659	659	613	694	612	373	333
Customers' other credit balances	262	281	142	137	120	176		
Money borrowed	1 337	882	638	290	218	240	504	276
Other liabilities	.	.	.	.	.	.	641	494
Aggregate indebtedness (excluding borrowing on exempt securities)	2 488	2 077	1 539	1 185	.	.	.	.
Net capital	935	803	507	411	.	.	315	280

VARIOUS ESTIMATES OF PRINCIPAL ASSETS AND LIABILITIES OF SECURITY BROKERS AND DEALERS: 1946

D-15

	Method I				Method II				Method III			
	Total	Unin- corpo- rated	In- corpo- rated	Propor- tion in- corpo- rated	Total	Unin- corpo- rated	In- corpo- rated	Propor- tion in- corpo- rated	Total	Unin- corpo- rated	In- corpo- rated	Propor- tion in- corpo- rated
	$ mill.			Percent	$ mill.			Percent	$ mill.			Percent
	1	2	3	4	5	6	7	8	9	10	11	12
Cash	622	479	143	23	656	516	140	21	687	547	140	20
Customers' debit balances	1 038	877	161	16	1 276	988	288 [1]	23	942	654	288 [1]	31
Government securities	810	497	313	39	1 182	471	711	60	.	.	711	.
Other securities	798	476	322	40	1 011	443	568	56	.	.	568	.
Customers' free credit balances	713	672	41	6	791				833			
					1 334		373 [2]	28	1 386		373 [2]	27
Customers' other	262	172	90	34	170				180			
Borrowed from banks	1 337	812	525	39	1 270	766	504 [3]	40	766	262	504 [3]	66
Capital	935	615	320	34	923	608	315	34	.	.	315	.

[1] Notes and accounts receivable.
[2] Accounts payable.
[3] Bonds, notes, and mortgages with maturity of less than one year.

717

Column 1 – 1897–1899: *Commercial and Financial Chronicle*, 1902, p. 70.
            1900–1933: *Historical Statistics*, p. 282. This series covers only reported full lot trading.

Column 2 – 1897–1919: Obtained by dividing col. 3 by col. 1. Refers to reported round lot trading only.
            1920–1924: Obtained by interpolating between 1919 and 1925 values with the help of Alfred
            Cowles and Associates index of common stock prices (cf. *Common Stock Indexes*, p. 67).
            1925–1933: Read off from chart in New York Stock Exchange, *The Exchange*, Jan. 1938.

Column 3 – 1897–1920: Estimates of *Commercial and Financial Chronicle* (cf. 1921, p. 204; 1902, p. 70).
            1921–1933: Col. 1 multiplied by col. 2.

VALUE OF STOCK TRADING ON NEW YORK STOCK EXCHANGE
1897 to 1933

Year	Number of shares traded	Average traded price	Value of reported trading	Year	Number of shares traded	Average traded price	Value of reported trading	Year	Number of shares traded	Average traded price	Value of reported trading
	mill.	$	$ bill.		mill.	$	$ bill.		mill.	$	$ bill.
	1	2	3		1	2	3		1	2	3
1897	77	64	5.0	1910	164	86	14.1	1923	236	60	14.2
1898	113	72	8.2	1911	127	87	11.0	1924	282	52	14.6
1899	176	76	13.4	1912	131	88	11.6	1925	454	61	27.6
1900	139	66	9.2	1913	83	86	7.2	1926	451	69	31.1
1901	265	77	20.4	1914	48	81	3.9	1927	577	71	41.0
1902	187	76	14.2	1915	173	73	12.7	1928	920	75	69.0
1903	159	69	11.0	1916	233	81	18.9	1929	1 125	77	86.6
1904	187	64	12.1	1917	186	84	15.6	1930	810	53	42.9
1905	261	82	21.3	1918	144	87	12.5	1931	577	35	20.2
1906	282	83	23.4	1919	317	82	25.9	1932	425	22	9.4
1907	195	76	14.8	1920	227	73	16.5	1933	655	23	15.1
1908	195	79	15.3	1921	173	58	10.0				
1909	212	90	19.1	1922	259	65	16.8				

INDIVIDUALS' SAVING THROUGH MORTGAGES ADJUSTED
FOR REDUCTION THROUGH FORECLOSURES AND WRITE-DOWNS
1921 to 1949

$ mill.

Year	All mortgages	Nonfarm mortgages					Farm mortgages
		Total	Residential			Nonresidential	
			Total	1- to 4-family	Multi-family		
	1	2	3	4	5	6	7
1921	268	218	199	106	93	19	50
1922	−17	147	205	143	62	−58	−164
1923	359	704	582	432	150	122	−345
1924	−272	339	353	226	127	−14	−611
1925	549	812	727	451	276	85	−263
1926	781	916	1 084	446	638	−168	−135
1927	1 320	1 326	1 207	541	666	119	−6
1928	1 646	1 572	1 473	659	814	99	74
1929	1 895	1 919	1 499	541	958	420	−24
1930	790	864	717	105	612	147	−74
1931	−169	−46	−100	−43	−57	54	−123
1932	−210	−3	−58	−85	27	55	−207
1933	−863	−505	−573	−299	−274	68	−358
1934	−482	−208	−219	102	−321	11	−274
1935	146	148	128	273	−145	20	−2
1936	112	215	17	137	−120	198	−103
1937	99	155	204	266	−62	−49	−56
1938	−197	−153	27	114	−87	−180	−44
1939	−288	−254	−59	6	−65	−195	−34
1940	−276	−239	−42	−5	−37	−197	−37
1941	84	120	75	92	−17	45	−36
1942	−226	−155	−185	−137	−48	30	−71
1943	−233	−177	−204	−34	−170	27	−56
1944	24	91	130	194	−64	−39	−67
1945	646	639	292	290	2	347	7
1946	1 574	1 479	874	1 036	−162	605	95
1947	1 676	1 617	981	938	43	636	59
1948	1 194	1 092	637	547	90	455	102
1949	607	514	100	30	70	414	93

Column 1 – Sum of cols. 2 and 7.

Column 2 – Sum of cols. 3 and 6.

Column 3 – Sum of cols. 4 and 5.

Column 4 – Table M-2, col. 4 plus: (a) 25 percent of Table M-23, col. 2, on assumption that one- to four-family dwellings foreclosed by individual mortgagees were resold on the basis of, on the average, 25 percent cash payment and 75 percent purchase money mortgage (average for properties sold by the Home Owners' Loan Corporation from 1936 through 1946 was 20 percent cash); and (b) Table M-26, col. 3.

Column 5 – The sum of Table M-2, col. 5, Table M-26, col. 4, and 25 percent of Table M-23, col. 3.

Column 6 – The sum of Table M-2, col. 6, Table M-26, col. 5, and 25 percent of Table M-23, col. 4.

Column 7 – Table M-2, col. 7 plus 30 percent of Table M-28, col. 7. This ratio is based on sales of 13 large insurance companies during the period 1928–1937.

INDIVIDUALS' SAVING THROUGH MORTGAGES NOT ADJUSTED FOR REDUCTION THROUGH FORECLOSURES AND WRITE-DOWNS: 1897 to 1949

$ mill.

Year	All mortgages	Nonfarm mortgages					Farm mortgages
		Total	Residential			Nonresidential	
			Total	1- to 4-family	Multi-family		
	1	2	3	4	5	6	7
1897	57	3	11	10	1	−8	54
1898	53	0	4	2	2	−4	53
1899	56	8	17	17	0	−9	48
1900	46	7	15	16	−1	−8	39
1901	50	11	17	12	5	−6	39
1902	52	10	19	15	4	−9	42
1903	67	21	24	17	7	−3	46
1904	61	16	18	13	5	−2	45
1905	65	28	36	34	2	−8	37
1906	40	23	29	27	2	−6	17
1907	66	21	12	3	9	9	45
1908	73	17	15	10	5	2	56
1909	56	36	39	35	4	−3	20
1910	202	30	30	27	3	0	172
1911	235	30	15	6	9	15	205
1912	241	30	17	8	9	13	211
1913	603	385	247	195	52	138	218
1914	459	302	197	156	41	105	157
1915	257	142	85	59	26	57	115
1916	462	258	162	124	38	96	204
1917	995	654	426	332	94	228	341
1918	389	261	159	103	56	102	128
1919	934	141	65	29	36	76	793
1920	1 960	1 126	679	503	176	447	834
1921	259	218	199	106	93	19	41
1922	−32	147	205	143	62	−58	−179
1923	338	704	582	432	150	122	−366
1924	−296	339	353	226	127	−14	−635
1925	525	812	727	451	276	85	287
1926	732	891	1 064	434	630	−173	−159
1927	1 260	1 290	1 179	523	656	111	−30
1928	1 580	1 530	1 439	637	802	91	50
1929	1 824	1 872	1 462	516	946	410	−48
1930	685	786	654	67	587	132	−101
1931	−379	−216	−228	−116	−112	12	−163
1932	−517	−244	−241	−188	−53	−3	−273
1933	−1 136	−746	−746	−397	−349	0	−390
1934	−731	−438	−381	12	−393	−57	−293
1935	−103	−82	−34	183	−217	−48	−21
1936	−70	52	−101	72	−173	153	−122
1937	−50	25	111	213	−102	−86	−75
1938	−308	−247	−47	72	−119	−200	−61
1939	−364	−315	−107	−22	−85	−208	−49
1940	−338	−289	−82	−27	−55	−207	−49
1941	58	102	62	84	−22	40	−44
1942	−250	−173	−198	−145	−53	25	−77
1943	−246	−186	−211	−39	−172	25	−60
1944	15	85	126	192	−66	−41	−70
1945	639	635	289	288	1	346	4
1946	1 568	1 476	872	1 035	−163	604	92
1947	1 670	1 614	979	937	42	635	56
1948	1 187	1 088	634	545	89	454	99
1949	599	509	97	28	69	412	90

TABLE M-2

Column 1 – 1897–1949: Sum of cols. 2 and 7.

Column 2 – 1897–1949: Sum of cols. 3 and 6.

Column 3 – 1897–1949: Sum of cols. 4 and 5.

Column 4 – 1897–1924: Annual differences in Table M-5, col. 2.
  1925–1949: Annual differences in Table M-9, col. 2 adjusted in 1933–1936 for mortgages exchanged for Home Owners' Loan Corporation bonds as estimated in Table M-21, cols. 6 and 7 plus 10 percent.

Column 5 – 1897–1924: Annual differences in Table M-6, col. 2.
  1925–1949: Annual differences in Table M-10, col. 2.

Column 6 – 1897–1924: Annual differences in Table M-7, col. 2.
  1925–1927: Annual differences in Table M-11, col. 2.
  1928–1949: Annual differences in Table M-12, col. 7.

Column 7 – 1897–1949: Annual differences in Table M-27, col. 6 plus col. 7 plus col. 8 adjusted in 1933–1936 for mortgages exchanged by individual mortgagees for bonds of Federal Farm Mortgage Corporation. The total of such exchanges may be estimated at about $500 million (cf. Department of Agriculture, Farm Credit Administration, *Farm Credit Quarterly*, Sept. 1936, p. 149) of which $30 million is allocated to 1933, $320 million to 1934, $130 million to 1935, and $20 million to 1936 on the basis of distribution of new issues of Federal Farm Mortgage Corporation bonds over the four-year period.

TABLE M-3

Column 1 – From Table R-34, col. 1.

Column 2 – Col. 1 minus col. 3.

Column 3 – Sum of cols. 4–15.

Column 4 – From Table L-24, col. 5.

Column 5 – From Table M-14, col. 2.

Column 6 – Table L-29, col. 4 minus Table A-61, col. 11.

Column 7 – From Table J-2, col. 2.

Column 8 – From Table I-5, col. 4.

Column 9 – Table I-10, col. 4 minus Table A-61, col. 8.

Column 10 – From Table V-55, col. 3.

Column 11 – From Table V-56, col. 3.

Column 12 – From Table I-14, col. 3.

Column 13 – From Table V-54, col. 3.

Column 14 – From Table M-20, col. 2.

Column 15 – From Table M-19, col. 2.

$ mill.

End of year	Total outstanding	Non-institutional holdings	Institutional holdings						
			Total	Commercial banks		Mutual savings banks	Savings and loan associations	Life insurance companies
				Operating	Closed			
	1	2	3	4	5	6	7	8
1896	4 239	2 325	1 914	335	–	706	429	322
1897	4 239	2 328	1 911	332	–	731	403	328
1898	4 269	2 328	1 941	342	–	757	396	328
1899	4 309	2 336	1 973	352	–	790	376	335
1900	4 409	2 343	2 066	376	–	839	371	357
1901	4 510	2 354	2 156	412	–	874	367	377
1902	4 662	2 364	2 298	464	–	922	378	402
1903	4 838	2 385	2 453	525	–	965	394	434
1904	5 047	2 401	2 646	596	–	1 020	423	463
1905	5 313	2 429	2 884	697	–	1 092	448	494
1906	5 612	2 452	3 160	778	–	1 175	487	559
1907	5 829	2 473	3 356	801	–	1 229	538	614
1908	6 045	2 490	3 555	847	–	1 294	575	650
1909	6 410	2 526	3 884	968	–	1 384	628	703
1910	6 785	2 556	4 229	1 057	–	1 476	690	784
1911	7 108	2 586	4 522	1 096	–	1 572	768	854
1912	7 451	2 616	4 835	1 153	–	1 679	847	913
1913	8 103	3 001	5 102	1 171	–	1 768	930	971
1914	8 672	3 303	5 369	1 236	–	1 809	1 013	1 034
1915	9 075	3 445	5 630	1 345	–	1 881	1 098	1 016
1916	9 606	3 703	5 903	1 377	–	1 994	1 175	1 053
1917	10 612	4 357	6 255	1 474	–	2 064	1 293	1 095
1918	11 058	4 618	6 440	1 546	–	2 038	1 387	1 124
1919	11 617	4 759	6 858	1 741	–	2 142	1 552	1 068
1920	13 516	5 885	7 631	1 900	–	2 366	1 860	1 085
1921	14 744	6 103	8 641	2 035	5	2 583	2 179	1 358
1922	16 197	6 250	9 947	2 499	5	2 878	2 468	1 534
1923	18 766	6 954	11 812	3 129	10	3 237	2 917	1 840
1924	21 335	7 293	14 042	3 828	15	3 660	3 519	2 203

End of year	Institutional holdings						
	Fraternal insurance organizations	Other insurance companies				Mortgage companies	Installment investment companies
		Fire and marine	Casualty and miscellaneous	Mutual accident	Savings bank life		
	9	10	11	12	13	14	15
1896	1	64	2	0	–	55	–
1897	1	58	2	1	–	55	–
1898	2	53	2	1	–	60	–
1899	2	54	3	1	–	60	–
1900	2	51	3	1	–	66	–
1901	3	51	3	1	–	68	–
1902	4	47	4	2	–	75	–
1903	4	48	4	2	–	77	–
1904	4	48	4	2	–	86	–
1905	5	51	5	2	–	90	–
1906	7	46	5	2	–	101	–
1907	8	53	6	2	–	105	–
1908	10	54	8	2	–	115	–
1909	10	56	10	3	0	122	–
1910	12	61	10	3	0	136	–
1911	13	64	11	2	0	142	–
1912	15	65	12	2	0	149	–
1913	18	66	14	2	0	162	–
1914	19	68	15	2	0	173	–
1915	22	68	16	2	0	182	–
1916	25	71	14	2	0	192	–
1917	28	71	14	3	1	212	–
1918	31	74	14	3	1	221	1
1919	28	75	15	3	1	232	1
1920	34	87	23	3	1	270	2
1921	39	84	27	3	1	324	3
1922	50	82	31	6	1	389	4
1923	55	86	36	6	2	488	6
1924	72	88	38	11	2	598	8

HOLDINGS OF MORTGAGES ON NONFARM
RESIDENTIAL REAL ESTATE BY HOLDER GROUPS: 1896 to 1924

$ mill.

End of year	Total out- standing	Non- institu- tional holdings	Institutional holdings							
			Total	Com- mercial banks	Mutual savings banks	Savings and loan associ- ations	Insurance companies			Mortgage companies
							Life	Fraternal	Other	
	1	2	3	4	5	6	7	8	9	10
1896	2 840	1 557	1 283	173	445	429	166	0	33	37
1897	2 840	1 568	1 272	172	461	403	169	0	30	37
1898	2 860	1 572	1 288	177	477	396	169	1	28	40
1899	2 887	1 589	1 298	182	498	376	172	1	29	40
1900	2 954	1 604	1 350	194	529	371	183	1	28	44
1901	3 022	1 621	1 401	213	551	367	194	2	28	46
1902	3 124	1 640	1 484	240	581	378	207	2	26	50
1903	3 241	1 664	1 577	271	608	394	223	2	27	52
1904	3 381	1 682	1 699	308	643	423	238	2	27	58
1905	3 560	1 718	1 842	360	688	448	254	3	29	60
1906	3 760	1 747	2 013	402	740	487	287	3	26	68
1907	3 905	1 759	2 146	414	774	538	316	4	30	70
1908	4 050	1 774	2 276	438	815	575	334	5	32	77
1909	4 295	1 813	2 482	500	872	628	361	5	34	82
1910	4 546	1 843	2 703	546	930	690	403	6	37	91
1911	4 762	1 858	2 904	567	990	768	439	7	38	95
1912	4 992	1 875	3 117	596	1 058	847	469	7	40	100
1913	5 429	2 122	3 307	605	1 114	930	499	9	41	109
1914	5 810	2 319	3 491	639	1 140	1 013	531	10	42	116
1915	6 080	2 404	3 676	695	1 185	1 098	522	11	43	122
1916	6 436	2 566	3 870	712	1 256	1 175	541	13	44	129
1917	7 110	2 992	4 118	762	1 300	1 293	563	14	44	142
1918	7 409	3 151	4 258	799	1 284	1 387	578	15	46	148
1919	7 783	3 216	4 567	900	1 349	1 552	549	14	47	155
1920	9 042	3 895	5 147	982	1 491	1 860	558	17	57	181
1921	9 952	4 094	5 858	1 055	1 627	2 179	698	20	58	219
1922	11 014	4 299	6 715	1 295	1 813	2 468	788	25	60	264
1923	12 836	4 881	7 955	1 623	2 039	2 917	946	28	65	334
1924	14 700	5 234	9 466	1 987	2 306	3 519	1 132	36	70	412

Column 1 – From Table R-34, col. 2.

Column 2 – Col. 1 minus col. 3.

Column 3 – Sum of cols. 4–10. Includes for 1918–1924 very small amounts of residential mortgages held by installment investment companies as shown in Table M-19, col. 3.

Column 4 – Obtained by applying to total nonfarm mortgage holdings of commercial banks, as shown in Table M-3, col. 4, a multiplier of 0.517, the 1925 value obtained from Table M-13, cols. 2 and 3. Includes for 1921–1924 very small amounts of residential mortgages held by closed banks as estimated in Table M-14, col. 3.

Column 5 – Same procedure as col. 4 but multiplier of 0.630.

Column 6 – Assumed equal to total mortgage loans as shown in Table M-3, col. 7.

Column 7 – Same procedure as cols. 4 and 5, but multiplier of 0.514.

Column 8 – Estimated at 0.500 of nonfarm mortgage loans of fraternal insurance organizations as shown in Table M-3, col. 9.

Column 9 – Same procedure as cols. 4 and 5, but multiplier of 0.500.

Column 10 – From Table M-20, col. 3.

$ mill.

End of year	Total out-standing	Non-institu-tional holdings	Institutional holdings							Mortgage companies
			Total	Com-mercial banks	Mutual savings banks	Savings and loan associ-ations	Insurance companies			
							Life	Fraternal	Other	
1	2	3	4	5	6	7	8	9	10	

End of year	1	2	3	4	5	6	7	8	9	10
1896	2 579	1 424	1 155	142	381	429	141	0	28	34
1897	2 573	1 434	1 139	140	393	403	143	0	26	34
1898	2 585	1 436	1 149	144	405	396	143	1	24	36
1899	2 604	1 453	1 151	147	422	376	145	1	24	36
1900	2 659	1 469	1 190	156	445	371	153	1	24	40
1901	2 705	1 481	1 224	169	461	367	161	2	23	41
1902	2 780	1 496	1 284	188	481	378	170	2	21	44
1903	2 868	1 513	1 355	210	499	394	182	2	22	46
1904	2 975	1 526	1 449	236	523	423	192	2	22	51
1905	3 115	1 560	1 555	272	554	448	203	2	23	53
1906	3 271	1 587	1 684	299	590	487	226	2	21	59
1907	3 378	1 590	1 788	304	611	538	247	3	24	61
1908	3 483	1 600	1 883	318	637	575	258	4	25	66
1909	3 672	1 635	2 037	358	675	628	276	4	26	70
1910	3 864	1 662	2 202	385	712	690	305	5	28	77
1911	4 024	1 668	2 356	395	750	768	329	5	29	80
1912	4 193	1 676	2 517	409	794	847	348	5	30	84
1913	4 533	1 871	2 662	410	828	930	366	7	30	91
1914	4 822	2 027	2 795	426	838	1 013	385	7	30	96
1915	5 016	2 086	2 930	457	861	1 098	374	8	31	101
1916	5 278	2 210	3 068	461	903	1 175	383	9	31	106
1917	5 795	2 542	3 253	485	924	1 293	394	10	31	116
1918	6 001	2 645	3 356	502	904	1 387	400	10	32	120
1919	6 265	2 674	3 591	556	939	1 552	376	10	32	125
1920	7 234	3 177	4 057	597	1 026	1 860	377	12	39	145
1921	7 862	3 283	4 579	620	1 093	2 179	461	13	39	173
1922	8 591	3 426	5 165	737	1 191	2 468	507	16	39	206
1923	9 884	3 858	6 026	891	1 307	2 917	593	18	41	257
1924	11 172	4 084	7 088	1 053	1 444	3 519	692	22	43	313

Column 1 – From Table R-34, col. 3.

Column 2 – Col. 1 minus col. 3.

Column 3 – Sum of cols. 4–10. Includes for 1918 to 1924 very small amounts of one- to four-family mortgages held by installment investment companies as shown in Table M-19, col. 4.

Columns 4 to 10 – Difference between appropriate columns of Tables M-4 and M-6. Assumption that all mortgage loans by savings and loan associations were on one- to four-family dwellings, while substantially correct, is not entirely true. After these estimates were completed some indication of distribution of mortgage loans by type of property became available from a sample of loans made by ninety-two associations between 1920 and 1927 representing something like 0.5 percent of total loans outstanding (cf. Edwards, E. E., *Urban Real Estate Financing by Savings and Loan Associations*, preliminary manuscript from Financial Research Program, National Bureau of Economic Research, Dec. 1950, tables 9, 10, and 33). These data indicate that mortgage loans on one- to four-family dwellings accounted throughout the period for about 90–95 percent of the total. Loans on apartment houses, mostly structures of small size, seem to have accounted for nearly 5 percent in the 1920's, while their share had declined to about 2 percent in the 1940's. Loans on farm properties averaged about 1 percent. Small remainder was divided among loans on offices, stores, hotels, institutional structures, industrial properties, and vacant lots. If these figures are at all representative of the distribution of all associations' loans, separate allowance for the 5–10 percent not secured by one- to four-family dwellings would make only very little difference in the calculations of mortgage loans of different types held by individuals. Allocation of all loans to those on one- to four-family dwellings, of course, does not introduce an error into an estimate of individuals' holdings of total mortgage loans.

HOLDINGS OF MORTGAGES ON MULTI-FAMILY DWELLINGS
BY HOLDER GROUPS: 1896 to 1924

$ mill.

End of year	Total outstanding	Non-institutional holdings	Institutional holdings						
			Total	Commercial banks	Mutual savings banks	Insurance companies			Mortgage companies
						Life	Fraternal	Other	
	1	2	3	4	5	6	7	8	9
1896	261	133	128	31	64	25	0	5	3
1897	267	134	133	32	68	26	0	4	3
1898	275	136	139	33	72	26	0	4	4
1899	283	136	147	35	76	27	0	5	4
1900	295	135	160	38	84	30	0	4	4
1901	317	140	177	44	90	33	0	5	5
1902	344	144	200	52	100	37	0	5	6
1903	373	151	222	61	109	41	0	5	6
1904	406	156	250	72	120	46	0	5	7
1905	445	158	287	88	134	51	1	6	7
1906	489	160	329	103	150	61	1	5	9
1907	527	169	358	110	163	69	1	6	9
1908	567	174	393	120	178	76	1	7	11
1909	623	178	445	142	197	85	1	8	12
1910	682	181	501	161	218	98	1	9	14
1911	738	190	548	172	240	110	2	9	15
1912	799	199	600	187	264	121	2	10	16
1913	896	251	645	195	286	133	2	11	18
1914	988	292	696	213	302	146	3	12	20
1915	1 064	318	746	238	324	148	3	12	21
1916	1 158	356	802	251	353	158	4	13	23
1917	1 315	450	865	277	376	169	4	13	26
1918	1 408	506	902	297	380	178	5	14	28
1919	1 518	542	976	344	410	173	4	15	30
1920	1 808	718	1 090	385	465	181	5	18	36
1921	2 090	811	1 279	435	534	237	7	19	46
1922	2 423	873	1 550	558	622	281	9	21	58
1923	2 952	1 023	1 929	732	732	353	10	24	77
1924	3 528	1 150	2 378	934	862	440	14	27	99

Column 1 – From Table R-34, col. 4.

Column 2 – Col. 1 minus col. 3.

Column 3 – Sum of cols. 4–9. Includes for 1918–1924 very small amounts of multi-family mortgages held by installment investment companies as shown in Table M-19, col. 5.

Columns 4 to 8 – Obtained by applying to total residential mortgage loans of each mortgagee (as shown in Table M-4) multipliers representing the product of: (a) the quotient of the 1925 share of multi-family in total residential mortgages for each group of mortgagees divided by 1925 share of total multi-family debt outstanding to total residential debt (this quotient is 1.96 for commercial banks, 1.56 for mutual savings banks, 1.62 for life insurance companies, and 1.60 for fraternal and other insurance companies); and (b) the year's ratio of multi-family to total residential mortgage debt (as estimated in Table R-34, col. 7).

Column 9 – From Table M-20, col. 5.

HOLDINGS OF MORTGAGES ON NONFARM NONRESIDENTIAL REAL ESTATE   M-7
BY HOLDER GROUPS: 1896 to 1924

$ mill.

End of year	Total outstanding	Non-institutional holdings	Institutional holdings						Mortgage companies
			Total	Commercial banks	Mutual savings banks	Insurance companies			
						Life	Fraternal	Other	
	1	2	3	4	5	6	7	8	9
1896	1 399	768	631	162	261	156	1	33	18
1897	1 399	760	639	160	270	159	1	31	18
1898	1 409	756	653	165	280	159	1	28	20
1899	1 422	747	675	170	292	163	1	29	20
1900	1 455	739	716	182	310	174	1	27	22
1901	1 488	733	755	199	323	183	1	27	22
1902	1 538	724	814	224	341	195	2	27	25
1903	1 597	721	876	254	357	211	2	27	25
1904	1 666	719	947	288	377	225	2	27	28
1905	1 753	711	1 042	337	404	240	2	29	30
1906	1 852	705	1 147	376	435	272	4	27	33
1907	1 924	714	1 210	387	455	298	4	31	35
1908	1 995	716	1 279	409	479	316	5	32	38
1909	2 115	713	1 402	468	512	342	5	35	40
1910	2 239	713	1 526	511	546	381	6	37	45
1911	2 346	728	1 618	529	582	415	6	39	47
1912	2 459	741	1 718	557	621	444	8	39	49
1913	2 674	879	1 795	566	654	472	9	41	53
1914	2 862	984	1 878	597	669	503	9	43	57
1915	2 995	1 041	1 954	650	696	494	11	43	60
1916	3 170	1 137	2 033	665	738	512	12	43	63
1917	3 502	1 365	2 137	712	764	532	14	45	70
1918	3 649	1 467	2 182	747	754	546	16	46	73
1919	3 834	1 543	2 291	841	793	519	14	47	77
1920	4 474	1 990	2 484	918	875	527	17	57	89
1921	4 792	2 009	2 783	985	956	660	19	57	105
1922	5 183	1 951	3 232	1 209	1 065	746	25	60	125
1923	5 930	2 073	3 857	1 516	1 198	894	27	65	154
1924	6 635	2 059	4 576	1 856	1 354	1 071	36	69	186

Column 1 – From Table R-34, col. 5.

Column 2 – Col. 1 minus col. 3.

Column 3 – Sum of cols. 4–9. Includes for 1920–1924 very small amounts of nonresidential mortgages held by installment investment companies as shown in Table M-19, col. 6.

Columns 4 to 8 – Difference between appropriate columns of Tables M-3 and M-4.

Column 9 – From Table M-20, col. 6.

Column 1 – 1925–1928: From Table R-34, col. 1.
            1929–1949: From Table R–35, col. 1.

Column 2 – 1925–1949: Col. 1 minus col. 3.

Column 3 – 1925–1949: Sum of cols. 4–15.

Column 4 – 1925–1949: From Table M-13, col. 2.

Column 5 – 1925–1949: From Table M–14, col. 2.

Column 6 – 1925–1942: From Table M-15, col. 2.

Column 7 – 1925–1949: From Table M-16, col. 2.

Column 8 – 1925–1949: From Table M-17, col. 2.

Column 9 – 1925–1948: From Table M-18, col. 2.

Column 10 – 1925–1949: From Table M-20, col. 2.

Column 11 – 1925–1949: From Table J-2, col. 2.

Column 12 – 1930–1946: Based on Table J-6, col. 6. See notes to Table M-9, col. 12.

Column 13 – 1925–1949: From Table M-19, col. 2.

Column 14 – 1933–1949: From Home Loan Bank Board, *Statistical Summary*, 1950, p. 14.

Column 15 – 1938–1946: Information supplied by Housing and Home Finance Agency.
             1947–1949: From *Daily Treasury Statement*, Mar. 15, 1948, 1949, and 1950.

HOLDINGS OF MORTGAGES ON NONFARM PROPERTIES
BY HOLDER GROUPS: 1925 to 1949

$ mill.

End of year	Total outstanding	Non-institutional holdings	Institutional holdings					
			Total	Commercial banks		Mutual savings banks	Life insurance companies	Fraternal insurance companies
				Operating	Closed			
	1	2	3	4	5	6	7	8
1925	24 462	8 105	16 359	4 383	20	4 030	2 739	88
1926	27 590	8 996	18 594	4 784	22	4 440	3 438	96
1927	30 829	10 286	20 543	5 046	18	4 885	4 033	112
1928	34 069	11 816	22 253	5 247	17	5 267	4 648	125
1929	35 849	12 488	23 361	5 266	15	5 367	5 219	139
1930	36 930	13 274	23 656	5 053	33	5 616	5 551	155
1931	36 111	13 158	22 953	4 487	107	5 847	5 684	162
1932	34 270	13 014	21 256	3 773	164	5 818	5 492	169
1933A	30 672	10 643	20 029	3 533	486	5 457	5 086	161
1933B	30 672	10 707	19 965	3 533	486	5 457	5 022	161
1934	30 066	9 863	20 203	2 998	388	5 260	4 683	144
1935	29 230	9 695	19 535	3 008	290	5 004	4 345	127
1936	28 958	9 811	19 147	3 131	210	4 875	4 236	124
1937	28 971	9 936	19 035	3 293	148	4 788	4 304	136
1938	29 160	9 789	19 371	3 488	108	4 751	4 515	139
1939	29 706	9 574	20 132	3 765	80	4 775	4 777	143
1940	30 552	9 385	21 167	4 103	56	4 802	5 110	148
1941	31 712	9 587	22 125	4 444	26	4 760	5 514	157
1942	31 218	9 414	21 804	4 311	4	4 581	5 868	168
1943	30 233	9 228	21 005	4 112	–	4 379	5 909	166
1944	30 042	9 313	20 729	4 026	–	4 269	5 972	169
1945	30 901	9 948	20 953	4 317	–	4 177	5 748	167
1946	37 116	11 424	25 692	6 596	–	4 412	6 332	173
1947	44 297	13 038	31 259	8 689	–	4 827	7 667	188
1948	51 301	14 126	37 175	10 057	–	5 549	9 782	235
1949	57 101	14 635	42 466	10 741	–	6 436	11 558	269

End of year	Institutional holdings						
	Fire, marine and other insurance companies	Mortgage companies	Savings and loan associations		Installment investment companies	Home Owners' Loan Corporation	Federal National Mortgage Association
			Operating	Closed			
	9	10	11	12	13	14	15
1925	149	734	4 204	–	10	–	–
1926	164	828	4 810	–	12	–	–
1927	174	771	5 488	–	16	–	–
1928	186	681	6 060	–	22	–	–
1929	194	627	6 507	–	27	–	–
1930	194	554	6 402	67	31	–	–
1931	183	451	5 890	108	34	–	–
1932	186	343	5 148	129	34	–	–
1933A	173	276	4 437	258	30	132	–
1933B	173	276	4 437	258	30	132	–
1934	153	241	3 710	224	23	2 379	–
1935	137	234	3 292	174	27	2 897	–
1936	126	261	3 237	135	49	2 763	–
1937	109	261	3 410	123	65	2 398	–
1938	102	292	3 555	90	80	2 169	82
1939	100	327	3 757	132	91	2 038	147
1940	97	371	4 084	154	105	1 956	181
1941	100	333	4 552	132	123	1 777	207
1942	96	210	4 556	100	132	1 567	211
1943	92	170	4 584	67	123	1 338	65
1944	86	129	4 800	21	114	1 091	52
1945	80	130	5 376	6	93	852	7
1946	88	177	7 141	3	128	636	6
1947	97	270	8 856	–	175	486	4
1948	114	364	10 305	–	201	369	199
1949	138	456	11 600	–	209	231	828

Column 1 – 1925–1928: From Table R-34, col. 3.
     1929–1949: From Table R-35, col. 3.

Column 2 – 1925–1949: Col. 1 minus col. 3.

Column 3 – 1925–1949: Sum of cols. 4–15.

Column 4 – 1925–1949: From Table M-13, col. 4.

Column 5 – 1925–1942: From Table M-14, col. 4.

Column 6 – 1925–1949: From Table M-15, col. 4.

Column 7 – 1925–1949: From Table M-16, col. 4.

Column 8 – 1925–1949: From Table M-17, col. 4.

Column 9 – 1925–1949: From Table M-18, col. 4.

Column 10 – 1925–1949: From Table M-20, col. 4.

Column 11 – 1925–1949: From Table J-2, col. 2. The Home Loan Bank Board (*Statistical Summary*, 1950, tables 4 and 10) regards total mortgage holdings of savings and loan associations as consisting exclusively of mortgages on one- to four-family dwellings. It is, however, known that savings and loan associations in some states also made farm mortgage loans, particularly in earlier part of the period. This was the case, for instance, in Pennsylvania and Ohio. In Ohio they were reported in 1916 to have held $22 million of farm mortgages (Sparks, Earl S., *History and Theory of Agricultural Credit in the United States*, 1932, p. 187). Holdings reported for Ohio alone were equivalent to 2 percent of all mortgage loans for the country as a whole. In absence of information for other states and probability that absolute and relative volume of farm mortgage loans declined during later part of the period, these loans have been neglected, i.e., regarded as on one- to four-family homes. It is also possible that small amounts of mortgage loans were made on multi-family dwellings and nonresidential buildings, but no information appears to be available on the amounts involved. (See note to Table M-5, cols. 4 to 10.)

Column 12 – 1930–1946: Total holdings of mortgages and real estate of closed associations as estimated in Table J-6, col. 6 have been split between mortgage loans and real estate in proportion prevailing for same year among operating associations (cf. Table J-2, cols. 2 and 4). This procedure probably results in some overstatement of mortgage holdings since it may be assumed that closed associations had to foreclose a larger proportion of their total mortgage loans than associations that continued to operate.

Column 13 – 1925–1949: From Table M-19, col. 4.

Column 14 – 1933–1949: From Home Loan Bank Board, *Statistical Summary*, 1949, p. 18, and 1950, p. 14.

Column 15 – 1938–1949: From "Balance Sheets of Corporations of the U.S. Government Including Certain Business-Type Activities of U.S. Government" as shown in *Daily Treasury Statement*.

BY HOLDER GROUPS: 1925 to 1949

$ mill.

End of year	Total outstanding	Non-institutional holdings	Institutional holdings						
			Total	Commercial banks		Mutual savings banks	Life insurance companies	Fraternal insurance companies	
				Operating	Closed				
	1	2	3	4	5	6	7	8	
1925	12 742	4 535	8 207	1 154	8	1 547	837	27	
1926	14 648	4 969	9 679	1 563	9	1 713	1 062	30	
1927	16 378	5 492	10 886	1 714	7	1 922	1 254	35	
1928	18 139	6 129	12 010	1 895	7	2 139	1 445	39	
1929	19 481	6 645	12 836	1 962	6	2 286	1 626	43	
1930	19 615	6 712	12 903	1 940	13	2 341	1 732	48	
1931	19 013	6 596	12 417	1 812	43	2 436	1 775	51	
1932	17 872	6 408	11 464	1 654	66	2 446	1 724	53	
1933	16 743	5 986	10 757	1 521	194	2 354	1 599	51	
1934	16 958	5 492	11 466	1 200	155	2 190	1 379	42	
1935	16 841	5 489	11 352	1 281	116	2 089	1 281	37	
1936	16 690	5 525	11 165	1 363	84	2 082	1 245	37	
1937	16 827	5 738	11 089	1 472	59	2 111	1 246	39	
1938	17 073	5 810	11 263	1 580	43	2 119	1 320	41	
1939	17 608	5 788	11 820	1 754	32	2 128	1 490	45	
1940	18 400	5 761	12 639	1 930	23	2 162	1 758	51	
1941	19 400	5 845	13 555	2 316	11	2 189	1 976	56	
1942	19 219	5 700	13 519	2 363	2	2 128	2 255	65	
1943	18 781	5 661	13 120	2 316	–	2 033	2 410	68	
1944	18 778	5 853	12 925	2 293	–	1 937	2 458	70	
1945	19 208	6 141	13 067	2 428	–	1 894	2 258	66	
1946	23 569	7 176	16 393	3 690	–	2 033	2 570	70	
1947	28 570	8 113	20 457	4 982	–	2 237	3 459	85	
1948	33 451	8 658	24 793	5 700	–	2 742	4 925	118	
1949	37 251	8 686	28 565	6 100	–	3 190	5 970	139	

End of year	Institutional holdings						
	Fire, marine and other insurance companies	Mortgage companies	Savings and loan associations		Installment investment companies	Home Owners' Loan Corporation	Federal National Mortgage Association
			Operating	Closed			
	9	10	11	12	13	14	15
1925	45	382	4 204	–	3	–	–
1926	49	440	4 810	–	3	–	–
1927	52	410	5 488	–	4	–	–
1928	56	363	6 060	–	6	–	–
1929	58	341	6 507	–	7	–	–
1930	58	294	6 402	67	8	–	–
1931	55	238	5 890	108	9	–	–
1932	56	179	5 148	129	9	–	–
1933	52	151	4 437	258	8	132	–
1934	46	136	3 710	224	5	2 379	–
1935	41	135	3 292	174	9	2 897	–
1936	38	150	3 237	135	31	2 763	–
1937	33	151	3 410	123	47	2 398	–
1938	31	171	3 555	90	62	2 169	82
1939	30	194	3 757	132	73	2 038	147
1940	29	224	4 084	154	87	1 956	181
1941	30	204	4 552	132	105	1 777	207
1942	29	129	4 556	100	114	1 567	211
1943	28	106	4 584	67	105	1 338	65
1944	26	81	4 800	21	96	1 091	52
1945	24	81	5 376	6	75	852	7
1946	26	113	7 141	3	105	636	6
1947	29	174	8 856	–	145	486	4
1948	34	237	10 305	–	164	369	199
1949	41	298	11 600	–	168	231	828

HOLDINGS OF MORTGAGES ON MULTI-FAMILY DWELLINGS
BY HOLDER GROUPS: 1925 to 1949

$ mill.

End of year	Total outstanding	Non-institutional holdings	Institutional holdings								
			Total	Commercial banks		Mutual savings banks	Insurance companies			Mortgage companies	Installment investment companies
				Operating	Closed		Life	Fraternal	Fire, marine, other		
	1	2	3	4	5	6	7	8	9	10	11
1925	4 247	1 426	2 821	1 075	4	993	571	18	30	128	2
1926	5 147	2 056	3 091	1 073	4	1 091	713	20	33	154	3
1927	6 058	2 712	3 346	1 110	4	1 185	834	23	35	151	4
1928	7 054	3 514	3 540	1 116	3	1 251	961	26	37	141	5
1929	8 089	4 460	3 629	1 100	3	1 232	1 078	29	39	141	7
1930	8 758	5 047	3 711	1 037	7	1 310	1 146	32	39	132	8
1931	8 569	4 935	3 634	891	21	1 364	1 173	33	37	107	8
1932	8 263	4 882	3 381	706	33	1 349	1 130	35	37	83	8
1933A	7 731	4 533	3 198	670	97	1 241	1 046	33	35	69	7
1933B	7 731	4 552	3 179	670	97	1 241	1 027	33	35	69	7
1934	7 181	4 159	3 022	599	78	1 228	991	31	31	58	6
1935	6 774	3 942	2 832	575	58	1 166	919	27	27	54	6
1936	6 530	3 769	2 761	589	42	1 117	897	26	25	59	6
1937	6 406	3 667	2 739	606	30	1 071	917	29	22	58	6
1938	6 281	3 548	2 733	635	22	1 053	906	28	20	63	6
1939	6 403	3 463	2 940	670	16	1 059	1 067	32	20	70	6
1940	6 464	3 408	3 056	724	11	1 056	1 129	33	19	78	6
1941	6 517	3 386	3 131	709	5	1 028	1 259	36	20	68	6
1942	6 441	3 333	3 108	649	1	981	1 370	39	19	43	6
1943	6 221	3 161	3 060	598	–	938	1 425	40	18	35	6
1944	6 053	3 095	2 958	577	–	933	1 361	38	17	26	6
1945	6 100	3 096	3 004	629	–	913	1 374	40	16	26	6
1946	6 400	2 933	3 467	968	–	952	1 451	40	18	30	8
1947	6 900	2 975	3 925	1 234	–	1 036	1 546	38	19	42	10
1948	7 600	3 064	4 536	1 451	–	1 123	1 829	44	23	54	12
1949	8 400	3 133	5 267	1 545	–	1 298	2 262	53	28	67	14

Column 1 – 1925–1928: From Table R-34, col. 4.
  1929–1949: From Table R-35, col. 4.

Column 2 – 1925–1949: Col. 1 minus col. 3.

Column 3 – 1925–1949: Sum of cols. 4–11.

Column 4 – 1925–1949: From Table M-13, col. 5.

Column 5 – 1925–1942: From Table M-14, col. 5.

Column 6 – 1925–1949: From Table M-15, col. 5.

Column 7 – 1925–1949: From Table M-16, col. 5.

Column 8 – 1925–1949: From Table M-17, col. 5.

Column 9 – 1925–1949: From Table M-18, col. 5.

Column 10 – 1925–1949: From Table M-20, col. 5.

Column 11 – 1925–1949: From Table M-19, col. 5.

BY HOLDER GROUPS; UNADJUSTED: 1925 to 1949

$ mill.

End of year	Total outstanding	Non-institutional holdings	Institutional holdings								
			Total	Commercial banks		Mutual savings banks	Insurance companies			Mortgage companies	Installment investment companies
				Oper-ating	Closed		Life	Frater-nal	Fire, marine, other		
	1	2	3	4	5	6	7	8	9	10	11
1925	7 473	2 144	5 329	2 154	8	1 490	1 331	43	74	224	5
1926	7 795	1 971	5 824	2 148	9	1 636	1 663	46	82	234	6
1927	8 393	2 082	6 311	2 222	7	1 778	1 945	54	87	210	8
1928	8 876	2 173	6 703	2 236	7	1 877	2 242	60	93	177	11
1929	8 279	1 383	6 896	2 204	6	1 849	2 515	67	97	145	13
1930	8 557	1 515	7 042	2 076	13	1 965	2 673	75	97	128	15
1931	8 529	1 627	6 902	1 784	43	2 047	2 736	78	91	106	17
1932	8 135	1 724	6 411	1 413	65	2 023	2 638	81	93	81	17
1933A	6 198	124	6 074	1 342	195	1 862	2 441	77	86	56	15
1933B	6 198	169	6 029	1 342	195	1 862	2 396	77	86	56	15
1934	5 927	212	5 715	1 199	155	1 842	2 313	71	76	47	12
1935	5 615	264	5 351	1 152	116	1 749	2 145	63	69	45	12
1936	5 738	517	5 221	1 179	84	1 676	2 094	61	63	52	12
1937	5 738	531	5 207	1 215	59	1 606	2 141	68	54	52	12
1938	5 806	431	5 375	1 273	43	1 579	2 289	70	51	58	12
1939	5 695	323	5 372	1 341	32	1 588	2 220	66	50	63	12
1940	5 688	216	5 472	1 449	22	1 584	2 223	64	49	69	12
1941	5 795	356	5 439	1 419	10	1 543	2 279	65	50	61	12
1942	5 558	381	5 177	1 299	1	1 472	2 243	64	48	38	12
1943	5 231	406	4 825	1 198	–	1 408	2 074	58	46	29	12
1944	5 211	365	4 846	1 156	–	1 399	2 153	61	43	22	12
1945	5 593	711	4 882	1 260	–	1 370	2 116	61	40	23	12
1946	7 147	1 315	5 832	1 938	–	1 427	2 311	63	44	34	15
1947	8 827	1 950	6 877	2 473	–	1 554	2 662	65	49	54	20
1948	10 250	2 404	7 846	2 906	–	1 684	3 028	73	57	73	25
1949	11 450	2 816	8 634	3 096	–	1 948	3 326	77	69	91	27

Column 1 – 1925–1928: From Table R-34, col. 5.
1929–1949: From Table R-35, col. 5.

Column 2 – 1925–1949: Col. 1 minus col. 3.

Column 3 – 1925–1949: Sum of cols. 4–11.

Column 4 – 1925–1949: From Table M-13, col. 6.

Column 5 – 1925–1942: From Table M-14, col. 6.

Column 6 – 1925–1949: From Table M-15, col. 6.

Column 7 – 1925–1949: From Table M-16, col. 6.

Column 8 – 1925–1949: From Table M-17, col. 6.

Column 9 – 1925–1949: From Table M-18, col. 6.

Column 10 – 1925–1949: From Table M-20, col. 6.

Column 11 – 1925–1949: From Table M-19, col. 6.

ADJUSTED ESTIMATES OF NONFARM NONRESIDENTIAL MORTGAGE DEBT
1928 to 1949

$ mill. (except cols. 9 and 10)

End of year	Total nonresidential debt			Institutional holdings	Noninstitutional holdings					Share of non-institutional holdings (percent)	
	Unadjusted Department of Commerce figures	Adjusted			Unadjusted	Adjusted				Unadjusted	Adjusted B
		A	B			A	B	C			
	1	2	3	4	5	6	7	8		9	10
1928	8 876	8 876	8 876	6 703	2 173	2 173	2 173	2 173		24.5	24.5
1929	8 279	9 479	9 479	6 896	1 383	2 583	2 583	2 027		16.7	27.2
1930	8 557	9 757	9 757	7 042	1 515	2 715	2 715	2 095		17.7	27.8
1931	8 529	9 729	9 629	6 902	1 627	2 827	2 727	2 088		19.1	28.3
1932	8 135	9 335	9 135	6 411	1 724	2 924	2 724	1 992		21.2	29.8
1933A	6 198	8 998	8 798	6 074	124	2 924	2 724	1 517		2.0	31.0
1933B	6 198	8 998	8 798	6 029	169	2 969	2 769	1 517		2.7	31.5
1934	5 927	8 727	8 427	5 715	212	3 012	2 712	1 451		3.6	32.2
1935	5 615	8 415	8 015	5 351	264	3 064	2 664	1 375		4.7	33.2
1936	5 738	8 538	8 038	5 221	517	3 317	2 817	1 405		9.0	35.0
1937	5 738	8 538	7 938	5 207	531	3 331	2 731	1 405		9.3	34.4
1938	5 806	8 606	7 906	5 375	431	3 231	2 531	1 421		7.4	32.0
1939	5 695	8 495	7 695	5 372	323	3 123	2 323	1 394		5.7	30.2
1940	5 688	8 488	7 588	5 472	216	3 016	2 116	1 393		3.8	27.9
1941	5 795	8 595	7 595	5 439	356	3 156	2 156	1 419		6.1	28.4
1942	5 558	8 358	7 358	5 177	381	3 181	2 181	1 361		6.9	29.6
1943	5 231	8 031	7 031	4 825	406	3 206	2 206	1 281		7.8	31.4
1944	5 211	8 011	7 011	4 846	365	3 165	2 165	1 276		7.0	30.9
1945	5 593	8 393	7 393	4 882	711	3 511	2 511	1 369		12.7	34.0
1946	7 147	9 947	8 947	5 832	1 315	4 115	3 115	1 750		18.4	34.8
1947	8 827	11 627	10 627	6 877	1 950	4 750	3 750	2 161		22.1	35.3
1948	10 250	13 050	12 050	7 846	2 404	5 204	4 204	2 509		23.5	34.9
1949	11 450	14 250	13 250	8 634	2 816	5 616	4 616	2 803		24.6	34.8

Column 1 – 1928: From Table R-34, col. 5.
   1929–1949: From Table R-35, col. 5.

Column 2 – 1928–1949: Col. 1 plus $1,200 million from 1929 to 1932 and $2,800 million from 1933 to 1949.

Column 3 – 1928–1949: Col. 2 reduced by an amount increasing regularly (excepting 1933) from $100 million in 1931 to $1,000 million in 1941.

Column 4 – 1928–1949: From Table M-11, col. 3.

Columns 5 to 7 – 1928–1949: Cols. 1 to 3, respectively, minus col. 4.

Column 8 – 1928–1949: Col. 1 multiplied by 0.2448, the ratio of col. 7 to col. 1 in 1928.

Column 9 – 1928–1949: Col. 5 divided by col. 1.

Column 10 – 1928–1949: Col. 7 divided by col. 3.

DISTRIBUTION OF HOLDINGS OF MORTGAGES
BY OPERATING COMMERCIAL BANKS: 1925 to 1949

$ mill.

End of year	Total	Nonfarm					Farm
		Total	Residential			Non-residential	
			Total	1- to 4-family	Multi-family		
	1	2	3	4	5	6	7
1925	5 490	4 383	2 229	1 154	1 075	2 154	1 107
1926	5 850	4 784	2 636	1 563	1 073	2 148	1 066
1927	6 058	5 046	2 824	1 714	1 110	2 222	1 012
1928	6 202	5 247	3 011	1 895	1 116	2 236	955
1929	6 170	5 266	3 062	1 962	1 100	2 204	904
1930	5 903	5 053	2 977	1 940	1 037	2 076	850
1931	5 326	4 487	2 703	1 812	891	1 784	839
1932	4 562	3 773	2 360	1 654	706	1 413	789
1933	4 150	3 533	2 191	1 521	670	1 342	617
1934	3 523	2 998	1 799	1 200	599	1 199	525
1935	3 523	3 008	1 856	1 281	575	1 152	515
1936	3 643	3 131	1 952	1 363	589	1 179	512
1937	3 816	3 293	2 078	1 472	606	1 215	523
1938	4 029	3 488	2 215	1 580	635	1 273	541
1939	4 323	3 765	2 424	1 754	670	1 341	558
1940	4 671	4 103	2 654	1 930	724	1 449	568
1941	5 002	4 444	3 025	2 316	709	1 419	558
1942	4 804	4 311	3 012	2 363	649	1 299	493
1943	4 574	4 112	2 914	2 316	598	1 198	462
1944	4 488	4 026	2 870	2 293	577	1 156	462
1945	4 836	4 317	3 057	2 428	629	1 260	519
1946	7 297	6 596	4 658	3 690	968	1 938	701
1947	9 503	8 689	6 216	4 982	1 234	2 473	814
1948	10 926	10 057	7 151	5 700	1 451	2 906	869
1949	11 646	10 741	7 645	6 100	1 545	3 096	905

Column 1 – From Table L-24, col. 3.

Column 2 – From Table L-24, col. 5.

Column 3 – Sum of cols. 4 and 5.

Column 4 – Home Loan Bank Board, *Statistical Summary*, 1949, p. 18.

Column 5 – Estimated at one-third of all nonfarm mortgage loans except those on one- to four-family dwellings (col. 2 minus col. 4). Ratio is based on relationship for mutual savings banks and life insurance companies.

Column 6 – Estimated at two-thirds of col. 2 minus col. 4.

Column 7 – From Table A-61, col. 9.

DISTRIBUTION OF HOLDINGS OF MORTGAGES
BY CLOSED COMMERCIAL BANKS: 1921 to 1943

$ mill.

End of year	Total	Nonfarm					Farm
		Total	Residential			Non-residential	
			Total	1- to 4-family	Multi-family		
1	2	3	4	5	6	7
1921	15	5	3	2	1	2	10
1922	20	5	3	2	1	2	15
1923	30	10	6	4	2	4	20
1924	40	15	9	6	3	6	25
1925	45	20	12	8	4	8	25
1926	52	22	13	9	4	9	30
1927	48	18	11	7	4	7	30
1928	42	17	10	7	3	7	25
1929	40	15	9	6	3	6	25
1930	63	33	20	13	7	13	30
1931	157	107	64	43	21	43	50
1932	224	164	99	66	33	65	60
1933	607	486	291	194	97	195	121
1934	484	388	233	155	78	155	96
1935	362	290	174	116	58	116	72
1936	262	210	126	84	42	84	52
1937	185	148	89	59	30	59	37
1938	135	108	65	43	22	43	27
1939	100	80	48	32	16	32	20
1940	70	56	34	23	11	22	14
1941	33	26	16	11	5	10	7
1942	5	4	3	2	1	1	1
1943	–	–	–	–	–	–	–

Column 1 – 1921–1943: From Table V-76, col. 5.

Column 2 – 1921–1943: Col. 1 minus col. 7.

Column 3 – 1921–1943: Sum of cols. 4 and 5.

Columns 4 to 6 – 1921–1943: Estimated at 40 percent, 20 percent, and 40 percent, respectively, of col. 2. These ratios are based on distribution of nonfarm mortgage loans of operating commercial banks in late 1920's (cf. Table M-13).

Column 7 – 1921–1932: Estimated roughly as declining from about two-thirds of col. 1 in early 1920's to about 30 percent in 1932. High ratios up to 1930 reflect fact that during that period a large part of closed banks were located in farm areas.
1933–1943: Estimated at 20 percent of col. 1, ratio prevailing around 1932 for operating commercial banks since by that time closed banks may be regarded as made up of a representative cross section of all banks.

DISTRIBUTION OF HOLDINGS OF MORTGAGES
BY MUTUAL SAVINGS BANKS: 1925 to 1949

$ mill.

End of year	Total	Nonfarm					Farm
		Total	Residential			Non-residential	
			Total	1- to 4-family	Multi-family		
	1	2	3	4	5	6	7
1925	4 101	4 030	2 540	1 547	993	1 490	71
1926	4 518	4 440	2 804	1 713	1 091	1 636	78
1927	4 970	4 885	3 107	1 922	1 185	1 778	85
1928	5 359	5 267	3 390	2 139	1 251	1 877	92
1929	5 460	5 367	3 518	2 286	1 232	1 849	93
1930	5 713	5 616	3 651	2 341	1 310	1 965	97
1931	5 948	5 847	3 800	2 436	1 364	2 047	101
1932	5 918	5 818	3 795	2 446	1 349	2 023	100
1933	5 551	5 457	3 595	2 354	1 241	1 862	94
1934	5 350	5 260	3 418	2 190	1 228	1 842	90
1935	5 085	5 004	3 255	2 089	1 166	1 749	81
1936	4 950	4 875	3 199	2 082	1 117	1 676	75
1937	4 857	4 788	3 182	2 111	1 071	1 606	69
1938	4 816	4 751	3 172	2 119	1 053	1 579	65
1939	4 836	4 775	3 187	2 128	1 059	1 588	61
1940	4 859	4 802	3 218	2 162	1 056	1 584	57
1941	4 812	4 760	3 217	2 189	1 028	1 543	52
1942	4 627	4 581	3 109	2 128	981	1 472	46
1943	4 420	4 379	2 971	2 033	938	1 408	41
1944	4 305	4 269	2 870	1 937	933	1 399	36
1945	4 208	4 177	2 807	1 894	913	1 370	31
1946	4 441	4 412	2 985	2 033	952	1 427	29
1947	4 855	4 827	3 273	2 237	1 036	1 554	28
1948	5 583	5 549	3 865	2 742	1 123	1 684	34
1949	6 472	6 436	4 488	3 190	1 298	1 948	36

Column 1 – From Table L-30, col. 1.

Column 2 – From Table L-30, col. 3.

Column 3 – Sum of cols. 4 and 5.

Column 4 – Home Loan Bank Board, *Statistical Summary*, 1949, p. 18, and 1950, p. 14.

Column 5 – Estimated at 40 percent of all nonfarm mortgage loans other than those on one- to four-family dwellings. This ratio is somewhat above the 34 percent ratio shown in data for a sample of mortgage loans made by mutual savings banks in Massachusetts between 1918 and 1931 (cf. Lintner, John, *Mutual Savings Banks in the Savings and Mortgage Markets*, p. 378) to take account of presumably greater importance of loans on multi-family buildings in New York banks.

Column 6 – Estimated at 60 percent of col. 2 minus col. 4 by procedure outlined under col. 5.

Column 7 – From Table L-30, col. 2.

DISTRIBUTION OF HOLDINGS OF MORTGAGES
BY LIFE INSURANCE COMPANIES: 1925 to 1949

$ mill.

End of year	Total	Nonfarm					Farm
		Total	Residential			Non-residential	
			Total	1- to 4-family	Multi-family		
	1	2	3	4	5	6	7
1925	4 769	2 739	1 408	837	571	1 331	2 030
1926	5 562	3 438	1 775	1 062	713	1 663	2 124
1927	6 206	4 033	2 088	1 254	834	1 945	2 173
1928	6 787	4 648	2 406	1 445	961	2 242	2 139
1929	7 337	5 219	2 704	1 626	1 078	2 515	2 118
1930	7 638	5 551	2 878	1 732	1 146	2 673	2 087
1931	7 721	5 684	2 948	1 775	1 173	2 736	2 037
1932	7 390	5 492	2 854	1 724	1 130	2 638	1 898
1933A	6 784	5 086	2 645	1 599	1 046	2 441	1 698
1933B	6 720	5 022	2 626	1 599	1 027	2 396	1 698
1934	5 985	4 683	2 370	1 379	991	2 313	1 302
1935	5 457	4 345	2 200	1 281	919	2 145	1 112
1936	5 252	4 236	2 142	1 245	897	2 094	1 016
1937	5 293	4 304	2 163	1 246	917	2 141	989
1938	5 498	4 515	2 226	1 320	906	2 289	983
1939	5 761	4 777	2 557	1 490	1 067	2 220	984
1940	6 126	5 110	2 887	1 758	1 129	2 223	1 016
1941	6 577	5 514	3 235	1 976	1 259	2 279	1 063
1942	6 911	5 868	3 625	2 255	1 370	2 243	1 043
1943	6 896	5 909	3 835	2 410	1 425	2 074	987
1944	6 906	5 972	3 819	2 458	1 361	2 153	934
1945	6 632	5 748	3 632	2 258	1 374	2 116	884
1946	7 222	6 332	4 021	2 570	1 451	2 311	890
1947	8 604	7 667	5 005	3 459	1 546	2 662	937
1948	10 818	9 782	6 754	4 925	1 829	3 028	1 036
1949	12 730	11 558	8 232	5 970	2 262	3 326	1 172

Column 1 – 1925–1949: Sum of cols. 2 and 7.

Column 2 – 1925–1933A: From Table I-5, col. 4.
1933B–1949: Sum of cols. 3 and 6.

Column 3 – 1925–1949: Sum of cols. 4 and 5.

Column 4 – 1925–1947: Home Loan Bank Board, *Statistical Summary*, 1949, p. 18. (Although column is headed "Insurance companies," it actually covers only life companies.)
1948–1949: Home Loan Bank Board, *Mortgage Investments of Life Insurance Companies*, 1949, p. 7.

Column 5 – 1925–1932: Estimated at 30 percent of all nonfarm mortgage loans other than on one- to four-family dwellings (col. 2 minus col. 4) on basis of relationship prevailing in 1928 for twenty-six large companies which accounted for about 85 percent of total mortgage loans (cf. *Temporary National Economic Committee Hearings*, part 10A, pp. 208–209).
1933–1937: Estimated at 30 percent of figures for all nonfarm mortgage loans other than on one-to four-family dwellings as given by Home Loan Bank Board, *Mortgage and Real Estate Investments of Life Insurance Companies*, 1947, table 6.
1938–1949: Home Loan Bank Board, *Mortgage Investments of Life Insurance Companies*, 1949, p. 7.

Column 6 – 1925–1932: Estimated at 70 percent of col. 2 minus col. 4 by procedure described under col. 5.
1933–1937: Estimated at 70 percent of source described under col. 5.
1938–1949: Same source as for col. 5.

Column 7 – 1925–1949: From Table A-61, col. 7.

$ mill.

End of year	Total	Nonfarm					Farm
		Total	Residential			Non-residential	
			Total	1- to 4-family	Multi-family		
	1	2	3	4	5	6	7
1925	98	88	45	27	18	43	10
1926	107	96	50	30	20	46	11
1927	124	112	58	35	23	54	12
1928	139	125	65	39	26	60	14
1929	154	139	72	43	29	67	15
1930	172	155	80	48	32	75	17
1931	179	162	84	51	33	78	17
1932	186	169	88	53	35	81	17
1933	177	161	84	51	33	77	16
1934	159	144	73	42	31	71	15
1935	140	127	64	37	27	63	13
1936	136	124	63	37	26	61	12
1937	149	136	68	39	29	68	13
1938	152	139	69	41	28	70	13
1939	157	143	77	45	32	66	14
1940	162	148	84	51	33	64	14
1941	172	157	92	56	36	65	15
1942	183	168	104	65	39	64	15
1943	181	166	108	68	40	58	15
1944	184	169	108	70	38	61	15
1945	182	167	106	66	40	61	15
1946	189	173	110	70	40	63	16
1947	205	188	123	85	38	65	17
1948	256	235	162	118	44	73	21
1949	293	269	192	139	53	77	24

Column 1 – From Table I-10, col. 4.

Column 2 – From Table I-10, col. 4 minus col. 5.

Column 3 – Sum of cols. 4 and 5.

Columns 4 to 6 – Estimated at same percentage of total nonfarm mortgages (col. 2) as applies for life insurance companies in same year (cf. Table M-16).

Column 7 – From Table I-10, col. 5.

Column 1 – Sum of mortgage holdings of fire and marine companies (Table V-55, col. 3), of casualty and miscellaneous companies (Table V-56, col. 3), of mutual accident and health associations (Table I-14, col. 3), and of savings bank life insurance departments (Table V-54, col. 3).

Column 2 – Assumed equal to col. 1.

Column 3 – Sum of cols. 4 and 5.

Columns 4 to 6 – Estimated at 30 percent (col. 4), 20 percent (col. 5), and 50 percent (col. 6) of total nonfarm mortgages. Ratios are based on distribution of nonfarm mortgage loans of other institutional lenders, particularly life insurance companies. It was, however, assumed that increase in share of loans on one- to four-family dwellings observable in other lender groups was absent, or small, in the case of fire, etc., insurance companies.

Column 1 – 1918–1949: From Table V-72, cols. 3 and 4.

Column 2 – 1918–1949: Assumed to be equal to col. 1.

Column 3 – 1918–1949: Sum of cols. 4 and 5.

Column 4 – 1918–1934: Estimated at about one-fourth of col. 1. This ratio, as well as those used in cols. 5 and 6, had to be estimated roughly in absence of information on properties underlying mortgage loans of installment investment companies in either their reports or in the Securities and Exchange Commission study (*Investment Trusts and Investment Companies, Companies Issuing Face Amount Installment Certificates*). Estimates were guided by fact that a very substantial proportion of mortgage loans of Investors Syndicate (which accounts for practically all mortgage loans of installment investment companies) were in individual loans of $ 50,000 or more (cf. Securities and Exchange Commission, *Investment Trusts and Investment Companies, Companies Issuing Face Amount Installment Certificates*, p. 42) and, hence, would have to be secured by either apartments or nonresidential properties.
1935–1949: Estimated on assumption that most changes in total mortgage loans after 1935 were attributable to loans on one- to four-family dwellings. For years 1936 to about 1945 an additional basis of estimation is provided by separately reported holdings of Federal Housing Administration insured mortgages by Investors' Syndicate (cf. Table V-72, col. 4) which were all secured by one- to four-family dwellings.

Column 5 – 1918–1934: Estimated at about one-fourth of col. 1.
1935–1945: Assumed unchanged from 1934.
1946–1949: Rough estimates guided by increase in total mortgage loans.

Column 6 – 1918–1934: Estimated at roughly one-half of col. 1.
1935–1945: Assumed unchanged from 1934.
1946–1949: Rough estimates guided by increase in total mortgage loans.

DISTRIBUTION OF HOLDINGS OF MORTGAGES BY FIRE, MARINE, CASUALTY, AND MISCELLANEOUS INSURANCE COMPANIES: 1925 to 1949

$ mill.

End of year	Total	Nonfarm					End of year	Total	Nonfarm				
		Total	Residential			Non-residential			Total	Residential			Non-residential
			Total	1- to 4-family	Multi-family					Total	1- to 4-family	Multi-family	
	1	2	3	4	5	6		1	2	3	4	5	6
1925	149	149	75	45	30	74	1938	102	102	51	31	20	51
1926	164	164	82	49	33	82	1939	100	100	50	30	20	50
1927	174	174	87	52	35	87	1940	97	97	48	29	19	49
1928	186	186	93	56	37	93	1941	100	100	50	30	20	50
1929	194	194	97	58	39	97	1942	96	96	48	29	19	48
1930	194	194	97	58	39	97	1943	92	92	46	28	18	46
1931	183	183	92	55	37	91	1944	86	86	43	26	17	43
1932	186	186	93	56	37	93	1945	80	80	40	24	16	40
1933	173	173	87	52	35	86	1946	88	88	44	26	18	44
1934	153	153	77	46	31	76	1947	97	97	48	29	19	49
1935	137	137	68	41	27	69	1948	114	114	57	34	23	57
1936	126	126	63	38	25	63	1949	138	138	69	41	28	69
1937	109	109	55	33	22	54							

DISTRIBUTION OF HOLDINGS OF MORTGAGES BY INSTALLMENT INVESTMENT COMPANIES: 1918 to 1949

$ mill.

End of year	Total	Nonfarm					End of year	Total	Nonfarm				
		Total	Residential			Non-residential			Total	Residential			Non-residential
			Total	1- to 4-family	Multi-family					Total	1- to 4-family	Multi-family	
	1	2	3	4	5	6		1	2	3	4	5	6
1918	1	1	1	1	0	0	1934	23	23	11	5	6	12
1919	1	1	1	1	0	0	1935	27	27	15	9	6	12
1920	2	2	1	1	0	1	1936	49	49	37	31	6	12
1921	3	3	2	1	1	1	1937	65	65	53	47	6	12
1922	4	4	2	1	1	2	1938	80	80	68	62	6	12
1923	6	6	3	2	1	3	1939	91	91	79	73	6	12
1924	8	8	4	2	2	4	1940	105	105	93	87	6	12
1925	10	10	5	3	2	5	1941	123	123	111	105	6	12
1926	12	12	6	3	3	6	1942	132	132	120	114	6	12
1927	16	16	8	4	4	8	1943	123	123	111	105	6	12
1928	22	22	11	6	5	11	1944	114	114	102	96	6	12
1929	27	27	14	7	7	13	1945	93	93	81	75	6	12
1930	31	31	16	8	8	15	1946	128	128	113	105	8	15
1931	34	34	17	9	8	17	1947	175	175	155	145	10	20
1932	34	34	17	9	8	17	1948	201	201	176	164	12	25
1933	30	30	15	8	7	15	1949	209	209	182	168	14	27

Column 1 – 1896–1939: Sum of cols. 2 and 7.

          1940–1947: Rough estimates based on balance sheets of mortgage companies as tabulated by Bureau of Internal Revenue (*Statistics of Income*, part II, various issues).

          1948–1949: Rough estimates based on trend of total nonfarm mortgage debt. After the estimates were completed it appeared that as of May 31, 1951 mortgage companies reported holdings of $492 million of real estate loans (*Federal Reserve Bulletin*, 1952, p. 633). Since both reported and tabulated holdings are not quite complete (*ibid.*, p. 620) these figures indicate that the estimates of col. 1 are only slightly, if at all, on the high side even though total mortgage loans outstanding increased by about 25 percent between the end of 1949 and May 31, 1951.

Column 2 – 1896–1909: Estimated as rising regularly from 1 percent of total nonfarm mortgage debt outstanding (Table R-34) in 1890 to 2 percent in 1910.

          The 1890 percentage is based on ratio of holdings of mortgage companies (excluding English debenture companies since it can be assumed that most of their mortgage holdings were on farm land) as estimated by D. M. Frederiksen ("Mortgage Banking in America," *Journal of Political Economy*, Mar. 1894, p. 208), slightly reduced to allow for holdings of farm mortgages, to total nonfarm mortgage debt in U.S.

          1910–1919: Estimated at 2 percent of nonfarm mortgage debt outstanding.

          1920–1925: Estimated to rise regularly from 2 to 3 percent of nonfarm mortgage debt.

          1926–1940: Estimated to decline from 3 percent in 1926 to 1.2 percent in 1940.

          1941–1949: Sum of cols. 3 and 6.

Column 3 – 1896–1949: Sum of cols. 4 and 5.

Columns 4 to 6 – 1896–1939: Same procedure as for col. 2 except that ratios were applied to mortgage debt outstanding on one- to four-family, multi-family, and nonresidential, respectively (see Tables R-34 and R-35).

          1940–1949: Col. 1 divided among one- to four-family, multi-family, nonresidential, and farm properties in proportion of total mortgage debt outstanding on each of the four types of properties (cf. Tables R-34, R-35, and A-61).

Column 7 – 1896–1913: Estimated at 5 percent of total farm mortgage debt outstanding (cf. Table A-61, col. 1) on basis of 1914 relationship.

          1914: Estimated on basis of data regarding activity of foreign mortgage companies in U.S. given by Lewis, Cleona, *America's Stake in International Investments*, p. 86, assuming that holdings of farm mortgages by domestic mortgage companies were small.

          1915–1916: Rough interpolation.

          1917: Same procedure as for 1914.

          1918–1920: Rough interpolation.

          1921–1937: Estimated at 1.6 percent of total farm mortgage debt outstanding on basis of 1938 relationship.

          1938–1949: Same method as cols. 4–6.

HOLDINGS OF MORTGAGES BY MORTGAGE COMPANIES

1896 to 1949

$ mill.

M-20

End of year	Total	Nonfarm					Farm
		Total	Residential			Non-residential	
			Total	1- to 4-family	Multi-family		
	1	2	3	4	5	6	7
1896	155	55	37	34	3	18	100
1897	158	55	37	34	3	18	103
1898	167	60	40	36	4	20	107
1899	171	60	40	36	4	20	111
1900	182	66	44	40	4	22	116
1901	188	68	46	41	5	22	120
1902	199	75	50	44	6	25	124
1903	206	77	52	46	6	25	129
1904	220	86	58	51	7	28	134
1905	229	90	60	53	7	30	139
1906	245	101	68	59	9	33	144
1907	254	105	70	61	9	35	149
1908	270	115	77	66	11	38	155
1909	282	122	82	70	12	40	160
1910	312	136	91	77	14	45	176
1911	338	142	95	80	15	47	196
1912	366	149	100	84	16	49	217
1913	397	162	109	91	18	53	235
1914	423	173	116	96	20	57	250
1915	412	182	122	101	21	60	230
1916	407	192	129	106	23	63	215
1917	412	212	142	116	26	70	200
1918	406	221	148	120	28	73	185
1919	402	232	155	125	30	77	170
1920	430	270	181	145	36	89	160
1921	495	324	219	173	46	105	171
1922	562	389	264	206	58	125	173
1923	659	488	334	257	77	154	171
1924	757	598	412	313	99	186	159
1925	889	734	510	382	128	224	155
1926	983	828	594	440	154	234	155
1927	927	771	561	410	151	210	156
1928	837	681	504	363	141	177	156
1929	781	627	482	341	141	145	154
1930	704	554	426	294	132	128	150
1931	597	451	345	238	107	106	146
1932	478	343	262	179	83	81	135
1933	399	276	220	151	69	56	123
1934	362	241	194	136	58	47	121
1935	353	234	189	135	54	45	119
1936	375	261	209	150	59	52	114
1937	372	261	209	151	58	52	111
1938	405	292	234	171	63	58	113
1939	409	327	264	194	70	63	82
1940	450	371	302	224	78	69	79
1941	400	333	272	204	68	61	67
1942	250	210	172	129	43	38	40
1943	200	170	141	106	35	29	30
1944	150	129	107	81	26	22	21
1945	150	130	107	81	26	23	20
1946	200	177	143	113	30	34	23
1947	300	270	216	174	42	54	30
1948	400	364	291	237	54	73	36
1949	500	456	365	298	67	91	44

743

TABLE M-21

Column 1 – Total of bonds issued from Housing and Home Finance Agency, *Second Annual Report*, p. 148 ("Disbursement to mortgagees in refinancing operations"). Total mortgages exchanged assumed to be about 10 percent in excess of bonds issued as on the average mortgagees received only slightly over 90 percent of the face value of the mortgages turned over to Home Owners' Loan Corporation. Distribution among years based on loans made as shown in the *Annual Reports* of the Home Owners' Loan Corporation. (Total for loans made through 1936 of $3,093 million is slightly in excess of Home Owners' Loan Corporation bonds issued as some of the loans were made for purposes other than refinancing.)

Columns 2 to 7 – Obtained by distributing annual total of col. 1 among different groups of mortgagees in accordance with their share in total bonds received in exchange for mortgages in the years 1933–1936 (cf. Housing and Home Finance Agency, *Second Annual Report*, p. 148).

TABLE M-22

Column 1 – From Home Loan Bank Board, *Statistical Summary*, 1949, p. 18, and 1950, p. 14.

Column 2 – Col. 1 multiplied by $6,000 per foreclosure. This figure is a rough estimate based on average value of mortgages on one- to four-family dwellings foreclosed by the Home Owners' Loan Corporation (as derived from data in the Corporation's *Annual Reports*) but substantially increased (by about 50 percent) to take account of higher average value of foreclosed multi-family and nonresidential properties. As most foreclosures resulted from mortgage loans made before 1931, average value per foreclosure would not be expected to reflect changes in real estate prices, at least not until the mid-1940's; and, hence, could be assumed to show substantial fluctuations only to extent that distribution of total foreclosures as between one- to four-family dwellings on the one hand and multi-family and nonresidential properties on the other hand changed.

Column 3 – From Table M-23, col. 1.

Column 4 – Col. 2 minus col. 3. Includes foreclosures by reporting institutions as well as by other nonindividual mortgagees.

EXCHANGE OF NONFARM MORTGAGES ON ONE- TO FOUR-FAMILY NONFARM M-21
DWELLINGS FOR HOME OWNERS' LOAN CORPORATION BONDS

1933 to 1936

$ mill.

Year	Home Owners' Loan Corporation bonds issued, total	Commercial banks	Savings and loan associations	Insurance companies	Finance and mortgage companies	Individuals	Estates
	1	2	3	4	5	6	7
1933	90	31	25	5	6	19	4
1934	1 850	628	518	112	132	386	74
1935	675	230	189	40	47	142	27
1936	135	46	38	8	10	28	5
Total bonds issued	2 750	935	770	165	195	575	110
Total mortgages exchanged	3 025	1 029	847	181	215	632	121

M-22

FORECLOSURES OF NONFARM MORTGAGES

1926 to 1949

$ mill. (except col. 1)

Year	Total foreclosures Number (000)	Value	Foreclosures By individuals	By all other mortgagees	Year	Total foreclosures Number (000)	Value	Foreclosures By individuals	By all other mortgagees
	1	2	3	4		1	2	3	4
1926	68	408	100	308	1938	118	708	180	528
1927	91	546	140	406	1939	100	600	140	460
1928	116	696	170	526	1940	76	456	100	356
1929	135	810	190	620	1941	59	354	70	284
1930	150	900	210	690	1942	42	252	70	182
1931	194	1 164	280	884	1943	25	150	40	110
1932	249	1 494	360	1 134	1944	17	102	30	72
1933	252	1 512	360	1 152	1945	13	78	20	58
1934	230	1 380	320	1 060	1946	10	60	15	45
1935	229	1 374	320	1 054	1947	11	66	15	51
1936	185	1 110	250	860	1948	13	78	20	58
1937	151	906	220	686	1949	18	108	25	83

745

Column 1 – 1926–1944: Sum of cols. 2–4.
  1945–1949: Rough estimates on basis described under cols. 2–4.

Columns 2 to 4 – 1926–1949: Roughly estimated on basis of following assumptions:
  (a) That individuals resorted to foreclosures, relatively to their holdings of mortgages on different types of real estate at end of 1930, to a somewhat lesser degree than institutions, (partly because of their relatively heavy holdings of second mortgages which became worthless), with result that their foreclosures during period from 1926 through 1949 amounted to about one-third of their maximum mortgage holdings.
  (b) That year-to-year movements of foreclosures by individuals of mortgages of each of three main types followed roughly those of total number of nonfarm foreclosures (cf. Home Loan Bank Board, *Statistical Summary*, 1949, p. 18).
  Estimates derived on these assumptions fall roughly along a line determined by the equation: foreclosures by individuals of all nonfarm mortgages ($ million) = 1.4 multiplied by number of nonfarm foreclosures (thousands).

Column 1 – Lintner, John, *Mutual Savings Banks in the Savings and Mortgage Markets*, p. 272.

Column 2 – From *Temporary National Economic Committee Hearings*, vol. 10A, p. 199.

Column 3 – Home Owners' Loan Corporation, unpublished data.

Column 4 – From *Temporary National Economic Committee Hearings*, vol. 10A, p. 165.

Column 5 – From Farm Credit Administration, *House Resolution 119*, Sept. 1944, pp. 92ff. Figures for 1942–1944 are averages of fiscal-year data.

FORECLOSURES OF NONFARM MORTGAGES BY INDIVIDUALS
1926 to 1949
$ mill.

Year	Total	1- to 4-family dwellings	Multi-family dwellings	Non-residential properties	Year	Total	1- to 4-family dwellings	Multi-family dwellings	Non-residential properties
	1	2	3	4		1	2	3	4
1926	100	50	30	20	1938	180	90	50	40
1927	140	70	40	30	1939	140	70	40	30
1928	170	90	50	30	1940	100	50	30	20
1929	190	100	50	40	1941	70	30	20	20
1930	210	110	60	40	1942	70	30	20	20
1931	280	150	80	50	1943	40	20	10	10
1932	360	190	100	70	1944	30	10	10	10
1933	360	190	100	70	1945	20	10	5	5
1934	320	160	90	70	1946	15	5	5	5
1935	320	160	90	70	1947	15	5	5	5
1936	250	120	70	60	1948	20	10	5	5
1937	220	110	60	50	1949	25	10	5	10

DATA ON INSTITUTIONAL FORECLOSURES
1925 to 1945
$ mill.

Year	Nonfarm mortgages			Farm mortgages		Year	Nonfarm mortgages			Farm mortgages	
	Massachusetts mutual savings banks	26 life insurance companies	Home Owners' Loan Corporation	26 life insurance companies	Federal land banks		Massachusetts mutual savings banks	26 life insurance companies	Home Owners' Loan Corporation	26 life insurance companies	Federal land banks
	1	2	3	4	5		1	2	3	4	5
1925	1	–	–		–	1936	44	164	163	71	57
1926	2	–	–	–	–	1937	33	109	290	45	37
1927	3	–	–	–	–	1938	29	69	227	38	32
1928	6	–	–	–	15	1939	32	–	184	–	48
1929	11	–	–	–	14	1940	38	–	69	–	26
1930	19	–	–	–	19	1941	31	–	51	–	20
1931	33	–	–	–	31	1942	25	–	19	–	14
1932	52	132	–	115	49	1943	17	–	9	–	7
1933	70	240	–	155	31	1944	19	–	3	–	4
1934	67	269	–	141	20	1945	15	–	1	–	–
1935	59	247	6	104	50						

COMPARISON OF DISTRIBUTION OF NONFARM FORECLOSURES
IN 1934 AND NONFARM MORTGAGE HOLDINGS IN 1930 and 1933

Percent

	Sample of foreclosures	Nonfarm mortgages outstanding, end of	
	1934	1930	1933
	1	2	3
Commercial banks	} 18.9	13.8	13.1
Mutual savings banks		15.2	17.8
Insurance companies	20.9	15.0	16.6
Savings and loan associations	18.3	17.5	15.3
Mortgage companies	4.0	1.5	.9
U.S. Government agencies	2.9	–	0.4
Individuals	29.7	} 37.0	} 35.9
Others	5.3		
All mortgagees	100.0	100.0	100.0

Column 1 – Based on sample of 5,175 foreclosures in 352 communities during the second half of 1934 (cf. Federal Home Loan Bank Administration, *Federal Home Loan Bank Review*, June 1935, p. 318).

Columns 2 and 3 – Derived from Table M-8.

ADJUSTMENT FOR WRITE-DOWNS ON NONFARM MORTGAGES
HELD BY NONINSTITUTIONAL MORTGAGEES: 1930 to 1940

$ mill.

Year	Total noninstitutional holdings	Estimated write-downs by individual mortgagees				Year	Total noninstitutional holdings	Estimated write-downs by individual mortgagees			
		Total	1- to 4-family	Multi-family	Non-residential			Total	1- to 4-family	Multi-family	Non-residential
	1	2	3	4	5		1	2	3	4	5
1930	12 881	25	10	10	5	1935	9 779	150	50	50	50
1931	13 216	100	35	35	30	1936	9 753	100	35	35	30
1932	13 086	150	55	55	40	1937	9 874	75	25	25	25
1933	11 828	150	50	50	50	1938	9 863	50	20	20	10
1934	10 285	150	50	50	50	1939	9 682	25	10	10	5
						1940	9 480	25	10	10	5

Column 1 – Averages of noninstitutional holdings of mortgages at beginning and end of year as shown in Table M-8, col. 2.

Column 2 – Estimated on assumption of total write-downs by individual mortgagees of $1 billion, and distribution within periods guided by foreclosures of nonfarm real estate by individuals, as shown in Table M-22, col. 3. Starting figure of $1 billion is a rough guess based on the assumption that write-downs by individual mortgagees were substantially larger than those by institutional holders of nonfarm mortgages, particularly because of their relatively larger holdings of junior liens.

Columns 3 to 5 – Col. 2 distributed on basis of noninstitutional holdings of mortgages on the three types of properties in 1930, as shown in Tables M-9, M–10, and M-12.

748

DISTRIBUTION OF HOLDINGS OF FARM MORTGAGES
1896 to 1949
$ mill.

| End of year | Total outstanding | Institutional holdings | Noninstitutional holdings | | | | | |
| | | | Total | Farmers | Nonfinancial corporations | Nonfarm individuals | Unincorporated business | Nonprofit institutions |
	1	2	3	4	5	6	7	8
1896	1 998	237	1 761	123	176	1 145	264	53
1897	2 072	245	1 827	128	183	1 187	274	55
1898	2 149	259	1 890	132	189	1 228	284	57
1899	2 229	280	1 949	137	195	1 267	292	58
1900	2 312	316	1 996	140	200	1 297	299	60
1901	2 397	354	2 043	143	205	1 328	306	61
1902	2 486	394	2 092	146	209	1 360	314	63
1903	2 578	430	2 148	150	215	1 396	322	65
1904	2 674	472	2 202	154	220	1 431	331	66
1905	2 773	527	2 246	157	224	1 460	337	68
1906	2 876	608	2 268	159	227	1 474	340	68
1907	2 983	662	2 321	162	232	1 509	348	70
1908	3 093	704	2 389	167	239	1 553	358	72
1909	3 208	794	2 414	169	242	1 569	362	72
1910	3 522	902	2 620	183	262	1 703	393	79
1911	3 930	1 062	2 868	201	287	1 864	430	86
1912	4 348	1 226	3 122	219	312	2 029	468	94
1913	4 707	1 323	3 384	237	338	2 200	508	101
1914	4 991	1 418	3 573	250	357	2 323	536	107
1915	5 256	1 544	3 712	260	371	2 413	557	111
1916	5 826	1 798	4 028	346	397	2 574	593	118
1917	6 537	2 010	4 527	462	439	2 842	654	130
1918	7 137	2 229	4 908	579	575	2 725	858	171
1919	8 449	2 563	5 886	789	550	3 563	821	163
1920	10 221	3 124	7 097	1 065	651	4 217	971	193
1921	10 702	3 550	7 152	1 073	657	4 249	979	194
1922	10 786	3 998	6 788	910	635	4 109	946	188
1923	10 665	4 466	6 199	731	591	3 822	880	175
1924	9 913	4 618	5 295	540	513	3 324	766	152
1925	9 713	4 862	4 851	417	479	3 099	714	142
1926	9 658	5 084	4 574	320	458	2 973	686	137
1927	9 757	5 220	4 537	318	453	2 949	681	136
1928	9 757	5 159	4 598	322	460	2 989	690	137
1929	9 631	5 091	4 540	318	454	2 951	681	136
1930	9 398	4 980	4 418	309	442	2 872	663	132
1931	9 094	4 873	4 221	295	422	2 744	633	127
1932	8 466	4 573	3 893	273	389	2 531	584	116
1933	7 685	4 299	3 386	237	338	2 201	508	102
1934	7 584	4 935	2 649	186	265	1 722	397	79
1935	7 423	4 956	2 467	173	247	1 603	370	74
1936	7 154	4 859	2 295	161	229	1 492	344	69
1937	6 955	4 751	2 204	154	220	1 433	331	66
1938	6 779	4 648	2 131	149	213	1 385	320	64
1939	6 586	4 514	2 072	145	207	1 347	311	62
1940	6 491	4 478	2 013	141	201	1 309	302	60
1941	6 372	4 412	1 960	137	196	1 274	294	59
1942	5 951	4 083	1 868	131	187	1 214	280	56
1943	5 389	3 594	1 795	126	179	1 167	269	54
1944	4 933	3 222	1 711	120	171	1 112	257	51
1945	4 682	2 966	1 716	120	172	1 116	257	51
1946	4 777	2 951	1 826	128	182	1 187	274	55
1947	4 882	2 988	1 894	132	190	1 231	284	57
1948	5 108	3 095	2 013	141	201	1 309	302	60
1949	5 413	3 291	2 122	149	212	1 379	318	64

TABLE M-27

Column 1 – From Table A-61, col. 1.

Column 2 – Col. 1 minus col. 3.

Column 3 – From Table A-61, col. 12.

Columns 4 to 8 – Estimated at 7 percent (col. 4), 10 percent (col. 5), 65 percent (col. 6), 15 percent (col. 7), and 3 percent (col. 8) of col. 3. Percentages are derived from distribution of farm mortgage holdings in 1927 developed by Wickens, D. L., *Farm Mortgage Credit*, (Department of Agriculture Technical Bulletin 288, Feb. 1932). To obtain classifications needed in this table, Wickens' data had to be rearranged, largely with help of rough estimates.
    From 1916–1925, however, proportion of col. 3 was first increased regularly to 15 percent in 1920–1921 and then decreased in the same way to take account of large volume of purchase money mortgages resulting from widespread farm land sales during and immediately after World War I. Relation of 1920–1921 top to level prevailing before 1916 and after 1926 was based on development in Story County, Iowa (cf. Murray, W., *An Economic Analysis of Farm Mortgages in Story County, Iowa, 1854-1931*, pp. 421–422). Percentages for cols. 5 to 8 were reduced correspondingly.

TABLE M-28

Column 1 – 1920–1944: From *Historical Statistics*, p. 95. Data for missing years supplied by Bureau of Agricultural Economics. Mar. 1 data shifted to end of preceding year.
    1945–1948: *Agricultural Statistics*, 1949, p. 569.
    1949: Department of Agriculture, *Current Developments in the Farm Real Estate Market*, August 1950, p. 6.

Column 2 – 1920–1949: Obtained by multiplying col. 1 by figures for total number of farms, as given for census years in *Agricultural Statistics*, 1949, p. 566; figures for intercensal years obtained by linear interpolation. Beginning-of-year census data shifted to end of preceding year.

Column 3 – 1920–1949: Estimated on assumption of an average value per foreclosure of $3,000. Figure is based on the average mortgage per farm in 1930 ($3,817; cf. *Statistical Abstract*, 1938, p. 613) as most foreclosures may be assumed to have originated in mortgages incurred in 1920's. Value used, however, is somewhat below average mortgage per farm as part of foreclosures may be assumed to have been due to nonmortgage debts which presumably on the average were substantially smaller than the average mortgage owned.

Column 4 – 1932–1938: Estimated at 150 percent of foreclosures by life insurance companies (twenty-six companies plus 20 percent) and federal land banks, as shown in Table M-22, on basis of relation in 1930 of their farm mortgages to farm mortgages held by all reporting institutions (cf. Table A-61).

Column 5 – 1932–1938: Col. 3 minus col. 4.

Column 6 – 1920–1931: Roughly estimated at about one-third of total foreclosures, partly on basis of relationship of 1932 to 1938.
    1932–1938: Assumed to be 60 percent of col. 5.
    1939–1949: Roughly estimated at about one-third of col. 3, except for years beginning with 1944 when proportion is assumed to have been higher.

Column 7 – 1920–1949: Assumed at about two-thirds of col. 6. Ratio is based on relationship between holdings of farm mortgages of different groups of mortgagees in 1927 (cf. Wickens, D. L., *Farm Mortgage Credit*, Department of Agriculture Technical Bulletin 288).

FORECLOSURES OF FARM MORTGAGES

1920 to 1949

Year	All farm foreclosures			Foreclosures by			
	Rate	Number	Value	Institutions	Others	Nonfarm individuals	
						Total	Excluding nonprofit institutions
	Per 1,000 farms	000	$ mill.				
	1	2	3	4	5	6	7
1920	4.0	26	78	.	.	30	20
1921	6.6	42	126	.	.	40	30
1922	11.7	75	225	.	.	70	50
1923	14.6	93	279	.	.	90	70
1924	16.7	106	318	.	.	100	80
1925	17.4	111	333	.	.	100	80
1926	18.2	115	345	.	.	100	80
1927	17.6	111	333	.	.	100	80
1928	14.8	93	279	.	.	100	80
1929	15.7	99	297	.	.	100	80
1930	18.7	120	360	.	.	120	90
1931	28.4	185	555	.	.	180	135
1932	38.8	256	768	281	487	292	219
1933	28.0	188	564	326	238	143	107
1934	21.0	143	429	284	145	87	65
1935	20.3	135	405	261	144	86	64
1936	18.1	118	354	213	141	85	64
1937	14.3	91	273	137	136	82	62
1938	13.5	84	252	127	125	75	56
1939	12.6	77	231	.	.	70	50
1940	10.5	64	192	.	.	60	40
1941	6.2	37	111	.	.	35	25
1942	4.4	26	78	.	.	30	20
1943	3.1	18	54	.	.	25	15
1944	1.9	11	33	.	.	15	10
1945	1.5	9	27	.	.	15	10
1946	1.1	7	21	.	.	15	10
1947	1.0	6	18	.	.	15	10
1948	1.2	7	21	.	.	15	10
1949	1.4	9	27	.	.	15	10

Column 1 – 1897–1949: Sum of cols. 2, 7, and 12 minus sum of cols. 8–11.

Column 2 – 1897–1949: Sum of cols. 3–6.

Column 3 – 1897–1949: Table A-6, col. 1 raised 55 percent in order to bring estimates in line with figures for value of farm buildings as given in *Census of Agriculture* (cf. Kuznets, S., *National Product since 1869*, pp. 202, 216; Burroughs, R. J., "The Agricultural Segment of the National Balance Sheet," *Studies in Income and Wealth*, vol. XII, p. 196) minus adjustment for fire losses from Table A-51, col. 6. For 1945 and later years, the level of the farm construction expenditure series was raised fairly substantially by the Bureau of Agricultural Economics to bring the figures into line with postwar surveys of farm construction activity (compare *Farm Income Situation*, Aug.–Sept. 1948, p. 20 with *Farm Income Situation*, July–Aug. 1949, p. 17 and July–Aug. 1951, p. 28). Thus the 55 percent correction for understatement introduced here probably is too large for the post-World War II period.

Column 4 – 1897–1949: Sum of Table A-16, col. 6, Table A-18, col. 6, Table A-19, col. 6, and Table A-20, col. 6 minus Table A-52, col. 6.

Column 5 – 1897–1949: Sum of Table A-21, col. 1 and Table A-29, col. 6 minus adjustment for fire losses which was obtained by subtracting from fire losses on durable goods (roughly estimated at 60 percent of total fire losses on household goods, Table A-50, col. 6) depreciation calculated at rate of 16.67 percent per year.

Column 6 – 1897–1949: From Table A-32, col. 1.

Column 7 – 1897–1916: First differences of Table A-53, col. 1.
1917–1927: Sum of first differences of Table A-53, cols. 2–4, 6–8, and Table V-4, col. 2. Figures in Table V-4, col. 2 adjust figures in Table A-53, col. 5, 1920–1922, for amounts farmers' receipts from sales fell short of the amount of par value paid.
1928–1949: First differences of Table A-53, col. 1.

Column 8 – 1897–1949: First differences of Table A-54, col. 1 minus Table A-57, col. 6.

Column 9 – 1897–1949: From Table A-65, col. 1.

Column 10 – 1897–1949: From Table A-13, col. 4.

Column 11 – 1897–1949: Derived from average of minimum and maximum decadal estimates given in Table A-15, cols. 10 and 11.

Column 12 – 1897–1949: From Table A-12, col. 6.

AGRICULTURAL SAVING; INVENTORY PROFITS INCLUDED

Original Cost Depreciation: 1897 to 1949

$ mill.

Year	Total	Tangible assets (excluding columns 10–12)					Financial assets	Financial liabilities	Debt write-down	Net purchases of farm land by nonfarm owners	Net sales proceeds from farm land subdivided	Dealers' commissions on sales of farms
		Total	Buildings	Equipment	Consumer durables	Inventories						
	1	2	3	4	5	6	7	8	9	10	11	12
1897	423	522	65	−27	6	478	43	90	1	42	15	6
1898	317	436	78	19	10	329	82	150	1	42	15	7
1899	531	647	79	51	24	493	119	184	1	43	15	8
1900	194	389	88	50	26	225	103	243	1	48	15	9
1901	204	426	102	65	37	222	112	274	2	54	15	11
1902	385	610	116	128	45	321	91	254	2	59	15	14
1903	−55	160	115	70	44	−69	59	206	2	64	15	13
1904	122	348	111	67	47	123	72	227	2	69	15	15
1905	436	684	117	76	57	434	157	327	2	74	15	13
1906	704	1 007	134	122	83	668	159	380	2	79	15	14
1907	195	396	135	121	76	64	87	203	2	85	15	17
1908	234	469	136	61	53	219	15	160	2	90	15	17
1909	933	1 289	164	97	94	934	142	407	2	95	15	21
1910	114	602	187	95	98	222	90	486	2	88	25	23
1911	−397	137	165	87	80	−195	65	503	2	90	25	21
1912	493	1 151	189	110	96	756	141	701	4	92	25	23
1913	294	819	183	86	69	481	106	532	4	94	25	24
1914	210	545	174	54	72	245	61	297	4	93	25	23
1915	182	580	185	13	105	277	272	565	4	100	25	24
1916	846	1 583	321	28	162	1 072	529	1 158	4	107	25	28
1917	4 252	4 791	506	134	411	3 740	1 220	1 651	4	117	25	38
1918	2 821	1 680	536	232	291	621	2 226	968	6	128	25	42
1919	−1 235	1 166	793	348	495	−470	701	2 976	6	156	25	61
1920	−4 807	−2 233	640	437	267	−3 577	−144	2 688	8	−226	25	65
1921	−3 661	−3 536	92	−189	−293	−3 146	−916	−673	83	−191	25	35
1922	990	922	156	−172	−37	975	−329	−270	55	−184	30	28
1923	740	319	226	−40	189	−56	−123	−426	46	−175	40	29
1924	1 758	437	187	−39	87	202	−94	−1 310	36	−174	60	27
1925	440	706	198	67	270	171	−83	−167	36	275	70	31
1926	14	75	173	119	129	−346	−51	−317	30	266	60	29
1927	831	995	255	109	−34	665	217	62	30	264	50	25
1928	835	986	206	94	116	570	235	81	30	267	30	22
1929	229	271	159	136	149	−173	−92	−346	30	268	20	22
1930	−2 330	−2 622	−30	4	−165	−2 431	−243	−577	42	7	10	17
1931	−2 160	−2 602	−179	−253	−333	−1 837	−527	−1 045	73	6	10	13
1932	−1 114	−2 131	−270	−382	−444	−1 035	−272	−1 388	106	4	0	11
1933	970	−130	−238	−328	−326	762	−28	−1 274	150	5	0	9
1934	660	52	−206	−158	−123	539	476	−277	151	5	0	11
1935	2 225	1 620	−105	40	18	1 667	537	−166	119	−5	0	16
1936	1 250	357	−64	202	91	128	590	−366	91	−6	0	22
1937	562	378	14	342	93	−71	325	110	59	−6	0	22
1938	86	−163	−48	179	−83	−211	174	−81	32	−5	0	21
1939	1 101	571	11	160	94	306	421	−103	20	−5	0	21
1940	1 112	662	54	253	70	285	585	234	18	−92	0	25
1941	5 015	3 567	158	453	281	2 675	1 346	9	15	−98	5	33
1942	7 724	4 329	77	363	147	3 742	2 508	−748	3	−108	5	39
1943	6 067	1 519	104	101	161	1 153	3 526	−848	2	−126	5	55
1944	4 711	131	95	553	−49	−468	3 779	−608	2	−141	5	59
1945	5 230	1 274	65	492	34	683	3 917	−52	2	76	10	75
1946	7 528	6 009	963	649	961	3 436	2 269	732	3	86	15	86
1947	7 944	7 512	1 571	1 316	1 306	3 319	1 279	816	4	93	15	81
1948	3 776	4 854	1 729	1 831	1 236	58	61	1 091	4	96	20	72
1949	700	1 429	1 532	1 823	1 118	−3 044	−13	666	4	93	20	67

Column 1 – Sum of cols. 2, 7, and 12 minus sum of cols. 8–11.

Column 2 – Sum of cols. 3–6.

Column 3 – Table A-6, col. 2 raised 55 percent minus Table A-51, col. 7 (cf. note to Table A-1, col. 3).

Column 4 – Sum of Table A-16, col. 7, Table A-18, col. 7, Table A-19, col. 7, and Table A-20, col. 7, minus Table A-52, col. 7.

Column 5 – Sum of Table A-22, col. 1 and Table A-29, col. 7 minus adjustment for fire losses which was estimated by subtracting from fire losses in 1929 prices (obtained by deflating the original cost series [cf. Table A-1, col. 5] by an index derived by dividing farm expenditures on new consumer durable goods, original cost, by expenditures in 1929 prices [cf. note to Table Q-15, col. 2]) depreciation in 1929 prices calculated at a rate of 16.67 percent per year.

Column 6 – From Table A-32, col. 4.

Column 7 – First differences of the deflated values of Table A-53, col. 1. Index used obtained by linking in 1913 Department of Labor consumers' price index for moderate income families in large cities (1913–1946, *Handbook of Labor Statistics*, 1947, Bulletin 916; 1947–1949, *Monthly Labor Review*, July 1950, p. 179) to cost-of-living index of Douglas, P.H., (*Real Wages in the U.S., 1890–1926*, pp. 38, 60), both indices first having been converted to 1929 = 100 (1920–1922 adjustment made, cf. notes to Table A-1, col. 7).

Column 8 – First differences of deflated values of Table A-54, col. 1 (using index described in notes to col. 7) minus deflated values of Table A-57, col. 6.

Column 9 – Table A-65, col. 1 deflated by index described in notes to col. 7.

Column 10 – Table A-13, col. 4 deflated by index of value of farm real estate per acre (March 1 figures taken as Dec. of preceding year) as given in Table A-12, col. 3. 1950 figure taken from Department of Agriculture, Bureau of Agricultural Economics, *Current Developments in the Farm Real Estate Market*, March 1950.

Column 11 – Table A-1, col. 11 deflated by index of value of farm real estate per acre (cf. col. 10).

Column 12 – Table A-12, col. 5 deflated by index described in notes to col. 7 less depreciation. Since proportion of dealers' commissions which is depreciable is so small, it was decided not to calculate depreciation in 1929 prices by same procedure as used for original cost (cf. Table A-12, col. 6) but rather to obtain estimates by applying to deflated values of commissions the ratio of depreciation in 1929 prices to expenditures in 1929 prices on farm construction.

Column 1 – Sum of cols. 2, 7, and 12 minus sum of cols. 8–11.

Column 2 – Sum of cols. 3–6.

Column 3 – Table A-6, col. 3 raised 55 percent minus Table A-51, col. 8 (cf. note to Table A-1, col. 3).

Column 4 – Sum of Table A-16, col. 8, Table A-18, col. 8, Table A-19, col. 8, and Table A-20, col. 8 minus Table A-52, col. 8.

Column 5 – Sum of Table A-23, col. 1 and Table A-29, col. 8 minus adjustment for fire losses which was estimated by subtracting from fire losses in original cost (cf. Table A-1, col. 5) replacement cost depreciation, obtained by multiplying depreciation in 1929 prices by index described in notes to Table A-2, col. 5.

Column 6 – From Table A-32, col. 7.

Columns 7 to 11 – Same as Table A-1, cols. 7–11 respectively.

Column 12 – Depreciation in 1929 prices, as described in notes to Table A-2, col. 12, multiplied by index (cf. notes to Table A-2, col. 7) and then subtracted from Table A-12, col. 5.

AGRICULTURAL SAVING; 1929 PRICES
1897 to 1949

$ mill.

Year	Total	Tangible assets (excluding columns 10–12)					Financial assets	Financial liabilities	Debt write-down	Net purchases of farm land by nonfarm owners	Net sales proceeds from farm land subdivided	Dealers' commissions on sales of farms
		Total	Buildings	Equipment	Consumer durables	Inventories						
	1	2	3	4	5	6	7	8	9	10	11	12
1897	60	263	161	−7	84	25	84	152	2	109	39	15
1898	501	792	181	73	69	469	194	356	2	106	38	17
1899	354	534	164	82	94	194	236	298	2	100	35	19
1900	179	411	179	49	62	121	137	265	2	92	29	19
1901	−334	16	204	95	64	−347	195	452	4	88	24	23
1902	1 005	1 324	220	192	71	841	123	337	4	103	26	28
1903	−10	163	200	93	60	−190	−5	62	4	104	24	26
1904	84	569	205	104	64	196	173	538	4	119	26	29
1905	95	575	198	99	75	203	324	676	4	125	25	26
1906	355	699	198	143	128	230	202	431	4	116	22	27
1907	−103	−117	176	123	83	−499	−34	−169	4	125	22	30
1908	−310	337	202	87	47	1	177	723	4	111	18	32
1909	59	675	243	135	174	123	279	800	4	112	18	39
1910	315	733	265	101	166	201	−57	265	4	104	29	41
1911	−741	−88	226	91	71	−476	−5	546	4	106	29	37
1912	238	1 280	267	127	104	782	223	1 165	7	105	29	41
1913	−624	−58	246	102	41	−447	60	526	7	105	28	40
1914	754	1 108	242	52	27	787	39	293	7	103	28	38
1915	184	677	239	−27	34	431	416	810	7	105	26	39
1916	−402	−37	376	−19	123	−517	506	780	6	104	24	43
1917	2 513	1 583	471	64	383	665	849	−163	5	104	22	49
1918	3 197	429	366	45	102	−84	1 637	−1 217	7	104	20	45
1919	−833	601	488	146	198	−231	−320	1 043	6	105	17	57
1920	−273	942	221	230	−143	634	−1 213	192	7	−164	18	51
1921	−3 160	−1 753	−64	−297	−472	−920	−211	1 280	80	−157	21	28
1922	−1 053	−264	20	−191	−167	74	−36	853	56	−156	25	25
1923	528	−88	62	−59	56	−147	−234	−751	46	−154	35	26
1924	673	−670	36	−78	−1	−627	−112	−1 364	36	−157	54	24
1925	403	304	51	37	206	07	226	561	35	253	64	26
1926	−5	−20	34	84	95	−233	−92	−425	29	255	58	24
1927	−240	103	124	87	−60	−48	321	352	30	257	49	24
1928	34	286	78	36	97	75	298	247	30	263	30	20
1929	115	168	30	98	135	−95	−86	−331	30	268	20	20
1930	−384	−447	−146	5	−135	−171	−97	−208	43	8	11	14
1931	−434	−35	−285	−254	−282	786	−15	288	82	8	13	7
1932	−468	−678	−389	−377	−391	479	317	−40	133	6	0	−8
1933	−459	−1 395	−348	−319	−251	−477	313	−833	199	7	0	−4
1934	−1 106	−2 135	−313	−145	−41	−1 636	386	−845	193	7	0	−2
1935	1 904	993	−189	63	143	976	500	−541	149	−7	0	12
1936	403	−746	−138	225	218	−1 051	656	−579	112	−8	0	18
1937	1 962	1 601	−68	357	188	1 124	111	−292	70	−8	0	20
1938	459	232	−121	177	−36	212	360	119	39	−7	0	18
1939	1 003	408	−48	185	154	117	644	52	25	−7	0	21
1940	1 238	657	−4	304	128	229	637	182	22	−123	0	25
1941	3 268	1 458	67	485	332	574	1 102	−576	17	−123	6	32
1942	5 214	1 565	−59	349	139	1 136	1 587	−1 919	3	−124	6	28
1943	4 347	6	−70	51	55	−30	2 780	−1 404	2	−126	5	38
1944	4 159	−180	−103	455	−165	−367	3 468	−716	2	−128	5	34
1945	3 368	−132	−140	395	−89	−298	3 309	−225	2	61	8	37
1946	1 789	1 584	392	548	734	−90	274	60	3	62	11	67
1947	−107	1 408	510	937	820	−859	−1 808	−313	3	63	10	56
1948	1 444	3 142	519	1 110	634	879	−1 391	276	3	63	13	48
1949	999	1 374	467	885	528	−506	240	580	3	63	14	45

A-3 AGRICULTURAL SAVING; INVENTORY PROFITS EXCLUDED

Replacement Cost Depreciation: 1897 to 1949

$ mill.

Year	Total	Tangible assets (excluding columns 10-12)					Financial assets	Financial liabilities	Debt write-down	Net purchases of farm land by nonfarm owners	Net sales proceeds from farm land subdivided	Dealers' commissions on sales of farms
		Total	Buildings	Equipment	Consumer durables	Inventories						
	1	2	3	4	5	6	7	8	9	10	11	12
1897	42	141	68	-3	25	51	43	90	1	42	15	6
1898	233	352	79	36	22	215	82	150	1	42	15	7
1899	107	223	74	45	31	73	119	184	1	43	15	8
1900	-29	166	86	29	25	26	103	243	1	48	15	9
1901	-350	-128	97	55	24	-304	112	274	2	54	15	11
1902	478	704	108	114	27	455	91	254	2	59	15	13
1903	-139	76	103	55	24	-106	59	206	2	64	15	13
1904	83	310	102	60	29	119	72	227	2	69	15	14
1905	98	346	103	60	37	146	157	327	2	74	15	13
1906	96	400	109	92	61	138	159	380	2	79	15	13
1907	-272	-70	103	85	47	-305	87	203	2	85	15	16
1908	27	263	112	53	37	61	15	160	2	90	15	16
1909	95	452	139	85	95	133	142	407	2	95	15	20
1910	-9	480	157	69	98	156	90	486	2	88	25	22
1911	-653	-119	134	64	65	-382	65	503	2	90	25	21
1912	268	926	158	92	80	596	141	701	4	92	25	23
1913	-661	-135	148	71	37	-391	106	532	4	94	25	23
1914	401	737	143	45	43	506	61	297	4	93	25	22
1915	207	605	147	-4	84	378	272	565	4	100	25	24
1916	-1 102	-364	260	-3	123	-744	529	1 158	4	107	25	27
1917	1 219	1 759	398	60	321	980	1 220	1 651	4	117	25	37
1918	1 501	362	373	56	75	-142	2 226	968	6	128	25	40
1919	-1 758	646	577	169	209	-309	701	2 976	6	156	25	58
1920	-1 634	945	325	264	-214	570	-144	2 688	8	-226	25	60
1921	-1 842	-1 712	-67	-307	-549	-789	-916	-673	83	-191	25	30
1922	-198	-262	20	-184	-171	73	-329	-270	55	-184	30	24
1923	331	-87	67	-71	42	-125	-123	-426	46	-175	40	26
1924	581	-737	39	-96	-13	-667	-94	-1 310	36	-174	60	24
1925	66	336	55	13	202	66	-83	-167	36	275	70	27
1926	-42	23	34	73	94	-178	-51	-317	30	266	60	25
1927	-114	51	124	67	-58	-82	217	62	30	264	50	24
1928	109	262	78	34	95	55	235	81	30	267	30	20
1929	127	171	30	98	135	-92	-92	-346	30	268	20	20
1930	-177	-465	-140	4	-132	-197	-243	-577	42	7	10	13
1931	9	-426	-236	-245	-248	303	-527	-1 045	73	6	10	6
1932	192	-807	-284	-350	-303	130	-272	-1 388	106	4	0	-7
1933	16	-1 072	-252	-287	-180	-353	-28	-1 274	150	5	0	-3
1934	-1 129	-1 725	-255	-136	-9	-1 325	476	-277	151	5	0	-1
1935	1 248	649	-151	54	121	625	537	-166	119	-5	0	10
1936	-22	-908	-114	208	181	-1 183	590	-366	91	-6	0	15
1937	1 291	1 112	-59	340	148	683	325	110	59	-6	0	17
1938	393	151	-104	168	-38	125	174	-81	32	-5	0	14
1939	827	301	-41	160	134	48	421	-103	20	-5	0	17
1940	947	502	-4	260	85	161	585	234	18	-92	0	20
1941	2 737	1 294	65	444	246	539	1 346	9	15	-98	5	28
1942	5 044	1 661	-66	333	37	1 357	2 508	-748	3	-108	5	27
1943	4 399	-133	-89	61	20	-125	3 526	-848	2	-126	5	39
1944	4 216	-340	-143	480	-225	-452	3 779	-608	2	-141	5	35
1945	3 612	-308	-206	419	-142	-379	3 917	-52	2	76	10	39
1946	3 327	1 818	637	591	767	-177	2 269	732	3	86	15	76
1947	1 419	996	1 063	1 146	1 003	-2 216	1 279	816	4	93	15	72
1948	3 969	5 052	1 167	1 531	885	1 469	61	1 091	4	96	20	67
1949	1 799	2 533	1 014	1 377	804	-662	-13	666	4	93	20	62

FARMERS' SHARE IN NATIONAL INCOME
1859 to 1910

Year	Realized national income	Realized private production income in agriculture	Share of agricultural income		Year	Realized national income	Realized private production income in agriculture	Share of agricultural income	
			Unadjusted	Adjusted				Unadjusted	Adjusted
	$ mill.		Percent			$ mill.		Percent	
	1	2	3	4		1	2	3	4
1859	4 311	1 264	29.3	21.0	1885			19.0	13.6
1860			28.5	20.4	1886			19.0	13.6
1861			27.8	19.9	1887			19.0	13.6
1862			27.1	19.4	1888			19.0	13.6
1863			26.4	18.9	1889	10 701	1 517	19.0	13.6
1864			25.7	18.4	1890			19.0	13.6
1865			25.0	17.9	1891			19.0	13.6
1866			24.3	17.4	1892			19.0	13.6
1867			23.6	16.9	1893			19.0	13.6
1868			22.9	16.4	1894			19.0	13.6
1869	6 827	1 517	22.2	15.9	1895			19.0	13.6
1870			21.9	15.7	1896			18.8	13.5
1871			21.6	15.5	1897			19.9	14.3
1872			21.3	15.3	1898			19.9	14.3
1873			20.9	15.0	1899	15 364	2 933	19.1	13.7
1874			20.6	14.8	1900	16 158	3 034	18.8	13.5
1875			20.3	14.6	1901	17 170	3 153	18.4	13.2
1876			19.9	14.3	1902	18 444	3 335	18.1	13.0
1877			19.6	14.1	1903	19 595	3 439	17.6	12.6
1878			19.3	13.8	1904	20 090	3 708	18.5	13.3
1879	7 227	1 371	19.0	13.6	1905	21 428	3 678	17.2	12.3
1880			19.0	13.6	1906	23 165	4 029	17.4	12.5
1881			19.0	13.6	1907	24 403	4 214	17.3	12.4
1882			19.0	13.6	1908	23 458	4 621	19.7	14.1
1883			19.0	13.6	1909	26 456	5 311	20.1	14.4
1884			19.0	13.6	1910	28 166	5 563	19.8	14.2

Columns 1 and 2 – 1859–1910: National Industrial Conference Board, *Conference Board Studies in Enterprise and Social Progress,* pp. 79, 95.

Column 3 – 1859–1910: Col. 2 divided by col. 1. Figures for intercensal years obtained by linear interpolation 1859–1879; kept unchanged at 19.0 (the 1879 and 1899 value) 1879–1895; and for 1896–1898 moved in accordance with the relationship of farm income, derived from Strauss F., and Bean, L., *Gross Farm Income and Indices of Farm Production and Prices in the United States, 1869–1937,* U.S. Department of Agriculture, Technical Bulletin 703, p. 24, to national income estimated by extrapolating the National Conference Board figure for 1899 (*op. cit.,* p. 79) by a combined index of wholesale prices (*Statistical Abstract,* 1947, p. 287), cost of living (Snyder, Carl, *Business Cycles and Business Measurements,* p. 290), and volume of production (Persons, Warren M., *Forecasting Business Cycles,* p. 170).

Column 4 – 1859–1909: Col. 3 multiplied by 0.717, ratio of 1910 value of Table A-5, col. 3 to that of col. 3. 1910: Table A-5, col. 3.

Column 1 – Derived from figures appearing in Department of Agriculture, Bureau of Agricultural Economics, *Farm Income Situation*, August 1950. Income of farm operators includes government payments and adjustment for change in inventories of crops and livestock, as estimated by Bureau of Agricultural Economics. (Note that Bureau of Agricultural Economics inventory change series is not same as that given in Table A-32, col. 7 as explained in notes to latter.)

Column 2 – Roughly estimated at 20 percent of farm operators' net income from agriculture. Estimates supplied by Bureau of Agricultural Economics indicated that nonfarm wage earnings of members of farm operators' families other than farm operator himself plus interest, dividends, and income from other sources received by such families totaled 27 percent of net income from agriculture received by farm operators in 1934 and 13 percent in 1947. Similar figures were not available for years prior to 1934, and this, coupled with fact that estimates of nonagricultural income of farm operators were exceedingly rough, led to the decision to use a simple average of the two percentages for all years back to 1910. Nonfarm wage earnings of farm operators, as estimated by Bureau of Agricultural Economics, were not taken into account in this percentage. If they had been included, percentage would have been about double. A very large part of such wages were probably earned by persons classified as "farm operators" only because they met the technical definition in the *Census of Agriculture*, while conducting very minor agricultural operations. Actually, their primary source of earnings was nonagricultural work so that they are not included here in the universe of "farm operators."

Column 3 – Col. 1 plus col. 2. These are necessarily rough estimates because of the approximate nature of the nonagricultural income shares in col. 2.

Column 1 – Sum of cols. 4 and 7.

Column 2 – Sum of cols. 5 and 8.

Column 3 – Sum of cols. 6 and 9.

Column 4 – Table A-7, col. 3 minus Table A-8, col. 4.

Column 5 – Table A-7, col. 4 minus Table A-8, col. 5.

Column 6 – Table A-7, col. 3 minus Table A-8, col. 6.

Column 7 – Table A-7, col. 5 minus Table A-8, col. 7.

Column 8 – Table A-7, col. 6 minus Table A-8, col. 8.

Column 9 – Table A-7, col. 5 minus Table A-8, col. 9.

FARMERS' SHARE IN NATIONAL INCOME
1910 to 1949

Percent of national income

Year	Net income of farm operators from agricultural sources	Net income of farm operators from nonagricultural sources	Net income of farm operators from agricultural and nonagricultural sources	Year	Net income of farm operators from agricultural sources	Net income of farm operators from nonagricultural sources	Net income of farm operators from agricultural and nonagricultural sources
	1	2	3		1	2	3
1910	11.8	2.4	14.2	1930	5.8	1.2	7.0
1911	10.4	2.1	12.5	1931	4.8	1.0	5.8
1912	10.9	2.2	13.1	1932	4.3	0.9	5.2
1913	10.1	2.0	12.1	1933	6.2	1.2	7.4
1914	10.8	2.2	13.0	1934	6.3	1.3	7.6
1915	10.0	2.0	12.0	1935	8.0	1.6	9.6
1916	9.8	2.0	11.8	1936	7.2	1.4	8.6
1917	14.1	2.8	16.9	1937	7.5	1.5	9.0
1918	15.0	3.0	18.0	1938	6.5	1.3	7.8
1919	13.3	2.7	16.0	1939	6.4	1.3	7.7
1920	9.7	1.9	11.6	1940	5.9	1.2	7.1
1921	5.1	1.0	6.1	1941	7.1	1.4	8.5
1922	6.7	1.3	8.0	1942	8.1	1.6	9.7
1923	6.7	1.3	8.0	1943	8.3	1.7	10.0
1924	6.7	1.3	8.0	1944	7.4	1.5	8.9
1925	8.0	1.6	9.6	1945	7.5	1.5	9.0
1926	7.1	1.4	8.5	1946	8.8	1.8	10.6
1927	6.9	1.4	8.3	1947	9.0	1.8	10.8
1928	7.2	1.4	8.6	1948	8.2	1.6	9.8
1929	6.8	1.4	8.2	1949	6.8	1.4	8.2

FARMERS' SAVING THROUGH CONSTRUCTION; UNADJUSTED
1897 to 1949

$ mill.

Year	Total			Residential buildings			Other buildings		
	Original cost	1929 prices	Replacement cost	Original cost	1929 prices	Replacement cost	Original cost	1929 prices	Replacement cost
	1	2	3	4	5	6	7	8	9
1897	43	108	45	24	60	24	19	48	21
1898	52	122	53	28	66	28	24	56	25
1899	54	113	51	29	62	27	25	51	24
1900	61	122	59	34	66	31	27	56	28
1901	70	139	66	37	75	35	33	64	31
1902	78	147	72	40	77	37	38	70	35
1903	76	131	67	39	70	35	37	61	32
1904	79	145	72	41	77	37	38	68	35
1905	78	130	68	41	71	36	37	59	32
1906	89	129	71	46	69	37	43	60	34
1907	92	119	70	48	65	37	44	54	33
1908	93	137	76	48	74	40	45	63	36
1909	109	159	91	56	84	47	53	75	44
1910	125	175	103	65	94	54	60	81	49
1911	111	150	89	57	81	47	54	69	42
1912	125	174	103	64	93	54	61	81	49
1913	121	160	96	62	87	51	59	73	45
1914	117	160	95	60	87	50	57	73	45
1915	120	151	93	62	83	50	58	68	43
1916	211	242	167	105	132	87	106	110	80
1917	329	299	252	147	141	114	182	158	138
1918	350	230	234	148	100	97	202	130	137
1919	515	306	361	214	122	143	301	184	218
1920	418	132	194	203	60	93	215	72	101
1921	68	−43	−45	32	−21	−22	36	−22	−23
1922	111	15	15	52	3	3	59	12	12
1923	155	40	43	73	14	16	82	26	27
1924	131	25	27	62	9	10	69	16	17
1925	139	38	39	68	18	18	71	20	21
1926	120	23	23	62	13	13	58	10	10
1927	173	82	82	83	36	36	90	46	46
1928	143	55	55	77	31	31	66	24	24
1929	114	26	26	66	21	21	48	5	5
1930	−4	−82	−79	24	−16	−16	−28	−66	−63
1931	−102	−168	−139	−25	−57	−47	−77	−111	−92
1932	−161	−230	−168	−60	−93	−67	−101	−137	−101
1933	−148	−213	−154	−54	−87	−62	−94	−126	−92
1934	−130	−198	−161	−47	−82	−67	−83	−116	−94
1935	−70	−123	−99	−22	−50	−40	−48	−73	−59
1936	−37	−83	−69	−8	−34	−28	−29	−49	−41
1937	8	−45	−40	16	−14	−12	−8	−31	−28
1938	−30	−76	−65	−6	−32	−27	−24	−44	−38
1939	9	−28	−24	20	0	0	−11	−28	−24
1940	35	−2	−2	58	40	35	−23	−42	−37
1941	101	40	39	92	58	57	9	−18	−18
1942	47	−46	−51	43	−9	−10	4	−37	−41
1943	68	−52	−66	28	−33	−42	40	−19	−24
1944	62	−75	−103	13	−52	−72	49	−23	−31
1945	43	−99	−146	4	−64	−96	39	−35	−50
1946	623	243	395	309	112	188	314	131	207
1947	1 020	319	664	503	147	318	517	172	346
1948	1 122	323	727	553	147	346	569	176	381
1949	993	290	630	493	137	305	500	153	325

FARMERS' EXPENDITURES ON NEW CONSTRUCTION
1897 to 1949

A-7

$ mill.

Year	Total Original cost	Total 1929 prices	Residential buildings Original cost	Residential buildings 1929 prices	Other buildings Original cost	Other buildings 1929 prices	Year	Total Original cost	Total 1929 prices	Residential buildings Original cost	Residential buildings 1929 prices	Other buildings Original cost	Other buildings 1929 prices
	1	2	3	4	5	6		1	2	3	4	5	6
1897	102	243	49	120	53	123	1924	298	287	133	127	165	160
1898	113	261	54	128	59	133	1925	311	303	141	138	170	165
1899	117	256	56	126	61	130	1926	297	291	137	134	160	157
1900	130	269	62	132	68	137	1927	355	354	160	159	195	195
1901	138	291	66	143	72	148	1928	331	332	156	156	175	176
1902	148	303	70	147	78	156	1929	307	307	147	147	160	160
1903	148	292	70	142	78	150	1930	193	201	107	111	86	90
1904	154	310	73	151	81	159	1931	97	116	59	71	38	45
1905	155	299	74	147	81	152	1932	37	52	24	34	13	18
1906	169	302	80	147	89	155	1933	49	68	29	40	20	28
1907	174	296	83	145	91	151	1934	66	81	36	44	30	37
1908	179	319	85	156	94	163	1935	126	154	61	75	65	79
1909	198	345	94	168	104	177	1936	161	193	76	91	85	102
1910	217	367	104	181	113	186	1937	207	231	100	111	107	120
1911	206	348	98	170	108	178	1938	171	200	79	93	92	107
1912	223	377	106	184	117	193	1939	212	248	106	125	106	123
1913	223	369	106	181	117	188	1940	240	275	145	166	95	109
1914	223	374	106	183	117	191	1941	310	318	182	185	128	133
1915	229	371	109	182	120	189	1942	260	234	135	120	125	114
1916	324	467	154	233	170	234	1943	284	228	121	96	163	132
1917	449	532	199	246	250	286	1944	283	206	108	78	175	128
1918	478	470	203	208	275	262	1945	267	182	100	66	167	116
1919	653	553	273	233	380	320	1946	856	527	409	244	447	283
1920	566	385	266	173	300	212	1947	1 272	610	611	282	661	328
1921	223	213	98	94	125	119	1948	1 397	621	671	285	726	336
1922	269	271	119	118	150	153	1949	1 292	595	621	279	671	316
1923	317	300	142	131	175	169							

Column 1 – 1897–1909: Estimated at 3.28 percent of gross farm income (Strauss, F. and Bean, L., *Gross Farm Income and Indices of Farm Production and Prices in the U.S., 1869–1937*, U.S. Department of Agriculture, Technical Bulletin 703, p. 24). Percentage obtained by averaging annual percentages for 1910–1915. Approximately same average percent would have been obtained if period 1910–1929 had been used.
1910–1914: Sum of cols. 3 and 5.
1915–1949: From Department of Commerce, *Construction and Construction Materials, Statistical Supplement*, May 1950, p. 8.

Column 2 – 1897–1949: Sum of cols. 4 and 6.

Column 3 – 1897–1909: Col. 1 multiplied by 47.6 percent, ratio of col. 3 to col. 1 in 1915.
1910–1914: Estimated at 56 percent of Bureau of Agricultural Economics series, the link relationship to Commerce figure from *Construction and Construction Materials* in 1915. Bureau of Agricultural Economics series, which includes repairs on residential buildings as well as new construction, from *Income Parity for Agriculture*, part II, section 5, p. 2.
1915–1949: Same source as for 1915–1949 in col. 1.

Column 4 – 1897–1949: Col. 3 deflated by Table A-30, col. 1.

Column 5 – 1897–1909: Col. 1 minus col. 3.
1910–1914: Same procedure as for 1910–1914 in col. 3 except that link relationship is 45 percent.
1915–1949: Same source as for 1915–1949 in col. 1.

Column 6 – 1897–1949: Col. 5 deflated by Table A-30, col. 2.

Column 1 – Sum of cols. 4 and 7.

Column 2 – Sum of cols. 5 and 8.

Column 3 – Sum of cols. 6 and 9. Note: Bureau of Agricultural Economics estimates of depreciation on farm buildings, computed annually since 1910 in current prices, as part of derivation of annual net income of farm operators (*Farm Income Situation*, Aug. 1950, table 9), are substantially higher than series given here largely because they include repairs.

Column 4 – Calculated from Table A-7, col. 3 assuming average life of sixty years. Farmers' expenditures on residential construction for years prior to 1897, which were required for estimating depreciation in 1897 and later years, were derived by: (1) applying index given in Table A-9, col. 5 to value for 1890–1899, which was obtained by same procedure as Table A-7, col. 1, 1897–1909; (2) roughly distributing decadal sums by taking annual average of decadal sums to represent mid-year of period and linear interpolating; (3) multiplying by 47.6 percent (cf. note to Table A-7, col. 3, 1897–1909); (4) assuming 1836–1839 values to be same as for 1840.

Column 5 – Calculated from Table A-7, col. 4 assuming average life of sixty years. Farmers' expenditures on residential construction for years prior to 1897 obtained by deflating expenditures in original cost, as derived by procedure described in col. 4 above, by price index from Table A-30, col. 1.

Column 6 – Col. 5 multiplied by price index from Table A-30, col. 1.

Column 7 – Calculated from Table A-7, col. 5 assuming average life of forty-five years. Farmers' expenditures on nonresidential construction for years prior to 1897 derived by same procedure as for col. 4 except that total expenditures multiplied by 52.4 percent.

Column 8 – Calculated from Table A-7, col. 6 assuming average life of forty-five years. Farmers' expenditures on nonresidential construction for years prior to 1897 obtained by deflating expenditures in original cost, as derived by procedure stated in col. 7, by price index from Table A-30, col. 2.

Column 9 – Col. 8 multiplied by price index from Table A-30, col. 2.

DEPRECIATION ON FARM CONSTRUCTION
1897 to 1949

$ mill.

Year	Total			Residential buildings			Other buildings		
	Original cost	1929 prices	Replacement cost	Original cost	1929 prices	Replacement cost	Original cost	1929 prices	Replacement cost
	1	2	3	4	5	6	7	8	9
1897	59	135	57	25	60	25	34	75	32
1898	61	139	60	26	62	26	35	77	34
1899	63	143	66	27	64	29	36	79	37
1900	65	147	71	28	66	31	37	81	40
1901	68	152	72	29	68	31	39	84	41
1902	70	156	76	30	70	33	40	86	43
1903	72	161	81	31	72	35	41	89	46
1904	75	165	82	32	74	36	43	91	46
1905	77	169	87	33	76	38	44	93	49
1906	80	173	98	34	78	43	46	95	55
1907	82	177	104	35	80	46	47	97	58
1908	86	182	103	37	82	45	49	100	58
1909	89	186	107	38	84	47	51	102	60
1910	92	192	114	39	87	50	53	105	64
1911	95	198	117	41	89	51	54	109	66
1912	98	203	120	42	91	52	56	112	68
1913	102	209	127	44	94	55	58	115	72
1914	106	214	128	46	96	56	60	118	72
1915	109	220	136	47	99	59	62	121	77
1916	113	225	157	49	101	67	64	124	90
1917	120	233	197	52	105	85	68	128	112
1918	128	240	244	55	108	106	73	132	138
1919	138	247	292	59	111	130	79	136	162
1920	148	253	372	63	113	173	85	140	199
1921	155	256	268	66	115	120	89	141	148
1922	158	256	254	67	115	116	91	141	138
1923	162	260	274	69	117	126	93	143	148
1924	167	262	271	71	118	123	96	144	148
1925	172	265	272	73	120	123	99	145	149
1926	177	268	274	75	121	124	102	147	150
1927	182	272	273	77	123	124	105	149	149
1928	188	277	276	79	125	125	109	152	151
1929	193	281	281	81	126	126	112	155	155
1930	197	283	272	83	127	123	114	156	149
1931	199	284	236	84	128	106	115	156	130
1932	198	282	205	84	127	91	114	155	114
1933	197	281	203	83	127	91	114	154	112
1934	196	279	227	83	126	103	113	153	124
1935	196	277	225	83	125	101	113	152	124
1936	198	276	230	84	125	104	114	151	126
1937	199	276	247	84	125	112	115	151	135
1938	201	276	236	85	125	106	116	151	130
1939	203	276	236	86	125	106	117	151	130
1940	205	277	242	87	126	110	118	151	132
1941	209	278	271	90	127	125	119	151	146
1942	213	280	311	92	129	145	121	151	166
1943	216	280	350	93	129	163	123	151	187
1944	221	281	386	95	130	180	126	151	206
1945	224	281	413	96	130	196	128	151	217
1946	233	284	461	100	132	221	133	152	240
1947	252	291	608	108	135	293	144	156	315
1948	275	298	670	118	138	325	157	160	345
1949	299	305	662	128	142	316	171	163	346

TABLE A-9

Column 1 – Obtained by averaging Census figures for beginning and end of decade (*Statistical Abstract*, 1922, p. 128), except for 1840–1849, which is rough estimate.

Column 2 – First differences of Census figures for beginning and end of decade.

Column 3 – Average of indices of cols. 1 and 2.

Column 4 – Obtained by extrapolating Bureau of Agricultural Economics index of farm construction costs (see Table A-30, cols. 1 and 2) by index derived by averaging indices of wholesale prices of building materials and of wage rates as given in Warren, G. F. and Pearson, F. A., *Gold and Prices*, pp. 30, 32, 317.

Column 5 – Col. 3 multiplied by col. 4.

TABLE A–10

Column 1 – 1919–1949: Sum of cols. 2–9.

Column 2 – 1919–1923: Rough estimates.
1924–1928: *Agricultural Finance Review*, Nov. 1945, p. 86.
1929–1949: *Agricultural Finance Review*, Nov. 1950, table 11.

Columns 3 and 4 – 1919–1923: Rough estimates.
1924–1928: Unpublished estimates of Farm Credit Administration.
1929–1949: Same source as for col. 2.

Column 5 – 1936–1949: *Agricultural Finance Review*, Nov. 1950, table 11.

Column 6 – 1919–1928: The 1929 value extrapolated by series derived as cumulation beginning with 1919 as zero of change in farm real estate holdings by legal reserve life insurance companies as derived from data given in *Life Insurance Fact Book*, 1949, p. 65.
1929–1949: *Agricultural Finance Review*, Nov. 1950, table 11.

Column 7 – 1919–1949: Assumed to be roughly 10 percent of total real estate holdings by fraternal life insurance companies (Table I-10, col. 3).

Column 8 – 1919–1935: Extrapolated on basis of "other real estate" of country member banks as given in *Banking and Monetary Statistics*, p. 98.
1936–1942: *Agricultural Finance Review*, Nov. 1948, p. 113.
1942–1949: Assumed to have declined gradually from 1942 level to zero.

Column 9 – 1923–1940: From Table R-58, col. 8.

FARMERS' EXPENDITURES ON NEW CONSTRUCTION

A-9

Period Totals: 1840 to 1899

Period	Number of existing farms	Number of additional farms	Farm construction activity	Farm construction costs	Total farm construction expenditures
	000		1890–1899 = 100.0		
	1	2	3	4	5
1840–49	1 274	350	27.2	66.4	18.1
1850–59	1 747	595	42.3	72.3	30.6
1860–69	2 352	616	49.1	105.5	51.8
1870–79	3 334	1 349	89.8	109.2	98.1
1880–89	4 287	556	65.3	102.5	66.9
1890–99	5 151	1 173	100.0	100.0	100.0

HOLDINGS OF FARM REAL ESTATE BY SELECTED LENDING AGENCIES

A-10

1919 to 1949

$ mill.

End of year	Total	Federal land banks	Joint stock land banks	Three state credit agencies	Federal Farm Mortgage Corporation	Life insurance companies	Fraternal order life insurance	Commercial banks	
								Operating	Closed
	1	2	3	4	5	6	7	8	9
1919	14	0	0	0	–	0	1	13	–
1920	17	0	0	0	–	1	1	15	–
1921	25	0	0	0	–	6	1	18	–
1922	41	2	1	1	–	10	1	26	–
1923	73	4	2	2	–	27	2	35	1
1924	82	5	3	4	–	25	2	41	2
1925	111	11	6	8	–	35	2	46	3
1926	139	17	9	12	–	49	3	46	3
1927	169	22	12	16	–	66	3	45	5
1928	195	26	15	20	–	85	3	44	2
1929	233	30	20	27	–	107	3	44	2
1930	265	37	22	34	–	123	3	43	3
1931	376	54	38	39	–	191	3	45	6
1932	557	83	72	47	–	288	4	55	8
1933	741	97	86	56	–	428	5	51	18
1934	877	97	82	60	–	558	6	59	15
1935	938	119	78	62	–	589	9	70	11
1936	1 002	129	73	68	10	634	10	70	8
1937	957	118	62	72	22	612	10	56	5
1938	945	115	54	72	35	607	10	49	3
1939	935	126	47	68	40	600	10	42	2
1940	830	109	36	61	33	548	9	33	1
1941	649	74	25	53	24	442	8	23	–
1942	485	40	18	44	20	336	7	20	–
1943	301	17	7	36	13	205	6	17	–
1944	188	7	4	33	6	119	5	14	–
1945	106	2	1	4	2	82	4	11	–
1946	52	0	1	4	1	34	4	8	–
1947	27	0	0	4	0	14	4	5	–
1948	16	0	0	4	0	6	4	2	–
1949	11	0	0	4	0	3	4	0	–

NET CHANGE (CASH BASIS) IN HOLDINGS OF FARM REAL ESTATE
BY SELECTED LENDING AGENCIES: 1920 to 1949

$ mill.

Year	Total	Federal land banks	Joint stock land banks	Three state credit agencies	Federal Farm Mortgage Corporation	Life insurance companies	Fraternal order life insurance	Commercial banks	
								Operating	Closed
	1	2	3	4	5	6	7	8	9
1920	3	0	0	0	–	1	0	2	–
1921	8	0	0	0	–	5	0	3	–
1922	16	2	1	1	–	4	0	8	–
1923	32	2	1	1	–	17	1	9	1
1924	9	1	1	2	–	–2	0	6	1
1925	29	6	3	4	–	10	0	5	1
1926	29	6	3	4	–	14	1	0	1
1927	33	6	4	4	–	17	0	–1	3
1928	30	5	4	4	–	19	0	–1	–1
1929	43	5	6	7	–	24	0	0	1
1930	44	9	3	7	–	20	0	3	2
1931	132	20	18	5	–	73	0	12	4
1932	217	35	37	8	–	105	1	28	3
1933	217	17	15	9	–	148	1	15	12
1934	168	3	–2	4	–	137	1	27	–2
1935	88	30	0	3	0	39	3	16	–3
1936	103	22	1	7	11	63	1	0	–2
1937	–19	1	–5	5	15	–19	0	–14	–2
1938	27	7	–3	1	21	9	0	–7	–1
1939	47	23	–1	–3	22	13	0	–7	0
1940	–49	–3	–4	–6	5	–31	–1	–9	0
1941	–125	–18	–2	–7	1	–87	–1	–10	–1
1942	–123	–21	0	–8	3	–93	–1	–3	–
1943	–163	–18	–8	–8	–4	–121	–1	–3	–
1944	–109	–9	–3	–3	–6	–84	–1	–3	–
1945	–85	–5	–3	–29	–4	–40	–1	–3	–
1946	–58	–2	0	0	–1	–52	0	–3	–
1947	–24	0	–1	0	–1	–19	0	–3	–
1948	–8	0	0	0	0	–5	0	–3	–
1949	0	0	0	0	0	2	0	–2	–

Column 1 – Sum of cols. 2–9.

Column 2 – First differences of Table A-10, col. 2 plus losses sustained in liquidation of loans, supplied by Farm Credit Administration.

Columns 3 and 4 – First differences of Table A-10, cols. 3–4, respectively, plus capital losses. Estimates for losses obtained by taking 1929 figures for farm loans held by respective institutions as base values and multiplying annually by ratios of losses sustained by federal land banks (cf. col. 2) to farm loans held in 1929.

Column 5 – First differences of Table A-10, col. 5 plus losses, supplied by Farm Credit Administration.

Column 6 – First differences of Table A-10, col. 6 minus 30 percent of Table I-7, col. 1. Percentage estimated on basis of data on mortgage holdings and foreclosures of largest life insurance companies (cf. Table M-24).

Column 7 – First differences of Table A-10, col. 7.

Column 8 – First differences of Table A-10, col. 8 plus Table R-57, col. 3.

Column 9 – First differences of Table A-10, col 9 plus Table R-59, col. 8.

Column 1 – 1897–1949: Based on census-year figures in *Agricultural Statistics*, 1947, p. 488. Estimates for intercensal years obtained by linear interpolation. Figures so obtained were converted to June 30 basis by two-year moving average.

Column 2 – 1897–1911: Derived from regression line fitted to number of farms changing ownership by voluntary sales and trades and index of prices of farm products for 1912–1920. Index of prices of farm products from Warren, G. F. and Pearson, F. A., *Gold and Prices*, pp. 30–32. Number of farms changing ownership by voluntary sales and trades from sources given in *Yearbook of Agriculture*, 1942.
　　1912–1941: Derived from Department of Agriculture, Bureau of Agricultural Economics data (*Agricultural Outlook*, Dec. 1946, p. 38).
　　1942–1949: Derived from Bureau of Agricultural Economics data (*Agricultural Finance Review, Supplement*, May 1950, p. 32).

Column 3 – 1897–1911: Derived from regression line fitted to index of value per acre and index of prices of farm products for 1890, 1900, 1910–1916. Index of prices of farm products from Warren and Pearson, *op. cit.* Index of value per acre for census years derived from figures for value of farm land and buildings and number of acres of land in farms as given in *Agricultural Statistics*, 1947, p. 488, linked in 1912 to index given in the *Farm Real Estate Situation, 1945–1946*. Value for 1911 obtained by linear interpolation.
　　1912–1945: Department of Agriculture, Bureau of Agricultural Economics, *Farm Real Estate Situation, 1945–1946*, pp. 44–45.
　　1946–1949: *Agricultural Finance Review, Supplement*, May 1950.

Column 4 – 1897–1949: Col. 1 multiplied by the product of cols. 2 and 3.

Column 5 – 1897–1949: Col. 4 multiplied by $25 million, estimated average commission for the years 1935–1939. This figure was obtained as follows:
　　(a) Value of land and buildings, obtained by averaging Census and Bureau of Agricultural Economics figures for 1935–1939 (*Statistical Abstract*, 1947, p. 581), is $34.0 billion.
　　(b) Average annual number of farms per thousand changing hands as a result of voluntary sales and trades, and of administrators' and executors' sales, is 37.4 (*Yearbook of Agriculture*, 1942).
　　(c) It is assumed, on the basis of information obtained from the Bureau of Agricultural Economics, that only about one-half of all transfers are handled through real estate dealers, the remainder representing direct transactions between buyer and seller.
　　(d) Average rate of dealers' commissions is estimated, again on basis of information from the Bureau of Agricultural Economics, at 4 percent.
　　(e) Combination of above yields an estimate of $25 million for dealers' commissions on real estate transfers for average of 1935–1939 ($ 34.0 billion multiplied by 0.0374 multiplied by 0.5 multiplied by 0.04).

Column 6 – 1897–1949: Col. 5 less depreciation. Depreciation obtained by: (1) multiplying col. 5 by percent of value of buildings to total value of land and buildings. (Value of buildings for 1890, 1900, 1912 and 1922 from Kuznets, S., *National Product since 1869*, p. 202, and for 1925, 1930, 1935, 1940, and 1945 residual of value of land and buildings given in *Agricultural Statistics*, 1942, p. 632, and 1947, p. 488, and value of land given in *Census of Agriculture*. Estimates of percent for intercensal years derived by linear interpolation); (2) fitting a straight line to the logarithims of values for 1897–1929 and extrapolating it back to 1847; (3) applying depreciation rate of 2 percent per year.

COMMISSIONS PAID TO REAL ESTATE DEALERS
IN CONNECTION WITH SALES OF FARMS: 1897 to 1949

Year	Land in farms	Rate of voluntary sales	Land prices	Value of sales	Total commissions to dealers	Commissions less depreciation	Year	Land in farms	Rate of voluntary sales	Land prices	Value of sales	Total commissions to dealers	Commissions less depreciation
	1935–1939 = 100				$ mill.			1935–1939 = 100				$ mill.	
	1	2	3	4	5	6		1	2	3	4	5	6
1897	74	80	48	28	7	6	1924	88	87	157	120	30	27
1898	76	81	53	33	8	7	1925	88	101	153	136	34	31
1899	78	82	55	35	9	8	1926	89	96	150	128	32	29
1900	79	85	59	40	10	9	1927	90	90	144	117	29	25
1901	80	86	72	50	12	11	1928	92	80	142	105	26	22
1902	80	90	85	61	15	14	1929	93	81	140	105	26	22
1903	81	88	79	56	14	13	1930	94	65	138	84	21	17
1904	81	90	85	62	16	15	1931	95	55	128	67	17	13
1905	81	88	80	57	14	13	1932	96	57	107	59	15	11
1906	82	89	82	60	15	14	1933	98	61	88	53	13	9
1907	82	92	94	71	18	17	1934	99	66	92	60	15	11
1908	83	92	94	72	18	17	1935	100	85	95	81	20	16
1909	83	96	112	89	22	21	1936	100	107	99	106	26	22
1910	83	99	117	96	24	23	1937	100	104	102	106	26	22
1911	84	95	117	93	23	21	1938	100	101	103	104	26	21
1912	85	102	117	101	25	23	1939	100	103	101	104	26	21
1913	86	101	121	105	26	24	1940	101	116	102	120	30	25
1914	86	95	124	101	25	23	1941	103	142	103	151	38	33
1915	87	96	124	104	26	24	1942	104	152	110	174	44	39
1916	88	105	131	121	30	28	1943	106	191	120	243	61	55
1917	89	125	142	158	40	38	1944	107	176	138	260	65	59
1918	89	126	156	175	44	42	1945	109	196	152	325	81	75
1919	90	166	169	252	63	61	1946	110	197	171	371	93	86
1920	90	148	205	273	68	65	1947	112	167	192	359	90	81
1921	89	90	190	152	38	35	1948	113	139	205	322	80	72
1922	89	83	168	124	31	28	1949	115	126	211	306	76	67
1923	88	89	163	128	32	29							

A-13   TABLE A–13

Column 1 – 1897–1899: Obtained by linear interpolation between Jan. 1, 1890 and Jan. 1, 1900 figures as given by *Census of Agriculture* (cf. *Historical Statistics*, p. 96).
1900–1908: Obtained by linear interpolation between Jan. 1, 1900 and Jan. 1, 1910 figures.
1909–1913: *Agricultural Statistics*, 1942, p. 635.
1914–1923: *Balance Sheet of Agriculture*, 1949, p. 18.
1924–1938: *Agricultural Statistics*, 1942, p. 635.
1939–1949: *Balance Sheet of Agriculture*, 1949, p. 18; *Agricultural Finance Review*, Nov. 1950, table 30.

Column 2 – 1897–1949: From Table A-61, col. 1.

Column 3 – 1897–1899: Assumed same as for 1899–1909.
1900–1949: First differences of percents given in Table A-14, col. 6, distributed evenly over given period.

Column 4 – 1897–1949: Obtained by multiplying col. 3 by value of farm land and buildings less mortgage debt (col. 1 minus col. 2).

Column 5 – 1897–1919: Not estimated but assumed to be negligible.
1920–1949: From Table A-11, col. 1.

Column 6 – 1897–1949: Col. 4 minus col. 5.

768

1897 to 1949

Year	Value of farm land and buildings (end of year)	Mortgage debt (end of year)	Change in ownership by nonfarmers	Net purchase or sale of farm land by nonfarmers		
				Total	Reporting institutions	Other
	$ mill.		Percent	$ mill.		
	1	2	3	4	5	6
1897	15 948	2 072	.30	42	–	42
1898	16 281	2 149	.30	42	–	42
1899	16 615	2 229	.30	43	–	43
1900	18 434	2 312	.30	48	–	48
1901	20 252	2 397	.30	54	–	54
1902	22 071	2 486	.30	59	–	59
1903	23 889	2 578	.30	64	–	64
1904	25 708	2 674	.30	69	–	69
1905	27 527	2 773	.30	74	–	74
1906	29 345	2 876	.30	79	–	79
1907	31 164	2 983	.30	85	–	85
1908	32 982	3 093	.30	90	–	90
1909	34 801	3 208	.30	95	–	95
1910	36 050	3 522	.27	88	–	88
1911	37 306	3 930	.27	90	–	90
1912	38 463	4 348	.27	92	–	92
1913	39 586	4 707	.27	94	–	94
1914	39 597	4 991	.27	93	–	93
1915	42 271	5 256	.27	100	–	100
1916	45 531	5 826	.27	107	–	107
1917	49 986	6 537	.27	117	–	117
1918	54 539	7 137	.27	128	–	128
1919	66 316	8 449	.27	156	–	156
1920	61 477	10 221	–.44	–226	3	–229
1921	54 017	10 702	–.44	–191	8	–199
1922	52 710	10 786	–.44	–184	16	–200
1923	50 468	10 665	–.44	–175	32	–207
1924	49 468	9 913	–.44	–174	9	–183
1925	49 052	9 713	.70	275	29	246
1926	47 634	9 658	.70	266	29	237
1927	47 495	9 757	.70	264	33	231
1928	47 880	9 757	.70	267	30	237
1929	47 880	9 631	.70	268	43	225
1930	43 993	9 398	.02	7	44	–37
1931	37 236	9 094	.02	6	132	–126
1932	30 724	8 466	.02	4	217	–213
1933	31 933	7 685	.02	5	217	–212
1934	32 859	7 584	.02	5	168	–163
1935	33 910	7 423	–.02	–5	88	–93
1936	34 757	7 154	–.02	–6	103	–109
1937	34 747	6 955	–.02	–6	–19	13
1938	33 931	6 779	–.02	–5	27	–32
1939	33 642	6 586	–.02	–5	47	–52
1940	33 497	6 491	–.34	–92	–49	–43
1941	35 331	6 372	–.34	–98	–125	27
1942	37 855	5 951	–.34	–108	–123	15
1943	42 532	5 389	–.34	–126	–163	37
1944	46 389	4 933	–.34	–141	–109	–32
1945	52 114	4 682	.16	76	–85	161
1946	58 604	4 777	.16	86	–58	144
1947	62 813	4 882	.16	93	–24	117
1948	65 168	5 108	.16	96	–8	104
1949	63 527	5 413	.16	93	0	93

NET PURCHASES OR SALES OF FARM LAND
BY NONINSTITUTIONAL NONFARM OWNERS
Selected Years: 1899 to 1949

End of year	Value of farms		Proportion of rented farms	Proportion of rented farms owned by persons not residing on farms	Proportion of all farms owned by nonfarm landlords	
	Total	Less mortgage debt			Unadjusted	Adjusted
	$ mill.		Percent			
	1	2	3	4	5	6
1899	16 615	14 386	38.2	62.8	24.0	31.7
1909	34 801	31 593	41.9	62.8	26.3	34.7
1919	66 316	57 867	45.7	61.9	28.3	37.4
1924	49 468	39 555	43.1	61.9	26.7	35.2
1929	47 880	38 249	46.0	63.6	29.3	38.7
1934	32 859	25 275	45.1	65.1	29.4	38.8
1939	33 642	27 056	44.0	66.7	29.3	38.7
1944	46 389	41 456	41.8	67.2	28.1	37.0
1949	63 527	58 114	42.5	67.2	28.6	37.8

Column 1 – 1899–1944: Value of farm land and buildings, as given by *Census of Agriculture* (cf. *Historical Statistics*, p. 96). Figures in this and cols. 2 and 3 refer to Jan. 1 of year following, except for 1909, 1929, and 1939, when they apply to mid-April of following year.
1949: From *Balance Sheet of Agriculture*, 1950, p. 2.

Column 2 – 1899–1949: Col. 1 minus Table A-61, col. 1.

Column 3 – 1899–1944: Proportion of total value of farm land and buildings operated by tenants and managers and by part-owners (portion rented by them) derived from Census data (cf. *Historical Statistics*, p. 96). For period 1899-1934, when separate figures are not given for value of farms owned by part-owners, proportion was assumed to be approximately same as ratio of value of rented to all land operated by part-owners in 1939. (Figures on acreage operated, available since 1924, indicate that during fifteen years preceding 1939 proportion of rented land operated by part-owners remained virtually unchanged.)
1949: Rough estimate. The results of the 1950 Census, which became available some time after these calculations had been completed, indicate that the proportion of rented farms is around 39 percent. This revision would affect proportionately the estimates of cols. 5 and 6. Examination of later issues of the *Balance Sheet of Agriculture* reveals that the values of cols. 1 and 2 for 1944 and 1949 have been considerably increased.

Column 4 – 1899: Assumed same as in 1909. No figures are available for this period, but some support for assumption that no substantial change in ratio occurred is given by fact that proportion of rented farms owned by landlords residing outside of the county in which the farm was situated was approximately same in 1920 with 19.6 percent (184 counties in 24 states) as in whole U.S. in 1900 with 21.2 percent (Turner, H. A., *The Ownership of Tenant Farms in the United States*, U.S. Department of Agriculture, Bulletin 1432, p. 23).
1909–1949: Proportion of net rent payments going to landlords not living on farms (average of year indicated and year following) derived from data in *Agricultural Statistics*, 1949, p. 635, for the years 1929–1939 and from Bureau of Agricultural Economics for years 1909–1924, 1944, and 1949. This figure is lower than proportion of rented farms owned by nonfarm landlords, measured by their value, since it does not include rent payments to nonfarm landlords living on farms.

Column 5 – 1899–1949: Col. 3 multiplied by col. 4.

Column 6 – 1899–1939: Col. 5 stepped up by 32 percent, ratio to nearest whole percent between values of col. 6 and col. 5 for 1944. This step-up is supposed to take account of fact that col. 5 does not include farms owned by nonfarmers residing on farms and of other discrepancies between the two sets of figures.
1944: Based on estimate that, in 1946, 66 percent measured by value, of individually owned farms were held by farmers and an additional estimated 1 percent by farm wives (Inman, B. T. and Fippin, W. H., *Farm Land Ownership in the United States*, p. 13); and that about 7 percent of farm land was in hands of nonindividual owners. (Derived from Inman and Fippin, *op. cit.*, p. 51, by weighting percentages of ownership for each state by Census value of farm land and buildings in states as given in *Agricultural Statistics*, 1947, p. 489.) Adjusted slightly to include nonfarm owners in residence on farms (cf. Inman and Fippin, *op. cit.*, p. 16).
1949: Col. 5 stepped up by 32 percent.

Selected Periods: 1890 to 1948

Year	Population			Total lots				Acreage purchased from farmers during period			
	Total	Farm	Non-farm	Number	Raw land equivalent		Total	Average price		Total consideration	
					Total	In-crease		Mini-mum	Maxi-mum	Mini-mum	Maxi-mum
	mill.				mill. acres			$		$ mill.	
	1	2	3	4	5	6	7	8	9	10	11
1890	62.9	27.6	35.3	14.1	2.8	.	.	.	.	.	.
1900	76.0	30.0	46.0	18.4	3.7	0.9	.50	51	350	26	175
1910	92.0	32.1	59.9	24.0	4.8	1.1	.63	102	400	64	252
1920	106.5	31.7	74.8	29.9	6.0	1.2	.71	108	600	77	426
1930	123.1	30.3	92.8	37.1	7.4	1.4	.81	82	900	66	729
1940	132.0	30.1	101.9	36.7	7.5	0.1	.05	63	500	3	25
1948	146.6	27.8	118.8	38.5	7.9	0.4	.24	81	800	19	192

Column 1 – 1890–1948: *Statistical Abstract*, 1949, pp. 6–7.

Column 2 – 1890, 1900: Estimated at 67.5 and 65.5 percent of rural population, rates obtained by extrapolation from those for 1910–1930 (*Historical Statistics*, p. 29).
1910–1948: *Statistical Abstract*, 1949, pp. 10, 20. Figures for 1910 refer to Jan. 1; those for 1920–1940 are averages of Jan. 1 data of year indicated and year following; that for 1948 applies to mid-April.

Column 3 – 1890–1948: Col. 1 minus col. 2.

Column 4 – 1890–1930: Estimated at 40 percent of col. 3 on basis of data given in Fisher, E. M., *Real Estate Subdividing and Population Growth in Nine Urban Areas*, appendix.
1940–1948: Rough estimates taking account of limited amount of development after 1930.

Column 5 – 1890–1948: Estimated on assumption of five lots per acre of raw land until 1930 and slightly lower figures for 1940 and 1948. These figures are based on information from experts not derived from statistical data.

Column 6 – 1900–1948: First differences of col. 5.

Column 7 – 1900–1948: Assumed at 50–60 percent of col. 6 based on fact that land in farms represented somewhat over one-half of entire land area of U.S. (cf. Reuss, L. A., "Land Utilization Data as Background Information for the National Balance Sheet and Approximations of the Value of Forest Land," *Studies in Income and Wealth*, vol. XII, p. 226).

Column 8 – 1900–1948: Weighted average value per acre of farm land in New England, Middle Atlantic, and East North Central States, where it can be assumed most of subdividing activity took place; derived from figures for total value of farm land and buildings and acreage of land in farms taken from *Statistical Abstract*, various issues.

Column 9 – 1900–1948: From Volume II, Table B-51, col. 5.

Column 10 – 1900–1948: Col. 7 multiplied by col. 8.

Column 11 – 1900–1948: Col. 7 multiplied by col. 9.

Column 1 – 1897–1928: From Table A-17, col. 8.
            1929–1949: Same source as given for 1910–1929 in Table A-17, col. 8.

Column 2 – 1897–1949: Col. 1 deflated by price index in Table A-30, col. 3.

Column 3 – 1897–1949: Calculated from Table A-17, cols. 9–11 and Table A-16, col. 1, assuming an average
            life of eight years for horse-drawn vehicles, five years for miscellaneous producer durable
            goods and fifteen years for farm equipment and machinery.

Column 4 – 1897–1949: Same procedure as for col. 3 except that expenditures were converted to 1929 prices
            by price index in Table A-30, col. 3 before making calculations.

Column 5 – 1897–1949: Col. 4 converted to current prices by price index in Table A-30, col. 3. Estimates by
            Bureau of Agricultural Economics of depreciation on farm machinery, computed annually
            since 1910 in current prices as part of derivation of annual net income of farm operators, are
            conceptually comparable with figures in col. 5. The two series correspond reasonably well for
            1910–1940, but after that year Bureau of Agricultural Economics series (*Farm Income Situa-
            tion*, Aug. 1950, table 9, p. 30) is substantially higher than the present series because Bureau of
            Agricultural Economics raised its estimates of value of machinery on farms which it used as
            basis for deriving depreciation charges but did not revise its annual series on farmers' expend-
            itures for machinery which are cumulated and used as basis for present estimates of depreci-
            ation. Bureau of Agricultural Economics estimates of depreciation on farm tractors are also
            higher than those shown in Table A-18 partly for same reason.

Column 6 – 1897–1949: Col. 1 minus col. 3.

Column 7 – 1897–1949: Col. 2 minus col. 4.

Column 8 – 1897–1949: Col. 1 minus col. 5.

FARMERS' SAVING THROUGH FARM MACHINERY [1]
1897 to 1949
$ mill.

Year	Expenditures		Depreciation			Saving		
	Original cost	1929 prices	Original cost	1929 prices	Replacement cost	Original cost	1929 prices	Replacement cost
	1	2	3	4	5	6	7	8
1897	143	303	171	311	146	−28	−8	−3
1898	189	389	170	316	153	19	73	36
1899	223	406	172	324	178	51	82	45
1900	228	380	177	331	199	51	49	29
1901	249	434	183	338	194	66	96	55
1902	320	542	192	350	206	128	192	114
1903	273	458	203	366	218	70	92	55
1904	281	485	212	378	219	69	107	62
1905	296	489	220	390	236	76	99	60
1906	354	548	232	406	262	122	142	92
1907	370	549	248	425	286	122	124	84
1908	324	531	262	443	271	62	88	53
1909	370	597	276	463	287	94	134	83
1910	379	580	291	483	316	88	97	63
1911	385	589	307	503	329	78	86	56
1912	417	637	322	521	341	95	116	76
1913	412	630	334	535	350	78	95	62
1914	378	578	343	542	354	35	36	24
1915	329	489	346	543	365	−17	−54	−36
1916	346	491	347	540	381	−1	−49	−35
1917	439	546	352	538	432	87	8	7
1918	494	488	365	535	542	129	−47	−48
1919	597	570	385	535	560	212	35	37
1920	670	618	416	542	588	254	76	82
1921	229	219	428	536	560	−199	−317	−331
1922	235	251	412	504	471	−177	−253	−236
1923	335	346	398	479	463	−63	−133	−128
1924	281	278	383	454	460	−102	−176	−179
1925	330	328	359	421	425	−29	−93	−95
1926	366	364	346	397	399	20	−33	−33
1927	353	349	341	384	389	12	−35	−36
1928	370	368	338	369	371	32	−1	−1
1929	390	390	341	361	361	49	29	29
1930	324	326	343	330	328	−19	−4	−4
1931	177	181	337	322	316	−160	−141	−139
1932	84	91	321	306	284	−237	−215	−200
1933	90	100	299	288	260	−209	−188	−170
1934	140	149	275	270	254	−135	−121	−114
1935	235	243	253	254	246	−18	−11	−11
1936	303	309	247	250	245	56	59	58
1937	393	393	257	260	260	136	133	133
1938	361	349	267	268	277	94	81	84
1939	318	314	271	272	276	47	42	42
1940	377	377	276	276	276	101	101	101
1941	499	493	284	284	288	215	209	211
1942	540	504	296	296	317	244	208	223
1943	405	365	306	303	337	99	62	68
1944	630	554	316	310	352	314	244	278
1945	749	651	339	327	376	410	324	373
1946	865	727	376	356	424	489	371	441
1947	1 262	938	439	403	542	823	535	720
1948	1 589	1 013	528	462	725	1 061	551	864
1949	1 652	936	628	518	914	1 024	418	738

[1] Excludes automobiles, trucks, and tractors.

Columns 1 to 3 – 1882–1929: Value of these commodities destined for domestic consumption at manufacturers' prices from Shaw, W. H., *Value of Commodity Output since 1869*, pp. 54–55, 58–59, 61, 69, stepped up to retail price level by applying markups based on Department of Commerce markup data for 1929 (43 percent for farm equipment, 24 percent for business horse-drawn vehicles, and 19 percent for miscellaneous producer durable goods) and adjusted for following estimated changes in inventories in period 1919–1929 (data for a similar adjustment in earlier years were not available) developed from data in Kuznets, S., *Commodity Flow and Capital Formation*:

1919	–3.3%	1924	–
1920	–	1925	–
1921	7.1%	1926	–0.5%
1922	2.8%	1927	1.5%
1923	–2.8%	1928	–
		1929	–1.8%

Column 4 – 1882–1929: Assumed equal to col. 1.

Column 5 – 1889–1919: Represents 55 percent of col. 2 for 1899–1908, 57 percent for 1909–1914, 78 percent for 1919, with percentages interpolated between 57 and 78 for 1915–1918. These percentages were based on relative magnitude of value of output of farm wagons and all business wagons in 1909, 1914, and 1919 from Bureau of the Census, *Census of Manufactures*, 1920, vol. x, p. 890.

Column 6 – 1892–1929: Represents percentages of col. 3 varying from 42 percent for 1892 to 8 percent for 1929. These percentages were derived from data from the *Census of Manufactures* for each census year 1889–1929 on value of output of various types of farm equipment which were included by Shaw in "miscellaneous producer durable goods" expressed as a percentage of Shaw's total for "miscellaneous producer durable goods." The types of farm equipment considered were (1) horse clothing, (2) horseshoes, (3) saddlery and harness, (4) whips, (5) horse blankets, and (6) wheelbarrows. For items 1–5, the percentage assumed to be purchased by farmers ranged from 75 in 1892 to 94 in 1929, based on the ratio of number of horses on farms to total number (derived from Bureau of Agricultural Economics data). Onehalf of wheelbarrows were assumed to be purchased by farmers, as estimated in *Income Parity for Agriculture*, part II, section 3, p. 62.

Column 7 – 1882–1929: Sum of cols. 4–6.

Column 8 – 1882–1909: Extrapolated back from 1910 on basis of col. 7.
1910–1929: From *Income Parity for Agriculture*, part II, section 3, p. 3, as revised and brought up to date by Bureau of Agricultural Economics and stepped-up to include Bureau of Agricultural Economics estimates of farmers' expenditures for harness and saddlery.

Columns 9 to 11 – 1882–1929: Col. 8 distributed among three categories on basis of proportions in cols. 4–6. This distribution was made because average length of life varies for the three categories (see note to Table A-16, col. 3).

SALES OF FARM MACHINERY [1]

1882 to 1929

$ mill.

Year	Total sales to all consumers			Sales to farmers (first approximation)				Sales to farmers (final estimates)	Sales to farmers distributed		
	Farm equipment	Business horse-drawn vehicles	Miscellaneous producer durables	Farm equipment	Business horse-drawn vehicles	Miscellaneous producer durables	Total		Farm equipment	Business horse-drawn vehicles	Miscellaneous producer durables
	1	2	3	4	5	6	7	8	9	10	11
1882	103.33	–	–	103.33	–	–	103.33	112	112	–	–
1883	105.71	–	–	105.71	–	–	105.71	114	114	–	–
1884	108.08	–	–	108.08	–	–	108.08	117	117	–	–
1885	110.47	–	–	110.47	–	–	110.47	120	120	–	–
1886	112.84	–	–	112.84	–	–	112.84	122	122	–	–
1887	115.22	–	–	115.22	–	–	115.22	125	125	–	–
1888	117.59	–	–	117.59	–	–	117.59	127	127	–	–
1889	119.96	35.20	–	119.96	19.36	–	139.32	151	130	21	–
1890	127.28	39.64	–	127.28	21.80	–	149.08	161	137	24	–
1891	107.72	41.50	–	107.72	22.82	–	130.54	141	116	25	–
1892	107.82	42.35	89.18	107.82	23.29	37.46	168.57	182	116	25	41
1893	101.83	39.79	85.36	101.83	21.88	35.85	159.56	173	110	24	39
1894	83.91	35.20	72.59	83.91	19.36	30.49	133.76	145	91	21	33
1895	84.83	31.84	77.06	84.83	17.51	32.37	134.71	146	92	19	35
1896	66.60	28.48	80.75	66.60	15.66	33.92	116.18	126	72	17	37
1897	83.53	30.00	76.36	83.53	16.50	32.07	132.10	143	90	18	35
1898	122.38	32.17	82.59	122.38	17.69	34.69	174.76	189	132	19	38
1899	142.08	40.35	99.86	142.08	22.19	41.94	206.21	223	154	24	45
1900	143.80	38.91	109.24	143.80	21.40	45.88	211.08	228	155	23	50
1901	157.86	49.86	106.53	157.86	27.42	44.74	230.02	249	171	30	48
1902	218.60	46.98	122.32	218.60	25.84	51.37	295.81	320	236	28	56
1903	171.89	46.59	131.41	171.89	25.62	55.19	252.70	273	186	28	59
1904	179.05	48.26	129.36	179.05	26.54	54.33	259.92	281	193	29	59
1905	186.19	53.48	137.62	186.19	29.41	57.80	273.40	296	202	32	62
1906	229.47	57.33	160.91	229.47	31.53	65.97	326.97	354	249	34	71
1907	231.07	61.44	187.89	231.07	33.79	77.03	341.89	370	250	37	83
1908	196.87	49.81	187.26	196.87	27.40	74.90	299.17	324	213	30	81
1909	238.08	53.28	183.91	238.08	30.37	73.56	342.01	370	257	33	80
1910	243.92	59.92	180.40	243.92	34.15	72.16	350.23	379	264	37	78
1911	240.47	54.75	175.03	240.47	31.21	68.26	339.94	385	273	35	77
1912	267.82	51.97	181.78	267.82	29.62	70.89	368.33	417	303	34	80
1913	289.50	49.41	192.40	289.50	28.16	73.11	390.77	412	305	30	77
1914	268.55	45.71	203.53	268.55	26.05	77.34	371.94	378	273	26	79
1915	293.35	42.18	167.35	293.35	25.73	60.25	379.33	329	255	22	52
1916	339.10	46.34	244.69	339.10	30.12	83.19	452.41	346	259	23	64
1917	357.44	63.31	346.94	357.44	43.68	111.02	512.14	439	306	38	95
1918	431.62	62.73	429.27	431.62	45.79	128.78	606.19	494	352	37	105
1919	475.41	52.72	401.91	475.41	41.21	116.55	633.08	597	448	39	110
1920	386.92	–	479.59	386.92	–	119.90	506.82	670	511	–	159
1921	379.96	–	265.92	379.96	–	53.18	433.14	229	201	–	28
1922	236.23	–	299.83	236.23	–	56.97	293.20	235	189	–	46
1923	438.58	–	349.43	438.58	–	62.90	501.48	335	293	–	42
1924	380.18	–	247.56	380.18	–	37.13	417.31	281	256	–	25
1925	438.28	–	357.46	438.28	–	46.47	484.75	330	298	–	32
1926	505.70	–	381.09	505.70	–	45.73	551.43	366	336	–	30
1927	494.03	–	384.54	494.03	–	46.14	540.17	353	323	–	30
1928	509.81	–	362.85	509.81	–	36.28	546.09	370	345	–	25
1929	542.77	–	432.05	542.77	–	34.56	577.33	390	367	–	23

[1] Excludes automobiles, trucks, and tractors.

Column 1 – From *Income Parity for Agriculture*, part II, section 3, p. 53, as revised and brought up to date by Bureau of Agricultural Economics. For 1942, includes sales of estimated 50,000 tractors out of dealers' stocks.

Column 2 – Col. 1 deflated by price index in Table A-30, col. 4.

Column 3 – Depreciation calculated from col. 1 assuming an average life of five years for tractors purchased in 1909–1919, ten years for those purchased in 1920–1929, and fifteen years for 1930 to date.

Column 4 – Depreciation calculated from col. 2 using same average life as in col. 3.

Column 5 – Col. 4 converted to current prices by price index in Table A-30, col. 4. See note to Table A-16, col. 5.

Column 6 – Col. 1 minus col. 3.

Column 7 – Col. 2 minus col. 4.

Column 8 – Col. 1 minus col. 5.

Column 1 – 1907–1909: Roughly extrapolated on basis of nonfarm expenditures for new trucks in Table P-5, col. 12.
1910–1949: From *Income Parity for Agriculture*, part II, section 3, p. 44, as revised and brought up to date by Bureau of Agricultural Economics, adjusted (raised) to represent gross purchases of new trucks, i.e., before value of trucks traded in are deducted.

Column 2 – 1907–1949: Col. 1 deflated by price index in Table A-30, col. 7.

Column 3 – 1907–1949: Depreciation calculated from col. 1 (using unrounded figures) assuming an average life of ten years.

Column 4 – 1907–1949: Depreciation calculated from col. 2 (using unrounded figures) assuming same average life as in col. 3.

Column 5 – 1907–1949: Col. 4 converted to current prices by price index in Table A-30, col. 7.

Column 6 – 1907–1949: Col. 1 minus col. 3.

Column 7 – 1907–1949: Col. 2 minus col. 4.

Column 8 – 1907–1949: Col. 1 minus col. 5.

FARMERS' SAVING THROUGH TRACTORS
1909 to 1949

$ mill.

Year	Expenditures		Depreciation			Saving		
	Original cost	1929 prices	Original cost	1929 prices	Replacement cost	Original cost	1929 prices	Replacement cost
	1	2	3	4	5	6	7	8
1909	2	1	0	0	0	2	1	2
1910	6	4	1	1	1	5	3	5
1911	8	5	2	2	3	6	3	5
1912	14	10	5	3	4	9	7	10
1913	10	7	7	5	7	3	2	3
1914	20	15	10	7	9	10	8	11
1915	28	22	14	10	13	14	12	15
1916	31	28	18	14	16	13	14	15
1917	53	57	24	21	20	29	36	33
1918	130	116	40	37	41	90	79	89
1919	179	154	68	61	71	111	93	108
1920	212	194	92	83	91	120	111	121
1921	83	85	101	92	90	−18	−7	−7
1922	80	129	101	94	58	−21	35	22
1923	97	146	91	91	61	6	55	36
1924	92	126	70	77	56	22	49	36
1925	119	156	62	76	58	57	80	61
1926	129	154	75	91	76	54	63	53
1927	155	190	89	109	89	66	81	66
1928	130	122	103	124	133	27	−2	−3
1929	181	181	119	139	139	62	42	42
1930	158	162	122	144	141	36	18	17
1931	76	79	116	138	133	−40	−59	−57
1932	32	35	111	131	121	−79	−96	−89
1933	30	34	104	120	107	−74	−86	−77
1934	83	91	98	110	101	−15	−19	−18
1935	153	174	96	105	92	57	69	61
1936	214	236	96	103	93	118	133	121
1937	271	296	98	104	95	173	192	176
1938	201	222	99	105	95	102	117	106
1939	200	244	97	106	87	103	138	113
1940	231	304	102	115	87	129	189	144
1941	302	378	120	138	110	182	240	192
1942	253	319	138	161	128	115	158	125
1943	138	180	151	177	136	−13	3	2
1944	359	407	168	197	174	191	210	185
1945	309	333	185	216	201	124	117	108
1946	371	422	200	233	205	171	189	166
1947	615	627	229	265	260	386	362	355
1948	866	799	276	310	336	590	489	530
1949	957	757	333	358	452	624	400	505

FARMERS' SAVING THROUGH NEW TRUCKS
1907 to 1949

$ mill.

Year	Expenditures		Depreciation			Saving		
	Original cost	1929 prices	Original cost	1929 prices	Replacement cost	Original cost	1929 prices	Replacement cost
	1	2	3	4	5	6	7	8
1907	1	0	1	0	0	0	0	1
1908	1	0	1	0	0	0	0	1
1909	2	1	1	1	2	1	0	0
1910	3	2	1	1	2	2	1	1
1911	4	3	1	1	1	3	2	3
1912	7	5	1	1	1	6	4	6
1913	7	6	2	1	1	5	5	6
1914	12	10	3	2	2	9	8	10
1915	20	17	5	3	4	15	14	16
1916	23	22	7	6	6	16	16	17
1917	26	26	9	8	8	17	18	18
1918	24	21	11	10	11	13	11	13
1919	40	30	15	13	17	25	17	23
1920	81	57	20	17	24	61	40	57
1921	56	49	27	22	25	29	27	31
1922	60	57	32	27	28	28	30	32
1923	57	57	37	32	32	20	25	25
1924	79	83	43	38	36	36	45	43
1925	85	92	50	46	42	35	46	43
1926	99	107	57	53	49	42	54	50
1927	93	100	64	61	57	29	39	36
1928	102	105	71	70	68	31	35	34
1929	102	102	78	76	76	24	26	26
1930	66	69	81	81	77	−15	−12	−11
1931	31	33	79	80	75	−48	−47	−44
1932	17	19	75	78	70	−58	−59	−53
1933	29	34	71	76	66	−42	−42	−37
1934	57	64	69	73	65	−12	−9	−8
1935	63	72	67	72	63	−4	0	0
1936	83	93	65	70	63	18	23	20
1937	87	91	64	69	66	23	22	21
1938	47	47	61	65	66	−14	−18	−19
1939	69	68	57	61	62	12	7	7
1940	75	71	55	59	62	20	12	13
1941	101	88	59	62	71	42	26	30
1942	0	0	62	64	77	−62	−64	−77
1943	23	19	61	62	77	−38	−43	−54
1944	34	26	59	59	76	−25	−33	−42
1945	20	15	56	55	73	−36	−40	−53
1946	90	65	54	50	69	36	15	21
1947	198	113	60	50	87	138	63	111
1948	274	141	77	56	109	197	85	165
1949	292	146	100	65	130	192	81	162

FARMERS' SAVING THROUGH USED TRUCKS
1917 to 1949

$ mill.

Year	Expenditures		Depreciation			Saving		
	Original cost	1929 prices	Original cost	1929 prices	Replacement cost	Original cost	1929 prices	Replacement cost
	1	2	3	4	5	6	7	8
1917	1	1	0	0	0	1	1	1
1918	1	1	0	0	0	1	1	1
1919	1	1	1	1	1	0	0	0
1920	4	3	1	1	1	3	2	3
1921	3	3	2	2	2	1	1	1
1922	2	2	2	2	2	0	0	0
1923	0	0	2	2	2	−2	−2	−2
1924	9	9	3	3	3	6	6	6
1925	9	10	4	4	4	5	6	5
1926	8	9	5	5	5	3	4	3
1927	8	9	6	7	7	2	2	1
1928	13	13	8	9	9	5	4	4
1929	12	12	10	10	10	2	2	2
1930	15	16	11	11	11	4	5	4
1931	7	7	11	12	11	−4	−5	−4
1932	4	4	11	11	10	−7	−7	−6
1933	6	7	10	10	9	−4	−3	−3
1934	11	12	9	9	8	2	3	3
1935	10	11	8	9	8	2	2	2
1936	18	20	9	10	9	9	10	9
1937	19	20	11	12	11	8	8	8
1938	10	10	13	14	14	−3	−4	−4
1939	13	13	14	15	15	−1	−2	−2
1940	18	17	15	15	16	3	2	2
1941	31	27	17	17	20	14	10	11
1942	90	68	25	22	29	65	46	61
1943	94	60	41	32	50	53	28	44
1944	135	78	61	44	76	74	34	59
1945	74	47	79	53	83	−5	−6	−9
1946	40	29	86	56	77	−46	−27	−37
1947	54	31	83	53	93	−29	−22	−39
1948	61	31	76	46	90	−15	−15	−29
1949	48	24	64	38	76	−16	−14	−28

Column 1 – Same source as Table A-19, col. 1 adjusted (lowered) to represent net purchases of used trucks, i.e. to subtract from gross purchases the value of all trucks traded in by farmers. (In determining farmers' expenditures for used trucks, Bureau of Agricultural Economics subtracts only trade-ins for purchases of used trucks; trade-ins for purchases of new trucks are subtracted from its series on farmers' purchases of new trucks. In col. 1, all of these trade-ins have been netted against purchases of used trucks.)

Column 2 – Col. 1 deflated by price index in Table A-30, col. 8.

Column 3 – Depreciation calculated from col. 1 (using unrounded figures) assuming an average life of five years.

Column 4 – Depreciation calculated from col. 2 (using unrounded figures) assuming same average life as in col. 3.

Column 5 – Col. 4 converted to current prices by price index in Table A-30, col. 8.

Column 6 – Col. 1 minus col. 3.

Column 7 – Col. 2 minus col. 4.

Column 8 – Col. 1 minus col. 5.

779

A-21   TABLE A–21

Column 1 – Sum of cols. 2–11.

Columns 2 to 11 – Table A-24, cols. 2–11 minus Table A-26, cols. 2–11, respectively. For scope of cols. 5 and 11 see Table Q–10.

A-22   TABLE A–22

Column 1 – Sum of cols. 2–11.

Columns 2 to 11 – Table A-25, cols. 2–11 minus Table A-27, cols. 2–11, respectively.

A-23   TABLE A–23

Column 1 – Sum of cols. 2–11.

Columns 2 to 11 – Table A-24, cols. 2–11 minus Table A-28, cols. 2–11, respectively.

A-24   TABLE A–24

Column 1 – 1897–1949: Sum of cols. 2–11.

Columns 2 to 7 – 1897–1949: Derived by applying to total expenditures on consumer durable goods (see notes to Table Q-5), the percentages given in Table A-4, col. 4, and Table A-5, col. 3.

Column 8 – 1897–1909: Extrapolated on basis of Table Q-5, col. 8.
1910–1949: From *Income Parity for Agriculture,* part II, section 3, p. 28, as revised and brought up to date by the Bureau of Agricultural Economics, adjusted (raised) to represent gross purchases of new cars, i.e. before value of cars traded in are deducted.

Columns 9 to 11 – 1897–1940: Same procedure as for cols. 2–7.

Original Cost Depreciation: 1897 to 1949

$ mill.

Year	Total	Fur-niture	Household appliances	House furnishings	China etc.	Musical instru-ments	Books	Passenger cars	Passenger car acces-sories	Medical appliances	Miscel-laneous
	1	2	3	4	5	6	7	8	9	10	11
1897	6	2	2	0	0	0	1	–	–	0	1
1898	10	2	1	0	2	1	2	–	–	0	2
1899	23	4	3	4	7	2	1	0	0	0	2
1900	26	4	3	5	8	4	1	2	0	0	–1
1901	37	7	4	6	10	5	2	1	0	0	2
1902	45	8	5	9	12	7	2	1	0	0	1
1903	44	10	4	8	13	8	2	0	0	0	–1
1904	48	11	3	7	14	7	2	3	0	0	1
1905	56	12	4	6	15	8	2	6	0	1	2
1906	82	18	6	11	22	11	1	10	0	0	3
1907	77	16	5	8	18	11	1	12	0	1	5
1908	52	12	3	3	6	6	2	18	0	1	1
1909	93	22	6	12	18	10	3	16	1	1	4
1910	97	22	6	11	18	9	2	21	1	1	6
1911	76	17	5	5	10	8	1	27	0	0	3
1912	93	22	10	8	13	13	2	23	0	0	2
1913	66	21	6	5	8	12	3	10	0	0	1
1914	66	19	4	3	1	10	2	28	0	2	–3
1915	93	11	3	–2	–7	7	2	83	0	3	–7
1916	148	22	8	9	13	12	2	79	1	3	–1
1917	377	55	32	47	59	28	10	121	3	12	10
1918	286	68	39	64	45	33	12	–23	1	28	19
1919	467	92	36	54	80	54	13	111	11	3	13
1920	270	79	38	50	39	40	7	6	7	–3	7
1921	–256	0	–11	–25	–40	–4	–6	–134	–4	–15	–17
1922	–27	12	–3	–7	–24	4	–3	20	–1	–11	–14
1923	167	20	6	6	–8	10	–3	148	1	–6	–7
1924	72	27	8	0	–17	18	0	47	0	–3	–8
1925	233	44	21	20	9	31	3	101	7	0	–3
1926	124	28	15	0	–2	28	0	57	3	0	–5
1927	–15	26	11	0	–8	18	3	–63	2	1	–5
1928	103	22	5	6	2	34	3	33	0	0	–2
1929	127	12	8	7	3	28	4	60	4	0	1
1930	–163	–23	–7	–17	–20	4	–2	–91	–1	–1	–5
1931	–314	–42	–19	–36	–40	–35	–6	–119	–5	–3	–9
1932	–410	–61	–31	–50	–48	–50	–12	–134	–7	–4	–13
1933	–301	–51	–17	–40	–38	–50	–8	–82	–3	–1	–11
1934	–145	–45	–8	–27	–28	–48	–6	23	1	1	–8
1935	–4	–21	11	–8	–9	–39	–1	53	7	5	–2
1936	55	–13	14	7	–4	–33	1	72	7	3	1
1937	81	–2	26	18	12	–26	5	29	7	5	7
1938	–73	–19	4	2	1	–33	0	–30	–2	0	4
1939	65	–7	10	13	7	–23	1	58	0	0	6
1940	52	–1	13	14	10	–13	1	24	–1	0	5
1941	237	36	48	45	43	10	6	22	8	5	14
1942	164	46	15	58	70	27	14	–95	4	9	16
1943	165	44	–29	61	81	3	22	–48	6	12	13
1944	8	33	–42	37	60	–9	24	–111	0	6	10
1945	109	55	–26	40	83	–3	30	–98	8	5	15
1946	879	160	108	131	175	95	49	34	58	12	57
1947	1 176	192	221	148	156	125	40	164	59	9	62
1948	1 070	189	199	123	120	103	26	212	41	7	50
1949	913	149	113	62	64	96	11	364	24	2	28

FARMERS' SAVING THROUGH MAIN TYPES OF CONSUMER DURABLE GOODS
1929 Prices: 1897 to 1949

$ mill.

Year	Total	Fur- niture	Household appliances	House furnishings	China etc.	Musical instru- ments	Books	Passenger cars	Passenger car acces- sories	Medical appliances	Miscel- laneous
	1	2	3	4	5	6	7	8	9	10	11
1897	84	27	13	8	13	3	5	–	–	1	14
1898	69	17	7	5	15	6	7	–	–	1	11
1899	94	21	12	15	25	6	6	0	0	0	9
1900	62	10	9	11	24	9	3	2	0	0	–6
1901	64	16	11	13	10	11	3	1	0	0	–1
1902	71	17	11	20	15	11	2	0	0	0	–5
1903	59	17	8	13	17	12	1	0	0	0	–9
1904	66	21	6	8	20	10	2	3	0	0	–4
1905	74	23	6	6	28	12	0	2	0	1	–4
1906	127	35	11	15	48	16	0	3	0	1	–2
1907	83	17	6	6	38	14	–2	4	0	1	–1
1908	46	10	1	3	22	8	–1	7	0	2	–6
1909	172	38	8	26	60	15	5	15	0	2	3
1910	165	30	8	22	63	13	2	19	0	1	7
1911	68	1	2	0	30	9	–2	29	0	0	–1
1912	100	2	11	8	31	19	0	32	1	–1	–3
1913	37	–10	2	0	12	17	0	22	0	0	–6
1914	21	–10	0	–1	–8	15	–1	35	0	2	–11
1915	22	–20	0	–11	–26	8	–2	86	1	3	–17
1916	109	–3	8	–7	–3	19	–3	103	2	4	–11
1917	348	48	40	14	23	48	6	157	2	12	–2
1918	98	34	35	7	–19	41	6	–31	1	26	–2
1919	182	30	26	2	17	53	4	54	9	–1	–12
1920	–136	–23	13	–22	–41	20	–5	–58	3	–8	–15
1921	–442	–55	–29	–58	–96	–20	–12	–125	–3	–15	–29
1922	–162	–35	–17	–27	–61	–7	–7	26	0	–11	–23
1923	28	–28	–11	–15	–51	–5	–6	157	2	–4	–11
1924	–21	–12	–7	–11	–49	3	–3	66	3	–1	–10
1925	165	10	9	10	–12	21	2	117	8	1	–1
1926	89	2	7	–2	–10	16	1	72	5	0	–2
1927	–41	6	4	2	–8	7	3	–56	2	1	–2
1928	84	4	2	13	4	18	5	40	0	–1	–1
1929	114	–1	6	15	8	18	5	57	3	0	3
1930	–133	–29	–6	–10	–13	20	–1	–87	–1	–2	–4
1931	–263	–36	–15	–24	–33	–20	–4	–117	–3	–3	–8
1932	–357	–51	–25	–37	–37	–40	–11	–134	–6	–4	–12
1933	–226	–37	–4	–28	–27	–36	–6	–77	–1	–1	–9
1934	–67	–32	8	–18	–18	–34	–4	32	3	2	–6
1935	118	10	32	3	3	–16	2	65	11	6	2
1936	178	22	36	18	3	–5	2	82	10	4	6
1937	180	29	48	21	20	6	7	22	10	5	12
1938	–19	8	14	5	7	–17	1	–43	–1	0	7
1939	132	24	21	16	10	4	2	46	0	1	8
1940	117	26	26	13	10	17	1	19	–2	0	7
1941	304	58	71	41	40	66	6	–7	9	5	15
1942	167	50	10	43	47	85	16	–106	–1	10	13
1943	84	44	–45	43	55	9	22	–64	2	10	8
1944	–110	18	–62	14	27	–30	24	–108	–3	5	5
1945	–35	29	–46	11	39	–22	29	–93	6	3	9
1946	696	108	80	72	96	192	43	5	46	10	44
1947	767	114	151	62	60	209	25	64	38	6	38
1948	580	90	123	41	32	147	11	86	20	4	26
1949	468	71	67	11	8	143	1	150	6	–1	12

FARMERS' SAVING THROUGH MAIN TYPES OF CONSUMER DURABLE GOODS A-23
Replacement Cost Depreciation: 1897 to 1949
$ mill.

Year	Total	Furniture	Household appliances	House furnishings	China etc.	Musical instruments	Books	Passenger cars	Passenger car accessories	Medical appliances	Miscellaneous
	1	2	3	4	5	6	7	8	9	10	11
1897	25	6	3	3	4	1	2	–	–	1	5
1898	22	5	2	2	5	2	2	–	–	0	4
1899	31	6	3	5	9	2	2	1	0	0	3
1900	25	4	3	4	9	4	1	2	0	0	-2
1901	24	5	3	4	5	5	1	1	0	0	0
1902	27	6	4	7	7	5	1	-1	0	0	-2
1903	24	6	3	5	8	7	0	-1	0	0	-4
1904	30	7	2	3	9	6	0	5	0	0	-2
1905	36	8	2	2	12	7	0	6	0	0	-1
1906	60	13	4	6	21	9	0	7	0	0	0
1907	46	7	2	2	16	8	-1	11	0	1	0
1908	35	4	0	1	9	4	0	19	0	1	-3
1909	93	15	4	11	23	8	2	26	1	1	2
1910	97	13	3	9	24	8	1	33	1	1	4
1911	60	0	2	0	12	6	-2	42	1	-1	0
1912	77	2	6	4	13	11	0	41	1	0	-1
1913	33	-6	1	0	5	10	0	26	0	0	-3
1914	36	-6	0	-1	-3	9	0	41	0	2	-6
1915	70	-13	0	-4	-11	5	-1	102	0	2	-10
1916	109	-2	4	-4	-1	11	-2	108	1	2	-8
1917	286	32	25	11	17	27	5	158	2	10	-1
1918	70	29	28	8	-17	28	5	-35	1	25	-2
1919	187	32	22	2	16	44	3	74	11	-2	-15
1920	-203	-40	14	-31	-48	22	-8	-83	5	-12	-22
1921	-515	-74	-30	-66	-107	-19	-15	-145	-4	-19	-36
1922	-166	-42	-18	-27	-58	-5	-7	28	0	-11	-26
1923	14	-34	-13	-17	-58	-5	-6	161	2	-5	-11
1924	-33	-14	-7	-12	-57	3	-2	65	2	-1	-10
1925	162	11	9	11	-13	20	2	114	8	1	-1
1926	87	2	7	-2	-10	16	1	70	4	1	-2
1927	-40	6	4	3	-8	6	4	-55	2	1	-3
1928	82	5	1	13	4	18	4	38	-1	0	0
1929	114	-1	6	15	8	18	5	57	3	0	3
1930	-130	-27	-5	-9	-12	14	-1	-83	-1	-2	-4
1931	-230	-30	-13	-21	-29	-10	-4	-110	-3	-3	-7
1932	-272	-33	-19	-27	-30	-15	-10	-121	-4	-4	-9
1933	-159	-23	-3	-20	-21	-12	-5	-67	0	-1	-7
1934	-33	-22	5	-15	-14	-12	-4	29	3	2	-5
1935	99	6	23	2	2	-6	1	58	7	5	1
1936	145	14	24	14	3	-1	2	74	8	3	4
1937	140	20	34	19	16	2	6	22	7	5	9
1938	-21	5	10	4	5	-6	1	-44	-2	0	6
1939	111	17	15	14	9	1	1	47	0	0	7
1940	73	18	18	12	9	6	1	6	-2	0	5
1941	213	45	50	38	36	23	5	-9	7	5	13
1942	75	44	8	45	51	32	14	-139	-1	9	12
1943	71	39	-38	46	61	4	21	-83	2	11	8
1944	-111	18	-56	16	33	-12	23	-140	-3	5	5
1945	-33	31	-45	13	51	-9	28	-121	5	4	10
1946	697	127	85	97	136	87	45	7	53	11	49
1947	886	148	186	96	98	108	30	115	50	6	49
1948	744	130	161	67	56	81	14	165	29	5	36
1949	632	99	84	18	14	78	1	314	9	-1	16

FARMERS' EXPENDITURES ON MAIN TYPES OF CONSUMER DURABLE GOODS
Original Cost: 1897 to 1949
$ mill.

Year	Total	Fur-niture	Household appliances	House furnishings	China etc.	Musical instru-ments	Books	Passenger cars	Passenger car acces-sories	Medical appliances	Miscel-laneous
	1	2	3	4	5	6	7	8	9	10	11
1897	114	22	8	22	25	6	7	–	–	2	22
1898	120	23	7	22	28	7	8	–	–	2	23
1899	136	25	9	26	33	8	8	1	0	2	24
1900	142	26	10	28	35	10	8	2	0	2	21
1901	157	29	11	29	38	12	9	3	0	2	24
1902	169	31	13	33	41	14	9	3	0	2	23
1903	172	33	12	33	43	16	9	3	0	2	21
1904	183	35	12	33	46	15	10	7	0	2	23
1905	199	37	13	33	50	17	10	12	0	3	24
1906	239	44	16	40	60	20	10	20	0	3	26
1907	250	43	16	39	60	21	10	29	0	4	28
1908	241	40	15	35	51	17	11	43	0	4	25
1909	298	51	18	46	65	21	13	50	1	5	28
1910	324	53	19	47	69	21	12	66	1	5	31
1911	326	49	19	42	64	21	11	87	1	4	28
1912	366	56	25	47	69	26	13	96	1	5	28
1913	355	56	22	45	67	26	14	92	1	5	27
1914	379	56	21	44	62	25	14	125	1	7	24
1915	446	49	21	40	55	23	14	215	1	8	20
1916	547	62	27	52	76	29	14	251	2	9	25
1917	853	98	53	93	126	47	23	352	4	20	37
1918	809	115	64	117	119	54	27	221	3	42	47
1919	1 078	144	65	115	162	78	29	405	15	22	43
1920	880	137	71	118	129	68	25	262	13	19	38
1921	334	62	25	46	52	26	13	84	4	8	14
1922	527	76	34	66	68	36	16	198	7	10	16
1923	721	86	44	81	84	43	16	324	10	11	22
1924	652	96	48	79	77	54	19	239	10	10	20
1925	843	117	64	104	106	70	23	306	16	11	26
1926	779	104	62	89	99	71	21	285	14	10	24
1927	660	105	61	90	93	65	24	174	14	11	23
1928	783	104	58	95	100	80	24	275	13	10	24
1929	827	96	63	94	97	83	25	315	18	11	25
1930	526	63	47	66	67	64	18	161	14	9	17
1931	339	44	33	45	44	28	14	103	9	7	12
1932	195	25	18	29	34	14	8	49	6	5	7
1933	253	33	30	35	40	14	11	66	9	7	8
1934	378	38	39	44	46	17	12	151	12	9	10
1935	503	62	59	59	61	24	17	176	17	13	15
1936	565	71	63	71	62	29	18	203	19	12	17
1937	599	81	76	80	76	35	22	170	21	15	23
1938	434	63	55	62	62	26	17	103	14	12	20
1939	555	72	60	70	64	32	17	189	17	13	21
1940	543	74	63	71	66	36	16	167	17	13	20
1941	746	111	100	105	101	55	21	177	27	19	30
1942	693	123	69	125	136	71	31	54	24	25	35
1943	711	123	26	138	158	47	42	86	27	30	34
1944	568	114	13	123	148	32	47	6	23	28	34
1945	678	137	28	134	182	36	57	0	33	30	41
1946	1 512	246	168	237	292	141	81	127	91	41	88
1947	1 934	286	296	272	296	183	78	275	107	41	100
1948	1 980	292	293	267	282	176	69	358	105	42	96
1949	1 987	261	223	224	246	185	59	564	104	40	81

Column 1 – Sum of cols. 2–11.

Columns 2 to 7 – Table A-24, cols. 2–7 deflated by respective price indices from Table Q-16.

Column 8 – Table A-24, col. 8 deflated by price index from Table A-30, col. 5.

Columns 9 to 11 – Table A-24, cols. 9–11 deflated by respective price indices from Table Q-16.

TABLE A–26   A-26

Column 1 – Sum of cols. 2–11.

Columns 2 to 11 – Depreciation calculated from Table A-24, cols. 2–11 assuming rates given in Table Q-12. Expenditures in years prior to 1897 which were required for estimating depreciation in 1897 and following years were derived in same manner as described for 1897–1949 in notes to Table A-24.

TABLE A–27   A-27

Column 1 – Sum of cols. 2–11.

Columns 2 to 11 – Depreciation calculated from Table A-25, cols. 2–11 assuming rates given in Table Q-12 (see note to Table A-26, cols. 2–11).

TABLE A–28   A-28

Column 1 – Sum of cols. 2–11.

Columns 2 to 11 – Table A-27, cols. 2–11 multiplied by respective price indices from Table Q-16, and from Table A-30, col. 5.

FARMERS' EXPENDITURES ON MAIN TYPES OF CONSUMER DURABLE GOODS
1929 Prices: 1897 to 1949

$ mill.

Year	Total	Fur-niture	Household appliances	House furnishings	China etc.	Musical instru-ments	Books	Passenger cars	Passenger car acces-sories	Medical appliances	Miscel-laneous
	1	2	3	4	5	6	7	8	9	10	11
1897	381	92	31	74	75	16	22	–	–	5	66
1898	377	84	27	73	79	19	25	–	–	5	65
1899	416	90	33	85	92	20	25	1	0	5	65
1900	394	81	31	83	95	23	23	2	0	5	51
1901	404	89	34	86	83	26	23	2	0	5	56
1902	422	92	36	95	90	27	23	2	0	5	52
1903	418	93	34	90	94	29	23	2	0	5	48
1904	435	99	33	88	101	28	24	5	0	5	52
1905	456	103	35	88	114	30	23	5	0	6	52
1906	525	118	42	99	140	35	23	8	0	6	54
1907	499	102	38	93	138	35	21	10	0	7	55
1908	474	97	35	92	127	30	22	15	0	8	48
1909	616	127	43	117	171	37	28	28	0	9	56
1910	636	122	44	117	183	37	25	39	0	9	60
1911	563	95	39	97	158	34	21	59	0	8	52
1912	620	97	49	106	167	45	23	75	1	7	50
1913	580	85	41	99	154	44	23	78	1	8	47
1914	586	86	39	99	139	44	22	105	1	10	41
1915	619	76	40	90	124	38	21	182	2	12	34
1916	747	93	48	94	148	51	20	239	3	13	38
1917	1 054	145	83	116	176	82	29	349	4	24	46
1918	858	134	82	111	136	78	30	196	3	43	45
1919	972	132	76	106	173	93	28	297	13	20	34
1920	653	80	66	80	111	64	19	182	9	14	28
1921	287	47	24	39	47	26	11	72	3	7	11
1922	507	65	35	65	72	40	15	186	7	9	13
1923	677	71	41	74	73	43	15	317	10	11	22
1924	629	86	45	75	67	53	18	244	11	10	20
1925	827	108	61	95	99	73	23	314	17	11	26
1926	783	100	61	83	98	72	22	295	16	10	26
1927	661	103	60	85	93	65	24	181	15	11	24
1928	787	102	59	93	99	80	25	282	14	10	23
1929	827	96	63	94	97	83	25	315	18	11	25
1930	573	66	49	68	71	91	19	168	15	9	17
1931	409	56	37	54	49	56	16	109	12	7	13
1932	269	39	23	40	43	39	9	54	8	5	9
1933	356	51	43	47	51	45	13	76	12	7	11
1934	494	54	57	54	58	50	15	167	16	10	13
1935	677	96	84	73	78	69	21	198	24	14	20
1936	755	109	91	87	76	83	21	225	26	13	24
1937	777	115	107	91	91	97	26	175	29	16	30
1938	574	92	76	74	77	76	20	100	21	13	25
1939	720	107	84	84	78	98	20	184	24	14	27
1940	722	109	92	81	77	111	19	170	23	14	26
1941	936	144	141	113	111	161	24	152	34	20	36
1942	825	140	85	121	125	188	36	42	25	26	37
1943	761	138	31	130	142	118	45	66	28	29	34
1944	574	114	14	107	122	79	50	4	24	27	33
1945	651	126	29	109	140	87	59	0	34	28	39
1946	1 426	209	158	176	206	313	78	90	80	38	78
1947	1 586	220	240	175	181	355	65	154	82	37	77
1948	1 487	202	224	162	162	318	54	186	74	36	69
1949	1 465	187	177	140	146	338	47	269	69	33	59

DEPRECIATION ON FARMERS' HOLDINGS OF MAIN TYPES OF CONSUMER DURABLE GOODS; ORIGINAL COST: 1897 to 1949

$ mill.

Year	Total	Furniture	Household appliances	House furnishings	China etc.	Musical instruments	Books	Passenger cars	Passenger car accessories	Medical appliances	Miscellaneous
	1	2	3	4	5	6	7	8	9	10	11
1897	108	20	6	22	25	6	6	–	–	2	21
1898	110	21	6	22	26	6	6	–	–	2	21
1899	113	21	6	22	26	6	7	1	0	2	22
1900	116	22	7	23	27	6	7	0	0	2	22
1901	120	22	7	23	28	7	7	2	0	2	22
1902	124	23	8	24	29	7	7	2	0	2	22
1903	128	23	8	25	30	8	7	3	0	2	22
1904	135	24	9	26	32	8	8	4	0	2	22
1905	143	25	9	27	35	9	8	6	0	2	22
1906	157	26	10	29	38	9	9	10	0	3	23
1907	173	27	11	31	42	10	9	17	0	3	23
1908	189	28	12	32	45	11	9	25	0	3	24
1909	205	29	12	34	47	11	10	34	0	4	24
1910	227	31	13	36	51	12	10	45	0	4	25
1911	250	32	14	37	54	13	10	60	1	4	25
1912	273	34	15	39	56	13	11	73	1	5	26
1913	289	35	16	40	59	14	11	82	1	5	26
1914	313	37	17	41	61	15	12	97	1	5	27
1915	353	38	18	42	62	16	12	132	1	5	27
1916	399	40	19	43	63	17	12	172	1	6	26
1917	476	43	21	46	67	19	13	231	1	8	27
1918	523	47	25	53	74	21	15	244	2	14	28
1919	611	52	29	61	82	24	16	294	4	19	30
1920	610	58	33	68	90	28	18	256	6	22	31
1921	590	62	36	71	92	30	19	218	8	23	31
1922	554	64	37	73	92	32	19	178	8	21	30
1923	554	66	38	75	92	33	19	176	9	17	29
1924	580	69	40	79	94	36	19	192	10	13	28
1925	610	73	43	84	97	39	20	205	9	11	29
1926	655	76	47	89	101	43	21	228	11	10	29
1927	675	79	50	90	101	47	21	237	12	10	28
1928	680	82	53	89	98	46	21	242	13	10	26
1929	700	84	55	87	94	55	21	255	14	11	24
1930	689	86	54	83	87	60	20	252	15	10	22
1931	653	86	52	81	84	63	20	222	14	10	21
1932	605	86	49	79	82	64	20	183	13	9	20
1933	554	84	47	75	78	64	19	148	12	8	19
1934	523	83	47	71	74	65	18	128	11	8	18
1935	507	83	48	67	70	63	18	123	10	8	17
1936	510	84	49	64	66	62	17	131	12	9	16
1937	518	83	50	62	64	61	17	141	14	10	16
1938	507	82	51	60	61	59	17	133	16	12	16
1939	490	79	50	57	57	55	16	131	17	13	15
1940	491	75	50	57	56	49	15	143	18	13	15
1941	509	75	52	60	58	45	15	155	19	14	16
1942	529	77	54	67	66	44	17	149	20	16	19
1943	546	79	55	77	77	44	20	134	21	18	21
1944	560	81	55	86	88	41	23	117	23	22	24
1945	569	82	54	94	99	39	27	98	25	25	26
1946	633	86	60	106	117	46	32	93	33	29	31
1947	758	94	75	124	140	58	38	111	48	32	38
1948	910	103	94	144	162	73	43	146	64	35	46
1949	1 074	112	110	162	182	89	48	200	80	38	53

DEPRECIATION ON FARMERS' HOLDINGS OF MAIN TYPES
OF CONSUMER DURABLE GOODS; 1929 PRICES: 1897 to 1949

$ mill.

Year	Total	Fur-niture	Household appliances	House furnishings	China etc.	Musical instru-ments	Books	Passenger cars	Passenger car acces-sories	Medical appliances	Miscel-laneous
	1	2	3	4	5	6	7	8	9	10	11
1897	297	65	18	66	62	13	17	–	–	4	52
1898	308	67	20	68	64	13	18	–	–	4	54
1899	322	69	21	70	67	14	19	1	0	5	56
1900	332	71	22	72	71	14	20	0	0	5	57
1901	340	73	23	73	73	15	20	1	0	5	57
1902	351	75	25	75	75	16	21	2	0	5	57
1903	359	76	26	77	77	17	22	2	0	5	57
1904	369	78	27	80	81	18	22	2	0	5	56
1905	382	80	29	82	86	18	23	3	0	5	56
1906	398	83	31	84	92	19	23	5	0	5	56
1907	416	85	32	87	100	21	23	6	0	6	56
1908	428	87	34	89	105	22	23	8	0	6	54
1909	444	89	35	91	111	22	23	13	0	7	53
1910	471	92	36	95	120	24	23	20	0	8	53
1911	495	94	37	97	128	25	23	30	0	8	53
1912	520	95	38	98	136	26	23	43	0	8	53
1913	543	95	39	99	142	27	23	56	1	8	53
1914	565	96	39	100	147	29	23	70	1	8	52
1915	597	96	40	101	150	30	23	96	1	9	51
1916	638	96	40	101	151	32	23	136	1	9	49
1917	706	97	43	102	153	34	23	192	2	12	48
1918	760	100	47	104	155	37	24	227	2	17	47
1919	790	102	50	104	156	40	24	243	4	21	46
1920	789	103	53	102	152	44	24	240	6	22	43
1921	729	102	53	97	143	46	23	197	6	22	40
1922	669	100	52	92	133	47	22	160	7	20	36
1923	649	99	52	89	124	48	21	160	8	15	33
1924	650	98	52	86	116	50	21	178	8	11	30
1925	662	98	52	85	111	52	21	197	9	10	27
1926	694	98	54	85	108	56	21	223	11	10	28
1927	702	97	56	83	101	58	21	237	13	10	26
1928	703	98	57	80	95	62	20	242	14	11	24
1929	713	97	57	79	89	65	20	258	15	11	22
1930	706	95	55	78	84	71	20	255	16	11	21
1931	672	92	52	78	82	76	20	226	15	10	21
1932	626	90	48	77	80	79	20	188	14	9	21
1933	582	88	47	75	78	81	19	153	13	8	20
1934	561	86	49	72	76	84	19	135	13	8	19
1935	559	86	52	70	75	85	19	133	13	8	18
1936	577	87	55	69	73	88	19	143	16	9	18
1937	597	86	59	70	71	91	19	153	19	11	18
1938	593	84	62	69	70	93	19	143	22	13	18
1939	588	83	63	68	68	94	18	138	24	13	19
1940	605	83	66	68	67	94	18	151	25	14	19
1941	632	86	70	72	71	95	18	159	25	15	21
1942	658	90	75	78	78	103	20	148	26	16	24
1943	677	94	76	87	87	109	23	130	26	19	26
1944	684	96	76	93	95	109	26	112	27	22	28
1945	686	97	75	98	101	109	30	93	28	25	30
1946	730	101	78	104	110	121	35	85	34	28	34
1947	819	106	89	113	121	146	40	90	44	31	39
1948	907	112	101	121	130	171	43	100	54	32	43
1949	997	116	110	129	138	195	46	119	63	34	47

DEPRECIATION ON FARMERS' HOLDINGS OF MAIN TYPES OF CONSUMER DURABLE GOODS; REPLACEMENT COST: 1897 to 1949

$ mill.

Year	Total	Fur-niture	Household appliances	House furnishings	China etc.	Musical instru-ments	Books	Passenger cars	Passenger car acces-sories	Medical appliances	Miscel-laneous
	1	2	3	4	5	6	7	8	9	10	11
1897	89	16	5	19	21	5	5	—	—	1	17
1898	98	18	5	20	23	5	6	—	—	2	19
1899	105	19	6	21	24	6	6	0	0	2	21
1900	117	22	7	24	26	6	7	0	0	2	23
1901	133	24	8	25	33	7	8	2	0	2	24
1902	142	25	9	26	34	9	8	4	0	2	25
1903	148	27	9	28	35	9	9	4	0	2	25
1904	153	28	10	30	37	9	10	2	0	2	25
1905	163	29	11	31	38	10	10	6	0	3	25
1906	179	31	12	34	39	11	10	13	0	3	26
1907	204	36	14	37	44	13	11	18	0	3	28
1908	206	36	15	34	42	13	11	24	0	3	28
1909	205	36	14	35	42	13	11	24	0	4	26
1910	227	40	16	38	45	13	11	33	0	4	27
1911	266	49	17	42	52	15	13	45	0	5	28
1912	289	54	19	43	56	15	13	55	0	5	29
1913	322	62	21	45	62	16	14	66	1	5	30
1914	343	62	21	45	65	16	14	84	1	5	30
1915	376	62	21	44	66	18	15	113	1	6	30
1916	438	64	56	23	77	18	16	143	1	7	33
1917	567	66	28	82	109	20	18	194	2	10	38
1918	739	86	36	109	136	26	22	256	2	17	49
1919	891	112	43	113	146	34	26	331	4	24	58
1920	1 083	177	57	149	177	46	33	345	8	31	60
1921	849	136	55	112	159	45	28	229	8	27	50
1922	693	118	52	93	126	41	23	170	7	21	42
1923	707	120	57	98	142	48	22	163	8	16	33
1924	685	110	55	91	134	51	21	174	8	11	30
1925	681	106	55	93	119	50	21	192	8	10	27
1926	692	102	55	91	109	55	20	215	10	9	26
1927	700	99	57	87	101	59	20	229	12	10	26
1928	701	99	57	82	96	62	20	237	14	10	24
1929	713	97	57	79	89	65	20	258	15	11	22
1930	656	90	52	75	79	50	19	244	15	11	21
1931	569	74	46	66	73	38	18	213	12	10	19
1932	467	58	37	56	64	29	18	170	10	9	16
1933	412	56	33	55	61	26	16	133	9	8	15
1934	411	60	34	59	60	29	16	122	9	7	15
1935	404	56	36	57	59	30	16	118	10	8	14
1936	420	57	39	57	59	30	16	129	11	9	13
1937	459	61	42	61	60	33	16	148	14	10	14
1938	455	58	45	58	57	32	16	147	16	12	14
1939	444	55	45	56	55	31	16	142	17	13	14
1940	470	56	45	59	57	30	15	161	19	13	15
1941	533	66	50	67	65	32	16	186	20	14	17
1942	618	79	61	80	85	39	17	193	25	16	23
1943	640	84	64	92	97	43	21	169	25	19	26
1944	679	96	69	107	115	44	24	146	26	23	29
1945	711	106	73	121	131	45	29	121	28	26	31
1946	815	119	83	140	156	54	36	120	38	30	39
1947	1 048	138	110	176	198	75	48	160	57	35	51
1948	1 236	162	132	200	226	95	55	193	76	37	60
1949	1 355	162	139	206	232	107	58	250	95	41	65

Column 1 – Same source as Table A-24, col. 8 adjusted (lowered) to represent net purchases of used cars, i.e. to subtract from gross purchases value of all cars traded in by farmers. (In determining farmers' expenditures for used cars Bureau of Agricultural Economics subtracts only trade-ins for purchases of used cars; trade-ins for purchases of new cars are subtracted from its series on farmers' purchases of new cars. In col. 1 all of these trade-ins have been netted against purchases of used cars.)

Column 2 – Col. 1 deflated by price index from Table A-30, col. 6.

Column 3 – Depreciation calculated from col. 1, assuming average life of five years.

Column 4 – Depreciation calculated from col. 2, using same average life as in col. 3.

Column 5 – Col. 4 converted to current prices by price index in Table A-30, col. 6.

Column 6 – Col. 1 minus col. 3.

Column 7 – Col. 2 minus col. 4.

Column 8 – Col. 1 minus col. 5.

FARMERS' SAVING THROUGH USED PASSENGER CARS
1905 to 1949
$ mill.

Year	Expenditures		Depreciation			Saving		
	Original cost	1929 prices	Original cost	1929 prices	Replacement cost	Original cost	1929 prices	Replacement cost
	1	2	3	4	5	6	7	8
1905	1	0	0	0	0	1	0	1
1906	1	0	0	0	0	1	0	1
1907	1	0	1	0	0	0	0	1
1908	2	1	1	0	0	1	1	2
1909	2	1	1	0	0	1	1	2
1910	3	2	2	1	2	1	1	1
1911	6	4	2	1	1	4	3	5
1912	6	5	3	2	3	3	3	3
1913	7	6	4	3	4	3	3	3
1914	12	10	6	4	5	6	6	7
1915	21	18	9	7	8	12	11	13
1916	26	25	12	11	12	14	14	14
1917	53	52	19	18	18	34	34	35
1918	31	27	26	24	27	5	3	4
1919	62	45	34	30	41	28	15	21
1920	37	26	40	34	49	−3	−8	−12
1921	4	3	40	33	38	−36	−30	−34
1922	26	24	35	28	30	−9	−4	−4
1923	58	57	35	28	29	23	29	29
1924	52	53	36	32	31	16	21	21
1925	78	80	40	38	37	38	42	41
1926	54	56	49	49	47	5	7	7
1927	35	36	54	55	53	−19	−19	−18
1928	70	72	57	58	57	13	14	13
1929	84	84	61	62	62	23	22	22
1930	61	64	62	64	61	−1	0	0
1931	42	44	60	61	58	−18	−17	−16
1932	24	27	57	59	53	−33	−32	−29
1933	26	30	52	54	47	−26	−24	−21
1934	67	74	46	49	44	21	25	23
1935	64	72	44	49	44	20	23	20
1936	85	94	49	54	49	36	40	36
1937	69	71	58	64	62	11	7	7
1938	55	53	65	70	72	−10	−17	−17
1939	100	97	71	75	77	29	22	23
1940	96	90	78	79	84	18	11	12
1941	130	111	86	83	97	44	28	33
1942	73	54	90	83	112	−17	−29	−39
1943	90	51	94	81	142	−4	−30	−52
1944	34	16	91	72	149	−57	−56	−115
1945	0	0	75	55	110	−75	−55	−110
1946	151	80	68	43	81	83	37	70
1947	215	97	84	44	98	131	53	117
1948	285	109	118	55	144	167	54	141
1949	377	132	171	72	205	206	60	172

Columns 1 and 2 – 1836–1839: Assumed to be same as in 1840.

    1840–1949: Bureau of Agricultural Economics index of farm construction costs (*Income Parity for Agriculture,* part II, section 5, p. 28, as revised and brought up to date by Bureau of Agricultural Economics, shifted to 1929 = 100) linked back of 1910 to an index derived by averaging indices of wholesale prices of building materials and of wage rates as given in Warren, G. F., and Pearson, F. A., *Gold and Prices,* pp. 30, 32, 317, shifted to 1929 = 100.

Column 3 – 1882–1890: Bureau of Labor Statistics index of wholesale prices of all commodities linked in 1891 to Mills' index.

    1891–1909: Index of wholesale prices of processed producer durable goods as estimated by Mills, F. C., *Economic Tendencies in the U.S.,* p. 585, linked in 1913 to Marshall and Stevens index of equipment costs (*Stevens' Valuation Quarterly,* Jan. 1949, pp. 60–64).

    1910–1949: Department of Agriculture, Bureau of Agricultural Economics series on farm machinery prices as given in *Agricultural Prices,* Jan. 31, 1950, p. 42, shifted to 1929 = 100.

Column 4 – 1909–1949: Index constructed from prices in *Income Parity for Agriculture,* part II, section 3, p. 53, as revised and brought up to date by Bureau of Agricultural Economics.

Column 5 – 1899–1909: Extrapolated from 1910 value by price index for nonfarm automobiles (cf. Table Q-16, col. 8).

    1910–1949: From p. 26 of same source as col. 4, as revised by Bureau of Agricultural Economics.

Column 6 – 1899–1949: W. H. Shaw's index for "motor vehicles" (*Value of Commodity Output since 1869*) linked in 1910 to index constructed from p. 26 of same source as col. 4, as revised by Bureau of Agricultural Economics.

Column 7 – 1902–1909: Extrapolated from 1910 value by price index for nonfarm trucks (cf. Table P-10, col. 11).

    1910–1949: From p. 43 of same source as col. 4, as revised by Bureau of Agricultural Economics.

Column 8 – 1909–1949: From p. 43 of same source as col. 4, as revised by Bureau of Agricultural Economics.

PRICE INDICES OF AGRICULTURAL DURABLE GOODS

1836 to 1949

1929 = 100.0

	Construction		Farm machinery		Construction		Farm machinery	Tractors	Automobiles		Trucks	
Year	Residential	Other buildings		Year	Residential	Other buildings			New	Used	New	Used
	1	2	3		1	2	3	4	5	6	7	8
1836	29.2	30.7	–	1893	43.0	45.4	54.6	–	–	–	–	–
1837	29.2	30.7	–	1894	41.6	43.8	49.4	–	–	–	–	–
1838	29.2	30.7	–	1895	41.3	43.6	48.9	–	–	–	–	–
1839	29.2	30.7	–	1896	41.6	43.8	48.6	–	–	–	–	–
1840	29.2	30.7	–	1897	41.0	43.2	47.0	–	–	–	–	–
1841	30.1	31.8	–	1898	42.2	44.5	48.5	–	–	–	–	–
1842	28.3	29.9	–	1899	44.6	47.0	55.0	–	165.0	165.1	–	–
1843	27.1	28.6	–	1900	46.9	49.5	59.9	–	165.0	165.1	–	–
1844	27.1	28.6	–	1901	46.1	48.6	57.4	–	165.0	165.1	–	–
1845	28.9	30.5	–	1902	47.5	50.1	59.0	–	162.9	163.1	207.3	–
1846	29.2	30.7	–	1903	49.2	51.9	59.6	–	163.2	163.4	207.7	–
1847	28.3	29.9	–	1904	48.4	51.0	57.9	–	148.9	149.0	189.4	–
1848	28.6	30.1	–	1905	50.4	53.2	60.5	–	224.9	225.2	184.8	–
1849	28.1	29.6	–	1906	54.6	57.5	64.7	–	261.1	261.4	187.5	–
1850	28.6	30.1	–	1907	57.3	60.3	67.3	–	300.6	301.0	185.5	–
1851	28.3	29.9	–	1908	54.6	57.5	61.0	–	300.5	300.9	177.2	–
1852	29.5	31.1	–	1909	55.8	58.8	61.9	148.8	181.8	182.1	168.6	168.9
1853	30.4	32.0	–	1910	57.5	60.6	65.4	148.8	167.9	168.1	167.8	168.1
1854	31.8	33.6	–	1911	57.5	60.6	65.4	148.8	147.5	147.7	147.1	147.4
1855	32.5	34.2	–	1912	57.5	60.6	65.4	139.5	128.4	128.6	128.7	128.9
1856	33.3	35.1	–	1913	58.6	62.4	65.4	144.2	118.0	118.1	118.4	118.4
1857	33.7	35.5	–	1914	58.0	61.2	65.4	134.9	120.0	120.1	119.5	119.7
1858	31.6	33.3	–	1915	59.8	63.6	67.3	130.2	118.0	118.1	118.4	118.4
1859	30.6	32.3	–	1916	66.1	72.7	70.6	111.6	104.8	104.9	104.6	104.6
1860	31.0	32.7	–	1917	81.0	87.3	80.4	93.0	100.9	101.0	101.1	101.3
1861	30.6	32.3	–	1918	97.7	104.8	101.3	111.6	112.8	112.8	112.6	112.8
1862	32.7	34.5	–	1919	117.2	118.8	104.6	116.3	136.4	136.5	134.5	134.9
1863	39.3	41.4	–	1920	153.4	141.8	108.5	109.3	143.6	143.7	141.4	141.4
1864	48.6	51.2	–	1921	104.6	104.8	104.6	97.7	116.0	116.1	113.8	113.8
1865	52.5	55.3	–	1922	101.1	98.2	93.5	61.9	106.2	106.2	104.6	104.6
1866	56.4	59.4	–	1923	108.0	103.6	96.7	66.5	102.3	102.3	100.0	100.0
1867	54.6	57.5	–	1924	104.6	103.0	101.3	73.0	97.7	97.7	95.2	95.4
1868	54.0	56.9	–	1925	102.3	103.0	100.7	76.3	97.4	97.4	92.2	92.4
1869	52.5	55.3	–	1926	102.3	101.8	100.7	83.7	96.4	96.4	92.6	92.8
1870	50.2	52.9	–	1927	100.6	100.0	101.3	81.4	96.4	96.4	93.1	93.4
1871	50.7	53.4	–	1928	100.0	99.4	100.7	107.0	97.7	97.7	96.8	97.0
1872	52.5	55.3	–	1929	100.0	100.0	100.0	100.0	100.0	100.0	100.0	100.0
1873	52.3	55.1	–	1930	96.6	95.8	99.3	97.7	95.6	95.7	95.5	95.7
1874	50.2	52.9	–	1931	82.8	83.6	98.0	96.3	94.4	94.4	94.1	94.4
1875	46.9	49.5	–	1932	71.3	73.3	92.8	92.6	90.2	90.1	89.2	89.5
1876	44.2	46.6	–	1933	71.8	72.7	90.2	88.8	86.8	86.8	86.2	86.2
1877	42.2	44.5	–	1934	81.6	81.2	94.1	91.6	90.3	90.5	89.0	89.1
1878	39.5	41.6	–	1935	81.0	81.8	96.7	87.9	88.8	88.8	87.6	87.8
1879	39.9	42.0	–	1936	83.3	83.6	98.0	90.7	90.3	90.5	89.6	89.8
1880	42.2	44.5	–	1937	89.7	89.1	100.0	91.6	96.9	97.0	95.2	95.4
1881	43.4	45.7	–	1938	84.5	86.1	103.3	90.7	102.9	103.0	101.0	101.3
1882	45.1	47.5	68.5	1939	84.5	86.1	101.3	81.9	102.8	103.0	101.0	101.3
1883	44.6	47.0	67.4	1940	87.4	87.3	100.0	76.0	107.0	106.9	105.5	105.6
1884	44.2	46.6	62.2	1941	98.3	96.4	101.3	79.9	117.1	117.1	115.2	115.5
1885	43.4	45.7	59.1	1942	112.1	109.7	107.2	79.3	130.1	134.5	119.8	132.9
1886	43.6	46.0	58.1	1943	126.4	123.6	111.1	76.7	130.1	175.0	124.3	156.6
1887	44.2	46.6	58.1	1944	138.5	136.4	113.7	88.3	130.1	206.6	128.7	172.4
1888	44.0	46.4	59.1	1945	150.6	143.6	115.0	92.9	130.1	200.7	133.3	156.9
1889	44.6	47.0	59.1	1946	167.8	158.2	119.0	88.0	141.4	188.8	137.8	138.2
1890	45.7	48.2	58.3	1947	216.7	201.8	134.6	98.1	178.3	221.7	174.7	175.0
1891	44.6	47.0	57.9	1948	235.6	215.8	156.9	108.4	192.8	261.5	194.5	194.7
1892	43.4	45.7	55.6	1949	222.4	212.1	176.5	126.3	210.0	284.9	199.5	200.0

Column 1 – Sums of cols. 2 and 3.

Column 2 – From Table A-45, col. 1.

Column 3 – From Table A-35, col. 1.

Note: These estimates agree very closely with Bureau of Agricultural Economics estimates given, for 1939 to date, in the *Balance Sheet of Agriculture* (cf. *Balance Sheet of Agriculture*, 1947, tables 1 and 9; 1948, tables 1 and 15; and 1950, tables 1 and 6) as shown below ($ million):

| End of year | Balance Sheet of Agriculture | | Saving Study | |
	Crops on farms (including crops on farms under Commodity Credit Corporation loans but excluding stocks held in bonded warehouses as security for Commodity Credit Corporation loans)	Livestock on farms	Crops on farms (plus corn and wheat on farms under Commodity Credit Corporation loans)	Livestock on farms
	1	2	3	4
1939	2 339	5 133	2 297	5 133
1940	2 493	5 325	2 469	5 325
1941	3 408	7 074	3 448	7 074
1942	4 585	9 642	4 689	9 642
1943	5 564	9 685	5 602	9 685
1944	5 770	9 012	5 748	9 012
1945	5 778	9 742	5 661	9 742
1946	6 823	11 977	6 852	11 977
1947	8 732	13 384	8 773	13 384
1948	7 631	14 657	7 650	14 657
1949	6 800	13 211	6 485	13 184

Differences in estimates for crops reflect the fact that certain of series shown here are based on slightly different Bureau of Agricultural Economics quantity and price series than those shown in *Balance Sheet*, e.g. Saving Study series includes cotton owned by farmers (not under Commodity Credit Corporation loans) but stored off farms, whereas such cotton is excluded from *Balance Sheet* figures. Moreover, Saving Study series includes a rough 5 percent increase to allow for minor crops for which long-time quantity and price series were not available (cf. Table A-35, col. 1) whereas *Balance Sheet* attempts to measure value of these minor crops more precisely. In col. 3 above, corn and wheat stored on farms under Commodity Credit Corporation loans (Table A-40) which are not included in Table A-31 have been added for comparability with crop series in col. 1. Col. 1 includes some minor crops on farms under Commodity Credit Corporation loans which are not included in col. 3. (Crops stored off farms that were under Commodity Credit Corporation loans are excluded from both Saving Study series and *Balance Sheet* figures given above, but they are included in some summary tables published in *Balance Sheet*.)

Column 4 – Sum of cols. 5 and 6.

Column 5 – From Table A-46, col. 1.

Column 6 – From Table A-36, col. 1.

LIVESTOCK AND CROP INVENTORIES; VALUE ON FARMS

Current and 1929 Prices: 1896 to 1949

$ mill.

End of year	Current prices			1929 prices			End of year	Current prices			1929 prices		
	Total	Live-stock	Crops	Total	Live-stock	Crops		Total	Live-stock	Crops	Total	Live-stock	Crops
	1	2	3	4	5	6		1	2	3	4	5	6
1896	3 012	1 981	1 031	8 200	5 635	2 565	1923	8 398	5 071	3 327	10 319	7 063	3 256
1897	3 490	2 355	1 135	8 225	5 817	2 408	1924	8 600	5 021	3 579	9 692	6 732	2 960
1898	3 819	2 603	1 216	8 694	5 998	2 696	1925	8 771	5 386	3 385	9 789	6 501	3 288
1899	4 312	3 028	1 284	8 888	6 266	2 622	1926	8 425	5 520	2 905	9 556	6 396	3 160
1900	4 537	3 117	1 420	9 009	6 450	2 559	1927	9 090	6 026	3 064	9 508	6 418	3 090
1901	4 759	3 213	1 546	8 662	6 518	2 144	1928	9 660	6 593	3 067	9 583	6 436	3 147
1902	5 080	3 399	1 681	9 503	6 625	2 878	1929	9 487	6 514	2 973	9 488	6 514	2 974
1903	5 011	3 365	1 646	9 313	6 707	2 606	1930	7 056	4 859	2 197	9 317	6 565	2 752
1904	5 134	3 370	1 764	9 509	6 719	2 790	1931	5 219	3 555	1 664	10 103	6 729	3 374
1905	5 568	3 748	1 820	9 712	6 723	2 989	1932	4 184	2 983	1 201	10 582	6 989	3 593
1906	6 236	4 276	1 960	9 942	6 762	3 180	1933	4 946	3 169	1 777	10 105	7 137	2 968
1907	6 300	4 199	2 101	9 443	6 721	2 722	1934	5 485	3 478	2 007	8 469	6 481	1 988
1908	6 519	4 316	2 203	9 444	6 626	2 818	1935	7 152	5 184	1 968	9 445	6 450	2 995
1909	7 453	4 914	2 539	9 567	6 506	3 061	1936	7 280	5 064	2 216	8 394	6 338	2 056
1910	7 675	5 266	2 409	9 768	6 577	3 191	1937	7 209	5 033	2 176	9 518	6 238	3 280
1911	7 480	5 037	2 443	9 292	6 484	2 808	1938	6 998	5 092	1 906	9 730	6 352	3 378
1912	8 236	5 648	2 588	10 074	6 513	3 561	1939	7 304	5 133	2 171	9 847	6 641	3 206
1913	8 717	6 148	2 569	9 627	6 687	2 940	1940	7 589	5 325	2 264	10 076	6 711	3 365
1914	8 962	6 292	2 670	10 414	6 999	3 415	1941	10 264	7 074	3 190	10 650	7 075	3 575
1915	9 239	6 357	2 882	10 845	7 246	3 599	1942	14 006	9 642	4 364	11 786	7 562	4 224
1916	10 311	7 064	3 247	10 328	7 396	2 932	1943	15 159	9 685	5 474	11 756	7 880	3 876
1917	14 051	8 553	5 498	10 993	7 601	3 392	1944	14 691	9 012	5 679	11 389	7 418	3 971
1918	14 672	9 022	5 650	10 909	7 597	3 312	1945	15 374	9 742	5 632	11 091	7 182	3 909
1919	14 202	8 480	5 722	10 678	7 376	3 302	1946	18 810	11 977	6 833	11 001	6 880	4 121
1920	10 625	6 380	4 245	11 312	7 201	4 111	1947	22 129	13 384	8 745	10 142	6 569	3 573
1921	7 479	5 070	2 409	10 392	7 181	3 211	1948	22 187	14 657	7 530	11 021	6 507	4 514
1922	8 454	5 366	3 088	10 466	7 216	3 250	1949	19 143	13 184	5 959	10 515	6 614	3 901

Column 1 – Sum of cols. 2 and 3.

Column 2 – From Table A-47, col. 1.

Column 3 – From Table A-37, col. 1.

Column 4 – Sum of cols. 5 and 6.

Column 5 – From Table A-48, col. 1.

Column 6 – From Table A-38, col. 1.

Column 7 – Sum of cols. 8 and 9.

Column 8 – From Table A-49, col. 1.

Column 9 – From Table A-39, col. 1.

Note: The Bureau of Agricultural Economics publishes an annual series on value of change in farm inventories, 1910 to date. (See, for example, Department of Agriculture, Bureau of Agricultural Economics, *Farm Income Situation*, Aug.-Sept. 1948, table 2.) That series differs conceptually from col. 7 of Table A-32 because it includes only the portion of the various crops on farms estimated to be stored for sale, whereas change in total farm inventories, whether for feed, seed, home consumption, or for sale, is included in Table A-32. (After the present estimates were completed the Bureau of Agricultural Economics published a revised series covering all crops—see *Farm Income Situation*, July–Sept. 1951.) The year-end prices used by Bureau of Agricultural Economics to value annual changes in farm inventories represent state prices weighted by annual changes in farm inventories in the several states; year-end prices used in present series are state prices weighted by farm inventories in the several states in the case of livestock, and by production or sales in the several states in the case of crops.

The Department of Commerce also publishes series on annual net change in farm inventories valued at end-of-year prices, for 1929 to date (*Survey of Current Business, National Income Supplement*, July 1947, and *Survey of Current Business*, July 1950, table 33) which agree conceptually with series shown here in Table A-32, col. 7. Some differences appear, however, because of differences in prices mentioned above and also because of minor differences in coverage of crop items and some statistical revisions incorporated in present series.

LIVESTOCK AND CROP INVENTORIES;
ANNUAL CHANGE IN VALUE ON FARMS, CURRENT AND 1929 PRICES, AND ANNUAL CHANGE IN QUANTITY ON FARMS VALUED AT END-OF-YEAR PRICES
1897 to 1949
$ mill.

Year	Annual change in value						Annual change in quantity valued at end-of-year prices		
	Current prices			1929 prices					
	Total	Livestock	Crops	Total	Livestock	Crops	Total	Livestock	Crops
	1	2	3	4	5	6	7	8	9
1897	478	374	104	25	182	−157	51	70	−19
1898	329	248	81	469	181	288	215	79	136
1899	493	425	68	194	268	−74	73	124	−51
1900	225	89	136	121	184	−63	26	76	−50
1901	222	96	126	−347	68	−415	−304	24	−328
1902	321	186	135	841	107	734	455	52	403
1903	−69	−34	−35	−190	82	−272	−106	49	−155
1904	123	5	118	196	12	184	119	22	97
1905	434	378	56	203	4	199	146	27	119
1906	668	528	140	230	39	191	138	53	85
1907	64	−77	141	−499	−41	−458	−305	21	−326
1908	219	117	102	1	−95	96	61	−15	76
1909	934	598	336	123	−120	243	133	−34	167
1910	222	352	−130	201	71	130	156	106	50
1911	−195	−229	34	−476	−93	−383	−382	−11	−371
1912	756	611	145	782	29	753	596	48	548
1913	481	500	−19	−447	174	−621	−391	153	−544
1914	245	144	101	787	312	475	506	245	261
1915	277	65	212	431	247	184	378	177	201
1916	1 072	707	365	−517	150	−667	−744	119	−863
1917	3 740	1 489	2 251	665	205	460	980	231	749
1918	621	469	152	−84	−4	−80	−142	11	−153
1919	−470	−542	72	−231	−221	−10	−309	−262	−47
1920	−3 577	−2 100	−1 477	634	−175	809	570	−147	717
1921	−3 146	−1 310	−1 836	−920	−20	−900	−789	−18	−771
1922	975	296	679	74	35	39	73	52	21
1923	−56	−295	239	−147	−153	6	−125	−108	−17
1924	202	−50	252	−627	−331	−296	−667	−257	−410
1925	171	365	−194	97	−231	328	66	−177	243
1926	−346	134	−480	−233	−105	−128	−178	−49	−129
1927	665	506	159	−48	22	−70	−82	30	−112
1928	570	567	3	75	18	57	55	13	42
1929	−173	−79	−94	−95	78	−173	−92	78	−170
1930	−2 431	−1 655	−776	−171	51	−222	−197	22	−219
1931	−1 837	−1 304	−533	786	164	622	303	60	243
1932	−1 035	−572	−463	479	260	219	130	76	54
1933	762	186	576	−477	148	−625	−353	31	−384
1934	539	309	230	−1 636	−656	−980	−1 325	−295	−1 030
1935	1 667	1 706	−39	976	−31	1 007	625	−27	652
1936	128	−120	248	−1 051	−112	−939	−1 183	−93	−1 090
1937	−71	−31	−40	1 124	−100	1 224	683	−98	781
1938	−211	59	−270	212	114	98	125	73	52
1939	306	41	265	117	289	−172	48	171	−123
1940	285	192	93	229	70	159	161	61	100
1941	2 675	1 749	926	574	364	210	539	364	175
1942	3 742	2 568	1 174	1 136	487	649	1 357	670	687
1943	1 153	43	1 110	−30	318	−348	−125	407	−532
1944	−468	−673	205	−367	−462	95	−452	−660	208
1945	683	730	−47	−298	−236	−62	−379	−275	−104
1946	3 436	2 235	1 201	−90	−302	212	−177	−510	333
1947	3 319	1 407	1 912	−859	−311	−548	−2 216	−585	−1 631
1948	58	1 273	−1 215	879	−62	941	1 469	−23	1 492
1949	−3 044	−1 473	−1 571	−506	107	−613	−662	289	−951

Crop inventory data published by U.S. Department of Agriculture for Jan. 1 are used here for Dec. 31 of previous year.

Columns 1 to 3 – 1896–1925: March 1 inventory and annual production series were available for this period but no data were available on inventories as of end of calendar year. For each of the three crops, estimates for Dec. 31 were derived from annual production, 1896–1925, and Mar. 1 inventories on farms 1897–1926, on basis of a regression line fitted to Jan. 1 and Mar. 1 inventories on farms for 1927–1932 expressed as percentages of preceding year's production. Regression equations thus derived: col. 1, $y = 36.96 + 0.4814x$; col. 2, $y = 3.14 + 1.4100x$; col. 3, $y = 47.01 + 0.3333x$ where x represents in each case Mar. 1 and y, Jan. 1 stocks as a percentage of preceding year's production. Mar. 1 stocks and annual production figures from Department of Agriculture, *Wheat and Rye Statistics* and *Corn Statistics*, Statistical Bulletins 12 and 28; *Agricultural Statistics*, 1941, tables 1, 49, and 75; *Agricultural Statistics*, 1943, tables 1, 35, 48; Kuznets, S., *Commodity Flow and Capital Formation*, vol. I, p. 423 (Mar. 1 stocks of wheat for 1925–1932, and of corn for 1929–1932); and from records of Crop Reporting Board, Department of Agriculture (Mar. 1 stocks of oats). Jan. 1 stocks for 1927–1932 from *Agricultural Statistics*, 1943, tables 8, 40, 52.

    1926–1949: Inventories on farms, as of end of calendar year, from *Agricultural Statistics*, 1943, tables 8, 40, 52, and *Agricultural Statistics*, 1947, tables 9, 51, 65, and from Bureau of Agricultural Economics releases on *Crop Production, Jan. 1, 1948, Jan. 1, 1949*, and *Jan. 1, 1950*, issued Jan. 9, 1948, Jan. 10, 1949, and Jan. 10, 1950, respectively, minus corn and wheat stored on farms under Commodity Credit Corporation loan from Table A-40, cols. 1 and 2.

Columns 4 and 5 – 1896–1908: Estimates were derived from production data for these years on basis of a regression line fitted to production and end-of-year stocks for following five-year period. Production series from *Agricultural Statistics*, 1941, tables 34 and 94, and end-of-year stocks from source given below. Regression equation thus derived: col. 4, $y = -39598.4 + 0.867309x$; col. 5, $y = 5029.6 + 0.460996x$ where x represents production and y, end-of-year stocks.

    1909–1932: Estimates of stocks on farms stored for sale from *Income Parity for Agriculture*, part I, sections 9 and 10, as revised by the Bureau of Agricultural Economics, were stepped up by that Bureau to include other stocks on farms on basis of relationship in later years between Jan. 1 total stocks on farms and Jan. 1 stocks on farms stored for sale.

    1933–1949: Inventories on farms from *Agricultural Statistics*, 1945, tables 25, 74, and 1947, tables 24, 75, and from Bureau of Agricultural Economics releases, *Stocks of Feed Grains*, issued Jan. 23, 1948, Apr. 25, 1949, and Apr. 25, 1950, and *Stocks of Wheat and Rye, Jan. 1, 1948, Jan. 1, 1949*, and *Jan. 1, 1950*, issued Jan. 23, 1948, Jan. 25, 1949, and Jan. 25, 1950. Inventory data include minor amount of crops on farms under Commodity Credit Corporation loans.

Columns 6 to 8, 10 and 11 – 1896–1907: Estimates for tobacco and, for 1896–1908, for cotton lint, buckwheat, and potatoes were derived from production data for these years on basis of regression line fitted to production and end-of-year stocks for following five-year period. Regression equations thus derived: col. 6, $y = -738.8 + 0.295338x$; col. 7, $y = -86.2 + 0.813022x$; col. 10, $y = 224.6 + 0.223746x$ (1,000 bales); and col. 11, $y = 17550.4 + 0.201407x$ where x represents, in each case, production and y, end-of-year stocks. Production series from *Agricultural Statistics*, 1941, tables 139, 151, 223, 335; and end-of-year stocks from source given below. In the case of cotton, bales were converted into pounds, assuming 500 lbs. per bale.

    1908–1949: Estimates for tobacco and, for 1909–1949, for the other crops in this heading, are Bureau of Agricultural Economics series on stocks on farms stored for sale from *Income Parity for Agriculture*, part I, various sections, as revised and brought up to date by Bureau of Agricultural Economics. These series exclude crops on farms under Commodity Credit Corporation loans.

Column 9 – 1896–1918: Estimated from production data for these years on basis of a regression line fitted to Jan. 1 inventories on farms for 1938–1948 and production in preceding year. Regression equation thus derived: $y = 7.3 + 0.622743x$, where x represents production and y, stocks. Production series from *Agricultural Statistics*, 1941, table 413, end-of-year stocks from sources given below. This method was tested by applying it to period 1919–1936, where it was found to yield estimates which were very close to those obtained by procedure utilizing May 1 inventory data described below. May 1 stocks were not available prior to 1920.

    1919–1936: Year-end inventories on farms were estimated from production data for these years and May 1 inventories on farms of following year on basis of a regression line fitted to Jan. 1 and May 1 inventories on farms, for 1938–1948, expressed as percentages of preceding year's production. Regression equation thus derived: $y = 70.60 - 0.0648x$ where x represents May 1 and y, Jan. 1 stocks as a percentage of preceding year's production. Production series and May 1 inventories on farms from *The Feed Situation*, May 1948, and October 1948 and *Agricultural Statistics*, 1941, table 413; Jan. 1 inventories on farms for 1938–1948 from Bureau of Agricultural Economics releases on *Revised Estimates of Stocks on Farms*, issued July 1947, and *Crop Production, Jan. 1, 1948*, issued Jan. 9, 1948.

    1937–1949: End-of-year inventories on farms from Bureau of Agricultural Economics releases on *Revised Estimates of Stocks on Farms*, issued July 1947, *Crop Production, Jan. 1, 1948*, issued Jan. 9, 1948, *Jan. 1, 1949*, issued Jan. 10, 1949, and *Jan. 1, 1950*, issued Jan. 10, 1950.

End of year	Corn	Wheat	Oats	Barley	Rye	Buck-wheat	Tobacco	Peanuts	Hay	Cotton lint	Potatoes
			000 bushels				000 pounds		000 tons	000 pounds	000 bushels
	1	2	3	4	5	6	7	8	9	10	11
1896	1 541 520	176 591	479 294	44 946	19 713	3 334	531 745	.	38 788	1 067 000	70 467
1897	1 215 361	213 772	497 715	49 366	19 380	3 490	485 598	.	42 026	1 331 500	57 464
1898	1 286 803	340 833	505 576	45 549	18 419	2 860	652 930	.	44 884	1 374 000	65 958
1899	1 342 731	278 463	554 338	62 884	17 016	2 568	621 352	.	40 873	1 158 000	72 448
1900	1 372 395	227 100	558 875	44 173	17 667	2 719	606 498	.	38 300	1 245 000	69 853
1901	823 399	280 992	458 532	67 774	19 216	3 734	633 792	.	40 327	1 176 000	59 325
1902	1 493 665	269 049	639 247	87 208	20 640	3 262	693 919	.	44 064	1 301 500	77 281
1903	1 287 085	213 783	520 036	89 921	18 367	3 474	707 634	.	46 897	1 214 500	73 196
1904	1 402 573	175 372	607 136	104 464	18 150	3 836	610 251	.	48 083	1 615 500	87 941
1905	1 557 582	253 951	666 502	109 266	19 400	3 986	677 138	.	48 712	1 295 500	78 114
1906	1 690 612	322 538	617 106	115 778	18 679	3 634	704 492	.	44 869	1 597 500	86 323
1907	1 376 913	229 290	471 313	91 004	18 051	3 462	633 849	.	48 531	1 355 000	84 644
1908	1 421 664	214 284	486 140	108 521	18 237	3 595	581 183	.	51 875	1 593 500	79 029
1909	1 422 939	252 296	599 017	105 000	19 000	3 776	755 352	127 980	61 547	1 219 000	95 955
1910	1 627 822	249 349	658 388	89 000	19 000	3 593	869 018	146 356	54 081	1 422 000	82 360
1911	1 361 232	191 559	510 152	85 000	18 000	3 326	707 264	132 565	47 474	1 851 500	79 359
1912	1 776 262	243 617	830 098	135 000	25 000	3 568	794 672	127 491	60 858	1 642 500	100 374
1913	1 321 496	237 946	619 426	96 000	22 000	2 270	627 649	137 690	55 226	1 726 500	86 918
1914	1 426 395	243 604	621 029	96 000	24 000	2 850	706 080	146 734	58 702	3 500 000	96 001
1915	1 644 411	376 879	864 320	108 000	25 000	2 699	771 917	169 039	64 202	1 670 500	79 053
1916	1 325 356	161 943	658 666	65 000	22 000	2 176	772 907	228 659	68 684	1 282 000	59 995
1917	1 736 271	171 897	861 328	89 000	34 000	2 826	831 733	294 409	60 209	1 370 000	91 784
1918	1 336 723	210 456	857 309	147 000	60 000	2 944	909 419	284 310	58 505	2 269 500	85 054
1919	1 542 421	269 969	648 469	54 000	62 000	2 506	793 360	185 107	64 695	1 625 500	63 402
1920	1 939 236	332 128	899 793	89 000	36 000	2 311	1 035 425	172 329	63 660	2 963 500	88 805
1921	1 762 678	214 809	625 490	57 000	36 000	2 159	565 677	177 521	59 268	1 223 000	83 521
1922	1 600 403	246 485	673 246	62 000	54 000	2 053	648 910	134 273	66 443	994 000	104 048
1923	1 684 098	213 778	718 762	62 000	35 000	1 909	821 273	161 460	62 438	894 500	97 605
1924	1 218 424	184 482	835 511	65 000	22 000	1 841	719 913	179 069	63 744	1 327 500	102 513
1025	1 717 761	162 227	841 474	70 000	24 000	1 887	700 030	209 190	55 061	1 731 500	73 783
1926	1 461 332	207 303	686 436	57 000	19 000	2 051	690 135	288 174	53 126	2 418 000	79 609
1927	1 424 215	201 532	626 387	76 000	23 000	2 138	460 941	347 174	58 632	1 467 000	97 900
1928	1 423 978	253 066	760 286	89 000	14 000	1 966	550 763	346 254	58 632	1 548 000	106 329
1929	1 387 581	216 841	642 422	65 000	9 000	1 735	674 509	405 419	61 067	1 236 000	81 869
1930	1 136 675	248 828	742 412	74 000	11 000	1 474	720 395	227 211	52 118	1 089 000	88 928
1931	1 558 153	322 062	655 997	46 000	12 000	1 375	802 903	476 004	52 532	2 197 000	102 523
1932	1 851 594	276 054	767 316	92 000	20 000	1 268	582 179	343 043	58 401	1 800 000	103 471
1933	1 448 293	185 302	458 398	66 000	10 400	1 278	724 785	286 941	52 511	1 977 500	95 440
1934	807 092	146 996	345 177	37 000	6 600	1 272	467 683	214 097	42 382	854 000	110 782
1935	1 385 878	163 703	778 151	166 000	24 500	1 316	427 468	436 117	62 898	750 000	100 863
1936	811 179	128 954	486 046	55 000	12 000	961	402 466	474 419	49 041	668 500	84 496
1937	1 662 090	208 071	708 546	86 000	18 300	999	566 959	490 987	55 501	1 377 000	110 956
1938	1 749 990	250 428	706 730	137 000	26 000	993	420 627	249 310	66 261	711 500	99 667
1939	1 717 214	192 786	602 698	134 300	21 000	600	528 658	255 692	63 520	479 500	93 008
1940	1 534 833	222 709	795 277	170 000	24 500	354	496 601	358 163	67 252	776 000	106 450
1941	1 797 447	253 184	751 016	195 300	22 400	370	381 534	163 826	67 580	861 500	98 884
1942	2 108 096	266 968	874 238	234 500	30 500	632	394 098	236 363	74 973	1 684 642	100 193
1943	1 930 464	294 522	702 858	152 000	13 500 ·	1 031	420 056	155 651	71 039	1 596 279	130 197
1944	2 065 790	338 297	734 449	135 200	9 250	1 314	709 604	162 467	70 180	1 402 046	103 273
1945	1 858 689	342 247	976 631	126 000	6 550	562	585 755	206 510	74 192	1 124 547	120 539
1946	2 136 640	355 957	892 282	110 000	4 000	810	825 947	206 045	69 675	1 320 754	127 932
1947	1 506 271	418 577	733 303	117 300	7 200	725	477 028	223 816	69 777	1 227 318	114 589
1948	2 517 630	351 219	928 377	156 357	8 749	674	458 148	257 719	67 196	1 591 038	100 155
1949	2 056 611	256 400	819 701	107 532	4 807	492	414 604	181 643	69 185	1 374 103	115 282

For crops, unlike livestock (see Table A-44), price series shown are U.S. prices derived by weighting state prices by production or sales in the several states; U.S. crop prices derived by weighting by inventories on farms in the several states were not available for this relatively long period.

Columns 1 to 7, 9 to 11 – 1896–1907: Prices as of Dec. 1 from *Agricultural Statistics*, 1941, tables 1, 34, 49, 75, 94, 139, 151, 223, 335, 413.

        1908–1935: Prices as of Dec. 15, from *Prices Received by Farmers for Crops, Livestock and Livestock Products, 1909–45*, Department of Agriculture, 1946, except for tobacco, and except for Dec. 1, 1908 price for cotton lint in col. 10 which was obtained from Bureau of Agricultural Economics. For tobacco, Dec. prices for 1908-1949 from *Income Parity for Agriculture*, part I, section 2, as revised and brought up to date by Bureau of Agricultural Economics.

        1936–1949: Prices as of Dec. 15, except for tobacco, from Department of Agriculture, Bureau of Agricultural Economics releases, *Crops and Markets*, Jan., 1948 and 1949 editions, and *Agricultural Prices*, issued Dec. 30, 1949. Hay price for 1949 extrapolated from 1948 on basis of price for baled hay.

Column 8 – 1909–1935: Prices as of Dec. 15 from Department of Agriculture, *Prices Received by Farmers for Crops, Livestock and Livestock Products, 1909–45*, 1946. (Dec. 1909 price for peanuts was obtained from Bureau of Agricultural Economics.)

        1936–1949: Prices as of Dec. 15, from Department of Agriculture, Bureau of Agricultural Economics releases, *Crops and Markets*, Jan. 1948, and 1949 editions, and *Agricultural Prices*, issued Dec. 30, 1949.

1896 to 1949

dollars

End of year	Corn	Wheat	Oats	Barley	Rye	Buck-wheat	Tobacco	Peanuts	Hay	Cotton lint	Potatoes
			per bushel				per pound		per ton	per pound	per bushel
	1	2	3	4	5	6	7	8	9	10	11
1896	0.214	0.721	0.183	0.296	0.369	0.390	0.055	.	7.60	0.0666	0.290
1897	0.260	0.809	0.210	0.343	0.426	0.419	0.074	.	7.21	0.0668	0.553
1898	0.285	0.579	0.251	0.389	0.441	0.448	0.061	.	6.52	0.0573	0.422
1899	0.298	0.588	0.245	0.388	0.495	0.561	0.071	.	8.20	0.0698	0.401
1900	0.350	0.621	0.253	0.407	0.501	0.558	0.067	.	9.78	0.0915	0.430
1901	0.600	0.631	0.397	0.454	0.550	0.563	0.072	.	9.88	0.0703	0.767
1902	0.401	0.630	0.305	0.453	0.500	0.595	0.069	.	9.05	0.0760	0.474
1903	0.419	0.693	0.337	0.447	0.535	0.608	0.067	.	9.18	0.1049	0.612
1904	0.436	0.926	0.309	0.412	0.692	0.625	0.078	.	8.82	0.0898	0.453
1905	0.406	0.747	0.288	0.394	0.603	0.583	0.082	.	8.49	0.1078	0.612
1906	0.391	0.660	0.317	0.418	0.585	0.594	0.096	.	10.40	0.0958	0.507
1907	0.505	0.866	0.444	. 0.665	0.726	0.699	0.100	.	11.60	0.1036	0.608
1908	0.606	0.932	0.476	0.560	0.735	0.750	0.102	.	9.06	0.0869	0.713
1909	0.601	1.010	0.415	0.558	0.733	0.700	0.101	0.045	10.48	0.1430	0.550
1910	0.481	0.884	0.338	0.588	0.724	0.660	0.083	0.045	11.92	0.1420	0.549
1911	0.620	0.877	0.450	0.866	0.830	0.732	0.095	0.044	14.02	0.0860	0.822
1912	0.488	0.761	0.320	0.502	0.650	0.664	0.099	0.046	11.45	0.1210	0.506
1913	0.694	0.804	0.392	0.530	0.630	0.760	0.104	0.048	12.06	0.1200	0.686
1914	0.653	1.032	0.444	0.543	0.884	0.772	0.081	0.043	10.80	0.0670	0.492
1915	0.598	0.974	0.376	0.532	0.844	0.801	0.087	0.042	9.97	0.1130	0.662
1916	0.894	1.553	0.519	0.876	1.203	1.150	0.142	0.047	10.74	0.1840	1.467
1917	1.314	2.014	0.702	1.201	1.682	1.614	0.216	0.071	17.32	0.2830	1.219
1918	1.406	2.045	0.708	0.915	1.512	1.647	0.258	0.061	19.64	0.2810	1.177
1919	1.374	2.234	0.743	1.254	1.428	1.484	0.306	0.091	20.00	0.3570	1.690
1920	0.668	1.464	0.458	0.678	1.258	1.268	0.157	0.047	16.43	0.1260	1.100
1921	0.428	0.930	0.306	0.428	0.696	0.824	0.187	0.035	11.29	0.1620	1.094
1922	0.676	1.032	0.403	0.556	0.707	0.890	0.202	0.050	11.82	0.2410	0.588
1923	0.722	0.945	0.426	0.576	0.639	0.947	0.176	0.062	13.15	0.3202	0.815
1924	1.056	1.411	0.506	0.762	1.127	1.046	0.187	0.056	12.69	0.2225	0.641
1925	0.707	1.537	0.391	0.584	0.868	0.879	0.169	0.041	13.40	0.1707	2.015
1926	0.645	1.228	0.411	0.564	0.824	0.835	0.141	0.047	13.47	0.1006	1.370
1927	0.751	1.139	0.481	0.715	0.878	0.810	0.196	0.052	10.55	0.1876	0.941
1928	0.761	0.982	0.425	0.550	0.872	0.887	0.222	0.051	11.23	0.1807	0.577
1929	0.780	1.081	0.436	0.546	0.884	0.959	0.191	0.038	11.04	0.1606	1.353
1930	0.649	0.613	0.323	0.388	0.411	0.797	0.147	0.032	11.33	0.0873	0.898
1931	0.345	0.441	0.230	0.357	0.368	0.419	0.085	0.014	8.71	0.0549	0.457
1932	0.188	0.316	0.130	0.193	0.211	0.383	0.114	0.012	6.14	0.0538	0.368
1933	0.420	0.673	0.314	0.406	0.519	0.513	0.105	0.026	7.69	0.0966	0.692
1934	0.853	0.906	0.539	0.797	0.744	0.561	0.148	0.033	13.86	0.1245	0.449
1935	0.530	0.889	0.255	0.375	0.400	0.516	0.152	0.030	7.20	0.1137	0.637
1936	0.956	1.145	0.484	0.861	0.900	0.797	0.246	0.036	11.08	0.1237	1.062
1937	0.485	0.836	0.291	0.508	0.592	0.643	0.170	0.032	8.79	0.0800	0.530
1938	0.431	0.536	0.244	0.365	0.323	0.529	0.162	0.033	6.81	0.0863	0.613
1939	0.503	0.824	0.347	0.438	0.523	0.617	0.154	0.034	7.71	0.0943	0.708
1940	0.545	0.715	0.323	0.416	0.413	0.542	0.158	0.032	7.53	0.0938	0.547
1941	0.669	1.022	0.452	0.561	0.578	0.649	0.232	0.048	9.43	0.1635	0.827
1942	0.802	1.103	0.474	0.622	0.563	0.796	0.317	0.062	10.46	0.1955	1.116
1943	1.110	1.430	0.769	1.050	1.070	1.320	0.407	0.071	15.20	0.1985	1.350
1944	1.060	1.450	0.694	0.982	1.060	0.973	0.424	0.082	16.50	0.2085	1.500
1945	1.090	1.540	0.703	1.080	1.430	1.240	0.426	0.083	15.40	0.2280	1.350
1946	1.220	1.930	0.808	1.360	2.180	1.450	0.413	0.089	17.70	0.2998	1.260
1947	2.370	2.790	1.180	2.000	2.450	2.010	0.443	0.101	18.10	0.3405	1.720
1948	1.230	2.050	0.765	1.130	1.470	1.100	0.396	0.105	19.10	0.2964	1.540
1949	1.130	1.930	0.699	1.090	1.260	0.902	0.409	0.104	17.60	0.2650	1.310

Column 1 – Sum of cols. 2–12 plus step-up of 5 percent of this total in order to adjust series for omission of corn silage and forage and sorghums for silage and forage for which long-time quantity and price series are not available.

Columns 2 to 11 – Quantities from Table A-33 multiplied by prices for corresponding crop and year from Table A-34.

Column 12 – Includes buckwheat and rice (1896–1949); dry edible beans, flaxseed, and cottonseed (1909–1949); and soybeans (1928–1949). (For buckwheat the data were taken from Tables A-33 and A-34.) A series of each of these crops was derived by multiplying quantities by prices similarly to cols. 2–11. Quantity series for 1909–1949 for these crops, except soybeans, derived from same sources as described in Table A-33, col. 10; for soybeans for 1928–1941, as described for 1909–1932 in Table A-33, col. 4, and for 1942–1949 from *Agricultural Statistics*, 1947 (table 188) and Bureau of Agricultural Economics releases on *Crop Production, Jan. 1, 1948, 1949* and *1950*. Quantity series for rice 1896–1908 obtained from regression line $y = -1497.2 + 0.343834x$ fitted to 1909–1913 data where x represents production (figures from *Agricultural Statistics*, 1941, p. 102) and y end-of-year stocks (*Income Parity for Agriculture*, part I, section 12). Price series for dry edible beans, flaxseed, cottonseed, and soybeans derived from same sources as described in Table A-34, col. 8. Prices for rice derived as follows: 1896–1903, estimated farm price per bushel for calendar year as given in Strauss, F. and Bean, L., *Gross Farm Income and Indices of Farm Production and Prices in the United States, 1869–1937*, p. 71, converted to Dec. 31 prices by arithmetic averaging and linked in 1904 to Dec. 1 prices as given in *Agricultural Statistics*, 1941, p. 102; 1904–1923, *Agricultural Statistics*, 1941, p. 102; 1924–1929, Bureau of Agricultural Economics estimates; 1930–1935, Dec. 15 prices from Department of Agriculture, *Prices Received by Farmers for Crops, Livestock and Livestock Products, 1909–45*, 1946; 1936–1949, Dec. 15 prices from *Crops and Markets, Jan. 1948* and *1949* editions, and *Agricultural Prices*, issued Dec. 30, 1949.

Note: For comparison with *Balance Sheet of Agriculture*, see note to Table A-31.

CROP INVENTORIES; VALUE ON FARMS

Current Prices: 1896 to 1949

$ mill.

End of year	Adjusted total	Corn	Wheat	Oats	Barley	Rye	Tobacco	Peanuts	Hay	Cotton lint	Potatoes	Miscel- laneous
	1	2	3	4	5	6	7	8	9	10	11	12
1896	1 031	330	127	88	13	7	29	–	295	71	21	1
1897	1 135	316	173	105	17	8	36	–	303	89	32	2
1898	1 216	366	197	127	18	8	40	–	293	79	28	2
1899	1 284	400	164	136	24	8	44	–	335	81	29	2
1900	1 420	480	141	141	18	9	41	–	375	114	30	3
1901	1 546	494	177	182	31	11	46	–	398	83	46	4
1902	1 681	599	170	195	39	10	48	–	399	99	37	5
1903	1 646	539	148	175	40	10	47	–	431	127	45	6
1904	1 764	612	162	188	43	13	48	–	424	145	40	5
1905	1 820	632	190	192	43	12	56	–	414	140	48	6
1906	1 960	661	213	196	48	11	68	–	467	153	44	6
1907	2 101	695	199	209	61	13	63	–	563	140	51	7
1908	2 203	862	200	231	61	13	59	–	470	138	56	8
1909	2 539	855	255	249	59	14	76	6	645	174	53	32
1910	2 409	783	220	223	52	14	72	7	645	202	45	31
1911	2 443	844	168	230	74	15	67	6	666	159	65	33
1912	2 588	867	185	266	68	16	79	6	697	199	51	31
1913	2 569	917	191	243	51	14	65	7	666	207	60	26
1914	2 670	932	252	276	52	21	57	6	634	235	47	31
1915	2 882	983	367	325	57	21	67	7	640	189	52	37
1916	3 247	1 185	251	342	57	26	110	11	738	236	88	48
1917	5 498	2 281	346	605	107	57	180	21	1 043	388	112	96
1918	5 650	1 879	430	607	135	91	235	17	1 149	638	100	100
1919	5 722	2 119	345	482	68	89	243	17	1 294	580	107	106
1920	4 245	1 296	486	412	60	45	163	8	1 046	373	98	56
1921	2 409	755	200	191	24	25	106	6	669	198	91	29
1922	3 088	1 082	254	271	34	38	131	7	785	240	61	38
1923	3 327	1 216	202	306	36	22	145	10	821	286	80	45
1924	3 579	1 287	260	423	50	25	135	10	809	295	66	49
1925	3 385	1 214	249	320	41	21	119	9	738	296	149	59
1926	2 905	943	255	282	32	16	97	14	716	243	109	60
1927	3 064	1 070	230	301	54	20	90	18	721	275	92	47
1928	3 067	1 084	249	323	49	12	122	18	658	280	61	65
1929	2 973	1 082	234	280	35	8	129	15	674	198	111	65
1930	2 197	738	153	240	29	4	106	7	590	95	80	50
1931	1 664	538	142	151	16	4	68	7	458	121	47	33
1932	1 201	348	87	100	18	4	66	4	359	97	38	23
1933	1 777	608	125	144	27	5	76	8	404	191	66	38
1934	2 007	689	133	186	29	5	69	7	587	106	50	50
1935	1 968	734	146	198	62	10	65	13	453	85	64	44
1936	2 216	776	148	235	47	11	99	17	543	83	90	61
1937	2 176	807	174	206	44	11	96	16	488	110	59	61
1938	1 906	754	134	172	50	8	68	8	451	61	61	48
1939	2 171	864	159	209	59	11	81	9	490	45	66	75
1940	2 264	837	159	257	71	10	79	12	506	73	58	94
1941	3 190	1 203	259	339	110	13	89	8	637	141	82	157
1942	4 364	1 691	295	414	146	17	125	15	784	329	112	228
1943	5 474	2 142	421	540	160	14	171	11	1 080	317	176	181
1944	5 679	2 190	491	510	133	10	301	13	1 158	292	155	156
1945	5 632	2 026	527	687	136	9	250	17	1 143	256	163	150
1946	6 833	2 607	687	721	150	9	341	18	1 233	396	161	185
1947	8 745	3 570	1 168	865	235	18	211	23	1 263	418	197	361
1948	7 530	3 097	720	710	177	13	181	27	1 283	472	154	337
1949	5 959	2 324	495	573	117	6	170	19	1 218	364	151	238

A-36

TABLE A-36

Column 1 – Sum of cols. 2–12 raised 5 percent (see note to Table A-35, col. 1).

Columns 2 to 11 – Quantities from Table A-33 multiplied by 1929 price for corresponding crop from Table A-34.

Column 12 – Includes buckwheat and rice (1896–1949); dry edible beans, flaxseed, and cottonseed (1909–1949); and soybeans (1928–1949). Series for each of these crops derived similarly to cols. 2–11 (see note to Table A-35, col. 12).

A-37

TABLE A-37

Columns 1 to 12 – From Table A-35, by subtracting value at end of preceding year from corresponding value at end of current year.

A-38

TABLE A-38

Columns 1 to 12 – From Table A-36, by subtracting value at end of preceding year from corresponding value at end of current year.

A-39

TABLE A-39

Column 1 – Sum of cols. 2–12 raised 5 percent (see note to Table A-35, col. 1).

Columns 2 to 11 – Annual change in quantity calculated from Table A-33, multiplied by end-of-year price for corresponding crop from Table A-34.

Column 12 – Includes buckwheat and rice (1897–1949); dry edible beans, flaxseed, and cottonseed (1910–1949); and soybeans (1929–1949). Series for each of these crops derived similarly to cols. 2–11 (see note to Table A-35, col. 12).

Note: For comparison with Bureau of Agricultural Economics and Commerce Department estimates see note to Table A-32.

804

CROP INVENTORIES; VALUE ON FARMS
1929 Prices: 1896 to 1949
$ mill.

End of year	Adjusted total	Corn	Wheat	Oats	Barley	Rye	Tobacco	Peanuts	Hay	Cotton lint	Potatoes	Miscel-laneous
	1	2	3	4	5	6	7	8	9	10	11	12
1896	2 565	1 202	191	209	25	17	102	–	428	171	95	3
1897	2 408	948	231	217	27	17	93	–	464	214	78	4
1898	2 696	1 004	368	220	25	16	125	–	496	221	89	4
1899	2 622	1 047	301	242	34	15	119	–	451	186	98	4
1900	2 559	1 070	245	244	24	16	116	–	423	200	94	5
1901	2 144	642	304	200	37	17	121	–	445	189	80	7
1902	2 878	1 165	291	279	48	18	133	–	486	209	105	7
1903	2 606	1 004	231	227	49	16	135	–	518	195	99	8
1904	2 790	1 094	190	265	57	16	117	–	531	259	119	9
1905	2 989	1 215	275	291	60	17	129	–	538	208	106	8
1906	3 180	1 319	349	269	63	17	135	–	495	257	117	8
1907	2 722	1 074	248	205	50	16	121	–	536	218	115	9
1908	2 818	1 109	232	212	59	16	111	–	573	256	107	9
1909	3 061	1 110	273	261	57	17	144	5	679	196	130	43
1910	3 191	1 270	270	287	49	17	166	6	597	228	111	38
1911	2 808	1 062	207	222	46	16	135	5	524	297	107	53
1912	3 561	1 385	263	362	74	22	152	5	672	264	136	56
1913	2 940	1 031	257	270	52	19	120	5	610	277	118	41
1914	3 415	1 113	263	271	52	21	135	6	648	562	130	51
1915	3 599	1 283	407	377	59	22	147	6	709	268	107	43
1916	2 932	1 034	175	287	35	19	148	9	758	206	81	40
1917	3 392	1 354	186	376	49	30	159	11	665	220	124	56
1918	3 312	1 043	227	374	80	53	174	11	646	364	115	67
1919	3 302	1 203	292	283	29	55	152	7	714	261	86	63
1920	4 111	1 513	359	392	49	32	198	7	703	476	120	66
1921	3 211	1 375	232	273	31	32	108	7	654	196	113	37
1922	3 250	1 248	266	294	34	48	124	5	734	160	141	41
1923	3 256	1 314	231	313	34	31	157	6	689	144	132	50
1924	2 960	950	199	364	35	19	138	7	704	213	139	51
1925	3 288	1 340	175	367	38	21	135	8	608	278	100	61
1926	3 160	1 140	224	299	31	17	132	11	587	388	108	73
1927	3 090	1 111	218	273	41	20	88	13	755	236	132	56
1928	3 147	1 111	274	331	49	12	105	13	647	249	144	62
1929	2 974	1 082	234	280	35	8	129	15	674	198	111	66
1930	2 752	887	269	324	40	10	138	9	575	175	120	74
1931	3 374	1 215	348	286	25	11	153	18	580	353	139	85
1932	3 593	1 444	298	335	50	18	111	13	645	289	140	79
1933	2 968	1 130	200	200	36	9	138	11	580	318	129	76
1934	1 988	629	159	150	20	6	89	8	468	137	150	77
1935	2 995	1 081	177	339	91	22	82	17	694	120	136	93
1936	2 056	633	139	212	30	11	77	18	541	107	114	76
1937	3 280	1 297	225	309	47	16	108	19	613	222	150	118
1938	3 378	1 365	270	308	75	23	80	10	732	114	135	105
1939	3 206	1 340	208	263	73	19	101	10	701	77	126	135
1940	3 365	1 197	241	347	93	22	95	14	742	125	144	185
1941	3 575	1 402	274	327	107	20	73	6	746	138	134	178
1942	4 224	1 644	289	381	128	27	75	9	828	270	136	236
1943	3 876	1 506	318	306	83	12	80	6	784	256	176	164
1944	3 971	1 611	366	320	74	8	136	6	775	225	140	121
1945	3 909	1 450	370	426	69	6	112	8	819	181	163	119
1946	4 121	1 667	384	389	60	4	158	8	769	212	173	101
1947	3 573	1 175	452	320	64	6	91	9	770	197	155	164
1948	4 514	1 963	380	405	85	8	88	10	742	256	136	226
1949	3 901	1 604	277	357	59	4	79	7	764	221	156	187

CROP INVENTORIES; ANNUAL CHANGE IN VALUE ON FARMS
Current Prices: 1897 to 1949

$ mill.

Year	Adjusted total	Corn	Wheat	Oats	Barley	Rye	Tobacco	Peanuts	Hay	Cotton lint	Potatoes	Miscel-laneous
	1	2	3	4	5	6	7	8	9	10	11	12
1897	104	−14	46	17	4	1	7	0	8	18	11	1
1898	81	51	24	22	1	0	4	0	−10	−10	−4	0
1899	68	33	−33	9	6	0	4	0	42	2	1	0
1900	136	80	−23	5	−6	1	−3	0	40	33	1	1
1901	126	14	36	41	13	2	5	0	23	−31	16	1
1902	135	105	−7	13	8	−1	2	0	1	16	−9	1
1903	−35	−60	−22	−20	1	0	−1	0	32	28	8	1
1904	118	73	14	13	3	3	1	0	−7	18	−5	−1
1905	56	20	28	4	0	−1	8	0	−10	−5	8	1
1906	140	29	23	4	5	−1	12	0	53	13	−4	0
1907	141	34	−14	13	13	2	−5	0	96	−13	7	1
1908	102	167	1	22	0	0	−4	0	−93	−2	5	1
1909	336	−7	55	18	−2	1	17	6	175	36	−3	24
1910	−130	−72	−35	−26	−7	0	−4	1	0	28	−8	−1
1911	34	61	−52	7	22	1	−5	−1	21	−43	20	2
1912	145	23	17	36	−6	1	12	0	31	40	−14	−2
1913	−19	50	6	−23	−17	−2	−14	1	−31	8	9	−5
1914	101	15	61	33	1	7	−8	−1	−32	28	−13	5
1915	212	51	115	49	5	0	10	1	6	−46	5	6
1916	365	202	−116	17	0	5	43	4	98	47	36	11
1917	2 251	1 096	95	263	50	31	70	10	305	152	24	48
1918	152	−402	84	2	28	34	55	−4	106	250	−12	4
1919	72	240	−85	−125	−67	−2	8	0	145	−58	7	6
1920	−1 477	−823	141	−70	−8	−44	−80	−9	−248	−207	−9	−50
1921	−1 836	−541	−286	−221	−36	−20	−57	−2	−377	−175	−7	−27
1922	679	327	54	80	10	13	25	1	116	42	−30	9
1923	239	134	−52	35	2	−16	14	3	36	46	19	7
1924	252	71	58	117	14	3	−10	0	−12	9	−14	4
1925	−194	−73	−11	−94	−9	−4	−16	−1	−71	1	83	10
1926	−480	−271	6	−47	−9	−5	−22	5	−22	−53	40	1
1927	159	127	−25	19	22	4	−7	4	5	32	−17	−13
1928	3	14	19	22	−5	−8	32	0	−63	5	−31	18
1929	−94	−2	−15	−43	−14	−4	7	−3	16	−82	50	0
1930	−776	−344	−81	−40	−6	−4	−23	−8	−84	−103	−31	−15
1931	−533	−200	−11	−89	−13	0	−38	0	−132	26	−33	−17
1932	−463	−190	−55	−51	2	0	−2	−3	−99	−24	−9	−10
1933	576	260	38	44	9	1	10	4	45	94	28	15
1934	230	81	8	42	2	0	−7	−1	183	−85	−16	12
1935	−39	45	13	12	33	5	−4	6	−134	−21	14	−6
1936	248	42	2	37	−15	1	34	4	90	−2	26	17
1937	−40	31	26	−29	−3	0	−3	−1	−55	27	−31	0
1938	−270	−53	−40	−34	6	−3	−28	−8	−37	−49	2	−13
1939	265	110	25	37	9	3	13	1	39	−16	5	27
1940	93	−27	0	48	12	−1	−2	3	16	28	−8	19
1941	926	366	100	82	39	3	10	−4	131	68	24	63
1942	1 174	488	36	75	36	4	36	7	147	188	30	71
1943	1 110	451	126	126	14	−3	46	−4	296	−12	64	−47
1944	205	48	70	−30	−27	−4	130	2	78	−25	−21	−25
1945	−47	−164	36	177	3	−1	−51	4	−15	−36	8	−6
1946	1 201	581	160	34	14	0	91	1	90	140	−2	35
1947	1 912	963	481	144	85	9	−130	5	30	22	36	176
1948	−1 215	−473	−448	−155	−58	−5	−30	4	20	54	−43	−24
1949	−1 571	−773	−225	−137	−60	−7	−11	−8	−65	−108	−3	−99

CROP INVENTORIES; ANNUAL CHANGE IN VALUE ON FARMS A-38
1929 Prices: 1897 to 1949

$ mill.

Year	Adjusted total	Corn	Wheat	Oats	Barley	Rye	Tobacco	Peanuts	Hay	Cotton lint	Potatoes	Miscellaneous
	1	2	3	4	5	6	7	8	9	10	11	12
1897	-157	-254	40	8	2	0	-9	–	36	43	-17	1
1898	288	56	137	3	-2	-1	32	–	32	7	11	0
1899	-74	43	-67	22	9	-1	-6	–	-45	-35	9	0
1900	-63	23	-56	2	-10	1	-3	–	-28	14	-4	1
1901	-415	-428	59	-44	13	1	5	–	22	-11	-14	2
1902	734	523	-13	79	11	1	12	–	41	20	25	0
1903	-272	-161	-60	-52	1	-2	2	–	32	-14	-6	1
1904	184	90	-41	38	8	0	-18	–	13	64	20	1
1905	199	121	85	26	3	1	12	–	7	-51	-13	-1
1906	191	104	74	-22	3	0	6	–	-43	49	11	0
1907	-458	-245	-101	-64	-13	-1	-14	–	41	-39	-2	1
1908	96	35	-16	7	9	0	-10	–	37	38	-8	0
1909	243	1	41	49	-2	1	33	5	106	-60	23	34
1910	130	160	-3	26	-8	0	22	1	-82	32	-19	-5
1911	-383	-208	-63	-65	-3	-1	-31	-1	-73	69	-4	15
1912	753	323	56	140	28	6	17	0	148	-33	29	3
1913	-621	-354	-6	-92	-22	-3	-32	0	-62	13	-18	-15
1914	475	82	6	1	0	2	15	1	38	285	12	10
1915	184	170	144	106	7	1	12	0	61	-294	-23	-8
1916	-667	-249	-232	-90	-24	-3	1	3	49	-62	-26	-3
1917	460	320	11	89	14	11	11	2	-93	14	43	16
1918	-80	-311	41	-2	31	23	15	0	-19	144	-9	11
1919	-10	160	65	-91	-51	2	-22	-4	68	-103	-29	-4
1920	809	310	67	109	20	-23	46	0	-11	215	34	3
1921	-900	-138	-127	-119	-18	0	-90	0	-49	-280	-7	-29
1922	39	-127	34	21	3	16	16	-2	80	-36	28	4
1923	6	66	-35	19	0	-17	33	1	-45	-16	-9	9
1924	-296	-364	-32	51	1	-12	-19	1	15	69	7	1
1925	328	390	-24	3	3	2	-3	1	-96	65	-39	10
1926	-128	-200	49	-68	-7	-4	-3	3	-21	110	8	12
1927	-70	-29	-6	-26	10	3	-44	2	168	-152	24	-17
1928	57	0	56	58	8	-8	17	0	-108	13	12	6
1929	-173	-29	-40	-51	-14	-4	24	2	27	-51	-33	4
1930	-222	-195	35	44	5	2	9	-6	-99	-23	9	8
1931	622	328	79	-38	-15	1	15	9	5	178	19	11
1932	219	229	-50	49	25	7	-42	-5	65	-64	1	-6
1933	-625	-314	-98	-135	-14	-9	27	-2	-65	29	-11	-3
1934	-980	-501	-41	-50	-16	-3	-49	-3	-112	-181	21	1
1935	1 007	452	18	189	71	16	-7	9	226	-17	-14	16
1936	-939	-448	-38	-127	-61	-11	-5	1	-153	-13	-22	-17
1937	1 224	664	86	97	17	5	31	1	72	115	36	42
1938	98	68	45	-1	28	7	-28	-9	119	-108	-15	-13
1939	-172	-25	-62	-45	-2	-4	21	0	-31	-37	-9	30
1940	159	-143	33	84	20	3	-6	4	41	48	18	50
1941	210	205	33	-20	14	-2	-22	-8	4	13	-10	-7
1942	649	242	15	54	21	7	2	3	82	132	2	58
1943	-348	-138	29	-75	-45	-15	5	-3	-44	-14	40	-72
1944	95	105	48	14	-9	-4	56	0	-9	-31	-36	-43
1945	-62	-161	4	106	-5	-2	-24	2	44	-44	23	-2
1946	212	217	14	-37	-9	-2	46	0	-50	31	10	-18
1947	-548	-492	68	-69	4	2	-67	1	1	-15	-18	63
1948	941	788	-72	85	21	2	-3	1	-28	59	-19	62
1949	-613	-359	-103	-48	-26	-4	-9	-3	22	-35	20	-39

CROP INVENTORIES; ANNUAL CHANGE IN QUANTITY ON FARMS
VALUED AT END-OF-YEAR PRICES: 1897 to 1949

$ mill.

Year	Adjusted total	Corn	Wheat	Oats	Barley	Rye	Tobacco	Peanuts	Hay	Cotton lint	Potatoes	Miscellaneous
	1	2	3	4	5	6	7	8	9	10	11	12
1897	−19	−85	30	4	2	0	−3	−	23	18	−7	0
1898	136	20	74	2	−1	0	10	−	19	2	4	0
1899	−51	17	−37	12	7	−1	−2	−	−33	−15	3	0
1900	−50	10	−32	1	−8	0	−1	−	−25	8	−1	0
1901	−328	−329	34	−40	11	1	2	−	20	−5	−8	2
1902	403	269	−8	55	9	1	4	−	34	10	9	1
1903	−155	−87	−38	−40	1	−1	1	−	26	−9	−2	1
1904	97	50	−36	27	6	0	−8	−	10	36	7	0
1905	119	63	59	17	2	1	5	−	5	−34	−6	1
1906	85	52	45	−16	3	0	3	−	−40	29	4	1
1907	−326	−158	−81	−65	−16	0	−7	−	42	−25	−1	1
1908	76	27	−14	7	10	0	−5	−	30	21	−4	0
1909	167	1	38	47	−2	1	18	−	101	−54	9	0
1910	50	99	−3	20	−9	0	9	1	−89	29	−7	−2
1911	−371	−165	−51	−67	−3	−1	−15	−1	−93	37	−2	8
1912	548	203	40	102	25	5	9	0	153	−25	11	−1
1913	−544	−316	−5	−83	−21	−2	−17	0	−68	10	−9	−7
1914	261	68	6	1	0	2	6	0	38	119	4	5
1915	201	130	130	91	6	1	6	1	55	−207	−11	−11
1916	−863	−285	−334	−107	−38	−4	0	3	48	−71	−28	−6
1917	749	540	20	142	29	20	13	5	−147	25	39	27
1918	−153	−562	79	−3	53	39	20	−1	−33	253	−8	17
1919	−47	283	133	−155	−117	3	−36	−9	124	−230	−37	−4
1920	717	265	91	115	24	−33	38	−1	−17	169	28	4
1921	−771	−76	−109	−84	−14	0	−88	0	−50	−282	−6	−25
1922	21	−110	33	19	3	13	17	−2	85	−55	12	5
1923	−17	60	−31	19	0	−12	30	2	−53	−32	−5	6
1924	−410	−492	−41	59	2	−15	−19	1	17	96	3	−1
1925	243	353	−34	2	3	2	−2	1	−116	69	−58	11
1926	−129	−165	55	−64	−7	−4	−2	4	−26	69	8	9
1927	−112	−28	−7	−29	14	4	−45	3	161	−178	17	−19
1928	42	0	51	57	7	−8	20	0	−109	15	5	2
1929	−170	−28	−39	−51	−13	−4	24	2	27	−50	−33	3
1930	−219	−163	20	32	3	1	7	−6	−101	−13	6	5
1931	243	145	32	−20	−10	0	7	3	4	61	6	3
1932	54	55	−15	14	9	2	−25	−2	36	−21	0	−2
1933	−384	−169	−61	−97	−11	−5	15	−1	−45	17	−6	−3
1934	−1 030	−547	−35	−61	−23	−3	−38	−2	−140	−140	7	1
1935	652	307	15	110	48	7	−6	7	148	−12	−6	3
1936	−1 090	−549	−40	−141	−96	−11	−6	1	−154	−10	−17	−15
1937	781	413	66	65	16	4	28	1	57	57	14	23
1938	52	38	23	0	19	2	−24	−8	73	−57	−7	−9
1939	−123	−16	−47	−36	−1	−3	17	0	−21	−22	−5	17
1940	100	−99	21	62	15	1	−5	3	28	28	7	34
1941	175	176	31	−20	14	−1	−27	−9	3	14	−6	−8
1942	687	249	15	58	24	5	4	4	77	161	1	56
1943	−532	−197	39	−132	−87	−18	11	−6	−60	−18	41	−80
1944	208	143	63	22	−16	−5	123	1	−14	−40	−40	−39
1945	−104	−226	6	170	−10	−4	−53	4	62	−63	23	−8
1946	333	339	26	−68	−22	−6	99	0	−80	59	9	−39
1947	−1 631	−1 494	175	−188	15	8	−155	2	2	−32	−23	137
1948	1 492	1 244	−138	149	44	2	−7	4	−49	108	−22	86
1949	−951	−521	−183	−76	−53	−5	−18	−8	35	−57	20	−40

CROP INVENTORIES; CORN AND WHEAT STORED ON FARMS
UNDER COMMODITY CREDIT CORPORATION LOANS: 1933 to 1949

End of year	Quantity		Current price		Value at current prices		Value at 1929 prices	
	Corn	Wheat	Corn	Wheat	Corn	Wheat	Corn	Wheat
	000 bushels		$ per bushel		$ mill.			
	1	α. 2	3	4	5	6	7	8
1933	32 352	–	0.420	0.673	14	–	25	–
1934	21 297	–	0.853	0.906	18	–	17	–
1935	14 613	–	0.530	0.889	8	–	11	–
1936	121	–	0.956	1.145	0	–	0	–
1937	9 100	–	0.485	0.836	4	–	7	–
1938	64 946	23 832	0.431	0 536	28	13	51	26
1939	191 440	36 588	0.503	0.824	96	30	149	40
1940	301 055	57 261	0.545	0.715	164	41	235	62
1941	204 843	118 591	0.669	1.022	137	121	160	128
1942	106 214	217 786	0.802	1.103	85	240	83	235
1943	2 398	87 829	1.110	1.430	3	126	2	95
1944	1 196	46 341	1.060	1.450	1	67	1	50
1945	271	18 784	1.090	1.540	0	29	0	20
1946	0	9 837	1.220	1.930	0	19	0	11
1947	12	10 089	2.370	2.790	0	28	0	11
1948	30 282	40 160	1.230	2.050	37	82	24	43
1949	344 668	70 830	1.130	1.930	389	137	269	77

Columns 1 and 2 – Estimates from Commodity Credit Corporation.

Columns 3 and 4 – From Table A-34, cols. 1 and 2.

Columns 5 and 6 – Cols. 1 and 2 multiplied by cols. 3 and 4.

Columns 7 and 8 – Cols. 1 and 2 multiplied by 1929 price from Table A-34, cols. 1 and 2.

Livestock inventory data published by U.S. Department of Agriculture for Jan. 1 are used here for Dec. 31 of previous year.

Columns 1 to 4 – 1896–1929: From Department of Agriculture, Bureau of Agricultural Economics, *Livestock on Farms, January 1, 1867–1935*, Jan. 1938.
   1930–1949: From Department of Agriculture, Bureau of Agricultural Economics, *Livestock on Farms, January 1*, issued Feb. 18, 1948 and Feb. 15, 1951. Cattle includes animals kept for milk and other cattle.

Column 5 – 1896–1922: Sum of cols. 6 and 7.
   1923–1939: From Department of Agriculture, *Meat Animals, Farm Production and Income, 1924–1944*, Sept. 1947.
   1940–1949: From Department of Agriculture, Bureau of Agricultural Economics, *Livestock on Farms, January 1*, issued Feb. 18, 1948, and Feb. 15, 1951.

Columns 6 and 7 – 1896–1928: From Department of Agriculture, Bureau of Agricultural Economics, *Livestock on Farms, January 1, 1867–1935*, Jan. 1938.
   1929–1947: From *Agricultural Statistics*, 1949, table 466.
   1948–1949: From Department of Agriculture, Bureau of Agricultural Economics, *Livestock on Farms, January 1*, issued Feb. 15, 1951.

Column 8 – 1896–1907: From Table A-42, col. 6.
   1908–1929: From Department of Agriculture, Bureau of Agricultural Economics, *Farm Production and Disposition of Chickens and Eggs, 1909–1924* and *1925–1937*, June 1939 and Dec. 1938.
   1930–1949: From Department of Agriculture, Bureau of Agricultural Economics, *Livestock on Farms, January 1*, issued Feb. 18, 1948 and Feb. 15, 1951.

Column 9 – 1928–1929: From Department of Agriculture, Bureau of Agricultural Economics, *Farm Production, Disposition and Income: Turkeys, 1929–1939*, April 1942.
   1930–1949: From Department of Agriculture, Bureau of Agricultural Economics, *Livestock on Farms, January 1*, issued Feb. 18, 1948 and Feb. 15, 1951.

LIVESTOCK INVENTORIES; NUMBER OF HEAD ON FARMS
1896 to 1949

thous.

End of year	All cattle	Hogs	Horses	Mules	All sheep	Stock sheep	Sheep and lambs on feed	Chickens	Turkeys
	1	2	3	4	5	6	7	8	9
1896	50 447	51 232	17 803	2 836	41 101	38 891	2 210	268 948	.
1897	52 868	53 282	17 698	2 918	43 222	40 097	3 125	268 368	.
1898	55 927	51 558	17 728	3 012	45 813	42 688	3 125	268 518	.
1899	59 739	51 055	17 856	3 139	48 105	45 065	3 040	288 787	.
1900	62 576	50 681	17 955	3 190	49 101	46 126	2 975	298 376	.
1901	64 418	47 858	17 968	3 264	49 236	46 196	3 040	291 932	.
1902	66 004	48 100	18 121	3 353	47 536	44 436	3 100	304 607	.
1903	66 442	51 623	18 331	3 465	45 458	41 908	3 550	309 495	.
1904	66 111	53 176	18 491	3 586	43 825	40 410	3 415	313 631	.
1905	65 009	53 633	18 806	3 680	45 525	41 965	3 560	329 453	.
1906	63 754	56 543	19 090	3 814	47 260	43 460	3 800	354 359	.
1907	61 989	58 388	19 444	3 949	48 195	45 095	3 100	342 630	.
1908	60 774	52 508	19 731	4 085	50 793	47 098	3 695	340 200	.
1909	58 993	48 072	19 972	4 239	50 239	46 939	3 300	355 988	.
1910	57 225	55 366	20 418	4 429	50 555	46 055	4 500	381 540	.
1911	55 675	55 394	20 726	4 551	47 897	42 972	4 925	367 266	.
1912	56 592	53 747	21 008	4 683	44 652	40 544	4 108	364 670	.
1913	59 461	52 853	21 308	4 870	43 089	38 059	5 030	366 505	.
1914	63 849	56 600	21 431	5 062	40 513	36 263	4 250	379 211	.
1915	67 438	60 596	21 334	5 200	40 010	36 260	3 750	369 458	.
1916	70 979	57 578	21 306	5 353	38 886	35 246	3 640	359 479	.
1917	73 040	62 931	21 238	5 485	39 664	36 704	2 960	363 372	.
1918	72 094	64 326	20 922	5 568	41 875	38 360	3 515	391 364	.
1919	70 400	60 159	20 091	5 651	40 743	37 328	3 415	381 109	.
1920	68 714	58 942	19 369	5 768	39 479	35 426	4 053	370 125	.
1921	68 795	59 849	18 764	5 824	36 922	33 365	3 557	394 950	.
1922	67 546	69 304	18 125	5 893	36 803	32 597	4 206	415 100	.
1923	65 996	66 576	17 378	5 907	37 139	32 859	4 280	434 853	.
1924	63 373	55 770	16 651	5 918	38 543	34 469	4 074	434 998	.
1925	60 576	52 105	16 083	5 903	40 363	35 719	4 644	438 000	.
1926	58 178	55 496	15 388	5 804	42 415	38 067	4 348	460 999	.
1927	57 322	61 873	14 792	5 656	45 258	40 689	4 569	474 997	.
1928	58 877	59 042	14 234	5 510	48 381	43 481	4 900	449 006	5 541
1929	61 003	55 705	13 742	5 382	51 565	45 577	5 988	468 491	5 969
1930	63 030	54 835	13 195	5 273	53 233	47 720	5 513	449 743	5 318
1931	65 801	59 301	12 664	5 148	53 902	47 682	6 220	436 815	5 946
1932	70 280	62 127	12 291	5 046	53 054	47 303	5 751	444 523	6 852
1933	74 369	58 621	12 052	4 945	53 503	48 244	5 259	433 937	6 309
1934	68 846	39 066	11 861	4 822	51 808	46 139	5 669	389 958	5 499
1935	67 847	42 975	11 598	4 628	51 136	45 435	5 701	403 446	5 731
1936	66 098	43 083	11 342	4 460	50 848	45 251	5 597	423 921	6 358
1937	65 249	44 525	10 995	4 250	51 063	44 972	6 091	389 624	6 096
1938	66 029	50 012	10 629	4 163	51 348	45 463	5 885	418 591	6 489
1939	68 309	61 165	10 444	4 034	52 107	46 266	5 841	438 288	8 569
1940	71 755	54 353	10 193	3 911	53 920	47 441	6 479	422 841	7 193
1941	76 025	60 607	9 873	3 782	56 213	49 346	6 867	476 935	7 485
1942	81 204	73 881	9 605	3 626	55 150	48 196	6 954	542 047	6 600
1943	85 334	83 741	9 192	3 421	50 782	44 270	6 512	582 197	7 429
1944	85 573	59 331	8 715	3 235	46 520	39 609	6 911	516 497	7 203
1945	82 434	61 301	8 053	3 010	42 436	35 599	6 837	530 203	8 493
1946	81 207	56 921	7 249	2 772	37 818	32 125	5 693	474 441	6 650
1947	78 126	55 028	6 589	2 541	34 827	29 976	4 851	461 550	4 450
1948	78 298	57 128	5 898	2 348	31 654	27 651	4 003	448 676	5 540
1949	80 052	60 502	5 274	2 149	30 743	27 099	3 644	480 834	5 986

LIVESTOCK INVENTORIES; NUMBER OF CHICKENS ON FARMS
1889 to 1919

thous. (except col. 2)

End of year	Census data	Adjustment (percent)	Adjusted Census data	Cases of eggs received at seven leading markets	Number of chickens on farms	
					Unadjusted	Adjusted
	1	2	3	4	5	6
1889	258 871	−25	194 153	5 000	194 153	.
1890				5 041	195 104	.
1891				5 665	209 629	.
1892				5 672	209 782	.
1893				6 383	226 322	.
1894				6 331	225 114	.
1895				7 240	246 269	.
1896				7 126	243 623	268 948
1897				7 104	243 098	268 368
1898				7 110	243 234	268 518
1899	233 566	12	261 594	7 899	261 594	288 787
1900				8 655	270 280	298 376
1901				8 147	264 443	291 932
1902				9 147	275 925	304 607
1903				9 532	280 352	309 495
1904				9 858	284 099	313 631
1905				11 106	298 431	329 453
1906				13 071	320 992	354 359
1907				12 146	310 367	342 630
1908				12 295	312 086	340 200
1909	280 341	15	322 392	13 193	322 392	355 988
1910				14 276	342 069	381 540
1911				13 699	331 598	367 266
1912				13 654	330 769	364 670
1913				13 277	323 924	.
1914				15 367	361 885	.
1915				15 120	357 408	.
1916				13 945	336 062	.
1917				13 639	330 506	.
1918				16 822	388 322	.
1919	359 537	−	−	15 237	359 537	.

Column 1 – 1889, 1899, 1909, 1919: Number of chickens on farms from Bureau of the Census, *Census of Agriculture*, 1920. Census inventory figures were used for Dec. 31 of preceding year.

Column 2 – 1889, 1899, 1909, 1919: Percentage adjustments to census data from Strauss, F. and Bean, L., *Gross Farm Income and Indices of Farm Production and Prices in the United States, 1869–1937*, Department of Agriculture, Technical Bulletin 703, Dec. 1940, p. 99. Adjustments are to allow for differences in census dates and for some differences in schedules.

Column 3 – 1889, 1899, 1909, 1919: Col. 1 increased by the product of col. 1 multiplied by col. 2.

Column 4 – 1889–1919: *Yearbook of the U.S. Department of Agriculture*, 1910, p. 645, and 1920, p. 740.

Column 5 – 1889–1919: Col. 3 with intercensal years interpolated on basis of col. 4 except for minor differences due to rounding. This is similar to method used by Department of Agriculture, Bureau of Agricultural Economics, in estimating chicken inventories for 1909–1919, which were based in part on receipts of eggs at leading markets (Department of Agriculture, *Farm Production and Disposition of Chickens and Eggs, 1909–1924*, June 1939).

Column 6 – 1896–1907: Col. 5 multiplied by 1.10395, which is the average of the ratios for 1908–1912 of col. 6 to col. 5.
1908–1912: From Table A-41, col. 8.

LIVESTOCK INVENTORIES; ESTIMATED PRICE PER CHICKEN
1896 to 1908

Year	Weight per chicken	Price pe pound	Average price		Year	Weight per chicken	Price per pound	Average price	
			Calendar year	Dec. 31				Calendar year	Dec. 31
	pounds	cents	dollars			pounds	cents	dollars	
	1	2	3	4		1	2	3	4
1896	4.00	7.2	0.288	0.292	1903	3.91	9.9	0.387	0.386
1897	4.00	7.4	0.296	0.294	1904	3.88	9.9	0.384	0.380
1898	4.00	7.3	0.292	0.304	1905	3.85	9.8	0.377	0.380
1899	4.00	7.9	0.316	0.308	1906	3.82	10.0	0.382	0.394
1900	4.00	7.5	0.300	0.305	1907	3.79	10.7	0.406	0.396
1901	3.97	7.8	0.310	0.336	1908	3.76	10.3	0.387	.
1902	3.94	9.2	0.362	0.374					

Columns 1 and 2 – From Strauss, F. and Bean, L., *Gross Farm Income and Indices of Farm Production and Prices in the United States, 1869–1937*, Department of Agriculture, Technical Bulletin 703, Dec. 1940, p. 101.

Column 3 – Col. 1 multiplied by col. 2.

Column 4 – Two-year moving average of col. 3.

Prices shown here are U.S. prices derived by weighting state prices by inventories on farms in the several states. In measuring value of inventories on farms and annual changes in inventories, these prices are more appropriate to use than prices derived by weighting by sales in the various states, such as are shown in monthly Bureau of Agricultural Economics releases, *Agricultural Prices*. Prices used here for Dec. 31 are those published by Department of Agriculture for Jan. 1 of following year.

Columns 1 to 4 – 1896–1949: Same sources as Table A-41, cols. 1–4.

Column 5 – 1919–1928: *From Income Parity for Agriculture*, part I, section 6.
      1929–1945: From *Agricultural Statistics*, 1949, table 466.
      1946–1949: By dividing farm value by number on farms as shown in Department of Agriculture, Bureau of Agricultural Economics, *Livestock on Farms, January 1*, issued Feb. 15, 1951.

Column 6 – 1896–1918, 1929: From Department of Agriculture, Bureau of Agricultural Economics, *Livestock on Farms, January 1, 1867–1935*, Jan. 1938.

Column 7 – 1896–1918: Estimated at 91.44 percent of col. 6, average of Jan. 1, 1920–1929 ratios of prices of sheep and lambs on feed to prices of stock sheep. Prices of sheep and lambs on feed Jan. 1, 1920–1929 derived by subtracting total value of stock sheep on farms from total value of all sheep on farms and dividing remainder by number of sheep and lambs on feed on farms. Total value of all sheep on farms, Jan. 1, 1920–1929, from Table A-45, col. 6; other series including prices of stock sheep for Jan. 1 1920–1929 from Department of Agriculture, Bureau of Agricultural Economics, *Livestock on Farms, January 1, 1867–1935*, Jan. 1938.
      1929: From *Agricultural Statistics*, 1949, table 466.

Column 8 – 1896–1907: From Table A-43, col. 4.
      1908–1949: Same sources as Table A-41, col. 8.

Column 9 – 1928–1949: Same sources as Table A-41, col. 9.

1896 to 1949

dollars

End of year	All cattle	Hogs	Horses	Mules	All sheep	Stock sheep	Sheep and lambs on feed	Chickens	Turkeys
	1	2	3	4	5	6	7	8	9
1896	18.62	4.36	30.92	40.49	.	1.84	1.68	0.292	.
1897	22.79	4.70	33.35	42.31	.	2.51	2.30	0.294	.
1898	24.53	4.67	36.61	43.52	.	2.80	2.56	0.304	.
1899	26.50	5.36	43.56	51.46	.	2.97	2.72	0.308	.
1900	22.68	6.08	53.03	63.47	.	2.96	2.71	0.305	.
1901	21.48	6.95	58.52	67.23	.	2.62	2.40	0.336	.
1902	21.55	7.69	62.27	71.73	.	2.62	2.40	0.374	.
1903	19.69	6.08	67.59	78.02	.	2.55	2.33	0.386	.
1904	18.39	5.89	69.73	87.06	.	2.77	2.53	0.380	.
1905	19.65	6.07	79.77	97.75	.	3.51	3.21	0.380	.
1906	20.91	7.54	92.85	111.46	.	3.81	3.48	0.394	.
1907	20.92	5.99	92.76	107.81	.	3.87	3.54	0.396	.
1908	21.99	6.45	95.13	108.20	.	3.42	3.13	0.438	.
1909	24.54	9.05	107.70	119.98	.	4.06	3.71	0.473	.
1910	27.22	9.33	111.11	125.73	.	3.83	3.50	0.456	.
1911	27.68	7.99	105.58	120.33	.	3.42	3.13	0.422	.
1912	33.07	9.89	110.58	124.10	.	3.87	3.54	0.465	.
1913	38.97	10.51	109.27	123.47	.	3.91	3.58	0.491	.
1914	40.67	9.95	103.23	112.19	.	4.39	4.01	0.465	.
1915	40.10	8.48	101.45	113.78	.	5.10	4.66	0.491	.
1916	43.34	11.82	102.64	118.45	.	7.06	6.46	0.594	.
1917	50.01	19.69	103.97	128.97	.	11.76	10.75	0.775	.
1918	54.65	22.18	97.94	135.58	.	11.49	10.51	0.955	.
1919	52.64	20.00	96.45	148.29	10.44	.	.	0.972	.
1920	39.07	13.63	84.48	117.37	6.26	.	.	0.893	.
1921	30.39	10.58	71.01	88.99	4.79	.	.	0.808	.
1922	31.66	12.29	70.49	86.87	7.48	.	.	0.746	.
1923	32.11	10.30	65.39	85.89	7.87	.	.	0.761	.
1924	31.72	13.15	64.28	82.91	9.66	.	.	0.793	.
1925	36.80	15.66	65.31	81.51	10.40	.	.	0.885	.
1926	39.98	17.19	63.73	74.51	9.65	.	.	0.906	.
1927	50.63	13.17	66.71	79.84	10.20	.	.	0.858	.
1928	58.47	12.93	69.68	82.45	10.57	.	.	0.911	3.55
1929	56.36	13.45	69.98	83.93	8.93	9.00	8.37	0.928	3.00
1930	38.99	11.35	60.64	69.23	5.35	.	.	0.703	2.60
1931	26.39	6.13	53.48	60.70	3.40	.	.	0.615	2.43
1932	19.74	4.21	54.12	60.42	2.91	.	.	0.449	1.41
1933	17.78	4.09	66.88	82.42	3.78	.	.	0.420	1.48
1934	20.20	6.31	77.05	99.34	4.31	.	.	0.544	2.18
1935	34.06	12.71	96.73	120.63	6.38	.	.	0.755	2.82
1936	34.06	11.89	99.14	130.25	6.00	.	.	0.656	2.06
1937	36.58	11.26	90.89	123.39	6.11	.	.	0.756	2.49
1938	38.44	11.18	84.32	118.58	5.74	.	.	0.700	2.56
1939	40.60	7.78	77.30	116.00	6.31	.	.	0.605	2.14
1940	43.20	8.34	68.20	107.00	6.73	.	.	0.654	2.26
1941	55.00	15.60	64.70	107.00	8.60	.	.	0.833	3.08
1942	69.30	22.50	79.80	127.00	9.66	.	.	1.040	4.47
1943	68.40	17.50	78.60	143.00	8.71	.	.	1.180	5.33
1944	66.90	20.60	64.90	134.00	8.57	.	.	1.210	5.78
1945	76.20	23.90	57.40	133.00	9.69	.	.	1.270	5.75
1946	97.40	36.00	59.20	141.00	12.62	.	.	1.440	6.47
1947	116.00	42.80	55.50	133.00	15.35	.	.	1.440	6.87
1948	135.00	38.20	52.30	117.00	17.19	.	.	1.660	8.70
1949	123.00	27.10	45.80	99.40	17.83	.	.	1.360	6.25

Column 1 – 1896–1949: Sum of cols. 2–6, 9–10.

Columns 2 to 5, 10 – 1896–1949: Same sources as Table A-41, cols. 1–4 and 9. Value of turkeys 1896–1927 not estimated but assumed to be small.

Column 6 – 1896–1918: Sum of cols. 7 and 8.
                1919–1928: From *Income Parity for Agriculture*, part I, section 6.
                1929–1949: From *Agricultural Statistics*, 1949, table 466, and Department of Agriculture, Bureau of Agricultural Economics, *Livestock on Farms, January 1*, issued Feb. 15, 1951.

Column 7 – 1896–1918: From Department of Agriculture, Bureau of Agricultural Economics, *Livestock on Farms, January 1, 1867–1935*, Jan. 1938.

Column 8 – 1896–1918: Table A-41, col. 7 multiplied by Table A-44, col. 7 except for minor differences due to rounding.

Column 9 – 1896–1907: Table A-41, col. 8 multiplied by Table A-44, col. 8 except for minor differences due to rounding.
                1908–1949: Same sources as Table A-41, col. 8.

Note: For comparison with *Balance Sheet of Agriculture* see note to Table A-31.

Current Prices: 1896 to 1949

$ mill.

End of year	Total	All cattle	Hogs	Horses	Mules	All sheep	Stock sheep	Sheep and lambs on feed	Chickens	Turkeys
	1	2	3	4	5	6	7	8	9	10
1896	1 981	939	223	550	115	75	71	4	79	—
1897	2 355	1 205	250	590	123	108	101	7	79	—
1898	2 603	1 372	241	649	131	128	120	8	82	—
1899	3 028	1 583	274	778	162	142	134	8	89	—
1900	3 117	1 420	308	952	202	144	136	8	91	—
1901	3 213	1 383	333	1 051	219	129	122	7	98	—
1902	3 399	1 422	370	1 128	241	124	117	7	114	—
1903	3 365	1 308	314	1 239	270	115	107	8	119	—
1904	3 370	1 216	313	1 289	312	121	112	9	119	—
1905	3 748	1 278	326	1 500	360	159	148	11	125	—
1906	4 276	1 333	426	1 773	425	179	166	13	140	—
1907	4 199	1 297	350	1 804	426	186	175	11	136	—
1908	4 316	1 336	339	1 877	442	173	161	12	149	—
1909	4 914	1 448	435	2 151	509	203	191	12	168	—
1910	5 266	1 558	516	2 269	557	192	176	16	174	—
1911	5 037	1 541	442	2 188	548	163	147	16	155	—
1912	5 648	1 871	532	2 323	581	171	157	14	170	—
1913	6 148	2 317	555	2 328	601	167	149	18	180	—
1914	6 292	2 597	563	2 212	568	176	159	17	176	—
1915	6 357	2 704	514	2 164	592	202	185	17	181	—
1916	7 064	3 076	681	2 187	634	272	249	23	214	—
1917	8 553	3 653	1 239	2 208	707	464	432	32	282	—
1918	9 022	3 940	1 426	2 049	755	478	441	37	374	—
1919	8 480	3 706	1 203	1 938	838	425	.	.	370	—
1920	6 380	2 685	804	1 636	677	247	.	.	331	—
1921	5 070	2 090	633	1 333	518	177	.	.	319	—
1922	5 366	2 139	852	1 278	512	275	.	.	310	—
1923	5 071	2 119	686	1 136	507	292	.	.	331	—
1924	5 021	2 010	733	1 070	491	372	.	.	345	—
1925	5 386	2 229	816	1 050	481	422	.	.	388	—
1926	5 520	2 326	954	981	432	409	.	.	418	—
1927	6 026	2 902	815	987	452	462	.	.	408	—
1928	6 593	3 443	764	992	454	511	.	.	409	20
1929	6 514	3 438	749	962	452	460	.	.	435	18
1930	4 859	2 457	622	800	365	285	.	.	316	14
1931	3 555	1 737	363	677	312	183	.	.	269	14
1932	2 983	1 387	262	665	305	154	.	.	200	10
1933	3 169	1 322	240	806	408	202	.	.	182	9
1934	3 478	1 391	247	914	479	223	.	.	212	12
1935	5 184	2 311	546	1 122	558	326	.	.	305	16
1936	5 064	2 251	512	1 124	581	305	.	.	278	13
1937	5 033	2 387	501	999	524	312	.	.	295	15
1938	5 092	2 538	559	896	494	295	.	.	293	17
1939	5 133	2 770	476	808	467	329	.	.	265	18
1940	5 325	3 103	453	695	419	363	.	.	276	16
1941	7 074	4 180	945	638	406	484	.	.	398	23
1942	9 642	5 625	1 662	766	462	533	.	.	564	30
1943	9 685	5 837	1 467	723	490	442	.	.	686	40
1944	9 012	5 722	1 224	565	434	399	.	.	626	42
1945	9 742	6 280	1 468	462	401	411	.	.	671	49
1946	11 977	7 907	2 049	429	390	477	.	.	682	43
1947	13 384	9 094	2 356	366	337	535	.	.	665	31
1948	14 657	10 552	2 184	309	274	544	.	.	746	48
1949	13 184	9 848	1 641	241	214	548	.	.	655	37

A-46   TABLE A–46

Column 1 – Sum of cols. 2–6 and 9–10.

Columns 2 to 5, 7 to 10 – Table A-41, cols. 1–4 and 6–9 multiplied by 1929 price for corresponding item from Table A-44, cols. 1–4 and 6–9 except for minor differences due to rounding. Value of turkeys 1896–1927 not estimated but assumed to be small.

Column 6 – Sum of cols. 7 and 8.

A-47   TABLE A–47

Column 1 – Sum of cols. 2–8.

Columns 2 to 8 – From Table A-45 by subtracting value at end of preceding year from corresponding value at end of current year.

A-48   TABLE A–48

Column 1 – Sum of cols. 2–8.

Columns 2 to 8 – From Table A-46, by subtracting value at end of preceding year from corresponding value at end of current year.

A-49   TABLE A–49

Column 1 – 1897–1949: Sum of cols. 2–6 and 9–10.

Columns 2 to 5, 7 to 10 – 1897–1949: Annual change in quantity calculated from Table A-41, cols. 1–4 and 6–9 multiplied by end-of-year price for corresponding item from Table A-44 except for minor differences due to rounding.

Column 6 – 1897–1918: Sum of cols. 7 and 8.
   1919–1949: Annual change in quantity calculated from Table A-41, col. 5 multiplied by end-of-year price from Table A-44, col. 5.

   Note: For comparison with Bureau of Agricultural Economics and Department of Commerce estimates see note to Table A-32.

818

LIVESTOCK INVENTORIES; VALUE ON FARMS

1929 Prices: 1896 to 1949

$ mill.

End of year	Total	All cattle	Hogs	Horses	Mules	All sheep	Stock sheep	Sheep and lambs on feed	Chickens	Turkeys
	1	2	3	4	5	6	7	8	9	10
1896	5 635	2 843	689	1 246	238	369	350	19	250	–
1897	5 817	2 980	717	1 239	245	387	361	26	249	–
1898	5 998	3 152	693	1 241	253	410	384	26	249	–
1899	6 266	3 367	687	1 250	263	431	406	25	268	–
1900	6 450	3 527	682	1 256	268	440	415	25	277	–
1901	6 518	3 631	644	1 257	274	441	416	25	271	–
1902	6 625	3 720	647	1 268	281	426	400	26	283	–
1903	6 707	3 745	694	1 283	291	407	377	30	287	–
1904	6 719	3 726	715	1 294	301	392	364	28	291	–
1905	6 723	3 664	721	1 316	309	407	377	30	306	–
1906	6 762	3 593	761	1 336	320	423	391	32	329	–
1907	6 721	3 494	785	1 361	331	432	406	26	318	–
1908	6 626	3 425	706	1 381	343	455	424	31	316	–
1909	6 506	3 325	647	1 398	356	450	422	28	330	–
1910	6 577	3 225	745	1 429	372	452	415	37	354	–
1911	6 484	3 138	745	1 450	382	428	387	41	341	–
1912	6 513	3 190	723	1 470	393	399	365	34	338	–
1913	6 687	3 351	711	1 491	409	385	343	42	340	–
1914	6 999	3 599	761	1 500	425	362	326	36	352	–
1915	7 246	3 801	815	1 493	436	358	326	32	343	–
1916	7 396	4 000	774	1 491	449	348	317	31	334	–
1917	7 601	4 117	846	1 486	460	355	330	25	337	–
1918	7 597	4 063	865	1 464	467	375	345	30	363	–
1919	7 376	3 968	809	1 406	474	365	336	29	354	–
1920	7 201	3 873	793	1 355	484	353	319	34	343	–
1921	7 181	3 877	805	1 313	489	330	300	30	367	–
1922	7 216	3 807	932	1 268	495	329	294	35	385	–
1923	7 063	3 720	895	1 216	496	332	296	36	404	–
1924	6 732	3 572	750	1 165	497	344	310	34	404	–
1925	6 501	3 414	701	1 125	495	360	321	39	406	–
1926	6 396	3 279	746	1 077	487	379	343	36	428	–
1927	6 418	3 231	832	1 035	475	404	366	38	441	–
1928	6 436	3 318	794	996	462	432	391	41	417	17
1929	6 514	3 438	749	962	452	460	410	50	435	18
1930	6 565	3 552	738	923	443	476	430	46	417	16
1931	6 729	3 709	798	886	432	481	429	52	405	18
1932	6 989	3 961	836	860	424	474	426	48	413	21
1933	7 137	4 191	788	843	415	478	434	44	403	19
1934	6 481	3 880	525	830	405	463	415	48	362	16
1935	6 450	3 824	578	812	388	457	409	48	374	17
1936	6 338	3 725	579	794	374	454	407	47	393	19
1937	6 238	3 677	599	769	357	456	405	51	362	18
1938	6 352	3 721	673	744	349	458	409	49	388	19
1939	6 641	3 850	823	731	339	465	416	49	407	26
1940	6 711	4 044	731	713	328	481	427	54	392	22
1941	7 075	4 285	815	691	317	502	444	58	443	22
1942	7 562	4 577	994	672	304	492	434	58	503	20
1943	7 880	4 809	1 126	643	287	453	398	55	540	22
1944	7 418	4 823	798	610	272	414	356	58	479	22
1945	7 182	4 646	824	564	253	378	321	57	492	25
1946	6 880	4 577	766	507	233	337	289	48	440	20
1947	6 569	4 403	740	461	213	311	270	41	428	13
1948	6 507	4 413	768	413	197	283	249	34	416	17
1949	6 614	4 512	814	369	180	275	244	31	446	18

LIVESTOCK INVENTORIES; ANNUAL CHANGE IN VALUE ON FARMS
Current Prices: 1897 to 1949

$ mill.

Year	Total	All cattle	Hogs	Horses	Mules	All sheep	Chickens	Turkeys
	1	2	3	4	5	6	7	8
1897	374	266	27	40	8	33	0	—
1898	248	167	−9	59	8	20	3	—
1899	425	211	33	129	31	14	7	—
1900	89	−163	34	174	40	2	2	—
1901	96	−37	25	99	17	−15	7	—
1902	186	39	37	77	22	−5	16	—
1903	−34	−114	−56	111	29	−9	5	—
1904	5	−92	−1	50	42	6	0	—
1905	378	62	13	211	48	38	6	—
1906	528	55	100	273	65	20	15	—
1907	−77	−36	−76	31	1	7	−4	—
1908	117	39	−11	73	16	−13	13	—
1909	598	112	96	274	67	30	19	—
1910	352	110	81	118	48	−11	6	—
1911	−229	−17	−74	−81	−9	−29	−19	—
1912	611	330	90	135	33	8	15	—
1913	500	446	23	5	20	−4	10	—
1914	144	280	8	−116	−33	9	−4	—
1915	65	107	−49	−48	24	26	5	—
1916	707	372	167	23	42	70	33	—
1917	1 489	577	558	21	73	192	68	—
1918	469	287	187	−159	48	14	92	—
1919	−542	−234	−223	−111	83	−53	−4	—
1920	−2 100	−1 021	−399	−302	−161	−178	−39	—
1921	−1 310	−595	−171	−303	−159	−70	−12	—
1922	296	49	219	−55	−6	98	−9	—
1923	−295	−20	−166	−142	−5	17	21	—
1924	−50	−109	47	−66	−16	80	14	—
1925	365	219	83	−20	−10	50	43	—
1926	134	97	138	−69	−49	−13	30	—
1927	506	576	−139	6	20	53	−10	—
1928	567	541	−51	5	2	49	1	20
1929	−79	−5	−15	−30	−2	−51	26	−2
1930	−1 655	−981	−127	−162	−87	−175	−119	−4
1931	−1 304	−720	−259	−123	−53	−102	−47	0
1932	−572	−350	−101	−12	−7	−29	−69	−4
1933	186	−65	−22	141	103	48	−18	−1
1934	309	69	7	108	71	21	30	3
1935	1 706	920	299	208	79	103	93	4
1936	−120	−60	−34	2	23	−21	−27	−3
1937	−31	136	−11	−125	−57	7	17	2
1938	59	151	58	−103	−30	−17	−2	2
1939	41	232	−83	−88	−27	34	−28	1
1940	192	333	−23	−113	−48	34	11	−2
1941	1 749	1 077	492	−57	−13	121	122	7
1942	2 568	1 445	717	128	56	49	166	7
1943	43	212	−195	−43	28	−91	122	10
1944	−673	−115	−243	−158	−56	−43	−60	2
1945	730	558	244	−103	−33	12	45	7
1946	2 235	1 627	581	−33	−11	66	11	−6
1947	1 407	1 187	307	−63	−53	58	−17	−12
1948	1 273	1 458	−172	−57	−63	9	81	17
1949	−1 473	−704	−543	−68	−60	4	−91	−11

1929 Prices: 1897 to 1949

$ mill.

Year	Total	All cattle	Hogs	Horses	Mules	All sheep	Chickens	Turkeys
	1	2	3	4	5	6	7	8
1897	182	137	28	−7	7	18	−1	—
1898	181	172	−24	2	8	23	0	—
1899	268	215	−6	9	10	21	19	—
1900	184	160	−5	6	5	9	9	—
1901	68	104	−38	1	6	1	−6	—
1902	107	89	3	11	7	−15	12	—
1903	82	25	47	15	10	−19	4	—
1904	12	−19	21	11	10	−15	4	—
1905	4	−62	6	22	8	15	15	—
1906	39	−71	40	20	11	16	23	—
1907	−41	−99	24	25	11	9	−11	—
1908	−95	−69	−79	20	12	23	−2	—
1909	−120	−100	−59	17	13	−5	14	—
1910	71	−100	98	31	16	2	24	—
1911	−93	−87	0	21	10	−24	−13	—
1912	29	52	−22	20	11	−29	−3	—
1913	174	161	−12	21	16	−14	2	—
1914	312	248	50	9	16	−23	12	—
1915	247	202	54	−7	11	−4	−9	—
1916	150	199	−41	−2	13	−10	−9	—
1917	205	117	72	−5	11	7	3	—
1918	−4	−54	19	−22	7	20	26	—
1919	−221	−95	−56	−58	7	−10	−9	—
1920	−175	−95	−16	−51	10	−12	−11	—
1921	−20	4	12	−42	5	−23	24	—
1922	35	−70	127	−45	6	−1	18	—
1923	−153	−87	−37	−52	1	3	19	—
1924	−331	−148	−145	−51	1	12	0	—
1925	−231	−158	−49	−40	−2	16	2	—
1926	−105	−135	45	−48	−8	19	22	—
1927	22	−48	86	−42	−12	25	13	—
1928	18	87	−38	−39	−13	28	−24	17
1929	78	120	−45	−34	−10	28	18	1
1930	51	114	−11	−39	−9	16	−18	−2
1931	164	157	60	−37	−11	5	−12	2
1932	260	252	38	−26	−8	−7	8	3
1933	148	230	−48	−17	−9	4	−10	−2
1934	−656	−311	−263	−13	−10	−15	−41	−3
1935	−31	−56	53	−18	−17	−6	12	1
1936	−112	−99	1	−18	−14	−3	19	2
1937	−100	−48	20	−25	−17	2	−31	−1
1938	114	44	74	−25	−8	2	26	1
1939	289	129	150	−13	−10	7	19	7
1940	70	194	−92	−18	−11	16	−15	−4
1941	364	241	84	−22	−11	21	51	0
1942	487	292	179	−19	−13	−10	60	−2
1943	318	232	132	−29	−17	−39	37	2
1944	−462	14	−328	−33	−15	−39	−61	0
1945	−236	−177	26	−46	−19	−36	13	3
1946	−302	−69	−58	−57	−20	−41	−52	−5
1947	−311	−174	−26	−46	−20	−26	−12	−7
1948	−62	10	28	−48	−16	−28	−12	4
1949	107	99	46	−44	−17	−8	30	1

LIVESTOCK INVENTORIES; ANNUAL CHANGE IN NUMBER OF HEAD ON FARMS VALUED AT END-OF-YEAR PRICES: 1897 to 1949

$ mill.

Year	Total	All cattle	Hogs	Horses	Mules	All sheep	Stock sheep	Sheep and lambs on feed	Chickens	Turkeys
	1	2	3	4	5	6	7	8	9	10
1897	70	55	10	−3	3	5	3	2	0	−
1898	79	75	−8	1	4	7	7	0	0	−
1899	124	101	−3	6	7	7	7	0	6	−
1900	76	64	−2	5	3	3	3	0	3	−
1901	24	40	−20	1	5	0	0	0	−2	−
1902	52	34	2	9	6	−4	−4	0	5	−
1903	49	8	21	14	9	−5	−6	1	2	−
1904	22	−6	9	11	10	−4	−4	0	2	−
1905	27	−22	3	25	9	6	6	0	6	−
1906	53	−26	22	26	15	6	5	1	10	−
1907	21	−37	11	33	15	4	6	−2	−5	−
1908	−15	−27	−38	27	15	9	7	2	−1	−
1909	−34	−44	−40	26	19	−2	−1	−1	7	−
1910	106	−48	68	49	24	1	−3	4	12	−
1911	−11	−43	0	32	15	−9	−10	1	−6	−
1912	48	30	−16	31	16	−12	−9	−3	−1	−
1913	153	112	−9	33	23	−7	−10	3	1	−
1914	245	178	37	13	22	−11	−8	−3	6	−
1915	177	144	34	−10	16	−2	0	−2	−5	−
1916	119	154	−36	−3	18	−8	−7	−1	−6	−
1917	231	103	105	−7	17	10	17	−7	3	−
1918	11	−52	31	−31	11	25	19	6	27	−
1919	−262	−89	−83	−80	12	−12	−	−	−10	−
1920	−147	−66	−16	−61	14	−8	−	−	−10	−
1921	−18	2	10	−43	5	−12	−	−	20	−
1922	52	−39	116	−45	6	−1	−	−	15	−
1923	−108	−50	−28	−49	1	3	−	−	15	−
1924	−257	−83	−142	−47	1	14	−	−	0	−
1925	−177	−103	−57	−37	−1	19	−	−	2	−
1926	−49	−96	58	−44	−7	20	−	−	20	−
1927	30	−43	84	−40	−12	29	−	−	12	−
1928	13	91	−36	−39	−12	33	−	−	−24	−
1929	78	120	−45	−34	−11	29	−	−	18	1
1930	22	79	−10	−33	−8	9	−	−	−13	−2
1931	60	73	27	−28	−8	2	−	−	−8	2
1932	76	88	12	−20	−6	−2	−	−	3	1
1933	31	73	−14	−16	−8	2	−	−	−5	−1
1934	−295	−112	−123	−15	−12	−7	−	−	−24	−2
1935	−27	−34	50	−26	−24	−4	−	−	10	1
1936	−93	−59	1	−25	−22	−2	−	−	13	1
1937	−98	−31	16	−31	−26	1	−	−	−26	−1
1938	73	30	61	−31	−10	2	−	−	20	1
1939	171	92	87	−14	−15	5	−	−	12	4
1940	61	149	−57	−17	−13	12	−	−	−10	−3
1941	364	235	98	−21	−14	20	−	−	45	1
1942	670	359	298	−21	−20	−10	−	−	68	−4
1943	407	282	173	−32	−29	−38	−	−	47	4
1944	−660	16	−503	−31	−25	−37	−	−	−79	−1
1945	−275	−239	47	−38	−30	−39	−	−	17	7
1946	−510	−120	−158	−48	−34	−58	−	−	−80	−12
1947	−585	−357	−81	−36	−31	−46	−	−	−19	−15
1948	−23	23	80	−36	−23	−55	−	−	−21	9
1949	289	216	91	−29	−20	−16	−	−	44	3

$ mill.

Year	Total farm fire losses	Resi- dences	Other farm build- ings	Farm equip- ment	Inven- tories	House- hold goods	Year	Total farm fire losses	Resi- dences	Other farm build- ings	Farm equip- ment	Inven- tories	House- hold goods
	1	2	3	4	5	6		1	2	3	4	5	6
1897	25.3	6.9	5.7	2.5	7.7	2.5	1924	77.6	21.3	17.5	7.8	23.2	7.8
1898	28.3	7.8	6.4	2.8	8.5	2.8	1925	81.0	22.3	18.3	8.1	24.2	8.1
1899	33.3	9.1	7.5	3.3	10.1	3.3	1926	75.5	20.7	16.9	7.6	22.7	7.6
1900	34.9	9.6	7.8	3.5	10.5	3.5	1927	76.3	21.0	17.2	7.6	22.9	7.6
1901	35.9	9.9	8.1	3.6	10.7	3.6	1928	84.4	23.2	19.0	8.4	25.4	8.4
1902	34.9	9.6	7.8	3.5	10.5	3.5	1929	91.9	25.3	20.7	9.2	27.5	9.2
1903	31.5	8.7	7.1	3.1	9.5	3.1	1930	106.0	29.2	23.8	10.6	31.8	10.6
1904	49.7	13.6	11.2	5.0	14.9	5.0	1931	102.4	28.2	23.0	10.2	30.8	10.2
1905	35.8	9.8	8.0	3.6	10.8	3.6	1932	102.6	28.2	23.0	10.3	30.8	10.3
1906	36.6	10.0	8.2	3.7	11.0	3.7	1933	82.9	22.8	18.6	8.3	24.9	8.3
1907	46.6	12.8	10.4	4.7	14.0	4.7	1934	74.6	20.5	16.7	7.5	22.4	7.5
1908	47.2	13.0	10.6	4.7	14.2	4.7	1935	60.4	16.6	13.6	6.0	18.2	6.0
1909	40.9	11.2	9.2	4.1	12.3	4.1	1936	80.7	22.2	18.2	8.1	24.1	8.1
1910	46.4	12.8	10.4	4.6	14.0	4.6	1937	65.7	18.0	14.8	6.6	19.7	6.6
1911	47.1	13.0	10.6	4.7	14.1	4.7	1938	73.3	20.1	16.5	7.3	22.1	7.3
1912	44.7	12.3	10.1	4.5	13.3	4.5	1939	76.8	21.1	17.3	7.7	23.0	7.7
1913	44.2	12.2	10.0	4.4	13.2	4.4	1940	72.6	19.9	16.3	7.3	21.8	7.3
1914	49.4	13.6	11.2	4.9	14.8	4.9	1941	69.9	19.2	15.8	7.0	20.9	7.0
1915	38.0	10.4	8.6	3.8	11.4	3.8	1942	64.7	17.8	14.6	6.5	19.3	6.5
1916	48.5	13.3	10.9	4.9	14.5	4.9	1943	75.4	20.8	17.0	7.5	22.6	7.5
1917	46.6	12.8	10.4	4.7	14.0	4.7	1944	77.4	21.3	17.5	7.7	23.2	7.7
1918	50.7	14.0	11.4	5.1	15.1	5.1	1945	80.3	22.1	18.1	8.0	24.1	8.0
1919	50.1	13.8	11.2	5.0	15.1	5.0	1946	82.0	22.6	18.4	8.2	24.6	8.2
1920	55.4	15.3	12.5	5.5	16.6	5.5	1947	99.0	27.2	22.3	9.9	29.7	9.9
1921	67.1	18.5	15.1	6.7	20.1	6.7	1948	99.0	27.2	22.3	9.9	29.7	9.9
1922	75.4	20.8	17.0	7.5	22.6	7.5	1949	95.0	26.1	21.4	9.5	28.5	9.5
1923	73.3	20.1	16.5	7.3	22.1	7.3							

Column 1 From Table R-70, col. 2.

Columns 2 to 6 – Total shown in col. 1 was distributed among buildings, equipment, inventories (crops and livestock), and household goods on basis of premium rates and percentage of total face value of policies ascribable to each group in Kentucky alone. Premium rates were reported by insurance companies and percentage of value in each group was based on 1945 *Census of Agriculture*. This information was taken from Botts, Ralph R. and Houseman, Earl E., *Method of Estimating Farm Fire Losses in the United States*, Bureau of Agricultural Economics, July 1948, p. 4, note 2. Loss ratio for each group was obtained as the product of premium rate and percentage of insured value for each group divided by gross premium rate (sum of foregoing products for all groups). As a result of this procedure, 10 percent of total farm losses were allocated to farm equipment, 10 percent to household goods, and 30 percent to crop and livestock inventories. The remaining 50 percent were distributed between dwellings and other farm buildings in ratio of 55 to 45 on basis of average relationship between remaining value in current prices of these two types of buildings.

Column 1 – Sum of Table A-50, cols. 2 and 3.

Column 2 – Components of col. 1 deflated by Table A-30, cols. 1 and 2, respectively.

Column 3 – Obtained by depreciating on linear basis components of col. 1 assuming a rate of 3.33 percent for residential and 4.35 percent for nonresidential farm buildings (cf. notes to Table R-72, col. 3).

Column 4 – Same procedure as for col. 3 except expenditure series given in col. 2 used.

Column 5 – Depreciation allowances on residential and nonresidential buildings in 1929 prices (col. 4) multiplied by appropriate index from Table A-30, cols. 1 and 2.

Column 6 – Col. 1 minus col. 3.

Column 7 – Col. 2 minus col. 4.

Column 8 – Col. 1 minus col. 5.

ADJUSTMENT TO SAVING THROUGH FARM CONSTRUCTION
DUE TO FIRE LOSSES: 1897 to 1949

$ mill.

Year	Fire losses		Depreciation			Net		
	Original cost	1929 prices	Original cost	1929 prices	Replacement cost	Original cost	1929 prices	Replacement cost
	1	2	3	4	5	6	7	8
1897	12.6	30.0	11.1	24.4	10.3	1.5	5.6	2.3
1898	14.2	32.9	11.3	25.1	10.9	2.9	7.8	3.3
1899	16.6	36.4	11.5	25.7	11.8	5.1	10.7	4.8
1900	17.4	36.3	11.9	26.5	12.8	5.5	9.8	4.6
1901	18.0	38.2	12.3	27.3	12.9	5.7	10.9	5.1
1902	17.4	35.8	12.6	28.0	13.6	4.8	7.8	3.8
1903	15.8	31.4	13.0	28.7	14.5	2.8	2.7	1.3
1904	24.8	50.1	13.4	29.6	14.7	11.4	20.5	10.1
1905	17.8	34.4	13.8	30.4	15.7	4.0	4.0	2.1
1906	18.2	32.6	14.2	30.9	17.3	4.0	1.7	0.9
1907	23.2	39.5	14.7	31.5	18.4	8.5	8.0	4.8
1908	23.6	42.2	15.2	32.3	18.1	8.4	9.9	5.5
1909	20.4	35.7	15.6	32.9	18.8	4.8	2.8	1.6
1910	23.2	39.5	16.1	33.5	19.8	7.1	6.0	3.4
1911	23.6	40.1	16.5	34.1	20.1	7.1	6.0	3.5
1912	22.4	38.1	17.1	34.7	20.5	5.3	3.4	1.9
1913	22.2	36.8	17.4	35.2	21.3	4.8	1.6	.9
1914	24.8	41.7	17.8	35.6	21.2	7.0	6.1	3.6
1915	19.0	30.9	18.1	35.8	22.0	0.9	−4.9	−3.0
1916	24.2	35.1	18.4	35.8	24.7	5.8	−0.7	−0.5
1917	23.2	27.7	18.8	35.9	30.1	4.4	−8.2	−6.9
1918	25.4	25.2	19.2	35.7	36.0	6.2	−10.5	−10.6
1919	25.0	21.2	19.6	35.4	41.7	5.4	−14.2	−16.7
1920	27.8	18.8	20.2	35.0	51.9	7.6	−16.2	−24.1
1921	33.6	32.1	20.8	34.8	36.4	12.8	−2.7	−2.8
1922	37.8	37.9	21.5	34.7	34.6	16.3	3.2	3.2
1923	36.6	34.5	22.3	34.8	37.0	14.3	−0.3	−0.4
1924	38.8	37.4	23.1	34.7	36.1	15.7	2.7	2.7
1925	40.6	39.6	24.0	34.7	35.6	16.6	4.9	5.0
1926	37.6	36.8	24.9	34.9	35.6	12.7	1.9	2.0
1927	38.2	38.1	25.6	35.0	35.1	12.6	3.1	3.1
1928	42.2	42.3	26.5	35.2	35.1	15.7	7.1	7.1
1929	46.0	46.0	27.6	35.5	35.5	18.4	10.5	10.5
1930	53.0	55.0	28.8	36.1	34.7	24.2	18.9	18.3
1931	51.2	61.6	29.9	36.8	30.6	21.3	24.8	20.6
1932	51.2	71.0	31.1	37.9	27.3	20.1	33.1	23.9
1933	41.4	57.4	32.1	39.0	28.1	9.3	18.4	13.3
1934	37.2	45.7	32.8	39.4	32.1	4.4	6.3	5.1
1935	30.2	37.1	33.2	39.5	32.2	−3.0	−2.4	−2.0
1936	40.4	48.4	33.8	39.8	33.2	6.6	8.6	7.2
1937	32.8	36.7	34.3	39.0	35.7	−1.5	−2.3	−2.9
1938	36.6	43.0	34.8	40.0	34.1	1.8	3.0	2.5
1939	38.4	45.1	35.4	40.3	34.4	3.0	4.8	4.0
1940	36.2	41.5	35.9	40.7	35.6	0.3	0.8	0.6
1941	35.0	35.9	36.4	40.8	39.7	−1.4	−4.9	−4.7
1942	32.4	29.2	36.7	40.9	45.4	−4.3	−11.7	−13.0
1943	37.8	30.3	37.2	40.9	51.2	0.6	−10.6	−13.4
1944	38.8	28.2	37.6	40.8	56.1	1.2	−12.6	−17.3
1945	40.2	27.3	38.0	40.6	59.8	2.2	−13.3	−19.6
1946	41.0	25.1	38.4	40.2	65.6	2.6	−15.1	−24.6
1947	49.5	23.7	39.0	39.7	83.2	10.5	−16.0	−33.7
1948	49.5	21.8	39.6	39.4	89.2	9.9	−17.6	−39.7
1949	47.5	21.8	40.2	39.0	84.9	7.3	−17.2	−37.4

Column 1 – From Table A-50, col. 4.

Column 2 – Col. 1 deflated by index derived by dividing farm expenditures on producer durable goods in original cost by expenditures in 1929 prices (cf. Tables A-16 to A-20).

Column 3 – Sum of depreciation of col. 1 during six years preceding date indicated (cf. notes to Table R-72, col. 2).

Column 4 – Same procedure as for col. 3 except expenditure series given in col. 2 used.

Column 5 – Col. 4 multiplied by price index determined in col. 2.

Column 6 – Col. 1 minus col. 3.

Column 7 – Col. 2 minus col. 4.

Column 8 – Col. 1 minus col. 5.

ADJUSTMENT TO SAVING THROUGH FARM EQUIPMENT
DUE TO FIRE LOSSES: 1897 to 1949

$ mill.

Year	Fire losses		Depreciation			Net		
	Original cost	1929 prices	Original cost	1929 prices	Replacement cost	Original cost	1929 prices	Replacement cost
	1	2	3	4	5	6	7	8
1897	2.5	5.3	3.1	5.9	2.8	−.6	−.6	−.3
1898	2.8	5.7	3.0	5.9	2.9	−.2	−.2	−.1
1899	3.3	5.9	2.9	5.8	3.2	.4	.1	.1
1900	3.5	5.8	2.9	5.7	3.4	.6	.1	.1
1901	3.6	6.2	3.0	5.7	3.3	.6	.5	.3
1902	3.5	5.9	3.1	5.7	3.4	.4	.2	.1
1903	3.1	5.2	3.2	5.8	3.5	−.1	−.6	−.4
1904	5.0	8.6	3.5	6.0	3.5	1.5	2.6	1.5
1905	3.6	5.9	3.7	6.3	3.8	−.1	−.4	−.2
1906	3.7	5.7	3.7	6.3	4.1	0	−.6	−.4
1907	4.7	6.9	3.8	6.3	4.3	.9	.6	.4
1908	4.7	7.6	4.0	6.5	4.0	.7	1.1	.7
1909	4.1	6.5	4.2	6.8	4.3	−.1	−.3	−.2
1910	4.6	6.9	4.3	6.7	4.5	.3	.2	.1
1911	4.7	6.9	4.3	6.7	4.6	.4	.2	.1
1912	4.5	6.6	4.5	6.8	4.6	0	−.2	−.1
1913	4.4	6.5	4.5	6.9	4.7	−.1	−.4	−.3
1914	4.9	7.1	4.5	6.8	4.7	.4	.3	.2
1915	3.8	5.2	4.5	6.6	4.8	−.7	−1.4	−1.0
1916	4.9	6.5	4.5	6.5	4.9	.4	0	0
1917	4.7	5.6	4.6	6.4	5.4	.1	−.8	−.7
1918	5.1	4.9	4.6	6.1	6.4	.5	−1.2	−1.3
1919	5.0	4.5	4.7	5.8	6.4	.3	−1.3	−1.4
1920	5.5	5.0	4.8	5.5	6.2	.7	−.5	−.7
1921	6.7	6.4	5.1	5.4	5.6	1.6	1.0	1.1
1922	7.5	8.6	5.5	5.7	5.0	2.0	2.9	2.5
1923	7.3	8.1	6.0	6.0	5.4	1.3	2.1	1.9
1924	7.8	8.4	6.4	6.5	6.1	1.4	1.9	1.7
1925	8.1	8.7	6.9	7.2	6.7	1.2	1.5	1.4
1926	7.6	8.0	7.3	7.8	7.4	.3	.2	.2
1927	7.6	8.1	7.6	8.2	7.7	0	−.1	−.1
1928	8.4	8.3	7.7	8.3	8.4	.7	0	0
1929	9.2	9.2	8.0	8.4	8.4	1.2	.8	.8
1930	10.6	10.8	8.3	8.6	8.5	2.3	2.2	2.1
1931	10.2	10.5	8.8	9.0	8.8	1.4	1.5	1.4
1932	10.3	9.0	9.2	9.2	8.5	1.1	−.2	1.8
1933	8.3	9.4	9.4	9.4	8.3	−1.1	0	0
1934	7.5	8.2	9.4	9.5	8.7	−1.9	−1.3	−1.2
1935	6.0	6.6	9.1	9.3	8.5	−3.1	−2.7	−2.5
1936	8.1	8.7	8.6	8.9	8.3	−.5	−.2	−.2
1937	6.6	6.8	8.1	8.4	8.1	−1.5	−1.6	−1.5
1938	7.3	7.4	7.5	8.0	7.9	−.2	−.6	−.6
1939	7.7	8.1	7.2	7.7	7.3	.5	.4	.4
1940	7.3	7.9	7.2	7.6	7.0	.1	.3	.3
1941	7.0	7.2	7.2	7.6	7.4	−.2	−.4	−.4
1942	6.5	6.4	7.2	7.5	7.6	−.7	−1.1	−1.1
1943	7.5	6.7	7.1	7.3	8.1	.4	−.6	−.6
1944	7.7	7.0	7.2	7.2	7.9	.5	−.2	−.2
1945	8.0	7.2	7.3	7.1	7.9	.7	.1	.1
1946	8.2	7.1	7.4	7.0	8.1	.8	.1	.1
1947	9.9	7.6	7.7	7.0	9.1	2.2	.6	.8
1948	9.9	6.7	8.2	7.0	10.4	1.7	−.3	−.5
1949	9.5	6.7	8.7	7.0	9.9	.8	−.3	−.4

Column 1 – 1896–1949: Sum of cols. 2–8.

Column 2 – 1896–1949: From Table A-55, col. 5.

Column 3 – 1896–1949: From Table A-56, col. 1.

Column 4 – 1896–1949: Cumulated from Table A-57, col. 7, estimating reserves at end of 1896 at $125 million.

Column 5 – 1917–1933: Cumulated from Table V-4, col. 2. The $150 million by which farmers' receipts from sales fell short of amount paid was arbitrarily distributed among the years 1920, 1921, and 1922.

          1934–1938: Extrapolated on the basis of the relationship of farmers' holdings to holdings of all individuals (cumulated from table 10, line 6a, Friend, I. and Natrella, V., *Individuals' Saving*, part II) in 1939.

          1939–1947: *Agricultural Finance Review*, Nov. 1949, tables 30 and 195.

          1948–1949: *Balance Sheet of Agriculture*, 1950, p. 6.

Column 6 – 1896–1949: From Table A-58.

Column 7 – 1896–1949: From Table M-27, col. 4.

Column 8 – 1920–1949: From Table F-28, col. 2.

FARMERS' FINANCIAL ASSETS
1896 to 1949
$ mill.

End of year	Total	Currency holdings	Bank deposits	Life insurance reserves	Government securities	Equity in cooperatives	Mortgage debt held by farmers	Equity in veterans' funds
	1	2	3	4	5	6	7	8
1896	814	306	200	125	–	60	123	–
1897	857	322	208	134	–	65	128	–
1898	939	330	262	145	–	70	132	–
1899	1 058	358	331	157	–	75	137	–
1900	1 161	374	398	169	–	80	140	–
1901	1 273	382	477	184	–	87	143	–
1902	1 364	394	532	199	–	93	146	–
1903	1 423	400	560	213	–	100	150	–
1904	1 495	395	608	231	–	107	154	–
1905	1 652	436	696	250	–	113	157	–
1906	1 811	452	810	270	–	120	159	–
1907	1 898	475	848	286	–	127	162	–
1908	1 913	430	878	305	–	133	167	–
1909	2 055	448	968	330	–	140	169	–
1910	2 145	448	1 014	353	–	147	183	–
1911	2 210	420	1 056	380	–	153	201	–
1912	2 351	436	1 130	406	–	160	219	–
1913	2 457	428	1 180	432	–	180	237	–
1914	2 518	402	1 211	455	–	200	250	–
1915	2 790	464	1 362	484	–	220	260	–
1916	3 319	528	1 686	519	–	240	346	–
1917	4 539	724	2 030	558	500	265	462	–
1918	6 765	961	2 440	595	1 900	290	579	–
1919	7 466	934	2 876	647	1 900	320	789	–
1920	7 272	924	2 782	698	1 450	350	1 065	3
1921	6 306	629	2 570	747	900	380	1 073	7
1922	5 927	678	2 661	807	450	410	910	11
1923	5 804	692	2 800	877	250	440	731	14
1924	5 710	678	2 900	947	150	470	540	25
1925	5 627	084	2 900	1 033	50	500	417	43
1926	5 576	644	2 900	1 126	0	525	320	61
1927	5 793	623	3 000	1 226	0	550	318	76
1928	6 028	620	3 100	1 332	0	575	322	79
1929	5 936	608	2 900	1 420	0	600	318	90
1930	5 693	586	2 600	1 500	0	600	309	98
1931	5 166	670	2 000	1 560	0	600	295	41
1932	4 894	710	1 700	1 580	0	600	273	31
1933	4 866	776	1 600	1 621	0	600	237	32
1934	5 342	772	2 000	1 707	0	640	186	37
1935	5 879	842	2 300	1 819	16	680	173	49
1936	6 469	904	2 600	1 943	53	720	161	88
1937	6 794	926	2 700	2 060	109	755	154	90
1938	6 968	898	2 700	2 175	163	790	149	93
1939	7 389	980	2 800	2 296	249	826	145	93
1940	7 974	1 088	3 000	2 425	352	875	141	93
1941	9 320	1 452	3 600	2 572	511	953	137	95
1942	11 828	2 050	4 700	2 721	1 061	1 044	131	121
1943	15 354	2 691	6 000	2 882	2 335	1 140	126	180
1944	19 133	3 176	7 500	3 064	3 714	1 264	120	295
1945	23 050	3 722	9 500	3 266	4 498	1 437	120	507
1946	25 319	3 996	10 900	3 469	4 504	1 625	128	697
1947	26 598	3 932	11 400	3 679	4 781	1 880	132	794
1948	26 659	3 730	11 000	3 891	5 024	2 041	141	832
1949	26 646	3 431	10 600	4 112	5 250	2 205	149	899

FARMERS' FINANCIAL LIABILITIES
1896 to 1949

$ mill.

End of year	Total	Real estate debt	Non-real estate debt		Tax accruals	End of year	Total	Real estate debt	Non-real estate debt		Tax accruals
			To principal credit institutions	To others					To principal credit institutions	To others	
	1	2	3	4	5		1	2	3	4	5
1896	2 725	1 998	310	310	107	1923	17 111	10 665	2 982	2 929	535
1897	2 816	2 072	318	318	108	1924	15 813	9 913	2 713	2 647	540
1898	2 967	2 149	355	355	108	1925	15 657	9 713	2 735	2 659	550
1899	3 152	2 229	407	407	109	1926	15 353	9 658	2 613	2 517	565
1900	3 397	2 312	488	488	109	1927	15 431	9 757	2 596	2 488	590
1901	3 673	2 397	583	583	110	1928	15 530	9 757	2 645	2 518	610
1902	3 929	2 486	662	662	119	1929	15 215	9 631	2 546	2 408	630
1903	4 138	2 578	716	716	128	1930	14 672	9 398	2 206	2 408	660
1904	4 368	2 674	783	783	128	1931	13 672	9 094	1 772	2 146	660
1905	4 698	2 773	898	898	129	1932	12 319	8 466	1 466	1 747	640
1906	5 082	2 876	1 038	1 038	130	1933	11 042	7 685	1 209	1 528	620
1907	5 294	2 983	1 086	1 086	139	1934	10 756	7 584	947	1 605	620
1908	5 461	3 093	1 110	1 110	148	1935	10 581	7 423	1 154	1 404	600
1909	5 872	3 208	1 250	1 250	164	1936	10 206	7 154	1 087	1 385	580
1910	6 364	3 522	1 338	1 338	166	1937	10 315	6 955	1 165	1 625	570
1911	6 873	3 930	1 380	1 380	183	1938	10 233	6 779	1 319	1 590	545
1912	7 579	4 348	1 520	1 520	191	1939	10 120	6 586	1 504	1 500	530
1913	8 119	4 707	1 597	1 597	218	1940	10 343	6 491	1 647	1 700	505
1914	8 425	4 991	1 606	1 606	222	1941	10 340	6 372	1 783	1 700	485
1915	8 995	5 256	1 748	1 748	243	1942	9 578	5 951	1 672	1 500	455
1916	10 154	5 826	2 034	2 034	260	1943	8 712	5 389	1 688	1 200	435
1917	11 807	6 537	2 489	2 489	292	1944	8 090	4 933	1 622	1 100	435
1918	12 776	7 137	2 666	2 662	311	1945	8 028	4 682	1 671	1 200	475
1919	15 751	8 449	3 455	3 454	393	1946	8 756	4 777	1 954	1 500	525
1920	18 445	10 221	3 871	3 870	483	1947	9 575	4 882	2 293	1 800	600
1921	17 793	10 702	3 300	3 281	510	1948	10 673	5 108	2 714	2 200	651
1922	17 531	10 786	3 137	3 088	520	1949	11 350	5 413	2.838	2 400	699

Column 1 – 1896–1949: Sum of cols. 2–5.

Column 2 – 1896–1949: From Table A-61, col. 1.

Column 3 – 1896–1949: From Table A-62, col. 1.

Column 4 – 1896–1922: Assumed equal to non-real estate debt to commercial banks, Table A-62, col. 2.
1923–1928: Estimated by multiplying non-real estate debt to banks, Table A-62, col. 2, by ratios of debt to "others" to debt to banks. Ratios obtained by rough linear interpolation between 1922 and 1929 figures.
1929: Burroughs, R. J., "The Agricultural Segment of the National Balance Sheet," *Studies in Income and Wealth*, vol. XII, p. 196.
1930–1938: Estimated on basis of linear interpolation between 1929 and 1939 ratios of receivables of farm machinery companies to farmers' debt to others. Figures for notes and accounts receivable of farm machinery companies taken from *Statistics of Income, Source Book.*
1939–1949: Annual editions of *Balance Sheet of Agriculture*, 1945–1949.

Column 5 – 1896–1949: From Table A-64, col. 4.

1896 to 1949

End of year	Currency outside banks	Farmers' share in national income	Farm share in total population	Currency holdings of farmers		End of year	Currency outside banks	Farmers' share in national income	Farm share in total population	Currency holdings of farmers	
				Estimate A	Estimate B					Estimate A	Estimate B
	$ mill.	Percent		$ mill.			$ mill.	Percent		$ mill.	
	1	2	3	4	5		1	2	3	4	5
1896	1 137	13.5	40.5	–	306	1923	3 922	8.0	27.3	–	692
1897	1 185	14.3	40.1	–	322	1924	3 899	8.0	26.8	–	678
1898	1 225	14.3	39.7	–	330	1925	3 808	9.6	26.3	–	684
1899	1 352	13.7	39.3	–	358	1926	3 789	8.5	25.5	–	644
1900	1 426	13.5	38.9	–	374	1927	3 717	8.3	25.2	–	623
1901	1 476	13.2	38.5	–	382	1928	3 703	8.6	24.9	–	620
1902	1 540	13.0	38.1	–	394	1929	3 709	8.2	24.6	600	608
1903	1 597	12.6	37.6	–	400	1930	3 702	7.0	24.7	–	586
1904	1 564	13.3	37.2	–	395	1931	4 368	5.8	24.9	–	670
1905	1 775	12.3	36.8	–	436	1932	4 615	5.2	25.6	–	710
1906	1 849	12.5	36.4	–	452	1933	4 736	7.4	25.4	–	776
1907	1 966	12.4	35.9	–	475	1934	4 719	7.6	25.1	–	772
1908	1 734	14.1	35.5	–	430	1935	4 928	9.6	24.6	–	842
1909	1 809	14.4	35.1	–	448	1936	5 527	8.6	24.1	–	904
1910	1 841	14.2	34.5	–	448	1937	5 666	9.0	23.7	–	926
1911	1 800	12.5	34.1	–	420	1938	5 753	7.8	23.4	–	898
1912	1 868	13.1	33.5	–	436	1939	6 388	7.7	23.0	1 000	980
1913	1 899	12.1	32.9	–	428	1940	7 329	7.1	22.6	1 100	1 088
1914	1 770	13.0	32.5	–	402	1941	9 615	8.5	21.7	1 500	1 452
1915	2 102	12.0	32.1	–	464	1942	13 943	9.7	19.7	2 000	2 050
1916	2 442	11.8	31.4	–	528	1943	18 816	10.0	18.6	2 700	2 691
1917	3 053	16.9	30.5	–	724	1944	23 525	8.9	18.1	3 300	3 176
1918	4 047	18.0	29.5	–	961	1945	26 490	9.0	19.1	4 000	3 722
1919	4 067	16.0	29.9	–	934	1946	26 730	10.6	19.3	4 000	3 996
1920	4 496	11.6	29.5	–	924	1947	26 476	10.8	18.9	3 900	3 932
1921	3 583	6.1	29.0	–	629	1948	26 079	9.8	18.8	3 800	3 730
1922	3 764	8.0	28.0	–	678	1949	25 415	8.2	18.8	3 700	3 431

Column 1 – 1896–1949: From Table L-2, col. 3.

Column 2 – 1896–1910: From Table A-4, col. 4.
          1911–1949: From Table A-5, col. 3.

Column 3 – 1896–1899: Extrapolated from 1900 figure.
          1900, 1909: Estimated on basis of Census data on proportion of rural population, 1900–1919.
          1901–1908: Linear interpolation between 1900 and 1909 figures.
          1910–1919: *Income Parity for Agriculture*, part v, section 1.
          1920–1928: Farm population from *Agricultural Statistics*, 1942, p. 643; total population arithmetic averages of July 1 estimates from *Statistical Abstract*, 1947, p. 9.
          1929–1949: *Agricultural Statistics*, 1947, p. 499, as revised and brought up to date by Bureau of Agricultural Economics.

Column 4 – 1929–1949: *Balance Sheet of Agriculture*, various issues.

Column 5 – 1896–1949: Arithmetic average of col. 1 multiplied by col. 2 and col. 1 multiplied by col. 3.

Column 1 – 1896–1922: Two-year moving average of col. 2.
             1923–1949: Sum of cols. 5 and 6.

Column 2 – 1896–1922: Extrapolated from 1923 value by col. 3.
             1923: Dec. value from col. 1 extrapolated to June by Bureau of Agricultural Economics monthly index of farmers' total deposits.

Column 3 – 1896–1923: Computed from data from Comptroller of the Currency on country national bank and state bank total individual deposits for the following seventeen agricultural states: Arkansas, Georgia, Idaho, Illinois, Iowa, Kansas, Louisiana, Minnesota, Mississippi, Missouri, Nebraska, North Carolina, North Dakota, South Carolina, South Dakota, Texas, and Wisconsin. The states were selected on the basis of their importance in annual cash income from farm production (as shown in Wall, Norman J., *Demand Deposits of Country Banks*, Department of Agriculture Technical Bulletin 575, Aug. 1937, and *Income Parity for Agriculture*, part VI, *State Estimates of Income and Production Expenses*), relative unimportance of industry outside of their reserve cities, and representativeness of the different agricultural regions. Country national bank data (available on worksheets in files of the National Bureau of Economic Research) were used for all seventeen states, and adjustments were made for the changing classification of reserve cities. State commercial bank data were not used for those states for which reserve city state banks were of importance, as shown in the National Monetary Commission, *Special Report from the Banks of the United States,* April 28, 1909, i.e. loan and trust company data for Louisiana, Missouri, and Wisconsin were not used since the same study showed that where they existed they were fundamentally big city institutions. For the few states and years where private banks were important rural institutions, their data were combined with those for state banks.

    Data for years obviously out of line with previous and succeeding years with respect to coverage were eliminated from all computations.

    Relatives for the combined data used for each state were then computed on the base 1923–1929 = 100 to provide an overlap with Bureau of Agricultural Economics index covering those years; the relatives for each state were combined finally by weights derived from those used by Wall (*op. cit.*, pp. 9, 11, 12).

Column 4 – 1923–1938: Department of Agriculture, Bureau of Agricultural Economics, *Impact of the War on the Financial Structure of Agriculture*, Miscellaneous Publication 567, p. 69.
             1939–1943: *Balance Sheet of Agriculture*, 1948, table 16, p. 26.

Column 5 – 1923–1942: Col. 4 values lowered by ratio of col. 5 to col. 4 in 1943 and rounded to nearest $100 mill.
             1943–1949: Federal Reserve Board estimates of farmers' demand deposits (*Federal Reserve Bulletin*, May 1949, p. 505; *The Balance Sheet of Agriculture*, 1949, p. 35, as brought up to date by Bureau of Agricultural Economics).

Column 6 – 1923–1938: Same source as col. 4.
             1939–1949: *Balance Sheet of Agriculture*, 1949, p. 35.

FARMERS' BANK DEPOSITS
1896 to 1949

$ mill. (except col. 3)

Year	Farmers' total deposits		Index of farmers' deposits (1923–29 =100.0)	Farmers' demand deposits		B.A.E. estimate of farmers' time deposits	Year	Farmers' total deposits		Index of farmers' deposits (1923–29 =100.0)	Farmers' demand deposits		B.A.E. estimate of farmers' time deposits
				Prelim. esti- mate	Final esti- mate						Prelim. esti- mate	Final esti- mate	
	Dec. 31	June 30	June 30	Dec. 31	Dec. 31	Dec. 31		Dec. 31	June 30	June 30	Dec. 31	Dec. 31	Dec. 31
	1	2	3	4	5	6		1	2	3	4	5	6
1896	200	199	6.9	–	–	–	1923	2 800	2 700	93.4	1 400	1 300	1 500
1897	208	202	7.0	–	–	–	1924	2 900	–	–	1 400	1 300	1 600
1898	262	214	7.4	–	–	–	1925	2 900	–	–	1 400	1 300	1 600
1899	331	309	10.7	–	–	–	1926	2 900	–	–	1 400	1 300	1 600
1900	398	353	12.2	–	–	–	1927	3 000	–	–	1 400	1 300	1 700
1901	477	442	15.3	–	–	–	1928	3 100	–	–	1 400	1 300	1 800
1902	532	512	17.7	–	–	–	1929	2 900	–	–	1 300	1 200	1 700
1903	560	552	19.1	–	–	–	1930	2 600	–	–	1 100	1 000	1 600
1904	608	569	19.7	–	–	–	1931	2 000	–	–	800	700	1 300
1905	696	648	22.4	–	–	–	1932	1 700	–	–	700	600	1 100
1906	810	743	25.7	–	–	–	1933	1 600	–	–	700	600	1 000
1907	848	876	30.3	–	–	–	1934	2 000	–	–	1 000	900	1 100
1908	878	821	28.4	–	–	–	1935	2 300	–	–	1 200	1 100	1 200
1909	968	934	32.3	–	–	–	1936	2 600	–	–	1 400	1 300	1 300
1910	1 014	1 003	34.7	–	–	–	1937	2 700	–	–	1 400	1 300	1 400
1911	1 056	1 026	35.5	–	–	–	1938	2 700	–	–	1 400	1 300	1 400
1912	1 130	1 087	37.6	–	–	–	1939	2 800	–	–	1 500	1 400	1 400
1913	1 180	1 174	40.6	–	–	–	1940	3 000	–	–	1 700	1 500	1 500
1914	1 211	1 185	41.0	–	–	–	1941	3 600	–	–	2 200	2 000	1 600
1915	1 362	1 237	42.8	–	–	–	1942	4 700	–	–	3 200	2 900	1 800
1916	1 686	1 486	51.4	–	–	–	1943	6 000	–	–	4 400	4 000	2 000
1917	2 030	1 885	65.2	–	–	–	1944	7 500	–	–	–	5 000	2 500
1918	2 440	2 174	75.2	–	–	–	1945	9 500	–	–	–	6 200	3 300
1919	2 876	2 706	93.6	–	–	–	1946	10 900	–	–	–	7 300	3 600
1920	2 782	3 047	105.4	–	–	–	1947	11 400	–	–	–	7 600	3 800
1921	2 570	2 518	87.1	–	–	–	1948	11 000	–	–	–	7 200	3 800
1922	2 661	2 622	90.7	–		..	1949	10 600	–	–	–	6 800	3 800

Column 1 – 1910–1949: Based on special tabulation by Life Insurance Association of America.

Column 2 – 1910–1949: Farm population and total population of fifteen key agricultural states (Arkansas
Georgia, Idaho, Iowa, Kansas, Louisiana, Minnesota, Mississippi, Nebraska, North Carolina
North Dakota, South Carolina, South Dakota, Texas, and Wisconsin) from population censuses of 1910, 1920, 1930, and 1940. Total population for 1935 and 1945 from intercensal year
estimates of the Bureau of the Census and farm population from *Census of Agriculture*, 1935
and 1945. Intercensal interpolations, 1910–1930 and 1946–1948, based on change in Bureau of
Agricultural Economics estimates of percentage of farm population in the U.S. Interpolations
between 1930, 1935, 1940, and 1945 Census data based on changes in Bureau of Agricultural
Economics estimates of percentage of farm population in west central states because percentages for these states at Census dates were very close to those for the fifteen selected states.

Column 3 – 1910–1949: Col. 1 multiplied by col. 2.

Column 4 – 1897–1909: Value for 1910 extrapolated by farmers' share in national income as given in Table
A-4, col. 4.
1910–1940: Obtained by multiplying 1941 value by col. 3.
1941: Based on relationship of premium payments by farm families (derived from Department of Agriculture's consumer expenditure study for 1941) to total premium payments
(see Table I-8).
1942–1949: Same procedure as for 1910–1940.

Column 5 – 1897–1949: Col. 4 multiplied by total domestic policyholders' saving (before adjustment for
changes in policy loans but including adjustment for capital gains and losses) as given in Table
I-1, col. 1 minus col. 7.

Column 6 – 1897–1949: Col. 4 multiplied by Table I-1, col. 1 minus col. 4.

Column 7 – 1897–1949: Col. 5 minus col. 6.

FARMERS' SAVING THROUGH LIFE INSURANCE
1897 to 1949

Year	Share of 15 agricultural states in premium reserves of 48 states	Proportion of farm population in 15 states		Farmers' share in total premium reserve accruals		Change in policy loans to farmers	Farmers' saving through life insurance
	1941 = 100.0			Percent	$ mill.		
	1	2	3	4	5	6	7
1897	.	.	.	12.0	10	1	9
1898	.	.	.	12.0	12	1	11
1899	.	.	.	11.5	13	1	12
1900	.	.	.	11.3	14	2	12
1901	.	.	.	11.1	17	2	15
1902	.	.	.	10.9	17	2	15
1903	.	.	.	10.6	17	3	14
1904	.	.	.	11.1	21	3	18
1905	.	.	.	10.3	22	3	19
1906	.	.	.	10.5	24	4	20
1907	.	.	.	10.4	25	9	16
1908	.	.	.	11.8	26	7	19
1909	.	.	.	12.1	29	4	25
1910	120.2	141.1	169.6	11.9	29	6	23
1911	120.9	140.4	169.7	11.9	33	6	27
1912	122.1	138.9	169.6	11.9	31	5	26
1913	123.2	137.3	169.2	11.8	34	8	26
1914	122.5	136.6	167.3	11.7	32	9	23
1915	118.4	135.8	160.8	11.3	34	5	29
1916	114.5	133.7	153.1	10.7	36	1	35
1917	113.7	130.9	148.8	10.4	41	2	39
1918	114.5	127.3	145.8	10.2	38	1	37
1919	115.2	129.8	149.5	10.5	51	−1	52
1920	118.8	129.1	153.4	10.7	57	6	51
1921	115.9	127.8	148.1	10.4	70	21	49
1922	115.2	124.5	143.4	10.0	68	8	60
1923	113.0	122.4	138.3	9.7	76	6	70
1924	109.4	120.8	132.2	9.3	82	12	70
1925	108.0	119.6	129.2	9.0	97	11	86
1926	105.7	116.8	123.5	8.6	106	13	93
1927	105.0	116.3	122.1	8.5	116	16	100
1928	105.0	115.8	121.6	8.5	124	18	106
1929	102.9	115.2	118.5	8.3	119	31	88
1930	102.9	113.7	117.0	8.2	114	34	80
1931	102.1	114.2	116.6	8.2	105	45	60
1932	101.4	116.0	117.6	8.2	55	35	20
1933	100.0	113.9	113.9	8.0	38	−3	41
1934	100.0	112.3	112.3	7.9	77	−9	86
1935	98.5	110.1	108.4	7.6	103	−9	112
1936	99.3	107.5	106.7	7.5	115	−9	124
1937	99.3	106.7	106.0	7.4	116	−1	117
1938	100.0	105.4	105.4	7.4	114	−1	115
1939	100.0	104.1	104.1	7.3	111	−10	121
1940	100.7	103.6	104.3	7.3	118	−11	129
1941	100.0	100.0	100.0	7.0	135	−12	147
1942	100.5	87.9	88.3	6.2	135	−14	149
1943	101.0	82.3	83.1	5.8	143	−18	161
1944	101.6	82.3	83.6	5.9	168	−14	182
1945	102.1	87.1	88.9	6.2	192	−10	202
1946	102.1	86.6	88.4	6.2	199	−4	203
1947	104.3	83.8	87.4	6.1	213	3	210
1948	104.3	82.0	85.5	6.0	219	7	212
1949	104.3	81.7	85.2	6.0	232	11	221

A-58

1896–1928: Rough estimates derived by interpolation between estimated values for 1900, 1912, 1922, and 1929 (Table A–59) and allowing for changes in equity in federal land banks, the only component for which annual data are available (cf. Table A–60).

1929: Burroughs, R. J., "The Agricultural Segment of the National Balance Sheet," *Studies in Income and Wealth*, vol. XII, table 1.

1930–1935: Interpolated between 1929 and 1936 figures on assumption that farmers' equity in cooperatives remained unchanged during the depression and that difference between the 1929 and 1936 totals can be prorated equally among years 1934–1936.

1936: From Table A–59, col. 1.

1937–1938: Obtained by linear interpolation between 1936 and 1939 figures.

1939–1949: *Agricultural Finance Review*, Nov. 1950, p. 110.

Note: All figures refer to the end of the year.

A-59

Column 1 – 1900, 1912, 1922: Rough estimates.
    1929: Burroughs, R. J., "The Agricultural Segment of the National Balance Sheet," *Studies in Income and Wealth*, vol. XII, table 1.
    1936: Sum of cols. 2–7.
    1939: *Balance Sheet of Agriculture*, 1948, table 20.

Column 2 – 1912, 1922: Rough estimates based on relation of volume of business in those years to that in 1929 (cf. Wanstall, Grace, *Statistics of Farmers' Marketing and Purchasing Cooperatives, 1945–1946*, Department of Agriculture, Farm Credit Administration, p. 5).
    1929: Obtained as residual between col. 1 and sum of cols. 3–7.
    1936: Department of Agriculture, Farm Credit Administration, *Statistical Handbook of Farmers' Cooperatives*, p. 161.
    1939: Same as col. 1.

Column 3 – 1912, 1922, 1929: Estimated on basis of data on capital invested in cooperative irrigation enterprises in 1910, 1920, and 1930 compiled by Bureau of the Census (cf. *Statistical Abstract*, 1948, p. 577).
    1936: Same source as for col. 2, pp. 259–260.
    1939: Same as col. 1.

Column 4 – 1912, 1922, 1929: Rough estimates based on data on total capital investment in small telephone companies and on receipts of all small telephone companies and of farmers' mutual telephone companies in *Census of Electrical Industries* for 1917, 1922, and 1927.
    1936: Assumed equal to value for 1939.
    1939: Same as col. 1.

Column 5 – 1912, 1922, 1929: Estimated on basis of insurance in force (cf. *Agricultural Finance Review*, Nov. 1948, p. 126).
    1936, 1939: Surplus and reserves as given in *Agricultural Finance Review, op. cit.*

Column 6 – 1936: Rough estimate.
    1939: Same as col. 1.

Column 7 – 1922, 1929, 1936, 1939: From Table A–60, col. 1.

FARMERS' EQUITY IN COOPERATIVES
1896 to 1949

A-58

$ mill.

1896	60	1910	147	1924	470	1937	755
1897	65	1911	153	1925	500	1938	790
1898	70	1912	160	1926	525	1939	826
1899	75	1913	180	1927	550	1940	875
1900	80	1914	200	1928	575	1941	953
1901	87	1915	220	1929	600	1942	1 044
1902	93	1916	240	1930	600	1943	1 140
1903	100	1917	265	1931	600	1944	1 264
1904	107	1918	290	1932	600	1945	1 437
1905	113	1919	320	1933	600	1946	1 625
1906	120	1920	350	1934	640	1947	1 880
1907	127	1921	380	1935	680	1948	2 041
1908	133	1922	410	1936	720	1949	2 205
1909	140	1923	440				

FARMERS' EQUITY IN COOPERATIVES
Selected Years: 1900 to 1939

A-59

$ mill.

End of year	Total	Marketing and purchasing associations	Mutual irrigation companies	Mutual telephone companies	Mutual fire insurance companies	Production credit associations	Federal land banks (including national farm loan associations)
	1	2	3	4	5	6	7
1900	80	.	.	.	.	–	–
1912	160	40	100	10	10	–	–
1922	410	160	170	15	25	–	40
1929	600	296	170	15	35	–	84
1936	720	288	190	23	35	20	164
1939	826	330	197	23	42	31	203

A-6

Column 1 – Sum of cols. 2–6.

Columns 2 to 6 – Department of Agriculture, Farm Credit Administration, *Combined Statements of Federal Land Banks*. Col. 6 includes deficits of $0.3 million in 1932 and $13.0 million in 1934.

FARMERS' EQUITY IN FEDERAL LAND BANKS
1917 to 1949

$ mill.

| End of year | Farmers' equity | Capital stock held by | | Legal reserves | Earned surplus | Other reserves and surplus |
		National farm associations	Others excluding U.S. Government			
	1	2	3	4	5	6
1917	1.6	1.5	0.1	–	–	–
1918	7.5	7.4	0.1	–	–	–
1919	14.9	14.1	0.1	–	–	0.7
1920	20.1	17.7	0.1	0.1	–	2.2
1921	25.2	21.1	0.1	1.5	–	2.5
1922	39.9	32.6	0.1	3.0	–	4.2
1923	50.0	40.9	0.2	4.6	–	4.3
1924	58.5	47.5	0.4	6.6	–	4.0
1925	65.2	51.9	0.5	8.3	–	4.5
1926	70.2	56.1	0.6	9.2	–	4.3
1927	77.2	60.7	0.7	11.0	–	4.8
1928	82.0	63.5	0.8	12.4	–	5.3
1929	83.8	64.6	0.8	13.0	–	5.4
1930	83.3	65.0	0.8	13.4	–	4.1
1931	81.3	64.6	0.8	13.1	–	2.8
1932	80.0	63.2	0.8	14.2	–	1.8
1933	84.8	65.6	1.1	13.2	–	4.9
1934	109.0	100.4	3.6	18.0	–	–13.0
1935	140.8	109.3	3.6	27.5	–	0.4
1936	163.8	111.0	3.5	35.4	–	13.9
1937	176.7	110.4	3.4	43.1	8.5	11.3
1938	192.2	109.7	3.6	49.9	5.0	24.0
1939	203.0	107.8	3.7	56.9	5.0	29.6
1940	215.9	107.0	3.6	64.6	6.0	34.7
1941	224.5	104.2	3.3	69.2	47.8	–
1942	228.0	97.4	3.0	73.9	53.7	–
1943	216.9	85.5	2.5	75.3	53.6	–
1944	217.1	73.6	2.0	80.5	61.0	–
1945	230.2	66.4	1.7	83.0	79.1	–
1946	240.5	60.7	1.2	85.5	93.1	–
1947	252.5	56.2	0.8	93.3	102.2	–
1948	257.1	55.1	0.8	94.8	106.4	–
1949	263.8	57.2	0.7	96.4	109.5	–

Columns 1 and 2 – 1896–1908: Obtained by geometric interpolation between 1890 and 1909, the 1890 figure based on relation between benchmark data derived from Censuses of 1890 and 1910 by Kuvin, L., *Private Long-Term Debt in U.S.*, p. 121. Approximately same figures would be obtained if 1909 figure had been extrapolated by farm construction expenditures.

　　1909–1928: Department of Agriculture, *Farm Mortgage Credit Facilities in the U.S.*, Miscellaneous Publication 478, p. 12.

　　1929–1933: Larsen, Harold C., *Distribution by Lender Groups of Farm Mortgage and Real Estate Holdings, January 1, 1930–1945*, Department of Agriculture, p. 7. Figures (as those in cols. 3 to 6) include purchase money mortgages and sales contracts.

　　1934–1949: *Agricultural Finance Review, Supplement*, May 1950, p. 12.

Column 3 – 1934–1949: Same sources as col. 1. Loans held by Federal Farm Mortgage Corporation were made on its behalf by Land Bank Commissioner.

Column 4 – 1917–1949: Same sources as col. 1. Joint-stock land banks have been in liquidation since May 12, 1933. Includes banks in receivership.

Column 5 – 1938–1949: Same sources as col. 1. Farmers Home Administration is successor to Farm Security Administration. Data for 1938–1940 include tenant purchase-loans. Thereafter data include farm-development (special real estate) loans beginning 1941, farm-enlargement loans beginning 1943, and project-liquidation loans beginning 1944. Data also include loans for these purposes from State Rural Rehabilitation Corporation trust funds.

Column 6 – 1917–1928: Wall, Norman J., *Outstanding Farm Mortgage Loans of Leading Lending Agencies*, Department of Agriculture, p. 38. The three state credit agencies are Department of Rural Credit of Minnesota, Bank of North Dakota, and Rural Credit Board of South Dakota. Rural Credit Board completed liquidation during 1945.

　　1929–1934: Bureau of Agricultural Economics worksheets.

　　1935–1945: Same sources as col. 1.

　　1946–1949: Included in col. 12.

Column 7 – 1896–1908: From Table I-5, col. 3.

　　1909–1949: Same sources as col. 1.

Column 8 – 1896–1924: Roughly estimated to be 10 percent of Table I-10, col. 4.

　　1925–1949: From Table I-10, col. 5.

Column 9 – 1896–1908: Two-year moving average of index, Table A-63, col. 3, applied to 1909 estimate.

　　1909–1933: Same source as col. 1 except that estimates of farm mortgage debt held by mutual savings banks (col. 11) subtracted.

　　1934–1949: Farm mortgages held by insured commercial banks (from *Annual Report of the Federal Deposit Insurance Corporation*) increased to account for other commercial banks on assumption that farm mortgages held by noninsured banks as percentage of farm mortgages held by insured commercial banks is double the ratio of total loans of noninsured to insured commercial banks (cf. Table L-26, col. 3). This assumption is based on relation prevailing from 1947 to 1949 (derived from *Annual Report of the Federal Deposit Insurance Corporation*).

　　Bureau of Agricultural Economics report cited in col. 1 gives farm mortgages held by insured commercial banks but not other commercial banks.

Column 10 – 1921–1942: From Table M-14, col. 7.

Column 11 – 1896–1949: From Table L-30, col. 2.

Column 12 – 1896–1949: Col. 1 minus sum of cols. 2–11.

FARM MORTGAGE DEBT; TOTAL OUTSTANDING AND AMOUNTS HELD BY PRINCIPAL LENDER GROUPS: 1896 to 1949

$ mill.

End of year	Total	Federal land banks	Federal Farm Mortgage Corporation	Joint stock land banks	Farmers Home Administration	Three state credit agencies	Insurance companies		Commercial banks		Mutual savings banks	Individuals and others
							Life	Fraternal order life	Operating	Closed		
	1	2	3	4	5	6	7	8	9	10	11	12
1896	1 998	–	–	–	–	–	120	0	85	–	32	1 761
1897	2 072	–	–	–	–	–	124	0	88	–	33	1 827
1898	2 149	–	–	–	–	–	127	0	98	–	34	1 890
1899	2 229	–	–	–	–	–	133	0	112	–	35	1 949
1900	2 312	–	–	–	–	–	144	0	134	–	38	1 996
1901	2 397	–	–	–	–	–	155	0	160	–	39	2 043
1902	2 486	–	–	–	–	–	171	0	182	–	41	2 092
1903	2 578	–	–	–	–	–	190	0	197	–	43	2 148
1904	2 674	–	–	–	–	–	209	1	216	–	46	2 202
1905	2 773	–	–	–	–	–	230	1	247	–	49	2 246
1906	2 876	–	–	–	–	–	268	1	286	–	53	2 268
1907	2 983	–	–	–	–	–	307	1	299	–	55	2 321
1908	3 093	–	–	–	–	–	340	1	305	–	58	2 389
1909	3 208	–	–	–	–	–	387	1	344	–	62	2 414
1910	3 522	–	–	–	–	–	423	1	412	–	66	2 620
1911	3 930	–	–	–	–	–	480	2	510	–	70	2 868
1912	4 348	–	–	–	–	–	550	2	599	–	75	3 122
1913	4 707	–	–	–	–	–	597	2	645	–	79	3 384
1914	4 991	–	–	–	–	–	670	2	658	–	88	3 573
1915	5 256	–	–	–	–	–	766	2	699	–	77	3 712
1916	5 826	–	–	–	–	–	861	3	867	–	67	4 028
1917	6 537	39	–	2	–	2	956	3	946	–	62	4 527
1918	7 137	157	–	8	–	13	1 018	3	973	–	57	4 908
1919	8 449	296	–	60	–	25	975	3	1 147	–	57	5 886
1920	10 221	356	–	78	–	33	1 206	4	1 390	–	57	7 097
1921	10 702	443	–	85	–	36	1 432	4	1 487	10	53	7 152
1922	10 786	656	–	219	–	40	1 556	6	1 455	15	51	6 788
1923	10 665	822	–	393	–	45	1 792	6	1 331	20	57	6 199
1924	9 913	923	–	446	–	73	1 943	8	1 136	25	64	5 295
1925	9 713	999	–	546	–	74	2 030	10	1 107	25	71	4 851
1926	9 658	1 069	–	633	–	73	2 124	11	1 066	30	78	4 574
1927	9 757	1 145	–	667	–	96	2 173	12	1 012	30	85	4 537
1928	9 757	1 183	–	657	–	94	2 139	14	955	25	92	4 598
1929	9 631	1 202	–	638	–	96	2 118	15	904	25	93	4 540
1930	9 398	1 197	–	606	–	96	2 087	17	850	30	97	4 418
1931	9 094	1 181	–	552	–	96	2 037	17	839	50	101	4 221
1932	8 466	1 147	–	475	–	87	1 898	17	789	60	100	3 893
1933	7 685	1 258	–	412	–	83	1 698	16	617	121	94	3 386
1934	7 584	1 947	617	277	–	66	1 302	15	525	96	90	2 649
1935	7 423	2 114	794	201	–	54	1 112	13	515	72	81	2 467
1936	7 154	2 148	841	163	–	40	1 016	12	512	52	75	2 295
1937	6 955	2 127	824	134	–	35	989	13	523	37	69	2 204
1938	6 779	2 088	774	115	10	32	983	13	541	27	65	2 131
1939	6 586	2 010	713	92	32	30	984	14	558	20	61	2 072
1940	6 491	1 957	685	73	65	29	1 016	14	568	14	57	2 013
1941	6 372	1 881	635	56	115	30	1 063	15	558	7	52	1 960
1942	5 951	1 718	544	37	157	29	1 043	15	493	1	46	1 868
1943	5 389	1 453	430	10	172	24	987	15	462	–	41	1 795
1944	4 933	1 210	347	5	193	20	934	15	462	–	36	1 711
1945	4 682	1 079	239	3	182	14	884	15	519	–	31	1 716
1946	4 777	977	147	2	189	–	890	16	701	–	29	1 826
1947	4 882	889	107	1	195	–	937	17	814	–	28	1 894
1948	5 108	868	78	–	189	–	1 036	21	869	–	34	2 013
1949	5 413	906	59	–	189	–	1 172	24	905	–	36	2 122

Column 1 – 1896–1933: Sum of cols. 2–8.
             1934–1949: *Agricultural Finance Review,* Nov. 1950, p. 96.

Column 2 – 1896–1909: From Table A-63, col. 1.
             1910–1933: *Agricultural Finance Review,* Nov. 1945, p. 2.
             1934–1949: Same source as col. 1.

Column 3 – 1934–1949: Same source as col. 1.

Column 4 – 1922–1933: *Agricultural Statistics,* 1942, p. 723.
             1934–1949: Same source as col. 1.

Column 5 – 1932–1933: *Agricultural Statistics,* 1949, p. 668.
             1934–1949: Same source as col. 1. Also includes flood damage, fire, and flood and windstorm restoration loans and loans made by Regional Agricultural Credit Corporation prior to its dissolution and transfer of its assets from Farm Credit Administration to Federal Housing Administration on Apr. 16, 1949.

Column 6 – 1922: *Historical Statistics,* p. 112. June 30 figures converted to Dec. 31 by arithmetic averaging.
             1923–1933; *Agricultural Statistics,* 1942, p. 703.
             1934–1949: Same source as col. 1.

Column 7 – 1934–1949: Same source as col. 1.

Column 8 – 1918–1927: Bureau of Agricultural Economics worksheets.

NON-REAL ESTATE LOANS TO FARMERS
AMOUNTS HELD BY PRINCIPAL CREDIT INSTITUTIONS
(Excluding Commodity Credit Corporation Guarantees and Loans): 1896 to 1949
$ mill.

End of year	Total	Commercial banks	Production credit associations	Federal intermediate credit banks	Farmers Home Administration			War Finance Corporation
					Disaster loans	Emergency crop and feed loans	Production and subsistence loans	
	1	2	3	4	5	6	7	8
1896	310	310	–	–	–	–	–	–
1897	318	318	–	–	–	–	–	–
1898	355	355	–	–	–	–	–	–
1899	407	407	–	–	–	–	–	–
1900	488	488	–	–	–	–	–	–
1901	583	583	–	–	–	–	–	–
1902	662	662	–	–	–	–	–	–
1903	716	716	–	–	–	–	–	–
1904	783	783	–	–	–	–	–	–
1905	898	898	–	–	–	–	–	–
1906	1 038	1 038	–	–	–	–	–	–
1907	1 086	1 086	–	–	–	–	–	–
1908	1 110	1 110	–	–	–	–	–	–
1909	1 250	1 250	–	..	–	–	–	–
1910	1 338	1 338	–	–	–	–	–	–
1911	1 380	1 380	–	–	–	–	–	–
1912	1 520	1 520	–	–	–	–	–	–
1913	1 597	1 597	–	–	–	–	–	–
1914	1 606	1 606	–	–	–	–	–	–
1915	1 748	1 748	–	–	–	–	–	–
1916	2 034	2 034	–	–	–	–	–	–
1917	2 489	2 489	–	–	–	–	–	–
1918	2 666	2 662	–	–	–	–	–	4
1919	3 455	3 454	–	–	–	–	–	1
1920	3 871	3 870	–	–	–	–	–	1
1921	3 300	3 281	–	–	–	–	–	19
1922	3 137	3 088	–	0	–	3	–	46
1923	2 982	2 944	–	9	–	2	–	27
1924	2 713	2 674	–	19	–	2	–	18
1025	2 735	2 699	–	20	–	2	–	8
1926	2 613	2 568	–	39	–	2	–	4
1927	2 596	2 552	–	42	–	2	–	0
1928	2 645	2 596	–	44	–	5	–	–
1929	2 546	2 491	–	47	–	8	–	–
1930	2 206	2 109	–	62	–	35	–	–
1931	1 772	1 650	–	72	–	50	–	–
1932	1 466	1 272	–	80	24	90	–	–
1933	1 209	913	–	60	145	91	–	–
1934	947	628	60	55	87	111	6	–
1935	1 154	735	93	47	43	172	63	–
1936	1 087	621	104	41	25	165	132	–
1937	1 165	683	137	40	16	172	118	–
1938	1 319	789	147	33	11	171	169	–
1939	1 504	900	153	32	8	168	242	–
1940	1 647	984	171	32	6	168	287	–
1941	1 783	1 073	186	37	6	164	317	–
1942	1 672	924	183	38	4	155	368	–
1943	1 688	936	197	34	33	146	343	–
1944	1 622	949	188	30	14	138	303	–
1945	1 671	1 034	195	26	7	129	279	–
1946	1 954	1 289	230	32	4	117	282	–
1947	2 293	1 593	289	38	3	106	265	–
1948	2 714	1 946	367	56	3	90	253	–
1949	2 838	2 049	387	51	13	71	267	–

Column 1 – 1896–1909: Arithmetic average of preceding and succeeding June 30 value from col. 2.
    1910: *Agricultural Finance Review*, Nov. 1945, p. 2.

Column 2 – 1896–1909: 1910 value extrapolated by index from col. 3.
    1910: Same source as col. 1.

Column 3 – 1896–1910: Computed from data obtained from Comptroller of the Currency reports on country
    national bank and state bank total loans and discounts for same group of seventeen key agri-
    cultural states used in index described in Table A-56, col. 3. Same methods of choosing types
    of banks to be included, screening data used, computing relatives, weighting and averaging as
    were described for deposit index of Table A-56, col. 3 were used in constructing index for
    loans and discounts.

Column 1 – 1896–1908: Col. 2 multiplied by col. 3.
    1909–1945: *Historical Statistics*, p. 98.
    1946–1949: *Agricultural Finance Review*, Nov. 1949, table 22.

Column 2 – 1896–1949: *Agricultural Finance Review*, Nov. 1949, table 23.

Column 3 – 1896–1899: Extrapolated on basis of 1900–1910 trend.
    1900: *Historical Statistics*, p. 96.
    1901–1909: Obtained by linear interpolation between 1900 and 1910 values.
    1910, 1920, 1925, 1930, 1935, 1940, 1945: *Historical Statistics*, p. 96.

Column 4 – 1897–1920: Identical with col. 1 on assumption that taxes levied in one calendar year are payable
    during next year and that tax arrears and defaults were small (cf. *Agricultural Statistics*, 1947,
    p. 563: "For the country as a whole levies and payments probably are about equal over long
    periods").
    1921–1946: Figures of col. 1 roughly adjusted on assumption that substantial extraordinary
    arrears developed between 1921 and 1934, part of which were made good from 1936 to 1941.
    Figures are intended to abstract from ordinary excess of taxes levied over taxes collected.
    1947–1949: Assumed equal to col. 1.

COMMERCIAL BANK NON-REAL ESTATE LOANS TO FARMERS
1896 to 1910

Year	Loans and discounts		June 30 index	Year	Loans and discounts		June 30 index
	Dec. 31	June 30			Dec. 31	June 30	
	$ mill.		1910 = 100.0		$ mill.		1910 = 100.0
	1	2	3		1	2	3
1896	310	320	23.9	1904	783	737	55.0
1897	318	300	22.4	1905	898	829	61.9
1898	355	336	25.1	1906	1 038	966	72.1
1899	407	374	27.9	1907	1 086	1 110	82.8
1900	488	440	32.8	1908	1 110	1 061	79.2
1901	583	536	40.0	1909	1 250	1 159	86.5
1902	662	630	47.0	1910	1 338	1 340	100.0
1903	716	695	51.9				

ACCRUED TAXES ON FARM REAL ESTATE
1896 to 1949

Year	Tax levy		Farm acreage	Accrued taxes adjusted, end of year	Year	Tax levy		Farm acreage	Accrued taxes adjusted, end of year
	Aggregate amount	Tax per acre				Aggregate amount	Tax per acre		
	$ mill.	Cents	Mill. acres	$ mill.		$ mill.	Cents	Mill. acres	$ mill.
	1	2	3	4		1	2	3	4
1896	107	13	823	107	1923	516	55		535
1897	108	13	827	108	1924	511	55		540
1898	108	13	831	108	1925	517	56	924	550
1899	109	13	835	109	1926	526	56		565
1900	109	13	839	109	1927	545	57		590
1901	110	13	843	110	1928	556	58		010
1902	119	14	847	119	1929	567	58		630
1903	128	15	851	128	1930	567	57	987	660
1904	128	15	855	128	1931	526	53		660
1905	129	15	859	129	1932	462	46		640
1906	130	15	863	130	1933	399	39		620
1907	139	16	867	139	1934	385	37		620
1908	148	17	871	148	1935	394	37	1 055	600
1909	164	19	875	164	1936	396	38		580
1910	166	19	879	166	1937	407	39		570
1911	183	21		183	1938	402	38		545
1912	191	21		191	1939	409	39		530
1913	218	24		218	1940	402	38	1 061	505
1914	222	24		222	1941	406	38		485
1915	243	26		243	1942	402	37		455
1916	260	28		260	1943	403	36		435
1917	292	31		292	1944	421	37		435
1918	311	33		311	1945	471	41	1 142	475
1919	393	41		393	1946	525	46		525
1920	483	51	956	483	1947	600	53		600
1921	510	54		510	1948	651	57		651
1922	509	54		520	1949	699	62		699

Column 1 – 1897–1949: Sum of cols. 2–4.

Column 2 – 1897–1920: Assumed to be negligible.

             1921–1941: Rough estimates. For years 1931–1937, total write-downs on mortgages were assumed to amount to about $400 million, starting from estimate of $100 million for write-downs in 1933–1935 in connection with refinancing of debt by Farm Credit Administration (Hart, A. G., *Debts and Recovery: A Study of Changes in the Internal Debt Structure from 1929 to 1937 and a Program for the Future*, pp. 153–154) and of similar write-downs of about $110 million under auspices of Farmers Home Administration between Sept. 1935 and March 1938, and making allowance for similar transactions in years 1931 and 1932, and for debt write-downs, primarily by noninstitutional mortgagees not connected with Farm Credit Administration, Federal Land Bank, or Farmers Home Administration operations. Estimates for 1921–1930 and for 1937–1941 are very rough and have been guided by movements of farm foreclosure rate (cf. *Historical Statistics*, p. 95).

             1942–1949: Assumed to be negligible.

Column 3 – 1897–1900: Assumed to be negligible.

             1901–1949: Obtained by applying to nonmortgage loans to farmers by commercial banks as shown in Table A-62, col. 2, an average loss rate of 0.1 percent for the years 1897–1920 and 1942–1949 as losses in these years of farm prosperity assumed to have been nominal. For period 1935–1941, loss rate was derived from data for country member banks of Federal Reserve System (*Federal Reserve Bulletin*, various issues) as it was assumed that these would come as near to rates applicable to nonmortgage bank loans to farmers as banking statistics, which do not segregate experience on this type of loan, permit. Since country member bank data were unavailable for the period 1921–1934, loss rate was obtained by taking net losses and charge-offs as percent of total loans for all member banks (*Banking and Monetary Statistics*, pp. 72, 262). Recoveries for period 1921–1926 which were not given separately in *Banking and Monetary Statistics* were estimated at roughly 20 percent, the average relationship of recoveries to losses in next three years.

Column 4 – 1897–1949: Loss rates used in col. 3 applied to farmers' non-real estate debt to other than financial institutions (Table A-54, col. 4).

WRITE-DOWNS OF FARM DEBT
1897 to 1949

$ mill.

A-65

Year	Total	Mortgage debt	Bank debt	Other debt	Year	Total	Mortgage debt	Bank debt	Other debt
	1	2	3	4		1	2	3	4
1897	1	–	–	1	1923	46	10	18	18
1898	1	–	–	1	1924	36	10	13	13
1899	1	–	–	1	1925	36	10	13	13
1900	1	–	–	1	1926	30	10	10	10
1901	2	–	1	1	1927	30	10	10	10
1902	2	–	1	1	1928	30	10	10	10
1903	2	–	1	1	1929	30	10	10	10
1904	2	–	1	1	1930	42	10	15	17
1905	2	–	1	1	1931	73	20	23	30
1906	2	–	1	1	1932	106	30	32	44
1907	2	–	1	1	1933	150	75	28	47
1908	2	–	1	1	1934	151	75	21	55
1909	2	–	1	1	1935	119	75	15	29
1910	2	–	1	1	1936	91	75	5	11
1911	2	–	1	1	1937	59	50	3	6
1912	4	–	2	2	1938	32	20	4	8
1913	4	–	2	2	1939	20	10	4	6
1914	4	–	2	2	1940	18	10	3	5
1915	4	–	2	2	1941	15	10	2	3
1916	4	–	2	2	1942	3	–	1	2
1917	4	–	2	2	1943	2	–	1	1
1918	6	–	3	3	1944	2	–	1	1
1919	6	–	3	3	1945	2	–	1	1
1920	8	–	4	4	1946	3	–	1	2
1921	83	5	39	39	1947	4	–	2	2
1922	55	5	25	25	1948	4	–	2	2
					1949	4	–	2	2

Column *1* – 1897–1949: Cols. 2–12, 16 less 13–15.

Column *2* – 1897–1949: Table A-7, col. 1 raised 55 percent (cf. notes to Table A-1, col. 3).

Column *3* – 1897–1949: Table A-24, col. 1 plus Table A-29, col. 1.

Column *4* – 1897–1949: Sum of Table A-16, col. 1, Table A-18, col. 1, Table A-19, col. 1, and Table A-20, col. 1.

Column *5* – 1897–1949: Table A-32, col. 7.

Column *6* – 1897–1949: First differences of Table A-53, col. 2.

Column *7* – 1897–1949: First differences of Table A-53, col. 3 minus Table L-23, cols. 4 and 8.

Column *8* – 1897–1949: Table I-8, col. 10 minus col. 11.

Column *9* – 1917–1934: Table V-4, col. 2.
1935–1949: Table V-3, col. 5.

CASH FLOW OF AGRICULTURAL SAVING
1897 to 1949

$ mill.

Year	Total	Tangible assets				Financial assets			
		Build-ings	Consumer durables	Equip-ment	Inven-tories	Cur-rency	Bank deposits	Life insurance reserves	Government securities
	1	2	3	4	5	6	7	8	9
1897	367	158	114	143	51	16	4	11	–
1898	577	175	120	189	215	8	49	12	–
1899	494	181	136	223	73	28	63	13	–
1900	399	202	142	228	26	16	61	14	–
1901	89	214	157	249	–304	8	71	16	–
1902	953	229	169	320	455	12	46	19	–
1903	354	229	172	273	–106	6	17	17	–
1904	587	239	183	281	119	–5	36	21	–
1905	623	240	200	296	146	41	75	20	–
1906	676	262	240	354	138	16	99	20	–
1907	370	270	251	371	–305	23	20	15	–
1908	654	277	243	325	61	–45	11	16	–
1909	747	307	300	374	133	18	68	21	–
1910	691	336	327	388	156	0	23	19	–
1911	117	319	332	397	–382	–28	18	21	–
1912	1 072	346	372	438	596	16	47	22	–
1913	214	346	362	429	–391	–8	23	21	–
1914	1 288	346	391	410	506	–26	3	20	–
1915	1 165	355	467	377	378	62	121	23	–
1916	–22	502	573	400	–744	64	291	30	–
1917	2 553	696	906	519	980	196	304	34	500
1918	3 199	741	840	649	–142	237	361	30	1 400
1919	294	1 012	1 140	817	–309	–27	378	54	0
1920	807	877	917	967	570	–10	–158	66	–400
1921	179	346	338	371	–789	–295	–276	54	–500
1922	1 490	417	553	377	73	49	30	61	–400
1923	2 058	491	779	489	–125	14	75	76	–200
1924	2 247	462	704	461	–667	–14	33	76	–100
1925	1 709	482	921	543	66	6	–67	92	–100
1920	1 611	460	833	602	–178	–40	–67	94	–50
1927	1 572	550	695	609	–82	–21	30	102	0
1928	1 847	513	853	615	55	–3	27	106	0
1929	1 863	476	911	685	–92	–12	–274	86	0
1930	1 487	299	587	563	–197	–22	–366	71	0
1931	1 472	150	381	291	303	84	–648	41	0
1932	1 549	57	219	137	130	40	–338	0	0
1933	1 343	76	279	155	–353	66	–129	26	0
1934	238	102	445	291	–1 325	–4	374	71	0
1935	2 513	195	567	461	625	70	276	95	16
1936	1 224	250	650	618	–1 183	62	279	104	36
1937	2 638	321	668	770	683	22	78	98	55
1938	1 710	265	489	619	125	–28	–22	90	52
1939	2 135	329	655	600	48	82	80	98	83
1940	2 284	372	639	701	161	108	181	107	98
1941	4 232	480	876	933	539	364	581	118	152
1942	6 725	403	766	883	1 357	598	1 081	119	541
1943	6 267	440	801	660	–125	641	1 282	133	1 261
1944	6 238	439	602	1 158	–452	485	1 480	150	1 353
1945	5 636	414	678	1 152	–379	546	1 975	163	740
1946	5 486	1 327	1 663	1 366	–177	274	1 371	175	–52
1947	4 331	1 972	2 149	2 129	–2 216	–64	468	171	210
1948	7 487	2 165	2 265	2 790	1 469	–202	–434	169	173
1949	5 734	2 003	2 364	2 949	–662	–299	–435	158	156

Column 10 – 1897–1949: First differences of Table A-53, col. 6.

Column 11 – 1897–1949: First differences of Table A-53, col. 7.

Column 12 – 1920–1949: Derived according to the procedure described in the notes to Table F-30.

Column 13 – 1897–1949: First differences of Table A-54, col. 2.

Column 14 – 1897–1949: First differences of Table A-54, cols. 3 and 4.

Column 15 – 1897–1949: Table A-1, sum of cols. 10 and 11

Column 16 – 1897–1949: Table A-12, col. 5.

CASH FLOW OF AGRICULTURAL SAVING
1897 to 1949
$ mill.

Year	Financial assets			Financial liabilities		Other intangible assets and liabilities	
	Equity in cooperatives	Mortgage debt held by farmers	Equity in veterans' funds	Mortgage debt	Non-real estate debt	Net proceeds from sale of land subdivided and purchase of farm land	Dealers' commissions on real estate
	10	11	12	13	14	15	16
1897	5	5	—	74	16	57	7
1898	5	4	—	77	74	57	8
1899	5	5	—	80	104	58	9
1900	5	3	—	83	162	63	10
1901	7	3	—	85	190	69	12
1902	6	3	—	89	158	74	15
1903	7	4	—	92	108	79	14
1904	7	4	—	96	134	84	16
1905	6	3	—	99	230	89	14
1906	7	2	—	103	280	94	15
1907	7	3	—	107	96	100	18
1908	6	5	—	110	48	105	18
1909	7	2	—	115	280	110	22
1910	7	14	—	314	176	113	24
1911	6	18	—	408	84	115	23
1912	7	18	—	418	280	117	25
1913	20	18	—	359	154	119	26
1914	20	13	—	284	18	118	25
1915	20	10	—	265	284	125	26
1916	20	86	—	570	572	132	30
1917	25	116	—	711	910	142	40
1918	25	117	—	600	350	153	44
1919	30	210	—	1 312	1 581	181	63
1920	30	276	7	1 772	832	—201	68
1921	30	8	9	481	—1 160	—166	38
1922	30	—163	6	84	—356	—154	31
1923	30	—179	6	—121	—314	—135	32
1924	30	—191	6	—752	—551	—114	30
1925	30	—123	4	—200	34	345	34
1926	25	—97	4	—55	—264	326	32
1927	25	—2	4	99	—46	314	29
1928	25	4	2	0	79	297	26
1929	25	—4	—11	—126	—209	288	26
1930	0	—9	—16	—233	—340	17	21
1931	0	—14	—117	—304	—696	16	17
1932	0	—22	—18	—628	—705	4	15
1933	0	—36	—6	—781	—476	5	13
1934	40	—51	—1	—101	—185	5	15
1935	40	—13	1	—161	6	—5	20
1936	40	—12	—7	—269	—86	—6	26
1937	35	—7	2	—199	318	—6	26
1938	35	—5	2	—176	119	—5	26
1939	36	—4	—1	—193	95	—5	26
1940	49	—4	—2	—95	343	—92	30
1941	78	—4	1	—119	136	—93	38
1942	91	—6	13	—421	—311	—103	44
1943	96	—5	55	—562	—284	—121	61
1944	124	—6	82	—456	—166	—136	65
1945	173	0	77	—251	149	86	81
1946	188	8	29	95	583	101	93
1947	255	4	15	105	639	108	90
1948	161	9	5	226	821	116	80
1949	164	8	—6	305	324	113	76

TABLE U-1

Column 1 – 1896–1915: Assumed to decline from 70 percent of nonfarm individuals' demand deposits in 1896 to 52.4 percent in 1915 (cf. Table L-5). Similarly calculated ratio for 1916 is 51.5 percent.

1916–1928: Obtained from a regression based on values for 1929 to 1941 (excluding 1931–1933) of cash holdings of a sample of small and middle size corporations (Lutz, F. A., *Corporate Cash Balances, 1914–1943*, pp. 119, 123) and figures shown in this column. Both series were expressed as indices on basis of 1939 = 100. Regression equation is $y = 40.6 + 0.6637x$ where x is index derived from sample figures and y index derived from figures in col. 1. Coefficient of correlation for 1929–1941 (excluding 1931–1933) is $+0.91$.

1929–1938: Obtained by applying to 1939 value an index derived from estimates of cash holdings by unincorporated business made by Shapiro, S., "The Distribution of Deposits and Currency in the United States, 1929–1939," *Journal of the American Statistical Association,* vol. 38, 1943, p. 441. Figures exclude professional services, finance, and public utilities.

1939–1949: Estimates of the Money Flow Study of the Federal Reserve Board. These figures are slightly smaller than figures for all nonfinancial unincorporated business published in *Federal Reserve Bulletin* (e.g. 1949, p. 794) because they also exclude lessors of real estate and finance companies.

Column 2 – 1917–1934: Rough estimates guided by the trend in holdings of nonfinancial corporations (Table V-73, col. 2).

1935–1949: Federal Reserve Board, Money Flow Study estimates.

Column 3 – 1896–1949: From Table D-1, col. 4.

Column 4 – 1926–1949: Derived from Table U-4, col. 9.

Column 5 – 1896–1949: From Table U-6, col. 7.

Column 6 – 1896–1949: From Table P-19, col. 3.

Column 7 – 1896–1949: Cumulated net expenditures (expenditures less accrued depreciation) on unincorporated equipment, original cost depreciation (see Table P-1, col. 3).

Column 8 – 1896–1949: Cumulated net expenditures on commercial and industrial construction (see Tables R-10 and R-13) split between corporate and unincorporated businesses on basis of Table R-29, cols. 3 and 4, interpolating linearly between decadal percentages. Also includes cumulated net expenditures on petroleum and mining development construction (see Tables R-14 and R-15) and net purchases of real estate from institutions.

Column 9 – 1896–1949: Mortgage debt and real estate bonds outstanding split between commercial and industrial construction and also between corporate and unincorporated businesses (see note to Table R-10, cols. 3 and 4 and Table R-13, col. 6). (Upon reexamination of the scanty material available it was found that these estimates are probably too high. Revised figures for selected benchmark dates will be found in Volume III, Table W-29. This revision will also have some effect on certain tables in Volume II, e.g. Tables B-70 to B-72.)

Column 10 – 1896–1949: From Table U-5, col. 3.

Column 11 – 1896–1949: Sum of cols. 1–3 and 5–8 minus cols. 9 and 10.

Column 12 – 1896–1925: Same as col. 11.

1926–1949: Col. 11 minus col. 3 plus col. 4.

PRINCIPAL BALANCE SHEET ITEMS OF UNINCORPORATED BUSINESS U-1

(Excluding Agriculture, Security Brokers and Dealers, and Professionals)

Original Cost Depreciation: 1896 to 1949

$ mill.

End of year	Assets								Liabilities		Net worth	
	Cash	U.S. Government securities	Consumer loans	Net receivables from Non-farmers	Net receivables from Farmers	Inventories	Equipment	Structures	Real estate debt	Bank loans	Estimate A	Estimate B
	1	2	3	4	5	6	7	8	9	10	11	12
1896	770	–	181	.	228	2 109	916	1 732	780	1 222	3 934	3 934
1897	820	–	201	.	229	1 975	862	1 827	782	1 345	3 787	3 787
1898	950	–	226	.	252	2 032	817	1 907	790	1 372	4 022	4 022
1899	1 240	–	247	.	285	2 516	806	1 986	800	1 534	4 746	4 746
1900	1 280	–	263	.	338	2 649	819	2 123	820	1 681	4 971	4 971
1901	1 500	–	284	.	400	2 445	831	2 248	840	1 880	4 988	4 988
1902	1 640	–	308	.	449	2 753	858	2 400	869	2 060	5 479	5 479
1903	1 680	–	330	.	477	2 670	903	2 502	902	2 279	5 381	5 381
1904	1 600	–	341	.	513	2 513	921	2 574	941	2 244	5 277	5 277
1905	2 020	–	366	.	583	2 623	969	2 661	987	2 453	5 782	5 782
1906	2 120	–	397	.	663	2 884	1 048	2 788	1 040	2 647	6 213	6 213
1907	1 860	–	419	.	678	3 007	1 148	2 956	1 078	2 561	6 429	6 429
1908	1 610	–	403	.	675	2 878	1 153	3 047	1 117	2 562	6 087	6 087
1909	1 640	–	444	.	748	2 973	1 180	3 145	1 180	2 712	6 238	6 238
1910	1 740	–	462	.	786	3 116	1 233	3 239	1 244	2 772	6 560	6 560
1911	1 820	–	487	.	797	2 993	1 263	3 309	1 301	2 862	6 506	6 506
1912	2 000	–	509	.	862	3 115	1 338	3 408	1 360	3 028	6 844	6 844
1913	2 190	–	520	.	891	3 282	1 434	3 545	1 466	3 051	7 345	7 345
1914	2 310	–	530	.	871	3 164	1 459	3 610	1 560	3 045	7 339	7 339
1915	2 730	–	544	.	937	3 403	1 498	3 660	1 628	3 561	7 583	7 583
1916	3 600	–	582	.	1 082	4 449	1 694	3 808	1 714	3 886	9 615	9 615
1917	3 500	300	583	.	1 296	5 905	2 036	3 948	1 869	4 457	11 242	11 242
1918	3 700	450	570	.	1 362	6 538	2 445	4 005	1 941	4 675	12 454	12 454
1919	4 100	900	613	.	1 773	7 988	2 744	4 173	2 056	5 634	14 601	14 601
1920	4 600	850	661	.	1 974	8 223	3 102	4 657	2 369	6 115	15 583	15 583
1921	4 100	850	617	.	1 644	6 401	3 189	5 023	2 522	5 126	14 176	14 176
1922	4 500	900	625	.	1 494	6 679	3 300	5 430	2 765	5 013	15 150	15 150
1923	4 400	850	646	.	1 376	7 317	3 596	5 896	3 190	5 610	15 281	15 281
1924	4 400	900	667	.	1 198	7 028	3 784	6 363	3 618	5 011	15 711	15 711
1925	4 600	900	745	.	1 146	7 155	4 004	6 888	4 265	5 161	16 012	16 012
1926	4 900	900	805	3 888	1 045	6 944	4 230	7 630	4 659	5 210	16 585	19 668
1927	4 700	1 000	781	3 968	999	6 612	4 342	8 304	5 107	4 965	16 666	19 853
1928	4 700	1 100	860	4 038	965	6 280	4 469	8 886	5 563	4 981	16 716	19 894
1929	4 900	1 000	997	4 148	869	6 426	4 717	9 422	5 886	5 093	17 352	20 503
1930	4 600	850	918	2 418	872	5 139	4 662	9 748	6 041	4 396	16 352	17 852
1931	3 700	800	840	248	756	3 997	4 391	9 736	6 326	3 534	14 360	13 768
1932	3 600	800	720	−1 382	582	3 033	3 953	9 492	6 144	2 858	13 178	11 076
1933	3 300	800	593	−839	472	3 092	3 579	9 195	6 016	2 068	12 947	11 515
1934	3 900	750	644	922	496	3 160	3 359	8 912	5 878	2 012	13 331	13 609
1935	3 900	700	736	1 844	384	3 385	3 291	8 626	5 730	1 929	13 363	14 471
1936	4 400	800	854	2 298	363	4 017	3 402	8 484	5 725	2 118	14 477	15 921
1937	4 200	900	925	2 078	446	4 263	3 612	8 458	5 675	2 311	14 818	15 971
1938	4 400	900	867	1 499	447	3 893	3 570	8 373	5 642	2 039	14 769	15 401
1939	4 600	900	911	1 451	398	4 145	3 633	8 333	5 554	2 117	15 249	15 789
1940	5 400	900	1 006	1 553	478	4 591	3 904	8 309	5 499	2 455	16 634	17 181
1941	6 000	1 400	1 071	1 431	459	5 644	4 357	8 352	5 479	3 127	18 677	19 037
1942	8 000	2 500	781	2 471	440	6 302	4 297	8 223	5 371	2 692	22 480	24 170
1943	10 800	3 900	696	2 749	349	6 411	4 175	8 062	5 225	2 634	26 534	28 587
1944	12 800	5 700	765	2 879	316	7 287	4 255	7 958	5 175	2 753	31 153	33 267
1945	15 500	7 000	832	2 347	358	7 829	4 586	7 978	5 250	3 178	35 655	37 170
1946	15 800	7 300	1 211	2 831	424	9 945	5 628	8 468	5 702	4 584	38 490	40 110
1947	15 900	7 300	1 523	2 697	484	11 517	7 195	8 789	6 205	5 897	40 606	41 780
1948	15 200	5 700	1 759	3 020	625	13 292	8 915	9 339	6 628	6 445	41 757	43 018
1949	15 000	5 500	1 966	4 014	705	11 885	10 394	9 772	6 981	6 163	42 078	44 126

PRINCIPAL BALANCE SHEET ITEMS OF UNINCORPORATED BUSINESS
Replacement Cost Depreciation
1896 to 1948
$ mill.

End of year	Equipment	Structures	Land	Net worth	End of year	Equipment	Structures	Land	Net worth
	1	2	3	4		1	2	3	4
1896	808	1 603	842	4 539	1923	3 713	8 861	4 127	22 490
1897	869	1 717	885	4 569	1924	3 831	9 290	4 699	23 384
1898	890	1 889	972	5 049	1925	4 002	9 755	5 449	24 326
1899	909	2 070	1 063	5 996	1926	4 180	10 316	6 281	28 585
1900	911	2 228	1 124	6 292	1927	4 273	10 884	7 223	29 587
1901	906	2 343	1 164	6 322	1928	4 420	11 263	7 480	29 702
1902	904	2 550	1 267	6 942	1929	4 562	11 100	7 335	29 361
1903	942	2 668	1 322	6 908	1930	4 295	10 623	5 731	24 091
1904	968	2 771	1 348	6 869	1931	3 850	9 418	4 108	17 017
1905	1 011	2 951	1 412	7 526	1932	3 368	8 757	3 124	12 880
1906	1 103	3 166	1 516	8 162	1933	3 204	9 326	3 482	14 753
1907	1 172	3 338	1 600	8 435	1934	3 159	9 712	3 867	18 076
1908	1 164	3 391	1 600	8 042	1935	3 132	9 680	3 954	19 320
1909	1 220	3 478	1 614	8 225	1936	3 417	10 025	4 237	21 714
1910	1 310	3 599	1 670	8 667	1937	3 775	10 348	4 348	22 372
1911	1 350	3 710	1 718	8 712	1938	3 722	10 300	4 213	21 693
1912	1 419	3 843	1 757	9 117	1939	3 840	10 537	4 164	22 364
1913	1 506	3 927	1 771	9 570	1940	4 240	11 028	4 309	24 545
1914	1 586	3 944	1 782	9 582	1941	4 887	11 861	4 567	27 643
1915	1 781	4 279	1 928	10 413	1942	4 914	12 350	4 665	33 579
1916	2 284	4 907	2 225	13 529	1943	4 703	12 554	4 624	38 231
1917	3 126	5 763	2 572	16 719	1944	4 695	12 937	4 629	43 315
1918	3 834	6 937	3 055	19 830	1945	5 191	14 301	4 765	48 863
1919	4 145	8 750	3 839	24 418	1946	6 917	16 956	5 452	55 339
1920	4 088	8 870	3 829	24 611	1947	9 189	19 445	5 868	60 298
1921	3 516	7 794	3 349	20 623	1948	10 984	20 430	5 913	62 091
1922	3 424	8 215	3 519	21 578					

Column 1 – Cumulated net expenditures, replacement cost depreciation, obtained by multiplying the 1929 cumulated values by the appropriate index on a year-end basis (see Table P-1, col. 11).

Column 2 – Same procedure as for Table U-1, col. 8 except cumulated net expenditures replacement cost depreciation used (cf. Tables R-12 and R-13).

Column 3 – Derived by applying to value of commercial and industrial structures proportions of land and allocating value between corporate and unincorporated businesses on basis of Table R-29, cols. 3 and 4, interpolating between decadal percentages.

Column 4 – Cols. 1–3 plus Table U-1, col. 12 minus cols. 7 and 8.

Original and Replacement Cost Depreciation

1897 to 1949

$ mill.

Year	Original cost		Replacement cost	Year	Original cost		Replacement cost
	A	B			A	B	
	1	2	3		1	2	3
1897	−151	−173	−154	1924	403	496	297
1898	231	230	232	1925	381	292	155
1899	719	369	359	1926	550	969	850
1900	220	254	235	1927	−66	121	15
1901	11	−50	−65	1928	−293	−279	−379
1902	485	265	250	1929	326	468	379
1903	−105	46	32	1930	−2 958	−2 203	−2 195
1904	−111	−206	−223	1931	−4 210	−3 599	−3 548
1905	498	512	490	1932	−3 173	−2 878	−2 746
1906	423	271	247	1933	−27	−552	−438
1907	208	152	121	1934	1 648	1 594	1 626
1908	−350	−312	−334	1935	510	460	478
1909	143	−148	−173	1936	1 151	1 031	1 036
1910	314	487	460	1937	−192	−221	−288
1911	−63	−4	−35	1938	−782	−561	−632
1912	329	122	93	1939	174	8	−57
1913	492	509	482	1940	1 211	1 159	1 061
1914	−15	96	74	1941	1 641	838	690
1915	260	52	11	1942	4 982	4 610	4 392
1916	2 017	898	812	1943	4 297	4 143	3 922
1917	1 617	366	201	1944	4 590	4 520	4 305
1918	1 202	543	269	1945	3 823	3 710	3 483
1919	2 122	1 537	1 191	1946	2 840	1 021	680
1920	967	2 132	1 705	1947	1 570	23	−517
1921	−1 451	364	118	1948	1 138	744	95
1922	933	689	542	1949	1 008	1 703	1 069
1923	−53	−95	−259				

Column 1 – 1897–1926: Sum of first differences of Table P-19, col. 3, Table P-1, col. 3, Table R-10, col. 7, Table R-13, col. 8, Table R-14, col. 9, Table R-15, col. 9, and first differences of Table U-1, cols. 1–5 minus Table U-5, col. 6.

1927–1949: Same procedure as for earlier period except Table U-4, col. 9 used instead of first differences of Table U-1, cols. 3 and 4.

Column 2 – 1897–1949: Col. 1 minus first differences of Table P-19, col. 3 plus Table P-19, col. 12, i.e. including inventory valuation adjustment.

Column 3 – 1897–1926: Sum of Table P-19, col. 12, Table P-1, col. 11, Table R-12, col. 7, Table R-13, col. 10, Table R-14, col. 11, Table R-15, col. 11, and first differences of Table U-1, cols. 1–5 minus Table U-5, col. 6.

1927–1949: Same procedure as for 1897–1926 except Table U-4, col. 9 used instead of first differences of Table U-1, cols. 3 and 4.

Column 1 – 1935–1938A: From Copeland, M. A., *A Study of Moneyflows in the United States*, pp. 128, 129.
1938B–1949: From Money Flow Study of the Federal Reserve Board.

Column 2 – 1936–1949: First differences of col. 1.

Column 3 – 1927–1932: Estimated at 28 percent of bad debt allowance of all corporations as reported in *Statistics of Income*, the ratio in all years from 1933 to 1936 between Securities and Exchange Commission estimates of debt write-down and that in *Statistics of Income*.
1933–1949: Friend, I. and Natrella, V., *Individuals' Saving*, part I, table 7.

Column 4 – 1936–1949: Col. 2 minus col. 3.

Column 5 – 1932–1949: Cumulation of col. 6 adjusted for bad debt write-down.

Column 6 – 1933–1949: From *Survey of Current Business*, Sept. 1949, p. 12; July 1950, p. 11 (sign reversed) as revised by SEC-Commerce. The July 1947 figures for "increase in net payables to other corporations and financial intermediaries" (*Survey of Current Business, National Income Supplement*, July 1947, p. 20) were corrected in *Survey of Current Business*, Sept. 1949, but were carried in their original version in *Survey of Current Business, National Income Supplement*, 1951.

Column 7 – 1926: From Tables U-9 and U-10 assuming 1926 relation between accounts and notes payable to be the same as in 1929.
1929, 1939, 1946: From Tables U-7, U-8, and U-9.

Column 8 – 1926–1946: Derived from col. 7. Figures are not adjusted for debt write-down.

Column 9 – 1927–1929: Obtained by interpolation between 1926 and 1929 values of col. 7 allowing for debt write-down.
1930–1932: Rough interpolation guided by values in col. 8 and allowing for debt write-down.
1933–1935: Assumed equal to col. 6 and first differences of Table D-1, col. 4.
1936–1949: Average of col. 4 and the sum of col. 6 and first differences of Table D-1, col. 4.

NET RECEIVABLES OF UNINCORPORATED BUSINESS FROM CORPORATIONS, FINANCIAL INTERMEDIARIES, AND NONFARMERS U-4
(Excluding Security Brokers and Dealers): 1926 to 1949

$ mill.

Year	Based on Money Flow Study estimates				SEC-Commerce estimates		Saving Study benchmark estimates		Final estimate (adjusted)
	Amount	Annual change			Amount	Annual adjusted change	Amount	Annual change	
		Unadjusted	Bad debt write-down	Adjusted					
	1	2	3	4	5	6	7	8	9
1926							1 272		
1927			230					277	−150
1928			220						−150
1929			260				1 549		−150
1930			270						−2 000
1931			330						−2 500
1932			370		−1 330				−2 000
1933			350		−670	320			193
1934A			330		1 050	1 380			1 431
1934B					1 900			−2 912	
1935	1 300		270		2 730	560			652
1936	1 400	100	250	−150	3 420	440			204
1937	1 100	−300	210	−510	3 210	−420			−430
1938A	1 600	500	190	310	1 620	−1 790			−769
1938B	500								
1939	500	0	200	−200	1 480	−340	−1 363		−248
1940	800	300	170	130	1 290	−360			−68
1941	1 300	500	210	290	470	−1 020			−332
1942	1 800	500	150	350	2 340	1 720			890
1943	1 900	100	120	−20	2 880	420		1 407	158
1944	1 700	−200	90	−290	3 280	300			40
1945	1 600	−100	80	−180	2 250	−1 110			−612
1946	2 500	900	100	800	1 940	−410	44		384
1947	2 600	100	100	0	1 270	−780			−234
1948	3 100	500	100	400	1 180	−190			223
1949	4 400	1 300	100	1 200	1 660	380			894

Column 1 – 1896–1949: From Table L-25, col. 6. Consumer loans before 1923 assumed to constitute 5.83 percent of other loans, the 1923 ratio.

Column 2 – 1896–1928: Assumed to move similarly to, but to decline somewhat more slowly than, estimated share of unincorporated business enterprises in total inventories (Table P-26), annual ratios being obtained by linear interpolation between quinquennial figures. This basis of estimation was selected because proportions were reasonably close in 1929, and it may be assumed that size of inventories was one of the most important determinants of volume of bank loans to unincorporated business enterprises.

 1929, 1939: Estimated on basis of 1946 ratio and movement of share of unincorporated business enterprises in total inventories (cf. Table P-26).

 1930–1938, 1940–1945: Interpolated between 1929, 1939, and 1946 values.

 1946: From statistics of member banks, *Federal Reserve Bulletin*, 1947, p. 259.

 1947–1949: Assumed unchanged from 1946 value.

Column 3 – 1896–1949: Col. 1 multiplied by col. 2.

Column 4 – 1897–1949: First differences of col. 3.

Column 5 – 1897–1915: Roughly estimated at 0.3 percent of bank loans to unincorporated business, this ratio apparently representing average loss ratio on bank loans for years not affected by depression in period after 1920.

 1916–1920: Rough estimates made on assumption that losses were very small during this prosperity period.

 1921–1941: Estimated to bear same ratio to total net losses of operating commercial banks (Table R-55, col. 6) as commercial short-term loans to unincorporated business enterprises (col. 3) bear to total loans and discounts of commercial banks (Table L-24, col. 2). This procedure assumes that loss ratio on nonmortgage short-term loans to unincorporated business was equal to average loss ratio on all loans and discounts.

 1942–1949: Assumed to be negligible.

Column 6 – 1897–1949: Col. 4 plus col. 5.

COMMERCIAL BANK DEBT OF UNINCORPORATED BUSINESS
1896 to 1949

$ mill.

Year	Total commercial loans by banks	Share of unincorporated business	Commercial loans to unincorporated business		Write-off on loans	Adjusted change
			Amount outstanding	Change		
	1	2	3	4	5	6
1896	2 247	0.544	1 222	.	.	.
1897	2 510	0.536	1 345	123	4	127
1898	2 599	0.528	1 372	27	4	31
1899	2 950	0.520	1 534	162	5	167
1900	3 284	0.512	1 681	147	5	152
1901	3 731	0.504	1 880	199	6	205
1902	4 154	0.496	2 060	180	6	186
1903	4 670	0.488	2 279	219	7	226
1904	4 676	0.480	2 244	−35	7	−28
1905	5 196	0.472	2 453	209	7	216
1906	5 704	0.464	2 647	194	8	202
1907	5 616	0.456	2 561	−86	8	−78
1908	5 719	0.448	2 562	1	8	9
1909	6 164	0.440	2 712	150	8	158
1910	6 417	0.432	2 772	60	8	68
1911	6 750	0.424	2 862	90	9	99
1912	7 279	0.416	3 028	166	9	175
1913	7 478	0.408	3 051	23	9	32
1914	7 612	0.400	3 045	−6	9	3
1915A	9 016	0.392	3 534	489	11	500
1915B	9 085	0.392	3 561			
1916	10 121	0.384	3 886	325	15	340
1917	11 855	0.376	4 457	571	10	581
1918	12 703	0.368	4 675	218	10	228
1919A	15 692	0.360	5 649	974	10	984
1919B	15 649	0.360	5 634			
1920	17 275	0.354	6 115	481	15	496
1921	14 729	0.348	5 126	−989	44	−945
1922	14 659	0.342	5 013	−113	41	−72
1923A	15 730	0.366	5 757	744	37	781
1923B	15 327	0.366	5 610			
1924	15 186	0.330	5 011	−599	27	−572
1925	15 930	0.324	5 161	150	24	174
1926	16 385	0.318	5 210	49	23	72
1927	15 915	0.312	4 965	−245	21	−224
1928A	16 587	0.306	5 076	111	19	130
1928B	16 277	0.306	4 981			
1929	16 978	0.300	5 093	112	23	135
1930	14 902	0.295	4 396	−697	32	−665
1931	12 187	0.290	3 534	−862	50	−812
1932	10 029	0.285	2 858	−676	71	−605
1933	7 387	0.280	2 068	−790	66	−724
1934A	7 304	0.275	2 009	−59	69	10
1934B	7 316	0.275	2 012			
1935	7 146	0.270	1 929	−83	32	−51
1936	7 992	0.265	2 118	189	19	208
1937	8 889	0.260	2 311	193	7	200
1938	7 998	0.255	2 039	−272	12	−260
1939	8 469	0.250	2 117	78	9	87
1940	9 628	0.255	2 455	338	6	344
1941	12 028	0.260	3 127	672	5	677
1942	10 196	0.264	2 692	−435	−	−435
1943	9 793	0.269	2 634	−58	−	−58
1944	10 048	0.274	2 753	119	−	119
1945	11 390	0.279	3 178	425	−	425
1946	16 198	0.283	4 584	1 406	−	1 406
1947	20 837	0.283	5 897	1 313	−	1 313
1948	22 775	0.283	6 445	548	−	548
1949	21 778	0.283	6 163	−282	−	−282

Column 1 – From Table A-54, col. 4.

Column 2 – Cumulated from Table A-57, col. 6 assuming policy loans at $5 million in 1896.

Column 3 – From Table D-1, col. 5.

Column 4 – Col. 5 multiplied by ratio of Table D-1, col. 2 to Table D-1, col. 1.

Column 5 – Col. 1 minus sum of cols. 2 and 3.

Column 6 – Col. 5 multiplied by share of unincorporated business in total trade inventories (Table P-26, complement of col. 3).

Column 7 – Sum of cols. 4 and 6.

UNINCORPORATED BUSINESS: NET RECEIVABLES FROM FARMERS
1896 to 1949
$ mill.

End of year	Total farmers' nonmortgage debt to others	Policy loans	Farm consumer debt		Other debt		Net receivables
			Total	To un- incorporated creditors	Total	To un- incorporated creditors	
	1	2	3	4	5	6	7
1896	310	5	33	16	272	212	228
1897	318	6	40	20	272	209	229
1898	355	7	46	22	302	230	252
1899	407	8	49	23	350	262	285
1900	488	10	53	24	425	314	338
1901	583	12	58	26	513	374	400
1902	662	14	63	28	585	421	449
1903	716	17	68	29	631	448	477
1904	783	20	76	32	687	481	513
1905	898	23	77	32	798	551	583
1906	1 038	27	88	35	923	628	663
1907	1 086	36	94	37	956	641	678
1908	1 110	43	107	41	960	634	675
1909	1 250	47	123	46	1 080	702	748
1910	1 338	53	131	47	1 154	739	786
1911	1 380	59	126	44	1 195	753	797
1912	1 520	64	144	49	1 312	813	862
1913	1 597	72	141	47	1 384	844	891
1914	1 606	81	159	51	1 366	820	871
1915	1 748	86	157	49	1 505	888	937
1916	2 034	87	172	52	1 775	1 030	1 082
1917	2 489	89	256	74	2 144	1 222	1 296
1918	2 662	90	280	78	2 292	1 284	1 362
1919	3 454	89	280	76	3 085	1 697	1 773
1920	3 870	95	231	60	3 544	1 914	1 974
1921	3 281	116	120	30	3 045	1 614	1 644
1922	3 088	124	167	40	2 797	1 454	1 494
1923	2 929	130	184	42	2 615	1 334	1 376
1924	2 647	142	195	43	2 310	1 155	1 198
1925	2 659	153	276	58	2 230	1 088	1 146
1926	2 517	166	272	55	2 079	990	1 045
1927	2 488	182	263	51	2 043	948	999
1928	2 518	200	311	58	2 007	907	965
1929	2 408	231	350	65	1 827	804	869
1930	2 408	265	255	49	1 888	823	872
1931	2 146	310	173	38	1 663	718	756
1932	1 747	345	110	29	1 292	553	582
1933	1 528	342	163	38	1 023	434	472
1934	1 605	333	192	42	1 080	454	496
1935	1 404	324	297	58	783	326	384
1936	1 385	315	332	59	738	304	363
1937	1 625	314	379	66	932	380	446
1938	1 590	313	296	51	981	396	447
1939	1 500	303	334	53	863	345	398
1940	1 700	292	362	55	1 046	423	478
1941	1 700	280	468	70	952	389	459
1942	1 500	266	304	56	930	384	440
1943	1 200	248	238	51	714	298	349
1944	1 100	234	236	51	630	265	316
1945	1 200	224	263	54	713	304	358
1946	1 500	220	498	88	782	336	424
1947	1 800	223	723	113	854	371	484
1948	2 200	230	821	121	1 149	504	625
1949	2 400	241	832	117	1 327	588	705

Line 1 – Estimates based on Department of Commerce (National Income Division) data on unincorporated cash and deposits (cf. note to Table U-8, line 1) through 1945, extrapolated to 1946 by same method as was used in the earlier years.

Line 2 – Method and sources similar to those utilized in 1939 (cf. note to Table U-8, line 2).

Line 3 – Estimates of Department of Commerce (*Survey of Current Business*, July 1950).

Line 4 – Estimated in same way as in 1939 (cf. Table U-8, line 2).

Line 5 – Preliminary estimates obtained by same method as used in 1939 (cf. Table U-8, line 5) adjusted downward to reflect postwar shift to the corporate form by many unincorporated firms after elimination of wartime excess profits tax. This adjustment was based on special tabulations by the Bureau of Internal Revenue which show, by asset size, number of partnerships and proprietorships incorporating during the 1946 tax year. Resulting estimates are quite close to those derived by use of unincorporated depreciation charges and ratios among small corporations of net capital assets to depreciation (cf. note to Table U-8, line 5).

Line 6 – Same methods as used in 1939 (cf. Table U-8, line 6).

Line 7 – Sum of lines 1–6.

Line 8 – Same methods as used in 1939 (cf. Table U-8, line 8).

Line 8a – Line 8 minus line 8b.

Line 8b – Total short-term and long-term bank debt from Friend and Natrella, *Individuals' Saving*, part I, table 6, line 4, distributed industrially according to data on unincorporated short-term and long-term debt outstanding on Nov. 20, 1946, shown in the Federal Reserve Bank Board bank loan survey of that date (*Federal Reserve Bulletin*, March, May 1947).

Line 9 – Same sources and methods as in line 8b. Long-term debt loans are those with maturities over one year.

Line 10 – Cf. note to Table U-8, line 10.

Line 11 – Cf. note to Table U-8, line 9, except that estimates were reduced by 40 percent (as compared to 20 percent in 1939) to take account of relatively greater importance of provision for income taxes among small corporations in later period.

Line 12 – Line 7 minus lines 8, 9, 10, and 11.

BENCHMARK BALANCE SHEET
OF UNINCORPORATED BUSINESS: End of 1946[1]

$ mill.

	Manu-facturing	Min-ing	Retail trade	Whole-sale trade	Serv-ices	Con-struc-tion	Transpor-tation and public utilities	Real estate	Other finance	Total
	1	2	3	4	5	6	7	8	9	10
1. Cash	528	148	4 350	538	490	280	134	1 080	254	7 802
2. Receivables										
a. Trade	1 015	146	2 230	1 090	135	578	230	662	405	6 491
b. Consumers			360		435				215	1 010
3. Inventories	988	61	6 772	1 468	320	339	28	29	14	10 019
4. Investments	199	49	690	192	188	81	63	497	346	2 305
5. Net capital assets	1 122	414	3 858	389	1 227	338	621	4 880	262	13 111
6. Other assets	250	49	675	144	213	69	70	263	93	1 826
7. Total assets	4 102	867	18 935	3 821	3 008	1 685	1 146	7 411	1 589	42 564
8. Notes and accounts payable	1 270	292	4 150	1 073	785	566	300	1 510	596	10 542
a. Accounts payable	565	214	3 514	275	604	324	195	1 390	376	7 457
b. Notes payable	705	78	636	798	181	242	105	120	220	3 085
9. Long-term bank debt	171	19	192	59	99	34	76	75	19	744
10. Mortgage debt	362	80	975	228	279	115	139	2 591	208	4 977
11. Other liabilities	393	97	925	287	260	139	84	503	137	2 825
12. Net worth	1 906	379	12 693	2 174	1 585	831	547	2 732	629	23 476

[1] Tables U–7 to U–10 exclude agriculture, security brokers and dealers, professionals, and personal holdings of entrepreneurs.

863

TABLE U–8

Line 1 – Figures on cash and bank deposits are based on data obtained from Department of Commerce, National Income Division. Estimates were derived by: (1) assuming that 1941 unincorporated ratios of cash to sales in each major industry group of *Statistics of Income* were same as ratios for small corporations (i.e., those with assets under $50,000) in the same industries; (2) extrapolating these ratios to 1939 by those of all corporations in the same industry; and (3) applying the ratios to the National Income Division's data on unincorporated sales in 1939. Sources of corporate data are *Statistics of Income*, Part II, 1939, 1941.

Line 2 – Estimates were derived by applying to unincorporated sales in 1939, ratios of receivables to sales existing among corporations with assets under $50,000 submitting 1939 balance sheets to the Bureau of Internal Revenue. For cols. 3 and 9 (retail trade and other finance and insurance) calculation was based on ratios for subgroups rather than on that for entire industry.

Line 3 – From *Survey of Current Business*, National Income Supplement, July 1947.

Line 4 – Estimated by same procedure as line 2.

Line 4a – Estimated from 1939 partnership returns to the Bureau of Internal Revenue. Interest receipts from U.S. Government obligations (reported in these returns) were divided by the average yield in 1939 of long-term government bonds to obtain an approximation to the value of holdings. These values were then blown up to cover all unincorporated firms by ratio of total unincorporated sales to sales by partnerships reporting to Bureau of Internal Revenue. In this blow-up it was assumed that partnerships held about three times as much investments per dollar of sales as did proprietorships, a ratio derived by fitting a curve to the relationship between average sales and the ratio of total investment to sales for each asset-size group of corporations reporting to Bureau of Internal Revenue in 1939.

Line 4b – Line 4 minus line 4a.

Line 5 – Estimated in same way as line 2 except for real estate firms. Net capital assets of latter group estimated by applying to mortgage debt of this group at end of 1939 (cf. line 12) ratio among small real estate corporations of net capital assets to long-term debt on Dec. 31, 1939.

As a check, another set of estimates of net capital assets of nonfinancial unincorporated firms was obtained by capitalizing unincorporated depreciation charges by ratios prevailing among small corporations of net capital assets to depreciation charges. (Data on unincorporated depreciation are based on estimates of the National Income Division derived by applying to depreciation charges by partnerships, as shown in supplement to Part I of *Statistics of Income*, 1939, ratio of total unincorporated receipts to partnership receipts.) Results of this method were within 1 percent of those obtained by first method but differences by industries ranged from zero to somewhat over 20 percent.

Line 6 – Estimated by same procedure as line 2.

Line 7 – Total of lines 1, 2, 3, 4, 5, and 6.

Line 8 – Estimated by same procedure as line 2.

Line 8a – Total unincorporated short-term commercial and industrial bank debt (col. 10) is an unpublished estimate of the Securities and Exchange Commission. Industrial breakdown is based on distribution of unincorporated commercial and industrial short-term loans outstanding on Nov. 20, 1946, according to Federal Reserve bank loan survey of that date (*Federal Reserve Bulletin*, Mar., May 1947).

Line 8b – Line 8 minus line 8a.

Line 9 – Same source and methods as in line 8a. Long-term loans are those with maturities over one year.

Line 10 – Estimates of unincorporated commercial and multi-family mortgage debt from the Department of Commerce (*Survey of Current Business*, Sept. 1946, Oct. 1949), were arbitrarily reduced to exclude professionals' and nonbusiness individuals' mortgage debt. One-fifth of the unincorporated mortgage debt on multi-family housing (as estimated in *Survey of Current Business*, Sept. 1946) was attributed to unincorporated real estate firms while the remainder was regarded as owed by nonbusiness individuals. Unincorporated commercial mortgage debt was attributed in its entirety to business. Its industrial distribution was derived by applying to long-term debt of small corporations the ratio of unincorporated sales to small corporations' sales.

Line 11 – Estimated in same way as line 4. Resulting estimates were then reduced by one-fifth on assumption that "other liabilities" of corporate firms would be overstated relative to unincorporated firms due to relatively greater provision for income taxes.

Line 12 – Line 7 minus lines 8, 9, 10, and 11.

BENCHMARK BALANCE SHEET
OF UNINCORPORATED BUSINESS: End of 1939

$ mill.

	Manu-facturing	Min-ing	Retail trade	Whole-sale trade	Serv-ices	Con-struc-tion	Transpor-tation and public utilities	Real estate	Other finance	Total
	1	2	3	4	5	6	7	8	9	10
1. Cash	140	38	673	187	126	114	33	227	121	1 659
2. Receivables	382	57	1 720	572	250	328	63	257	779	4 408
3. Inventories	387	33	2 757	765	104	99	6	15	–	4 166
4. Investments	42	18	154	53	55	48	12	193	319	894
a. U.S. Government	12	2	34	20	33	12	3	179	133	428
b. Other	30	16	120	33	22	36	9	14	186	466
5. Net capital assets	590	229	2 065	264	652	239	196	3 870	265	8 370
6. Other assets	57	18	224	44	72	33	19	100	114	681
7. Total assets	1 598	393	7 593	1 885	1 259	861	329	4 662	1 598	20 178
8. Notes and accounts payable	660	180	2 900	690	526	433	127	790	696	7 002
a. Notes payable	276	40	260	315	70	90	40	40	100	1 231
b. Accounts payable	384	140	2 640	375	456	343	87	750	596	5 771
9. Long-term bank debt	60	10	70	25	35	20	25	10	25	280
10. Mortgage debt	245	97	995	170	314	145	88	2 114	210	4 378
11. Other liabilities	38	32	292	66	58	53	23	206	36	804
12. Net worth	595	74	3 336	934	326	210	66	1 542	631	7 714

BENCHMARK BALANCE SHEET
OF UNINCORPORATED BUSINESS: End of 1929

$ mill.

	Manufacturing	Mining	Trade	Services	Construction	Transportation and public utilities	Real estate	Other finance	Total
	1	2	3	4	5	6	7	8	9
1. Cash	164	49	856	228	193	30	277	117	1 914
2. Accounts receivable	401	29	3 276	417	758	89	565	681	6 216
3. Inventories	531	89	5 410	105	291	12	–	–	6 438
4. Investments	125	32	436	367	139	34	270	382	1 785
5. Net capital assets	735	415	2 460	609	984	270	5 325	535	11 333
6. Other assets	95	20	405	130	105	25	100	100	980
7. Total assets	2 051	634	12 843	1 856	2 470	460	6 537	1 815	28 666
8. Notes and accounts payable									
a. Accounts payable	664	181	4 352	665	873	150	1 185	750	4 667
b. Notes payable									4 153
9. Mortgage debt	309	131	1 733	378	425	102	2 897	300	6 275
10. Other liabilities	88	35	498	162	142	44	100	100	1 169
11. Net worth	990	287	6 260	651	1 030	164	2 355	665	12 402

Line 1 – Same source and methods as used in the estimates of 1939 cash holdings (cf. Table U-8, line 1).

Line 2 – Due to absence of data from *Statistics of Income* on corporations with assets under $50,000 prior to 1931 and to changeover from consolidated to unconsolidated company reporting in 1934, a different and probably less reliable method had to be used to estimate net accounts receivable of nonfinancial unincorporated business. It was assumed that 1931 receivables/sales ratios of unincorporated firms in each industry were the same as those of small corporations with assets under $50,000 reporting to Bureau of Internal Revenue in 1931 in the same industry. These ratios were then extrapolated back to 1929 on basis of similar ratios of all corporations reporting to Bureau of Internal Revenue and extrapolated ratios applied to 1929 receivables. Receivables of real estate and other finance firms were assumed to bear same relationship to sales as shown in 1946 unincorporated estimates.

Line 3 – Figures underlying *Survey of Current Business, National Income Supplement,* July 1947, table 33.

Lines 4 and 6 – Estimated by same procedure as line 2. However, since small corporation data in 1931 did not separate these two types of assets, they were extrapolated together to 1929 and then segregated according to their distribution among all corporations in same industry in 1929. Investments by real estate dealers and other finance groups were estimated by applying to their 1929 receipts ratio of their investments to receipts in 1946.

Line 5 – Derived by applying ratios of net capital assets to depreciation (based on corporate data) to unincorporated depreciation charges. Unincorporated depreciation figures are based on estimates of the National Income Division. Ratios were first determined for all corporations in each industry and then adjusted by 1939 relationship of the ratio of small corporations to those of all corporations. Unincorporated real estate and financial firms' net capital assets were estimated from mortgage estimates (cf. note to line 9 below) on assumption that their ratios to mortgage debt were the same as that for the total nonfinancial group.

Line 7 – Sum of lines 1–6.

Line 8a – Estimated in same way as line 2.

Line 8b – While no attempt was made to estimate notes payable (i.e., bank debt) in each industry, total for all unincorporated commercial and industrial unincorporated enterprises at end of 1929 is estimated at $4,153 million.

Line 9 – Same sources and methods as 1926 estimates (cf. Table U-10, line 9).

Line 10 – Other liabilities of nonfinancial industries were estimated in same way as accounts receivable (cf. note to line 2) and then reduced by 20 percent to allow for lower relative provisions for income taxes among unincorporated firms. Estimates for the financial groups are arbitrary.

Line 11 – Line 7 minus lines 8, 9, and 10.

$ mill.

	Manu-facturing	Min-ing	Trade	Serv-ices	Con-struc-tion	Transpor-tation and public utilities	Real estate and other finance	Total
	1	2	3	4	5	6	7	8
1. Cash	170	65	755	150	235	35	380	1 790
2. Receivables	410	35	2 900	180	700	50	1 210	5 485
3. Inventories	585	115	5 010	95	315	15	–	6 135
4. Investments	130	50	580	305	85	50	630	1 830
5. Net capital assets	785	640	2 000	425	905	305	5 680	10 740
6. Other assets	95	30	365	115	120	35	195	955
7. Total assets	2 175	935	11 610	1 270	2 360	490	8 095	26 935
8. Notes and accounts payable	720	235	3 700	545	805	110	1 850	7 965
9. Mortgage debt	285	185	790	195	340	55	3 095	4 945
10. Other liabilities	145	85	545	125	180	160	195	1 435
11. Net worth	1 025	430	6 575	405	1 035	165	2 955	12 590

Lines 1 to 5, 8 and 10 – All estimates for nonfinancial industries derived by following method: (1) Unincorporated sales in 1929 (from estimates based on data obtained from the National Income Division, Department of Commerce) extrapolated to 1926 by change in net profits of sole proprietorships with net income over $5,000 reporting to Bureau of Internal Revenue on Form 1040 (*Statistics of Income*, 1926, 1929); (2) ratio of each asset and liability to sales among unincorporated firms in 1929 (as estimated in Table U-9) extrapolated to 1926 by change from 1929 to 1926 in similar ratios for all corporations reporting to Bureau of Internal Revenue; and (3) estimated 1926 ratios applied to unincorporated sales in 1926.

Net capital assets in real estate and other finance groups estimated from their mortgage debt (line 9) on assumption that 1926 ratios were same as in 1929.

Line 6 – Assumed to bear same ratios to sales (cf. note to line 1) as in 1929.

Line 7 – Sum of lines 1–6.

Line 9 – By use of data from the National Income Division, Department of Commerce, estimate of total unincorporated mortgage debt (*Survey of Current Business*, Oct. 1949) was broken down into commercial, multi-family, and one to four-family debt. Eighty percent of multi-family and all of one- to four-family mortgage debt was allocated to individuals, and a small amount of commercial mortgages attributed to professionals. Industry breakdown was based on a preliminary distribution derived by applying to unincorporated sales, on an industry-by-industry basis, estimated ratio of long-term debt to sales among small corporations. In deriving these ratios, 1931 ratios of corporations with assets under $50,000 were extrapolated by similar ratios of all corporations (*Statistics of Income*, part 2, 1926, 1931).

Line 11 – Line 7 minus lines 8–10.

Column 1 – 1897–1926: Sum of cols. 2–7, 9 less cols. 10 and 11.
　　　　　 1927–1949: Sum of cols. 2–6, 8 and 9 less cols. 10 and 11.

Column 2 – 1897–1949: Table R-10, col. 1 less col. 5 plus Table R-13, col. 1. Does not include small portion of Table R-14, col. 1 and Table R-15, col. 1 which should be added.

Column 3 – 1897–1949: Sum of unincorporated business expenditures on producer durable goods obtained as sum of Table P-12, col. 1, Table P-13, col. 1, and Table P-16, col. 3.

Column 4 – 1897–1949: From Table P-19, col. 12.

Column 5 – 1897–1949: First differences of Table U-1, col. 1 less interest payments from Table L-23, col. 5.

Column 6 – 1917–1949: First differences of Table U-1, col. 2.

Column 7 – 1897–1923: First differences of Table D-1, col. 4.
　　　　　 1924–1949: First differences of Table D-2, col. 4 less annual change in finance charges included in reported debt outstanding, from Table D-7, col. 4.

Column 8 – 1927–1949: First differences of Table U-1, col. 4.

Column 9 – 1897–1949: First differences of Table U-6, col. 6.

Column 10 – 1897–1949: Table U-5, col. 4.

Column 11 – 1897–1949: Table R-10, sum of cols. 3 and 4 plus Table R-13, col. 6.

1897 to 1949

$ mill.

Year	Total	Nonresidential real estate	Producer durables	Inventories	Demand deposits	U.S. Government securities	Consumer loans	Net receivables	Farm receivables	Debt to banks	Change in real estate debt
	1	2	3	4	5	6	7	8	9	10	11
1897	16	158	82	−156	40	−	20	.	−3	123	2
1898	419	145	88	56	119	−	25	.	21	27	8
1899	556	146	118	134	276	−	21	.	33	162	10
1900	436	205	139	167	24	−	16	.	52	147	20
1901	134	198	136	−265	203	−	21	.	60	199	20
1902	456	227	159	88	120	−	24	.	47	180	29
1903	231	180	167	68	19	−	22	.	27	219	33
1904	−16	155	141	−252	−100	−	11	.	33	−35	39
1905	700	169	170	124	398	−	25	.	69	209	46
1906	482	223	215	109	74	−	31	.	77	194	53
1907	353	255	232	67	−285	−	22	.	14	−86	38
1908	−100	183	143	−91	−272	−	−16	.	−7	1	39
1909	67	189	168	−196	10	−	41	.	68	150	63
1910	718	189	203	316	79	−	18	.	37	60	64
1911	244	169	188	−64	58	−	25	.	15	90	57
1912	370	198	243	−85	156	−	22	.	61	166	59
1913	777	236	280	184	164	−	11	.	31	23	106
1914	373	169	221	−7	92	−	10	.	−24	−6	94
1915	343	156	243	31	388	−	14	.	68	489	68
1916	1 193	250	418	−73	830	−	38	.	141	325	86
1917	664	240	595	205	−144	300	1	.	193	571	155
1918	897	158	702	−26	155	150	−13	.	61	218	72
1919	1 907	274	630	865	351	450	43	.	383	974	115
1920	2 613	581	735	1 400	446	−50	48	.	247	481	313
1921	922	496	499	−7	−559	0	−44	.	−299	−989	153
1922	1 238	543	544	34	348	50	8	.	−159	−113	243
1923	497	611	762	596	−153	−50	21	.	−121	744	425
1924	1 087	625	699	−248	−52	50	20	.	−178	−599	428
1925	964	795	774	38	147	0	74	.	−67	150	647
1926	1 714	921	825	208	244	0	58	.	−99	49	394
1927	1 155	878	743	−145	−257	100	−23	80	−41	−245	448
1928	785	807	793	−318	−59	100	76	70	−41	111	456
1929	1 615	765	953	288	138	−100	130	110	−104	112	323
1930	−929	573	702	−532	−354	−150	−74	−1 730	20	−697	155
1931	−2 211	537	463	−531	−932	−50	−72	−2 170	−105	−862	285
1932	−1 454	18	260	−669	−125	0	−110	−1 630	−166	−676	−182
1933	803	−30	268	−466	−311	0	−127	543	−119	−790	−128
1934	2 891	−28	379	14	598	−50	49	1 761	20	−59	−138
1935	1 607	−41	500	175	−2	−50	85	922	−128	−83	−148
1936	2 128	96	671	512	500	100	110	454	−21	189	−5
1937	825	200	795	217	−200	100	74	−220	76	193	−50
1938	499	146	560	−149	200	0	−45	−579	16	−272	−33
1939	1 059	189	673	86	200	0	43	−48	−51	78	−88
1940	2 196	204	902	394	800	0	91	102	77	338	−55
1941	1 929	269	1 118	250	600	500	63	−122	−34	672	−20
1942	5 692	114	613	286	2 000	1 100	−276	1 040	−4	−435	−108
1943	5 150	77	523	−45	2 800	1 400	−80	278	−87	−58	−146
1944	5 443	109	699	806	2 000	1 800	69	130	−32	119	−50
1945	4 604	225	943	429	2 700	1 300	67	−532	39	425	75
1946	1 949	698	1 696	297	300	300	374	484	32	1 406	452
1947	1 068	523	2 335	25	100	0	302	−134	35	1 313	503
1948	1 958	725	2 667	1 381	−700	−1 600	226	323	133	548	423
1949	3 163	624	2 644	−712	−200	−200	196	994	84	−282	353

Column 1 – Sum of Table P-2, col. 1, Table P-13, col. 6, Table P-14, col. 6, Table P-16, col. 7, minus Table P-18, col. 6.

Column 2 – Col. 1 minus sum of cols. 3 and 4.

Column 3 – Sum of Table P-12, col. 6, Table P-13, col. 6, Table P-16, col. 7, minus adjustment for fire losses (generally about 15 percent of Table P-18, col. 6; ratio based on share of unincorporated in total business expenditures on producer durable goods [see Table P-12, col. 1]).

Column 4 – Expenditures, estimated to be 20 percent of institutional expenditures on new construction, (see Table R-17, col. 1) minus depreciation, obtained by depreciating expenditure series on a linear basis assuming average life of 12 years.

Column 5 – Sum of Table P-3, col. 1, Table P-13, col. 7, Table P-14, col. 7, Table P-17, col. 5, minus Table P-18, col. 7.

Column 6 – Col. 5 minus sum of cols. 7 and 8.

Column 7 – Sum of Table P-12, col. 7, Table P-13, col. 7, Table P-17, col. 5, minus adjustment for fire losses in 1929 prices (see Table P-18, col. 7).

Column 8 – Institutional expenditures on equipment in original cost (cf. note to col. 4) deflated by index derived by dividing nonfarm expenditures on producer durable goods, original cost, by expenditures in 1929 prices and depreciated.

Column 9 – Sum of Table P-4, col. 1, Table P-13, col. 8, Table P-14, col. 8, Table P-17, col. 9, minus Table P-18, col. 8.

Column 10 – Col. 9 minus sum of cols. 11 and 12.

Column 11 – Sum of Table P-12, col. 8, Table P-13, col. 8, Table P-17, col. 9, minus adjustment for fire losses (see Table P-18, col. 8).

Column 12 – Depreciation in 1929 prices multiplied by index described in note to col. 8 and subtracted from original cost expenditure series (see note to col. 4).

SAVING THROUGH PRODUCER DURABLE GOODS BY CORPORATIONS, UNINCORPORATED BUSINESS, AND NONPROFIT INSTITUTIONS 1897 to 1949

$ mill.

Year	Original cost				1929 prices				Replacement cost			
	Total	Business		Non-profit insti-tutions	Total	Business		Non-profit insti-tutions	Total	Business		Non-profit insti-tutions
		Cor-porate	Unin-corpo-rated			Cor-porate	Unin-corpo-rated			Cor-porate	Unin-corpo-rated	
	1	2	3	4	5	6	7	8	9	10	11	12
1897	52	105	−54	1	195	297	−108	6	76	116	−42	2
1898	89	133	−45	1	202	308	−108	2	88	133	−46	1
1899	238	249	−11	0	460	510	−49	−1	215	236	−21	0
1900	354	335	13	6	683	685	−13	11	326	321	0	5
1901	339	322	12	5	652	653	−10	9	308	305	−1	4
1902	416	382	27	7	824	781	29	14	387	365	15	7
1903	499	451	45	3	1 070	987	77	6	487	448	36	3
1904	305	286	18	1	581	575	7	−1	276	271	5	0
1905	476	425	48	3	923	853	67	3	441	406	34	1
1906	660	573	79	8	1 275	1 134	127	14	620	547	66	7
1907	792	681	100	11	1 435	1 268	150	17	724	632	83	9
1908	171	164	5	2	286	308	−24	2	137	141	−5	1
1909	312	282	27	3	471	456	12	3	246	230	15	1
1910	488	433	53	2	769	706	62	1	412	371	41	0
1911	349	319	30	0	387	383	10	−6	235	225	13	−3
1912	619	541	75	3	901	807	93	1	517	456	61	0
1913	780	676	96	8	1 161	1 025	128	8	660	573	83	4
1914	306	282	25	−1	342	340	9	−7	196	184	16	−4
1915	335	301	39	−5	199	216	−2	−15	165	163	12	−10
1916	1 243	1 046	196	1	1 259	1 089	179	−9	917	783	141	−7
1917	2 201	1 856	342	3	1 733	1 495	250	−12	1 562	1 345	227	−10
1918	2 765	2 356	409	0	1 441	1 258	201	−18	1 664	1 474	211	−21
1919	1 836	1 531	299	6	497	447	63	−13	614	550	79	−15
1920	2 085	1 729	358	−2	612	543	87	−18	696	601	117	−22
1921	530	437	87	6	−245	−186	−52	−7	−250	−187	−55	−8
1922	587	458	111	18	197	133	52	12	222	154	56	12
1923	1 631	1 311	296	24	1 119	872	230	17	1 137	883	236	18
1924	1 177	961	188	28	727	561	143	23	746	579	144	23
1925	1 356	1 098	220	38	889	670	184	35	911	690	186	35
1926	1 508	1 244	226	38	1 071	826	208	37	1 071	830	205	36
1927	1 057	908	112	37	645	508	99	38	638	503	97	38
1928	1 096	940	127	29	716	568	117	31	728	580	117	31
1929	1 818	1 546	248	24	1 411	1 152	234	25	1 411	1 152	234	25
1930	485	522	−55	18	327	305	−1	23	305	284	−1	22
1931	−878	−602	−271	−5	−925	−708	−219	2	−839	−646	−194	1
1932	−1 905	−1 435	−438	−32	−1 987	−1 566	−393	−28	−1 653	−1 299	−331	−23
1933	−1 792	−1 369	−374	−49	−1 818	−1 450	−320	−48	−1 481	−1 179	−263	−39
1934	−1 096	−830	−220	−46	−1 171	−937	−187	−47	−1 065	−856	−167	−42
1935	−481	−372	−68	−41	−445	−386	−18	−41	−443	−390	−17	−36
1936	433	353	111	−31	586	446	171	−31	480	359	148	−27
1937	1 091	903	210	−22	997	808	213	−24	919	741	201	−23
1938	−146	−88	−42	−16	−310	−225	−67	−18	−328	−246	−64	−18
1939	265	215	63	−13	143	101	56	−14	95	54	54	−13
1940	1 382	1 116	271	−5	1 127	897	237	−7	1 148	919	236	−7
1941	2 411	1 954	453	4	1 957	1 583	373	1	2 022	1 633	388	1
1942	126	194	−60	−8	−418	−260	−146	−12	−425	−242	−170	−13
1943	−446	−308	−122	−16	−893	−679	−196	−18	−958	−713	−225	−20
1944	798	726	80	−8	302	312	0	−10	330	346	−5	−11
1945	2 362	2 030	331	1	1 718	1 489	230	−1	1 905	1 652	254	−1
1946	6 042	4 963	1 042	37	4 329	3 567	737	25	5 238	4 293	913	32
1947	8 701	7 077	1 567	57	4 953	4 027	894	32	7 182	5 814	1 320	48
1948	9 632	7 819	1 720	93	4 930	3 999	881	50	7 745	6 253	1 410	82
1949	7 613	6 011	1 479	123	3 687	2 904	714	69	5 831	4 543	1 175	113

P-2 TABLE P–2

Columns 1 to 13 – Table P-5, cols. 1–13 minus Table P-7, cols. 1–13.

P-3 TABLE P–3

Columns 1 to 13 – Table P-6, cols. 1–13 minus Table P-8, cols. 1–13.

P-4 TABLE P–4

Columns 1 to 13 – Table P-5, cols. 1–13 minus Table P-9, cols. 1–13.

Original Cost Depreciation: 1897 to 1949
$ mill.

Year	Total	Industrial machinery and equipment	Electrical equipment	Office machinery	Nonresidential furniture and equipment	Railway and transit equipment	Ships and boats	Business horse-drawn vehicles	Aircraft	Professional and scientific equipment	Tools	Trucks	Miscellaneous
	1	2	3	4	5	6	7	8	9	10	11	12	13
1897	47	27	10	0	0	15	1	-3	–	0	-1	0	-2
1898	88	35	16	1	-2	31	5	-1	–	0	1	0	2
1899	241	103	29	4	3	73	15	2	–	1	2	0	9
1900	358	174	34	8	8	91	25	2	–	2	4	0	10
1901	344	145	33	6	14	84	41	6	–	2	4	1	8
1902	419	175	39	7	20	121	35	4	–	2	5	1	10
1903	498	197	45	7	27	165	35	4	–	2	4	1	11
1904	317	105	33	3	25	114	25	3	–	1	2	1	5
1905	472	173	36	8	34	178	26	4	–	2	2	1	8
1906	717	259	56	16	48	286	24	4	–	4	3	1	16
1907	778	249	59	16	41	343	34	4	–	3	6	0	23
1908	154	52	28	1	21	35	1	0	–	1	-3	1	17
1909	287	160	43	10	36	17	2	-1	–	3	3	4	10
1910	464	212	62	14	37	117	4	2	–	3	3	3	3
1911	329	160	52	8	32	53	9	-1	–	2	-1	19	-4
1912	592	185	67	11	40	242	9	-3	–	3	2	37	-1
1913	755	195	73	13	37	393	11	-2	–	4	4	26	1
1914	288	93	52	6	27	75	6	-1	–	8	1	3	18
1915	294	154	57	16	9	-15	28	0	–	11	3	25	6
1916	1 174	505	110	42	24	284	62	3	–	11	20	58	55
1917	2 140	919	148	70	41	609	76	4	–	26	31	120	96
1918	2 760	1 076	150	74	45	752	79	5	–	64	59	330	126
1919	1 772	825	152	30	78	325	83	-7	6	25	24	165	66
1920	2 011	1 018	200	66	139	331	85	-20	4	33	21	78	56
1921	536	304	132	-11	109	57	87	-17	2	9	-5	-94	-37
1922	557	399	121	-7	132	-23	35	-15	3	7	-20	-47	-28
1923	1 536	715	189	14	220	356	8	-12	2	11	-1	15	19
1924	1 130	493	215	10	266	180	3	-10	1	10	-2	9	-45
1925	1 270	627	210	18	261	19	-10	-7	1	13	2	89	47
1926	1 425	687	251	19	253	59	18	-3	5	18	3	55	60
1927	1 041	530	229	21	257	-36	3	-1	5	16	-1	-27	45
1928	1 059	621	285	25	227	-131	-10	–	25	18	15	-35	19
1929	1 753	893	314	21	276	-26	5	–	21	29	6	153	61
1930	572	252	197	-30	155	-37	37	–	-7	10	-14	12	-3
1931	-741	-240	72	-60	10	-330	10	–	-15	-12	-33	-76	-67
1932	-1 737	-677	-74	-74	-110	-366	-55	–	-22	-31	-40	-166	-122
1933	-1 701	-661	-108	-64	-134	-377	-59	–	-10	-35	-25	-127	-101
1934	-1 066	-453	-54	-42	-86	-282	-49	–	2	-29	-5	-31	-37
1935	-550	-201	6	-14	-75	-263	-60	–	-1	-16	9	46	19
1936	303	199	57	13	-44	-152	-11	–	-1	-3	19	149	77
1937	971	427	206	44	9	-4	-3	–	9	23	26	150	84
1938	-125	-26	56	26	-44	-226	52	–	3	5	2	11	16
1939	241	146	118	29	-26	-185	16	–	9	25	5	73	31
1940	1 306	667	309	51	25	-31	70	–	21	27	23	92	52
1941	2 307	1 145	381	91	102	83	115	–	12	45	51	182	100
1942	362	446	89	45	-1	80	148	–	-19	7	-15	-327	-91
1943	-247	143	-26	-15	-53	-99	220	–	-22	12	-4	-242	-161
1944	981	608	293	33	-43	0	167	–	-18	52	70	-69	-112
1945	2 518	1 350	393	82	28	3	181	–	-1	59	44	372	7
1946	5 876	.	.	.	.	.	.	.	.	.	.	.	.
1947	8 278	.	.	.	.	.	.	.	.	.	.	.	.
1948	9 155	.	.	.	.	.	.	.	.	.	.	.	.
1949	6 967	.	.	.	.	.	.	.	.	.	.	.	.

873

1929 Prices: 1897 to 1949

$ mill.

Year	Total	Industrial machinery and equipment	Electrical equipment	Office machinery	Nonresidential furniture and equipment	Railway and transit equipment	Ships and boats	Business horse-drawn vehicles	Aircraft	Professional and scientific equipment	Tools	Trucks	Miscellaneous
	1	2	3	4	5	6	7	8	9	10	11	12	13
1897	188	64	23	-2	39	63	2	-4	–	0	-1	0	4
1898	198	48	32	-1	17	93	18	-5	–	-1	2	0	-5
1899	461	157	56	2	30	170	37	0	–	1	4	0	4
1900	688	311	68	12	25	203	57	0	–	3	5	0	4
1901	659	255	66	8	42	176	87	7	–	2	5	0	11
1902	828	334	81	14	49	246	74	6	–	4	8	0	12
1903	1 068	436	100	16	61	338	73	4	–	4	7	0	29
1904	607	175	67	5	57	224	52	3	–	1	4	1	18
1905	919	323	74	17	75	344	51	5	–	5	4	1	20
1906	1 401	524	118	36	95	540	43	6	–	8	6	1	24
1907	1 418	453	116	30	57	641	60	5	–	6	10	0	40
1908	270	107	63	4	20	36	-5	-3	–	2	-5	0	51
1909	433	240	81	15	57	-5	2	-3	–	6	5	2	33
1910	737	346	117	24	43	175	5	1	–	5	5	3	13
1911	354	156	83	6	9	90	6	-3	–	3	-2	7	-1
1912	866	271	121	17	9	437	4	-6	–	4	4	14	-9
1913	1 132	342	115	25	-13	668	5	-4	–	6	8	11	-31
1914	316	83	78	8	-24	136	-4	-1	–	13	3	2	22
1915	142	92	78	15	-49	-49	28	1	–	15	8	13	-10
1916	1 171	557	127	49	-27	280	59	5	–	12	26	26	57
1917	1 652	816	130	59	-16	485	42	3	–	22	19	55	37
1918	1 417	646	105	36	-29	381	11	-5	–	47	36	131	58
1919	446	354	97	-7	-31	-24	7	-16	5	11	4	83	-37
1920	577	481	123	26	-38	-59	12	-24	3	17	-1	74	-37
1921	-232	-94	80	-34	-12	-128	34	-21	2	3	-7	-14	-41
1922	162	174	85	-11	36	-162	3	-18	3	8	-12	60	-4
1923	1 007	456	136	10	113	132	-20	-14	3	10	3	133	45
1924	657	232	166	8	188	17	-24	-11	2	11	0	92	-24
1925	780	390	167	21	202	-120	-36	-7	1	14	2	98	48
1926	957	468	201	23	221	-77	-7	-3	5	20	1	46	59
1927	600	329	191	22	231	-191	-22	-1	5	19	-2	-18	37
1928	667	426	249	25	207	-264	-33	–	25	21	15	-12	8
1929	1 346	700	277	17	263	-174	-17	–	21	30	6	165	58
1930	406	206	183	-34	150	-173	19	–	-6	13	-13	47	14
1931	-790	-246	78	-62	27	-451	-3	–	-14	-10	-29	-36	-44
1932	-1 811	-685	-81	-74	-82	-475	-69	–	-22	-30	-38	-152	-103
1933	-1 732	-645	-125	-57	-96	-481	-72	–	-8	-32	-22	-103	-91
1934	-1 146	-502	-69	-35	-47	-367	-60	–	4	-24	-5	1	-42
1935	-535	-215	10	-6	-24	-340	-70	–	-2	-8	10	95	15
1936	427	231	66	22	16	-215	-16	–	-2	8	20	215	82
1937	871	313	222	56	50	-76	-10	–	10	38	21	179	68
1938	-270	-125	64	37	-6	-288	46	–	3	15	-3	-26	13
1939	128	34	138	38	10	-242	10	–	11	42	2	49	36
1940	1 064	504	337	60	50	-89	62	–	25	41	19	55	0
1941	1 885	869	377	106	89	7	94	–	10	57	48	141	87
1942	-172	218	61	38	-46	-14	107	–	-22	-11	-19	-378	-106
1943	-693	-27	-60	-27	-94	-159	152	–	-25	-6	-7	-274	-166
1944	482	410	243	24	-88	-73	104	–	-20	32	60	-97	-113
1945	1 089	1 089	323	74	-25	-58	108	–	-3	39	38	284	0
1946	4 230	.	.	.	.	.	.	.	.	.	.	.	.
1947	4 696	.	.	.	.	.	.	.	.	.	.	.	.
1948	4 659	.	.	.	.	.	.	.	.	.	.	.	.
1949	3 349	.	.	.	.	.	.	.	.	.	.	.	.

874

Replacement Cost Depreciation: 1897 to 1949

$ mill.

Year	Total	Industrial machinery and equipment	Electrical equipment	Office machinery	Nonresidential furniture and equipment	Railway and transit equipment	Ships and boats	Business horse-drawn vehicles	Aircraft	Professional and scientific equipment	Tools	Trucks	Miscellaneous
	1	2	3	4	5	6	7	8	9	10	11	12	13
1897	73	27	10	-1	12	26	1	-2	–	0	-1	0	1
1898	86	22	15	-1	6	40	8	-3	–	0	1	0	-2
1899	215	77	28	1	10	78	17	0	–	1	2	0	1
1900	327	151	33	6	10	94	26	0	–	2	3	0	2
1901	311	122	32	4	16	83	41	4	–	1	3	1	4
1902	390	157	39	6	19	118	35	4	–	2	4	1	5
1903	486	192	45	7	24	162	35	3	–	2	4	1	11
1904	288	83	32	2	23	109	25	2	–	1	2	2	7
1905	438	152	35	8	30	170	25	3	–	3	2	2	8
1906	676	243	56	17	40	274	22	4	–	4	3	2	11
1907	710	221	57	15	27	330	31	3	–	3	5	0	18
1908	122	48	29	2	9	19	-2	-2	–	1	-3	1	20
1909	216	121	41	8	26	-2	1	-2	–	3	3	4	13
1910	382	174	59	12	21	95	3	0	–	3	3	7	5
1911	206	87	47	3	5	45	3	-2	–	2	-1	17	0
1912	481	142	64	9	5	227	2	-4	–	2	2	36	-4
1913	626	171	66	12	-9	367	3	-3	–	3	4	27	-15
1914	166	44	45	4	-17	68	-2	0	–	8	1	5	10
1915	110	56	47	9	-33	-25	18	1	–	10	4	28	-5
1916	830	367	91	32	-19	195	44	3	–	9	16	59	33
1917	1 478	662	114	48	-12	434	41	2	–	20	16	122	31
1918	1 635	649	104	36	-26	448	15	-5	–	53	-17	324	54
1919	546	371	101	-7	-36	-31	10	-19	6	13	4	177	-43
1920	639	529	139	28	-63	-84	17	-30	4	21	-1	127	-48
1921	-236	-98	84	-35	-16	-127	41	-23	2	4	-7	-21	-40
1922	177	157	83	-10	42	-141	3	-17	3	7	-11	65	-4
1923	1 016	437	141	9	133	141	-20	-14	3	10	3	130	43
1924	672	225	170	8	204	17	-24	-10	2	10	0	92	-22
1925	700	378	169	20	212	-112	-36	-6	1	14	2	110	47
1926	959	456	207	22	222	-73	-7	-3	5	20	1	52	57
1927	595	321	191	22	232	-188	-22	-1	5	19	-2	-19	37
1928	679	421	249	24	208	-247	-33	–	25	21	15	-12	8
1929	1 346	700	277	17	263	-174	-17	–	21	30	6	165	58
1930	378	189	173	-34	149	-171	19	–	-5	13	-12	44	13
1931	-718	-214	67	-63	25	-412	-3	–	-11	-10	-27	-32	-38
1932	-1 499	-556	-66	-72	-70	-383	-60	–	-16	-29	-34	-128	-85
1933	-1 407	-523	-105	-48	-77	-383	-63	–	-6	-27	-20	-80	-75
1934	-1 042	-470	-61	-30	-40	-327	-56	–	3	-21	-4	1	-37
1935	-521	-202	8	-6	-20	-322	-66	–	-2	-6	9	73	13
1936	345	216	58	20	13	-205	-15	–	-2	6	18	164	72
1937	803	325	201	49	44	-76	-10	–	9	31	21	144	65
1938	-291	-131	57	31	-6	-290	47	–	3	12	-3	-23	12
1939	80	36	122	32	9	-248	11	–	9	32	2	43	32
1940	1 087	537	307	52	46	-94	64	–	22	31	20	51	51
1941	1 947	961	365	91	90	8	104	–	10	45	50	135	88
1942	-142	245	62	35	-52	-17	131	–	-23	-11	-22	-378	-112
1943	-725	-30	-63	-25	-105	-205	197	–	-26	-6	-8	-275	-179
1944	537	453	258	23	-100	-94	140	–	-21	34	67	-101	-122
1945	2 079	1 205	352	71	-28	-75	152	–	-3	41	42	322	0
1946	5 100	.	.	.	.	.	.	.	.	.	.	.	.
1947	6 777	.	.	.	.	.	.	.	.	.	.	.	.
1948	7 279	.	.	.	.	.	.	.	.	.	.	.	.
1949	5 216	.	.	.	.	.	.	.	.	.	.	.	.

Column 1 – 1897–1945: Sum of cols. 2–13.

       1946–1949: Estimated on basis of data obtained, prior to the 1953 revision, from National Income Division, Department of Commerce. Revised figures of expenditures on producer durable equipment by type are given in *Survey of Current Business*, Nov. 1953, pp. 18–19.

Columns 2 to 7 – 1897–1928: Shaw's estimates of output of producer durable goods (*Value of Commodity Output since 1869*, pp. 52–61, 69) adjusted for inventory changes and linked to Department of Commerce figures. This procedure was extended backwards for years prior to 1897 whenever it was required for calculation of depreciation. Annual estimates for years 1870–1878 and 1880–1888 were obtained by interpolation between Shaw's figures. Inventory changes for years prior to 1919 were assumed to be negligible. For years 1919–1929 following percentage changes were derived from estimates by S. Kuznets (cf. *Commodity Flow and Capital Formation*, p. 307) and assumed to be same for all commodities.

1919	–3.3%	1924	0.0%
1920	0.0%	1925	0.0%
1921	7.1%	1926	–0.5%
1922	2.8%	1927	1.5%
1923	–2.8%	1928	0.0%

       No adjustment was needed from 1929–1949 as estimates of Department of Commerce reflect, in principle at least, sales to users rather than manufacturers' output.

       1929–1945: *Survey of Current Business, National Income Supplement*, various issues. Col. 2 is a consolidation of individual items of special industrial machinery, mining machinery, construction machinery, metal-working machinery, pumps and pumping equipment, general and miscellaneous machinery, engines and turbines, and durable containers. Government purchases allocated among industrial machinery and equipment, electrical apparatus, professional and scientific equipment and tools according to percentage distribution of total expenditures on these items. Data for remaining items are reported exclusive of government purchases.

Column 8 – 1897–1945: Table A-17, col. 2 minus col. 10.

Column 9 – 1897–1945: Same procedure as for cols. 2–7.

Columns 10 and 11 – 1897–1928: Extrapolated on basis of Table A-17, col. 3 minus col. 11, linked in 1929 to Department of Commerce series.

       1929–1945: Same procedure as for cols. 2–7.

Column 12 – 1897–1945: Obtained by: (1) increasing W. H. Shaw's estimates of expenditures on business motor vehicles (*Value of Commodity Output since 1869*) by 24 percent, estimate of new truck markup by National Income Division; (2) adjusting for percentage changes in inventories (cf. notes to col. 2); (3) linking 1929 to Department of Commerce estimates; and (4) deducting farmers' expenditures. For period 1910–1945 farmers' expenditures estimated on basis of underlying data of *Income Parity for Agriculture*, part II, section 3, pp. 35–47, as revised and brought up to date by Bureau of Agricultural Economics. The series represents gross expenditures by farmers for new trucks before deduction of allowance for trade-ins of old trucks. Figures for period 1899–1909 obtained by extrapolating on basis of estimate of farmers' expenditures on trucks obtained by multiplying adjusted Shaw series by ratio of farm income to total national income (Table A-4, col. 4, and Table A-5, col. 3).

Column 13 – 1897–1945: Same procedure as for cols. 10 and 11.

EXPENDITURES BY NONFARM PRODUCERS ON MAIN TYPES OF DURABLE GOODS; ORIGINAL COST: 1897 to 1949

$ mill.

Year	Total	Industrial machinery and equipment	Electrical equipment	Office machinery	Nonresidential furniture and equipment	Railway and transit equipment	Ships and boats	Business horse-drawn vehicles	Aircraft	Professional and scientific equipment	Tools	Trucks	Miscellaneous
	1	2	3	4	5	6	7	8	9	10	11	12	13
1897	427	186	15	9	46	94	20	12	–	2	8	0	35
1898	476	199	21	10	45	114	13	24	–	2	9	0	39
1899	643	273	35	13	51	159	35	16	–	3	11	0	47
1900	783	355	42	18	57	181	46	16	–	4	13	0	51
1901	791	337	42	17	64	178	63	20	–	4	14	1	51
1902	898	379	50	20	71	220	59	19	–	5	17	1	57
1903	1 008	414	57	21	80	271	60	19	–	5	18	1	62
1904	860	334	47	18	80	227	52	19	–	4	17	2	60
1905	1 047	413	52	25	91	299	54	21	–	6	18	2	66
1906	1 333	515	74	35	107	417	53	23	–	8	21	2	78
1907	1 445	522	79	38	103	489	64	24	–	8	25	2	91
1908	860	338	51	25	85	191	33	20	–	6	17	3	91
1909	1 024	456	68	36	102	177	37	20	–	9	23	6	90
1910	1 239	523	89	43	106	283	40	23	–	9	24	11	88
1911	1 137	487	82	39	103	225	42	20	–	9	21	25	84
1912	1 442	528	100	45	114	423	43	18	–	10	24	49	88
1913	1 656	555	109	50	114	589	46	19	–	12	27	46	89
1914	1 237	470	91	46	107	283	42	20	–	17	25	28	108
1915	1 283	548	99	57	91	198	65	20	–	21	28	57	99
1916	2 238	925	156	89	109	506	101	23	–	23	48	102	156
1917	3 343	1 387	200	126	129	851	118	25	–	40	65	185	217
1918	4 180	1 609	209	142	138	1 023	124	26	–	84	105	441	279
1919	3 417	1 422	218	109	176	621	131	14	7	51	84	332	252
1920	3 860	1 677	273	156	245	645	137	–	6	63	93	291	274
1921	2 543	1 013	213	88	224	385	143	–	5	44	77	148	203
1922	2 659	1 144	209	98	255	313	94	–	7	45	65	212	217
1923	3 745	1 506	284	127	355	708	69	–	8	53	81	292	262
1924	3 432	1 337	320	129	416	551	66	–	8	56	77	282	190
1925	3 654	1 524	326	141	428	404	54	–	8	63	79	350	277
1926	3 921	1 639	378	143	437	455	84	–	13	73	79	320	300
1927	3 667	1 536	368	147	458	370	70	–	15	75	76	249	303
1928	3 815	1 686	437	154	446	281	59	–	38	78	95	253	288
1929	4 672	2 031	480	154	514	391	75	–	41	91	88	458	349
1930	3 641	1 453	376	107	411	387	109	–	17	75	68	335	303
1931	2 364	997	260	75	278	94	83	–	9	54	45	243	226
1932	1 330	573	119	53	164	52	18	–	1	35	30	128	157
1933	1 280	592	87	52	141	33	12	–	8	29	34	142	150
1934	1 849	809	143	64	192	118	21	–	15	33	44	227	183
1935	2 319	1 083	207	83	208	125	9	–	8	44	51	287	214
1936	3 181	1 511	264	103	246	230	57	–	7	55	61	380	267
1937	3 931	1 763	422	129	307	383	65	–	19	80	74	397	292
1938	2 912	1 312	281	109	261	162	122	–	15	62	57	284	247
1939	3 347	1 478	352	115	285	200	88	–	23	80	65	379	282
1940	4 514	2 008	555	145	341	353	145	–	39	82	88	435	323
1941	5 684	2 533	644	200	425	463	194	–	35	103	127	565	395
1942	3 849	1 890	366	170	329	461	233	–	6	68	66	52	208
1943	3 219	1 609	258	119	277	287	312	–	0	77	79	84	117
1944	4 445	2 095	588	174	282	385	267	–	0	124	165	226	139
1945	6 077	.	.	.	.	.	.	.	.	.	.	.	.
1946	9 707	.	.	.	.	.	.	.	.	.	.	.	.
1947	12 669	.	.	.	.	.	.	.	.	.	.	.	.
1948	14 326	.	.	.	.	.	.	.	.	.	.	.	.
1949	12 909	.	.	.	.	.	.	.	.	.	.	.	.

P-6   TABLE P-6

Column 1 – 1897–1945: Sum of cols. 2–13.
        1946–1949: Expenditures, original cost, by type (rough estimates based on National Income
        Division, Department of Commerce data) deflated by appropriate price index given in
        Table P-10.

Columns 2 to 13 – 1897–1945: Table P-5, cols. 2–13 deflated by appropriate price index from Table P-10.

P-7   TABLE P-7

Column 1 – Sum of cols. 2–13. Figures for 1946–1949 derived by same procedure from rough estimates of
        expenditures (see Table P-5).

Columns 2 to 13 – Table P-5, cols. 2–13 depreciated on basis of following average lengths of life:

Industrial machinery and equipment	20
Electrical equipment	30
Office machinery	8
Nonresidential furniture and equipment	20
Railway and transit equipment	28
Ships and boats	30
Business horse-drawn vehicles	8
Aircraft	5
Professional and scientific equipment	10
Tools	5
Trucks	6
Miscellaneous producer durable equipment	5

These estimates based on data in Department of the Treasury, Bureau of Internal Revenue,
Bulletin F.

P-8   TABLE P-8

Column 1 – Sum of cols. 2–13. Figures for 1946–1949 derived by same procedure from rough estimates of
        expenditures (see Table P-6).

Columns 2 to 13 – Table P-6, cols. 2–13 depreciated on a linear basis assuming length of life given in notes
        to Table P-7.

EXPENDITURES BY NONFARM PRODUCERS ON MAIN TYPES
OF DURABLE GOODS; 1929 PRICES: 1897 to 1949

$ mill.

Year	Total	Industrial machinery and equipment	Electrical equipment	Office machinery	Nonresidential furniture and equipment	Railway and transit equipment	Ships and boats	Business horse-drawn vehicles	Aircraft	Professional and scientific equipment	Tools	Trucks	Miscellaneous
	1	2	3	4	5	6	7	8	9	10	11	12	13
1897	1 089	438	35	21	152	227	49	22	–	5	18	0	122
1898	1 111	434	45	22	134	263	56	21	–	4	20	0	112
1899	1 403	556	71	26	150	349	77	25	–	6	23	0	120
1900	1 674	732	86	37	149	392	100	24	–	8	25	0	121
1901	1 701	702	87	35	171	376	133	31	–	8	27	0	131
1902	1 928	806	105	43	183	459	124	31	–	10	32	0	135
1903	2 239	939	128	48	200	566	126	30	–	11	34	0	157
1904	1 843	705	98	38	201	468	108	29	–	8	33	1	154
1905	2 220	875	109	53	225	604	110	32	–	12	35	1	164
1906	2 787	1 108	157	75	251	822	105	35	–	16	40	1	177
1907	2 906	1 072	161	78	218	951	125	35	–	15	46	1	204
1908	1 835	751	112	56	185	366	62	28	–	12	32	1	230
1909	2 056	905	134	71	226	333	70	28	–	17	43	3	226
1910	2 431	1 038	175	85	217	524	74	32	–	17	45	5	219
1911	2 109	873	146	70	186	451	76	28	–	16	39	10	214
1912	2 683	1 011	190	86	188	815	76	25	–	18	45	19	210
1913	3 020	1 110	190	100	168	1 073	78	26	–	21	51	19	184
1914	2 264	880	158	86	158	562	70	28	–	29	48	12	233
1915	2 133	910	163	95	134	386	103	29	–	33	54	26	200
1916	3 232	1 402	218	135	156	726	137	33	–	32	77	45	271
1917	3 833	1 710	228	155	167	952	122	32	–	45	77	83	262
1918	3 750	1 601	210	141	155	871	93	24	–	74	103	178	300
1919	2 902	1 358	208	104	153	481	91	11	6	42	79	155	214
1920	3 123	1 525	241	142	147	452	97	–	5	51	79	170	214
1921	2 374	977	204	85	172	387	121	–	5	40	76	102	205
1922	2 808	1 263	215	108	221	358	91	–	7	48	70	195	232
1923	3 730	1 572	273	133	302	664	69	–	8	53	82	298	276
1924	3 468	1 381	312	133	384	563	66	–	8	57	77	284	203
1925	3 682	1 574	323	146	407	435	54	–	8	63	79	312	281
1926	3 957	1 683	367	147	435	486	84	–	13	73	78	282	309
1927	3 700	1 571	368	150	456	376	70	–	15	75	76	239	304
1928	3 861	1 705	438	156	444	302	59	–	38	79	95	262	283
1929	4 672	2 031	480	154	514	391	75	–	41	91	88	458	349
1930	3 846	1 578	398	107	413	391	112	–	18	77	69	360	323
1931	2 674	1 147	301	75	298	103	89	–	11	56	49	280	265
1932	1 599	707	147	55	192	64	21	–	1	37	33	151	191
1933	1 575	730	103	61	178	41	14	–	11	33	39	184	181
1934	2 076	863	160	74	229	132	23	–	18	39	47	286	205
1935	2 626	1 156	242	95	257	132	10	–	9	54	56	375	240
1936	3 582	1 613	302	117	304	241	61	–	8	69	66	499	302
1937	4 093	1 700	466	148	346	378	65	–	21	100	73	493	303
1938	3 015	1 253	316	130	298	160	121	–	17	78	55	319	268
1939	3 478	1 405	398	136	322	195	87	–	27	106	63	429	310
1940	4 508	1 885	609	169	372	335	140	–	45	107	85	471	290
1941	5 467	2 292	665	233	422	411	175	–	37	129	122	590	391
1942	3 468	1 684	360	183	296	375	191	–	6	66	59	52	196
1943	2 865	1 446	243	126	248	223	241	–	0	74	71	84	109
1944	3 988	1 893	553	183	249	299	198	–	0	118	148	219	128
1945	5 414	2 611	648	244	306	294	206	–	11	133	140	606	215
1946	7 949	.	.	.	.	.	.	.	.	.	.	.	.
1947	8 732	.	.	.	.	.	.	.	.	.	.	.	.
1948	9 125	.	.	.	.	.	.	.	.	.	.	.	.
1949	8 242	.	.	.	.	.	.	.	.	.	.	.	.

DEPRECIATION ON NONFARM PRODUCERS' HOLDINGS OF MAIN TYPES OF DURABLE GOODS; ORIGINAL COST: 1897 to 1949

$ mill.

Year	Total	Industrial machinery and equipment	Electrical equipment	Office machinery	Nonresidential furniture and equipment	Railway and transit equipment	Ships and boats	Business horse-drawn vehicles	Aircraft	Professional and scientific equipment	Tools	Trucks	Miscellaneous
	1	2	3	4	5	6	7	8	9	10	11	12	13
1897	380	159	5	9	46	79	19	15	–	2	9	0	37
1898	388	164	5	9	47	83	19	14	–	2	8	0	37
1899	402	170	6	9	48	86	20	14	–	2	9	0	38
1900	425	181	8	10	49	90	21	14	–	2	9	0	41
1901	447	192	9	11	50	94	22	14	–	2	10	0	43
1902	479	204	11	13	51	99	24	15	–	3	12	0	47
1903	510	217	12	14	53	106	25	15	–	3	14	0	51
1904	543	229	14	15	55	113	27	16	–	3	15	1	55
1905	575	240	16	17	57	121	28	17	–	4	16	1	58
1906	616	256	18	19	59	131	29	19	–	4	18	1	62
1907	667	273	20	22	62	146	30	20	–	5	19	2	68
1908	706	286	23	24	64	156	32	20	–	5	20	2	74
1909	737	296	25	26	66	160	35	21	–	6	20	2	80
1910	775	311	27	29	69	166	36	21	–	6	21	4	85
1911	808	327	30	31	71	172	33	21	–	7	22	6	88
1912	850	343	33	34	74	181	34	21	–	7	22	12	89
1913	901	360	36	37	77	196	35	21	–	8	23	20	88
1914	949	377	39	40	80	208	36	21	–	9	24	25	90
1915	989	394	42	41	82	213	37	20	–	10	25	32	93
1916	1 064	420	46	47	85	222	39	20	–	12	28	44	101
1917	1 203	468	52	56	88	242	42	21	–	14	34	65	121
1918	1 420	533	59	68	93	271	45	21	–	20	46	111	153
1919	1 645	597	66	79	98	296	48	21	1	26	60	167	186
1920	1 849	659	73	90	106	314	52	20	2	30	72	213	218
1921	2 007	709	81	99	115	328	56	17	3	35	82	242	240
1922	2 102	745	88	105	123	336	59	15	4	38	85	259	245
1923	2 209	791	95	113	135	352	61	12	6	42	82	277	243
1924	2 302	844	105	119	150	371	63	10	7	46	79	273	235
1925	2 384	897	116	123	167	385	64	7	7	50	77	261	230
1926	2 496	952	127	124	184	396	66	3	8	55	76	265	240
1927	2 626	1 006	139	126	201	406	67	1	10	59	77	276	258
1928	2 756	1 065	152	129	219	412	69	–	13	60	80	288	269
1929	2 919	1 138	166	133	238	417	70	–	20	62	82	305	288
1930	3 069	1 201	179	137	256	424	72	–	24	65	82	323	306
1931	3 105	1 237	188	135	268	424	73	–	24	66	78	319	293
1932	3 067	1 250	193	127	274	418	73	–	23	66	70	294	279
1933	2 981	1 253	195	116	275	410	71	–	18	64	59	269	251
1934	2 915	1 262	197	106	278	400	70	–	13	62	49	258	220
1935	2 869	1 284	201	97	283	388	69	–	9	60	42	241	195
1936	2 878	1 312	207	90	290	382	68	–	8	58	42	231	190
1937	2 960	1 336	216	85	298	387	68	–	10	57	48	247	208
1938	3 037	1 338	225	83	305	388	70	–	12	57	55	273	231
1939	3 106	1 332	234	86	311	385	72	–	14	55	60	306	251
1940	3 208	1 341	246	94	316	384	75	–	18	55	65	343	271
1941	3 377	1 388	263	109	323	380	79	–	23	58	76	383	295
1942	3 487	1 444	277	125	330	381	85	–	25	61	81	379	299
1943	3 466	1 466	284	134	330	386	92	–	22	65	83	326	278
1944	3 464	1 487	295	141	325	385	100	–	18	72	95	295	251
1945	3 559	1 540	313	152	320	375	108	–	13	82	112	316	228
1946	3 831	.	.	.	.	.	.	.	.	.	.	.	.
1947	4 391	.	.	.	.	.	.	.	.	.	.	.	.
1948	5 171	.	.	.	.	.	.	.	.	.	.	.	.
1949	5 942	.	.	.	.	.	.	.	.	.	.	.	.

DEPRECIATION ON NONFARM PRODUCERS' HOLDINGS
OF MAIN TYPES OF DURABLE GOODS; 1929 PRICES: 1897 to 1949

$ mill.

Year	Total	Industrial machinery and equipment	Electrical equipment	Office machinery	Nonresidential furniture and equipment	Railway and transit equipment	Ships and boats	Business horse-drawn vehicles	Aircraft	Professional and scientific equipment	Tools	Trucks	Miscellaneous
	1	2	3	4	5	6	7	8	9	10	11	12	13
1897	901	374	12	23	113	164	47	26	–	5	19	0	118
1898	913	386	13	23	117	170	38	26	–	5	18	0	117
1899	942	399	15	24	120	179	40	25	–	5	19	0	116
1900	986	421	18	25	124	189	43	24	–	5	20	0	117
1901	1 042	447	21	27	129	200	46	24	–	6	22	0	120
1902	1 100	472	24	29	134	213	50	25	–	6	24	0	123
1903	1 171	503	28	32	139	228	53	26	–	7	27	0	128
1904	1 236	530	31	33	144	244	56	26	–	7	29	0	136
1905	1 301	552	35	36	150	260	59	27	–	7	31	0	144
1906	1 386	584	39	39	156	282	62	29	–	8	34	0	153
1907	1 488	619	45	48	161	310	65	30	–	9	36	1	164
1908	1 565	644	49	52	165	330	67	31	–	10	37	1	179
1909	1 623	665	53	56	169	338	68	31	–	11	38	1	193
1910	1 694	692	58	61	174	349	69	31	–	12	40	2	206
1911	1 755	717	63	64	177	361	70	31	–	13	41	3	215
1912	1 817	740	69	69	179	378	72	31	–	14	41	5	219
1913	1 888	768	75	75	181	405	73	30	–	15	43	8	215
1914	1 948	797	80	78	182	426	74	29	–	16	45	10	211
1915	1 991	818	85	80	183	435	75	28	–	18	46	13	210
1916	2 061	845	91	86	183	446	78	28	–	20	51	19	214
1917	2 181	894	98	96	183	467	80	29	–	23	58	47	242
1918	2 333	955	105	105	184	490	82	29	–	27	67	47	242
1919	2 456	1 004	111	111	184	505	84	27	1	31	75	72	251
1920	2 546	1 044	118	116	185	511	85	24	2	34	80	96	251
1921	2 606	1 071	124	119	184	515	87	21	3	37	83	116	246
1922	2 646	1 089	130	119	185	520	88	18	4	40	82	135	236
1923	2 723	1 116	137	123	189	532	89	14	5	43	79	165	231
1924	2 811	1 149	146	125	196	546	90	11	6	46	77	192	227
1925	2 902	1 184	156	125	205	555	90	7	7	49	77	214	233
1926	3 000	1 215	166	124	214	563	91	3	8	53	77	236	250
1927	3 100	1 242	177	128	225	567	92	1	10	56	78	257	267
1928	3 194	1 279	189	131	237	566	92	–	13	58	80	274	275
1929	3 326	1 331	203	137	251	565	92	–	20	61	82	293	291
1930	3 440	1 372	215	141	263	564	93	–	24	64	82	313	309
1931	3 464	1 393	223	137	271	554	92	–	25	66	78	316	309
1932	3 410	1 392	228	129	274	539	90	–	23	67	71	303	294
1933	3 307	1 375	228	118	274	522	86	–	19	65	61	287	272
1934	3 222	1 365	229	109	276	499	83	–	14	63	52	285	247
1935	3 161	1 371	232	101	281	472	80	–	11	62	46	280	225
1936	3 155	1 382	236	95	288	456	77	–	10	61	46	284	220
1937	3 222	1 387	244	92	296	454	75	–	11	62	52	314	235
1938	3 285	1 378	252	93	304	448	75	–	14	63	58	345	255
1939	3 350	1 371	260	98	312	437	77	–	16	64	61	380	274
1940	3 444	1 381	272	109	322	424	78	–	20	66	66	416	290
1941	3 582	1 423	288	127	333	404	81	–	27	72	74	449	304
1942	3 640	1 466	299	145	342	389	84	–	28	77	78	430	302
1943	3 558	1 473	303	153	342	382	89	–	25	80	78	358	275
1944	3 506	1 483	310	159	337	372	94	–	20	86	88	316	241
1945	3 545	1 522	325	170	331	352	98	–	14	94	102	322	215
1946	3 719	.	.	.	.	.	.	.	.	.	.	.	.
1947	4 036	.	.	.	.	.	.	.	.	.	.	.	.
1948	4 466	.	.	.	.	.	.	.	.	.	.	.	.
1949	4 893	.	.	.	.	.	.	.	.	.	.	.	.

TABLE P-9

Column 1 – Sum of cols. 2–13. Figures for 1946–1949 derived by same procedure. See Tables P-8 and P-10.

Columns 2 to 13 – Table P-8, cols. 2–13 multiplied by appropriate price index from Table P-10.

DEPRECIATION ON NONFARM PRODUCERS' HOLDINGS OF MAIN TYPES OF DURABLE GOODS; REPLACEMENT COST: 1897 to 1949

$ mill.

Year	Total	Industrial machinery and equipment	Electrical equipment	Office machinery	Nonresidential furniture and equipment	Railway and transit equipment	Ships and boats	Business horse-drawn vehicles	Aircraft	Professional and scientific equipment	Tools	Trucks	Miscellaneous
	1	2	3	4	5	6	7	8	9	10	11	12	13
1897	354	159	5	10	34	68	19	14	–	2	9	0	34
1898	390	177	6	11	39	74	16	16	–	2	8	0	41
1899	428	196	7	12	41	81	18	16	–	2	9	0	46
1900	456	204	9	12	47	87	20	16	–	2	10	0	49
1901	480	215	10	13	48	95	22	16	–	3	11	0	47
1902	508	222	11	14	52	102	24	15	–	3	13	0	52
1903	522	222	12	14	56	109	25	16	–	3	14	0	51
1904	572	251	15	16	57	118	27	17	–	3	15	0	53
1905	609	261	17	17	61	129	29	18	–	3	16	0	58
1906	657	272	18	18	67	143	31	19	–	4	18	0	67
1907	735	301	22	23	76	159	33	21	–	5	20	2	73
1908	738	290	22	23	76	172	35	22	–	5	20	2	71
1909	808	335	27	28	76	179	36	23	–	6	21	4	77
1910	857	349	30	31	85	188	37	23	–	6	21	4	83
1911	931	400	35	36	98	180	39	22	–	7	22	8	84
1912	961	386	36	36	109	196	41	22	–	8	22	13	92
1913	1 030	384	43	38	123	222	43	22	–	9	23	19	104
1914	1 071	426	46	42	124	215	44	20	–	9	24	23	98
1915	1 173	492	52	48	124	223	47	19	–	11	24	29	104
1916	1 408	558	65	57	128	311	57	20	–	14	32	43	123
1917	1 865	725	86	78	141	417	77	23	–	20	49	63	186
1918	2 545	960	105	106	164	575	109	31	–	31	122	117	225
1919	2 871	1 051	117	116	212	652	121	33	1	38	80	155	295
1920	3 221	1 148	134	128	308	729	120	30	2	42	94	164	322
1921	2 779	1 111	129	123	240	512	102	23	3	40	84	169	243
1922	2 482	987	126	108	213	454	91	17	4	38	76	147	221
1923	2 729	1 069	143	118	222	567	89	14	5	43	78	162	219
1924	2 760	1 112	150	121	212	534	90	10	6	46	77	190	212
1925	2 855	1 146	157	121	216	516	90	6	7	49	77	240	230
1926	2 962	1 183	171	121	215	528	91	3	8	53	78	268	243
1927	3 072	1 215	177	125	226	558	92	1	10	56	78	268	266
1928	3 136	1 265	188	130	238	528	92	–	13	57	80	265	280
1929	3 326	1 331	203	137	251	565	92	–	20	61	82	293	291
1930	3 263	1 264	203	141	262	558	90	–	22	62	80	291	290
1931	3 082	1 211	193	138	253	506	86	–	20	64	72	275	264
1932	2 829	1 129	185	125	234	435	78	–	17	64	64	256	242
1933	2 687	1 115	192	100	218	416	75	–	14	56	54	222	225
1934	2 891	1 279	204	94	232	445	77	–	12	54	48	226	220
1935	2 840	1 285	199	89	228	447	75	–	10	50	42	214	201
1936	2 836	1 295	206	83	233	435	72	–	9	49	43	216	195
1937	3 128	1 438	221	80	263	459	75	–	10	49	53	253	227
1938	3 203	1 443	224	78	267	452	75	–	12	50	60	307	235
1939	3 267	1 442	230	83	276	448	77	–	14	48	63	336	250
1940	3 427	1 471	248	93	295	447	81	–	17	51	68	384	272
1941	3 737	1 572	279	109	335	455	90	–	25	58	77	430	307
1942	3 991	1 645	304	135	381	478	102	–	29	79	88	430	320
1943	3 944	1 639	321	144	382	492	115	–	26	83	87	359	296
1944	3 908	1 642	330	151	382	479	127	–	21	90	98	327	261
1945	3 998	1 685	354	163	376	453	137	–	15	100	114	366	235
1946	4 607	.	.	.	.	.	.	.	.	.	.	.	.
1947	5 892	.	.	.	.	.	.	.	.	.	.	.	.
1948	7 047	.	.	.	.	.	.	.	.	.	.	.	.
1949	7 693	.	.	.	.	.	.	.	.	.	.	.	.

Column 1 – 1877–1888: Shaw's implicit index of producer durable goods prices (cf. Shaw, W. H., *Value of Commodity Output since 1869*, pp. 294–295 for 1869, 1879, and 1889; price index for years between from National Bureau of Economic Research worksheets), as recomputed to 1929 base by National Bureau of Economic Research, linked in 1889 to his index of prices for industrial machinery and equipment (group 25a).

1889–1938: Shaw's index of prices for industrial machinery and equipment shifted to 1929 base.

1939–1946: Value of 1938 extrapolated by a weighted average of Bureau of Labor Statistics indices of prices of general and auxiliary machinery and equipment, standard machine tools, and construction machinery, assigning to them weights of 75 percent, 15 percent, and 10 percent respectively on basis of average expenditures for period for corresponding items.

1947–1949: Value for 1946 extrapolated by Marshall and Stevens index of comparative equipment cost (cf. *Stevens' Valuation Quarterly*).

Column 2 – 1867–1868: Assumed equal to 1869 value.

1869–1888: Shaw's recomputed implicit index of producer durable goods prices linked in 1889 to his price index for electrical equipment (group 26).

1889–1938: Shaw's price index for electrical equipment shifted to 1929 base.

1939–1949: Weighted average of Interstate Commerce Commission cost indices for telegraph and telephone lines (account 26), signals and interlockers (account 27), power plants (account 29), power transmission systems (account 31), and power plant machinery (account 45), using weights estimated by the Commission shifted to 1929 base (cf. Interstate Commerce Commission, Bureau of Valuation, Engineering Section, *Railroad Construction Indices*, Aug. 1, 1950).

Column 3 – 1889–1929: Same as col. 1.

1930–1942: Shavell's wholesale price index for office machinery (group 52) shifted to 1929 base (*Survey of Current Business*, May 1943, p. 19).

1943–1949: Value for 1942 extrapolated by Bureau of Labor Statistics index of wholesale prices of manufactured products (*Survey of Current Business*, various issues).

Column 4 – 1877–1888: Same procedure as col. 1, linked in 1889 to Shaw's index of prices for office and store furniture and fixtures (group 29).

1889–1929: Shaw's price index for office and store furniture and fixtures shifted to 1929 base.

1930–1942: Shavell's price index for nonresidential furniture and equipment (group 53) shifted to 1929 base.

1943–1949: Value for 1942 extrapolated by Bureau of Labor Statistics wholesale price index of house furnishings goods (*Survey of Current Business*, various issues).

Column 5 – 1869–1888: Shaw's recomputed implicit price index of producer durable goods linked in 1889 to his price index for locomotives and railroad cars (group 30).

1889–1929: Shaw's price index for locomotives and railroad cars shifted to 1929 base.

1930–1942: Shavell's price index for locomotives and railroad cars (group 60) shifted to 1929 base.

1943–1949: Weighted average of Interstate Commerce Commission indices for steam locomotives (account 51), other locomotives (account 52), freight train cars (account 53), and passenger train cars (account 54) using weights estimated by the Commission linked to index for 1942 (cf. *Railroad Construction Indices*, Aug. 1, 1950).

884

INDICES OF PRICES OF PRODUCER DURABLE GOODS
1867 to 1949

1929 = 100.0

Year	Industrial machinery and equipment	Electrical equipment	Office machinery	Nonresidential furniture and equipment	Railway and transit equipment	Ships and boats	Business horse-drawn vehicles	Aircraft	Professional and scientific equipment	Tools	Trucks	Passenger cars	Miscellaneous
	1	2	3	4	5	6	7	8	9	10	11	12	13
1867	–	81.2	–	–	–	84.2	–	–	–	–	–	–	–
1868	–	81.2	–	–	–	84.2	–	–	–	–	–	–	–
1869	–	81.2	–	–	84.5	84.2	–	–	–	–	–	–	–
1870	–	72.2	–	–	74.4	74.0	–	–	–	–	–	–	–
1871	–	68.8	–	–	70.9	70.6	–	–	–	–	–	–	–
1872	–	75.9	–	–	78.2	77.8	–	–	–	–	–	–	–
1873	–	77.6	–	–	79.9	79.6	–	–	–	–	–	–	–
1874	–	71.5	–	–	73.6	73.3	–	–	–	–	–	–	–
1875	–	68.7	–	–	70.7	70.4	–	–	–	–	–	–	–
1876	–	61.8	–	–	63.6	63.3	–	–	–	–	–	–	–
1877	54.4	54.9	–	51.7	56.5	56.2	–	–	–	–	–	–	–
1878	48.9	49.3	–	46.5	50.8	50.5	–	–	–	–	–	–	–
1879	47.1	47.5	–	44.8	48.9	48.7	–	–	–	–	–	–	–
1880	55.2	55.7	–	52.5	57.3	57.1	–	–	–	–	–	–	–
1881	51.2	51.7	–	48.8	53.2	53.0	–	–	–	–	–	–	–
1882	52.5	53.0	–	50.0	54.5	54.3	–	–	–	–	–	–	–
1883	50.3	50.7	–	47.9	52.2	52.0	–	–	–	–	–	–	–
1884	45.2	45.6	–	43.0	47.0	46.8	–	–	–	–	–	–	–
1885	43.5	43.9	–	41.4	45.2	45.0	–	–	–	–	–	–	–
1886	43.1	43.5	–	41.0	44.8	44.6	–	–	–	–	–	–	–
1887	43.4	43.8	–	41.3	45.1	44.9	–	–	48.9	–	–	–	–
1888	44.3	44.7	–	42.2	46.0	45.8	–	–	49.9	–	–	–	–
1889	43.7	44.1	43.7	41.6	45.4	45.2	65.0	–	49.2	–	–	–	–
1890	44.3	44.8	44.3	40.9	45.4	45.2	64.8	–	49.0	–	–	–	–
1891	40.3	40.7	40.3	40.9	44.6	44.4	59.1	–	44.7	47.7	–	–	34.4
1892	39.9	40.3	39.9	40.9	44.1	43.9	58.2	–	44.0	47.5	–	–	32.0
1893	40.0	40.3	40.0	37.9	43.1	42.9	57.0	–	43.1	46.4	–	–	29.1
1894	42.5	42.9	42.5	37.2	42.3	42.1	56.8	–	43.0	46.4	–	–	34.0
1895	35.0	35.3	35.0	34.1	41.0	40.9	52.1	–	39.4	45.6	–	–	34.0
1896	31.0	31.3	31.0	30.4	40.8	40.6	46.9	–	35.5	45.5	–	–	31.9
1897	42.5	42.9	42.5	30.3	41.4	41.2	55.1	–	41.7	45.6	–	–	28.8
1898	45.8	46.2	45.8	33.6	43.4	43.2	61.3	–	46.4	45.4	–	–	34.8
1899	49.1	49.5	49.1	34.0	45.5	45.3	65.2	–	49.3	48.3	261.8	185.9	39.3
1900	48.5	49.0	48.5	38.2	46.2	46.0	65.8	–	49.8	51.8	261.8	185.9	42.2
1901	48.0	48.4	48.0	37.4	47.4	47.2	65.4	–	49.5	52.2	261.8	185.9	39.0
1902	47.0	47.4	47.0	38.7	47.9	47.7	60.6	–	50.4	52.6	258.5	183.6	42.1
1903	44.1	44.5	44.1	40.0	47.9	47.7	62.8	–	47.5	52.9	258.9	183.9	39.6
1904	47.4	47.8	47.4	39.9	48.5	48.3	65.6	–	49.6	51.5	236.2	167.7	38.9
1905	47.2	47.7	47.2	40.4	49.5	49.3	65.8	–	49.8	52.0	230.4	253.5	40.3
1906	46.5	47.0	46.5	42.7	50.7	50.5	66.5	–	50.3	53.0	233.8	294.3	44.0
1907	48.7	49.1	48.7	47.2	51.4	51.2	68.6	–	51.9	54.3	231.3	338.8	44.7
1908	45.0	45.5	45.0	46.0	52.2	52.0	71.6	–	49.3	53.6	220.9	338.6	39.6
1909	50.4	50.8	50.4	45.2	53.1	52.8	72.3	–	52.7	53.3	210.2	204.9	39.8
1910	50.4	50.9	50.4	48.8	54.0	53.7	72.7	–	53.1	53.2	209.2	189.2	40.2
1911	55.8	56.3	55.8	55.4	49.9	55.2	71.7	–	56.1	53.7	255.4	179.5	39.3
1912	52.2	52.6	52.2	60.8	51.9	56.7	71.7	55.9	55.9	53.3	254.0	149.6	41.9
1913	50.0	57.5	50.0	67.7	54.9	58.7	71.7	57.0	57.0	53.0	243.3	144.1	48.4
1914	53.4	57.7	53.4	67.9	50.4	59.7	70.4	57.8	57.8	52.4	230.8	122.1	46.3
1915	60.2	60.8	60.2	67.9	51.3	62.9	68.7	63.7	63.7	52.2	220.9	112.8	49.6
1916	66.0	71.7	66.0	69.9	69.7	73.5	70.4	71.2	71.2	62.1	227.0	105.0	57.6
1917	81.1	87.8	81.1	77.1	89.4	96.5	78.2	88.2	88.2	84.1	224.0	107.8	82.8
1918	100.5	99.7	100.5	89.2	117.4	133.5	107.6	114.0	114.0	101.6	248.1	118.2	92.9
1919	104.7	105.0	104.7	115.3	129.2	144.1	122.6	122.6	122.6	106.1	214.8	139.2	117.5

Column 6 – 1867–1868: Same as for 1869.
    1869–1888: Same index as for col. 2 linked in 1889 to Shaw's price index for ships and boats (group 31).
    1889–1929: Shaw's price index for ships and boats shifted to 1929 base.
    1930–1949: Interstate Commerce Commission cost index for floating equipment (account 56) shifted to 1929 base.

Column 7 – 1889–1906: Shaw's recomputed implicit price index for producer durable goods linked in 1907 to his price index for carriages and wagons (group 20c).
    1907–1919: Shaw's price index for carriages and wagons linked in 1919 to his recomputed price index of producer durable goods.
    1920–1927: Shaw's recomputed price index for producer durable goods.

Column 8 – 1912–1929: Shaw's recomputed price index for producer durable goods.
    1930–1949: Bureau of Labor Statistics wholesale price index of all manufactured products shifted to 1929 base.

Column 9 – 1887–1929: Shaw's recomputed price index for producer durable goods.
    1930–1942: Shavell's price index for professional and scientific equipment (group 55) shifted to 1929 base.
    1943–1949: Value for 1942 extrapolated by Bureau of Labor Statistics index of wholesale prices of manufactured products.

Column 10 – 1892–1929: Shaw's index of prices of carpenters' and mechanics' tools (group 35) shifted to 1929 base.
    1930–1942: Shavell's index of prices of tools (group 56) shifted to 1929 base.
    1943–1948: Weighted average of Bureau of Labor Statistics indices of wholesale prices of axes, chisels, files, hammers, hatchets, planes, hand saws, and vises using 1944 relative importance as weights and linked to value for 1942.
    1949: Wholesale prices of iron and steel products linked to 1948.

Column 11 – 1899–1903: Shaw's price index for motor vehicles (group 20a) linked in 1904 to his index for business motor vehicles (group 32a).
    1904–1925: Shaw's price index for business motor vehicles linked in 1926 to Bureau of Labor Statistics index of wholesale prices of trucks.
    1926–1949: Bureau of Labor Statistics index of wholesale prices of trucks shifted to 1929 base.

Column 12 – 1899–1925: Shaw's price index for motor vehicles (group 20a) linked in 1926 to Bureau of Labor Statistics index of wholesale prices of passenger cars.
    1926–1949: Bureau of Labor Statistics index of wholesale prices of passenger cars shifted to 1929 base.

Column 13 – 1892–1929: Shaw's price index for miscellaneous subsidiary durable equipment (group 36) shifted to 1929 base.
    1930–1942: Shavell's price index for miscellaneous durable equipment (group 57) shifted to 1929 base.
    1943–1949: Value for 1942 extrapolated by Bureau of Labor Statistics index of wholesale prices of manufactured products.

General Note: The Department of Commerce deflators for 1929–1949 *(Survey of Current Business. 1951 National Income Supplement*, p. 146) were not available at the time the estimates were made. For a discussion of the differences see Volume II, Chapter XIV, Section 2e.

1867 to 1949

1929 = 100.0

Year	Industrial machinery and equipment	Electrical equipment	Office machinery	Nonresidential furniture and equipment	Railway and transit equipment	Ships and boats	Business horse-drawn vehicles	Aircraft	Professional and scientific equipment	Tools	Trucks	Passenger cars	Miscellaneous
	1	2	3	4	5	6	7	8	9	10	11	12	13
1920	110.0	113.3	110.0	166.4	142.7	140.6	123.8	123.8	123.8	117.9	170.8	156.9	128.3
1921	103.7	104.3	103.7	130.5	99.4	117.7	109.0	109.0	109.0	101.8	145.7	140.1	98.9
1922	90.6	97.2	90.6	115.2	87.4	102.9	94.7	94.7	94.7	92.3	108.7	113.8	93.7
1923	95.8	104.2	95.8	117.4	106.6	100.0	99.8	99.8	99.8	99.3	98.0	106.2	95.0
1924	96.8	102.6	96.8	108.4	97.8	100.0	99.1	99.1	99.1	100.5	99.2	105.0	93.4
1925	96.8	100.9	96.8	105.2	92.9	100.0	99.4	99.4	99.4	100.2	112.1	102.9	98.7
1926	97.4	102.9	97.4	100.5	93.7	100.0	99.9	99.9	99.9	101.1	113.6	97.7	97.2
1927	97.8	100.0	97.8	100.5	98.5	100.0	99.5	99.5	99.5	99.9	104.1	94.7	99.6
1928	98.9	99.7	98.9	100.4	93.2	100.0	–	99.1	99.1	99.8	96.7	97.2	101.8
1929	100.0	100.0	100.0	100.0	100.0	100.0	–	100.0	100.0	100.0	100.0	100.0	100.0
1930	92.1	94.4	100.0	99.6	99.0	97.1	–	93.1	97.0	98.1	93.1	94.2	93.7
1931	86.9	86.5	100.4	93.3	91.3	93.0	–	81.5	97.1	92.7	86.9	90.0	85.3
1932	81.1	81.0	96.7	85.3	80.7	87.0	–	74.4	95.2	90.4	84.5	87.7	82.4
1933	81.1	84.1	84.8	79.4	79.7	87.0	–	74.6	86.7	88.0	77.2	84.5	82.7
1934	93.7	89.3	86.0	84.0	89.2	93.0	–	82.8	85.0	93.1	79.3	89.5	89.1
1935	93.7	85.7	87.7	81.0	94.7	94.1	–	87.0	81.3	91.5	76.5	85.8	89.3
1936	93.7	87.3	87.8	80.8	95.5	94.1	–	86.8	80.2	92.4	76.2	85.0	88.5
1937	103.7	90.6	87.2	88.8	101.2	100.6	–	92.3	79.7	101.1	80.6	91.3	96.5
1938	104.7	89.0	83.8	87.7	101.0	100.6	–	87.0	79.7	103.6	88.9	96.8	92.0
1939	105.2	88.4	84.5	88.6	102.5	100.6	–	85.1	75.6	103.5	88.4	94.4	91.1
1940	106.5	91.2	85.6	91.6	105.4	103.5	–	86.3	76.8	103.1	92.4	97.7	93.8
1941	110.5	96.9	86.0	100.6	112.6	110.6	–	94.3	80.0	103.9	95.7	105.0	101.0
1942	112.2	101.6	92.9	111.3	123.0	121.8	–	104.3	102.6	112.6	100.1	115.4	106.1
1943	111.3	106.1	94.3	111.6	128.8	129.4	–	105.9	104.1	111.5	100.3	115.4	107.7
1944	110.7	106.3	95.0	113.4	128.8	134.7	–	106.7	104.9	111.5	103.4	115.4	108.5
1945	110.7	108.9	95.9	113.6	128.8	140.0	–	107.7	105.9	111.5	113.6	115.6	109.5
1946	120.4	123.2	109.4	121.3	148.8	150.6	–	122.9	120.8	119.2	121.6	136.4	124.9
1947	147.2	138.5	137.6	142.5	158.8	161.8	–	154.5	151.9	137.9	136.6	157.6	157.1
1948	159.1	144.4	150.2	157.1	168.8	164.7	–	168.6	165.9	150.9	153.3	171.4	171.5
1949	157.5	147.9	142.5	157.8	174.8	165.3	–	160.0	157.3	161.1	154.8	182.1	162.7

Lines 1a, 2a, and 3a – 1881–1912: Obtained from first differences of value of equipment (i.e. net expenditures), in 1929 prices, as estimated by Kuznets, S., *National Product since 1869*, table IV-6a, p. 219.
    1919–1938: Gross capital expenditures as estimated by Kuznets, *op. cit.*, table IV-8, p. 224.

Line 1b – 1881–1900: Rough estimates based on extrapolation.
    1901–1938: Estimated on basis of share of corporations in value of output as reported by Bureau of the Census for census years.

Line 1c – 1881–1938: Line 1a multiplied by line 1b.

Line 1d – 1881–1938: Line 1a minus line 1c.

Line 2b – 1881–1938: Rough estimate based on corporate share in inventories (cf. Table P-26). For 1919–1938 a lower figure—about 50 percent—would be obtained by weighting the shares of corporations in tangible assets, as estimated in National Resources Committee, *The Structure of the American Economy*, p. 375, by capital assets of corporations as reported in *Statistics of Income*.

Line 2c – 1881–1938: Line 2a multiplied by line 2b.

Line 2d – 1881–1938: Line 2a minus line 2c.

Line 3b – 1881–1938: Based on assumption that share of unincorporated enterprises is negligible except for road transportation.

Line 3c – 1881–1938: Line 3a multiplied by line 3b.

Line 3d – 1881–1938: Line 3a minus line 3c.

Lines 4a, 4b, and 4c – 1881–1938: Sum of corresponding lines under 1, 2, and 3.

Selected Periods: 1881 to 1938

	1881–1890	1891–1900	1901–1912	1919–1938
1. *Manufacturing and mining*				
a. Total percentage	37.6	43.5	43.5	45.1
b. Corporate share	0.60	0.70	0.85	0.95
c. Corporate percentage	22.6	30.5	37.0	42.8
d. Unincorporated percentage	15.0	13.0	6.5	2.3
2. *Trade, services, and construction*				
a. Total percentage	36.3	11.9	14.8	35.8
b. Corporate share	0.20	0.30	0.40	0.65
c. Corporate percentage	7.3	3.6	5.9	23.3
d. Unincorporated percentage	29.0	8.3	8.9	12.5
3. *Public utilities*				
a. Total percentage	26.1	44.6	41.7	19.1
b. Corporate share	0.99	0.99	0.99	0.99
c. Corporate percentage	25.8	44.1	41.3	18.9
d. Unincorporated percentage	0.3	0.5	0.4	0.2
4. *All industries*				
a. Total percentage	100.0	100.0	100.0	100.0
b. Corporate percentage	55.7	78.2	84.2	85.0
c. Unincorporated percentage	44.3	21.8	15.8	15.0

889

Column 1 – Obtained by multiplying total business expenditures on producer durable goods, excluding passenger cars, by share of unincorporated business, estimated on basis of data given in Table P-11, as declining regularly from 60 percent in 1870 to 15 percent in 1910, and remaining at about 15 percent through 1949.

Column 2 – Obtained by dividing col. 1 by index derived by dividing original cost of nonfarm expenditures on producer durable goods, excluding automobiles, (cf. Table P-5, col. 1) by expenditures in 1929 prices (cf. Table P-6, col. 1).

Column 3 – Obtained by depreciating col. 1, assuming life of fifteen years, which is approximately the weighted average of lengths of life used in computing depreciation on various types of producer durable goods (cf. notes to Table P-7).

Column 4 – Calculated by depreciating expenditure series given in col. 2.

Column 5 – Col. 4 multiplied by index described in note to col. 2.

Column 6 – Col. 1 minus col. 3.

Column 7 – Col. 2 minus col. 4.

Column 8 – Col. 1 minus col. 5.

SAVING BY UNINCORPORATED BUSINESS P-12
THROUGH PURCHASE OF NONFARM PRODUCER DURABLE GOODS
(Excluding Passenger Cars): 1897 to 1949

$ mill.

Year	Expenditures		Depreciation			Saving		
	Original cost	1929 prices	Original cost	1929 prices	Replacement cost	Original cost	1929 prices	Replacement cost
	1	2	3	4	5	6	7	8
1897	82	209	137	318	125	−55	−109	−43
1898	88	205	133	314	134	−45	−109	−46
1899	117	254	128	303	139	−11	−49	−22
1900	138	286	125	298	139	13	−12	−1
1901	135	282	123	292	136	12	−10	−1
1902	149	315	121	285	133	28	30	16
1903	166	363	121	286	129	45	77	37
1904	139	294	120	283	132	19	11	7
1905	167	349	121	282	133	46	67	34
1906	209	431	124	286	137	85	145	72
1907	223	442	130	296	147	93	146	76
1908	130	274	134	302	142	−4	−28	−12
1909	153	302	136	299	149	17	3	4
1910	183	358	142	306	156	41	52	27
1911	168	311	147	311	168	21	0	0
1912	213	396	154	318	171	59	78	42
1913	244	445	164	332	182	80	113	62
1914	182	334	171	343	187	11	−9	−5
1915	190	316	175	346	208	15	−30	−18
1916	332	480	183	354	245	149	126	87
1917	498	571	201	369	322	297	202	176
1918	624	573	228	384	428	396	189	196
1919	508	432	256	396	466	252	36	42
1920	576	466	282	405	501	294	61	75
1921	377	352	301	406	435	76	−54	−58
1922	392	415	312	401	380	80	14	12
1923	554	552	332	411	413	222	141	141
1924	506	512	358	427	423	148	85	83
1925	538	542	382	441	437	156	101	101
1926	577	582	410	455	451	167	127	126
1927	538	543	431	469	465	107	74	73
1928	561	568	453	478	471	108	90	90
1929	690	690	480	494	494	210	196	196
1930	535	566	508	512	485	27	54	50
1931	347	392	520	518	458	−173	−126	−111
1932	196	235	511	504	419	−315	−269	−223
1933	191	235	487	482	392	−296	−247	−201
1934	276	310	465	468	417	−189	−158	−141
1935	346	392	450	460	406	−104	−68	−60
1936	474	534	445	463	411	29	71	63
1937	586	610	455	478	459	131	132	127
1938	433	448	458	484	468	−25	−36	−35
1939	498	518	453	473	455	45	45	43
1940	673	672	457	481	481	216	191	192
1941	848	815	471	494	514	377	321	334
1942	575	518	481	500	555	94	18	20
1943	482	429	480	495	556	2	−66	−74
1944	665	597	476	487	543	189	110	122
1945	909	810	488	492	552	421	318	357
1946	1 448	1 185	537	527	643	911	658	805
1947	1 888	1 301	630	588	853	1 258	713	1 035
1948	2 130	1 357	751	662	1 039	1 379	695	1 091
1949	1 911	1 221	870	730	1 143	1 041	491	768

Column 1 – Obtained by allocating 90 percent of total expenditures on new passenger cars to consumers, two-thirds of remaining 10 percent to unincorporated business, and one-third to corporations. For total expenditures on new passenger cars, 1929–1949, the figures of Department of Commerce, which already exclude government purchases, were taken. Figures for earlier years were obtained by increasing Shaw's estimates (*Value of Commodity Output since 1869*, p. 68) by 45 percent, which is Department of Commerce estimate for new car markup in 1929, adjusting for inventory changes (cf. Table P-5, col. 2) and linking them to Commerce figures. Proportion of passenger cars allocated to business was derived on assumption that, if business use of passenger cars by farmers, professionals, and traveling salesmen—which under the definition used here is regarded as individual and not as business expenditure—was eliminated from Department of Commerce allocation of 30 percent of total expenditures, resultant percentage would be about 10 percent. Share of unincorporated in business expenditure was derived from Public Roads Administration data which showed that 9.8 percent of individual owners of passenger cars in twenty-six states in 1943, classified by occupation, was "proprietors." Since the statistics did not specifically classify owners of nearly one-fifth of all cars, and since it may be assumed that passenger cars owned and operated by unincorporated business enterprises are of slightly higher average size and are utilized more intensively and replaced more rapidly than those owned by individuals, share of unincorporated business enterprises in expenditures on new passenger cars should be somewhat in excess of 10 percent. On the other hand, some—and probably a considerable proportion—of the cars whose owners were classified as "proprietors" were for private rather than for business use and were owned by individuals rather than by unincorporated firms. It therefore appeared that an allocation of 10 percent was more likely to overstate than to understate proportion of new passenger cars acquired by unincorporated business and used exclusively or predominantly in their business operations, and a ratio of around 7 percent was more appropriate to use. On basis of data concerning number of taxicabs operated in an organized way (Cab Research Bureau, Inc. data cited in Automobile Manufacturers Association, *Automobile Facts and Figures*, 1950) it was evident that number of taxicabs operated by unincorporated businesses, including those not in organized fleets, was so small that it could not significantly affect proportion of passenger cars used by unincorporated business.

Column 2 – Col. 1 deflated by price index given in Table P-10, col. 12.

Column 3 – Expenditure series given in col. 1 depreciated assuming average life of six years.

Column 4 – Same procedure as for col. 3 except expenditure series given in col. 2 used.

Column 5 – Col. 4 multiplied by Table P-10, col. 12.

Column 6 – Col. 1 minus col. 3.

Column 7 – Col. 2 minus col. 4.

Column 8 – Col. 1 minus col. 5.

892

1899 to 1949

$ mill.

Year	Expenditures		Depreciation			Saving		
	Original cost	1929 prices	Original cost	1929 prices	Replacement cost	Original cost	1929 prices	Replacement cost
	1	2	3	4	5	6	7	8
1899	1	0	0	0	0	1	0	1
1900	1	0	0	0	0	1	0	1
1901	1	1	0	0	0	1	1	1
1902	1	1	1	1	2	0	0	−1
1903	1	1	1	1	2	0	0	−1
1904	2	1	1	1	2	1	0	0
1905	3	1	1	1	3	2	0	0
1906	6	2	2	1	3	4	1	3
1907	9	3	3	1	3	6	2	6
1908	13	4	5	2	7	8	2	6
1909	15	7	7	3	6	8	4	9
1910	20	11	9	4	8	11	7	12
1911	20	11	12	5	9	8	6	11
1912	30	20	15	8	12	15	12	18
1913	36	25	20	11	16	16	14	20
1914	38	32	25	15	18	13	17	20
1915	52	46	29	21	24	23	25	28
1916	85	81	38	30	32	47	51	53
1917	96	89	50	43	46	46	46	50
1918	74	62	60	53	63	14	9	11
1919	118	85	71	61	85	47	24	33
1920	153	97	87	71	111	66	26	42
1921	118	85	102	80	112	16	5	6
1922	147	129	113	87	99	34	42	48
1923	200	188	126	99	105	74	89	95
1924	184	175	144	117	123	40	58	61
1925	224	218	162	137	141	62	81	83
1926	237	243	178	161	157	59	82	80
1927	194	205	101	183	173	3	22	21
1928	217	223	203	201	195	14	22	22
1929	243	243	213	213	213	30	30	30
1930	153	163	214	217	203	−61	−54	−50
1931	106	118	201	207	186	−95	−89	−80
1932	58	66	177	185	162	−119	−119	−104
1933	71	85	151	159	134	−80	−74	−63
1934	95	106	131	140	125	−36	−34	−30
1935	141	163	113	123	106	28	40	35
1936	179	211	106	121	103	73	90	76
1937	185	203	115	132	121	70	71	64
1938	113	117	126	143	138	−13	−26	−25
1939	156	165	138	154	145	18	11	11
1940	204	209	154	169	165	50	40	39
1941	242	231	171	183	192	71	48	50
1942	17	15	167	173	200	−150	−158	−183
1943	18	16	139	141	163	−121	−125	−145
1944	8	7	116	116	134	−108	−109	−126
1945	4	4	95	93	108	−91	−89	−104
1946	208	153	83	75	102	125	78	106
1947	400	254	96	73	115	304	181	285
1948	482	281	148	97	166	334	184	316
1949	684	375	242	149	271	442	226	413

Column 1 – See note to Table P-13, col. 1.

Column 2 – Col. 1 deflated by price index given in Table P-10, col. 12.

Column 3 – Expenditure series given in col. 1 depreciated assuming average life of six years.

Column 4 – Same procedure as for col. 3 except expenditure series given in col. 2 used.

Column 5 – Col. 4 multiplied by Table P-10, col. 12.

Column 6 – Col. 1 minus col. 3.

Column 7 – Col. 2 minus col. 4.

Column 8 – Col. 1 minus col. 5.

SAVING BY CORPORATE BUSINESS THROUGH PASSENGER CARS
1899 to 1949

$ mill.

Year	Expenditures		Depreciation			Saving		
	Original cost	1929 prices	Original cost	1929 prices	Replacement cost	Original cost	1929 prices	Replacement cost
	1	2	3	4	5	6	7	8
1899	0	0	0	0	0	0	0	0
1900	0	0	0	0	0	0	0	0
1901	0	0	0	0	0	0	0	0
1902	0	0	0	0	0	0	0	0
1903	1	0	1	0	0	0	0	1
1904	1	1	1	0	0	0	1	1
1905	2	1	1	0	0	1	1	2
1906	3	1	1	0	0	2	1	3
1907	4	1	1	1	3	3	0	1
1908	6	2	2	1	3	4	1	3
1909	7	4	3	1	2	4	3	5
1910	10	5	5	2	4	5	3	6
1911	10	6	6	3	5	4	3	5
1912	15	10	8	4	6	7	6	9
1913	18	13	10	6	9	8	7	9
1914	19	16	12	8	10	7	8	9
1915	26	23	15	10	11	11	13	15
1916	42	40	19	15	16	23	25	26
1917	48	45	25	21	23	23	24	25
1918	37	31	30	26	31	7	5	6
1919	59	42	35	30	42	24	12	17
1920	77	49	43	36	56	34	13	21
1921	59	42	51	40	56	8	2	3
1922	73	64	56	44	50	17	20	23
1923	100	94	63	50	53	37	44	47
1924	92	88	72	58	61	20	30	31
1925	112	109	81	69	71	31	40	41
1926	119	121	89	80	78	30	41	41
1927	97	102	96	91	86	1	11	11
1928	108	111	102	100	97	6	11	11
1929	122	122	106	107	107	16	15	15
1930	77	82	107	108	101	-30	-26	-24
1931	53	59	101	104	94	-48	-45	-41
1932	29	33	88	92	81	-59	-59	-52
1933	36	42	76	80	68	-40	-38	-32
1934	47	53	66	70	63	-19	-17	-16
1935	70	82	56	62	53	14	20	17
1936	90	106	53	60	51	37	46	39
1937	93	102	57	66	60	36	36	33
1938	57	58	63	72	70	-6	-14	-13
1939	78	82	69	77	73	9	5	5
1940	102	104	77	85	83	25	19	19
1941	121	115	86	92	97	35	23	24
1942	9	7	83	86	99	-74	-79	-90
1943	9	8	70	70	81	-61	-62	-72
1944	4	3	58	58	67	-54	-55	-63
1945	3	2	47	47	54	-44	-45	-51
1946	104	76	41	38	52	63	38	52
1947	200	127	48	36	57	152	91	143
1948	241	141	74	48	82	167	93	159
1949	342	188	121	75	137	221	113	205

Column 1 – 1902–1920: Automobile Manufacturers Association, *Automobile Facts and Figures*, 1948, p. 4, col. 1.
1921–1941: *Ibid.*, p. 7.

Column 2 – 1902–1941: *Ibid.*, p. 17.

Column 3 – 1903–1941: Col. 2 minus sum of current year and preceding year values of col. 1.

Column 4 – 1919–1929: 1930 figure extrapolated by ratio of all used cars sold as estimated by National Automobile Dealers' Association (see Smith, Theodore H., *Marketing Used Automobiles*, p. 16, table 3, col. 2).
1930–1938: Estimates of Automobile Manufacturers Association, *ibid.*, appendix E, p. 267, col. 45.
1939: Estimates for 1938 extrapolated on basis of estimate by Automobile Manufacturers Association of all used cars sold as percent of new cars sold (see Automobile Manufacturers Association, *Automobile Facts and Figures*, 1940, p. 35).
1940–1941: Rough estimates.

Column 5 – 1902–1918: 29 percent of col. 3 based on average 1919–1930 relationship of col. 5 to col. 3.
1919–1941: Col. 1 multiplied by col. 4.

Column 6 – 1902–1941: Wholesale value of production in U.S. plants divided by factory sales (see Automobile Manufacturers Association, *Automobile Facts and Figures*, 1948, p. 4).

Column 7 – 1925–1938: Smith, Theodore H., *Marketing Used Automobiles*, appendix E, p. 265, col. 9. It is assumed here that finance companies purchase notes on used cars at approximately wholesale level.

Column 8 – 1902–1924: Estimated roughly as 50 percent of wholesale price of new cars, based on average relationship during period 1925–1931.
1925–1933: Estimate for 1934 extrapolated by col. 7.
1934–1941: From bar chart in Automobile Manufacturers Association, *op. cit.*, 1942, p. 14.

Column 9 – 1902–1941: Assumed to be 20 percent of col. 8.

Column 10 – 1902–1941: Col. 5 multiplied by col. 9.
1942–1949: Estimated on basis of data obtained from National Income Division, Department of Commerce.

DEALERS' MARGINS ON USED CARS

1902 to 1949

Year	Factory sales of new passenger cars	Passenger car registration		Used passenger cars sold		Average wholesale price of new car	Average price of used car		Used car margin	
		Actual	Adjusted	Proportion of new passenger cars sold	Number		Wholesale	Retail	Average	Total
	Thous.			Percent	Thous.	$				$ mill.
	1	2	3	4	5	6	7	8	9	10
1902	9	23		.	2	1 155	.	578	116	0
1903	11	33	13	.	4	1 157	.	578	116	0
1904	22	55	22	.	6	1 055	.	528	106	1
1905	24	77	31	.	9	1 595	.	798	160	1
1906	33	106	49	.	14	1 851	.	926	185	3
1907	43	140	64	.	19	2 131	.	1 066	213	4
1908	64	194	87	.	25	2 130	.	1 065	213	5
1909	124	306	118	.	34	1 095	.	548	110	4
1910	181	458	153	.	44	1 190	.	595	119	5
1911	199	619	239	.	69	1 129	.	565	113	8
1912	356	902	347	.	101	941	.	470	94	9
1913	462	1 190	372	.	108	867	.	434	87	9
1914	548	1 664	654	.	190	768	.	384	77	15
1915	896	2 332	888	.	258	643	.	322	64	17
1916	1 526	3 368	946	.	274	604	.	302	60	16
1917	1 746	4 727	1 455	.	422	603	.	302	60	25
1918	943	5 555	2 866	.	831	850	.	425	85	71
1919	1 652	6 679	4 084	64	1 057	827	.	414	83	88
1920	1 906	8 132	4 574	71	1 353	949	.	475	95	129
1921	1 417	9 212	5 889	77	1 091	707	.	354	71	77
1922	2 169	10 704	7 118	75	1 627	657	.	329	66	107
1923	3 450	13 253	7 634	75	2 588	606	.	303	61	158
1924	2 969	15 436	9 017	100	2 969	618	.	309	62	184
1925	3 419	17 440	11 052	108	3 693	658	280	316	63	233
1926	3 495	19 221	12 307	98	3 425	698	277	313	63	216
1927	2 604	20 142	14 043	130	3 385	737	286	323	65	220
1928	3 397	21 308	15 307	128	4 348	675	307	346	69	300
1929	4 136	23 060	15 527	141	5 832	621	297	335	67	391
1930	2 537	22 973	16 300	180	4 567	591	280	316	63	288
1931	1 839	22 330	17 954	182	3 347	563	268	302	60	201
1932	1 062	20 832	17 931	224	2 379	545	241	272	54	128
1933	1 475	20 586	18 049	175	2 581	485	220	248	50	129
1934	1 994	21 472	18 003	164	3 270	527	226	255	51	167
1935	3 042	22 495	17 459	152	4 624	526	237	280	56	259
1936	3 458	24 108	17 608	164	5 671	549	258	320	64	363
1937	3 643	25 391	18 290	176	6 412	573	279	380	76	487
1938	1 811	25 167	19 713	236	4 274	618	275	335	67	286
1939	2 702	26 140	21 627	202	5 458	616	.	350	70	382
1940	3 608	27 372	21 062	200	7 216	638	.	345	69	498
1941	3 682	29 524	22 234	200	7 364	679	.	380	76	560
1942	.	.	.	.	.	.	.	.	.	417
1943	.	.	.	.	.	.	.	.	.	462
1944	.	.	.	.	.	.	.	.	.	529
1945	.	.	.	.	.	.	.	.	.	606
1946	.	.	.	.	.	.	.	.	.	800
1947	.	.	.	.	.	.	.	.	.	937
1948	.	.	.	.	.	.	.	.	.	1 094
1949	.	.	.	.	.	.	.	.	.	981

897

TABLE P–16

Column 1 – From Table P-15, col. 10.

Column 2 – Assumed at 20 percent of gross expenditures on used cars by farmers (cf. Table A-29).

Column 3 – Estimated at roughly 5 percent of total margin on nonfarm purchases of used cars (col. 1 minus col. 2) on assumption that producer's share in used cars is about half as large as in new cars.

Column 4 – Col. 1 minus sum of cols. 2 and 3.

Column 5 – Computed on basis of three-year life expectancy, roughly half assumed life expectancy of new cars used in business.

Column 6 – Computed on basis of varying life expectancy as follows:

> 1904–1919 – three years
> 1920–1929 – four years
> 1930–1949 – six years

These life expectancies are roughly half as large as assumed life expectancies of new cars bought by consumers.

Column 7 – Col. 3 minus col. 5.

Column 8 – Col. 4 minus col. 6.

TABLE P–17

Column 1 – Table P-10, col. 12 applied to Table P-16, col. 3.

Column 2 – Table P-10, col. 12 applied to Table P-16, col. 4.

Column 3 – See notes to Table P-16, col. 5; computed on basis of life expectancy of three years.

Column 4 – See notes to Table P-16, col. 6 for basis of computations.

Column 5 – Col. 1 minus col. 3.

Column 6 – Col. 2 minus col. 4.

Column 7 – Col. 3 multiplied by Table P-10, col. 12.

Column 8 – Col. 4 multiplied by Table P-10, col. 12.

Column 9 – Table P-16, col. 3 minus col. 7 of this table.

Column 10 – Table P-16, col. 4 minus col. 8 of this table.

TABLE P–18

Column 1 – Sum of Table R-71, cols. 7 and 10, using unrounded figures.

Column 2 – Col. 1 deflated by index derived by dividing nonfarm expenditures on producer durable goods, original cost, by expenditures in 1929 prices.

Column 3 – Sum of depreciation on fire losses, as given in col. 1, during six years preceding year indicated.

Column 4 – Same procedure as col. 3 except that absolute figures are taken from col. 2.

Column 5 – Col. 4 multiplied by index described in col. 2.

Column 6 – Col. 1 minus col. 3.

Column 7 – Col. 2 minus col. 4.

Column 8 – Col. 1 minus col. 5.

Original Cost: 1904 to 1949

$ mill.

Year	Dealers' margin on used cars bought by				Depreciation		Saving	
	All groups	Farmers	Business	Nonfarm consumers	Business	Nonfarm consumers	Business	Nonfarm consumers
	1	2	3	4	5	6	7	8
1904	1	0	0	1	0	0	0	1
1905	1	0	0	1	0		0	0
1906	3	0	0	3	0	1	0	2
1907	4	1	0	3	0	2	0	1
1908	5	1	0	4	0	3	0	1
1909	4	1	0	3	0	3	0	0
1910	5	1	0	4	0	4	0	0
1911	8	2	0	6	0	4	0	2
1912	9	2	0	7	0	5	0	2
1913	9	2	0	7	0	6	0	1
1914	15	3	1	11	0	8	1	3
1915	17	6	1	10	1	9	0	1
1916	16	8	1	7	1	9	0	-2
1917	25	12	1	12	1	10	0	2
1918	71	8	4	59	2	18	2	41
1919	88	17	4	67	3	36	1	31
1920	129	12	6	111	4	58	2	53
1921	77	4	4	69	5	69	-1	0
1922	107	10	5	92	5	68	0	24
1923	158	16	8	134	5	85	3	49
1924	184	15	9	160	7	108	2	52
1925	233	21	12	200	8	130	4	70
1926	216	18	11	187	10	158	1	29
1927	220	14	11	195	11	178	0	17
1928	300	23	15	262	12	198	3	64
1929	391	27	20	344	14	229	6	115
1930	288	20	14	254	16	245	-2	9
1931	201	13	10	178	15	233	-5	-55
1932	128	8	6	114	12	200	-6	-86
1933	129	8	6	115	9	144	-3	-29
1934	167	17	8	142	7	122	1	20
1935	259	18	13	228	8	153	5	75
1936	363	23	18	322	11	178	7	144
1937	487	21	24	442	16	205	8	237
1938	286	17	14	255	18	239	-4	16
1939	382	27	19	336	19	269	0	67
1940	498	25	25	448	19	313	6	135
1941	560	30	28	502	22	361	6	141
1942	417	19	21	377	24	389	-3	-12
1943	462	24	23	415	24	391	-1	24
1944	529	8	26	495	24	409	2	86
1945	606	0	30	576	25	449	5	127
1946	800	30	40	730	29	492	11	238
1947	937	46	47	844	35	544	12	300
1948	1 094	63	55	976	43	623	12	353
1949	981	87	49	845	49	708	0	137

899

SAVING THROUGH DEALERS' MARGINS ON USED CARS
1929 Prices and Replacement Cost: 1904 to 1949

$ mill.

Year	1929 prices						Replacement cost			
	Dealers' margin on used cars bought by		Depreciation		Saving		Depreciation		Saving	
	Business	Nonfarm consumers	Business	Nonfarm consumers	Business	Nonfarm consumers	Business	Nonfarm consumers	Business	Nonfarm consumers
	1	2	3	4	5	6	7	8	9	10
1904	0	1	0	0	0	1	0	0	0	1
1905	0	0	0	0	0	0	0	0	0	1
1906	0	1	0	1	0	0	0	3	0	0
1907	0	1	0	1	0	0	0	3	0	0
1908	0	1	0	1	0	0	0	3	0	1
1909	0	1	0	1	0	0	0	2	0	1
1910	0	2	0	1	0	1	0	2	0	2
1911	0	3	0	2	0	1	0	4	0	2
1912	0	5	0	3	0	2	0	4	0	3
1913	0	5	0	4	0	1	0	6	0	1
1914	1	9	0	5	1	4	0	6	1	5
1915	1	9	1	7	0	2	1	8	0	2
1916	1	7	1	8	0	−1	1	8	0	−1
1917	1	11	1	9	0	2	1	10	0	2
1918	3	50	1	16	2	34	1	19	3	40
1919	3	48	2	29	1	19	3	40	1	27
1920	4	71	3	43	1	28	5	67	1	44
1921	3	49	3	48	0	1	4	67	0	2
1922	4	81	4	48	0	33	5	55	0	37
1923	8	126	4	66	4	60	4	70	4	64
1924	9	152	6	92	3	60	6	97	3	63
1925	12	194	8	120	4	74	8	123	4	77
1926	11	191	10	152	1	39	10	149	1	38
1927	12	206	11	176	1	30	10	167	1	28
1928	15	270	12	200	3	70	12	194	3	68
1929	20	344	14	234	6	110	14	234	6	110
1930	15	270	16	251	−1	19	15	236	−1	18
1931	11	198	16	241	−5	−43	14	217	−4	−39
1932	7	130	13	209	−6	−79	11	183	−5	−69
1933	7	136	10	154	−3	−18	8	130	−2	−15
1934	9	159	8	136	1	23	7	122	1	20
1935	15	266	9	171	6	95	8	147	5	81
1936	21	379	13	202	8	177	11	172	7	150
1937	26	484	18	235	8	249	16	215	8	227
1938	14	263	20	270	−6	−7	19	261	−5	−6
1939	20	356	20	299	0	57	19	282	0	54
1940	26	459	20	343	6	116	20	335	5	113
1941	27	478	22	385	5	93	23	404	5	98
1942	18	327	24	399	−6	−72	28	460	−7	−83
1943	20	360	23	384	−3	−24	27	443	−4	−28
1944	23	429	21	388	2	41	24	448	2	47
1945	26	498	22	413	4	85	25	477	5	99
1946	29	535	25	431	4	104	34	588	6	142
1947	30	536	27	443	3	93	43	698	4	146
1948	32	569	29	468	3	101	50	802	5	174
1949	27	464	30	496	−3	−32	55	903	−6	−58

$ mill.

Year	Fire losses		Depreciation			Net		
	Original cost	1929 prices	Original cost	1929 prices	Replacement cost	Original cost	1929 prices	Replacement cost
	1	2	3	4	5	6	7	8
1897	23	59	28	66	26	−5	−7	−3
1898	26	61	27	65	28	−1	−4	−2
1899	30	65	26	64	29	4	1	1
1900	32	68	27	63	30	5	5	2
1901	33	71	27	63	29	6	8	4
1902	32	69	29	65	30	3	4	2
1903	29	64	30	66	30	−1	−2	−1
1904	45	96	32	69	32	13	27	13
1905	33	69	34	72	34	−1	−3	−1
1906	103	213	40	85	41	63	128	62
1907	42	83	47	98	49	−5	−15	−7
1908	43	88	48	101	49	−5	−13	−6
1909	37	72	50	103	53	−13	−31	−16
1910	42	80	50	102	54	−8	−22	−12
1911	43	77	51	101	56	−8	−24	−13
1912	41	73	46	90	50	−5	−17	−9
1913	40	70	41	78	45	−1	−8	−5
1914	44	76	41	76	44	3	0	0
1915	34	54	41	73	46	−7	−19	−12
1916	42	58	41	70	50	1	−12	−8
1917	49	55	41	66	58	8	−11	−9
1918	61	55	43	63	70	18	−8	−9
1919	54	45	46	59	71	8	−14	−17
1920	78	61	50	56	71	28	5	7
1921	86	77	57	57	63	29	20	23
1922	86	88	65	61	60	21	27	26
1923	92	91	73	66	67	19	25	25
1924	94	94	79	73	73	15	21	21
1925	96	96	85	80	80	11	16	16
1926	97	98	90	88	87	7	10	10
1927	79	80	91	91	89	−12	−11	−10
1928	76	77	90	90	89	−14	−13	−13
1929	74	74	87	88	88	−13	−14	−14
1930	79	84	85	86	81	−6	−2	−2
1931	70	79	81	83	74	−11	−4	−4
1932	60	72	76	80	67	−16	−8	−7
1933	38	46	70	75	61	−32	−29	−23
1934	39	44	63	69	61	−24	−25	−22
1935	35	40	57	64	56	−22	−24	−21
1936	37	42	50	57	50	−13	−15	−13
1937	38	40	44	51	49	−6	−11	−11
1938	37	38	39	44	43	−2	−6	−6
1939	40	42	37	41	39	3	1	1
1940	43	43	38	41	41	5	2	2
1941	47	45	39	41	43	8	4	4
1942	50	45	41	42	47	9	3	3
1943	60	53	44	43	48	16	10	12
1944	72	65	49	47	52	23	18	20
1945	81	72	55	51	57	26	21	24
1946	96	78	63	57	70	33	21	26
1947	119	81	74	63	92	45	18	27
1948	122	77	86	68	108	36	9	14
1949	114	71	97	73	117	17	−2	−3

Column 1 – 1896–1917: Table P-20, col. 7.
      1918–1928: Table P-25, col. 2.
      1929, 1939: Cobren, G. M., "The Non-Farm Business Inventory Component of National Wealth," *Studies in Income and Wealth,* vol. xii, table 1.
      1930–1938, 1940–1949: Estimated on basis of data obtained from National Income Division, Department of Commerce. Cobren's figures tie in with this series.

Column 2 – 1896–1918: Table P-20, col. 4.
      1919–1928: From Table P-25, col. 4.
      1929–1949: Estimated on basis of data obtained from National Income Division, Department of Commerce.

Column 3 – 1896–1917: Table P-20, col. 6.
      1918–1928: Col. 1 minus col. 2.
      1929–1949: Estimated on basis of data obtained from National Income Division, Department of Commerce.

Column 4 – 1896–1917: Values of col. 1 divided by average of wholesale price index of Bureau of Labor Statistics for Oct., Nov., and Dec.
      1918–1928: Kuznets, S., *National Income and Its Composition, 1919–1938,* vol. ii, table vii multiplied by 0.948 to link with estimates based on Department of Commerce figures (cf. Table P-25).
      1929–1949: Estimated on basis of data obtained from National Income Division, Department of Commerce. Values shifted from 1939 to 1929 prices. The 1934 figure in line A is based on consolidated reports (comparable to 1933 and previous years), that in line B on unconsolidated reports (comparable to 1935 and later years).

Column 5 – 1896–1917: Values of col. 2 divided by Bureau of Labor Statistics index (cf. col. 4).
      1918–1928: Col. 4 multiplied by Table P-25, col. 3.
      1929–1949: Same source as for col. 4.

Column 6 – 1896–1949: Col. 4 minus col. 5.

Column 7 – 1897–1918: Obtained from estimates of book value of inventories shown in cols. 1, 2, and 3 by following steps:
      (1) Reduction of book values into 1929 prices by means of division by the fourth quarter average of Bureau of Labor Statistics wholesale price index reduced to 1929 basis.
      (2) Conversion of first differences of year-end inventories in 1929 prices to current prices by means of multiplication with the annual average of Bureau of Labor Statistics on 1929 base.
      (3) Subtraction of annual change in the year-end book value of inventories from the annual change inventory in current prices, obtained by step (2). Difference is the measure of inventory valuation adjustment, or inventory profit or loss.
      Procedure is basically same as that used by the Department of Commerce (cf. Cobren, *op. cit.,* and Kuznets, S., *Commodity Flow and Capital Formation,* p. 404) except that they apply the adjustment industry by industry and vary the assumed average age of the inventories (here set at one to one and a half months since average of prices for fourth quarter of year is used as deflator and price index) to conform as nearly as possible to the conditions assumed to exist in each industry.
      1919–1928: Kuznets, S., *National Income and Its Composition, 1919–1938,* vol. ii, table vii.
      1929–1941: *Survey of Current Business, National Income Supplement,* July 1947, table 22.
      1942–1949: *Survey of Current Business,* July 1950, p. 26.

Column 8 – 1897–1918: Same procedure as for col. 7.
      1919–1928: Col. 7 multiplied by Table P-25, col. 3.
      1929–1949: Same sources as for col. 7.

Column 9 – 1897–1949: Col. 7 minus col. 8.

Columns 10 to 12 – 1897–1949: First differences of cols. 1–3 plus cols. 7–9, respectively, except for 1941, col. 12, which was taken from *Survey of Current Business,* July 1950, p. 11. Discrepancy due to break in the unrevised and revised series.

NONFARM BUSINESS INVENTORIES
1896 to 1949
$ mill.

Year	Current prices			1929 prices			Inventory valuation adjustment			Adjusted change in value of inventories		
	Total	Corporations	Unincorporated business	Total	Corporations	Unincorporated business	Total	Corporations	Unincorporated business	Total	Corporations	Unincorporated business
	1	2	3	4	5	6	7	8	9	10	11	12
1896	3 979	1 870	2 109	7 895	3 710	4 185	.	.	.	−226	−70	−156
1897	3 798	1 823	1 975	7 432	3 567	3 865	−45	−23	−22	185	129	56
1898	3 984	1 952	2 032	7 796	3 820	3 976	−1	0	−1	185	129	56
1899	5 032	2 516	2 516	8 442	4 221	4 221	−694	−344	−350	354	220	134
1900	5 406	2 757	2 649	9 194	4 689	4 505	69	35	34	443	276	167
1901	5 094	2 649	2 445	8 434	4 386	4 048	−129	−68	−61	−441	−176	−265
1902	5 857	3 104	2 753	8 914	4 724	4 190	−466	−246	−220	297	209	88
1903	5 804	3 134	2 670	9 346	5 047	4 299	323	172	151	270	202	68
1904	5 585	3 072	2 513	8 659	4 763	3 896	−211	−116	−95	−430	−178	−252
1905	5 962	3 339	2 623	9 301	5 209	4 092	28	14	14	405	281	124
1906	6 707	3 823	2 884	9 907	5 647	4 260	−352	−200	−152	393	284	109
1907	7 159	4 152	3 007	10 375	6 017	4 358	−132	−76	−56	320	253	67
1908	7 020	4 142	2 878	10 293	6 073	4 220	85	47	38	−54	37	−91
1909	7 433	4 460	2 973	9 858	5 915	3 943	−721	−430	−291	−308	−112	−196
1910	7 990	4 874	3 116	11 206	6 836	4 370	439	266	173	996	680	316
1911	7 876	4 883	2 993	11 251	6 976	4 275	145	86	59	31	95	−64
1912	8 419	5 304	3 115	11 240	7 081	4 159	−551	−344	−207	−8	77	−85
1913	9 117	5 835	3 282	12 254	7 843	4 411	44	27	17	742	558	184
1914	9 040	5 876	3 164	12 573	8 172	4 401	305	194	111	228	235	−7
1915	10 009	6 606	3 403	13 067	8 624	4 443	−609	−401	−208	360	329	31
1916	13 481	9 032	4 449	13 217	8 855	4 362	−3 337	−2 218	−1 119	135	208	−73
1917	18 453	12 548	5 905	14 151	9 623	4 528	−3 820	−2 569	−1 251	1 152	947	205
1918	21 226	14 688	6 538	15 789	10 926	4 863	−2 101	−1 442	−659	672	698	−26
1919	26 627	18 639	7 988	18 378	12 865	5 513	−1 950	−1 365	−585	3 451	2 586	865
1920	28 066	19 843	8 223	21 459	15 172	6 287	3 977	2 812	1 165	5 416	4 016	1 400
1921	22 458	16 057	6 401	21 828	15 607	6 221	6 370	4 555	1 815	762	769	−7
1922	24 026	17 347	6 679	22 377	16 156	6 221	−877	−633	−244	691	657	34
1923	27 100	19 783	7 317	25 107	18 328	6 779	−156	−114	−42	2 918	2 322	596
1924	26 721	19 693	7 028	24 876	18 334	6 542	157	116	41	−222	26	−248
1925	28 058	20 903	7 155	25 880	19 281	6 599	−350	−261	−89	987	949	38
1926	28 112	21 168	6 944	27 341	20 588	6 753	1 695	1 276	419	1 749	1 541	208
1927	27 666	21 054	6 612	27 637	21 032	6 605	784	597	187	338	483	−145
1928	27 195	20 915	6 280	27 206	20 921	6 285	60	46	14	−411	−93	−318
1929	28 427	22 001	6 426	28 427	22 001	6 426	614	472	142	1 846	1 558	288
1930	24 071	18 932	5 139	28 223	22 338	5 885	4 015	3 260	755	−341	191	−532
1931	19 387	15 390	3 997	26 384	21 121	5 263	3 025	2 414	611	−1 659	−1 128	−531
1932	15 558	12 525	3 033	22 993	18 645	4 348	1 342	1 047	295	−2 487	−1 818	−669
1933	16 888	13 796	3 092	21 051	17 337	3 714	−2 668	−2 143	−525	−1 338	−872	−466
1934A	17 766	14 606	3 160	21 210	17 488	3 722	−679	−625	−54	199	185	14
1934B	17 766	14 606	3 160	21 069	17 347	3 722	−679	−625	−54	199	185	14
1935	18 425	15 040	3 385	21 598	17 682	3 916	−277	−227	−50	382	207	175
1936	21 381	17 364	4 017	23 966	19 467	4 499	−858	−738	−120	2 098	1 586	512
1937	23 183	18 920	4 263	25 774	21 049	4 725	−60	−31	−29	1 742	1 525	217
1938	20 927	17 034	3 893	24 514	19 975	4 539	1 184	963	221	−1 072	−923	−149
1939	22 144	17 999	4 145	24 919	20 262	4 657	−880	−714	−166	337	251	86
1940	24 375	19 784	4 591	27 226	22 127	5 099	−200	−148	−52	2 031	1 637	394
1941	31 217	25 573	5 644	30 768	25 416	5 352	−3 261	−2 617	−644	3 581	3 172	250
1942	33 548	27 246	6 302	32 312	26 497	5 815	−1 576	−1 204	−372	755	469	286
1943	33 972	27 561	6 411	32 175	26 391	5 784	−927	−773	−154	−503	−458	−45
1944	34 067	26 780	7 287	31 802	25 296	6 506	−357	−287	−70	−262	−1 068	806
1945	34 146	26 317	7 829	30 846	23 963	6 883	−677	−564	−113	−598	−1 027	429
1946	47 492	37 547	9 945	36 098	28 894	7 204	−7 012	−5 193	−1 819	6 334	6 037	297
1947	56 204	44 687	11 517	37 337	30 084	7 253	−7 304	−5 757	−1 547	1 408	1 383	25
1948	62 983	49 691	13 292	39 673	31 601	8 072	−2 426	−2 032	−394	4 353	2 972	1 381
1949	56 978	45 093	11 885	37 547	29 929	7 618	2 928	2 233	695	−3 077	−2 365	−712

903

Column 1 – 1896–1918: From Table P-21, col. 3.

Column 2 – 1896–1918: Col. 1 applied to 1918 value of corporate nonfarm inventories, excluding railroads, of $14,030 million. Value is obtained by subtracting from Kuznets' adjusted estimate of $14,688 million (cf. Table P-25, col. 4) the value of railroad inventories as given in col. 3.

Column 3 – 1896–1918: From Table P-24, col. 3. Figures for 1896–1915 obtained by averaging the June 30 values for current and following year.

Column 4 – 1896–1918: Sum of cols. 2 and 3.

Column 5 – 1896–1918: Based on Table P-26, col. 6.

Column 6 – 1896–1917: Obtained by multiplication of col. 4 with the ratio of col. 5 to its complement. 1918: From Table P-25, col. 5.

Column 7 – 1896–1918: Sum of cols. 4 and 6.

Column 1 – 1899–1913: From Table P-22, col. 5.
1914–1918: Based on inventories of eighty-one large manufacturing corporations (National Bureau of Economic Research, *Corporate Financial Data for Studies in Business Finance,* unpublished, table B-27).

Column 2 – 1903–1918: From Table P-23, col. 3.

Column 3 – 1896–1898: Based on index of railroad inventories as shown in Table P-24, col. 3 (averaging June 30 values for current and following year for the period 1896–1915) linked to col. 3 in 1899.
1899–1902: Based on col. 1, linked to col. 3, in 1903.
1903–1918: Arithmetic average of cols. 1 and 2.

End of year	Index of corporate inventories (excluding railroads)	Value of corporate inventories			Share of unincorporated business in total inventories	Value of unincorporated business inventories	Value of total inventories
		Excluding railroads	Railroads	Total			
	1914 = 100.0	$ mill.			Percent	$ mill.	
	1	2	3	4	5	6	7
1896	32.1	1 800	70	1 870	53	2 109	3 979
1897	31.3	1 755	68	1 823	52	1 975	3 798
1898	33.5	1 879	73	1 952	51	2 032	3 984
1899	43.2	2 422	94	2 516	50	2 516	5 032
1900	47.2	2 647	110	2 757	49	2 649	5 406
1901	45.2	2 535	114	2 649	48	2 445	5 094
1902	52.9	2 966	138	3 104	47	2 753	5 857
1903	53.0	2 972	162	3 134	46	2 670	5 804
1904	51.9	2 910	162	3 072	45	2 513	5 585
1905	56.4	3 163	176	3 339	44	2 623	5 962
1906	64.3	3 606	217	3 823	43	2 884	6 707
1907	69.8	3 914	238	4 152	42	3 007	7 159
1908	69.8	3 914	228	4 142	41	2 878	7 020
1909	75.5	4 234	226	4 460	40	2 973	7 433
1910	82.6	4 632	242	4 874	39	3 116	7 990
1911	82.6	4 632	251	4 883	38	2 993	7 876
1912	89.6	5.024	280	5 304	37	3 115	8 419
1913	98.8	5 540	295	5 835	36	3 282	9 117
1914	100.0	5 608	268	5 876	35	3 164	9 040
1915	112.8	6 325	281	6 606	34	3 403	10 009
1916	155.0	8 692	340	9 032	33	4 449	13 481
1917	214.4	12 023	525	12 548	32	5 905	18 453
1918	250.2	14 030	658	14 688	31	6 538	21 226

Percent (1914 = 100.0)

End of year	Index based on selected large manufacturing corporations	Index based on Massachusetts corporations	Combined index	End of year	Index based on selected large manufacturing corporations	Index based on Massachusetts corporations	Combined index
	1	2	3		1	2	3
1896	.	.	32.1	1908	77.9	61.8	69.8
1897	.	.	31.3	1909	80.7	70.3	75.5
1898	.	.	33.5	1910	89.1	76.1	82.6
1899	50.9	.	43.2	1911	86.4	78.8	82.6
1900	55.7	.	47.2	1912	92.9	86.3	89.6
1901	53.3	.	45.2	1913	104.6	93.0	98.8
1902	62.4	.	52.9	1914	100.0	100.0	100.0
1903	62.5	43.4	53.0	1915	113.5	112.0	112.8
1904	59.2	44.6	51.9	1916	155.7	154.3	155.0
1905	67.3	45.6	56.4	1917	220.0	208.7	214.4
1906	74.2	54.4	64.3	1918	276.3	224.2	250.2
1907	79.4	60.1	69.8				

Columns 1 to 3 – Data for following individual companies from annual volumes of *Moody's Manuals*:

	First year included	
	Inventories	Cash
Alaska Packers Association	1905	1905
American Agricultural Chemical Co.	1904	1904
American Beet Sugar Co.	1909	1909
American Can Co.	1903	1903
American Car & Foundry Co.	1903	1903
American Cotton Oil Co.	1903	1903
American Express Co.	1910	
American Hide & Leather Co.	1904	1904
American Locomotive Co.	1903	1903
American Malting Co.	1904	1904
American Ship Building Co.	1903	1903
American Snuff Co.	1905	1905
American Sugar Refining Corp.	1899	1907
American Thread Co.	1900	1900
American Tobacco Co.	1904	1904
American Woolen Co.	1901	1901
American Writing Paper Co.	1900	1900
Armour & Co.	1909	1909
Associated Oil Co.	1906	1906
Bethlehem Steel Co.	1905	1905
Cambria Steel Co.	1902	1902
Central Leather Co. (U.S. Leather)	1899	1899
Colorado Fuel & Iron Co.	1905	
Corn Products Refining Co.	1906	1906
Crucible Steel Co. of America	1902	1902
Cudahy Packing Co.	1909	1909
Diamond Match Co.	1900	1900
Distillers Securities Corp.	1903	1903
Eastman Kodak Co.	1904	1904
Electric Storage Battery Co.	1904	1904
General Asphalt Co.	1903	1903
General Chemical Co.	1903	1903
General Electric Co.	1900	1900
Goff, D., & Sons	1908	1908
Harbison-Walker Refractories, Inc.	1908	1906
International Silver Co.	1901	1901
Lackawanna Steel Co.	1906	1906
Lehigh Coal and Navigation Co.	1905	
Mergenthaler Linotype Co.	1900	1900
National Biscuit Co.	1899	1899
National Lead Co.	1899	1899
Newport News Shipbuilding & Drydock Co.	1906	1906
New York Dock Co.	1909	
Otis Elevator Co.	1905	1905
Pacific Coast Co.	1904	
Pittsburg Brewing Co.	1904	1904
Pressed Steel Car Co.	1901	1901
Railway Steel-Spring Co.	1902	1902
Swift & Co.	1899	1899
Texas Co.	1908	1908
Union Bag & Paper Co.	1903	1903
United States Cast Iron Pipe & Foundry	1902	1902
United States Realty & Improvement	1905	
United States Steel Corp.	1901	1901
Utah Copper Co.	1908	
Virginia-Carolina Chemical Co.	1902	1902
Westinghouse Air Brake Co.	1902	1902
Westinghouse Electric & Manufacturing Co.	1908	1908

Column 4 – Obtained by dividing value in col. 3 by preceding year's value in col. 2.

Column 5 – Obtained from col. 4.

1899 to 1918

End of year	Companies	Inventories of reporting companies	Inventories of companies reporting in preceding year	Link relatives	Index of inventories	End of year	Companies	Inventories of reporting companies	Inventories of companies reporting in preceding year	Link relatives	Index of inventories
	Number	$ mill.		Percent	1914 = 100.0		Number	$ mill.		Percent	1914 = 100.0
	1	2	3	4	5		1	2	3	4	5
1899	5	46.7	.	.	50.9	1909	57	555.8	515.6	103.6	80.7
1900	10	70.9	51.1	109.4	55.7	1910	58	613.3	613.2	110.3	89.1
1901	14	183.6	67.8	95.7	53.3	1911	58	594.6	594.6	97.0	86.4
1902	20	221.5	215.1	117.1	62.4	1912	58	639.7	639.7	107.5	92.9
1903	29	258.3	222.0	100.2	62.5	1913	58	720.3	720.3	112.6	104.6
1904	37	286.5	244.7	94.7	59.2	1914	58	688.4	688.4	95.6	100.0
1905	44	341.9	325.5	113.6	67.3	1915	58	702.4	702.4	102.0	102.0
1906	49	390.1	377.1	110.3	74.2	1916	58	916.1	916.1	130.5	133.1
1907	49	417.4	417.4	107.0	79.4	1917	58	1297.6	1297.6	141.6	188.5
1908	53	497.6	409.3	98.1	77.9	1918	58	1631.8	1631.8	125.8	237.1

907

Column 1 – National Bureau of Economic Research, *Corporate Financial Data for Studies in Business Finance* (unpublished), table B-27. Figures include all Massachusetts domestic corporations, except railroads, public utilities, and banks.

Column 2 – Column 1 multiplied by 15.5; multiplier obtained by dividing difference between 1918 figure in Table P-25, col. 4 and 94.8 percent of Kuznets' current inventory valuation for "Transportation and Other Public Utilities" (cf. *National Income and Its Composition, 1919–1938*, vol. II, table VII) by 1918 inventory of Massachusetts corporations as shown in col. 1.

Column 3 – Derived from col. 2.

Column 1 – 1896–1918: From annual volumes of *Statistics of Railways* except for 1910. Figure for 1910 is obtained by linear interpolation between adjacent years, as annual report for 1910 (page 78) combined inventories with other "working assets."

Column 2 – 1896–1910: Allowance for nonoperating subsidiaries and Class II and Class III roads and switching and terminal companies based on proportion of inventories of these groups to Class I roads in 1915 and 1916, when separate figures for each group are given in *Statistics of Railways*.
1911–1914: Figures for Class III roads and switching and terminal companies estimated on basis of 1915–1916 relationship, those for nonoperating subsidiaries and Class II roads being given in *Statistics of Railways*.
1915–1916: From *Statistics of Railways*.
1917–1918: Figures for nonoperating subsidiaries and switching and terminal companies from *Statistics of Railways*, those for Class II and Class III roads estimated on basis of 1915–1916 relationship to Class I roads.

Column 3 – 1896–1918: Col. 1 plus col. 2.

ESTIMATES OF CORPORATE INVENTORIES
BASED ON MASSACHUSETTS CORPORATIONS: 1903 to 1918

End of year	Inventories of Massachusetts corporations	Total corporate inventories (excluding railroads and public utilities)		End of year	Inventories of Massachusetts corporations	Total corporate inventories (excluding railroads and public utilities)	
	$ mill.	$ mill.	1914 = 100.0		$ mill.	$ mill.	1914 = 100.0
	1	2	3		1	2	3
1903	174	2 697	43.4	1911	316	4 898	78.8
1904	179	2 774	44.6	1912	346	5 363	86.3
1905	183	2 836	45.6	1913	373	5 782	93.0
1906	218	3 379	54.4	1914	401	6 216	100.0
1907	241	3 736	60.1	1915	449	6 960	112.0
1908	248	3 844	61.8	1916	619	9 594	154.3
1909	282	4 371	70.3	1917	837	12 974	208.7
1910	305	4 728	76.1	1918	899	13 934	224.2

INVENTORIES OF RAILROADS
1896 to 1918

$ mill.

Date	Class I roads	Other roads	All roads		Date	Class I roads	Other roads	All roads
	1	2	3			1	2	3
June 30, 1896	69	4	73		June 30, 1908	226	12	238
,, 1897	64	3	67		,, 1909	207	11	218
,, 1898	67	3	70		,, 1910	222	12	234
,, 1899	72	4	76		,, 1911	238	12	250
,, 1900	107	6	113		,, 1912	239	13	252
,, 1901	103	5	108		,, 1913	293	14	307
,, 1902	115	6	121		,, 1914	270	13	283
,, 1903	148	8	156		,, 1915	241	12	253
,, 1904	159	8	167		,, 1916	296	13	309
,, 1905	149	8	157		Dec. 31, 1916	324	16	340
,, 1906	185	10	195		,, 1917	503	22	525
,, 1907	227	12	239		,, 1918	631	27	658

Column 1 – 1918–1929: Kuznets, S., *National Income*, pp. 903–910.

Column 2 – 1918–1927: Col. 1 multiplied by 0.948, the 1928 relation between Kuznets' and Department of Commerce figures for total nonfarm inventories.
1928–1929: Obtained from Department of Commerce figures (1929 shown in Cobren, G. M., "The Non-Farm Business Inventory Component of National Wealth," *Studies in Income and Wealth*, vol. XII, table I).

Column 3 – 1918: Obtained by extrapolation.
1919: From Table P-26, col. 6.
1920–1927: Obtained by linear interpolation.
1928–1929: Same source as for col. 2.

Column 4 – 1918–1929: Col. 2 multiplied by col. 3, using unrounded figures.
Column 5 – 1918–1929: Col. 2 minus col. 4.

Column 1 – 1899–1919: Share of corporations in value of output as reported by Bureau of Census, linked in 1929 to Cobren's figure.
1924: Kuznets, S., *Commodity Flow*, pp. 412, 418, linked in 1929 to Cobren's figure.
1929–1939: Cobren, G. M., "The Non-Farm Business Inventory Component of National Wealth," *Studies in Income and Wealth*, vol. XII, p. 381.
1946: Estimated on basis of data obtained from Department of Commerce.

Column 2 – 1899–1919: Estimated on basis of Census data on value of output for 1902, 1909, and 1919, linked in 1929 to Cobren's figure.
1924: Rough estimate.
1929–1946: Same source as for col. 1.

Column 3 to 5 – 1899–1924: Rough estimates.
1929–1946: Same source as for col. 1.

Column 6 – 1899–1924: Roughly weighted average of group ratios.
1929–1946: Same source as for col. 1.

DERIVATION OF NONFARM BUSINESS INVENTORIES
1918 to 1929

End of year	Total inventories		Proportion of corporate inventories	Estimated inventories	
	Kuznets	Linked to Department of Commerce		Corporations	Unincorporated business
	$ mill.		Percent	$ mill.	
	1	2	3	4	5
1918	22 390	21 226	69.2	14 688	6 538
1919	28 088	26 627	70.0	18 639	7 988
1920	29 605	28 066	70.7	19 843	8 223
1921	23 690	22 458	71.5	16 057	6 401
1922	25 344	24 026	72.2	17 347	6 679
1923	28 587	27 100	73.0	19 783	7 317
1924	28 187	26 721	73.7	19 693	7 028
1925	29 597	28 058	74.5	20 903	7 155
1926	29 654	28 112	75.3	21 168	6 944
1927	29 184	27 666	76.1	21 054	6 612
1928	28 692	27 195	76.9	20 915	6 280
1929	30 380	28 427	77.4	22 001	6 426

SHARE OF CORPORATIONS IN TOTAL NONFARM BUSINESS INVENTORIES
Selected Years: 1899 to 1946

Percent

Year	Manufacturing	Mining	Trade	Construction and service	Public utilities (including railroads)	Total
	1	2	3	4	5	6
1899	68	81	25	30	100	50
1904	76	83	30	35	100	55
1909	82	86	35	40	100	60
1914	86	87	40	45	100	65
1919	91	88	45	50	100	70
1924	94	89	50	57	100	74
1929	96	89	56	64	100	78
1939	97	91	60	72	100	81
1946	96	85	57	62	100	79

TABLE C–1

Column 1 – 1897–1915: Table C-4, col. 1.
1916–1921: Table C-27, col. 1.
1922–1946: Table C-32, col. 1.
1947–1949: Assumed to change in same proportions as Department of Commerce estimate of corporate saving (*Survey of Current Business*, July 1950, p. 19). These estimates were made before the Bureau of Internal Revenue figures, shown in Table C-32, became available. Since the two sets of figures differ only slightly, revision to the Bureau of Internal Revenue series was not considered necessary.

Column 2 – 1897–1949: Table C-2, col. 1.

Column 3 – 1897–1949: Table C-3, sum of cols. 2 and 3.

Column 4 – 1897–1949: Table C-3, cols. 5–7 minus World War II adjustments (cf. Table C-36, col. 8) minus col. 4.

Column 5 – 1897–1949: Col. 1 plus col. 2.

Column 6 – 1897–1949: Col. 1 plus col. 2 minus col. 3.

Column 7 – 1897–1949: Col. 1 plus the sum of cols. 2 and 4 minus col. 3.

Columns 8 to 11 – 1897–1949: Cols. 1, 5, 6, and 7, respectively, multiplied by the difference between 100 percent and the share of foreign stockholders as shown in Table C-50, col. 4.

Column 12 – 1897–1949: Col. 11 plus Table C-51.

TABLE C–2

Column 1 – 1897–1949: Sum of cols. 3 and 4 minus sum of cols. 2, 5, and 6.

Column 2 – 1897–1915: Not applicable since this item is already excluded from estimates for total.
1916–1920: From Table C-38, col. 6.
1921–1949: From Table C-38, col. 3.

Column 3 – 1914–1949: From Table C-37, col. 3.

Column 4 – 1897–1915: Not applicable since estimates for these years are not based on corporation income tax returns.
1916–1928: From Table C-34, col. 5.
1929–1947: From Table C-34, col. 4.
1948–1949: Rough estimates assuming about same ratio between reported and unreported profit as in previous years.

Column 5 – 1897–1917: From Table C-44, col. 3.
1918–1949: Not applicable.

Column 6 – 1897–1942: From Table C-35.
1943–1949: Not applicable.

TABLE C–3

Column 1 – 1897–1949: Sum of cols. 5, 6, and 7 minus cols. 2, 3, and 4. Includes following special World War II deductions taken from Table C-36, col. 8.

1941	$ 9 mill.
1942	434 mill.
1943	555 mill.
1944	–349 mill.
1945	–12 mill.

Column 2 – 1897–1949: Table P-19, col. 8 with sign reversed.

Column 3 – 1915–1948: Sum of Table C-40, col. 1 and Table C-37, col. 4.
1949: Rough preliminary estimate. Figure later reported as 917.

Column 4 – 1897–1949: From Table C-41, col. 8.

Column 5 – 1897–1949: From Table C-47, col. 8.

Column 6 – 1897–1949: From Table C-49, col. 9.

Column 7 – 1897–1949: From Table C-46, col. 6.

CORPORATE SAVING, REPORTED AND ADJUSTED

1897 to 1949

$ mill.

Year	Reported saving	Adjustments			Adjusted saving			Domestic stockholders' share in				
		For coverage and comparability	For capital gains and losses	Other	For coverage and comparability	Also for capital gains and losses	Also for other adjustments	Reported saving	Adjusted saving			
									For coverage and comparability	Also for capital gains and losses	Also for other adjustments	Also for reinvested foreign earnings
	1	2	3	4	5	6	7	8	9	10	11	12
1897	374	−82	23	34	292	269	303	344	269	247	279	294
1898	454	−82	0	13	372	372	385	418	343	342	355	370
1899	996	−84	344	8	912	568	576	918	841	524	531	546
1900	758	−87	−35	6	671	706	712	700	619	652	657	672
1901	832	−91	68	7	741	673	680	769	685	622	628	648
1902	1 089	−95	246	13	994	748	761	1 007	919	692	704	724
1903	1 023	−99	−172	29	924	1 096	1 125	947	856	1 015	1 042	1 067
1904	625	−103	116	−6	522	406	400	579	484	376	371	396
1905	802	−107	−14	−11	695	709	698	744	645	658	648	678
1906	1 073	−112	200	−8	961	761	753	997	893	707	700	730
1907	1 018	−117	76	−31	901	825	794	947	838	767	738	773
1908	576	−123	−47	−94	453	500	406	536	422	466	378	413
1909	1 061	−128	430	−97	933	503	406	989	870	469	378	418
1910	1 074	−132	−266	−68	942	1 208	1 140	1 002	879	1 127	1 064	1 104
1911	719	−138	−86	−97	581	667	570	672	543	623	532	577
1912	1 074	−136	344	−38	938	594	556	1 004	877	555	520	565
1913	861	−130	−27	168	731	758	926	805	683	709	866	916
1914	556	−121	−194	107	435	629	736	522	408	591	691	741
1915	1 694	−116	401	58	1 578	1 177	1 235	1 606	1 496	1 116	1 171	1 246
1916	4 908	570	2 318	87	5 478	3 160	3 247	4 712	5 259	3 034	3 117	3 192
1917	4 715	608	2 669	−138	5 323	2 654	2 516	4 545	5 131	2 558	2 425	2 525
1918	1 923	575	1 442	−723	2 498	1 056	333	1 861	2 418	1 022	322	422
1919	4 316	697	1 465	−1 095	5 013	3 548	2 453	4 195	4 873	3 449	2 384	2 484
1920	1 424	655	−2 812	−1 414	2 079	4 891	3 477	1 387	2 025	4 764	3 387	3 437
1921	−2 622	232	−4 755	−1 047	−2 390	2 365	1 318	−2 562	−2 335	2 311	1 288	1 338
1922	1 746	289	733	−408	2 035	1 302	894	1 706	1 988	1 272	873	948
1923	2 528	320	214	−297	2 848	2 634	2 337	2 465	2 777	2 568	2 279	2 354
1	1 575	327	84	−428	1 902	1 818	1 390	1 536	1 854	1 773	1 355	1 455
1925	2 957	384	661	−350	3 341	2 680	2 330	2 880	3 254	2 610	2 269	2 369
1926	2 336	392	−876	−248	2 728	3 604	3 356	2 275	2 657	3 510	3 269	3 394
1927	1 114	365	−97	−300	1 479	1 576	1 276	1 085	1 441	1 535	1 243	1 368
1928	2 400	498	604	−285	2 898	2 294	2 009	2 335	2 820	2 232	1 955	2 105
1929	2 156	589	344	−351	2 745	2 401	2 050	2 089	2 660	2 327	1 986	2 136
1930	−4 247	330	−3 547	−213	−3 917	−370	−583	−4 111	−3 792	−358	−564	−514
1931	−7 327	175	−3 815	−138	−7 152	−3 337	−3 475	−7 085	−6 916	−3 227	−3 360	−3 360
1932	−8 001	97	−2 606	135	−7 904	−5 298	−5 163	−7 721	−7 627	−5 113	−4 982	−5 032
1933	−4 480	263	721	87	−4 217	−4 938	−4 851	−4 310	−4 058	−4 750	−4 667	−4 687
1934	−2 485	361	578	−113	−2 124	−2 702	−2 815	−2 391	−2 043	−2 599	−2 708	−2 718
1935	−1 253	421	465	−42	−832	−1 297	−1 339	−1 204	−800	−1 246	−1 287	−1 287
1936	−799	371	1 186	140	−428	−1 614	−1 474	−761	−408	−1 538	−1 405	−1 405
1937	−960	440	173	109	−520	−693	−584	−912	−494	−658	−553	−553
1938	−1 742	352	−880	−102	−1 390	−510	−612	−1 664	−1 327	−487	−584	−574
1939	199	503	794	−22	702	−92	−114	190	670	−88	−109	−89
1940	711	351	−512	71	1 062	1 574	1 645	682	1 018	1 509	1 578	1 618
1941	2 806	416	1 662	10	3 222	1 560	1 570	2 711	3 112	1 507	1 517	1 697
1942	5 525	−742	1 030	−990	4 783	3 753	2 763	5 365	4 644	3 644	2 683	2 863
1943	6 473	−537	650	−1 120	5 936	5 286	4 166	6 298	5 776	5 143	4 054	4 234
1944	5 606	−456	354	−41	5 150	4 796	4 755	5 455	5 011	4 667	4 627	4 787
1945	4 470	−609	1 208	−304	3 861	2 653	2 349	4 349	3 757	2 581	2 286	2 507
1946	9 022	−452	6 465	−255	8 570	2 105	1 850	8 778	8 339	2 048	1 800	2 103
1947	12 239	−477	6 683	−1 121	11 762	5 079	3 958	11 921	11 456	4 947	3 855	4 254
1948	13 282	−382	3 012	−1 266	12 900	9 888	8 622	12 950	12 578	9 641	8 406	8 975
1949	9 500	−565	−1 733	−1 460	8 935	10 668	9 208	9 263	8 712	10 401	8 978	9 473

ADJUSTMENTS TO REPORTED CORPORATE SAVING
FOR COVERAGE AND COMPARABILITY: 1897 to 1949

$ mill.

Year	Total	Life insurance companies	Federal Reserve banks	Un-reported profits	Unreported depreciation in transportation and public utilities	Unreported depreciation of railways on way and structures
	1	2	3	4	5	6
1897	−82	−	−	−	36	46
1898	−82	−	−	−	36	46
1899	−84	−	−	−	37	47
1900	−87	−	−	−	39	48
1901	−91	−	−	−	42	49
1902	−95	−	−	−	45	50
1903	−99	−	−	−	49	50
1904	−103	−	−	−	52	51
1905	−107	−	−	−	55	52
1906	−112	−	−	−	59	53
1907	−117	−	−	−	63	54
1908	−123	−	−	−	69	54
1909	−128	−	−	−	73	55
1910	−132	−	−	−	76	56
1911	−138	−	−	−	81	57
1912	−136	−	−	−	78	58
1913	−130	−	−	−	72	58
1914	−121	−	0	−	62	59
1915	−116	−	0	−	56	60
1916	570	−81	1	599	51	60
1917	608	−138	2	572	44	60
1918	575	−188	47	402	−	62
1919	697	−175	71	514	−	63
1920	655	−161	83	474	−	63
1921	232	94	16	374	−	64
1922	289	131	0	485	−	65
1923	320	152	2	535	−	65
1924	327	152	−3	548	−	66
1925	384	158	2	606	−	66
1926	392	158	9	608	−	67
1927	365	162	5	588	−	66
1928	498	140	22	684	−	68
1929	589	127	22	763	−	69
1930	330	121	−2	523	−	70
1931	175	107	−7	360	−	71
1932	97	113	11	272	−	73
1933	263	33	−1	371	−	74
1934	361	52	6	482	−	75
1935	421	26	0	523	−	76
1936	371	38	0	486	−	77
1937	440	6	2	519	−	75
1938	352	−8	1	417	−	74
1939	503	−19	2	555	−	73
1940	351	−35	6	382	−	72
1941	416	−35	1	445	−	65
1942	−742	1 058	3	363	−	50
1943	−537	1 082	28	517	−	−
1944	−456	1 146	40	650	−	−
1945	−609	1 237	131	497	−	−
1946	−452	1 266	81	733	−	−
1947	−477	1 345	8	860	−	−
1948	−382	1 400	18	1 000	−	−
1949	−565	1 437	22	850	−	−

ECONOMIC ADJUSTMENTS TO REPORTED CORPORATE SAVING
1897 to 1949
$ mill.

Year	Total	Inventory gains and losses	Capital gains and losses	Excess depreciation adjustment	Excess development costs in mining	Excess capital expenditures charged to current expenses	Excess depletion
	1	2	3	4	5	6	7
1897	11	23	–	–29	7	11	–13
1898	13	0	–	–5	8	15	–15
1899	–336	344	–	17	15	30	–20
1900	41	–35	–	32	17	43	–22
1901	–61	68	–	27	16	41	–23
1902	–233	246	–	30	19	51	–27
1903	201	–172	–	27	26	60	–30
1904	–122	116	–	35	24	32	–27
1905	3	–14	–	51	22	50	–32
1906	–208	200	–	71	26	75	–38
1907	–107	76	–	101	33	78	–41
1908	–47	–47	–	72	25	–15	–32
1909	–527	430	–	94	28	6	–37
1910	198	–266	–	105	29	28	–20
1911	–11	–86	–	139	28	12	2
1912	–382	344	–	140	37	50	15
1913	195	–27	–	–6	51	75	36
1914	301	–194	–	–23	39	12	33
1915	–343	401	0	25	43	3	37
1916	–2 231	2 218	100	258	75	125	145
1917	–2 807	2 569	100	670	125	212	195
1918	–2 165	1 442	0	1 377	154	188	312
1919	–2 560	1 365	100	1 426	119	–31	243
1920	1 398	–2 812	0	1 884	226	–104	348
1921	3 708	–4 555	–200	1 205	79	–131	210
1922	–1 141	633	100	778	111	14	245
1923	–511	114	100	936	128	118	393
1924	–512	–116	200	888	106	17	337
1925	–1 011	201	400	869	137	28	354
1926	628	–1 276	400	925	154	95	428
1927	–203	–597	500	847	85	86	376
1928	–889	–46	650	831	51	109	386
1929	–695	–472	816	876	54	52	419
1930	3 334	–3 260	–287	554	22	–29	348
1931	3 677	–2 414	–1 401	261	–57	–22	202
1932	2 741	–1 047	–1 559	–117	–21	–147	186
1933	–634	2 143	–1 422	–104	–62	–140	185
1934	–691	625	–47	203	–52	–92	234
1935	–507	227	238	230	–21	–53	262
1936	–1 046	738	448	230	25	17	328
1937	–64	31	142	488	85	118	394
1938	778	–963	83	458	50	–22	328
1939	–816	714	80	462	53	58	329
1940	583	148	–660	528	72	171	356
1941	–1 652	2 617	–955	734	87	258	408
1942	–2 020	1 204	–174	966	0	–25	435
1943	–1 770	773	–123	997	23	–75	484
1944	–395	287	67	988	137	–74	535
1945	–1 512	564	644	1 026	148	42	520
1946	–6 720	5 193	1 272	1 530	157	516	602
1947	–7 804	5 757	926	2 677	195	453	908
1948	–4 278	2 032	980	3 268	328	549	1 125
1949	273	–2 233	500	3 018	314	306	938

TABLE C–4

Column 1 – Table C-5, col. 1 minus Table C-6, col. 1.

Column 2 – Table C-9, col. 12 multiplied by Table C-12, col. 5.

Column 3 – Table C-5, col. 3 minus Table C-6, col. 3.

Column 4 – Table C-7, col. 4.

Column 5 – Table C-25, col. 11.

Column 6 – Table C-5, col. 6 minus Table C-6, col. 6.

Column 7 – Table C-5, col. 7 minus Table C-6, col. 7.

TABLE C–5

Column 1 – 1897–1915: Sum of cols. 2–7.

Column 2 – 1897–1915: From Table C-9, col. 12.

Column 3 – 1897–1901: Extrapolated from 1902 figure on assumption of same rate of growth as prevailed from 1902–1907.
1902, 1907, 1912: From Table C-20, col. 1. Based on *Census of Electrical Industries*.
1903–1906, 1908–1911, 1913–1915: Interpolated between 1902 and 1907, 1907 and 1912, 1912 and 1917, respectively, by assuming even rate of growth between benchmarks. (Figure for 1917 is also based on *Census of Electrical Industries* and is taken from Table C-20, col. 1.)

Column 4 – 1897–1915: From Table C-7, col. 1.

Column 5 – 1897–1915: From Table C-25, col. 9.

Column 6 – 1897–1915: Estimated from regression equation $y = 0.21625x + 126.61$ where x represents the net earnings of manufacturing and mining corporations and y, the net earnings of construction, trade, service, and miscellaneous corporations fitted to the data for the period 1917–1929.

Column 7 – 1897–1915: Includes net earnings of agricultural corporations; corporations in the transportation and public utilities group other than electrical utilities and railroads; and corporations in the finance group other than banking. It was assumed that the net earnings of these corporations amounted to 5 percent of those of all other corporations.

CORPORATE SAVING BY MAJOR INDUSTRIAL GROUPS
1897 to 1915
$ mill.

Year	All corporations	Manufac-turing and mining	Electrical utilities	Railroads	Commercial banks	Construction, trade, service, and miscellaneous	All other corporations
	1	2	3	4	5	6	7
1897	374	153	22	32	3	147	17
1898	454	192	24	56	7	154	21
1899	996	561	26	97	37	228	47
1900	758	351	29	105	64	173	36
1901	832	396	31	129	60	177	39
1902	1 089	594	35	137	76	195	52
1903	1 023	544	39	128	80	183	49
1904	625	252	43	115	66	119	30
1905	802	374	47	137	64	142	38
1906	1 073	540	52	165	95	170	51
1907	1 018	495	56	166	95	157	49
1908	576	263	57	46	71	112	27
1909	1 061	534	58	168	83	167	51
1910	1 074	574	59	136	88	166	51
1911	719	368	59	67	69	122	34
1912	1 074	590	60	128	68	161	67
1913	861	512	61	56	67	124	41
1914	556	338	62	−30	42	118	26
1915	1 694	1 054	62	187	56	254	81

NET CORPORATE EARNINGS BY MAJOR INDUSTRIAL GROUPS
1897 to 1915
$ mill.

Year	All corporations	Manufac-turing and mining	Electrical utilities	Railroads	Commercial banks	Construction, trade, service, and miscellaneous	All other corporations
	1	2	3	4	5	6	7
1897	775	295	56	124	74	190	36
1898	911	361	62	160	80	205	43
1899	1 581	801	69	222	114	300	75
1900	1 522	693	77	254	150	276	72
1901	1 750	808	85	300	173	301	83
1902	2 434	1 303	95	328	184	408	116
1903	2 460	1 278	106	337	219	403	117
1904	2 095	989	118	345	203	340	100
1905	2 393	1 157	131	393	221	377	114
1906	2 894	1 424	146	455	296	435	138
1907	2 972	1 410	161	518	309	432	142
1908	2 423	1 108	169	406	259	366	115
1909	2 994	1 429	178	535	273	436	143
1910	3 285	1 595	187	573	302	472	156
1911	2 921	1 368	196	503	293	422	139
1912	3 382	1 701	206	519	301	494	161
1913	3 553	1 862	215	473	305	529	169
1914	2 714	1 312	224	362	277	410	129
1915	4 110	2 257	233	523	286	615	196

GROSS DIVIDEND PAYMENTS BY MAJOR INDUSTRIAL GROUPS
1897 to 1915

$ mill.

Year	All corporations	Manufac- turing and mining	Electrical utilities	Railroads	Commercial banks	Construction, trade, service, and miscellaneous	All other corporations
	1	2	3	4	5	6	7
1897	401	142	34	92	71	43	19
1898	457	169	38	104	73	51	22
1899	585	240	43	125	77	72	28
1900	764	342	48	149	86	103	36
1901	918	412	54	171	113	124	44
1902	1 345	709	60	191	108	213	64
1903	1 437	734	67	209	139	220	68
1904	1 470	737	75	230	137	221	70
1905	1 591	783	84	256	157	235	76
1906	1 821	884	94	290	201	265	87
1907	1 954	915	105	352	214	275	93
1908	1 847	845	112	360	188	254	88
1909	1 933	895	120	367	190	269	92
1910	2 211	1 021	128	437	214	306	105
1911	2 202	1 000	137	436	224	300	105
1912	2 308	1 111	146	391	233	333	94
1913	2 692	1 350	154	417	238	405	128
1914	2 158	974	162	392	235	292	103
1915	2 416	1 203	171	336	230	361	115

Column 1 – 1897–1915: Sum of cols. 2–7.

Column 2 – 1897–1915: Table C-5, col. 2 minus Table C-4, col. 2.

Column 3 – 1897–1901: Extrapolated from 1902 figure on assumption of same rate of growth as prevailed from 1902 to 1907.
1902, 1907, 1912: From Table C-20, col. 2. Based on *Census of Electrical Industries*.
1903–1906, 1908–1911, 1913–1915: Interpolated between 1902 and 1907, 1907 and 1912, 1912 and 1917, respectively, by assuming even rate of growth between benchmarks. (Figure for 1917 is based on *Census of Electrical Industries* as shown in Table C-20, col. 2.)

Column 4 – 1897–1915: Table C-7, col. 3.

Column 5 – 1897–1915: Table C-25, col. 10.

Column 6 – 1897–1915: Assumed to be 30 percent of col. 2, the average relationship derived from 1917–1922 data.

Column 7 – 1897–1915: Assumed to be 5 percent of the sum of cols. 2–6.

918

EARNINGS, DIVIDENDS, AND SAVING OF STEAM RAILROADS
1897 to 1949

$ mill.

Year	Net income Excluding defaulted bond interest	Net income Including defaulted bond interest	Dividends	Saving Excluding defaulted bond interest	Saving Including defaulted bond interest	Year	Net income Excluding defaulted bond interest	Net income Including defaulted bond interest	Dividends	Saving Excluding defaulted bond interest	Saving Including defaulted bond interest
	1	2	3	4	5		1	2	3	4	5
1897	124	.	92	32	.	1924	632	.	391	241	.
1898	160	.	104	56	.	1925	783	.	414	369	.
1899	222	.	125	97	.	1926	896	.	475	421	.
1900	254	.	149	105	.	1927	753	.	565	188	.
1901	300	.	171	129	.	1928	868	.	518	350	.
1902	328	.	191	137	.	1929	992	1 002	570	422	432
1903	337	.	209	128	.	1930	587	602	602	−15	0
1904	345	.	230	115	.	1931	172	199	407	−235	−208
1905	393	.	256	137	.	1932	−124	−87	151	−275	−238
1906	455	.	290	165	.	1933	27	97	161	−134	−64
1907	518	.	352	166	.	1934	23	103	215	−192	−112
1908	406	.	360	46	.	1935	53	155	206	−153	−51
1909	535	.	367	168	.	1936	225	335	220	5	115
1910	573	.	437	136	.	1937	148	252	231	−83	21
1911	503	.	436	67	.	1938	−88	46	138	−226	−92
1912	519	.	391	128	.	1939	143	269	182	−39	87
1913	473	.	417	56	.	1940	247	413	220	27	193
1914	362	.	392	−30	.	1941	566	690	243	323	447
1915	523	.	336	187	.	1942	1 008	1 080	258	750	822
1916	746	.	371	375	.	1943	960	1 047	268	692	779
1917	668	.	388	280	.	1944	744	796	296	448	500
1918	449	.	344	105	.	1945	510	554	299	211	255
1919	505	.	340	165	.	1946	340	388	287	53	101
1920	489	.	336	153	.	1947	545	571	284	261	287
1921	356	.	359	−3	.	1948	780	787	340	440	447
1922	441	.	344	97	.	1949	503	515	312	191	203
1923	642	.	368	274	.						

Column 1 – 1897–1915: Earnings for fiscal year ending June 30 divided between July/December and January/June on basis of earnings of sample of Class I railroads as published in *Commercial and Financial Chronicle*, March issues. Calendar-year figures are totals of semiannual estimates so obtained.
1916–1949: From Table C-8, col. 2.

Column 2 – 1929–1949: Col. 1 plus defaulted bond interest which had been deducted as expense and is the difference between interest accruals and interest payments. For amounts of defaulted bond interest which is available only since 1929 see *Statistics of Railways*, 1939, p. 106, 1947, p. 117, and 1949, p. 114.

Column 3 – 1897–1915: Two-year moving averages of amounts in Table C-8, col. 4.
1916–1949: From Table C-8, col. 4.

Column 4 – 1897–1949: Col. 1 minus col. 3.

Column 5 – 1929–1949: Col. 2 minus col. 3.

TABLE C-8

Column 1 – 1896–1899: From Stevens, W. H. and Hobbs, E. S., *Analysis of Steam Railway Dividends, 1890–1941*, p. 84.

1900–1949: From *Statistics of Railways*, 1949, p. 157.

Column 2 – 1896–1907: Same as col. 1.

1908–1912: Col. 1 multiplied by 1.015 in order to include switching and terminal companies, which have been excluded beginning with 1908. It is estimated on basis of figures in the 1917 issue of *Statistics of Railways* that switching and terminal companies account approximately for 1.5 percent of net income and dividends.

1913: Col. 1 multiplied by 1.02, to include switching and terminal companies and Class III railroads, which have also been omitted in 1913. It is estimated on basis of figures in 1917 issue of *Statistics of Railways* that Class III railroads account for about 0.5 percent of total net income and dividends.

1914–1949: Amounts in col. 1 multiplied by 1.015 (see note for 1908–1912).

Column 3 – 1896–1949: Same source as col. 1. Stock dividends have been excluded as follows:

Year	$ mill.	Year	$ mill.
1908	2	1926	2
1910	5	1927	7
1915	8	1928	1
1916	2	1930	10
1921	102	1932	2
1923	50	1936	15
1925	2	1943	1

(See *Analysis of Steam Railway Dividends, 1890–1941*, p. 38, and *Statistics of Railways*, 1946, p. 110, table 123, note 1.)

Column 4 – 1896–1949: Same adjustments as col. 2.

Column 5 – 1896–1949: Col. 2 minus col. 4.

DERIVATION OF EARNINGS AND DIVIDENDS OF STEAM RAILROADS
1896 to 1949

$ mill.

Year	Net income	Net income adjusted	Dividends	Dividends adjusted	Retained earnings adjusted	Year	Net income	Net income adjusted	Dividends	Dividends adjusted	Retained earnings adjusted
	1	2	3	4	5		1	2	3	4	5
Fiscal year						1921	351	356	354	359	-3
1896	95	95	88	88	7	1922	434	441	339	344	97
1897	86	86	87	87	-1	1923	632	642	362	368	274
1898	147	147	96	96	51	1924	623	632	385	391	241
1899	177	177	111	111	66	1925	771	783	408	414	369
1900	253	253	140	140	113	1926	883	896	468	475	421
1901	273	273	157	157	116	1927	742	753	557	565	188
1902	315	315	185	185	130	1928	855	868	510	518	350
1903	338	338	197	197	141	1929	977	992	561	570	422
1904	317	317	222	222	95	1930	578	587	593	602	-15
1905	365	365	238	238	127	1931	169	172	401	407	-235
1906	434	434	273	273	161	1932	-122	-124	149	151	-275
1907	488	488	308	308	180	1933	27	27	159	161	-134
1908	444	451	389	395	56	1934	23	23	212	215	-192
1909	441	448	321	326	122	1935	52	53	203	206	-153
1910	583	592	401	407	185	1936	222	225	217	220	5
1911	547	555	460	467	88	1937	146	148	228	231	-83
1912	453	460	400	406	54	1938	-87	-88	136	138	-226
1913	547	558	369	375	183	1939	141	143	179	182	-39
1914	395	401	452	459	-58	1940	243	247	217	220	27
1915	355	360	320	325	35	1941	558	566	239	243	323
1916	671	681	342	347	334	1942	993	1 008	254	258	750
Calendar Year						1943	946	960	264	268	692
						1944	733	744	292	296	448
1916	735	746	365	371	375	1945	502	510	295	299	211
1917	658	668	382	388	280	1946	335	340	283	287	53
1918	442	449	339	344	105	1947	537	545	280	284	261
1919	497	505	335	340	165	1948	768	780	335	340	440
1920	482	489	331	336	153	1949	496	503	307	312	191

921

TABLE C–9

Column 1 – 1899, 1904, 1909: Estimated on basis of sum of estimates for manufacturing (Table C-13, col. 10) and mining (based on Table C-17, col. 10).
1916: Table C-28, sum of cols. 3 and 4.

Column 2 – 1897–1901, 1904: Based on earnings as given in Cowles, Alfred and Associates, *Common Stock Indexes*, E-2 series, pp. 420–421.

Column 3 – 1901–1914: Based on Table C-10, cols. 2 and 3.

Column 4 – 1911–1916: Based on Table C-11, col. 1.

Column 5 – 1897–1901: Benchmark for 1899 extended in both directions on basis of col. 2.

Column 6 – 1900, 1901, 1904: Benchmark for 1904 extended back for 1900 and 1901 on basis of col. 2.

Column 7 – 1901: Weighted average of cols. 5 and 6, respective weights being 60 percent and 40 percent.
1902–1903: Figure for 1901 extended on basis of index in col. 3.

Column 8 – 1901–1908: Benchmark for 1904 extended in both directions on basis of index in col. 3.

Column 9 – 1905–1911: Benchmark for 1909 extended in both directions on basis of index in col. 3.

Column 10 – 1911: Same as col. 9.
1912–1915: Figure for 1911 extended on basis of index in col. 4.

Column 11 – 1911–1916: Benchmark for 1916 extended back on basis of index in col. 4.

Column 12 – 1897–1899: Same as col. 5.
1900: Weighted average of cols. 5 and 6, the respective weights being 80 percent and 20 percent.
1901–1904: Weighted average of cols. 7 and 8, respective weights being 75 percent and 25 percent for 1901, 50–50 percent for 1902, 25–75 percent for 1903, and 0–100 percent for 1904.
1905–1909: Weighted average of cols. 8 and 9, respective weights being 80–20 percent for 1905, 60–40 percent for 1906, 40–60 percent for 1907, 20–80 percent for 1908, and 0–100 percent for 1909.
1910: Same as in col. 9.
1911–1916: Weighted average of cols. 10 and 11, respective weights being 5/6–1/6 for 1911, 4/6–2/6 for 1912, 3/6–3/6 for 1913, 2/6–4/6 for 1914, 1/6–5/6 for 1915, and 0–1 for 1916.

TABLE C–10

Columns 1 to 7: Data for individual corporations from *Moody's Manuals*, various issues. (For list see notes to Table P-22.) Figures for U.S. Steel Corporation and Standard Oil Company, though available have been excluded. Figures for 1905–1910 include forty-three corporations whose fiscal years center about Dec. 31, and twenty-four corporations whose fiscal years center around June 30. Data for the latter group of corporations were adjusted to Dec. 31 basis by using a two-year moving average. Those for 1910–1914 are limited to corporations whose fiscal years end on or close to Dec. 31.

CORPORATE EARNINGS IN MANUFACTURING AND MINING 1897 to 1916

$ mill. (except cols. 2–4)

Year	Bench- marks	Indexes of earnings			Interpolation on basis of Cowles		Interpolation on basis of sample of corporations			Interpolation on basis of Muller		Final estimate of net earnings
		Cowles 1909 =100.0	Sample 1909 =100.0	Muller 1916 =100.0								
	1	2	3	4	5	6	7	8	9	10	11	12
1897		34.6			295							295
1898		42.4			361							361
1899	801	94.0			801							801
1900		63.0			537	1 317	—	683				693
1901		63.0	48.7		537	1 317	849	683				808
1902			82.8				1 443	1 162				1 303
1903			85.9				1 498	1 205				1 278
1904	989	47.3	70.5			989		989				989
1905			82.2					1 153	1 175			1 157
1906			100.8					1 414	1 440			1 424
1907			99.4					1 394	1 420			1 410
1908			77.8					1 091	1 112			1 108
1909	1 429		100.0						1 429			1 429
1910			111.6						1 595			1 595
1911			100.8	22.0					1 440	1 440	1 005	1 368
1912			115.4	28.9						1 892	1 320	1 701
1913			111.4	33.5						2 193	1 530	1 862
1914			91.7	25.1						1 643	1 146	1 312
1915				46.1						3 017	2 105	2 257
1916	4 566			100.0							4 566	4 566

EARNINGS, DIVIDENDS, AND SAVING OF A SAMPLE OF INDUSTRIAL CORPORATIONS: 1899 to 1914

$ mill. (except col. 1)

Year	Number of corporations	Earnings		Dividends		Saving	
		Current year	Preceding year for same corporations	Current year	Preceding year for same corporations	Current year	Preceding year for same corporations
	1	2	3	4	5	6	7
1899	8	6.5	.	3.2	.	3.3	.
1900	8	7.1	6.5	4.8	3.2	2.3	3.3
1901	21	20.9	24.2	14.3	14.9	6.7	9.3
1902	39	53.6	31.6	27.0	14.8	26.6	16.8
1903	55	78.6	75.6	45.6	41.6	33.0	34.0
1904	65	74.2	90.4	52.0	45.4	22.1	45.0
1905	67	91.8	78.7	59.1	56.5	32.8	22.2
1906	67	112.5	91.8	65.4	59.1	47.1	32.8
1907	67	110.9	112.5	68.0	65.4	43.0	47.1
1908	67	86.8	110.9	64.1	68.0	22.7	43.0
1909	67	111.6	86.8	65.5	64.1	46.1	22.7
1910	55	59.7	53.5	38.3	33.5	21.5	20.0
1911	55	54.0	59.7	39.5	38.3	14.5	21.5
1912	55	61.8	54.0	40.1	39.5	21.7	14.5
1913	55	59.6	61.8	41.3	40.1	18.3	21.7
1914	55	49.1	59.6	40.7	41.3	8.3	18.3

C-11 | TABLE C-11

Columns 1, 2, 5, and 6: Muller, J. P., *Analysis of Financial Statistics*, pp. 414–415.
　　　Number of corporations included not given in source. From detailed listing it is evident that number increased during period, and that about seven hundred corporations were included for one or more years.

Column 3 – Col. 1 minus col. 2.

Column 4 – Col. 3 divided by col. 1.

C-12 | TABLE C-12

Column 1 – 1897–1915: The difference between earnings-price ratios (R-2 series) and yields of stocks (Yea-2 series) expressed as percent of the earnings-price ratios (see Cowles, Alfred and Associates, *Common Stock Indexes*, pp. 404 and 485, respectively).

Column 2 – 1897–1915: Derived from col. 1.

Column 3 – 1901–1914: Derived from link relatives of ratios obtained by dividing col. 6 by col. 2 and col. 7 by col. 3 of Table C-10.

Column 4 – 1911–1915: Table C-11, col. 4.

Column 5 – 1897–1900: The 1901 figure in col. 5 multiplied by index of col. 2.
　　　1901–1910: The 1911 figure of col. 5 multiplied by index in col. 3.
　　　1911–1915: Same as col. 4.

C-13 | TABLE C-13

Columns 1 and 2 – 1899–1919: Estimated from sources listed in Table C-16, col. 1. All columns of this table include figures for manufactured gas companies.

Column 3 – 1899–1919: Col. 1 multiplied by 0.025/0.975. Numerator of this ratio is based on the assumption, supported by data in *Statistics of Income*, 1922–1924, that nonoperating income constitutes about 2.5 percent of total receipts. Denominator in turn adjusts the "value of product" to a "total receipts" basis. Amounts shown include dividends received.

Column 4 – 1899, 1904: Not applicable.
　　　1909, 1914: Estimated at about 50 percent of total corporate tax collections on the basis of relationship for other years (see *Statistics of Income*, part 2, 1940, p. 282).
　　　1919: *Statistics of Income*, 1919, p. 12.

Column 5 – 1899–1919: Table C-15, col. 4.

Column 6 – 1899–1909: No allowance as it is assumed that in most cases deductions for depletion commenced in 1913 in connection with corporate income tax computations.
　　　1914, 1919: Estimated at about 45 percent of total depletion charges in manufacturing and mining, which were in turn estimated from relationship to both value and volume of minerals output.

Column 7 – 1899–1919: Table C-15, col. 5.

Column 8 – 1899–1919: Table C-14, col. 7 multiplied by percent of value added by manufacturing corporations, which was obtained as follows: 1899, decreasing percentage of value of product (Table C-16, col. 1) by same absolute difference as the corresponding percentages in 1904 and 1909; 1900, 1914, 1939, dividing the absolute amounts of value added by manufacturing corporations (col. 2) by value added by all industries (figures obtained from sources listed in Table C-16, col. 1, 1919–1929, interpolating between the 1914 and 1939 percentages).

Column 9 – 1899–1919: Sum of cols. 2 and 3 minus sum of cols. 4–8. Includes dividends received.

Column 10 – 1899–1919: Estimated at 92 percent of col. 9 in order to reduce earnings to level of estimate for 1919 by Kuznets (*National Income*, p. 312 for corporate saving; p. 870 for gross dividends paid).

924

EARNINGS AND DIVIDENDS OF SELECTED INDUSTRIAL CORPORATIONS   C-11
1911 to 1920

Year	Net income	Dividends	Retained net income	Proportion of net income retained	Surplus	Capital stock
	$ mill.			Percent	$ mill.	
	1	2	3	4	5	6
1911	428	313	115	26.9	990	5 142
1912	562	367	195	34.7	1 270	5 903
1913	652	473	179	27.5	1 382	6 515
1914	488	362	126	25.8	1 494	6 790
1915	899	479	420	46.7	2 042	7 335
1916	1 948	789	1 159	59.5	3 288	8 310
1917	1 947	992	955	49.0	4 441	9 137
1918	1 513	897	616	40.7	5 173	9 587
1919	1 522	723	799	52.5	6 003	10 076
1920	1 558	1 043	515	33.1	6 490	11 340

CORPORATE SAVING RATIOS   C-12
1897 to 1915

Year	Based on Cowles		Based on sample	Based on Muller	Final estimate	Year	Based on Cowles		Based on sample	Based on Muller	Final estimate
	Percent	1901 = 100.0	1911 = 100.0	Percent	Percent		Percent	1901 = 100.0	1911 = 100.0	Percent	Percent
	1	2	3	4	5		1	2	3	4	5
1897	56.8	105.6	–	–	51.7	1907	59.0	109.7	130.5	–	35.1
1898	58.3	108.4	–	–	53.1	1908	37.1	69.0	88.1	–	23.7
1899	76.8	142.8	–	–	70.0	1909	63.2	117.5	139.0	–	37.4
1900	55.5	103.2	–	–	50.6	1910	48.2	89.6	133.8	–	36.0
1901	53.8	100.0	182.0	–	49.0	1911	28.5	53.0	100.0	26.9	26.9
1902	63.7	118.4	169.6	–	45.6	1912	41.1	76.4	130.5	34.7	34.7
1903	46.2	85.9	158.4	–	42.6	1913	49.0	91.1	114.2	27.5	27.5
1904	56.5	105.0	94.8	–	25.5	1914	29.0	53.9	62.8	25.8	25.8
1905	67.9	126.2	120.0	–	32.3	1915	68.4	127.1	–	46.7	46.7
1906	70.7	131.4	140.9	–	37.9						

NET EARNINGS OF MANUFACTURING CORPORATIONS   C-13
Selected Years: 1899 to 1919

$ mill.

Year	Value of product	Value added	Non-operating income	Corporate income taxes	Depreciation	Depletion	Interest payments	Other expenses	Net earnings	Adjusted net earnings
	1	2	3	4	5	6	7	8	9	10
1899	7 602	3 130	195	–	130	–	276	2 135	784	721
1904	10 904	4 526	280	–	205	–	321	3 334	946	870
1909	16 341	6 582	419	11	319	–	369	4 864	1 438	1 323
1914	20 183	8 093	518	20	419	29	406	6 340	1 397	1 285
1919	54 744	21 661	1 404	1 359	863	154	470	16 228	3 991	3 659

TABLE C–14

C-14

Column 1 – 1899–1909: *Census of Manufactures,* 1910, vol. VIII, p. 129.
   1914, 1919: *Census of Manufactures,* 1920, vol. VIII, p. 14.

Column 2 – 1899: Not available. Factory rent expenses included in all other expenses.
   1904, 1909: Same as col. 1.
   1914, 1919: Same as col. 1. Includes only contract work. Factory rent expenses not available separately.

Column 3 – 1899: Not available separately. Included in other expenses.
   1904: Same as col. 1. Excludes Internal Revenue taxes as they are included in other expenses and are not listed separately.
   1909: Same as col. 1. An estimated $11 million of 1 percent excise taxes of corporations were excluded and are shown separately in Table C-13.
   1914, 1919: Same as col. 1. Corporate income taxes which were estimated at $20 million for 1914 and which are available in *Statistics of Income,* 1919, were deducted and are shown separately in Table C-13.

Column 4 – 1899: Same as col. 1. Includes taxes and factory rent.
   1904: Same as col. 1. Includes Internal Revenue taxes.
   1909: Same as col. 1.
   1914, 1919: Col. 7 multiplied by col. 6.

Column 5 – 1899: Not available since other expenses include factory rent.
   1904, 1909: Sum of cols. 3 and 4 as percent of col. 7.
   1914, 1919: Not available since estimates for other expenses had to be constructed.

Column 6 – 1899: Not available. See col. 5.
   1904: Not available since other expenses include Internal Revenue taxes.
   1909: Col. 4 as percent of col. 7.
   1914, 1919: Roughly the same percentage was assumed as for 1909 in view of the relative constancy of percentages in col. 5 for 1904 and 1909.

Column 7 – 1899–1909: Sum of cols. 1–4.
   1914, 1919: Based on the assumption that the sum of cols. 1–3 constitute about 79 percent (the difference between 100 percent and the percentage in col. 6) of all expenses.

C-15

TABLE C–15

Columns 1 and 2 – 1899–1919: *Census of Manufactures,* 1920, vol. VIII, p. 14.

Column 3 – 1899–1919: Derived from col. 2.

Column 4 – 1899–1914: Col. 3 applied to 1919 figure.
   1919: Derived by subtracting an estimate for depletion from the combined amount of depreciation and depletion reported in *Statistics of Income.* Depletion in manufacturing was estimated to be roughly 45 percent of total depletion, which in turn was estimated from a relation to both the value and volume of minerals output (see Table C-46).

Column 5 – 1899–1914: Col. 6 applied to 1919 figure.
   1919: As reported in *Statistics of Income.*

Column 6 – 1899–1919: Based on estimates of interest on long-term debt in manufacturing as given by Kuvin, L., *Private Long-Term Debt in the United States,* 1936, p. 44. The estimate for 1899 was obtained by extrapolation from Kuvin's figure for 1900.

EXPENSES OF ALL MANUFACTURING ESTABLISHMENTS

Selected Years: 1899 to 1919

$ mill. (except cols. 5 and 6)

Year	Wages and salaries	Contract work and factory rent	Taxes	Other expenses	Other expenses and taxes as percent of all expenses	Other expenses as percent of all expenses	All expenses
	1	2	3	4	5	6	7
1899	2 389	–	–	905	–	–	3 294
1904	3 184	217	59	1 177	26.7	–	4 637
1909	4 366	286	340	1 309	26.2	20.8	6 301
1914	5 354	199	562	1 626	–	21.0	7 741
1919	13 425	464	932	3 940	–	21.0	18 761

DEPRECIATION CHARGES AND INTEREST PAYMENTS
OF MANUFACTURING CORPORATIONS

Selected Years: 1899 to 1919

Year	Capital in manufacturing			Depreciation	Interest payments	
	Total	Corporate				
	$ mill.	$ mill.	1919 = 100.0	$ mill.	$ mill.	1919 = 100.0
	1	2	3	4	5	6
1899	8 975	5 816	15.1	130	276	58.7
1904	12 676	9 114	23.7	205	321	68.4
1909	18 428	14 226	37.0	319	369	78.6
1914	22 791	18 666	48.5	419	406	86.4
1919	44 467	38 464	100.0	863	470	100.0

927

Column 1 – 1899–1909: *Census of Manufactures*, 1910, vol. VIII, p. 135.
            1914: *Abstract of the Census of Manufactures*, 1914, p. 374.
            1919: *Census of Manufactures*, 1920, vol. VIII, pp. 14, 108.
            1929: *Census of Manufactures*, 1930, vol. I, pp. 15, 95.
            1939: *Census of Manufactures*, 1940, vol. I, pp. 19, 229.
            1947: Estimated at 0.3 percent below share in value added (*Census of Manufactures*, 1947, vol. I, p. 149), the relationship obtaining in 1939.

Columns 2 to 4 – 1902: *Census of Mines and Quarries*, p. 65 (figure in col. 2 is estimate).
            1909: *XIIIth Census*, vol. XI, p. 33.
            1919: *XIVth Census*, vol. XI, p. 29.
            1929: *XVth Census, Mines and Quarries*, p. 14. (figures in cols. 2 and 3 are estimates).
            1939: *Mineral Industries*, vol. I, p. 113.
            1947: Rough estimates (cf. U.S. Congress, House of Representatives, *Special Depletion Allowances for Mineral Properties*, Feb. 1950, p. 5: "it is estimated that corporations account for more than 80 percent...of all depletion deductions," most of which arise in production of oil and gas).

Column 1 – 1902–1919: Table C-18, col. 2.

Column 2 – 1902–1919: Col. 1 divided by 0.925. It is assumed here, with some support from *Statistics of Income*, 1922–1924, that nonoperating income constitutes about 7.5 percent of total receipts and hence "value of product," 92.5 percent of total receipts.

Column 3 – 1902: Not applicable.
            1909: Rough estimate.
            1919: *Statistics of Income*.

Column 4 – 1902–1919: Table C-18, col. 6.

Column 5 – 1902, 1909: Not applicable since depletion charges are assumed to have started in 1913 in connection with income tax.
            1919: See note for Table C-18, col. 6.

Column 6 – 1902–1919: Table C-18, col. 8.

Column 7 – 1902: Same as Table C-19, col. 7 since it applies only to corporations.
            1909, 1919: Table C-19, col. 7 multiplied by Table C-18, col. 3.

Column 8 – 1902–1919: Col. 2 minus sum of cols. 3–7.

Column 9 – 1902–1919: Col. 8 plus 20 percent to raise series to level of 1919, as estimated by Kuznets, S., *National Income*, pp. 312, 867.

SHARE OF CORPORATIONS IN VALUE OF OUTPUT IN MANUFACTURING AND MINING

Selected Years: 1899 to 1947

Percent

Year	Manu-facturing	Mining			Year	Manu-facturing	Mining		
		All	Oil and gas	Other			All	Oil and gas	Other
	1	2	3	4		1	2	3	4
1899	66.6	.	.	.	1919	87.7	93.6	88.9	95.5
1902	.	85.0	.	85.9	1929	92.1	93.0	87.7	95.6
1904	73.7	.	.	.	1939	92.6	91.2	87.5	94.0
1909	79.0	91.4	80.6	93.3	1947	91.6	92.0	85.0	95.0
1914	83.2	.	.	.					

NET EARNINGS OF MINING CORPORATIONS

Selected Years: 1902, 1909, 1919

$ mill.

Year	Value of product	Total receipts	Corporate income taxes	Depre-ciation	Depletion	Interest payments	Other expenses	Net earnings	Adjusted net earnings (excluding depletion)
	1	2	3	4	5	6	7	8	9
1902	696	752	–	88	–	15	550	99	119
1909	1 132	1 224	1	148	–	35	952	88	106
1919	2 955	3 195	75	294	181	79	2 381	185	220

C-18   TABLE C–18

Columns 1 and 2 – 1902–1919: Bureau of Census, *Census of Mines and Quarries*, volume for corresponding
         year.

Column 3 – 1902–1919: Col. 2 as percent of col. 1.

Column 4 – 1902–1919: Based on values for 1900, 1912, and 1922 as estimated by Kuznets, S., *National
         Product since 1869*, pp. 202, 213, by assuming a constant rate of increase between census years.

Column 5 – 1902–1919: Col. 3 multiplied by col. 4. Assumes that value of buildings and equipment is pro-
         portional to value of product.

Column 6 – 1902, 1909: Index in col. 7 applied to 1919 estimate.
         1919: Derived by deducting estimated depletion from depreciation and depletion combined
         as reported in *Statistics of Income*. Depletion in mining enterprises was estimated to be
         about 55 percent of total depletion, which in turn was estimated on the basis of relationship
         to value and volume of minerals output.

Column 7 – 1902–1919: Index of col. 5.

Column 8 – 1902: Same as col. 1. Represents interest on bonds. Other interest included in "miscellaneous
         expenses."
         1909: Index in col. 9 applied to 1919 estimate.
         1919: Reported in *Statistics of Income*.

Column 9 – 1902–1919: Based on interest on long-term debt in mining as estimated by Kuvin, L., *Private
         Long-Term Debt and Interest in the United States*, p. 44.

C-19   TABLE C–19

Columns 1, 2, and 4 – 1902–1919: Bureau of the Census, *Census of Mines and Quarries*, volume for corres-
         ponding years. Includes only corporate expenses for 1902.

Column 3 – 1902: Included in miscellaneous expenses (col. 6).
         1909–1919: Same source as col. 1.

Column 5 – 1902: Included in miscellaneous expenses (col. 6).
         1909–1919: Same source as col. 1.

Column 6 – 1902: Same source as col. 1. Includes also rents, royalties, and taxes.
         1909: Same source as col. 1.
         1919: Assumed to be 4 percent of total expenses (col. 7) as in 1909.

Column 7 – 1902–1909: Sum of cols. 1–6.
         1919: Derived by assuming that the expenses listed in cols. 1–5 constitute 96 percent of
         all expenses.

C-20   TABLE C–20

Columns 1 to 5 – Sum of corresponding columns of Tables C-21, C-22, C-23, and C-24. Figures include central
         electric light and power stations, street and electric railways, telephones, and telegraphs.
         Values for col. 5 are at cost.

930

VALUE OF PRODUCT, DEPRECIATION, AND INTEREST PAID
OF MINING ENTERPRISES

Selected Years: 1902, 1909, 1919

Year	Value of product			Value of buildings and equipment		Corporate depreciation		Interest paid	
	Total	Corporate		Total	Corporate				
	$ mill.	$ mill.	Percent	$ mill.	$ mill.	$ mill.	1919=100.0	$ mill.	1919=100.0
	1	2	3	4	5	6	7	8	9
1902	797	696	87.3	820	716	88	29.9	15	25.0
1909	1 238	1 132	91.4	1 320	1 206	148	50.3	35	44.4
1919	3 158	2 955	93.6	2 560	2 396	294	100.0	79	100.0

EXPENSES OF MINING ENTERPRISES

Selected Years: 1902, 1909, 1919

$ mill.

Year	Salaries and wages	Materials, supplies, fuel, and power	Royalties and rents	Contract work	Taxes (excluding federal income tax)	Miscellaneous expenses	Total
	1	2	3	4	5	6	7
1902	354	111	–	20	–	65	550
1909	640	248	64	29	17	44	1 042
1919	1 445	677	175	79	66	102	2 544

EARNINGS AND CORPORATE SAVING OF ELECTRIC UTILITIES

Selected Years: 1902 to 1922

$ mill.

Year	Net income	Gross dividends	Corporate saving	Depreciation	Plant and equipment
	1	2	3	4	5
1902	95	60	35	29	3 202
1907	161	105	56	56	5 722
1912	206	146	60	84	8 000
1917	253	190	63	117	9 748
1922	392	260	132	204	11 745

TABLE C-21

C-21

Columns 1, 2, and 5 – 1902–1922: *Census of Electrical Industries, Electric Stations,* 1902, 1907, 1912, 1917, and 1922. Figures include both operating and holding companies. Combined income account, excluding intercorporate payments and receipts for leases.

Column 3 – 1902, 1907: Rough estimate.
 1912, 1917, 1922: Same source as for col. 1.

Column 4 – 1902–1922: Col. 1 plus col. 3 minus col. 2.

Column 6 – 1902–1922: Col. 4 minus col. 5.

Column 7 – 1902, 1907: Assumed at 0.85 percent of col. 8, the percentage indicated by 1912 data. In these two years, depreciation, if and when charged, was included with "miscellaneous expenses."
 1912, 1917, 1922: Same source as for col. 1.

Column 8 – 1902–1922: Same source as for col. 1. Amount represents value of plant and equipment (including land) at cost. In most cases this amount is net of depreciation.

TABLE C-22

C-22

Columns 1 and 4 – 1902–1922: *Census of Electrical Industries, Telegraph* for 1902, 1907, 1912, 1917, and 1922. Figures include land telegraph, ocean cable, and wireless.

Column 2 – 1902–1922: Same source as for col. 1. Does not include depreciation charges for 1902 and 1907. Includes sinking fund charges for 1912, which are negligible.

Column 3 – 1902–1907: Col. 1 minus cols. 2 and 6 except for rounding. Does not include net income of wireless companies, which was negligible for these years.
 1912: Col. 1 minus col. 2. Does not include net income of wireless companies, which was negligible for this year.
 1917–1922: Col. 1 minus col. 2 plus net income of wireless companies, which was estimated to be $2 million in 1917 and amounted to $3 million in 1922.

Column 5 – 1902–1922: Col. 3 minus col. 4.

Column 6 – 1902–1907: Assumed to be 2.5 percent of col. 7, or half the 1917 percentage. This lower rate of depreciation was based on the assumption that exclusion of depreciation from expenses was partly offset by more liberal allowances for maintenance charges.
 1912, 1922: Assumed to be 5 percent of col. 7, the percentage indicated by 1917 data.
 1917: Same source as for col. 1.

Column 7 – 1902–1922: Same source as for col. 1. Amount represents value at cost and includes land. In most cases amount is net of depreciation.

932

EARNINGS AND CORPORATE SAVING
OF COMMERCIAL CENTRAL ELECTRIC STATIONS
Selected Years: 1902 to 1922

$ mill.

Year	Gross income	Expenses	Charges for sinking fund	Net income	Dividends	Corporate saving	Depreciation	Plant and equipment
	1	2	3	4	5	6	7	8
1902	78.7	62.8	0.5	16.4	6.2	10.2	4.1	483.0
1907	157.8	121.3	0.8	37.3	19.3	18.0	9.0	1054.0
1912	274.5	214.4	1.5	61.6	34.6	27.0	18.0	2099.0
1917	480.9	391.1	4.2	94.0	64.6	29.4	26.3	2933.0
1922	979.0	786.0	5.1	198.1	129.2	68.9	59.3	4229.0

EARNINGS AND CORPORATE SAVING OF TELEGRAPH COMPANIES

Selected Years: 1902 to 1922

$ mill.

Year	Gross income	Expenses	Net income	Dividends	Corporate saving	Depreciation	Plant and equipment
	1	2	3	4	5	6	7
1902	40.9	30.9	6.0	6.3	−0.3	4.0	162.0
1907	51.6	41.9	4.7	7.5	−2.8	5.2	210.0
1912	64.7	58.4	6.3	6.2	0.1	11.2	223.0
1917	109.7	91.9	19.8	9.8	10.0	12.2	243.0
1922	151.9	128.0	26.9	10.7	16.2	16.0	327.0

TABLE C-23

Columns 1, 2, and 4 – 1902–1922: *Census of Electrical Industries, Telephones* for 1902, 1907, 1912, 1917, and 1922.

Column 3 – 1902–1922: Col. 1 minus col. 2.

Column 5 – 1902–1922: Col. 3 minus col. 4.

Column 6 – 1902, 1907, 1912: Assumed at 4.4 percent of col. 7, the percentage indicated by 1917 data. 1917, 1922: Same source as for col. 1.

Column 7 – 1902–1922: Same source as for col. 1. Amount represents value at cost and also includes land. In most cases amount is net of depreciation.

TABLE C-24

Columns 1 and 2 – 1902–1922: *Census of Electrical Industries, Street and Electric Railways*, 1902, 1907, 1912, 1917, and 1922. Figures include both operating and holding companies. Combined income account, excluding intercorporate payments and receipts for leases. For 1902 and 1907 $4 and $7 million added to published figures to take account of charges for sinking fund included in reported gross income from 1912 on.

Column 3 – 1902–1922: Col. 1 minus col. 2 and minus net income of municipal railways. The last item was $4 million in 1922, $2 million in 1917, and negligible for earlier years.

Column 4 – 1902–1922: Same source as for col. 1.

Column 5 – 1902–1922: Col. 3 minus col. 4.

Column 6 – 1902–1907: Assumed to be 0.16 percent of col. 7, percentage indicated by 1912 data, since in these two years depreciation, if and when charged, was included with "miscellaneous expenses." 1912–1922: Same source as for col. 1.

Column 7 – 1902–1922: Same source as for col. 1. Amount represents value at cost and includes land. In most cases amount is net of depreciation.

EARNINGS AND CORPORATE SAVING OF TELEPHONE COMPANIES
Selected Years: 1902 to 1922

$ mill.

Year	Gross income	Expenses	Net income	Dividends	Corporate saving	Depreciation	Plant and equipment
	1	2	3	4	5	6	7
1902	86.5	64.9	21.6	15.0	6.6	17.1	389.0
1907	183.8	140.2	43.6	23.7	19.9	36.1	820.0
1912	254.0	203.0	51.0	34.1	16.9	47.5	1081.0
1917	373.0	314.0	59.0	42.3	16.7	63.0	1436.0
1922	657.0	560.0	97.0	66.0	31.0	94.0	2130.0

EARNINGS AND CORPORATE SAVING OF ELECTRIC AND STREET RAILWAYS
Selected Years: 1902 to 1922

$ mill.

Year	Gross income	Expenses	Net income	Dividends	Corporate saving	Depreciation	Plant and equipment
	1	2	3	4	5	6	7
1902	254.5	203.1	51.4	33.0	18.4	3.5	2168.0
1907	437.2	361.4	75.8	54.5	21.3	5.8	3638.0
1912	586.0	499.0	87.0	71.0	16.0	7.4	4597.0
1917	731.0	649.0	80.0	73.0	7.0	15.9	5136.0
1922	1050.0	976.0	70.0	54.0	16.0	35.0	5059.0

Column 1 – 1896–1905: March 1 interpolated from estimates for Aug. 31 as given in *Annual Report of the Comptroller of the Currency*, 1937.
1906: March 1, *ibid*.
1907–1915: June 30, *ibid*.

Column 2 – 1896–1905: Year ending March 1 of following year (see *Annual Report of the Comptroller of the Currency*, 1920, vol. I). Not adjusted to calendar year basis.
1906–1908: Interpolated estimates for year ending Aug. 31 based on *Annual Report of the Comptroller of the Currency*, 1937.
1909–1915: Amounts represent averages of successive June 30 figures from *Annual Report of the Comptroller of Currency*, 1920, vol. I, as reprinted in *Banking and Monetary Statistics*, p. 261.

Column 3 – 1896–1915: Col. 2 expressed as percent of col. 1.

Column 4 – 1896–1915: Same sources as for col. 2.

Column 5 – 1896–1915: Col. 4 expressed as percent of col. 1.

Column 6 – 1896–1915: Col. 2 minus col. 4, using unrounded figures.

Column 7 – 1896–1915: Col. 3 minus col. 5.

Column 8 – 1896–1915: Figures for all reporting banks less mutual savings banks as given in *Annual Report of the Comptroller of the Currency*, 1920, vol. I.

Column 9 – 1896–1915: Percentages of col. 3 applied to col. 8, using unrounded figures.

Column 10 – 1896–1915: Percentages of col. 5 applied to col. 8, using unrounded figures.

Column 11 – 1896–1915: Col. 9 minus col. 10.

C-26   TABLE C–26

Column 1 – 1909–1915: *Statistics of Income*, 1943, part 2, table 15, p. 340. Net income data for the years 1909–1912 include only net income of corporations with net income of $5,000 or more; those for the years 1913–1915 include net income of all corporations with net income.

Column 2 – 1909–1915: Adjusted to include net income of all corporations with net income of less than $5,000 in the years 1909–1912 (see col. 1). The adjustment was based on assumption that net income of corporations with net income of $5,000 or more constituted about 96 percent of net income of all corporations with net income.

Column 3 – 1909–1915: Derived as follows: first, a line of regression, $\log y = 4.64435 - 0.0321838x$, was computed for the years 1916–1929, where y represented ratio of deficit of all corporations to net income before taxes (*Statistics of Income* data) and x represented Persons' index (*Forecasting Business Cycles*) of production and trade (expressed in percent of trend); then, another line of regression, $D = -5.21648 + 0.274066t$, was computed for the deviations of the actual ratios from the trend of the computed ratios over time; next, the two regression lines were extrapolated back to 1909 and the results combined to yield estimated ratios. For the years 1909–1912, these estimated ratios were used without any further adjustments. For the years 1913–1915, however, an additional adjustment was necessary to take account of the inclusion of dividends received in the given net income figures. On the basis of later years, it was estimated that the ratio of deficit to net income, including dividends received, was about 75 percent of the ratio computed after excluding dividends received. This percentage was then applied to the ratios computed from the two regression lines to yield the final estimates for 1913–1915.

Column 4 – 1909–1915: Col. 2 multiplied by the difference of col. 3 from unity.

Column 5 – 1909–1915: Col. 4 minus taxes, as given in *Statistics of Income*, 1943, part 2, p. 340 (cf. col. 1).

Column 6 – 1909–1915: Based on estimates of net dividends by Martin, R. F., *National Income in the United States 1799–1938*, p. 42.

Column 7 – 1909–1912: Sum of cols. 5 and 6.
1913–1915: Same as col. 5.

EARNINGS, DIVIDENDS, AND CORPORATE SAVING OF COMMERCIAL BANKS
1896 to 1915

C-25

$ mill.

Year	National banks							All commercial banks			
	Capital and surplus	Net earnings		Dividends		Corporate saving		Capital and surplus	Net earnings	Dividends	Corporate saving
		Absolute amount	Ratio of capital and surplus	Absolute amount	Ratio of capital and surplus	Absolute amount	Ratio of capital and surplus				
	$ mill.	$ mill.	Percent	$ mill.	Percent	$ mill.	Percent	$ mill.			
	1	2	3	4	5	6	7	8	9	10	11
1896	901	49	5.4	43	4.8	5	0.6	1 446	78	69	9
1897	882	46	5.2	44	5.0	2	0.2	1 423	74	71	3
1898	871	49	5.7	45	5.2	4	0.5	1 404	80	73	7
1899	856	70	8.2	47	5.5	23	2.7	1 390	114	77	37
1900	873	88	10.0	50	5.8	38	4.2	1 497	150	86	64
1901	913	99	10.9	65	7.1	34	3.8	1 586	173	113	60
1902	1 010	103	10.2	60	6.0	43	4.2	1 802	184	108	76
1903	1 090	117	10.7	74	6.8	43	3.9	2 048	219	139	80
1904	1 149	105	9.2	71	6.2	34	3.0	2 206	203	137	66
1905	1 198	114	9.5	81	6.7	33	2.8	2 332	221	157	64
1906	1 263	146	11.6	99	7.9	47	3.7	2 554	296	201	95
1907	1 419	156	11.0	109	7.6	48	3.4	2 811	309	214	95
1908	1 483	131	8.8	95	6.4	36	2.4	2 931	259	188	71
1909	1 528	143	9.3	100	6.5	43	2.8	2 924	273	190	83
1910	1 634	156	9.5	110	6.7	45	2.8	3 179	302	214	88
1911	1 692	153	9.1	118	6.9	36	2.2	3 231	293	224	69
1912	1 728	155	9.0	120	7.0	35	2.0	3 347	301	233	68
1913	1 778	155	8.7	120	6.8	35	1.9	3 504	305	238	67
1914	1 782	138	7.8	117	6.6	21	1.2	3 566	277	235	42
1915	1 791	142	7.9	114	6.4	28	1.5	3 606	286	230	56

NET EARNINGS OF CORPORATIONS
ESTIMATED FROM BUREAU OF INTERNAL REVENUE DATA: 1909 to 1915

C-26

$ mill.

Year	Corporations with net income		Ratio of deficit to net income	Net earnings of all corporations		Estimated dividends received by corporations	Net earnings including dividends received
	As reported	Adjusted		Before taxes	After taxes		
	1	2	3	4	5	6	7
1909	3 590	3 740	0.26	2 768	2 747	301	3 048
1910	3 761	3 918	0.22	3 056	3 022	393	3 415
1911	3 503	3 649	0.30	2 554	2 525	418	2 943
1912	4 151	4 324	0.20	3 459	3 424	405	3 829
1913	4 714	4 714	0.16	3 960	3 917	408	3 917
1914	3 940	3 940	0.36	2 522	2 483	388	2 483
1915	5 310	5 310	0.24	4 036	3 979	351	3 979

937

TABLE C-27

Columns 1 to 10 – Table C-28 minus Table C-29.

TABLE C-28

Column 1 – 1916–1921: Estimate of Ebersole, J. F., Burr, S., and Peterson, G. M., excluding special exemptions of life insurance companies ("Income Forecasting By the Use of Statistics of Income Data," *Review of Economic Statistics*, vol. XI, 1929, pp. 180, 181, line 54 minus line 45).
1922: *Statistics of Income.*

Column 2 – 1916–1922: Net income minus deficit minus tax as given in *Statistics of Income*, adjusted in 1918–1921 by adding dividends received and tax exempt interest. Dividends received were derived from estimates of gross and net dividends shown in Table C-30. No adjustment for dividends received was necessary for 1916 and 1917, as they were already included in reported income. Tax exempt interest was derived by applying the 1922 percentage distribution by industry division (as reported in *Statistics of Income*, 1922) to the given or estimated totals (see Ebersole, Burr, and Peterson, *op. cit.*, line 15).

Column 3 – 1916–1922: Same source as for col. 2.

Column 4 – 1916–1922: Same source as for col. 2 except that 1916 data were adjusted to make group more comparable with later data by excluding building construction, contract construction, and engineering.

Column 5 – 1916–1922: Same source as for col. 2.

Column 6 – 1916: No separate estimate made as *Statistics of Income*, 1916, does not classify this group separately, and contract construction, building construction, and engineering, which were originally included in manufacturing, did not seem upon examination to constitute entire major industry division of "construction." Hence it was thought best to consolidate data for these minor divisions with those of trade, finance, service, and miscellaneous, especially as 1916 data for latter also seemed to be inconsistent with later years. Finally adjustments were made to the combined net income of these groups to include tax exempt interest as indicated in col. 2 and to exclude special exemption of life insurance companies from finance as noted in col. 8.
1917–1922: Same source as for col. 2.

Column 7 – 1916: See col. 6 for same year.
1917–1922: Same source as for col. 2.

Column 8 – 1916: See col. 6 for same year. Special exemption of life insurance companies was eliminated from net income of finance division to make data comparable with 1921 and later years. For estimates of this exemption cf. Ebersole, Burr, and Peterson, *op. cit.*, line 45.
1917–1920: Same source as for col. 2 with additional elimination of special exemption of life insurance companies, as noted for 1916.
1921–1922: Same source as for col. 2.

Column 9 – 1916: See col. 6 for same year.
1917–1922: Same source as for col. 2. An additional adjustment was made for the years 1918–1921 to include personal service corporations as these were exempt by law from filing corporation income tax returns. Estimates of net income of these corporations were made by Ebersole, Burr, and Peterson, (*op. cit.*, line 40 minus line 52).

Column 10 – 1916: See col. 6 for same year.
1917–1922: Same source as for col. 2.

Note: Details may not add to total because of rounding.

938

CORPORATE SAVING BY MAJOR INDUSTRIAL GROUPS
1916 to 1922
$ mill.

Year	Total	Agri-culture	Mining	Manu-facturing	Trans-portation and other public utilities	Con-struction	Trade	Finance	Service	Miscel-laneous
	1	2	3	4	5	6	7	8	9	10
1916	4 908	0	325	2 587	871			1 125		
1917	4 715	2	221	2 968	538	64	698	322	0	−98
1918	1 923	−21	−9	1 218	184	38	277	55	45	137
1919	4 316	26	−5	2 619	463	68	726	318	117	−16
1920	1 424	−35	136	896	254	35	9	122	84	−78
1921	−2 622	−77	−449	−1 758	81	−25	−462	87	38	−57
1922	1 746	−22	−153	1 023	294	−1	307	270	26	3

NET CORPORATE EARNINGS BY MAJOR INDUSTRIAL GROUPS
1916 to 1922
$ mill.

Year	Total	Agri-culture	Mining	Manu-facturing	Trans-portation and other public utilities	Con-struction	Trade	Finance	Service	Miscel-laneou
	1	2	3	4	5	6	7	8	9	10
1916	7 908	46	714	3 852	1 441			1 855		
1917	8 340	61	709	4 469	1 183	74	1 115	730	31	−32
1918	4 964	22	344	2 506	696	50	662	420	74	191
1919	7 292	53	220	3 919	993	83	1 136	708	147	33
1920	4 855	−8	392	2 454	784	58	404	622	169	−21
1921	517	−50	−209	−345	581	10	−129	587	108	−36
1922	5 183	5	70	2 528	944	37	629	862	82	27

Column 1 – 1916–1921: Sum of net dividends paid and dividends received, as estimated by Ebersole, J. F., Burr, S., and Peterson, G. M. ("Income Forecasting by the Use of Statistics of Income Data," *Review of Economic Statistics*, vol. XI, 1929).
1922: *Statistics of Income*.

Column 2 – 1916–1918: Relationship of net to gross dividends prevailing in 1922 applied to estimates for net dividends. An adjustment was then made to bring estimates into line with total in col. 1.
1919–1921: Assumed to be the same as in 1922. This parallels the assumption of Kuznets (see *National Income*, p. 316) regarding net dividends in agriculture.
1922: Same source as col. 1.

Column 3 – 1916–1918: Based on estimates by King (*The National Income and Its Purchasing Power*, tables XXXIV and XXXV, pp. 182, 184, respectively) linked to 1919 value. An adjustment was then made to bring estimates into line with total in col. 1, having due regard to level of net dividends.
1919–1921: Based on estimates by Kuznets (see *National Income*, p. 867) linked to 1922 value. Adjustment was then made to bring estimates into line with total in col. 1, having due regard to level of net dividends.
1922: Same source as for col. 1.

Column 4 – 1916–1922: Same sources and procedure as for col. 3.

Column 5 – 1916–1921: Same procedure as for col. 2, 1916–1918.
1922: Same source as for col. 1.

Column 6 – 1916–1921: Same source as for col. 2, 1916–1918. It was assumed that net dividends were 65 percent of gross dividends.
1922: Same source as for col. 1.

Column 7 – 1916–1921: Same procedure as for col. 2, 1916–1918. It was assumed here that gross dividends were 7 percent higher than net dividends.
1922: Same source as for col. 1.

Column 8 – 1916–1921: Same procedure as for col. 2, 1916–1918. Net dividends were assumed at 62 percent of gross dividends.
1922: Same source as for col. 1.

Column 9 – 1916–1918: Approximately follows movement of net dividends.
1919–1921: Kuznets, *National Income*, p. 889, with slight adjustment in 1919.
1922: Same source as for col. 1.

Column 10 – 1916–1921: Approximately follows movement of gross dividends with adjustments to bring estimates into line with total of col. 1.
1922: Same source as for col. 1.

C-30   TABLE C–30

Columns 1 to 10 – Table C-29 minus Table C-31.

GROSS DIVIDEND PAYMENTS BY MAJOR INDUSTRIAL GROUPS
1916 to 1922
$ mill.

Year	Total	Agri-culture	Mining	Manu-facturing	Con-struction	Trans-portation and other public utilities	Trade	Finance	Service	Miscel-laneous
	1	2	3	4	5	6	7	8	9	10
1916	3 000	46	389	1 265	3	570	308	346	23	50
1917	3 625	59	488	1 501	10	645	417	408	31	66
1918	3 041	43	353	1 288	12	512	385	365	29	54
1919	2 976	27	225	1 300	15	530	410	390	30	49
1920	3 431	27	256	1 558	23	530	395	500	85	57
1921	3 139	27	240	1 413	35	500	333	500	70	21
1922	3 437	27	223	1 505	38	650	322	592	56	24

DIVIDENDS RECEIVED BY CORPORATIONS
BY MAJOR INDUSTRIAL GROUPS: 1916 to 1922

$ mill.

Year	Total	Agri-culture	Mining	Manu-facturing	Con-struction	Trans-portation and other public utilities	Trade	Finance	Service	Miscel-laneous
	1	2	3	4	5	6	7	8	9	10
1916	500	4	36	114	1	189	12	125	2	17
1917	600	8	55	83	2	232	32	158	3	27
1918	421	3	35	54	3	155	23	127	3	18
1919	376	3	20	41	2	155	10	130	1	14
1920	531	3	36	73	5	187	13	186	5	23
1921	509	3	47	90	7	169	13	170	4	6
1922	803	3	84	197	5	250	20	226	7	11

Column 1 – 1916–1922: Estimates by Ebersole, J. F., Burr, S., and Peterson, G. M. ("Income Forecasting by the Use of Statistics of Income Data," *Review of Economic Statistics,* vol. XI, 1929, pp. 180, 181).

Columns 2 to 9 – 1916–1918: Derived by linking the data developed by Robert F. Martin to the 1919 estimates (cf. *National Income in the United States,* table 13, p. 42) and then adjusting to the given totals of col. 1 by distributing the differences proportionately.
1919–1921: Derived by linking the data developed by Kuznets (*National Income,* table 54, p. 316) to the 1922 data.
1922: From *Statistics of Income.*

Column 10 – 1916–1918, 1921: Estimated by assuming the same percentage change from preceding year as for the sum of all other industry divisions, except as otherwise indicated.
1919–1920, 1922: From *Statistics of Income.*

Columns 1 to 10 – 1922–1945: *Statistics of Income,* various issues. Total for 1942 (col. 1) is less than sum of amounts for industry divisions because of $16 million of taxes which were deducted from total but could not be allocated by industry division. Figures for 1928, 1929, 1930, 1934 are revised Bureau of Internal Revenue data.
1946–1948: *Treasury Department Press Releases S-1051* (April 21, 1949), *S-2449* (Sept. 22, 1950), and *S-2808* (Sept. 20, 1951).

Note: Details may not add to total because of rounding.

NET DIVIDEND PAYMENTS BY MAJOR INDUSTRIAL GROUPS
1916 to 1922

C-31

$ mill.

Year	Total	Agri-culture	Mining	Manu-facturing	Con-struction	Trans-portation and other public utilities	Trade	Finance	Service	Miscel-laneous
	1	2	3	4	5	6	7	8	9	10
1916	2 500	42	353	1 151	2	381	296	221	21	33
1917	3 025	51	433	1 418	8	413	385	250	28	39
1918	2 620	40	318	1 234	9	357	362	238	26	36
1919	2 600	24	205	1 259	13	375	400	260	29	35
1920	2 900	24	220	1 485	18	343	382	314	80	34
1921	2 630	24	193	1 323	28	331	320	330	66	15
1922	2 634	24	139	1 308	33	400	302	366	49	13

CORPORATE SAVING BY MAJOR INDUSTRIAL GROUPS: 1922 to 1948
(Bureau of Internal Revenue Data)

C-32

$ mill.

Year	Total	Agri-culture	Mining	Manu-facturing	Con-struction	Trans-portation and other public utilities	Trade	Finance	Service	Miscel-laneous
	1	2	3	4	5	6	7	8	9	10
1922	1 746	−22	−153	1 023	−1	294	307	270	26	3
1923	2 528	9	−292	1 413	20	607	460	246	43	21
1924	1 575	−28	−296	766	46	367	306	367	44	3
1925	2 957	−17	−69	1 338	37	505	394	713	55	0
1926	2 336	−17	−98	1 096	50	572	236	481	23	−8
1927	1 114	−29	−273	447	45	146	173	618	−7	−3
1928	2 400	−17	−154	944	33	380	278	931	7	−3
1929	2 156	−11	−166	1 214	31	448	69	561	15	−6
1930	−4 247	−64	−305	−1 737	−14	−609	−640	−789	−80	−12
1931	−7 327	−106	−392	−2 807	−76	−957	−985	−1 781	−207	−16
1932	−8 001	−98	−306	−2 942	−131	−1 091	−1 037	−1 904	−477	−13
1933	−4 480	−48	−254	−933	−87	−848	−266	−1 681	−357	−5
1934	−2 485	−47	−213	−474	−53	−727	−100	−625	−239	−6
1935	−1 253	−26	−211	−71	−35	−770	−71	152	−212	−10
1936	−799	−32	−143	166	−24	−476	5	−89	−201	−6
1937	−960	−34	−140	116	−19	−457	−50	−198	−171	−7
1938	−1 742	−27	−194	−435	−9	−610	−137	−256	−58	−15
1939	199	−17	−123	736	−6	−254	137	−227	−35	−13
1940	711	−19	−144	1 364	14	−121	276	−573	−21	−65
1941	2 806	8	−86	2 657	63	137	632	−575	9	−41
1942	5 525	14	−74	2 921	98	923	669	927	88	−25
1943	6 473	20	−31	3 419	62	915	768	1 198	129	−8
1944	5 606	25	−29	2 625	23	532	795	1 498	141	−3
1945	4 470	42	−36	1 320	22	149	905	1 921	153	−7
1946	9 022	82	−6	3 632	111	105	2 627	2 164	305	2
1947	12 269	79	182	6 177	209	396	2 870	2 082	274	3
1948	13 281	77	275	6 659	300	791	2 553	2 420	212	−7

943

Column 1 – Sum of earnings of the following industry divisions: electric light and power; manufactured gas; steam railways; pullman and railway express; street railways; water transportation; telephone; telegraph; pipe lines. The earnings of each industry division were obtained as follows:

1922–1937: The sum of gross dividends paid and net savings as estimated by Kuznets (*National Income*) except for the adjustments and additions which are indicated in notes to cols. 2 and 3. Net earnings in 1937 for electric light and power industry were taken from Federal Power Commission data (cf. *Statistics of Electrical Utilities in the U.S.*, 1947, p. XVIII).

1938–1947: (a) Electric light and power from same source as for 1937.

(b) Manufactured gas: *Statistics of Income, Source Book*, up to 1945; extrapolated for 1946–1947 on basis of Department of Commerce estimates (cf. *Survey of Current Business*, July 1948, p. 20).

(c) Steam railroads, pullman, and railway express: Interstate Commerce Commission data (*Statistics of Railways*, 1946, and unpublished data).

(d) Street railways: extrapolated on basis of same sources as b.

(e) Water transportation: same as b.

(f) Telephone: sum of gross dividends and net saving.

(g) Telegraph: Federal Communications Commission data (cf. *Statistics of Communications Industry in the U.S.*).

(h) Pipe lines: based on Interstate Commerce Commission data up to 1946 and extrapolated for 1947 as in b.

Column 2 – Sum of gross dividend payments of the same industries as enumerated in notes to col. 1, which were obtained as follows:

1922–1937: Estimated by Kuznets (cf. *National Income* pp. 880–886) except for the following additions and adjustments:

(a) Steam railroads, pullman, and railway express: estimates were made of gross dividends paid for pullman and railway express industries on basis of data from Interstate Commerce Commission and on basis of net dividends paid and added to Kuznets' estimates of gross dividends paid in railroads (*ibid.*, pp. 605 and 882).

(b) Pipe lines: estimated on basis of net dividends paid (*ibid.*, p. 660) for 1920–1921 and from 1922 on basis of Interstate Commerce Commission data.

(c) Electric light and power: Federal Power Commission data for 1937.

1938–1947: Same as col. 1 except that gross dividends for telephone industry are extrapolated on basis of Federal Communication Commission data (cf. *Statistics of Communications Industry in the U.S.*).

Column 3 – Sum of net saving of the same industries as enumerated in notes to col. 1, which were obtained as follows:

1922–1937: Estimated by Kuznets (*op. cit.*, pp. 673–674) except for the following adjustments:

(a) Electric light and power: adjusted to exclude saving of unincorporated business.

(b) Water transportation: same as (a).

(c) Electric light and power: based on Federal Power Commission data for 1937.

1938–1947: Difference between net earnings and gross dividends except for telephone industry, where net saving was directly extrapolated on basis of Federal Communications Commission data.

Columns 4 and 5 – 1922–1947: From *Statistics of Income*, various issues.

Column 6 – 1922–1947: From Table C-32, col. 6.

Columns 7 to 9 – 1922–1947: Differences between cols. 4 and 1, 5 and 2, and 6 and 3, respectively. Computed from unrounded figures.

944

COMPARISON OF BUREAU OF INTERNAL REVENUE AND AGENCY DATA ON NET EARNINGS, DIVIDENDS, AND CORPORATE SAVING OF PUBLIC UTILITIES: 1922 to 1947

$ mill.

Year	Agency data			Bureau of Internal Revenue data			Difference		
	Earnings	Dividends	Saving	Earnings	Dividends	Saving	Earnings	Dividends	Saving
	1	2	3	4	5	6	7	8	9
1922	904	677	227	944	650	294	40	−27	67
1923	1 209	762	447	1 270	663	607	61	−99	160
1924	1 202	831	372	1 292	925	367	90	94	−5
1925	1 599	955	644	1 512	1 007	505	−87	52	−139
1926	1 698	1 011	687	1 849	1 277	572	151	266	−115
1927	1 640	1 197	442	1 753	1 607	146	113	410	−296
1928	1 926	1 228	699	2 033	1 653	380	107	425	−319
1929	2 262	1 506	756	2 541	2 093	448	279	587	−308
1930	1 820	1 688	131	1 615	2 224	−609	−205	536	−740
1931	1 276	1 479	−203	840	1 797	−957	−436	318	−754
1932	759	1 235	−476	222	1 313	−1 091	−537	78	−615
1933	789	980	−190	152	1 000	−848	−637	20	−658
1934A	774	991	−217				−280	230	−510
1934B	768	983	−215	494	1 221	−727	−274	238	−512
1935	827	1 045	−218	514	1 284	−770	−313	239	−552
1936	1 218	1 007	211	860	1 336	−476	−358	329	−687
1937	1 202	1 080	123	904	1 361	−457	−298	281	−580
1938	883	948	−64	507	1 117	−610	−376	169	−546
1939	1 276	1 062	214	955	1 209	−254	−321	147	−468
1940	1 468	1 160	308	954	1 075	−121	−514	−85	−429
1941	1 749	1 134	615	1 224	1 087	137	−525	−47	−478
1942	2 041	991	1 050	2 053	1 130	923	12	139	−127
1943	2 079	957	1 122	2 091	1 176	915	12	219	−207
1944	1 810	1 095	715	1 759	1 227	532	−51	132	−183
1945	1 571	1 005	566	1 392	1 243	149	−179	238	−417
1946	1 616	1 192	424	1 448	1 343	105	−168	151	−319
1947	1 719	1 220	499	1 704	1 308	396	−15	88	−103

ADDITIONAL CORPORATE PROFITS DISCLOSED
BY BUREAU OF INTERNAL REVENUE AUDIT: 1916 to 1947

$ mill.

Year	Reported additional profits before tax	Estimated additional profits before tax		Reported additional profits after tax	Estimated additional profits after tax	
		Method I	Method II		Method I	Method II
	1	2	3	4	5	6
1916	–	611	596	–	599	584
1917	–	715	664	–	572	531
1918	–	647	582	–	402	362
1919	–	668	637	–	514	490
1920	–	597	566	–	474	449
1921	–	446	441	–	374	370
1922	–	552	533	–	485	469
1923	–	609	580	–	535	510
1924	–	623	593	–	548	522
1925	–	693	672	–	606	588
1926	–	699	685	–	608	596
1927	–	675	663	–	588	577
1928	–	733	733	–	684	684
1929	854	–	–	763	–	–
1930	590	–	–	523	–	–
1931	405	–	–	360	–	–
1932	316	–	–	272	–	–
1933	432	–	–	371	–	–
1934	560	–	–	482	–	–
1935	610	–	–	523	–	–
1936	584	–	–	486	–	–
1937	629	–	–	519	–	–
1938	505	–	–	417	–	–
1939	673	–	–	555	–	–
1940	571	–	–	382	–	.
1941	918	–	–	445	–	–
1942	919	–	–	363	–	–
1943	1 300	–	–	517	–	–
1944	1 670	–	–	650	–	–
1945	1 100	–	–	497	–	–
1946	1 150	–	–	733	–	–
1947	1 350	–	–	860	–	–

Columns 1 and 4 – 1929–1947: Survey of Current Business, National Income Supplement, July 1947 and July 1950, table 38; The figures are based on Bureau of Internal Revenue data.

Column 2 – 1916–1928: Estimated from the 1929–1941 regression of reported additional profits before tax on compiled net profits before tax of all corporations. The regression equation (in $ mill. and designating additional profits by y, and compiled net profits by x) is $y = 0.02796x + 433$; $r = 0.939$.

Column 3 – 1916–1928: Estimated from the 1929–1941 regression of reported additional profits before tax on compiled profits before tax of corporations with net income. The regression equation (in $ mill. and designating additional profits by y' and compiled profits of corporations with net income by z) is $y' = 0.03492z + 290$: $\bar{r} = 0.921$.

Columns 5 and 6 – 1916–1928: Obtained by multiplying cols. 2 and 3 respectively with 1.00 minus the average proportion of compiled net profits taken by taxes for corporations with net income, both taken from *Statistics of Income.*

UNRECORDED DEPRECIATION OF RAILWAYS
ON WAY AND STRUCTURES
(Excluding Track): 1897 to 1942

$ mill.

Year	Amount	Year	Amount	Year	Amount	Year	Amount
1897	46	1909	55	1921	64	1932	73
1898	46	1910	56	1922	65	1933	74
1899	47	1911	57	1923	65	1934	75
1900	48	1912	58	1924	66	1935	76
1901	49	1913	58	1925	66	1936	77
1902	50	1914	59	1926	67	1937	75
1903	50	1915	60	1927	66	1938	74
1904	51	1916	60	1928	68	1939	73
1905	52	1917	60	1929	69	1940	72
1906	53	1918	62	1930	70	1941	65
1907	54	1919	63	1931	71	1942	50
1908	54	1920	63				

1897–1914: Extrapolated on assumption of increase of $0.8 million per year, the average for 1915–1935.

1915–1941: Stevens, W. H. S. and Hobbs, E. S., *Analysis of Steam Railway Dividends 1890–1941*, Interstate Commerce Commission statement 4368, Nov. 1943, mimeographed, p. 95, col. 10.

1942: Rough estimate constructed to bring total depreciation allowances on way and structures (recorded and unrecorded) in 1942 to the midpoint between the 1941 and the 1943 values. (Recorded depreciation allowances on way and structures of Class I roads, according to *Statistics of Railways*, table 89, increased from $7 million in 1940 to $14 million in 1941 and $41 million in 1942 and then jumped, with the compulsory introduction of such allowances to $103 million in 1943 slowly rising to $121 million in 1946.)

C-36

TABLE C–36

Columns 1 to 3 – Bureau of Internal Revenue data (cf. *Survey of Current Business, National Income Number,* July 1947, table 38; July 1950, p. 27). Figures cover only refunds not reported on original tax returns.

Columns 4 to 6 – Department of Commerce estimates (*ibid.*). For 1945 included in depreciation and amortization allowances reported in *Statistics of Income.*

Column 7 – Same source as for cols. 1–3.

Column 8 – Sum of cols. 3 and 6 minus col. 7; in 1942 includes deduction for war losses (*Survey of Current Business, loc. cit.*).

C-37

TABLE C–37

Columns 1 and 2 – 1914–1941: *Banking and Monetary Statistics,* p. 356. 1942–1949: *Federal Reserve Bulletin,* Feb. issues. Net earnings are after all payments to and from contingency reserves.

Column 3 – 1914–1949: Col. 1 minus col. 2.

Column 4 – 1927–1941: *Annual Report of the Board of Governors of the Federal Reserve System.* 1942–1949: *Federal Reserve Bulletin,* Feb. issues. Net capital gains, all on U.S. Government securities, are included in col. 1.

SPECIAL WORLD WAR II DEDUCTIONS FROM REPORTED INCOME
1941 to 1945

$ mill.

Year	Renegotiation refunds			Emergency amortization acceleration				Total
	Gross	Taxes	Net	Gross	Taxes	Net	Carry back tax refund	
	1	2	3	4	5	6	7	8
1941	–	–	–	18	9	9	–	9
1942	1 783	1 316	467	145	101	44	–	434
1943	2 893	2 141	752	337	248	89	286	555
1944	1 478	1 106	372	912	699	213	934	–349
1945	522	395	127	–	–	–	139	–12

SAVING OF FEDERAL RESERVE BANKS
1914 to 1949

$ mill.

Year	Net earnings	Dividends	Saving	Net capital gains	Year	Net earnings	Dividends	Saving	Net capital gains
	1	2	3	4		1	2	3	4
1914	0	0	0	–	1932	20	9	11	4
1915	0	0	0	–	1933	8	9	–1	1
1916	3	2	1	–	1934	15	9	6	8
1917	9	7	2	–	1935	9	9	0	7
1918	53	6	47	–	1936	8	8	0	9
1919	76	5	71	–	1937	10	8	2	2
1920	89	6	83	–	1938	9	8	1	8
1921	22	6	16	–	1939	10	8	2	4
1922	6	6	0	–	1940	14	8	6	12
1923	9	7	2	–	1941	9	8	1	1
1924	4	7	–3	–	1942	12	9	3	3
1925	9	7	2	–	1943	37	9	28	36
1926	16	7	9	–	1944	50	10	40	3
1927	13	8	5	0	1945	141	10	131	3
1928	30	8	22	0	1946	92	11	81	2
1929	32	10	22	0	1947	20	12	8	3
1930	8	10	–2	3	1948	30	12	18	6
1931	3	10	–7	3	1949	34	12	22	32

Column 1 – 1916–1925: Table C-39, col. 6.

        1926–1945: From *Statistics of Income, Source Book*; beginning with 1942 the special exemption of life insurance companies is included in the data on corporate income reported in *Statistics of Income*, though excluded for purpose of taxation.

        1946–1947: Estimated on basis of figures for mutual life insurance companies (*Survey of Current Business*, July 1950, p. 27) which in 1943–1945 accounted for about 94 percent of total.

        1948–1949: Rough estimate based on trend in preceding years.

Column 2 – 1916–1925: Assumed to be zero as in 1926.

        1926–1945: Same source as for col. 1.

        1946–1948: From *Spectator Life Insurance Yearbook*.

        1949: Institute of Life Insurance estimates.

Column 3 – 1916–1949: Col. 1 minus col. 2.

Column 4 – 1916–1920: Estimates of Ebersole, J. F., Burr, S., and Peterson, G. M. ("Income Forecasting by the Use of Statistics of Income Data," *Review of Economic Statistics*, vol. xi, 1929, table I, pp. 180–181, line 45).

Column 5 – 1916–1920: Col. 1 minus col. 4. This adjustment will make net profit estimates of this table consistent with those of Table C-28.

Column 6 – 1916–1920: Col. 3 minus col. 4. This adjustment will make saving estimates of this table consistent with those of Table C-27.

ADJUSTMENT OF REPORTED CORPORATE SAVING
FOR SAVING OF LIFE INSURANCE COMPANIES
1916 to 1949

$ mill.

· Year	Net profit (less tax)	Cash dividends	Compiled saving	Special exemption	Adjusted net profits	Adjusted compiled saving
	1	2	3	4	5	6
1916	48	0	48	129	−81	−81
1917	4	0	4	142	−138	−138
1918	−32	0	−32	156	−188	−188
1919	13	0	13	188	−175	−175
1920	60	0	60	221	−161	−161
1921	94	0	94	−	−	−
1922	131	0	131	−	−	−
1923	152	0	152	−	−	−
1924	152	0	152	−	−	−
1925	158	0	158	−	−	−
1926	158	0	158	−	−	−
1927	162	0	162	−	−	−
1928	149	9	140	−	−	−
1929	148	21	127	−	−	−
1930	144	23	121	−	−	−
1931	125	18	107	−	−	−
1932	125	12	113	−	−	−
1933	48	15	33	−	−	−
1934	64	12	52	−	−	−
1935	36	10	26	−	−	−
1936	53	15	38	−	−	−
1937	26	20	6	−	−	−
1938	8	16	−8	−	−	−
1939	5	24	−19	−	−	−
1940	−13	22	−35	−	−	−
1941	−20	15	−35	−	−	−
1942	1 074	16	1 058	−	−	−
1943	1 124	42	1 082	−	−	−
1944	1 175	29	1 146	−	−	−
1945	1 269	32	1 237	−	−	−
1946	1 300	34	1 266	−	−	−
1947	1 380	35	1 345	−	−	−
1948	1 440	40	1 400	−	−	−
1949	1 500	63	1 437	−	−	−

Column 1 – 1916–1926: Statutory net income minus deficit minus total tax. Based on *Statistics of Income*, except for 1917 and 1925, for which years such data were not available. Estimates for these years were based on linear interpolations.

Column 2 – 1916–1926: Estimated at 6 percent of holdings of stock (cf. Table I-6, cols. 6 and 7) as life insurance companies held primarily preferred stock.

Column 3 – 1916–1926: Estimated by applying to holdings of U.S. Government and state and municipal bonds (cf. Table I-6, cols. 1 and 2) yield rates shown in *Banking and Monetary Statistics*, pp. 468, 475. (For 1916–1918 same yield was assumed as in 1919.)

Column 4 – 1916–1921: Col. 2 plus percentage of col. 3, as portion of tax exempt interest was included in net income, being only exempt from normal tax but subject to the excess profits tax. The percentages varied for each year as follows: 1918, 61.1; 1919, 37.5; 1920, 45.5; and 1912, 48.2; and were based on data for all corporations as reported in *Statistics of Income*.
1922–1926: Sum of cols. 2 and 3.

Column 5 – 1916–1926: Col. 4 raised about 6 percent to bring it up to the 1926 level of reported tax exempt income.

Column 6 – 1916–1926: Col. 1 plus col. 5.

Column 1 – 1915–1927: A rough estimate based on relationships prevailing from 1929–1940 between corporate net capital gains and: (a) individual net capital gains; and (b) ratio between stock price index for current year and average for preceding three years. After considerable experimentation with formal correlations, they were abandoned in favor of a judgment estimate rounded to the nearest $100 million.

Consideration was also given to using estimates of net corporate capital gains derived by Kuznets, in *National Income*, p. 895. Kuznets' figures are averages of two estimates. The first is obtained by applying to estimated individuals' net gain on capital assets the geometric mean of the ratio of corporate to individual net gain in 1929 and 1935–1937. The second is based on the net profits of real estate and holding corporations, reported in *Statistics of Income*, and the geometric mean of the ratio of corporate capital gains to them in 1929–1934. These estimates were rejected partly because their rationale did not seem quite satisfactory, and partly because the method yields an estimate for 1928 of $1,188 million, while the reported figure for corporate capital gains (without deduction of the unknown amount of corporate capital losses for that year, which, however, must have been small) amounts to only $722 million. From this and other comparisons the conclusion was reached that the level of Kuznets' estimates is substantially too high.

1928: Based on reported figure of corporate gross capital gains of $722 million and the assumption that corporate capital losses were relatively small.

1929–1944: Bureau of Internal Revenue data taken from Seltzer, *The Nature and Tax Treatment of Capital Gains and Losses*, table 151. Figures represent the difference between capital gains and losses of all corporations. From 1928–1931, all capital gains and losses, both long- and short-term, were recognized by the Bureau of Internal Revenue. In 1932–1933 net loss from sale of stocks and bonds, other than government securities, held for two years or less, could not be deducted except by banks and trust companies. From 1934 through 1939, net loss deduction was limited to $2,000 per corporation except for banks and trust companies; limitation did not apply in 1938–1939 to losses suffered on depreciable property. Losses on transactions of eighteen months or less were not deductible in 1940 and 1941, nor were any net losses from sale of capital assets in 1942 to 1944.

1945–1948: From *Statistics of Income*.

Columns 2 and 3 – 1929–1948: Same source as for col. 1.

DERIVATION OF COMPILED NET PROFITS OF LIFE INSURANCE COMPANIES   C-39

1916 to 1926

$ mill.

Year	Compiled net income	Dividends received	Interest on government bonds received	Tax exempt income		Compiled net profits
				Unadjusted	Adjusted	
	1	2	3	4	5	6
1916	37.1	5.0	10.4	10.4	11.0	48.1
1917	−11.3	5.1	14.5	14.5	15.3	4.0
1918	−59.7	5.3	33.9	25.9	27.5	−32.2
1919	−9.9	5.3	44.5	22.0	23.3	13.4
1920	30.0	5.3	50.8	28.4	30.1	60.1
1921	62.2	4.7	53.2	30.4	32.2	94.4
1922	71.3	4.5	51.3	55.8	59.2	130.5
1923	95.3	4.8	48.8	53.6	56.8	152.1
1924	100.3	4.9	43.8	48.7	51.7	152.0
1925	107.7	5.9	41.1	47.0	49.9	157.6
1926	115.0	6.3	34.3	40.7	43.2	158.2

CORPORATE NET CAPITAL GAINS   C-40

1915 to 1948

$ mill.

Year	All corporations	Financial corporations	Nonfinancial corporations	Year	All corporations	Financial corporations	Nonfinancial corporations
	1	2	3		1	2	3
1915	0	.	.	1932	−1 563	−530	−1 033
1916	100	.	.	1933	−1 423	−511	−912
1917	100	.	.	1934	−55	−1	−54
1918	0	.	.	1935	231	41	190
1919	100	.	.	1936	439	94	345
1920	0	.	.	1937	140	83	57
1921	−200	.	.	1938	75	2	73
1922	100	.	.	1939	76	−4	80
1923	100	.	.	1940	−672	−273	−399
1924	200	.	.	1941	−956	−522	−434
1925	400	.	.	1942	−177	−41	−136
1926	400	.	.	1943	−159	−94	−65
1927	500	.	.	1944	64	−34	98
1928	650	.	.	1945	641	504	137
1929	816	241	575	1946	1 270	748	522
1930	−290	−74	−216	1947	923	464	459
1931	−1 404	−456	−948	1948	974	436	538

953

Column 1 – 1897–1939: Table C-42, col. 6.
           1940–1947: Table C-42, col. 6 minus col. 5.
           1948–1949: Department of Commerce estimates derived from *Survey of Current Business*, July
           1950, tables 5, 6, pp. 10–11.

Column 2 – 1897–1942: Sum of Table C-44, col. 3 and Table C-35.

Column 3 – 1897–1949: The ratio of depreciation allowances on producer durable goods (see Tables P-7, P-9)
           and nonresidential, exclusive of institutional, construction (see Tables R-10, R-12, R-13, R-16),
           based on original cost, to those based on reproduction cost. For the period 1913–1920 the ratios
           were roughly increased by 15 percent to allow for the provision in the income tax law which
           permitted depreciation charges to be based either on original cost or 1913 replacement value,
           whichever was higher. This percent was derived by computing depreciation allowances ad-
           justed for the 1913 value for certain corporate expenditures and comparing them with the
           unadjusted figures.

Column 4 – 1897–1949: Col. 1 divided by col. 3.

Column 5 – 1897–1942: Col. 2 divided by col. 3.

Column 6 – 1897–1949: Col. 4 minus col. 1.

Column 7 – 1897–1942: Col. 5 minus col. 2.

Column 8 – 1897–1949: Sum of cols. 6 and 7.

1897 to 1949

$ mill. (except col. 3)

| Year | Estimated depreciation Original cost | | Trans- formation index (percent) | Estimated depreciation Current cost | | Excess of current over original cost depreciation | | |
	Reported	Unreported in transportation and public utilities		Reported	Unreported in transportation and public utilities	Reported	Unreported in transportation and public utilities	Total
	1	2	3	4	5	6	7	8
1897	297	82	108.2	274	76	−23	−6	−29
1898	322	82	101.4	318	81	−4	−1	−5
1899	348	84	96.1	362	87	14	3	17
1900	381	87	93.5	407	93	26	6	32
1901	410	91	94.9	432	96	22	5	27
1902	444	95	94.7	469	100	25	5	30
1903	483	99	95.6	505	104	22	5	27
1904	526	103	94.8	555	109	29	6	35
1905	574	107	93.1	617	115	43	8	51
1906	625	112	91.3	685	123	60	11	71
1907	681	117	88.8	767	132	86	15	101
1908	735	123	92.2	797	133	62	10	72
1909	796	128	90.8	877	141	81	13	94
1910	840	132	90.2	931	146	91	14	105
1911	883	138	88.0	1 003	157	120	19	139
1912	937	136	88.5	1 059	154	122	18	140
1913	1 000	130	100.5	995	129	−5	−1	−6
1914	1 069	121	102.0	1 048	119	−21	−2	−23
1915	1 145	116	98.0	1 168	118	23	2	25
1916	1 544	111	86.5	1 785	128	241	17	258
1917	1 801	104	74.0	2 434	141	633	37	670
1918	2 333	62	63.5	3 674	98	1 341	36	1 377
1919	1 989	63	59.0	3 371	107	1 382	44	1 426
1920	2 193	63	54.5	4 024	116	1 831	53	1 884
1921	2 339	64	66.6	3 512	96	1 173	32	1 205
1922	2 660	65	77.8	3 419	84	759	19	778
1923	2 712	65	74.8	3 626	87	914	22	936
1924	2 824	66	76.5	3 692	86	868	20	888
1925	2 895	66	77.3	3 745	85	850	19	869
1926	3 270	67	78.3	4 176	86	906	19	925
1927	3 346	66	80.1	4 177	82	831	16	847
1928	3 597	68	81.5	4 413	83	816	15	831
1929	3 871	69	81.8	4 732	84	861	15	876
1930	3 986	70	88.0	4 530	80	544	10	554
1931	4 003	71	94.0	4 259	76	256	5	261
1932	3 693	73	103.2	3 578	71	−115	−2	−117
1933	3 496	74	103.0	3 394	72	−102	−2	−104
1934	3 362	75	94.4	3 561	79	199	4	203
1935	3 352	76	93.7	3 577	81	225	5	230
1936	3 286	77	93.6	3 511	82	225	5	230
1937	3 342	75	87.5	3 819	86	477	11	488
1938	3 352	74	88.2	3 800	84	448	10	458
1839	3 443	73	88.4	3 895	83	452	10	462
1940	3 520	72	87.2	4 037	83	517	11	528
1941	3 765	65	83.9	4 487	77	722	12	734
1942	3 914	50	80.4	4 868	62	954	12	966
1943	3 916	−	79.7	4 913	−	997	−	997
1944	3 950	−	80.0	4 938	−	988	−	988
1945	3 977	−	79.5	5 003	−	1 026	−	1 026
1946	4 199	−	73.3	5 729	−	1 530	−	1 530
1947	5 220	−	66.1	7 897	−	2 677	−	2 677
1948	6 150	−	65.3	9 418	−	3 268	−	3 268
1949	6 750	−	69.1	9 768	−	3 018	−	3 018

Column 1 – 1897–1898: Same rate of change was assumed as for 1900–1904.

        1899–1914: For figures for census years (1899, 1904, 1909, and 1914) see Table C-13, col. 5. Figures for other years estimated by assuming constant rate of change between census years.

        1915–1917: Interpolated between 1914 and 1918 figures on basis of depreciation reported by a group of large corporations (National Bureau of Economic Research, *Corporate Financial Data...*, sec. A, p. 139).

        1918–1924: Derived by subtracting estimated depletion from combined depreciation and depletion reported in *Statistics of Income*. Depletion in manufacturing was estimated at 45 percent of total depletion, which in turn was estimated from relationship to value and volume of minerals output (cf. Tables C-43 and C-46).

        1925–1947: *Statistics of Income*, various issues.

Column 2 – 1897–1917: Same method as for col. 1 (for figures for 1902, 1909, and 1919 see Table C-17, col. 4). Figures for col. 2 shown before and after 1908 are not comparable but those for sum of cols. 1 and 2 probably are.

        1918–1924: Same method as for col. 1. Depletion in mining estimated to be 55 percent of total depletion.

        1925–1947: Same source as for col. 1.

Column 3 – 1897–1916: From Table C-44, col. 7.

        1917: Same method as for col. 1.

        1918–1925: Data reported in *Statistics of Income* raised to account for 18.8 percent of total depreciation and depletion (cf. Table C-43).

        1926–1947: Same source as for col. 1.

Column 4 – 1897–1916: Estimated at 48 percent of depreciation in manufacturing (col. 1) on basis of 1917–1921 average relationship.

        1917–1947: Col. 6 minus sum of cols. 1, 2, 3, and 4, or sum of depreciation allowances for all other groups as reported in *Statistics of Income*.

Column 5 – 1940–1947: *Statistics of Income*, various issues.

Column 6 – 1897–1917: Sum of cols. 1, 2, 3, and 4.

        1918–1925: Amounts reported in *Statistics of Income* raised to include unreported depreciation for transportation and public utilities (cf. col. 3; also Table C-43, col. 5).

        1926–1947: Same source as for col. 1.

ESTIMATED (1897 to 1917) OR REPORTED (1918 to 1947)

$ mill.

Year	Manufacturing	Mining	Transportation and public utilities	Other industries	Accelerated depreciation of war facilities	Total depreciation
	1	2	3	4	5	6
1897	108	61	76	52	—	297
1898	118	66	81	57	—	322
1899	130	71	85	62	—	348
1900	143	76	93	69	—	381
1901	156	82	97	75	—	410
1902	170	88	104	82	—	444
1903	187	94	112	90	—	483
1904	205	101	122	98	—	526
1905	224	109	133	108	—	574
1906	245	117	145	118	—	625
1907	268	126	158	129	—	681
1908	292	136	167	140	—	735
1909	319	148	176	153	—	796
1910	337	154	187	162	—	840
1911	355	160	197	171	—	883
1912	375	166	216	180	—	937
1913	396	172	242	190	—	1 000
1914	419	179	270	201	—	1 069
1915	450	186	293	216	—	1 145
1916	700	193	315	336	—	1 544
1917	850	201	342	408	—	1 801
1918	1 082	209	518	524	—	2 333
1919	863	294	437	395	—	1 989
1920	935	306	504	448	—	2 193
1921	1 019	347	495	478	—	2 339
1922	1 187	365	564	544	—	2 660
1923	1 195	384	606	527	—	2 712
1924	1 210	408	614	592	—	2 824
1925	1 363	280	625	627	—	2 895
1926	1 509	233	720	808	—	3 270
1927	1 588	231	794	733	—	3 346
1928	1 667	207	898	825	—	3 597
1929	1 753	228	983	907	—	3 871
1930	1 819	194	1 023	950	—	3 986
1931	1 726	194	1 123	960	—	4 003
1932	1 571	166	1 062	894	—	3 693
1933	1 523	153	996	824	—	3 496
1934	1 317	175	1 005	865	—	3 362
1935	1 288	164	1 033	867	—	3 352
1936	1 304	168	937	877	—	3 286
1937	1 376	171	908	887	—	3 342
1938	1 393	169	892	898	—	3 352
1939	1 442	162	936	903	—	3 443
1940	1 530	167	900	923	8	3 528
1941	1 632	180	1 006	947	114	3 879
1942	1 754	163	1 076	921	411	4 325
1943	1 826	146	1 059	885	691	4 607
1944	1 825	146	1 124	855	981	4 931
1945	1 827	147	1 165	838	1 951	5 928
1946	1 909	155	1 167	968	64	4 263
1947	2 352	193	1 435	1 240	59	5 279

TABLE C–43

Column 1 – Statistics of Income, various issues.

Column 2 – Col. 1 minus col. 3.

Column 3 – From Table C-46, col. 5.

Column 4 – Col. 1 raised to include unreported depreciation allowances for transportation and public utilities. Depreciation for that group is raised to account for 18.8 percent of total depreciation and depletion.

Column 5 – Col. 4 minus col. 3.

TABLE C-44

Columns 1 to 3 – 1897–1917: Difference of corresponding items in cols. 4–7 and 8–11.

Column 4 – 1897–1908: Depreciation ratio for 1908 applied to book values of investment in plant and equipment as reported in Interstate Commerce Commission, *Statistics of Railways.*
1909–1917: Based on data in *Statistics of Railways.* Reported amounts for fiscal years were averaged to obtain calendar year estimates and then raised by 4 percent to cover Class II and Class III railroads and switching and terminal companies.

Column 5 – 1902–1907, 1912, 1917: Based on *Census of Electrical Industries* (see Table C-20, col. 4).
Other years: Interpolated and extrapolated assuming constant rate of change between census years.

Column 6 – 1897–1917: Col. 7 minus sum of cols. 4 and 5.

Column 7 – 1897–1917: Sum of cols. 4 and 5 multiplied by 1.5, thus assuming on basis of relationship in 1919, 1922, and 1926, that "other" depreciation constitutes about one-third of total.

Column 8 – 1897–1917: The 1919 rate of depreciation applied to value of real estate improvements and equipment at book value. (Amount of depreciation underlying this rate was derived by raising amount reported in *Statistics of Railways* by 4 percent to include Class II and Class III railroads and switching and terminal companies.) Values for 1900, 1912, and 1922 (not shown in this table) are from Kuznets, *National Product since 1869,* pp. 202, 213; for other years, interpolated and extrapolated on assumption of constant rate of change between census years.

Column 9 – 1897–1917: Table C-45, col. 9.

Column 10 – 1897–1917: Same as col. 6.

Column 11 – 1897–1917: Sum of cols. 8–10.

SEGREGATION OF DEPRECIATION AND DEPLETION ALLOWANCES
1918 to 1925

$ mill.

Year	Depreciation and depletion reported	Depreciation unadjusted	Depletion	Depreciation and depletion adjusted	Depreciation adjusted
	1	2	3	4	5
1918	2 415	1 992	423	2 756	2 333
1919	2 074	1 739	335	2 324	1 989
1920	2 514	2 026	488	2 681	2 193
1921	2 573	2 280	293	2 632	2 339
1922	2 889	2 551	338	2 998	2 660
1923	3 116	2 603	513	3 225	2 712
1924	3 187	2 744	443	3 267	2 824
1925	3 330	2 858	472	3 367	2 895

ADJUSTMENT OF DEPRECIATION ALLOWANCES IN TRANSPORTATION
AND PUBLIC UTILITIES TO 1919 OR 1922 RATES: 1897 to 1917

$ mill.

Year	Adjustment			Actual depreciation allowances				Adjusted depreciation allowances			
	Steam railroads	Electric utilities and other	Total	Steam railroads	Electric utilities	Other	Total	Steam railroads	Electric utilities	Other	Total
	1	2	3	4	5	6	7	8	9	10	11
1897	24	12	36	37	14	25	76	61	26	25	112
1898	24	12	36	38	16	27	81	62	28	27	117
1899	24	13	37	38	19	28	85	62	32	28	122
1900	25	14	39	40	22	31	93	65	36	31	132
1901	27	15	42	40	25	32	97	67	40	32	139
1902	29	16	45	41	29	34	104	70	45	34	149
1903	31	18	49	42	33	37	112	73	51	37	161
1904	32	20	52	44	38	40	122	76	58	40	174
1905	33	22	55	46	43	44	133	79	65	44	188
1906	34	25	59	48	49	48	145	82	74	48	204
1907	36	27	63	50	56	52	158	86	83	52	221
1908	39	30	69	51	61	55	167	90	91	55	236
1909	42	31	73	52	66	58	176	94	97	58	249
1910	43	33	76	54	71	62	187	97	104	62	263
1911	46	35	81	55	77	65	197	101	112	65	278
1912	44	34	78	61	84	71	216	105	118	71	294
1913	35	37	72	73	89	80	242	108	126	80	314
1914	25	37	62	86	95	89	270	111	132	89	332
1915	20	36	56	94	102	97	293	114	138	97	349
1916	15	36	51	102	109	104	315	117	145	104	366
1917	9	35	44	111	117	114	342	120	152	114	386

959

Columns 1 to 4 – 1896–1922: Obtained for 1903–1921 by interpolation from Census figures (cf. Tables C-21, C-22, C-23, and C-24) assuming equal rates of growth between census years, and for 1897–1901 by extrapolation of rates of growth prevailing from 1902 to 1907.

Column 5 – 1896–1921: Obtained by applying 1922 depreciation rate to col. 1.
1922: From Table C-24, col. 6.

Column 6 – 1896–1921: Obtained by applying 1922 depreciation rate to col. 2.
1922: From Table C-21, col. 6.

Column 7 – 1896–1921: Obtained by applying 1922 depreciation rate to col. 3.
1922: From Table C-23, col. 6.

Column 8 – 1896–1921: Obtained by applying 1922 depreciation rate to col. 4.
1922: From Table C-22, col. 6.

Column 9 – 1896–1922: Sum of cols. 5–8.

1922 Rates: 1896 to 1922

$ mill.

Year	Plant and equipment				Depreciation allowances				
	Electric railways	Central electric stations	Telephone	Telegraph	Electric railways	Central electric stations	Telephone	Telegraph	Total
	1	2	3	4	5	6	7	8	9
1896	1 165	189	159	119	.	.	.	.	.
1897	1 292	221	185	125	9	3	8	6	26
1898	1 433	259	214	132	10	3	9	6	28
1899	1 589	302	249	139	11	4	10	7	32
1900	1 762	354	289	146	12	5	12	7	36
1901	1 955	413	335	154	13	5	15	7	40
1902	2 168	483	389	162	14	6	17	8	45
1903	2 405	565	452	171	16	7	20	8	51
1904	2 667	660	524	180	18	9	22	9	58
1905	2 958	771	608	189	20	10	26	9	65
1906	3 280	902	706	199	22	12	30	10	74
1907	3 638	1 054	820	210	24	14	35	10	83
1908	3 812	1 210	867	213	26	16	39	10	91
1909	3 945	1 388	916	215	27	19	41	10	97
1910	4 186	1 593	968	218	28	22	43	11	104
1911	4 387	1 829	1 023	220	30	25	46	11	112
1912	4 597	2 099	1 081	223	31	28	48	11	118
1913	4 700	2 244	1 144	227	33	31	51	11	126
1914	4 805	2 400	1 211	231	33	34	54	11	132
1915	4 913	2 566	1 282	235	34	36	57	11	138
1916	5 023	2 743	1 357	239	35	38	60	12	145
1917	5 136	2 933	1 436	243	36	41	63	12	152
1918	5 120	3 156	1 554	258	36	44	69	12	161
1919	5 105	3 395	1 681	274	36	47	74	13	170
1920	5 089	3 653	1 819	290	35	50	80	14	179
1921	5 074	3 930	1 968	308	36	55	86	15	192
1922	5 059	4 229	2 130	327	35	59	94	16	204

TABLE C–46

Column 1 – 1897–1948: Department of the Interior, Bureau of Mines, *Minerals Yearbook*, 1948, p. 19.
Figures cover output of mines and quarries.
1949: Rough preliminary estimate.

Column 2 – 1913–1918: Extrapolated on basis of Barger, H. and Schurr, S., *The Mining Industries, 1899–1939*, p. 14.
1919–1949: Index of minerals production of Federal Reserve Board (*Federal Reserve Bulletin*, 1950, p. 1377).

Column 3 – 1916–1924: Values read off from correlation chart between depletion allowances as reported to Bureau of Internal Revenue (col. 5) and value of minerals output (col. 1) for the years 1925–1939.

Column 4 – 1916–1924: Values read off from correlation chart between depletion allowances as reported to Bureau of Internal Revenue (col. 5) and volume of minerals output (col. 2) for the years 1925–1939.

Column 5 – 1897–1909: It was assumed that corporate reports made no allowance for depletion (cf. Tables C-13 and C-17). While this assumption is too sweeping, the error involved in its use does not affect the final estimates of corporate saving as an offsetting adjustment is made in col. 6.
1910–1912: Obtained by interpolation between 1909 and 1913 values.
1913–1915: Estimated at 3.5 percent of value of minerals output (col. 1). This estimate was based on the facts that depletion was limited in the revenue acts for 1913–1915 to 5 percent of the value of output at the mine; and that value of minerals output as reported by the Bureau of Mines, which includes intercompany sales, exceeded the Bureau of Census figures of the (unduplicated) value of output by roughly 40 percent.
1916–1924: Average of cols. 3 and 4, except for 1916 and 1917. This procedure was adopted because there was reason to assume, on basis of wording of depletion provisions in relevant revenue acts, that depreciation allowances reported to the Bureau of Internal Revenue depended partly on volume and partly on value of output. For 1916 and 1917, value obtained by averaging cols. 3 and 4 was reduced by $100 million each in order to effect a smoother transition from values before 1916 to those after 1917 and to obtain a more plausible series for depreciation in mining which, for the period from 1917–1924, must be derived by subtracting estimate for depletion from combined figure for depreciation and depletion, as reported to the Bureau of Internal Revenue.
1925–1947: *Statistics of Income*, various issues.
1948–1949: Rough preliminary estimates.

Column 6 – 1897–1909: Estimated on assumption that "economic" rate of depletion was 2 percent of value of output as in later part of period.
1910–1924: Difference between col. 5 and 2 percent of value of output.
1925–1949: Assumed at 75 percent of depletion allowances reported in income tax reports (col. 5). This ratio is based on data discussed in Volume II, Chapter XVI.

INCLUDED IN REPORTS (1897 to 1914) AND INCOME TAX RETURNS (1915 to 1949)

Year	Value of minerals output	Volume of minerals output	Reported depletion allowances			Excess allowances
			Based on value of output	Based on volume of output	Final estimate	
	$ mill.	1935-1939 = 100			$ mill.	
	1	2	3	4	5	6
1897	652	–	–	–	–	–13
1898	727	–	–	–	–	–15
1899	1 010	–	–	–	–	–20
1900	1 109	–	–	–	–	–22
1901	1 155	–	–	–	–	–23
1902	1 328	–	–	–	–	–27
1903	1 495	–	–	–	–	–30
1904	1 359	–	–	–	–	–27
1905	1 624	–	–	–	–	–32
1906	1 901	–	–	–	–	–38
1907	2 070	–	–	–	–	–41
1908	1 592	–	–	–	–	–32
1909	1 887	–	–	–	–	–37
1910	1 988	–	–	–	20	–20
1911	1 924	–	–	–	40	2
1912	2 238	–	–	–	60	15
1913	2 434	66	–	–	85	36
1914	2 111	61	–	–	75	33
1915	2 395	67	–	–	85	37
1916	3 508	77	340	290	215	145
1917	4 992	81	465	325	295	195
1918	5 541	82	510	335	423	312
1919	4 624	71	430	240	335	243
1920	6 981	83	635	340	488	348
1921	4 139	66	390	195	293	210
1922	4 647	71	435	240	338	245
1923	5 987	98	550	475	513	393
1924	5 306	89	495	390	443	337
1925	5 678	92	–	–	472	354
1926	6 214	100	–	–	571	428
1927	5 530	100	–	–	502	376
1928	5 385	99	–	–	515	386
1929	5 888	107	–	–	559	419
1930	4 765	93	–	–	463	348
1931	3 167	80	–	–	268	202
1932	2 462	67	–	–	247	186
1933	2 555	76	–	–	246	185
1934	3 325	80	–	–	312	234
1935	3 650	86	–	–	349	262
1936	4 557	99	–	–	437	328
1937	5 413	112	–	–	524	394
1938	4 363	97	–	–	437	328
1939	4 914	106	–	–	438	329
1940	5 614	117	–	–	475	356
1941	6 878	125	–	–	544	408
1942	7 576	129	–	–	579	435
1943	8 072	132	–	–	644	484
1944	8 417	140	–	–	712	535
1945	8 141	137	–	–	693	520
1946	8 896	134	–	–	802	602
1947	12 484	149	–	–	1 210	908
1948	15 670	155	–	–	1 500	1 125
1949	12 500	135	–	–	1 250	938

Column 1 – The sum of capital expenditures charged to current operating expense by oil and metal mining corporations, obtained by allocating to corporations on the basis of Table C-16, cols. 3 and 4 (linearly interpolating between benchmark year percentages) a share of total development costs charged to current expense.

       Estimates for development costs by oil companies were derived for the period 1897–1928 by applying to figures of the value of output (Table R-33, col. 1) a ratio which rises regularly from 18 percent, the 1929 relationship, to a peak of 23 percent in 1919 and remains constant for preceding years. Figures for the period 1929–1949 were estimated on basis of data obtained from National Income Division, Department of Commerce.

       Total capital expenditures charged to current operating expense by metal mining companies were estimated to be 2 percent of the value of metal and coal production (1897–1944, *Historical Statistics*, pp. 141, 142; 1945–1948, *Statistical Abstract*, pp. 689, 704; 1949, Bureau of Mines preliminary figures).

Column 2 – The corporate capital expenditures series described in col. 1 deflated by Table R-20, col. 3.

Column 3 – Obtained by depreciating corporate capital expenditures by oil companies, original cost (col. 1) assuming for 1897–1929 a twenty-year life period, and for 1930–1949 twenty-five years, and expenditures by metal companies (col. 1), assuming a forty-year life period.

Column 4 – Same procedure as for col. 3 except expenditures series given in col. 2 used.

Column 5 – Components of col. 4 multiplied by Table R-20, col. 3.

Column 6 – Col. 1 minus col. 3.

Column 7 – Col. 2 minus col. 4.

Column 8 – Col. 1 minus col. 5.

964

ADJUSTMENT FOR DEVELOPMENT COST IN MINING
CHARGED TO CURRENT EXPENSE BY CORPORATIONS: 1897 to 1949

$ mill.

Year	Development cost charged to current expense		Depreciation allowances			Excess charges		
	Original cost	1929 prices	Original cost	1929 prices	Replacement cost	Original cost	1929 prices	Replacement cost
	1	2	3	4	5	6	7	8
1897	15	36	9	19	8	6	17	7
1898	17	39	9	20	9	8	19	8
1899	25	54	9	21	10	16	33	15
1900	28	58	10	23	11	18	35	17
1901	28	60	11	24	12	17	36	16
1902	31	64	12	26	12	19	38	19
1903	39	78	13	28	13	26	50	26
1904	39	79	15	31	15	24	48	24
1905	39	76	15	33	17	24	43	22
1906	45	85	17	36	19	28	49	26
1907	54	100	18	39	21	36	61	33
1908	48	89	20	42	23	28	47	25
1909	52	98	22	45	24	30	53	28
1910	55	102	24	48	26	31	54	29
1911	55	101	25	51	27	30	50	28
1912	67	121	28	55	30	39	66	37
1913	84	151	31	59	33	53	92	51
1914	74	136	33	64	35	41	72	39
1915	81	147	36	69	38	45	78	43
1916	122	195	39	75	47	83	120	75
1917	184	259	45	83	59	139	176	125
1918	231	279	53	93	77	178	186	154
1919	224	217	62	102	105	162	115	119
1920	371	285	74	111	145	297	174	226
1921	199	200	87	120	120	112	80	79
1922	235	245	96	129	124	139	116	111
1923	268	263	105	137	140	163	126	128
1924	257	251	115	147	151	142	104	106
1925	299	289	128	157	162	171	132	137
1926	328	317	141	169	174	187	148	154
1927	268	263	153	179	183	115	84	85
1928	244	238	162	188	193	82	50	51
1929	250	250	172	196	196	78	54	54
1930	209	227	179	203	187	30	24	22
1931	122	140	185	206	179	−63	−66	−57
1932	131	180	188	209	152	−57	−29	−21
1933	105	131	190	210	167	−85	−79	−62
1934	131	150	190	210	183	−59	−60	−52
1935	173	189	194	212	194	−21	−23	−21
1936	224	242	199	215	199	25	27	25
1937	303	301	204	217	218	99	84	85
1938	268	269	207	219	218	61	50	50
1939	277	271	209	219	224	68	52	53
1940	306	289	209	221	234	97	68	72
1941	335	296	209	220	248	126	76	87
1942	268	220	210	220	268	58	0	0
1943	299	237	211	219	276	88	18	23
1944	421	322	214	217	284	207	105	137
1945	449	325	218	218	301	231	107	148
1946	503	313	223	215	346	280	98	157
1947	600	318	230	215	405	370	103	195
1948	774	376	246	217	446	528	159	328
1949	762	374	263	220	448	499	154	314

TABLE C–48

Lines 1a and 1b – 1946–1947: From *Special Depletion Allowances for Mineral Properties* (exhibit 2 to accompany statement of Secretary of the Treasury John W. Snyder before the Committee on Ways and Means, House of Representatives, Feb. 3, 1950), tables 4 and 5. Figures are based on about 350 selected corporations, but seem to be only a few percent short of total for all corporations.

Line 1c – 1946–1947: Sum of lines 1a and 1b.

Lines 2a and 2b – 1946–1947: From Pogue, J. and Cocqueron, F., *Financial Analysis of Thirty Oil Companies*, 1946, 1947 (table 9), deducting 15 and 16 percent, respectively, for expenditures outside the U.S. (the ratio of total property expenditures abroad) and assuming on the basis of crude oil production that the thirty companies included represent 55 percent of the industry.

    1948–1949: *Ibid.*, 1948, 1949 (tables 10,15), assuming companies included represent 55 percent of the industry (separate figures are available for these years for expenditures in the U.S.).

Line 2c – 1946–1949: Same procedure as for lines 2a and 2b for 1948–1949.

Line 2d – 1946–1949: Sum of lines 2a, 2b and 2c.

Line 3 – 1946–1949: Estimated on basis of data obtained from National Income Division, Department of Commerce.

Line 4 – 1946–1947: Line 1c plus 20 percent to take account of corporations not included and of unincorporated enterprises divided by line 2d.

Line 5 – 1946–1947: Line 1a increased by 20 percent (cf. line 4) divided by line 3.

Line 6 – 1946–1947: Line 1a increased by 20 percent (cf. line 4), divided by value of output at wells of crude oil (*Statistical Abstract*, 1949, p. 790).

DEVELOPMENT AND EXPLORATION COSTS
CHARGED TO CURRENT INCOME IN THE OIL AND NATURAL GAS INDUSTRY
1946 to 1949

$ mill. (except lines 4–6)

	1946	1947	1948	1949
1. Deductions in income tax reports				
a. Development cost	381	471	.	.
b. Exploration cost and losses on abandonment	161	200	.	.
c. Total	542	671	.	.
2. Deductions in published reports				
a. Intangible development cost	25	35	55	45
b. Dry holes	150	170	250	235
c. Exploration	175	225	295	295
d. Total	350	430	600	575
3. Estimated on basis of Department of Commerce data of intangible development cost	500	575	755	765
4. Ratio of tax to published deductions	1.86	1.87	.	.
5. Ratio of reported to estimated intangible development cost	0.91	0.98	.	.
6. Ratio of reported development cost to value of crude oil production	0.19	0.16	.	.

Column 1 – 1887–1928: Estimated at 20 percent of nonfarm expenditures on producer durable goods excluding motor vehicles (Table P-5, col. 1) on basis of approximate average relationship for 1924–1941.

        1929–1949: Capital outlays charged to current expense as given in *Survey of Current Business*, July 1950, p. 10, less estimates of development cost in oil and gas well drilling charged to current expense (see notes to Table C-47, col. 1).

Column 2 – 1887–1949: Col. 1 multiplied by share of corporations in total capital outlay, estimated for 1909–1949 to be 85 percent and to have fallen in preceding years to 60 percent in 1887 (see discussion in Volume II, Chapter XVI).

Column 3 – 1887–1890: Col. 2 deflated by index of prices, published in 1893 by the Committee on Finance, United States Senate, on an 1860 base and recomputed by the Bureau of Labor Statistics on a 1926 base (see *Handbook of Labor Statistics*, 1941, vol. I) linked in 1891 to Mills' index (*Economic Tendencies in the U.S.: Aspects of Pre-War and Post-War Changes*, p. 585). The original indexes are unweighted arithmetic averages of prices.

        1891–1912: Col. 2 deflated by index of wholesale prices of processed producer durable goods as estimated by F. C. Mills linked in 1913 to Marshall and Stevens index (see *Economic Tendencies in the United States*, p. 585).

        1913–1949: Col. 2 deflated by index of equipment costs as estimated by Marshall and Stevens (see *Stevens' Valuation Quarterly*, Jan. 1949, pp. 60–64 and current issues) shifted to 1929 base.

Column 4 – 1897–1949: Col. 2 depreciated assuming a depreciation period of ten years.

Column 5 – 1897–1949: Same procedure as for col. 4 except expenditure series given in col. 3 used.

Column 6 – 1897–1949: Col. 5 multiplied by Table R-20, col. 3.

Column 7 – 1897–1949: Col. 2 minus col. 4.

Column 8 – 1897–1949: Col. 3 minus col. 5.

Column 9 – 1897–1949: Col. 2 minus col. 6.

ADJUSTMENT FOR CAPITAL EXPENDITURES
CHARGED TO CURRENT EXPENSE BY CORPORATIONS: 1887 to 1949

$ mill.

Year	Estimated capital expenditures charged to current expense			Estimated depreciation allowances on capitalized expenditures of corporations			Excess charges		
	Total	Corporations		Original cost	1929 prices	Replacement cost	Original cost	1929 prices	Replacement cost
	Original cost	Original cost	1929 prices						
	1	2	3	4	5	6	7	8	9
1887	84	50	88	.	.	.	.	.	.
1888	88	55	95	.	.	.	.	.	.
1889	93	61	105	.	.	.	.	.	.
1890	93	64	112	.	.	.	.	.	.
1891	97	70	123	.	.	.	.	.	.
1892	102	75	137	.	.	.	.	.	.
1893	100	76	137	.	.	.	.	.	.
1894	73	56	115	.	.	.	.	.	.
1895	85	66	138	.	.	.	.	.	.
1896	94	74	155	.	.	.	.	.	.
1897	85	68	148	66	124	57	2	24	11
1898	95	77	162	68	130	62	9	32	15
1899	129	105	194	71	138	75	34	56	30
1900	157	129	219	76	147	86	53	72	43
1901	158	130	230	83	158	89	47	72	41
1902	179	149	257	89	170	98	60	87	51
1903	201	167	285	98	183	107	69	102	60
1904	172	144	254	106	197	112	38	57	32
1905	209	176	297	116	212	126	60	85	50
1906	266	223	346	129	230	148	94	116	75
1907	289	243	368	146	250	165	97	118	78
1908	171	144	240	158	265	159	−14	−25	−15
1909	204	173	285	164	274	167	9	11	6
1910	246	209	326	172	283	181	37	43	28
1911	222	189	313	179	293	177	10	20	12
1912	279	237	384	186	303	187	51	81	50
1913	324	275	436	196	317	200	79	119	75
1914	242	206	350	204	330	194	2	20	12
1915	245	208	342	209	337	205	−1	5	3
1916	427	363	531	218	348	238	145	183	125
1917	635	540	609	240	370	328	300	239	212
1918	779	662	554	280	397	474	382	157	188
1919	617	524	395	324	418	555	200	−23	−31
1920	714	607	364	361	426	711	246	−62	−104
1921	479	407	324	392	428	538	15	−104	−131
1922	489	416	447	412	432	402	4	15	14
1923	691	587	552	436	441	469	151	111	118
1924	630	536	468	468	453	519	68	15	17
1925	661	562	490	503	466	534	59	24	28
1926	720	612	562	533	475	517	79	87	95
1927	684	581	556	547	474	495	34	82	86
1928	712	605	576	547	472	496	58	104	109
1929	626	532	532	544	480	480	−12	52	52
1930	514	437	461	536	492	466	−99	−31	−29
1931	471	400	478	527	504	422	−127	−26	−22
1932	254	216	300	517	505	363	−301	−205	−147
1933	266	226	299	489	485	366	−263	−186	−140
1934	336	286	353	458	466	378	−172	−113	−92
1935	393	334	393	434	456	387	−100	−63	−53
1936	486	413	465	413	446	396	0	19	17
1937	639	543	565	401	442	425	142	123	118
1938	442	376	410	388	434	398	−12	−24	−22
1939	527	448	485	372	423	390	76	62	58
1940	675	574	609	375	428	403	199	181	171
1941	834	709	703	397	447	451	312	256	258
1942	563	479	442	426	465	504	53	−23	−25
1943	527	448	410	450	478	523	−2	−68	−75
1944	552	469	421	470	487	543	−1	−66	−74
1945	707	601	534	493	497	559	108	37	42
1946	1 439	1 223	912	546	527	707	677	385	516
1947	1 619	1 376	840	629	563	923	747	277	453
1948	1 900	1 615	912	732	602	1 066	883	310	549
1949	1 689	1 436	819	844	644	1 130	592	175	306

Column 1 – 1897–1915: Estimated as five-sixths of gross dividend payments as given in Table C-6, col. 1.
1916–1921: Net dividend payments as given in Table C-31, col. 1.
1922–1948: Net dividend payments as reported in *Statistics of Income*.
1949: Preliminary Bureau of Internal Revenue figure.

Column 2 – 1897, 1914: Obtained by applying to estimates of foreign holdings of stocks and direct investments (cf. Table K-2, cols. 4 to 6) yield rates of 3.9 percent (1897) and 5 percent (1914) for stocks (taken from Cowles, Alfred and Associates, *Common Stock Indexes*, 1939, pp. 372, 373), and of 5 percent for direct investments.
1898–1913: Obtained by applying yield rates described above to estimated value of foreign holdings of common stock and direct investments, derived by moving 1897 estimate in accordance with an index of common stock prices (*ibid.*, p. 66) and adding estimated net foreign purchases or sales of stock (cf. Tables K-2 and K-3).
1915–1918: Interpolated between values for 1914 and 1919, taking into account such factors as liquidation of American securities by British Treasury (cf. Lewis, Cleona, *America's Stake in International Investments*, p. 544) and of German and other enemy alien-held securities by the Alien Property Custodian (*ibid.*, p. 536).
1919–1935: Based on rough breakdown of Department of Commerce estimates of total income interest, dividends, and branch profits of foreign investments in the U.S. (cf. *United States in the World Economy*, table 1).
1936–1945: Based on withholding tax returns filed with Bureau of Internal Revenue.

Column 3 – 1897–1945: Col. 2 divided by col. 1.
1946: Estimated to continue at approximately 1945 value.
1947–1949: See note for col. 4, 1946–1949.

Column 4 – 1897: Rough estimate (deviates from the value in col. 3, which is regarded as too high as a result of incomparability, for the early part of the period covered, between cols. 1 and 2).
1898–1912: Obtained by linear interpolation between the 1897 and 1913 estimates.
1913: Estimated on the basis of the 1914 value, taking account of the substantial net sales of American stocks by foreign holders during the year 1914.
1914–1945: Same as col. 3.
1946–1949: Estimated on basis of balance in foreigners' transactions in stock as shown in Table K-2, cols. 4 and 5.

1897–1919: Obtained by arbitrary allocation of estimated total of $1,000 million over period. Total represents about one-fourth of book value of American investment in foreign subsidiaries at end of 1919 as estimated by Department of Commerce (*Survey of Current Business*, Jan. 1951, p. 22, table 1). Proportion of one-fourth is based on the fact that from 1940–1949 about one-half of the increase in total American investment represented reinvested earnings, and the assumption that the proportion was substantially lower before 1929. (The Department's estimate covers all corporations incorporated outside the U.S. in which American corporations or individuals own 25 percent or more of the stock.)
1920–1929: Obtained by allocating about one-fourth of increase in book value of American investment in foreign subsidiaries between 1919 and 1929 (*ibid.*) over period.
1930–1939: Assumed negligible for period as a whole since total American investment in foreign subsidiaries during this period is estimated (*ibid.*) to have declined by $400 million or 5 percent, probably as a result of liquidation; distribution among years is arbitrary.
1940–1944: Figures supplied by Department of Commerce.
1945–1947: Department of Commerce, Office of Business Economics, *The Balance of International Payments of the U.S., 1946–48*, p. 256.
1948–1949: *Survey of Current Business*, Jan. 1951, p. 22, table 3.

FOREIGNERS' SHARE IN CORPORATE SAVING: 1897 to 1949 — C-50

Year	Dividend payments		Foreigners' share in		Year	Dividend payments		Foreigners' share in	
	Total	To foreign shareholders	Dividend payments	Corporate saving		Total	To foreign shareholders	Dividend payments	Corporate saving
	$ mill.		Percent			$ mill.		Percent	
	1	2	3	4		1	2	3	4
1897	334	41	12.3	8.0	1924	3 424	85	2.5	2.5
1898	381	42	11.0	7.9	1925	4 014	104	2.6	2.6
1899	487	45	9.2	7.8	1926	4 439	115	2.6	2.6
1900	637	60	9.4	7.7	1927	4 766	126	2.6	2.6
1901	765	59	7.7	7.6	1928	5 157	139	2.7	2.7
1902	1 121	66	5.9	7.5	1929	5 763	176	3.1	3.1
1903	1 197	77	6.4	7.4	1930	5 631	179	3.2	3.2
1904	1 225	70	5.7	7.3	1931	4 182	139	3.3	3.3
1905	1 326	70	5.3	7.2	1932	2 626	91	3.5	3.5
1906	1 517	85	5.6	7.1	1933	2 101	80	3.8	3.8
1907	1 628	101	6.2	7.0	1934	2 672	102	3.8	3.8
1908	1 539	90	5.8	6.9	1935	2 927	115	3.9	3.9
1909	1 611	92	5.7	6.8	1936	4 702	220	4.7	4.7
1910	1 842	106	5.8	6.7	1937	4 832	240	5.0	5.0
1911	1 835	108	5.9	6.6	1938	3 222	146	4.5	4.5
1912	1 923	111	5.8	6.5	1939	3 841	176	4.6	4.6
1913	2 243	120	5.3	6.5	1940	4 068	166	4.1	4.1
1914	1 798	109	6.1	6.1	1941	4 466	151	3.4	3.4
1915	2 013	105	5.2	5.2	1942	4 262	125	2.9	2.9
1916	2 500	100	4.0	4.0	1943	4 394	118	2.7	2.7
1917	3 025	109	3.6	3.6	1944	4 628	123	2.7	2.7
1918	2 620	84	3.2	3.2	1945	4 663	125	2.7	2.7
1919	2 600	74	2.8	2.8	1946	5 523	.	2.7	2.7
1920	2 900	74	2.6	2.6	1947	6 425	.	2.6	2.6
1921	2 630	61	2.3	2.3	1948	7 156	.	2.5	2.5
1922	2 634	60	2.3	2.3	1949	7 821	.	2.5	2.5
1923	3 299	81	2.5	2.5					

REINVESTED EARNINGS OF FOREIGN SUBSIDIARIES OF AMERICAN CORPORATIONS: 1897 to 1949 — C-51

$ mill.

Year	Amount	Year	Amount	Year	Amount
1897	15	1914	50	1932	−50
1898	15	1915	75	1933	−20
1899	15	1916	75	1934	−10
1900	15	1917	100	1935	0
1901	20	1918	100	1936	0
1902	20	1919	100	1937	0
1903	25	1920	50	1938	10
1904	25	1921	50	1939	20
1905	30	1922	75	1940	40
1906	30	1923	75	1941	180
1907	35	1924	100	1942	180
1908	35	1925	100	1943	180
1909	40	1926	125	1944	160
1910	40	1927	125	1945	221
1911	45	1928	150	1946	303
1912	45	1929	150	1947	399
1913	50	1930	50	1948	569
		1931	0	1949	495

Column 1 – 1897–1928: Table F-10, col. 11 minus Table F-11, col. 11.
        1929–1942: Col. 2 minus net (difference) of first differences of Table F-26, col. 1 and Table F-27, col. 4.

Column 2 – 1897–1928: Col. 1 plus net of first differences of Table F-26, col. 1 and Table F-27, col. 4.
        1929–1949: Sum of Table F-22, col. 13 and first differences of Table F-26, cols. 2 and 4 minus first differences of Table F-27, col. 4.

Column 3 – 1897–1928: Table F-10, col. 11 minus F-11, col. 12.
        1929–1942: Col. 4 minus net of first differences of Table F-26, col. 1 and Table F-27, col. 4.

Column 4 – 1897–1928: Col. 3 plus net of first differences of Table F-26, col. 1 and Table F-27, col. 4.
        1929–1949: Sum of Table F-22, col. 14 and first differences of Table F-26, cols. 2 and 4 minus first differences of Table F-29, col. 4.

Column 5 – 1897–1928: Table F-2, col. 11 minus col. 12.
        1929–1942: Col. 6 minus net of first differences of Table F-26, col. 1 and Table F-27, col. 4.

Column 6 – 1897–1928: Col. 5 plus net of first differences of Table F-26, col. 1 and Table F-27, col. 4.
        1929–1949: Sum of Table F-12, col. 12 and first differences of Table F-26, cols. 2 and 4 minus first differences of Table F-27, col. 4.

Column 7 – 1897–1928: Col. 5 changed to a replacement cost basis by substituting for cols. 2, 4, and 6 comparable series on replacement cost basis obtained by subtracting from expenditure series depreciation charges given in Table F-11, col. 10.
        1929–1942: Col. 8 minus net of first differences of Table F-26, col. 1 and Table F-27, col. 4.

Column 8 – 1897–1928: Col. 7 plus net of first differences of Table F-26, col. 1 and Table F-27, col. 4.
        1929–1949: Table F-12, col. 12 changed to replacement cost basis by substituting for cols. 2 and 4 comparable series on replacement cost basis (for total amounts involved see Table F-22, col. 12) plus first differences of Table F-26, col. 2 and 4 minus first differences of Table F-27, col. 4.

Income Account and Balance Sheet Methods: 1897 to 1949

$ mill.

Year	Income account method				Balance sheet method			
	Original cost depreciation		Replacement cost depreciation		Original cost depreciation		Replacement cost depreciation	
	Tax and interest accruals							
	Excluded	Included	Excluded	Included	Excluded	Included	Excluded	Included
	1	2	3	4	5	6	7	8
1897	−30	−30	−29	−29	23	23	24	24
1898	−117	−117	−117	−117	−106	−106	−106	−106
1899	18	18	18	18	13	13	13	13
1900	86	86	84	84	34	34	32	32
1901	105	105	104	104	92	92	91	91
1902	77	77	77	77	64	64	64	64
1903	45	45	44	44	56	56	55	55
1904	−3	−3	−5	−5	−1	−1	−3	−3
1905	27	27	28	28	37	37	38	38
1906	105	105	103	103	123	123	121	121
1907	103	103	99	99	103	103	99	99
1908	−63	−63	−66	−66	−36	−36	−39	−39
1909	19	41	19	41	23	45	23	45
1910	71	85	68	82	77	91	74	88
1911	75	69	71	65	74	68	70	64
1912	101	136	98	133	98	133	95	130
1913	50	71	46	67	86	107	82	103
1914	35	58	32	55	6	29	3	26
1915	21	145	16	140	26	150	21	145
1916	24	627	12	615	18	621	6	609
1917	−5 333	−2 901	−5 358	−2 926	−5 238	−2 806	−5 263	−2 831
1918	−13 442	−12 274	−13 474	−12 306	−12 698	−11 530	−12 730	−11 562
1919	−4 782	−5 974	−4 820	−6 012	−4 584	−5 776	−4 622	−5 814
1920	1 313	398	1 258	343	1 121	206	1 066	151
1921	1 281	393	1 243	355	475	−413	437	−451
1922	460	365	431	336	325	230	296	201
1923	788	1 018	749	979	770	1 000	731	961
1924	793	703	756	666	923	833	886	796
1925	241	554	195	508	752	1 065	706	1 019
1926	1 311	1 437	1 276	1 402	1 081	1 207	1 046	1 172
1927	642	772	609	739	1 045	1 175	1 012	1 142
1928	719	987	684	952	802	1 070	767	1 035
1929	1 205	1 091	1 176	1 062	1 242	1 128	1 213	1 099
1930	820	−117	794	−143	776	−161	751	−186
1931	−1 111	−1 731	−1 133	−1 753	−1 291	−1 911	−1 313	−1 933
1932	−1 178	−1 199	−1 191	−1 212	−1 199	−1 220	−1 212	−1 233
1933	−1 202	−922	−1 217	−937	−1 388	−1 108	−1 404	−1 124
1934	−2 716	−2 268	−2 739	−2 291	−2 582	−2 134	−2 604	−2 156
1935	−2 081	−1 579	−2 104	−1 602	−2 053	−1 551	−2 077	−1 575
1936	−4 369	−3 382	−4 394	−3 407	−4 499	−3 512	−4 524	−3 537
1937	−719	−752	−756	−789	−722	−755	−759	−792
1938	−1 635	−2 491	−1 671	−2 527	−1 748	−2 604	−1 784	−2 640
1939	−2 996	−2 546	−3 030	−2 580	−3 141	−2 691	−3 175	−2 725
1940	−2 945	−929	−2 983	−967	−3 000	−984	−3 039	−1 023
1941	−10 562	−3 141	−10 613	−3 192	−10 454	−3 033	−10 504	−3 083
1942	−37 262	−34 129	−37 335	−34 202	−36 475	−33 342	−36 549	−33 416
1943	.	−46 756	.	−46 843	.	−46 676	.	−46 763
1944	.	−54 841	.	−54 930	.	−54 442	.	−54 532
1945	.	−48 806	.	−48 907	.	−48 713	.	−48 814
1946	.	−1 741	.	−1 875	.	−1 606	.	−1 740
1947	.	6 642	.	6 440	.	6 517	.	6 315
1948	.	5 413	.	5 161	.	5 624	.	5 373
1949	.	−1 796	.	−2 050	.	−1 783	.	−2 037

Column 1 – From Table F-3, col. 12.

Column 2 – From Table F-4, col. 12.

Column 3 – Expenditures are taken from series H 27–32 and H 33–35, "Federal Expenditures for Public Works: 1791 to 1919" and "Construction Expenditures—For Public Works by Permanent Construction Agencies: 1920 to 1939," in *Historical Statistics of the United States 1789–1945*, pp. 169–170. Figures in col. 3 are exclusive of expenditures for military and naval public works as given in Public Works Administration worksheets and federal grants-in-aid for highways (figures taken from budget reports). Total for fiscal year 1904 excludes $50 million for purchase of Panama Canal, included in col. 5. Expenditures for six-month periods were assumed at half fiscal year totals.

Column 4 – Col. 3 distributed according to purpose of expenditures (Public Works Administration worksheets) and depreciated assuming average life of eighty years for conservation, fifty years for public buildings, twenty-five years for highways, and eighty years for construction outside continental U.S.

Column 5 – Obtained by summarizing expenditures as shown in annual *Combined Statements of Receipts and Disbursements* for machinery, equipment, furniture, horses and wagons, autos, books, land, etc. Included are $50 million for purchase of Panama Canal in fiscal year 1904, $25 million for Danish West Indies in fiscal year 1917, and $6 million for Cape Cod Canal in fiscal years 1928 and 1929. Figures are exclusive of amounts for land and fixed equipment for public works included in col. 3. They also exclude expenditures of Departments of War and the Navy. Figures are subject to understatement since not all capital expenditures were reported separately. Summary figures for 1923–1929 for "plant and equipment", and "land, structures, improvements to land, and fixed equipment" from *Budget of the United States Government* for 1928, 1929, and 1930 could not be segregated to reconcile with public works totals in col. 3, but comparison indicates that sum of cols. 3 and 5 gives a reasonable estimate of combined expenditures for construction, equipment, land, etc.

Column 6 – Col. 5 less depreciation charges on equipment obtained by depreciating equipment expenditures on linear basis assuming average life of twelve years.

Column 7 – From Table F-5, col. 10.

Column 8 – From Table F-6, col. 6.

Column 9 – From Table F-7, col. 4.

Column 10 – From Table F-8, col. 5.

Column 11 – Sum of cols. 1, 2, 4, and 6.

Column 12 – Sum of cols. 7–10.

SAVING OF FEDERAL GOVERNMENT
Balance Sheet Method: 1896 to 1928
$ mill.

Semi-annual period ending	General fund assets	Government corporation assets	General government public works		Land purchases and		General fund liabilities	Government corporation liabilities	Public debt	Other liabilities	Net change in	
			Undepreciated	Depreciated	Undepreciated equipment	Depreciated equipment					Assets	Liabilities
	1	2	3	4	5	6	7	8	9	10	11	12
1896 Dec.	−4	–		6	–	–	34	–	−2	−1	2	31
1897 June	12	–	10	6	1	–	7	–	6	−1	18	12
Dec.	9	–	13	8	–	–	−8	–	8	0	17	0
1898 June	−51	–	13	8	1	–	−15	–	−2	0	−43	−17
Dec.	96	–	10	6	–	–	−9	–	191	0	102	182
1899 June	−27	–	11	6	1	–	1	–	13	1	−21	15
Dec.	152	–	13	9	–	–	131	–	−19	0	161	112
1900 June	39	–	14	9	1	–	91	–	−55	0	48	36
Dec.	21	–	16	12	–	–	35	–	−24	0	33	11
1901 June	41	–	16	11	1	–	18	–	−17	1	52	2
Dec.	36	–	12	7	–	–	39	–	−39	1	43	1
1902 June	40	–	12	7	1	–	15	–	−5	1	47	11
Dec.	56	–	16	10	–	–	54	–	−16	0	66	38
1903 June	32	–	16	11	1	–	11	–	−3	0	43	8
Dec.	39	–	20	14	–	–	46	–	−15	1	53	32
1904 June	−34	–	20	15	51	50	42	–	−8	2	31	36
Dec.	23	2	23	17	1	1	39	4	−4	0	43	39
1905 June	−45	−1	24	17	1	0	−27	−1	0	1	−29	−27
Dec.	43	1	34	27	1	1	29	1	3	0	72	33
1906 June	63	1	34	28	1	0	31	0	8	1	92	40
Dec.	157	1	39	33	1	1	84	1	31	5	192	121
1907 June	47	2	40	33	1	0	35	1	−27	5	82	14
Dec.	91	0	49	42	1	1	89	0	7	3	134	99
1908 June	18	1	50	42	1	0	57	−4	24	4	61	81
Dec.	−10	−1	48	41	1	1	58	0	−11	0	31	47
1909 June	−103	0	49	40	1	0	−41	0	−19	0	−63	−60
Dec.	11	1	48	40	1	0	27	0	−2	1	52	26
1910 June	−9	0	48	39	1	0	–	−1	1	2	30	2
Dec.	62	0	49	40	1	0	47	0	6	0	102	53
1911 June	67	2	49	40	2	1	53	0	1	1	110	55
Dec.	48	1	49	40	4	3	33	0	41	−1	92	73
1912 June	32	1	49	39	4	3	28	0	−1	−2	75	25
Dec.	49	1	53	43	1	0	47	1	−3	0	93	45
1913 June	30	1	54	43	2	1	6	0	2	−1	75	7
Dec.	30	1	51	40	4	2	59	0	−4	0	73	55
1914 June	−38	1	52	41	5	3	−20	0	−2	0	7	−22
Dec.	−45	−1	52	40	2	1	21	0	−1	−2	−5	18
1915 June	152	0	52	40	2	0	144	1	4	−3	192	146
Dec.	208	0	35	23	1	0	231	1	10	9	231	251
1916 June	213	3	23	16	1	−1	88	0	23	9	231	120
Dec.	233	0	36	29	1	0	354	0	2	−1	262	355
1917 June	1 153	2	37	23	27	25	207	−1	1 749	−1	1 203	1 954
Dec.	−189	144	36	23	1	0	60	43	4 358	4	−22	4 465
1918 June	787	455	36	22	1	−1	15	179	4 863	5	1 263	5 062
Dec.	−549	741	35	21	2	0	−33	475	8 672	−2	213	9 112
1919 June	11	192	35	21	3	1	−128	−193	4 246	−1	225	3 924
Dec.	−534	−184	35	20	3	1	−278	−39	502	3	−697	188
1920 June	−745	−242	35	19	3	1	−138	−31	−1 385	4	−967	−1 550
Dec.	233	35	42	26	10	8	90	36	−361	−1	302	−236
1921 June	541	25	43	16	10	7	488	62	−42	−1	589	507
Dec.	300	86	25	19	1	−1	428	139	−554	−2	404	11
1922 June	−68	42	24	10	2	−1	153	194	−489	−1	−17	−143
Dec.	446	−22	29	14	4	1	191	−13	59	3	439	240
1923 June	−47	−72	29	14	5	2	129	−36	−617	3	−103	−521
Dec.	133	95	39	23	3	0	187	121	−407	−2	251	−101
1924 June	153	42	40	23	4	1	237	63	−638	−3	219	−341
Dec.	134	45	51	34	3	0	55	69	−278	4	213	−150
1925 June	−245	9	51	35	4	1	−123	36	−468	3	−200	−552
Dec.	125	36	37	21	3	0	2	46	−263	−3	182	−218
1926 June	−29	38	36	22	3	0	93	44	−600	−2	31	−465
Dec.	−93	35	34	21	4	1	−104	44	−562	1	−36	−621
1927 June	−13	17	34	19	5	1	−12	33	−558	2	24	−535
Dec.	−128	7	41	26	4	1	−139	38	−477	−2	−94	−580
1928 June	−265	0	41	24	11	7	−284	15	−434	−2	−234	−705
Dec.	−3	18	56	39	6	3	−4	16	−287	1	57	−274

Table F-3 is a summary of assets held by the Treasury as reported in *Daily Treasury Statement*, p. 1, for June 30 and Dec. 31 (or end-of-month-statements) for 1896–1928. For the years 1896–1899 the *Statement* is referred to as *Statement of Condition of the U.S. Treasury and the Receipts and Expenditures of the Government*. The distinction observed at present on the *Daily Treasury Statement* between gold, silver, and the general fund (with only net balances of each of the two former accounts carried forward to the latter) is not followed. Both gold and silver are listed on a gross basis with liabilities related to those assets shown in Table F–5.

Column 1 – Total of gold bullion and gold coin in the gold section of the general fund. Figures have been adjusted to include gold reserve from 1900–1915. The manner of presenting gold reserve fund on the asset side of the *Daily Treasury Statement* varies. For the years 1896–1899, a footnote states that "net gold coin and bullion includes $150 million reserve for redemption of U.S. notes..." indicating that gold reserve is included in other gold figures. For the years 1900–1915, gold reserve fund is not included in gold coin and bullion shown in gold section and reserve has been added to gold shown on the *Statement*. Beginning with 1916, gold reserve is again included in gold coin and gold bullion as reported on the asset side of the gold section of the *Statement*.

Column 2 – Total of silver dollars, silver dollars of 1890, and standard silver dollars as shown in the asset side of the silver section of the general fund. Decrease in the figures in 1919–1920 (as well as the negative figure for June 30, 1920, in col. 6) is due to the fact that silver dollars were melted and sold to India under provisions of the Pittman Act at prices in excess of cost of the metal to the Treasury. Hence, col. 2 includes what is actually a capital gain to the U.S. Government.

Column 3 – As reported on the asset side of the general fund.

Column 4 – Sum of items reported on the asset side of the general fund.

Column 5 – Seigniorage receipts for fiscal years were tabulated from *Combined Statement of Receipts and Disbursements of the United States* for years shown; semiannual figures were estimated at half fiscal year total. The figures shown in col. 5 are semiannual figures cumulated since 1896.

Column 6 – Sum of cols. 2–4 minus col. 5.

Column 7 – Sum of following items in the general fund: United States notes, Federal Reserve notes, or Federal Reserve Bank notes; National Bank notes; Treasury notes; certified checks on banks; gold certificates; silver certificates; currency certificates; and minor coin.

Columns 8 and 9 – As reported in the *Daily Treasury Statement*.

Column 10 – Sum of deposits in federal land banks, in foreign depositories, national banks, the Philippine Treasury (all three to the credit of the Treasurer and other government officials), and in special depository accounts for sales of Liberty Bonds and Certificates of Indebtedness, and income and excess profits taxes.

Column 11 – Sum of cols. 1 and 6–10.

Column 12 – Successive semiannual differences of col. 11.

GENERAL FUND ASSETS

1896 to 1928

$ mill.

Semi-annual period ending	Gold at cost	Silver at monetary value	Subsidiary silver coin	Silver bullion at cost and at recoinage value	Seigniorage on silver	Silver at cost	Minor coin and currency	Unclassified	Deposits in Federal Reserve banks	Deposits in other depositories	Total general fund assets	Semi-annual change in general fund assets
	1	2	3	4	5	6	7	8	9	10	11	12
1896 Dec.	175	385	14	111	5	505	150	1	–	16	847	-4
1897 June	178	400	16	105	9	512	152	0	–	17	859	12
Dec.	197	394	11	102	12	495	109	17	–	50	868	9
1898 June	202	405	12	98	14	501	77	1	–	36	817	-51
Dec.	282	405	6	93	17	487	49	1	–	94	913	96
1899 June	272	417	6	85	20	488	46	1	–	79	886	-27
Dec.	398	413	3	81	25	472	66	16	–	86	1 038	152
1900 June	421	430	7	70	30	477	75	2	–	102	1 077	39
Dec.	478	433	4	61	36	462	56	0	–	102	1 098	21
1901 June	494	454	11	47	43	469	73	1	–	102	1 139	41
Dec.	540	457	7	39	48	455	61	–	–	119	1 175	36
1902 June	559	471	14	30	54	461	68	–	–	127	1 215	40
Dec.	617	470	6	24	58	442	61	–	–	151	1 271	56
1903 June	634	487	9	15	62	449	65	–	–	155	1 303	32
Dec.	686	477	8	13	65	433	51	–	–	172	1 342	39
1904 June	680	496	12	5	69	444	64	–	–	120	1 308	-34
Dec.	697	487	9	5	71	430	87	–	–	117	1 331	23
1905 June	705	492	13	0	73	432	69	–	–	80	1 286	-45
Dec.	765	484	7	1	74	418	76	–	–	70	1 329	43
1906 June	802	490	7	0	76	421	70	–	–	99	1 392	63
Dec.	894	483	4	1	80	408	83	–	–	164	1 549	157
1907 June	904	487	8	0	85	410	96	–	–	186	1 596	47
Dec.	949	477	4	3	90	394	80	–	–	264	1 687	91
1908 June	1 002	491	24	0	96	419	115	–	–	169	1 705	18
Dec.	1 034	496	18	4	99	419	115	–	–	127	1 695	-10
1909 June	1 041	496	27	0	103	420	53	–	–	78	1 592	-103
Dec.	1 032	494	16	3	105	408	109	–	–	54	1 603	11
1910 June	1 043	496	20	4	107	413	81	–	–	57	1 594	-9
Dec.	1 103	493	15	3	109	402	97	–	–	54	1 656	62
1911 June	1 161	495	21	4	112	408	92	–	–	62	1 723	67
Dec.	1 183	494	18	2	115	399	135	–	–	54	1 771	48
1912 June	1 206	499	26	2	119	408	136	–	–	53	1 803	32
Dec.	1 255	494	18	1	122	391	153	–	–	53	1 852	49
1913 June	1 260	497	21	2	125	395	118	–	–	109	1 882	30
Dec.	1 201	404	14	2	128	382	139	–	–	100	1 912	30
1914 June	1 276	498	22	3	131	392	100	–	–	106	1 874	-38
Dec.	1 184	499	21	3	133	390	174	–	–	81	1 829	-45
1915 June	1 381	505	26	4	135	400	101	–	–	99	1 981	152
Dec.	1 692	502	19	5	137	389	42	1	15	50	2 189	208
1916 June	1 801	502	17	6	140	385	33	0	111	72	2 402	213
Dec.	2 175	496	3	7	145	361	26	1	28	44	2 635	233
1917 June	2 323	496	4	6	151	355	31	0	306	773	3 788	1 153
Dec.	2 364	490	2	7	162	337	47	1	109	741	3 599	-189
1918 June	2 478	422	15	13	173	277	60	3	26	1 542	4 386	787
Dec.	2 546	318	3	12	179	154	74	8	157	898	3 837	-549
1919 June	2 523	227	11	16	185	69	152	6	105	993	3 848	11
Dec.	2 268	207	3	14	191	33	166	25	110	712	3 314	-534
1920 June	2 170	135	7	19	197	-36	63	13	44	315	2 569	-745
Dec.	2 221	171	5	38	203	11	39	25	143	363	2 802	233
1921 June	2 670	214	10	56	210	70	26	21	80	476	3 343	541
Dec.	3 023	289	12	37	221	117	30	9	131	333	3 643	300
1922 June	3 157	313	18	44	232	143	28	13	56	178	3 575	-68
Dec.	3 284	374	13	28	245	170	28	3	34	502	4 021	446
1923 June	3 364	426	12	30	258	210	19	7	47	327	3 974	-47
Dec.	3 554	422	7	33	262	200	24	6	64	259	4 107	133
1924 June	3 785	428	8	31	266	201	26	9	46	193	4 260	153
Dec.	3 835	442	7	23	270	202	22	4	71	260	4 394	134
1925 June	3 691	453	7	16	274	202	28	4	42	182	4 149	-245
Dec.	3 694	455	6	15	279	197	22	2	38	321	4 274	125
1926 June	3 713	465	6	8	284	195	25	62	19	231	4 245	-29
Dec.	3 657	469	3	8	288	192	21	3	29	250	4 152	-93
1927 June	3 651	476	5	7	293	195	26	0	38	229	4 130	-13
Dec.	3 503	447	2	6	296	159	29	3	34	283	4 011	-128
1928 June	3 215	480	3	8	300	191	28	13	24	275	3 746	-265
Dec.	3 206	482	2	5	302	187	23	2	39	286	3 743	-3

Assets shown in Table F-4 are those of following government corporations, obtained from annual financial statements of the corporation as of date indicated below, or from Senate Document 172, part 2, 76th Congress, 3rd Session, *Financial Statements of Certain Government Agencies*, Feb. 15, 1940:

(a) Panama Railroad Company: annual report with financial statement as of June 30 for years 1917–1928, as of Dec. 31 for 1904–1905, and as of Oct. 31, 1906–1916; also financial statements as of June 30 from Senate Document No. 172.

(b) Inland Waterways Corporation: financial statements as of Dec. 31, 1924–1928, from Senate Document No. 172.

(c) Federal land banks: financial statement as of Dec. 31, 1918, 1920, and 1922–1928, and Nov. 30, 1919 and 1921, as published in various issues of *Statistical Abstract*.

(d) Federal intermediate credit banks: financial statement as of Dec. 31, 1923–1928, as published in various issues of *Statistical Abstract*.

(e) U.S. Emergency Fleet Corporation: annual report of U.S. Shipping Board with financial statement for U.S. Emergency Fleet Corporation as of Oct. 31, 1917, and June 30, 1918–1928.

(f) War Finance Corporation: annual reports, with financial statements as of Nov. 30, 1918–1928, and tabulations showing balances outstanding on advances for agricultural and livestock purposes as of June 30 and Dec. 31, 1921–1929.

(g) U.S. Food Administration Grain Corporation: financial statements as of Feb. 20, 1919, June 30, 1919 and Aug. 31, 1921, from unpublished reports on examination of accounts, by various accounting firms, in custody of National Archives.

(h) U.S. Sugar Equalization Board Incorporated: financial statements as of Dec. 31, 1918–1923, and June 30, 1919–1922 from unpublished reports on audit of accounts, by various auditing firms, in custody of National Archives.

(i) U.S. Housing Corporation: report of U.S. Housing Corporation, Organizations, policies, transactions: *War Emergency Construction* (housing war workers). Photostat copies of financial statements as of Dec. 31, 1918–1919, and June 30, 1919–1928, made available by New York office of Home Owners' Loan Corporation.

Where financial statements are as of June 30, estimates for Dec. 31 were obtained by averaging figures for June preceding and following. Similarly, where financial statements are as of Dec. 31, figures for June 30 were obtained by averaging the two Dec. figures. Where reports relate to other dates, figures for June 30 and Dec. 31 were obtained by interpolation.

In the case of U.S. Housing Corporation, figures on fixed assets are shown at total cost minus sale price of those sold, with no adjustment for $29 million losses on property sold in 1919. For example, balance sheet for Dec. 31, 1919, shows projects at construction cost of $51 million, whereas published report referred to above indicates that value of property on hand as of Jan. 1, 1920, was $22 million, with loss on property sold amounting to $29 million.

Assets for all agencies are shown gross of reserves for depreciation, losses, etc., where statistics permit.

Figures begin with 1904 when U.S. acquired stock of Panama Railroad Company with purchase of Panama Canal.

Depreciation of fixed assets calculated on linear basis, assuming average life of fifty years.

$ mill.

Semi-annual period ending	Loans (except interagency)			Other invest-ments	Cash other than with Treasury	Accounts receiv-able and accrued assets	Inven-tories	Fixed assets	Depre-ciated fixed assets	Other assets	Total assets	Semi-annual change in assets
	Farm mort-gage	Other agri-cultural	Other									
	1	2	3	4	5	6	7	8	9	10	11	12
1904 June	–	–	–	1	0	0	0	12	12	–	13	
Dec.	–	–	–	1	1	0	0	13	13	–	15	2
1905 June	–	–	–	1	0	0	0	13	13	–	14	–1
Dec.	–	–	–	1	0	0	1	13	13	–	15	1
1906 June	–	–	–	1	0	1	1	14	13	–	16	1
Dec.	–	–	–	1	0	1	1	15	14	–	17	1
1907 June	–	–	–	1	1	1	1	16	15	–	19	2
Dec.	–	–	–	1	1	1	1	16	15	–	19	0
1908 June	–	–	–	0	1	1	2	17	16	–	20	1
Dec.	–	–	–	0	1	1	1	17	16	–	19	–1
1909 June	–	–	–	0	1	1	1	18	16	–	19	0
Dec.	–	–	–	0	2	1	1	18	16	–	20	1
1910 June	–	–	–	0	2	1	1	18	16	–	20	0
Dec.	–	–	–	0	2	1	1	18	16	–	20	0
1911 June	–	–	–	0	4	1	1	18	16	–	22	2
Dec.	–	–	–	2	3	1	1	18	16	–	23	1
1912 June	–	–	–	2	3	1	2	19	16	–	24	1
Dec.	–	–	–	2	3	1	2	20	17	–	25	1
1913 June	–	–	–	2	3	1	2	21	18	–	26	1
Dec.	–	–	–	2	3	1	2	22	19	–	27	1
1914 June	–	–	–	2	4	1	2	23	19	–	28	1
Dec.	–	–	–	2	3	1	2	23	19	–	27	–1
1915 June	–	–	–	2	3	1	2	23	19	–	27	0
Dec.	–	–	–	2	2	1	2	24	20	–	27	0
1916 June	–	–	–	2	4	1	2	25	21	–	30	3
Dec.	–	–	–	2	3	1	3	26	21	–	30	0
1917 June	–	–	–	2	1	1	4	27	22	2	32	2
Dec.	–	–	–	2	2	1	72	28	23	76	176	144
1918 June	94	–	–	2	3	56	300	29	23	153	631	455
Dec.	157	3	37	2	5	209	564	48	42	353	1 372	741
1919 June	220	3	74	3	4	387	253	73	66	554	1 564	192
Dec.	282	2	101	18	3	406	213	84	77	278	1 380	–184
1920 June	316	1	111	33	4	418	178	84	76	1	1 138	–242
Dec.	350	1	123	60	6	421	142	78	69	1	1 173	35
1921 June	391	1	120	87	8	428	103	69	59	1	1 198	25
Dec.	433	83	113	44	10	468	73	68	58	2	1 284	86
1922 June	536	115	74	2	9	489	43	67	56	2	1 326	42
Dec.	639	149	36	2	8	384	30	66	54	2	1 304	–22
1923 June	720	109	34	2	10	276	16	66	54	11	1 232	–72
Dec.	800	110	31	3	16	264	14	67	54	35	1 327	95
1924 June	864	106	25	3	18	248	12	67	53	40	1 369	42
Dec.	928	103	23	3	22	222	11	77	63	39	1 414	45
1925 June	967	99	24	3	21	195	11	79	64	39	1 423	9
Dec.	1 006	96	25	4	20	191	9	80	64	44	1 459	36
1926 June	1 042	99	25	5	21	185	8	81	64	48	1 497	38
Dec.	1 078	101	25	5	24	178	8	83	65	48	1 532	35
1927 June	1 117	90	19	6	26	172	8	84	66	45	1 549	17
Dec.	1 156	77	13	8	28	154	8	84	65	47	1 556	7
1928 June	1 175	79	15	7	25	133	8	97	77	37	1 556	0
Dec.	1 195	82	18	7	23	129	8	109	88	24	1 574	18

Table F-5 presents liabilities of the Treasury as reported in the *Daily Treasury Statement* for June 30 and Dec. 31 (or end-of-month statements) for 1896–1928. For the years 1896–1899, the *Statement* is referred to as *Statement of Condition of the U.S. Treasury and the Receipts and Expenditures of the Government*. The distinction observed at present on the *Daily Treasury Statement* between gold, silver, and the general fund (with only net balances of each of the two former accounts carried forward to the latter) is not followed. Both gold and silver are listed on a gross basis with liabilities related to these assets shown in this table.

Although the Post Office Department deposits with the Treasurer of the United States, the transactions do not affect the balance of the Treasury and, hence, figures on liabilities exclude deposits of the Post Office Department and postmasters. For the same reason the deposits of clerks of court, disbursing officers etc., are excluded from liabilities.

Column 1 – Includes gold certificates and currency certificates outstanding.

Column 2 – As shown in *Daily Treasury Statements*.

Column 3 – Includes deposits for Federal Reserve notes, 5 percent fund; Federal Reserve Bank notes, 5 percent fund, lawful money; and retirement of additional circulating notes (act of May 30, 1918). For the years 1909–1915 figures for National Bank notes are shown on the *Daily Treasury Statement* for both the redemption fund and notes in process of redemption; figure shown in col. 3 is the net of the two figures.

Column 4 – For years 1896–1899 the gold reserve ($100 million fund) is not included on the *Daily Treasury Statement* as a liability of the Treasury since it is included in the public debt. Beginning with 1900, the fund is carried as a liability of the Treasury on *Daily Treasury Statement*, including both gold coin and gold bullion. For purposes of this study the gold reserve fund is also carried as a liability of the Treasury for 1896–1899, and the public debt has been reduced by the amount of the gold reserve.

Column 5 – Includes silver certificates and Treasury notes of 1890 outstanding.

Column 6 – As shown in *Daily Treasury Statements*.

Column 7 – Includes Board of Trustees, Postal Savings System, 5 percent reserve and other deposits of the system.

Column 8 – Exchanges, miscellaneous items, etc.

Column 9 – Sum of cols. 1–8.

Column 10 – Semiannual differences of col. 9.

GENERAL FUND LIABILITIES

1896 to 1928

$ mill.

Semi-annual period ending	Gold certificates outstanding	Gold fund, Federal Reserve banks	Redemption fund, Federal Reserve and other notes	Gold reserve fund	Silver certificates and Treasury notes of 1890 outstanding	Treasurer's checks outstanding	Deposits of Postal Savings System with Treasury	Uncollected items, exchanges, etc.	Total general fund liabilities	Semi-annual change in general fund liabilities
	1	2	3	4	5	6	7	8	9	10
1896 Dec.	90	–	9	100	491	4	–	2	696	34
1897 June	101	–	7	100	490	3	–	2	703	7
Dec.	83	–	8	100	494	8	–	2	695	–8
1898 June	64	–	8	100	500	6	–	2	680	–15
Dec.	58	–	10	100	495	6	–	2	671	–9
1899 June	55	–	9	100	500	5	–	3	672	1
Dec.	197	–	9	100	489	5	–	3	803	131
1900 June	232	–	12	150	492	5	–	3	894	91
Dec.	264	–	14	150	490	8	–	3	929	35
1901 June	289	–	14	150	483	8	–	3	947	18
Dec.	317	–	14	150	495	7	–	3	986	39
1902 June	347	–	13	150	484	5	–	2	1 001	15
Dec.	384	–	15	150	494	9	–	3	1 055	54
1903 June	409	–	15	150	484	7	–	1	1 066	11
Dec.	447	–	17	150	488	8	–	2	1 112	46
1904 June	494	–	16	150	483	9	–	2	1 154	42
Dec.	525	–	17	150	488	12	–	1	1 193	39
1905 June	518	–	18	150	474	5	–	1	1 166	–27
Dec.	528	–	21	150	484	10	–	2	1 195	29
1906 June	560	–	21	150	484	9	–	2	1 226	31
Dec.	639	–	25	150	483	11	–	2	1 310	84
1907 June	678	–	22	150	482	11	–	2	1 345	35
Dec.	767	–	28	150	477	10	–	2	1 434	89
1908 June	823	–	23	150	479	13	–	3	1 491	57
Dec.	858	–	29	150	496	14	–	2	1 549	58
1909 June	853	–	4	150	488	11	–	2	1 508	–41
Dec.	875	–	6	150	491	11	–	2	1 535	27
1910 June	863	–	12	150	493	17	–	0	1 535	0
Dec.	923	–	8	150	489	11	–	1	1 582	47
1911 June	995	–	14	150	467	9	–	0	1 635	53
Dec.	1 011	–	0	150	492	13	–	2	1 668	33
1912 June	1 040	–	14	150	485	7	–	0	1 696	28
Dec.	1 084	–	1	150	494	12	–	2	1 743	47
1913 June	1 087	–	9	150	487	16	–	0	1 749	6
Dec.	1 116	–	45	150	492	6	1	–2	1 808	59
1914 June	1 081	–	51	150	493	6	2	5	1 788	–20
Dec.	968	–	188	152	483	4	2	12	1 809	21
1915 June	1 174	–	116	153	495	5	4	6	1 953	144
Dec.	1 475	–	49	153	488	3	4	12	2 184	231
1916 June	1 566	–	42	153	493	3	4	11	2 272	88
Dec.	1 922	–	48	153	479	4	4	16	2 626	354
1917 June	1 592	528	58	153	480	3	6	13	2 833	207
Dec.	1 343	808	91	153	474	7	6	11	2 893	60
1918 June	1 037	1 196	114	153	384	4	7	13	2 908	15
Dec.	885	1 334	199	153	267	4	8	25	2 875	–33
1919 June	748	1 415	227	153	172	1	8	23	2 747	–128
Dec.	665	1 222	252	153	151	3	8	15	2 469	–278
1920 June	584	1 184	261	153	121	1	8	19	2 331	–138
Dec.	533	1 254	302	153	154	1	8	16	2 421	90
1921 June	716	1 538	288	153	204	0	4	6	2 909	488
Dec.	710	1 934	245	153	281	0	7	7	3 337	428
1922 June	695	2 109	216	153	306	0	7	4	3 490	153
Dec.	708	2 236	219	153	346	3	7	9	3 681	191
1923 June	737	2 285	207	153	413	2	7	6	3 810	129
Dec.	977	2 220	219	153	411	2	7	8	3 997	187
1924 June	1 218	2 261	172	153	409	1	8	12	4 234	237
Dec.	1 509	1 987	187	153	440	1	7	5	4 289	55
1925 June	1 608	1 753	189	154	447	2	7	6	4 166	–123
Dec.	1 712	1 649	192	154	448	2	7	4	4 168	2
1926 June	1 681	1 717	178	154	459	1	8	63	4 261	93
Dec.	1 680	1 629	206	154	466	1	7	14	4 157	–104
1927 June	1 625	1 712	166	155	471	6	7	3	4 145	–12
Dec.	1 617	1 557	185	155	474	7	8	3	4 006	–139
1928 June	1 514	1 388	176	156	473	5	7	3	3 722	–284
Dec.	1 413	1 449	200	156	476	11	9	4	3 718	–4

Liabilities shown are those of following corporations:

Pamama Railroad Company
Inland Waterways Corporation
Federal land banks
Federal intermediate credit banks
U.S. Emergency Fleet Corporation
War Finance Corporation
U.S. Food Administration Grain Corporation
U.S. Sugar Equalization Board Incorporated
U.S. Housing Corporation.

Figures were obtained from financial statements in annual reports of the corporations and, in some cases, from Senate Document No. 172, Part 2, 76th Congress, 3rd Session, *Financial Statements of Certain Government Agencies*, Feb. 15, 1940. In general the financial statements are as of June 30 or Dec. 31 (see notes to Table F-4 for date and source of financial statements).

Where financial statements are as of June 30, figures for Dec. 31 were obtained by averaging the two June figures. Similarly, where financial statements are as of Dec. 31, figures for June 30 were obtained by averaging the two Dec. figures. Where reports relate to other dates, figures for June 30 and Dec. 31 were obtained by interpolation. Figures are shown gross of reserves where statistics permit.

Column 1 – Figures begin with 1904 when U.S. acquired capital stock of Panama Railroad Company with purchase of Panama Canal. Includes bonds, debentures, and notes payable of Panama Railroad Company, Inland Waterways Corporation, federal land banks, federal intermediate credit banks, and U.S. Grain Corporation.

Column 2 – Consists largely of interest payable on securities (in col. 1) of federal land banks and federal intermediate credit banks.

Column 3 – Includes accounts payable, deposit liabilities, deferred credit items, and miscellaneous other items of indebtedness to public of all corporations listed above. Largest items are liabilities of U.S. Emergency Fleet Corporation, including accounts payable, uncompleted voyages, charter hire payable, and other commitments.

Column 4 – Includes capital stock of federal land banks owned by National Farm Loan Associations, borrowers, and individual subscribers.

Column 5 – Sum of cols. 1–4.

Column 6 – Successive differences of col. 5.

1904 to 1928

$ mill.

Semi-annual period ending	Obligations held by public	Accrued liabilities	Accounts payable and other liabilities	Paid-in capital, privately held	Total liabilities	Semi-annual change in liabilities
	1	2	3	4	5	6
1904 June	–	–	–	–	–	–
Dec.	4	–	–	–	4	4
1905 June	3	–	–	–	3	–1
Dec.	3	–	1	–	4	1
1906 June	3	–	1	–	4	0
Dec.	3	–	2	–	5	1
1907 June	3	–	3	–	6	1
Dec.	3	–	3	–	6	0
1908 June	–	–	2	–	2	–4
Dec.	–	–	2	–	2	0
1909 June	–	–	2	–	2	0
Dec.	–	–	2	–	2	0
1910 June	–	–	1	–	1	–1
Dec.	–	–	1	–	1	0
1911 June	–	–	1	–	1	0
Dec.	–	–	1	–	1	0
1912 June	–	–	1	–	1	0
Dec.	–	–	2	–	2	1
1913 June	–	–	2	–	2	0
Dec.	–	–	2	–	2	0
1914 June	–	–	2	–	2	0
Dec.	–	–	2	–	2	0
1915 June	–	–	3	–	3	1
Dec.	–	–	4	–	4	1
1916 June	–	–	4	–	4	0
Dec.	–	–	4	–	4	0
1917 June	–	–	3	–	3	–1
Dec.	–	–	46	–	46	43
1918 June	–	–	225	–	225	179
Dec.	451	1	240	8	700	475
1919 June	273	1	222	11	507	–193
Dec.	286	1	167	14	468	–39
1920 June	310	2	109	16	437	–31
Dec.	334	3	118	18	473	36
1921 June	385	3	127	20	535	62
Dec.	435	3	214	22	674	139
1922 June	538	4	299	27	868	194
Dec.	643	6	173	33	855	–13
1923 June	727	9	46	37	819	–36
Dec.	843	12	44	41	940	121
1924 June	905	13	41	44	1 003	63
Dec.	969	14	41	48	1 072	69
1925 June	1 007	14	37	50	1 108	36
Dec.	1 049	15	37	53	1 154	46
1926 June	1 090	16	37	55	1 198	44
Dec.	1 132	18	35	57	1 242	44
1927 June	1 165	18	33	59	1 275	33
Dec.	1 198	19	34	62	1 313	38
1928 June	1 213	20	32	63	1 328	15
Dec.	1 230	21	28	65	1 344	16

Column 1 – Figures on gross public debt as of June 30 are taken from an historical table in the *Annual Report of the Secretary of the Treasury* for the fiscal year ended June 30, 1930, pp. 560–561. Figures as of Dec. 31, 1896–1915 are from "Statement of the Public Debt" in the *Daily Treasury Statements*, issues of Dec. 31; for 1916–1930 they are from *Banking and Monetary Statistics*, p. 509. For 1896–1899 published figures include the gold reserve fund ($100 million); after 1899 the fund in omitted from the public debt and is carried under liabilities on the *Daily Treasury Statement*. To obtain uniformity over the period the published public debt has been adjusted in 1896–1899 to exclude the gold reserve fund of $100 million and liabilities (Table F-5, col. 4) have been increased by the same amount.

Column 2 – Figures as of June 30 for 1916–1930 are from *Banking and Monetary Statistics*, p. 512, adjusted to exclude investment of trust funds in government securities since these funds are included in this study under "Direct federal debt held by public." For years prior to 1916 no figures are shown in *Banking and Monetary Statistics*. Prior to 1916, according to information from Treasury, federal agencies either held no part of the public debt or their holdings were not more than $1 million. Estimates for Dec. 31 are averages of figures for June 30 preceding and following. Federal Reserve banks are not included among government corporations and credit agencies.

Column 3 – Col. 1 minus col. 2. Figures include that part of the public debt held by Federal Reserve banks and the Postal Savings System and investments of government trust funds.

Column 4 – Successive differences of col. 3.

1896 to 1928

$ mill.

Semi-annual period ending	Gross federal debt	Federal debt held by government corporations and credit agencies (excluding trust funds)	Direct federal debt held by public (including trust funds)	Semi-annual net change in direct federal debt held by public	Semi-annual period ending	Gross federal debt	Federal debt held by government corporations and credit agencies (excluding trust funds)	Direct federal debt held by public (including trust funds)	Semi-annual net change in direct federal debt held by public
	1	2	3	4		1	2	3	4
1896 Dec.	1 121	–	1 121	–2	1913 June	1 193	–	1 193	2
1897 June	1 127	–	1 127	6	Dec.	1 189	–	1 189	–4
Dec.	1 135	–	1 135	8	1914 June	1 188	1	1 187	–2
1898 June	1 133	–	1 133	–2	Dec.	1 187	1	1 186	–1
Dec.	1 324	–	1 324	191	1915 June	1 191	1	1 190	4
1899 June	1 337	–	1 337	13	Dec.	1 201	1	1 200	10
Dec.	1 318	–	1 318	–19	1916 June	1 225	2	1 223	23
1900 June	1 263	–	1 263	–55	Dec.	1 227	2	1 225	2
Dec.	1 239	–	1 239	–24	1917 June	2 976	2	2 974	1 749
1901 June	1 222	–	1 222	–17	Dec.	7 357	25	7 332	4 358
Dec.	1 183	–	1 183	–39	1918 June	12 244	49	12 195	4 863
1902 June	1 178	–	1 178	–5	Dec.	21 076	209	20 867	8 672
Dec.	1 162	–	1 162	–16	1919 June	25 482	369	25 113	4 242
1903 June	1 159	–	1 159	–3	Dec.	25 834	219	25 615	502
Dec.	1 144	–	1 144	–15	1920 June	24 298	68	24 230	–1 385
1904 June	1 136	–	1 136	–8	Dec.	23 978	109	23 869	–361
Dec.	1 132	–	1 132	–4	1921 June	23 976	149	23 827	–42
1905 June	1 132	–	1 132	0	Dec.	23 438	165	23 273	–554
Dec.	1 135	–	1 135	3	1922 June	22 964	180	22 784	–489
1906 June	1 143	–	1 143	8	Dec.	22 995	152	22 843	59
Dec.	1 174	–	1 174	31	1923 June	22 350	124	22 226	–617
1907 June	1 147	–	1 147	–27	Dec.	21 916	97	21 819	–407
Dec.	1 154	–	1 154	7	1924 June	21 251	70	21 181	–638
1908 June	1 178	–	1 178	24	Dec.	20 979	76	20 903	–278
Dec.	1 167	–	1 167	11	1925 June	20 516	81	20 435	–468
1909 June	1 148	–	1 148	–19	Dec.	20 248	76	20 172	–263
Dec.	1 146	–	1 146	–2	1926 June	19 643	71	19 572	–600
1910 June	1 147	–	1 147	1	Dec.	19 075	65	19 010	–562
Dec.	1 153	–	1 153	6	1927 June	18 510	58	18 452	–558
1911 June	1 154	–	1 154	1	Dec.	18 036	61	17 975	–477
Dec.	1 195	–	1 195	41	1928 June	17 604	63	17 541	–434
1912 June	1 194	–	1 194	–1	Dec.	17 310	56	17 254	–287
Dec.	1 191	–	1 191	–3					

Miscellaneous other liabilities consist of Treasury balances in trust funds not invested in securities of U.S. Government. These balances, like trust fund investments, represent liabilities to public. The figures as of June 30, 1896–1911, were obtained from *Annual Treasury Department Statement of Balances, Appropriations and Disbursements*. Beginning with 1912, statements were changed to *Combined Statement of Receipts, Disbursements and Balances*. Estimates as of Dec. 31 were obtained by averaging figures for June 30 preceding and following.

Column 1 – Figures include balances in principal of Indian trust funds deposited in Treasury and drawing 4 percent interest, balances of interest funds, and small balances (if any) in these accounts to credit of disbursing officers. The 1896–1907 principal and interest were combined in trust fund totals for the various tribes. Beginning with 1908, principal is reported as trust fund account and interest as general permanent account. Both interest and principal are included in col. 1.

Column 2 – Includes balances in accounts held for military and naval personnel, such as "Pay of the Army, deposit fund," "Pay of the Navy, deposit fund," Army, Navy, and Marines allotments of pay, and funds for the Soldiers' Home.

Column 3 – Includes balances of small funds held for individuals by Department of the Treasury, Department of State, Smithsonian Institution, Department of the Interior exclusive of Indian accounts, District of Columbia funds, and small balances of major trust funds held by disbursing officers and not included in the investment totals.

Column 4 – Sum of cols. 1–3. Dec. data obtained by linear interpolation between June figures.

Column 5 – Successive differences of col. 4.

986

1896 to 1928

$ mill.

Semi-annual period ending	Balances of trust funds in Treasury					Semi-annual period ending	Balances of trust funds in Treasury				
	Indian trust funds	Military and naval personnel	Other	Total	Semi-annual net change		Indian trust funds	Military and naval personnel	Other	Total	Semi-annual net change
	1	2	3	4	5		1	2	3	4	5
1896 Dec.				33	-1	1913 June	47	7	4	58	-1
1897 June	29	3	0	32	-1	Dec.				58	0
Dec.				32	0	1914 June	47	7	4	58	0
1898 June	29	3	0	32	0	Dec.				56	-2
Dec.				32	0	1915 June	43	7	3	53	-3
1899 June	30	3	0	33	1	Dec.				62	9
Dec.				33	0	1916 June	46	22	3	71	9
1900 June	30	3	0	33	0	Dec.				70	-1
Dec.				33	0	1917 June	43	23	3	69	-1
1901 June	30	4	0	34	1	Dec.				73	4
Dec.				35	1	1918 June	40	35	3	78	5
1902 June	32	4	0	36	1	Dec.				76	-2
Dec.				36	0	1919 June	34	38	3	75	-1
1903 June	32	4	0	36	0	Dec.				78	3
Dec.				37	1	1920 June	35	43	4	82	4
1904 June	34	5	0	39	2	Dec.				81	-1
Dec.				39	0	1921 June	29	42	9	80	-1
1905 June	35	5	0	40	1	Dec.				78	-2
Dec.				40	0	1922 June	26	43	8	77	-1
1906 June	36	5	0	41	1	Dec.				80	3
Dec.				46	5	1923 June	30	43	10	83	3
1907 June	39	9	3	51	5	Dec.				81	-2
Dec.				54	3	1924 June	24	42	12	78	-3
1908 June	45	9	4	58	4	Dec.				82	4
Dec.				58	0	1925 June	31	45	9	85	3
1909 June	46	8	4	58	0	Dec.				82	3
Dec.				59	1	1926 June	25	41	14	80	-2
1910 June	49	8	4	61	2	Dec.				81	1
Dec.				61	0	1927 June	27	40	16	83	2
1911 June	51	7	4	62	1	Dec.				81	-2
Dec.				61	-1	1928 June	24	41	14	79	-2
1912 June	48	7	4	59	-2	Dec.				80	1
Dec.				59	0						

987

Individuals' equity in trust funds administered by Treasury under various acts is regarded as equal to investments held by Treasury on behalf of these funds and their beneficiaries. Figures as of June 30 were taken from *Annual Report of the Secretary of the Treasury* (in early years referred to as *Annual Report on the State of Finances*). With exception of Indian trust funds, figures are taken from that section of *Annual Report of the Secretary of the Treasury* relating to "Trust funds administered by the Treasury," and include investments only. Balances, if any, to credit of disbursing officers are included in Table F-8, col. 3. In some cases where both "par value" (or "face value") and "principal cost" were shown, figures tabulated are "principal costs." Figures as of Dec. 31 were obtained by averaging June 30 figures. This is subject to error since it is conceivable that "lump" investments rather than "continuous" investments may have been made.

Column 6 – Beginning with 1927 fund was invested in government securities and loans to veterans. Loans to veterans are shown in col. 6 but are excluded from total in col. 10.

Column 7 – Beginning with 1919 some Indian trust funds were invested in government securities. Amounts in col. 7 are taken from tabulation in *Annual Report of the Secretary of the Treasury* of special trust funds in custody of Treasurer and are exclusive of Treasury balances of Indian trust funds included in Table F-8.

Column 10 – Sum of cols. 1–5 and 7. Dec. figures obtained by linear interpolation between June figures.

Column 11 – Successive differences of col. 10.

ADMINISTERED BY UNITED STATES TREASURY: 1918 to 1928

$ mill.

Semi-annual period ending	Civil Service Retire-ment and Disability Fund	Foreign Service Retire-ment and Disability Fund	District of Columbia Teachers' Retire-ment Fund	Adjusted Service Certif-icate Fund	U.S. Government Life Insurance Fund		Indian trust funds	Alien Property Custodian	German Special Deposit Account	Invest-ments of trust funds	Semi-annual change in invest-ments of trust funds
					Invest-ments	Loans to vet-erans					
	1	2	3	4	5	6	7	8	9	10	11
1918 June	–	–	–	–	–	–	3	39	–	3	3
Dec.										6	3
1919 June	–	–	–	–	–	–	9	101	–	9	3
Dec.										15	6
1920 June	–	–	–	–	11	–	10	156	–	21	6
Dec.										36	15
1921 June	8	–	0	–	35	–	9	158	–	52	16
Dec.										70	18
1922 June	18	–	1	–	60	–	9	164	–	88	18
Dec.										105	17
1923 June	26	–	1	–	87	–	8	174	–	122	17
Dec.										140	18
1924 June	33	–	1	0	117	–	7	165	–	158	18
Dec.										230	72
1925 June	44	0	1	95	149	–	14	177	–	303	73
Dec.										390	87
1926 June	54	0	1	204	187	–	32	179	–	478	88
Dec.										551	73
1927 June	68	0	2	313	210	21	31	180	12	624	73
Dec.										681	57
1928 June	83	0	2	402	219	74	32	156	85	738	57
Dec.										808	70

Table F-10 presents semi-annual estimates of current receipts of federal government derived by excluding from total receipts (a) those receipts of a noncurrent or capital nature; and (b) those treated in this study as transactions of the "public" or of state and local governments.

Fiscal-year totals (as of June 30) were taken from *Treasury Statement of Receipts and Disbursements* and *Combined Statement of Receipts, Disbursements and Balances.* Six-month totals from July 1 through Dec. 31 were obtained from *Daily Statement of the United States Treasury* (referred to as *Daily Treasury Statement*) where published. Where detailed items were not shown on *Daily Treasury Statement*, fiscal year total was distributed equally between the two six-month periods.

Column 1 – Total of "ordinary" receipts, excluding public debt receipts and postal revenues under control of Postmaster General except surplus of such receipts over postal expenditures. Figures are on a warrants-issued basis through fiscal year 1918, after which they are on cash-receipts basis, revised to *Daily Treasury Statement* basis. Beginning with *Combined Statement* for fiscal year 1923, cash receipts previously credited against expenditures are included in both receipts and expenditures to adjust figures to actual receipts and expenditure basis. This adjustment to receipts is made under two headings, "Proceeds of railroad securities owned by the government" and "Receipts from miscellaneous sources." Totals in col. 1 have been adjusted to include miscellaneous receipts (tolls, etc.) of Panama Canal for those years (1916–1920) in which these receipts were not included in "ordinary" receipts in *Combined Statement.*

Column 2 – Receipts of Federal Reserve System are deducted since in this study the System is treated as part of the private sector of the economy.

Column 3 – Receipts of District of Columbia, including trust fund receipts, are deducted since in this study the District is included with state and local governments.

Column 4 – Trust fund receipts, exclusive of those of District of Columbia in col. 3, are deducted. Such receipts include premiums on insurance funds, employee deductions for retirement, receipts of Indian trust funds, deposit funds for military and naval personnel, etc.

Column 5 – Deducted as capital receipt.

Column 6 – Receipts deducted as being in nature of capital gains.

Column 7 – Receipts from sale of federal land bank bonds.

Column 8 – Redemption of capital stock of federal land banks, federal intermediate credit banks, and war emergency corporations (U.S. Grain Corporation, U.S. Sugar Equalization Board, Inc.). In fiscal year 1919, $1 billion was appropriated for "Operations under the wheat price guarantee." Expenditures for fiscal year 1920 include $350 million for "Operations under wheat price guarantee," offset in some years by receipts of $350 million from decrease of capital stock of U.S. Grain Corporation and return of fund to Treasury. In 1921, $647 million was returned to surplus, with no receipts or expenditures shown. Remaining $3 million was used in 1921 for administrative expenses. See negative expenditures in Table F-11, col. 4 for return of capital stock of War Finance Corporation.

Column 9 – Receipts 1896–1909 consist of repayments by Central Pacific and other railroads. Figures in later years include return or advances made to reclamation fund and repayment of housing loans.

Column 10 – Receipts on account of railroad securities were credited as offsets to appropriation accounts instead of being listed as receipts, being added to both receipts and expenditures to adjust to actual receipts and expenditures bases (see notes to col. 1). Proceeds include interest on loans to carriers after termination of federal control; repayment of loans by carriers to government for improvements to railroads while under federal control; and receipts from sale of these obligations by government to private investors. Interest figures should not be deducted as capital receipts, but it has not been possible in all cases to segregate interest payments from capital proceeds.

Column 11 – Col. 1 minus cols. 2–10.

CURRENT RECEIPTS OF FEDERAL GOVERNMENT
1897 to 1928

$ mill.

Semi-annual period ending	Total receipts	Federal Reserve Board	District of Columbia	Trust funds (excluding District of Columbia)	Sale of public lands	Seign-iorage	Sale of farm loan bonds	Redemp-tion of capital stock	Repay-ment of loans	Proceeds of railroad securities	Cur-rent re-ceipts
	1	2	3	4	5	6	7	8	9	10	11
1897 June	190	–	2	1	1	4	–	–	1	–	181
Dec.	208	–	2			2	–	–	65	–	139
1898 June	197	–	2	1	1	3	–	–	–	–	190
Dec.	246	–	2	1	1	3	–	–	6	–	233
1899 June	270	–	2	1	1	3	–	–	6	–	257
Dec.	285	–	2	1	1	5	–	–	2	–	274
1900 June	282	–	2	1	2	5	–	–	2	–	270
Dec.	292	–	2	1	1	6	–	–	2	–	280
1901 June	296	–	2	2	2	7	–	–	3	–	280
Dec.	285	–	2	1	2	5	–	–	–	–	275
1902 June	278	–	2	2	2	6	–	–	–	–	266
Dec.	289	–	2	2	4	4	–	–	2	–	275
1903 June	271	–	3	2	5	4	–	–	2	–	255
Dec.	278	–	3	3	4	3	–	–	3	–	262
1904 June	263	–	3	3	4	3	–	–	3	–	247
Dec.	278	–	3	3	2	2	–	–	5	–	263
1905 June	266	–	3	2	3	2	–	–	5	–	251
Dec.	297	–	3	3	2	1	–	–	2	–	286
1906 June	298	–	3	4	3	2	–	–	3	–	283
Dec.	328	–	3	4	4	4	–	–	2	–	311
1907 June	335	–	3	5	4	5	–	–	3	–	315
Dec.	317	–	3	5	5	5	–	–	2	–	297
1908 June	284	–	4	5	5	6	–	–	3	–	261
Dec.	293	–	3	4	4	3	–	–	2	–	277
1909 June	311	–	4	4	4	4	–	–	3	–	292
Dec.	327	–	3	4	3	2	–	–	–	–	315
1910 June	349	–	4	4	3	2	–	–	–	–	336
Dec.	341	–	4	5	3	2	–	–	–	–	327
1911 June	360	–	4	6	3	3	–	–	–	–	344
Dec.	330	–	4	5	2	3	–	–	–	–	316
1912 June	362	–	5	5	3	4	–	–	–	–	345
Dec.	355	–	4	5	1	3	–	–	–	–	342
1913 June	369	–	5	6	2	3	–	–	–	–	353
Dec.	353	–	4	5	1	3	–	–	–	–	340
1914 June	382	–	5	6	2	3	–	–	–	–	366
Dec.	317	0	5	4	1	2	–	–	–	–	305
1915 June	381	0	5	5	1	2	–	–	–	–	368
Dec.	326	0	5	6	1	2	–	–	–	–	312
1916 June	457	0	5	6	1	2	–	–	–	–	443
Dec.	369	0	5	8	1	5	–	–	–	–	350
1917 June	755	1	5	8	1	6	–	–	–	–	734
Dec.	569	1	5	9	1	11	3	–	–	–	539
1918 June	3 611	1	6	10	1	12	4	–	–	–	3 577
Dec.	1 612	1	6	11	1	6	3	–	–	–	1 584
1919 June	3 026	2	6	12	1	6	3	1	–	–	2 995
Dec.	3 230	1	6	20	1	6	–	–	–	–	3 196
1920 June	3 474	2	7	21	1	6	–	351	–	–	3 086
Dec.	2 968	2	8	29	1	6	–	30	–	–	2 892
1921 June	2 617	3	8	29	2	7	–	101	–	–	2 467
Dec.	2 314	2	8	28	–	11	22	–	–	–	2 243
1922 June	1 790	1	8	28	1	11	22	26	–	–	1 693
Dec.	1 871	1	9	13	–	13	18	–	–	80	1 737
1923 June	2 142	1	10	60	1	13	19	28	1	19	1 990
Dec.	1 969	1	9	16	–	4	–	–	–	18	1 921
1924 June	2 039	1	10	54	1	4	–	1	1	76	1 891
Dec.	1 810	1	11	16	–	4	6	–	–	111	1 661
1925 June	1 911	1	11	65	1	5	7	1	1	33	1 786
Dec.	1 910	1	13	18	–	5	14	–	–	20	1 839
1926 June	2 053	1	14	65	1	5	14	–	1	17	1 935
Dec.	2 032	1	15	22	–	4	30	–	–	32	1 928
1927 June	2 096	1	16	67	1	5	31	–	1	58	1 916
Dec.	1 983	1	16	32	–	3	–	–	–	86	1 845
1928 June	2 055	1	17	67	0	3	–	–	1	68	1 898
Dec.	1 868	1	16	26	0	2	–	–	–	5	1 818

Table F-11 shows adjustments made to total expenditures to obtain estimates of current expenditures. Expenditures for fiscal years were tabulated from *Combined Statement of Receipts and Disbursements*. Total expenditures for six-month period ending Dec. 31 were obtained from *Daily Treasury Statement*. Except for a few other series shown in detail in *Daily Treasury Statement*, totals as of Dec. 31 were estimated at half the annual total. Prior to fiscal year 1919, figures are on a warrants-issued basis. Beginning in 1919 they have been adjusted to *Daily Treasury Statement* cash basis.

Column 1 – Figures include "ordinary" (general) expenditures, expenditures in special accounts, and trust-account expenditures. They are exclusive of those for debt retirement. Postal expenditures, except for the deficit, are excluded. Beginning with 1923, cash receipts credited in prior years against expenditures are included in both receipts and expenditures to adjust figures to actual receipt and actual expenditure basis. Such adjustments were made under two headings, "Proceeds of railroad securities owned by the government," and "Receipts from miscellaneous sources." For fiscal years 1909–1919, expenditures by Panama Canal, excluded from the total in *Statement*, have been included in col. 1.

Column 2 – Expenditures by District of Columbia, including those from trust funds, have been excluded since in this study figures for District are included in totals for state and local governments.

Column 3 – Expenditures by trust funds (exclusive of those of District of Columbia, included in col. 3) are excluded as part of the private sector. Federal current payments to trust funds, however, are included in current expenditures (e.g. payments to adjusted service certificate fund, federal contribution to civil service retirement and disability fund, etc.).

Column 4 – Includes subscriptions to capital stock of federal land banks, federal intermediate credit banks, and war emergency corporations of World War I (U.S. Grain Corporation, War Finance Corporation, and U.S. Sugar Equalization Board, Inc.). Negative expenditures in this column in 1925 and 1926 reflect return of capital stock to Treasury by War Finance Corporation and U.S. Sugar Equalization Board. Capital stock of Panama Railroad Company was acquired with purchase of the Panama Canal (col. 10) in fiscal year 1904.

Column 5 – Includes loans for construction and reconditioning of vessels (Smith G. and Betters, P., *U.S. Shipping Board, Service Monograph of the U.S. Government*, no. 63, Brookings Institution, Institute of Government Research, p. 285). Also includes loans of War Finance Corporation (*Annual Reports*) and loans to railroads which were made after termination of federal control, under Section 210 of the Transportation Act of 1920. Revolving fund of $300 million was set up for these loans, and repayments were credited to the account. Proceeds of these loans (interest and repayments) were included in adjustment figures under "Proceeds of railroad securities" which were added to both receipts and expenditures to place them on an actual basis. Expenditures shown in col. 7 are gross. Figures on new loans and repayments were obtained from *Annual Reports of the Secretary of the Treasury*. (See notes to Table F-10, col. 10.)

Column 6 – War Finance Corporation, *Annual Reports*.

Column 7 – Public works (civil) are deducted as capital expenditures (see notes to Table F-2, col. 3).

Column 8 – Equipment, land, acquisition of territory, etc., are deducted as capital expenditures (see notes to Table F-2, col. 5).

Column 9 – Sum of depreciation allowances on fixed assets of government corporations, general government construction, and equipment, original cost basis (see Tables F-4, col. 9 and F-2, cols. 4 and 6).

Column 10 – Same procedure as for col. 9 except replacement cost depreciation used, which was obtained by multiplying by appropriate price index depreciation in 1929 prices derived from deflated expenditure series. Expenditures for fixed assets, conservation, public buildings, and construction outside continental U.S. deflated by index of public construction (Table R-20, col. 8), highway outlays by a special index (Table R-20, col. 6), and equipment expenditures by an index derived by dividing nonfarm producer durable expenditures original cost (see Table P-5, col. 1) by expenditures in 1929 prices (see Table P-6, col. 1) and extrapolating for years prior to 1897 by an index of wholesale prices of all commodities, as given in Warren, G. F. and Pearson, F. H., *Gold and Prices*, p. 50.

Column 11 – Col. 1 plus col. 9 minus sum of cols. 2 to 8. Expenditures by Federal Reserve banks, have been excluded since in this study the System is included in the private sector. Also purchase of farm loan bonds are excluded. Amounts involved are $65 million in June 1918, $4 million in Dec. 1918, $93 million in June 1919, $27 million in June 1920, and $9 million in June 1921.

Column 12 – Same procedure as for col. 11 except col. 10 rather than col. 9 added.

992

CURRENT EXPENDITURES OF FEDERAL GOVERNMENT
1897 to 1928

F-11

$ mill.

Semi-annual period ending	Total ex-pend-itures	District of Co-lumbia	Trust funds	Subscrip-tion to capital stock	Loans	Purchase and sale of U.S. obli-gations	Public works (civil)	Equip-ment, land acqui-sition	Depreciation charges		Current expenditures	
									Orig-inal cost	Re-place-ment cost	Original cost depre-ciation basis	Re-place-ment cost basis
	1	2	3	4	5	6	7	8	9	10	11	12
1897 June	169	4	4	–	–	–	10	1	5	5	155	155
Dec.	208	3	2	–	–	–	13	–	5	4	195	194
1898 June	235	3	3	–	–	–	13	1	6	6	221	221
Dec.	330	3	2	–	–	–	10	–	4	4	319	319
1899 June	275	4	3	–	, –	–	11	1	6	5	262	261
Dec.	264	3	1	–	–	–	13	–	4	5	251	252
1900 June	224	4	2	–	–	–	14	1	6	6	209	209
Dec.	273	4	2	–	–	–	16	–	4	6	255	257
1901 June	237	5	2	–	–	–	16	1	6	7	219	220
Dec.	242	2	2	–	–	–	12	–	5	5	231	231
1902 June	229	3	2	–	–	–	12	1	6	6	217	217
Dec.	264	4	3	–	–	–	16	–	6	6	247	247
1903 June	242	5	3	–	–	–	16	1	6	7	223	224
Dec.	269	4	2	–	–	–	20	–	6	6	249	249
1904 June	313	5	3	–	–	–	20	51	6	7	240	241
Dec.	300	6	3	–	–	–	23	1	6	7	273	274
1905 June	267	6	3	–	–	–	24	1	8	7	241	240
Dec.	305	6	2	–	–	–	34	1	7	7	269	269
1906 June	264	6	3	–	–	–	34	1	8	8	228	228
Dec.	303	5	3	–	–	–	39	1	6	8	261	263
1907 June	276	6	3	–	–	–	40	1	8	9	234	235
Dec.	327	6	3	–	–	–	49	1	7	10	275	278
1908 June	332	6	4	–	–	–	50	1	9	10	280	281
Dec.	373	7	3	–	–	–	48	1	7	9	321	323
1909 June	321	8	4	–	–	–	49	1	11	10	270	269
Dec.	367	6	3	–	–	–	48	1	9	10	318	319
1910 June	327	6	3	–	–	–	48	1	10	12	279	281
Dec.	365	6	6	–	–	–	49	1	10	11	313	314
1911 June	326	6	7	–	–	–	49 ·	2	10	12	272	274
Dec.	369	6	7	–	–	–	49	4	10	12	313	315
1912 June	321	7	7	–	–	–	49	4	12	13	266	267
Dec.	376	6	7	–	–	–	53	1	11	13	320	322
1913 June	369	7	7	–	–	–	54	2	12	14	311	313
Dec.	386	6	6	–	–	–	51	4	13	15	332	334
1914 June	349	7	7	–	–	–	52	5	14	16	292	294
Dec.	396	7	4	–	–	–	52	2	13	14	344	345
1915 June	365	7	7	–	–	–	52	2	14	16	311	313
Dec.	382	7	4	–	–	–	35	1	13	16	348	351
1916 June	360	7	5	–	–	–	35	1	9	14	321	326
Dec.	493	7	10	–	–	–	36	1	9	16	448	455
1917 June	1 593	7	10	9	–	–	37	27	16	28	1 518	1 530
Dec.	5 213	7	44	50	–	–	36	1	14	27	5 088	5 101
1918 June	8 579	7	44	55	19	65	36	1	17	32	8 303	8 318
Dec.	10 638	8	124	90	20	70	35	2	16	33	10 300	10 317
1919 June	8 314	9	125	378	30	150	35	3	17	37	7 507	7 527
Dec.	3 847	10	19	150	30	150	35	3	17	35	3 466	3 484
1920 June	2 295	10	20	350	17	–199	35	3	19	46	2 049	2 076
Dec.	2 508	11	36	–	10	–200	42	10	19	47	2 616	2 644
1921 June	1 961	12	36	–	223	–18	43	10	21	39	1 664	1 682
Dec.	1 838	12	37	–	32	–18	25	1	18	38	1 765	1 785
1922 June	1 522	12	38	–	34	–	24	2	18	32	1 427	1 441
Dec.	1 628	12	41	–	17	–	29	4	19	34	1 543	1 558
1923 June	1 665	13	42	12	–38	–	29	5	18	39	1 619	1 640
Dec.	1 580	13	45	–	–5	–	39	3	20	38	1 504	1 522
1924 June	1 461	13	45	12	14	–	40	4	21	39	1 353	1 371
Dec.	1 504	17	44	–	2	–	51	3	20	39	1 406	1 425
1925 June	1 561	17	44	–499	8	–	51	4	20	44	1 955	1 979
Dec.	1 531	17	45	–	19	–	37	3	20	42	1 429	1 451
1926 June	1 563	17	55	–	–4	–	36	3	18	35	1 473	1 490
Dec.	1 146	14	46	–11	–4	–	34	4	17	35	1 079	1 097
1927 June	1 828	15	46	1	0	–	34	5	19	35	1 744	1 760
Dec.	1 469	15	52	–	0	–	41	4	19	36	1 375	1 392
1928 June	1 636	15	52	–	2	–	41	11	22	39	1 536	1 553
Dec.	1 569	15	49	–	2	–	56	6	21	39	1 461	1 479

993

Column 1 – From Table F-13, col. 12.

Column 2 – From Table F-14, col. 15.

Column 3 – From Table F-15, col. 5.

Column 4 – From Table F-16, col. 11.

Column 5 – From Table F-17, col. 6.

Column 6 – Sum of cols. 1–5.

Column 7 – From Table F-18, col. 10.

Column 8 – From Table F-19, col. 5.

Column 9 – Sum of Table F-20, col. 7 and Table F-15, col. 7.

Column 10 – From Table F-21, col. 5.

Column 11 – Sum of cols. 7–10.

Column 12 – Col. 6 minus col. 11.

SAVING OF FEDERAL GOVERNMENT
Balance Sheet Method: 1929 to 1949

$ mill.

Semi-annual period ending	General fund assets	Government corporation assets	Exchange Stabilization Fund assets	General government acquisition of land, structures, equipment	Other assets	Total assets	General fund liabilities	Direct debt held by public	Government corporation liabilities	Other liabilities	Total liabilities	Net saving
	1	2	3	4	5	6	7	8	9	10	11	12
1929 June	183	17	–	65	81	346	65	–379	–14	–	–328	674
Dec.	–142	87	–	82	2	29	73	–627	5	–	–549	578
1930 June	293	101	–	94	–153	335	152	–118	25	–	59	276
Dec.	11	143	–	99	–271	–18	32	–154	28	–	–94	76
1931 June	349	116	–	116	–165	416	172	772	18	–	962	–546
Dec.	–124	64	–	122	–168	–106	–128	1 132	–32	–	972	–1 078
1932 June	–651	825	–	140	–68	246	–582	1 562	–24	–	956	–710
Dec.	317	462	–	147	–31	895	181	1 321	–19	–	1 483	–588
1933 June	449	515	–	137	44	1 145	132	1 730	–1	–	1 861	–716
Dec.	249	578	–	147	99	1 073	–6	1 285	323	–	1 602	–529
1934 June	2 641	2 767	129	155	88	5 780	1 929	2 937	1 793	–	6 659	–879
Dec.	437	1 751	11	175	116	2 490	531	1 336	2 122	–	3 989	–1 499
1935 June	22	788	9	203	48	1 070	1 111	252	461	–	1 824	–754
Dec.	1 807	210	4	229	147	2 397	1 549	1 854	98	–	3 501	–1 104
1936 June	1 121	197	3	235	166	1 722	739	3 689	219	–	4 647	–2 925
Dec.	–48	–181	11	249	265	296	788	603	47	1	1 439	–1 143
1937 June	617	–75	8	225	35	810	19	1 468	–83	3	1 407	–597
Dec.	753	295	10	215	31	1 304	391	806	142	24	1 363	–59
1938 June	822	193	57	204	–263	1 013	1 609	–151	250	–9	1 699	–686
Dec.	2 039	267	14	186	–190	2 316	1 237	2 213	348	33	3 831	–1 515
1939 June	1 581	92	–47	161	8	1 795	1 849	1 010	650	–27	3 482	–1 687
Dec.	1 376	142	–4	207	345	2 066	1 749	1 450	–49	17	3 167	–1 101
1940 June	1834	9	27	131	486	2 487	2 580	1 038	–147	–19	3 452	–965
Dec.	2071	518	–17	239	1 492	4 303	2 052	2 104	687	115	4 958	–655
1941 June	1 263	456	0	172	2 077	3 968	591	3 835	600	178	5 204	1 236
Dec.	1 154	1 243	4	302	3 086	5 789	247	8 895	519	383	10 044	–4 255
1942 June	–329	1 295	0	292	4 059	5 317	235	14 378	–1 049	1 228	14 792	–9 475
Dec.	7539	2 494	–2	323	5 329	15 683	–124	35 650	554	2 261	38 341	–22 658
1943 June	–1 305	3 475	2	318	4 171	6 661	–308	28 269	30	1 025	29 016	–22 355
Dec.	2 167	–682	8	172	1 819	3 484	–587	29 078	–481	118	28 128	–24 644
1944 June	7 093	805	9	83	–1 971	6 019	–733	35 040	–864	–108	33 335	–27 316
Dec.	1 324	–142	19	104	–1 681	–376	–617	29 521	–2 129	311	27 086	–27 462
1945 June	1 988	–1 677	14	99	–1 154	–730	–310	28 003	–1 043	466	27 116	–27 846
Dec.	1 294	–822	–11	41	–2 356	–1 854	88	19 419	–413	–878	18 216	–20 070
1946 June	–11 534	–751	11	119	–1 869	–14 024	360	–8 767	19	–2 323	–10 711	–3 313
Dec.	–10 573	393	–3	177	26	–9 980	616	–10 379	–229	–860	–10 852	872
1947 June	–342	2 446	6	141	1 779	4 030	1 872	–870	–597	–218	187	3 843
Dec.	1 183	182	1	236	668	2 270	1 013	–1 295	–112	–17	–411	2 681
1948 June	2 694	–522	4	263	416	2 855	697	–4 603	–333	–46	–4 285	7 140
Dec.	–72	1 023	–2	463	703	2 115	1 019	337	649	15	2 020	95
1949 June	–519	884	4	404	–1 304	–531	343	–164	–1	–278	–100	–431
Dec.	1 127	1 676	–6	607	–316	3 088	78	4 297	163	–55	4 483	–1 395

Table F-13 presents and summarizes data on various liquid assets held by Treasury, as reported in *Daily Treasury Statement*, p. 1. With following qualifications, all figures represent simple transcriptions from June and Dec. end-of-month *Statements:*

(1) Distinction observed in Treasury accounting between gold, silver, and general fund proper (with only net balances of each of the two former accounts carried forward to the latter) is not followed here. Both gold and silver are listed in this table on gross basis, and liabilities explicitly related to these assets in *Treasury Statement* are carried separately in Table F-18. This consolidation, of course, results in omission here of those gold and silver items of official "general fund" statement which are carried forward from the distinct gold and silver statements.

(2) Gold and silver are here to be carried at cost rather than at monetary value, as in *Daily Treasury Statement*. Both valuations are specified in Table F-13, however, along with adjustment between them (derivations of desired cost values are described below).

(3) For convenience some of the detailed items appearing in *Daily Treasury Statement* are combined under summary headings in Table F-13. All such combinations are indicated in the annotations which follow.

Column 1 – Gold at monetary value as shown in *Daily Treasury Statement* less increment from dollar devaluation in 1934. Since increment on gold was in the nature of a capital gain, it is eliminated from value of gold held by Treasury in order to avoid distortion of the estimates of federal government saving.

Virtually entire increment occurred in first half of 1934. Most of it represented a write-up in book value of existing gold stock, but substantial additional amounts resulted from a corresponding write-up of gold required by law to be delivered to Treasury. A trickle of late deliveries brought further small increments for several years.

Receipts accruing to Treasury from revaluation of gold in terms of dollars were reserved for specified purposes and reported separately in *Daily Treasury Statement*.

Column 2 – Total of silver dollars and bullion at monetary value shown on asset side of silver section of general fund section of *Daily Treasury Statement*.

Column 3 – As reported on asset side of general fund section of *Daily Treasury Statement*.

Column 4 – Sum of items thus designated in *Daily Treasury Statement*.

Column 5 – Cumulative from Dec. 31, 1896. Cumulative difference between cost and book value of silver revalued for monetary purposes. As in the case of increment on gold, write-up of silver to monetary value gives rise to Treasury receipts in the nature of capital gains which must be eliminated from saving estimates by restoration of cost valuation for silver held by government.

Data tabulated in col. 5 are cumulated seigniorage "receipts" as reported by Treasury. Through first half of 1934, fiscal year seigniorage (in rather trivial amounts) is ascertained from *Annual Reports of the Secretary of the Treasury* and allocated arbitrarily in equal parts to the two semi-annual periods involved. Subsequent to June 30, 1934 seigniorage is explicitly reported in *Daily Treasury Statement*, and semi-annual data may be readily compiled from the Jan. and July mid-month *Statements*. In these documents, seigniorage appears under two separate headings: (1) in miscellaneous receipts when it results from silver operations relating to purchases of newly mined domestic silver or from coinage of subsidiary silver coins; and (2) in trust-account receipts when it results from silver operations with respect to silver acquired under Silver Purchase Act of 1934 or Nationalization Order of Aug. 9, 1934. The two types of seigniorage are combined in col. 7.

Column 6 – Sum of cols. 2–4 minus col. 5.

Column 7 – Combination of items taken directly from end-of-month *Daily Treasury Statements*, specifically, minor coin, United States notes, Federal Reserve notes, Federal Reserve Bank notes, and National Bank notes held by Treasury.

Column 8 – Simply a suspense account for items properly debitable to some other Treasury account but not yet distributed; data are taken directly from *Daily Treasury Statement*.

Column 9 – As reported in end-of-month *Daily Treasury Statements*. Until adoption of a system of telegraphic notification in 1947, these balances differed slightly from Federal Reserve Bank records as of same dates.

Column 10 – Sum of following deposit items as they appear in *Daily Treasury Statement:* "Special depositaries, account of sales of government securities"; "National and other bank depositaries"; "Foreign depositaries"; and "Philippine treasury."

In connection with last two items, it should be noted that only dollar deposits with these agencies are reported. Treasury treats acquisition of foreign deposits or currency as an expenditure at the time dollars are disbursed in exchange for them and hence does not regard such holdings as general fund assets. This defect is remedied by inclusion of changes in foreign currency and deposits held by federal government among items comprising Table F-12, col. 5. (See Table F-17, col. 4 and notes thereto.)

Column 11 – Sum of cols. 1 and 6–10.

Column 12 – Successive differences of col. 11.

996

1928 to 1949

$ mill.

Semi-annual period ending	Gold at cost	Silver at monetary value	Subsidiary silver coin	Silver bullion at cost or at recoinage value	Seigniorage cumulative from Dec. 31 1896	Silver at cost	Minor coin and currency	Unclassified collections, etc.	Deposits in Federal Reserve banks	Deposits in other depositories	Total general fund assets	Semi-annual change in general fund assets
	1	2	3	4	5	6	7	8	9	10	11	12
1928 Dec.	3 206	482	2	5	302	187	23	2	39	285	3 742	–
1929 June	3 278	488	3	7	305	193	21	3	44	386	3 925	183
Dec.	3 331	494	3	5	309	193	46	2	46	165	3 783	–142
1930 June	3 493	495	5	7	313	194	28	2	32	327	4 076	293
Dec.	3 518	496	7	7	313	197	32	1	30	309	4 087	11
1931 June	3 696	498	6	12	314	202	28	1	64	445	4 436	349
Dec.	3 557	499	7	14	314	206	26	1	53	469	4 312	–124
1932 June	2 958	501	8	18	314	213	25	1	29	435	3 661	–651
Dec.	3 161	501	13	18	314	218	30	2	49	518	3 978	317
1933 June	3 234	507	9	26	315	227	47	1	51	867	4 427	449
Dec.	3 202	507	10	36	315	238	46	20	77	1 093	4 676	249
1934 June	5 045	505	4	46	316	239	45	3	97	1 888	7 317	2 641
Dec.	5 421	720	4	86	449	361	46	4	157	1 765	7 754	437
1935 June	6 302	823	5	134	514	448	54	14	118	840	7 776	22
Dec.	7 310	1 086	4	261	661	690	28	4	600	951	9 583	1 807
1936 June	7 794	1 217	5	325	729	818	22	2	862	1 206	10 704	1 121
Dec.	8 443	1 282	6	347	783	852	26	3	276	1 056	10 656	–48
1937 June	9 502	1 341	5	375	818	903	22	3	141	702	11 273	617
Dec.	9 943	1 442	5	427	888	986	24	3	181	889	12 026	753
1938 June	10 146	1 541	9	481	944	1 087	23	3	929	660	12 848	822
Dec.	11 694	1 640	4	535	1 001	1 178	20	15	1 033	947	14 887	2 039
1939 June	13 293	1 733	4	586	1 057	1 266	17	18	1 022	852	16 468	1 581
Dec.	14 826	1 892	6	615	1 113	1 400	20	17	673	908	17 844	1 376
1940 June	17 146	1 851	4	644	1 150	1 349	19	17	254	893	19 678	1 834
Dec.	19 178	1 893	2	657	1 197	1 355	20	20	405	771	21 749	2 071
1941 June	19 807	1 928	4	665	1 238	1 359	19	19	1 024	784	23 012	1 263
Dec.	19 919	1 960	4	660	1 298	1 326	24	30	966	1 901	24 166	1 154
1942 June	19 920	1 985	13	660	1 340	1 318	52	25	603	1 919	23 837	–329
Dec.	19 909	1 984	9	628	1 381	1 240	58	30	1 516	8 623	31 376	7 539
1943 June	19 570	1 974	38	592	1 417	1 187	76	56	1 038	8 144	30 071	–1 305
Dec.	19 121	1 924	14	570	1 437	1 071	95	39	1 408	10 504	32 238	2 167
1944 June	18 356	1 910	21	458	1 460	929	91	24	1 442	18 489	39 331	7 093
Dec.	17 802	1 897	13	406	1 500	816	146	28	1 335	20 528	40 655	1 324
1945 June	17 396	1 887	25	325	1 537	700	136	29	1 500	22 882	42 643	1 988
Dec.	17 248	2 061	11	188	1 683	577	119	47	1 674	24 272	43 937	1 294
1946 June	17 453	2 260	15	103	1 839	539	107	54	1 006	13 244	32 403	–11 534
Dec.	17 712	2 255	14	93	1 878	484	121	37	682	2 794	21 830	–10 573
1947 June	18 449	2 266	20	92	1 899	479	86	62	1 202	1 210	21 488	–342
Dec.	19 937	2 275	13	91	1 915	464	87	39	968	1 176	22 671	1 183
1948 June	20 715	2 290	11	92	1 936	457	86	31	2 051	2 025	25 365	2 694
Dec.	21 426	2 300	5	89	1 964	430	65	31	1 213	2 128	25 293	–72
1949 June	21 649	2 315	15	89	1 982	437	67	26	541	2 054	24 774	–519
Dec.	21 610	2 325	11	94	1 993	437	73	13	935	2 833	25 901	1 127

FEDERAL GOVERNMENT CORPORATION AND CREDIT AGENCY ASSETS
1928 to 1949

$ mill.

Semi-annual period ending	Farm mortgage loans	Other agricultural loans	Loans to home owners	Loans to states, municipalities etc.	Other loans except interagency	Total loans except interagency	Other investments, except interagency
	1	2	3	4	5	6	7
1928 Dec.	1 195	81	–	–	114	1 390	7
1929 June	1 205	68	–	–	124	1 397	6
Dec.	1 199	154	–	–	130	1 483	6
1930 June	1 193	248	–	–	134	1 575	5
Dec.	1 190	383	–	–	137	1 710	4
1931 June	1 184	487	–	–	141	1 812	3
Dec.	1 168	538	–	–	161	1 867	3
1932 June	1 147	603	–	–	908	2 658	4
Dec.	1 124	649	–	–	1 309	3 082	4
1933 June	1 118	747	–	–	1 661	3 526	34
Dec.	1 346	627	–	50	1 729	3 752	250
1934 June	2 084	417	834	61	2 305	5 701	830
Dec.	2 607	346	2 394	122	1 818	7 287	935
1935 June	2 872	495	2 658	185	1 717	7 927	956
Dec.	2 933	444	2 903	192	1 615	8 087	958
1936 June	3 037	558	2 960	193	1 465	8 213	878
Dec.	3 045	526	2 787	207	1 385	7 950	867
1937 June	3 059	573	2 580	196	1 395	7 803	869
Dec.	3 049	552	2 466	173	1 430	7 670	840
1938 June	3 047	595	2 344	141	1 452	7 579	874
Dec.	2 914	621	2 303	176	1 482	7 496	877
1939 June	2 915	677	2 263	224	1 327	7 406	868
Dec.	2 853	698	2 242	296	1 378	7 467	822
1940 June	2 857	776	2 236	278	1 371	7 518	787
Dec.	2 874	778	2 204	382	1 428	7 666	763
1941 June	2 909	877	2 129	529	1 418	7 862	702
Dec.	2 828	913	2 056	570	1 887	8 254	718
1942 June	2 728	980	1 974	586	1 880	8 148	660
Dec.	2 556	956	1 873	562	1 938	7 885	699
1943 June	2 399	1 028	1 612	499	1 919	7 457	609
Dec.	2 177	1 070	1 504	481	1 882	7 114	523
1944 June	2 015	1 034	1 394	471	1 927	6 841	455
Dec.	2 049	983	1 237	510	1 703	6 482	424
1945 June	1 947	986	1 048	489	1 487	5 957	375
Dec.	1 757	1 022	915	484	1 451	5 629	325
1946 June	1 695	1 130	783	467	1 819	5 894	439
Dec.	1 577	1 187	685	460	2 497	6 406	581
1947 June	1 543	1 335	660	469	2 822	6 829	3 603
Dec.	1 439	1 478	556	474	3 330	7 277	3 581
1948 June	1 411	1 721	633	506	3 461	7 732	3 555
Dec.	1 390	1 826	767	507	3 404	7 894	3 545
1949 June	1 410	2 065	980	408	3 297	8 160	3 534
Dec.	1 417	2 138	1 251	409	3 439	8 654	3 518

998

$ mill.

Semi-annual period ending	Cash other than with Treasury	Accounts receivable and accrued assets except interagency	Inventories	Fixed assets, undepreciated	Fixed assets, depreciated	Other assets except interagency	Total assets except interagency	Semiannual change in total assets
	8	9	10	11	12	13	14	15
1928 Dec.	23	53	2	113	88	2	1 565	
1929 June	24	58	3	114	92	2	1 582	17
Dec.	23	58	3	117	94	2	1 669	87
1930 June	28	64	3	119	94	1	1 770	101
Dec.	28	68	3	125	99	1	1 913	143
1931 June	27	73	3	138	111	0	2 029	116
Dec.	21	78	3	150	121	0	2 093	64
1932 June	23	100	2	161	131	0	2 918	825
Dec.	28	124	2	172	140	0	3 380	462
1933 June	28	158	2	178	144	3	3 895	515
Dec.	49	187	3	187	152	80	4 473	578
1934 June	81	117	331	192	155	25	7 240	2 767
Dec.	77	148	255	219	179	110	8 991	1 751
1935 June	105	194	292	258	216	89	9 779	788
Dec.	55	261	289	275	231	108	9 989	210
1936 June	60	281	247	374	326	181	10 186	197
Dec.	86	301	218	503	451	132	10 005	−181
1937 June	66	301	130	723	664	97	9 930	−75
Dec.	60	287	330	1 009	942	96	10 225	295
1938 June	70	292	392	1 239	1 161	50	10 418	193
Dec.	69	335	697	1 257	1 167	44	10 685	267
1939 June	64	383	781	1 354	1 252	23	10 777	92
Dec.	96	388	937	1 298	1 182	27	10 919	142
1940 June	108	428	880	1 291	1 163	44	10 928	9
Dec.	97	526	1 308	1 185	1 045	41	11 446	518
1941 June	94	644	1 234	1 425	1 268	98	11 902	456
Dec.	89	607	1 787	1 736	1 561	129	13 145	1 243
1942 June	99	815	2 079	2 552	2 331	308	14 440	1 295
Dec.	137	1 133	2 980	3 814	3 543	557	16 934	2 494
1943 June	1 363	1 870	2 983	5 570	5 188	939	20 409	3 475
Dec.	137	2 034	2 655	6 656	6 160	1 104	19 727	−682
1944 June	117	2 088	3 110	7 094	6 438	1 483	20 532	805
Dec.	128	951	3 665	7 398	6 582	2 158	20 390	−142
1945 June	143	911	2 808	7 917	6 926	1 593	18 713	−1 677
Dec.	202	1 124	2 584	8 071	6 904	1 123	17 891	−822
1946 June	214	1 019	1 651	8 080	6 880	1 043	17 140	−751
Dec.	232	1 084	1 544	8 152	6 919	767	17 533	393
1947 June	175	865	1 164	8 032	6 766	577	19 979	2 446
Dec.	165	789	1 268	7 940	6 642	439	20 161	182
1948 June	96	653	687	7 693	6 365	551	19 639	−522
Dec.	114	616	2 033	7 681	6 323	137	20 662	1 023
1949 June	121	624	2 700	7 651	6 264	143	21 546	884
Dec.	118	656	3 736	7 691	6 275	265	23 222	1 676

999

Table F-14 presents and summarizes data on the wide variety of assets held by federal corporations and credit agencies. Since these figures are intended to form an integral part of a consolidated financial statement for the entire federal government, no interagency claims are knowingly included.

Extreme statistical difficulties were encountered in the compilation of these series for the 1929–1949 span, and it is probable that some of them have not been resolved satisfactorily. Because of the proliferation of government corporations and credit agencies engaged in quasi-business-type activities during the depression and war years, it has been essential in the absence of an exhaustive first-hand study of the subject to place chief reliance in such comprehensive summary data as are available. Specifically, the summary balance sheets of government corporations and credit agencies which have appeared periodically in the *Daily Treasury Statement* since 1934 are the primary sources of data presented. Unfortunately, these balance sheets have not been compiled upon a uniform basis throughout the period under review. There have been serious discontinuities and inconsistencies both with respect to agencies covered and with respect to classification of assets and liabilities reported.

From time to time agencies already in operation have been added to the group covered by the Treasury financial statements, apparently as a result of fortuitous administrative decisions. Where the agencies so added have been of trivial consequence statistically, no attempt has been made to adjust for the resultant discontinuity, but in a few cases—notably those of federal war housing programs—it has been necessary to incorporate data on principal assets (from independent sources) for periods prior to inclusion of the agencies in the Treasury list. It may be remarked in passing that the list itself involves some anomalies. The Tennessee Valley Authority, for example, is included but the big western power projects are not. No effort is made here to expand coverage to activities never reported in the *Daily Treasury Statement* balance sheets, however analogous they may be to covered activities. Such programs are taken into account in these estimates as part of the various "general government" components of Table F-12.

Inconsistencies over time with respect to classification of assets (or liabilities) have forced the adoption of a "lowest common denominator" approach in establishing the categories tabulated (as well as in Table F-20). Where the lowest common denominator has proven too unsatisfactory for present purposes (e.g., in the case of tangible assets), resort has been had to independent sources of information to establish more meaningful categories. Particular instances of this sort are cited in the detailed notes.

Since the summary corporation and credit agency balance sheets were not published by the Treasury until 1934, prior-year data had to be developed from other sources. This problem was substantially simplified by the fact that not many of the organizations in question came into existence before 1934. Annual data for most of those which did were found in Senate Document 172, 76th Congress, *Financial Statements of Government Corporations and Certain Other Agencies.* Information on various lending activities not covered by the Senate Document was obtained from *Annual Reports of the Secretary of the Treasury.* Semi-annual figures have been arbitrarily interpolated (prior to 1934) for those agencies whose operations were not of significant magnitude, but are taken from original agency reports in several more important cases—notably the Reconstruction Finance Corporation (which published detailed quarterly financial statements), the federal intermediate credit banks, and the federal land banks.

In derivation of all the series relating to government corporations and credit agencies, an effort has been made to eliminate discontinuities and inconsistencies between reports as of different dates. However, exhaustive investigation of even the published reports of each individual agency was not feasible, and adjustments have been confined to major instances where prima facie evidence indicated defects in the Treasury statements. Even where the general nature of such defects was known, it has not always been possible, with reasonable expenditure of time and effort, to obtain adequate information for proper adjustment. Nevertheless, it is believed that on the whole, a satisfactory degree of uniformity has been achieved.

With reference to cols. 1–6 it should be noted that interagency loans are excluded in the process of consolidation. All loans are here tabulated before deduction of valuation reserves. For some periods, the Treasury balance sheets reported only the net values of loans outstanding, but in these cases the valuation reserves (arbitrarily interpolated in part) have been added back.

The breakdown by type of loan given in cols. 1–5 follows the classification under which loans have been reported in the *Daily Treasury Statement* balance sheets since Dec. 1944. This classification could not be extended cleanly to earlier periods on a uniform basis because of divergent classifications in the original Treasury financial statements, but a fairly close approximation has been achieved through regrouping of items as reported prior to Dec. 1944.

Column 1 – Comprises loans of this type held by federal land banks, Federal Farm Mortgage Corporation, and Farmers Home Administration (successor to Farm Security Administration and Resettlement Administration).

Column 2 – Consists of agricultural loans other than farm mortgages, principally by Farm Credit Administration, federal intermediate credit banks, Rural Electrification Administration, and banks for cooperatives. Commodity Credit Corporation crop loans were regarded as physical assets; hence amounts of such loans held directly by the Commodity Credit Corporation since 1934 and by banks under Commodity Credit Corporation guarantee since 1946 as reported in the *Daily Treasury Statement* were deducted from loans (col. 2) and transferred to inventories (col. 10). Amounts of bank-held loans for period 1934-1945, which are not covered in *Daily Treasury Statement*, were derived primarily from Bureau of Agricultural Economics data and added to col. 10.

Column 3 – Predominantly those of Home Owners' Loan Corporation; Federal National Mortgage Association and Reconstruction Finance Corporation Mortgage Company have accounted for most of the rest.

Column 4 – Chiefly Federal Public Housing Administration and Federal Works Agency loans; Reconstruction Finance Corporation has also made loans to political subdivisions as have a few other agencies. Some $300 million of loans to states by Reconstruction Finance Corporation in 1932 and 1933 are not reflected in col. 4 since they were later retroactively classified as relief grants—Reconstruction Finance Corporation being reimbursed by Treasury—and hence are conveniently regarded as originally such for present purposes.

Column 5 – Includes all other government corporation and credit agency loans, most important among which are those of Reconstruction Finance Corporation to businesses. Attention may be called to the fact that certain direct loans by Treasury are shown under this caption. World War I loans to railroads, for example, appear during earlier years. British loan of $3750 million, however, has been excluded.

Column 6 – Sum of cols. 1–5. Represents a firm aggregate taken directly from summary balance sheets, whereas preceding columns represent a not wholly satisfactory breakdown of the established total by type of loan.

Column 7 – Until 1946, represents mainly holdings of equity securities such as preferred stock of banks and trust companies and stock of production credit associations; some corporate bonds are also included. All data are before deduction of valuation reserves. Great increase in 1947 is accounted for by Treasury's subscription to capital of International Bank and International Monetary Fund.

(Notes to Part 2 on pages 1002–1003.)

Column 8 – Deposits with private banks and till cash as reported in combined (or individual agency prior to June 1934) balance sheets.

Figure of $1,363 million on June 30, 1943, looks implausibly out of line with balances as of other dates. A satisfactory explanation, however, is found in the fact that Commodity Credit Corporation had just received $1.1 billion from Department of Agriculture lend-lease allocation, partly in payment for commodities already procured by Commodity Credit Corporation as purchasing agent and partly as an advance against further procurement. Excess cash balance was quickly reduced to normal proportions, but this did not happen to have occurred by June 30

Column 9 – Sum of accounts, notes, and accrued interest receivable according to classifications employed in *Daily Treasury Statement* balance sheets. All values are taken before deduction of valuation reserves.

Columns 10 and 11 – Cols. 10 and 11 are best discussed jointly since it is here that classifications found in *Daily Treasury Statement* balance sheets for all but recent years were most inadequate.

We may dispose first of figures from Dec. 31, 1944 through Dec. 31, 1949 to which the above remark is not applicable. During this recent period, Treasury financial statements of government corporations and credit agencies provide a fairly clear segregation of tangible assets, further subdivided into "Commodities, supplies, and materials" and "Land, structures, and equipment." Former is directly utilizable in col. 10 and latter plus "Acquired security or collateral" (largely real estate and other assets obtained through foreclosure on loans) meets requirements for col. 11 as far as classification is concerned. (There are deficiencies of other sorts, to be discussed below.) All these tangible assets are reported, beginning Dec. 1944, both gross and net of depreciation and valuation reserves, so that there is no problem in obtaining the desired gross values.

Prior to Dec. 1944, however, *Daily Treasury Statement* balance sheets were compiled in terms of a classification which seriously obscured important segments of fixed assets through unidentifiable merging with intangibles and which completely obscured any distinction between fixed assets and the most important inventories. Relevant categories of those earlier balance sheets were as follows:

(1) Real estate and other business property
    a. Real estate and equipment
    b. Vessels and rolling stock
    c. Stores and supplies
(2) Real estate and other property held for sale
(3) Other assets.

The distinction between (1) and (2) is baffling since the content of these series by no means conforms to the literal implication of the distinction. Item (1c) in some years represents only a minute fraction of inventories, the overwhelming bulk of which are unidentifiably combined with assorted fixed assets in (2). Again, item (1b) largely fails to cover the only important holdings of vessels with which the statements are concerned, namely, those of the U.S. Maritime Commission and War Shipping Administration, which are buried among "other assets" (3). (U.S. Maritime Commission vessels eventually are excluded from saving in this study as representing essentially military assets.)

In the face of these irrationalities of classification, the following expedient was adopted for all dates from June 1934 through June 1944: Items (1) and (2) were combined to develop a series which represented total physical assets of the agencies covered. Then the inventory share of this total was ascertained partly by the use of independent data. The "stores and supplies" item mentioned above was substantially satisfactory until Dec. 1938, although meaningless thereafter. By linking to it a series on semi-annual net changes in government enterprise inventories, as estimated from data of the National Income Division of the Department of Commerce, it was possible to fill in the missing inventory data through June 1944. Extension of this approach through Dec. of that year revealed a small discrepancy in comparison with the first inventory figure reported under the revised balance sheet classification, but the results on the whole were quite satisfactory. With the inventory component of physical assets established (col. 10), fixed assets were simply obtained as a residual (entered in col. 11) after elimination of certain Maritime Commission and Reconstruction Finance Corporation assets here viewed as military. To col. 10 were added amounts deducted from col. 2 representing Commodity Credit Corporation loans.

Several deficiencies remained in the fixed asset series, however. One was that they were reported only net of depreciation reserves prior to Dec. 31, 1944. Given the amount of such reserves as of that date, it is not difficult to interpolate them for prior periods by reference to changes in the stock of fixed assets. The estimated reserves are added to reported net values in deriving data for col. 11.

Another serious deficiency in the fixed asset series was that certain very large public war housing programs were not included in the *Daily Treasury Statement* until June 1945. To eliminate the discontinuity created by sudden introduction of these programs, col. 11 includes an addition of the relevant assets for prior periods. The required data were obtained by cumulating corresponding construction expenditure estimates of the Office of Domestic Commerce of the Department of Commerce.

To the fixed asset series thus derived Reconstruction Finance Corporation plant and equipment investment in selected industries is added. Figures for the period 1940 through June 1945 are based on War Production Board, *Facts for Industry*, data. Selected industries include: iron and steel, basic and semifinished; nonferrous metals, basic and semifinished; machine tools; machinery and electrical appliances; synthetic rubber; chemicals (other than explosives), coal, and petroleum products; food processing; and "other manufacturing"—and exclude: explosive and ammunition loading; ship construction and repair; aircraft, engines, parts, and accessories; combat and other motorized vehicles; guns and ammunition; and aviation gasoline. Figures for second half of 1945 are rough estimates based on Reconstruction Finance Corporation balance sheets, and consider relationship between balance sheet totals and *Facts for Industry* data up to that point.

Column 12 – Col. 11 depreciated on linear basis, assuming average life of fifty years for fixed assets of government corporations, forty years for Reconstruction Finance Corporation plant, and twelve years for Reconstruction Finance Corporation equipment investment in civilian industries.

Column 13 – Consists of "deferred and undistributed charges" and "other assets" as reported in *Daily Treasury Statement* balance sheets except for elimination of vessels and other fixed assets of Maritime Commission and War Shipping Administration included in this category for some periods.

Column 14 – Sum of cols. 6–10, 12, and 13.

Column 15 – Successive differences of col. 14.

The Exchange Stabilization Fund is an entity distinct from the Treasury whose current operations are not by and large reflected in Treasury accounting. It is, of course, a federal agency, and account must be taken in this study of its assets and liabilities. Table F-15 presents and summarizes data on those assets and liabilities of the fund which are not elsewhere covered.

The major part of its assets has consisted of gold on deposit with the Treasury. This has already been incorporated in Table F-12, col. 1, and proper consolidation requires omission of such gold here, at the same time disregarding (in Table F-12, col. 7) the Treasury's liability to the fund for the deposit. Cash on deposit with the Treasury is ignored for the same reason. Holdings by the fund of U.S. Government securities are also excluded here, being netted out of public debt obligations (Table F-12, col. 8) in the process of consolidation, as indicated in the notes to Table F-19.

Similarly, on the liability side of the account neither the paid-in capital nor the earnings of the fund are counted here, nor is the Treasury's equity in the organization separately recorded among general fund assets.

Basic data for all dates subsequent to June 30, 1938 and for June 30 of each preceding year are taken from balance sheets of the Exchange Stabilization Fund as reported periodically in Department of the Treasury, *Treasury Bulletin*. Prior to 1938 balance sheets were published only as of June 30, and figures for each Dec. 1934–1937 are interpolated arbitrarily.

Column 1 – Consists very largely of gold held for account of Exchange Stabilization Fund by Federal Reserve Bank of New York. Small amounts of other gold are included at some dates, and certain silver holdings are included in 1934.

Column 2 – Consists mainly of cash on deposit with Federal Reserve Bank of New York, but other working balances outside Treasury are also included.

Column 3 – Largely accounts receivable arising from gold and foreign exchange operations.

Column 4 – The sum of cols. 1–3. Gold and cash on deposit with Treasury, as noted in introduction, are excluded as are fund's holdings of U.S. Government securities.

Column 5 – Successive differences of col. 4.

Column 6 – Consists solely of accounts payable, incurred largely in connection with gold and foreign exchange operations.

Column 7 – Successive differences of col. 6.

EXCHANGE STABILIZATION FUND ASSETS AND LIABILITIES
1934 to 1949
$ mill.

Semi-annual period ending	Gold other than with Treasury	Cash and deposits except with Treasury	Due from foreign banks or governments	Total assets except interagency	Net change in assets	Liabilities except interagency	Change in liabilities
	1	2	3	4	5	6	7
1934 June	51	78	–	129	129	–	–
Dec.	25	115	–	140	11	–	–
1935 June	0	149	–	149	9	–	–
Dec.	29	124	–	153	4	–	–
1936 June	59	97	–	156	3	–	–
Dec.	114	53	–	167	11	–	–
1937 June	169	5	1	175	8	–	–
Dec.	108	53	24	185	10	–	–
1938 June	93	101	48	242	57	–	–
Dec.	129	78	49	256	14	1	1
1939 June	85	105	19	209	–47	0	–1
Dec.	156	30	19	205	–4	2	2
1940 June	86	127	19	232	27	23	21
Dec.	48	143	24	215	–17	1	–22
1941 June	89	107	19	215	0	0	–1
Dec.	37	155	27	219	4	2	2
1942 June	22	178	19	219	0	2	0
Dec.	12	195	10	217	–2	0	–2
1943 June	11	202	6	219	2	0	0
Dec.	43	181	3	227	8	0	0
1944 June	21	207	8	236	9	0	0
Dec.	12	218	25	255	19	0	0
1945 June	81	164	24	269	14	6	6
Dec.	18	230	10	258	–11	0	–6
1946 June	71	194	4	269	11	0	0
Dec.	177	80	9	266	–3	0	0
1947 June	151	19	102	272	6	4	4
Dec.	114	38	121	273	1	1	–3
1948 June	208	12	57	277	4	3	2
Dec.	155	64	56	275	–2	0	–3
1949 June	171	52	56	279	4	3	3
Dec.	136	87	50	273	–6	0	–3

The purpose of Table F-16 is to derive estimates of acquisition of land, structures, and equipment (other than military) not taken into account elsewhere in the calculation of federal saving.

The decision to exclude military assets is partly a matter of doubt on conceptual grounds with respect to treatment of military assets and partly a matter of expediency arising from the extreme difficulty of securing satisfactory statistical data sufficiently comprehensive and consistent with other portions of the accounts.

Column 1 – Purports to measure federal acquisition of land other than by government corporations. Data are based on material compiled by National Income Division of the Department of Commerce in the process of measuring the "government purchases" component of gross national product. National Income Division data, in turn, are based upon Bureau of the Budget tabulations of obligations by object of expenditure for period 1929–1940, and thereafter from records of Department of Justice, based upon its participation in title clearance, condemnation proceedings, etc.

Column 2 – Based upon estimates of federal new construction activity compiled by Construction Division, Office of Domestic Commerce, Department of Commerce. For present purposes latter series is overstated by inclusion of large amounts of government corporation capital outlays already reflected in Table F-14, col. 11. To avoid duplication, construction expenditures of Tennessee Valley Authority, Federal public housing agencies, and Reconstruction Finance Corporation are deducted from Office of Domestic Commerce estimates in deriving col. 2.

Annual figures for Tennessee Valley Authority and housing agencies are provided by Construction Division for all years under consideration, and semiannual data are available from same source beginning in 1939. Semiannual data prior to 1939 are arbitrarily interpolated; this is true of the total as well as of the corporation components. No large error is believed to result from this arbitrary allocation.

In addition to the foregoing government corporation items, federal expenditures on war and atomic energy plants (if *Construction and Construction Materials, Statistical Supplement,* May 1950, figures are used) and on military and naval construction are deducted. Both series, the former in combination with Reconstruction Finance Corporation war plant construction, are taken directly from estimates published by the Construction Division except that semiannual amounts have been arbitrarily interpolated prior to 1939.

Column 3 – Col. 2 distributed according to purpose of expenditure (as given in *ibid.,* May 1949—May 1950 for 1948 and 1949 figures only, although there were minor revisions for prior years, as well as the addition of Atomic Energy Commission item not previously covered which, however, need not be taken into account here, being regarded as representing military expenditures) and depreciated assuming average life of eighty years for conservation, fifty years for public buildings, and twenty-five years for highways.

Column 4 – These data are taken from compilations by Bureau of the Budget representing a breakdown of obligations by object of expenditure. For fiscal years 1929–1940 these tabulations were published in annual Budget documents. For subsequent fiscal years such tables have not been included in the Budget, but are available in the files of the Bureau.

Until 1940 the relevant category is no. 30 in Budget-General Accounting Office object classification code; subsequently, under a revised object code, no. 09 represents obligations for equipment. Comparability of these object classifications is somewhat doubtful, but not sufficiently so, prima facie, to impugn validity of linking the two series.

Two other qualifications may be noted. First, there is the fact that for 1934 and 1935 the table from which these data are drawn is unfortunately restricted to obligations under general appropriations. Large amounts of "emergency and relief" obligations are omitted from object breakdown. Secondly, tabulations for 1941 and 1942 do not include Department of War military activities. Because of the decision not to capitalize any military expenditures, latter omission causes no trouble. A crude attempt to repair the former is undertaken, however (see note to col. 8).

Column 5 – For fiscal years 1929–1940 series represents the result of a laborious extraction of object-code no. 30 items from detailed Bureau of the Budget estimates of obligations by appropriation title. In this extraction items of less than $50,000 have been ignored as a matter of expediency, but no material deficiency is believed to result.

For 1933–1935 the figures carried here, like those in col. 4, exclude emergency and relief appropriations. In 1941 and 1942 no figure is given, but this is immaterial in view of omission of Department of War military activities from col. 4. For 1943–1950 the data come from summary of obligations under Department of War military activities appropriations available in Bureau of the Budget files.

Column 6 – Figures for 1929–1940 are extracted from detailed Budget estimates in same fashion as Department of War figures. In 1933 and 1934 emergency and relief items are again excluded. For 1941–1950 the Budget Bureau summaries provide the desired information.

1006

$ mill.

Period ending	Semiannual periods			Fiscal years		
	General government purchase of land	Gross new construction	Construction less depreciation charges	Total budgetary obligations for equipment	War and Air Force Departments obligations for equipment	Navy Department obligations for equipment
	1	2	3	4	5	6
1929 June	14	57	43	106	24	59
Dec.	14	79	60			
1930 June	15	87	70	113	24	62
Dec.	16	93	74			
1931 June	17	110	91	105	28	47
Dec.	15	121	100			
1932 June	11	144	123	98	23	49
Dec.	9	155	132			
1933 June	10	145	121	90	20	44
Dec.	10	157	132			
1934 June	11	165	139	94	9	74
Dec.	14	183	153			
1935 June	17	199	169	195	24	136
Dec.	20	218	186			
1936 June	25	217	183	319	56	184
Dec.	35	223	187			
1937 June	37	209	171	293	71	163
Dec.	38	204	165			
1938 June	37	205	164	325	69	214
Dec.	35	190	148			
1939 June	26	167	123	765	112	543
Dec.	16	223	177			
1940 June	12	152	104	921	376	374
Dec.	19	254	205			
1941 June	38	178	127	6 400	–	5 799
Dec.	73	266	214			
1942 June	117	184	130	15 698	–	11 218
Dec.	89	240	184			
1943 June	50	290	232	54 408	34 347	13 692
Dec.	37	167	108			
1944 June	47	91	30	37 604	27 086	9 925
Dec.	66	101	39			
1945 June	50	116	54	23 259	18 154	4 065
Dec.	24	76	13			
1946 June	19	128	64	1 887	1 388	1 045
Dec.	16	190	124			
1947 June	–	174	107	2 148	711	1 258
Dec.	–	270	201			
1948 June	–	282	211	3 384	2 008	1 128
Dec.	–	465	391			
1949 June	–	437	359	2 917	1 449	1 102
Dec.	–	659	577			
1950 June				3 803	2 526	968

Column 7 – These are eliminated here, in the case of Tennessee Valley Authority, because of its inclusion among the government corporations whose assets are reflected in Table F-12, col. 2, and, in the case of the Maritime Commission, because of the decision to view its assets as military. Until 1940, the data come from detailed Budget appropriation schedules; subsequently they are taken from unpublished summaries to which several references have already been made.

It may be worth noting that negative entry in 1946 represents a net excess of cancellations of obligations previously incurred over new obligations. This causes no difficulty in the present context since the objective is only to eliminate from col. 3 whatever Maritime Commission component may be included.

Column 8 – Col. 4 minus sum of cols. 5–7 with following exception: in 1933–1935, as noted previously, no tabulation of emergency and relief obligations by object is available; col. 8 for these two years includes a crudely interpolated estimate of missing nonmilitary emergency and relief items.

Column 9 – In the absence of data on a less than fiscal year basis, semiannual timing is established arbitrarily by application to col. 8 of a trapezoidal interpolation formula designed to produce smooth progressions.

Since budget object breakdown ran in terms of expenditures until 1931, interpolated semiannual estimates through June of that year may be allocated directly to halves of the respective fiscal years. Subsequent budgets, however, contained object breakdowns only in terms of obligations, which tend to precede associated expenditures. Since it is expenditure series which is desired for present purposes, question is raised as to length of time elapsed between obligation and expenditure, which varies materially depending upon nature of purchases under consideration. Without satisfactory information regarding weighted average lag, but simply as a concession to the idea that it exists, a period of six months (probably too long) is assumed in establishing timing of the equipment series used here beginning with fiscal year 1932. Gap in the last half of 1931 resulting from substitution of obligations for expenditures as basis for budget tabulations is interpolated arbitrarily.

Column 10 – Col. 9 depreciated on linear basis, assuming average life of twelve years.

Column 11 – Sum of cols. 1, 3, and 10.

$ mill.

| Period ending | Fiscal years | | Semiannual periods | | |
| | U.S. Maritime Commission and T.V.A. obligations for equipment | General government obligations for equipment exclusive of War and Navy Departments | General government acquisition of equipment other than military | | General government acquisition of land, structures, and equipment |
			Gross expenditures	Expenditures less depreciation charges	
	7	8	9	10	11
1929 June	–	23	12	8	65
Dec.			13	8	82
1930 June	–	27	14	9	94
Dec.			15	9	99
1931 June	–	30	15	8	116
Dec.			13	7	122
1932 June	–	26	13	6	140
Dec.			13	·6	147
1933 June	–	26	13	6	137
Dec.			13	5	147
1934 June	–	30	13	5	155
Dec.			17	8	175
1935 June	–	60	27	17	203
Dec.			33	23	229
1936 June	–	79	40	27	235
Dec.			39	27	249
1937 June	–	59	32	17	225
Dec.			27	12	215
1938 June	2	40	20	3	204
Dec.			20	3	186
1939 June	47	63	30	12	161
Dec.			33	14	207
1940 June	99	72	36	15	131
Dec.			36	15	239
1941 June	532	69	30	7	172
Dec.			39	15	302
1942 June	4 332	148	71	45	292
Dec.			77	50	323
1943 June	6 244	125	67	36	318
Dec.			58	27	172
1944 June	520	73	40	6	83
Dec.			33	–1	104
1945 June	969	71	31	–5	99
Dec.			40	4	41
1946 June	–698	152	75	36	119
Dec.			77	37	177
1947 June	22	157	78	34	141
Dec.			79	35	236
1948 June	26	222	101	52	263
Dec.			121	72	463
1949 June	181	185	100	45	404
Dec.			85	30	607
1950 June	82	227			

Table F-17 brings together changes in miscellaneous assets and assorted balancing items not elsewhere classified in this set of accounts. With one or two exceptions, series shown here are completely unrelated to each other; they are combined within a single table only as a matter of convenience in simplifying Table F-12.

Column 1 – Timing of certain taxes included among government receipts in Table F-22 (and reflected, respectively, in business and personal sector accounts of this study) differs from cash basis according to which general fund assets of Treasury are reported in Table F-12, col. 1.

In calculation of corporate saving, corporate profits taxes are, it may be presumed, entered on an accrued liability basis, and refunds of such taxes are netted out of liabilities at time of accrual. This basis of recording corporate profits taxes is also reflected in the revenue-expenditure calculation of government saving shown in Table F-22. In order to bring balance sheet calculation of government saving into reconcilement with revenue-expenditure computation and estimates of corporate saving used in this study, excess during each period of tax liabilities over cash receipts less cash refunds must be added to the change in other assets.

A qualification, to be discussed more thoroughly in notes to col. 3, may be mentioned here. Cash receipts from corporate profits taxes as recorded by Treasury are overstated, in a sense, by inclusion of levies on excess profits subsequently eliminated through renegotiation of war contracts. These receipts are retrospectively ascribable to renegotiation but have not been reclassified as such in Treasury records. As a result of this overstatement of cash corporate profits tax receipts, col. 1 is understated; but a compensating error is made in col. 3, as discussed more fully in the notes thereto.

A relatively minor difference between cash receipts as reported by Treasury and tax receipts as reflected in Table F-22 occurs also in the case of personal income taxes withheld by employers. These are reflected in Table F-22 (and in the personal sector account of this study) at time of withholding. General fund assets, however, reflect them at time of deposit by employers with Treasury—which tends to be several weeks or a month after actual withholding (and, in the case of small firms, may even be several months). These withholdings during the interval between collection from individuals and deposit with Treasury should be treated as accounts payable by business and as current receivables by federal government. Net difference for any period, therefore, between personal tax payments as reflected in Table F-22 and cash receipts by Treasury must be recorded among the changes in consolidated federal government assets.

Data on cash receipts from all income taxes and cash payments of refunds by Treasury are readily available on a semiannual basis in *Daily Treasury Statement*. These, of course, are consistent with changes in liquid assets of general fund. Data on corporate profits tax liabilities, personal income tax payments by individuals, and personal income tax refunds are based on data from Department of Commerce, National Income Division. The two latter series are estimated semiannually for entire 1929–1949 span. Corporate profits tax liabilities have been measured on a less-than-annual basis only since 1939; a semiannual series for prior years is established for present purposes by application of a trapezoidal interpolation formula to the given annual data.

Col. 1, then, is the difference between the sum of corporate profits tax liabilities and personal income taxes less refunds on a national income accounting basis, and the sum of withholding and other income taxes less refunds as reported by *Daily Treasury Statement*.

Column 2 – The fact that the federal government makes advances and prepayments in the course of its procurement programs, which it does not carry as receivables, constitutes another deviation from business accounting methods. It also creates a discrepancy between the books of Treasury (which are on a cash basis) and those of private business (which are on an accrual basis). A prepayment results in recording of an expenditure by Treasury without a corresponding current receipt by business; delivery of goods against such a prepayment (upon which business sales are recorded), on the other hand, gives rise to a business receipt not reflected at that time among Treasury expenditures.

A specific adjustment has been made in government expenditures as reflected in Table F-22 to convert government accounts to a basis paralleling those of business. A corresponding adjustment is required in the balance sheet calculation inasmuch as general fund assets reflect only cash disbursements. Thus the appropriate adjustment is the addition to consolidated federal government assets as of any date of the outstanding balance of advances and prepayments, i.e., the addition of the net change for any period in such advances and prepayments to the net change in other assets as recorded in Table F-12.

Data for this adjustment are taken from Securities and Exchange Commission, "Working Capital of U.S. Corporations," *Statistical Series Release 797*, Dec. 31, 1947. These releases are not available prior to 1940, and after 1946 no longer include requisite item of U.S. Government share of current payables. No adjustment, therefore, is attempted except for years 1940–1946. Amounts involved in other years, however, are probably small.

Securities and Exchange Commission releases provide data only annually for years 1941–1943;

(Notes continued on page 1012.)

MISCELLANEOUS OTHER ASSETS OF FEDERAL GOVERNMENT
1929 to 1949
$ mill.

Semi-annual period ending	Excess of tax accruals over cash receipts less refunds	Net change in U.S. Government advances and prepayments	Excess of gross renegotiation accruals over cash receipts from renegotiation of war contracts	Net change in international claims not else-where classified	Adjustment for selected capital gains and losses (net)	Total
	1	2	3	4	5	6
1929 June	81	–	–	–	–	81
Dec.	2	–	–	–	–	2
1930 June	–153	–	–	–	–	–153
Dec.	–271	–	–	–	–	–271
1931 June	–165	–	–		–	–165
Dec.	–168	–	..	–	–	–168
1932 June	–68	–	–	–	–	–68
Dec.	–31	–	–	–	–	–31
1933 June	44	–	–	–	–	44
Dec.	99	–	–	–	–	99
1934 June	88	–	–	–	–	88
Dec.	116	–	–	–	–	116
1935 June	48	–	–	–	–	48
Dec.	147	–	–	–	–	147
1936 June	166	–	–	–	–	166
Dec.	265	–	–	–	–	265
1937 June	35	–	–	–	–	35
Dec.	31	–	–	–	–	31
1938 June	–263	–	–	–	–	–263
Dec.	–190	–	–	–	–	–190
1939 June	8	–	–	–	–	8
Dec.	345	–	–	–	–	345
1940 June	445	42	–	–1	–	486
Dec.	935	558	–	–1	–	1 492
1941 June	1 900	177	–	–	–	2 077
Dec.	3 063	23	–	–	–	3 086
1942 June	1 842	508	1 659	50	–	4 059
Dec.	2 500	692	2 080	57	–	5 329
1943 June	2 358	164	1 612	37	–	4 171
Dec.	1 002	36	744	37	–	1 819
1944 June	–2 240	0	162	107	–	–1 971
Dec.	–1 341	–400	–80	140	–	–1 681
1945 June	–609	–300	–410	165	–	–1 154
Dec.	–2 206	–600	–482	932	–	–2 356
1946 June	–1 679	–600	–360	706	64	–1 869
Dec.	843	–200	–179	507	–945	26
1947 June	2 053	–	–100	–9	–165	1 779
Dec.	1 366	–	–83	55	–670	668
1948 June	547	–	–80	54	–105	416
Dec.	928	–	–50	–22	–153	703
1949 June	–1 122	–	–26	12	–168	–1 304
Dec.	–434	–	–14	188	–56	–316

a semiannual series for these years is interpolated in such fashion as to match the timing of the adjustment applied in deriving National Income Division estimates of government purchases as reflected in Table F-22.

Column 3 – Large scale retroactive renegotiation of procurement contracts during the war years has created a rather complicated situation with respect to estimates of government saving. In the accounts of National Income Division, both federal expenditures and corporate profits are adjusted to reflect full effect of renegotiation at time of original purchases subsequently subjected to renegotiation. In Treasury accounts, changes in general fund assets reflect following relevant transactions: Full amount of payments at original contract prices appears in Treasury expenditures at time of disbursement. Where renegotiation occurs prior to the filing of a definitive tax return, Treasury receives in cash the difference between original and renegotiated prices. Where renegotiation occurs after filing of a definitive tax return and payment of taxes thereon the business repays Treasury the difference between determined excess profit and credit allowed for previous overpayment of taxes. Excess tax payments are not reclassified by Treasury although they might properly be regarded as part of the renegotiation settlement.

Given this combination of original excess prices, overpayments of taxes related to excess profits, and additional cash proceeds arising from renegotiation, it is necessary, in order to match Table F-22 and corporate saving on the basis of national income measures, to add to the change in general fund assets for each period the difference between the gross amount of excess profits determined by renegotiation (by which government purchases and corporate profits in the national income accounts have been adjusted) and proceeds of renegotiation (including overpayment of taxes) received by Treasury.

In actual computation of col. 3, however, only proceeds of renegotiation in excess of associated tax credits are known. Since the subtrahend in the calculation is thus understated by amount of overpayments on definitive tax returns filed prior to determination of excess profits, col. 3 is overstated by the same amount, and a cumulative error of very considerable magnitude results. However, the subtrahend involved in the computation of col. 1 of this table is overstated (and col. 1 itself understated) by an identical amount. Therefore, cols. 1 and 3, taken together, produce correct results.

Information on the gross amount of excess profits determined by renegotiation comes from the records of National Income Division. Cash proceeds from renegotiation are obtainable by fiscal years from the Bureau of the Budget. They are not identifiable in *Daily Treasury Statement* but constitute a large enough component of "other miscellaneous receipts" to permit use of the latter loosely as an interpolating series.

Column 4 – Transactions recorded here represent estimated semiannual changes in both long- and short-term claims of U.S. Government on foreign governments, banks, etc., not already recorded among the more formal international assets appearing in Table F-12, col. 2. An important reason for the magnitude of net changes shown here during the war years is the fact that Treasury, in its general fund statement, does not regard foreign deposits or currency as assets. *Daily Treasury Statement* records dollar disbursements in exchange for such items as expenditures at the time of dollar disbursement, whether or not expenditures in foreign currencies have actually occurred.

Data shown here are based on detailed balance of payments worksheets of International Economics Division, Office of Business Economics, Department of Commerce. An effort has been made to avoid duplication with loans and accounts receivable of government corporations. Since balance of payments records are on a transaction basis rather than an agency basis, there is no firm assurance that all elements of duplication have been avoided.

Column 5 – This column does not undertake to present an exhaustive calculation of capital gains or losses. Some, such as seigniorage on gold and silver are covered elsewhere. The need for others, such as those on loans by government corporations and credit agencies, is obviated by the policy adopted here of carrying assets before deduction of valuation reserves. Disregard of such write-downs is, in effect, an automatic adjustment for "unrealized" portion of capital losses on assets in question. Although many loans are very heavily reserved to reflect official judgment that collection is unlikely, relatively few have actually been written completely off the books, so that we thus account for the greater share of appropriate capital loss adjustment. Nothing is done about realized losses on loans except in 1946 and 1947, as noted below.

Only two specific items in the nature of capital gains or losses are taken into account in col. 5. These, which are too large to be ignored, are: (1) losses from charge-offs of assets (largely fixed) of government corporations in 1946 and 1947; and (2) "capital gains" equal to proceeds from sales of surplus property not reflected among the tangible asset components of this study.

Basic data for item (1) above come from the quarterly consolidated income and expense statements of government corporations and credit agencies published for recent years in *Treasury Bulletin*. What is incorporated in col. 5 is the net excess during 1946 and 1947 of losses and charge-offs over gains on sale of assets as reported in these financial statements. Magnitude of item was not sufficient to warrant adjustment during period July 1944 through Dec. 1945. Unfortunately, income and expense statements from which necessary data come are not available in utilizable form for prior years. Accordingly, the adjustment has been ignored until 1946, when postwar sales of defense facilities and materials introduced heavy capital losses. However, to the extent that these were connected with assets either not capitalized in this study or, if capitalized, not written down upon sale or other disposition, the capital loss in item (1) is more than offset by a "capital gain" in item (2), below. Item (2) is essentially a balancing item covering certain deficiencies in the present tabulation of federal assets, tangible components of which fail to reflect sales (except by government corporations, and then only in part).

To understand the required adjustment, it is necessary to consider the treatment of general government (as distinguished from government enterprise) sales in Table F-22, i.e., in the national income accounts. All foreign sales, together with domestic sales of inventory—or consumption-type materials—are netted out of government expenditures in computation of the federal component of gross national product. Hence they are, in effect, treated as current receipts in the revenue-expenditure measure of federal saving, and no explicit adjustment of Table F-12 is required to achieve consistency between the two saving estimates. (The broader question of inadequacies resulting from absence of a general government inventory account is ignored.)

Receipts from domestic sales of fixed assets do not appear in the national income accounts but do affect the general fund balance in Table F-12. With respect to these items there should properly be a reduction of general government tangible assets equal to the book value of assets sold and a balancing capital loss equal to difference between book value and sales proceeds. In the present statistics, however, vast amounts of fixed assets sold as surplus property either have never been capitalized, due to exclusion of military assets from government saving, or, even though originally capitalized, have not been written down to reflect disposals. In particular, no allowance has been made for sales of such general government holdings of land, structures, and equipment as have been capitalized. (None of the relevant items are identifiable in surplus property disposal statistics of War Assets Administration.)

As a substitute for the appropriate entries suggested above, an amount representing estimated proceeds of surplus property sales neither reflected in fixed asset accounts nor treated in Table F-22 as current receipts has been entered as a "capital gain," i.e., as a deduction from the net change in assets. This "capital gain" adjustment has the same effect upon the measurement of saving (apart from statistical imperfections) as would the proper combination of asset reduction and capital losses but is otherwise without meaning except as a balancing item. It is measured by the excess of general government receipts from domestic surplus property sales over the amounts netted out of the federal expenditure component of gross national product. The subtrahend in this computation is based on National Income Division records, while the minuend is derived from *Daily Treasury Statement* reports of surplus property sales proceeds, adjusted for certain government corporation and foreign sale items included.

The whole adjustment is highly unsatisfactory but is adopted, in default of adequate information for more accurate accounting, because the magnitudes involved are too great to be ignored and because it has at least the merit of reconciling federal saving estimates of Table F-12 with those derived in Table F-22.

Column 6 – Sum of cols. 1–5.

Table F-18 presents and summarizes data on various relevant general fund liabilities of Treasury as reported in *Daily Treasury Statement*, p. 1. With a few qualifications all figures represent transcriptions from June and December end-of-month statements.

As noted in the discussion of general fund assets (Table F-13) the distinction observed in Treasury accounting between gold, silver, and the general fund proper is not followed here. Liabilities of these three separate sections of the Treasury's general fund statement are reported on a consolidated basis, which of course results in the omission from liabilities of the net balances of gold and silver accounts carried forward in the standard statement to the general fund proper.

The following items of liability carried in *Daily Treasury Statement* are omitted from col. 9 for reasons given below:

(1) *Exchange Stabilization Fund carried in gold section.* This item represents gold belonging to Exchange Stabilization Fund but held on deposit with Treasury. Since Exchange Stabilization Fund is regarded as a separate entity in Treasury accounting practice, Treasury carried the deposit as a liability. However, in a consolidated nonduplicating balance sheet for the federal government as a whole, this gold, having been recorded along with other Treasury holdings in Table F-12, col. 1, must be omitted from general fund liabilities and also from assets of Exchange Stabilization Fund (see notes to Table F-15).

(2) *Liabilities of general fund to Post Office Department.* The situation here is similar to that noted in connection with the Exchange Stabilization Fund. The Post Office Department, in general, is an entity distinct from the Treasury. Only deficiency appropriations to, or return of excess postal revenues by, the Post Office Department affect reported Treasury receipts, expenditures, or general fund balance. The Post Office Department does, however, deposit funds with the Treasurer of the United States which, although included among general fund assets, are prevented from affecting the balance by the recording of a contra-liability on the books of the Treasury. For present purposes, proper consolidation is best achieved by ignoring this liability. Identical results would obtain, so far as federal saving estimates are concerned, if instead the additional assets of the Post Office Department were recorded, but this would create overstatement on both sides of the consolidated account.

(3) *General fund liabilities to postmasters, clerks of courts, disbursing officers, etc.* The "postmaster" component constitutes the overwhelming bulk of this account and is subject to precisely the considerations outlined above in connection with the Post Office Department item. Analogous consideration apply to the remaining components, and the entire item is omitted from the consolidated statement of liabilities.

Columns 1 and 2 – *Daily Treasury Statement*, gold account, p. 1.

Column 3 – For most years this item consists simply of the gold-account liability, "Redemption fund–Federal Reserve notes." With it for some of the early years, however, are combined certain liabilities appearing in the general fund statement proper. The additional items so combined are "deposits for redemption of national bank notes," "deposits for retirement of additional circulating notes," and "deposits for redemption of Federal Reserve Bank notes."

Column 4 – *Daily Treasury Statement*, gold account, p. 1; must be carried as liability to maintain consistency with official public debt statements, which show certain obligations net of this reserve.

Column 5 – Combination of the two items specified as reported in silver section of general fund statement.

Column 6 – *Daily Treasury Statement*, general fund proper, p. 1.

Column 7 – Combination of the two items listed in general fund statement under Board of Trustees, Postal Savings System, i.e., the 5 percent reserve and other deposits. Unlike Post Office Department, Postal Savings System is not among federal entities consolidated herein but is treated in this study as a part of the banking system. Deposits of System with Treasury, therefore, are to be regarded as Treasury liabilities to the public.

Column 8 – For most years simply a suspense account for items properly creditable to some other Treasury account but not yet distributed. Data are taken directly from general fund statement.

In addition, there is added on Dec. 31, 1946, and subsequent dates balance of clearing account for outstanding checks, outstanding accrued interest on public debt (which is not a full accrual of interest, of course, but simply measures the "float" of interest due on coupon bonds not yet presented for payment), and telegraphic reports. This clearing account was established in 1946 in order to permit immediate charging of certain budgetary expenditures upon issuance of Treasury checks (instead of upon payment as had theretofore been the rule). Later, it also became involved in a scheme of telegraphic reporting of receipts and, still later, in a system of charging interest on coupon bonds to budgetary expenditures when due instead of when paid. Individual general fund assets and liabilities, however, are still subject to debit or credit only upon advice of clearance of checks or receipts of covering warrants. The clearing account, then, represents the lag between issuance and payment of checks, between due dates and presentation for payment of interest coupons, and between telegraphic advice of receipts and full documentation by which resultant credits can be distributed to appropriate accounts. Transactions in the clearing account are treated in *Daily Treasury Statement* itself as an adjustment of current receipts or expenditures, but, in the present context, it is better to regard the balance of the account as an additional liability in the balance sheet. Balances can readily be cumulated from net receipts or expenditures recorded in *Daily Treasury Statement*.

Column 9 – Sum of cols. 1–8.

Column 10 – Successive differences of col. 9.

1014

GENERAL FUND LIABILITIES
1928 to 1949
$ mill.

Semi-annual period ending	Gold certificates outstanding outside of Treasury	Gold certificate fund, Federal Reserve System	Redemption fund, Federal Reserve and other notes	Gold reserve	Silver certificates and Treasury notes of 1890 outstanding	Treasurer's checks outstanding	Deposits of Postal Savings System with Treasury	Uncollected items, exchanges, etc.	Total general fund liabilities (except inter-agency)	Semi-annual change in general fund liabilities
	1	2	3	4	5	6	7	8	9	10
1928 Dec.	1 413	1 449	200	156	476	11	9	4	3 718	
1929 June	1 384	1 562	197	156	470	4	8	2	3 783	65
Dec.	1 321	1 774	101	156	491	1	9	3	3 856	73
1930 June	1 490	1 796	65	156	488	1	10	2	4 008	152
Dec.	1 790	1 527	61	156	490	1	13	2	4 040	32
1931 June	1 702	1 777	59	156	494	1	22	1	4 212	172
Dec.	1 751	1 565	84	156	495	2	28	3	4 084	−128
1932 June	1 491	1 236	90	156	488	1	38	2	3 502	−582
Dec.	1 329	1 577	77	156	492	0	49	3	3 683	181
1933 June	1 231	1 771	88	156	481	1	82	5	3 815	132
Dec.	1 159	1 768	98	156	494	1	112	21	3 809	−6
1934 June	959	3 973	63	156	496	10	68	13	5 738	1 929
Dec.	931	4 324	53	156	702	5	91	7	6 269	531
1935 June	788	5 510	35	156	811	6	66	8	7 380	1 111
Dec.	124	7 538	18	156	997	4	84	8	8 929	1 549
1936 June	2 916	5 291	14	156	1 135	76	74	6	9 668	739
Dec.	2 910	6 036	13	156	1 235	7	89	10	10 456	788
1937 June	2 904	6 020	10	156	1 306	8	64	7	10 475	19
Dec.	2 898	6 304	9	156	1 401	7	72	19	10 866	391
1938 June	2 894	7 820	9	156	1 509	13	68	6	12 475	1 609
Dec.	2 891	8 972	10	156	1 592	10	63	18	13 712	1 237
1939 June	2 887	10 699	9	156	1 704	7	70	29	15 561	1 849
Dec.	2 885	12 384	10	156	1 778	5	61	31	17 310	1 749
1940 June	2 882	14 928	11	156	1 830	9	68	6	19 890	2 580
Dec.	2 880	16 935	10	156	1 872	4	75	10	21 942	2 052
1941 June	2 878	17 497	9	156	1 915	7	67	4	22 533	591
Dec.	2 877	17 675	14	156	1 944	12	84	18	22 780	247
1942 June	2 875	17 735	15	156	1 969	17	214	34	23 015	235
Dec.	2 874	17 708	30	156	1 974	18	82	49	22 891	−124
1943 June	2 873	17 355	55	156	1 918	35	109	82	22 583	−308
Dec.	2 871	16 717	233	156	1 837	57	93	32	21 996	−587
1944 June	2 869	15 784	410	156	1 814	73	114	43	21 263	−733
Dec.	2 868	15 035	594	156	1 802	30	122	39	20 646	−617
1945 June	2 868	14 540	699	156	1 816	68	143	46	20 336	−310
Dec.	2 867	14 247	800	156	2 047	53	153	101	20 424	88
1946 June	2 866	14 532	756	156	2 243	35	162	34	20 784	360
Dec.	2 865	14 772	794	156	2 217	25	169	402	21 400	616
1947 June	2 863	16 514	710	156	2 232	24	198	575	23 272	1 872
Dec.	2 862	17 995	687	156	2 248	24	184	129	24 285	1 013
1948 June	2 861	18 827	616	156	2 260	23	189	50	24 982	697
Dec.	2 859	19 520	631	156	2 280	24	194	337	26 001	1 019
1949 June	2 858	19 841	589	156	2 267	17	199	417	26 344	343
Dec.	2 857	19 807	554	156	2 304	18	168	558	26 422	78

The direct federal debt held by the public, of course, represents the overwhelming proportion of federal liabilities to the public. Except for the fact that interagency holdings of public debt obligations are eliminated in the process of consolidation, and, with the further exception of one adjustment in 1936, the figures derived in this table are simply changes in direct U.S. Government debt outstanding.

It may be worth noting that, for the purposes of this study, certain federal trust funds holding very substantial amounts of U.S. securities are regarded as components of individuals' saving rather than the government sector. Obligations held by such trust funds accordingly are not among the interagency items deducted.

Column 1 – Taken directly from "Monthly Public Debt Statement," *Daily Treasury Statement* (or from convenient summaries thereof in *Banking and Monetary Statistics*).

Column 2 – Obtained from summary balance sheets of government corporations and credit agencies published periodically in *Daily Treasury Statement* since 1934 and prior to that date compiled from individual agency balance sheets. These data are a by-product of the more comprehensive analyses of government corporation and credit agency financial statements undertaken in connection with the derivation of Table F-12, cols. 2 and 9.

Column 3 – As in the case of government corporations, these figures are the by-product of a more elaborate investigation (see Table F-15). They come from balance sheets of the fund as reported in Department of the Treasury, *Treasury Bulletin*. For some of the earlier years, as explained in notes to Table F-15, only fiscal year-end balance sheets were available. December figures during those years were arbitrarily interpolated.

Column 4 – Col. 1 minus sum of cols. 2 and 3.

Column 5 – Successive differences of col. 4. However, in June 1936 $500 million were added to col. 4; in Dec. 1936, $500 million were subtracted from col. 4. This is a special adjustment arising out of a rather confused set of transactions occurring in 1936–1937 between Treasury, Adjusted Service Certificate Fund, and Government Life Insurance Fund. About $500 million of loans by the Government Life Insurance Fund to veterans of World War I on the security of their Adjusted Service Certificates were canceled by law in 1936. Legislation provided that Adjusted Service Certificate Fund should reimburse Government Life Insurance Fund in full for the canceled loans and that Treasury should provide funds to Adjusted Service Certificate Fund to meet this obligation. Because of delays in determination of amount involved, payment was not actually made until June 1937, when it was effected through issuance to Government Life Insurance Fund of special public debt obligations. In the meantime, Government Life Insurance Fund continued to carry the Adjusted Service Certificate secured loans as assets, although veterans had been relieved of any obligation therefor. Loans were thus, in effect, claims upon Treasury. Both estimates of individuals' saving in other parts of this study and federal saving estimates given in Table F-22 impute a federal payment in connection with these canceled loans in the first half of 1936. To match these results, $500 million of public debt obligations have been imputed one year in advance of their actual issuance. This procedure, in effect, follows Government Life Insurance Fund itself in regarding its canceled loans as a claim on Treasury during the interval before their replacement by formal issuance of U.S. Government securities. A more detailed description of this set of transactions is provided in the detailed notes to the estimates of individuals' equity in assets of federal trust funds held on their behalf (cf. notes to Table F-23, col. 8).

$ mill.

Semi-annual period ending	Gross federal debt	Federal debt held by government corporations and credit agencies	Federal debt held by Exchange Stabilization Fund	Direct federal debt held by public as reported	Semi-annual change in direct federal debt held by public
	1	2	3	4	5
1928 Dec.	17 310	29	–	17 281	
1929 June	16 931	29	–	16 902	–379
Dec.	16 301	26	–	16 275	–627
1930 June	16 185	28	–	16 157	–118
Dec.	16 026	23	–	16 003	–154
1931 June	16 801	26	–	16 775	772
Dec.	17 826	19	–	17 807	1 132
1932 June	19 487	118	–	19 369	1 562
Dec.	20 805	115	–	20 690	1 321
1933 June	22 539	119	–	22 420	1 730
Dec.	23 814	109	–	23 705	1 285
1934 June	27 053	373	38	26 642	2 937
Dec.	28 479	469	32	27 978	1 336
1935 June	28 701	444	27	28 230	252
Dec.	30 557	449	24	30 084	1 854
1936 June	33 779	486	20	33 273	3 689
Dec.	34 407	506	25	33 876	603
1937 June	36 425	551	30	35 844	1 468
Dec.	37 279	606	23	36 650	806
1938 June	37 165	651	15	36 499	–151
Dec.	39 427	710	5	38 712	2 213
1939 June	40 440	713	5	39 722	1 010
Dec.	41 942	758	12	41 172	1 450
1940 June	42 968	748	10	42 210	1 038
Dec.	45 025	701	10	44 314	2 104
1941 June	48 961	802	10	48 149	3 835
Dec.	57 938	884	10	57 044	8 895
1942 June	72 422	990	10	71 422	14 378
Dec.	108 170	1 088	10	107 072	35 650
1943 June	136 696	1 345	10	135 341	28 269
Dec.	165 877	1 448	10	164 419	29 078
1944 June	201 003	1 524	20	199 459	35 040
Dec.	230 630	1 630	20	228 980	29 521
1945 June	258 682	1 679	20	256 983	28 003
Dec.	278 115	1 683	30	276 402	19 419
1946 June	269 422	1 767	20	267 635	–8 767
Dec.	259 149	1 873	20	257 256	–10 379
1947 June	258 286	1 880	20	256 386	–870
Dec.	256 900	1 789	20	255 091	–1 295
1948 June	252 292	1 784	20	250 488	–4 603
Dec.	252 800	1 955	20	250 825	337
1949 June	252 770	2 089	20	250 661	–164
Dec.	257 130	2 152	20	254 958	4 297

Table F-20 presents and summarizes data on liabilities of federal corporations and credit agencies to the public. Since these figures are intended to form an integral part of a consolidated financial statement for the entire federal government, no interagency liabilities are knowingly included.

The sources of data and many of the problems of a general nature are identical with those discussed in the introduction to Table F-14. On the whole, the compilation of data on liabilities of government corporations and credit agencies has been more straightforward than in the case of their assets. However, two instances of rather substantial departure from reported liabilities deserve special mention.

The first relates to reserves for uncollectible items and other operating reserves carried as liabilities in *Daily Treasury Statement* balance sheets. Such reserves largely reflect agency estimates of unrealized capital losses, which should not affect estimate of saving. Accordingly, no such reserves are knowingly carried as liabilities in Table F-20.

A similar attitude is taken toward deferred income and undistributed credits as reported by the agencies. Some portion of these deferred credit items may correspond to deferred debit entries in the books of private business or may otherwise be properly distributable to liability accounts. To the extent that this is so, they should be carried here as liabilities. The preponderant items, however, are not of this type. Most of the undistributed credits reported seem to represent legitimate income set aside through deferment for one special reason or another. Since it is not possible to distinguish the various types of transactions reflected here, it seems, on balance, that the least error will be made by treating the entire category as an element of surplus. Accordingly, no liability is here carried with respect to deferred and undistributed credits.

Column 1 – Total (exclusive of interagency holdings) of bonds, debentures, and notes payable guaranteed by U.S., as reported in *Daily Treasury Statement* balance sheets. The large amounts of guaranteed obligations held by Treasury and by other federal agencies are, of course, omitted in process of consolidation.

Column 2 – Total of nonguaranteed securities outstanding, exclusive of interagency holdings, as reported in periodic balance sheets. There is no fundamental reason in present context for distinguishing between guaranteed and nonguaranteed obligations, but it is readily done on basis of classifications employed in Treasury financial statements and may assist in clarifying comparisons with certain types of public debt statistics inclusive of guaranteed obligations.

Column 3 – Consists at most dates almost entirely of accrued interest payable on securities in cols. 1 and 2. Interest payable to Treasury or to other federal agencies is, of course, omitted. At some dates also includes rather large amounts of accrued warehouse and related charges incurred by Commodity Credit Corporation.

Column 4 – Includes accounts payable, trust and deposit liabilities, and miscellaneous other items of indebtedness to the public. A further breakdown of this item would be desirable for all years but is possible only since Dec. 1944. Earlier balance sheets combine under single classification virtually all liabilities except those embodied in form of security issues.

It should be noted that miscellaneous liability category as reported in *Daily Treasury Statement* balance sheets has at some dates included certain large reserves or elements of deferred income. For example, Federal Deposit Insurance Corporation followed for a time the practice of regarding their entire earnings as reserves for contingencies and these were carried among "other liabilities" rather than as surplus or even as deferred credits. Adjustment has been made to exclude from col. 4 all known items of a similar nature. This adjustment may be incomplete since it is confined to cases where prima facie evidence has indicated that magnitude involved would warrant further investigation.

At certain dates miscellaneous "other liabilities" group has also erroneously included large interagency trust and deposit liabilities. Correction is made to eliminate these from col. 4. The column also includes amounts of bank-held loans which are not covered in *Daily Treasury Statement* for period 1934–1945 but which were derived from Bureau of Agricultural Economics data.

Column 5 – Represents that portion of paid-in capital of mixed ownership agencies which is held by the public. Data are provided in analyses of ownership accompanying *Daily Treasury Statement* balance sheets. No consideration is given here to private equity in undistributed earnings of organizations in question.

Column 6 – Sum of cols. 1–5.

Column 7 – First differences of col. 6.

LIABILITIES OF FEDERAL GOVERNMENT CORPORATIONS AND CREDIT AGENCIES: 1928 to 1949

$ mill.

Semi-annual period ending	Guaranteed obligations held by public	Other bonds, notes and debentures held by public	Accrued liabilities, except interagency	Accounts payable and other liabilities except interagency	Paid-in capital privately held	Total liabilities except interagency	Semiannual net change in liabilities except interagency
	1	2	3	4	5	6	7
1928 Dec.	–	1 229	20	7	64	1 320	
1929 June	–	1 211	21	9	65	1 306	–14
Dec.	–	1 219	19	8	65	1 311	5
1930 June	–	1 242	20	8	66	1 336	25
Dec.	–	1 271	20	7	66	1 364	28
1931 June	–	1 284	20	12	66	1 382	18
Dec.	–	1 257	20	8	65	1 350	–32
1932 June	–	1 235	20	6	65	1 326	–24
Dec.	–	1 215	19	9	64	1 307	–19
1933 June	–	1 202	19	12	73	1 306	–1
Dec.	180	1 313	20	32	84	1 629	323
1934 June	600	2 085	35	423	279	3 422	1 793
Dec.	3 082	1 773	42	339	308	5 544	2 122
1935 June	3 948	1 469	48	225	315	6 005	461
Dec.	4 331	1 307	54	101	310	6 103	98
1936 June	4 508	1 364	56	94	300	6 322	219
Dec.	4 473	1 398	76	137	285	6 369	47
1937 June	4 493	1 298	76	131	288	6 286	–83
Dec.	4 465	1 331	76	264	292	6 428	142
1938 June	4 695	1 304	57	329	293	6 678	250
Dec.	4 847	1 282	58	544	294	7 025	347
1939 June	5 331	1 341	53	657	294	7 676	651
Dec.	5 574	1 307	52	397	295	7 625	–51
1940 June	5 398	1 295	53	415	296	7 457	–168
Dec.	5 789	1 373	52	654	298	8 166	709
1941 June	6 247	1 425	54	742	299	8 767	601
Dec.	6 209	1 346	56	1 372	301	9 284	517
1942 June	4 461	1 385	40	2 049	300	8 235	–1 049
Dec.	4 116	1 381	37	2 960	297	8 791	556
1943 June	3 881	1 311	35	3 300	294	8 821	30
Dec.	3 793	1 319	33	2 903	292	8 340	–481
1944 June	1 588	1 406	21	4 173	288	7 476	–864
Dec.	1 537	1 395	38	2 092	285	5 347	–2 129
1945 June	502	1 163	34	2 314	285	4 298	–1 049
Dec.	555	1 113	22	1 913	288	3 891	–407
1946 June	325	1 234	225	1 835	291	3 910	19
Dec.	261	1 252	190	1 682	296	3 681	–229
1947 June	83	1 235	77	1 382	303	3 080	–601
Dec.	82	1 370	39	1 307	173	2 971	–109
1948 June	68	1 526	43	817	182	2 636	–335
Dec.	38	1 647	34	1 376	193	3 288	652
1949 June	26	1 548	165	1 345	200	3 284	–4
Dec.	28	1 489	186	1 537	210	3 450	166

Table F-21 brings together changes in miscellaneous liabilities and assorted balancing items not elsewhere classified in this set of accounts. The series shown here are unrelated to each other and are combined within a single table only for convenience in simplifying Table F-12.

Column 1 – This deposit liability is established because of decision to treat certain federal pension, insurance, and veterans' funds holding assets on behalf of individuals as components of individuals' rather than of government saving. These federal trust funds thus become a segment of the public in present context and deposits maintained by them with Treasury, although covered in general fund in ordinary Treasury accounting, must here be regarded as liabilities to the public.

Since the trust funds have normally followed a policy of investing available funds immediately in interest-bearing U.S. Government securities, working balances tended to be nominal prior to advent of the large social security funds. Deposit liabilities to the funds prior to 1936 are ignored on grounds of inconsequentiality. For subsequent periods data as of each June 30 for each of principal funds are taken from their financial statements as given in *Annual Reports of the Secretary of the Treasury*. December figures may be readily interpolated through reference to trust fund receipts and expenditures as reported in *Daily Treasury Statement*.

Column 2 – There are a number of instances in which Treasury receives from various classes of individuals sums of money not in the nature of revenues but to be held in a purely custodial capacity. During the war years such deposits became rather large as a result of various transactions involving military personnel. Soldiers' deposit system operated by Army, together with similar Navy programs and arrangements for deposits of personal funds by overseas personnel, gave rise to large increase in Treasury's liability to individuals. Following the war, of course, correspondingly large payments were made when personal funds were returned to depositors.

In Treasury accounting practice, receipts of this type are included in general fund and repayments are shown as expenditures reducing general fund balance. It is necessary here, however, to establish a liability in connection with such deposits in order to avoid counting as federal assets funds which the Treasury holds only as trustee. Accurate data on fiscal year basis are available from trust account detail in *Combined Statement of Receipts, Expenditures and Balances*. Equally accurate information on less-than-annual basis is not available since trust accounts in question are merged in *Daily Treasury Statement* with various other miscellaneous trust accounts. They constitute, however, a large enough share of "other miscellaneous" group to warrant using latter as interpolator in deriving the desired semiannual series for periods when its magnitude was greatest. Semiannual timing is arbitrary for other periods.

Column 3 – Represent accounts payable by government to businesses which have delivered goods on credit. In revenue-expenditure calculation of saving (Table F-22) an adjustment of federal purchases has been made to take account of difference between accrual accounting employed by business and cash accounting practice of Treasury. Similar adjustment must be made in balance sheet tabulation if it is to be consistent with alternative federal saving estimate and with business accounting method applied throughout this study.

Data shown in col. 3 are taken from Securities and Exchange Commission, "Working Capital of U.S. Corporations," *Statistical Series Releases*. These releases were not available for years prior to 1940 and do not contain data pertinent to present adjustment after 1946; hence, item is ignored for those periods. Securities and Exchange Commission estimates were quarterly beginning in 1944 but annual previously; a semiannual series for 1941–1943 is interpolated in such fashion as to match the timing of adjustment applied in deriving National Income Division estimates of government purchases.

Column 4 – Transactions reported here represent estimated semiannual changes in short-term liabilities of U.S. Government to foreign governments, banks, etc. Data are based on detailed balance of payments worksheets of Office of Business Economics, Department of Commerce.

Balance-of-payments data are available less than annually only beginning in 1945, before which semiannual figures represent arbitrary interpolations from given annual totals. Prior to 1940 there were no relevant transactions of substantial magnitude, and the item is ignored.

Column 5 – Sum of cols. 1–4.

1936 to 1949

$ mill.

Semi-annual period ending	Semiannual net change				
	In major deposits of trust funds with Treasury	In deposits of individuals in certain Treasury accounts	In government payables to private corporations	In international liabilities not elsewhere classified	In miscellaneous liabilities not elsewhere classified
	1	2	3	4	5
1936 June	–	–	–	–	–
Dec.	1	–	–	–	1
1937 June	3	–	–	–	3
Dec.	24	–	–	–	24
1938 June	–9	–	–	–	–9
Dec.	33	–	–	–	33
1939 June	–27	–	–	–	–27
Dec.	17	–	–	–	17
1940 June	–16	–	–	–3	–19
Dec.	19	–	100	–4	115
1941 June	5	–	150	23	178
Dec.	9	–	350	24	383
1942 June	12	7	1 200	9	1 228
Dec.	29	23	2 200	9	2 261
1943 June	–18	32	1 000	11	1 025
Dec.	47	59	–	12	118
1944 June	–25	95	–200	22	–108
Dec.	–4	165	–100	250	311
1945 June	67	431	–600	568	466
Dec.	38	58	–1 400	426	–878
1946 June	81	–431	–1 700	–273	–2 323
Dec.	–85	–197	–300	–278	–860
1947 June	–14	–43	–	–161	–218
Dec.	8	–10	–	–15	–17
1948 June	22	–16	–	–52	–46
Dec.	53	–10	–	–28	15
1949 June	–60	–8	–	–210	–278
Dec.	27	–15	–	–67	–55

SAVING OF FEDERAL GOVERNMENT
Income Account Method: 1929 to 1949

$ mill.

Year	Receipts (National Income definition)	Expenditures (National Income definition)	Federal surplus (National Income definition)	Surplus of federal social insurance funds	Federal general government surplus (National Income definition)	Miscellaneous adjustments for classification or timing	Government corporation capital formation
	1	2	3	4	5	6	7
1929	3 833	2 648	1 185	101	1 084	2	10
1930	3 053	2 777	276	99	177	53	4
1931	2 049	4 142	−2 093	89	−2 182	530	4
1932	1 705	3 170	−1 465	72	−1 537	−6	1
1933	2 673	3 983	−1 310	58	−1 368	−67	104
1934	3 543	6 393	−2 850	49	−2 899	−194	179
1935	3 978	6 516	−2 538	62	−2 600	−97	74
1936	5 026	8 501	−3 475	281	−3 756	−822	25
1937	7 049	7 225	−176	1 452	−1 628	220	240
1938	6 491	8 451	−1 960	1 084	−3 044	47	414
1939	6 742	8 955	−2 213	1 145	−3 358	24	228
1940	8 685	10 094	−1 409	1 180	−2 589	6	602
1941	15 656	20 545	−4 889	1 788	−6 677	−369	1 038
1942	23 199	56 148	−32 949	2 459	−35 408	−1 177	3 307
1943	39 590	85 979	−46 389	3 703	−50 092	326	2 542
1944	41 590	95 594	−54 004	4 336	−58 340	1 895	1 684
1945	43 021	84 840	−41 819	4 714	−46 533	−291	−717
1946	39 672	37 060	2 612	3 500	−888	−1 088	−799
1947	43 968	31 113	12 855	3 522	9 333	−3 007	−17
1948	43 916	35 493	8 423	2 846	5 577	−477	1 224
1949	39 207	41 370	−2 163	2 066	−4 229	−310	1 717

Table F-22 shows the derivation of estimates of federal government saving, computed as the excess of current revenue over current expenditure. These estimates represent an adaptation of data on government receipts and expenditures compiled and published by the National Income Division, Department of Commerce, in *Survey of Current Business, National Income Supplement*, July 1947 and July 1950 issues. They are used in preference to the figures provided by the *Budget*, the *Daily Treasury Statement*, or other fiscal documents, because they offer a much closer initial approximation to the ultimate goal of the present effort. The National Income Division figures, of course, are themselves based very largely on such fiscal documents, especially the *Daily Treasury Statement*. Their use is simply a shortcut in which advantage is taken of the substantial agreement between measures relevant to national income accounting and the objectives of the present study.

This is true for two reasons. In the first place, the National Income accounts already represent a consolidated statement of federal government transactions whereas no single fiscal document adequately covering entities distinct from Treasury is available. Secondly, intangible capital transactions such as government borrowing, lending, and repayments by or to Treasury, as well as transactions involving land and existing fixed assets, are outside the scope of the National Income accounts. Capital gains and losses are likewise excluded. Thus, in adapting these data, only a single primary problem is faced that of capitalizing (i.e. excluding from current expenditures) purchases of new tangible assets and of depreciating them.

Apart from that primary problem, the process of adaptation involves several adjustments of classification and a few important alterations of timing. For example, the Adjusted Service Certificate Fund, to be treated here as one of the federal trust funds representing individuals' saving, is not among the social insurance funds for which separate data are available in the National Income statistics. Similarly the Postal Savings System, here regarded as part of the banking system, is treated by the National Income Division as a federal agency. Reclassification of the Adjusted Service Certificate Fund sharply alters the timing of certain large federal expenditures in a few years. Another important change in timing is the substitution in 1946 and 1947 of issuance of Armed Forces leave bonds for cash redemptions, the latter being counted as transfer payments in National Income estimates of federal expenditures. Still another important alteration of timing has to do with expenditures of the Maritime Commission and is of a purely statistical nature. It is discussed in the notes to col. 6, as are miscellaneous additional adjustments of a minor character. The first five columns of Table F-22 present in summary fashion the relevant National Income statistics on federal government operations, with the annual surplus (or deficit) exclusive of social insurance funds shown in col. 5. Assorted adjustments of classification or timing, are combined in col. 6. Cols. 7-10 represent measures of the various capital outlays to be excluded from current expenditures, and included in saving, for present purposes. These

Income Account Method: 1929 to 1949

$ mill.

Year	General government construction (except military)	General government acquisition of equipment (except military)	Government purchases of silver and minor coin metals (net)	Depreciation charges		Federal government net saving	
				Original cost	Replacement cost	Original cost depreciation	Replacement cost depreciation
	8	9	10	11	12	13	14
1929	136	25	2	44	73	1 215	1 186
1930	180	29	2	49	75	396	370
1931	231	28	1	56	78	−1 444	−1 466
1932	299	26	1	61	74	−1 277	−1 290
1933	302	26	12	68	83	−1 059	−1 074
1934	348	30	101	77	100	−2 512	−2 535
1935	417	60	347	87	110	−1 886	−1 909
1936	440	79	199	103	128	−3 938	−3 963
1937	413	59	165	122	159	−653	−690
1938	395	40	200	140	176	−2 088	−2 124
1939	390	63	163	153	187	−2 643	−2 677
1940	406	72	102	164	202	−1 565	−1 603
1941	444	69	80	184	235	−5 599	−5 650
1942	424	148	46	260	333	−32 920	−32 993
1943	457	125	−33	404	491	−47 079	−47 166
1944	192	73	−170	511	600	−55 177	−55 266
1945	192	71	−183	548	649	−48 009	−48 110
1946	318	152	4	275	409	−2 576	−2 710
1947	444	157	28	289	491	6 649	6 447
1948	747	222	33	302	554	7 024	6 772
1949	1 096	185	30	328	582	−1 839	−2 093

do not include acquisition of military assets, which is regarded as part of current expenditure. The final results of these tabulations after imputation of depreciation charges and without consideration of saving in the form of military assets appear in cols. 13 and 14.

Column 1 – Total of federal revenues according to National Income definitions; includes personal tax and nontax receipts, indirect business tax and nontax accruals, corporate profits tax accruals, and contributions to social insurance funds. Data are taken from table 8 of *Survey of Current Business, National Income Supplement*, July 1947, and July 1950.

Column 2 – Aggregate of federal expenditures according to National Income definitions; includes purchases of goods and services, transfer payments, net interest paid and subsidies less current surplus of government enterprises. The data come from table 9 of *Survey of Current Business, National Income Supplement*, July 1950.

Column 3 – This is the surplus in terms of National Income definitions, equal to col. 1 minus col. 2. It includes federal social insurance funds, which are regarded as part of government sector in standard National Income accounts. Separate data on social insurance funds, however, have been published by National Income Division to facilitate rearrangement according to alternative view of social insurance funds as a component of the personal sector.

Column 4 – As defined in National Income measurement; data are taken from table 10 of *Survey of Current Business, National Income Number*, July 1950.

Column 5 – Col. 3 minus col. 4.

Column 6 – Sum of seven items discussed separately below:
(1) National Income Division has not treated Adjusted Service Certificate Fund as a social insurance fund but as a general government agency. Transfers by Treasury to the Fund have accordingly been ignored, and expenditures by the Fund itself appear in federal expenditures as transfer payments. Not only benefit payments as such but loans by the Fund to veterans of World War I on security of their Adjusted Service Certificates are so regarded because of subsequent cancellation of these loans by act of Congress. Additional amounts lent by Government Life Insurance Fund on security of Adjusted Service Certificates received same treatment.
In this study, Adjusted Service Certificate Fund is regarded as a component of individuals'

saving. To make estimates of federal saving consistent with resultant personal saving measures, it is necessary to eliminate from federal expenditures all items counted by National Income Division and to substitute transfers from Treasury to the Fund. In this connection it is necessary to advance by one year the timing of a transfer of $500 million actually shown in Treasury records in June 1937. This transfer was made to permit Adjusted Service Certificate Fund to reimburse Government Life Insurance Fund for canceled Adjusted Service Certificate secured loans held by the latter. (This transaction is discussed briefly in notes to Table F-19, col. 5 and more fully in annotation of estimates of individuals' equity in federal trust funds in Table F-23.)

(2) In the government interest component of National Income series, interest paid by Treasury to Adjusted Service Certificate Fund is an intragovernmental transaction and does not affect the federal surplus. If Adjusted Service Certificate Fund is regarded as a component of individuals' saving, as it is here, this interest becomes a payment to the public and must be added to federal expenditures, i.e. deducted from federal saving.

(3) An analogous adjustment is required in the case of interest paid by Treasury to Postal Savings System. This is an intragovernmental transfer in National Income accounts but becomes a payment to the public upon reclassification of Postal Savings System as part of the banking system.

(4) National Income Division has disregarded issuance of armed forces leave bonds to veterans of World War II but has counted cash redemption of these obligations as transfer payments at time of redemption. In this study, armed forces leave bonds are regarded as assets of individuals and (as in official public debt statements) as liabilities of federal government. Accordingly, it is necessary to substitute issuance for redemption of these bonds among federal expenditures entering present calculation of saving.

(5) In 1932 and 1933, Reconstruction Finance Corporation made large loans to states for relief purposes. These were ignored by National Income Division as capital transactions. Subsequently, however, loans were canceled, and Reconstruction Finance Corporation reimbursed by Treasury, so that in retrospect they may be regarded as grants-in-aid. The loans are not counted as assets in Table F-12, col. 2, and consistency requires that they be expensed here.

(6) In 1933 and 1934, National Income series reflects certain Civil Works Administration expenditures with timing different from that reported in *Daily Treasury Statement*. That adjustment is here reversed so as to restore consistency with general fund asset changes recorded in Table F-12.

(7) Decision not to capitalize tangible assets of Maritime Commission means, in effect, that net increments in these assets as reported in Treasury balance sheets of government enterprises are charged to current expense in Table F-12. In reconciling preliminary results of Table F-22 with those of F-12 a serious incompatibility of timing between Maritime Commission fixed asset acquisitions as indicated by government enterprise balance sheets and corresponding expenditures of Maritime Commission as estimated by the National Income Division became evident, although the two series matched reasonably well on a cumulative basis. Since the enterprise balance sheet series is linked to various claims and liabilities remaining in Table F-12, cols. 2 and 9, while the National Income Division series is independent of other elements of Table F-22, the difficulty has been resolved by substituting the former for the latter in Table F-22. Specifically, this is done by entering in col. 6 for years 1940–1946 net difference between National Income Division series and sum of increments in Maritime Commission fixed assets and estimated ship losses. This solution tends, of course, to impair the independence of the two sets of saving estimates, but it seems preferable to ignoring an identified, but unexplained, statistical discrepancy of large size. The substitution should not be taken to imply greater reliability of enterprise balance sheet figures (reverse may well be the case) but is dictated simply by their interrelationships with other data in Table F-12, in contrast to independence of National Income Division series.

Column 7 – Consists of gross acquisitions of new fixed assets by government enterprises other than Maritime Commission and part of Reconstruction Finance Corporation, together with the net change in their inventories (including, for technical reasons, certain large crop loans of Commodity Credit Corporation). Series represents capital outlays of government corporations included in federal purchases of goods and services but to be excluded from expenditures (and added to federal government saving) for present purposes. Estimates are based on data from National Income Division.

Column 8 – These outlays are included in National Income estimates of federal purchases but must be capitalized here. Series is described in notes to Table F-16, col. 2.

Column 9 – Again, these outlays are included among federal expenditures by National Income Division but must be capitalized in present calculation. Series is described in notes to Table F-16, cols. 4–9

Column 10 – Acquisition of monetary metals is treated in Treasury accounting practice as a shift among general fund assets rather than as an expenditure. National Income Division has expensed these items (on net basis), but it is appropriate here to restore original Treasury accounting in order to maintain consistency with Table F-12. Estimates are based on data from National Income Division.

Column 11 – Sum of depreciation allowances on fixed assets, general government construction, and equipment, original cost basis (see notes to Table F-14, col. 12, and Table F-16, cols. 3 and 10).

Column 12 – Sum of depreciation allowances on fixed assets, general government construction, and equipment, replacement cost basis (see note to Table F-11, col. 12. Expenditures for Reconstruction Finance Corporation civilian plants deflated by Table R-20, col. 3.)

Column 13 – Sum of cols. 5–10 minus col. 11.

Column 14 – Sum of cols. 5–10 minus col. 12.

INDIVIDUALS' EQUITY IN FEDERAL PERSONAL SECTOR TRUST FUNDS
1928 to 1949

$ mill.

Semi-annual period ending	Total special issues of U.S. securities held by federal agencies and trust funds	Special issues held by government corporations and Postal Savings System	Special issues held by personal sector funds	Total public issues of U.S. securities held by federal agencies and trust funds	Public issues held by federal agencies other than personal sector funds	Public issues held by personal sector funds
	1	2	3	4	5	6
1928 Dec.	481	–	481	341	236	105
1929 June	607	–	607	309	178	131
Dec.	628	–	628	271	156	115
1930 June	764	–	764	237	138	99
Dec.	781	–	781	202	115	87
1931 June	291	–	291	173	99	74
Dec.	393	–	393	205	131	74
1932 June	309	–	309	299	227	72
Dec.	351	–	351	300	222	78
1933 June	323	–	323	372	284	88
Dec.	371	–	371	428	341	87
1934 June	396	35	361	920	825	95
Dec.	557	145	412	952	853	99
1935 June	633	225	408	1 013	908	105
Dec.	729	200	529	1 161	1 012	149
1936 June	1 126	200	926	1 332	1 140	192
Dec.	1 132	200	932	1 484	1 257	227
1937 June	1 558	125	1 433	1 684	1 423	261
Dec.	2 227	130	2 097	1 744	1 464	280
1938 June	2 676	130	2 546	1 791	1 507	284
Dec.	3 156	157	2 999	1 873	1 558	315
1939 June	3 770	229	3 541	1 835	1 520	315
Dec.	4 231	143	4 088	2 031	1 687	344
1940 June	4 775	153	4 622	2 028	1 683	345
Dec.	5 370	169	5 201	1 986	1 620	366
1941 June	6 120	183	5 937	2 105	1 733	372
Dec.	6 982	133	6 849	2 277	1 889	388
1942 June	7 885	156	7 729	2 455	1 937	518
Dec.	9 032	158	8 874	2 906	2 160	746
1943 June	10 871	408	10 463	3 220	2 418	802
Dec.	12 703	275	12 428	3 800	2 899	901
1944 June	14 287	393	13 894	4 633	3 102	1 531
Dec.	16 326	536	15 790	5 347	3 366	1 981
1945 June	18 812	598	18 214	6 122	3 675	2 447
Dec.	20 000	510	19 490	7 031	4 040	2 991
1946 June	22 332	951	21 381	6 789	3 862	2 927
Dec.	24 585	1 201	23 384	6 329	3 874	2 455
1947 June	27 366	2 116	25 250	5 443	2 983	2 460
Dec.	28 955	2 468	26 487	5 397	2 545	2 852
1948 June	30 211	2 576	27 635	5 538	2 419	3 119
Dec.	31 714	2 635	29 079	5 603	2 483	3 120
1949 June	32 776	2 831	29 945	5 498	2 381	3 117
Dec.	33 896	2 848	31 048	5 450	2 337	3 113

The federal government administers a number of programs in which funds collected from the public or transferred from the Treasury are placed in trust accounts, to be held or invested (and ultimately disbursed) on behalf of specified classes of beneficiaries. Although such beneficiaries exercise very little control over the disposition of the funds in question and although contributions are in most cases compulsory, the fact remains that the government's role is basically that of custodian. Accordingly, it is desirable for many purposes to distinguish transactions of and balances in such funds from those associated with general government activities.

INDIVIDUALS' EQUITY IN FEDERAL PERSONAL SECTOR TRUST FUNDS

1928 to 1949

F-23
(Part 2)

$ mill.

Semi-annual period ending	Cash balances of principal funds	Other assets of Government Life Insurance and Adjusted Service Certificate Funds	Adjusted Service Certificate and Government Life Insurance Fund policy loans	Individuals' equity in federal personal sector funds	Semiannual net change in individuals' equity in federal personal sector funds
	7	8	9	10	11
1928 Dec.	0	194	92	688	
1929 June	0	236	134	840	152
Dec.	0	292	190	845	5
1930 June	0	382	280	965	120
Dec.	0	424	322	970	5
1931 June	0	1 262	1 160	467	−503
Dec.	0	1 382	1 280	569	102
1932 June	0	1 566	1 464	483	−86
Dec.	0	1 669	1 567	531	48
1933 June	0	1 743	1 641	513	−18
Dec.	0	1 785	1 683	560	47
1934 June	0	1 805	1 703	558	−2
Dec.	0	1 854	1 752	613	55
1935 June	0	1 878	1 776	615	2
Dec.	0	1 888	1 816	750	135
1936 June	0	183	131	1 170	420
Dec.	1	174	132	1 202	32
1937 June	4	176	134	1 740	538
Dec.	28	182	140	2 447	707
1938 June	19	189	147	2 891	444
Dec.	52	193	151	3 408	517
1939 June	25	196	154	3 923	515
Dec.	42	195	153	4 516	593
1940 June	26	195	153	5 035	519
Dec.	45	195	153	5 654	619
1941 June	50	196	154	6 401	747
Dec.	59	195	153	7 338	937
1942 June	71	194	152	8 360	1 022
Dec.	100	188	146	9 762	1 402
1943 June	82	183	141	11 389	1 627
Dec.	129	150	136	13 472	2 083
1944 June	104	146	132	15 543	2 071
Dec.	100	141	127	17 885	2 342
1945 June	167	119	119	20 828	2 943
Dec.	205	117	117	22 686	1 858
1946 June	286	116	116	24 594	1 908
Dec.	201	114	114	26 040	1 446
1947 June	187	113	113	27 897	1 857
Dec.	195	112	112	29 534	1 637
1948 June	217	116	116	30 971	1 437
Dec.	270	119	119	32 469	1 498
1949 June	210	122	122	33 272	803
Dec.	237	124	124	34 398	1 126

The view taken in this study is that changes in assets of federal trust funds are best regarded as a component of personal saving rather than of government saving. Thus transactions of the general government with the trust funds are treated as dealings with the public, and liabilities to them as liabilities to the public. (Presentation of separate data, however, readily permits an alternative consolidation of these entities with the government sector, in which all transactions, claims, and liabilities between the two groups would be viewed as intragovernmental.)

In Table F-23 and supporting Tables F-24 and F-25 the term "personal sector trust funds" is used to designate the federal trust accounts segregated from general government operations for inclusion with individuals' saving. Generally speaking, they include all agencies engaged in the conduct of insurance, pension, or analogous programs in which assets in the nature of reserves are held on behalf of individual participants or beneficiaries, viz.:

    (1) Federal Old-Age and Survivors Insurance Trust Fund
    (2) Railroad Retirement Account
    (3) Unemployment Trust Fund
    (4) Civil Service, Foreign Service, Alaska Railroad, and Canal Zone retirement funds
    (5) Government Life Insurance Fund
    (6) National Service Life Insurance Fund
    (7) Adjusted Service Certificate Fund
    (8) Indian tribal funds
    (9) Various petty funds (of which the Ainsworth Library Fund and the National Institute of Health Gift Fund may be cited as illustrative). Careful investigation might result in a different classification for many of these minor funds but is scarcely warranted because of their quantitative insignificance.

A residual approach has been adopted in measuring the bulk of individuals' equity in these funds. Data on total federal agency holdings of both public and special issues of U.S. Government securities are rather readily available. Since most of such agencies fall within the personal sector group and since in turn investments of personal sector trust funds are restricted for the most part to public debt obligations, a substantial portion of their assets may be ascertained by subtracting from the totals amounts held by nonpersonal sector agencies. These steps are indicated separately for special and for public issues in Table F-23, cols. 1–6. The derivation of the series to be deducted is shown in the supporting Table F-24.

The residual is subject to a slight hazard of reporting discrepancies between nonpersonal sector values implicit in the starting totals and those compiled directly (from different sources) for deduction. Probability of error from this cause is believed low, however, and the method has the great practical advantage of avoiding a laborious fund-by-fund compilation.

Once public debt holdings of the personal sector funds have been determined, completion of the estimates of individuals' equity in them is not difficult since only a few other types of investment are legally permissible. These consist of cash balances on deposit with the Treasury, minor holdings of government corporation securities by the Government Life Insurance Fund, and several types of loans to veterans by that and the Adjusted Service Certificate Fund. The last-mentioned loans are in the nature of a memorandum entry, as they do not contribute to individuals' equity in the funds when the latter are consolidated with borrowers' liabilities in the measurement of total individuals' saving. While such loans are included in the tabulation of total fund assets in Table F-23, they are netted out in arriving at individuals' equity therein. Presentation of the gross data with respect to these loans, however, permits proper treatment of them should it be desired to show saving of the funds and of individuals as such in separate sectors.

The final result of Table F-23 is a measure of changes in individuals' equity in federal personal sector trust funds consistent with the measures of general government saving shown elsewhere in this study.

Column 1 – Inasmuch as special issues of U.S. securities are not sold to the public, data shown in this column represent entire amounts of such issues outstanding as of dates indicated. Information comes basically from detailed analyses of public debt published monthly in *Daily Treasury Statement*. For most of period under review, actual transcription has been made from convenient summaries of public debt statements in Department of the Treasury, *Treasury Bulletin* and in *Banking and Monetary Statistics*. Series is quite straightforward except as noted in following paragraph.

In June 1936 there was outstanding a large volume of loans from both Adjusted Service Certificate Fund and Government Life Insurance Fund to veterans of World War I on security of their adjusted service certificates. In conjunction with legislation enacted in that month to authorize exchange of the certificates for non-negotiable (but immediately redeemable) bonds of same face value, Adjusted Service Certificate secured loans and most accrued interest thereon were canceled, with provision for corresponding reduction in value of adjusted service bonds issued to those veterans who had pledged their certificates as collateral for loans. An appropriation was made to Adjusted Service Certificate Fund to enable it to meet all obligations imposed by this legislation, one of which was reimbursement in full to Government Life Insurance Fund for canceled Adjusted Service Certificate loans in its portfolio. Difficulties in computation of sum due (which was to include all accrued interest) delayed payment until June 1937, when it was effected through issuance to Government Life Insurance Fund of special public debt obligations amounting to 500 million dollars. Government Life Insurance Fund itself continued to carry its adjusted service certificate loans as assets until actual receipt of the special public debt issues, but, since original borrowers had been relieved by law of any liability a year earlier, it is clear that during interim the loans should be regarded as a claim on U.S. Government. Col. 1, therefore, reflects as of June 30 and Dec. 31, 1936, $500 million of special issues not officially recorded by Treasury until June 1937.

Column 2 – Government corporations and Postal Savings System are the only holders of special issues not belonging to personal sector group of federal trust funds. Former are included in consolidated federal government statement, while latter is regarded as part of the banking system. Their holdings must, of course, be eliminated in deriving a measure of public debt held on behalf of individuals by federal trust funds. Data are readily available in monthly public debt statements and summaries thereof in Department of the Treasury, *Treasury Bulletin.*

Government corporations and credit agencies owning special issues during period under review were Federal Deposit Insurance Corporation, Federal Savings and Loan Insurance Corporation, and Federal Housing Administration. Their combined holdings are shown in Table F-24, col. 2, and a separate series for Postal Savings System appears in col. 5 of same table.

Column 3 – Col. 1 minus col. 2. Shows, as of each date indicated, amount of assets held for individuals by federal trust funds in form of special public debt issues.

Column 4 – Figures exclude Federal Reserve bank holdings. For all dates subsequent to Dec. 31, 1937' and for June 30 of 1937 and each prior year, they are taken directly from the analyses of ownership of public debt published periodically in Department of the Treasury, *Treasury Bulletin.* Successive revisions of Treasury series make it difficult to ensure absolute consistency over entire period, but it is believed that this objective has been very nearly achieved. December data for 1937 and prior years are subject to a slightly wider margin of error since lack of Treasury compilations as of earlier calendar year-ends necessitated a partial interpolation. Great bulk of public issues held during these years by federal agencies and trust funds was in hands of government corporations and Postal Savings System, for which precise Dec. figures are available. (See discussion of Table F-24, cols. 1–6.) Remainder was held by Government Life Insurance Fund, Civil Service Retirement Fund, and an assortment of Indian and miscellaneous minor funds. Dec. interpolations were made separately for each fund for which accurate fiscal year-end data were given in *Annual Reports of the Secretary of the Treasury* and collectively for a small residual group of minor funds. Results are satisfactory for purpose at hand. While much of the missing information could doubtless be obtained from individual agency records, resultant improvements in the series could scarcely be proportionate to the effort expended in such refinement.

Column 5 – From Table F-24, col. 9; individual components of series are discussed in notes to that table.

Column 6 – Col. 4 minus col. 5. Shows, as of each date indicated, amount of direct public debt other than special issues held on behalf of individuals by federal trust funds.

Column 7 – Represent deposits with U.S. Treasury to credit of selected funds. Figures are somewhat incomplete but not, it is believed, with respect to any consequential sums. Cash balances actually taken into account, beginning with Dec. 31, 1936, are those of Old-Age, Railroad Retirement, Unemployment, Civil Service Retirement, and National Service Life Insurance Funds.

Data for the first three are as reported in social security statements of accounts published in *Treasury Bulletin,* with following qualification: in some instances, statements cited include as assets the unexpended balances of appropriations not yet transferred to the funds. While this may be regarded as entirely proper for some purposes, it is inconsistent with accounting practices followed in compiling *Daily Treasury Statement,* upon which federal government estimates given in another section of this study are largely based. Unexpended appropriation balances, therefore, are excluded from col. 7.

With respect to Civil Service Retirement and National Service Life Insurance funds, cash balances as of each June 30 are taken from statements of condition of trust funds published in *Annual Reports of the Secretary of the Treasury.* December values have been ascertained by adding in each case the net excess of receipts over expenditures (including investments) for the last half of the year as reported in the *Daily Treasury Statement.*

Cash balances of other funds since 1936 and those of all funds at earlier dates have been ignored here simply because of their smallness. The funds invariably follow a practice of immediate investment of all resources except minimum working balances, and prior to the advent of social security programs working balance requirements were extremely modest. A spot check of dates between 1928 and 1936 indicated that this item could safely be neglected during those years.

Column 8 – From Table F-25, cols. 6, 8–10. Most of the federal trust funds are prohibited by law from making investments other than in U.S. Government securities. There are, however, a few exceptions which are taken into account under this heading. Items included are as follows: (a) adjusted service certificate secured loans to World War I veterans by Adjusted Service Certificate Fund; (b) similar loans by the Government Life Insurance Fund; (c) Government Life Insurance Fund policy loans; and (d) federal land bank bonds held by Government Life Insurance Fund.

Column 9 – It will be observed that the first three items included in col. 8 involved loans made by the funds to individuals. If these borrowings are not taken into account elsewhere in measuring personal debt, they must be treated here as a reduction in individuals' equity in the assets of federal trust funds. Col. 9 equals col. 8 minus federal land bank bonds held by Government Life Insurance Fund, or to Table F-25, sum of cols. 8–10.

Column 10 – Sum of cols. 3, 6–8 minus col. 9.

Column 11 – Successive differences of col. 10.

The primary object of this table is to show the derivation of Table F-23, col. 5, viz. public issues of U.S. securities held by federal agencies other than the personal sector trust funds. As a by-product, it also shows (in cols. 2 and 5) a breakdown of data appearing in Table F-23, col. 2.

A parenthetical reference to the disposition of the public debt holding summarized in this table may be in order. Those of government corporations and credit agencies (col. 1) and of Exchange Stabilization Fund (col. 7) are netted out of gross public debt in the process of consolidation, as these entities are regarded as part of the general government sector. The Postal Savings System is treated as an element in the banking system; hence its public debt holdings (col. 4) remain in general government liabilities. U.S. obligations held by the Alien Property Custodian and by German Special Deposit Account (col. 8) are regarded as owned by federal agencies (cf. Table V-2, col. 4) and therefore are left in outstanding general government liabilities.

Column 1 – From June 30, 1934 through Dec. 31, 1949, summary totals are readily available from balance sheets of government corporations and credit agencies published periodically in *Daily Treasury Statement*. In one instance (June 30, 1942) a minor adjustment has been made because of divergent reporting dates for some of the constituent corporations.

Prior to June 30, 1934, series has been compiled from individual corporation balance sheets given in Senate Document 172, 76th Congress, supplemented by quarterly reports of Reconstruction Finance Corporation and by financial statements for federal land banks and federal intermediate credit banks in *Annual Reports of the Secretary of the Treasury*. Beginning June 30, 1947, federal land bank holdings are excluded since, upon retirement of U.S.-owned capital of the banks, Treasury ceased including them as federal agencies in its analyses of ownership of the public debt (Table F-23, col. 4).

Column 2 – Figures pertain only to Federal Deposit Insurance Corporation, Federal Savings and Loan Insurance Corporation, and Federal Housing Administration and come from monthly analyses of the public debt, as indicated in discussion of Table F-23, col. 2.

Column 3 – Col. 1 minus col. 2.

Column 4 – Taken from Postal Savings statements in *Banking and Monetary Statistics* for all dates through Dec. 31, 1941, and from corresponding statements in *Federal Reserve Bulletins* for subsequent dates.

Column 5 – From "Monthly Public Debt Statements," *Daily Treasury Statement*.

Column 6 – Col. 4 minus col. 5.

Column 7 – Obtained from balance sheets of the Exchange Stabilization Fund published periodically in Department of the Treasury, *Treasury Bulletin*. Dec. values have been interpolated for a few early years when only fiscal year-end statements were published.

Column 8 – June 30 data may be found in statements of the condition of these funds in *Annual Reports of the Secretary of the Treasury*. December values have been interpolated by averaging fiscal year-end holdings except in a few instances where they were actually reported in Department of the Treasury, *Treasury Bulletin*, analyses of ownership of the public debt.

Column 9 – Sum of cols. 3, 6–8.

DERIVATION OF SELECTED ITEMS OF INDIVIDUALS' EQUITY IN PERSONAL SECTOR TRUST FUNDS: 1928 to 1949

$ mill.

Semi-annual period ending	Total direct public debt held by government corporations and credit agencies	Special issues held by Federal Deposit Insurance Corporation, Federal Savings and Loan Insurance, Federal Housing Administration, and Federal Home Loan Bank Board	Total public issues held by government corporations and credit agencies	Total direct public debt held by Postal Savings System	Special issues held by Postal Savings System	Public issues held by Postal Savings System	U.S. securities held by Exchange Stabilization Fund	Public issues held by Alien Property Custodian Fund and German Special Deposit Account	Total public issues held by federal agencies other than personal sector trust funds
	1	2	3	4	5	6	7	8	9
1928 Dec.	29	–	29	25	–	25	–	182	236
1929 June	29	–	29	26	–	26	–	123	178
Dec.	26	–	26	26	–	26	–	104	156
1930 June	28	–	28	26	–	26	–	84	138
Dec.	23	–	23	27	–	27	–	65	115
1931 June	26	–	26	27	–	27	–	46	99
Dec.	19	–	19	70	–	70	–	42	131
1932 June	118	–	118	71	–	71	–	38	227
Dec.	115	–	115	71	–	71	–	36	222
1933 June	119	–	119	131	–	131	–	34	284
Dec.	109	–	109	200	–	200	–	32	341
1934 June	373	0	373	418	35	383	38	31	825
Dec.	469	100	369	467	47	420	32	32	853
1935 June	444	100	344	630	125	505	27	32	908
Dec.	449	100	349	706	100	606	24	33	1 012
1936 June	486	100	386	800	100	700	20	34	1 140
Dec.	506	100	406	892	100	792	25	34	1 257
1937 June	551	95	456	933	30	903	30	34	1 423
Dec.	606	100	506	931	30	901	23	34	1 464
1938 June	651	85	566	936	45	891	15	35	1 507
Dec.	710	105	605	965	52	913	5	35	1 558
1939 June	713	101	612	1 011	128	883	5	20	1 520
Dec.	758	71	687	1 046	72	974	12	14	1 687
1940 June	748	56	692	1 078	97	981	10	–	1 683
Dec.	701	72	629	1 078	97	981	10	–	1 620
1941 June	802	95	707	1 104	88	1 016	10	–	1 733
Dec.	884	70	814	1 128	63	1 065	10	–	1 889
1942 June	937	100	837	1 146	56	1 090	10	–	1 937
Dec.	1 088	101	987	1 220	57	1 163	10	–	2 160
1943 June	1 345	209	1 136	1 471	199	1 272	10	–	2 418
Dec.	1 448	87	1 361	1 716	188	1 528	10	–	2 899
1944 June	1 524	125	1 399	1 951	268	1 683	20	–	3 102
Dec.	1 630	130	1 500	2 252	406	1 846	20	–	3 366
1945 June	1 679	134	1 545	2 574	464	2 110	20	–	3 675
Dec.	1 683	54	1 629	2 837	456	2 381	30	–	4 040
1946 June	1 767	169	1 598	3 026	782	2 244	20	–	3 862
Dec.	1 873	263	1 610	3 182	938	2 244	20	–	3 874
1947 June	1 777	488	1 289	3 302	1 628	1 674	20	–	2 983
Dec.	1 685	586	1 099	3 308	1 882	1 426	20	–	2 545
1948 June	1 684	664	1 020	3 291	1 912	1 379	20	–	2 419
Dec.	1 854	768	1 086	3 244	1 867	1 377	20	–	2 483
1949 June	2 004	879	1 125	3 188	1 952	1 236	20	–	2 381
Dec.	2 047	966	1 081	3 118	1 882	1 236	20	–	2 337

The primary objective of this table is to show the derivation of Table F-23, cols. 8 and 9. Additional information is incorporated, however, and the table is so arranged as to show semiannually the net change in individuals' equity in the three veterans' funds.

Columns 1 to 3 – Special public debt issues held, respectively, by Adjusted Service Certificate Fund, Government Life Insurance Fund, and National Service Life Insurance Fund all come directly, or via Department of the Treasury, *Treasury Bulletin*, from monthly public debt statements. Note that col. 2, as of June 30 and Dec. 31, 1936, includes an imputed claim upon Treasury for special issues not actually transferred to Government Life Insurance Fund until June 1937 (this imputation is described and explained in notes to Table F-23, col. 1).

Column 4 – Fiscal year-end data for all years provided by statements of the condition of Fund appearing in *Annual Reports of the Secretary of the Treasury*. December figures for certain years have appeared in Department of the Treasury, *Treasury Bulletin*, and for others may be derived from estimates appearing in Copeland's National Bureau of Economic Research Technical Paper 5, *Concerning a New Federal Financial Statement*. Remaining December amounts have been interpolated arbitrarily between known June 30 values, a procedure which, in view of the stability of Fund's operation, cannot have resulted in error of more than a few million dollars.

Column 5 – Sum of cols. 1-4.

Column 6 – Fiscal year-end information from statements of the condition of Fund appearing in *Annual Reports of the Secretary of the Treasury*. Inasmuch as amount held changed only a few times in the course of nineteen years, there is no hazard in the interpolation of most Dec. 31 values. Several are arbitrary, but in connection with most important reductions in Fund's holdings of federal land bank bonds, call dates were given in *Annual Report of the Secretary of the Treasury* so that interpolated figures are exact.

Column 7 – In principle, cash balances with Treasury of other two veterans' funds should be included here, but they are neglected because of quantitative insignificance. National Service Life Insurance series shown is described in notes to Table F-23, col. 7, of which it is a part.

Column 8 – These loans were not authorized until Feb. 1931, and outstanding balances were canceled by law in June 1936. (A brief summary of the nature of the loans is given in conjunction with discussion of Table F-23, col. 1.) Outstanding amounts on Dec. 31, 1932-1935 are as reported by Veterans' Administration to Securities and Exchange Commission. Balances at June 30, 1934 and 1935, are taken from *Annual Reports of the Secretary of the Treasury* and those as of remaining dates indicated are derived from information on net loan disbursements furnished to National Income Division by Veterans' Administration.

Column 9 – Unlike Adjusted Service Certificate Fund, Government Life Insurance Fund had been authorized to make loans to veterans on security of their adjusted service certificates prior to 1931 (beginning in 1927 to be exact). December data for 1932-1935 are as reported by Veterans' Administration to Securities and Exchange Commission, while June figures for each of those years as well as for 1931 are found in Government Life Insurance Fund statements contained in *Annual Reports of the Secretary of the Treasury*. Remaining balances are derived from information on net loan disbursements furnished by Veterans' Administration to Department of Commerce, National Income Division.

Column 10 – Statements of condition of Fund in *Annual Reports of the Secretary of the Treasury* provide June 30 data for all years except 1929-1931, when they are there shown only in combination with adjusted service certificate loans. Policy loans as of June 30 of each of those years, however, may be obtained as residuals through use of adjusted service certificate loan series given in preceding column. December balances for all years are arbitrarily interpolated—a procedure rendered quite feasible by the smooth progressions apparent in fiscal year-end series.

Column 11 – Sum of cols. 5-10.

Column 12 – Col. 11 minus sum of cols. 8-10.

INDIVIDUALS' EQUITY IN VETERANS' FUNDS
1928 to 1949

$ mill.

Semiannual period ending	Special issues held by Adjusted Service Certificate Fund	Special issues held by Government Life Insurance Fund	Special issues held by National Service Life Insurance Fund	Public issues held by Government Life Insurance Fund	Total direct public debt held by veterans' funds	Federal Land Bank bonds held by Government Life Insurance Fund	Cash balance of National Service Life Insurance Fund	Adjusted service certificate loans to veterans by		Government Life Insurance Fund policy loans	Total assets of veterans' funds	Individuals' equity in veterans' funds
								Adjusted Service Certificate Fund	Government Life Insurance Fund			
	1	2	3	4	5	6	7	8	9	10	11	12
1928 Dec.	393	–	–	114	507	102	–	–	87	5	701	609
1929 June	513	–	–	112	625	102	–	–	129	5	861	727
Dec.	504	–	–	94	598	102	–	–	157	33	890	700
1930 June	629	–	–	75	704	102	–	–	218	62	1 086	806
Dec.	620	–	–	52	672	102	–	–	252	70	1 096	774
1931 June	122	–	–	28	150	102	–	767	314	79	1 412	252
Dec.	199	–	–	28	227	102	–	860	329	91	1 609	329
1932 June	105	–	–	28	133	102	–	1 007	355	102	1 699	235
Dec.	127	–	–	28	155	102	–	1 089	367	111	1 824	257
1933 June	92	–	–	28	120	102	–	1 127	395	119	1 863	222
Dec.	126	–	–	35	161	102	–	1 155	407	121	1 946	263
1934 June	118	–	–	42	160	102	–	1 153	428	122	1 965	262
Dec.	158	–	–	52	210	102	–	1 188	440	124	2 064	312
1935 June	156	–	–	61	217	102	–	1 185	466	125	2 095	319
Dec.	247	–	–	107	354	72	–	1 216	473	127	2 242	426
1936 June	127	500	–	140	767	52	–	–	2	129	950	819
Dec.	53	500	–	177	730	42	–	–	2	130	904	772
1937 June	38	500	–	211	749	42	–	–	2	132	925	791
Dec.	31	500	–	231	762	42	–	–	2	138	944	804
1938 June	26	523	–	238	787	42	–	–	3	144	976	829
Dec.	22	507	–	272	801	42	–	–	3	148	001	843
1939 June	20	537	–	274	831	42	–	–	3	151	1 027	873
Dec.	15	503	–	304	822	42	–	–	3	150	1 017	864
1940 June	11	524	–	304	839	42	–	–	3	150	1 034	881
Dec.	10	506	–	324	840	42	–	–	3	150	1 035	882
1941 June	19	531	3	327	880	42	1	–	3	151	1 077	923
Dec.	19	507	10	339	875	42	–	–	3	150	1 070	917
1942 June	18	537	39	375	969	42	10	–	3	149	1 173	1 021
Dec.	18	526	146	434	1 124	42	16	–	3	143	1 328	1 182
1943 June	18	538	352	435	1 343	42	7	–	3	138	1 533	1 392
Dec.	18	508	731	522	1 779	14	2	–	3	133	1 931	1 795
1944 June	17	502	1 213	558	2 290	14	19	–	4	128	2 455	2 323
Dec.	20	543	1 804	555	2 922	14	14	–	4	123	3 077	2 950
1945 June	14	589	3 187	552	4 342	–	44	–	–	119	4 505	4 386
Dec.	13	605	3 850	546	5 014	–	53	–	–	117	5 184	5 067
1946 June	12	684	5 240	478	6 414	–	63	–	–	116	6 593	6 477
Dec.	12	1 236	5 675	–	6 923	–	51	–	–	114	7 088	6 974
1947 June	12	1 254	6 474	–	7 740	–	52	–	–	113	7 905	7 792
Dec.	6	1 252	6 655	–	7 913	–	26	–	–	112	8 051	7 939
1948 June	6	1 286	6 935	–	8 227	–	28	–	–	116	8 371	8 255
Dec.	6	1 284	7 013	–	8 303	–	21	–	–	119	8 443	8 324
1949 June	6	1 318	7 288	–	8 612	–	20	–	–	122	8 754	8 632
Dec.	5	1 268	7 696	–	8 969	–	24	–	–	124	9 117	8 993

Column 1 – 1909–1943: Sum of cols. 2–4.

Column 2 – 1912–1927: Assumed equal to tax liabilities in personal income tax returns for year (cf. *Statistical Abstract*, 1931, p. 191). Figures include taxes due from sole proprietors and partners in other unincorporated business enterprises which cannot be separated.

1928–1941: Assumed equal to income tax payments less refunds during following year, as shown in Department of Commerce, *Survey of Current Business, National Income Supplement*, July 1947, p. 21.

1942: Very rough estimate. (Other methods are not usable for this year because of shift to partial collection at source system and partial forgiveness of taxes for 1942.)

1943–1947: Rough estimates which make allowance for changes in scope and method of withholding payments, particularly in 1942–1945.

1948: Rough estimate, considerably reduced from 1947 because of heavy refunds resulting from reduction in income tax rates.

1949: Rough estimate.

Column 3 – 1909–1928: Assumed equal to 1.05 times corporate income tax liabilities (including war and excess profits tax) as shown in income tax reports (cf. *Historical Statistics*, p. 308), the ratio obtaining for 1929 between this series and that used from 1929 on.

1929–1943: Cumulated from Table F-17, col. 1. Not estimated for later years because of sizable cumulative amount of overstatement of cash receipts from corporate profits tax; see notes to Table F-17, cols. 1 and 3.

Column 4 – 1916–1927: Assumed equal to average payments on account of estate and (since 1933) gift taxes during current and following fiscal year (*Statistical Abstract*, 1931, p. 187). Figure so obtained for 1928 ($63 million) is virtually identical with that in Department of Commerce series used from 1928 on.

1928–1949: Assumed equal to payments during following calendar year from *Survey of Current Business, National Income Supplement*, July 1947, p. 21, and July 1950, p. 12.

Column 1 – 1916–1948: From *Annual Report of the Secretary of the Treasury* for the fiscal year ended June 30, 1948, p. 539. Figures include increase in redemption value of savings bonds; discount on unmatured issues of Treasury bills. They exclude guaranteed debt. Figures refer to fiscal year ending June 30 of indicated year.

1949–1950: From *Treasury Bulletin*, various issues.

Column 2 – 1916–1933: Derived from col. 1 on basis of average amounts of public debt outstanding, disregarding minor fluctuations.

1934–1948: Derived from monthly figures on interest on direct national debt (*Banking and Monetary Statistics*, pp. 513–514; *Federal Reserve Bulletin*, various issues).

1949–1950: From *Treasury Bulletin*.

Column 3 – 1935–1940: Rough estimates.

1941–1950: Obtained by deducting cumulated figures for accrued interest on savings bonds as of Dec. 31 from those as of June 30 of following year (cf. Department of the Treasury, *Treasury Bulletin*, various issues, e.g. Oct. 1949, p. 26).

Column 4 – 1916–1933: Estimated at one-half of col. 2 for following year (this implies assumptions of [a] semiannual coupons and [b] regular distribution of coupon dates over year). Figures include interest on special issues held by federal agencies and trust funds.

1934–1950: Obtained by deducting from col. 2 interest accruals on savings bonds as shown in col. 3 and taking one-half of difference. Figures, therefore, include relatively small amounts accrued on Treasury bills.

NET TAX ACCRUALS OF FEDERAL GOVERNMENT
1909 to 1949

$ mill.

End of year	Total	Personal income tax	Corporate income tax	Estate and gift tax	End of year	Total	Personal income tax	Corporate income tax	Estate and gift tax
	1	2	3	4		1	2	3	4
1909	22	–	22	–	1929	2 358	1 044	1 253	61
1910	36	–	36	–	1930	1 416	531	829	56
1911	30	–	30	–	1931	821	295	496	30
1912	65	28	37	–	1932	820	354	397	69
1913	86	41	45	–	1933	1 107	438	540	129
1914	109	68	41	–	1934	1 557	565	744	248
1915	233	173	60	–	1935	2 052	727	939	386
1916	900	692	181	27	1936	3 072	1 300	1 370	402
1917	3 442	1 128	2 249	65	1937	3 051	1 225	1 436	390
1918	4 680	1 270	3 317	93	1938	2 203	849	983	371
1919	3 488	1 075	2 284	129	1939	2 684	1 007	1 336	341
1920	2 573	720	1 706	147	1940	4 711	1 594	2 716	401
1921	1 700	830	737	133	1941	12 184	4 034	7 679	471
1922	1 570	632	823	115	1942	15 482	3 000	12 021	461
1923	1 785	695	984	106	1943	19 346	3 400	15 381	565
1924	1 685	650	926	109	1944	.	3 900	.	663
1925	1 988	649	1 229	110	1945	.	3 300	.	734
1926	2 099	727	1 292	80	1946	.	4 000	.	830
1927	2 219	970	1 188	61	1947	.	4 000	.	900
1928	2 482	1 178	1 243	61	1948	.	2 500	.	754
					1949	.	2 700	.	700

INTEREST ACCRUED ON DIRECT OBLIGATIONS
OF FEDERAL GOVERNMENT: 1916 to 1950

$ mill.

Year	Interest paid or accrued			Accrued interest on obligations other than savings bonds	Year	Interest paid or accrued			Accrued interest on obligations other than savings bonds
	Total	Total	On savings bonds			Total	Total	On savings bonds	
	Fiscal year	Second half of fiscal year		End of preceding year		Fiscal year	Second half of fiscal year		End of preceding year
	1	2	3	4		1	2	3	4
1916	23	12	–	6	1934	757	403	–	202
1917	25	13	–	70	1935	821	407	0	204
1918	198	140	–	180	1936	748	393	0	197
1919	619	360	–	250	1937	867	464	5	230
1920	1 024	500	–	250	1938	926	494	10	242
1921	997	500	–	250	1939	941	515	15	250
1922	989	500	–	265	1940	1 041	587	25	281
1923	1 055	530	–	230	1941	1 110	620	37	292
1924	939	460	–	215	1942	1 260	735	48	344
1925	882	430	–	205	1943	1 813	1 091	74	509
1926	831	410	–	195	1944	2 610	1 508	128	690
1927	788	390	–	180	1945	3 622	2 124	220	952
1928	732	360	–	170	1946	4 747	2 748	309	1 220
1929	679	340	–	165	1947	4 958	2 722	360	1 181
1930	659	330	–	155	1948	5 188	2 937	422	1 258
1931	611	310	–	150	1949	5 339	2 922	477	1 223
1932	600	300	–	175	1950	5 750	3 191	539	1 326
1933	689	350	–	195					

Column 1 – 1920–1927: Table F-9, col. 4 plus col. 5. Dec. 31 figures obtained by averaging data for June 30
        preceding and following.
        1928–1949: From Table F-25, col. 12.

Column 2 – 1920–1949: Estimated from 1943 on at 10 percent of col. 1, based on proportion of veterans living
        on farms and of agriculture in total labor force. For previous years proportion was obtained
        by linear interpolation between 10 percent in 1943 and 15 percent in 1918, latter estimate
        based on fact that proportion of farm population in 1918 was about 50 percent higher than in
        1945 (cf. *Historical Statistics*, p. 29; *Agricultural Statistics*, 1949, p. 499).

Column 3 – 1920–1949: Col. 1 minus col. 2.

Column 4 – 1920–1949: Derived from col. 2.

Column 5 – 1920–1949: Derived from col. 3.

1920 to 1949

$ mill.

| End of year | Total equity | Farmers | Non-farmers | Change in equity | | End of year | Total equity | Farmers | Non-farmers | Change in equity | |
				Farmers	Non-farmers					Farmers	Non-farmers
	1	2	3	4	5		1	2	3	4	5
1920	23	3	20	3	20	1935	426	49	377	12	102
1921	48	7	41	4	21	1936	772	88	684	39	307
1922	74	11	63	4	22	1937	804	90	714	2	30
1923	102	14	88	3	25	1938	843	93	750	3	36
1924	180	25	155	11	67	1939	864	93	771	0	21
1925	318	43	275	18	120	1940	882	93	789	0	18
1926	457	61	396	18	121	1941	917	95	822	2	33
1927	572	76	496	15	100	1942	1 182	121	1 061	26	239
1928	609	79	530	3	34	1943	1 795	180	1 615	59	554
1929	700	90	610	11	80	1944	2 950	295	2 655	115	1 040
1930	774	98	676	8	66	1945	5 067	507	4 560	212	1 905
1931	329	41	288	−57	−388	1946	6 974	697	6 277	190	1 717
1932	257	31	226	−10	−62	1947	7 939	794	7 145	97	868
1933	263	32	231	1	5	1948	8 324	832	7 492	38	347
1934	312	37	275	5	44	1949	8 993	899	8 094	67	602

Column 1 – 1896–1949: Col. 2 minus tax liabilities on farm real estate (Table A-54, col. 5).

Column 2 – 1896–1949: Sum of cols. 3–9.

Column 3 – 1912–1949: From Table F-26, col. 2.

Column 4 – 1916–1949: From Table F-26, col. 4.

Column 5 – 1914–1927: Estimated at one-half of total income tax collections during following year (*Historical Statistics*, p. 317), which is roughly the relationship prevailing in later years. Figures for 1915–1917 and 1919–1920, obtained by linear interpolation.
  1928–1948: Assumed equal to payments in following calendar year as shown in *Survey of Current Business, National Income Supplement*, July 1947, p. 22, and July 1949, p. 12.
  1949: Rough preliminary estimate.

Column 6 – 1914–1927: *Historical Statistics*, p. 317. Figures for 1915–1917 and 1919–1920 obtained by linear interpolation.
  1928–1949: Same source and procedure as col. 5.

Column 7 – 1896–1927: Rough estimates based on movement of total propertyax collections (*Historical Statistics*, p. 317). Figures for 1915–1917 and 1919–1920 obtained by linear interpolation.
  1928–1949: Same source and procedure as col. 5.

Column 8 – 1896–1929: Rough estimates for years 1890, 1901, 1912, and 1929 obtained by applying to figures for state and local revenue from property taxes (*Historical Statistics*, p. 314) estimated share of individuals' investment in real estate. Figures for other years obtained by linear interpolation.
  1930–1941: Assumed unchanged from the 1929 value.
  1942–1948: Same procedure as for 1896–1929 but based on changes in figures for state and local government receipts from property taxes as reported in *Survey of Current Business*, July 1950, p. 12.
  1949: Rough estimate based on trend of preceding years.

Column 9 – 1930–1941: Obtained by multiplying ratio of extraordinary tax arrears to total collections by $3 billion, which is approximately the amount of property taxes on nonfarm real estate payable annually by individuals 1930–1941, the period in which most of the arrears may be assumed to have originated (see col. 8). Ratio of extraordinary tax arrears based on the ratio of total collections to year's levy for cities of over 50,000 population as given in Bird, F. L., *Trend of Tax Delinquency, 1930–1940*, pp. 17 and 30, *1930–1944*, p. 14, assuming that deviations of the collection rate from 98 percent represent extraordinary arrears as a deficiency of 2 percent is regarded by Bird as normal.

NET TAX LIABILITIES OF NONFARM INDIVIDUALS
1896 to 1949

$ mill.

End of year	Net tax liabilities		Federal taxes		State and local taxes				
	Nonfarm individuals	All individuals	Personal income	Gift and death	Personal income	Gift and death	Personal property	Real estate	Extra-ordinary tax arrears
	1	2	3	4	5	6	7	8	9
1896	435	542	–	–	–	–	33	509	–
1897	452	560	–	–	–	–	33	527	–
1898	471	579	–	–	–	–	34	545	–
1899	489	598	–	–	–	–	34	564	–
1900	508	617	–	–	–	–	35	582	–
1901	525	635	–	–	–	–	35	600	–
1902	532	651	–	–	–	–	37	614	–
1903	538	666	–	–	–	–	39	627	–
1904	555	683	–	–	–	–	42	641	–
1905	569	698	–	–	–	–	44	654	–
1906	584	714	–	–	–	–	46	668	–
1907	592	731	–	–	–	–	49	682	–
1908	598	746	–	–	–	–	51	695	–
1909	598	762	–	–	–	–	53	709	–
1910	612	778	–	–	–	–	56	722	–
1911	611	794	–	–	–	–	58	736	–
1912	647	838	28	–	–	–	60	750	–
1913	758	976	41	–	–	–	70	865	–
1914	935	1 157	68	–	1	29	80	979	–
1915	1 149	1 392	173	–	7	33	85	1 094	–
1916	1 808	2 068	692	27	13	37	90	1 209	–
1917	2 381	2 673	1 128	65	19	42	95	1 324	–
1918	2 661	2 972	1 270	93	25	46	100	1 438	–
1919	2 564	2 957	1 075	129	33	52	115	1 553	–
1920	2 282	2 765	720	147	41	59	130	1 668	–
1921	2 500	3 010	830	133	49	66	150	1 782	–
1922	2 395	2 915	632	115	46	75	150	1 897	–
1923	2 557	3 092	695	106	50	79	150	2 012	–
1924	2 633	3 173	650	109	52	86	150	2 126	–
1925	2 768	3 318	649	110	67	91	160	2 241	–
1926	2 940	3 505	727	80	81	106	155	2 356	–
1927	3 291	3 881	970	61	92	128	160	2 470	–
1928	3 666	4 276	1 178	61	139	165	148	2 585	–
1929	3 621	4 251	1 044	61	110	182	154	2 700	–
1930	3 078	3 738	531	56	74	168	149	2 700	60
1931	2 890	3 550	295	30	64	137	144	2 700	180
1932	3 239	3 879	354	69	67	110	129	2 700	450
1933	3 737	4 357	438	129	87	97	126	2 700	780
1934	4 122	4 742	565	248	121	109	129	2 700	870
1935	4 406	5 006	727	386	167	116	130	2 700	780
1936	4 979	5 559	1 300	402	204	129	134	2 700	690
1937	4 767	5 337	1 225	390	208	137	137	2 700	540
1938	4 255	4 800	849	371	201	122	137	2 700	420
1939	4 347	4 877	1 007	341	214	115	140	2 700	360
1940	4 862	5 367	1 594	401	235	115	142	2 700	180
1941	7 326	7 811	4 034	471	264	110	142	2 700	90
1942	6 264	6 719	3 000	461	303	110	145	2 700	–
1943	6 891	7 326	3 400	565	340	124	147	2 750	–
1944	7 593	8 028	3 900	663	376	140	149	2 800	–
1945	7 142	7 617	3 300	734	376	152	155	2 900	–
1946	8 303	8 828	4 000	830	451	176	171	3 200	–
1947	8 794	9 394	4 000	900	526	179	189	3 600	–
1948	7 447	8 098	2 500	754	664	174	206	3 800	–
1949	7 745	8 444	2 700	700		1 044		4 000	–

Column 1 – 1920–1949: Sum of cols. 2–6 less sum of cols. 7–10.

Columns 2, 3, and 6 – 1936–1949: *Survey of Current Business*, various issues.

Column 4 – 1920–1928: Average of overlapping fiscal-year figures from *Statistical Abstract*, 1931, p. 167.
1929–1949: Same source as col. 2.

Column 5 – 1920–1928: Estimated by multiplying Government Life Insurance premiums, derived by averaging overlapping fiscal-year figures from *Statistical Abstract*, 1938, p. 152, by assumed share of nonfarm veterans (see note to Table F-28, col. 3).
1929–1949: Same method as above, using premiums from *Survey of Current Business*, various issues.

Column 7 – 1920–1928: Average of overlapping fiscal-year figures from *Statistical Abstract*, 1938, p. 159. In this period only federal civilian retirement payments are included.
1929–1949: Same source as col. 2, including benefits from social insurance funds paid by the federal government, excluding Government Life Insurance.

Column 8 – 1920–1928: Same method as col. 5, using figures from *Statistical Abstract*, 1938, p. 149.
1929–1949: Same source and method as col. 5.

Column 9 – 1928–1949: Annual change in Government Life Insurance policy loans, derived from Table F-25, col. 10, multiplied by assumed share of nonfarm veterans (see note to Table F-28, col. 3).

Column 10 – 1924–1928: Same method as col. 5 using figure from *Statistical Abstract*, 1938, p. 149.
1929–1935: Same source and method as col. 5.
1936: Same source and method as col. 5 excluding amounts paid on redemption of adjusted service bonds, from figures supplied by Bureau of Public Debt.
1937–1949: Assumed negligible since redemptions of adjusted service bonds constituted almost the entire amount of adjusted service benefits in this period. These redemptions are included with other cash transactions in U.S. Government securities and so are excluded here.

$ mill.

Year	Contributions						Receipts			
	Total	Old Age and Survivors' Insurance	Railroad Retirement Fund	Federal Civilian Employee Retirement Fund	Govern-ment Life Insurance	Unem-ployment Insurance	Social insurance funds	Government Life Insurance		Adjusted compen-sation benefits
								Benefits	Policy loans	
	1	2	3	4	5	6	7	8	9	10
1920	41	–	–	6	39	–	3	1	–	–
1921	64	–	–	14	60	–	7	3	–	–
1922	42	–	–	14	41	–	8	5	–	–
1923	40	–	–	14	41	–	9	6	–	–
1924	41	–	–	16	45	–	10	7	–	3
1925	33	–	–	18	47	–	12	8	–	12
1926	28	–	–	21	50	–	14	10	–	19
1927	32	–	–	25	58	–	16	13	–	22
1928	27	–	–	27	62	–	17	18	4	23
1929	–62	–	–	29	58	–	18	23	24	84
1930	–93	–	–	30	58	–	22	25	32	102
1931	–823	–	–	31	57	–	27	29	18	837
1932	–131	–	–	32	55	–	32	35	18	133
1933	–52	–	–	30	52	–	42	35	9	48
1934	–31	–	–	30	55	–	52	37	3	24
1935	–23	–	–	32	53	–	57	32	3	16
1936	–74	–	–	34	54	9	61	30	3	77
1937	328	288	62	37	54	32	106	32	7	0
1938	–160	261	54	39	53	44	566	36	9	0
1939	–206	291	58	42	53	41	627	62	2	0
1940	–292	329	67	50	50	44	765	67	0	0
1941	–28	419	80	66	58	56	654	53	0	0
1942	284	532	98	159	163	74	698	50	–6	0
1943	1 116	625	129	257	546	88	478	60	–9	0
1944	1 356	648	140	282	839	90	548	104	–9	0
1945	767	630	140	295	927	79	1 064	245	–5	0
1946	–610	687	163	262	555	44	2 029	295	–3	0
1947	–319	780	271	246	453	33	1 787	317	–2	0
1948	–429	839	283	275	373	18	1 893	318	6	0
1949	–1 678	816	277	350	341	11	3 084	385	4	0

Column 1 – 1939–1946: Obtained by distributing increase between 1939 and 1946 in the original cost of durable military assets (Goldsmith, "The Growth of Reproducible Wealth of the United States of America from 1805 to 1950," *Income and Wealth*, series II, table III, col. 3) among individual years on basis of: (a) expenditures on munitions and war construction (*Budget of U.S. Government*, 1947, p. 752); (b) proportion of value of output of aircraft, ships, guns, combat and motor vehicles, and communications and electronic equipment to total munitions production (War Production Board, *Industrial Mobilization of War*, vol. I, p. 962), and (c) index of volume of munitions production (*Survey of Current Business, Statistical Supplement*, 1947, p. 15).

        1947–1949: Sum of expenditures on aircraft procurement; construction of ships; other major procurement; military public works; stockpiling; civilian components and research and development expenditures (using only one-half of the last two items) in *Budget of U.S. Government*, 1949, p. M-14; 1950, p. M-20; 1951, p. M-28.

Column 2 – 1939–1945: Derived from col. 1 on assumption that level of munitions prices in 1944, when quantity production was established, was comparable to 1929 price level of nonmilitary commodities (the index of civilian prices of metals and metal products, then under control, was only 3 percent above the 1929 level in 1944), but the prices of military commodities declined, in comparison to the 1944 level, by about 10 percent a year from 1942 through 1945.

        1946–1949: Derived on assumption that prices of military assets moved in relation to 1946 level like Bureau of Labor Statistics index of wholesale prices of (civilian) metals and metal products.

Column 3 – 1939–1949: Obtained by depreciating col. 1 (and corresponding rough estimates for 1930–1938) at a rate of 9 percent required to reach 1946 benchmark of Reeve, J. and Associates ("Government Component in the National Wealth," *Studies in Income and Wealth*, vol. XII, p. 502). This is probably the lowest rate that can be considered and a somewhat higher over-all rate, up to about 15 percent, may take account more adequately of obsolescence on some types of equipment, particularly aircraft.

Column 4 – 1939–1949: Same rate of depreciation as used in col. 3 but applied to col. 2.

Column 5 – 1939–1945: Assumed equal to col. 4.

        1946–1949: Col. 4 multiplied by annual average of Bureau of Labor Statistics index of wholesale prices of metals and metal products shifted to 1944 basis.

Column 6 – 1939–1949: Col. 1 minus col. 3.

Column 7 – 1939–1949: Col. 2 minus col. 4.

Column 8 – 1939–1949: Col. 1 minus col. 5.

NET AND GROSS EXPENDITURES
ON DURABLE REPRODUCIBLE MILITARY ASSETS: 1939 to 1949

$ bill.

Year	Expenditures on durable military assets		Depreciation allowances			Net expenditures		
	Current	1929 prices	Original cost	1929 prices	Replacement cost	Original cost	1929 prices	Replacement cost
	1	2	3	4	5	6	7	8
1939	0.5	0.4	0.5	0.4	0.4	0	0	0.1
1940	0.7	0.6	0.5	0.4	0.4	0.2	0.2	0.3
1941	3.5	2.9	0.6	0.5	0.5	2.9	2.4	3.0
1942	13.5	11.0	1.3	1.1	1.1	12.2	9.9	12.4
1943	21.0	18.9	2.8	2.4	2.4	18.2	16.5	18.6
1944	21.0	21.0	4.6	4.1	4.1	16.4	16.9	16.9
1945	13.5	15.0	6.0	5.6	5.6	7.5	9.4	7.9
1946	2.9	2.9	6.7	6.3	7.0	−3.8	−3.4	−4.1
1947	2.0	1.6	6.9	6.5	9.1	−4.9	−4.9	−7.1
1948	2.4	1.7	7.0	6.6	10.4	−4.6	−4.9	−8.0
1949	3.2	2.2	7.2	6.7	11.0	−4.0	−4.5	−7.8

Column 1 – From Table G-2, col. 2.

Column 2 – From Table G-2, col. 4.

Column 3 – Col. 1 minus col. 2.

Column 4 – Table G-6, sum of cols. 7–9.

Column 5 – Sum of the depreciation allowances, replacement cost, on highways, equipment, and other capital outlay which were obtained by multiplying depreciation allowances, in 1929 prices, by appropriate index. Highway construction outlay, original cost, as given in Table G-6, col. 7 was deflated to 1929 prices by index given in Table R-20, col. 6; equipment outlays from Table G-6, col. 9 by an index derived by dividing nonfarm producer durable expenditures original cost by expenditures in 1929 prices and extrapolating for the years prior to 1897 by the index of whole-sale prices, all commodities, as given in Warren, G. F. and Pearson, F. H., *Gold and Prices*, p. 50; other capital outlay from Table G-6, col. 8 by the index for public construction (Table R-20, col. 8). Depreciation calculated by assuming an average life of twenty-five years for streets and highways, twelve years for equipment, and fifty years for other capital outlays.

Column 6 – Col. 3 minus col. 4.

Column 7 – Col. 3 minus col. 5.

Income Account: 1897 to 1949

$ mill.

Year	Total revenue	Current expenditures	Gross saving	Depreciation allowances		Net saving	
				Original cost	Replacement cost	Original cost basis	Replacement cost basis
	1	2	3	4	5	6	7
1897	754	658	96	46	42	50	54
1898	762	658	104	49	48	55	56
1899	770	649	121	54	56	67	65
1900	816	685	131	58	62	73	69
1901	894	683	211	63	66	148	145
1902	910	753	157	68	74	89	83
1903	950	755	195	74	81	121	114
1904	939	778	161	82	88	79	73
1905	982	876	106	90	99	16	7
1906	1 022	815	207	97	114	110	93
1907	1 090	891	199	107	130	92	69
1908	1 217	992	225	116	132	109	93
1909	1 227	961	266	127	146	139	120
1910	1 365	1 064	301	139	163	162	138
1911	1 422	1 109	313	151	176	162	137
1912	1 470	1 165	305	164	190	141	115
1913	1 472	1 158	314	175	208	139	106
1914	1 549	1 240	309	187	212	122	97
1915	1 626	1 323	303	202	230	101	73
1916	1 736	1 382	354	214	283	140	71
1917	1 876	1 459	417	228	358	189	59
1918	1 994	1 597	397	241	434	156	−37
1919	2 190	1 753	437	253	484	184	−47
1920	2 466	2 114	352	269	623	83	−271
1921	2 747	2 478	269	291	522	−22	−253
1922	3 681	2 919	762	318	497	444	265
1923	3 942	3 100	842	349	586	493	256
1924	4 330	3 325	1 005	387	607	618	398
1925	4 714	3 574	1 140	432	625	708	515
1926	5 188	3 869	1 319	477	652	842	667
1927	5 621	4 152	1 469	524	691	945	778
1928	5 988	4 407	1 581	575	715	1 006	866
1929	5 959	4 632	1 327	624	752	703	575
1930	6 675	5 080	1 595	675	766	920	829
1931	6 731	5 316	1 415	727	748	688	667
1932	6 245	5 280	965	765	668	200	297
1933	5 093	4 341	752	787	768	−35	−16
1934	5 638	4 547	1 091	798	857	293	234
1935	6 216	4 811	1 405	804	840	601	565
1936	6 296	5 135	1 161	812	872	349	289
1937	6 785	5 710	1 075	824	910	251	165
1938	7 175	6 222	953	839	894	114	59
1939	7 404	6 486	918	855	906	63	12
1940	7 615	6 731	884	880	936	4	−52
1941	8 151	6 584	1 567	897	1 035	670	532
1942	8 162	6 583	1 579	901	1 207	678	372
1943	8 336	6 530	1 806	896	1 296	910	510
1944	8 581	6 785	1 796	886	1 244	910	552
1945	9 042	6 985	2 057	871	1 229	1 186	828
1946	9 728	7 791	1 937	859	1 351	1 078	586
1947	10 973	9 040	1 933	856	1 553	1 077	380
1948	12 312	10 107	2 205	874	1 731	1 331	474
1949	14 000	12 000	2 000	913	1 756	1 087	244

Columns 1 and 3 – 1897: Estimated on assumption that difference between 1897 and 1898 values is equal to that between 1898 and 1899 values.

　　　　1898–1901: Obtained by using 1902 as benchmark and applying the increase of revenue and expenditures of cities over 25,000 as published in the Department of Commerce, Bureau of Labor, *Bulletin,* 1899–1902. Increases for 1897–1898 were assumed equal to those of 1898-1899.

　　　　1902–1940: *Financial Statistics of Cities,* and Bureau of the Census, *Historical Review of State and Local Government Finances,* for annual data; Bureau of the Census, *Wealth, Debt and Taxation* for decennial Census data. Figures for the years 1914, 1920, and 1921 were obtained by linear interpolation. Data for 1902–1903 for cities over 25,000; 1904–1931 for cities over 100,000 population. An estimate for 1932 for cities of 30,000 to 100,000, required in order to make estimates for total local governments possible, was made by using the changes in revenue and expenditures of city governments proper (excludes outlying districts) of the cities over 100,000, 1931–1932, as the basis of an extrapolation.

Columns 2 and 4 – 1902, 1913, 1932: From Bureau of the Census, *Wealth, Debt and Taxation,* various issues.

　　　　1897–1901, 1903–1912, 1914–1931, 1933–1939: Cols 1 and 3, respectively, multiplied by the ratios obtained by linear interpolation between the ratio of revenue or expenditures of all local governments and those of large cities for benchmark years. For the period 1897–1901, the 1902 ratio was used.

　　　　1940: The 1940 benchmark figure estimated by extrapolation, using the data of the general government, 1942 and 1940, of cities over 100,000 (exclusive overlying units) as published in Bureau of the Census, *Historical Review of State and Local Government Finances,* and the enterprise data of cities over 100,000 as published for 1942 in *City Finances,* 1942 and for 1940 in *Financial Statistics of Cities,* 1940. The ratio 1940 to 1942 was applied to the aggregate of total local government data for 1942, consisting of the general government data (revised) of the *Historical Review* and enterprise data published in *Governmental Finances in the United States,* 1942.

　　　　1941–1949: From Table G-3, lines 8 and 12.

REVENUE AND CURRENT EXPENDITURES OF LOCAL GOVERNMENTS G-2
1897 to 1949

$ mill.

Year	Revenue		Expenditures		Year	Revenue		Expenditures	
	Large cities	All local govern-ments	Large cities	All local govern-ments		Large cities	All local govern-ments	Large cities	All local govern-ments
	1	2	3	4		1	2	3	4
1897	367	754	310	658	1924	2 323	4 330	1 812	3 325
1898	371	762	310	658	1925	2 509	4 714	1 938	3 574
1899	375	770	306	649	1926	2 739	5 188	2 089	3 869
1900	397	816	323	685	1927	2 946	5 621	2 232	4 152
1901	435	894	322	683	1928	3 114	5 988	2 359	4 407
1902	443	910	355	753	1929	3 075	5 959	2 468	4 632
1903	470	950	362	755	1930	3 418	6 675	2 695	5 080
1904	472	939	379	778	1931	3 420	6 731	2 808	5 316
1905	502	982	434	876	1932	3 149	6 245	2 776	5 280
1906	531	1 022	411	815	1933	2 507	5 093	2 197	4 341
1907	576	1 090	457	891	1934	2 711	5 638	2 218	4 547
1908	654	1 217	518	992	1935	2 921	6 216	2 265	4 811
1909	671	1 227	511	961	1936	2 893	6 296	2 336	5 135
1910	760	1 365	576	1 064	1937	3 050	6 785	2 513	5 710
1911	806	1 422	612	1 109	1938	3 157	7 175	2 651	6 222
1912	849	1 470	655	1 165	1939	3 190	7 404	2 679	6 486
1913	866	1 472	664	1 158	1940	3 214	7 615	2 698	6 731
1914	903	1 549	708	1 240	1941	.	8 151	.	6 584
1915	940	1 626	751	1 323	1942	.	8 162	.	6 583
1916	995	1 736	781	1 382	1943	.	8 336	.	6 530
1917	1 066	1 876	821	1 459	1944	.	8 581	.	6 785
1918	1 124	1 994	894	1 597	1945	.	9 042	.	6 985
1919	1 224	2 190	977	1 753	1946	.	9 728	.	7 791
1920	1 367	2 466	1 173	2 114	1947	.	10 973	.	9 040
1921	1 510	2 747	1 369	2 478	1948	.	12 312	.	10 107
1922	2 007	3 681	1 605	2 919	1949	.	14 000	.	12 000
1923	2 132	3 942	1 697	3 100					

Line 1 – 1941: Extrapolated by applying ratio of cities over 100,000 for 1941 and 1942 to benchmark figures
 for total local government revenue of 1942. Data obtained from Bureau of the Census, *Historical
 Review of State and Local Government Finances*, 1948.
 1942: Same source as 1941.
 1943–1944: Same procedure and source as 1941; however, computation was based on all cities over
 25,000 and all counties.
 1945–1946: From *Governmental Revenue*, 1946 and 1947.
 1947–1949: Included in over-all estimate, line 8.

Line 2 – 1941: Procedure same as line 1; data obtained from *City Finances*, 1941 and 1942.
 1942: From Bureau of the Census, *Governmental Finances in the United States*, 1942.
 1943–1946: Procedure same as line 1, 1943 and 1944; data obtained from *City Finances* for the
 respective year.
 1947–1949: Included in over-all estimate, line 8.

Line 3 – 1941–1946: Obtained by deducting from total of Table G-19, col. 1 data for states, published in
 State Finances for the respective years.
 1947–1949: Included in over-all estimate, line 8.

Line 4 – 1941–1946: Obtained by deducting from total of Table G-19, col. 3 data for states, published in
 State Finances for the respective years.
 1947–1949: Included in over-all estimate, line 8.

Line 5 – 1941–1946: Obtained by applying annual ratio of sinking fund earnings to sinking fund assets of
 cities over 250,000 (as published in *City Finances* for the respective years) to total local government sinking fund assets.
 1947–1949: Included in over-all estimate, line 8.

Line 6 – 1941–1946: Covers only cities over 25,000 inhabitants; obtained from *City Finances* for the
 respective years. Assumed negligible for other local governments.
 1947–1949: Included in over-all estimates, line 8.

Line 7 – 1941–1946: Same method as in line 2.

Line 8 – 1941–1946: Sum of lines 1–6 minus line 7.
 1947–1949: Extrapolated by applying 1946–1947 ratio for cities over 25,000 to total local
 government estimates of 1946; data obtained from *City Finances*, 1946–1949. Estimate was
 based on total general revenue, enterprise revenue, pension assessments, and enterprise contributions to general fund. Total revenue data were checked against Bureau of the Census general
 revenue data as published in *Governmental Revenue*, various issues.

Lines 9 and 10 – 1941–1946: Same procedure and sources as line 1.
 1947–1949: Included in over-all estimate, line 12.

Line 11 – 1941–1946: Same as line 3.
 1947–1949: Included in over-all estimate, line 12.

Line 12 – 1941–1946: The sum of lines 9–11.
 1947–1949: Same method as in line 8; estimates based on current expenditure (operation and interest) of general government and enterprises.

REVENUE AND CURRENT EXPENDITURES OF LOCAL GOVERNMENTS
1941 to 1949

$ mill.

	1941	1942	1943	1944	1945	1946	1947	1948	1949
Revenue									
1. General government	7 080	7 040	7 050	7 251	7 667	8 295	.	.	.
2. Enterprises	991	1 026	1 190	1 252	1 313	1 375	.	.	.
3. Pension assessment	50	49	52	54	55	60	.	.	.
4. Pension fund earnings	29	30	32	34	35	38	.	.	.
5. Sinking fund earnings	45	47	44	45	40	41	.	.	.
6. Miscellaneous trust fund earnings	8	8	8	9	9	9	.	.	.
7. Less contributions from enterprises	52	38	40	64	77	90	.	.	.
8. Total	8 151	8 162	8 336	8 581	9 042	9 728	10 973	12 312	14 000
Current Expenditures									
9. General government	5 764	5 707	5 593	5 766	5 935	6 620	.	.	.
10. Enterprises	716	770	824	893	916	1 024	.	.	.
11. Pension benefits	104	106	113	126	134	147	.	.	.
12. Total	6 584	6 583	6 530	6 785	6 985	7 791	9 040	10 107	12 000

Column 1 – 1897–1940: Same sources and procedures as Table G-2, cols. 1 and 4.

Column 2 – 1902, 1913, 1932: From Bureau of the Census, *Wealth, Debt and Taxation,* various issues.

        1897–1901, 1903–1912, 1914–1931, 1933–1939: Col. 1 multiplied by the ratio obtained by linear interpolation between the ratio of capital outlays of all local governments and those of large cities (col. 1) for benchmark years. For the period 1897–1901, the 1902 ratio was used. In deriving the 1940 ratio the New York subway purchase outlay of $327 million was omitted. For 1932 ratio was taken for the capital outlay of cities of 30,000 and over.

        1940: Estimated by extrapolation, using the data of general governments (exclusive of overlapping units) as published in *Historical Review* and the enterprise data of cities over 100,000 as published in *City Finances,* 1942 and *Financial Statistics of Cities,* 1940. The ratio for 1940 to 1942 was applied to the aggregate of total local government. 1942 data from *Historical Review* and the enterprise data from Bureau of the Census, *Governmental Finances in the United States,* 1942.

        1941–1949: From Table G-5, col. 3.

Column 1 – 1940–1942: Data for cities over 100,000 (city corporations only) obtained from *Historical Review of State and Local Government Finances,* 1948 for general government, and from *City Finances,* 1940, 1941, and 1942 for enterprises. Expenditures for the New York subway purchase in 1940 were excluded from the estimate and added after the "blow-up."

        1942–1947: Data for cities over 25,000 obtained from Bureau of the Census, *Historical Review of State and Local Government Finances,* and from Bureau of the Census, *Large City Finances,* 1943–1947.

        1947–1949: Data for cities over 250,000 obtained from Bureau of the Census, *Large City Finances,* 1947, 1948, and 1949.

Column 2 – 1940–1947: Figures of col. 1 expressed as indices on 1942 basis.

        1948, 1949: Same method using 1947 cities over 250,000 = 100.

Column 3 – 1940–1948: Col. 2 applied to 1942 benchmark figure, obtained from Bureau of the Census, *Historical Review of State and Local Government Finances* for general government, and *Governmental Finances in the United States,* 1942 for enterprises. (The 1940 figure excludes $327 million for New York subway purchase.) For 1940 an additional correction was made to allow for the extended highway, hospital, health center, and airport programs partly financed by federal grants.

        1949: Rough estimate.

CAPITAL OUTLAY OF LOCAL GOVERNMENTS
1897 to 1949

G-4

$ mill.

Year	Large cities (1)	All local governments (2)	Year	Large cities (1)	All local governments (2)	Year	Large cities (1)	All local governments (2)
1897	96	152	1915	330	514	1933	355	665
1898	103	163	1916	288	453	1934	304	578
1899	109	173	1917	287	457	1935	358	691
1900	119	189	1918	278	447	1936	438	858
1901	132	209	1919	256	416	1937	535	1 064
1902	130	206	1920	353	580	1938	519	1 047
1903	177	279	1921	450	746	1939	640	1 309
1904	183	288	1922	618	1 035	1940	684	1 746
1905	187	293	1923	664	1 123	1941	.	1 068
1906	196	306	1924	963	1 646	1942	.	747
1907	244	380	1925	974	1 681	1943	.	486
1908	275	427	1926	830	1 446	1944	.	344
1909	260	402	1927	1 092	1 921	1945	.	433
1910	279	430	1928	1 037	1 842	1946	.	725
1911	317	487	1929	967	1 734	1947	.	1 262
1912	304	465	1930	1 115	2 018	1948	.	1 981
1913	311	474	1931	936	1 709	1949	.	2 910
1914	320	493	1932	655 [1]	1 207			
			1932	557 [2]				

[1] Cities over 30,000.
[2] Cities over 100,000.

DERIVATION OF CAPITAL OUTLAY OF LOCAL GOVERNMENTS
1940 to 1949

G-5

$ mill. (except col. 2)

Year	Large cities (1)	Index of large cities' outlay (2)	Total local capital outlay (3)	Year	Large cities (1)	Index of large cities' outlay (2)	Total local capital outlay (3)
Cities over 100,000							
1940	487	190	1 419	1945	178	58	433
1941	367	143	1 068	1946	300	97	725
1942	256	100	747	1947	520	169	1 262
Cities over 25,000				Cities over 250,000 (General government and enterprises)			
1942	308	100	747	1947	338	100	1 262
1943	201	65	486	1948	531	157	1 981
1944	143	46	344	1949	732	217	2 910

1051

Column 1 – 1897–1949: Table G-4, col. 2.

Column 2 – 1897–1914: Obtained by applying the annual ratio of highway capital outlays of cities over 30,000 (25,000 up to 1904) to their total capital outlay to col. 1. City data obtained for 1898–1901 from the Department of Commerce, Bureau of Labor, *Bulletin* (1897 assumed to bear same relation to 1898 as 1898 to 1899); 1903–1913 from *Financial Statistics of Cities*; 1914 by linear interpolation.

      1915–1926: Obtained by deducting state highway capital outlay as shown in Table G-16, col. 2 from highway construction cost estimates of Department of Commerce, *Construction and Construction Materials, Statistical Supplement*, May 1948, p. 19.

      1927–1946: Obtained by computing the average percentage of local highway construction cost estimates of Department of Commerce to total capital outlay as reported by the Bureau of the Census for whole periods (1927–1933; 1934–1939; 1940–1946) and applying the average to the annual figures of col. 1. This procedure was necessary to take account of the lag between actual construction outlays and payments as shown in local accounts and, therefore, in Bureau of the Census statistics.

      1947: Obtained by extrapolation, using the big-city ratios of highway to total capital outlay as shown in *City Finances*, 1946 and 1947, and applying it to 1946 highway and total capital outlay.

      1948, 1949: Same method as in 1947, by using data published in Bureau of the Census, *Large City Finances*, 1947, 1948, and 1949.

Column 3 – 1897–1949: Col. 1 minus col. 2.

Column 4 – 1897–1949: Roughly estimated on the basis of individual budget reports as 7 percent of col. 3.

Column 5 – 1897–1949: Roughly estimated on the basis of individual budget reports as 10 percent of col. 3.

Column 6 – 1897–1949: Col. 3 minus cols. 4 and 5.

Column 7 – 1897–1949: Depreciation calculated from col. 2, assuming an average life of twenty-five years. Highway capital outlay prior to 1897 was assumed at 25 percent of total public construction expenditures.

Column 8 – 1897–1949: Depreciation calculated from col. 6 assuming an average life of fifty years. Non-highway capital outlay 1847–1896 was assumed at 75 percent of total public construction expenditures.

Column 9 – 1897–1949: Depreciation calculated from col. 5 assuming an average life of twelve years. Expenditures for equipment prior to 1897 obtained by same method as col. 5.

COMPONENTS OF CAPITAL OUTLAY OF LOCAL GOVERNMENTS
1897 to 1949

$ mill.

Year	Capital expenditures						Depreciation, original cost		
	Total	Street and highway	Other				Street and highway	Other structures	Equipment
			Total	Land	Equipment	Structures			
	1	2	3	4	5	6	7	8	9
1897	152	35	117	8	12	97	14	24	8
1898	163	40	123	9	12	102	15	26	8
1899	173	40	133	9	13	111	17	28	9
1900	189	43	146	10	15	121	18	30	10
1901	209	44	165	12	16	137	20	33	10
1902	206	64	142	10	14	118	22	35	11
1903	279	87	192	13	19	160	24	38	12
1904	288	104	184	13	18	153	28	41	13
1905	293	100	193	14	19	160	32	44	14
1906	306	98	208	15	21	172	35	47	15
1907	380	129	251	18	25	208	40	51	16
1908	427	128	299	21	30	248	44	55	17
1909	402	133	269	19	27	223	49	60	18
1910	430	142	288	20	29	239	54	65	20
1911	487	165	322	23	32	267	60	70	21
1912	465	158	307	21	31	255	66	75	23
1913	474	156	318	22	32	264	71	80	24
1914	493	173	320	22	32	266	77	85	25
1915	514	244	270	19	27	224	85	90	27
1916	453	275	178	12	18	148	94	93	27
1917	457	293	164	11	16	137	105	96	27
1918	447	266	181	13	18	150	115	99	27
1919	416	378	38	3	4	31	127	100	26
1920	580	534	46	3	5	38	144	101	24
1921	746	652	94	7	9	78	167	102	22
1922	1 035	586	449	31	45	373	190	106	22
1923	1 123	473	650	46	65	539	210	115	24
1924	1 646	588	1 058	74	106	878	230	129	28
1925	1 681	622	1 059	74	106	879	252	146	34
1926	1 446	640	806	56	81	669	276	161	40
1927	1 921	692	1 229	86	123	1 020	300	178	46
1928	1 842	663	1 179	83	118	978	324	197	54
1929	1 734	624	1 110	78	111	921	346	216	62
1930	2 018	726	1 292	90	129	1 073	369	235	71
1931	1 709	615	1 094	77	109	908	392	255	80
1932	1 207	435	772	54	77	641	408	270	87
1933	665	239	426	30	43	353	417	279	91
1934	578	127	451	32	45	374	419	286	93
1935	691	152	539	38	54	447	419	293	92
1936	858	189	669	47	67	555	420	302	90
1937	1 064	234	830	58	83	689	422	314	88
1938	1 047	230	817	57	82	678	425	327	87
1939	1 309	288	1 021	71	102	848	428	341	86
1940	1 746	402	1 344	94	134	1 116	434	360	86
1941	1 068	246	822	58	82	682	436	376	85
1942	747	172	575	40	58	477	433	387	81
1943	486	112	374	26	37	311	428	393	75
1944	344	79	265	19	26	220	419	397	70
1945	433	100	333	23	33	277	404	400	67
1946	725	167	558	39	56	463	386	406	67
1947	1 262	317	945	66	94	785	371	416	69
1948	1 981	426	1 555	109	156	1 290	364	435	75
1949	2 910	648	2 262	123	178	1 961	365	465	83

Column 1 – 1896–1936: Sum of cols. 2–4.
            1937–1949: From Table G-8, col. 1.

Column 2 – 1896–1949: From Table G-10, col. 5.

Column 3 – 1896–1949: From Table G-11, col. 4.

Column 4 – 1896–1936: From Table G-9, col. 3.
            1937–1949: Col. 1 minus the sum of cols. 2 and 3.

Column 5 – 1896–1949: Sum of cols. 6–8.

Column 6 – 1896–1899: Rough estimates.
            1900–1949: Cumulated from Table G-6, col. 4; 1900 assumed at $300 million.

Column 7 – 1896–1949: The sum of the cumulated net street and highway expenditures, equipment expend-
            itures, and other local capital outlay. Cumulated net expenditures (expenditures less ac-
            crued depreciation) derived by cumulating net expenditures for the years prior to 1896; the
            year with which cumulation starts depends on estimated length of life of asset involved (see
            Table G-6, cols. 7–9).

Column 8 – 1896–1931: *Financial Statistics of Cities*, various issues, except for 1914, 1920, and 1921, which
            were obtained by linear interpolation. For content of this series and reason for not depre-
            ciating it see Table G-17, col. 8. The large increase between 1911 and 1912 was due to the fact
            that New York City bought $89 million of such assets with investment fund money, and
            Boston and Chicago bought their transit systems for $22 and $8 million, respectively. Figures,
            which covered all cities over 30,000, have not been raised as investments in real property
            by cities under 30,000 may be assumed negligible.
            1932–1940: Only cities over 100,000 included.
            1941–1949: Increases were assumed at $50 million a year.

Column 9 – 1896–1949: Col. 1 plus col. 5.

Column 10 – 1896–1949: From Table G-21, col. 2.

Column 11 – 1896–1949: Col. 9 minus col. 10.

Column 12 – 1896–1949: Col. 11 minus col. 3.

NET WORTH OF LOCAL GOVERNMENTS
1896 to 1949
$ mill.

End of year	Liquid assets				Fixed assets				Total assets	Total liabil-ities	Net worth	
	Total	Sinking funds	Trust funds	Invest-ment funds and cash	Total	Land	Capital outlay depreciated, original cost basis	Invest-ment in real property			Total	Ex-cluding trust funds
	1	2	3	4	5	6	7	8	9	10	11	12
1896	442	219	43	180	1 418	220	1 158	40	1 860	1 450	410	367
1897	442	219	43	180	1 536	240	1 256	40	1 978	1 520	458	415
1898	442	219	43	180	1 661	260	1 361	40	2 103	1 593	510	467
1899	442	231	43	168	1 791	280	1 471	40	2 233	1 670	563	520
1900	461	262	43	156	1 932	300	1 592	40	2 393	1 750	643	600
1901	480	251	43	186	2 081	312	1 726	43	2 561	1 834	727	684
1902	618	295	47	276	2 220	322	1 854	44	2 838	1 924	914	867
1903	637	306	49	282	2 425	335	2 046	44	3 062	2 050	1 012	963
1904	742	321	55	366	2 634	348	2 239	47	3 376	2 176	1 200	1 145
1905	764	340	58	366	2 837	362	2 428	47	3 601	2 302	1 299	1 241
1906	794	370	58	366	3 046	377	2 622	47	3 840	2 465	1 375	1 317
1907	819	389	64	366	3 365	395	2 877	93	4 184	2 685	1 499	1 435
1908	856	419	65	372	3 676	416	3 167	93	4 532	2 999	1 533	1 468
1909	942	459	69	414	3 953	435	3 423	95	4 895	3 179	1 716	1 647
1910	1 067	500	75	492	4 241	455	3 694	92	5 308	3 468	1 840	1 765
1911	1 192	549	79	564	4 577	478	4 007	92	5 769	3 769	2 000	1 921
1912	1 256	592	82	582	5 026	499	4 287	240	6 282	4 030	2 252	2 170
1913	1 281	599	82	600	5 325	521	4 564	240	6 606	4 075	2 531	2 449
1914	1 361	653	90	618	5 664	543	4 848	273	7 025	4 492	2 533	2 443
1915	1 438	708	88	642	5 994	562	5 141	291	7 432	4 923	2 509	2 421
1916	1 528	764	92	672	6 285	574	5 368	343	7 813	5 291	2 522	2 430
1917	1 630	830	98	702	6 562	585	5 586	391	8 192	5 654	2 538	2 440
1918	1 764	912	102	750	6 773	598	5 779	396	8 537	6 051	2 486	2 384
1919	1 889	987	110	792	6 982	601	5 939	442	8 871	6 344	2 527	2 417
1920	2 278	1 072	132	1 074	7 317	604	6 247	466	9 595	7 229	2 366	2 234
1921	2 661	1 158	153	1 350	7 796	611	6 695	490	10 457	8 146	2 311	2 158
1922	3 140	1 339	175	1 626	8 537	642	7 381	514	11 677	9 093	2 584	2 409
1923	3 254	1 445	201	1 608	9 333	688	8 109	536	12 587	9 779	2 808	2 607
1924	3 598	1 565	239	1 794	10 623	762	9 294	567	14 221	10 466	3 755	3 516
1925	3 892	1 680	268	1 944	11 891	836	10 469	586	15 783	11 152	4 631	4 363
1926	4 319	1 831	304	2 184	12 918	892	11 382	644	17 237	11 838	5 399	5 095
1927	4 404	1 980	342	2 082	14 369	978	12 693	698	18 773	12 774	5 999	5 657
1928	4 857	2 103	382	2 372	15 823	1 061	13 877	885	20 680	13 589	7 091	6 709
1929	5 307	2 220	420	2 667	16 989	1 139	14 909	941	22 296	14 501	7 795	7 375
1930	5 484	2 408	459	2 617	18 554	1 229	16 162	1 163	24 038	15 579	8 459	8 000
1931	4 647	1 611	515	2 521	19 622	1 306	17 067	1 249	24 269	16 582	7 687	7 172
1932	4 072	1 465	558	2 049	19 390	1 360	17 455	575	23 462	16 680	6 782	6 224
1933	4 340	1 475	597	2 268	19 288	1 390	17 303	595	23 628	16 391	7 237	6 640
1934	5 116	1 500	639	2 977	19 081	1 422	17 051	608	24 197	15 976	8 221	7 582
1935	5 613	1 472	684	3 457	18 965	1 460	16 900	605	24 578	16 165	8 413	7 729
1936	5 798	1 504	733	3 561	19 327	1 507	16 899	921	25 125	16 350	8 775	8 042
1937	5 618	1 503	779	3 336	19 630	1 565	17 081	984	25 248	16 130	9 118	8 339
1938	5 882	1 489	830	3 563	19 952	1 622	17 232	1 098	25 834	16 053	9 781	8 951
1939	5 737	1 478	860	3 399	20 373	1 693	17 615	1 065	26 110	16 385	9 725	8 865
1940	5 864	1 486	955	3 423	21 289	1 787	18 387	1 115	27 153	16 766	10 387	9 432
1941	5 899	1 497	1 000	3 402	21 510	1 845	18 500	1 165	27 409	16 646	10 763	9 763
1942	5 712	1 514	1 070	3 128	21 406	1 885	18 306	1 215	27 118	16 131	10 987	9 917
1943	6 109	1 537	1 160	3 412	21 046	1 911	17 870	1 265	27 155	15 243	11 912	10 752
1944	6 906	1 559	1 290	4 057	20 554	1 930	17 309	1 315	27 460	14 433	13 027	11 737
1945	7 727	1 582	1 400	4 745	20 166	1 953	16 848	1 365	27 893	13 864	14 029	12 629
1946	8 369	1 590	1 500	5 279	20 082	1 992	16 675	1 415	28 451	13 706	14 745	13 245
1947	9 021	1 647	1 590	5 784	20 538	2 058	17 015	1 465	29 559	14 414	15 145	13 555
1948	9 844	1 763	1 730	6 351	21 695	2 167	18 013	1 515	31 539	15 916	15 623	13 893
1949	10 251	1 885	1 903	6 463	23 707	2 290	19 852	1 565	33 958	17 588	16 370	14 467

Column 1 – 1896–1936: From Table G-7, col. 1.
            1937–1949: Sum of cols. 2–6.

Column 2 – 1896–1898: Assumed equal to 1899.
            1899–1901: Obtained by applying ratio of cash to total liquid assets for big cities, as given in Department of Commerce, Bureau of Labor, *Bulletin*, 1899–1901, to col. 1.
            1902–1927: Same method as for 1899–1901; data obtained from *Financial Statistics of Cities* except 1914, 1920, and 1921, which were obtained by linear interpolation.
            1928–1933: Same procedure as 1934–1949 except that the Dec. 31 figures for demand and time deposits of state and local governments in member banks (*Banking and Monetary Statistics*, p. 78) were linked to the Dec. 31, 1934, figures for demand and time deposits of state and local governments in insured commercial banks.
            1934–1949: Total state and local deposits in insured commercial banks (*Banking and Monetary Statistics*, and *Federal Reserve Bulletin*, various issues) as of Dec. 31 raised 5.5 percent, minus state deposits (Table G-17, col. 2, converted to year-end basis by simple arithmetic averaging). Total deposit figures were raised 5.5 percent on assumption that vault cash equalled 2 percent, deposits of state and local governments in uninsured banks, 2.5 percent, and working funds of enterprises, 1 percent.

Column 3 – 1896–1936: Obtained by applying ratio of own securities to total liquid assets for big cities to col. 1; data from *Financial Statistics of Cities*. For the years 1896–1901, col. 3 includes col. 4.
            1937–1940: Obtained by linear interpolation between the 1936 and 1941 values.
            1941–1949: Data on state and local governmental securities held in sinking funds and trust and investment funds (*Annual Report of the Secretary of the Treasury*, 1948, pp. 629–630), minus state figures as given in Table G-17, cols. 3 and 4, converted to year-end basis by simple arithmetic averaging and raised 5 percent because of apparent underestimation of Treasury figures.

Column 4 – 1896–1901: Included in col. 3.
            1902–1936: Col. 1 minus sum of cols. 2, 3, 5, and 6.
            1937–1940: Derived from big-city data (*Financial Statistics of Cities*).
            1941–1949: Included in col. 3.

Column 5 – 1896–1917: Assumed to be negligible.
            1918–1936: Rough estimates, assuming most of changes in sum of cols. 4 and 5 from 1918–1922 to be attributable to U.S. Government securities, and U.S. Government securities after 1922 to decline from about 60 percent of total of cols. 3 and 4 (cf. Hardy, C. O., *Tax-Exempt Securities and Surtax*, p. 51) to about 30 percent in 1936.
            1937–1949: Same source and procedure as col. 3, 1941–1949, except that data on U.S. Government securities held in sinking funds and investment funds of state and local governments were used, averaged to obtain year-end figures, minus Table G-17, col. 5.

Column 6 – 1896–1931: Estimated on the basis of big-city data at 4.5 percent of total liquid assets.
            1932–1940: Obtained by applying ratio of other liquid assets to total liquid assets for big cities to col. 1.
            1941–1949: Rough estimates.

LIQUID ASSETS OF LOCAL GOVERNMENTS
1896 to 1949

$ mill.

End of year	Total	Cash	Own securities	Other state and local government securities	U.S. Government securities	Other liquid assets
	1	2	3	4	5	6
1896	442	88	334	–	–	20
1897	442	88	334	–	–	20
1898	442	88	334	–	–	20
1899	442	88	334	–	–	20
1900	461	82	358	–	–	21
1901	480	101	357	–	–	22
1902	618	191	371	28	–	28
1903	637	185	349	74	–	29
1904	742	251	406	52	–	33
1905	764	251	414	65	–	34
1906	794	245	457	57	–	35
1907	819	235	487	60	–	37
1908	856	246	508	64	–	38
1909	942	279	558	63	–	42
1910	1 067	326	632	62	–	47
1911	1 192	375	691	73	–	53
1912	1 256	383	741	76	–	56
1913	1 281	397	814	12	–	58
1914	1 361	392	873	35	–	61
1915	1 438	383	921	70	–	64
1916	1 528	407	966	87	–	68
1917	1 630	451	1 016	90	–	73
1918	1 764	437	979	69	200	79
1919	1 889	450	1 220	65	70	84
1920	2 278	633	1 368	75	100	102
1921	2 661	820	1 520	81	120	120
1922	3 140	1 005	1 667	127	200	141

End of year	Total	Cash	Own securities	Other state and local government securities	U.S. Government securities	Other liquid assets
	1	2	3	4	5	6
1923	3 254	973	1 816	134	185	146
1924	3 598	1 144	2 002	131	160	161
1925	3 892	1 272	2 198	113	135	174
1926	4 319	1 408	2 390	162	165	194
1927	4 404	1 300	2 600	156	150	198
1928	4 857	1 525	2 742	196	175	219
1929	5 307	1 744	2 936	213	175	239
1930	5 484	1 678	3 168	221	170	247
1931	4 647	1 512	2 358	333	235	209
1932	4 072	1 240	2 311	213	140	168
1933	4 340	1 422	2 334	269	150	165
1934	5 116	2 014	2 426	325	170	181
1935	5 613	2 482	2 468	314	150	199
1936	5 798	2 636	2 481	335	145	201
1937	5 618	2 589	2 284	427	134	184
1938	5 882	2 847	2 244	405	196	190
1939	5 737	2 711	2 252	336	250	188
1940	5 864	2 865	2 274	255	306	164
1941	5 899	2 818	2 465		416	200
1942	5 712	2 627	2 478		407	200
1943	6 109	2 700	2 350		859	200
1944	6 906	2 818	2 067		1 821	200
1945	7 727	3 292	1 823		2 312	300
1946	8 369	3 884	1 709		2 376	400
1947	9 021	4 471	1 713		2 337	500
1948	9 844	5 068	1 782		2 394	600
1949	10 251	5 137	1 920		2 444	750

INVESTMENT FUND AND TREASURY CASH OF LOCAL GOVERNMENTS
1896 to 1949

End of year	Large cities $ mill.	Index of large cities 1913 = 100	All local governments $ mill.	End of year	Large cities $ mill.	Index of large cities 1913 = 100	All local governments $ mill.
	1	2	3		1	2	3
1896	71	30	180	1923	632	268	1 608
1897	71	30	180	1924	705	299	1 794
1898	71	30	180	1925	765	324	1 944
1899	67	28	168	1926	860	364	2 184
1900	62	26	156	1927	819	347	2 082
1901	74	31	186	1928	854	362	2 372
1902	109	46	276	1929	866	367	2 667
1903	110	47	282	1930	932	395	2 617
1904	145	61	366	1931	879	372	2 521
1905	145	61	366	1932	639	271	2 049
1906	145	61	366	1933	627	266	2 268
1907	145	61	366	1934	745	316	2 977
1908	147	62	372	1935	869	368	3 457
1909	162	69	414	1936	874	370	3 561
1910	193	82	492	1937	.	.	3 336
1911	222	94	564	1938	.	.	3 563
1912	230	97	582	1939	.	.	3 399
1913	236	100	600	1940	.	.	3 423
1914	243	103	618	1941	.	.	3 402
1915	252	107	642	1942	.	.	3 128
1916	264	112	672	1943	.	.	3 412
1917	275	117	702	1944	.	.	4 057
1918	294	125	750	1945	.	.	4 745
1919	312	132	792	1946	.	.	5 279
1920	422	179	1 074	1947	.	.	5 784
1921	532	225	1 350	1948	.	.	6 351
1922	640	271	1 626	1949	.	.	6 463

Column 1 – 1896–1897: Estimated as equal to 1898.

1898–1901: From Department of Commerce, Bureau of Labor, *Bulletin*.

1902–1931: *Financial Statistics of Cities*, various issues. Figures do not cover real property of investment funds.

1932–1936: Since the Bureau of the Census after 1931 no longer included data on cities under 100,000, estimates were needed for cities between 30,000 and 100,000 to maintain comparability of the data after 1931 with those of previous years. This was achieved by multiplying the figures for cities over 100,000, as given in *Financial Statistics of Cities*, 1932–1939 by 1.21, the ratio existing in 1931 between cities over 30,000 and over 100,000 inhabitants.

Column 2 – 1896–1936: Col. 1 divided by its 1913 value.

Column 3 – 1896–1927: Col. 2 times 600, the estimated value for the only benchmark year available, 1913. For this year data were available in Bureau of the Census, *Wealth, Debt and Taxation* for cities over 2,500 and counties. These were increased by 10 percent for smaller governmental units omitted.

1928–1936: Demand and time deposits of state and local governments reported since 1928 by Federal Reserve Board and Federal Deposit Insurance Corporation showed up to 1943 amounts much higher than corresponding data for state and local government cash deposit assets, estimated on basis of state and big-city cash data. Therefore, data of the Federal Reserve Board were substituted for cash portion of original estimates for period 1928–1943 (Table G-8, col. 2), when estimates based on the Bureau of the Census and deposits reported by the Federal Reserve Board started to agree. As the state figures represented actual financial data from original statements, it was assumed that the apparent underestimate in the combined state and local government figures was entirely attributable to local governments. Difference between data in deposits of the Federal Reserve Board reports and original estimates for state plus local cash was, therefore, added to original estimate of local cash and investment funds, derived in the same way as for 1897–1927.

1937–1949: From Table G-7, col. 4.

1896 to 1950

$ mill.

End of year	Large cities	New York City	Other large cities	Bench-mark totals	Total including New York City	End of year	Large cities	New York City	Other large cities	Bench-mark totals	Total including New York City
	1	2	3	4	5		1	2	3	4	5
1896	209				219	1924	1 264	751	513		1 565
1897	209				219	1925	1 355	812	543		1 680
1898	209				219	1926	1 469	878	591		1 831
1899	220				231	1927	1 582	948	634		1 980
1900	250				262	1928	1 683	1 026	657		2 103
1901	239				251	1929	1 777	1 100	677		2 220
1902	281			295	295	1930	1 933	1 221	712		2 408
1903	290				306	1931	1 137	441	696		1 611
1904	303				321	1932	1 051	455	596	1 465	1 465
1905	320				340	1933	1 064				1 475
1906	347				370	1934	1 089				1 500
1907	364				389	1935	1 075				1 472
1908	390				419	1936	1 106				1 504
1909	425				459	1937	1 112				1 503
1910	462				500	1938	1 108				1 489
1911	504				549	1939	1 107				1 478
1912	543				592	1940	1 120			1 486	1 486
1913	547			599	599	1941				1 497	1 497
1914	588				653	1942				1 514	1 514
1915	630				708	1943				1 537	1 537
1916	671				764	1944				1 559	1 559
1917	719				830	1945				1 582	1 582
1918	780				912	1946				1 590	1 590
1919	834				987	1947				1 647	1 647
1920	895				1 072	1948				1 763	1 763
1921	955				1 158	1949				1 885	1 885
1922	1 091	647	444	1 339	1 339	1950				2 031	2 031
1923	1 173	698	475		1 445						

Columns 1 and 2 – 1896–1897: Assumed equal to 1898.

1898–1901: From Department of Commerce, Bureau of Labor, *Bulletin*.

1902–1940: *Financial Statistics of Cities*, except 1914, 1920, and 1921, which were obtained by linear interpolation. Estimate of sinking fund assets for 1940 includes sinking fund assets of public service enterprises.

Column 3 – 1922–1932: Col. 1 minus col. 2.

Column 4 – 1902, 1913, 1922, 1932: Bureau of the Census, *Wealth, Debt and Taxation* for the respective years. 1940–1950: Bureau of the Census, *Governmental Debt in the United States*, 1950, p. 7. 1943 and 1944 interpolated between 1942 and 1945 by linear interpolation.

Column 5 – 1896–1922: Col. 1 multiplied by the ratio between sinking fund assets of all local governments (col. 4) and that of large cities (col. 1). For years between benchmark dates the ratios were obtained by linear interpolation, and for 1897–1901 the 1902 ratio was used.

1923–1932: Calculated by the same method as 1896–1922 except that the sinking fund assets ot New York City (col. 2) were excluded from the benchmark data before obtaining the ratios and readded to the derived estimates.

1933–1940: Calculated by the same method as 1896–1922.

1941–1950: Same as col. 4.

TRUST FUNDS OF LOCAL GOVERNMENTS
1896 to 1949

$ mill.

End of year	Large cities			All local governments	End of year	Large cities			All local governments
	All over 100,000	37 Largest cities	Index 1941 = 100			All over 100,000	37 Largest cities	Index 1941 = 100	
	1	2	3	4		1	2	3	4
1896	40		4	43	1923	189		20	201
1897	40		4	43	1924	224		24	239
1898	40		4	43	1925	251		27	268
1899	40		4	43	1926	285		30	304
1900	40		4	43	1927	321		34	342
1901	40		4	43	1928	358		38	382
1902	44		5	47	1929	394		42	420
1903	46		5	49	1930	431		46	459
1904	52		6	55	1931	483		51	515
1905	54		6	58	1932	523		56	558
1906	54		6	58	1933	560		60	597
1907	60		6	64	1934	599		64	639
1908	61		7	65	1935	642		68	684
1909	65		7	69	1936	688		73	733
1910	70		7	75	1937	731		78	779
1911	74		8	79	1938	779		83	830
1912	77		8	82	1939	807		86	860
1913	77		8	82	1940	896		96	955
1914	84		9	90	1941	938	821	100	1 000
1915	83		9	88	1942	.	882	107	1 070
1916	86		9	92	1943	.	953	116	1 160
1917	92		10	98	1944	.	1 058	129	1 290
1918	96		10	102	1945	.	1 150	140	1 400
1919	103		11	110	1946	.	1 230	150	1 500
1920	.		.	132	1947	.	1 309	159	1 590
1921	.		.	153	1948	.	1 421	173	1 730
1922	164		17	175	1949	.			1 903

Column 1 – 1896–1899: Assumed unchanged at level of 1900.

   1900–1901: From Department of Commerce, Bureau of Labor, *Bulletin*.

   1902–1941: From *Financial Statistics of Cities*, various issues; and Bureau of the Census, *City Finances*. 1941 adjusted to include amount in trust funds of overlying areas (cf. *Retirement Systems for State and Local Government Employees: 1941*, State and Local Government Special Study 17, p. 92).

Column 2 – 1941–1945: *City Finances*, various issues.

   1946–1948: *Large City Finances*, various issues.

Column 3 – 1896–1941: Based on col. 1.

   1942–1948: Based on col. 2.

Column 4 – 1896–1941: Col. 4 multiplied by 1.066 according to the 1941 ratio of big-city data to total local trust funds (cf. *Retirement Systems for State and Local Government Employees: 1941*, State and Local Government Special Study 17, and *City Finances*, 1941) except for 1920 and 1921, which were obtained by linear interpolation.

   1942–1948: Col. 3 applied to 1941 figure.

   1949: Rough estimate.

COMPARISON OF NET SAVING OF STATE AND LOCAL GOVERNMENTS G-12
Income Account and Balance Sheet, Methods
Original Cost: 1897 to 1949

$ mill.

Year	Local governments			State governments			Year	Local governments			State governments		
	Income account	Balance sheet	Difference	Income account	Balance sheet	Difference		Income account	Balance sheet	Difference	Income account	Balance sheet	Difference
	1	2	3	4	5	6		1	2	3	4	5	6
1897	50	48	2	2	−5	7	1924	618	947	−329	268	365	−97
1898	55	52	3	2	−6	8	1925	708	876	−168	364	434	−70
1899	67	53	14	2	−2	4	1926	842	768	74	434	416	18
1900	73	80	−7	9	26	−17	1927	945	600	345	466	470	−4
1901	148	84	64	10	15	−5	1928	1 006	1 092	−86	499	498	1
1902	89	187	−98	11	1	10	1929	703	704	−1	531	532	−1
1903	121	98	23	14	17	−3	1930	920	664	256	552	576	−24
1904	79	188	−109	7	10	−3	1931	688	−772	1 460	394	452	−58
1905	16	99	−83	12	16	−4	1932	200	−905	1 105	63	297	−234
1906	110	76	34	17	24	−7	1933	−35	455	−490	−29	260	−289
1907	92	124	−32	16	24	−8	1934	293	984	−691	161	269	−108
1908	109	34	75	22	30	−8	1935	601	192	409	416	460	−44
1909	139	183	−44	28	26	2	1936A	349	362	−13	607	574	33
1910	162	124	38	32	26	6	1936B	349	362	−13	774	742	32
1911	162	160	2	30	30	0	1937	251	343	−92	985	927	58
1912	141	252	−111	28	35	−7	1938	114	663	−549	815	844	−29
1913	139	279	−140	34	11	23	1939	63	−56	119	768	688	80
1914	122	2	120	44	−2	46	1940	4	662	−658	1 048	1 058	−10
1915	101	−24	125	40	50	−10	1941	670	376	294	1 435	1 469	−34
1916	140	13	127	44	72	−28	1942	678	224	454	1 840	1 775	65
1917	189	16	173	66	78	−12	1943	910	925	−15	2 168	2 268	−100
1918	156	−52	208	82	114	−32	1944	910	1 115	−205	2 338	2 470	−132
1919	184	41	143	100	114	−14	1945	1 186	1 002	184	1 881	1 908	−27
1920	83	−161	244	126	120	6	1946	1 078	716	362	1 442	1 398	44
1921	−22	−55	33	152	163	−11	1947	1 077	400	677	1 654	1 482	172
1922	444	273	171	202	212	−10	1948	1 331	478	853	1 536	1 416	120
1923	493	224	269	241	250	−9	1949	1 087	747	340	1 436	1 358	78

Column 1 – 1897–1949: From Table G-1, col. 6.

Column 2 – 1897–1949: Annual change in Table G-7, col. 11. Decline in 1932 overstated due to break in Table G–7, col. 8.

Column 3 – 1897–1949: Col. 1 minus col. 2.

Column 4 – 1897–1949: From Table G-13, col. 9.

Column 5 – 1897–1935: Table G-16, col. 9; first differences converted from fiscal- to calendar-year basis by arithmetic averaging.
1936–1949: Same procedure as for 1897–1935 plus first differences of G-16, col. 11; this sum converted to calendar-year basis by arithmetic averaging.

Column 6 – 1897–1949: Col. 4 minus col. 5

Column 1 – 1897–1901: Extrapolated on the basis of 1902 values in Department of Commerce and Labor, Census Office, *Wealth, Debt and Taxation*, (1907) with the help of data for large cities published in Department of Commerce, Bureau of Labor, *Bulletin*, 1898–1901. Change from 1897 to 1898 assumed equal to that from 1898 to 1899.

        1902: *Wealth, Debt and Taxation*, (1907).

        1903–1912: Interpolated between Census data for 1902 and 1913 (*Wealth, Debt and Taxation*, 1913) with the help of annual city data from *Financial Statistics of Cities*, 1902–1912.

        1913: From Bureau of the Census, *Wealth, Debt and Taxation*, 1913.

        1914: Obtained by linear interpolation between 1913 and 1915 values.

        1915–1919: *Financial Statistics of States*, various issues.

        1920–1921: Interpolated on basis of 1919 and 1922 Census data with the help of figures for state revenue from Ellis, P. W., *The World's Biggest Business*, p. 62.

        1922–1932: *Financial Statistics of States*, various issues. The unpublished 1932 figure was obtained from the Bureau of the Census.

        1933–1936: Obtained by adding to state tax collection data (Bureau of the Census, *Historical Review of State and Local Finances*, 1933–1936, p. 20) estimates for other revenues, derived by a linear interpolation of these revenues between their 1932 and 1937 values (*Financial Statistics of States*, 1932 and 1937).

        1937–1939: *Financial Statistics of States*, various issues. Amounts for general fund and for enterprises which the Bureau of the Census reported separately from 1937 on were added from same source.

        1940–1950: *State Finances*, 1940 and 1950, and *Historical Review of State and Local Finances*, total of figures for general fund, state enterprises, trust fund finances, and sinking fund earnings (for details see Table G-14).

Column 2 – 1897–1932: Same source as for col. 1.

        1933–1936: Ellis' data for total expenditures were converted into current expenditures by the following steps:

        (1) Capital expenditures as given in Table G-15 were deducted.

        (2) An adjustment for the revenue of alcoholic beverage monopolies was made by interpolating between 0 in 1932 and the actual figure for 1937.

        (3) Ellis' figure for state aid to local governments was incomplete as it did not include federal aid to states passed on to local governments. Hence Ellis' figure for state aid was deducted from his figure for total state expenditures and in its place a Bureau of the Census figure was added. As the Census figure for state aid to local governments was available only for 1937 (Bureau of the Census, *Historical Review of State and Local Government Finances*, p. 20) 1933–1936 data for state aid had to be obtained from an extrapolation of the Bureau of the Census data on the basis of Ellis' figure for total state revenues.

        (4) An adjustment was made for Ellis' underestimation for shared taxes as evidenced by Bureau of the Census, *ibid.*, 1933–1936, pp. 19 and 20.

        1937–1950: Same procedure as for col. 1.

Column 3 – 1897–1950: Col. 1 minus col. 2.

Column 4 – 1897–1950: Table G-15, cols. 5 and 6.

Column 5 – 1897–1950: Sum of the depreciation allowances, replacement cost, on highways and other capital outlays derived from the expenditures series given in Table G-15, cols. 2 and 3 according to the method described in the notes to Table G-1, col. 5.

Column 6 – 1897–1950: Col. 3 minus col. 4.

Column 7 – 1897–1950: Col. 3 minus col. 5.

Column 8 – 1937–1950: Bureau of the Census, *Historical Review of State and Local Government Finances*, p. 19; *State Finances*, various issues.

Columns 9 to 12 – 1897–1949: Cols. 6 and 7 and the residuals of cols. 6 and 7 minus col. 8 respectively converted to a calendar year basis by arithmetic averaging.

GROSS AND NET SAVING OF STATE GOVERNMENTS
Income Account: 1897 to 1950
$ mill.

Fiscal year	Total revenue	Current expenditure	Gross saving	Depreciation Original cost depreciation	Depreciation Replacement cost depreciation	Net saving Original cost depreciation	Net saving Replacement cost depreciation	Unemployment compensation funds	Net saving, calendar year Original cost depreciation Including	Original cost depreciation Excluding	Replacement cost depreciation Including	Replacement cost depreciation Excluding
	1	2	3	4	5	6	7	8	9	10	11	12
1897	151	149	2	0	0	2	2	–	2	2	2	2
1898	153	151	2	0	0	2	2	–	2	2	2	2
1899	154	152	2	0	0	2	2	–	2	2	2	2
1900	164	162	2	0	0	2	2	–	9	9	9	9
1901	177	161	16	0	0	16	16	–	10	10	10	10
1902	182	178	4	0	0	4	4	–	11	11	11	11
1903	201	183	18	0	0	18	18	–	14	14	14	14
1904	201	191	10	0	0	10	10	–	7	7	7	7
1905	213	209	4	0	0	4	4	–	12	12	10	10
1906	226	207	19	0	2	19	17	–	17	17	15	15
1907	245	230	15	0	2	15	13	–	16	16	14	14
1908	278	261	17	0	2	17	15	–	22	22	20	20
1909	285	258	27	1	2	26	25	–	28	28	28	28
1910	323	290	33	2	2	31	31	–	32	32	32	32
1911	343	309	34	2	2	32	32	–	30	30	30	30
1912	361	330	31	3	3	28	28	–	28	28	28	28
1913	368	335	33	4	4	29	29	–	34	34	34	34
1914	413	368	45	6	6	39	39	–	44	44	44	44
1915	458	400	58	9	9	49	49	–	40	40	40	40
1916	467	425	42	12	12	30	30	–	44	44	44	44
1917	523	450	73	14	16	59	57	–	66	66	62	62
1918	588	499	89	15	21	74	68	–	82	82	74	74
1919	675	569	106	17	26	89	80	–	100	100	87	87
1920	870	740	130	20	36	110	94	–	126	126	110	110
1921	1 020	850	170	27	43	143	127	–	152	152	140	140
1922	1 160	962	198	36	45	162	153	–	202	202	193	193
1923	1 247	957	290	48	57	242	233	–	241	241	230	230
1924	1 370	1 068	302	62	74	240	228	–	268	268	258	258
1925	1 485	1 111	374	79	87	295	287	–	364	364	357	357
1926	1 655	1 126	529	96	102	433	427	–	434	434	430	430
1927	1 758	1 208	550	114	117	436	433	–	466	466	465	465
1928	1 935	1 305	630	134	133	496	497	–	499	499	502	502
1929	2 059	1 402	657	155	149	502	508	–	531	531	540	540
1930	2 243	1 501	742	182	169	560	573	–	552	552	572	572
1931	2 324	1 567	757	212	185	545	572	–	394	394	436	436
1932	2 150	1 662	488	244	188	244	300	–	63	63	120	120
1933	2 289	2 138	151	269	210	–118	–59	–	–29	–29	13	13
1934	2 609	2 261	348	288	263	60	85	–	161	161	182	182
1935	3 017	2 445	572	310	292	262	280	–	416	416	435	435
1936	3 608	2 702	906	335	316	571	590	–	774	607	792	624
1937	4 563	3 223	1 340	362	346	978	994	335	985	592	1 010	617
1938	5 168	3 788	1 380	388	353	992	1 027	452	815	414	856	454
1939	5 222	4 172	1 050	412	365	638	685	351	768	418	818	467
1940	5 695	4 359	1 336	437	386	899	950	350	1 048	608	1 087	646
1941	6 074	4 416	1 658	460	434	1 198	1 224	531	1 435	787	1 412	764
1942	6 829	4 673	2 156	484	555	1 672	1 601	765	1 840	941	1 709	810
1943	7 196	4 686	2 510	503	693	2 007	1 817	1 032	2 168	982	1 970	784
1944	7 580	4 733	2 847	518	724	2 329	2 123	1 340	2 338	1 022	2 150	834
1945	7 918	5 044	2 874	526	696	2 348	2 178	1 294	1 881	1 136	1 697	952
1946	8 562	6 616	1 946	532	730	1 414	1 216	197	1 442	1 233	1 198	990
1947	9 868	7 851	2 017	548	837	1 469	1 180	220	1 654	1 321	1 309	976
1948	11 725	9 307	2 418	579	980	1 839	1 438	446	1 536	1 305	1 108	877
1949	12 427	10 570	1 857	625	1 080	1 232	777	15	1 436	1 328	976	869
1950	13 733	11 416	2 317	678	1 141	1 639	1 176	200	.	.	.	.

Lines 1–4 – 1940–1949: *State Finances,* issues of the respective years.

Line 5 – 1940–1949: *State Finances,* 1940–1942, 1944. Other years assumed equal to 1944 except for 1947–1949, which are rough estimates.

Line 6 – 1940–1949: 1940–1944 same source as line 1 except 1943, obtained by linear interpolation. Data for 1945–1949 estimated on basis of Table G-19, cols. 7 and 8.

Line 7 – 1940–1949: Same source as for line 5.

Lines 8–10 – 1940–1949: Same source as for line 1.

Line 11 – 1940–1949: Same source as for line 5.

Line 12 – 1940–1949: Line 1 minus line 2 plus the sum of lines 3–11.
     1950: Estimated according to tax increases 1949 to 1950, derived from data given in *State Tax Collections in 1950,* p. 3.

Lines 13–17 – 1940–1950: Same source as for line 1.

Lines 18–20 – 1940–1950: Same source as for line 5.

Line 21 – 1940–1950: Same source as for line 6.

Line 22 – 1940–1950: Same source as for line 5.

Line 23 – 1940–1950: Rough estimate on basis of previous year's figures for items for which no information was available.

Line 24 – 1940–1950: Sum of lines 13–23.

REVENUE AND EXPENDITURES OF STATE GOVERNMENTS
1940 to 1950

$ mill.

Item	Fiscal year										
	1940	1941	1942	1943	1944	1945	1946	1947	1948	1949	1950
Revenue											
1. General government	5 145	5 492	6 178	6 358	6 691	6 820	7 293	8 529	10 367	11 000	.
2. Contributions from enterprises	63	69	76	96	73	85	120	134	171	174	.
3. Pension assessments	56	60	65	70	76	89	110	145	182	222	.
4. Alcoholic beverage monopoly	280	327	373	516	526	680	847	849	852	849	.
5. Other enterprises	14	47	42	42	42	42	42	50	50	50	.
6. Workmen compensation assessment and earnings of funds	95	67	104	135	135	135	135	145	145	150	.
7. School trust fund receipts	48	47	49	60	55	55	55	70	70	75	.
8. Sinking fund earnings		14	16	13	16	16	16	16	16	17	.
9. Unemployment compensation fund earnings	– 110	46	58	70	86	110	128	130	143	157	.
10. Pension fund earnings	–	31	8	14	12	42	42	50	53	62	.
11. Miscellaneous fund earnings	10	12	12	14	14	14	14	18	18	19	.
12. Total	5 695	6 074	6 829	7 196	7 580	7 918	8 562	9 868	11 725	12 427	13 733
Expenditures											
13. Operation	1 745	1 790	1 916	1 968	2 102	2 254	2 577	3 317	4 351	4 972	5 370
14. Unemployment compensation	556	417	369	210	65	70	965	880	756	973	1 028
15. Aid to other governments	1 627	1 670	1 791	1 778	1 850	1 881	2 086	2 607	3 167	3 544	3 933
16. Interest	123	117	110	99	87	80	70	63	71	76	88
17. Alcoholic beverage monopoly		252	288	408	422	530	630	710	690	694	694
18. Other enterprises		22	25	23	23	23	23	15	15	15	15
19. School trust fund expenditures	237	11	22	11	11	11	11	20	20	20	20
20. Pension fund		58	65	71	70	52	91	105	105	141	141
21. Workmen compensation	71	71	75	93	93	93	93	120	120	125	125
22. Miscellaneous expenditures	–	8	12	10	10	10	10	14	14	15	15
23. Underestimation of trust fund	–	–	–	15	–	40	60	–	–	–	–
24. Total	4 359	4 416	4 673	4 686	4 733	5 044	6 616	7 851	9 309	10 575	11 429

Column 1 – 1897–1899: No data on capital outlay are available for these years. Review of budgetary statements of the larger states indicated that the annual amounts were probably below $1 million.

  1900–1912: Benchmark data for all states are available from Bureau of the Census, *Wealth, Debt and Taxation,* for the years 1902 and 1913. Data for other years obtained by applying the ratio of big-city capital outlay to total city expenditures, from *Financial Statistics of Cities,* to total state expenditures.

  1913–1932: *Financial Statistics of States.* Figures for 1914, 1920, and 1921 obtained by linear interpolation between adjacent years. For 1932 unpublished Census data used.

  1933–1936: As the relevant figures were not collected by the Bureau of the Census, the Department of Commerce estimates of new construction expenditures of nonfederal governments were used as a basis (cf. *Construction and Construction Materials, Statistical Supplement,* May 1948). To these estimates, 20 percent was added as allowance for the purchase of land, buildings, and equipment, estimated from the average of 1932 and 1937. From the total amounts, local capital outlay, as given in Table G-4, was deducted. As the Department of Commerce data are estimated on a calendar year basis, a two-year moving average of the residual was used as the estimate of state government capital outlay for the fiscal year.

  1937–1940: *Financial Statistics of States,* various issues.

  1941–1950: *State Finances,* various issues. Figures for total outlay given in *State Finances* were increased by an estimate for outlays of public service enterprises.

Column 2 – 1897–1932: Same sources and procedure as col. 1.

  1933–1936: Estimated by applying ratio of highway capital expenditures, obtained by linear interpolation between 1932 and 1937 values, to figures of col. 1.

  1937–1950: Same sources and procedure as col. 1.

Column 3 – 1897–1950: Col. 1 minus col. 2.

Column 4 – 1897–1950: Assumed at 7 percent of col. 3 (see Table G-6, col. 4).

Column 5 – 1897–1950: Depreciation calculated from col. 2 assuming an average life of twenty-five years.

Column 6 – 1897–1950: Depreciation calculated from col. 3 assuming an average life of fifty years.

1897 to 1950

$ mill.

Fiscal year	Repro-ducible capital outlay	High-way capital outlay	Other capital outlay	Pur-chase of land	Depreciation, original cost		Fiscal year	Repro-ducible capital outlay	High-way capital outlay	Other capital outlay	Pur-chase of land	Depreciation, original cost	
					High-way outlay	Other capital exclud-ing land						High-way outlay	Other capital exclud-ing land
	1	2	3	4	5	6		1	2	3	4	5	6
1897	0	0	0	0	0	0	1924	445	335	110	8	50	12
1898	0	0	0	0	0	0	1925	503	389	114	8	65	14
1899	0	0	0	0	0	0	1926	488	355	133	9	79	17
1900	1	0	1	0	0	0	1927	519	404	115	8	95	19
1901	1	0	1	0	0	0	1928	585	452	133	9	112	22
1902	2	1	1	0	0	0	1929	659	533	126	9	131	24
1903	1	0	1	0	0	0	1930	789	635	154	11	155	27
1904	7	4	3	0	0	0	1931	942	757	185	13	182	30
1905	5	2	3	0	0	0	1932	844	628	216	15	210	34
1906	3	2	1	0	0	0	1933	546	415	131	9	231	38
1907	1	0	1	0	0	0	1934	589	459	130	9	248	40
1908	10	5	5	0	0	0	1935	613	490	123	9	267	43
1909	10	5	5	0	1	0	1936	820	672	148	10	289	46
1910	23	12	11	1	1	1	1937	716	601	115	8	314	48
1911	24	12	12	1	1	1	1938	701	567	134	9	337	51
1912	29	15	14	1	2	1	1939	764	559	205	14	358	54
1913	48	24	24	2	3	1	1940	737	556	181	13	379	58
1914	72	36	36	3	4	2	1941	690	566	124	9	399	61
1915	95	54	41	3	6	3	1942	639	527	112	8	420	64
1916	85	33	52	4	8	4	1943	500	416	84	6	438	65
1917	68	20	48	3	9	5	1944	345	282	63	4	451	67
1918	66	22	44	3	9	6	1945	290	223	67	5	458	68
1919	71	37	34	2	11	6	1946	390	266	124	9	462	70
1920	131	106	25	2	13	7	1947	1 000	670	330	23	473	75
1921	202	175	27	2	19	8	1948	1 500	1 018	482	34	496	83
1922	318	244	74	5	27	9	1949	1 900	1 330	570	40	531	94
1923	353	275	78	5	38	10	1950	2 200	1 438	762	53	576	102

Column 1 – 1896–1950: Total of cols. 2–4.

Column 2 – 1896: Rough estimate based on annual differences, 1897–1898.
　1897–1913: Bureau of the Census, *Wealth, Debt and Taxation*, 1913, p. 38.
　1914–1950: *Financial Statistics of States* and *State Finances*, 1914–1947, except for the years
　　1914, 1920, 1921, and 1933–1936, for which the figures were obtained by linear interpolation.

Column 3 – 1896–1940: Same source and procedure as col. 2.
　1941–1950: From Table G-18, line 12.

Column 4 – 1896–1940: Same source and procedure as col. 2.
　1941–1950: From Table G-18, line 6.

Column 5 – 1896–1950: Sum of cols. 6–8.

Column 6 – 1896–1950: Derived by cumulating net expenditures (i.e., expenditures less accrued deprecia-
　tion) for the years up to and including 1897. The year with which cumulation starts depends
　on length of life of the commodity involved (see notes to Table G-15, cols. 5 and 6).

Column 7 – 1896–1911: Roughly estimated at $200 million throughout the period.
　1912–1950: Table G-15, col. 4 cumulated plus an allowance of $200 million for land already in
　the possession of state governments in 1911.

Column 8 – 1896–1914: Assumed unchanged at $500 million since the reported values for the period 1915–
　1922 fluctuated around that figure without trend.
　1915–1940: *Financial Statistics of States*, various issues. The reported figures presumably include
　real property owned by state governments as well as that held in their trust and investment
　funds. They include agricultural properties, forests, unimproved land, and buildings. The
　figures seem to represent a combination of original cost values, depreciated cost values, and
　adjusted values. The series, therefore, would not seem to be an appropriate object of system-
　atic depreciation.
　1941–1950: Increase of $25 million annually assumed.

Column 9 – 1896–1950: Col. 1 plus col. 5 minus Table G-21, col. 1.

Column 10 – 1896–1950: Col. 9 minus col. 3.

Column 11 – 1896–1950: *Historical Review of State and Local Government Finances.*

NET WORTH OF STATE GOVERNMENTS
1896 to 1950
$ mill.

End of fiscal year	Liquid assets				Fixed assets				Excess of assets over liabilities		Unemployment compensation fund assets
	Total	Sinking funds	Trust funds	Investment funds and cash	Total	Capital outlay depreciated	Land	Investment in real property	Total	Excluding trust funds	
	1	2	3	4	5	6	7	8	9	10	11
1896	273	26	168	79	700	0	200	500	747	579	–
1897	282	28	171	83	700	0	200	500	745	574	–
1898	291	30	174	87	700	0	200	500	737	563	–
1899	295	33	173	89	700	0	200	500	734	561	–
1900	298	30	174	94	701	1	200	500	734	560	–
1901	345	34	212	99	702	2	200	500	785	573	–
1902	334	35	191	108	704	4	200	500	764	573	–
1903	348	35	195	118	705	5	200	500	787	592	–
1904	359	37	203	119	712	12	200	500	798	595	–
1905	369	39	214	116	717	17	200	500	808	594	–
1906	392	43	226	123	720	20	200	500	831	605	–
1907	415	45	240	130	721	21	200	500	856	616	–
1908	439	51	255	133	731	31	200	500	880	625	–
1909	477	59	277	141	740	40	200	500	917	640	–
1910	493	67	297	129	761	61	200	500	931	634	–
1911	533	71	325	137	783	83	200	500	969	644	–
1912	557	76	333	148	810	109	201	500	991	658	–
1913	606	77	353	176	856	153	203	500	1 039	686	–
1914	589	82	347	160	925	219	206	500	1 013	666	–
1915	580	88	348	144	1 035	305	209	521	1 035	687	–
1916	603	91	375	137	1 113	378	213	522	1 113	738	–
1917	677	105	392	180	1 161	432	216	513	1 180	788	–
1918	739	127	414	198	1 229	483	219	527	1 268	854	–
1919	812	147	434	231	1 291	537	221	533	1 409	975	–
1920	936	174	467	295	1 382	648	223	511	1 496	1 029	–
1921	1 060	201	500	359	1 537	823	225	489	1 648	1 148	–
1922	1 182	227	533	422	1 803	1 105	230	468	1 822	1 289	–
1923	1 255	255	562	438	2 237	1 410	235	592	2 073	1 511	–
1924	1 426	311	608	507	2 636	1 793	243	600	2 323	1 715	–
1925	1 481	367	649	465	3 067	2 217	251	599	2 803	2 154	–
1926	1 590	355	692	543	3 459	2 609	260	590	3 191	2 499	–
1927	1 753	402	741	610	3 876	3 014	268	594	3 634	2 893	–
1928	1 890	411	800	679	4 384	3 465	277	642	4 130	3 330	–
1929	2 039	444	848	747	4 892	3 969	286	637	4 631	3 783	–
1930	2 130	449	914	767	5 509	4 576	297	636	5 195	4 281	–
1931	2 204	496	971	737	6 244	5 306	310	628	5 782	4 811	–
1932	2 133	521	915	697	6 861	5 906	325	630	6 098	5 183	–
1933	2 256	549	996	711	7 138	6 183	334	621	6 376	5 380	–
1934	2 379	577	1 077	725	7 439	6 484	343	612	6 617	5 540	–
1935	2 503	606	1 158	739	7 742	6 787	352	603	6 914	5 756	–
1936	2 626	634	1 239	753	8 228	7 272	362	594	7 536	6 297	–
1937	2 748	663	1 319	766	8 589	7 626	370	593	8 061	6 742	335
1938	3 018	690	1 547	781	8 893	7 939	379	575	8 602	7 055	787
1939	3 101	681	1 684	736	9 187	8 291	393	503	8 945	7 261	1 138
1940	3 044	663	1 546	835	9 549	8 591	406	552	9 067	7 521	1 698
1941	3 653	495	2 041	1 117	9 813	8 821	415	577	10 053	8 012	2 145
1942	4 148	438	2 166	1 544	10 001	8 976	423	602	10 938	8 772	2 764
1943	4 942	663	2 292	1 987	10 029	8 973	429	627	12 062	9 770	3 687
1944	5 961	685	2 586	2 690	9 885	8 800	433	652	13 078	10 492	5 159
1945	6 978	686	2 857	3 435	9 679	8 564	438	677	14 232	11 375	6 457
1946	8 172	657	3 215	4 300	9 571	8 422	447	702	15 385	12 170	6 666
1947	9 508	660	3 421	5 427	10 071	8 874	470	727	16 601	13 180	6 886
1948	10 393	718	3 823	5 852	11 051	9 795	504	752	17 722	13 899	7 293
1949	10 785	869	4 272	5 644	12 391	11 070	544	777	19 152	14 880	7 167
1950	11 394	1 000	4 742	5 652	13 991	12 592	597	802	20 062	15 320	7 669

Column 1 – 1897–1950: From Table G-16, col. 1.

Column 2 – 1897–1913: From Bureau of the Census, *Wealth, Debt and Taxation*, 1913, p. 38.
1914: Obtained by linear interpolation between 1913 and 1915.
1915–1940: *Financial Statistics of States*, various issues, except for the years 1920, 1921, and 1932–1936, which were obtained by linear interpolation.
1941–1950: Col. 1 minus sum of cols. 3–6.

Column 3 – 1897–1914: No separate data were available for these years; the average ratio between cols. 3 and 4 existing in the years 1915–1919 was assumed to have also prevailed from 1897–1914.
1915–1940: *Financial Statistics of States*, except for the years 1920, 1921, and 1933–1936, which were obtained by linear interpolation.
1941–1944: *State Finances*, various issues. Value for 1943 was obtained by linear interpolation.
1945–1950: Estimated from col. 4 by applying the 1944 ratio between cols. 4 and 3.

Column 4 – 1897–1914: Same source and procedure as col. 2.
1915–1940: Col. 1 minus the sum of cols. 2, 3, 5, and 6.
1941–1944: Same source and procedure as col. 3.
1945–1950: Total state and local securities owned by states as given in Bureau of the Census, *Governmental Debt in the United States*, 1950, p. 10, minus col. 3.

Column 5 – 1897–1916: Included with col. 4; amounts probably negligible.
1917–1922: Linear interpolation between rough estimates of 0 in 1916 and 35 in 1923.
1923: Hardy, C. O., *Tax-Exempt Securities and Surtax*, p. 51.
1924–1939: Estimated at rising from 7 percent of cols. 4 and 5 in 1923 to 13 percent in 1940.
1940–1944: *State Finances*, various issues, except 1943, which was obtained by linear interpolation.
1945–1950: Bureau of the Census, *Governmental Debt in the United States*, 1950, p. 9.

Column 6 – This column includes nongovernmental securities, mortgages, and other credit instruments.
1897–1913: Same source as col. 2.
1914: Col. 1 minus the sum of cols. 2–4.
1915–1938: *Financial Statistics of States* excepts for the years 1920, 1921, and 1933–1936, which were obtained by linear interpolation.
1939–1944: *State Finances*, various issues, except 1943, which was obtained by linear interpolation.
1945–1950: Estimated as unchanged from 1944.

LIQUID ASSETS OF STATE GOVERNMENTS
1897 to 1950

$ mill.

End of fiscal year	Total	Cash	States' own securities	Other state and local government securities	U.S. Government securities	Other liquid assets	End of fiscal year	Total	Cash	States' own securities	Other state and local government securities	U.S. Government securities	Other liquid assets
	1	2	3	4	5	6		1	2	3	4	5	6
1897	282	44	49	147	—	42	1924	1 426	544	118	515	40	209
1898	291	48	50	149	—	44	1925	1 481	493	131	578	45	234
1899	295	50	51	155	—	39	1926	1 590	563	143	591	50	243
1900	298	55	42	126	—	75	1927	1 753	627	153	646	60	267
1901	345	59	58	175	—	53	1928	1 890	671	148	713	70	288
1902	334	67	50	149	—	68	1929	2 039	737	157	761	75	309
1903	348	80	50	151	—	67	1930	2 130	756	153	811	85	325
1904	359	81	52	157	—	69	1931	2 204	733	160	868	95	348
1905	369	78	54	163	—	74	1932	2 133	640	168	872	100	353
1906	392	84	57	173	—	78	1933	2 256	676	177	924	105	374
1907	415	91	60	182	—	82	1934	2 379	712	186	972	115	394
1908	439	94	63	191	—	91	1935	2 503	748	195	1 025	120	415
1909	477	102	70	210	—	95	1936	2 626	784	204	1 072	130	436
1910	493	90	75	227	—	101	1937	2 748	826	213	1 113	140	456
1911	533	98	82	245	—	108	1938	3 018	883	237	1 243	155	500
1912	557	109	84	253	—	111	1939	3 101	841	283	1 266	160	551
1913	606	137	88	264	—	117	1940	3 044	937	285	1 140	174	508
1914	589	143	84	258	—	104	1941	3 653	1 394	292	1 260	287	420
1915	580	149	87	242	—	102	1942	4 148	1 766	276	1 264	416	426
1916	603	148	85	262	0	108	1943	4 942	2 250	255	1 189	844	404
1917	677	191	89	278	5	114	1944	5 961	2 367	237	1 105	1 871	381
1918	739	216	94	301	10	118	1945	6 978	2 424	185	863	3 106	400
1919	812	240	96	322	15	139	1946	8 172	2 812	133	622	4 205	400
1920	936	310	98	358	20	150	1947	9 508	3 467	142	663	4 836	400
1921	1 060	380	100	394	25	161	1948	10 393	3 532	151	702	5 608	400
1922	1 182	452	102	425	30	173	1949	10 785	3 839	172	800	5 574	400
1923	1 255	461	103	468	35	188	1050	11 394	4 213	210	981	5 590	400

TRUST AND INVESTMENT FUND ASSETS OF STATE GOVERNMENTS
1941 to 1950

$ mill.

Item	1941	1942	1943	1944	1945	1946	1947	1948	1949	1950
	Investment fund and treasury cash (fiscal year)									
1. Total revenue	5 458	6 142	6 321	6 649	6 775	7 247	8 540	10 026	10 986	11 863
2. New borrowing	315	148	48	28	14	73	742	799	588	1 328
3. Total receipts	5 773	6 290	6 369	6 677	6 789	7 320	9 282	10 825	11 574	13 191
4. Total expenditures	5 491	5 863	5 926	5 974	6 044	6 455	8 155	10 400	11 782	13 183
5. Difference (gross)	282	427	443	703	745	865	1 127	425	−208	8
6. New investment fund, end of fiscal year	1 117	1 544	1 987	2 690	3 435	4 300	5 427	5 852	5 644	5 652
	Trust funds (end of fiscal year)									
7. Pension	930	1 006	1 083	1 241	1 390	1 607	1 790	2 093	2 437	.
8. Workmen's compensation	250	261	324	389	417	438	461	506	550	.
9. School	701	745	775	813	850	900	900	950	1 000	.
10. Other trust funds	120	104	50	63	100	150	150	154	160	.
11. Enterprises	40	50	60	80	100	120	120	120	125	.
12. Total	2 041	2 166	2 292	2 586	2 857	3 215	3 421	3 823	4 272	.

Lines 1 to 4 – 1941–1950: *State Finances,* various issues.

Line 5 – 1941–1950: Line 3 minus line 4.

Line 6 – 1941–1950: Line 5 cumulated from 1940 value of $835 mill. *(State Finances).*

Line 7 – 1941–1949: Same source as line 1.

Line 8 – 1941–1949: From Table G-19, col. 11: figures converted to fiscal-year basis.

Lines 9 to 11 – 1941–1944: Same source as line 1.
  1945–1949: Increases are rough estimates based on general increase of revenue and expenditure.

Line 12 – 1941–1949: Sum of lines 8–12.

STATE AND LOCAL GOVERNMENT EMPLOYEE RETIREMENT AND STATE-ADMINISTERED WORKMEN'S COMPENSATION FUNDS
1896 to 1949
$ mill.

End of calendar year	State and local government employee retirement funds						Workmen's compensation funds				
	Assessments	Government contributions	Investment income	Benefits	Fund increase	Fund assets	Assessments	Investment income	Benefits	Fund increase	Fund assets
	1	2	3	4	5	6	7	8	9	10	11
1896	.	.	.	.	.	2	.	.	.	.	.
1897	.	.	.	.	.	2	.	.	.	.	.
1898	.	.	.	.	.	3	.	.	.	.	.
1899	.	.	.	.	.	4	.	.	.	.	.
1900	.	.	.	.	.	5	.	.	.	.	.
1901	.	.	.	.	.	6	.	.	.	.	.
1902	.	.	.	.	.	7	.	.	.	.	.
1903	.	.	.	.	.	8	.	.	.	.	.
1904	.	.	.	.	.	9	.	.	.	.	.
1905	.	.	.	.	.	10	.	.	.	.	.
1906	.	.	.	.	.	11	.	.	.	.	.
1907	.	.	.	.	.	12	.	.	.	.	.
1908	.	.	.	.	.	14	.	.	.	.	.
1909	.	.	.	.	.	15	.	.	.	.	.
1910	.	.	.	.	.	16	.	.	.	.	.
1911	.	.	.	.	.	16	.	.	.	.	.
1912	.	.	.	.	.	17	.	.	.	.	.
1913	.	.	.	.	.	17	.	.	.	.	3
1914	.	.	.	.	.	15	.	.	.	.	5
1915	3	12	0	12	3	18	7	0	5	2	7
1916	3	12	0	12	3	21	11	0	7	4	11
1917	4	14	0	14	4	25	12	0	8	4	15
1918	5	14	0	14	5	30	19	1	11	9	24
1919	6	17	0	17	6	36	19	1	12	8	32
1920	12	22	1	22	13	49	22	1	14	9	41
1921	17	28	1	28	18	67	23	2	16	9	50
1922	22	34	4	31	26	93	19	3	19	3	53
1923	27	40	5	40	32	125	24	4	21	7	60
1924	31	42	6	42	37	162	30	5	29	6	66
1925	33	45	8	45	41	203	28	6	34	0	66
1926	36	50	10	50	46	249	33	6	39	0	66
1927	39	55	13	55	52	301	48	6	46	8	74
1928	44	60	16	60	60	361	47	7	48	6	80
1929	47	72	16	72	63	424	48	7	48	7	87
1930	51	78	19	78	70	494	42	7	48	1	88
1931	55	84	21	86	74	568	39	7	48	−2	86
1932	57	96	24	95	82	650	30	6	45	−9	77
1933	63	107	28	110	88	738	36	5	42	−1	76
1934	65	118	31	119	95	833	48	6	43	11	87
1935	70	127	35	127	105	938	57	6	48	15	102
1936	76	131	39	137	109	1 047	69	6	54	21	123
1937	86	141	43	144	126	1 173	84	7	60	31	154
1938	96	147	48	151	140	1 313	75	7	63	19	173
1939	105	152	53	157	153	1 466	78	8	61	25	198
1940	112	155	59	163	163	1 629	81	8	63	26	224
1941	115	165	66	175	171	1 800	98	8	73	33	257
1942	122	185	69	194	182	1 982	111	8	78	41	298
1943	133	202	74	213	196	2 178	119	11	86	44	342
1944	144	212	78	223	211	2 389	128	14	94	48	390
1945	159	225	82	240	226	2 615	111	15	99	27	417
1946	238	250	86	260	314	2 929	114	15	108	21	438
1947	285	290	91	297	369	3 298	121	16	114	23	461
1948	348	360	101	326	483	3 781	147	18	120	45	506
1949	368	392	115	357	518	4 299	170	20	130	60	566

TABLE G–19

Column 1 – 1915–1928: Estimated on basis of data obtained from National Income Division, Department of Commerce.
1929–1949: *Survey of Current Business, National Income Supplement*, July 1947; July 1950.

Column 2 – 1915–1928: Assumed equal to col. 4, on basis of relationship in 1929–1935.
1929–1949: Same source as for col. 1.

Column 3 – 1915–1949: Same source as for col. 1.

Column 4 – 1915–1949: Same source as for col. 1.

Column 5 – 1915–1949: Total of cols. 1–3 minus col. 4.

Column 6 – 1896–1914: Rough extrapolation of 1915 value based on the fact that pension systems began during the 1890's but grew only slowly until World War I.
1915–1940: Obtained by deducting cumulatively annual fund increases, as shown in col. 5, from 1941 benchmark figure published in Bureau of Census, *Retirement Systems for State and Local Government Employees: 1941*, State and Local Government Special Study 17, table 15.
1941–1949: Obtained by adding cumulatively annual fund increase to 1941 benchmark value.

Columns 7 to 9 – 1915–1949: Estimated on basis of data obtained from National Income Division, Department of Commerce, except for 1941, 1942 and 1944, for which data were available in Bureau of Census, *States Finances*.

Column 10 – 1915–1949: Sum of cols. 7 and 8 minus 9.

Column 11 – 1913–1949: Same method as applied in col. 6, using 1944 as benchmark figure.

TABLE G–20

Column 1 – 1896–1949: Sum of cols. 2–5.

Column 2 – 1914–1927: Assumed equal to payments in following year as reported in *Historical Statistics*, p. 314. Figures for 1915–1917, and 1919–1920 obtained by linear interpolation.
1928–1948: Assumed equal to personal income tax receipts and corporate profit tax accruals in following year as shown in *Survey of Current Business, National Income Supplement*, July 1947, p. 22, and July 1950, p. 12.
1949: Rough estimate guided by trend in preceding years.

Column 3 – 1914–1949: Same sources as for col. 2.

Column 4 – 1896–1927: Linear interpolation between benchmark years 1890, 1901, 1912, 1914, 1918, 1922, and 1926 (*Historical Statistics*, p. 314).
1928–1949: Same procedure as for col. 2. Sum of personal and real property taxes.

Column 5 – 1896–1927: Linear interpolation between benchmark years 1890, 1901, 1912, 1931 (*Historical Statistics*, p. 314).
1928–1949: Included in col. 4.

1074

NETTAX ACCRUALS OF STATE AND LOCAL GOVERNMENTS
1896 to 1949

$ mill.

End of year	Total	State governments			Local governments	End of year	Total	State governments			Local governments
		Income tax	Gift and death taxes	Property taxes	Property taxes			Income tax	Gift and death taxes	Property taxes	Property taxes
	1	2	3	4	5		1	2	3	4	5
1896	597	–	–	77	520	1924	3 540	103	86	362	2 989
1897	619	–	–	78	541	1925	3 751	134	91	366	3 160
1898	640	–	–	79	561	1926	3 968	162	106	370	3 330
1899	662	–	–	80	582	1927	4 174	184	128	362	3 500
1900	684	–	–	81	603	1928A	4 473	284	165	353	3 671
1901	706	–	–	82	624	1928B	5 140	284	165		4 691
1902	740	–	–	87	653	1929	5 271	208	182		4 881
1903	775	–	–	93	682	1930	5 005	149	168		4 688
1904	809	–	–	98	711	1931	4 826	121	137		4 568
1905	843	–	–	103	740	1932	4 327	126	110		4 091
1906	877	–	–	108	769	1933	4 317	187	97		4 033
1907	912	–	–	114	798	1934	4 513	252	109		4 152
1908	946	–	–	119	827	1935	4 628	324	116		4 188
1909	980	–	–	124	856	1936	4 794	369	129		4 296
1910	1 015	–	–	130	885	1937	4 893	342	137		4 414
1911	1 049	–	–	135	914	1938	4 901	357	122		4 422
1912	1 083	–	–	140	943	1939	5 075	413	115		4 547
1913	1 277	–	–	163	1 114	1940	5 218	512	115		4 591
1914	1 501	2	29	186	1 284	1941	5 257	608	110		4 539
1915	1 700	14	33	199	1 454	1942	5 510	761	110		4 639
1916	1 900	26	37	212	1 625	1943	5 635	799	124		4 712
1917	2 100	38	42	224	1 796	1944	5 762	831	140		4 791
1918	2 299	50	46	237	1 966	1945	5 981	838	152		4 991
1919	2 520	66	52	266	2 136	1946	6 748	1 055	176		5 517
1920	2 743	82	59	295	2 307	1947	7 511	1 196	179		6 136
1921	2 966	98	66	324	2 478	1948	7 999	1 294	174		6 531
1922	3 169	93	75	353	2 648	1949	8 468	1 394	174		6 900
1923	3 355	101	79	357	2 818						

Column 1 – 1896: Estimated on basis of annual differences, 1897–1898.

    1897–1913: Bureau of the Census, *Wealth, Debt and Taxation*, 1913, p. 38. Data for this and later periods until 1941 refer to end of fiscal year of the various states, generally or slightly before June 30. From 1941 on all data are as of June 30.

    1914: Obtained by linear interpolation between 1913 and 1915.

    1915–1928: From *Financial Statistics of States*, except for 1920–1921, obtained by linear interpolation between 1919 and 1922.

    1929–1939: *Survey of Current Business*, Sept. 1947.

    1940–1947: Bureau of the Census, *Historical Review of State and Local Government Finances*.

    1948–1950: Bureau of the Census, *Governmental Debt in 1950*, p. 5.

Column 2 – 1896–1902: Obtained by geometric interpolation between 1890 and 1902 figures, *Historical Statistics of the U.S. 1789–1945*, p. 314, linked to benchmark 1902 figure from Bureau of the Census, *Wealth, Debt and Taxation*. Data refer through 1939 to end of fiscal year, generally on or about Dec. 31; from 1940 on to June 30, figures being averaged to obtain Dec. 31 estimates.

    1903–1913: Extrapolated from benchmark figure for 1913 Bureau of the Census, *Wealth, Debt and Taxation* by means of big-city data obtained from *Financial Statistics of Cities*.

    1914–1922: Same procedure with 1922 as the benchmark year. Data for 1914, 1920, and 1921 obtained by linear interpolation.

    1923–1925: Obtained by linear interpolation between 1922 and 1926 data.

    1926–1940: *Federal, State and Local Government Fiscal Relations*, p. 358.

    1941–1947: Bureau of the Census, *Historical Review of State and Local Government Finances*.

    1948–1949: Bureau of the Census, *Government Debt in 1950*, p. 5.

$ mill.

Year	State	Local	Year	State	Local	Year	State	Local
	1	2		1	2		1	2
1896	226	1 450	1915	580	4 923	1933	3 018	16 391
1897	237	1 520	1916	603	5 291	1934	3 201	15 976
1898	254	1 593	1917	658	5 654	1935	3 331	16 165
1899	261	1 670	1918	700	6 051	1936	3 318	16 350
1900	265	1 750	1919	694	6 344	1937	3 276	16 130
1901	262	1 834	1920	822	7 229	1938	3 309	16 053
1902	274	1 924	1921	949	8 146	1939	3 343	16 385
1903	266	2 050	1922	1 163	9 093	1940	3 526	16 766
1904	273	2 176	1923	1 419	9 779	1941	3 413	16 646
1905	278	2 302	1924	1 739	10 466	1942	3 211	16 131
1906	281	2 465	1925	1 745	11 152	1943	2 909	15 243
1907	280	2 685	1926	1 858	11 838	1944	2 768	14 433
1908	290	2 999	1927	1 995	12 774	1945	2 425	13 864
1909	300	3 179	1928	2 144	13 589	1946	2 358	13 706
1910	323	3 468	1929	2 300	14 501	1947	2 978	14 414
1911	347	3 769	1930	2 444	15 579	1948	3 722	15 916
1912	376	4 030	1931	2 666	16 582	1949	4 024	17 588
1913	423	4 075	1932	2 896	16 680	1950	5 323	
1914	501	4 492						

Column 1 – 1897–1918: Sum of: (1) Merchandise trade proper, as published in *Monthly Summary of Foreign Commerce* and *Statistical Abstract*. (2) Silver, from same sources. In certain years data were adjusted to agree with those published in *The United States in the World Economy*. (3) Non-monetary gold, equivalent to "net exports and monetary use of gold" as formerly used in the national product compilations of the Department of Commerce. Gold exports and imports are shown in various issues of *Monthly Summary of Foreign Commerce* and, from 1914–1941, in *Banking and Monetary Statistics*. Changes in gold stock, 1914–1941 appear in the latter volume and in the *Federal Reserve Bulletin* for subsequent dates. Gold stock figures have been adjusted to include certain government holdings, such as those of the Exchange Stabilization Fund, which are not included in the official monetary stock. Data prior to 1914 are from *Annual Reports, Director of the Mint*.

    1919–1945: Official balance of payments estimates of U.S. Department of Commerce, especially *The United States in the World Economy*, and *International Transactions of the United States during the War, 1940–1945*, pp. 221–222, table XXVI.

    1946–1949: *The Balance of International Payments of the United States, 1946–1948*, and *Survey of Current Business*, June 1950.

Column 2 – 1897–1914: Dickens, Paul D., *The Transition Period in American International Financing: 1897–1914* (unpublished doctoral dissertation, George Washington University, 1933), p. 272. Payments to foreigners revised on basis of newer yields and interest data.

    1915–1918: Receipts of income on U.S. investments abroad, 1915–1918, were roughly interpolated from Dickens' estimate of $145 million for 1914 and Department of Commerce estimate of $544 million in 1919. Estimates used in millions of dollars were: 1915, 200; 1916, 250; 1917, 350; and 1918, 450. According to Williams, John, "The Balance of International Payments of the United States for the Year 1920," *The Review of Economic Statistics*, June 1921, supplement 1, p. 202, interest on loans placed in American market during the war amounted to $59 million in 1915, 118 in 1916, 131 in 1917, and 93 in 1918. Also interest of $106 million was paid to U.S. Government on its war loans in 1918. (Treasury data, cited in Moulton, H. G. and Pasvolsky, Leo, *War Debts and World Prosperity*, p. 483.) This would leave the following amounts, which do not seem unreasonable, for income on investments outstanding in 1914 and on direct investments made during the war (in millions of dollars): 1915, 141; 1916, 142; 1917, 219; and 1918, 251.

    On payments side for same war years, Williams estimates as follows: "…the interest paid on foreign capital owned abroad [was] $86 million in the last half of 1914, $72 million in the first half of 1915, $128 million for the twelve months June 31, 1915 to July 31, 1916, and $54 million for the last half of 1916; for 1917 and 1918, the interest would not be less than $100 million a year." These figures were raised to 175, 150, 125, and 125, respectively, to take care of higher investment figures assumed herein.

    1919–1949: Official balance of payments estimates as given in sources indicated in col. 1.

Column 3 – 1897–1915: Dickens, *op. cit.*

    1916–1918: Estimates of Bullock, L., Williams, J., and Tucker, R., "The Balance of Trade of the United States, 1789–1919," *The Review of Economic Statistics*, July 1919, pp. 248–250, have been employed. Since there are some unexplained discrepancies between text and tables in this account, values of exports carried in U.S. bottoms and of imports carried in foreign bottoms have been multiplied by 30 percent and 15 percent, respectively, to obtain freight receipts and payments, respectively. Net of these two items was reduced by 20 percent to allow for port expenditures, and a debit of $87 million in 1917 and $174 million in 1918 for chartering foreign ships was added. The computation is summarized in following table:

Year	Exports in U.S. ships ($ mill.)	Imports in foreign ships ($ mill.)	Freight earned on exports (col. 1 × 30 %)	Freight paid on imports (col. 2 × 15 %)	col. 3 + col. 4 less 20% for port expenditures	Foreign charter	Net
	1	2	3	4	5	6	7
1916	499	1550	150	−233	−66	–	−66
1917	795	1706	239	−256	−14	−87	−101
1918	969	1850	291	−278	10	−174	−164

    It should be noted that Williams' 1919 estimate is substantially below that of Department of Commerce; this may indicate that his net debits in earlier years were too high.

    1919–1949: Official balance of payments estimates.

NET FOREIGN INVESTMENT OF THE UNITED STATES
1897 to 1949

K-1

$ mill.

Year	Adjusted balance of trade in commodities	Net income from			Private remittances	Balance of other current items	Estimated change in net foreign investment	
		Foreign investments	Freight and shipping	Tourism			Current year	Cumulated from Dec. 31, 1896
	1	2	3	4	5	6	7	8
1897	433	−112	−24	−73	−85	−	139	139
1898	698	−108	−21	−76	−85	−	408	547
1899	560	−103	−18	−88	−85	−	266	813
1900	754	−99	−36	−112	−95	−	412	1 225
1901	673	−88	−25	−122	−104	−	334	1 559
1902	477	−80	−24	−115	−105	−	153	1 712
1903	556	−72	−26	−118	−115	−	225	1 937
1904	501	−71	−24	−127	−127	−	152	2 089
1905	536	−69	−27	−142	−133	−	165	2 254
1906	556	−62	−34	−164	−147	−	149	2 403
1907	582	−66	−41	−179	−177	−	119	2 522
1908	721	−71	−30	−193	−192	−	235	2 757
1909	335	−64	−35	−210	−187	−	−161	2 596
1910	386	−64	−49	−227	−204	−	−158	2 438
1911	652	−76	−54	−248	−224	−	50	2 488
1912	666	−74	−78	−257	−212	−	45	2 533
1913	771	−73	−63	−261	−207	−	167	2 700
1914	415	−55	−71	−233	−170	−	−114	2 586
1915	1 873	64	−53	−136	−150	−	1 598	4 184
1916	3 137	132	−66	−101	−150	−	2 952	7 136
1917	3 392	250	−101	−66	−180	−	3 295	10 431
1918	3 329	350	−164	−39	−268	−1 018	2 190	12 621
1919	4 896	589	291	−67	−832	−1 053	3 824	16 445
1920	3 097	476	271	−123	−634	−243	2 844	19 289
1921	2 014	340	60	−124	−450	−227	1 613	20 902
1922	745	565	−55	−182	−314	−114	645	21 547
1923	393	710	−30	−189	−328	−79	477	22 024
1924	1 057	622	−46	−226	−339	−81	987	23 011
1925	720	742	−73	−264	−373	−68	684	23 695
1926	422	753	−45	−262	−361	−62	445	24 140
1927	742	741	−57	−286	−355	−69	716	24 856
1928	1 090	805	−88	−327	−346	−122	1 012	25 868
1929	884	809	−119	−344	−343	−116	771	26 639
1930	825	745	−152	−334	−306	−88	690	27 329
1931	374	546	−119	−247	−279	−78	197	27 526
1932	324	392	−84	−194	−217	−52	169	27 695
1933	226	322	−46	−133	−191	−28	150	27 845
1934	475	302	−63	−137	−162	14	429	28 274
1935	−58	366	−67	−144	−162	11	−54	28 220
1936	44	299	−89	−180	−176	9	−93	28 127
1937	270	282	−130	−213	−175	28	62	28 189
1938	1 070	385	−36	−173	−153	16	1 109	29 298
1939	938	311	−64	−155	−151	9	888	30 186
1940	1 411	354	69	−95	−178	−52	1 509	31 695
1941	1 857	357	219	−142	−180	−837	1 274	32 969
1942	5 222	355	426	−73	−124	−5 729	77	33 046
1943	9 688	353	767	−89	−250	−12 338	−1 869	31 177
1944	11 380	411	908	−108	−357	−13 924	−1 690	29 487
1945	6 807	357	889	−147	−473	−8 505	−1 072	28 415
1946	6 504	594	821	−205	−679	−2 224	4 811	33 226
1947	9 877	897	1 027	−206	−665	−2 035	8 895	42 121
1948	5 594	1 091	657	−292	−652	−4 475	1 923	44 044
1949	5 193	994	521	−325	−515	−5 446	422	44 466

1079

Column 4 – 1897–1914: Dickens, *op. cit.*, p. 275, calendar year figures having been derived from his fiscal-year data by averaging successive fiscal year figures.

        1915–1918: Interpolated between Dickens' 1914 estimate and Department of Commerce estimate for 1919. Number of citizens and alien residents arriving or departing, whichever was smaller, was used for estimates of U.S. expenditures abroad; and number of alien visitors arriving or departing, whichever was smaller, for estimates of foreign expenditures in U.S. Fiscal-year figures, from *Annual Reports of the Commissioner-General of Immigration*, cited in Department of Commerce, *Oversea Travel and Travel Expenditures in the Balance of International Payments of the U.S., 1919–1938*, p. 14, were averaged to obtain calendar-year data. Extrapolations were made forward from Dickens' figure and backward from Department of Commerce figures; averages of resulting estimates were used. Maximum variation between the two methods in any one year was $11 million.

        1919–1949: Official balance of payments estimates.

Column 5 – 1897–1914: Dickens, *op. cit.*, pp. 281–282, converted to calendar years by averaging successive fiscal-year estimates.

        1915–1918: Annual estimate of $150 million was used; this was figure used by the Harvard group (see *Review of Economic Statistics*, July 1919, p. 251). In addition, data on foreign remittances by American Red Cross were available for 1917–1918 (see *Review of Economic Statistics*, June 1921, supplement, p. 187).

        1919–1949: Official balance of payments estimates.

Column 6 – 1918–1949: In 1918 consisted solely of foreign currencies purchased for U.S. armed forces as reported in *Review of Economic Statistics*, June 1921, supplement, p. 202. For all other years, data were taken from Department of Commerce publications cited in col. 1.

Column 7 – 1897–1949: Sum of cols. 1–6.

Column 8 – 1897–1949: Col. 7 cumulated.

TABLE K-2

Column 1 – 1897–1949: Col. 2 plus col. 8.

Column 2 – 1897–1949: Sum of cols. 3–7.

Column 3 – 1897–1914: Dickens, Paul D., *The Transition Period in American International Financing: 1897 to 1914*, p. 131.

        Flotations broken down between stocks and bonds as given by Dickens. Transactions in outstanding securities assumed to be 30 percent stocks and 70 percent bonds, based on estimates of outstanding investments, except for 1904–1908, when proportion of stocks was assumed to be larger.

        1915–1918: Estimates based largely on Loree's study of changes in foreign holdings of railroad securities during this period, cited, e.g., in Bullock, C., Williams, J., and Tucker, R., "The Balance of Trade in the United States: 1789–1919," *Review of Economic Statistics*, July 1919, p. 245–246. Breakdown between stocks and bonds also based largely on Loree's study.

        1919–1939: *The United States in the World Economy*, table III (in back of volume). Breakdown between stocks and bonds for 1919–1922 based on Loree's study. For 1922–1929 it was assumed that 90 percent of foreign purchases were stocks and 10 percent bonds on basis of estimates of value of outstanding holdings, taking account of price changes. For 1930–1939 proportions were assumed to be 93 percent stocks and 7 percent bonds.

        1940–1944: Department of Commerce, *International Transactions of the United States During the War, 1940–1945*, p. 93. Breakdown between stocks and bonds for 1940–1949 based on various monthly issues of the Department of the Treasury, *Treasury Bulletin*, as given in section on capital movements under section I, historical summary, table 4, adjusted to include small amounts of long-term credit in col. 3, and vestings of enemy-owned bonds and stocks in cols. 3, 4, and 5, respectively.

        1945: Department of Commerce, *The Balance of International Payments of the United States, 1946–1948*, p. 130.

        1946–1949: *Survey of Current Business*, June 1950, p. 11, *et seq.*, and underlying detailed data in files of Department of Commerce.

Column 4 – 1897–1929: Rough estimates obtained by assuming that about one-third of total net change in foreign transactions of stocks (see notes to col. 3) is attributable to preferred stocks, the ratio being based on relation between foreigners' holdings of American preferred and common stock (cf. Lewis, Cleona, *America's Stake in International Investments*, p. 558). Figures were modified in a few years on basis of available information on offerings of preferred stock to foreigners, as given in Dickens, *op. cit.*

1930–1939: Annual movements based on data on changes in holdings between benchmark years as shown in Lewis, *loc. cit.* and in Department of Commerce, *Foreign Investments in the United States*, 1937–1939, taking account of fluctuations in preferred stock prices.

1940–1949: Roughly estimated at 10 percent of total net change of stocks, approximately the proportion of foreigners' holdings of preferred to total stocks.

Column 5 – 1897–1949: Total net change in foreign transactions of stocks minus col. 4.

Columns 6 and 7 – 1940–1949: Same source as for col. 3.

Column 8 – 1897–1913: No estimates available.

1914–1922: Sum of cols. 9–15.

1923–1949: Equivalent to "net movement of foreign short-term capital in the United States," as reported in official balance of payments estimates. (See notes to Table K-1, col. 1.)

Column 9 – 1914–1949: From balance sheets of Federal Reserve banks, as published in *Banking and Monetary Statistics*, pp. 33ff., and in *Federal Reserve Bulletin*, various issues (see also notes to Table K-4, col. 3).

Column 10 – 1914–1928: Estimated roughly on basis of residual estimate in balance of payments, computed without reference to this entry. After estimating total movement of short-term capital, 60 percent of net movement was arbitrarily allocated to col. 10 plus col. 11. Remainder was divided between cols. 9 and 14, with col. 9 being known.

1929–1949: From Table K-4, col. 8.

Column 11 – 1929–1949: From Table K-4, col. 9. Not separable from col. 10, 1914–1928.

Column 12 – 1936–1949: Department of the Treasury, *Treasury Bulletin*, various issues. Series includes only those securities held in custody accounts with American banks and bankers, including the Federal Reserve banks.

Column 13 – 1935–1949: Includes only deposits of Philippine government with U.S. Treasury for 1935–1945 as published in Department of the Treasury, *Treasury Bulletin*, July 1946, p. 89. Data for 1946–1949 were furnished by Treasury and include a small account for another country. Series excludes other short-term Treasury liabilities to foreigners which appear in balance of payment statistics for recent years and are included in col. 15.

Column 14 – 1918–1922: Estimated net inflow of U.S. currency, 1923–1935, is assumed to have been made possible by an equivalent amount of exports during years 1918–1922, distributed about evenly over this period.

1923–1949: From official balance of payments estimates.

Column 15 – 1914–1922: See note to col. 10.

1923–1949: Col. 8 minus sum of cols. 9–14.

NET CHANGE IN ASCERTAINABLE FOREIGN INVESTMENTS
IN THE UNITED STATES: 1897 to 1949

$ mill.

Year	Grand total	Long-term assets Total	Bonds	Stocks Preferred	Stocks Common	Direct investments	Other
	1	2	3	4	5	6	7
1897	0	0	0	0	0	–	–
1898	–8	–8	–13	2	3	–	–
1899	–45	–45	–47	1	1	–	–
1900	–75	–75	–56	–5	–14	–	–
1901	–33	–33	–25	–2	–6	–	–
1902	–30	–30	–31	0	1	–	–
1903	20	20	30	–3	–7	–	–
1904	59	59	34	8	17	–	–
1905	56	56	–19	25	50	–	–
1906	114	114	91	7	16	–	–
1907	136	136	156	–7	–13	–	–
1908	89	89	97	–3	–5	–	–
1909	171	171	148	7	16	–	–
1910	345	345	321	8	16	–	–
1911	171	171	135	12	24	–	–
1912	232	232	175	40	17	–	–
1913	252	252	200	17	35	–	–
1914	18	–432	–296	–80	–56	–	–
1915	–339	–789	–592	–70	–127	–	–
1916	–1 291	–391	–274	–40	–77	–	–
1917	364	–36	–25	–4	–7	–	–
1918	422	0	0	0	0	–	–
1919	–585	–215	–160	–20	–35	–	–
1920	–548	–278	–210	–22	–46	–	–
1921	32	–4	–4	0	0	–	–
1922	28	7	7	0	0	–	–
1923	387	338	34	90	214	–	–
1924	413	185	19	50	116	–	–
1925	241	301	30	80	191	–	–
1926	550	95	10	25	60	–	–
1927	884	–50	–5	–15	–30	–	–
1928	346	463	46	125	292	–	–
1929	554	358	36	100	222	–	–
1930	–222	66	5	–50	111	–	–
1931	–1 199	66	5	–50	111	–	–
1932	–699	–26	–2	–100	76	–	–
1933	–289	165	12	–50	203	–	–
1934	111	–15	–1	0	–14	–	–
1935	968	320	22	30	268	–	–
1936	976	600	42	60	498	...	–
1937	556	245	17	20	208	–	–
1938	374	57	4	5	48	–	–
1939	1 173	–86	–6	–8	–72	–	–
1940	1 263	–90	–46	–19	–170	–	145
1941	–727	–327	–45	–22	–201	–79	20
1942	98	–84	26	2	19	–96	–35
1943	1 159	–63	71	–4	–39	–52	–39
1944	684	175	246	–4	–31	–16	–20
1945	2 086	–103	–16	–10	–87	19	–9
1946	–986	–347	–270	–7	–60	–4	–6
1947	243	–96	66	–16	–145	12	–13
1948	379	–170	–49	–15	–132	36	–10
1949	45	126	97	–3	–23	72	–17

NET CHANGE IN ASCERTAINABLE FOREIGN INVESTMENTS IN THE UNITED STATES: 1897 to 1949

$ mill.

Year	Short-term assets							
	Total	Deposits in Federal Reserve banks	Deposits of		U.S. Government securities	Deposits with U.S. Treasury	U.S. currency	Other
			Foreign banks	Other foreigners				
			In commercial banks					
	8	9	10	11	12	13	14	15
1897	–	–	–	–	–	–	–	–
1898	–	–	–	–	–	–	–	–
1899	–	–	–	–	–	–	–	–
1900	–	–	–	–	–	–	–	–
1901	–	–	–	–	–	–	–	–
1902	–	–	–	–	–	–	–	–
1903	–	–	–	–	–	–	–	–
1904	–	–	–	–	–	–	–	–
1905	–	–	–	–	–	–	–	–
1906	–	–	–	–	–	–	–	–
1907	–	–	–	–	–	–	–	–
1908	–	–	–	–	–	–	–	–
1909	–	–	–	–	–	–	–	–
1910	–	–	–	–	–	–	–	–
1911	–	–	–	–	–	–	–	–
1912	–	–	–	–	–	–	–	–
1913	–	–	–	–	–	–	–	–
1914	450	0	270	–	–	–	–	180
1915	450	0	270	–	–	–	–	180
1916	–900	0	–540	–	–	–	–	–360
1917	400	3	240	–	–	–	–	157
1918	422	93	240	–	–	–	22	67
1919	–370	–23	–240	–	–	–	30	–137
1920	–270	–68	–180	–	–	–	30	–52
1921	36	6	0	–	–	–	30	0
1922	21	–9	0	–	–	–	30	0
1923	49	1	15		–	–	01	–28
1924	228	15	288	–	–	–	–12	–63
1925	–60	–10	–158	–	–	–	–16	124
1926	455	38	164	–	–	–	9	244
1927	934	–42	264	–	–	–	–18	730
1928	–117	1	–15	–	–	–	–9	–94
1929	196	–	101	–9	–	–	6	98
1930	–288	–	87	–69	–	–	5	–311
1931	–1 265	73	–361	–73	–	–	7	–911
1932	–673	–60	–169	–63	–	–	–78	–303
1933	–454	–15	–109	–56	–	–	–71	–203
1934	126	15	35	66	–	–	–25	35
1935	648	10	378	38	–	28	–1	195
1936	376	70	3	165	2	31	25	80
1937	311	73	71	–71	87	33	–3	121
1938	317	27	54	222	–89	–3	15	91
1939	1 259	198	311	335	10	3	131	271
1940	1 353	736	–45	40	–4	–11	38	599
1941	–400	–359	–61	45	176	43	34	–278
1942	182	19	169	–66	409	22	71	–442
1943	1 222	567	69	–74	575	3	59	23
1944	509	–156	49	163	–10	104	84	275
1945	2 189	–342	345	216	682	195	68	1 025
1946	–639	–354	114	246	–205	–194	61	–307
1947	339	256	57	–263	539	85	71	–406
1948	549	191	132	–11	113	4	42	78
1949	–81	145	56	–38	–18	–271	66	–21

Column 1 – 1897–1949: Sum of cols. 2, 3, and 6–9.

Column 2 – 1897–1914: Dickens, Paul D., *The Transition Period in American International Financing*: *1897–1914*, p. 91. Division between direct investments and other revised on basis of material in appendix A.
    1919–1939: *The United States in the World Economy*, table III (in back of volume).
    1940–1944: Department of Commerce, *International Transactions of the United States during the War, 1940–1945*, p. 93.
    1945: Department of Commerce, *The Balance of International Payments of the United States, 1946–1948*, p. 130.
    1946–1949: Department of Commerce, *Survey of Current Business*, June 1950, p. 11, *et seq.*

Column 3 – 1897–1914: Dickens, *op. cit.*
    1915–1918: New foreign issues from Department of Commerce, *Handbook of American Underwriting of Foreign Securities*, 1930. Amortizations included in 1917–1918 only to extent paid out of war loan proceeds and reported in *Annual Report of the Secretary of the Treasury*, 1920, pp. 332ff. No estimate for transactions in outstanding securities.
    1919–1949: Official balance of payments estimates as given in sources indicated in col. 1.
    Figures are net of brokers' and underwriters' commissions on all security transactions.

Columns 4 and 5 – 1897–1914: All transactions assumed to involve bonds.
    1915–1942: New issues distributed between stocks and bonds on basis of sources cited in col. 3 and official balance of payments estimates. Transactions in outstanding securities were divided between bonds and stocks in such a way as to be as consistent as possible with estimates for value of total holdings outstanding in 1912, 1922, and 1929 (see notes to Table K-7, lines 3–5). In practice, it appeared, after allowing for security price changes, necessary to assume U.S. purchases of foreign shares amounted to $500 million in 1915–1922 and to a like sum in 1923–1929. Breakdown for individual years between stocks and bonds was, therefore, made proportional to over-all ratio for those periods except for 1919 and 1920, when independent data indicated a higher proportion for stocks.
    1943–1949: Department of the Treasury, *Treasury Bulletin*, August 1950, p. 57, adjusted for unrecorded transactions according to official balance of payments estimates. Col. 4 includes some long-term banking and commercial loans in 1940–1949.

Column 6 – 1917–1918: *Combined Annual Reports of the World War Foreign Debt Commission*, 1927, p. 318ff.
    1919–1949: Official balance of payments estimates. Includes total paid subscriptions to International Bank and Fund.

Columns 7 and 8 – 1923–1949: Official balance of payments estimates.

Column 9 – 1897–1914: *Annual Report of the Director of the Mint*, various issues.
    1915–1918: *Banking and Monetary Statistics*, p. 536.
    1919–1949: Official balance of payments estimates.

Column 10 – 1897–1899: *Annual Report of the Secretary of the Treasury*, 1901.
    1900–1918: Exports and imports, *Statistical Abstract*, 1946, pp. 890–891; earmarking, domestic and foreign, *Annual Report of the Board of Governors of the Federal Reserve System Covering Operations for the Year 1930*, pp. 67–68.
    1919–1949: Official balance of payments estimates.

Column 11 – 1897–1949: Net domestic production (or consumption) is assumed to equal difference between changes in gold stock and net international transactions, i.e., it is a residual series assumed to measure the excess (or deficit) of domestic mining production over domestic nonmonetary use.

NET CHANGE IN ASCERTAINABLE U.S. INVESTMENTS ABROAD
1897 to 1949

$ mill.

Year	Total	Long-term assets					Short-term assets		Gold		
		Direct invest-ments	Other investments				Private loans	Govern-ment loans	Total stock	Im-ported stock	Domes-tically produced stock
			Total securities	Bonds and notes	Stocks	Govern-ment loans					
	1	2	3	4	5	6	7	8	9	10	11
1897	59	5	5	5	–	–	–	–	49	–5	54
1898	234	40	0	0	–	–	–	–	194	137	57
1899	109	20	23	23	–	–	–	–	66	–5	71
1900	234	56	87	87	–	–	–	–	91	13	78
1901	273	89	123	123	–	–	–	–	61	–3	64
1902	176	65	40	40	–	–	–	–	71	8	63
1903	112	81	–40	–40	–	–	–	–	71	21	50
1904	94	80	–11	–11	–	–	–	–	25	–36	61
1905	210	46	93	93	–	–	–	–	71	3	68
1906	217	92	–46	–46	–	–	–	–	171	109	62
1907	219	89	–24	–24	–	–	–	–	154	88	66
1908	179	48	87	87	–	–	–	–	44	–31	75
1909	94	88	24	24	–	–	–	–	–18	–89	71
1910	161	124	–34	–34	–	–	–	–	71	0	71
1911	213	95	28	28	–	–	–	–	90	20	70
1912	290	139	70	70	–	–	–	–	81	19	62
1913	190	138	27	27	–	–	–	–	25	–28	53
1914	–10	76	14	14	–	–	–	–	–100	–165	65
1915	1 289	–	790	703	87	–	–	–	499	421	78
1916	1 595	–	1 064	947	117	–	–	–	531	524	7
1917	4 562	–	594	529	65	3 656	–	–	312	233	79
1918	4 429	–	396	353	43	4 028	–	–	5	–26	31
1919	2 331	94	75	65	10	2 328	–	–	–166	–164	–2
1920	662	154	400	343	57	176	–	–	–68	–50	–18
1921	1 293	111	477	428	49	–30	–	–	735	686	49
1922	1 060	153	669	597	72	–31	–	–	269	235	34
1923	689	148	235	201	34	–91	82	–	315	295	20
1924	1 222	182	703	602	101	–28	109	–	256	216	40
1925	790	268	603	515	88	–27	46	–	–100	–102	2
1926	920	351	470	401	69	–30	36	–	93	72	21
1927	1 177	351	636	543	93	–46	349	–	–113	–154	41
1928	1 254	558	752	642	110	–49	231	–	–238	–272	34
1929	941	602	34	29	5	–38	200	–	143	120	23
1930	788	294	70	60	10	–77	191	–	310	278	32
1931	–910	222	–350	–351	1	–21	–628	–	–133	–176	43
1932	–457	16	–267	–267	0	–32	–227	–	53	11	42
1933	–118	–32	80	80	0	–	–35	–	–131	–173	42
1934	985	17	–202	–202	0	–	–96	–	1 266	1 178	88
1935	1 282	–34	–82	–82	0	–	–424	–	1 822	1 720	102
1936	1 040	12	–189	–202	13	–	–55	–	1 272	1 147	125
1937	1 043	–35	–241	–241	0	–	–45	–	1 364	1 271	93
1938	1 732	–16	–24	–24	0	–	–27	–	1 799	1 657	142
1939	2 850	–9	–104	–104	0	–	–211	–	3 174	3 018	156
1940	4 049	–32	–36	–36	0	51	–177	–	4 243	4 095	148
1941	1 023	–47	–19	–19	0	381	–21	10	719	572	147
1942	167	–19	84	84	0	10	–96	211	–23	–115	92
1943	–676	–98	58	57	1	124	12	–15	–757	–735	–22
1944	–1 043	–71	63	67	–4	162	85	68	–1 350	–1 305	–45
1945	1 022	100	354	316	38	842	96	178	–548	–463	–85
1946	4 004	183	–124	–129	5	3 262	310	–250	623	708	–85
1947	10 118	724	86	101	–15	6 849	189	108	2 162	2 143	19
1948	3 314	945	116	101	15	999	116	–92	1 530	1 523	7
1949	1 443	834	–34	–16	–18	470	–164	173	164	190	–26

Column 1 – 1922–1923: Department of Commerce, *The Balance of International Payments of the United States*, 1924, p. 22.

1924: *Ibid.*, 1925, p. 26.

1925–1933: Department of Commerce estimates. Data vary somewhat in coverage from year to year, especially between 1923 and 1924. No adjustment has been made to correct the error in annual movement resulting from changes in coverage.

1934–1949: Department of the Treasury, *Treasury Bulletin*, various issues. After 1946 this series includes foreign deposits with Treasury. For 1946–1949 such deposits, amounting to $326, $411, $415, and $144 million, have been deducted from published figures of $4694, $4809, $5210, and $5074 million, respectively. Amounts were furnished by Treasury. Although Department of the Treasury, *Census of Foreign-Owned Assets in the U.S.*, pp. 41, 42, indicates that total foreign deposits in June 1941 were 8.3 percent higher than reported in regular foreign deposit series, no adjustment has been made herein.

Column 2 – 1922–1949: Both Commerce and Treasury series include "deposits" with institutions, principally agencies of foreign banks and certain firms like American Express and others, which are not banks in the sense of having to file condition statements with appropriate banking authorities. These "deposits" have, therefore, to be eliminated. This has been done on the basis of data collected by Department of Commerce for 1922–1933, and from data furnished Federal Reserve Bank of New York for 1935–1949. Adjustment is incomplete for latter period in that similar institutions in other than New York Federal Reserve District have not been eliminated. Amounts involved are insignificant, however. For 1922–1933 it was not possible to avoid eliminating (i.e. including in this item) deposits with certain private banks, principally J. P. Morgan & Co. Figure for 1934 was interpolated.

Column 3 – 1922–1949: Taken from balance sheets published in *Banking and Monetary Statistics* and in *Federal Reserve Bulletin*. Deposits of international institutions, as reported in Department of the Treasury, *Treasury Bulletin*, are almost entirely with Federal Reserve banks but are not reported as foreign deposits in condition statements of such banks. Amounts involved, $372 million in 1947, $314 million in 1948, and $333 million in 1949, have been added to published figures of foreign deposits with Federal Reserve banks.

Column 4 – 1922–1949: Col. 1 minus cols. 2 and 3.

Column 5 – 1928–1949: Foreign bank deposits in U.S. banks. Figures are taken from condition statements of banks and undoubtedly have a somewhat larger coverage than col. 4, at least from 1934 on. From 1932 to 1947, data were taken from Friend, I. and Natrella, V., *Individuals' Saving*, part II. 1948 and 1949 data were provided by Securities and Exchange Commission. From 1928 to 1931, data are for member banks only. Principal omission due to this factor is undoubtedly foreign bank deposits with domestic private banks. Data for member banks appear in *Banking and Monetary Statistics*, p. 78. The 1928 figure includes estimate of $62 million for time deposits and corresponds to the ratio on June 29 and Oct. 4, 1929, first dates for which segregation was made. Foreign bank deposits with nonmember banks in 1932 and 1933 were $11 million and $10 million, respectively, but may have been much higher in the late 1920's. However, break in series between 1931 and 1932 has been disregarded in calculating annual movements.

Column 6 – 1935–1949: This item, applicable from 1935 on, represents balances of foreign branches of domestic banks with their own head offices. These are reported not as deposits but as other liabilities in condition statements (*Banking and Monetary Statistics*, p. 63) but would have been included as deposits of foreigners in Treasury series. Data from Friend and Natrella, *op. cit.* The 1948 and 1949 figures were provided by Securities and Exchange Commission.

Column 7 – 1922–1949: Col. 4 minus cols. 5 and 6 leaves, at least approximately, amount of deposits of foreigners that would be included in category, "Individuals, partnerships, corporations, etc." in condition statements.

Column 8 – 1929–1949: First differences of sum of cols. 5 and 6. Figure for 1928 not included for reason given below.

Column 9 – 1923–1949: First differences of col. 7 except for 1928, when first difference of col. 5 was not included since data do not represent a change from zero.

Column 10 – 1923–1949: Sum of cols. 8 and 9.

FOREIGN DEPOSITS IN THE UNITED STATES
1922 to 1949

$ mill.

Year	Total foreign deposits	Deposits with non-banking institutions	Foreign deposits with Federal Reserve banks	Foreign deposits in banks	Foreign inter-bank deposits	Deposits of foreign branches of domestic banks in home office	Deposits of foreign individuals, partner-ships, and corporations	Change in deposits of foreign banks	Change in deposits of foreign individuals	Total net change
	1	2	3	4	5	6	7	8	9	10
1922	488	60	3	425	.	—	425	.	.	.
1923	505	61	4	440	.	—	440	.	15	15
1924	909	162	19	728	.	—	728	.	288	288
1925	1 005	427	8	570	.	—	570	.	−158	−158
1926	1 335	555	46	734	.	—	734	.	164	164
1927	1 846	843	5	998	.	—	998	.	264	264
1928	1 680	691	6	983	597	—	386	.	−15	−15
1929	1 710	629	6	1 075	698	—	377	101	−9	92
1930	1 640	541	6	1 093	785	—	308	87	−69	18
1931	1 025	287	79	659	424	—	235	−361	−73	−434
1932	715	269	19	427	255	—	172	−169	−63	−232
1933	389	123	4	262	146	—	116	−109	−56	−165
1934	496	114	19	363	181	—	182	35	66	101
1935	1 056	248	29	779	508	51	220	378	38	416
1936	1 325	279	99	947	498	64	385	3	165	168
1937	1 437	318	172	947	515	118	314	71	−71	0
1938	1 824	402	199	1 223	570	117	536	54	222	276
1939	2 902	636	397	1 869	848	150	871	311	335	646
1940	3 627	630	1 133	1 864	771	182	911	−45	40	−5
1941	3 156	534	774	1 848	743	149	956	−61	45	−16
1942	3 305	561	793	1 951	844	217	890	169	−66	103
1943	3 913	607	1 360	1 946	926	204	816	69	−74	−5
1944	4 031	669	1 204	2 158	995	184	979	49	163	212
1945	4 426	845	862	2 719	1 313	211	1 195	345	216	561
1946	4 368	781	508	3 079	1 443	195	1 441	114	246	360
1947	4 398	761	764	2 873	1 445	250	1 178	57	−263	−206
1948	4 795	846	955	2 994	1 565	262	1 167	132	−11	121
1949	4 930	818	1 100	3 012	1 492	391	1 129	56	−38	18

AMERICAN STOCKHOLDERS' SHARE IN SAVING OF FOREIGN CORPORATIONS OTHER THAN SUBSIDIARIES OF AMERICAN CORPORATIONS
1897 to 1949

$ mill.

Year	Holdings of foreign stocks excluding direct investments	Share in undistributed earnings	Year	Holdings of foreign stocks excluding direct investments	Share in undistributed earnings	Year	Holdings of foreign stocks excluding direct investments	Share in undistributed earnings
	1	2		1	2		1	2
1897		1	1915		5	1933		30
1898		1	1916		7	1934		30
1899		1	1917		9	1935		30
1900	40	1	1918		10	1936		30
1901		1	1919		10	1937		30
1902		1	1920		11	1938		32
1903		2	1921		12	1939	1 700	34
1904		2	1922	700	14	1940		36
1905		2	1923		18	1941		38
1906		2	1924		22	1942		40
1907		2	1925		26	1943		42
1908		3	1926		30	1944		44
1909		3	1927		34	1945		47
1910		4	1928		39	1946	2 500	50
1911		4	1929	2 200	44	1947		55
1912	200	4	1930		30	1948		60
1913		4	1931		30	1949		60
1914		4	1932		30			

Column 1 – 1900: Rough estimate based on estimate of holdings of foreign bonds and stocks in Table K-7. 1912, 1922, 1929, 1939, 1946: From Table K-7, line 5.

Column 2 – 1897–1946: Derived by assuming on basis of average dividend yield of 4 percent and average corporate saving rate of one-third that undistributed earnings amounted to 2 percent of col. 1 in years for which estimates of holdings are available, and then interpolating between value so obtained, generally by linear method, but occasionally by also taking account of volume of purchases of foreign stock as shown in Table K-3, col. 5.
1947–1949: Assumed to rise slowly from 1946 level.

Selected Dates: 1900 to 1946

$ mill.

End of year	1900	1912	1914	1922	1929	1939	1946
Private debts or issues							
1. Direct investments	428	812	875	975	1 400	2 790	2 560
2. Railway bonds	1 209	2 247	2 156	422	225	225	262
3. Other bonds	518	671	644	95	225	225	263
4. Railway stocks	592	1 027	820	231	409	341	331
5. Other stocks	254	461	368	449	2 591	2 759	2 679
6. Other long-term claims	.	.	.	163	750	2 015	1 490
7. Total long-term claims	3 001	5 218	4 863	2 335	5 600	8 355	7 585
8. Deposits in banks	{ 250	450	450 }	425	1 075	1 869	3 079
9. Other short-term claims				63	2 000	1 751	2 056
10. Total short-term claims	250	450	450	488	3 075	3 620	5 135
11. Real assets	.	.	.	.	435	435	475
12. Total private liabilities and securities	3 251	5 668	5 313	2 823	9 110	12 410	13 195
Government liabilities							
13. Long-term bonds	.	.	.	.	125	250	315
14. Currency	.	.	.	.	.	220	620
15. Deposits	.	.	.	.	.	165	325
16. Short-term public debt issues	.	.	.	.	.	10	1 633
17. Other short-term liabilities	.	.	.	.	.	.	592
18. Total government liabilities	.	.	.	.	125	645	3 485
19. *Total liabilities and securities*	3 251	5 668	5 313	2 823	9 235	13 055	16 680

Line 1 – 1900: Total foreign long-term investments in U.S. on Jan. 1, 1897, were estimated at $2,800 million by Dickens, Paul D., in *The Transition Period in American International Financing: 1897–1914.* It was arbitrarily estimated that $300 million of this constituted direct investments.

1912: Interpolated between 1900 and 1914.

1914: Estimated at $875 million on July 1, 1914, using round figure of $5 billion for total long-term investments in U.S. and calculating security holdings as outlined below.

1922: Lewis' estimate for 1924, unadjusted. (Lewis, Cleona, *America's Stake in International Investments*, p. 558.)

1929, 1939, 1946: Sammons, Robert L., "Foreign Investment Aspects of the Measurement of National Wealth," *Studies in Income and Wealth*, vol. XII, pp. 566–567.

Line 2 – 1900: Total for 1897 estimated at $2,800 million (see line 1). Dickens' tabulations of American security offerings abroad for each year 1897–1914 show that, of total offerings during this period, 69 percent were railroad issues and 90 percent were bonds or notes, many of relatively short maturity. After deducting amortization, 84 percent of gross increase in foreign holdings (i.e. before deducting repatriations through securities market) consisted of bonds. On the other hand, Loree's railroad data (see below) with common stock at market value yield an estimate of 27 percent for stocks, and British Dollar Securities Committee shows 25 percent for rail stocks and about 30 percent for others. After making a rough allowance of $300 million for direct investments, remaining $2.5 billion is then divided as follows, using a 25 percent stock ratio:

	Stocks		Bonds		Total	
	percent	$ mill.	percent	$ mill.	percent	$ mill.
Rails		437		1313	70	1750
Other		188		562	30	750
Total	25	625	75	1875	100	2500

Bacon's method gives neither par nor market value (Bacon, N. T., "American International Indebtedness," *Yale Review*, Nov. 1900) although probably nearer the former, at least with regard to bonds. In view of the rough character of the estimates, it has been assumed that value is market for stocks and par for bonds. Classifying all direct investments as stock gives total of $925 million.

Total for 1897 was then extrapolated to 1900 on basis of Dickens' estimates, assuming 75 percent of transactions in outstanding securities to have been bond transactions. Total bonds of $1,727 million split in ratio of 70 : 30 between railway bonds and other bonds.

1912: Same as 1900 except 1914 ratios of 77 : 23 used to allocate total of $2,918 million between railroad and other securities.

1914: Relatively complete report on foreign holdings of railroad securities on Jan. 31, 1915, by Loree (cited in Lewis and in Department of Commerce, Bureau of Foreign and Domestic Commerce, *Foreign Investments in the U.S.*, p. 24), puts total at $2,704 million, par value. Adding $150 million for nominee holdings (Dickens' estimate) gives $2,854 million par value, or $2,644 million at market. Rails comprised 75 percent of American securities made available during the war to British Dollar Securities Committee. At this ratio total investments in securities would have been about $3,525 million, or $4,125 million on July 1, 1914, assuming a liquidation in the interim of $600 million. (Dickens' estimate for total holdings on that date was $4.4 billion; Lewis' was $6,750 million. Figure adopted herein is $5 billion, including $825 million for direct investments.) Loree and American Dollar Securities Committee (British) are surprisingly close on proportion of stocks (with common at market) to total foreign holdings of railway securities, Loree showing 27 percent and Committee 25 percent. For other issues, stock ratio was somewhat higher in Committee's figure. On this basis, foreign holdings in the U.S. on July 1, 1914, may be estimated as follows:

	$ mill.	Percent of total, excluding direct
Railway stocks ($\frac{1}{4}$)	773	
Railway bonds ($\frac{3}{4}$)	2320	
Total rails	3093	75.0
Other stocks ($\frac{1}{3}$)	344	
Other bonds ($\frac{2}{3}$)	688	
Total other	1032	25.0
Total portfolio	4125	100.0
Direct	875	
Total investments	5000	
Total stocks	1117	
Total bonds	3008	
	4125	

This estimate yields figure of $1,117 million for stocks as of July 1, 1914, or about $1 billion for year-end. It may be compared with figure of $1,188 million for end of year, arrived at by taking previously estimated 1897 figure of $625 million and adjusting it for changes in price of stocks and for annual capital movements based on Dickens' study.

Similarly, figure of $3,180 million for bonds is obtained, using 1897 estimate and Dickens' annual movement. The two methods may be compared as follows:

	$ mill.	
	1914 as above	1897 plus Dickens
Stocks	1117	1188
Bonds	3008	3180
	4125	4368

Difference is certainly less than the margin of error in estimates. Rough extrapolation to Dec. 31, 1914, gives $2,800 million for all bonds, divided 77 : 23 according to July 1 ratio of railroad and other bonds.

1922: Lewis' 1924 estimate for total holdings (excluding direct investments) adjusted back to 1922 on basis of balance of payments estimates, yielding total of $1,360 million. This has been divided among various classes of securities on basis of her 1924 distribution, according to which railway bonds were 31 percent of total.

1929: Sammons gives total bonds, excluding governments, at $450 million, market value. Divided 50 : 50 between rails and other on basis of 1934 distribution of 47 : 53 (par value basis) as given in Department of Commerce, Bureau of Foreign and Domestic Commerce, *Foreign Investments in the United States*, p. 19.

1939: Same procedure as for 1929.

1946: Same procedure as for 1929. Total was $525 million.

Line 3 – 1900–1946: See line 2. Other was 7 percent of total in 1924.

Line 4 – 1900: See line 2 for breakdown of 1897 holdings, showing railway stocks at 70 percent of total stock holdings. Total extrapolated to 1900 on basis of Dickens' estimates, assuming 25 percent of transactions in outstanding securities were stock transactions, and adjusted for changes in market value of all stocks as given by indices of Cowles, Alfred and Associates, *Common Stock Indexes*, 1939. Total in 1900 was $846 million.

1912: Same as 1900 except 1914 ratio of 69 : 31 of railroad to other stocks used. Total was $1,488 million.

1914: See line 2 for July 1, 1914, estimate. Extrapolation to Dec. 31 gives total for all stocks of $1,188 million, divided 69 : 31, according to July 1 ratio of railroad to other stocks.

1922: See line 2. Railway stocks were 17 percent of total.

1929: Sammons' estimate for all stocks was $3,000 million, Lewis', $2,934 million. Lewis' estimate for railway stocks used, unadjusted.

1939: Sammons' estimate for all stocks was $3,100 million. Lewis' 1936 estimate shows 11 percent rails; 1939 estimate divided on this basis.

1946: Same as 1939. Total was $3,010 million.

Line 5 – 1900–1914: See line 4.

1922: See line 4. Other stocks were 33 percent of total in 1924.

1929, 1939, 1946: See line 4.

Line 6 – 1922: See line 2. Miscellaneous claims were 12 percent of total in 1924.

1929–1946: Sammons, *op. cit.*

Line 7 – 1900–1946: Sum of lines 1–6.

Line 8 – 1900: Lewis' estimate for Dec. 31, 1897.

1912, 1914: Lewis' estimate for July 1, 1914.

1922–1946: From Table K-4, col. 4.

Line 9 – 1922: From Table K-4, cols. 2 and 3.

1929: Sammons, appendix table 4, lines 3 and 4, minus line 8 above.

1939: Sammons, appendix table 5, lines 3 and 4 (excluding federal government liabilities), minus line 8 above.

1946: Same source as for 1939.

Line 10 – 1900–1946: Sum of lines 8 and 9.

Line 11 – 1929–1946: Sammons, *op. cit.*

Line 12 – 1900–1946: Sum of lines 7, 10, and 11.

Lines 13 to 15 – 1929–1946: Sammons, *op. cit.*

Line 16 – 1939–1946: Department of the Treasury, *Treasury Bulletin*.

Line 17 – 1946: Sammons, *op. cit.*, short-term liabilities of federal government, excluding deposits and less public debt holdings as given in line 16.

Line 18 – 1929–1946: Sum of lines 13–17.

Line 19 – 1900–1946: Sum of lines 12 and 18.

Line 1 – 1900: Lewis, Cleona, *America's Stake in International Investments*, p. 605. Figure for 1897 adjusted to 1900 on basis of data on annual capital movements in Dickens, Paul D., *The Transition Period in American International Financing: 1897–1914*, p. 91.

1912: Same procedure as for 1900. Lewis' estimate is for July 1, 1914. One-half of annual movement in 1914 allocated to first half of year.

1922: Lewis' 1924 estimate, adjusted on basis of annual capital movement figures in Department of Commerce, *The United States in the World Economy*, table III.

1929, 1939, 1946: Sammons, Robert L., "Foreign Investment Aspects of the Measurement of National Wealth," in *Studies in Income and Wealth*, vol. XII. Estimates in this volume have not been adjusted for recent revisions in balance of payments data, but differences would not be substantial.

Line 2 – 1900–1946: Same sources and procedure as line 1.

Lines 3 to 5 – 1900: Same sources and procedure as line 1.

1912: Same sources and procedure as line 1 except that Lewis' estimate for foreign shares has been raised somewhat to fit in better with estimates shown in this table for later years.

1922: Lewis' figure for this year, adjusted from her estimate for 1924, would be $3,627 million, of which some $200 million would be foreign shares. These totals appear to be too low to be consistent with balance of payments data on annual security transactions 1912–1922, or with data developed by Department of the Treasury in its comprehensive *Census of American-Owned Assets in Foreign Countries*, published in 1947. For these reasons, as well as to allow for changes in security prices, Lewis' totals were raised to $4,000 million for bonds and $700 million for stocks. These adjustments are no more than rough estimates, however, in as much as there are no independent data on breakdown of security transactions between bonds and stocks prior to 1943.

1929–1946: Sammons, *op. cit.*

Line 6 – 1929–1946: Sammons, *op. cit.*

Line 7 – 1929–1946: Same source as line 6.

Line 8 – 1900–1946: Sum of lines 1–7.

Lines 9 and 10 – 1922: Same source and procedure as line 1.

1929–1946: Sammons, *op. cit.*

Line 11 – 1922–1946: Line 9 plus line 10.

Line 12 – 1900–1946: Line 8 plus line 11.

Line 13 – 1922–1929: Taken as net amount disbursed less repayments, as shown in Table K-3. Thus allowance is not made for unpaid interest or for interest payments later credited to principal in funding agreements.

1939–1946: Sammons, *op. cit.*

Line 14 – 1946: Sammons, *op. cit.*

Line 15 – 1946: Sammons, *op. cit.*

Line 16 – 1922–1946: Sum of lines 13–15.

Line 17 – 1900–1946: Line 12 plus line 16.

U.S. ASSETS ABROAD

Selected Dates: 1900 to 1946

$ mill.

End of year	1900	1912	1922	1929	1939	1946
Private assets						
1. Direct investments, subsidiaries	751	2 476	5 059	5 530	4 760	6 050
2. Direct investments, branches				2 320	1 990	2 220
3. Foreign dollar bonds	159	623	4 000	6 465	1 685	1 535
4. Other foreign bonds				910	915	1 395
5. Foreign stocks		200	700	2 200	1 700	2 500
6. Other long-term assets	.	.	.	735	775	875
7. Tangible assets	.	.	.	1 035	1 185	1 185
8. Total long-term assets	910	3 299	9 759	19 195	13 010	15 760
9. Deposits			609	210	400	450
10. Other short-term claims	.	.		1 565	650	775
11. Total short-term claims	.	.	609	1 775	1 050	1 225
12. Total private assets	910	3 299	10 368	20 970	14 060	16 985
Government assets						
13. Government loans	.	.	10 127	9 818	40	4 775
14. Short-term claims	.	.	.	.	.	480
15. Tangible assets	.	.	.	.	.	2 600
16. Total government assets	.	.	10 127	9 818	40	7 855
17. *Total assets*	910	3 299	20 495	30 788	14 100	24 840

BIBLIOGRAPHY

This bibliography is limited to material specifically referred to in text or tables of this volume. Reference is to table numbers in case of material cited in notes to tables, and to page numbers for publications cited in the Introduction.

NON-U.S. GOVERNMENT PUBLICATIONS

Author	Title	Table or page number
American Life Convention and Life Insurance Association of America	*Investment Bulletin.* No. 26, Nov. 12, 1948 and No. 78, Nov. 7, 1950. Mimeographed releases.	V-53
American Telephone and Telegraph Company	*Annual Report to the Stockholders.* Boston: A. Mudge and Co.	I-18, V-29, V-30
Automobile Manufacturers Association	*Automobile Facts and Figures.* Detroit: Automobile Manufacturers Association.	P-13, P-15
Bacon, N. T.	"American International Indebtedness," *Yale Review*, Volume IX. New Haven: Tuttle, Morehouse and Taylor, Nov. 1900.	K-6
Barger, H. and Schurr, S.	*The Mining Industries, 1899–1939: A Study of Output, Employment and Productivity.* New York: National Bureau of Economic Research, Inc., 1944.	C-46
Bergson, Abram	"Soviet National Income and Product in 1937," *Quarterly Journal of Economics*, Volume LXIV. Cambridge, Mass.: Harvard University Press, Aug. 1950.	p. 35
Best, A. M., Company, Inc.	*Best's Life Insurance Reports upon All Legal Reserve Companies Transacting Business in the United States and Canada, and Fraternal Societies and Assessment Associates Operating in the United States.* New York, 1906.	I-2
Bird, F. L.	*Trend of Tax Delinquency, 1930–1940.* New York: Dun and Bradstreet, Inc., Municipal Service Bureau, 1941; also *1930–1944* (1945).	F-29
Boeckh, E. H. and Associates	*Building Costs.* Washington: E. H. Boeckh and Associates, various issues.	R-20
Boulding, K. E.	*A Reconstruction of Economics.* New York: J. Wiley and Sons, Inc., 1950.	p. 201
Bridge, Lawrence	"The Financing of Investment by New Firms," *Conference on Research in Business Finance.* New York: National Bureau of Economic Research, Inc., 1952.	V-43
Brown, Benjamin	*The Brown Book of Life Insurance Economics.* Mass.: B. F. Brown.	I-1

Author	Title	Table or page number
Bullock, C., Williams, J., and Tucker, R.	"The Balance of Trade of the United States, 1789–1919," *The Review of Economic Statistics*. Cambridge, Mass.: Harvard University Press, July 1919.	K-1, K-2
Burns, A. F.	*Production Trends in the United States since 1870.* New York: National Bureau of Economic Research, Inc., 1934.	R-33
Burns, A. F. and Mitchell, W. C.	*Measuring Business Cycles.* New York: National Bureau of Economic Research, Inc., 1946.	pp. 75, 164, 168, 171, 182, 187
Burroughs, R. J.	"The Agricultural Segment of the National Balance Sheet," *Studies in Income and Wealth*, Volume XII. New York: National Bureau of Economic Research, Inc., 1950.	A-1, A-54, A-58, A-59
Canada, Bureau of Statistics	*Canada Yearbook.* Ottawa.	I-4
Canada, Superintendent of Insurance	*Abstract of Statements of Insurance Companies in Canada.* Ottawa, 1947.	I-3
„	*Annual Report.* Ottawa	I-4
Clark, Colin	*The Conditions of Economic Progress.* London: Macmillan and Co., 1951.	p. 67
Clark, Evans, ed.	*The Internal Debts of the United States.* New York: Macmillan Co. for Twentieth Century Fund, 1933.	R-41
Cobren, G. M.	"The Non-Farm Business Inventory Component of National Wealth," *Studies in Income and Wealth*, Volume XII. New York: National Bureau of Economic Research, Inc., 1950.	P-19, P-25, P-26
Colean, M. L.	*American Housing—Problems and Prospects.* New York: Twentieth Century Fund, 1944.	R-25
Commager, H. S.	*The American Mind.* New Haven, Conn.: Yale University Press, 1950.	p. 19
Commercial and Financial Chronicle	New York: William B. Dana Co.	V-12, V-18, V-25, V-45, V-20, V-21, V-22, V-23, V-24, V-34, C-7, R-42, D-16
Connecticut, Bank Commission	*Annual Report of the Superintendent of Banks.*	V-54
Copeland, M. A.	*Concerning a New Federal Financial Statement.* Technical Paper 5. New York: National Bureau of Economic Research, Inc., 1947.	F-25
„	*A Study of Moneyflows in the United States.* New York: National Bureau of Economic Research, Inc., 1952.	U-4
Cowles, Alfred and Associates	*Common Stock Indexes*, 2nd edition. Bloomington, Ind.: Principia Press, Inc., 1939.	D-16, C-9, C-12, C-50, K-6
Dewhurst, J. F. and Associates	*America's Needs and Resources.* New York: Twentieth Century Fund, 1947.	Q-12

1096

Author	Title	Table or page number
Dickens, P. D.	*The Transition Period in American International Financing: 1897–1914.* Washington, D.C.: George Washington University, 1933. Unpublished doctoral dissertation.	K-1, K-2, K-3, K-6 K-7
Dobrovolsky, Sergei	*Corporate Income Retention, 1915–43.* New York: National Bureau of Economic Research, Inc., 1951.	p. 112
Douglas, P. H.	*Real Wages in the U.S. 1890–1926.* Boston and New York: Houghton Mifflin Co., 1930.	A-2, R-5, R-8, R-11, R-18
Dun and Bradstreet	*Statistical Review.* New York: Dun and Bradstreet.	V-43
Dupriez, L. H.	*Des Mouvements Economiques Généraux,* Volume I. Louvain: Institut de Recherches Economiques et Sociales, 1951.	p. 65
Durand, J. D.	*The Labor Force in the U.S., 1890–1960.* New York: Social Science Research Council, 1948.	S-3
Ebersole, J. F., Burr, S., and Peterson, G. M.	"Income Forecasting by the Use of Statistics of Income Data," *The Review of Economic Statistics,* Volume XI. Cambridge, Mass.: Harvard University Press, Nov. 1929.	C-28, C-29, C-31, C-38
Edwards, E. E.	*Urban Real Estate Financing by Savings and Loan Associations.* New York: National Bureau of Economic Research, Inc., preliminary manuscript, 1950.	M-5
Electrical World	New York: McGraw-Hill Co.	V-34, V-41
Ellis, P. W.	*The World's Biggest Business.* New York: National Industrial Conference Board, Inc., 1944.	G-13
Epstein, L. A.	"Consumers' Tangible Assets," *Studies in Income and Wealth,* Volume XII. New York: National Bureau of Economic Research, Inc., 1950.	Q-12
Evans, G. H.	*Business Incorporations in the United States, 1800–1943.* New York: National Bureau of Economic Research, Inc., 1948.	V-43
The Exchange	New York: New York Stock Exchange.	D-10, D-16, V-44
Fisher, E. M.	*Urban Real Estate Markets: Characteristics and Financing.* New York: National Bureau of Economic Research, Inc., 1951.	R-32, R-41
,,	*Real Estate Subdividing Activity and Population in Nine Urban Areas.* Ann Arbor: University of Michigan School of Business Administration, Bureau of Business Research, 1928.	A-15
Fisher, J. A.	"Postwar Changes in Income and Savings among Consumers in Different Age Groups," *Econometrica,* Volume 20. Baltimore, Md.: Waverly Press, Inc., 1952.	p. 214

Author	Title	Table or page number
Fisher, J. A.	*The Economics of an Aging Population: A Study of the Income, Spending and Saving Patterns of Consumer Units in Different Age Groups, 1935–1936, 1945 and 1946.* New York: Columbia University, 1950. Unpublished doctoral dissertation.	p. 214
,,	"Income, Spending and Saving Patterns of Consumer Units in Different Age Groups," *Studies in Income and Wealth*, Volume xv. New York: National Bureau of Economic Research, Inc., 1952.	p. 214
Fraternal Monitor	*Statistics of Fraternal Societies.* Rochester, New York.	I-9, I-10, I-11, I-12
Frederiksen, D. M.	"Mortgage Banking in America," *Journal of Political Economy*, Volume ii. Chicago: University of Chicago Press, March 1894.	R-34, M-20
Friend, Irwin	*Activity in Over-the-Counter Markets.* Philadelphia: University of Pennsylvania Press, 1951.	V-44
Friend, Irwin and Natrella, Vito	*The Volume and Composition of Individuals' Saving.* Preliminary mimeographed version. (Now published as *Individuals' Saving: Volume and Composition*, by Irwin Friend with the assistance of Vito Natrella, John Wiley and Sons, Inc., New York, 1954.)	L-4, L-7, L-10, J-2, J-3, I-11, V-2, V-6, V-11, V-13, V-14, V-16, V-38, V-48, V-50, V-73, D-6, D-10, U-4, K-4, A-33
Garvy, George	"The Role of Dissaving in Economic Analysis," *Journal of Political Economy*, Volume lvi. Chicago: University of Chicago Press, Oct. 1948.	p. 5
Goldsmith, R. W.	"The Growth of Reproducible Wealth of the United States of America from 1805 to 1950," *Income and Wealth of the United States, Series II.* Cambridge, Eng.: Bowes and Bowes, 1952.	F-31, pp. 83, 192, Z-9
,,	"Trends and Structural Changes in Saving in the Twentieth Century," *Saving in the Modern Economy.* Minneapolis: University of Minnesota Press, 1953.	p. 12
,,	"Measuring National Wealth in a System of Social Accounting," *Studies in Income and Wealth*, Volume xii. New York: National Bureau of Economic Research, Inc., 1950.	p. 192
,,	"A Perpetual Inventory of National Wealth," *Studies in Income and Wealth*, Volume xiv. New York: National Bureau of Economic Research, Inc., 1951.	p. 191
Gould, J. M.	*Output and Productivity in the Electric and Gas Utilities, 1899–1942.* New York: National Bureau of Economic Research, Inc., 1946.	L-17
Gray, J. and Terborgh, G. W.	*First Mortgages in Urban Real Estate Finance.* Washington, D. C.: Brookings Institution, 1929.	R-43

Author	Title	Table or page number
Hansen, A. H.	*Business Cycles and National Income.* New York: W. W. Norton and Co., 1951.	p. 171
Hardy, C. O.	*Odd Lot Trading on the New York Stock Exchange.* Washington, D. C.: Brookings Institution, 1939.	V-44
,,	*Tax-Exempt Securities and Surtax.* New York: Macmillan Co., 1926.	G-8, G-17, V-73
Hart, A. G.	*Debts and Recovery: A Study of Changes in the Internal Debt Structure from 1929 to 1937 and a Program for the Future.* New York: Twentieth Century Fund, Committee on Debt Adjustment, 1938.	J-3, J-5, A-65
,,	"Uses of National Wealth Estimates and the Structure of Claims," *Studies in Income and Wealth,* Volume XII. New York: National Bureau of Economic Research, Inc., 1950.	p. 201
Hart, O. H.	*A Study of the Investment Performance of the Eighteen Largest Domestic Life Insurance Companies in Bonds and Stocks, 1929–1949.* New Haven, Conn.: Yale University, 1946. Unpublished doctoral dissertation.	V-53
Hickman, W. Braddock	*The Volume of Corporate Bond Financing since 1900.* Princeton, N. J.: Princeton University Press for National Bureau of Economic Research, Inc., 1953.	V-14, V-15
Hoad, W. M.	*Real Estate Prices.* Ann Arbor: University of Michigan. Unpublished thesis.	R-32
Hollander, Jacob	"Bank Loans and Stock Exchange Speculation," *Publications of National Monetary Commission,* Volume XX, Part V. Washington, D.C.: Government Printing Office, 1911.	V-44
Illinois, Auditor's Office	*Monthly Bulletin, Banking Department.*	L-40, L-41
Indiana, Department of Banking	*Annual Report of Financial Institutions.*	L-40
Institute of Life Insurance	*Life Insurance Fact Book.* New York: Institute of Life Insurance, Statistical Division.	A-10, I-2, I-3, I-8, R-63
,,	*Tally.* New York: Institute of Life Insurance, Statistical Division.	I-8
Iowa, Banking Department	*Report, Des Moines.*	L-40, L-41
Johnson, E. A. and Laird, J.	"Long-term Real Estate Securities," *Journal of Land and Public Utility Economics,* Volume XII. Chicago: A. W. Shaw and Co., Feb. 1936.	R-42
Journal of Commerce	New York: Journal of Commerce Corporation.	V-20, V-22, V-23, V-24, V-34, R-70
Katona, George	*Psychological Analysis of Economic Behavior.* New York: McGraw-Hill Book Co., 1951.	p. 5

Author	Title	Table or page number
Keller, Rev. Edward A.	*A Study of the Physical Assets Sometimes Called Wealth of the United States, 1922–33.* Notre Dame, Ind.: Notre Dame University, Bureau of Economic Research, 1939.	Q-12, R-44
Kendrick, John	"National Productivity and Its Long-Term Projection," *Long-Range Economic Projection:* Studies in Income and Wealth, Volume XVI. Princeton, N.J.: Princeton University Press for National Bureau of Economic Research, Inc., 1954.	p. 67
King, W. I.	*The National Income and Its Purchasing Power.* New York: National Bureau of Economic Research, Inc., 1930.	C-29
Klein, L. R.	"Assets, Debts and Economic Behavior," *Studies in Income and Wealth,* Volume XIV. New York: National Bureau of Economic Research, Inc., 1951.	p. 201
Kolster, Genevieve	"Chicago Real Estate Bonds, 1919–1938," *Journal of Land and Public Utility Economics.* Chicago: A. W. Shaw and Co., Feb. and May 1939.	R-43
Kuvin, Leonard	*Private Long-Term Debt and Interest in the United States.* New York: National Industrial Conference Board, Inc., 1936.	R-34, C-15, C-18, A-61
Kuznets, Simon	*Commodity Flow and Capital Formation.* New York: National Bureau of Economic Research, Inc., 1938.	Q-5, P-5, P-19, P-26, A-17, A-33
,,	"Long-Term Changes in the National Income of the United States of America since 1870," *Income and Wealth of the United States, Series II.* Cambridge, Eng., Bowes and Bowes, 1952.	pp. 67, 87
,,	*National Income and Its Composition, 1919–1938.* New York: National Bureau of Economic Research, Inc., 1941.	C-13, C-17, C-29, C-31, C-33, C-40, P-19, P-23, P-25, P-33, S-3
,,	*National Product since 1869.* New York: National Bureau of Economic Research, Inc., 1946.	R-10, R-13, R-74, R-27, P-11, C-18, C-44, A-1, A-12, p. 85, 87, Z-10
,,	*Secular Movements in Production and Prices.* Boston and New York: Houghton Mifflin Co., 1930.	p. 51
,,	*Shares of Upper Income Groups in Income and Savings.* Occasional Paper No. 35. New York: National Bureau of Economic Research, Inc., 1950.	p. 163
Latimer, M. W.	*Industrial Pension Systems in the United States and Canada.* New York: Industrial Relations Counselors, Inc., 1932.	I-15
Latimer, M. W. and Tufel, Karl	*Trends in Industrial Pensions.* New York: Industrial Relations Counselors, Inc., 1940.	I-15

Author	Title	Table or page number
Leven, M., Moulton, H. G., and Warburton, C.	*America's Capacity to Consume.* Washington, D.C.: Brookings Institution, 1934.	p. 162
Lewis, Cleona	*America's Stake in International Investments.* Washington, D.C.: Brookings Institution, 1938.	M-20, C-50, K-2, K-6, K-7
Lintner, John	*Mutual Savings Banks in the Savings and Mortgage Markets.* Boston: Harvard University, Division of Research, Graduate School of Business Administration, 1948.	J-10, R-61, R-62, M-15, M-24
Livermore, Shaw	"Loans on Securities, 1921–1932," *The Review of Economic Statistics*, Volume xiv. Cambridge, Mass.: Harvard University Press, Nov. 1932.	D-9
Long, Clarence	*Building Cycles and the Theory of Investment.* Princeton, N.J.: Princeton University Press, 1940.	R-22, R-25, R-27, R-31
Lough, W. H.	*High-Level Consumption, Its Behaviour, Its Consequences.* New York: McGraw-Hill Book Co., Inc., 1935.	Q-11
Lutz, F. A.	*Corporate Cash Balances, 1914–43: Manufacturing and Trade.* New York: National Bureau of Economic Research Inc., 1945.	L-14, U-1
Mack, Ruth	"Economics of Consumption," *A Survey of Contemporary Economics*, Volume ii. Homewood, Ill.: R. D. Irwin, 1952.	p. 21
Maisel, S. J.	"Housebuilding in the San Francisco Bay Area," *Journal of Political Economy*, Volume lix. Chicago: University of Chicago Press, Apr. 1951.	R-30
Martin, R. F.	*National Income in the United States, 1799–1938.* New York: National Industrial Conference Board, 1939.	R-21, D-2, C-26, C-31 pp. 87, 109, Z-2, Z-7
Massachusetts, Commissioner of Banks	*Annual Report.*	L-31, L-32, L-35, L-38, L-40, L-41, L-42, J-9, J-11
Massachusetts, Commissioner of Insurance	*Annual Report.*	V-54
Michigan, Banking Department	*Annual Report.*	L-40, L-41
Mills, F. C.	*Economic Tendencies in the U.S.: Aspects of Pre-War and Post-War Changes.* New York: J. J. Little and Ives Co., 1932.	A-30, C-49
Minnesota, Department of Banking	*Annual Report.*	L-40, L-41, V-72
Mitchell, W. C.	*What Happens during Business Cycles: A Progress Report.* New York: National Bureau of Economic Research, Inc., 1951.	pp. 164, 187

Author	Title	Table or page number
Moody's Investors Service, Ltd.	*Moody's Manual of Investments, American and Foreign.* New York: Moody's Investors Service.	I-18, L-15, L-17, L-18, L-20, C-10, V-19, V-22, V-27, V-28, V-30, V-34, V-35, V-36, V-37, V-41, V-60, V-62, V-72, P-22
Morgan, J. N.	"The Structure of Aggregate Personal Saving," *Journal of Political Economy*, Volume LIX. Chicago: University of Chicago Press, Dec. 1951.	pp. 109, 128
Moulton, H. G. and Pasvolsky, Leo	*War Debts and World Prosperity.* Washington, D. C.: Brookings Institution, 1932.	K-1
Muller, J. P.	*Analysis of Financial Statistics.* Washington, D.C.: Bankers Railway Bulletin, 1920–1921.	C-11
Murray, W. G.	*An Economic Analysis of Farm Mortgages in Story County, Iowa 1854–1931.* Research Bulletin No. 156. Ames, Iowa: Agricultural Experiment Station, Iowa State College of Agriculture and Mechanic Arts, 1933.	M-27
National Association of Mutual Savings Banks	*Mutual Savings Bank Earnings.* New York, 1945, 1946, 1947.	L-31, L-32, L-34, L-38
National Board of Fire Underwriters	*Statistics of Fires in American Cities Having a Population of 20,000 and Upward—1928. Report of the Committee on Statistics and Origins of Fires.* New York, 1929.	R-71
National Bureau of Economic Research, Inc.	*Corporate Financial Data for Studies in Business Finance.* New York. Unpublished.	L-16, D-21, D-23, C-42
National Fire Protection Association	"Buildings and Contents Losses," *Quarterly of the National Fire Protection Association.* Hartford, Conn.: National Fire Protection Association, 1938.	R-71
National Industrial Conference Board	*Conference Board Studies in Enterprise and Social Progress.* New York: National Industrial Conference Board, 1939.	A-4
,,	*Employee Stock Purchase Plans in the United States.* New York: National Industrial Conference Board, 1928.	V-42
New York Stock Exchange	*Annual Reports of the President.* New York: New York Stock Exchange.	V-45
New York Stock Exchange Yearbook	New York: New York Stock Exchange, Department of Public Relations.	V-44, V-45, V-47
New York, Superintendent of Insurance	*Annual Report.*	L-21, I-10, I-11, I-12, V-55, V-56, V-58, V-59
Nugent, Rolf	*Consumer Credit and Economic Stability.* New York: Russell Sage Foundation, 1939.	D-3, D-4, D-6

1102

Author	Title	Table or page number
Ohio, Department of Commerce, Division of Banks	*Report.*	L-40, L-41
O'Leary, J. J.	*1949 Record of Life Insurance Investments.* New York: Life Insurance Association of America, 1949.	I-6
Persons, Charles	"Credit Expansion, 1920 to 1929 and Its Lessons," *Quarterly Journal of Economics*, Volume XLV. Cambridge, Mass.: Harvard University Press, Nov. 1930.	R-41
Persons, W. M.	*Forecasting Business Cycles.* New York: J. Wiley and Sons, Inc., 1931.	A-4, C-26, D-2
Pogue, Joseph and Cocqueron, Frederick	*Financial Analysis of Thirty Oil Companies.* New York: Chase National Bank, Petroleum Department.	C-48
Poor, H. U. and H. W.	*Poor's Manual of Railroads.* New York: H. U. and H. W. Poor.	V-27, V-28
Poor's Railroad Manual Company	*Poor's Manual of Public Utilities: Street Railway, Gas, Electric, Water, Power, Telephone and Telegraph Companies.* 1st–6th annual numbers. New York: Poor's Railroad Manual Company, 1913–1918.	V-34
Reeve, J. and Associates	"Government Component in the National Wealth," *Studies in Income and Wealth*, Volume XII. New York: National Bureau of Economic Research, Inc., 1950.	L-3, F-31
Reuss, L. A.	"Land Utilization Data as Background Information for the National Balance Sheet and Approximations of the Value of Forest Land," *Studies in Income and Wealth*, Volume XII. New York: National Bureau of Economic Research, Inc., 1950.	A-15
Rhode Island, Bank Commissioner	*Annual Report Showing the Condition of State Banks, Savings Banks, Trust Companies and Loan and Investment Companies.*	L-40, L-41
Ripley, W. Z.	*Railroads: Finance and Organization.* New York: Longmans, Green and Co., 1915.	V-28
Rollins, Montgomery	*Convertible Securities.* 2nd edition, revised and enlarged. Boston: Financial Publishing Co., 1913.	V-28
Rose, D. C.	*A Scientific Approach to Investment Management.* New York: Harper and Bros., 1928.	V-55, V-56
Sammons, R. L.	"Foreign Investment Aspects of Measuring National Wealth," *Studies in Income and Wealth*, Volume XII. New York: National Bureau of Economic Research, Inc., 1950.	K-6, K-7
Sanders, T. H.	*Effects of Taxation on Executives.* Boston: Harvard University, Division of Research, Graduate School of Business Administration, 1951.	p. 18

Author	Title	Table or page number
Schwartz, Anna and Oliver, Elma	*Currency Held by the Public, the Banks and the Treasury: Monthly, Dec. 1917–Dec. 1944.* Technical Paper No. 4. New York: National Bureau of Economic Research, Inc., 1947.	L-2
Seltzer, L. H.	*The Nature and Tax Treatment of Capital Gains and Losses.* New York: National Bureau of Economic Research, Inc., 1951.	C-40
Shapiro, S.	"The Distribution of Deposits and Currency in the United States, 1929–1939," *Journal of the American Statistical Association*, Volume XXXVIII. Menasha, Wisc.: American Statistical Association, Dec. 1943.	L-12, U-1
Shaw, W. H.	*Value of Commodity Output since 1869.* New York: National Bureau of Economic Research, Inc., 1947.	A-17, A-30, P-5, P-10, P-13, Q-5, Q-16
Simon, H. H., Shephard, R. W., and Sharp, F. W.	*Fire Losses and Fire Risks.* Berkeley, Calif.: University of California, Bureau of Public Administration, 1943.	R-71
Smith, D. H. and Betters, P. V.	*The United States Shipping Board. Service Monograph of the U.S. Government,* No. 63. Washington, D.C.: Brookings Institution, 1931.	F-11
Smith, T. H.	*Marketing Used Automobiles.* Columbus, Ohio: Ohio State University, Bureau of Business Research, 1941.	P-15
Snyder, Carl	*Business Cycles and Business Measurements: Studies in Quantitative Economics.* New York: Macmillan Co., 1927.	A-4, D-2
Sparks, E. S.	*History and Theory of Agricultural Credit in the United States.* New York: Thomas Y. Crowell Co., 1932.	M-9
Spectator Company	*Compendium of Official Life Insurance Reports.* New York: Spectator Co.	I-5
,,	*The Spectator Insurance Yearbook.* Philadelphia: Spectator Co.	V-36, V-37, V-55, V-56, C-38, R-70, I-1, I-2, I-3, I-5, I-6, I-8, I-10, I-14
Spengler, Joseph	"Population Movements and Investments," *Journal of Finance*, Volume VI. Chicago: American Finance Association, Dec. 1951.	p. 19
Stalson, J. O.	*Marketing Life Insurance; Its History in America.* Cambridge, Mass.: Harvard University Press, 1942.	I-3
Stevens' Valuation Quarterly	Chicago: Marshall and Stevens, Jan. 1949.	R-20, R-22, P-10, A-30, C-49
Studenski, Paul	"Methods of Estimating National Income in Soviet Russia," *Studies in Income and Wealth*, Volume VIII. New York: National Bureau of Economic Research, Inc., 1946.	p. 35

Author	Title	Table or page number
Thompson, W. S. and Whelpton, P. K.	*Population Trends in the United States.* New York: McGraw-Hill Book Co., Inc., 1933.	R-21, S-3
United States Savings and Loan League	*Savings and Loan Annals.* Chicago: United States Savings and Loan League.	J-2, J-5, J-7
Wall Street Journal	New York: J. Hillyer.	R-41
Warren, G. F. and Pearson, F. H.	*Gold and Prices.* New York: J. Wiley and Sons, Inc., 1935.	F-11, R-20, R-22, G-1, A-9, A-12, A-30, Q-15
Wenzlick, Roy and Company	*Real Estate Analyst.* St. Louis: Roy Wenzlick and Co.	R-32
Wickens, D. L.	*Residential Real Estate: Its Economic Position as Shown by Values, Rents, Family Incomes, Financing, and Construction, Together with Estimates for All Real Estate.* New York: National Bureau of Economic Research, Inc., 1941.	R-35, R-36, R-38, R-40
Williams, John	"The Balance of International Payments of the United States for the Year 1920," *The Review of Economic Statistics*, Supplement 1. Cambridge, Mass.: Harvard University Committee on Economic Research, Statistical Service, June 1921.	K-1

1105

All United States Government publications are published by the Government Printing Office, Washington 25, D.C., unless it is otherwise stated. Listing is alphabetical, but words such as Department, Bureau, and Office are ignored.

Author	Title	Table or page number
Department of Agriculture	*Agricultural Statistics.*	A-12, A-13, A-14, A-33, A-34, A-35, A-41, A-44, A-45, A-55, A-62, A-64, F-28, M-28
,,	*Yearbook of the U.S. Department of Agriculture.*	A-12, A-42
Bureau of Agricultural Economics	*Agricultural Finance Review.*	A-10, A-53, A-58, A-59, A-62, A-63, A-64
,,	*Agricultural Finance Review, Supplement,* May 1950.	A-12, A-53, R-70
,,	*Agricultural Outlook.*	A-12
,,	*Agricultural Prices; Prices Received and Paid by Farmers and Parity Prices.*	A-30, A-34, A-35, A-44
,,	*The Balance Sheet of Agriculture.*	A-13, A-14, A-31, A-35, A-45, A-53, A-54, A-55, A-56, A-59, V-3
,,	*Corn Statistics, Statistical Bulletin No. 28.* 1941.	A-33
,,	*Crops and Markets,* Volume 25 and 26. Jan. 1948 and Jan. 1949.	A-34, A-35
,,	*Crop Production.*	A-33, A-35
,,	*Current Developments in the Farm Real Estate Market.*	M-28, A-2
,,	*Farm Income Situation.*	A-5, A-8, A-16, A-32
,,	*Farm Production and Disposition of Chickens and Eggs, 1909–1924* and *1925–1937.*	A-41, A-42
,,	*Farm Production, Disposition and Income: Turkeys, 1929–1939.* Apr. 1942.	A-41
,,	*The Farm Real Estate Situation, 1945–1946.* Circular No. 754. 1947.	A-12
,,	*The Feed Situation.*	A-33

Author	Title	Table or page number
Department of Agriculture, Bureau of Agricultural Economics	*Impact of the War on the Financial Structure of Agriculture.* Misc. Publication No. 567. 1944.	A-56
,,	*Income Parity for Agriculture,* Part I: *Farm Income,* Section 2: *Income from Tobacco.* May 1933. Preliminary.	A-33, A-34
,,	*Income Parity for Agriculture,* Part I: *Farm Income,* Section 6: *Income from Sheep and Lambs, Wool and Mohair, 1909–1938.* March 1939.	A-44, A-45
,,	*Income Parity for Agriculture,* Part II: *Expenses of Agricultural Production,* Section 3: *Purchases, Depreciation and Value of Farm Automobiles, Motortrucks, Tractors and Other Farm Machinery, 1910–1939.* 1940.	A-17, A-18, A-19, A-24, A-30, P-5
,,	*Income Parity for Agriculture,* Part II: *Expenses of Agricultural Production,* Section 5: *Expenditures for and Depreciation of Permanent Improvements on Farms, 1910–1940.* March 1941.	A-7, A-30
,,	*Income Parity for Agriculture,* Part V: *Population, Farms, and Farmers,* Section I: *Farm Population, Non-farm Population and Number of Farms in the United States, 1910–1939.* Dec. 1939.	A-55
,,	*Income Parity for Agriculture,* Part VI: *State Estimates of Income and Production Expenses.* Oct. 1945.	A-56
,,	*Livestock on Farms, January 1, 1867–1935.* Jan. 1935.	A-41, A-44
,,	*Livestock on Farms, January 1, 1948* and *January 1, 1951.*	A-41, A-44, A-45
,,	*Meat Animals, Farm Production and Income, 1924–1944. Revised Estimates by States.* 1947.	A-41
,,	*Prices Received by Farmers for Crops, Livestock and Livestock Products, 1909–1945.* Reprinted from *Crops and Markets,* as revised, 1946.	A-34, A-35
,,	*Revised Estimates of Stocks on Farms.* July 1947.	A-33
,,	*Stocks of Feed Grains.*	A-33
,,	*Stocks of Wheat and Rye.*	A-33
,,	*Wheat and Rye Statistics.* Statistical Bulletin No. 12. 1941.	A-33
Farm Credit Administration	*Annual Report.*	V-77
,,	*Combined Statements of the Federal Land Banks.*	V-78, A-60
,,	*Farm Credit Quarterly.*	M-2
,,	*A Statistical Handbook of Farmers' Cooperatives.* Bulletin No. 26, Nov. 1938.	A-59

Author	Title	Table or page number
Farm Credit Administration and Federal Deposit Insurance Corporation	*Annual Report of Operations of Federal Credit Unions.*	L-40, L-41, L-42
Botts, R. R. and Houseman, E. E.	*Method of Estimating Farm Fire Losses in the United States.* Department of Agriculture, Bureau of Agricultural Economics, July 1948.	A-50, R-70
Cooper, M., Barton, G. T., and Brodel, A. P.	*Progress of Farm Mechanization.* Misc. Publication No. 630, Department of Agriculture, Bureau of Agricultural Economics, Oct. 1947.	p. 100
Horton, D. C.	*Regional Variations in the Sources and in the Tenure Distribution of Farm Mortgage Credit Outstanding, January 1, 1935.* Department of Agriculture, Bureau of Agricultural Economics, Feb. 1938.	L-30
Horton, D. C., Larsen, H. C., and Wall, N. J.	*Farm Mortgage Credit Facilities in the U.S.* Misc. Publication No. 478, Department of Agriculture, Bureau of Agricultural Economics, 1942.	A-61
Inman, B. T., and Fippin, W. H.	*Farm Land Ownership in the United States.* Department of Agriculture, Bureau of Agricultural Economics, 1949.	A-14
Larsen, H. C.	*Distribution by Lender Groups of Farm Mortgage and Real Estate Holdings, January 1, 1930–1945.* Department of Agriculture, Bureau of Agricultural Economics, 1945.	A-61
Strauss, F. and Bean, L.	*Gross Farm Income and Indices of Farm Production and Prices in the U.S. 1869–1937.* Technical Bulletin No. 703, Department of Agriculture, Dec. 1940.	A-4, A-7, A-35, A-42, A-43, p. 100
Turner, H. A.	*The Ownership of Tenant Farms in the United States.* Bulletin No. 1432, Department of Agriculture, 1926.	A-14
Wall, N. J.	*Demand Deposits of Country Banks.* Technical Bulletin No. 575, Department of Agriculture, Aug. 1937.	A-56
,,	*Outstanding Farm Mortgage Loans of Leading Lending Agencies.* Department of Agriculture, Bureau of Agricultural Economics, 1937.	A-61
Wanstall, Grace	*Statistics of Farmers' Marketing and Purchasing Cooperatives, 1945–1946.* Misc. Bulletin No. 119, Department of Agriculture, Farm Credit Administration, June 1948.	A-59
Wickens, D. L.	*Farm Mortgage Credit.* Technical Bulletin No. 288, Department of Agriculture, Feb. 1932.	M-27, M-28
Bureau of the Budget	*Budget of the United States Government.*	F-2, F-31
Department of Commerce, Bureau of the Census	*Abstract of the Census of Manufacturers, 1914.* 1917.	C-16

Author	Title	Table or page number
Department of Commerce, Bureau of the Census	*Census of Agriculture*.	A-1, A-5, A-12, A-13, A-14, A-42, A-50, A-57
,,	*Census of Electrical Industries*. (Title varies.)	C-5, C-6, C-21, C-22, C-23, C-24, C-44, A-59, L-17, L-20, V-17, V-31, V-32, V-33, V-34
,,	*Census of Housing*.	R-15, R-23, R-25, R-33, R-36, R-37, R-38, R-39, R-40
,,	*Census of Manufactures*.	A-17, C-14, C-15, C-16, L-15, L-16
,,	*Census of Mines and Quarries*.	C-16, C-18, C-19, R-33
,,	*Census of Religious Bodies*.	R-44
,,	*Census of Business*.	D-6
,,	*City Finances*.	G-2, G-3, G-4, G-5, G-11
,,	*Financial Statistics of Cities*.	G-2, G-4, G-6, G-7, G-8, G-9, G-10, G-11, G-13, G-15, G-21
,,	*Financial Statistics of States*.	G-13, G-15, G-16, G-17, G-21
,,	*Governmental Debt in the United States*.	G-10, G-17, G-21
,,	*Governmental Finances in the United States*.	G-2, G-3, G-4, G-5
,,	*Governmental Revenue*.	G-3
,,	*Historical Review of State and Local Government Finances*. State and Local Government Special Study No. 25. 1948.	G-2, G-3, G-4, G-5, G-21, G-13
,,	*Historical Statistics of the U.S. 1789–1945*. 1949.	V-2, V-44, R-15, R-27, R-33, R-36, R-70, D-16, M-28, F-2, F-26, F-28, C-47, F-29, G-20, G-21, A-13, A-14, A-15, A-62, A-64, A-65, p. 106, Z-1, Z-2, S-3
,,	*Large City Finances*.	G-5, G-6, G-11
,,	*Mineral Industries, 1939. General Summary and Industry Statistics*. Volume I. 1944.	C-16

Author	Title	Table or page number
Department of Commerce, Bureau of the Census	*Retirement Systems for State and Local Government Employees: 1941.* State and Local Government Study No. 17. 1943.	G-19, G-11
,,	*State Finances.*	G-3, G-13, G-14, G-15, G-16, G-17, G-18
,,	*State Tax Collections in 1950.*	G-14
,,	*Statistical Abstract of the United States.*	A-4, A-9, A-15, A-55, A-59, A-12, C-47, C-48, D-2, D-4, F-4, F-26, J-2, K-1, K-3, Q-13, R-15, R-33, F-30, R-70, R-72, V-2, V-5, I-8, M-28, pp. 106, 222, Z-1, Z-2, S-3
,,	*Total Estimated Value and Total Monthly Rent of Dwelling Units for U.S. by Region, Urban and and Rural, 1940.* Release Series H 1943 No. 1, Sept. 11, 1943.	R-36
,,	*Wealth, Debt and Taxation,* 1907.	G-2, G-4, G-9, G-10, G-13, G-15, G-16, G-17, G-21
,,	*Eleventh Census of the United States, 1890. Report on Real Estate Mortgages in the United States.* Volume XII. 1895.	R-34
,,	*Thirteenth Census of the United States, 1909.* Volume XI.	C-16
,,	*Fourteenth Census of the United States, 1919.* Volume XI.	C-16
,,	*Fifteenth Census of the United States, 1930.* Volume XI.	C-16
Bureau of Foreign and Domestic Commerce	*The Balance of International Payments of the United States.*	C-51, K-1, K-2, K-3, K-4
,,	*Construction and Construction Materials, Industry Report, Statistical Supplement, Volume and Costs.*	G-6, G-15, F-16, A-7, R-4, R-10, R-13, R-16, R-20, R-25, R-28, R-33
,,	*Foreign Investments in the United States.*	K-2, K-6
,,	*Handbook of American Underwriting of Foreign Securities.* 1930.	K-3
,,	*International Transactions of the United States during the War, 1940–1945.* 1948.	K-1, K-2, K-3
,,	*Monthly Summary of Foreign Commerce.*	K-1

Author	Title	Table or page number
Department of Commerce, Bureau of Foreign and Domestic Commerce	*National Income, July 1947. A Supplement to the Survey of Current Business.*	A-32, C-34, C-36, F-22, F-26, F-29, G-19, G-20, Q-13, Q-14, Q-16, P-5, P-19, R-33, R-34, U-4, U-8, U-9, R-44
,,	*National Income, 1951. A Supplement to the Survey of Current Business.*	U-4, p. 164
,,	*Oversea Travel and Travel Expenditures in the Balance of International Payments of the U.S. 1919–1938.* Economic Series, No. 4. 1939.	K-1
,,	*Statistical Supplement to the Survey of Current Business.*	V-31, V-43, V-44, V-45
,,	*Survey of Current Business.*	I-8, C-51, G-19, G-21, K-1, K-2, K-3, P-10, Q-16, R-24, R-29, R-35, U-8, U-10, U-4, V-43, F-30, Z-7
,,	*Survey of Current Business,* July 1948, July 1949, and July 1950, *National Income Number.*	A-32, C-1, C-33, C-36, C-38, C-41, C-49, F-22, F-26, F-29, G-19, G-20, P-19, U-7, Q-5, Q-13
,,	*The United States in the World Economy, 1919–1939.* 1943.	C-50, K-1, K-2, K-3, K-7
Bureau of Labor	*Bulletin.*	G-1, G-6, G-8, G-9, G-10, G-13
Horton, D. C.	*Long-Term Debt in the United States.* Department of Commerce, Bureau of Foreign and Domestic Commerce, 1937.	R-34, R-41
Bureau of Education, Statistical Division	*Biennial Survey of Education.*	R-44
Federal Communications Commission	*Report on the American Telephone and Telegraph Company. Corporate Financial History.* 1935.	V-29, V-30
,,	*Statistics of Communications Industry in the U.S.*	C-33, V-30

Author	Title	Table or page number
Federal Deposit Insurance Corporation	*Annual Report of the Federal Deposit Insurance Corporation.*	L-5, L-6, L-8, L-23, L-24, L-26, L-33, L-37, V-74, R-55, D-8, D-9, A-61
,,	*Assets and Liabilities of Operating Insured Banks.*	L-26, L-32, L-33, R-54, V-74
Federal Home Loan Bank Administration	*Annual Report of Federal Home Loan Bank Administration.*	R-54, J-11
,,	*Federal Home Loan Bank Review.* June 1935.	M-25
Federal Intermediate Credit Banks	*Annual Report.*	F-14, F-24
Federal Power Commission	*Statistics of Electrical Utilities in the U.S.*	C-33, V-33, V-34
Federal Reserve System, Board of Governors	*Annual Reports of the Board of Governors of the Federal Reserve System.*	C-37, K-3
,,	*Banking and Monetary Statistics.* Washington: National Capital Press, Nov. 1943.	A-10, A-65, C-25, C-37, C-39, D-8, D-9, D-10, D-12, F-19, F-23, F-24, F-7, F-27, K-1, K-2, K-3, K-4, L-2, L-4, L-5, L-6, L-8, L-23, L-24, L-26, L-28, L-43, R-54, R-55, V-4, V-48, V-50, V-59, V-74, G-8
,,	*Federal Reserve Bulletin.*	A-65, D-4, D-8, D-9, D-12, C-37, F-27, G-8, K-1, K-2, K-4, F-24, L-2, L-4, L-5, L-6, L-8, L-24, L-26, L-41, L-43, R-32, R-36, R-40, V-35, V-48, V-74, U-1, U-5, U-7, U-8, C-46, D-14, D-15, pp. 5, 6, 18, 129, 130, 163, 206, 216, 217, 222

Author	Title	Table or page number
Federal Trade Commission	*Investigation of the Telephone Industry in the United States. Report of the Federal Communications Commission on the Investigation of the Telephone Industry in the United States. Made pursuant to Public Resolution No. 8., 74th Congress. 1939.*	I-18
Home Owners' Loan Corporation	*Annual Report.*	M-21, M-22
Housing and Home Finance Agency, Office of the Administrator	*Second Annual Report. 1949.*	M-21
	The Housing Situation. The Factual Background. June 1948.	R-24
Office of Housing Economics	*Housing Statistics Handbook. 1948.*	R-23, R-24
Home Loan Bank Board	*Combined Financial Statements, Members of the Federal Home Loan Bank System, 1948 and 1949.*	J-5, J-8, J-11
,,	*Home Loan Bank Review, Statistical Supplement. 1947.*	J-4, J-5
,,	*Mortgage Investments of Life Insurance Companies, 1949. June 13, 1950.*	R-63, M-16
,,	*Mortgage and Real Estate Investments of Life Insurance Companies, 1947. July 6, 1948.*	R-63, M-16
,,	*Report of Home Loan Bank Board for the Year Ending December 31, 1949. 1950.*	J-2, J-5
,,	*Safeguarding the Nation's Homes.* New York: Rodgers, Kellogg, Stillson Co., 1936.	J-10
,,	*Statistical Summary.*	R-34, R-37, R-54, R-61, M-9, M-13, M-15, M-16, M-22, M-23, J-2, J-3, J-4, J-5, M-8, p. 197
,,	*Trends in the Savings and Loan Field.*	J-2, J-3, J-4, J-5
Bureau of Immigration	*Annual Report of the Commissioner General of Immigration.*	K-1
Department of the Interior, Bureau of Mines	*Mineral Resources of the United States.*	R-33
,,	*Minerals Yearbook*	R-33, C-46
Interstate Commerce Commission, Bureau of Transport Economics and Statistics	*Annual Report on the Statistics of Railways in the United States.*	L-13, L-17, L-19, L-20, V-12, V-26, V-27, P-24, V-28, C-7, C-8, C-33, C-35, C-44
,,	*Receivership and Trusteeships, 1894–1942.* Statement 4341.	V-27

Author	Title	Table or page number
Interstate Commerce Commission, Bureau of Valuation, Engineering Section	*Railroad Construction Indices.* Aug. 1, 1950.	P-10
Locklin, D. P.	*Statistical Analysis of 31 Reorganizations of Class I Railways, 1914–1933.* Washington, D.C.: Interstate Commerce Commission, Bureau of Statistics, 1934.	V-27
Stevens, W. H. S. and Hobbs, E. S.	*Analysis of Steam Railway Dividends, 1890–1941.* Statement 4368, Interstate Commerce Commission, Bureau of Transport Economics and Statistics, Nov. 1943.	V-28, C-8, C-35
Department of Labor, Bureau of Labor Statistics	*Consumers' Cooperatives and Credit Unions: Operations in 1946.* Bulletin No. 922, 1948.	L-41, L-42
,,	*Handbook of Labor Statistics, 1947.* Bulletin No. 916.	A-2, C-49
,,	*Monthly Labor Review.*	R-30, A-2
,,	"Operations of Credit Unions in 194.," *Monthly Labor Review,* Sept. 1949 and Sept. 1950.	L-41
,,	*New Housing in Metropolitan Areas, 1949–1951.* Bulletin No. 115, Sept. 1952.	R-30
,,	*Release No. 4924.* Mimeographed.	V-43
,,	*Release No. 5812.* Mimeographed.	V-43
Berman, Edward	*Massachusetts System of Savings Bank Life Insurance.* Bulletin No. 615, Department of Labor, Bureau of Labor Statistics, 1935.	V-54
,,	*Operation of Savings Bank Life Insurance in Massachusetts and New York.* Bulletin 688, Department of Labor, Bureau of Labor Statistics, 1931.	V-54
Schumm, G. A.	*Construction Industry in the United States.* Bulletin 786, Department of Labor, Bureau of Labor Statistics, 1944.	R-25
National Resources Committee	*The Structure of the American Economy.* 1939–1940.	P-11
Chawner, Lowell	*Residential Building. Housing Monograph Series No. 1.* National Resources Committee, Industrial Committee, 1939.	R-25
National Resources Planning Board	*Family Expenditures in the United States.* 1941.	p. 162
Panama Railroad Company	*Annual Reports of the Board of Directors of the Panama Railroad Company to the Stockholders for the Fiscal Year Ending June 30.* New York: Martin B. Brown Co.	F-4, F-6

Author	Title	Table or page number
Securities and Exchange Commission	*Annual Report.*	V-44
,,	*Investment Trusts and Investment Companies. Report of the Securities and Exchange Commission Pursuant to Section 30 of the Public Utility Holding Act of 1935.* 1939 and 1940.	V-38, V-39, V-40, V-60, V-61, V-62, V-63, V-65, V-67, V-69, V-70, V-72, M-19
,,	*Statistical Bulletin.*	V-38, V-39, V-44, V-60, V-61, V-62, p. 164
,,	*Survey Series No. 141.* November 26, 1948.	D-14, D-15
,,	"Working Capital of U.S. Corporations," *Statistical Series Release.*	F-17, F-21
Temporary National Economic Committee	*Verbatim Record of the Proceedings of the Temporary National Economic Committee.* Washington, D. C.: Bureau of National Affairs, 1939–1941.	R-63, M-16, M-24
Department of the Treasury, Division of Bookkeeping and Warrants	*Statement of Balances, Appropriations and Expenditures of the Government for the Fiscal Year Ended June 30.*	F-8, F-10
,,	*Combined Statement of Receipts and Disbursements of the United States.* (Title varies slightly from year to year.)	F-2, F-3, F-8, F-10, F-11, F-21
Office of the Comptroller of the Currency	*Annual Report of the Comptroller of the Currency.*	D-8, D-9, V-54, V-74, V-76, L-2, L-4, L-5, L-6, L-8, L-23, L-24, L-28, L-29, L-30, L-31, L-38, L-42
Committee on Inter-governmental Fiscal Relations	*Federal, State and Local Government Fiscal Relations,* 1943.	G-21
Bureau of Internal Revenue	*Bulletin "F." Income Tax Depreciation and Obsolescence; Estimated Useful Lives and Depreciation Rates.* Revised, Jan. 1942.	Q-12, P-7
,,	*Press Service No. S-1051, No. S-1057, No. S-2449, No. S-2808.*	D-13, D-14, D-15, C-32
,,	*Statistics of Income.*	L-13, L-16, L-17, L-20, L-21, L-22, V-17, V-43, V-73, R-69, D-6, M-20, U-4, U-8, U-9, U-10, P-11, C-13, C-14, C-15, C-17,

Author	Title	Table or page number
Department of the Treasury, Bureau of Internal Revenue	*Statistics of Income.*	C-18, C-26, C-28, C-29, C-31, C-32, C-34, C-33, C-39, C-40, C-42, C-43, C-46, C-50, C-36, C-38, p. 6, Z-2, Z-7
,,	*Statistics of Income, Source Book.*	V-37, L-22, V-36, V-35, C-33, C-38, D-13, A-54
Bureau of the Mint	*Annual Report.*	K-1, K-3
Office of the Secretary of the Treasury	*Annual Report of the Secretary of the Treasury on the State of Finances.*	F-7, F-9, F-13, F-14, F-11, F-21, F-23, F-24, F-25, F-27, K-3, V-2, V-11, V-49, G-8
,,	*Census of American-Owned Assets in Foreign Countries. 1947.*	K-7
,,	*Census of Foreign-Owned Assets in the United States. 1945.*	L-7, K-4
,,	*Daily Statement of the United States Treasury.*	V-5, V-11, V-49, L-2, R-55, M-8, M-9, F-3, F-5, F-7, F-10, F-11, F-13, F-14, F-17, F-18, F-19, F-20, F-21, F-22, F-23, F-24,
,,	*Treasury Bulletin.*	F-17, F-19, F-23, F-24, F-25, F-27, K-2, K-3, K-4, K-6, V-2, V-6, V-23, D-1
U.S. Congress, House of Representatives	*High Cost of Housing.* House Document 647. 80th Congress, 29th Session. 1948.	R-32
,,	*House Resolution 119.* Sept. 1944. Mimeographed.	M-24
,,	*Report of the Special Commissioner of Revenue, 1869* (David Wells) House Document 27. 41st Congress, 2nd Session.	p. 83
,,	*Report of the Joint Commission of Agricultural Inquiry.* Hearings before the Joint Commission of Agricultural Inquiry, Volume II. 67th Congress, 1st Session. 1922.	L-23
,,	*Special Depletion Allowances for Mineral Properties.* Exhibit 2 to accompany statement of Secretary Snyder before the Committee on Ways and Means, House of Representatives, Feb. 3, 1950.	C-16, C-48

1116

Author	Title	Table or page number
U.S. Congress, Senate	*Financial Statements of Certain Government Agencies.* Senate Document 172, Part 2. 76th Congress, 3rd Session. Feb. 15, 1940.	F-4, F-6, F-14
,,	*Operation of the National and Federal Reserve Banking Systems.* Hearings before a Subcommittee of the Committee on Banking and Currency. 71st Congress, 3rd Session.	D-8
,,	*Special Report from the Banks of the United States.* Prepared by the National Monetary Commission. Senate Document No. 225. 61st Congress, 2nd Session. Apr. 28, 1909.	L-23, L-38, V-74, A-56
,,	*Stock Exchange Practices.* Hearings before the Committee on Banking and Currency. 73rd Congress, 2nd Session. 1934.	V-44, V-46, D-8
,,	*Taxation and Tax Exemption.* Senate Document 148. 68th Congress, 1st Session. 1923.	V-73
U.S. Housing Corporation	*War Emergency Construction.*	F-4, F-6
U.S. Shipping Board	*Annual Report of U.S. Shipping Board with Financial Statement for U.S. Emergency Fleet Corporation* as of October 31, 1917 and June 30, 1918–1930.	F-4, F-6
War Finance Corporation	*Annual Reports, with Financial Statements,* as of November 30, 1918–1930.	F-4, F-6, F-11
War Production Board	*Facts for Industry.*	F-14
,,	*Industrial Mobilization for War.*	F-31
World War Foreign Debt Commission	*Combined Annual Reports of the World War Foreign Debt Commission, with Additional Information Regarding Foreign Debts Due United States, Fiscal Years 1922, 1923, 1924, 1925 and 1926.*	K-3

INDEX TO INTRODUCTION

References to tables are indicated by a "t" following the page number,
those to charts by a "c" following the page number.

1119

INDEX TO TABLES OF ANNUAL ESTIMATES OF SAVING

Cash (*continued*):

    Postal Savings System, L–43

    savings and loan associations, J–2, J–6

    security brokers an dealers, D–13

    state governments, G–17

    unincorporated business, U–1

  personal saving through, T–6

  see also Currency, Deposits

Casualty and miscellaneous insurance companies:

  assets of, by type, V–56

  common stock holdings of, V–52

  corporate and foreign bond holdings of, V–50

  mortgage holdings of, by type of property, M–3, M–8, M–18

  nonfarm real estate holdings of, R–46 to R–53, R–66

  preferred stock holdings of, V–51

  state and local government bond holdings of, V–50

  stock—

    cash issues of, V–19, V–37

    net purchases and sales of, V–57 to V–59

  U.S. Government bond holdings of, V–49

Commercial banks, closed:

  assets of, by type, V–76

  common stock holdings of, V–52

  corporate and foreign bond holdings of, V–50

  deposits in, L–8

    by type of holder, L–9, L–10

  farm mortgage holdings of, A–61

  farm real estate holdings of, A–10, A–11

  losses of, on real estate, R–59

  mortgage holdings of, by type of property, M–14

  nonfarm individuals' saving through deposits of, L–1

  nonfarm mortgage holdings of, M–8

  nonfarm real estate holdings of, by type of real estate, R–46 to R–53, R–60

  real estate holdings of, by type, R–58

  state and local government bond holdings of, V–49

  U.S. Government bond holdings of, V–48

Commercial banks, operating:

  assets of, by type, L–24, L–25

  capital gains and losses of, R–45, R–57

    by type of security, V–75

  common stock—

    cash issues of, V–35

    changes in holdings of, V–52

  consumer credit extended by, D–4

  corporate and foreign bond holdings of, V–50

  demand deposit liabilities of, L–4

    by type of holder, L–5

Commercial banks, operating (*continued*):

  dividend payments by, C–6, C–25

  earnings of, C–5, C–25

  farm mortgage holdings of, A–61

  farm real estate holdings of, A–10, A–11

  foreign deposit liabilities of, L–7

  individuals' saving through common stock issues of, V–19

  interest paid on deposits by, L–23

  loans made by, non-real estate, A–62, A–63, L–25

  loans made by, real estate, L–24, M–13

  loans to unincorporated business by, U–5

  nonfarm individuals' saving through deposits of, L–1

  nonfarm mortgage holdings of, M–3, M–8

    by type of real estate, R–37, R–38, M–4 to M–11

  nonfarm real estate holdings of, by type of real estate, R–46, R–47 to R–53

  real estate holdings of, by type, R–54

  saving by, C–4, C–25

  saving through deposits of, T–6, T–8, T–10

  security holdings of, by type, V–74

  state and local government bond holdings of, V–49

  step-up ratios for insured commercial banks, L–26

  U.S. Government bond holdings of, V–48

Commercial and industrial buildings:

  construction cost index, R–20

  holdings of, by type of institution, R–49, R–53 R–54, R–58, R–61, R–63, R–65, R–66

  individuals' saving connected with foreclosure on, R–45

  individuals' share in total holdings of, R–29

  unincorporated business saving through, R–1, R–2, R–10 to R–13

Commissions:

  earned by dealers—

    on farm real estate transfers, A–1 to A–3, A–12, A–66

    on individuals' stock transactions, V–1, V–44, V–46

    on nonfarm real estate transfers, R–32

Commodity Credit Corporation:

  crop inventories stored under loans of, A–40

  obligations of, V–5

Consumer durables:

  agricultural—

    depreciation on, A–26 to A–28

    expenditures on, A–24, A–25

    saving through, A–1 to A–3, A–21 to A–23, A–29, A–66

1131

Federal government corporations and agencies:
  assets of, F-4, F-14
  demand deposit holdings of, L-5
  liabilities of, F-6, F-20
  not fully guaranteed obligations of, V-5
Federal government trust funds:
  individuals' equity in, F-9, F-23, F-24
  state and local government bond holdings of,
    V-49
  U.S. Government bond holdings of, V-48
  veterans' funds, individuals' equity in, F-25,
    F-28
Federal Home Loan Bank Board, obligations of,
    V-5
Federal Home Loan Banks:
  advances to savings and loan associations by,
    J-5
  stock of, held by savings and loan associations,
    J-2
Federal Intermediate Credit Banks:
  non-real estate loans to farmers of, A-62
  obligations of, V-5
Federal land banks:
  assets and liabilities of, by type, V-78
  bond issues of, V-14
  corporate bond holdings of, V-50
  farm mortgage holdings of, A-61
  farm real estate holdings of, A-10, A-11
  farmers' equity in, A-60
  U.S. Government bond holdings of, V-48
Federal National Mortgage Association:
  nonfarm mortgage holdings of, M-8, M-9
Federal Reserve banks:
  corporate and foreign bond holdings of, V-50
  saving by, C-37
  stock of, held by commercial banks, V-74
  Treasury deposits with, F-3, F-13
  U.S. Government bond holdings of, V-48
Fire losses:
  agricultural, R-70
    by type, A-50
  agricultural saving adjusted for, A-1 to A-3,
    A-51, A-52
  nonfarm, R-70
    by type, R-71
  on consumer durables, saving adjusted for,
    Q-15
  on dwellings, saving adjusted for, R-72
  on nonresidential buildings, saving adjusted
    for, R-73
  on producer durables, saving adjusted for, P-18
Fire and marine insurance companies:
  assets of, by type, V-55
  cash holdings of, L-21

Fire and marine insurance companies (*continued*):
  common stock holdings of, V-52
  corporate and foreign bond holdings of, V-50
  individuals' saving through new common
    stock issues of, V-19
  mortgage holdings of, by type of property, M-3,
    M-8, M-18
  nonfarm real estate holdings of, R-46, R-50
    by type of real estate, R-47 to R-53, R-66
  preferred stock holdings of, V-51
  state and local government bond holdings of,
    V-49
  stock—
    cash issues of, V-37
    net purchases and sales of, V-57 to V-59
  U.S. Government bond holdings of, V-48
Float: *see* Bank and mail float
Foreign corporations:
  individuals' saving through new common
    stock issues of, V-19
  saving through, T-6, T-8, K-5
  security issues of, offered in United States, V-16
Foreign investment:
  foreign assets in the United States, K-6
  foreign investment in the United States, an-
    nual net changes in, K-2
  net foreign investment of the United States,
    K-1
  United States assets abroad, K-7
  United States investment abroad, annual net
    changes in, K-3
Foreigners:
  common stock holdings of, V-52
  corporate bond holdings of, V-50
  corporate saving, foreigners' share in, C-50
  currency holdings of, L-3
  debit balances with brokers of, D-1
  demand deposit holdings of, L-5, L-7
  deposit holdings of, L-5 to L-7, K-4
  preferred stock holdings of, V-51
  saving through United States life insurance
    companies by, I-3
  securities sold privately to, V-16
  time deposit holdings of, L-6, L-7
  U.S. Government bond holdings of, V-48
Fraternal life insurance organizations:
  assets of, by type, I-10
  capital gains and losses of, I-12, I-13
  common stock holdings of, V-52
  corporate and foreign bond holdings of, V-50
  farm mortgage holdings of, A-61
  farm real estate holdings of, A-10, A-11
  individuals' saving through, I-9, T-10
  mortgage holdings of, by type of property, M-17

1132

Public utility and transportation corporations (*continued*):
  inventory holdings of, P–24
  preferred stock cash issues of, V–27, V–32
  saving by, C–4
  saving by, C–27, C–32
  through construction expenditures, R–16
  telegraph companies, earnings and saving of, C–22
  telephone companies, earnings and saving of, C–23
  see also Bell System
Purchases: *see* Expenditures

Railroads: *see under* Public utility and transportation corporations
Real estate:
  agricultural saving through, A–1 to A–3, A–6, A–66, T–6
  dealers' commissions on transfers of, R–32, A–12
  expenditures on, R–27, R–28
  farm real estate, holdings of, by type of holder, R–46
    net change in holdings, R–50, R–56, R–60, R–64
  fire losses on, R–71 to R–73, A–51
  holdings of, by—
    commercial banks, by type, R–54
    fraternal orders, R–65
    life insurance companies, R–63
    mutual savings banks, R–61
    property insurance companies, R–66
    unincorporated business, U–1, U–2
  mortgage debt on residential and nonresidential, R–34, R–35, R–39, R–40
  nonfarm real estate—
    personal saving through, by type of real estate, R–1, R–2
  owner-occupied and rented real estate, basic data on, R–36
  real estate bonds—
    amount of, outstanding, R–41, R–43
    issues and retirements of, R–41, R–42
  see also Commercial and industrial buildings *and* Homes *and* Multi-family dwellings
Retirement funds: *see* Pension and retirement funds

Saving, national, by principal saver groups:
  business accounting concept, T–2, T–5
  cash flow concept, T–3
  deflators of, T–16
  social accounting concept, T–1, T–4, T–12 to T–15

Saving, national, by principal saver groups (*continued*):
  refer also to specific components of saving, e.g. Producer durables; *and to particular saver groups, e.g.* Corporations
Saving, personal, T–1 to T–5, T–12 to T–15
  by major components, T–6, T–7
Savings and loan associations:
  assets of, by type, J–2, J–3, J–6
  capital gains and losses of, J–9, J–10
  credit union holdings of savings and loan shares, L–41
  income account of, J–8
  liabilities and surplus of, J–5, J–7
  mortgage holdings of, R–37, R–38, M–5, M–9
  nonfarm mortgage holdings of, M–3, M–4, M–8
  real estate holdings of, R–46, R–47, R–50, R–51, R–67
  saving through, T–6, T–8, T–10, J–1, J–11
  state and local government bond holdings of, V–49
  U.S. Government bond holdings of, V–48
Savings banks: *see* Mutual savings banks
Savings bank life insurance departments:
  assets of, by type, V–54
  corporate and foreign bond holdings of, V–50
  U.S. Government bond holdings of, V–48
Securities:
  borrowing on, by individuals, D–8
  loans on, by commercial banks, L–25, V–76
  nonfarm individuals' saving through, V–1
  retirements of, V–13
  see also Stocks *and* Bonds *and* Industrials
Security brokers and dealers:
  assets and liabilities of, by type, D–13 to D–15
  balances with, New York Stock Exchange member firms, D–12
  foreigners' debit balances with, D–11
  loans and borrowing on securities, D–8 to D–10
State governments:
  assets and liabilities of, G–16
  capital outlays of, G–15
  expenditures of, G–14
  liquid assets of, G–17
  revenues of, G–14
  saving by, G–13
  trust fund assets administered by, G–18, G–19
  see also State and local governments
State and local governments:
  debt of, outstanding, G–21
  demand deposit holdings of, L–5
  saving by, T–1 to T–3, T–12 to T–14
    comparison of alternate estimating methods, G–12

1137

State and local governments (*continued*):
  saving through bonds of, T–6, T–8, T–10
  saving through pension and retirement funds of, T–6, T–8, T–10
  state and local government bond holdings of, V–49
  tax accruals of, G–20
  time deposit holdings of, L–6
  U.S. Government bond holdings of, V–48
  see also State governments *and* Local governments
Stocks:
  Bell System issues of, V–29, V–30
  brokers' and dealers' commissions and spread in transactions in, V–44, V–46
  cash issues of, V–22
  common—
    all listed issues of, by character of issue, V–23
    commercial bank issues of, V–35
    individuals' saving through, V–10, V–19 to V–21
    institutional holdings of, V–52
  fire and marine insurance companies' net purchases and sales of, V–57 to V–59
  holdings of, by—
    casualty and miscellaneous insurance companies, V–56
    commercial banks, V–74
    fire and marine insurance companies, V–55
    fraternal orders, I–10
    investment companies, V–60, V–62, V–69, V–72
    life insurance companies, I–6
    mutual savings banks, L–30
    private pension funds, I–16, I–17
  investment companies' issues and retirements of, V–38
    cash issues of, representing individuals' saving, V–40
  life insurance companies' cash issues of, V–36
  new corporations, individuals' purchases of stock of, V–43
  preferred—
    all listed issues of, by character of issue, V–23
    individuals' saving through, V–9, V–17, V–20, V–21
    institutional holdings of, by type of institution, V–51
    net issues of, V–18

Stocks (*continued*):
  retirements of, V–25
  property insurance companies' cash issues of, V–37
  railroad cash issues of, V–27, V–28, V–32
  retirements of, V–13
  saving through, T–6, T–8, T–10, V–1
  taxes on transactions in, V–47
  transactions in, on New York Stock Exchange, D–16
  see also Industrials *and* Securities
Surplus: *see* Liabilities

Tax accruals:
  accrued on farm real estate, A–64
  of federal government, F–26
  of nonfarm individuals, F–29
  of state and local governments, G–20
  saving through, T–6, T–8
Taxes:
  on security transactions, V–1, V–47
  World War II refunds, C–36
Trade corporations:
  cash holdings of, L–16
  dividends paid by, C–29, C–31
  dividends received by, C–30
  earnings of, net, C–28
  saving by, C–27, C–32
Transportation corporations: *see* Public utility and transportation corporations
Trucks: *see* Automotive vehicles

Unincorporated business:
  assets and liabilities of, by type, U–1, U–2, U–7 to U–10
  cash flow saving by, U–11
  consumer credit extended by, D–6
  debt of, to commercial banks, U–5
  expenditures on new construction of, R–27, R–28
  interest earned on deposit holdings of, L–23
  net worth changes of, U–3, T–1 to T–3, T–12 to T–14, U–11
  receivables of—
    from corporations, U–4
    from farmers, U–6
  saving of, through—
    mining development, R–15
    oil and gas well drilling, R–14
    passenger cars, P–13
    producer durables, P–1, P–2
U.S. Government: *see* Federal government